PRAISE FOR THE NEW KINDRED SPIRITS

"I doubt that there is an ethanol category (potable alcohol) world-wide that F. Paul Pacult has not evaluated exhaustively. Pacult has developed relationships with the world's top distillers over the last thirty years that have given him up close and personal access to the explosion of alcohol beverage offerings over that time. This is especially true over the last twenty years that have defined an unprecedented golden age of fine spirits. As a bartender, the two previous *Kindred Spirits* have been my go-to guides to the right spirits to define the flavor profile I want to achieve in my cocktails. And now *The New Kindred Spirits* expands that knowledge base to previously little-known spirit categories and to the emerging category of artisanal distilleries."

—Dale DeGroff, aka "Kingcocktail" and author of *The New Craft of the Cocktail*

"Fuelled by a genuine passion for distilled spirits and more than two decades on, F. Paul Pacult's *The New Kindred Spirits* continues to answer the need for credible and thoughtful guidance on how to unlock the world of spirits for our greater enjoyment. Paul's independent views and meticulous tasting regimen deliver critiques to trust for the most advanced connoisseur through to the keenest of casual spirits hobbyists. By drawing back the curtain on where tasting notes come from Paul makes the reading of each spirit review all the more meaningful, inviting us each to develop our own vocabulary around the spirits we enjoy and would recommend to friends."

—Charlotte Voisey, global head of brand ambassador advocacy at
William Grant & Sons Inc.

"F. Paul Pacult is the leading spirits authority in the world . . . I've often heard Paul say that we are living in the 'Golden Age' of spirits. Well, *The New Kindred Spirits* is the Gold Standard for the Golden Age, a complete guide to understanding and selecting your tipple of choice, or the best base for your favorite cocktail . . . Whether you want to learn more about a specific spirit, or want to better understand the categories of spirits, history and production, or perhaps you are seeking accurate, professional recommendations of the world's greatest spirits, this book provides everything that professionals and consumers alike need to understand the spirit world."

—Steve Olson, global mezcal advocate for Del Maguey Single Village Mezcal

"When it comes to tasting and analyzing spirits, there is only one person I look to, and his name is F. Paul Pacult. In *The New Kindred Spirits*, Paul not only gives his expert review on thousands of spirits, but he teaches us how to properly taste and judge the spirits we buy. Paul is meticulous with his process and has been for decades. *The New Kindred Spirits* is a must-buy for professionals and novices alike."

—Julie Reiner, author of *The Craft Cocktail Party:
Delicious Drinks for Every Occasion*, cofounder of Social Hour Cocktails,
co-owner of Clover Club and Leyenda in Brooklyn, NY

THE NEW KINDRED SPIRITS

ALSO BY F. PAUL PACULT

Kindred Spirits: The Spirit Journal Guide to the World's Distilled Spirits and Fortified Wines (Hyperion, 1997)

The Beer Essentials: The Spirit Journal Guide to Over 650 of the World's Beers (Hyperion, 1997)

American Still Life: The Jim Beam Story and the Making of the World's #1 Bourbon (John Wiley & Sons, 2003)

A Double Scotch: How Chivas Regal and The Glenlivet Became Global Icons (John Wiley & Sons, 2005)

Kindred Spirits 2: 2,400 Reviews of Whiskey, Brandy, Vodka, Tequila, Rum, Gin, and Liqueurs from F. Paul Pacult's Spirit Journal 2000–2007 (Spirit Journal, Inc. 2008)

Buffalo, Barrels & Bourbon: The Story of How Buffalo Trace Distillery Became the World's Most Awarded Distillery (John Wiley & Sons, available September 8, 2021)

THE NEW KINDRED SPIRITS

More Than 2,000 All-New Whiskey, Brandy, Agave
Spirits, Gin, Vodka, Rum, Amari, Bitters, and
Liqueur Reviews from *F. Paul Pacult's Spirit Journal*

F. PAUL PACULT

Matt Holt Books
An Imprint of BenBella Books, Inc.
Dallas, TX

BenBella Books, Inc.
10440 N. Central Expressway
Suite 800
Dallas, TX 75231
benbellabooks.com
Send feedback to feedback@benbellabooks.com

BenBella is a federally registered trademark. MATT HOLT and logo are trademarks of BenBella Books.

Printed in the United States of America
10 9 8 7 6 5 4 3 2 1

Library of Congress Control Number: 2020058101
ISBN 9781950665969 (trade paper)

Editing by Alexa Stevenson
Copyediting by Scott Calamar
Proofreading by Jenny Bridges and Sarah Vostok
Text design and composition by Aaron Edmiston and Jessika Rieck
Cover design by Sarah Avinger
Cover photography by Upsplash/Andres Haro Dominguez
Printed by Lake Book Manufacturing

*This book is dedicated to the international community
of distillers and master blenders.*

*On a personal note, a shout-out is required to recognize the generous
individuals, absent and present, who each significantly contributed to
my understanding of the discipline of the evaluation of distilled spirits:*

*Yann Fillioux, France
Bernard Hine, France
Michael Jackson, United Kingdom
Elmer T. Lee, Kentucky
Dr. Bill Lumsden, Scotland
Booker Noe, Kentucky
Jim McEwan, Scotland
Richard Paterson, Scotland
Alain Royer, France
Colin Scott, Scotland
Pierrette Trichet, France*

CONTENTS

INTRODUCTION

THE DYNAMIC LANDSCAPE OF SPIRITS FROM 2008-2021: MAINSTREAM BRANDS, ARTISANAL SPIRITS, AND COCKTAILS

When Hyperion published the initial *Kindred Spirits* in 1997, it was an immediate success because there was nothing in the global book marketplace like it. *KS* answered a dire need for credible, accurate ratings and detailed descriptions of whiskeys, brandies, vodkas, tequilas, gins, et al. With the publication in 2008 of *Kindred Spirits 2,* the landscape had changed, in that spirits had at last taken hold in North America, and so the gist of KS2 was as much informational as it was about evaluations of pure spirits. In other words, the requirements and expectations of consumers had grown in scope as they evolved from being relatively ignorant about spirits in 1997 to being more acutely aware a decade down the road and, therefore, in need of more meaningful data.

Now, in 2021, with the publication of *The New Kindred Spirits*, the playing field is burgeoning with fresh historical information, emerging and shape-shifting categories, the exhilarating craft-distillation phenomenon (now with a reported 2,000+ micro distilleries in the US alone), and the whirlwind two-decades-long effect of the cocktail culture. So, what's necessary in this dynamic environment is a moderately overhauled journalistic approach that includes fundamental categorical data at each chapter's beginning, in addition to the updated ratings and reviews. With the explosion both in the United States and around the world of artisanal distilleries has come a deluge of new spirits to accompany a growing list of mainstream brands. This significant product growth has been paralleled by the advances seen in social media and technology, as Twitter, Facebook, Instagram, LinkedIn, Pinterest, smartphones, tablets, and more have furthered the public dialogue about spirits through blogs and personal observations that have careened through cyberspace.

Will all spirits that are available in the United States at the moment be reviewed here in *The New Kindred Spirits*? No. I'd like to say, "yes," but with the mushrooming of arcane, regional spirits, some of the more obscure craft spirits may be missing. TNKS offers a comprehensive representation of many of the most impactful distillates that are currently available on a broad basis. Some of the reviewed spirits have been evaluated multiple times to gauge consistency, with the latest rating being the analysis of record.

Are all products reviewed in *The New Kindred Spirits* available in the USA? The majority should be, even if some are restricted to certain areas of the nation or are only sold at the distillery. If a spirit is not available in the USA, that is indicated in the review. Bear in mind that some reviewed spirits might be of painfully small inventories if they were limited-edition bottlings, single barrels, or a surprise offering that was discovered in a warehouse. I have tried to indicate within the review when the quantities are miniscule. A few inclusions might not be available at all upon publication due to a time lag between when the review was created and the time of printing. That is unavoidable.

Do spirits that were reviewed in *Kindred Spirits* and/or *Kindred Spirits 2* reappear in *The New Kindred Spirits*? Yes, they might. That is due to our policy of retasting spirits to see if any changes have occurred since the last evaluation. I usually wait for between three to five years to conduct a retasting of any spirit. Formulas are modified on occasion to meet the needs of changing demographics. The alteration in spirits is nowhere near the annual change in wine, but be aware that spirits producers carefully monitor the shifting tides of consumer trends and will change a recipe if they think that bigger sales will occur because of a product's facelift.

Does *The New Kindred Spirits* address cocktails at all? The primary purpose of this book is to offer candid opinions on unadulterated spirits and how they look, smell, taste, and feel on their own. I do, at rare times, mention cocktail instances for certain spirits. To be clear, TNKS is not a cocktail-oriented book.

What is it that makes *The New Kindred Spirits* unique? Three pivotal attributes make TNKS different from all other spirits books.

One: In twenty-eight years of publication, *F. Paul Pacult's Spirit Journal* never accepted advertising, which means that the ratings and reviews that you read within this compilation are totally independent and unbiased.

Two: Since 1989, when I started writing about spirits for the *New York Times Magazine* and two years before the initial issue of *F. Paul Pacult's Spirit Journal*, I have employed the same evaluation regimen, day in, day out, over the course of 30,000+ formal spirits reviews and thirty years. The consistency of this personal procedure has enabled me to perceive spirits within identical parameters for three decades, thereby ensuring reliability and continuity of my viewpoint. Whether one agrees with my viewpoint or not is another matter. I'm sure some people don't, and that's cool.

Three: Over the years of carefully analyzing tens of thousands of spirits, I have constructed a voluminous mental library of sensory impressions that somehow have stayed with me. I believe that it was spawned from the continuous repetition of process and has thus served as a cornerstone for my reviews through the years. I have also taken great lengths to become familiar with the unique identifying aromas of spices, fruits, vegetables, candies, pastries, plants/flowers, tree barks, herbs, nuts, seeds, household goods (leather, books, cleaning fluids, fabric), atmospheres (library, attic, basement), and climatic events (rainfall, drying leaves). In other words, I have learned to pay attention to everyday smells, no matter the circumstance, to convey my impressions in terms that nearly anyone can relate to.

These three items—independence, strict regimen, and mental library—form the foundation of my approach to reviewing spirits with full respect accorded producers and their products and with dedication to saving consumers time and money by identifying the wonderful, the average, and the poor distillates. Reviewing, say, four to six gins from 8:30 AM until 11:30 AM on a frigid, snowy January morning lacks broad scale attraction, not to mention romance.

What it comes down to is this: I like being in this trade for its life-affirming aspect. It's been a supreme pleasure being able to inform responsible, legal-age imbibers about what's good to buy, to honor the important history of spirits production, distillation, and maturation, and to pay unbiased homage to the hundreds of dedicated, talented women and men who produce the potables that, on occasion, propel one's soul skyward. It is, on fortuitous occasion, that one transcendent five star spirit in a morning of tasting that suddenly makes my mission worthwhile, almost like an epiphany.

Here's hoping that, because of *The New Kindred Spirits,* you'll taste the best spirits of your life for years to come.

F. Paul Pacult
Ulster County, New York, USA
2021

TASTING ANALYTICALLY, RATINGS, AND ENHANCING YOUR DRINKING PLEASURE

Tasting distilled spirits formally, either for a review or as part of a consultation, is the hardest job that I do. By spirits, of course, I refer to brandies, liqueurs, whiskeys, gins, tequilas, mezcals, vodkas, or rums, meaning the potables that undergo first fermentation, then distillation, and sometimes maturation in wood barrels. The amount of concentration required to properly and meticulously identify subtle characteristics in spirits is enormous.

Analyzing spirits is far more demanding in nature and practice than scrutinizing wine, sake, or beer, all of which are fermented beverages. This is primarily due to the elevated alcohol-by-volume levels of the majority of distilled liquids. Fermented libations typically range from as low as 3 percent alcohol (light beer) up to 17 to 18 percent in the case of some very strong ales and wines.

Drinkable liquids that are fermented (beer or wine) and then heated, vaporized, and cooled in a traditional pot (think your teakettle) are made in individual batches that after two distillations range generally from 50 to 72 percent alcohol. This is pot still distillation. The more modern column still system (continuous distillation) creates liquids that can range from a low of 30 to 32 percent alcohol all the way up to 95.57 percent alcohol when the gases contain the same degree of ethanol as the liquid, becoming neutral grain spirit or NGS. High alcohol content automatically makes spirits significantly more complex than their fermented cousins.

That said, consumers, too, can learn several sequential steps that, when used properly, will increase their enjoyment of spirits without a great deal of rigor or pain. There is no magic to transforming oneself into even a moderately astute judge of spirits. Much of the process of becoming a better taster involves three fundamental components: one, the common sense utilization of one's senses, knowing what they do and getting them to work in unison; two, repetitive tasting practice, using a tasting system that works specifically for you; and three, first recognizing and then reeducating your inherent memory abilities and acknowledging how they are tethered to your senses, in particular, your most primal sense, smell.

All that I am talking about is deeper personal appreciation, not fanaticism, snobbery, or, worst of all, showboating. Face it, we've all been exposed to pontificating, insecure twits who, in effusive fits when tasting a wine, an ale, or a whiskey, spout absurd, often anthropomorphic terms (i.e., muscular, brooding, buxom) and philosophical drivel. When some idiot utters something like, "This single malt is more Ariana Grande while that one is more Rihanna," I leave the room. Keener appreciation is never about elitism or exclusivity. It is always about heightened personal enjoyment, sharing, inclusion, and sensible communication in understandable terms.

Knowing the Ground Rules
Proper environment
One's evaluation environment should be clean, well-lit, and appropriate to the task at hand. My formal reviews are conducted solely in my office at the *Spirit Journal* HQ in New York's Hudson Valley and never outside that space, but that's for a highly regimented professional. For your informal purposes, choose a cozy sitting room, den, dining room, or kitchen where you and your friends will be comfortable.

Glassware

Glassware is a key element. Never, ever use plastic cups because plastic can impart unpleasant odors and flavors to delicate beverages. Plastic is a petroleum-based product, so need I elaborate? I utilize the same small-volume, thin crystal glasses for all spirit categories, a combination of stemmed *copitas*, small wineglasses, six-ounce Riedel Vinum Port glasses, and five-ounce Glencairn whisky glasses that I wash myself by hand without the use of detergent. My tasting glasses are air-dried because sometimes even cotton towels and/or paper towels can leave residue or fibers that can later be mistaken as sediment. I wipe the outside after they have dried to remove spots. I haven't used fishbowl-like snifters for well over twenty-five years because they tend to diffuse key aromatic properties. Chimney-shaped glasses funnel aromas upward, which, for me, is desirable. For your purposes at home, just use six- or eight-ounce white wine glasses, which will handily serve all spirit varieties well. For whiskeys and brandies, you might consider using rocks glasses.

Spitting, numbers, timing, amounts

I believe in spitting ALWAYS in order to avoid even light inebriation and, therefore, I use opaque plastic sixteen-ounce beer cups for spittoons. Swallowing samples is ultimately counterproductive to becoming a better taster. One has to remain clearheaded and mentally agile. As a matter of policy, I never sample more than eight spirits in any one session and mostly hold the total to six per morning. Amateurs should heed that advice and, in my opinion, should refrain from overburdening anyone's taste buds or sensibilities, including their own. No more than one to two ounces (or about fifty milliliters) per sample are needed for a thorough evaluation.

I usually taste early in the morning, normally from 8:30 AM to around noon, which most people understandably blanch at. But I am a card-carrying morning person, so that time suits me best. An unadulterated, fresh, morning palate is preferred for my purposes but is clearly impractical for informal tastings. For most consumers, weekend afternoons or evenings are easier to hold tastings. Have plenty of water available. I like still water in between tastes, which cleanses the palate well. Sometimes, however, a low-sodium fizzy water, in particular, San Pellegrino or Perrier, also works well. Mild cheeses are recommended for serving with spirits, such as Muenster or Monterey Jack. Bread or unsalted water crackers (Carr's are best) are also excellent alcohol absorbers.

If I begin to experience palate fatigue, meaning the inability to use all my senses, I stop for the day. I also taste products from the same category in one session. Don't mix, say, two blanco tequilas, three Canadian whiskys, and two London dry gins. Doesn't work. Keep like with like for the purpose of context and focus.

Ratings and the positive effects of group discussion

What my critiques come down to are these two salient points: First, does this product stack up well in relation to the specific category's established, contemporary standards? And, second, would I recommend this product to a friend, reader, or colleague? Nothing is more important than the second question. All criticism forums, meaning book reviews, movie reviews, car reviews, etc., boil down to this query.

For three decades, I have employed a **one to five star rating system**, with one being the lowest score and five the highest. **Price does not affect the final score**. Here's what they signify:

★ red-flags that particular product's quality as being woefully below the established standard for the category. One star products are what I consider to be undrinkable, unbalanced, and are deemed as **Not Recommended**. They can smell and taste rancid, attic-like, musty, moldy, or unclean. These are very different traits to something like botanical, herbal, vegetal, mossy/earthy, oily, or dusty, which actually can all be considered good attributes, depending on the category.

★★ indicate an item that is average when judged against its peers and is, therefore, **Not Recommended**. These spirits may be drinkable and without severe failings, but in the end they are uninspiring and lacking any special merit. I would not tell a friend to buy them.

★★★ mean that the character profile of this item is better than average and exceeds what would be considered as the norm for product quality of this category. Three star products are always **Recommended**. I would advise a friend to hunt them down.

★★★★ point out products that exceed what is thought to be far better than average. Four star ratings spotlight a product of authentic quality and distinct personality. These high-quality items come **Highly Recommended**. I would, with gusto, counsel my friends to buy these products.

★★★★★ celebrate a watershed, benchmark product whose seamless quality is as ideal as an item can get within that category. These are the iconic, flawless products that can be thought of as defining a spirits category due to their harmonious natures in which all the chemical components—alcohol, acids, base materials, pH, wood use, if any—are perfectly integrated through outstanding base material selection, fermentation, distillation, maturation, filtration, blending, and/or other production techniques. These hallmark spirits receive my **Highest Recommendation**.

I encourage weekend or casual tasters to use some sort of scoring system (100-point scale or 1 to 10 are also fine) to render some sort of informal ranking. A rating system provides a point of debate among the tasters, and the more debate the better in order to establish the group's quality standards. In fact, I always urge consumers to taste in groups because hearing what other people are experiencing is the best way to learn and to develop a personal vocabulary. Group tasting opens vistas and can bolster or counter your own viewpoint, both of which are useful.

Alcohol by volume, or abv, and adding water issues

As part of every review I conduct, the abv is cited for your informational purposes. Be aware of the abv of every entered spirit so that you can set the order of tasting, lowest abv to highest, youngest spirit to oldest.

Typically, when you come across whiskey, rum, or brandy abv that's wildly divergent from the standard 40 to 43 percent abv level, such as 59.2 percent, 63.3 percent, or 49.9 percent, it nearly always signals a "cask strength" spirit. This means that the spirit was drawn from the barrel or holding tank and bottled without dilution to a lower range of strength. Make sure that these are last in the lineup. If you place them before spirits with lower abv, they will eclipse the lighter spirits. Also, I urge at-home tasters to add flat (noneffervescent) bottled mineral water to the cask-strength spirits in a ratio of ½ ounce of mineral water to every 1½ ounces of spirit. Dilution accomplishes two things: one, it stimulates aroma because water separates the molecules, thereby releasing more aroma, and, two, the reduced strength makes it easier to assess the spirit's characteristics.

The Value and Purpose of an Evaluation Regimen

I take twenty to thirty minutes for every formal product evaluation, which is excessive for at-home tasters, who shouldn't need more than three to five minutes for each spirit. That is one reason why I am an admittedly deliberate critic. Your purpose is pure enjoyment, and therefore is much less strenuous. Discovery should be fun, not demanding. Perhaps the biggest factor in becoming a good taster, whether you are a professional or not, is to formulate and then follow a tasting routine. One's personal system should never waver once you've found one that's comfortable.

The four-sense system I've used for the past three decades, but that you should moderate for your own reasons of comfort and convenience, goes as follows:

Sight: First, but not the most vital stage, is looking at the spirit under a bright "daylight" lamp. At this point, I'm gauging the clarity (is it opaque or translucent?), the overall cleanliness (do I see any floating sediment and if so, what does it appear to be: fabric, cork, minerals, oils?), and, of course, the color (brown, yellow, red, green, blue, and their various multitudinous shades). Google "shades of brown or orange" or "yellow or red" for more breakdowns. Most of all, does it own an appealing appearance? This stage should not consume more than ten to fifteen seconds.

Smell: Next comes the most pivotal phase of the whole exercise, the one that, for me, makes up the majority of my final score. Smell is our most primal sense (olfaction). The olfactory cortex is located in the segment of the brain called the limbic system, which impacts creativity, memory, and emotions. It is the only sense that triggers the eerie feeling of déjà vu. Smell directs and impacts the sense of taste by up to 80 to 90 percent, according to some studies, and furthermore, due to its fundamental status, allows us to identify danger, mates, and food.

Here's how it all works in a nutshell: While the tongue and approximately ten thousand taste buds in humans can only identify five fundamental flavors (sweet, sour, bitter, salty, umami), most human olfactory mechanisms can, if trained, recognize up to ten thousand singular odor molecules. Inhaling a spirit draws hundreds, more likely thousands, of tiny odor molecules into the nasal cavity. When they land on our moist, mucus-coated, one-square-inch, subdermal receptors (nasal epitheliums), those receptors instantaneously relay data to the olfactory cortex, which causes a reaction of, "Hey, I recognize that rose petal scent and I like it" or, "Whoa, that smells like Uncle Ned's work shoes, which I don't like very much."

Our brain's limbic system is directly connected to the body's apparatus (pituitary gland and hypothalamus) that controls the hormones that stimulate sensations we all uniformly experience, such as appetite, stress, body temperature, and the ability to concentrate. That is why the sense of smell is so potent, so intimate every minute of every day we are conscious, and why it is the most critical part of your spirit evaluations.

Step-by-step, here's how I do what I do: I smell every item in three stages. I take a series of gentle sniffs right after the pour, holding the glass just beneath my nose, lips parted to help circumvent the rush of alcohol. I allow it to sit undisturbed for another three minutes, and at the five-minute mark I take deeper, longer inhalations. It often takes a spirit that's been trapped within a bottle several minutes to adjust to its new environment. Then, at the ten-minute mark, I take parting whiffs just in case I missed anything in the first two nosing passes. In all, I spend from five to fifteen minutes total smelling each spirit. In some instances, I will return to the smelling phase after the tasting phase to double-check an observation or to erase a doubt.

I think of aromatic profile, as I do my gustatory, or flavor, profile, in the following foundational, associative categories:

Bakery Shop
Yeasty, biscuity, bread dough, cookie dough, pizza dough, cake batter, cake frosting, gingerbread, pretzel dough, honey, mincemeat, refined sugar, brown sugar, almond paste, nougat, praline, treacle, carob, flaky pastry, meringue, white flour, whole wheat, whole grain, French baguette, salt/saline, prune Danish, bear claw pastry, sourdough

Baking Spices/Herb
Vanilla extract/bean, cinnamon, clove, allspice, nutmeg, ginger, mace

Beans/Legumes
Cola nut, coffee bean, cocoa/cacao, chickpea, split pea, lentil, soy, kidney, pinto, tofu, cubeb, carob, chicory, sorghum, lima

Bitter
Soy sauce, hoisin, vinegar

Candy/Candy Shop
Refined sugar, brown sugar, honey, caramel, toffee, saltwater taffy, marshmallow, hard candy, cake frosting, molasses, apple butter, candy bar, marzipan, fudge, milk chocolate, dark chocolate, espresso, latte, malted milk ball

Cooking Spice/Seed/Herb
Black pepper, sage, thyme, rosemary, basil, parsley, coriander, paprika, ginger, chive, cumin, turmeric, sea salt, marjoram, dill, aniseed, saffron, bay laurel, cardamom, *savory,* cilantro, angelica, cubeb, cayenne, mint, fennel, lemongrass

Dairy
Milk, yogurt, salted/unsalted butter, buttermilk, egg yolk, egg white, hard/dry cheese (Parmigiano-Reggiano), soft cheese (Brie, Limburger, Gouda), milk shake, malted milk, rotten egg, meringue, hard-boiled egg

Floral/Flower/Plant
Violet, rose, jasmine, honeysuckle, orange blossom, lavender, lemon blossom, geranium, *dried*, *fresh*, vines/brambles/leaves, morning glory, marigold, hydrangea, hops, elderflower, damp leaves, tomato vines, verbena, gentian, prickly pear, pineapple sage

Fruit/Wine
Orchard—Pear, apple, plum/quince, cherry, nectarine, peach, kiwi, pomegranate, lychee, fig, date, avocado
Vine/bramble—Grape, all berries (currants included), juniper, prickly pear, tomato, tomato vine, tomatillo, rhubarb, green melon, watermelon, pumpkin
Tropical or subtropical/citrus orchard and fruits—orange, lemon, grapefruit, pineapple, lime, tangerine, guava, banana, papaya, star fruit, mango
Status—*Fresh*, *ripe*, *dried*, pulp, peel/zest, *green*, *baked*, *overripe*, marmalade

Grains/Cereal
Wheat, white rice, brown rice, rye, corn/maize, cornstarch, polenta, tamale, cornmeal/masa, snack cracker, breakfast cereal, graham cracker, *malty*, malted milk ball, *waxy*, popcorn, grain husk, kernel

Meat/Fat
Pork, pork rind, BBQ sauce, grilled meats, sausage, bacon, bacon fat, lard, baked ham, vegetable cooking oil, olive oil, salted/unsalted butter, brown butter

Mineral/Elemental/Atmospheric
Stony, limestone, chalk/*chalky*, nickel, lead/lead pencil, *salty*, flint/*flinty*, arid desert, rainfall, cement sidewalks, sand/wet sand, barnyard, rubber tire, inner tube, parchment, onionskin, cardboard, wax paper, sealing wax, candle, attic, leather, old books/library, lumberyard, *musty*, *dusty*, TCA (trichloroanisole)/*corked*, damp basement, mold/*moldy*

Nuts
Almond, walnut, hazelnut, pistachio, nut butter/Nutella, peanut, nougat, nut paste, peanut butter, peanut oil, cashew, macadamia

Sea/Weather
Salt air, seaweed, salted fish/kippers, wet sand, rain/fog, dew

Seeds
Poppy, sesame, caraway, pumpkin, grains of paradise

Smoke/Burnt/Carbonic
Campfire, wood smoke, burnt tobacco, peat, creosote, ashes, soot, grilled meat,

BBQ sauce, s'mores, pipe tobacco, cigar tobacco, carbon, burnt matches/sulphur, toasted marshmallow, burnt toast, charcoal briquette, rotten egg, potash, ammonia

Sweet
Sugar, sugarcane, honey, molasses, sugar beet, brown sugar, turbinado sugar, demerara sugar, powdered sugar, agave syrup, oloroso sherry, port, Madeira, corn syrup, maple, maple syrup, mead, caramel, toffee, fudge

Tea
Chamomile, green tea, black tea, orange pekoe, Earl Grey, peppermint, Lapsang souchong

Vegetation/Plant/Root
Forest floor/*woodsy*, mushroom, lichen, *mossy*, *earthy*, wet leaves, tobacco leaf, black tea, green tea, bark, peat, maple syrup/tree sap, pine forest, autumn leaves, damp soil, wormwood, eucalyptus, prickly pear, beet, spearmint, lemongrass, sarsaparilla, rose hips, mint, juniper, hyssop, hay, straw, grass, ginger root, licorice, bison grass
Kale, broccoli, asparagus, artichoke, green pepper, chili pepper, vegetable cooking oil, palm oil, tomato, tomato paste, tomatillo, green beans, spinach, chive, onion, spring onion, leek, cauliflower, cabbage, eggplant, vinegar, green olive, brine, parsnip, sweet potato, potato, cucumber, artichoke, celery, rhubarb

Wine/Vinification
Grapy, grape must, grape skins, grape pulp, *stemmy*, *viny*, oloroso sherry, port, Madeira, noble rot (botrytis cinerea)

Wood/Trees
Oak, cedar/pine, *resiny*, *oily*, *fatty*, sawdust, plank, maple/tree sap, plywood, old barn, woodshed, coconut, vanilla, bark, root beer, spruce, sandalwood, madrone, Douglas fir, marula

For your personal purposes, I suggest smelling each spirit in your flight in two stages: immediately following the pour and then at the three-minute mark. If you want to, you can always go back and sniff it again after you've smelled the other spirits in your flight. IMPORTANT: First smell spirits in the flight one after the other before moving on to taste. Smelling provides context that tasting could never do.

Taste: Immediately following the smelling stage of the entire flight, I take a small sip of the first entry and let the liquid rest at the tip of my tongue for a few seconds, then spit it out. Then I take a second sip, which is the vital one since the first sip acts only as palate cleanser. This is the palate entry stage. This initial impression should remind me at least a little of what was occurring in the smell. If I detected odors of, say, fruit, for instance, there should be some flavor evidence of orchard (pear, apple, plum, cherry) or vine (grape, strawberry, blackberry, blueberry, currant, raspberry, kiwifruit) or tropical fruit (orange, lemon, banana, pineapple, lime, tangerine, guava). Sometimes taste doesn't jibe with smell. Smell and taste are usually in harmony (75 to 80 percent of the time, I reckon), but on occasion show little resemblance.

If smell and taste do not mesh, it doesn't necessarily mean the spirit is out of whack. What you experienced in the nose might even return in the aftertaste, which often occurs. So, when smell and taste aren't reflective of each other, I suggest that you keep moving forward.

After another minute, I take a larger sip and let that amount rest on the tongue for ten to twenty seconds. This allows the whole of the tongue to be saturated. This midpalate phase makes or breaks the mouth experience. And it's here where the rating begins to firm up. I spend up to ten minutes tasting several times. You should figure on five minutes max. Some spirits, like cask-strength whiskeys, need another round of sniffing and tasting when mineral water is added. A rigid format trains your taste buds to work together with your olfactory cortex, creating one unified impression. The key to becoming a good communicator is to describe what you smell and taste in relatable terms.

Touch: The feel of a spirit, the textural experience, is the last piece of information that I need to render a final decision. Is the spirit oily, thin/watery, syrupy, biting, silky smooth, sharp/raw, aggressive, fiery? Any or all of these attributes can affect the score by as much as one star. Also, how long does the taste last in the throat? Extended length usually means a heavier, fuller spirit and is often highly desirable, unless the taste is horribly wrong and flawed.

Savor: By *savor* I simply mean to sit back and enjoy—or not—the entire experience of all the senses over a few moments. The key is to ponder the following questions: Do I like this product? If I do like it, to what degree of enthusiasm do I like it? If I don't care for it, to what degree do I dislike it?

For you as an at-home taster, this entire process requires no more than five to seven minutes per spirit, give or take two minutes. One needn't be a biochemist, a Master Sommelier, or a Mensa candidate to derive maximum pleasure. Success in spirits analysis requires, above all:

Repetition of a regimen that's comfortable for you
Strict adherence to that format
Recall (creating your mind's accessible collection of deep impressions)
Conducive, well-lighted, calm environment (a vital, if overlooked aspect)
Clean, category-appropriate glassware
Keen, penetrating, steady observation

Summation: Making Sense of It All

Practicing your tasting with friends is highly suggested because it is always more valuable to be exposed to varying viewpoints in your tasting journey. Oftentimes, someone next to me will cite an attribute that maybe I couldn't clearly identify, and when they mention it ("Hey, that's like cumin!"), it suddenly clicks into place and makes sense. Tasting by oneself is tedious; take it from me.

Tasting on a regular basis helps to build the sensory collection of key impressions that is absolutely necessary for successful critical analysis. If I have learned anything over three decades of tasting experience, it is that without a rich storehouse of reference data, accurate and reliable analysis simply won't happen, no matter how talented the taster in terms of technique. When you rate a spirit four or five stars, go back to it and pick out the three or four characteristics that make it so delightful (floral, fruity, sweet, ripe, stony, honeyed, you get the idea), then dog-ear those benchmark attributes and file them away for future use.

Every little bit of information will eventually create a master plan for you that will work because you'll have made it your own process. Greater technical application brings deeper enjoyment and appreciation.

SPIRITS PRODUCTION AND HISTORICAL FUNDAMENTALS

Throughout medieval Europe, specifically the post–Roman Empire period of 476–1453 CE (Common Era), Christian monks and nuns populated the abbeys and monasteries that linked the continent. These devout men and women were often the champions of the production of fermented liquids, such as beer and wine. Later, they learned that if you boil beer and/or wine and condense the vapors generated by the intense heat, the resultant liquid—clear and potent—could be utilized in the application of the healing arts.

Many of the Latin-speaking clergy of the era called the shimmering liquids *aqua vitae* (pronounced *ah-kwa VEE-tay*). In Ireland and Scotland, where Gaelic was spoken nearly exclusively, ancient distillers identified the local grain-based potables as *uisge beatha* (pronounced *ush-keh BAY-ah*). In France, the heady, grape- and fruit-based libations were referred to as *eau-de-vie* (pronounced *ohh-duh-vee*). In Eastern Europe and western Russia, inhabitants cherished them as *zhizennia voda* (pronounced *zhe-neh-nee-yah WOH-dah*). All of these regional monikers had one thing in common: they all meant "water of life."

The reference is correlated, in part, to the uniformly difficult, unsanitary living conditions throughout Europe that at their worst resulted in plagues that decimated the continent, in particular, in the fourteenth century CE. Polluted water sources and filthy village streets proved to be incubators of grave and infectious diseases spread rapidly by vermin. Physicians and Christian monks possessed little medical knowledge to relieve suffering except for distilled spirits, their *aqua vitae*, which as medicine helped ease some discomfort.

"Water of life" is also a reference to the search by some medieval alchemists and philosophers who utilized distillation practices in their quest for a unifying compound that would act as a conduit between things earthbound and the ethereal realm. Distillation's earliest usage, however, was far more likely to be medicinal in nature.

These names identified the fermented and distilled liquids that by the fifteenth century (1400s) had become inextricably linked to German, Polish, French, Italian, English, Irish, Spanish, Russian, Scottish, Dutch, Greek, Armenian, Slavic, and Scandinavian tribal societies from the Baltic Sea to the Mediterranean Sea to the northern Atlantic Ocean to Eurasia's vast steppes.

Fermentation and Distillation

But what did the evocative phrase "water of life" mean? The meaning has everything to do with how distilled liquids were initially perceived and then how they changed over 2,500 years. Two mandatory transformative biochemical processes create the beverages that we're addressing: **fermentation** and **distillation**. Eons before the discovery of the process of distillation, which most likely occurred in or around the region of what is today Pakistan and northern India or, possibly, in China, Eurasian farmers used fermentation to convert commonplace fruit juices, especially grape juice, and grain mashes from barley, wheat, and rye into low-alcohol (5 to 12 percent ales) beverages. When universally available microorganisms—yeast cells—consume innate sugars in either fruit juices or mashes of grain, then alcohol, carbon dioxide, and heat are automatically and naturally generated.

Fermentation, a natural biochemical process, is spontaneously triggered whenever sugary liquids collide and mingle with either airborne or purposely injected yeasts. Wild yeast cells are prevalent in Earth's lower atmosphere. Because fruit juices are bursting with innate sugars, wines can, under the right circumstances, produce themselves.

With beer, the procedure is a bit more complicated, in that the starches in the grains must first be converted to sugar through dampening, which stimulates partial germination. Once the grain starches have transformed to sugars, the resultant beige, soupy mashes start to bubble and change when yeast cells are introduced. Thus, beer really does need an assist from mankind in order to happen. And for at least five thousand years, civilized societies have obliged by creating ales and lagers and barley wines. That, in layman's terms, is what happens in fermentation, the necessary first step in the process of making distilled liquids.

In the historical sense, beer and wine, two low-alcohol beverages, have very likely existed since before recorded history. Early agrarian communities like those in ancient Egypt, India, China, and Mesopotamia from 3000 BCE (Before Common Era) and before have displayed indisputable archeological and recorded evidence (numerous hieroglyphs in Egypt's tombs and temples; India's Upanishads; Mesopotamia's cuneiform tablets; dried residues from prehistoric China) of winemaking and brewing. Pinpointing exactly when fermentation took flight within the framework of an ancient community must be left to speculation.

Distillation: Historians and archeologists are still debating when this human-devised second step may have first bubbled up to the surface. Archeological digs in the 1960s conducted in the ancient Greek-Indian city of Shaikhan Dheri in Pakistan unearthed compelling evidence of terra-cotta pot stills that suggested the existence of small-scale commercial distilleries being active circa 300–150 BCE. Similar findings near modern-day Peshawar, a city in northern Pakistan located near the Khyber Pass, have appeared in various reports. Adding to the debate are textual interpretations in India's Vedic literature that appear to support the archeological discoveries of the twentieth century, drawing tantalizing attention to the period of around 500 BCE as a possible launching date for distillation.

But then there are scriptural reports emanating from China that point to that ancient culture as being active in the distillation of wine. And what about early, pre-Columbian evidence of agave-based distillation in southern Mexico? And then there are the hazy reports concerning a possibly Hellenistic Jewish mystic by the name of Maria who dabbled and wrote about the alchemist's arts and is credited with inventing the double boiler? The mind boggles at the possible discoveries yet to emerge, assuming they ever do. What is clear is that there still remains much evidence that must be unearthed and verified before a definitive conclusion about the earliest distillation efforts can be determined. For the moment, then, just how does distillation work? How do low-alcohol beers and wines evolve into high-alcohol spirits?

The term "distillation" is derived from the Latin verb *destillare*, which means "to drip down" or "to drip off." At its most fundamental, distillation is a purification process that utilizes concentrated, sustained heat to boil fermented liquids, such as beer and wine, for the express purpose of separating the alcohol from the water, oils, fats, and other chemical compounds (congeners) of the base materials. Alcohol boils at 173.1 degrees Fahrenheit while water boils at 212 degrees Fahrenheit, so alcohol turns gaseous before water turns to steam. This procedure works best when carried out in a kettle, or any variety of bulbous mechanical contraption, in which intense, concentrated heat can be generated and in which the vapors can be captured. Potbellied kettles, made from malleable metals, are referred to as "pot stills." (More on pot stills and how they developed straight ahead.)

As the alcohol changes from liquid into warm vapor, it rises in the pot still's upper chambers and is guided through channels, whereupon it either falls back for more distillation (reflux), or cools and condenses (drips down) back into clear liquid form. It is the intense heat of distillation that strips away impurities (oils, esters, congeners, fats) in fermented liquids, thereby leaving behind the liquid's essence. With each round of distillation, the liquid gets less contaminated and the percentage of alcohol is elevated, increasing the potency as it purifies.

Off the Boil: What Happens in Distillation

From distillation's earliest days more than two thousand years ago up until the first quarter of the nineteenth century, there was only one way to distill liquids: the tried-and-true pot still method. For the last thirteen hundred years, potbellied, kettle-like pot stills have been made from a variety of metals and woods. Copper has been preferred for spirits such as Scotch whisky, Irish whiskey, and cognac because it is strong, easier to shape than other metals, durable (lasts far longer than stainless steel does), and conducts heat evenly.

The concept of pot still distillation is direct in its simplicity. Here's how it works, step-by-step:

1. The distiller pumps fermented liquid (beer or wine) into the lower chamber of the pot still.
2. The pot still is heated from beneath via gas, steam, or flame, gradually bringing the alcohol to a boil at 173.1 degrees Fahrenheit, whereupon it vaporizes and rises.
3. The vapors ascend into the upper region of the pot still chamber and either drop back down for further heating (reflux) or flow through a "swan neck" pipe at the top of the pot still. (The pipe is referred to as such for its resemblance to its namesake.)
4. The vapors drift from the swan neck through to cooled coils where they condense, turning back into liquid form (spirits), purer, clearer, and higher in alcohol than when they started.
5. The distiller carefully selects the middle part of the distillation run, the best portion or so-called "heart" (similar to the best cuts of meats, like the center cuts, tenderloins, filets, etc.), and separates that prime segment from the rest of the run. Single distillation results in a spirit ranging in alcohol degrees from 25 to 32 percent.
6. The lesser, more impure parts of the distillation run, the "heads" and the "tails," are often put through another distillation to purify them to the desired degree.
7. Many single-batch spirits are distilled again in other smaller pot stills to elevate levels of purity and alcohol. Second distillation results in a spirit ranging in alcohol degrees from 55 to 72 percent.

Once this basic sequence of "individual batch distilling" is completed, the pot still requires cleaning before the next batch of fermented liquid can be placed into its chamber. The resultant spirits are typically high in quality and distinctive in character. Fresh, virgin spirits smelled right off a pot still are pleasantly fragrant in a floral or fruity sense. They are also crystal clear in appearance. This age-old method, while expensive and labor intensive, remains an irreplaceable source for thousands of the world's finest distilled spirits. But even though it's the original way of distilling liquids, the pot still individual batch method isn't the only way to produce quality spirits.

Beginning in the first decades of the Industrial Revolution, an innovative, more efficient, and less expensive type of industrial distillation was introduced in 1813 in France by researcher Jean Baptiste Cellier-Blumenthal, who introduced the concept of ledges within the necks of stills. In late 1820s Scotland, distiller Robert Stein, who made whisky at the Kilbagie Distillery in Clackmannanshire, took Cellier-Blumenthal's design and added perforated plates to devise the first patented (1827) model of the single-column method in the form of a metal columnar still, which ran continuously and didn't need to be stopped and cleaned. Shortly thereafter, another insightful inventor-distiller, Irishman Aeneas Coffey, toiling in Dublin, Ireland, at the Dock Distillery, took Stein's design and added more height to the cylindrical column, thereby increasing the purity of the distillate as well as the volume of the output.

Here's how Coffey's revolutionary still design worked: The base of the column was called the "analyzer," and the top tier was known as the "rectifier." Every section enclosed a series of chambers that were separated by perforated metal plates. As alcohol vapors rose through each plate, more impurities (congeners, esters, fusel oils) collided with the plates and fell back down the chamber, allowing purer vapors to advance up the chamber. Coffey discovered that the taller the column, the cleaner the resultant spirit. Coffey patented his design in 1830. Within a decade, other distillers added another column to Coffey's basic design and were soon making ethereal spirits of remarkable purity, quality, and lightness with a double-column system. Soon, this newfangled type of still was being referred to as "patent still," "Coffey still," or "column still."

What was obvious to the distilling community across the world by the 1850s and 1860s was that this new, efficient, industrial, low-cost, continuously functioning process, the precise opposite of customary stop-and-start, labor-intensive pot still distillation, was the wave of the future for creating large volumes of spirits. Nowadays, the process called "continuous distillation" is practiced in every nation that produces spirits and is the distillation of choice for the majority of lighter, mostly unaged spirits like rum, gin, vodka, and cachaça.

Many distillers use both methods, frequently in tandem, to produce high-grade spirits that contain elements of each system. A prime example of a world-class spirit with international acceptance that combines both pot still and column still spirits is blended Scotch whisky from Scotland. Master blenders from renowned companies such as Chivas Brothers, Dewar's, Ballantine's, Berry Bros. & Rudd, Compass Box, and Johnnie Walker, to name only a few, marry multiple whiskies from column stills made in large industrial complexes and single malt whiskies made in pot stills at smaller distilleries to arrive at a highly palatable marriage of the two styles.

The 156-year period of 1865 to the present day is considered to be the modern age of spirits. Both distillation processes are vital components to the contemporary worldwide distilling industry. As the world has supposed become "smaller," the spirits industry has become larger.

Which Style of Distillation Is Better?

Naturally, the question arises regarding the differences in quality and character between customary pot still and modern continuous still distillation and whether one style produces better spirits than the other. From my point of view, I know that spirits derived by continuous distillation can be every bit as exotic and tantalizing as those from the batch method of pot still distillation. The misconception that continuous distillation is responsible only for high-volume, high-alcohol distillate (NGS) that acts only like water that stretches the soup is wrong. There are many examples of excellent spirits being made through column stills, such as bourbon, vodka, gin, Armagnac, rum, straight rye, and more.

The argument in favor of continuous still distillation's quality can best be understood by blended Scotch and Irish whiskey brands like Bell's, Johnnie Walker, Chivas Regal, Dewar's, Buchanan's, Ballantine's, Black Bush, and Jameson. These extremely high-quality whiskeys are marriages of grain whiskeys made in continuous stills and malt whiskeys produced in copper pot stills. The Scots and Irish would not break with tradition and offer poor-tasting whiskeys if they felt that continuous still whiskeys weren't every bit as tasty as the single malts from pot stills.

It is better to think of continuous and pot still distillations as simply being two varieties of still that each have inherent value and worth yet are different. It's kind of like a painter having multiple colors on his/her palette with which to create lovely images. The enlightened approach is to appreciate what both varieties of distillation bring to the banquet.

USEFUL INFORMATION ABOUT BARRELS AND WOOD MATURATION

Aging wines and spirits in barrels is as much a centuries-old practicality as it is a tradition. A potable that has not been matured in wood is invariably different than one that has spent time within the confines of an oak barrel. When one ponders this global custom, a flurry of questions arises. When were barrels first used for maturing beverages? From all the varieties of hard woods available in the world, why is oak the near-universal choice for winemakers and distillers? What happens to beverages once they are inside the barrel? Why are barrels set on fire on the inside during production? Perhaps most salient of all from a serious drinker's perspective is: What in the blazes is "the angel's share"?

Trade: The Underlying Reason for Barrels

Barter was the original form of trade, in which goods were exchanged for other goods. Oils were exchanged for timber, say, or beans and produce were traded for tools. Sometimes goods were exchanged for services, like when lamp oils were exchanged for road builders or maybe architectural expertise.

By 12,000 BCE, trade was common, mostly for hard and sharp obsidian for making tools and utensils for hunting, building, cooking, shipbuilding, and weapons. Obsidian was often traded for flint, with which to make fire. Later, precious and semiprecious stones like lapis lazuli became highly coveted for jewelry and were widely traded between Afghanistan, Babylonia, and Egypt. By 1000 BCE, the fabled Silk Road stretched 6,000 overland miles, bringing cargoes of herbs, gems, livestock, horses, weapons, and spices from China and India to Persia, Greece, and the Mediterranean cultures. From 1500 BCE to 500 CE, the Phoenicians, Greeks, Romans, and Egyptians each practiced trade and commercial shipping throughout the Mediterranean region and far beyond until Rome's collapse in the fifth century CE. The Mediterranean Sea was an accommodating waterway in which shippers could hug the coastline for long distances, stopping port by port to sell wares and pick up new cargo.

Commonplace items that were traded throughout the Mediterranean region included olives, olive oil, salted fish, nails, timber, coins, perfumes, palm oil, lamp oil, liniments, medicines, cloth, linen, wine, mustard, pickled foods, vinegar, beans/legumes, wheat, flour, precious metals and gems, powders, and sulfur. The Phoenicians, Egyptians, and Mesopotamians all utilized clay/earthenware jugs called *amphorae* to transport goods. Amphorae were sealed with pine tar and stowed on ships. Amphorae, however, eventually gave way to wood barrels as transport vessels. Fifth-century Greek historian Herodotus believed that Sumerian traders used the first barrels made from palm wood to move goods to the Harappan civilization that dwelled in the Indus River Valley.

Barrel making became prevalent in ancient Gaul, a large area that encompassed present-day Luxembourg, Belgium, France, northern Italy, and most of Switzerland. Those who made cylindrical wood vessels called "barrels" were referred to as *cuparius* because barrels themselves were known as *cupals*. In English, that translates to "cooper." Today, anyone named Cooper or Hooper is likely descended from this ancient line of craftsmen.

The Amphora vs. Wood Barrel Debate

So, what is a barrel? Barrels are cylindrical and hollow containers formed from wood planks, known as *staves*, that are fastened together by metal, twine, or wooden hoops, making them watertight. Barrels are shaped like wheels for a simple and practical reason: ease of movement when they are filled. Barrels are round so that one man could fill the hold of commercial ship simply by rolling the barrels up a plank and onto the deck of the ship. Barrels were also preferred over amphorae by shippers because if the ship sank, barrels were more likely to float, thereby saving at least a portion of the cargo. Amphorae, made from clay, usually sank like stones. Wood barrels largely replaced clay amphorae by the second century BCE. As trade exploded from Asia to Europe, and as shipping lanes became crowded with commercial vessels in the Mediterranean Sea, barrel making grew in importance.

Storing beverages in wood barrels accomplishes two biochemical things:

1. Affords gradual and steady contact with oxygen
2. Imparts various chemical compounds to the stored liquid that alter the character, often for the better (softening, rounding, coloring, deepening of aromatic properties)

Palm wood, the first wood variety used for cooperage, was very hard and not easy to bend and was saturated with resins/oils/sap. Oak is essentially pure wood, relatively free of resins, which are more prevalent in northern hemisphere genera, such as pine/cedar, palm, maple, redwood, elm, birch, acacia, and chestnut. Oak, a hard wood, became the wood of choice for coopers, perhaps influenced by shipbuilders, who easily bent oak when the staves were heated over open-pit fires. Curved planks were used to form the hulls of boats.

Types of Oak
American White Oak: Quercus Alba (White) and Quercus Garryana (Common)
Quercus garryana comes mainly from Oregon. Quercus alba comes from forests in Minnesota, Missouri, Indiana, and Wisconsin. Quercus alba is the favored type by the beverage industry. American white oak character is dense, yet wide grain, fast growing, with a low degree of tannins that impart attributes of sweetness, vanilla, coconut, dill, and spice. American white oak is more intensely flavored, denser than French because it has four times the amount of lactones but fewer tannins.

French Oak: Quercus Petraea (White) and Quercus Robur (Common)
More defined by forest than American oak, which is regional identified by the state.
Forests of central France: Allier, Nevers, Tronçais (Quercus petraea)
Forest of northeast France: Vosges (Quercus petraea)
Forest southwest/central France, east of Cognac: Limousin (Quercus robur)
QP and QR character features: Tight grain, medium-fast growing, relatively low degree of tannins, less dense than American oak and imparts attributes of medium sweetness, lots of vanilla, silky texture, toasted almond, peaches, kiwi, and jasmine. French oak is tighter grained and therefore less watertight than American oak. French oak composition obliges French coopers to split oak along the grain. Since French oak must be split by hand, only 20 to 25 percent of the oak tree can be utilized. American oak trees use twice as much oak volume and are therefore less costly. French oak is normally open-air seasoned for twenty-four to thirty-six months in wood yards.

Slavonian Oak: Northeast Croatia (Quercus robur and Quercus petraea)
Hungarian Oak: Quercus robur and Quercus petraea
Russian Oak: Quercus robur and Quercus petraea
Slavonian, Hungarian, and Russian oaks are utilized for larger storage vats, or tanks, that can be reused many times. Eastern European oak characteristics include tight grain, low tannins, and low aromatics.

What Occurs Inside the Barrel

Maturing anything in barrels comes down to one consideration: **surface area to volume ratio**. Smaller barrels have higher SA-to-VR and vice versa, so barrel size is crucial. Storage or maturation of a potable liquid in oak is all about making sure that the liquid has direct contact with the oak surface. Smaller barrels "convert" liquids quicker due entirely to higher surface area to volume ratio, meaning aging and conversion to matured liquids happens faster. A typical wine barrel is 55 to 59 gallons or 225 liters US and Europe. The Bordeaux variety of 59 gallons developed originally because the French government taxed wine producers on all barrels larger than that size.

Evaporation/climatic issues/absorption

The "angel's share" is the natural evaporation amount of barreled liquid per annum, meaning, the percentage of loss due to natural evaporation. In low-humidity climates, angel's share is mostly water. In high-humidity climates, angel's share is mostly alcohol. The difference between aging in the tropics, for example, as opposed to Scotland or Ireland is staggering. Evaporation in Scotland and Ireland is 2 to 3 percent per year while in tropical and subtropical climates, evaporation can be as high as 10 to 12 percent per year.

Alcohol expands in heat/humidity and contracts in cool temperatures

In expansion, the alcohol invades the wood to deeper levels; when cooler, the alcohol contracts, withdrawing from the wood. The release of alcohol/ethanol into the environment causes a dark-colored fungus, called *baudoinia compniacensis,* to grow on walls, doors, ceilings, all exterior surfaces.

Placement in a storage warehouse/cellar

Because heat rises, rows of barrels closer to the warehouse floor are generally in a cooler zone than higher rows closer to ceiling. Beverages in higher reaches of the warehouse tend to mature faster than ones in lower reaches. Open-air warehouse barrels have cyclical aging tenures dictated by climatic cycles while those in controlled-climate structures mature evenly. Is one placement better than the other? No. Just different. Dirt floors are preferred because dirt floors help maintain steadier humidity levels and are frequently watered down to promote more humidity, which keeps the barrels more watertight.

Duration of time in barrel

On average, following the first year of maturation in a new oak barrel, 33 percent of chemical properties are leeched out. By end of second year, 50 percent are leeched out. Every year of usage means a lessening of oak impact until barrels just become storage vessels after roughly fifteen years of continuous maturation.

Barrels that age straight bourbon are plentiful because by law they are utilized only once
Ex-bourbon barrels are in wide use from Ireland (whiskey) and Scotland (whisky) to the Caribbean region (rum) to Mexico (tequila). The advantages are manifold. Ex-bourbon barrels are pre-seasoned and therefore the roughest compounds are already leeched out. They are readily available and therefore more reasonable than French oak barrels, sherry butts (barrels), or port pipes (barrels).

Toasting and Charring
Toasting barrels probably started by accident in some cooperage in ancient Gaul. The idea was likely to either soften the staves for bending or to rid the wood of pests. When the resultant wine was tasted by the receiver on the other end of the commercial transaction, they were likely startled at how much better the aged wine was in a toasted barrel than that from a non-toasted barrel. Wine barrels are usually toasted while many barrels used for aging spirits, like whiskey, are more deeply charred.

Barrel reusage
Scraping the interior of used barrels to dispense with deposits rejuvenates the interior. Re-toasting or re-charring the interior is popular to prolong usage time.

Wine barrels
    Toast 1: Moderate surface toast/barely seared.
    Toast 2: Heavy toast/light char—1/64-inch to 1/32-inch depth.

Bourbon whiskey barrel charring USA
    Level 1: Light char/heavy toast—1/32-inch depth.
    Level 2: Medium char—1/16-inch depth.
    Level 3: Medium to heavy char—1/16-inch depth; tightly spaced alligator cracking appears.
    Level 4: Heavy char—1/16-inch to 1/8-inch depth; wide-spaced alligator cracking/sugars caramelize (a.k.a. red layer).
    Level 5: Craft distillers very heavy char—1/8-inch depth; peeling of alligator skin/sugars caramelize.

Conclusion
Maturing beverage alcohol in oak barrels is a major part of production and influences the final products that we all enjoy to a significant degree.

A NOTE ON SUGGESTED RETAIL PRICES

THE LISTED BOTTLE PRICES REFLECT THE YEAR IN WHICH THE REVIEW WAS PUBLISHED. THEY MAY VARY FROM CURRENT PRICES.

THE WORLD'S WHISKEYS

All whiskeys produced the world over are made up of a trio of fundamental base materials: grain, yeast, and water. On the surface this sounds like the ingredients for baking bread. Or, for that matter, beer. For good reason. Grain, which is sometimes malted, yeast, and water are the constituents of both bread and beer. Maybe that's why some whiskeys own bread-like, doughy, or yeasty aromatic and taste qualities.

But with just three primary ingredients, why is whiskey such a complicated beverage category? The whiskey category's wide latitude of types from various regions of the globe is best explained through a half-dozen pivotal factors that influence the telltale characteristics:

First, the choice of grain(s), meaning that specific kinds of grains (rye, wheat, corn a.k.a. maize, barley, oats, spelt) create specific varieties of aromas and tastes that are considered germane to certain subcategories. To illustrate, straight bourbon whiskey is sweeter than, say, single malt Scotch whisky because corn contains more sugar in its makeup than does barley.

Second, the management and selection of oak barrels, in terms of barrel variety and the duration of the maturation period. Most distillers will tell you that the period of oak barrel aging and the variety and history of the barrel influence the aroma and taste of whiskey by 60 percent to 80 percent.

Third, the origin, quality, and preservation of the water source. Yes, water is a key element, in that, even though whiskeys are fermented first and then distilled, water can and does affect the final outcome and is why so many distilleries fiercely protect their water sources.

Fourth, the terroir effect, if any, on the whiskey, meaning the environmental influence of the whiskey's place of origin. This is a controversial point, but there can be a strong case made for certain whiskeys being directly influenced by the location of the distillery or, more importantly, the aging warehouses.

Fifth, the variety of distillation utilized, meaning customary, labor-intensive, batch-by-batch pot still or efficient column still distillation or even a blend of both. This key factor is often misunderstood not only by the drinking public but by beverage tradespeople as well. One method isn't better than the other. They merely provide different types of unaged spirit that eventually become whiskey.

And sixth, the whiskey production laws and standards of the originating nation or region.

These half-dozen aspects are crucial to each whiskey type's underlying personality and degree of quality. The best way to understand the centuries-old universe of whiskey is to take a tour of the world's foremost whiskey-making nations. In addition to recognizing the six factors of quality, it's likewise good to understand a few other fundamental facts. For instance, the word "whiskey" is derived from the ancient Gaelic term for "water of life," *uisge beatha*. Making matters somewhat confusing is how different nations prefer to spell "whiskey." Ireland and the USA, with some exceptions like Maker's Mark bourbon, prefer the employment of the *e*, while Canada, Japan, and Scotland drop the *e*. The plurals then become "whiskeys" for whiskey and "whiskies" for whisky. When referring to the worldwide industry, I choose to use "whiskey."

WHISKY–SCOTLAND

The idea of creating *F. Paul Pacult's Spirit Journal* bloomed in 1990 after I started writing about Scotch whisky for the *New York Times Sunday Magazine* in late 1989. The huge success of *Sunday Magazine* special sections on Scotch and Scotland and eventually other spirits compelled me to shift my focus from writing and teaching about wine to writing about distilled spirits. After I'd written a handful of *Times Sunday Magazine* articles, my old second-floor office on First Avenue in Manhattan was littered with bottles of cognac, bourbon, Armagnac, rum, tequila, Irish whiskey, vodka, gin, and Scotch. Distillers, who for the first time felt that they had an American journalist who was willing to write on a regular basis about their beverages, sent me scores of distillates. In the fading moments of the 1980s, wine was the uncontested adult beverage darling of the media. Spirits, by contrast, were viewed as passé or, worse, as the crude distant cousin of wine. But while over the past quarter century we've striven at *F. Paul Pacult's Spirit Journal* to supply ample coverage of all spirit categories, I admit that when the time comes for me to review the new Scotches we've received for each quarterly edition, I silently delight at the task, usually saving them for last as a sort of reward.

The reasons for my fascination with Scotch whisky are numerous and complex; they are simultaneously deeply personal and professional. Besides being the topic of my first professional foray into spirits journalism, I have come to love Scotland, both the reality and the myth, its hospitable people, and its breathtaking landscape. My enthusiasm was immediate on my first research trip to Scotland in the spring of 1989 and has in the subsequent twenty-eight trips never waned or flagged. Yes, I take particular delight in visiting my friends and distilling colleagues in lovely Cognac and bucolic Armagnac, exhilarating Jalisco, enchanting Ireland, charming Kentucky and Tennessee, the addictive Caribbean, plus California, New York's Hudson Valley, and other locales.

But the landscape of Scotch whisky has changed dramatically since 1989, when all one would see in a liquor store were a few blended Scotches, like Cutty Sark, Black & White, J&B, Dewar's, and maybe Johnnie Walker Red Label, and possibly two or three single malts, typically Glenfiddich and The Glenlivet. Today, stroll into any Binny's in the Chicago area or Park Avenue Liquor in New York City or Spec's in Houston, and their shelves are lined top to bottom with legions of blended Scotch, the occasional blended malt, but almost always with rows of single malt Scotches from every whisky district, Highland or island, vintage and with age statements, cask strength and single barrel, wood finished and non-chill filtered, distillery, and merchant bottlings. The category is exhausting and exhaustive in 2021.

Scotch Whisky Defined

Scotch whisky is the grain-based alcoholic beverage **made only in Scotland**, using the three primary ingredients of yeast, grain (barley, corn, or wheat, depending on the whisky type), and water that is first fermented, then distilled. In order to be lawfully called Scotch whisky, the fermented liquid must be distilled at less than 94.8 percent alcohol; must be matured in oak barrels of less than 700 liters in size; must be aged exclusively within the borders of Scotland for no less than three years in an excise warehouse; must have no substance added except water or plain caramel coloring (for appearance adjustment only, not flavoring); and must be offered at a minimum alcoholic strength of 40 percent.

Types and Classifications

Since the invention of the continuous still in the late 1820s, there have been **two distinct varieties** of raw whisky made in Scotland. **Single malt Scotch whisky** is made in one or more individual batches only from malted barley at a single distillery using the traditional, labor intensive, onion-shaped, copper pot still method. **Grain whisky** is made in large volumes from corn or wheat in towering, multi-plated, cylindrical, stainless steel stills via the industrial, but efficient, continuous distillation process. Single malt whiskies are complex, intensely flavorful, and aromatic while grain whiskies are more ethereal, crisp, and light.

These two fundamental types of Scotch whisky, in turn, create the five classifications of Scotch:

Single malt Scotch whisky is produced from 100 percent malted barley whisky of one distillery, distilled in a pot still, and labeled under the originating distillery name;

Single grain Scotch whisky made at one distillery, is distilled either in pot stills or a column still and is comprised of malted barley, with or without whole grains of other malted or unmalted cereals, like wheat or corn, but does not comply with the definition of single malt whisky;

Blended malt Scotch whisky (a.k.a. vatted malt) is made from 100 percent malted barley whiskies produced at two or more malt distilleries;

Blended Scotch whisky is comprised of a combination of any number of single malt and grain whiskies and labeled under a brand name rather than a distillery name, for example, Dewar's, J&B, Cutty Sark;

Blended grain Scotch whisky is a marriage of single grain whiskies that have been distilled at more than one grain distillery.

Scotch Whisky Beginnings

Some historians speculate that Christian monks exported the system of distillation from Ireland to Argyll, Scotland, by the fourteenth century, possibly earlier. The initial substantiation of its existence on the island of Britain, however, didn't occur until the waning years of the fifteenth century. A Scottish Exchequer Roll recorded in 1494 that a clerical member, Friar John Cor, of the Benedictine Lindores Abbey in Fife, made a rather sizable purchase of barley malt in the amount of "viii bolls" for the purpose of making "aquavitae." Since a boll amounted to 140 pounds, eight bolls of malted barley topped the scales at well over half a ton. As writer Michael Brander, author of *The Original Scotch* (1975, p. 5) states, ". . . it is clear at once that this was no small operation. Half a ton of malt producing probably in the region of seventy gallons of spirit was not required for private consumption. Obviously the monastic establishment . . . was distilling on no mean scale . . ."

By the middle of the sixteenth century, public perceptions of *uisge beatha* had begun to change. In addition to *uisge beatha* being widely employed as a medicinal liquid, it started likewise to be viewed as a social libation. Legislative initiatives introduced in the Scottish Parliament in 1555 and 1579 suggest that the use of malted barley for the production of *uisge beatha* had greatly accelerated across Scotland in the second half of the sixteenth century. The two Acts each addressed, in part, the mandatory shifting of malted barley use for making bread and brown ale and away from the distilling of *uisge beatha*. Poor harvests and subsequent food shortages were the reasons given by Parliamentarians for the restrictive legislation.

Doubtless, the staunchly independent Highland and island Scots scoffed at the dictates of a governing body with which they felt no connection. These initial sixteenth-century Parliamentary edicts were the first of what would eventually become an onerous litany of regulation and taxation measures concerning distilling that would give rise to an unprecedented era of illegal distilling and smuggling that wouldn't settle down until the mid-1820s.

The Scots' first generations of *uisge beathas* were distant shadows of what was to come. After all, the farmer-distillers were unschooled, and the conditions, materials, and equipment were unsophisticated and frequently unhygienic. Production was minute in comparison to modern times because the era's pot stills ranged in size from a scant four to five gallons only up to, rarely, fifty gallons. Stills were small so they could be quickly disassembled and hidden from excisemen looking to either shut them down or tax them.

At their finest, Scotland's early whiskies were probably raw, unaged, pungent, high-alcohol spirits that provided a quick buzz and a brief respite from the day in, day out hardships and tedium of Middle Ages Scotland. At their worst, they were bad tasting, fierce brews. Because of the lack of regulation, alcohol poisoning was common and sometimes resulted in unpleasant deaths. Scotch whisky's authentic trendsetters, superstar personalities, and innovators didn't begin appearing until the late 1600s (Ferintosh, Scotland's first legal distillery, started distilling on a large scale in the 1670s) and early 1700s.

Production

Grain, water, and yeast. These are the three easily obtainable raw materials that constitute any whiskey made anywhere in the world, including the most prized and popular whiskey of all, Scotch whisky. At first blush, the value of this trio of commonplace substances seems modest. Though humble in worth, these individual ordinary elements become complex and extraordinary once they are carefully combined and processed.

Customarily, barley has been the requisite grain for making malt whisky in Scotland. This is not because barley was the only grain that grew well in Scotland's difficult, sometimes atrocious, climate. Oats, rye, and wheat grew, as well. Farmer-distillers in the early period of distillation selected an ancient strain of barley that had four rows of spikelets, called *bere*, as their grain of choice. An alternative variety was two-row barley, which made smoother ales and whiskies according to some distillers, but *bere* proved to be first among equals. This was for two reasons. *Bere's* reliably large crop yields in poor soils and rainy climates, and its early ripening tendency accommodates farmers. Before being milled, the barley is allowed to partially germinate, thereby stimulating the grain's natural starches. This partial germination breaks down the cell walls and is called "malting." Next, the malted barley is dried in kilns to halt the growth of the natural starches. The dried malted barley is then ground into powdery grist.

Water from a trusted source, such as a burn (stream) or a spring, is boiled and mixed with the malted barley grist in large metal vessels called "mash tuns." Mashing converts the starches into maltose, a natural sugar. The soupy result is a walnut-colored, sweet-smelling liquid called "wort." The wort is pumped into another metal tank, the "washback," and yeast is injected. The introduction of yeast triggers fermentation. Over forty-eight hours the innate sugar—the maltose—is transformed into carbon dioxide and alcohol. Fermentation changes the base materials into a low-alcohol (7 to 8 percent), fragrant "wash" that is, for all intents and purposes, beer.

The "wash beer" is then moved to a kettle-like copper pot still, the "wash still," and is set to boil. During the tumultuous first distillation, the vapors are forced to pass through a cold, coiled pipe, or condenser, a.k.a., "worm." Since alcohol boils at 173.1 degrees Fahrenheit and water boils at 212 degrees Fahrenheit, the wash's alcohol vaporizes well before the water, causing a separation of properties. The alcohol vapors return to liquid form while traveling through the icy cold worm. The moderate alcohol liquid (20 to 24 percent alcohol), or "low wines," is pumped into the "spirits still" for its second distillation for further purification and to elevate the alcohol level. Following the second distillation, the condensed vapors become a high-alcohol (70 to 72 percent), limpid distillate, the "spirit." (*Note*: Auchentoshan in the Scottish Lowlands does three distillations.)

After the second distillation, the biochemically altered base ingredients smell, feel, and taste like anything but simple water, grain, and yeast. Through malting, mashing, fermentation, and double distillation in pot stills, the grain, water, and yeast unite to become one liquid substance: pure grain alcohol. The resultant transparent-as-rainwater liquid of two distillations in a pot still is deceptively compelling. When drawn fresh off the still, virgin spirit smells strikingly similar to a damp garden in June. Dewy scents of fresh flowers, green vegetation, and pine rush at you one moment, then yeasty odors of bread dough or dry breakfast cereal tickle your attention the next. The potent, 70 to 72 percent alcohol, immature fluid burns the tongue initially if tasted undiluted. But as the taste buds adjust to the virgin alcohol's racy nature, layers of ripe fruit and grain flavors emerge. Even at this nascent stage, one can project how the razor-edged charms of the spirit can with maturation, mellowing, and time be transformed into an alcoholic beverage of unusual virtuosity, nuance, and complexity.

What Is "Cask Strength"?
Cask strength means a whisky that is undiluted and bottled straight from the barrel. The majority of Scotch whiskies are reduced in strength from roughly 62 to 65 percent barrel strength down to the standard 40 to 46 percent bottle strength for the purpose of being more palatable to the majority of imbibers. Cask strength whiskies offer bigger aromas and flavors since there is no water dilution, unless you want to dilute them yourself. Many drinkers feel that cask strength whiskies are more authentic due to the fact that there is one less point of human intervention in their process.

How Are Blended Scotches Different from Single Malt Scotches?
Blending whiskies in Scotland has been around in earnest since the 1860s and 1870s when

popular merchants of the day in Edinburgh, Glasgow, Aberdeen, and London bought whiskies-in-barrel from malt distillers and grain whisky from grain producers, and then aged, blended, and bottled the whiskies under their own banner. Merchants like John Dewar, Johnnie Walker, the Chivas Brothers, Arthur Bell, George Ballantine, John Begg, and James Buchanan forever altered the Scotch whisky landscape with their blended Scotch creations. They were visionaries. Because of them, Scotch whisky became a global phenomenon by the late 1800s as the British Empire expanded its reach.

The fortunate marriage of idiosyncratic single malts with the lighter, more malleable grain whiskies produced in the Scottish Lowlands offered drinkers the chance to enjoy the finest spirits in the world at affordable prices and with the assurance of consistency, which is something that malt whisky distillers couldn't provide since their output was so small and fragmented. Today, blended Scotch comprises over 90 percent of all Scotch made and is lorded over by large companies like Bacardi, Pernod Ricard, Diageo, and more. Producers of grain whiskies are centered in the following locations: Cameronbridge in Fife (owned by Diageo), North British in Edinburgh (Diageo/Edrington), Strathclyde in Glasgow (Pernod Ricard), Invergordon in Easter Ross (Emperador), Girvan in South Ayrshire (William Grant), Loch Lomond in Alexandria (Loch Lomond Distillery), and Glen Turner/Starlaw in Livingston (La Martiniquaise). Yet, much to my surprise with all the data that's available through so many avenues, there remains a cloud of inferiority, a boneheaded prejudice about blended Scotch that is simply unwarranted. The reality is, it's harder to create a Scotch whisky blend than it is a single malt. It takes an amazing amount of sensory skill for a master blender to create one whisky from as many as fifty to one hundred whiskies and have it be consistent from batch to batch.

Here's my final word on this topic: I consider blended Scotches like Johnnie Walker Platinum, Johnnie Walker Gold Label Reserve, Cutty Sark Prohibition Edition, Dewar's 18 Year Old, and Chivas Regal Gold Signature 18 to be as good as most single malts one can buy.

SMSW = Single Malt Scotch Whisky

Aberfeldy 12 Year Old Highland SMSW 40% abv, $45.
Brilliant topaz/amber color; excellent purity. Owns an accessible, pleasing fruitcake opening nose that boasts of aromas like dried pineapple, coconut, kiwi, and apricot, along with waxy, cereal grain scents; secondary sniffs pick up more of the malted barley presence and thereby turns a touch drier than the riper first whiffs. Entry is gently sweet, polite, medium bodied, fruity, and muesli-like; midpalate reinforces the entry findings, adding the astringency of oaky tannin, which balances the fruitiness. An appealing entry-level malt and, as such, an undemanding place to start one's malt journey.
2016 Rating: ★ ★ ★/Recommended

Aberlour 12 Year Old Non-Chill Filtered Speyside SMSW 48% abv, $55.

Attractive burnt-orange/copper color; flawless, sediment-free appearance. The full-on barley malt frontline notes are like shortbread and cake batter, with keenly dry supporting nuances of brewer's yeast, beer/wort, ginger root, birch beer; later sniffs following more air contact bring out traces of grape jam, sherry, cigarette ash, raisin bread. Entry is significantly sweeter and rounder than the dusty dry bouquet as the sherry cask impact kicks in with full measure; midpalate features the sherry influence in spades as the taste profile shifts from fruity to raisin- and prune-like. Aftertaste is very long, succulent, toasty, and obvious in its sherry cask usage. A big-hearted, mood-on-its-sleeve malt whisky that would never be accused of being subtle but that's its virtue.

2015 Rating: ★ ★ ★ ★/Highly Recommended

Aberlour 16 Year Old Double Cask Matured Speyside SMSW 40% abv, $90.

Bright cinnamon/ginger color; unblemished clarity. There's a noticeable orchard fruit juiciness in the initial whiffs after the pour that I find downright charming in this malt; later sniffs encounter deeper, grainier fragrances, including graham cracker, spice cake, cinnamon bun. Entry is unabashedly sweet, maple-like, buttery, creamy, peppery, prune-like, fig-like; midpalate mirrors the entry sensations to a tee, adding pecan pie, pipe tobacco, campfire ash, oloroso sherry. Aftertaste highlights the maple and sherry aspects as the taste profile crescendos in the extended finish. A terrific example of the bigger, brawnier side of Speyside.

2015 Rating: ★ ★ ★ ★/Highly Recommended

Aberlour A'Bunadh Non-Chill Filtered Cask Strength Matured in Spanish Oloroso Sherry Butts, Batch No. 50, Speyside SMSW 59.6% abv, $85.

Gorgeous henna/deep-russet color; sediment-free purity. This opening aroma is so over-stuffed with attributes that it's almost impossible to flag them all, but here goes: toasted malt, serious sawdust/wood plank, gum, dry stone, loose leaf tobacco, cigar box, black pepper-corn, clove, mace, kid leather glove, praline, nougat, candied almond, dates, figs—this is an aromatic banquet that defies adequate description, though I've tried my best. Entry explodes on the tongue in flavor tsunamis of sherry oak, honey wheat toast, cigar tobacco, maple syrup, dark caramel, fudge, high-cocoa-content dark chocolate, chocolate-covered raisins; midpalate features all of the above plus the welcome warmth of the cask strength, which doesn't annihilate the taste buds as much as it cradles them. Concludes brawny, robust, honey- and maple-like as the abv calms down, allowing the sweet, succulent flavors to shine. Truly magnificent.

2015 Rating: ★ ★ ★ ★ ★/Highest Recommendation

anCnoc 12 Year Old Highland SMSW 43% abv, $53.

Amber color; ideal purity. First, I notice a slightly salty/saltine cracker aroma, then I pick up notes of allspice, mace, and fried egg/egg yolk; later sniffs detect more of the malted barley/breakfast cereal thrust that's off-dry, lightly toasted, and candied. Entry is chewy in texture, sweeter than the aroma in a sugar-cookie manner; midpalate reflects the entry impressions, adding light touches of toffee, fresh honey, and malted milk ball. Finishes medium long, roasted, and agreeably friendly. A pleasing, straightforward inland beginner malt.

2018 Rating: ★ ★ ★/Recommended

anCnoc 18 Year Old Highland SMSW 46% abv, $149.

Caramel color; unblemished clarity. This aroma is 180 degrees different from that of the affable 12 year old, primarily due to a substantial increase in oak-driven woodiness/sappiness, which expresses itself in the earthy, furniture polish–like, lumberyard aromas of resin, tree bark, and sawdust; later whiffs encounter less assertive scents of unsalted butter, vegetable oil, newly tanned leather, and green, uncured tobacco. Entry exhibits candy-shop flavors of nougat, almond paste, walnut butter, cinnamon, clove, and marzipan; midpalate is malty, candied, bittersweet, and like roasted grain. Aftertaste is medium long, toffee-like, honeyed, and a touch smoky and pipe tobacco–like.

2018 Rating: ★ ★ ★/Recommended

anCnoc 24 Year Old Highland SMSW 46% abv, $170.

Tawny-brown color; impeccable purity. This atypical opening aroma is all about arid landscape, dry earth, stone, and toasted grain; further aeration brings out the fine graininess that's like unsweetened breakfast cereal and whole wheat bread. Entry flavors explode on the tongue as gigantic, sweet fruit, and Asian cooking tastes envelope the palate in waves of hoisin, soy sauce, white raisins, dried yellow plums, and apricots; midpalate follows up with more nuanced tastes that highlight the Asian cuisine aspects while intensifying the ripe, dried fruits, thereby creating a succulence that is beguiling and irresistibly luscious. Aftertaste is unabashedly sweet, savory, slightly spiced, and tropical fruit ripe, lasting long.

2018 Rating: ★ ★ ★ ★/Highly Recommended

anCnoc blas Highland SMSW 54% abv, $75.

Old gold color; free of sediment. I like the initial ethereal whiffs of light toffee, malted milk ball candy, poppy seed, and gentian; secondary sniffs encounter spicy, peppery aromas that are mature and vivid. Entry is solid in structure, moderately oily in texture, tobacco-like, and vegetal; midpalate features flavors of sweet malt, brown sugar, bacon fat, pineapple sage, and geranium. Aftertaste is medium long, pleasantly fat in texture, and deeply malty. I rode the three star/four star fence a bit, then the delightfully malty aftertaste put me firmly in four star territory.

2018 Rating: ★ ★ ★ ★/Highly Recommended

anCnoc Cutter Highland SMSW 46% abv, $79.

Produced at Knockdhu Distillery at 20.5 ppm (phenols, the chemical compounds within peat smoke). The sauvignon blanc–like, straw-yellow color catches the light and is quite pretty; unblemished and sediment-free. The lively peat-reek is apparent right from the initial whiffs after the pour, and there are also background scents of lemon zest, new leather, pine cone, and wood shavings; following more air contact, the smoky peat grows in intensity in a comforting campfire-smoke manner that's kind of tobacco-like, salty, sweet, and "green." Entry mirrors the bouquet, especially in the sweet smokiness that's now reminiscent of pipe tobacco and hickory-smoked pork sausages, all of which I find appealing; midpalate highlights the smoky sweetness that is now like brown sugar and saltwater taffy. Finishes medium long, less smoky than the aroma or midpalate, and far more settled and calmer in

demeanor. There are many fine attributes here, but the core beneath the peatiness seems a little hollow, though not enough for dismissal.
2017 Rating: ★★★/Recommended

anCnoc Rascan Highland SMSW 46% abv, $85.

Citrine color; superb purity. I pick up early fragrances of salted fish, olive brine, creosote, dill pickle, dill, and cigarette ash; later inhalations after more aeration detect hearty aromas of peat-reek, fireplace embers, and sooty chimney. Entry is lively, off-dry, intensely malty, even a dash citrusy (lemon peel, lemongrass), all of which I find delightful; midpalate features as much of the malted barley as the wood smoke, lemongrass, and citrus rind, as this single malt finds a charming balance from among its range of taste elements. Finishes cleanly, with a vivacious aftertaste that's acidic, tart, lightly smoked, and fruity. anCnoc at its snappy, zesty, peated finest.
2018 Rating: ★★★★/Highly Recommended

Ardbeg An Oa Islay SMSW 46.6% abv, $60.

Dandelion/corn-yellow color; spotless purity. Wow, this first aroma briskly ascends into the nasal cavity in potent waves of seaweed, Lapsang souchong tea, dry stones, road tar, smoked bacon, and cigarette ashes; secondary inhalations detect slightly milder, calmer notes of freshly dug peat, kippers, sooty campfire smoke, and anchovy. Entry is crackling with wood fire smoke, seared meat off the BBQ, tomato sauce, and caramelized onion; midpalate tastes include earthy, mossy, sautéed mushroom–like tastes that are woodsy and off-dry due primarily to the BBQ sauce–like underpinning flavor that, with time, comes to be the dominant in-mouth factor, leading ultimately to the heavily smoked, ash-like, carbolic aftertaste. As with all Ardbegs, An Oa provides an exhilarating sensory journey.
2017 Rating: ★★★★/Highly Recommended

Ardbeg Auriverdes Islay SMSW 49.9% abv, $100.

Only 1,100 cases available globally. True-to-Ardbeg color of old gold/amber; spotless purity. The opening nosing passes encounter enticing scents of smoldering campfire, kippers, lemon peel, baked nectarine, baked pineapple, tobacco leaf—an amazing array of out-front odors; second-stage inhalations after further air contact detect more subtle versions of the opening fragrances, but with notes of pine needle, asparagus, bay leaf, and coffee bean added for good measure. Entry is all about road tar, creosote, pipe tobacco, mocha flavors that are oily, keenly peppery/spicy, oddly floral; midpalate tastes put the spotlight on tobacco, wood smoke, smoked fish. Finishes absurdly extended, oily, leaner than some Ardbegs, but lusciously spicy all the same.
2014 Rating: ★★★★/Highly Recommended

Ardbeg Corryvreckan Islay SMSW 57.1% abv, $90.

Amber/bronze color; impeccable purity. Early sniffs detect traces of green tea, loose tobacco leaf, grain kernel, and graham cracker aromas; later inhalations unearth oily scents of furniture polish, oak resin, pickle brine, and kippers. Entry is firmly structured, oily, aridly dry, astringent, tannic, and grainy; midpalate offers greater depth of flavor, as the taste profile expands to include dried fruits (apricot, apple), winter holiday fruitcake, candied nuts, and cinnamon. Aftertaste is slightly honeyed, woody, and piquant. The elevated abv is never an issue since the flavor integration is so complete.

2018 Rating: ★ ★ ★ ★/Highly Recommended

Ardbeg Dark Cove Islay SMSW 46.5% abv, $70.

Mature color of brilliant amber/saffron; excellent clarity. First aromatic impressions are of dark chocolate, oloroso sherry, dates, figs, and black raisins; secondary notations are of marzipan, praline, nougat, fudge, as the dried fruits settle down. Entry is rich, cocoa-like, chocolatey, cigar-like, moderately smoky, with deft touches of iodine and sea breeze; mid-palate is deep, complex, rich in texture, caramelized onion–like, savory, and bittersweet. Finishes long and fathomless, toasted and bittersweet.

2016 Rating: ★ ★ ★ ★/Highly Recommended

Ardbeg Perpetuum Islay SMSW 47.4% abv, $100.

The otherwise pretty flax/pale-gold color is marred by too much sediment, which shouldn't be there. Opening aromatics are textbook Ardbeg, as the ashtray-like smokiness/peatiness runs into a citrusy character that then crashes with a salted fish/kipper component that circles back with the smoldering road tar/cigar tobacco, making for a delightful south shore of Islay nasal slugfest; another few minutes of air contact bring up egg cream, egg white, creosote, dying campfire to round out the experience. Entry is pleasingly sweet, malty, smoky, peaty, rich yet delicate; midpalate echoes the entry findings, but discovers a vein of saltiness that had not previously been evident even amidst the bonfires of seaweed. Aftertaste is surprisingly sedate, malty, brown-sugar sweet, and very extended.

2015 Rating: ★ ★ ★ ★ ★/Highest Recommendation

Ardbeg Supernova Committee Release Islay SMSW 55% abv, $160.

Brilliant wheat-field gold color; impeccable purity. Opening aroma is of dying camp-fire, dried sage, nickel, dry earth, drying leaves, seaweed, eucalyptus; secondary whiffs pick up burnt match, iodine, kippers, cigar tobacco, egg whites, brewer's yeast. Entry is vegetal, oily, smoky, charcoal sweet, buttery, salty; midpalate features all of the entry impressions but they are heightened by a honeyed sweetness that suddenly underpins the flavor profile all the way through the lap-it-up finish.

2014 Rating: ★ ★ ★ ★ ★/Highest Recommendation

Ardbeg Ten Islay SMSW 46% abv, $56.

Flax/citron color; excellent purity. I've always admired this peaty, saline, sea breeze–like, highly vegetal, and dill-like opening aroma that's akin to a good-natured slap in the face; next stop is the second nosing passes that bring out more of the campfire smoke, filled ash-tray, malted barley, and iodine/medicine chest than the first whiffs. Entry is round, supple in texture, featuring piquant, slightly prickly tastes of green melon, tobacco leaf, marshmallow, lemon curd, and chamomile; midpalate is toasty, roasted, astringent, acidic, yet nimble, grainy, malty, tart, and crisp all at the same time. Ends dry, lean, narrowly focused, and tobacco-like. Rated four stars in *Kindred Spirits 2* and remains a solid member of the Ardbeg portfolio.

2019 Rating: ★ ★ ★ ★/Highly Recommended

Ardbeg Traigh Bhan 19 Year Old Islay SMSW 46.2% abv, $300.

Like so many Ardbeg expressions, the color is green-gold and olive brine–like; shows pristine clarity. Initial sniffs encounter fragrances akin to saline solution, smoked fish, iodine, medicine chest, and fresh pineapple, the last a curiously attractive characteristic; secondary nosings after more time in the glass find astringent aromas of creosote, oak resin/sap, tropical fruits, cigarette ash, and shoe polish. Entry is lean in texture, deeply salty, nougat-like, and nutty; midpalate is sprightly, salty, peaty, more fresh tobacco–like and green than deeply smoky. This whisky's best moment is the silky, saline, sticky toffee finish.
2020 Rating: ★ ★ ★ ★/Highly Recommended

Ardbeg Uigeadail Islay SMSW 54.2% abv, $80.

Topaz color; totally free of sediment. Wow, up front I get traces of campfire smoke, stewed prunes, cigar tobacco, salted fish, hard-boiled egg, and seaweed aromas that some-how all work together in harmony; secondary inhalations feature heavyweight scents of BBQ sauce, tomatillo, wet cement, cigar smoke, black tea, and chalk. Entry is larger than life, heavily toasted, and charred, yet it's well-mannered and narrowly focused on the peat-reek smokiness; midpalate is this malt's finest moment as all the various taste elements meet at the middle, creating a splendid flavor display that's salty, deeply resiny/oily, creosote-like, smoked fish–like, and very much like Lapsang souchong black tea. Finishes brightly, long, densely smoked, and yet entirely elegant. A classic Ardbeg.
2018 Rating: ★ ★ ★ ★ ★/Highest Recommendation

Auchentoshan American Oak Lowlands SMSW 40% abv, $40.

Fourteen-karat-gold color; superb purity. Initial whiffs detect vibrant malty notes that are desert dry, vegetal, peppery, grainy, earthy; next round of inhalations encounter margin-ally sweeter, mash-like, doughy scents, with a hint of vanilla. Entry is grainy/malty, tangy, rich from the ex-bourbon maple/vanilla aspect; midpalate reflects the entry flavors, add-ing orange peel, light caramel, praline, almond paste. Aftertaste is long, mildly honeyed, peppercorn-like. I like the piquancy and harmonious nature of this Lowlands malt.
2014 Rating: ★ ★ ★ ★/Highly Recommended

Auchentoshan Virgin Oak Lowlands SMSW 46% abv, $130.

Amber/old gold color; some tendrils of sediment seen. I smell linen, fabric, cotton, can-dle wax, parchment in the opening sniffs; later inhalations detect more accentuated aromas of baked pears, cardamom, ginger, milkweed. Entry is sweet yet a touch raw and spirity, even astringent; midpalate shows the class of this Lowlands malt palace (Scotland's only triple distillation distillery) as the taste profile goes for grace, understatement, and a featherlight touch of green apple. Ends on a fruity note that's ripe. Lovely.
2014 Rating: ★ ★ ★ ★/Highly Recommended

Aultmore 12 Year Old Speyside SMSW 46% abv, $45.

Pale-yellow/chardonnay-like color; impeccable clarity. The opening, superficial smell of flaked, dried coconut is remarkable, as is the other, deeper scent of lightly sweetened breakfast cereal; secondary whiffs pick up both fragrances noted in the initial passes and add delicate odors of pear tart, heather honey, and allspice. Entry is gentle, pleasantly sweet,

approachable, silky in its light-to-medium-bodied texture; midpalate is as good-natured as the entry, showing a bit more waxiness, astringency from the oak. Finishes brief in the throat, slightly oily in texture, and drier than the entry. An entry-level, young, and accessible malt.
2016 Rating: ★ ★ ★ /Recommended

Aultmore 18 Year Old Speyside SMSW 46% abv, $n/a

Straw/wheat-field golden color; ideal purity. Right off the crack of the aromatic bat I get ripe orchard fruit fragrances, especially pear and quince, along with distant baking spices such as allspice and nutmeg; in the second passes, the fruit and spices are joined by malted milk balls and sweetened oatmeal/porridge aromas, making for a highly pleasing bouquet. Entry is delightfully sweet and sour, fruity and grainy, piquant, and satiny, with a bit of alcohol feistiness; midpalate sees the flavor components merge into a tangy taste profile that suddenly turns dry, earthy, and a touch baked. Ends on a tangy note that's mineral-like and desert dry. Hadn't expected the midpalate and finish stages to take such a sharp turn into arid landscape territory, away from the ripe pear fruit plumpness of the opening phases.
2020 Rating: ★ ★ ★ /Recommended

Balblair 1983 Highland SMSW 46% abv, $499.

Gamboge color; pristine clarity. This first nosing pass reminds me a bit of the 2005, in that there is clear, uncompromising evidence of malted barley, oak-influenced vanillin and tannin, dried fruits (plums, banana), and lard/fat; later inhalations pick up enhanced scents of pecan pie, almond paste, nougat, candy bar, oatmeal cookies, and buttermilk. Entry is pleasingly chewy in texture, almost fat, with lovely roasted/toasted flavors of marshmallow, sweetened breakfast cereal, bear claw pastry, and brown sugar; midpalate mirrors the entry findings, adding succulent flavors of nougat, praline, and walnut butter. Aftertaste is long, oily, woody, and grainy. A mature single malt that still has plenty of youthful vigor.
2018 Rating: ★ ★ ★ ★ /Highly Recommended

Balblair 1990 Highland SMSW 46% abv, $229.

Deep tawny/mahogany color; flawless purity; visually appealing. Opening sniffs pick up muted aromas of candied peanuts, walnut butter, tomato paste, and cardamom; secondary inhalations after more air contact detect nuances of teak, cherrywood, and cinnamon; this is not a generous, outspoken bouquet by any means and it takes patience to gather the scant aromatic evidence that exists. Entry is nut-like, almost candied, heavily toasted, robust, and spiced with various baking and cooking spices, including nutmeg, clove, bay leaf, cardamom, and cinnamon; midpalate offers round, nearly chewy flavors that are more bittersweet than sweet and like high-cocoa-content dark chocolate and even, to a lesser degree, coffee bean. Aftertaste is perhaps the best stage as the flavors mount, including pipe tobacco, black cherry, BBQ sauce, and tomato paste, and unite in an alluring finish. Still, the flurry of activity in the midpalate and finish aren't enough to earn a fourth rating star.
2018 Rating: ★ ★ ★ /Recommended

Balblair 1999 Highland SMSW 46% abv, $129.

Aureolin color; sediment-free. Smells initially of sawdust, oak plank, green tobacco, and flaxseed oil; later inhalations, following more aeration, encounter subtle notes of mushroom, lichen/moss, forest floor, vegetation, and parchment. Entry is dry, arid, grainy, acidic, and crisp on the tongue, showing little in the way of spice, oak resin, or fat; midpalate shows more oak influence as the taste profile turns more resiny/sap-like, all of which underscores the dry breakfast cereal/graininess. Finishes lean, a little toasty, parched, tart, and angular.

2018 Rating: ★★★/Recommended

Balblair 2005 Highland SMSW 46% abv, $69.

Citron/metallic-gold color; unblemished purity. I immediately get evolved aromatic notes of cocoa bean, dark chocolate, espresso, and Cocoa Puffs breakfast cereal in the opening whiffs; with more air contact, the aroma turns fried bread–like, bacon-y, fudge-like, and rich in malted barley fragrance; it's a pleasing, slightly fat bouquet that I like a lot. Entry echoes the bouquet, in that it is deeply grainy/malty, tending towards sweet, buttered biscuit–like, sausage-like, and plump on the tongue as the lipids (fats) from the oak barrels make their presence known; midpalate turns a bit leaner and more peppery/spicy, and that makes me reach for the fourth rating star because those developments bring balance and harmony to the in-mouth stages. Ends crisp, bittersweet, deeply cereal-like and malty, and just plain delicious.

2018 Rating: ★★★★/Highly Recommended

Ballantine's 12 Year Old Blended Scotch Whisky 40% abv, $25.

Note: Ballantine's is a blend of more than fifty single malts, with Miltonduff and Glenburgie being the primary malts, and at least four grain whiskies.

This Pernod Ricard–owned blended Scotch brand enjoys a wide global audience that annually purchases 6.9 million cases, as of 2017 statistics. Earth yellow color; impeccably pure. There are nuances of baking spice here in the opening whiffs, including vanilla, cinnamon, and mace; later inhalations following more time in the glass expose delicate scents of sweet malted grains, breakfast cereal with fruit, and unsweetened coconut; in all, an understated, polite bouquet. Entry is gently sweet and honeyed, with background flavors of caramel corn, vanilla extract, cake frosting, and honey wheat bread; midpalate provides a toasty, slightly roasted nutty flavor profile that's more bakery/pastry-like than candy-shop sweet. Ends longer and crisper in the throat than I expected, providing a grainy, yeasty, nutty, and dry finale.

2018 Rating: ★★★/Recommended

Ballantine's 17 Year Old Blended Scotch Whisky 40% abv, $100.

Amber/orange-peel color; perfect clarity. Offers tannic, edgy, oaky, and resiny opening aromas that are lean and tree bark–like; secondary passes pick up more of the cereal grain and barley-influenced maltiness provided by the single malt components of the blend; overall, however, to my surprise, I find this nose lacking in character. Entry is clean, acidic, leaner than I recalled, and metallic/earthy in the first tastes; midpalate is where the best virtues are noticed as the creamy malt character comes more into play, featuring toasted cereal, wheat bread, and brown sugar flavors that salvage the in-mouth phase. Aftertaste is savory, silky in the throat, keenly malty, and elegant.

2018 Rating: ★★★/Recommended

Ballantine's Finest Blended Scotch Whisky 40% abv, $16.

Sandy-brown color; sediment-free clarity. The malty, pumpernickel-like opening aroma is pleasing in its buttery, graham cracker–like suppleness; more aeration stimulates added scents of nutmeg, peanut butter, tomatillo, and clove. Entry is subtle, deeply crisp, spicy (black pepper), and a touch like marasca cherry; midpalate turns more to the grain whisky influence and away from the alluring spice and fruit aspects as the taste profile suddenly goes flat and waxy. Finishes short, mineral-like, and mediocre. Up to the midpalate stage, I was pondering an upgrade to three stars but the slippage in quality at midpalate and then the aftertaste kept the assessment at two stars.

2018 Rating: ★ ★/Not Recommended

Balvenie Caribbean Cask 14 Year Old Speyside SMSW 43% abv, $60.

Harvest gold color; superb clarity. I find aromatic hints of sprouted malt, shortbread, and floor maltings in the first whiffs after the pour; later inhalations pick up more dynamic scents, including lychee, leather, and prickly pear. Entry approaches being bittersweet as the zesty, piquant taste profile turns slightly sweeter, biscuity, and mildly honeyed; midpalate stage is where this single malt does its best work as the flavor profile bursts open with vivid tastes of marzipan, nougat, dark chocolate, toffee, hot cocoa, and dark honey. The dazzling display of flavor continues into the long, peppery aftertaste.

2019 Rating: ★ ★ ★ ★/Highly Recommended

Balvenie DoubleWood 12 Year Old Speyside SMSW 43% abv, $50.

Jonquil/golden-poppy color; flawlessly pure. I've always admired this malt-driven, completely dry opening aroma of warm buttermilk biscuits, malted milk balls, grain kernels, and oak resins; secondary whiffs after more air contact discover deeper scents of ginger snap cookies, vanilla wafers, and dried flowers; a lovely, textbook Speyside bouquet. Entry is tart to the point of being astringent and thereby cleansing and tangy, showing a larger percentage of malt than oak; midpalate provides a highlight reel of breakfast cereal and malted milk ball flavors that jibe nicely, going deep into the elegant, slightly piquant and peppery aftertaste. Continues to be, in my view, one of Scotland's top ten 12 year old single malts. Just plain delicious.

2019 Rating: ★ ★ ★ ★/Highly Recommended

Balvenie DoubleWood 17 Year Old Speyside SMSW 43% abv, $130.

Fulvous/tangerine-peel color; pristine clarity. To my surprise, this opening fragrance is 95 percent mute, bordering on neutral, and I can't help but think, *What gives?* Allowing for ample aeration time, I return to inhaling this mysterious creature gaining only scant, elusive aromas of parchment and cellophane; *Huh?* Entry offers moderately expressive flavors of vanilla bean from oak and Danish pastry and almond paste from the malt; midpalate features a bit more animation in the squeaky dry forms of unsweetened breakfast cereal, Fig Newton cookies, prune, and black raisins. Aftertaste is medium long, dry to bittersweet, and loaded with dried black fruits. Even though there ends up being enough pleasant attributes for a recommendation, the lack of bouquet and the late start in the taste stages lead me to suggest that instead of buying this, purchase two or three bottles of the DoubleWood 12 and avoid the disappointment.

2019 Rating: ★ ★ ★/Recommended

Balvenie PortWood 21 Year Old Speyside SMSW 40% abv, $180.

Butterscotch color; sediment-free clarity. I like this animated but narrowly focused opening nose that's equal parts grain cereal, leather-bound books, citrus peel, and graham cracker; later inhalations following more aeration unearth faint fragrances of candle wax, grape skin, and oatmeal but nothing more. Entry is awash with vibrant tastes of black raisins, figs, dates, candied walnut, and baking spices galore, especially allspice, clove, and cinnamon; midpalate does a good job enhancing all the entry stage impressions and adding a succulence to the texture that rounds out the experience deep into the finish. Bravo to this Balvenie.

2019 Rating: ★ ★ ★ ★/Highly Recommended

Balvenie Single Barrel 15 Year Old Speyside SMSW 47.5% abv, $80.

Lovely, warm, mahogany color; unblemished purity. I'm a bit stunned by the intensely woody/oaky opening aroma that's all about sawdust, sawed planks, and plywood rather than the malt, grain, floral aspects more typical to Speyside bouquets; more time in the glass doesn't pry open any other aromatic features beyond the severity of the oak barrel to make the bouquet more balanced. Entry, to my relief, offers more character variety than the one-note nose in the bakery-like forms of prune Danish, bear claw, and cinnamon bun flavors; midpalate accentuates the entry findings with tart tastes of burnt orange peel and toasted marshmallow. Finishes well in long, dry, oaky, and slightly candied tastes. I nearly bestowed only two stars on this whisky and would have if the flavor and finish stages hadn't come to the rescue. This Balvenie expression has a notorious history of inconsistency, so be aware.

2019 Rating: ★ ★ ★/Recommended

Ben Nevis 10 Year Old Highland SMSW 46% abv, $95.

Solid topaz color; impeccably clean and pure. I like this pencil eraser, rubbery, cigarette tobacco–like, brown rice–like first aroma that turns peppery and spicy with more aeration, even a bit like scallions/spring onion, onion grass; secondary whiffs after more air contact encounter moderately engaging scents of deep-fried pork rind, yellow onion, sawdust, wood plank, and malted barley. Entry highlights toasted sourdough bread, brown butter, brown rice, baker's yeast, sour mash; midpalate echoes the entry but aims for a slightly sweeter place, if a little hollow, that reaches into the aftertaste in a mildly sweet breakfast cereal manner. Comes up just short of being recommendable.

2016 Rating: ★ ★/Not Recommended

Ben Nevis 15 Year Old Oloroso Sherry Cask Highland SMSW 66.1% abv, $315.

The oloroso effect is apparent even in the cinnamon/ginger/henna color; superb clarity. The sherry impact is huge in the initial nosing passes after the pour as aromas of dried fruits—raisins, figs, apricots—waft up from the glass in thick waves along with fragrances of pipe tobacco, bacon fat, BBQ sauce, soy sauce, and fish oil that all vie for dominance; the cluster of competing aromas appears to merge with more air contact into a cohesive bouquet that's focused on cigarette ash, old leather books, egg cream, toasted marshmallow. Entry is more narrowly defined than the cacophonous aroma as the taste profile is squarely concentrated on the grapy/pruny sherry aspect, which is medium sweet and ripe; midpalate shines brightly with oloroso sherry, orange peel, marzipan, honey flavors that last deep into the bittersweet finish.

2016 Rating: ★ ★ ★ ★/Highly Recommended

BenRiach 10 Year Old Speyside SMSW 43% abv, $53.

Maize color; spotlessly pure. First inhalations identify soft aromas of just-baked multigrain bread, egg yolk, yeast, puff pastry, and lemon drop; following more air contact, the aroma features the same impressions as in the opening whiffs, adding black pepper and buttermilk-biscuit batter scents. Entry shows a lightning-like flash of the black pepper piquancy right from the first moment and that aspect dominates the initial impressions, perhaps to a fault as the exclusivity of it keeps the taste focus narrow; midpalate mirrors the entry, and that isn't a great development because there's little flavor expansion or dimension other than the severe pepperiness. A one-note song that doesn't work for me.

2019 Rating: ★ ★/Not Recommended

BenRiach 20 Year Old Speyside SMSW 46% abv, $175.

Bronze color; ideal clarity. Up front, I get spiced apple pastry, clove, mace, allspice, brown butter, and tomato paste aromas that have already melded together; secondary whiffs detect a greater presence of the oak barrel in the succulent forms of butterscotch, graham cracker, and caramel-corn candy. Entry is rich in texture, deeply woody/oaky/maple-like, with tastes of toffee, turbinado sugar, brown rice, and cocoa powder; midpalate echoes the entry stage impressions, adding caramelized onion, praline, nougat, dark honey, and rancio/sautéed mushrooms. Ends long, darkly sweet, and dark chocolate–like.

2019 Rating: ★ ★ ★ ★/Highly Recommended

BenRiach 25 Year Old Speyside SMSW 46.8% abv, $320.

Burnt sienna color; perfectly pure and free of sediment. I love the chocolatey first aromas that are reminiscent of cream caramel candies, chocolate cake frosting, and cocoa powder; secondary whiffs after more air contact encounter nutty fragrances that merge nicely with the buttery candy-shop core scents. Entry flavors mirror the aromatic impressions, holding on to the dark-chocolate sweetness and buttercream richness; midpalate doubles down on the candied aspects, going perhaps a little nuttier than the entry. Aftertaste features candied walnut, buttercream, maple syrup, and dark honey tastes that are round and supple.

2019 Rating: ★ ★ ★ ★/Highly Recommended

BenRiach Authenticus 25 Year Old Peated Speyside SMSW 46% abv, $250.

Bronze/burnished-orange color; pristine clarity. Out of the gate, the phenolic aroma profile is contained, keenly leathery, deeply resiny, sap-like; subsequent whiffs pick up long-dead campfire, ashtray remnants, plus subdued road tar, asphalt notes. Entry focused tightly on the malt, which is deeply flavorful, roasted, nutty, disarming; midpalate highlights the sweet malt aspect in spades, turning the flavor profile into a praline-like, marzipan explosion in the resiny aftertaste.

2014 Rating: ★ ★ ★ ★/Highly Recommended

BenRiach Authenticus 30 Year Old Speyside SMSW 46% abv, $570.

Tawny/sinopia color; unblemished clarity. Up front, the aromas are mature, oaky, dry overall, and moderately spicy; later sniffs pick up bigger, more characterful fragrances of sea salt, mushroom/fungi, attic, leather-bound books, toasted almonds, and malted milk ball candy. Entry is superbly chiseled in flavor, as lean and assertive tastes of malted barley, brown sugar, toasted walnut, baked pineapple, and honey buns impress the taste buds; midpalate echoes the entry findings, throwing in baked orchard fruits (pear, nectarine), sweetened muesli, white raisin, and apple strudel flavors that crescendo in the lovely, robust aftertaste. Rarely do I like older (25+ years) single malts as much as I like this beauty.
2019 Rating: ★ ★ ★ ★ ★/Highest Recommendation

BenRiach Cask Strength Batch 2 Speyside SMSW 60.6% abv, $95.

Orange peel/tangerine color; unblemished appearance. Initial aromatics offer dry traces of tropical fruits, vinyl, parchment, grain husk, and floor wax in equal measure; after more aeration, the aroma remains dry, showing solid fragrances of sawdust, vegetable cooking oil (canola especially), soybean, and sealing wax. Entry is full-bodied, slightly prickly and warm from the abv, grainy, snack cracker–like, lightly toasted, and cleansing; midpalate expands the flavor profile, adding carob, coffee bean, sea salt, oak resin/tree sap, and black tea tastes. Concludes warm but neither hot nor fiery, biscuity, grainy, malty, and dry.
2019 Rating: ★ ★ ★/Recommended

BenRiach Peated Cask Strength Batch 2 Speyside SMSW 60% abv, $106.

Flax/jasmine color; pristine appearance. The opening inhalations are treated to moderate strength peat-reek in the acceptable forms of kerosene, iodine, medicine chest, salted bread, cigar box, and chimney soot; later whiffs pick up much of the same impressions, throwing in burnt match, kindling, Lapsang souchong tea, metal, flint, and dry soil. Entry is succulent in its brown-sugar sweetness, grainy, fruity, ripe, and honeyed; midpalate features hints of black raisins, Fig Newton, dates, mincemeat pie, and prune Danish. Finishes very long, moderately smoky, delicately sweet, and lean and clean in texture.
2019 Rating: ★ ★ ★ ★/Highly Recommended

BenRiach Curiositas 10 Year Old Peated Speyside SMSW 46% abv, $58.

Mustard/saffron color; flawless clarity. I like the peat-driven opening aromas of chimney soot, cigarette ashes, salted bread, charcoal briquette, and scrambled eggs; secondary whiffs detect burnt matches, roasted barley malt, burnt toast, and salted butter. Entry tastes of super-roasted barley malt, cigar smoke, seared meat, and roasted almond; midpalate is lean, grainier than the smoke-filled entry, and keenly peppery/spicy and zesty. Finishes long, intensely smoky, and sooty.
2019 Rating: ★ ★ ★/Recommended

BenRiach Horizons 12 Year Old Triple Distilled Speyside SMSW 50% abv, $80.

Brick/burnt sienna color; superb clarity. I get dates, black raisins, mincemeat, black truffle, wet soil aromas in the first fragrances; further air contact unleashes toffee, honey, candied almond, prune Danish aromas that are bakery-shop welcoming and warm. Entry is succulent, deeply malty (chocolate-covered malted milk balls), nougat, nutty, confectioner-like;

midpalate offers a silky viscosity, mild smokiness, dense grain/deep-roasted malt, pistachio. Ends caramel-like, grainy/cereally, candy bar–like. Lusciously smoked, but multilayered and intriguing from start to finish.
2014 Rating: ★ ★ ★ ★ ★/Highest Recommendation

BenRiach Septendecim 17 Year Old Speyside SMSW 46% abv, $80.
Pretty hay/straw-gold color; impeccable clarity. Heavily peated opening aromas are like rubber inner tube, pencil eraser, chimney flue, cigar box, filled ashtray, then in the second nosings following more air contact there's a flurry of orchard fruit tartness that counters the smokiness in a pleasing manner. Entry is astringent with extreme smokiness and ash as the flavor profile features relatively few aspects save for the peat-reek; midpalate echoes the entry, adding only meager traces of baked apple, baked pineapple, lemon zest, and black pepper to uplift the peat-reek to a higher level of enjoyment deep into the tobacco-like aftertaste.
2015 Rating: ★ ★ ★ ★/Highly Recommended

BenRiach Solstice Second Edition 17 Year Old Peated/Port Finish Speyside SMSW 50% abv, $100.
Pale amber/old gold color; excellent, sediment-free purity. Oh my, big league phenols here as the initial whiffs encounter medicine cabinet, olive brine, seaweed, dill-like aromas that are firm and assertive; next level of bouquet goes more for pipe tobacco, ashes, iodine, campfire embers, outdoor wood smoke. Entry features drying tastes of cigarette ashes, toasted marshmallow; midpalate highlights the resiny oak, hard cheese, dried porcini mushrooms, dry grain/malt, and is oily on the palate. Concludes mildly smoked, kippery.
2014 Rating: ★ ★ ★ ★/Highly Recommended

BenRiach Temporis Peated 21 Year Old Speyside SMSW 46% abv, $265.
Harvest gold/wheat-field color; flawless purity. Opening sniffs encounter engagingly dry and lightly smoked scents of Arbroath smokie (the delicious smoked haddock from the eastern mainland Scottish village of Arbroath), sea breeze, campfire embers, cigar box, and cured tobacco leaf; secondary whiffs pick up large aromatic footprints of Lapsang souchong tea, vinyl, iodine, and grapefruit. Entry is lusciously sweet in its opulent smokiness, honeyed, and is akin to flavored pipe tobacco; midpalate is succulent in its dried-fruit character, with engaging flavors of mincemeat, BBQ sauce, demerara sugar, dried orange peel, and dark chocolate. Ends extended in the throat, only moderately smoky, lush in texture, and bittersweet.
2019 Rating: ★ ★ ★ ★ ★/Highest Recommendation

Benromach 10 Year Old Speyside SMSW 43% abv, $60.
Lovely, bright amber/khaki color; flawless purity. First sniffs pick up a wide array of dry fragrance, from lead pencil to leather chair to dried black tea leaf to oilskin to turnips; secondary passes pick up more scents, especially malted milk balls, barley kernel, unsalted snack cracker, unbuttered toast. Entry flavors include scone, dry breakfast cereal, wheat cracker; midpalate offers the most sensory impact as the taste profile expands into a fruitier and spicier space than the aroma or the entry, offering dried banana, cinnamon bun, vanilla bean, and ginger snap cookie. Aftertaste adds a nice resiny oak note that's keenly spicy.
2017 Rating: ★ ★ ★/Recommended

Benromach 15 Year Old Speyside SMSW 46% abv, $100.

Very pretty burnt sienna color; some sediment seen floating in the core. This early, at-arms-length nose is biscuity, toasted, arid, and resinous, yet distant; more aeration stimulates little more in the way of animation, except for earthy notes of moss and dry leaves; it's an elusive, veiled bouquet. Entry tastes are compact, bittersweet, roasted, almost akin to BBQ sauce, with flavors of tomato paste, bonfire smoke, pork rind, bacon, honey; midpalate expands on all the entry impressions, throwing in mace, sage, espresso. Finishes long, oily, medium bodied, bittersweet, and beany. Had the bouquet offered more substance, this single malt could easily have been rated four stars.

2017 Rating: ★★★/Recommended

Benromach 35 Year Old Speyside SMSW 43% abv, $680.

Sepia/ginger color; perfect purity. I'm admittedly and publicly skeptical of just about any whisky from anywhere that's more than twenty-five years old, and this opening aroma is one of the reasons why—the first impressions (which are crucial!) are of attic, dust, old fabric, old library books, you get the picture; secondary whiffs after more air contact show some improvement, in that there's greater evidence of malted barley, breakfast cereal, but even these scents are worn out. Entry offers a little more animation as the taste profile showcases mildly potent flavors of dry breakfast cereal, toasted almond, caramel, crème brûlée; to my surprise, midpalate finds the flavors building in intensity, highlighting the caramel element, especially. After a burst of energy in the midpalate, the aftertaste returns to the tired flavors of grain and spice—in the end offering little more than fond memories of more youthful years.

2017 Rating: ★★/Not Recommended

Benromach Imperial Proof 10 Year Old Speyside SMSW 57% abv, $90.

Sorrel/amber color; impeccable purity. Whoa, this opening aroma is top loaded with round, supple, dynamic grainy/floral fragrances, including graham cracker, porridge, honey wheat toast, dried hops, carnation, dried violet petals; secondary inhalations pick up traces of the 57 percent abv, but in measured degrees and that buttresses the surface aromas that now integrate into one aromatic thrust. Entry is saucy, zesty, tangy, slightly prickly, campfire warm, densely grainy, honeyed, toasty, spectacularly luscious; midpalate keeps the hits coming as the flavor profile now goes deep in buttery/creamy texture that blankets the palate in layers of caramelized sugar taste. Finishes fathomless, endless, smoky sweet.

2017 Rating: ★★★★★/Highest Recommendation

Benromach Organic 2010 Speyside SMSW 43% abv, $70.

Topaz color; completely sediment-free appearance. There's a pleasing fruitiness/ambrosial quality in the first inhalations after the pour that reminds me of nectarine, Bosc pear and/or quince; the orchard fruit aspect remains evident in the second passes following more aeration, plus I encounter additional scents of parchment, green tomato, and heather. Entry features the semidry, surprisingly evolved flavors of dried fruits (nectarine and pear, in particular), green tobacco, crème caramel; midpalate flavors are sturdy, sweeter than the those at entry, honeyed, biscuity, sugar cookie–like, and maple-like. Finishes medium long, gently sweet, sappy. Shockingly evolved for such a young malt whisky.

2017 Rating: ★★★★/Highly Recommended

Benromach Peat Smoke 2006 Speyside SMSW 46% abv, $70.

Flax/straw-yellow color; unblemished clarity. Yes, indeed, there is undeniable evidence of salty, briny, medicine chest, iodine-like peat but it's not of the barn-burning variety that crosses one's eyes—it's more akin to sea breeze, oyster shell, seaweed; secondary sniffs encounter smoky aromas of a light touch, including dried tobacco, cigar tobacco, filled ashtray, heather, and cereal. Entry is pleasingly sweet, mildly salty, briny, with deft flavors of dill, fennel; midpalate is toasty, honeyed, malty, complex, yet lithe in texture. Aftertaste features the delicate smokiness admired in the entry. It's the gracefulness of the peat presence that makes this malt so alluring and characterful.

2017 Rating: ★★★★/Highly Recommended

Big Smoke 46 Islay Blended Malt Scotch Whisky 46% abv, $60.

Lovely pale-straw/champagne color; good clarity. Opening sniffs have little trouble picking up clear evidence of campfire embers, kippers, black tea leaves, bacon fat; secondary inhalations discover traces of linseed oil, cooking oil, sweet pipe tobacco, and charcoal briquettes. Entry is sweet and sappy, with an edge of fruitiness, in particular, kiwi, grilled pineapple that brings an acidic freshness to the flavor; midpalate is smokier than the entry and also slightly sweeter in a tobacco, BBQ sauce, charred-meat manner. Aftertaste is long, peppery, mildly smoky, grainy sweet, oaky, and spicy (clove). A good but not great blended malt that highlights Islay's gentler side without sacrificing the island's thumbprint smokiness.

2016 Rating: ★★★/Recommended

Big Smoke 60 Islay Blended Malt Scotch Whisky 60% abv, $85.

The color is maize/marigold; excellent clarity. There's a latent potency in this initial aroma that lies just beneath the surface as the elevated abv comes into play in the early nosings, offering dusty, dry, and inviting smells of malted barley, breakfast cereal, biscuit batter, and ripe tropical fruit; following more time in the glass, the aroma becomes more overt in the forms of new leather, egg white, yeast, sea salt, olive brine, birch tar oil, and chalk. Entry is generously warm, smoky, moderately toasty, chewy in texture, and salty; midpalate echoes the entry impressions and adds an elegance that was missing from the Big Smoke 46 in terms of creamy, lush texture (that 60 percent abv at work!) and bountifully impactful flavors of sea salt, pipe smoke, buttercream. Finishes with a sense of luxury and a quiet power that's posh while all the time being properly smoky, peaty Islay.

2016 Rating: ★★★★/Highly Recommended

Black Bull 12 Year Old Blended Scotch Whisky 50% abv, $55.

Deep-topaz/amber color; not flawless clarity, as minuscule tendrils are seen—does not affect the score. The aromatic depth in the first whiffs after the pour is inviting as subtle scents of sawn lumber, almond paste, dry cereal, and butcher's wax paper rule the moment; more air contact releases meaty aromas of cooking oil, black pepper, dried flowers, English toffee, nougat, and peanuts. Entry is rich in texture, slightly sweet, resiny, maple-like, cherry-like, and laced with baking spices (clove, vanilla); midpalate affirms all the entry impressions and piles on bakery-shop flavors of marzipan, prune Danish, and vanilla wafer.

Aftertaste is medium long, sweet but not cloying, honeyed, woody, leathery, toasty, and marshmallow-like. This is a serious mouthful of blended Scotch splendor.
2016 Rating: ★ ★ ★ ★/Highly Recommended

Black Bull 21 Year Old Blended Scotch Whisky 50% abv, $180.
Why this 21 year old blend would be lighter in color than its sibling 12 year old is something of a mystery, but it is, by several shades of amber/old gold; sediment-free purity makes it shine. To my surprise, the opening aromatics on this older blend aren't as deep as the Kyloe or the 12 year old, and I am forced to take extra time in an attempt to dig up some early fragrance, which is spirity, clean, and quite woody/plank-like; following further aeration, the aroma offers more nuanced scents, in stingy measure, of candle wax/paraffin and flaxseed oil. Entry is more animated than the bouquet as tart flavors of orchard fruits (apple, nectarine) rule the moment, providing an obvious crispness that's refreshing; mid-palate offers tastes of oaky vanilla, clove, caramel, and maple fudge that extend long into the satisfying aftertaste. It took too long to get running, but once it did, the quality of the blend comes out, especially in the midpalate and finish. I'd gravitate to the 12 year old and the Kyloe.
2016 Rating: ★ ★ ★/Recommended

Black Bull Kyloe Blended Scotch Whisky 50% abv, $30.
Flax/gold color, which is pretty, shows inconsequential sediment floating in the core. I like the initial aromatic burst that's juicy (pear, kiwi), acidic, floral (honeysuckle, jasmine), and keenly dry and crisp; after more time in the glass the elemental aroma transforms into a graceful, round bouquet that highlights ripe yellow fruits (pear, banana), worn saddle leather, spring flower garden (sweet pea), and dry breakfast cereal/muesli—this is a deliciously compelling bouquet. Entry offers bright flavors of wheat snack crackers, unsweetened breakfast cereal, ripe tropical fruits (banana, guava, and pineapple), and light honey; midpalate mirrors all the entry impressions and adds fine touches of tree sap/resin and baking spices (nutmeg, allspice) that work well with the abv level, which is never an issue. Finishes a little quick, considering the evident quality of the blend.
2016 Rating: ★ ★ ★ ★/Highly Recommended

Bladnoch Adela 15 Year Old Oloroso Sherry Cask Matured Lowlands SMSW 46.7% abv, $110.
Fulvous/tawny-brown color; pristine purity. The influence of the oloroso sherry cask is immediate and undeniable, as the nose unfolds in waves of plump, raisiny/pruny scents that complement the malted barley; later sniffs pick up traces of florist shop, marmalade, candied fruits, and toffee. Entry is like blackberry jam on toast, prunes, black raisin bran, treacle, and dark honey; midpalate is long, sensual in texture, pipe tobacco–like, fruit salad–like, and round and peppery (black peppercorn). Finishes deeply raisiny, burnt, baked, and sweet.
2017 Rating: ★ ★ ★/Recommended

Bladnoch Bourbon Expression 10 Year Old Lowlands SMSW 46.7% abv, $60.
Straw-yellow color; unblemished clarity. Initial whiffs detect lightly spiced aromas of spice cake, damp forest, mushrooms/fungi, and wet straw; secondary inhalations introduce

attic- and old furniture–like notes that are dry and dusty. Entry offers round, cookie batter–like, doughy flavor notes that alleviate some of the aromatic doldrums; midpalate is doughy, bread-like, chewy in texture, and semisweet. Aftertaste highlights the modest virtues of the midpalate, extending them into a long grainy/malty finish that doesn't show enough core structure and panache to make this malt recommendable.

2019 Rating: ★★/Not Recommended

Bladnoch Samsara Lowlands SMSW 46.7% abv, $80.

Lovely topaz/amber color; exceptional purity. Opening fragrances are all about the barley malt, as soft waves of dry breakfast cereal perfume offer delicately spiced scents of black tea (Darjeeling), toasted almond, and candied walnut; the second phase of nosing finds the aroma fading slightly, becoming more mineral-like, stony, sandy, and arid. Entry is bone-dry, astringent, acidic, crisp, and sharp as a razor; midpalate features deeply toasted cereal notes that leave little room for other flavors, save for a cooking oil taste. Aftertaste is lean, stone-dry on the tongue, stingy, and narrowly focused.

2017 Rating: ★★/Not Recommended

Bowmore 12 Year Old Islay SMSW 40% abv, $52.

Mango/amber color; spotless clarity. The opening whiffs provide a saline-soaked gale of Loch Indaal sea breeze that's simultaneously attractive and jolting as the depth and density of the ocean is undeniably memorable; once past the bracing first inhalations and allowing for more air contact, the second wave of fragrances include smoldering campfire smoke, kippers/salted fish, dill, and olive brine in equal measure. Entry is keenly salty, mildly oaky and resiny, smoky, and chockfull of cigar tobacco astringency; midpalate builds upon the entry profile, adding fleeting tastes of smoked honey ham, pork rind, and smoked sausages. Finishes medium long and not as salt-driven as the entry and midpalate.

2018 Rating: ★★★★/Highly Recommended

Bowmore 18 Year Old Islay SMSW 43% abv, $130.

Burnt sienna color; ideal purity. I love this harmonious opening bouquet that's mildly salty/sea breeze–like, nutty (salted peanuts), buttery (salted creamery butter), dill-like, and pickle-like; it doesn't clobber you like the vigorous 12 year old first nosing and that's the blessing of maturity; secondary inhalations detect deep fragrances of green tobacco, salted chocolate candies, vegetable cooking oil, sap, vanilla bean/vanillin, and oak plank. Entry is deliciously cocoa-like, with expressive supporting flavors of espresso, black bean, sherry, baked dark fruits (cherries, plums), and black pepper; midpalate mirrors the entry impressions, adding delicate touches of dark, old honey and bittersweet chocolate. Aftertaste is extended, dark-chocolate bittersweet, and plush in texture. Flawless brilliance and a model of balance.

2018 Rating: ★★★★★/Highest Recommendation

Bowmore 18 Year Old The Vintner's Trilogy—Manzanilla Cask Islay SMSW 52.5% abv, $127.

Gamboge color; impeccable clarity. Up front, there is scant evidence of the lofty abv except for a mild prickliness that mingles nicely with fragrances of ripe grapes, grape preserves, toasted malt, and marshmallow; secondary whiffs pick up additional aromas including cookie batter, brown sugar, salted butter, oyster sauce, and soybean. Entry is generous in flavor and in oily texture as the flavor profile turns sweeter than I had anticipated it would, but pleasingly so in a bakeshop manner, full of tangy spices, like clove, allspice, and nutmeg, and fruitiness, such as baked pineapple and baked apple; midpalate takes on a more integrated demeanor as the fruit and spice taste elements merge with the malted barley graininess and sherry cask in a display of harmony that's bound together by the elevated alcohol level. The result of the midpalate convergence is a swank finish that's long, acceptably prickly, warming in the throat, more bittersweet than sweet, astringent, and zesty. A feast for those malt lovers who like cask strength offerings.

2018 Rating: ★★★★★/Highest Recommendation

Bowmore 25 Year Old Islay SMSW 43% abv, $425.

Tawny/ochre color; sediment-free clarity. I like the delicacy of the initial inhalations as the aromatic profile features integrated fragrances of Arbroath smokies, cigar tobacco, black peppercorn, and cinnamon; secondary inhalations after more aeration introduce deep-level aromas of oak panel, dill, flaxseed oil, anise, and tree sap/resin. Entry tastes are flush with a suitably oily texture that underpins the flavors of wood smoke, oloroso sherry, prune juice, dates, black olive, and treacle; midpalate serves to reinforce the entry impressions, adding bittersweet dark chocolate and candied cherry tastes that delight. Ends up very long in the throat, sinewy in texture, sweeter and fruitier than either the entry or midpalate and just luscious. While I prefer single malts from Scotland in the twelve- to twenty-year range, this Bowmore 25 remains a standard bearer for Islay.

2018 Rating: ★★★★★/Highest Recommendation

Bowmore 26 Year Old The Vintner's Trilogy—French Oak Barrique Islay SMSW 52.5% abv, $540.

Persimmon/tangelo color; immaculate purity. I find this opening aroma to be a little bit sweaty and "off," so I allow for more aeration time before resuming; following the added air-contact period, I still find a trace of tankiness (metallic) or sweatiness (bacteria) that's not as pronounced as in the initial sniffs; secondary aromas include matchstick, sea salt, salted popcorn, and breakfast cereal. Entry is assertive with barrel-driven oiliness/fat (the oak lipids) and flavors of black peppercorn, black olive, pipe tobacco, and candied fruits (orange, cherry); midpalate splendor erases much of the concern due to the bouquet as it features sterling, crisp, and edgy flavors of oak barrel, resin/tree sap, cocoa powder, espresso, coffee bean, and bittersweet chocolate. Aftertaste highlights the beaniness found in the midpalate, as well as the depth of the oily texture. Made an impressive comeback in the mouth after teetering on the brink in the bouquet.

2018 Rating: ★★★★/Highly Recommended

Bowmore 27 Year Old The Vintner's Trilogy—Port Cask Islay SMSW 48.3% abv, $520.

Matured in ex-bourbon barrels for thirteen years, then in port pipes for fourteen years. Cocoa-brown/mahogany color; superbly clean. First whiffs offer saline-driven notes of sea breeze, seaweed, medicine cabinet, creosote, linseed oil, green tobacco, and apple tart; secondary inhalations after more aeration bring out the winey, prune-like nuances brought about by the port pipes, thereby turning the maritime early aroma into an integrated, sophisticated bouquet that amalgamates the salt air, the suggestion of peat, the dry malt, and the succulence of the ripe-grape portiness. Entry soars into the flavor stratosphere, offering pitch-perfect maritime tastes of salted caramel, candied apple, pipe tobacco, campfire smoke, and smoked haddock; midpalate features more of the port influence, especially in the roundness of the black raisin, dates, mincemeat flavor that is lightly doused with sea salt. Finishes long, salty, smoky, and ripe with grapy fruit. I can't imagine it being any better.

2018 Rating: ★★★★★/Highest Recommendation

Bowmore Darkest 15 Year Old Islay SMSW 43% abv, $76.

Tawny/rust color; flawlessly pure. The sherry finish is immediately apparent in the very first sniff, as subsequent opening inhalations unearth other scents, namely cocoa powder, salted dark chocolate candies, salted fudge, and brown butter; secondary whiffs pick up fragrances of rock salt, oloroso sherry, and mincemeat as the latter aromas dissipate a bit too quickly. Entry is toasty, tart in a bittersweet manner, prune- and date-like, moderately salty, and lighter in texture than I recall from 2004; midpalate is lean, bittersweet, moderately chocolatey, and pastry-like (chocolate croissants). Finish is refined, elegant, bittersweet, and cocoa-like, with a medium weighted texture. While certainly very tasty, this incarnation is not as luscious and flat-out yummy as I recall Darkest of the past being.

2018 Rating: ★★★★/Highly Recommended

Bowmore Mizunara Cask Finish Islay SMSW 53.9% abv, $1,000.

Two thousand bottles available worldwide. Bright topaz/amber color is dazzling and pure. This opening nose is as different as any malt nose I've smelled of late, with the aromatic lead being taken by a bean-like scent (not cinnamon or vanilla but more coffee- or cocoa-like) that's dry, yet tangy and very peppery and parchment-like; secondary passes discover tobacco leaf, bay leaf, oak resin, sap, road tar fragrances. Entry is totally different than the aroma as the flavor profile highlights ripe red fruits (cherry, red plum), malted milk balls, oloroso sherry, honeysuckle; midpalate is rich in texture, a bit spiky in abv fire, toasty, semisweet, caramel-like, mildly salty. Finishes long, astringent, with not-so-subtle tastes of roasted meat, tomato paste, BBQ sauce, honey. One of the best examples of how the aroma/bouquet sometimes seems totally out of sync with the flavor, yet the final result is a superbly satisfying whisky all the same. While not my favorite Bowmore, a worthy, succulent addition to the portfolio.

2016 Rating: ★★★★/Highly Recommended

Bowmore The Devil's Casks Small Batch Release Islay SMSW 56.9% abv, $90.

Henna/auburn/chestnut-brown color; minor sediment seen. Goodness gracious, great balls of sherry and peat-reek in the first whiffs; later inhalations unearth (with no trouble) heaps of iodine, sea salt, kippers, campfire embers, creosote. Entry is acutely medicinal, instantly peaty/smoky, tobacco-like, salty, yet BBQ-sauce sweet; midpalate confirms the entry findings and adds tomato paste, hard cheese, oloroso sherry, marzipan, praline. Concludes sinewy, smoky, oily/viscous.

2014 Rating: ★★★★/Highly Recommended

Bruichladdich Bere Barley 2008 Dunlossit Estate Islay SMSW 50% abv, $129.

Jasmine color; shows a slight haziness. Whoa, there's all sorts of floor wax, furniture polish, candle wax, parchment, cedar, and pine tar–like scents in this elemental opening aroma; additional time in the glass allows for more of the barley grain to emerge from behind the waxy curtain and that event adds notes of dry cereal, muesli, grain husk, and safflower oil to the bouquet. Entry is nuttier than the aroma, high in acid and lignin, clean and tight in texture, and strikingly similar to Scottish shortbread in flavor; midpalate brings out more of the buttery aspect that eclipses the grain kernel/beaniness that dominated the entry point. Finishes medium long, astringent, mouth drying, and parched.

2019 Rating: ★ ★ ★/Recommended

Bruichladdich Black Art 1990 Unpeated Islay SMSW 46.9% abv, $399.

Brandy-like tawny/copper color; flawless clarity. First nosing pass discovers fragrances of pine tar, tree bark, nougat, walnut butter, and black tea; later sniffs after allowing for more air contact detect deeper aromas, including caulk, dry sand, pebbles, saddle leather, and carob. Entry features a rich, creamy texture that supports the flavors of coffee latte, caramel candies, dark chocolate, honey, and saltwater taffy; midpalate mirrors the entry, going deeper and further in length, as the texture turns oily, sap-like, and tapioca-like. Ends finely, alluring, and decidedly bittersweet.

2019 Rating: ★ ★ ★ ★/Highly Recommended

Bruichladdich Islay Barley 2010 Unpeated Islay SMSW 50% abv, $79.

Jonquil/amber color; spotlessly clean. Ooooh, I like these first inhalations, in which the interplay of the fruity grain and the seaside salinity paints a lovely aromatic picture of grace and balance; second-stage whiffs pick up the citrus peel/apple skin tartness that, with time, turns more in the direction of a flower-shop bouquet. Entry is reminiscent of toasted bread, sugar cookie, vanilla wafer, and butter brickle; midpalate turns on the maritime sea-air charm, as the graininess turns just slightly salty, paving the way for the near-succulent, baking spice (vanilla, allspice, clove) aftertaste. Lovely. Complete.

2019 Rating: ★ ★ ★ ★ ★/Highest Recommendation

Bruichladdich The Classic Laddie Scottish Barley Unpeated Islay SMSW 50% abv, $57.

Straw-yellow color; pristine appearance. I pick up frontline aromas of poppy seed, vanilla custard, malted milk balls, and steamed white rice; second passes unearth more lively scents, including tomato vine, sawdust, oak plank, unsweetened breakfast cereal, white flour, and French baguette. Entry flavor dries out the palate on contact, as the tart taste profile leans heavily in the direction of breakfast cereal and astringency in abundance; midpalate stays the grainy, kernel-like, poppy seed–like character that's stone dry, yet firm, highly acidic, and tannic. Finishes cleanly, medium long, with big green tea and tobacco notes in the pleasing finale.

2019 Rating: ★ ★ ★ ★/Highly Recommended

Bruichladdich The Organic 2009 Mid Coul Farms, Dalcross Islay SMSW 50% abv, $85.

Brut champagne-like/aureolin color; perfect purity. This curiously infectious initial

aroma is akin to meringue, egg whites, bubble gum, and macaroons; more aeration brings out the dry, almost citrus-like graininess that's fresh, fruit peel–like, and floral. Entry is borderline sweet, deeply grainy, graham cracker–like, and cereally, slightly honeyed, and biscuit batter–like; midpalate sees the 50 percent abv dominate perhaps a little too much, as the alcohol heat diminishes some of the pleasant graininess but not enough so that the aftertaste is negatively affected, which it is not. A grain train malt.
2019 Rating: ★ ★ ★/Recommended

Buchanan's Deluxe 12 Year Old Blended Scotch Whisky 40% abv, $31.

Buchanan's agonizing plastic pour system with an inserted ball is the most ill-conceived pouring system in the entire Scotch whisky category. The blends themselves are among the finest available but that's not the issue. The stupidly designed pouring system takes forever to get even a one-ounce pour, and if I owned an establishment, that alone would prevent me from having them on my backbar. Hello Diageo: you're big, brawny and resourceful. Wake up and smell the twenty-first century. Your inane system for Buchanan's is woefully antiquated and detrimental to the brand. Golden wheat-field color; pristine appearance. The gently sweet breakfast cereal aroma is welcoming, grainy, malty, and bakery-shop pleasant; secondary whiffs detect scents of baked pear, white raisins, and kiwi. Entry is sweeter than the bouquet implies it would be and is toasty, mildly nutty, and Fig Newton–like; midpalate offers more of the grain whisky aspect as the flavor profile turns lean, a bit astringent, and woody/resiny. Finishes medium long, acidic, tart, crisp, and delightful. Excellent value.
2019 Rating: ★ ★ ★/Recommended

Buchanan's Master Blended Scotch Whisky 40% abv, $50.

Jonquil/butterscotch color; excellent purity. In the opening sniffs I pick up grain-driven first aromas, mostly bread dough, wheat bread, graham cracker, and new honey; later inhalations after more air contact discover deeper fragrances of orchard fruits (pears, red apple), toffee, marshmallow, and nougat. Entry flavors include a deep maltiness that tells me of the richness of the single malt elements; midpalate features even denser grain/malt impressions that remind me most of bear claw pastry, prune Danish, and pear tart. Aftertaste is medium long, satiny in texture, delicately sweet, and elegant.
2019 Rating: ★ ★ ★ ★/Highly Recommended

Buchanan's Select 15 Year Old Blended Scotch Whisky 40% abv, $50.

Marigold color; flawless clarity. Initial inhalations encounter vivacious aromas of lemon peel, green tea, brown butter, caramel, and carob; later whiffs after more air contact recognize deeper fragrances, including sweetened coconut, spiced banana, and sawdust. Entry is lushly textured, semisweet, cocoa-like, and splendidly woody and vanilla bean–like; midpalate features the silky, opulent texture upon which the flavors of dried fruits, bacon fat, pork rind, toffee, and espresso abound. Finishes long, creamy, warming in the throat, and plush.
2019 Rating: ★ ★ ★ ★/Highly Recommended

Buchanan's Special Reserve 18 Year Old Blended Scotch Whisky 40% abv, $75.

Pretty burnt-orange/pumpkin color; impeccably clean and free of sediment. Opening nosing passes pick up integrated aromas of coffee bean, sawdust/oak plank, honey-doused breakfast cereal/muesli, toasted marshmallow, and baked pear; secondary inhalations are treated to even deeper, more concentrated aromas of light smoke, pipe tobacco, peach tart, and gingerbread. Entry echoes the latter stage aromatics, offering harmonious, sturdy, lushly textured tastes of caramel candy, candied walnut, brown sugar, and very mature rum; midpalate features the satiny texture whose fullness makes for the ideal platform for the bakery-like, dried fruit, puff pastry–like flavors. Lavish finish ends the experience on the highest note possible. One of the ten best blended Scotches in the marketplace.

2019 Rating: ★★★★★/Highest Recommendation

Bunnahabhain 12 Year Old Islay SMSW 46.3% abv, $65.

Old gold/marigold color; sediment-free and pure. This opening aroma is round, toasted, slightly honeyed, and oaky/woody; in later whiffs, the primary fragrance is the peated malt, but even that is on a lower par than other Islay malts, such as Ardbeg, Lagavulin, or Laphroaig, ending in a tree sap– and campfire embers–like scent that's delicately smoked. Entry is medium rich, totally dry and astringent, lightly grainy/cereal-like, and low on the peat-o-meter; midpalate reflects the entry impressions, especially the astringency that dries out the palate. Ends medium long, ethereal in smokiness, and keenly woody.

2020 Rating: ★★★★/Highly Recommended

Bunnahabhain Stiùireadair Islay SMSW 46.3% abv, $47.

Amber/golden-grain color; ideal clarity. The first inhalations are all about smoke, namely, wood smoke, as well as iodine, medicine chest, and cigarette ashes; secondary passes detect more delicate, ripe fruitiness (peach, nectarine) than actual peat-reek or smoke, resulting in a pleasant bouquet. Entry reflects the orchard fruit appeal found in the latter stage of nosing, as well as a candy-shop taste of nougat, candied nuts, and brown sugar; midpalate is a mirror image of the entry, but perhaps with a bit more smokiness, oak resin, and sea salt. Finishes in a medium-long manner, with a late-hour display of salted caramel.

2020 Rating: ★★★/Recommended

Caol Ila 14 Year Old Unpeated Style Islay SMSW 59.3% abv, $110.

Gold/marigold color; sediment-free. Smells decidedly chewy, sherry sweet, grapy ripe, and floral in the opening sniffs done right after the pour; another seven minutes on, I note mushroom, moss, damp earth, and baked pear fragrances that dominate the latter nosing stage. Entry is buttery/creamy in texture, supple, and fruity succulent; midpalate features ripe white grapes, candied pears, white raisins, and butterscotch flavors—the abv never gets in the way. Finishes sweet, sherried, and juicy.

2013 Rating: ★★★★/Highly Recommended

Chivas Regal 12 Year Old Blended Scotch Whisky 40% abv, $52.

Pretty topaz/old gold color; admirable purity. Up-front aromas include holiday spice cake that's loaded with dried fruits (apricot, pineapple), baking spices (clove, allspice), nuts (walnut), and brown sugar; later whiffs detect gently sweet grain scents that are pleasantly juicy and almost citrusy in their crisp cleanness. Entry is mature, firmly structured, grounded in single malt smoothness and substance; midpalate is honey sweet, marzipan-like, but the

grain whisky aspect that underpins the in-mouth stage is sturdy and solid all through the finish. Years ago I described this fine Scotch whisky as "a blend for grown-ups." I stick with that concise description because this is a complex, intricate whisky that only a seasoned palate could enjoy.
2015 Rating: ★★★★/Highly Recommended

Chivas Regal 18 Year Old Gold Signature Blended Scotch Whisky 40% abv, $75.
The depth of the bay/sorrel color is fascinating; impeccable purity. Opening aroma highlights the savory malt whisky component as the multilevel fragrance offers first dry breakfast cereal, graham cracker, then pipe tobacco, old saddle leather, and bakeshop spices galore (cinnamon, nutmeg); second inhalations encounter crisp citrus notes initially, then older, fully ripened fragrances of dried heather, old library, minerals, campfire embers, and a slight salinity to make up one of the finest Scotch whisky aromas of all time. Entry is supple, creamy, sturdy, gently honey sweet but simultaneously clean and crisp; midpalate is where the full-scale splendor does its most notable work in the forms of barley malt dryness, dried fruits (raisin, peach), candied walnut, vanilla bean, praline—a masterpiece taste profile of harmony, integration, and peak maturity. Finish owns that rare marriage of finesse and power that so few spirits possess. Still the pinnacle achievement of master blender Colin Scott.
2015 Rating: ★★★★★/Highest Recommendation

Chivas Regal Mizunara Oak Special Edition Blended Scotch Whisky 40% abv, $45.
Bright amber/topaz color; pristine clarity. Up front, I pick up pleasing and evolved aromas of coconut, brown sugar, and chocolate-covered cherry; secondary inhalations after more air contact discover deeper scents, including roasted grain, spice cake, and allspice. Entry is subtle in its complexity as the surface flavor of milk chocolate dances on the oily texture that caps the denser, bittersweet core tastes of oak resin, maple, toasted malt, and praline; midpalate stage offers finely tuned and nimble tastes of pecan pie, banana bread, and graham cracker. Finishes in the dazzling form of cocoa bean and dark chocolate, with deft dashes of clove and nutmeg. A concert of flavor from the genius of master blender Colin Scott. Superb value! Buy at least two bottles.
2018 Rating: ★★★★/Highly Recommended

Chivas Regal Ultis Blended Malt Scotch Whisky 40% abv, $200.
Malts come from the Speyside distilleries of Braeval, Longmorn, Tormore, Strathisla, and Allt-á-Bhainne. Simply put, one of the most attractive whiskies I've reviewed recently; the pristine ginger/cinnamon color sparkles under the examination lamp. First nosings detect earthy scents of autumn leaves, seasoned oak, sawdust, soft maple, and a delicate trace of clove; later sniffs encounter black pepper, dried violets, moss/lichen, fungi/mushroom, and slightly smoky malted barley. Entry showcases the sturdy side of Speyside malts as the taste profile goes resiny, woody, and oily, as well as biscuity, cookie dough–like, and gently honeyed; midpalate mirrors the entry impressions, throwing in black tea, citrus, baked pineapple for good measure. Aftertaste is toasty, long, leaner than the midpalate, acidic, and therefore fresh, suddenly fruity and ripe, but dry and gently spiced. Longtime subscribers

know my love for Chivas Regal 18 but I believe that this more austere expression is the 18's equal in terms of character and quality.
2017 Rating: ★ ★ ★ ★ ★/Highest Recommendation

Compass Box "Flaming Heart" Edition #4, Blended Malt Scotch Whisky 48.9% abv, $110.

Combination of Islay, Speyside, Island, and Northern Highlands malts with the majority hailing from Islay's southern shore and the Highlands distillery village of Brora. Pretty, impeccably clean, gamboge/gold color. The dying campfire odor of Islay leads the aromatic pack as the opening fragrance turns saltier, peaty, medicinal as oxygen stimulates the molecules; after more aeration, the aromatic properties become more vertical in their chimney smoke, cigar ash, sea breeze–like manner. Entry features Islay peat and smokiness on the salty surface, but there's also a good amount of Highland flower and Speyside maltiness that lie underneath the megaphone-like Islay brashness; midpalate finds that the smoke fades away, allowing for the floral and grain aspects to gain ground as the taste profile turns to dried fruits, especially prune, raisin, and date. Finishes peppery, astringent, crisp, razor-edged, zesty, and keenly dry and dusty.
2016 Rating: ★ ★ ★ ★/Highly Recommended

Compass Box "This is not a luxury Whisky" Blended Scotch Whisky 53.1% abv, $200.

A blend of 79 percent Glen Ord single malt aged in first fill sherry butt, 10.1 percent Strathclyde grain whisky/refill American oak hogshead, 6.9 percent Girvan grain whisky/refill American oak hogshead, and 4 percent Caol Ila single malt/refill American oak hogshead. Deep amber color; flawless purity. Early on, I smell grass, lima bean, soybean, tofu/bean curd in abundance; the intense beaniness doesn't abate with more air contact but actually gets denser and more vibrant, adding vegetal notes, in particular, cauliflower. Entry is off-dry to semisweet, astringent, and therefore fresh and slightly biting, powerful yet supple and round, caramel-like, grainy/corny, with a touch of maple syrup—a remarkably complex and multilayered flavor profile; midpalate echoes the entry impressions, adding honey-flavored cereal, praline. Aftertaste is semisweet, lip-smackingly delicious, toasted, raisiny. The abv never gets in the way and acts as the ideal underwriter of the whole in-mouth experience.
2016 Rating: ★ ★ ★ ★ ★/Highest Recommendation

Cooper's Choice 1997 Benrinnes Bourbon Cask Matured Speyside SMSW 46% abv, $125.

Citrine/buff color; excellent clarity. The first nosings on this older Speyside malt reveal a bit of reluctance, but I persevere knowing after twenty-eight years of evaluations that occasionally malts of twenty years and up need more time to aerate; this bouquet benefited from a few more minutes in the glass now exposing arid fragrances of dry sand, baked clay, thistle, and sagebrush, with sedate background notes of malt and dry cereal. Entry flavors are far more expressive than the aroma, giving off dry, snappy tastes of malted milk balls and baking spices such as clove, nutmeg, vanilla, and cinnamon; midpalate brings in the oak aspect, which is toasty, tannic, and therefore bitter. Concludes brief, tightly wound, and a little stingy. Not the best Benrinnes I've reviewed but recommendable all the same.
2017 Rating: ★ ★ ★/Recommended

Cooper's Choice 2003 MacDuff Sherry Cask Matured Speyside SMSW 46% abv, $124.

Khaki/olive color; excellent purity. The first nosing passes pick up very dry grain notes that remind me of uncooked oatmeal, muesli, and scones; later whiffs pick up additional notes of salt air, brown butter, bacon fat, and lanolin. Entry is piquant in its acute pepperiness, plus there's a distant wine-like aspect that rounds out some of the black pepper tanginess; midpalate highlights the interplay between the dry malt and the slightly sweet sherry cask, making a pleasant impression that lasts long into the aftertaste.

2019 Rating: ★ ★ ★/Recommended

Cooper's Choice 2006 Royal Brackla Marsala Cask Finish Speyside SMSW 46% abv, $79.

Fawn color; I see coils of oil swirling in the core of this whisky, but in all it's pure and sediment-free. The effect of the marsala cask finishing is immediately ascertained in the first whiff, emitting mildly fruity scents—orange blossom, pears, and white raisins; later sniffs pick up traces of malty grain and snack crackers, but it's the marsala impact that remains the leading aromatic force ten minutes on. Entry flavor exposes a fruit-laden taste that's properly malty and grainy, giving the entry phase a noticeable balance; midpalate is marginally rounder than the entry stage, providing a lushness of texture that supports the grapy/pruny, but superficial, wafer-thin flavor. Aftertaste, where this malt crumbles, turns unexpectedly bittersweet, grainy, earthy, harsh, tannic, and prickly. The awkward, raw-in-the-throat finish isn't an appropriate summing up of the otherwise pleasant aroma and flavor, thereby dropping it to Not Recommended status. Pass on it. You'll hate the aftertaste, as I did.

2017 Rating: ★ ★/Not Recommended

Cooper's Choice 2009 Inchfad (Loch Lomond Distillery) Bourbon Cask Matured Highland SMSW 46% abv, $72.

Ochre color; pristine clarity. The opening aroma is a curious mix of grain feed, seared meat, black tea, chimney, and Nutella; further sniffings after more air contact discover incongruous fragrances of lard, saltwater taffy, sautéed mushrooms, and oak plank. Entry is keenly bitter to bittersweet, burnt-grain–like, metallic/rusty/ore-like, heavily toasted, and baked orchard fruit–like; midpalate unites the various taste factions, but the resultant taste profile isn't one that I especially like. Concludes raw, a touch too harsh for my liking, and feral.

2019 Rating: ★ ★/Not Recommended

Cooper's Choice 2009 Laggan Mill Bourbon Cask Islay SMSW 46% abv, $74.

Tea-green/straw color; flawless purity. The sprightly first aromas are doused with seaweed, salted almonds, campfire smoke, iodine, medicine chest, and cigarette ashes, all in moderate measure, not gangbusters; secondary inhalations pick up deeper fragrances of peated malt, Lapsang souchong tea, lemon drops, creosote, and peppermint. Entry is beautifully harmonious, lightly smoked, dill-like, with background flavors of green olive and pickle brine; midpalate is soaked with the Lapsang souchong tea as well as pipe tobacco ash and kippers. Finishes as vibrant in the throat as it began in the nose, featuring pungent tastes of sea salt and charred marshmallow.

2017 Rating: ★ ★ ★ ★/Highly Recommended

Cooper's Choice Bunnahabhain 16 Year Old Sherry Cask Islay SMSW 46% abv, $120.
One hundred percent sherry oak cask. Attractive sepia/topaz color; completely sediment-free. Wow, the upshot on the opening nosing pass is a robust maltiness that's hearty, floral, slightly salty, briny, with a hint of oloroso sherry lurking in the background; more aeration brings about a seductive fruitiness that's raisiny, dried, and pruny—this is not your typical ethereal Bunnahabhain, mates. Entry is brazenly raisiny, bittersweet, honeyed, and supple in texture; midpalate builds upon the entry impressions, adding notes of candied peach, almond paste, cinnamon, clove, and hazelnut. Aftertaste is prickly, sherried, with a dash of mincemeat as a farewell wave. Bunnahabhain loyalists, used to its more delicate malts, might not respond to the richness of this edition. I, for one, like it immensely and believe it to be a fascinating new direction for this excellent Islay malt distillery.
2017 Rating: ★ ★ ★ ★/Highly Recommended

Cooper's Choice Croftengea 10 Year Old Speyside SMSW 46% abv, $80.
A Loch Lomond Distillery malt matured in ex-bourbon barrel. Very pale ecru/bisque/tarnished-silver color; absolute clarity. I find the first aromas to be racy, clean, acidic, citrusy, vegetal, tobacco ash–like, and grainy all at the same time and in equal measure; secondary sniffs encounter many of the same first-round impressions of youthful vigor, fueled by cereal-like malt and cigar tobacco fragrances—while the label claims "Heavily Peated," I do not find the bouquet overly smoky. Entry is keenly fresh, carbolic, seaweed-like, and zesty, and it's here, at last, where the peat smoke comes, although not in tsunami-like waves but rather in nuances of tobacco ash, sea salt, salted fish, and iodine; what I notice most at midpalate is the rich creaminess of the silky texture that blankets the palate in layers of flavor. Aftertaste is vigorous, piney, moderately salty, and controlled in its smokiness. This is a solid, young, and pleasant malt of dimension and depth that is worth buying.
2017 Rating: ★ ★ ★ ★/Highly Recommended

Copper Dog Speyside Blended Malt Scotch Whisky 40% abv, $33.
Made exclusively from undisclosed Speyside malts. Pretty topaz/amber color; superb clarity. Holy jeepers, Batman, this opening bouquet epitomizes Speyside's floral side as alluring fragrances of heather, dried moss, and field grains mingle with scents reminiscent of unsweetened breakfast cereal, floor malting, graham cracker, and shredded wheat; after the chockfull initial inhalations, the bouquet settles into a softly sweet mode that's firm in structure and almost fruity (white raisins come to mind). Entry features a sweeter, biscuit-like opening flavor that spotlights the graham cracker impression found in the aroma, making it the temporary centerpiece; midpalate turns richer than the entry as the underlying texture goes buttery/creamy and meringue-like and slightly spiced with hints of clove and nutmeg. Finishes medium long, honey sweet, lightly toasted. PHENOMENAL VALUE! You'd have to be slightly crazy not to buy a couple of bottles immediately.
2017 Rating: ★ ★ ★ ★/Highly Recommended

Craigellachie 13 Year Old Speyside SMSW 46% abv, $55.
Jonquil/gold color; sediment-free. I like this sturdy, barley malt, snack cracker opening aroma due primarily to its dusty dryness and arid earth character; secondary inhalations find

more nuttiness and light spice (mace), though in general this bouquet is straightforward. Entry offers a supple, round, succulent taste profile that's sweet, cereal-like, and reminiscent of malted milk ball candy; midpalate underlines the pleasant grainy/malty sweetness that typifies inland single malts. Aftertaste shows a bit more textural layering that sends the flavor into honeyed territory. Could not be anything other than a Speyside single malt.
2016 Rating: ★ ★ ★/Recommended

Craigellachie 17 Year Old Speyside SMSW 46% abv, $n/a.
Caramel color; pristinely clean. First olfactory impressions are of malted barley, sweetened breakfast cereal, corn muffins, spice cake, and toffee; later whiffs detect more of the oak influence, especially in the aspects of coconut, vanilla bean, and honey. Entry is lusciously sweet but neither candied nor unctuous, as the taste menu expands with presence on the tongue to include caramel, coffee bean, and bittersweet chocolate; midpalate reflects the entry findings, adding stewed prune, black plums, and black raisins. Concludes lush, gently sweet and ripe, woody/oaky, and sumptuously decadent in texture. Yummy and rich.
2020 Rating: ★ ★ ★ ★/Highly Recommended

Cutty Sark Prohibition Edition Blended Scotch Whisky 50% abv, $37.
Pretty eighteen-karat-gold color; crystalline clarity. The opening inhalations pick up plenty of toasted cereal, brown butter, baker's yeast, and dried violet notes that are pungent without being aggressive; further aeration brings out supple, nearly succulent notes of peanut butter, lanolin, vegetable oil, apricot jam. Entry is sweet, ripe, fruity, slightly saline, grapy; midpalate is honeyed, fruity (as in compote), raisiny, oaky, warming in the throat. Concludes medium long, oily, bittersweet.
2020 Rating: ★ ★ ★ ★/Highly Recommended

Cutty Sark Tam o'Shanter Blended Scotch Whisky 46.5% abv, $300.
Brilliant deep-topaz/umber color; flawlessly free of sediment/haze. I like the initial aromatic rush of roasted grain, dried fruits (orange, tangerine), allspice, clove; later sniffs pick up meatier layers of cookie dough, spice cake, oak plank, mango. Entry is bakery-shop sweet (shortbread), spicy (vanilla, clove), succulent, biscuity; midpalate is long, viscous, woody, intensely nutty, focused, orangey/orange blossom, sherried. Extended finish is slightly smoky, tobacco-like. A superb blend that deserves its fifth rating star.
2014 Rating: ★ ★ ★ ★ ★/Highest Recommendation

Dalmore 12 Year Old Highland SMSW 40% abv, $65.
Beautiful copper-kettle color; superb purity. I pick up lots of dried fruits in the first inhalations after the pour, primarily black raisins, prunes, plus succulent bits of spice cake, cookie batter, vanilla, nutmeg; secondary sniffs detect raisin bread, cinnamon rolls, candied almond. The taste profile features candied nuts, dried fruits (now pineapple, nectarine), and praline; midpalate is succulent, honeyed, and clearly impacted by oloroso sherry butts from González Byass—this is a big-hearted, unabashedly sweet and maple-like malt that's round and supple, even slightly fat.
2016 Rating: ★ ★ ★ ★/Highly Recommended

Dalmore 15 Year Old Highland SMSW 40% abv, $110.

Deep henna/burnt sienna color; flawless purity. I get a little bit of butterscotch and treacle in this opening nose, also a bit of egg cream and cocoa bean; second passes pick up a nougat-like richness that's more bittersweet than sweet, but the sherry influence is unmistakable. Entry features the cocoa aspect but now it's more like cocoa butter in its acute bittersweet manner; midpalate highlights the dark chocolate–like bitterness that's round and intensely kernel-like, and I also pick up chocolate-covered cherry. Aftertaste offers an array of finishing flavors, including toffee, cinnamon, clove, caramelized sugar, crème brûlée. Really tasty. My only issue is that I'd prefer to see this massive malt with a higher abv, like maybe 45 percent or 46 percent.

2016 Rating: ★ ★ ★ ★/Highly Recommended

Dalmore 18 Year Old Highland SMSW 43% abv, $200.

Pretty bronze/chestnut color; excellent clarity. Wow, the nuttiness is intense and more peanut- and peanut butter–driven than anything else; second inhalations detect the intensifying nuttiness, coupled with notes of rubber tire, rubber pencil eraser, malted barley, toasted cereal, rice cakes, brown rice. Entry features tastes of bacon fat, pork rind, sausages, chocolate-covered peanuts; midpalate mirrors the entry, adding vegetable oil, candle wax, black raisins, dates. Aftertaste is medium long, off-dry, silky in texture.

2016 Rating: ★ ★ ★ ★/Highly Recommended

Dalmore Cigar Malt Reserve Highland SMSW 44% abv, $180.

Burnt-orange color; totally sediment-free. The first nosing passes are treated to a cornucopia of dried-fruit richness, from baked apple to candied peach to chocolate-covered orange peel; secondary whiffs pick up additional scents of prunes, figs, dates, and black raisins that catapult the bouquet forward. Entry is resiny, honeyed, maple-like, and fudgy; midpalate mirrors the entry, adding caramel and a rum-like tanginess that does indeed make it worthy of a Cuban cigar.

2019 Rating: ★ ★ ★ ★/Highly Recommended

Dalmore Port Wood Reserve Highland SMSW 46.5% abv, $100.

Rich mahogany color; pristine clarity. First sniffs detect subtle aromas of pipe tobacco, dried plums, and stewed prunes; secondary inhalations after more air contact find mature, wine-like, and nutty aromas that are refined and multilayered. Entry features distinctly semisweet, tobacco-like, earthy/herbal, and raisiny flavors that are luscious and baked; midpalate stage is like a symphony of semisweet, fruity, herbal, and elemental flavors that merge into a singular taste that's bittersweet, piquant, and ambrosial. Ends long in the throat, peppery, buttery (brown butter), honeyed, and resiny/oily. Lovely.

2018 Rating: ★ ★ ★ ★/Highly Recommended

Deanston Virgin Oak Highland SMSW 46.3% abv, $33.

Pale-yellow/flax/muscadet color; unblemished clarity. I respond favorably to this bouquet's lemongrass, citrusy up-front aroma, but even more so to its keen freshness; later whiffs pick up bigger grain/breakfast cereal notes that are yeasty, doughy, early morning bakery-shop–like. Entry is off-dry, biscuity (continuing the dough theme), fruity, nougaty/

nutty; midpalate echoes most of the entry assets and brings in toasted marshmallow. Oak resin aspect shows up in finish, but doesn't obstruct.

2014 Rating: ★ ★ ★/Recommended

Deveron 12 Year Old Speyside SMSW 40% abv, $45.

Amber/fawn color; flawless purity. First nosing passes pick up floral notes of lemon blossom, honeysuckle, plus ethereal touches of citrus zest, sesame seed, black pepper; secondary sniffs encounter little more in the way of bouquet layering or depth. Entry echoes the delicacy of the aroma in the soft, candy-shop flavors of English toffee, marzipan, nougat; midpalate highlights the candy-bar aspect, as the flavor turns drier than the entry due to the oak resins, especially tannic acid that narrows the flavor focus. Concludes short to medium long, nutty, candy bar–like, gently sweet, and a bit rice pudding–like.

2016 Rating: ★ ★ ★/Recommended

Dewar's 8 Year Old Caribbean Smooth Rum Cask Finish Blended Scotch Whisky 40% abv, $22.

Finished in rum cask. Goldenrod/marigold color; crystalline clarity. I like the carefree, frisky opening aroma, which is immediately malty and grainy, but then turns slightly nutty (almond butter), buttery, and candy bar–like; after more aeration, the aroma becomes more grounded and settled as a malted milk, graham cracker character emerges, bringing with it serious fragrances of oaky vanilla and honey. Entry is far sweeter, toastier, and more honeyed than the bouquet implies it would be, and that makes for a shift in expectations; midpalate follows suit with the entry, staying the amicably sweet, honey bun–like, and toasted-grain path. Smiley-face finish is medium long, chewy, and simple. Merely okay.

2019 Rating: ★ ★/Not Recommended

Dewar's 8 Year Old Ilegal Smooth Mezcal Cask Finish Blended Scotch Whisky 40% abv, $22.

Jonquil-yellow color; very clean. Opening nosing passes detect fruity, tart, slightly salty aromas that do have a touch of agave pineapple-like aspect to them; secondary whiffs turn a bit sweeter as the fruit component goes riper and more compote-like. Entry provides a pleasing melange of barley spirit flavor mixed with oak resin and agave smokiness; midpalate turns up the volume on the malted barley grain element, which extends deep into the medium-long aftertaste. Had my doubts as to whether or not this idea would work but it does. Nevertheless, Scotch purists beware!

2020 Rating: ★ ★ ★/Recommended

Dewar's Double Double 21 Year Old Blended Scotch Whisky 46% abv, $90/375ml.

Finished in oloroso sherry cask. Butterscotch color; clean and pure. I like the moderately plump opening aromas of oatmeal, brown sugar, candied orange peel, and cinnamon stick; later inhalations pick up enticing bakery-shop hints of Walkers Shortbread, pain au chocolat, and pecan pie that dominate the lesser scents of dried fruits. Entry is bittersweet, dense with malted barley richness and flavor, moderately spicy and peppery, but overall very nice; midpalate is where the oloroso sherry comes into clear play, as the taste profile turns drier than the entry and deeply fruity and nutty, specifically, figs and walnuts. Ends on a weirdly tobacco-like note of misplaced astringency that majorly detracts from the positives of the bouquet, entry, and midpalate stages. Up to the horrendous finish, it was posting four stars as a final rating. An unfortunately late crash and burn.

2019 Rating: ★ ★/Not Recommended

Dewar's Double Double 27 Year Old Blended Scotch Whisky 46% abv, $160/375ml.
Finished in palo cortado sherry cask. Gamboge color; unblemished purity. Raisins, plums, prune Danish, and Oreo cookie–like smells dominate the opening nosing passes; later whiffs pick up additional elemental aromas, including sawdust, oak plank, dry earth, and saddle leather. Entry offers mildly pleasant flavors of oak resin, maple fudge, malted milk balls covered in chocolate, and honey-sweetened breakfast cereal; midpalate turns more bitter, oaky, resiny, sap-like, and syrupy. Aftertaste is medium long, woody, slightly salty, and tangy.

2019 Rating: ★ ★ ★/Recommended

Dewar's Double Double 32 Year Old Blended Scotch Whisky 46% abv, $250/375ml.
Finished in Pedro Ximénez sherry cask. Burnt sienna color; a bit of floating debris noticed but not enough for concern. Initial sniffs discover odd fragrances of Saran Wrap and vinyl, but then those quickly blow off, leaving behind aromas of candle wax, matchstick, and paraffin; secondary inhalations detect ordinary fragrances of oak, tree bark, cinnamon, and unbuttered toast. Entry is nicely sweet and succulent, doubtless from the PX; midpalate highlights the ambrosial qualities that remind me of prunes, Fig Newtons, mincemeat pie, and powdered sugar. Ends ripe, pruny, raisiny, and tart.

2019 Rating: ★ ★ ★/Recommended

Dewar's The Ancestor 12 Year Old Blended Scotch Whisky 40% abv, $29.
Earth yellow color; excellent purity. Up front in the aroma, there's a warm, deeply toasted graininess that I like for its delicacy and dryness; secondary scents include sawdust, wood plank, unsweetened breakfast cereal, unsalted grain snack crackers, and unbuttered wheat toast; there's a complexity here that's understated and calm. Entry is off-dry, biscuity, firm in structure, acidic, fresh, crisp, and deeply grainy; midpalate goes even more dry as the taste profile suggests a higher level of malt inclusion in the depth of this flavor's dryness. Aftertaste builds upon the gains of the midpalate, going flintier and slightly smoky in the final stage. A substantial leap forward in sophistication from the White Label.

2018 Rating: ★ ★ ★/Recommended

Dewar's The Monarch 15 Year Old Blended Scotch Whisky 40% abv, $55.
Wheat-field/harvest gold color; impeccably clean. This opening nose is generous, off-dry, nutty, and leathery; after more air contact, the nose offers deeper scents of baked wheat bread, graham cracker, figs, and caramel. Entry is gently spiced with touches of cinnamon and clove that accentuate the graininess and the bread dough aspects; midpalate features a pleasingly midweight texture that's creamy and supple and a delicately sweet flavor profile that's reminiscent of Honey Nut Cheerios cereal. Finishes long in the throat, chewy in texture, like sugar-sweetened breakfast cereal and mincemeat and bear claw pastry.

2018 Rating: ★ ★ ★/Recommended

Dewar's The Signature 25 Year Old Blended Scotch Whisky 40% abv, $200.

Ochre/tawny color; immaculate clarity. I like this opening nose of mature whisky as it exudes graininess, cooking spice (cardamom), library/book leather, vanilla snap cookies, and hay; with more aeration the aroma turns bread dough–like, slightly oaky/woody, and malty. Entry is all about the integrated, sublime tastes of honey-flavored cereal, succulent candied fruits (pear especially), candied walnut, and caramel; midpalate comes packaged in a creamy, buttery texture that wraps around the walnut paste, dried apple, and toffee flavor like a glove. Aftertaste highlights the texture's viscosity and pleasing oil level as the pastry-like, bacon fat, apple strudel flavors soar. Simply superb at every stage.

2018 Rating: ★ ★ ★ ★ ★/Highest Recommendation

Dewar's The Vintage 18 Year Old Blended Scotch Whisky 40% abv, $80.

Fulvous/bronze color; ideal purity. The high level of malt whisky (Aultmore, Aberfeldy, MacDuff, Royal Brackla, Craigellachie) is apparent right from the start in this floral, dried-fruit opening nose that's leathery, lightly toasted, and dry; later inhalations following more aeration unveil complex, multilayered aromas that include grain husk, hay, toasted oats, and wheat bread. Entry opens up new areas of sensory intrigue as the starting flavor goes in a much more honeyed direction than the tightly wound bouquet, introducing expansive, off-dry tastes of all-bran cereal, cinnamon bun, candied cherry, and cola; midpalate echoes the entry, adding deeper flavors of brown sugar, prune Danish, and spiced and baked banana. Ends up tasting of prune Danish as much as anything, and that's all right by me. A serious, genuinely lovely, and mature blended Scotch that's worth the search.

2018 Rating: ★ ★ ★ ★/Highly Recommended

Dewar's White Label Blended Scotch Whisky 40% abv, $23.

Sandy-brown color; flawless clarity. Opening aromas are biscuit-like, chocolatey, semisweet, deeply grainy, and sweetened breakfast cereal–like; secondary inhalations after more aeration time introduce scents of book leather, flaxseed, and honey wheat cereal. Entry is sweet, candy-like, nutty, and friendly, just as a frontline blended should be; midpalate adequately mirrors the sugary entry flavor, going even a bit sweeter, which is now getting out of my comfort zone as the flavor profile gets imbalanced, losing the breakfast cereal element to candy bar, honey, and brown sugar. Finishes too much like candy, and that's a sign of overcompensation to me. It's certainly drinkable, especially if you have a sweet tooth—the drinkability is not in question as much as the unnecessarily high degree of sweetness.

2018 Rating: ★ ★/Not Recommended

Diageo Special Releases Collection 2016 Auchroisk 25 Year Old/Distilled 1990 Speyside SMSW 51.2% abv, $450.

Attractive straw-yellow color; sediment-free appearance. First inhalations don't pick up a great deal of aroma, except for candle wax and linseed oil; secondary whiffs after more air contact detect reluctant scents of eggshell, dried flowers, sesame seed, white-flour dinner buns, and newly tanned leather. Entry is measured, lightweight, gently sweet and biscuit-like, lightly honeyed, and floral; midpalate echoes the entry impressions, throwing

in quicksilver tastes of heather, honey, sugar cookie, oaky vanillin. Finishes pleasantly sweet, slightly tangy, and showing a bit of lemon drop at the very end.
2017 Rating: ★ ★ ★/Recommended

Diageo Special Releases Collection 2016 Brora 38 Year Old/Distilled 1977 Highland SMSW 48.6% abv, $2,200.
Bright amber/old-straw color; unblemished clarity. There's a distinctive sea breeze, gentle maritime, saltine cracker–like opening fragrance that's delicate yet persistent in its reach; more air contact allows this bouquet to expand its boundaries to include citric acid/lemon, apple tart, sawdust. Entry features a desert-dry frontline flavor that's supported by a concentrated explosion of campfire spirit that brings with it a light smokiness loaded with wood-ash astringency; midpalate offers graceful, mature, and settled flavors of malted milk, pickle brine, smoked fish, and pipe tobacco. Finishes medium long, mildly briny, and suddenly spicy with feathery notes of vanilla. I have always liked the maritime malts from the closed (1983) Sutherland coast distillery.
2017 Rating: ★ ★ ★ ★/Highly Recommended

Diageo Special Releases Collection 2016 Cambus 40 Year Old/Distilled 1975 Single Grain Scotch Whisky 52.7% abv, $1,150.
Brilliant sepia/topaz color; impeccable clarity. Opening inhalations are all about graham cracker, canola oil, dried herbs (thyme, bay leaf, especially), and dried apple; after more aeration time, the aroma evolves nicely into a round, grainy/fruity bouquet that's understated, with nuances of green tobacco, fungi/mushrooms, and fennel. Entry is accentuated by a burst of fruit salad, loaded with apricot, pomegranate, and nectarine flavors that are ripe but not sweet since the acidity level remains high, keeping the taste fresh (remarkable for its age); midpalate reflects many of the entry impressions, adding a jammy component that's strikingly marmalade-like. Finishes long, fruity, contained, still squeaky-clean with acidity. Stunningly fresh and animated for its age.
2017 Rating: ★ ★ ★ ★ ★/Highest Recommendation

Diageo Special Releases Collection 2016 Caol Ila 15 Year Old/Distilled 2000 Islay SMSW 61.5% abv, $140.
Fino sherry color of straw/jonquil; perfect purity. The soft smokiness is barely perceptible, but it's positively present in the form of cigar box and cedar/pine forest aromas that highlight the barrel resins and the salty air of Islay; the aroma doesn't grow all that much with additional aeration time and that's disappointing. Entry is sturdily oily and viscous, giving off flavors of saltwater taffy, salted caramel, and buttermilk biscuit; midpalate remains as rich as the entry findings and goes a bit further with the delicately smoked malt, creating a toasted marshmallow-like flavor that extends deep into the aftertaste. A handsome Islay malt that's succulent and lip-smacking.
2017 Rating: ★ ★ ★ ★/Highly Recommended

Diageo Special Releases Collection 2016 Cragganmore Speyside SMSW 55.7% abv, $600.
Vividly gold, old sauternes–like color; unblemished clarity. Normally one of the

more refined and floral Speyside aromas, this dried fruit–like opening fragrance is elegant and accented with sweetened breakfast cereal, dried banana, and slivered almond; secondary inhalations following more aeration bring into focus a multilayered bouquet, featuring wood chips, sawdust, cherrywood, marzipan, nougat, and coconut candy bar—a study in aromatic understatement and majesty. Entry is tightly wound, unexpectedly prickly, fruity to the point of being mildly ambrosial, and campfire warm, and all of these factors provide a robust flavor ride that's outstanding and vibrant; midpalate ups the ante by highlighting the spirity (55.7 percent) embers-like warmth that comes off charred, woody, and therefore sweet and caramelized. Finishes long, toasty/roasted, malted milk sweet, and luscious.

2017 Rating: ★ ★ ★ ★ ★/Highest Recommendation

Diageo Special Releases Collection 2016 Glenkinchie 24 Year Old/Distilled 1991 Lowlands SMSW 57.2% abv, $450.

Pretty gamboge/old yellow color; excellent purity. First sniffs encounter weighty, substantial, and dry aromas of muesli, bran flakes, saddle leather, camphor; secondary nosing passes, following more aeration, find deeper scents of green vegetable (asparagus, especially), baked apple, apple peel, and poppy seed. Entry is lush (a surprise from this normally bantam-weight malt), significantly sweeter than the bouquet implies, laced with tangy baking spices, such as mace and allspice, and even a touch like custard/egg white; midpalate accentuates some of the entry impressions, in particular, the custard aspect, which now comes off like vanilla crème brûlée. Aftertaste is medium long, moderately sweet and ripe, with toasted flavors of brown sugar and honey.

2017 Rating: ★ ★ ★ ★/Highly Recommended

Diageo Special Releases Collection 2016 Lagavulin 12 Year Old 200th Anniversary Islay SMSW 55.7% abv, $135.

Pale electrum/Manzanilla sherry–yellow color; superb clarity. This unique aroma carries Lagavulin's aromatic thumbprint of contained smokiness, kippers, and smoldering campfire that is more astringent and sulfuric than flat-out dry, fishy, peaty, or grainy; further aeration brings out nuances of green tobacco, wood ash, cigarette ash, campfire embers, seared meat, sandalwood, wood-pipe cherry tobacco, and rubber tire. Entry is silky to the touch, densely smoky and peat-reek filled, sweet, oily, incredibly smooth; midpalate highlights the sweet pipe-tobacco smoke to its limits and the buttery texture, which I find utterly delicious in its sumptuousness. Finishes long, fathomlessly deep, delicately smoky, and timeless. For me, Lagavulin means sophistication, class, elegance, terroir, and controlled power. This edition has it all.

2017 Rating: ★ ★ ★ ★ ★/Highest Recommendation

Diageo Special Releases Collection 2016 Linkwood 37 Year Old/Distilled 1978 Speyside SMSW 50.3% abv, $900.

Maize/old gold color; impeccable purity. There's an acute spiciness/tanginess in the first whiffs after the pour that remind me of (spicy) cinnamon and clove and (tangy) mature spirit—but there're also traces of yeast, mash, and vegetable cooking oil; secondary passes unearth low-key scents of cereal, buttermilk biscuit, sand/glass, and greenhouse—definitely a bouquet whose calling card is subtlety. Entry is maple-like, sappy, resiny, honeyed, and vanilla cookie–like; midpalate features all of the entry impressions but now they seem punchier and more vivid in scope, offering a wide landscape of bakery-shop flavors that are baked and "browned." Aftertaste features the vanilla sugar-cookie taste and pleasantly sweet character. I liked this malt but didn't find it highly compelling.

2017 Rating: ★★★/Recommended

Diageo Special Releases Collection 2016 Mannochmore 25 Year Old/Distilled 1990 Speyside SMSW 53.4% abv, $400.

Resplendent bay/sorrel color; sediment-free purity. I immediately respond to the winter holiday fruitcake aromas of candied nuts, dried pineapple, white raisins, and dried apricot that abound in the initial aromatic encounter; further aeration brings out baking spices, especially nutmeg and clove, along with brown sugar, orange peel. Entry is unabashedly maple-like, honeyed, and bakeshop–driven as the taste profile focuses tightly on cinnamon bun, Danish pastry, and almond butter flavors that are oily, beany, and succulent; midpalate remains true to the entry impressions, amplifying the nuttiness and the pastry and espresso aspects. Aftertaste is medium long, intensely dried fruit–like, coconut-like and sweetly grainy. Might be too sweet, oak-influenced for some malt drinkers who prefer dry, barley-driven malts but I found it pleasant.

2017 Rating: ★★★★/Highly Recommended

Diageo Special Releases Collection 2016 Port Ellen 37 Year Old/Distilled 1978 Islay SMSW 55.2% abv, $4,000.

Bright amber/saffron color; flawlessly clean. I get unusual and downplayed first-time fragrances of steel wool, limestone, chalky soil, dry sand, barnyard, barley kernel, toasted whole wheat bread, sycamore; later whiffs pick up a whole other menu of fragrances, including fresh-ground black peppercorn, hemp, menthol cigarette smoke, sage, bay leaf, angelica. Entry is decidedly sweeter than the bouquet let on, featuring delicious and dry notes of charcoal, seared meat, bacon fat, smoked sausage; midpalate highlights the meatiness as well as the wood-fire smoke that accounts for the soft imprint of sweetness at this stage. Aftertaste is eternally long, ashy, moderately smoked and meaty, and lusciously memorable.

2017 Rating: ★★★★★/Highest Recommendation

Diageo Special Releases Collection 2014 Benrinnes 21 Year Old Speyside SMSW 56.9% abv, $400.

Bright deep-straw color; superb clarity. Opening nose is lush, full-bodied, robust, intensely grainy/malty, husk-like, with background notes of baked pumpernickel bread; with more air contact, the aroma blossoms into a wood edgy bouquet of sawdust, freshly sawn oak plank, and lemon drop; this is a dry, pedal-to-the-metal bouquet of elegance and understated power. Entry tastes are sweeter than I expected, resiny, chewy in texture, with defined flavor aspects of dried apricot, toasted marshmallow, chocolate-covered raisins; midpalate explodes with even deeper flavors, including brown butter, honey, deeply roasted malt, and oloroso sherry that dazzle long into the slightly salty, heated, spirity aftertaste. A magnificent whisky whose heartiness grows with every step.

2015 Rating: ★★★★★/Highest Recommendation

Diageo Special Releases Collection 2014 Brora 35 Year Old Highland SMSW 48.6% abv, $1,250.

Brilliant eighteen-karat-gold color that's remarkably light considering the age of this whisky; flawless purity. I smell peach, pear, baker's wax paper, candle wax, sawdust in the first whiffs; in the second pass, aromas of flax, textile fiber, grain husk, brown rice dominate this stage, but in a delicate manner that's composed, understated, graceful. Entry is gently sweet, a bit sherried, and like toffee; midpalate is even more intensely sweet, fruity (nectarine), and even candied as an attractive nut-like element takes charge of the flavor profile, driving it deep into the nougaty, candy bar, dried-orchard fruit finish. What's so appealing about this elegant malt is its polite style that demands little but gives so much.

2015 Rating: ★★★★★/Highest Recommendation

Diageo Special Releases Collection 2014 Caol Ila 30 Year Old Islay SMSW 55.1% abv, $700.

Pristine topaz/amber color; excellent purity. The first sniffs detect balanced but assertive aromas of cigar tobacco, cigar box, sea salt, green vegetable, grass, low-level peat-reek; additional time in glass brings out campfire smoke (embers, not flames), deeper tobacco leaf, saltine cracker, sautéed seaweed, medium-level peat-reek. Entry screams "Islay" immediately as the smokiness/campfire element becomes the lead factor within tightly wound flavors of kippers, dry-roasted peanut, oak resins, and polymers; midpalate takes a left turn on the sweetness scale as the flavor profile goes biscuity, honeyed, almost sherried. Aftertaste accentuates the sweet smokiness mostly, making for scrumptious savoring.

2015 Rating: ★★★★★/Highest Recommendation

Diageo Special Releases Collection 2014 Caol Ila Unpeated 15 Year Old Islay SMSW 60.39% abv, $120.

Seriously pretty jonquil/gamboge color; impeccable clarity. Wow, there's a seductive ripe orchard fruit (pear, red apple) fragrance in the first inhalations that's lightly spiced (nutmeg, mace) and very attractive; considering the abv level (60.39 percent), there is no spirit burn or aggression at all even after further aeration—in fact, what is going on aromatically is remarkably sedate, under the radar, floral, spring garden–like, fruity, genteel. Entry unleashes a torrent of biscuity, cookie batter, spice-driven (now cinnamon) flavors that are underpinned by a wave of spirit warmth that's delightfully comforting rather than aggressive; midpalate echoes the entry, adding tastes of brown sugar, high-cocoa-content bittersweet chocolate, and marshmallow that last deep into the bittersweet, candy-shop aftertaste. The elevated abv registers in spades in the mouth and extends deeply into the finish, but it always stays in check and never burns and appears raw.

2015 Rating: ★★★★/Highly Recommended

Diageo Special Releases Collection 2014 Clynelish Select Reserve Highland SMSW 54.9% abv, $800.

Attractive wheat-field gold color; perfect purity. First whiffs encounter touches of moss/lichen, grass, yellow plum, white raisins; secondary inhalations following more air contact see the orchard fruit aspect heighten and deepen as fragrances of quince, yellow pear, white peach accelerate. Entry is startlingly sweet, brown sugar–like, cocoa bean–like, even a little like sweetened coconut, treacle; midpalate mirrors the entry findings as the taste profile reflects more of a cookie/biscuit batter likeness than orchard fruit, which has faded completely. Aftertaste is solid, unabashedly sweet, almost syrupy/sappy, grainy/malty, acutely honeyed. I like this malt, but the road it takes from aroma through flavor through finish has more wiggles than a snake moving in the grass, and I find it disconcerting. While good and tasty, to be sure, the reason for the so-so (but Recommended) score is that there's no overall direction or running theme to this malt.

2015 Rating: ★★★/Recommended

Diageo Special Releases Collection 2014 Cragganmore 25 Year Old Speyside SMSW 51.4% abv, $500.

Striking amber/fourteen-karat-gold color; flawless clarity. First nosings discover toasty grainy/malty aromas that have spice aspects (vanilla bean, clove), a modest element of ripe fruit (white raisins, quince), chewing gum, tart lemon zest; further aeration brings out scents of candied almond, black cherry, sawdust, malt, salt, grape juice. Entry accentuates the fruitiness (raisins, quince especially), then changes course and focuses on the oak aspect as a sweet resiny/sap-like element arises; midpalate returns to the ripe fruit that reemerges with gently ripe, tangy, off-dry tastes that last medium long in the finish. I felt from the start that there is a hint of hollowness in the core here as opposed to so many other wonderful Cragganmores I've evaluated and scored highly over the past quarter century.

2015 Rating: ★★★/Recommended

Diageo Special Releases Collection 2014 Lagavulin 12 Year Old Islay SMSW 54.4% abv, $130.

Bisque/ecru/brut champagne–like color; crystalline clarity. Offers keenly smoky, peaty, salty aromas right out of the gate as well as baked pear, pipe tobacco, new leather; secondary whiffs detect black peppercorn, egg white, meringue, yeast, cigarette ash, smoldering embers. Entry is surprisingly sweet to bittersweet, with trailing tastes of ash, peat, tobacco leaf, salted fish, seaweed; midpalate echoes the entry findings to a tee, adding marshmallow, dried flowers, all wrapped in a waxy texture. Aftertaste is long, intensely smoky, ash-like, supple, more sweet than bittersweet, honeyed. All components are working in harmony. No loose layers or sharp edges. The biggest bargain of this collection.

2015 Rating: ★★★★/Highest Recommendation

Diageo Special Releases Collection 2014 Port Ellen 35 Year Old Islay SMSW 56.5% abv, $3,300.

Bright saffron color; bits of sediment are seen under the examination lamp. I smell lead pencil, nickel, baked rye bread, oatmeal, cigar ash in the opening salvo of nosings as well as traces of bacon fat, pork rind, brown butter; secondary sniffs come across with hints of roasted almond, dying campfire, candle wax, malted barley. Entry is amazingly rich in texture, resiny (is there rancio?), nutty, acutely oaky, grainy, dry to off-dry, succulent, seemingly endless in multilayered flavor profile; midpalate is, again, a supreme textural pleasure as the bountiful blanket of substance underpins the opulent flavors of buttered toast, chocolate-covered raisins, honey, oloroso sherry, dates, figs that all last

far into the semisweet aftertaste. The Port Ellen expression that will always serve as my distillery benchmark.
2015 Rating: ★ ★ ★ ★ ★/Highest Recommendation

Diageo Special Releases Collection 2014 Rosebank 21 Year Old Lowlands SMSW 55.1% abv, $500.
Really pretty eighteen-karat-gold color; excellent clarity. There's a piquancy in the first whiffs that is enticingly fresh, acidic, and fruity, almost juicy; after further aeration time the bouquet turns more subtle, waxy, leathery, and unsweetened breakfast cereal–like. Entry is peppery (like the aroma), nutty, astringent, and therefore fresh and tangy; midpalate is long, grainy, concentrated on the barley malt, cereal-like, mildly toasty, and pleasingly sharp on the tongue, which I take as a positive of this whisky's nimble cask strength. Finishes medium long, astringent, clean, lean, bordering on austere.
2015 Rating: ★ ★ ★ ★/Highly Recommended

Diageo Special Releases Collection 2014 Strathmill 25 Year Old Speyside SMSW 52.4% abv, $475.
Maize/gold color; superb clarity. Opening smells include honeysuckle, gum, parsley, bay leaf, steamed white rice; later sniffs encounter candied nuts, holiday fruitcake, dried apricot, prunes, black raisins, red cherry. Entry is gently sweet but with a metallic/tinny background taste that baffles me; midpalate remains unfavorably metallic and then unfortunately turns sharp and raw in the throat. Finishes well and balanced, recouping some of the hits it takes in the entry and midpalate, but there's not enough redemption here for a recommendation.
2015 Rating: ★ ★/Not Recommended

Diageo Special Releases Collection 2014 The Singleton of Glendullan 38 Year Old Speyside SMSW 59.8% abv, $1,250.
Deep straw/gold color; pristine purity. Early sniffs pick up aromas of butcher's wax paper, grain husk, textile fiber, palm fronds; secondary inhalations detect moderately deeper scents of barley malt, cereal grain, oatmeal, citrus peel, oak plank, wood resins. Entry is significantly sweeter than the bouquet, offering animated flavors of toasted marshmallow, baked pineapple, apple pie; midpalate reflects the entry findings and adds vanilla bean, cocoa bean, espresso, toffee, light caramel. Finishes deliciously in a whirlwind of biscuity, bakery-shop tastes.
2015 Rating: ★ ★ ★ ★/Highly Recommended

Dimensions 1989 Bunnahabhain 24 Year Old Islay SMSW 47% abv, $189.
Pale straw-yellow color shows too much sediment. First nosing passes detect aromas of dry earth, honeysuckle, prickly pear, herbs, and esters, but hardly any phenolic presence at all; later inhalations find an overall fading of bouquet particulars except for the alcohol, which remains a constant. Entry features nimble, fruity, juicy flavors of white grape, malted barley, cereal, salt, and oak resin; midpalate reflects some of the entry findings with the white grape and salt falling off, but leaving behind the toastiness of the barley malt and a textural oiliness that's moderately pleasing. Aftertaste seems to pick up a little vigor as the

flavor profile comes alive once again, highlighting the wood and the barley malt dryness. An up-and-down malt whose inconsistency keeps you guessing. A good, but not outstanding, Bunnahabhain.

2016 Rating: ★ ★ ★ /Recommended

Dimensions 1990 Tormore 24 Year Old Speyside SMSW 54.5% abv, $160.

Pretty gamboge/oaked chardonnay color; unblemished clarity. I get lots of nuttiness (walnut, hazelnut) from the first sniffs after the pour, and that blossoms into scents of orange peel, candle wax, and parchment; secondary inhalations following more air contact bring out deeper malty notes that are almost chewy and spice cake–like. Entry is alluringly sweet, honeyed, nutty, buttercream-like, cocoa butter–like, and richly creamy in texture; midpalate reinforces all the entry findings and adds lush flavors that are almost rum-like in their sweet intensity. Finishes long, sweet, raisiny, pruny, honeyed, and succulent.

2016 Rating: ★ ★ ★ ★ /Highly Recommended

Dimensions 1992 Glentauchers 21 Year Old Speyside SMSW 53% abv, $150.

Jonquil yellow color is attractive and pure. I like the intensely grainy/barley malt opening aroma that's dry and buttermilk biscuit–like; more aeration brings out traces of herbs (sage, bay leaf), new leather, breakfast cereal, and a deft touch of orange/citrus peel. Entry is sweet, honeyed, almost sherried, plummy, raisiny, grassy, and mildly tobacco-like; midpalate echoes the entry findings and adds an acute malted milk quality that is accentuated by the 53 percent abv through to the aftertaste, which is drier than the midpalate, more angular and lean than creamy or lush in texture, acidic, and therefore fresh if a bit prickly, ethanolic, and warming in the throat. All in all, a zesty malt with a lot of living to do.

2016 Rating: ★ ★ ★ ★ /Highly Recommended

Dimensions 1992 Longmorn 21 Year Old Speyside SMSW 53.8% abv, $170.

Copper/bronze color; flawless purity. This opening aroma has all sorts of scents to choose from, including hay, barley malt, leather saddle, field grass, heather, toffee, coconut, vanilla wafer, and that's just for starters; later whiffs pick up more evolved scents of honey wheat toast, cookie batter, oaky vanilla, clove, and nougat; it's an aromatic banquet. Entry is rich, bittersweet, toasty, oaky, maple-like, pleasantly spicy, and a touch jammy; midpalate is lusciously ambrosial, bakery-shop sweet, marmalade-like, mincemeat pie–like, juicy, oaky, and stunningly tasty. Aftertaste lasts deep as integrated, harmonious flavors come together for a flurry of honeyed, oloroso sherry–like splendor. The greatness of this distillery never ceases to amaze me.

2016 Rating: ★ ★ ★ ★ ★ /Highest Recommendation

Douglas Laing's Big Peat Islay Blended Malt Scotch Whisky 46% abv, $70.

Forty phenolic parts per million (meaning that it's quite smoky). Ecru/pale-yellow/brut champagne color; ideal clarity. Immediately, I pick up rubber tire, pencil eraser, seaweed, iodine, Band-Aid in the first inhalations after the pour; second tier sniffings discover hemp, rope, smoked salmon, bonfires. Entry is far more smoky than the bouquet, and suddenly the peat-reek is in control of the flavor profile to the at-present exclusion of other taste possibilities; midpalate is sweeter than the entry, malty, breakfast cereal–like, toasty, tobacco

ash—like, sooty, and carbolic. Concludes long, peaty, smoky, ashy, salty, but delicately sweet and malty through the peat-induced histrionics.
2016 Rating: ★ ★ ★ ★/Highly Recommended

Douglas Laing's Epicurean Blend Blended Scotch Whisky 43% abv, $80.

Contains a high percentage of malts, 90 percent. Pretty golden/straw-yellow color; flawless purity. Offers lovely, melded out-of-the-gate aromas of crisp breakfast cereals, mown grass, dried flowers, and baking spices (clove and vanilla); seven more minutes of air contact round out the already toasty and delicate bouquet that now features light caramel, Cheerios cereal, and Christmas cake spices. Entry is buttery in texture and nutty; midpalate glides gracefully into flavor heights of dried fruits, marmalade, spice cake, and sugar biscuits. Finishes a bit metallic, off-dry to moderately sweet, toasty, and slightly sherried. A sophisticated blend of high malt content that is worth every penny.
2013 Rating: ★ ★ ★ ★/Highly Recommended

Douglas Laing's Rock Oyster 18 Year Old Maritime Blended Malt Scotch Whisky 46.8% abv, $115.

The single malts come from Islay, Orkney, Jura, and Arran. Jonquil/ripe corn color; ideal clarity. I pick up a less phenolic/pickle relish initial aroma than from the Sherry Edition, as this first fragrance is more settled, integrated, mature, and sublime, emitting light-fingered scents of pine/cedar, sugar cookie batter, clove, hazelnut, and malted milk ball; secondary sniffs pick up additional, gently sweet aromas of pipe tobacco, jasmine, tomato paste, and dried apricot. Entry is flush with tarragon, beet sugar, dark honey, crème caramel, and grape preserve flavors; midpalate echoes the entry findings, adding candy-shop notes of chocolate caramel and high-cocoa-content dark chocolate. Aftertaste is lush, layered, mellow, and bittersweet. A seductive maritime blended malt in its prime.
2018 Rating: ★ ★ ★ ★/Highly Recommended

Douglas Laing's Rock Oyster Sherry Edition Maritime Blended Malt Scotch Whisky 46.8% abv, $59.

Like the 18 year old from Rock Oyster, the single malts hail from the islands of Islay, the Orkneys, Arran, and Jura. Rich goldenrod color; flawlessly clean and pure. The briny, pickle relish—like opening aroma is rife with sea air, salted fish/anchovy, loose leaf tobacco, and soy sauce; later inhalations after more air contact discover tangy, saline-driven, earthy scents of bog myrtle, bonfire, and Lapsang souchong tea, with fruity background traces of prunes and figs. Entry is moderately salty, green olive—like, toasted, and smoked; midpalate features a broader pallet of tastes, including sweetened black tea, charcoal, cigar tobacco, honey, cocoa butter, espresso, egg white, and custard. Concludes medium long in the throat, semisweet, mildly candied, piquant, and campfire-embers smoky. Seems youthful in its aggression.
2018 Rating: ★ ★ ★/Recommended

Douglas Laing's Scallywag 13 Year Old Speyside Blended Malt Scotch Whisky 46% abv, $79.

Lovely copper color; spotless clarity. In the opening nosing passes, I detect up-front aromas of burnt match, lemon meringue, prune Danish, fortified wine (sherry especially), and rosehips; further aeration brings out an aromatic wealth of honeysuckle, marmalade, kiwi, stewed apples, milk chocolate, and mince-pie scents. Entry confirms the sherry presence noted in the early stage bouquet, as luxurious, layered flavors of black raisins, dates, candied nuts, and gingerbread vie for dominance; midpalate highlights the prune Danish aspect, in particular, since the flavor profile veers in the direction of bakery-shop treats, those stuffed with candied and dried fruits and nut pastes. Concludes in a succulent, ambrosial manner as the midpalate directed. A seriously yummy, near-decadent, Speyside blended malt.

2018 Rating: ★ ★ ★ ★/Highly Recommended

Douglas Laing's Scallywag Speyside Blended Malt Scotch Whisky 46% abv, $70.
This blended malt includes single malts from Mortlach, The Macallan, and The Glenrothes. This color is topaz/sepia and sediment-free. Initial aromatic impressions include hazelnut, linseed oil, candle wax, and cotton fiber; secondary passes pick up deeper notes of hay, mulch, mown grass, heather. Entry is sweeter and more focused than the aroma as deeply cereal-like, malty, and mash-like flavors come alive; midpalate highlights the cereal but also adds touches of woodiness in the forms of vanilla, toffee, sponge cake, clove, and black peppercorn. Finishes complex, medium bodied, medium long, and drier than the entry. A handsome mélange of Speyside offerings.

2016 Rating: ★ ★ ★ ★/Highly Recommended

Douglas Laing's Timorous Beastie 18 Year Old Highland Blended Malt Scotch Whisky 46.8% abv, $109.
Pear-yellow color; pristine clarity. Right from the first whiff, I get floral/spring-garden scents of violet, pea pod, moss, and fresh topsoil that intermingle admirably with wood-influenced fragrances, such as oak resin, Madeira cake, and coffee grounds; later inhalations bring up alluring inland malt aromas of cardboard, ink, damp earth, and sweetened breakfast cereal. Entry immediately displays a raft of pleasant flavors, like sweet corn, bittersweet chocolate, toasted marshmallow, and brown sugar; midpalate impressions begin with astringent, acidic, and therefore cleansing flavors of citric acid (lemon zest), orange marmalade, and candied apple, and then conclude with beeswax, charred oak, maple, and brown sugar flavors. Finishes medium long, more bittersweet than sweet, candied, and like holiday fruitcake.

2018 Rating: ★ ★ ★ ★/Highly Recommended

Douglas Laing's Timorous Beastie Highland Blended Malt Scotch Whisky 46.8% abv, $60.
This blended malt includes single malts from Blair Atholl, The Dalmore, Glengoyne, and Glen Garioch. Color is strikingly pale and flaxen; perfect clarity. First aromatic impressions are of fresh fruit (apple, pear, apricot), baking spices (clove, cinnamon), and flowers (honeysuckle, orange blossom) that all seem to merge nicely; secondary whiffs encounter slightly sweeter, rounder, and a bit more dried-out scents of raisins, figs that add complexity to the bouquet. Entry is stunningly sweet and biscuity, as flavors of honey, Madeira cake, sugar cookie, and spice cake vie for dominance; midpalate features more of the spice cake as

a slight bitterness begins to prevail. Aftertaste is medium long, medium-oily texture, drier than the entry.

2016 Rating: ★ ★ ★/Recommended

Duncan Taylor 1981 Miltonduff 31 Year Old Speyside SMSW 50% abv, $400.
Slightly turbid flax color; mild haziness. There are pronounced tropical fruit aromas, to wit, banana and guava, up front in the early sniffings after the pour, and the 50 percent abv is likewise evident and moderately prickly; with more air contact, the elevated abv maintains its sturdy stature as added scents of creosote, matchstick, furniture polish counter the fading fruitiness. Entry is as prickly as the aroma, with the alcohol flashing on the tongue immediately, then fading away by midpalate, which is chewy, semisweet, grainy/malty, husk-like, toffee-like, and lightly honeyed. Aftertaste is medium long, velvety in texture, still a little bit peppery/piquant, but showing its age at the edges.

2016 Rating: ★ ★ ★/Recommended

Exceptional Grain by Sutcliffe & Son Blended Grain Scotch Whisky 43% abv, $90.
Straw-yellow color; impeccably clean and pure. First nosing passes detect grain husk/chaff, dried hops, unsweetened breakfast cereal, and spice cake; secondary inhalations after more air contact confront surprisingly underdeveloped fragrances of baking spice (allspice, especially), cornmeal, and unsalted snack cracker. Entry is pleasantly grainy, dry, acidic, cleansing, but overall lacking in memorable flavor character and depth; midpalate point turns up the volume on the flavor profile by expanding its boundaries with keenly dynamic tastes of graham cracker, toasted almond, and linseed oil. Finishes nicely in a slightly astringent manner that maintains the whisky's freshness factor. Recommended on the basis of the solid midpalate and aftertaste.

2017 Rating: ★ ★ ★/Recommended

Exceptional Grain by Sutcliffe & Son Small Batch Blended Malt Scotch Whisky 43% abv, $110.
Shimmering topaz/old gold color; unblemished purity. I pick up all sorts of exotic yet comforting and familiar aromas in the initial whiffs, including cotton fiber, textiles, unsalted butter, seeds, lemon drop, soft spices like ginger, cinnamon, nutmeg, barley malt, even Walkers Shortbread; second passes after more aeration unearth fresh honey, vanilla bean, tobacco. Entry is lithe, silky in texture, embers-like in its warming on the tongue, toasted, bread-like; midpalate features more of the malted barley in all of its roasted, slightly smoky, delicately sweet and sappy splendor. Finish is elegant yet potent, sweeter than the midpalate since the sherry impact shines through at last. Glorious in its subtlety and understatement.

2015 Rating: ★ ★ ★ ★ ★/Highest Recommendation

Exclusive Malts 2007 8 Year Old Cask #1603 Islay SMSW 57.1% abv, $150.
Light, pale-flax/chardonnay color; excellent clarity. Oh, I like the tangy, keenly peppery, medicine chest–like, sea-breeze-in-your-face opening scents that could only originate from one place in the world—Islay; further on down the sniffing line, following more air contact, the aroma detonates in heady waves of bonfire, Lapsang souchong, creosote, cigarette ashes,

and bog myrtle. Entry echoes the latter-stage bouquet in terms of the depth of tanginess and brininess, as the zesty flavor profile bursts with saltine cracker, seaweed, shellfish, smoked fish, and green tobacco tastes; midpalate goes in a decidedly sweeter direction than the entry, and this unexpected development adds to the overall complexity of this fathomless malt. Aftertaste shines brightly with sweetened black tea, toasted honey wheat bread flavors that are smoky and full of seaside character. What makes this Islay malt so sizzling is the youthfulness that pushes forward the beguiling fragrances and flavors.
2017 Rating: ★ ★ ★ ★ ★/Highest Recommendation

Exclusive Malts 1980 35 Year Old Blended Scotch Whisky 46% abv, $190.

Very pretty, deep-copper, burnt-orange color; ideal purity. I pick up mature, men's club, library-like aromas that speak to me of old leather-bound books, oatmeal with honey, pipe tobacco, sweetened breakfast cereal, black raisins, and toasted bread; secondary inhalations add notes of treacle, praline, hazelnut, and marzipan. Entry is round, supple in texture, sherried, pruny sweet, and roasted; midpalate features most of the sweet, maple-like flavors that are viscously creamy in texture, lightly smoked, and deeply caramelized. Finishes long, thick, woody, candied, sherried, and stately. For those whisky lovers who like fat, unctuous whisky, this is a dandy and a clear recommendation. I, however, prefer my blends to show a bit more dexterity.
2017 Rating: ★ ★ ★/Recommended

Glen Garioch 1986 Vintage 25 Year Old Small Batch Release No. 1 Highland SMSW 54.6% abv, $250.

Misty gold color; good purity. Matured in North American oak. I pick up lots of ripe fruits (dried apricot mostly), breakfast cereal, and hay/straw, along with a faint hint of smoke; further down the aromatic line after seven more minutes of air contact, the bouquet blossoms into an elegant Highland aromatic banquet that features the grain above all else, but includes supporting roles for dried fruits, unsalted butter, and walnuts. Entry is toasted, grainy, gently sweet, and honeyed. One of my favorites from this overlooked malt distillery. Breathtaking and elegant.
2013 Rating: ★ ★ ★ ★ ★/Highest Recommendation

Glen Garioch Virgin Oak Highland SMSW 48% abv, $110.

Rich topaz color; minor sediment seen. This aroma is reluctant to come out in the initial sniffs, except for a cheesecloth, fiber-like scent; additional air contact leads nowhere, other than to a textile/fibrous aroma that's of no standing. Entry is honey sweet, with medium viscosity, seed-like (poppy), peppery; midpalate reflects entry and adds red apple, baked pear, baking spices (clove, nutmeg). Concludes medium long, off-dry, caramel-like.
2014 Rating: ★ ★ ★/Recommended

Glen Grant 12 Year Old Speyside SMSW 43% abv, $47.

Reviews of this elusive distillery have been rare in the *Spirit Journal*, amounting to a handful of merchant bottlings from many years ago. I've visited this lovely distillery twice, liking it both times. I like the bright amber/old gold/sauternes-like color; spotless purity. Smells right out of the aromatic gate of malted milk balls candy, toasted cereal, citrus, and oak resin; secondary sniffs encounter porridge, dried hops, stewed prunes. Entry is completely dry and tannic, leathery, ginger-like, and toasted; midpalate highlights all the entry findings and adds meringue. Closes out with a gentleness that's dry, nutty, elegant, and oaky. I'm delighted to see this wonderfully delicate Speyside malt back in circulation.

2017 Rating: ★ ★ ★/Recommended

Glen Grant 18 Year Old Speyside SMSW 43% abv, $120.

The pale-flax/bisque color belies the age statement; excellent, flawless purity. Oh man, this opening aroma is like strolling into a florist's shop as the verdant, blossoming, "green," spring-garden bouquet could only hail from inland Speyside; but as the second sniffing passes find there's likewise a bundle of other aromas to enjoy, especially cooking oil, spring forest, green vegetable (cucumber, asparagus), cereal grains/malt, and gentle spice. Entry flexes a bit of muscle as the delicacy found in the aroma becomes meatier and more complex on the palate as flavors of oak resin, mace, and clove are underpinned by a solid texture; midpalate reflects the entry findings as the flavor turns rounder, more supple, and grainier. Finishes with a charming rush of maltiness that closes the experience with style.

2017 Rating: ★ ★ ★ ★/Highly Recommended

Glen Grant Five Decades Speyside SMSW 46% abv, $150.

Pretty, bright chardonnay-yellow color; superb clarity. Deep aromas in opening sniffs of butcher's wax, grain kernel, salted snack cracker/saltine, cake frosting; later inhalations discover seemingly incongruous yet harmonious layers of vanilla, pound cake, cumin, cardamom, fennel, celery, sea salt. Entry is succulent, intensely ripe, biscuity/doughy; midpalate is roasted, mildly salty, grainy, drier than entry, oaky/woody, beany, moderately floral (dried flowers in your yearbook). Delicately honeyed in aftertaste.

2014 Rating: ★ ★ ★ ★/Highly Recommended

Glen Scotia 10 Year Old Peated Campbeltown SMSW 46% abv, $60.

Buff/citrine color; some particles seen but not enough for concern. The initial whiffs detect soft, tobacco ashy and wood smoke–like scents that are more like iodine than sea salt as they remind me of a doused campfire; following more air contact, the medicine-chest aroma stays the course in the forms of Band-Aid and iodine, but it now also adds earthy fragrances such as green tea, chai, dry leaves, and moss. Entry is lean, agile, and nicely smoky/peaty as the taste profile includes off-dry, earthy flavors of cigarette tar, seaweed, and chocolate caramels dusted with sea salt; midpalate features all of the entry impressions plus subtle carbonic notes of cigar tobacco, charcoal, and kippers. Ends on a sweet smoky note that ably sums up the whole experience.

2018 Rating: ★ ★ ★ ★/Highly Recommended

Glen Scotia 15 Year Old Campbeltown SMSW 46% abv, $70.

Bronze/burnt sienna color; perfect purity. Early on in the first whiffs I detect nuanced bakery-shop notes of cookie batter, bread dough, but also mashed potato, Horlicks, chaff, and grain husk; later inhalations after more aeration discover very soft fragrances of black tea, scones, and oatmeal. Entry tastes include sweetened breakfast cereal, toasted marshmallow, and sugar-frosted pound cake; midpalate echoes the entry findings and throws in flavors

of orange peel, maple, oak resins, and gingerbread for kicks. Aftertaste is generous, more semisweet than flat-out sweet, deeply malty, and roasted.
2018 Rating: ★ ★ ★/Recommended

Glen Scotia 18 Year Old Campbeltown SMSW 46% abv, $110.

Aged in American oak, then finished in oloroso sherry butts. Fulvous/tawny color; superb clarity. I get a bit of sea-breeze saltiness in the opening sniffs, but then that fades, leaving behind a pleasant maltiness that's subtle and gently sweet in a breakfast cereal manner; further air contact unleashes spicy scents of allspice, clove, and cinnamon that are pastry-like, intensely fruity, and elegant. Entry goes in a ripe, succulent direction as the sweet raisin bran–like taste headlines the first flavors, pretty much eclipsing anything else; midpalate continues the grainy/cereal-like sweetness that maintains its lead position, reducing other flavor aspects like prune, fig, and treacle to mere glimpses. Finishes malty, oaky, maple-like, and raisin-like sherry sweet.
2018 Rating: ★ ★ ★/Recommended

Glen Scotia Double Cask Campbeltown SMSW 46% abv, $80.

Double Cask is aged in mature American oak and Pedro Ximénez sherry casks. Cocoa-brown color; inconsequential, minor sediment seen under the examination lamp. The unmistakably raisiny/dried-fig influence of the PX sherry is underscored right from the first sniffs following the pour; secondary inhalations pick up less pungent aromas of malted milk ball, dark toffee, chocolate milk, and crème caramel; it's an attractive bouquet that leans heavily towards the sweeter side of the dry/sweet scale. Entry is unabashedly sweet and biscuity, giving off dense and deeply bittersweet flavors of sherry, chocolate-covered orange peel, praline, marzipan, and candied walnut. Finishes full and viscous on the tongue and sweet and candy-like in the throat. Recommendable with a caution, as it is meant only for those whisky lovers who really hanker for sherry influence in their single malts.
2018 Rating: ★ ★ ★/Recommended

Glen Scotia Victoriana Campbeltown SMSW 51.5% abv, $90.

Earth yellow/amber color; spotless purity. The initial inhalations pick up mere traces of sawdust, pumpernickel, malted milk balls, Horlicks/Ovaltine, and mown hay; secondary sniffs detect deeper fragrances of oak plank (polymers and lipids), glue, newly tanned leather, whole wheat bread, and unsalted butter. Entry is alluringly sweet but neither cloying nor unctuous, as the malted barley calls the gustatory shots by maintaining its natural crispness and acidity; midpalate is razor edged with elevated spirit but not in the least biting or hot as the flavor profile unfolds tastes of malted milk ball, bittersweet chocolate, and praline. Ends drier than the midpalate and, therefore, with crispness and vitality.
2018 Rating: ★ ★ ★ ★/Highly Recommended

Glencadam 10 Year Old Highland SMSW 46% abv, $55.

Bright fino sherry–yellow color; impeccable purity. First scents after the pour are all about new saddle leather/leather gloves, sour malted barley, new spirit, grapefruit, then the later sniffs detect more of the grapefruit and a touch of lime but the oak remains hidden while the barley dances a jig. Entry reinforces the grapefruit/tropical fruit asset while the midpalate goes more grainy/malty and sap-like, almost but not quite succulent. Finishes medium long, slightly resiny, leathery, lean but not austere, and pleasingly youthful and sprightly.

2015 Rating: ★★★/Recommended

Glencadam The Re-Awakening 13 Year Old Highland SMSW 46% abv, $65.

Attractive jonquil/ripe corn–yellow/gold color; flawless purity. Up front, I get pleasant aromas of dried hops, dried fruits (white raisins, pineapple, apricot), toasted almond, and winter holiday fruitcake; later whiffs detect lemon zest, tangerine, and carnation. Entry is tangy, spicy, woody/resiny, and maple-like; midpalate features deeply cereal-like tastes of graham cracker, sweetened breakfast cereal, cinnamon bun, and clove. Aftertaste is medium long, satiny smooth, moderately spicy, and a touch baked. I like the 46 percent abv, which ably supports the inherent fruitiness of the whisky.

2017 Rating: ★★★/Recommended

Glencadam 15 Year Old Highland SMSW 46% abv, $85.

Straw-yellow/goldenrod color; excellent clarity. Opening sniffs encounter sturdy, concentrated, malty notes that are dry to off-dry and slightly citrusy; later whiffs pick up a small element of oak, vanilla, almond paste, but overall the bouquet is more violin than tuba. Entry is medium-rich, toasted, roasted, grainy, malty, and highly piquant/peppery; midpalate is long, floral, toasted, malty. Finishes medium long, very creamy, chewy, delightfully spicy, warming in the throat.

2015 Rating: ★★★★/Highly Recommended

Glencadam 21 Year Old Highland SMSW 46% abv, $199.

Attractive eighteen-karat-gold appearance that's unblemished by sediment. Opening nosings are treated to dry, slightly spicy aromas of poppy seed, sawdust, oak plank, toasted bread; secondary inhalations get beeswax, sap, oak resins. Entry is succulent, charmingly viscous, spicy, warming, medium toasty; midpalate features deep, oaky flavors that are resiny, sappy, complex, lasting far into the aftertaste where the ultra-creamy texture reigns supreme.

2015 Rating: ★★★★/Highly Recommended

GlenDronach Allardice 18 Year Old Highland SMSW 46% abv, $150.

Chestnut-brown color; excellent purity. Up front, I get pronounced aromas of demerara sugar, margarine, salted butter, lard, bacon fat, and grain husk; later sniffs after more air contact unearth additional fragrances of sawdust, praline, nougat, saltwater taffy, and tomato paste. Entry is dense, deeply flavored with molasses, honey, brown sugar, raisins, dried plums, and hoisin; midpalate is toasted/roasted, a bit like fruity pipe tobacco, toasted marshmallow, and caramelized sugar. Aftertaste is long, languid, honeyed, semisweet, and cocoa-like.

2019 Rating: ★★★★/Highly Recommended

GlenDronach Original 12 Year Old Highland SMSW 43% abv, $67.

Earth yellow/sandy-brown color; impeccable purity. Initial nosing passes pick up slightly distant aromas of dry earth, oak floor plank, and heather; later sniffs following more

air contact discover hints of toasted grain, unsweetened breakfast cereal, buttermilk biscuit, and baker's yeast. Entry is rich and creamy in texture, candied and caramel-like, fat and bacon-y; midpalate is where all the flavor action is with this Highland malt as the layers of taste unfold in succulent waves of caramelized onion, butterscotch, salted brown butter, maple syrup, and vanilla wafer. Finishes medium long and more peppery than the midpalate, as the taste profile turns right, turning more bitter and oaky.
2018 Rating: ★ ★ ★/Recommended

GlenDronach Parliament 21 Year Old Highland SMSW 48% abv, $210.

Tawny/bronze color; perfectly sediment-free. First inhalations detect attic-like scents of old books/library, saddle leather, old furniture, oak plank, and parchment; further aeration stimulates zestier fragrances of peach cobbler, pear tart, white raisins, and dried pineapple. Entry bursts onto the palate in expressive flavors of buttered honey wheat toast, pancakes with maple syrup, toasted almond, and candied fruits (pineapple especially); midpalate soars into the flavor stratosphere, highlighting the dried fruits and pancakes with maple tastes in particular. Ends on a semisweet note of succulence, honeyed density, and grilled pineapple. The perfect mature Highland malt at the perfect abv.
2019 Rating: ★ ★ ★ ★ ★/Highest Recommendation

GlenDronach The Revival 15 Year Old Highland SMSW 46% abv, $84.

Tawny/persimmon color; impeccably clean. My first impressions aromatically are of maturity, sherry cask, honey, charred marshmallow, and spiced baked apple; secondary passes encounter a buttercream richness that can only be inspired by the sherry oak. Entry is luscious, though not unctuous right from the get-go, giving off heavily baked flavors of gingerbread, cinnamon roll, and cherry pie; midpalate echoes the entry impressions but adds a healthy dose of baked apple, baked pineapple, chocolate-covered orange peel, and pear strudel, to boot. Finishes long, campfire embers smoky, tobacco-like, honeyed, and delicious, making no excuses for the eclipsing power of the 100 percent sherry cask maturation.
2019 Rating: ★ ★ ★ ★/Highly Recommended

Glenfiddich 12 Year Old Speyside SMSW 40% abv, $40.

Pale harvest gold color; impeccable purity. I like the rich malty opening aroma that's flecked with accentuating notes of citrus, banana, pineapple, and key lime; more aeration stimulates fragrances of kiwi, flint, guava, and honeysuckle; a definably inland single malt Scotch bouquet. Entry flavors, however, turn so stony, flinty, kernel- and chalk-like that all of the alluring fruitiness fades quickly into the background and eventually off the stage entirely; midpalate serves only to reinforce the earthy, soil-like metal tastes, and that I find unacceptable. What started out so pleasing in the nose ended up so regrettably banal in the mouth and throat.
2019 Rating: ★ ★/Not Recommended

Glenfiddich 14 Year Old Bourbon Barrel Reserve Speyside SMSW 43% abv, $65.

Goldenrod color; totally sediment-free and clean. Up front, I pick up aromatics that are rife with baking spices, especially vanilla bean and mace, as well as flashes of malted barley and oatmeal; secondary sniffs following more aeration detect subtle, if vegetal, scents of hominy, green tobacco, and green tea. Entry features earthy, slightly baked/grilled flavors of spiced (nutmeg) apple, toffee, buttermilk, and roasted cereal grain; midpalate ups the ante on the baked aspects, as the spiced apple with nutmeg component becomes the headlining taste. Finishes medium long, but rather hollow, dry, tart, and intensely spicy.

2019 Rating: ★★/Not Recommended

Glenfiddich 15 Year Old Speyside SMSW 40% abv, $65.

Saffron color; flawless clarity. The opening inhalations encounter brisk, mildly malty, and delicately sweet and ripe aromas that bring to mind white raisins, Anjou pear, and pipe tobacco; later whiffs pick up added, if meek, fragrances of baked pear, quince, and prickly pear. Entry is succulent, pleasantly fruity, a touch grilled/roasted, and nutty; midpalate flavor thrust is all about roasted fruits, in particular, pears and nectarines, plus it exhibits light touches of oloroso sherry, white raisins, and flan. Concludes nicely, with round, succulent tastes of raisins, dried apricot, and sweetened breakfast cereal.

2019 Rating: ★★★/Recommended

Glenfiddich 23 Year Old Grand Cru Speyside SMSW 40% abv, $300.

Harvest gold color; sediment-free. Opening sniffs detect subtle scents of rum or brandy cake, brownies, fudge, figs, and chocolate-covered raisins; later inhalations encounter mineral-like scents that match up well with the bakery-shop and candied notes, including lead pencil, dry soil, and toasted bread. Entry highlights the fruity aspects, especially the prunes and dried figs, but the entire spectrum of flavor is wide and deep; midpalate features an astounding array of honeyed flavors, including seasoned oak, biscuits covered in honey, butterscotch, and toasted honey wheat bread. Finishes long, luxurious, delicately sweet, supple and round in texture, and plummy. Delicious in a gentle manner.

2020 Rating: ★★★★★/Highest Recommendation

Glenfiddich Fire & Cane Speyside SMSW 43% abv, $55.

Sunglow/mustard color; pristine clarity. Initial inhalations after the pour discover understated aromas including refined sugar, saddle leather, grain kernel, and meringue; secondary whiffs after more air contact pick up mature yet vigorous scents of peach pit, geranium, sweet pea, and wet soil. Entry is a bit hollow in its core, but the silkiness of the texture makes me take notice going into the midpalate, which is mildly fruity (I mean, which Glenfiddich isn't fruity?), grainy, and breakfast cereal–like. Aftertaste shows a bit of zesty heat that I like, and it's this tangy, biscuity, pleasing ending that finds me bestowing a third rating star.

2019 Rating: ★★★/Recommended

Glenfiddich IPA Experiment India Pale Ale Cask Finish Speyside SMSW 43% abv, $70.

Jasmine/flax color; superb clarity. Opening fragrances are yeasty, sourdough-like, lemony, and piquant; secondary sniffs detect aromas of dry grain, malted barley, chalk, and dry soil. Entry is much sweeter than the bouquet implies, featuring a satin-like texture that supports bone-dry, biscuit-like flavors that are grainy, snack cracker–like, and mildly fruity;

midpalate highlights the biscuity aspect (buttermilk), as well as taste notes of graham cracker, gingerbread, and wheat toast. Finishes medium long, dry, deeply grainy, and buttery.
2019 Rating: ★ ★ ★/Recommended

Glenglassaugh 30 Year Old Highland SMSW 44.8% abv, $420.
Caramel color; flawlessly pure. First aromatic impressions are of toasted oats, baked bread, orange marmalade, and candied almond; after more aeration, the aroma turns woodier and more like candle wax. Entry flavors include a luscious texture that's creamy and rich as well as tastes of walnut butter, cinnamon, clove, baked ham, sweetened breakfast cereal, and dried apricot; midpalate echoes all of the entry findings, adding tight flavors of praline, black pepper, and black coffee. Ends gloriously rich, nutty, oaky, tree bark–like, zesty, and integrated. Shows remarkable vivacity, poise, and harmony for a three-decade-old whisky.
2019 Rating: ★ ★ ★ ★ ★/Highest Recommendation

Glenglassaugh 40 Year Old Highland SMSW 42.5% abv, $1,670.
Maroon color; excellent purity. Opening aroma is a little weird and slightly off, I believe, so I give it more time to collect itself; second passes are only a little better as the primary aromas include candle wax, parchment, old attic, and leather boots. Entry flavors offer ample redemption for the lackluster bouquet, mostly in the forms of grilled pork, bacon fat, vegetable cooking oil, and toasted wheat bread flavors; midpalate is heavily toasted, a little smoky, and black tea–like. Ends oaky, resiny, acidic, and therefore dry. Well past its prime. Take a pass.
2019 Rating: ★ ★/Not Recommended

Glenglassaugh Evolution Highland SMSW 50% abv, $60.
Citron/flax color; ideal purity. The first nosing passes pick up a more assertive alcohol presence that is deeply grainy/cereal-like but likewise fresh, crisp, and latently fruity; later sniffs after more air contact detect traces of plastic, vinyl, parchment, and wax paper that don't detract from the cereal and fruit. Entry is dry, crisp, tannic, and mildly astringent while also being waxy and plastic-like; midpalate highlights the grain/cereal the most. Finishes medium long, a touch warm from the abv, and resiny.
2019 Rating: ★ ★ ★/Recommended

Glenglassaugh Revival Highland SMSW 46% abv, $60.
Goldenrod color; pristine clarity. Opening scents are wonderfully round, tobacco-like, campfire embers–like, toffee-like, and just downright cotton-candy luscious; further aeration brings out more of the candy-store sweetness, as the aroma turns more like dried orange peel covered in dark chocolate and mincemeat; this is a truly lovely bouquet. Entry is rich in texture, bittersweet in flavors of cocoa powder, espresso, chocolate-covered coffee beans, caramelized onion, and turbinado sugar; midpalate mirrors the entry, offering slightly drier tastes that bring out the oak aspect in the form of vanilla frosting. Aftertaste is long, buttery, creamy, nutty, and bittersweet.
2019 Rating: ★ ★ ★ ★/Highly Recommended

Glenglassaugh Torfa Highland SMSW 50% abv, $65.

Pale straw-yellow color; sediment-free purity. Right from the initial whiffs there are piquant phenolic features of campfire embers, wood smoke, Lapsang souchong tea, medicine chest, and filled ashtray that wake up the olfactory mechanism in a hurry; secondary sniffs find a calmer, more settled aroma that highlights seaweed, moss/lichen, forest mushrooms, and malted milk balls. Entry is decidedly smoky sweet with not-so-subtle tastes of BBQ sauce, tomato paste, pipe tobacco, and English toffee; midpalate is ripe, brown rice–like, soy sauce–like, toasted, buttery/oily, and reminiscent of smoked salmon. Concludes long in the throat, tangy, salty, peppery, and custard-like. Really nice expression of this fast-rising malt distillery.

2017 Rating: ★ ★ ★ ★/Highly Recommended

Glengoyne 10 Year Old Highland SMSW 43% abv, $45.

Mustard color; bright, superb purity. I immediately like this open, straightforward aroma that sports equal parts malted milk balls, graham cracker, tree bark, eucalyptus, and cedar plank; secondary sniffs pick up deeper fragrances of bacon fat, lard, buttered and toasted wheat bread, and apple strudel. Entry features semisweet flavors that are bark-like (cinnamon), heavily toasted (marshmallow), grainy (malted barley), and spicy (oak-driven vanilla bean); midpalate mirrors the entry stage, adding succulent honey bun and maple syrup flavors. Finishes long, acutely bittersweet, toasted, grainy, and honeyed. A racy youngster that delivers the goods.

2019 Rating: ★ ★ ★ ★/Highly Recommended

Glengoyne 12 Year Old Highland SMSW 43% abv, $50.

Jonquil color; clean and clear of sediment. First nosing passes unearth zesty aromas of saddle leather, baked sourdough bread, and beeswax; later inhalations after more air contact yield only soft, plush scents of brown sugar, green tea, and cigar tobacco. Entry is pleasingly easy and approachable in its grainy, candy-shop sweetness; midpalate introduces more significant grain/barley malt character, as the flavor profile turns concentrated and biscuity. Concludes medium long, a bit leaner than I thought it might end, honeyed, and snack cracker–like.

2019 Rating: ★ ★ ★/Recommended

Glengoyne 18 Year Old Highland SMSW 43% abv, $130.

Marigold color; lovely clarity. Opening aroma offers tightly wound, narrowly focused scents of butterscotch, praline, nut butter, and toasted wheat bread; later sniffs encounter meaty fragrances such as bacon fat, pork rind, and grilled meat, as well as tobacco leaf. Entry is succulent, deeply honeyed, rich in texture, and very nougaty; midpalate echoes the entry, highlighting the sweet toffee-like top note. Ends with satisfying tastes of honey-dipped almonds, cinnamon bun, and candied orange peels.

2019 Rating: ★ ★ ★ ★/Highly Recommended

Glengoyne Cask Strength Highland SMSW 59.1% abv, $90.

Caramel-brown color; flawless clarity. The opening nosing passes pick up a remarkable fruitiness that's like dried pineapple and/or dried apricot; secondary inhalations following more aeration strengthen the fruit component while adding zesty aromas of malted barley, honey and buttermilk biscuits, peach pie, and white raisins. Entry is succulent, warm from the elevated abv, piquant, peppery, toasted, and grainy; midpalate highlights the entry impressions, throwing in a deeply wood-like, resiny oakiness that comes to define the latter flavor stage. Aftertaste introduces an alcohol-generated warmth that envelops the entire palate, squeezing out any other flavor option.

2019 Rating: ★★★/Recommended

Glenmorangie Bacalta Private Edition Baked Malmsey Madeira Casks Highland SMSW 46% abv, $100.

Very eye-appealing warm amber color; flawless purity. The first sniffs pick up front-loaded aromas of unsalted butter, charred oak, dry-roasted peanuts, oven-baked ham with pineapple, and burnt toast; after more aeration, the aroma transforms into a settled, focused bouquet that features melded scents of caramelized onion, roasted peppers, raisins, and roasted almonds. Entry highlights the baked Madeira cask, as the flavor profile turns winey, grapy, pruny, and decidedly jammy/preserves-like; midpalate changes direction a bit as the taste becomes drier, nicely bittersweet, intensely roasted, and even a tad like smoked bacon. The symphony of flavors continues long into the supple, viscous finish. This malt never loses the inherent delicacy that is Glenmorangie's trademark, but the forcefulness of the sultry wood nearly eclipses its exquisiteness. That said, I find this a charming expression from one of my favorite malt distilleries.

2017 Rating: ★★★★/Highly Recommended

Glenmorangie Companta Private Edition Highland SMSW 46% abv, $99.

Extra maturation in French oak wine casks from Burgundy and Côtes du Rhône. Burnt-orange/bright new-copper color; immaculate purity. Opening nose is juicy, full of marzipan and crème caramel splendor and suppleness; later inhalations discover butterscotch, wet earth/moss/lichen, mildly peppery fragrances that supplement the juiciness. Entry is like toasted marshmallow, salty, floral, candied; midpalate reflects all the entry impressions and adds brown sugar, chocolate-covered cherries, cocoa butter, nougat. Ends sweet, ripe, ambrosial.

2014 Rating: ★★★★★/Highest Recommendation

Glenmorangie Ealanta Highland SMSW 46% abv, $125.

Bright fourteen-karat-gold color; impeccable clarity. Opening inhalations encounter angular aromas of textile fibers, butcher's wax paper, and unsweetened coconut; later sniffs following further air contact discover intensely nutty, woody, wet pavement and resinous aromas that meld ideally into an elegant bouquet. Entry is deliciously toasty and sinewy in texture, with roasted pork tenderloin flavor aspects that are mildly charred; midpalate flavor profile is more in the dried-fruit (pineapple, peach) vein than meat and offers sumptuous tastes of salted butter and cream. Aftertaste is sensationally long, biscuity, fruity, ripe, and tangy. I just run out of superlatives when discussing Glenmorangie and the level of whisky making that happens there. Really astonishing.

2015 Rating: ★★★★★/Highest Recommendation

Glenmorangie Extremely Rare 18 Year Old Highland SMSW 43% abv, $119.
Saffron/mustard color; ideal clarity. I like the light-footed opening aromas of dry break-fast cereal, oatmeal cakes, and dried apricot; after more aeration, the aroma opens up only a notch more, as now I pick up ethereal fragrances of baked pear, egg cream soda, and vanilla wafer. Entry accurately reflects the bouquet impressions, featuring dry cereal, dried fruit (apricot still), and almond paste pastry; midpalate settles into a more characterful taste pro-file that's rife with oaky acids, vegetable cooking oil, unsalted butter, and bread crust notes. Ends in a crescendo of dry-as-a-bone leanness that remains as narrowly focused as the mid-palate and utterly clean. A mature malt that doesn't hammer you with multilayered flavor bombs; instead, it's trim, tightly wound, and svelte.
2019 Rating: ★ ★ ★ ★/Highly Recommended

Glenmorangie Finest Reserve 19 Year Old Highland SMSW 43% abv, $149.
Sunglow/jonquil color; perfectly clean and clear of sediment. This initial aroma is plum-like, not exactly ambrosial but effectively fruity nonetheless and a bit bakery shop–like with notable scents of bear claw pastry and pear strudel; secondary inhalations mirror the first round of sniffing. Entry is rich in texture, creamy, lightly toasted, and marshmallow-like; midpalate turns the taste semisweet, honeyed, and gingerbread-like. Finishes very long, chewy, spicy, and near luscious.
2019 Rating: ★ ★ ★ ★/Highly Recommended

Glenmorangie Lasanta 12 Year Old Sherry Cask Finish Highland SMSW 43% abv, $40.
Marigold/harvest gold color; immaculate purity. Up-front aromas speak of raisins, gooey pastries, cinnamon, nutmeg, and French toast; second nosing passes after more air contact discover delicate traces of beeswax, saddle leather, old honey, and soy sauce fra-grances. Entry is dense with dried fruits, including dates, figs, and black raisins, candied almond, and winter holiday spice cake; midpalate tastes like roasted pineapple, dried black fruits, and bacon fat. Ends on a bright, moderately succulent note.
2019 Rating: ★ ★ ★/Recommended

Glenmorangie Milsean Private Edition Extra Matured in Re-Toasted Wine Casks Highland SMSW 46% abv, $99.
Pretty light-amber/sepia color; superb clarity. Initial nosing passes detect very delicate fragrances of sawdust, brown butter, toasted almond, sea salt, unsweetened breakfast cereal; secondary sniffs encounter smells of linseed oil, vegetable oil, candle wax, oak resins, seared plank. Entry is sweeter, much more definitive than the aroma in that you can tell immediately that this is a malted barley whisky, which wasn't clear in the opening bouquet; midpalate is a touch hot, toasty, vibrantly resiny, sap-like. One of my least favorite Glenmorangies in a long while. Good enough to be recommended, but I don't feel the usual post-evaluation elation.
2016 Rating: ★ ★ ★/Recommended

Glenmorangie Nectar D'Or 12 Year Old Sauternes Cask Finish Highland SMSW 46% abv, $77.
Amber/old gold color; pristine purity. Everything about this opening aroma is golden and does justice to the name, in particular, the "nectar" aspect, as it offers a stunning array of

fresh (kiwi) and dried (pineapple, banana) fruit fragrances, as well as hints of honeysuckle and jasmine; secondary whiffs pick up additional scents, including unsalted butter, buttercream, and scrambled eggs. Entry features a supple, satin-like texture that supports the distinctively ripe and firm fruit flavors that mingle so gracefully with the malted barley base; midpalate is creamy, rich, luxuriously textured, and radiant with fruit flavors that scintillate. Finishes as elegantly and stately as it begins. Rated five stars in *Kindred Spirits 2* and remains, for my money, the quintessential barrel finish single malt Scotch. There has been, there is, none better.
2019 Rating: ★ ★ ★ ★ ★/Highest Recommendation

Glenmorangie Original 10 Year Old Highland SMSW 43% abv, $40.

Flax/maize color; immaculate cleanliness. First inhalations pick up delicate scents of hyssop, cocoa powder, yellow raisins (sultanas), and white chocolate; later whiffs pick up more of the malted barley in the form of malted milk balls, with supplemental fragrances of green vegetation, green tea, and tobacco. Entry is acutely piquant, gentian-like, and edgy, as the flavor profile speaks more of leanness and cleansing acidity than either barley malt or oak barrel; midpalate maintains the razor-like crispness found at the entry stage, which wipes the palate clean. This is an admirable ten-year-old malt whose breezy character is a direct reflection of Glenmorangie's skyscraper-like pot stills.
2019 Rating: ★ ★ ★/Recommended

Glenmorangie Quinta Ruban 14 Year Old Port Cask Finish Highland SMSW 43% abv, $59.

Indian-red/carrot-orange color; unblemished clarity. Wow, I like this saucy, zesty, deeply raisiny opening aroma that is hearty and elegant in equal parts; after more aeration, the aroma shows even deeper complexity, as the flavor profile swings from ambrosia to breakfast cereal doused with honey; memorable and a step forward with the addition of two more years of maturation. Entry is richly textured, piquant and peppery, fruity, raisiny, and ripe yet dry and crisp with acidity; midpalate soars with succulent flavors of candied walnut, figs, dates, caramel, and chocolate-covered orange peel. Finishes fathomlessly deep and long. A rival to Nectar D'Or. Fabulously luscious.
2019 Rating: ★ ★ ★ ★ ★/Highest Recommendation

Glenmorangie Signet Highland SMSW 46% abv, $199.

Persimmon color; flawlessly clean. Opening whiffs detect multiple layers of aromatic splendor, including waves of dried pear, dried pineapple, saltwater taffy, yogurt, and buttermilk; second nosing passes after more air contact encounter deeper scents of baked/dried orchard fruits, dairy products (soft cheese, egg white), and ore/flint. Entry is round and supple in texture, decidedly piquant and peppery, nut-like (candied walnut, almond paste), and succulent; midpalate dives deeper, offering candy-shop flavors of butter brickle, butterscotch, chocolate candies with cream centers, and hot cocoa. Concludes long, bittersweet, and fudgy.
2019 Rating: ★ ★ ★ ★/Highly Recommended

Glenmorangie Tusail Highland SMSW 46% abv, $99.

Bright amber/topaz color; sediment-free purity. Starts out aromatically in an off-dry manner that's full of burnt toast, baked peach and nectarine, dill, rosemary; secondary inhalations detect hints of black raisins, figs, mincemeat, clove, roasted barley. Entry is lean, almost austere in its dryness and acidity, but then at midpalate there's a burst of dried fruit flavors (pear, quince, grapes) that mingle nicely with the sap-like oakiness that's gently sweet and tangy. Finishes medium long, vegetal, herbaceous, woody.

2015 Rating: ★ ★ ★ ★/Highly Recommended

Glenrothes 10 Year Old Speyside SMSW 40% abv, $45.

Harvest gold color; superb clarity. Initial inhalations don't pick up much aroma, except for delicate touches of salted butter and lard; secondary whiffs collect soft, baking spice hints of clove, vanilla bean, and nutmeg, as well as spiced apple, spiced pear, and kiwi. Entry offers an immediately rich texture that's voluminous, oily, creamy, and tasting of fudge, dark chocolate, and candied walnut; midpalate echoes the entry, adding full doses of honeyed cereal, oloroso sherry, egg cream, cocoa powder, and buttermilk biscuit. Aftertaste maintains the voluptuousness found in the entry and midpalate, a flavor profile that's all about bakery-shop tastes that remind me of prune Danish, bear claw, chocolate croissant, and fudge brownies. Decadent, opulent, and full-throttle semisweet richness. A swaggering, remarkably meaty ten-year-old Speyside single malt.

2018 Rating: ★ ★ ★ ★/Highly Recommended

Glenrothes 12 Year Old Speyside SMSW 40% abv, $55.

Gorgeous cocoa-brown color; impeccably clean and free of sediment. This curious first nosing pass intrigues me by offering oddly appealing aromas of candle wax, black peppercorn, paraffin, mushroom, lichen/moss, and damp leaves in autumn; secondary whiffs detect more typical Speyside scents, such as heavily toasted malt, black raisins, jasmine, and brown sugar. Entry is all about the malted barley, as deeply grainy flavors, like oatmeal, graham cracker, muesli, and bran come across broadly and with conviction; midpalate reinforces the entry impressions, as it highlights the rich sweetness of the malt in tastes that bring to mind caramel, dark-chocolate candies with nuts, Cocoa Puffs cereal, and candied walnut. Ends on a bittersweet note that's fudgy and oily to the feel. In all, a masterfully constructed twelve-year-old with the heart of a lion.

2018 Rating: ★ ★ ★ ★/Highly Recommended

Glenrothes 18 Year Old Speyside SMSW 43% abv, $130.

Marigold/earth-brown color; flawless purity. The initial smells call to mind elemental, earthy aromas of buttered corn tortillas, clove, nutmeg, spiced baked apple, and raisin bran cereal; next set of inhalations after more air contact discover deeper, forest-like fragrances, including tree sap, sugar maple, cinnamon bark, and pistachio. Entry features a full-throttle viscosity to the texture that's oily and creamy while the flavor profile reveals a bittersweet taste that's one part honey and one part coffee bean; midpalate highlights the richness of the mouthfeel that wraps around the succulent tastes of espresso, hot chocolate, high-cocoa-content dark chocolate, and dried fruits (prune, date, black raisin). Gloriously opulent texture makes the finish a grand event as the flavors dance atop the satiny texture, making the aftertaste memorable. Glenrothes at its majestic peak.

2018 Rating: ★ ★ ★ ★ ★/Highest Recommendation

Glenrothes 25 Year Old Speyside SMSW 43% abv, $500.

Earth yellow/bronze color; excellent purity. Up-front aromas offer slight scents of plastic, grain husk, linseed oil, and worn leather; later inhalations following more aeration unearth faint wax-like, sawdust, barrel-stave aromas that lack grain presence or other customary Speyside traits (floral, fruit), and I come away from both aromatic stages disappointed and feeling that this malt might be past its sell-by date. Entry picks up the pace substantially in terms of bringing the expected Speyside in-mouth character into play as round, supple, and peppery opening tastes support the core flavors of toasted malt, salted butter, oloroso sherry, black raisin, and mincemeat; midpalate stage adds large dollops of honey, candied peanut, chocolate cake frosting, and treacle. Finishes grandly in a blanket of creamy texture that envelops the bittersweet, candy-shop flavors. Had the aroma been more than anemic, I'd have easily bestowed a fourth rating star. My suggestion is to instead purchase three bottles of the Glenrothes 18.
2018 Rating: ★ ★ ★/Recommended

Glenrothes Bourbon Cask Reserve Speyside SMSW 40% abv, $60.

Bright straw-yellow/jonquil color; quite a bit of fiber-like sediment seen under the examination lamp. This first aroma is surprisingly muted and inanimate, giving off only a distant graininess that is nondescript and dry; following several more minutes of aeration, the secondary whiffs pick up low-intensity aromas of beeswax, cardboard, green vegetable, waxy legumes. Entry is politely low-key, offering mere nuances of kiwi fruit, applesauce, salted caramel, malted milk balls; midpalate is this whisky's best phase as the flavor profile picks up steam finally, highlighting barley malt, cornmeal, vanilla, coconut. Concludes rather brief, off-dry, suddenly resiny, sap-like, and grainy.
2015 Rating: ★ ★ ★/Recommended

Glenrothes Sherry Cask Reserve Speyside SMSW 40% abv, $60.

Highly attractive saffron/amber color; like its siblings the Vintage Reserve and Bourbon Cask Reserve, there is floating sediment. Initial nosings are treated to round, delicately sweet and honeyed aromas that have oloroso sherry splashed all over them; second-stage whiffs unearth more robust scents, including buttercream, demerara sugar, prune, fig, maple sugar. Entry offers succulent, creamy, vanilla bean tastes that are bold yet settled; midpalate reinforces the entry impressions and adds deeply lush flavors of chocolate-covered raisins, cocoa butter, hot chocolate, espresso, dates, soft cheese. Finish is deep, extended, nutty, pruny, baked.
2015 Rating: ★ ★ ★ ★ ★/Highest Recommendation

Glenrothes Vintage Reserve Speyside SMSW 40% abv, $54.

Pretty flax/gamboge color; minuscule, cloth-like tendrils seen floating. Opening inhalations are treated to an entire battery of luscious aromas, such as buttery shortbread biscuits, allspice, cinnamon, brown sugar, honey; later sniffs detect hints of butterscotch, sourdough, cola, baker's yeast, white raisins. Entry is supple, silky in texture, delicately sweet in a bakeshop manner, nutty/nougat-like; midpalate is balanced, succulent, more nutty than ambrosial though there are underlying elements of dried fruits. Aftertaste is medium long, moderately sweet and honeyed, quite peppery.
2015 Rating: ★ ★ ★ ★/Highly Recommended

Glenrothes Whisky Maker's Cut Speyside SMSW 48.8% abv, $80.

Burnt sienna color; flawless clarity. Wow, this opening nosing pass introduces bright, fruity (pear, nectarine), dry spice (black pepper), bean-like (cacao, in particular), and floral (honeysuckle, jasmine) notes that are animated and vigorous and lovely; secondary sniffs pick up scents of bacon fat, pork rind, honey, and cocoa powder. Entry echoes the second aromatic stage to a tee as the entry flavors are fat, chewy, oily, and decadent, just like the latter bouquet; midpalate is cocoa-like, fudge-like, and pecan pie–like as the texture especially advances the taste profile in waves of creaminess. Finishes long, rich, sweet, and oaky/maple-like.

2018 Rating: ★ ★ ★ ★/Highly Recommended

Gordon & MacPhail's Connoisseurs Choice Ledaig 16 Year Old Mull SMSW 46% abv, $77.

Produced at the Tobermory Distillery on the Isle of Mull. The color is nine-karat-gold bright and a brut champagne look-alike; flawless purity. There's a lushness in the opening sniffs that's pleasing in its buttery character but beneath that lie fragrances of dried flowers, fall garden, tilled earth, and salt lick; later inhalations pick up feathery scents of malted milk balls, cotton fiber, and oatmeal. Entry is gently sweet, grainy/malty, spicy, zesty, acidic, fresh, and delicately salty; midpalate offers much the same as the entry in a sweet cereal way that's pleasing but neither profound nor dense. Aftertaste is longer than I thought it would be, showing more substance than anticipated and is intensely grainy/breakfast cereal–like. I like this maritime malt as I have nearly all Tobermory whiskies over the years.

2017 Rating: ★ ★ ★/Recommended

Gordon & MacPhail's The MacPhail's Collection Glenrothes 8 Year Old Speyside SMSW 43% abv, $59.

Gamboge/straw-yellow color; spotless clarity. First off, I pick up mustard seed, poppy seed, hemp, salt lick, filament, and beeswax that all dance atop a foundational fragrance of dry breakfast cereal; further on down the aromatic road following more aeration, there are distinctive scents of electrical cord, snuffed candle, burnt matches, and lead pencil. Entry plays up the malty cereal component to the degree that all other competing flavors fall off and get out of the way of the dry-as-a-desert malted barley; midpalate echoes the entry impressions, bringing in a resinous oaky quality that dries out the palate even more. Aftertaste is chewy, intensely oaky, sap-like, resiny. There is no getting away from the immaturity of this malt and, if it were mine, I'd give it another four years at the minimum to develop.

2017 Rating: ★ ★/Not Recommended

Gordon Graham's Black Bottle Blended Scotch Whisky 40% abv, $22.

Pretty, deep-topaz color; impeccable purity. This is a clinic on how blended Scotch should smell, with one part rich, toasty barley malt and one part fresh, breakfast cereal–like graininess that come together in harmony—opening aroma is marginally salty, showing just a trace of kippers-like smokiness; secondary inhalations after aeration encounter delicately sweet, leathery, slightly oily, legume-like, beany fragrances that somehow all work together. Entry flavors are all about campfire embers, wood smoke, sweet peatiness, oak, dried herbs (sage, rosemary), toasted marshmallow; midpalate echoes the entry impressions to a tee,

adding bacon fat, nutmeg, cinnamon accentuating tastes. Composed finish features the now subdued smokiness in its regal aftertaste.
2014 Rating: ★★★★/Highly Recommended

Haig Club Clubman Single Grain Scotch Whisky 40% abv, $25.
Clear and clean appearance; citrine-yellow color. First nosing passes pick up unsalted snack cracker and breakfast-cereal aromas that are compact, herbal, and dry; later inhalations encounter deeper grain-associated scents, most tellingly, grain husk and toasted wheat bread. Entry is pleasantly crisp, desert dry, and razor edged, as the grain-driven astringency comes into play; midpalate features subtle dashes of honey and lemon-zest flavors that underpin the primary taste of dry, toasted grain. I like this line extension more than the original Haig Club since it has greater dimension in the mouth.
2020 Rating: ★★★/Recommended

Haig Club Single Grain Scotch Whisky 40% abv, $65.
Brilliant, new, honey-gold color that's attractive and inviting. I smell opening slightly sour scents of lemon drop, lemon zest, hay, grass, green vegetation in the first sniffs, then with a touch more airing, the bouquet turns grainy with a little bit of fading. Entry is off-dry, notably fruity but at this stage more pear/plum-like than citrusy; midpalate is where I have questions as the flavor turns metallic, coin-like, austere, kernel-like, resiny, and this is due to the intensity and narrow focus of the grain. Finishes clean, lean, tightly wound, but limited in scope. This is a middling single grain whisky that, given its meager assets, is severely over-priced and would be more appropriate at $25.
2015 Rating: ★★/Not Recommended

Highland Park 12 Year Old Viking Honour Orkneys SMSW 43% abv, $55.
Old gold color; impeccably clean. I love this balanced, utterly charming opening aroma that's noted for its gently salty, deeply malty/grainy, and off-dry fragrance that actually owns a bit of orange-peel zestiness; secondary inhalations following more air contact discover faint hints of egg white, meringue, and vanilla custard. Entry features sublime and balanced flavors of sweet malted grain, honey, sherry, white raisins, white peach, and unsweetened breakfast cereal; midpalate serves to bolster the entry impressions as the taste attributes deepen and broaden, creating a flavor profile that's in complete harmony, meaning biscuity, off-dry, moderately oily in texture, lightly salty, and grainy. An affordably priced maritime masterpiece from the Orkney Islands—perhaps the finest twelve-year-old single malt Scotland has to offer.
2018 Rating: ★★★★★/Highest Recommendation

Highland Park 18 Year Old Viking Pride Orkneys SMSW 43% abv, $140.
I once called this Highland Park expression "the greatest distilled spirit in the world." Gamboge/orange-peel color; flawless, sediment-free clarity. First nosing passes encounter fully evolved and in-sync aromas of malted barley, baked banana, spiced orchard fruits (pear, apple), mace, and green melon; after several more minutes of aeration, the aroma transforms into a bountiful, off-dry bouquet that offers integrated scents of tree sap, honey, malted barley, unsweetened breakfast cereal, salted snack crackers, and doused campfire. Entry is

supremely satisfying, as tight, dense, and focused flavors of graham cracker, breakfast cereal with honey, malted milk ball covered in chocolate, and cigar tobacco work in harmony; midpalate accentuates the entry impressions, adding touches of olosoro sherry, caramel, vanilla custard, egg cream, and lemon barley cake. Finishes long, moderately oily in texture, off-dry to semisweet, mildly salty/maritime, toasty, and marshmallow-like. Question: Is HP 18 still my all-time favorite distilled spirit of any category? Answer: YES.
2018 Rating: ★ ★ ★ ★ ★/Highest Recommendation

Highland Park Dark Origins Orkneys SMSW 46.8% abv, $80.
Auburn/bronze color; flawless clarity. Mamma mia, I smell all sorts of slightly sour bakeshop things, such as baker's yeast, bread dough, starch, white flour, egg yolk; later inhalations introduce seductive aromas of citrus, vinegar, malted barley, sea salt, light toffee. Entry is toasted, semisweet, cereal-like, honeyed, caramel-like; midpalate soars with succulent flavors of raisins, stewed plums, salted sourdough bread, dried flowers. Ends on a sensationally luscious oloroso sherry note that points to the sherry cask aging. Utterly beguiling.
2016 Rating: ★ ★ ★ ★ ★/Highest Recommendation

Highland Park Fire Edition 15 Year Old Orkneys SMSW 45.2% abv, $300.
Deep topaz/bronze color; unspoiled purity. "Fire" is the appropriate name for this malt as the opening nosing passes discover immediate and impactful aromas of peat moss, cigarette ashes, bacon fat, vegetable cooking oil, brown butter, smoked salmon, and smoky black tea; another round of inhalations after more air contact bring in scents of roasted almond, roasted pork tenderloin, sandy beach, toasted crumpet, and fireplace soot. Entry is subtle in its textural richness, oily, and clean as the taste profile bursts forth with expressive flavors of birch, maple syrup, hot cross buns, black pepper, honey wheat bread toast; midpalate is alive with vivid flavors of sea salt, salted fish, cigar tobacco, and chives. Finishes extra long, silky, delicately sweet but really more bittersweet, beany, espresso-like, and totally yummy.
2017 Rating: ★ ★ ★ ★ ★/Highest Recommendation

Highland Park Full Volume Orkneys SMSW 47.2% abv, $100.
Distilled in 1999/bottled 2017. One hundred percent ex-bourbon barrels. Amber/buff color; flawless purity. Initial whiffs detect aromatic shades of vanilla bean, seaweed, subtle but potent abv heat, and hints of malted milk balls; secondary inhalations following more aeration discover slight traces of olive brine, sea salt, and kelp; one of the more nuanced HP bouquets of recent memory. Entry is more in line with Highland Park's personality as the flavor profile boasts lots of seaweed, mild, almost sweet smokiness akin to pipe tobacco, vanilla custard, and holiday fruitcake studded with candied apricot, walnuts, and pineapple; midpalate soars with mellow, mature, bakery-shop tastes of prunes, old honey, pralines, and almond butter. Concludes long in the throat, moderately toasted, citrusy, fresh, and maritime salty.
2018 Rating: ★ ★ ★ ★/Highly Recommended

Highland Park Ice Edition 17 Year Old Orkneys SMSW 53.9% abv, $300.
Matured exclusively in ex-bourbon barrels. Pale marigold/jonquil color; flawless clarity. Opening inhalations detect delicate scents of pine needle, sea breeze, saltwater taffy, dried

flowers, sautéed spinach, oak resins; the "greenness" of the bouquet, meaning the vegetal quality, remains solidly in charge, but the saline aspects pick up acceleration with more air contact, as does a whiff of new leather—a deceptively complex bouquet whose subtlety shouldn't be taken for simplicity. Entry is salty, maple-like, quite spicy, substantial, lightly oily; midpalate takes a citrusy turn that makes the midstage flavor profile more tart than the entry. Finishes long, silky, obviously maritime influenced, and wonderfully gentle, considering the abv level. Does Highland Park ever take a misstep? No.

2016 Rating: ★★★★★/Highest Recommendation

Highland Park Loki—Valhalla Collection Orkneys SMSW 48.7% abv, $249.

Marigold-yellow color; impeccable purity. Right out of the aromatic gate, there is strong evidence of sea breeze saltiness and seaweed tanginess, but neither interferes with the other; additional time in glass allows for more grainy/malty scents to gather that integrate perfectly with the maritime salinity, loose leaf tobacco, and sugar cookie underpinning fragrances. Entry is lemony, mildly smoky, peaty, and breakfast cereal–like; midpalate is long, languid, ideally oily, salty, vegetal, almondy, and like high-cocoa-content dark chocolate; the midpalate stage is monumentally wonderful and complete. Aftertaste is mildly smoky, fruity, and nougaty. A distillery that, for me, holds the key to all the mysteries of malt whisky distilling and maturation.

2016 Rating: ★★★★★/Highest Recommendation

Highland Park Magnus Orkneys SMSW 40% abv, $40.

Bright, spotless amber/dusty-gold color. The initial inhalations are treated to billowing waves of spicy barley malt and sandalwood aromas that build with intensity as they aerate—this animated, expansive bouquet could only be from one maritime malt distillery; later sniffs encounter fruity aromas of baked pear, nectarine, and grilled banana that float atop the base scents of bittersweet barley malt, pumpernickel dough, and latte. Entry mirrors the bouquet up to a point but then trailblazes its own salty in-mouth path that highlights the spicy barley malt and maritime breeze more than the fruit aspect, as the nosings did; midpalate is cereal dry, kernel-like, husk-like, salty, and yeasty sour but, then, the taste profile enters the aftertaste phase and turns decidedly nutty (walnut), intensely woody, and resiny bitter. In all, a splendid way to spend $40.

2017 Rating: ★★★★/Highly Recommended

Highland Park Odin 16 Year Old Orkneys SMSW 55.8% abv, $350.

Gorgeous new copper/burnished-orange color of palo cortado sherry; flawless clarity. I encounter deep scents of malted barley, malted milk balls candy, hints of oloroso sherry, fresh pineapple, pine nuts; secondary whiffs detect more of the barley grain in graham cracker form as the bouquet turns slightly sweeter, spicier (nutmeg, mace, allspice), and fruitier (yellow plum, white grapes, lemon). Entry is staggeringly profound, sherried, intensely grainy, dry to off-dry, complex and multilayered, toasted, slightly smoky; midpalate mirrors the entry but adds exhilarating layers of fresh honey, black peppercorn, candied apple that extend the spicy, herbal aftertaste stage well beyond normal limits. This is a

banquet of Orkney Islands bounty that ranks with HP 18, HP 25, HP Dark Origins, and others. Scotland's greatest malt distillery does it again. BAM!
2015 Rating: ★ ★ ★ ★ ★/Highest Recommendation

Highland Park The Dark 17 Year Old Orkneys SMSW 52.9% abv, $300.

Saffron color; impeccably clean. I immediately respond to the aromatic complexity, as the malted barley is apparent right from the initial whiff as are succulent notes of bakery treats like shortbread, gingerbread cake, and prune Danish; with more aeration, the aroma builds in power and depth, as all the splendor of the first nosing doubles down into deeper, slighter sweeter fragrances of raisin bran cereal, rum ball candy, and toffee. Entry is lip-smacking, dried fruit–like (black raisins, figs, dates, prunes), toasted, salty, honeyed, and lusciously textured; midpalate reflects all the entry findings and adds marzipan, crème brûlée, dried orange rind, and oloroso sherry. The rich aftertaste is all about the sherry oak impact, as evidenced by the raisiny, plummy primary tastes that linger and delight deep in the throat.
2018 Rating: ★ ★ ★ ★ ★/Highest Recommendation

Highland Park The Light 17 Year Old Orkneys SMSW 52.9% abv, $300.

Marigold/wheat-field gold color; flawless purity. First inhalations detect immediate yet gentle maritime saltiness as well as tantalizing traces of pineapple, kiwi, and guava that encourage further sniffing; secondary whiffs after additional aeration encounter a reprise of the tropical fruit more than the salinity. Entry is lean, nimble, and razor-edge crisp as the sky-high acidity rules the early stage in-mouth moment; midpalate offers a bit more flavor range as the acidity turns less piercing, thereby allowing the malted barley and savory oak aspects to emerge, creating a more balanced flavor profile. Aftertaste retains the attractive leanness found in the nose and entry stages as the firmness of the spirit comes into play in forms of deep graininess and resinous oak.
2018 Rating: ★ ★ ★/Recommended

Highland Park Valkyrie Orkneys SMSW 45.9% abv, $80.

Bright amber color; perfect clarity. The opening nosing passes discover delicate notes of aged parmesan cheese, sea breeze, smoked fish, toasted multigrain bread, and black tea; after ten more minutes of air contact, the alluring aromatics open up, revealing India ink, Horlicks, dry stone, malt kiln, potato scone, and damp logs. Entry is semisweet, astringent, dense, intensely grain-driven, and mildly salty/maritime; midpalate is lovely and scrumptious in its elegance and harmony as zesty/tangy tastes of breakfast cereal, salted butter, cocoa, cigar smoke, and butter cookie merge into one bittersweet flavor in the extended finish, which is soothing and integrated. Highland Park continues to lead Scotland's single malt category with one stunning offering after another.
2017 Rating: ★ ★ ★ ★ ★/Highest Recommendation

Hunter Laing Distiller's Art Benrinnes 1997 18 Year Old Speyside SMSW 49.4% abv, $86.

Chardonnay-like straw-yellow color; ideal purity. This supple opening aroma from

Benrinnes is subtle, delicately sweet, grainy/malty, fruity (kiwi), and delightfully mature, steady, and stable; later sniffs pick up nicely defined and integrated fragrances of green vegetation, springtime woods, candle wax, oak resins, sour apple candy and cooking oil—a finer bouquet than that of the erratic Benrinnes 7 YO. Entry is composed, elegant, gently sweet, and grainy (sweet corn), with early-on flavors of toasted malt, cinnamon, nutmeg, Jamaican jerk; midpalate echoes the entry and adds toasted marshmallow, toasted crumpet, cereal grain, honey wheat bread. Finishes medium long, drier than the entry and midpalate, acidic, fresh, lightly toasted.

2017 Rating: ★ ★ ★/Recommended

Hunter Laing Distiller's Art Benrinnes 2009 7 Year Old Speyside SMSW 56.1% abv, $52.

Ecru/oyster-shell color; sediment-free clarity. There are distinctly feinty smells in the initial whiffs that point to new cowhide, leather upholstery, mead, sesame seed, and tobacco ashes; secondary inhalations after more time in the glass pick up textile fiber, cotton fiber, steel wool, nickel, shale fragrances. Entry is much sweeter—stunningly so—than the bouquet implies, as densely grainy, sweet, sap-like flavors abound and dominate the palate; midpalate stage is more settled than the rambunctious entry, and that's largely because the spirit aspect calms down as it integrates with the flavors. Aftertaste is long, deeply grainy/cereal-like, with hints of maple and oak resins. My belief is that this roller-coaster-ride whisky has been released too early. If it were mine, I'd allow it to sit in cask for three to four more years, minimum.

2017 Rating: ★ ★/Not Recommended

Hunter Laing Distiller's Art Blair Athol 1995 20 Year Old Sherry Cask Highland SMSW 57.2% abv, $93.

Sherry cask influence immediately seen in the bright amber/old gold color; I see oils floating in the sediment-free core; pretty appearance. Opening inhalations detect traces of egg white, yeast, sourdough bread, carnation, citric acid, lemon zest; secondary sniffs following more air contact encounter drier scents of dry stone, arid desert, sand, metal, India ink. Entry is stony/flinty, dry, tired, rustic, brambles-like, musty; midpalate mirrors the entry (unfortunately), adding only an unpleasant waxiness that's stale, deeply flawed, and overly wooded. Aftertaste highlights all the low points of this sorry-ass malt. Rarely have I had, since 1989, a Blair Athol that I've liked . . . including this bottom-feeding dud. Buy this and I'll cut you from my will.

2017 Rating: ★/Not Recommended

Hunter Laing Distiller's Art Bunnahabhain 1995 20 Year Old Islay SMSW 56.1% abv, $221.

Topaz/old sauternes color; pristine clarity. There's just the barest hint of salinity here as the primary fragrance is, without doubt, the dry-as-a-bone malted barley, snack-cracker aroma; deeper inhalations after more air contact unearth brittle scents of malted milk ball, peanuts, and graham cracker. Entry is razor edged with cask strength spirit (56.1 percent), slightly yeasty, doughy, biscuity, and acidic; midpalate maintains the sharpness of the spirit, which begins to integrate with the grain and wood aspects, creating an experience that's frisky and slightly feral for the usually sublime and low-key Bunnahabhain. Finishes long, spirity, dry, acidic, and cleansing.

2017 Rating: ★ ★ ★/Recommended

Hunter Laing Distiller's Art Caol Ila 1984 32 Year Old Islay SMSW 50.9% abv, $259.

Amber/nine-karat-gold color; ideal clarity. The sea breeze, seashell, and anchovy-like frontline aromas are keenly salty, brisk, and iodine-like; later sniffs after more time in the glass discover creosote, olive brine, and smoked fish aromas that come to define the bouquet. Entry is emblematic Caol Ila in that there's an early rush of peat-reek, then the malted grain takes charge in a drying-out process that is the entry highlight; midpalate shows more cookie batter, almond-like, black tea/Lapsang souchong flavors that eclipse the sea salt and peatiness by the time the finish begins its highly astringent journey into the throat. I found this Caol Ila immensely satisfying due to its build up to the A1 aftertaste.

2017 Rating: ★ ★ ★ ★/Highly Recommended

Hunter Laing Distiller's Art Craigellachie 1995 20 Year Old Sherry Cask Speyside SMSW 50.4% abv, $94.

The deep chestnut/bay color is dazzling, as is the purity. First nosings detect not-so-subtle aromas of bacon fat, pork rind, brown butter, caramelized onion, and prickly spirit; next wave of inhalations find a more composed aroma as the spirit quiets down, allowing the oak influence to emerge, in particular, as vanilla bean, clove, allspice, and hard cheese. Entry is very cheese-like, sappy, spicy (vanilla extract, nutmeg), and honeyed as the sherry cask imprint gains in strength and influence; midpalate is like (Mexican) mole sauce, cocoa bean, and praline, chocolatey, lightly toasted, with a hint of marzipan. Concludes medium long, satiny in texture but neither creamy nor viscous, nutty, toasty, bread-like, and winey from the sherry cask. Like most malts from this distillery, I have reservations about it, especially in the core, which I find a touch hollow. The sherry cask pulls it through, however, with enough superficial verve to make it worth the experience for a Speyside malt.

2017 Rating: ★ ★ ★/Recommended

Hunter Laing Distiller's Art Girvan 1990 25 Year Old Single Grain Scotch Whisky 57.1% abv, $129.

Color is jonquil/fourteen-karat-gold; sediment-free clarity. First nosing passes detect animated and deep smells of sweet corn, porridge, bran flakes, and Honey Nut Cheerios cereal—a genuine grain-a-thon, at least at this point; further inhalations after more air contact discover smoked and feinty scents of plastic rope, smoked cheese (Gouda), burnt matches, rubber tires. Entry is stone dry at first, moderately toasty/roasted, almost like roast pork, and grainy; at midpalate, the taste profile turns bittersweet, like baked ham studded with cloves, meaty, and caramelized onion–like. Finish is heavily smoked like a tomato paste–based BBQ sauce, burnt/charred, but now flat-out bitter. One positive is that the lofty abv never dominates.

2017 Rating: ★ ★ ★/Recommended

Hunter Laing Distiller's Art Laphroaig 2001 15 Year Old Sherry Cask Islay SMSW 57.2% abv, $192.

Old gold/amber color; perfect purity. Wow, the lactic acidity in the opening inhalations is astoundingly milk-like and creamy, rich and bountiful, grainy, and batter-like; more aeration brings out a spiciness that's peppery, semisweet, green tobacco–like, and zesty, making the latter-stage nosings comforting and pleasing. Entry mirrors the second stage of nosing as the acute acidity cleanses the palate first, then provides plenty of tangy flavors, including smoked salmon, kippers, tar, and charred meat; midpalate comes across as being marginally sweeter than the entry, and that's due directly to the oaky vanilla (vanillin) that headlines this stage. Aftertaste is medium long, mildly smoky, pipe tobacco–like, pork rind–like, bacony.
2017 Rating: ★ ★ ★ ★/Highly Recommended

Hunter Laing Distiller's Art Macallan 1993 23 Year Old Speyside SMSW 54.5% abv, $991.

Topaz/sepia color is sediment-free and pristine. There's an aspect of burnt toast with marmalade in the initial whiff that I like, but then traces of dried orange peel, kiwi, and custard round out the frontline inhalations in typical Macallan style; secondary sniffs showcase the 54.5 percent abv in a smoldering campfire manner, and the later inhalations unearth honey, brown butter, brown sugar, and caramel. Entry is sumptuous, delicately sweet, sturdy, oily, creamy in texture, sherried, and tasty; midpalate reflects the entry findings and throws in Madeira cake, black raisins, candied apple, maple syrup, and black pepper. Finishes as lavish and robust as it started at entry, flashing luscious flavors of linseed oil, cocoa, espresso, hot chocolate, candied almond. I know it's pricey but, man, what a lovely Mac.
2017 Rating: ★ ★ ★ ★ ★/Highest Recommendation

Hunter Laing Distiller's Art North British 1996 19 Year Old Single Grain Scotch Whisky 53.4% abv, $105.

Greenish/straw-yellow/flax-like color; unblemished purity. This single grain opening aroma is tropical fruit–like (guava, papaya), gently sweet, a touch toasted, and honeyed; with more aeration the tropical fruit turns to orchard fruit, especially peach and pear, along with a bit of sulphur, fireworks, and cordite. Entry is steely/flinty, stone-like, earthy, espresso-like, maple-like, and sappy, as the fruit components disappear in favor of cereal and wood influences. Aftertaste is beany, semidry, grainy, brown rice–like, pleasantly silky in texture. A solid entry into the growing single grain Scotch subcategory.
2017 Rating: ★ ★ ★ ★/Highly Recommended

James MacArthur 6 Year Old Islay SMSW 45% abv, $105.

Chardonnay-yellow color; flawless purity. Here, the initial nosings are treated to pungent, smoky, peaty, can-only-hail-from-Islay aromas that bring to mind cigarette ashes, kippers, iodine, medicine chest, Band-Aids, sea breeze, tidal pools; secondary sniffs detect deeper scents, mostly pipe tobacco, saltwater taffy, olives in brine. Entry is mildly grainy, youthful, but pleasingly briny/salty/olive-like; midpalate is sweet, deeply malty, moderately salty, smoky, and briny. Finishes medium long, smoky, cigar box–like, ashy, campfire embers–like.
2016 Rating: ★ ★ ★/Recommended

James MacArthur Bunnahabhain 5 Year Old Islay SMSW 45% abv, $65.

Pale-yellow/ecru/tarnished-silver tint; excellent clarity. This opening nosing is rife with fresh-off-the-still flowery scents, all dewy, spring-like, and blossomy, as well as deft touches of sea salt and damp grain; later sniffs pick up more of the wet malt, wet sand, seaside, and cement aromas that all point to immaturity and lack of wood maturation time. Entry is gently sweet in a grainy, cereal-like manner that also flashes a flavor of tropical fruits (bananas, guavas); midpalate reacts like any young malt whisky in that the flavor profile is vibrantly spiky, intensely spirity, grainy sweet, and a little reminiscent of American moonshine. A mere slip of a single malt from Islay.

2016 Rating: ★ ★ ★/Recommended

Johnnie Walker Black Label 12 Year Old Blended Scotch Whisky 40% abv, $30.

Attractive gamboge/old gold hue; impeccable purity. Lovely first aromas include deep-roasted grain, toasty breakfast cereals, sea salt, and oak plank; more air contact releases dried apricot and walnut notes that round off the already splendid bouquet. Entry is moderately oily (though not creamy), nutty, malty, and toffee bittersweet; midpalate is medium long, significantly drier than the entry, oaky, gently smoky, and sophisticated in its integration. Concludes with elegance, maritime saltiness, and a chewy texture that I find delectable. Along with Chivas Regal 12 and Dewar's 12, JW Black is a benchmark Scotch whisky twelve-year-old expression and a tremendous value.

2018 Rating: ★ ★ ★ ★/Highly Recommended

Johnnie Walker Blue Label Blended Scotch Whisky 40% abv, $225.

Golden wheat field/golden color is very attractive and free of any hint of sediment. Immediately, I pick up a seaside saltiness (might that be Talisker single malt?) that is bedeviling in its attraction, but there are additional opening scents like nougat, bread dough, rum ball candy, pipe tobacco, and nutmeg to boot; after more aeration, secondary inhalations discover dry malted barley, a trace of campfire smoke, baked pear, and pine nut. Entry is delicate, creamy in texture, and maple-fudge sweet; midpalate is its "reaching-the-summit" moment in which fine, expressive layers of bittersweet flavor, most notably candied almond, spice cake, salted chocolates, and marzipan, merge into a singular flavor that's deeply satisfying, long in the throat, gently smoked, and maritime salty. Either this latest standard version is better than the earlier incarnations, or I have finally bought into the marketing. I trust that it's the former. Whichever the situation, this is truly a magnificent blended Scotch, if massively expensive.

2018 Rating: ★ ★ ★ ★ ★/Highest Recommendation

Johnnie Walker Blue Label Ghost and Rare Blended Scotch Whisky 46% abv, $400.

Pretty and clean bronze color. I have to exhibit some patience with this opening aroma since it comes off as being reluctant and latent, unwilling to offer much so I move on; later sniffs following further aeration pick up feathery hints of chalky soil, sawdust on the floor, wax paper, and porridge/oatmeal; for this kind of money, I want more aroma, please and thank you. Entry is mouth filling with inland Highland single malt graininess/breakfast cereal flavors that are tightly wound, dry as a bone, keenly peppery, piquant, and densely oaky; midpalate is zesty, tangy, highly spiced, and arid as the taste profile features vivid flavors of buttery Scottish shortbread, cinnamon bun, prune Danish, hazelnut, and oak-influenced vanilla bean. Concludes long, piquant and peppery, cocoa-like, and intensely grainy. The lack of bouquet aside (that killed the possibility of a fifth star), this is a stunning in-mouth experience from entry through the languid, luxurious aftertaste.

2018 Rating: ★ ★ ★ ★/Highly Recommended

Johnnie Walker Double Black Blended Scotch Whisky 40% abv, $32.

Marginally darker, more topaz in color than the regular JW Black; flawless clarity. Peatier, a smidgen sweeter, more charcoal-like/BBQ-smoked than the standard JW Black; the Double Black aroma is noticeably fatter, more buttery, resiny, and more oak barrel–driven than the more angular, grainy, and maritime-influenced regular JW Black. Entry is medium smoky, astringent and dry, oaky and delightfully round; midpalate displays a measure of soft peatiness and green olive brine that's appealing, but there are also tastes of dried fruit (pear, quince), candied almond, and spearmint aspects that work in harmony with the texture. Concludes in a sweet, ripe fruit, and pipe tobacco manner. A significant departure from standard JW Black, which is leaner and drier but just as yummy as this tasty blend.

2018 Rating: ★ ★ ★ ★/Highly Recommended

Johnnie Walker Gold Label Reserve Blended Scotch Whisky 40% abv, $87.

Saffron/maize color; impeccable purity. I get wheelbarrows of saltwater taffy, buttered almonds, plain omelet, soft cheese, black pepper in the first sniffs; later whiffs confirm the initial round and add toffee, marzipan, brown sugar, cornflower notes. Entry shows some peat, minor salinity, oaky resin, honey; midpalate reinforces the entry impressions, adding sesame, mace aspects. Finishes buttery, creamy textured, semisweet, fruity.

2015 Rating: ★ ★ ★ ★/Highly Recommended

Johnnie Walker Green Label 15 Year Old Blended Malt Scotch Whisky 43% abv, $65.

The amber color is bright under the examination lamp and there is no sediment seen; flawless purity and very oily—which I like very much. I have always admired the moderately smoky, salty aroma (that's the Talisker and Caol Ila) of JW Green, yet this version seems a little sweeter and maltier than the previous incarnation, which makes me wonder if there's more Speyside (Linkwood and Cragganmore) malt included in the recipe than in the earlier expression; later inhalations reinforce the findings of first whiffs as the second wave showcases a honeyed sweetness that dominates the bouquet. Entry is sublimely oily in the mouth, giving structure and a sturdy core to the flavor profile right off the crack of the bat; midpalate features a multitude of taste offerings, from pine to light peatiness to cookie batter to marzipan to dried apricot to cigar box. Concludes full-bodied, creamy in the throat, decidedly sweet with a savory, full-throated accent of Speyside. Aside from the discontinued JW Gold 18 (five stars), my favorite Johnnie Walker.

2017 Rating: ★ ★ ★ ★ ★/Highest Recommendation

Johnnie Walker Platinum Label 18 Year Old Blended Scotch Whisky 40% abv, $110.

Replaces one of my all-time favorite Scotches, the five star (in the *Spirit Journal*) Johnnie Walker Gold. Amber/old gold color; excellent purity. Opening nose is pleasantly biscuity and cookie dough–like, with nuances of nutmeg, old saddle leather, and tropical fruits;

further air contact gives rise to a floral, grainy, inland Scotland bouquet that speaks of Spey-side more than any other whisky district. Entry is grainy sweet, with integrated flavors of graham cracker and spice cake; midpalate mirrors the entry, adding touches of oak resin, salt, and hard cheese. Finishes well and elegantly.
2015 Rating: ★ ★ ★ ★ ★/Highest Recommendation

Johnnie Walker Red Label Blended Malt Scotch Whisky 40% abv, $23.

Bright amber color; excellent clarity. First nosings pick up very ripe scents of sour malt, wort, banana, kiwi, poached pear, and unsweetened breakfast cereal; second passes turn even more sour and malty as the aroma features the pungency of the included single malts more than the grain whiskies, and that's a plus. Entry is dry as a bone, spicy, and tart and it's here where the grain whiskies come into play, adding an acute flavor of grain husk and toasted snack cracker that provides the platform for the malt elements which are resiny, malty, and a trace salty; midpalate is where this blend does its finest work, emitting astringent flavors of cereal grains, cooking oils, and black peppercorn. It finishes with a faint honey-like aftertaste that accentuates the inherent dryness.
2018 Rating: ★ ★ ★/Recommended

Johnnie Walker Select Casks 10 Year Old Rye Cask Finish Blended Scotch Whisky 46% abv, $45.

Deep-amber/topaz color; excellent clarity. There's a dry-as-stone grain/cereal scent in the first whiffs that I find alluring, if one-dimensional; later inhalations after more air con-tact attempt to round out the aroma by adding delicate touches of banana, bran, and muesli but, overall, I find the mildly pleasant bouquet not as compelling as, say, Johnnie Walker Black. Entry offers nicely structured flavors of sweetened breakfast cereal, malted milk, all-spice, and meringue; midpalate accurately reflects the entry impressions, throwing in an oaky/resiny aspect, which helps to deepen the texture. Aftertaste is polite, pleasant.
2017 Rating: ★ ★ ★/Recommended

Jura Origin 10 Year Old Jura SMSW 43% abv, $45.

Old gold/amber color; perfectly sediment-free. Opening nose is a little closed off at first blush, then it unfolds a bit, offering ethereal scents of walnut butter, egg yolk, white pepper; secondary sniffs encounter malted barley cakes, white pepper, toasted sourdough bread. Entry is sap-like, resiny, juicy, ripe, fruity, raisiny, oaky, maple-like; midpalate features elements of fudge, cinnamon bun, clove, ham, honey. Aftertaste is zesty, tangy, mildly salty, grainy sweet, and oily in texture. A delicate maritime malt that's as much a Highland malt as it is island.
2016 Rating: ★ ★ ★ ★/Highly Recommended

Jura 12 Year Old Jura SMSW 40% abv, $50.

Carrot-orange color; superbly clean. Up front, the aroma is more akin to Highland than island/maritime character for me, as the initial whiffs encounter ripe pear and pipe tobacco notes that are neither smoky nor salty; secondary inhalations do pick up subtle hints of campfire embers, but not a smokefest, as well as honey-like oloroso sherry and chocolate-covered banana scents. Entry is stunningly sweet, honeyed, and sherried, with no

traces of peat-reek or smokiness; midpalate stays the course with the honey flavor, but now it's more grainy and sweetened cereal–like. Aftertaste is long and decidedly drier than the midpalate, as the flavor profile turns more bittersweet than honey sweet and that's a plus for me.
2020 Rating: ★★★/Recommended

Jura Tide 21 Year Old Jura SMSW 46.7% abv, $200.
Ochre/fulvous color; flawless purity. First up, I get oloroso sherry, bordering on cream sherry, up and down the initial nosings; later inhalations detect more butterscotch and nutty butter brickle candy than sherry mixed with a few aromatic tendrils of burnt lemon peel, sea salt, and mineral oil. Entry features a salty opening taste that's supported by flavors resembling hoisin sauce, bean curd, brown sugar, and fudge; midpalate echoes the entry impressions to a tee, leading to a satisfying aftertaste that's chewy in texture, moderately oily, slightly smoky, and off-dry.
2020 Rating: ★★★★/Highly Recommended

Jura Superstition Lightly Peated Jura SMSW 43% abv, $60.
Beautiful bronze/russet color; flawless purity. Opening whiffs detect a lightly sap-like first aroma that's followed quickly by delicately sweet barley malt/malted milk ball, buttered roll fragrance that's underpinned by a feathery-light saline smokiness; secondary inhalations pick up sweetened breakfast cereal, brown butter, sea salt. Entry is salty but savory, with supplemental flavors of pretzel, nougat, cocoa bean that orbit the primary taste of heavily toasted malted barley; midpalate features more of the oak presence in the forms of baking spice (allspice, vanilla) and maple. Aftertaste shines brightly beneath the flavor beacons of sweetened breakfast cereal, toasted marshmallow, honey, salted toffee. Really tasty and vibrant.
2016 Rating: ★★★★/Highly Recommended

Kilchoman 100% Islay SMSW 50% abv, $100.
Very pale tarnished-silver/Manzanilla sherry yellow; perfectly clean. This Kilchoman aroma offers rubber pencil eraser, electric cables, soft barley malt, and snack cracker scents in the opening whiffs that are understated; later sniffs detect delicate fragrances of sandy beach, sea breeze, beeswax. Entry is more assertive than the laid-back aroma, highlighting defined tastes of pickle brine, lightly peated malted barley, smoked salmon, toasted marshmallow; midpalate mirrors the entry, adding gently sweet flavors of malted milk and Horlicks. Ends on a sweet note that's lightly toasted and toffee-like.
2017 Rating: ★★★/Recommended

Kilchoman 7th Edition Islay SMSW 50% abv, $100.
Flax/buff color; sediment-free purity. I pick up a steely, flinty, mineral-like aroma in the very first sniff that's earthy, dry, and chalky/limestone-like, then a few more inhalations register traces of malted barley, textile fiber/nylon, and beeswax; after more time in the glass, the bouquet turns a bit vegetal (waxy beans, peas), glue-like, salty, and almost piney. Entry features a pleasing grain density that's dry, kernel-like, grassy, vegetal, viscous, and oily; midpalate heightens the oily texture, but also adds a crisp acidity that's drying/astringent in the

mouth, resiny, salty, and grainy. Finishes as astringently as the midpalate, and while wholly recommendable for how clean it is, I feel that it's two-dimensional and, therefore, in need of more core substance in order to qualify for a fourth rating star.

2017 Rating: ★★★/Recommended

Kilchoman Evolution Sherry Finish Islay SMSW 58% abv, $140.
  Amber/bronze color; pristine clarity. This first nosing features scents of furniture polish, lumberyard, charred oak stave, and assertive spirit; I feel that to do this malt's bouquet justice, it's advisable to allow it to air out so I do; after over ten minutes of air contact, I detect fragrances of bay leaf, Italian parsley, a campfire that's been extinguished for two days, filled ashtray, and pine tar. Entry is sweeter than the aroma as tastes of dark honey, caramelized mushrooms, brown sugar, chocolate Bundt cake, and treacle present an entirely different picture than the aroma; midpalate is pruny and laced with caramel, nougat, candy bar, and chocolate-covered raisin flavors, clearly from the sherry butt finish. Sherry influence lasts deep into the pruny, fig-like aftertaste that carries with it a barely noticeable undercurrent of pipe tobacco, burnt marshmallow, and BBQ sauce.

2017 Rating: ★★★★/Highly Recommended

Kilchoman Loch Gorm Sherry Cask Matured Islay SMSW 46% abv, $90.
  Tan/khaki color; some minor sediment spotted beneath the examination lamp—not an issue. First aromatic impressions are of shiitake mushroom, granola, bran, Honey Nut Cheerios, bacon fat, and leather upholstery; the next aromatic stage after more air contact discovers maritime fragrances, including seaweed, salted nuts, kippers, bog myrtle, Assam black tea, and cigarette ashes. Entry is intensely black tea–like, not exactly sweet but more like sweetened dry cereal (the sherry cask maybe?) or granola with coconut, and only mildly smoky/peaty; midpalate is keenly smokier, tomato sauce-, soy sauce-, and tobacco-like, all the while maintaining its salty, maritime brininess. Finishes long, peaty, charcoal-like, and markedly sooty. For a mere 46% abv, it's quite assertive and prickly on the tongue.

2017 Rating: ★★★★/Highly Recommended

Kilchoman Machir Bay Islay SMSW 46% abv, $60.
  Flax/straw-yellow color; can see oils swirling in the core, which is sediment-free. Up front, I detect strong and defined notes of dried bay leaf, seaweed, cabbage, starch, and dry stone—it's a bone-dry, herbal, vegetal aroma pointing to a maritime location on Islay; secondary whiffs pick up sandy beach, arid calcareous soil/limestone, hemp/rope, textile fiber, shellfish. Entry is piquant, intensely nutty, slightly prickly, with tastes of dill, brine, pickles, almond paste, sea salt, and it's so acidic that it cleanses the palate; midpalate highlights the salinity, dill, and almond in a wonderful display of melded flavors that lead into the finish, which is medium long, vegetal, ultra clean, tight, and efficiently delicious. This whisky has no rough edges or wasted traits or twists and turns. A nimble, compact Islay malt that's economically forward and seaside splendid.

2017 Rating: ★★★★/Highly Recommended

Kilchoman Sanaig Islay SMSW 46% abv, $75.
  Bright dusty-amber color; impeccably pure. Wow, this opening aroma offers deep

layers of caramelized onion, sautéed mushrooms, fungi, forest floor, oloroso sherry, toasted bread, and lead pencil; after a few more minutes of air contact, the bouquet reveals hints of salted caramel, saltwater taffy, textile fiber, and walnut—this is a seriously multilayered maritime bouquet. Entry is, like the bouquet, rich, winey, sherried, toasted, lightly salted, and composed; midpalate reflects the entry findings, throwing in traces of salted fish, campfire smoke that you can taste, charred meat, pork rind, bacon fat. Aftertaste is lush in texture, deeply oily, and is tightly wound, honeyed, and gently sweet and salty.

2017 Rating: ★ ★ ★ ★ ★/Highest Recommendation

Kilchoman Sauternes Cask Matured Islay SMSW 50% abv, $120.
Limited release in September 2016 of six thousand bottles. Beautiful ginger/fawn color; unblemished clarity. The initial nosing passes pick up delectable fragrances of milk chocolate, creamery butter, lightly spiced and mature white wine, and cigar tobacco; secondary inhalations encounter almond paste/nougat, candy bar, brown sugar, and dried fruits like dates, prunes, and raisins. Entry is stony/flinty dry at first, then the flavor profile expands to include black tea with honey, marmalade, candied fruits (pineapple, apricot); midpalate stays the course on the dried fruits and marmalade as the sauternes cask impact comes to fruition. Concludes medium long in the throat, delicately fruity/winey, with whispers of malted barley, bran, muesli, and honey wheat bread. A lovely Islay malt by any measure and the 50 percent abv never is an issue.

2017 Rating: ★ ★ ★ ★/Highly Recommended

Kilkerran 12 Year Old Campbeltown SMSW 46% abv, $75.
Green olive/citron color; immaculately clean. Initial whiffs detect floral/spring garden/ green tea aromas that are earthy, dewy, lightly spiced, and markedly tangy in the most positive sense; after more air contact, the aroma becomes an elegant bouquet that features blossoming vegetation and a light dose of sea salt/seaweed that adds a luster and complexity. Entry is intensely peated, iodine-like, smoky, and tobacco-like and that development I didn't see coming based on the light-fingered aroma; midpalate continues the peat-a-thon, as the flavor profile turns even more concentrated, campfire smoke–like, ashy/sooty, and saline. Aftertaste highlights the charred burnt-toast taste that runs rampant through the entry and midpalate stages.

2019 Rating: ★ ★ ★/Recommended

Lagavulin 16 Year Old Islay SMSW 43% abv, $90.
Burnt-orange/burnt sienna color; pristine clarity. Immediately, I pick up vibrant but merged scents of kippers, olive brine, dill, sea salt, pipe tobacco, and toasted cereal; after additional air contact, the aroma profile turns more towards the peat-reek, featuring vivid fragrances of caramelized onion, toasted marshmallow, honey biscuit, and chimney smoke. Entry is lush, oily, buttery, chalky, and piquant, highlighting round, supple, and heavily smoked flavors of charred meats, charcoal, tobacco ash, and baked fruits; midpalate reinforces the entry findings as the smokiness turns sweeter and more bakery shop–like in that

the spiciness now leans towards allspice, clove, and nutmeg. Ends long in the throat, sinewy in texture, and delicately sweet and smoked. An icon.
2018 Rating: ★ ★ ★ ★ ★/Highest Recommendation

Lagavulin 8 Year Old 200th Anniversary Edition Islay SMSW 48% abv, $70.

The color is pale ecru/bisque/champagne and is pristinely clean. The heavenly peatiness comes alive in the aromatic and carbolic specter first as Band-Aid, iodine, and hospital corridor, then it morphs into campfire smoke, kippers, dried seaweed, and earthy moss fragrances that could only hail from Islay; the aroma ramps up with more aeration as the profile turns more focused on dill, fennel, pickle brine, and sea salt smells. Entry mirrors the bouquet as the flavor profile goes a notch sweeter, more buttermilk biscuit batter–like, toasty, bacon-like, peppery, and salty; midpalate provides the taste buds with an animated peat-reek banquet that's on the sweeter side of the dryness/sweetness scale, with traces of clover honey and dark caramel that extend deep into the lovely, gently smoky finish. The youthful vigor of this tangy Lagavulin is what makes it so pleasing.
2017 Rating: ★ ★ ★ ★/Highly Recommended

Lagavulin 8 Year Old Limited Edition Islay SMSW 48% abv, $66.

The flax/jasmine-colored appearance is flawlessly clean and free of sediment. This opening nose is understated, exhibiting surprisingly gentle scents of canola oil, fruity young spirit, and green tobacco; secondary inhalations following more air contact discover sea salt, salted fish, and green vegetables (brussels sprouts). Entry is polite, lusciously oily and creamy, with background notes of campfire smoke, kippers, cigarette ash, and chalk; midpalate is where the biggest gains are realized as the harmonious flavor profile shows not only smoky restraint but also the rare teaming of polish and density of the malted barley. Concludes long, but moderately peaty/fumy/smoky as final lap hints of baked pineapple and apple strudel make last-minute appearances that round off the entire understated experience. Sensationally delicious.
2018 Rating: ★ ★ ★ ★ ★/Highest Recommendation

Laphroaig 10 Year Old Islay SMSW 43% abv, $50.

Amber/topaz color; superb clarity. First nosings encounter none-too-subtle aromas of road tar/asphalt, sea salt, and iodine; subsequent whiffs add notes of salted fish, deviled egg, and paprika. Entry is smoky/peaty, decidedly bittersweet, nutty, and oily; midpalate is medicinal, iodine-like, peaty, toasty, and moderately salty. While I prefer other expressions of Laphroaig, I've come around to this one.
2015 Rating: ★ ★ ★/Recommended

Laphroaig 15 Year Old Islay SMSW 43% abv, $80.

The color is textbook marigold/gamboge; flawless clarity. Initial nosings detect disparate aromas of steel wool, grapefruit juice, nickel, arid soil, parchment; another few minutes of air contact release scents of barley malt, seaweed, drying kelp, hemp, but little smoke or peatiness. Entry is where the peat is discovered as it punches its way into the flavor profile, creating a first-taste impression of sour tobacco, salt air, road tar, cigarette ash; midpalate is

more lush, silky in texture, malty sweet, round, and supple. Aftertaste is very long, delicately smoky, and charming.
2015 Rating: ★ ★ ★ ★/Highly Recommended

Laphroaig 16 Year Old Islay SMSW 48% abv, $90.
Hay/citron color; impeccably pure. Wildly creosote-like and briny in the initial whiffs after the pour; I mean, this smoky, salty aroma fills my office with scents of kippers, dead grass, damp hay, cigarette ashtray, and chimney soot. Entry is absurdly tannic, ribald, chewing tobacco–like, sea breeze–like, and woody; midpalate taste profile takes no prisoners as the elevated abv asserts itself on the palate while the flavor profile goes rubbery, lead pencil–like, minerally, flinty, toasted, and gamey. Everything you'd expect from this seaside malt distillery.
2020 Rating: ★ ★ ★/Recommended

Laphroaig 18 Year Old Islay SMSW 48% abv, $85.
Deep-gold/jonquil color; impeccably clean. Initial whiffs are confronted with assertive spirit and oddly incongruous but integrated aromas of bread dough, iodine/antiseptic, saltine crackers, and beeswax; secondary inhalations discover additional aromatic layers including salted butter, peanuts, and dried sage. Entry is astringent, but simultaneously semisweet, oily, and oaky; midpalate brings on assertive flavors of vanilla bean, candied almond, brown butter, and sweetened breakfast cereal. Finishes sweetly and elegantly, yet with power.
2016 Rating: ★ ★ ★ ★/Highly Recommended

Laphroaig 27 Year Old Islay SMSW 41.7% abv, $750.
Mustard/butterscotch color; flawless purity. Opening inhalations are treated to biscuit-like scents of spiced cookie dough, vegetable cooking oil, poppy seed, pastry dough, and lard; following more aeration time, the bouquet offers scents of lightly toasted bread, lead pencil, digestive biscuits, dried tea leaves, cardboard, and eucalyptus. Entry is animated and vibrant with dry flavors of malted milk balls, oatmeal, spiced cookies (cinnamon, nutmeg), and bran; midpalate is woodier than the entry, which brings along a bittersweet burnt-sugar taste that's moderately caramelized, honeyed, raisiny, and baked. Concludes with a zesty aftertaste that's rife with burnt marshmallow and toasted bun flavors that are only marginally smoky/peaty. The maturity has reduced the peat impact to the point where it's a pleasing snuffed campfire-like background element, allowing the grain, lipids (fatty acids), and the oak to do most of the talking.
2017 Rating: ★ ★ ★ ★/Highly Recommended

Laphroaig 32 Year Old Islay SMSW 46.7% abv, $1,200.
Ochre/deep amber color; impeccably clean. Wow, there's a burst of estery, tropical fruit aroma up front (banana, pineapple) that sets the early stage in an unexpected manner—I was certain that the wood aspect would be dominant when, in fact, it is the fruity grain that leads the way; secondary whiffs find that the aroma stays the course with the fruit still headlining. Entry is ripe, sweet, just a touch smoky, fruity, honeyed; midpalate is firmly structured, more oaky now than fruity and that is expressed mostly in a honey-like, tree sap

manner that is lush and opulent. Aftertaste reflects the midpalate perfectly, adding a little more astringency to keep the focus on the wood element.

2016 Rating: ★ ★ ★ ★/Highly Recommended

Laphroaig Cairdeas 2014 Amontillado Edition Islay SMSW 51.4% abv, $75.

Amber/topaz hue; perfect clarity. Smells right out of the aromatic gate of smoked fish, smoked cheese, iodine, dried seaweed, medicine cabinet, honey; second sniffs pick up deeper scents of toasted barley, pipe tobacco, smoldering embers, filled ashtray, old leather books, sea salt. Entry is appealingly smoky, bittersweet, fruity as in baked pineapple and banana; midpalate reflects the entry findings and adds a twist of lemongrass. Finishes long, smoky, delicately sweet.

2014 Rating: ★ ★ ★ ★/Highly Recommended

Laphroaig Cairdeas 2015 Islay SMSW 51.5% abv, $90.

One hundred percent floor maltings from distillery; aged for twelve years in ex-bourbon casks; distilled in small pot stills. Chardonnay straw-yellow color; excellent clarity. First sniffs pick up nail polish, acetate, sea salt, cardboard; secondary nosing passes reveal aromas that remind me of waxy orchard fruits, like apple and pear, but the acetate turns more like turpentine, Band-Aids, and medicine cabinet. Entry is very medicinal/clinical, sweet and sour, savory, tobacco-like, sage-like; midpalate is languid, malty, chewy in texture, bittersweet, gum-like. Aftertaste features wax candy, cigarette ash, grainy sweet.

2016 Rating: ★ ★ ★/Recommended

Laphroaig Cairdeas Triple Wood Islay SMSW 59.5% abv, $80.

Cocoa-brown color; flawless clarity. Wow, the high degree of oak/wood/sawdust fragrance in this opening inhalation is astounding and bracing; secondary sniffs after more aeration encounter a wider aromatic menu that includes used saddle leather, old library, musty attic, parchment, and cigar tobacco. Entry defies the narrowly focused bouquet, as the flavor roster includes candied walnut, winter holiday fruitcake, dried pineapple and apricot, white raisins, and lots of tannic acid; midpalate features succulent tastes of ripe tropical fruits (banana, pineapple), toasted wheat bread, honey, and candied nuts. Ends long, luxurious, and succulent.

2019 Rating: ★ ★ ★ ★/Highly Recommended

Laphroaig Cairdeas Port Wood Edition Islay SMSW 51.3% abv, $75.

Lovely burnt-orange/new copper/pale ale color; unblemished clarity. Aromas of pine tar, steamed brown rice, tofu, and soy sauce open up the nosing proceedings; another seven minutes of air contact stimulate further scents, including cigar box, peat, salted fish, cinnamon, paprika, and sea salt. Entry is smoky/peaty yet sweet, malty/grainy yet winey; midpalate reflects the entry and adds to the mix pleasing tastes of pipe tobacco, cooking oil, ash, and tree sap. Port impact comes alive in the winey aftertaste.

2015 Rating: ★ ★ ★ ★/Highly Recommended

Laphroaig Cairdeas Quarter Cask 2017 Release Islay SMSW 57.2% abv, $80.

Jonquil/yellow-gold color; perfect clarity. My initial olfactory impressions during the

first whiffs are of baked pineapple, grilled peach, apple pastry, Band-Aid, and steel medicine cabinet, but it's the nuances of fruit that linger; second sniffs discover sea salt, pickle brine, green olive, saltine cracker, cheese, clover honey, and leather armchair. Entry is alive with green tobacco topside flavors that are embellished by traces of salted butter, lime, multigrain toast, malted milk, and acetone; midpalate is crisply acidic and cleansing, but also squeaky tart, piquant, spicy (black pepper, savory), woody/oaky/resiny, and herbal (lemongrass, cardamom, licorice). Finishes medium long, not as smoky as other, more peat-intensive Laphroaigs, but altogether lovely, poised, ashy, and elegant.
2017 Rating: ★ ★ ★ ★/Highly Recommended

Laphroaig Cask Strength 10 Year Old Islay SMSW 55.3% abv, $60.

Rich golden/amber color; superb purity. Significant smokiness/peatiness in the opening sniffs, but there is also ample evidence of pine/cedar, dried fruits (apples, pears), and nuts (walnuts)—an amazing first nosing; after eight minutes of further aeration, the bouquet settles in, offering striking notes of lemon curd, vanilla pudding, apple butter, and roasted almond. Entry is chockfull of brown butter, honey, dried fruit, and nutty flavors; midpalate is long, juicy, tart, intensely smoky with sweet pipe tobacco–like elements, and toasty. Remarkably round, chewy, and savory in the oily, charred finish.
2016 Rating: ★ ★ ★ ★ ★/Highest Recommendation

Laphroaig Quarter Cask Double Cask Matured Islay SMSW 48% abv, $55.

Bright golden color; flawless purity. Initial sniffs pick up truckloads of seaweed, salt air, dried flowers, and peat-reek, as one would expect; later sniffings detect deeper layers of dried fruits, wheat bread, seeds, cigarette tobacco, and kippers. Entry is acutely dry and grainy, then in midpalate the taste profile expands to include gently sweetened pipe tobacco, lead, smoked meats, sap, toffee, and deep-roasted barley malt.
2015 Rating: ★ ★ ★ ★/Highly Recommended

Ledaig 10 Year Old Mull SMSW 46.3% abv, $55.

Rich golden chardonnay yellow color; excellent purity. Lovely piquant, briny, salty opening aromas that could only be maritime influenced; secondary whiffs following nine minutes of aeration encounter deeper scents of seaweed, kippers, and malted barley. Entry is briny, olive-like and toasty; midpalate is the best phase as the animated taste profile includes tobacco leaf, ash, Marmite, and caramelized onion. Aftertaste is biscuity, lean, and smoky.
2015 Rating: ★ ★ ★ ★/Highly Recommended

Loch Lomond 12 Year Old Highland SMSW 46% abv, $35.

Pretty bronze color; excellent sediment-free clarity. Similar to its sibling, the LL Original, there's a paucity of aromatic animation in the opening inhalations, so I allow it additional time to mingle with air; more time helps in stimulating a few delicate (read: featherweight) scents like lemon drop, parchment, onionskin, beeswax, and textile fiber/nylon. Entry is considerably fuller and more expressive than the bouquet as round, supple flavors of wood smoke, toasted malt, shortbread, and salted butter provide plenty of sensual "grip"; the midpalate stage is this malt's best moment as the flavor profile expands to include

peanut butter, buttered mashed potato, dark caramel, and lightly smoked malt, all wrapped in a silky cocoon of texture. Aftertaste highlights roasted malt and pipe tobacco tastes. Had the aroma displayed more vitality, it would have earned a fourth rating star.
2018 Rating: ★ ★ ★/Recommended

Loch Lomond 18 Year Old Highland SMSW 46% abv, $80.

Attractive copper/cocoa-brown color; impeccably clean. All that I unearth in the up-front nosings are ethereal hints of candle wax/paraffin, lychee, and textile fiber so I leave it alone for ten minutes; following the additional aeration time, I pick up deeper impressions of dry sand/arid landscape, bay leaf, savory, and geranium. Entry is dappled with mineral-like, nutty, low-intensity graininess; midpalate shows a brighter personality as candy-shop flavors of sweetened coconut, milk chocolate, and nougat showcase the toasted malt base. The bittersweet, caramelized aftertaste is its finest moment, but it's not enough to elevate the final score beyond three rating stars.
2018 Rating: ★ ★ ★/Recommended

Loch Lomond Inchmurrin Madeira Wood Finish Highland SMSW 46% abv, $79.99.

Brilliant new copper/cinnamon color; excellent purity. I like this opening aroma that's assertive, deeply malty, and a little bit winey, with touches of walnut, pineapple, kiwi, and lime; following more air contact, the bouquet remains vibrant, juicy, fruity, and malty, showing off delicate hints of poppy seed, black pepper, linseed oil. Entry is richly textured, bittersweet like pralines, jammy, honeyed, dense in its maltiness, and wonderfully winey; midpalate reflects all the entry impressions, solidifying them within the volume of the satiny texture. Finishes as lusciously as it began at entry: creamy, oily, pruny, fruitcake-like, nutty, and honeyed. A phenomenally delicious malt whisky.
2017 Rating: ★ ★ ★ ★ ★/Highest Recommendation

Loch Lomond Original Highland SMSW 40% abv, $25.

Light-catching amber color; pristine purity. On the first nosing passes after the pour, I don't encounter a great deal of animated aromas, so I decide to set it aside for a few minutes to aerate; after several minutes of further air contact, I detect faint traces of cookie batter, snack cracker, saddle leather, and fresh linen. Entry flavors offer hints of toasted marshmallow, truffle oil, roasted grain, and toasted multigrain bread; midpalate features the dry to off-dry bread-like graininess, which is like grain kernels and oatmeal. Ends up toasty, mildly spicy, and pleasantly malty. A simple, middle-of-the-road, entry-level inland malt that is affordably priced, but hollow overall.
2018 Rating: ★ ★/Not Recommended

Loch Lomond Single Grain Scotch Whisky 46% abv, $33.

Bright corn-yellow/marigold color; flawless purity. Opening smells are easy, friendly, cereal-like, and almost like wheat snack crackers plus there's a citrusy quality that's almost grapefruit-like; further time in the glass allows the aroma to develop a bit more, giving off fresh, uncomplicated fragrances of mown grass, wheat field, citrus grove, flint, dry stones, arid desert, sage, cucumber. Entry is youthful, simple, grainy sweet, and like sweetened breakfast cereal; midpalate echoes the entry, as the easy-as-Sunday-morning character is pleasingly friendly, grainy, straightforward, and inviting. Finishes medium long, gently sweet.

2017 Rating: ★ ★ ★/Recommended

Longmorn 16 Year Old Speyside SMSW 48% abv, $110.
Old gold/amber color; impeccable purity. A Speyside aromatic clinic for malt whisky, which highlights toasted malt/cereal grain underpinning scents that are accentuated with surface fragrances of cocoa bean, vanilla bean, butterscotch, and nougat—utterly sensational opening bouquet; seven more minutes of exposure to air unleashes irresistible and multilayered scents of almond paste, candy bar, sawdust, and marzipan. Entry is supple, honeyed, complex, and concentrated on the grain; midpalate flavor profile is tight, focused on the malt and oak, spicy/peppery, and sublimely delicious. One of the greatest inland single malts from Scotland, period. A genuine classic from this mysteriously and regrettably neglected distillery.

2017 Rating: ★ ★ ★ ★ ★/Highest Recommendation

Longrow Peated Campbeltown SMSW 46% abv, $74.
Straw color; sediment-free clarity. The opening smokiness from peat comes off sweet, wispy, and almost honeyed; more aeration calms the smokiness down a notch, as now the malted barley aspect emerges in the form of sweetened breakfast cereal (Honey Nut Cheerios) bringing with it a leavening of the entire aroma. Entry is generous in its grainy sweetness, delicate in its wood smoke and tobacco ash elements, and zesty primarily due to an underlying spiciness that's vanilla- and allspice-like; midpalate features more of the spice and the barley malt than the peat-reek, and so it's at this juncture when the most charm is apparent. Aftertaste is very long, narrow focused, lean, and intensely tobacco-like.

2019 Rating: ★ ★ ★ ★/Highly Recommended

Macallan 12 Year Old Double Cask Speyside SMSW 43% abv, $65.
Bronze color; impeccably pure. Up front, I get a stunning menu of aromas such as ripe cherries, toffee, citrus zest, sawdust, oak resins, almond paste, and stewed prunes; secondary whiffs pick up additional scents, including black peppercorn, allspice, mace, marzipan, and cocoa bean. Entry is creamy and honeyed in texture, toasted and slightly smoked, and loaded with BBQ sauce, tomato paste, grilled sausage, and hoisin-like flavors that are dazzling and rich; midpalate echoes the entry, throwing in bittersweet and roasted flavors of toasted marshmallow, pipe tobacco, chocolate-covered walnut, fudge, and hot cocoa. Finishes long, creamy, bittersweet, resiny, oaky, vanilla bean–like, and prune Danish–like. So much happening here on so many levels that it's hard to write them all down. The finest twelve-year-old Macallan to date and a superb value.

2018 Rating: ★ ★ ★ ★ ★/Highest Recommendation

Macallan Director's Edition Speyside SMSW 40% abv, $60.
Bright fourteen-karat-golden color; sediment-free. First whiffs encounter soft biscuity/cookie batter notes as well as some floral/spring forest scents akin to lichen/moss; after seven minutes of aeration, a big dose of sherry wood comes through followed by traces of citrus/lemon and grape preserve notes—this is BIG FRUIT territory aromatically and totally

beguiling. Entry broadcasts "oloroso and PX sherry" immediately, with aspects of toasted marshmallow, dark caramel, cocoa bean, and vanilla bean; midpalate profile sees the sherry bomb diminish a bit, allowing for tastes of honey and grapes to shine. Gorgeously rich and sumptuous aftertaste that is succulent, ripe, and grapy. A traditional type of The Macallan that will thrill old-time admirers.

2015 Rating: ★ ★ ★ ★ ★/Highest Recommendation

Macallan Edition No. 2 Speyside SMSW 45.2% abv, $100.

Stunningly pretty burnt sienna/bronze color; flawlessly pure. Oh man, there's oloroso sherry and honey written all over the very first aromatics, along with crème caramel, English toffee, and baked ham studded with cloves; secondary whiffs after more air contact discover delicate scents of dried tropical fruits (pineapple, banana), chestnut purée, cigar box, and pipe tobacco. Entry is surprisingly forward with astringent and trimmed flavors of oaky resins, cinnamon, and green tobacco; midpalate echoes the entry impressions as the flavor profile remains leaner than the aroma had implied it would be yet succulent all the same. Aftertaste sums up the experience nicely by promoting the deftness of the dried tropical fruits laced with dense spicy oak and black pepper. Not the robust Macallan of the Sherry Series or even to some extent the Fine Oak Series, but a nimble, intensely spiced Mac whose elegance wins the day and the four stars.

2017 Rating: ★ ★ ★ ★/Highly Recommended

Macallan M Speyside SMSW 44.5% abv, $6,000.

Auburn/sienna color; impeccably pure appearance. First nosing passes discover ripe, sturdy fragrances of black raisin, nutmeg, allspice, prune Danish, almond paste, pretzel, and nougat; secondary inhalations are treated to supple, lush scents of tree bark, sarsaparilla, meadowsweet, maple syrup, hard cheese, and oloroso sherry; a timeless, definitive Macallan bouquet. Entry is baked, roasted, and lightly spiced with complex flavors of cola nut, baked pineapple, star anise, and lemon verbena; while the entry phase is all about flavor profile, the midpalate is more focused on the layered, creamy, dark caramel texture that is far beyond luscious as it almost approaches being caramelized; an amazing, one-of-a-kind in-mouth experience. Aftertaste is tobacco-like, slightly smoky, buttery and oily feeling, raisin- and prune-like, and just altogether magnificent.

2018 Rating: ★ ★ ★ ★ ★/Highest Recommendation

Macallan Rare Cask Batch No. 2 2017 Release Speyside SMSW 43% abv, $350.

Beautiful cocoa-brown color; flawlessly clean. Oh my, the first nosing pass picks up luscious scents of brown sugar, cotton candy, butterscotch, figs, black raisins, and apple butter; later inhalations following more aeration are treated to lush, candy-like, and bakery-shop aromas of oloroso sherry, glazed donut, honey, bacon fat, and vegetable cooking oil. Entry is front-loaded with exquisitely balanced flavors, especially honey, oloroso sherry, winter holiday fruitcake, dried pear and pineapple, candied almonds, caramelized onion, and treacle; midpalate echoes the entry perfectly, adding a firmer texture that's oily and fat without being unwieldy or flabby. Aftertaste sums up the entire experience with elegance and power, being sweet yet clean and agile. Lovely from stem to stern.

2018 Rating: ★ ★ ★ ★ ★/Highest Recommendation

Macallan Sherry Oak 18 Year Old Speyside SMSW 43% abv, $285.

Copper/ochre color; flawless purity. Right up front, I detect alluring smells of bacon fat, toasted marshmallow, baked pumpernickel bread, toffee, baked orchard fruits (pears, plums), and cream sherry; secondary sniffs pick up subtler, gently sweet notes of smoldering campfire, treacle, dark caramel, BBQ sauce, tomato paste, honeysuckle, and dark cocoa powder. Entry is juicy, citrusy/orangey, and raisin-like to the taste but it's the creamy mouthfeel that makes the experience so special; midpalate features distinct notes of caramelized Vidalia onion, burnt toast, crème caramel/flan, prune, date, and dark honey. Ends supremely assertive yet polite, dark and plush, and majestic. An all-time Speyside crown jewel that has come to define The Macallan in the minds and hearts of thousands of its worldwide fans. Some might say that it's an old-fashioned style. I would argue that this lofty degree of quality never goes out of style and that this malt is as contemporary as any other eighteen-year-old out there.
2018 Rating: ★★★★★/Highest Recommendation

Macallan Sherry Oak 40 Year Old Speyside SMSW 45% abv, $8,700.

Chestnut-brown color; impeccably clean. Up front, I immediately get prune, blueberry, black plum, black raisin, and marasca cherry fragrances that combine with the old oak, vanilla bean, and rancio back notes to provide a graceful, mature opening aroma that still carries a youthful vigor; secondary whiffs detect deeper, more layered, herbal aromas, especially walnut, hyssop, and rose hip. Entry is medium weight in texture, moderately oily and resiny, nutty (walnut again, plus pistachio), and persimmon-like; midpalate mirrors the entry, adding slightly salty notes of oak sap/tree bark and Parmigiano-Reggiano. Finishes medium long, lean, earthy, dry cheese–like, and a little wood-like, which is to be expected. Pretty damn wonderful for an ancient Speyside malt.
2018 Rating: ★★★★/Highly Recommended

Macallan Triple Cask 15 Year Old Speyside SMSW 43% abv, $145.

Straw/citron color; superbly clear. Right off the crack of the aromatic bat I get toasted wheat bread, meringue, egg white, and baked tropical fruit (banana, pineapple) aromas that are vividly expressive and semisweet; after more aeration, the bouquet turns more raisin-like/pruny, ambrosial, and honeyed; this bouquet focuses mostly on fruit rather opposed to grain, oak, or alcohol. Entry is succulent, far woodier than the bouquet in an oily/resiny/tree sap sense, and is also within the realm of candy-shop tastes, especially candied nuts (walnut, hazelnut) and chocolate-covered malt balls; midpalate brings the various components together in a streamlined flavor profile that has now become spare, nut-like, and a bit flinty/earthy. Finishes in a size-zero manner, highlighting the crispness of the malted barley. Not sure if the slender, pencil-leg physique of this malt will satisfy old-guard Macallan admirers.
2018 Rating: ★★★/Recommended

Malt Whisky Company Braes of Glenlivet 1994 20 Year Old Speyside SMSW 53.5% abv, $250.

One of only 182 bottles available, so rarity factor is high. Last time I rated a Braes of Glenlivet (a.k.a. Braeval) merchant bottling was back in 2008. Chivas Brothers opened this relatively new distillery in 1973. Color is gamboge/flax; excellent purity. Initial nosing passes encounter low-key aromas of oak resins, tannin, vanilla, Highland flowers, fresh honey; secondary inhalations following more aeration discover marshmallow, cotton candy fragrances that meld nicely with the floral element. Entry is delicately sweet, deeply grainy, malty, flowery, slightly spicy (clove, allspice), and appealing; midpalate is acutely spicy, embers warm from the cask strength abv, and intensely floral, but it's the silky, oily texture that I respond to so favorably. Lush, sensuous finish. A genuine Speyside beauty.

2016 Rating: ★ ★ ★ ★/Highly Recommended

McDonald's Glencoe Highland SMSW 58% abv, $92.

Made at Ben Nevis Distillery in Scotland's western Highlands. The umber/topaz color is bright and the purity is pristine. I like the opening nose due to its unfailingly pure, slightly floral and fruity barley malt/dry cereal aroma that could be nothing else but malt whisky; aeration brings out a distinct muesli-like secondary aroma that's chockfull of dried fruits (pear, apricot), maple, honey, oats, sunflower seeds. Entry is generously sweet, honeyed, silky textured, pipe tobacco–like, with a highly appealing foundational flavor of malted milk ball candy; midpalate offers surprisingly evolved (considering the youngish age) tastes of maple syrup on pancakes, vanilla extract, caramelized onion. Midpalate flavors last deep into the long aftertaste. An excellent, rum cake–like dram.

2016 Rating: ★ ★ ★ ★/Highly Recommended

McDonald's Traditional Ben Nevis Highland SMSW 46% abv, $105.

Made at Ben Nevis Distillery in Scotland's western Highlands. Beautiful new-copper color; unblemished clarity. First whiffs pick up lightly toasted cereal grain aromas that are off-dry and a little waxy; further aeration fails to stimulate more in the aromatics, so I move on. Entry features pleasantly "roasted" tastes of baked apple, apple strudel, pear tart, sweetened breakfast cereal; midpalate echoes the entry to a tee, highlighting the brown sugar/baked fruit sweetness. Aftertaste is medium long, gently sweet, juicy.

2016 Rating: ★ ★ ★/Recommended

Monkey Shoulder Blended Malt Scotch Whisky 43% abv, $30.

A lovely blend of single malts from William Grant & Sons. Pretty brass color; superb clarity. Out of the sniffing gate, it smells of brown rice, breakfast cereal, malt, and cardboard; subsequent inhalations discover deeper scents, including malted milk balls, allspice, clove, and mincemeat. Entry features deeply grainy tastes that are dry; midpalate is toasty, nutty/nougat-like, and just a touch fruity (tropical fruit). Concludes dusty dry, medium long, and woody.

2020 Rating: ★ ★ ★ ★/Highly Recommended

Mortlach 18 Year Old Speyside SMSW 43.4% abv, $299.

Brilliant amber/burnished-orange color; flawless clarity. This Mortlach aroma is dusty dry, waxy, grain husk–like, tofu-like, fibrous, brown rice–like; later whiffs encounter minerals, nickel, breakfast cereal. Entry features Mighty Malts flavor that is lovely, dry, balanced, chewy in texture, nutty; midpalate impressions mirror those of the entry, adding raisin bread

toast, lemon marmalade, honey. Concludes like dried apricot, tobacco smoke, roasted malt, malted milk balls. Supple, succulent, luscious. Mortlach in its prime.
2015 Rating: ★★★★★/Highest Recommendation

Mortlach 25 Year Old Speyside SMSW 43.4% abv, $650.

Similar amber/bronze color to the 18; impeccable, sediment-free purity. I smell grass, hay field, textile fiber, unsalted snack cracker, new leather. Entry is malty, breakfast cereal–like, nearing semisweet status, biscuity; midpalate is all of the above and more, including saltwater taffy, tobacco leaf, dates, figs, dried berries. Finishes long, satiny, minerally, focused, seductive. Though I preferred the 18-year-old expression, this 25 packs a wallop.
2015 Rating: ★★★★/Highly Recommended

Mortlach Cowie's Blue Seal 20 Year Old Speyside SMSW 43.4% abv, $200.

Caramel color; ideally free of sediment. There are hop-like/floral and dried-fruit aspects to this first nosing pass that are fresh and lively considering the age; after more aeration, the aroma settles into a wood/bakery shop/earthy/mineral mode that's dry overall, but also baked, nut-like, and leathery. Entry is tightly wound, crisp, caramel cream candy–like, and a lot like BBQ sauce/tomato paste, brown sugar; midpalate sorts through the various entry findings and turns harmonious, one-pointed, bittersweet, succulent, and piquant and peppery. Ends on a peanut butter/roasted walnut note that's delicious, supple, and powerful.
2019 Rating: ★★★★★/Highest Recommendation

Mortlach Distiller's Dram 16 Year Old Speyside SMSW 43.4% abv, $100.

Cocoa-brown color; unblemished clarity. Oh my, I get all sorts of tobacco-related aromas in the first passes, including cigar box, pipe tobacco, and ashes, as well as dried cherries, mincemeat pie, and bear claw pastry; secondary whiffs after more air contact encounter bigger, more mature fragrances, namely oak plank, sawdust, candle wax, café latte, carob, and allspice. Entry is sensationally harmonious, spicy (allspice, mace, clove), fruity (dried apricot, kiwi), toasted marshmallow, and coffee bean; midpalate unites the disparate flavors found at entry into a singular taste that's roasted, grainy, a touch salty, bittersweet, balanced, and succulent. Aftertaste is textbook Speyside afterglow, gift wrapped in a creamy texture. This is a Speyside masterpiece that is in its prime right now. The term "majestic" comes to mind.
2019 Rating: ★★★★★/Highest Recommendation

Mortlach Rare Old Speyside SMSW 43.4% abv, $130.

Pretty topaz color; unblemished clarity. First nosing impressions are of toasted malt, Triscuit snack crackers, oats, hard cheese; secondary sniffs detect lard, dry cement/sand, baked pear, nougat, walnut butter, quince. Entry offers substantial grainy/malty, dry, nutty flavors that dance upon a medium-bodied viscosity; midpalate highlights the roasted malt, which tastes similar to toasted honey wheat bread. Aftertaste is long, supple, minerally, earthy, tobacco-like. What I like the most is the Speyside "grip" of it. Sturdy, no nonsense style of serious malt whisky that is sometimes lost today among all the wood finishes, cask strength, quarter cask, and fairy-dusted entries.
2016 Rating: ★★★★/Highly Recommended

Mortlach Wee Witchie 12 Year Old Speyside SMSW 43.4% abv, $50.

Marigold/gamboge color; flawlessly pure. Right out of the gate, I pick up biscuit-like scents that remind me most of buttermilk pancake batter, sourdough bread, toasted almond, and lemon curd; after more aeration, the aroma mirrors the initial impressions, adding sultanas, pimento, paraffin, and Parmesan. Entry is sultry, deeply peppery and piquant, dry as the desert, yet bountifully grainy/malty, oaky, and bittersweet; midpalate is flecked with butterscotch, toffee, cinnamon bun, and orange marmalade flavors that supplement the density of the barley malt core taste. Finishes long, drier than the midpalate, slightly salty and smoky, and luxuriously textured. Long a favored distillery within the Scotch industry, is this currently Speyside's best twelve-year-old? I cannot think of a better one.

2019 Rating: ★ ★ ★ ★/Highly Recommended

Naked Grouse Blended Malt Scotch Whisky 43% abv, $n/a.

A blend of single malts from superstar malt distilleries like Highland Park, The Macallan, Glenturret, and The Glenrothes; matured initially in first-fill and refill American and European oak casks, then finished in first-fill oloroso sherry butts for a half year. Bright color is topaz/cocoa-brown; immaculate purity. Initial whiffs detect succulent aromas of malted milk balls, candied almond, nougat, milk chocolate, and sweetened breakfast cereal (Honey Nut Cheerios); following another ten minutes of aeration, the oloroso sherry works its magic in the aromatic forms of banana bread, spice cake, black raisins, cocoa bean, caramelized onion, and dark honey. Entry is off-dry at first but then quickly turns candy-shop bittersweet, as layers of baking spices (cinnamon, vanilla bean, clove, nutmeg) merge with sweet malted barley, praline, marzipan, meringue, and brown sugar; midpalate sees the entry impressions integrate, causing an explosion of decadent flavors that spill out long past this point into the rich, creamy, extended finish. A spectacular blended malt of the first rank.

2018 Rating: ★ ★ ★ ★ ★/Highest Recommendation

Oban 14 Year Old Highland SMSW 43% abv, $75.

Pretty amber/topaz hue; good clarity. First whiffs pick up lovely, round fragrances of Walkers Shortbread, oatmeal, breakfast cereal, all with a delicate touch of sea salt; secondary sniffs are more malt-driven and totally dry. Entry is supple, complex, intensely barley-like, discernibly honeyed, yet that deft trace of salinity remains just off to stage left out of the limelight; midpalate is richer, toastier than the entry, more concentrated on the malt, again exhibiting that subtle flick of sea air. Ends medium long as it fades just a little in the aftertaste.

2016 Rating: ★ ★ ★/Recommended

Oban 18 Year Old Highland SMSW 43% abv, $140.

Gamboge/bronze color; impeccably pure. Opening inhalations pick up light touches of malted milk, malted barley, oatmeal, unsweetened breakfast cereal–like aromas that early on are integrated; more time in the glass allows for the fragrances to rally a bit more as they now offer larger, more pronounced scents of seaweed, sea air, pine board, and barley cakes. Entry is smoky, toasted, bittersweet, and alluringly tobacco-like; midpalate is the moment of truth for this malt as the flavor profile explodes on the tongue, offering succulent tastes of toasted cereal, toffee, malted barley, honey buns, and bear claw pastry, all wrapped in a

luscious, scoop-it-out-with-a-spoon texture that redefines the term "lush." The most memorable Oban, in my opinion.
2020 Rating: ★ ★ ★ ★ ★/Highest Recommendation

Oban Little Bay Highland SMSW 43% abv, $75.
The unblemished purity is showcased by the richness of the bronze color; a very pretty malt. First nosings detect a smattering of marine saltiness that is almost smoky but eventually is more like salted caramel; secondary passes after more aeration discover sea breeze, sweet grain, malted milk, root beer, and oaky sawdust. Entry is succulent, ripe, fruity, candy shop–like in its toffee leaning; midpalate highlights the sweet maltiness that's accented by a controlled saline aspect that carries the flavor profile deep into the roasted meat-like finish that flashes a touch of tomato paste.
2017 Rating: ★ ★ ★ ★/Highly Recommended

Octave 1992 Strathmill 21 Year Old Speyside SMSW 47.4% abv, $160.
Straw/maize color; excellent purity. This opening aroma is soft, plump, a bit fatty, and very wax paper–like, allowing for a smidgen of barley malt scent; more time in the glass doesn't serve to release much more fragrance as the existing aromas meld into a mildly pleasing, spicy bouquet that's neither sweet nor dry but is moderately biscuity and doughy. Entry is bittersweet, mineral-like, showing quick glimpses of nutmeg and clove; midpalate features zesty, grainy/malty, bakery-shop flavors that are high on spice and low on fruit. Finishes quite short, malty/grainy, bittersweet, tangy, and a touch sharp in the throat.
2016 Rating: ★ ★ ★/Recommended

Octomore Masterclass 08.1 Super Heavy Peated Islay SMSW 59.3% abv, $150.
Citrine color; unblemished purity. There's a fierce up-front, overflowing ashtray nose on this street brawler that's generous, deeply smoky, charred, creosote-like, and more like salted fish than grilled meat, but the primary message here is the 167 ppm of phenols; second passes pick up some nasal cavity stinging from the intense peat-reek that's akin to deeply inhaling a smoldering chimney's wood smoke. Entry attacks the taste buds in wave after feral wave of campfire smoke, cigar tobacco, and sooty flavors that jar the palate; midpalate turns tangy, piquant, peppery, and quite satisfying if you relish this variety of ultra-smoky Islay malt. Finishes astringent, metallic tasting, and carbon-like. For me, I believe I would have enjoyed this more had the abv been turned down to 48–50 percent.
2019 Rating: ★ ★ ★/Recommended

Old Pulteney 12 Year Old Highland SMSW 43% abv, $45.
Bright saffron color; unblemished purity. Right up front I get strong scents of caraway seed, poppy seed, and black peppercorn that are zesty, defined, and tangy; after more air contact, the bouquet turns malty and breakfast cereal–like, especially akin to lightly sweetened oatmeal. Entry is satiny and creamy in texture, toffee sweet, fudge brownie–like, and plump with oily viscosity; midpalate features the thick texture that carries along the biscuit-like, cereally, malted milk flavor that's more like pastry shop than candy shop. Aftertaste is firm in structure, acidic so therefore fresh, and rich in grainy/cereal surface tastes that now turn brown-sugar sweet. Lots happening here. All of it scrumptious. A splendid,

robust twelve-year-old from mainland Scotland's northern Highlands that deserves a wider audience.

2018 Rating: ★ ★ ★ ★/Highly Recommended

Old Pulteney 1983 Vintage 33 Year Old Highland SMSW 46% abv, $999.

Seriously beautiful rust/henna color; flawlessly pure. I can't honestly report that I'm getting a lot in the first nosing passes after the pour except for a parchment, butcher's wax paper aroma; allowing for more air contact, I have to work hard to identify the small array of scents, including peas, sawdust, and vinyl. Entry is hearty, rich, zesty, crisp, spicy, and tart, all while concealing gustatory specifics; midpalate sees the taste profile develop more as the flavor menu offers traces of caramel, praline, almond paste, walnut, bear claw pastry, and mincemeat. Ends intensely nutty, nougat-like, and bittersweet. This malt could not open up for whatever reason (too old?) and that, as a result, makes it not recommendable.

2018 Rating: ★ ★/Not Recommended

Old Pulteney 25 Year Old Highland SMSW 46% abv, $599.

Fulvous/tangerine color; sediment-free clarity. While I'd expect to encounter serious woodiness from a single malt this mature, what I get in the initial sniffs instead are round, supple, and dry aromas of salted snack cracker, candle wax, and flaxseed oil; later whiffs pick up nuances of grain husk, kernels, and milk chocolate–covered malted milk ball candy. Entry is dense with oak resin, maple, and slightly sooty flavors that are mildly salty and oily; midpalate is this malt's best moment as the various flavors merge into a singular taste that's dry, oaky, malty, and waxy. Aftertaste reflects the midpalate stage, adding only a carbon-like smokiness that's more ash-like than sooty. My concern about this malt and why it didn't receive a fourth rating star is that the cereal/barley aspect is significantly overshadowed by the oak.

2018 Rating: ★ ★ ★/Recommended

Old Pulteney Navigator Highland SMSW 46% abv, $55.

Harvest gold color; ideal clarity. I get a curious first aroma following the pour that's dry, citrusy (lemongrass), waxy, and textile-like; second nosing passes after more aeration bring out a seed-like, husk-like aroma that's dry, resiny, and flaxen, but I fail to pick up much in malt/grain or fruitiness. Entry is keenly citrusy, acidic, crisp, and nimble; midpalate highlights the emergence of the moderately sweet malted barley/breakfast cereal aspect that lends gravitas to the in-mouth experience. Finishes medium long, grainy, off-dry, and a bit salty.

2018 Rating: ★ ★ ★/Recommended

Port Askaig 8 Year Old Islay SMSW 45.8% abv, $65.

Citrine/maize color; impeccable clarity. In the up-front inhalations, I get pleasant, clean notes of fruit (pear, yellow plum) and sea salt crispness that are nimble and clean; later sniffs pick up gentle aromas of cigarette tobacco, green tea, eucalyptus, and dill; this is a well-managed bouquet that's agile and understated. Entry is lithe, gently smoked, and tobacco-like, with subtle hints of dried fruits and cooking spices (bay leaf, fennel), and malted milk balls; midpalate is toasted marshmallow–like, mildly smoked, off-dry, and

spiced with chili pepper. Finishes brief, delicately smoked, and atypically polite for an Islay malt and THAT is what makes it so charming and welcome.
2018 Rating: ★ ★ ★ ★/Highly Recommended

Port Askaig Islay SMSW 55% abv, $75.

Pale yellow color is strikingly fino sherry–like; impeccably pure. The aroma comes out swinging with razor-edged fragrances of citrus peel, egg white, yeast, sourdough bread, meringue, and spirity heat, but the spirit quickly calms down, allowing the other scents to emerge; secondary inhalations encounter more integrated aromas, such as green pepper, toasted almond, salted fish, green tobacco, and pickle brine. Entry is warming, to be sure, but hardly aggressive as the taste profile features a buttery texture and slightly smoked flavors of charred oak, maple (perhaps from ex-bourbon barrel?), vanilla bean, coffee bean/ espresso, and margarine; midpalate sees the taste profile settle in, becoming much more harmonious as the flavor highlights include baked fruits (banana, pineapple), baking spices like cinnamon, clove, and mace, and pleasing wood notes of maple and resin. Long, tobacco-like finish is creamy. Taken altogether, the aromatics and the in-mouth stages are beautifully rendered.
2017 Rating: ★ ★ ★ ★ ★/Highest Recommendation

Port Charlotte 10 Year Old Heavily Peated Islay SMSW 50% abv, $65.

Saffron color; minor sediment seen. This opening fragrance is only moderately smoky/ peaty and actually allows for a large measure of maltiness to shine through the light veil of gently sweet smoke, making for enjoyable early-on sniffing; later whiffs after more aeration discover grittier, earthier aromas, especially charcoal briquette, smoked fish (think: Arbroath smokies from eastern Scotland for those of you lucky enough to have eaten them), fruit-laced pipe tobacco, and chocolate-covered cherries. Entry taste offers a harmonious range of tangy flavors, including caramelized onion, sautéed mushrooms, smoked haddock, and roasted and candied walnut; midpalate findings echo those of the entry, with the emphasis laid heavily upon the sweet, cherrywood-like smoke, the zesty saltiness, and the ripe fruitiness. A total joy that could only be generated from one place on Earth—Islay.
2019 Rating: ★ ★ ★ ★/Highly Recommended

Port Charlotte Islay Barley 2011 Heavily Peated Islay SMSW 50% abv, $70.

Jasmine/straw color; some sediment seen that looks like cork particles. What I find so appealing about this opening scent is the harmony between the sweet-smelling malted barley and the medium-range impact of the fruity, cherrywood-like smoke; with more air contact, the interplay of the barley with the gently sweet, ripe fruit smoke continues to deepen. Entry provides a satiny, buttery texture upon which the engaging flavors of maple, toasted marshmallow, grilled pineapple, and grilled apricot cause a sensation in the mouth; midpalate is alluringly fruity, ripe, almost candied, and curiously reminiscent of honey baked ham. Finishes moderately smoky, gently sweet and pineapple-like, and sinewy in texture.
2019 Rating: ★ ★ ★ ★/Highly Recommended

Port Dundas 12 Year Old Single Grain Scotch Whisky 40% abv, $45.

In 2009, Diageo closed its Port Dundas distillery, located in Glasgow, in order to shift

grain whisky production to its newly expanded Cameronbridge distillery. In 2011, the building that housed Port Dundas was demolished. Once the largest whisky distillery in Scotland, by 1885 Port Dundas's trio of column stills and five pot stills were accounting for over two million gallons of grain whisky per year made from American corn, rye, and barley. Here is a twelve-year-old remnant of the last remaining stocks. Marigold color; ideal clarity. The initial nosing passes pick up crisp, off-dry scents of nutmeg, patent leather, soy sauce, soybean, and cigarette tobacco; second-stage inhalations detect a greater impact of the wood aging, especially in the lightly spiced forms of vanilla bean and lanolin. Entry reflects the character of the bouquet in the crispness of the acidity, which maintains the structure; mid-palate is clean, dense with graininess and bakery-shop flavors (dried apricot, marmalade, pie crust). Finishes measured, tightly wound, and lean as the high degree of acidity continues its march through the levels of aftertaste.
2018 Rating: ★ ★ ★/Recommended

Pure Scot Virgin Oak 43 Blended Scotch Whisky 43% abv, $40.

Pretty bronze color; pristine clarity. I smell caramel, Horlicks, and malted milk balls right out of the aromatic gate; later inhalations find pungent fragrances of cigar box, pipe tobacco, baked apricot, honeysuckle, and jasmine. Entry is keenly spicy (cinnamon, allspice, mace), baked/toasted, pleasantly acidic and crisp, with small doses of oak resin and bacon fat; midpalate reflects the entry to a tee, adding pecan pie and nougat flavors that thrive deep into the pleasant aftertaste. Hits most of the right notes and I especially like the 86 proof, which adds a sense of muscle to the core.
2017 Rating: ★ ★ ★/Recommended

Royal Brackla 12 Year Old Speyside SMSW 40% abv, $65.

Deep-ochre/sepia color; superb purity. Initial nosings detect caramel, grainy, snack cracker aromas that have a certain fruitiness that's more dried than fresh, as well as a vegetal, woodsy/forest-like quality that's a bit mossy; the aroma fades a little bit with more air contact and becomes indistinctive and amorphous. Entry features a touch more gravitas as the taste profile rounds out with substantial flavors of toffee, Danish pastry, caramelized sugar, cinnamon, vanilla; midpalate highlights the sinewy texture, which is satiny and medium bodied, which nicely supports the bakery-shop tastes. Aftertaste is medium long, delicately sweet, affably pleasant, if lacking in profundity.
2016 Rating: ★ ★ ★/Recommended

Scapa 16 Year Old Orkneys SMSW 40% abv, $75.

Brilliant old yellow/gold color; very minor sediment. I love the rubber tire, wet forest floor opening aroma on this elegant malt because then after another six minutes it turns concentrated in the graininess and shows a traceable hint of salinity (keep in mind the Scapa aging warehouses overlook the sea). But I think that this malt's strong suit is its lush, mildly salty/biscuit and malty entry flavor that is supple, round, and slightly honeyed. Concludes medium long and mildly oaky/resiny. A sturdy maritime-influenced malt of growing caliber.
2016 Rating: ★ ★ ★ ★/Highly Recommended

SIA Blended Scotch Whisky 43% abv, $50.

Marigold-yellow color; dazzling clarity. Initial nosings detect brisk breakfast cereal aromas, as well as toffee, lemon meringue fragrances; additional air contact stimulates dried apricot, new leather, marshmallow aromas. Entry is intensely grainy, lead pencil–like, earthy, semisweet, slightly metallic; midpalate highlights dry, tobacco-like flavors that leave behind a snack cracker taste that's a trace salty. Ends on a deeply grainy, wheat-like note. Good blended Scotch is always welcome, even though I think this one is too pricey.

2014 Rating: ★ ★ ★/Recommended

Spey River 12 Year Old Speyside SMSW 40% abv, $39.

Attractive gold color; excellent purity. Owns a moderately animated opening aroma that is citrusy, grainy, and slightly almond-like; further aeration stimulates integrated but restrained aromas of lemon curd, egg white, and dry breakfast cereal; pleasant but reined in. Entry is proper in its grainy sweetness, biscuit/cookie-like, and mildly spiced; midpalate is sweeter than the entry, keenly grainy, devoid of the fruitiness found in the bouquet, and slightly oaky/resiny. Finishes medium long, roasted, and nicely grainy. Very pleasant middle-of-the-road, beginner malt that plays everything safe and guarded, but shows more than ample charm.

2015 Rating: ★ ★ ★/Recommended

Spey River Double Cask Maturation Speyside SMSW 40% abv, $45.

Bright amber color is clean and clear of floating debris. I get all green/vegetal aromas up front, then the aroma takes a left turn after about one minute and becomes malty, doughy, cookie batter, and breakfast cereal–like; further aeration stimulates deft herbal traces of sage, parsley, basil that nicely support the graininess and doughy virtues. Entry is solid, sturdy, honey sweet, and intensely biscuity; midpalate is elegant, satiny in texture, even lush in its keenly raisin-like richness. Aftertaste highlights the ambrosial aspect, which creates a succulence that's disarming and regal. A terrifically appealing single malt.

2015 Rating: ★ ★ ★ ★/Highly Recommended

Speyburn 10 Year Old Speyside SMSW 40% abv, $30.

Sunglow-yellow color; flawless clarity. Wow, the buttermilk biscuit–like opening aroma is savory, doughy, a touch citrusy, and mild; later sniffs pick up deeper notes of dry, husk-like malted barley, lemon chiffon, citron, and apricot. Entry is firm, multilayered, off-dry, toasted bread–like, margarine-like, oily in texture, and solid in structure; midpalate is alive with vivid barley malt, biscuit-like, and breakfast cereal flavors that lean to dryness and yet own a zesty bittersweet back note taste that underlines the cereal aspect very nicely. Finishes maple-like, tree sap–like, resiny, oaky, peppery, and vanilla-like. A comely, affordable ten-year-old that runs with the best of them from Speyside.

2018 Rating: ★ ★ ★ ★/Highly Recommended

Speyburn 15 Year Old Speyside SMSW 46% abv, $65.

Pretty amber/sandy-brown color; superb purity. The alluring opening scents are chockfull of floral notes (jasmine and honeysuckle, especially) plus a deeply grainy/malty fragrance that's slightly off-dry, elegant, and keenly biscuity and cookie batter–like; with more aeration, there's a baking spice buildup that highlights mace, allspice, and clove along with traces of black tea and uncured tobacco; a lovely, stately inland bouquet. Entry is supple, moderately oily in texture and drier, more bittersweet than the aroma implies it would be; midpalate stage offers slightly prickly, piquant flavors that are intensely malty, and the overall bearing is understated and graceful. Aftertaste follows suit with the midpalate, offering polished, well-mannered flavors of malted barley, digestive biscuits, and dry breakfast cereal. Not a bruising, hearty inland malt but one that wins high marks for its quiet assertiveness and balance. I like the 46 percent abv, too, which pushes the deep Speyside maltiness forward.

2017 Rating: ★ ★ ★ ★/Highly Recommended

Speyburn Arranta Casks Speyside SMSW 46% abv, $45.

Saffron/goldenrod color; unblemished purity. I like this opening bouquet, as the highlight moment is the toasted malt element that's off-dry, breakfast cereal–like, and spicy (nutmeg, clove); secondary inhalations after more air contact discover deeper, nut-like scents, such as pecan pie, toasted walnut, and praline. Entry features a drier than expected, zesty, and spicy taste profile that's fruity, nutty, and pastry-like; midpalate shows a flavor profile that reminds me a little of ginger snap cookies and vanilla wafers. Finishes medium long, satiny, off-dry, and full of baking spices (allspice, mace, and clove, especially).

2018 Rating: ★ ★ ★ ★/Highly Recommended

Speyburn Bradan Orach Speyside SMSW 40% abv, $25.

Jonquil color; excellent purity. I like this flowery, vegetal opening nose that is initially quite woodsy, brambly, vine-like, and forest-like, then it quickly shifts into more of a bakery-shop mode, offering delicate scents of clove, allspice, baked apricot and nectarine, and brown sugar; secondary whiffs detect more of the spiced, baked orchard fruit that remind me of fruit-filled strudels. Entry is crackling with spicy, cinnamon bun, and mincemeat-like flavors that run drier than I would expect, and that's its strength in the opening in-mouth stage; midpalate is larger in sweetness as a demerara sugar-like flavor rules this phase. Aftertaste highlights the bakery-shop, brown-sugar-tinged, baked fruit flavor that turns bittersweet in the throat.

2018 Rating: ★ ★ ★/Recommended

Talisker 10 Year Old Skye SMSW 45.8% abv, $80.

Sinopia color; pristine clarity. Right from the first whiffs, this nose is vibrant with maritime saltiness but not so much that it's overbearing because it's not; later inhalations pick up an array of seaside and Highland aromas including deeply roasted barley malt, sea breeze, heather, oak resins, bacon fat, and pie crust. Entry flavors are complex, lush in texture, slightly spiced (nutmeg), and bread dough–like (pumpernickel, especially); midpalate offers a full range of succulent flavors such as honey-flavored breakfast cereal, toasted marshmallow, black tea, caramel, and heavily roasted malted barley. The finish is medium long, just slightly salty, flowery/woodsy, and tobacco-like.

2018 Rating: ★ ★ ★ ★/Highly Recommended

Talisker 18 Year Old Skye SMSW 45.8% abv, $160.

Marigold color; pristine clarity. Right from the get-go, there are dazzling, can't-get-enough sea breeze, salted peanut, seaweed, and kipper aromas that can only be Scottish maritime in nature; secondary inhalations add nuances of oak resin/sap and salted caramel to the already highly complex bouquet. Entry is stunningly "moreish," floral and sweet, honeyed, and oaky; midpalate is savory, salty, cereal-like, nutty, and earthy/flinty. Aftertaste is extended, narrowly focused on the maritime impact, malty, oily, peppery, and drier than the entry or midpalate.

2020 Rating: ★ ★ ★ ★/Highly Recommended

Talisker Storm Skye SMSW 45.8% abv, $66.

Bright deep straw/eiswein color; minor sediment seen. Roasted chestnuts, toasted marshmallow, sea breeze, light tobacco smoke fragrances all appear in fine form in opening whiffs; later inhalations uncover roasted peppers, low-intensity peat, almond paste. Entry sings with light peat animation and moderately sweet flavors of prunes, black raisins, pipe tobacco; midpalate reflects all the entry's glories and piles on light caramel, saltwater taffy, sea salt. Finishes oily, infinitely long, gently smoky/peaty. Wow, this is maritime single malt at its seductive best.

2016 Rating: ★ ★ ★ ★ ★/Highest Recommendation

Tamdhu 10 Year Old Sherry Cask Speyside SMSW 43% abv, $68.

The sherry cask influence is immediately seen in the topaz/sepia color; flawless purity. Right off the crack of the aromatic bat I get black tea, chalky aromas that are dry and earthy, subtly spiced, and herbaceous; with more air contact, the aroma evolves into a bouquet that's peppery, fruity (pomegranate, star fruit), and herbal (sassafras, coriander), with a background note of old saddle leather. Entry is lush in texture, slightly smoky, grainy/cereal-like, and intense with jammy fruit flavors, especially quince and gooseberry; midpalate ratchets up the spice element (coriander and black pepper), as the taste profile remains fruity but turns perceptibly drier, more bitter, and more acidic as the finish sees all flavor components merge into a singular taste that's bittersweet, resiny, maple-like. Really nice.

2017 Rating: ★ ★ ★ ★/Highly Recommended

Tamdhu 15 Year Old Speyside SMSW 46% abv, $90.

Burnt-orange color; perfectly sediment-free. The opening whiffs are treated to round, supple, and mature aromas of butterscotch, brown butter, praline, walnut, and bitter cacao; second passes after more aeration encounter very dense aromas of pain au chocolat, dark chocolate, candied raisins, and orange blossom. Entry features deep flavors of maple syrup, French toast, chocolate fudge, and cake frosting; midpalate highlights the concentrated cocoa-like tastes that are reminiscent of candy bars with nougat, almond paste, and hot cocoa. Finishes long, drier than the midpalate, bittersweet, and BBQ sauce–like.

2019 Rating: ★ ★ ★ ★/Highly Recommended

Tamdhu Batch Strength (Batch 001) Speyside SMSW 58.8% abv, $90.

Bright amber/sorrel color; pristine clarity. This is a lovely opening aroma all about inland single malt that is delightfully grainy, toffee-like, candied, cinnamon bun–like, toasty/

roasted, BBQ sauce–like, pork roast with pineapple, and, most charming of all, accessible; after more aeration, traces of dried flowers (violet, jasmine) and dried fruits (pear, black plum) come into play and mingle with the cereal grain richness, making me wonder why this distillery isn't better known in the USA. This elegant bouquet is so well integrated the elevated abv isn't a factor in the least. The entry ripples with nuanced undertones of spirit, which never overshadow the tastes of raisins, prunes, stewed apple, dried apricot, winter holiday fruitcake, candied walnut, and honey; midpalate echoes the entry, but here the lofty abv makes itself known a bit more by providing a soothing campfire warmth that extends through the luscious aftertaste. A malt whisky experience that builds with time in the glass to a stunning crescendo in the finish.

2017 Rating: ★ ★ ★ ★ ★/Highest Recommendation

Tamnavulin Double Cask Speyside SMSW 40% abv, $40.

Bronze/caramel color; unblemished purity. Opening aromatic impressions are muted, showing just a whisper of maltiness but little more; secondary inhalations following additional air contact don't register anything greater than low-volume muesli and dried orchard fruit fragrances. Entry, in direct opposition to the vastly understated aroma, is vivid, generous, and loaded with candy-shop sweetness and nut-like tastes; midpalate stage features traces of oaky vanilla, sweetened breakfast cereal, cinnamon bun, bear claw pastry, and dried dates. Closes in a rush of semisweet honey-like flavor that's lush and decadent.

2019 Rating: ★ ★ ★/Recommended

The Glenlivet 12 Year Old Speyside SMSW 40% abv, $50.

One of the most beloved, sophisticated malt whiskies of all time. Rated four stars in 1999 and 2007. Sepia/topaz color; impeccable clarity. The understated aroma, especially right after the pour, is dry, grainy, delicate, slightly woody, and a shrine to malted barley; after more aeration time, the aroma becomes a well-rounded, substantial bouquet that maintains its dry tendency without sacrificing the firm, kernel-like fragrance of the barley malt. Entry flavor echoes the dryness of the bouquet in soft waves of breakfast cereal, bread dough, baker's yeast, and nut bread; midpalate continues the dry flavor profile that is so pleasing and deceptively powerful, so deeply malty and integrated. Finishes long, just a notch sweeter than the midpalate: nutty, flowery, herbal, and majestic. A true adult beverage of gravitas and elegance.

2020 Rating: ★ ★ ★ ★/Highly Recommended

The Glenlivet 15 Year Old The French Oak Reserve Speyside SMSW 40% abv, $70.

Pretty, new-copper color; impeccably clean and sediment-free. What's so dazzling about this initial aroma is the softly spicy, peppery, clove-like scents that set the stage for deep fragrances of baked pear, malted milk balls, cocoa bean, fudge; second sniffs encounter deeper notes of breakfast cereal, multigrain bread dough, dried flowers, plus a distant oakiness that's vanilla-like. Entry offers keenly spicy tastes of winter holiday spice cake, blackberry scones, loose leaf tobacco, black tea; midpalate soars with buoyant flavors of buttercream, shortbread, brown sugar, oaky resin. Aftertaste is medium long, acutely spicy, toasty, roasted, grainy, mature.

2017 Rating: ★ ★ ★ ★/Highly Recommended

The Glenlivet 18 Year Old Speyside SMSW 43% abv, $100.

Deep cinnamon/ginger color; unblemished purity. This hearty opening aroma is animated, pleasingly grainy/malty, fruity (dates, prunes), floral (honeysuckle), medium dry and even a touch baked (caramelized); second inhalations bring out bread pudding, dark honey, cocoa butter, chocolate fudge, cake frosting. Entry explodes on the tongue with swashbuckling flavors of cinnamon, clove, vanilla bean, treacle, buttercream, high-cocoa-content dark chocolate; midpalate mirrors the entry to a tee, adding barley malt biscuits, butterscotch, baked pineapple, bacon fat, rancio. Finishes gloriously rich, honey sweet but not cloying. Batten down the hatches for this one.

2019 Rating: ★ ★ ★ ★ ★/Highest Recommendation

The Glenlivet Cognac Cask Selection 14 Year Old Speyside SMSW 40% abv, $53.

Ochre/marigold color; impeccable purity. This raisiny, apple tart–like opening aroma is stunningly fruity, ripe, and ambrosial; more air contact unleashes a soaring, streamline grain/malt note that's bone-dry, biscuity, and latently spicy. Entry is as dry as a desert, earthy, flinty, and yet pleasingly oaky and fruity; midpalate features a larger menu of flavors than the entry, mostly in the near-succulent forms of baked pineapple, candied walnut, orchard fruit pits and peels, nutmeg, and saltwater taffy. Finishes a bit more honeyed than the arid landscape-like midpalate. A dandy limited release from The Glenlivet.

2019 Rating: ★ ★ ★ ★/Highly Recommended

The Glenlivet Founder's Reserve Speyside SMSW 40% abv, $62.

New review of this no-age-statement offering that will replace the vaunted, iconic 12 Year Old in some markets. Pretty amber/burnt sienna color; flawless purity. There's a lively breakfast cereal graininess in the very first sniffs that is both fruity and delicately sweet; with more time in the glass, the aroma opens up more to offer vividly ambrosial fragrances of pear and nectarine. Entry is honey sweet, intensely barley-like, slightly caramelized, peppery, nearly succulent; midpalate is nicely toasty and continues to be honey sweet, all the while maintaining its concentrated graininess. Finishes on the sweeter, juicier side of the dryness/sweetness scale, and I can't help but think "young consumer demographic."

2017 Rating: ★ ★ ★/Recommended

The Glenlivet Nàdurra Oloroso Matured Speyside SMSW 60.7% abv, $80.

Lovely topaz/amber tone, with old gold core highlights. Prune, black raisin, malted milk ball, toasted marshmallow, vanilla extract reign in the first and second nosing passes; a robust bouquet of bakery and fruit stand notes. Entry opens with luxurious texture that sets the stage for semisweet flavors of dried red fruits/berries, harmonious, with a back note of campfire warmth at midpalate. Finishes drier than the midpalate stage, yet is biscuity, doughy, dense, malty. Its undiluted cask strength serves as the foundation for the rainbow of vivid aromas and flavors that are deeply influenced by the oloroso sherry barrel finish, which brings to mind raisins, plums, and prunes. This fully integrated malt is the real deal.

2014 Rating: ★ ★ ★ ★/Highly Recommended

The Glenlivet Nàdurra Peated Whisky Cask Finished Batch No. PW0715 Speyside SMSW 61.5% abv, $62.

A singular, cask strength malt whisky that has scored very well in different incarnations over the years (Triumph 1991—five stars/16 Year Old—four stars). Striking pale-gold/straw-yellow color; impeccable clarity. First nosing passes detect early tantalizing fragrances of campfire smoke, smoked fish, seaweed, olive brine, green olive, unsweetened breakfast cereal; following more air contact, the aroma turns slightly sweeter and more grain-driven as the peatiness gradually fades leaving behind zesty scents of malted barley, green pepper, creosote, vegetable oil. Entry flashes the peat influence immediately as the flavor profile highlights the tobacco smoke, kippers, sea salt, olive brine while the graininess takes a back seat; midpalate continues the smoke-a-thon as the peat-reek maintains its status as the lead flavor while the other taste aspects stand in the wings. Finishes long, moderately smoky, very cigar tobacco–like, roasted. I think the peat-reek while flavorful and deep was allowed to run amok without allowing this whisky's other virtues to emerge.
2016 Rating: ★ ★ ★/Recommended

The Lost Distillery Company Series No. 3 Gerston Blended Malt Whisky 46% abv, $63.

Earth yellow/citrine color; ideal clarity. There's not a flurry of aromas emanating from the glass in the initial whiffs except for candle wax, parchment, and textile fiber; later inhalations following more aeration discover cigar box, fresh tobacco leaf, bay leaf, and cinnamon. Entry is mildly toasty, toffee-like, marshmallow-y, and reminiscent of steamed white rice mixed with soy sauce; midpalate shows a richer, creamier side as the taste profile turns more honey-like, spicy, and even a touch burnt/baked. Finishes brief, fruity/estery, grainy, and semisweet.
2017 Rating: ★ ★ ★/Recommended

Tullibardine 20 Year Old Speyside SMSW 43% abv, $160.

The topaz/sandy-brown hue is free of sediment and pretty. The opening whiffs are treated to gentle and clean aromas of barley floor maltings, cracked grain kernels, porridge, bread dough, and flowers/hops; secondary inhalations find additional scents of orchard fruits (pear, quince), green vegetable (snow peas), and parchment. Entry offers trim, seed-like (pumpkin), highly acidic flavors that are crisp, willowy, and a bit razor edged; at midpalate, the taste profile features a little more chewiness in the texture and overall slightly more substance in the forms of unsweetened breakfast cereal, malted milk ball, and vegetable oil tastes. In the aftertaste, I still don't get a sense of two decades in oak casks, as the finish remains spare, but there is no denying that this malt is limber and clean as a whistle.
2018 Rating: ★ ★ ★/Recommended

Tullibardine 25 Year Old Speyside SMSW 43% abv, $300.

This amber color is a shade darker than that of the 20 Year Old and is equally pristine. Oh, now what I find here in this opening aroma is far more biscuity, buttermilk-like, and round than in the rawboned 20 Year Old; secondary whiffs pick up hints of baking spices, in particular, clove and cinnamon, as well as toasted oats, muesli, dried orchard fruits, and a delicate touch of honey. Entry is buttery, creamy in texture and loaded with caramel, date, fig, and raisiny flavors that show the oak impact nicely; midpalate is medium hefty in texture, sinewy, honeyed, and moderately candied. Concludes medium long, pleasantly toasted and tobacco-like, and appreciably raisin- and fig-like. Well done, here.

2018 Rating: ★ ★ ★ ★/Highly Recommended

Tullibardine 500 Sherry Finish Speyside SMSW 43% abv, $65.

Color is fawn/nut brown; excellent purity. First nosing passes pick up dry but faint scents of malted barley, beeswax, parchment, manila envelope, sesame seed; later inhalations following more time in the glass detect a strengthening of the aromatics that are now showcasing unsweetened breakfast cereal, bread dough, yeast, and unsalted snack crackers. Entry is desert dry, bitter, kernel-like, woody/oaky, tart, yet generously textured; midpalate stage features dry flavors, headlined by malted barley, just-baked multigrain bread, boiled pork, gravy. Aftertaste is multilayered, long, complex, grainy, biscuity, and divinely rich and buttery. At first, I didn't think that I'd like it as much as I ended up liking it. It grows in the glass, but the key to this malt is the dazzling, enveloping texture.

2017 Rating: ★ ★ ★ ★/Highly Recommended

Wemyss Malts Coastal Orchard Single Cask Release 1997 Clynelish Highland SMSW 46% abv, $150.

Saffron/amber color; sediment-free purity. First whiffs pick up distant traces of apple and pear aromas that are more peel-like than pulpy or juicy; in the second passes, I detect hints of rubber pencil eraser, damp straw, saltine cracker, and paraffin. Entry is chunkier and more animated than the fey, wispy bouquet as front-loaded flavors of roasted malt, honey wheat bread, baked apple, and sweet/ripe mincemeat make the case for profundity; midpalate goes drier than the entry, highlighting the malty grain/breakfast cereal core flavor that's off-dry, dense, and appealingly oily in texture. Aftertaste features all of the midpalate phase attributes that are underscored by the firm, slightly prickly alcohol. I've long been an ardent fan of this northern Highland malt distillery, and this expression speaks well of it.

2018 Rating: ★ ★ ★ ★/Highly Recommended

Wemyss Malts Hike to the Haven Single Cask Release 1990 Bunnahabhain Islay SMSW 46% abv, $205.

Flax/gold color; ideally pure. There's a steely, flinty, dry limestone-like element in the initial inhalations that is desert dry and even a dash like lemony cleaning fluid; after more aeration, the bouquet doesn't open up much beyond the first impressions when normally a Bunnahabhain aroma would include floral, malty, and sometimes fruity aspects. Entry offers a bit more animation than the stingy bouquet as dry-as-a-bone tastes of malty cereal, unsalted snack cracker, and bread dough do their best to impress; the midpalate only features astringent, steely, tongue-on-stone tastes that do little to alleviate the paucity of character. The finish does a bit better by offering a pleasing sugar cookie–like flavor that's more in line with this distillery's profile. Even though it ends up being a drinkable malt of modest virtue, I feel that the hollowness of the character, which by some might

be erroneously viewed as Bunnahabhain's customary litheness, is simply unacceptable. Therefore, no recommendation.
2018 Rating: ★★/Not Recommended

Wemyss Malts Italian Bakery Delight Single Cask Release 1997 Glenrothes Speyside SMSW 46% abv, $150.
Maize/citron color; pristine clarity. There are high-toned floral notes in the opening sniffs that are part hyacinth, part heather, and part hops, but then in the secondary passes after more time in the glass, the flower garden turns into fruit market as the bouquet becomes fruity, featuring lemon peel, citric acid, and sour apple/apple strudel and puff pastry; it's an interesting and pleasing bouquet. This malt is crisp, yeasty, hoppy, and engagingly beer-like in the lean, brittle entry phase; midpalate adds soft voices of cereal, malted milk ball, and toffee but overall stays rather severe as the high degree of acidity remains firmly in charge of the in-mouth stages. Finishes steely, clean, fresh, flowery, and texturally lean.
2018 Rating: ★★★/Recommended

Wemyss Malts Peat Chimney 12 Year Old Blended Malt Scotch Whisky 40%; $62.
Marigold/amber color; impeccable clarity. Smells of cigarette ashes, peated grain, peated water, and baked fruits in the initial whiffs after the pour; seven more minutes in glass release sweetened breakfast cereal aromas, along with lesser scents of cake batter, wood plank, and smoked fish. Entry is nicely structured, gently sweet, moderately smoky, and delightfully grainy; midpalate showcases raisins, dates, and peated grain, not in an overabundance but in a measured manner that works nicely deep into the medium-long finish.
2020 Rating: ★★★/Recommended

Wemyss Malts Spice King 12 Year Old Blended Malt Scotch Whisky 40% abv, $62.
Lovely topaz color; excellent purity. Opening nosing passes detect rich, aristocratic aromas of fruit-filled breakfast cereal and subtle baking spices (clove, nutmeg); further aeration stimulates a wood plank aspect that nicely melds with the grain and dried fruits. Entry is luscious, smoky, and fruity ripe; midpalate features sweet grains, dried apricot and pear, nutmeg, and milk chocolate. Finishes long, spicy, and oily textured.
2020 Rating: ★★★★/Highly Recommended

Wemyss Malts The Hive 12 Year Old Blended Malt Scotch Whisky 40% abv, $62.
The pretty golden sunset color is spoiled a bit by sediment. Wow, I smell bubble gum, confectioners' sugar, freshly cut hay, dry earth, and sawdust in the first inhalations after the pour; then following seven minutes of further air contact, the aroma bursts open with juicy, fruity, bakery goods scents that are delightful in their straightforward manner. Entry is semi-sweet, ripe, fruity, and definitely honey-like; midpalate is mildly woody/oaky and bakery sweet. Uncomplicated quality, sturdy, and grainy sweet.
2020 Rating: ★★★/Recommended

WHISKEY—IRELAND

The first millennium Scottish Gaels who inhabited Ireland were known to be avid and adept brewers of dark ales made from oats and barley. Once distillation was introduced to the island, circa 1050–1100 CE, some brewers became distillers as well. There exists a vague if tantalizing passage from the reports of English soldiers who occupied parts of twelfth-century Ireland under the command of England's King Henry II. The reports spoke of the Scots-Gaels producing a strong beverage made from "boiling," implying distillation. It stands to reason that the Scots-Gaels were likely boiling their ales in crude pot stills to produce crystalline *uisge beathas* (waters of life).

Whatever the situation, by the 1500s, small-scale distilling was widespread in Ireland. By the mid-nineteenth century, there were eighty-eight licensed distilleries operating throughout the island. During the 1800s, Irish whiskey was considered the international gold standard and was admired worldwide. North America evolved into Ireland's prime export destination as drinkers of Irish descent in Canada and the United States yearned for a taste of their beloved Éire.

Trouble for the Irish distilling industry began first with the outbreak of World War I, which closed down shipping lanes in the northern Atlantic Ocean because of U-boat activity, and then the Irish War of Independence and the Irish Civil War. Once the domestic hostilities abated in 1923, America was in the throes of Prohibition as dictated by the Eighteenth Amendment, which made the production, sale, and transportation of alcohol illegal within the USA. Prohibition ran from 1919 to 1933, when it was repealed by the Twenty-first Amendment. This infamous "double whammy" effectively shut down Ireland's main whiskey export market and virtually destroyed the entire Irish whiskey trade in the process.

Then came the Great Depression, followed by World War II. By the end of the Second World War, Americans had largely forgotten about Irish whiskey and turned instead to American-made blended whiskeys and bourbon, as well as Scotch whisky.

But tides turn and fortunes change in the cyclical world of beverage alcohol. By the grace of its storied heritage and the quality of Irish whiskey being made in the twenty-first century, Ireland is enjoying a whiskey renaissance of staggering magnitude. In 2010, only four distilleries were operating: Cooley, Old Bushmills, Kilbeggan, and Midleton. By the close of 2019, there were thirty-one fully operating, licensed distilleries on the island, with several more under construction.

Types and Classifications

There are four basic types of Irish whiskey.

Pure pot still whiskey. Made from 100 percent barley, which is both malted and unmalted, and distilled in one pot still. A variety that is unique to Ireland, pure pot still whiskey is very potent and robust.

Single malt whiskey. This type is made from 100 percent malted barley in a pot still in a single distillery and is known for its distinctive flavors.

Single grain whiskey. Produced in column stills, grain whiskey is made from wheat or corn and is normally lighter than single malt or pure pot still whiskeys.

Blended whiskey. This variety is a combination of grain and single malt whiskeys.

Irish Whiskey Production

To be legally labeled as Irish whiskey, the whiskey must be distilled and matured in the Republic of Ireland or Northern Ireland.

The whiskey must be distilled from a yeast-fermented mash of cereal grains to an alcohol by volume degree of less than 94.8 percent.

Irish whiskey must be matured in wooden casks not exceeding 185 gallons for a minimum of three years. A distinguishing characteristic of Irish whiskeys is that most are distilled three times to promote extra smoothness and drinkability.

Barr an Uisce 1803 16 Year Old Single Malt Irish Whiskey 46% abv, $120.

Maize color; flawlessly clean and pure. I like the first aromas after the pour, which are more fruity (quince, kiwi, lychee) than woody or alcohol prone, and therefore fresh and engaging; secondary inhalations detect ethereal hints of breakfast cereal and tree sap, both of which bring greater character depth to the fruit fragrance. Entry is sleek, lithe in texture, dry as a bone, and deeply grainy/dry breakfast cereal–like; midpalate is arid, crisp, woodier than the entry stage, and therefore more complex. Ends in an elegant, stone dry, woody, and caramelized manner that's satisfying and hearty.
2019 Rating: ★ ★ ★ ★/Highly Recommended

Bushmills 10 Year Old Single Malt Irish Whiskey (Northern Ireland) 40% abv, $40.

Flax/straw-yellow color; impeccable clarity. The juicy, vividly grainy/malty opening aroma is delightfully harmonious, youthful, animated in its advanced fruitiness; later sniffs detect orange/tangerine, sawdust, sugar biscuits, and a deft trace of honey. Entry is malty sweet, intensely grainy, resinous; midpalate features the oak and the dry-as-a-bone grain. Finish is a lopsided grainfest that concludes desert dry, earthy, minerally. Excellent value.
2019 Rating: ★ ★ ★ ★/Highly Recommended

Bushmills 16 Year Old Single Malt Irish Whiskey (Northern Ireland) 40% abv, $150.

Triple distilled, 100 percent malted barley. Matured in three types of wood barrels—ex-bourbon and ex-sherry for at least sixteen years, then for a few months in ex-port barrels. The tawny/copper color is dazzling and completely particle-free. The ambrosial opening aroma is state-of-the-art, brimming with raisins, peach, nectarine, lychee, grapefruit, and cinnamon; secondary sniffs detect more wonderful aromas, including fresh honey from the hive, ripe white grapes, dates, prune Danish, nougat, baked banana, and sweetened breakfast cereal—for me, my all-time favorite Irish whiskey bouquet to date. Entry is lithe yet substantial, gently sweet and ripe, but not for a moment cloying or syrupy, and divinely fruity and nimble, as ample acidity maintains the acute freshness; midpalate echoes the entry impressions, throwing in more of the malted barley oiliness that is rampant in the texture's creaminess. Aftertaste is polite, delicate even, yet shows a mature elegance that shines a spotlight on the astuteness of the Old Bushmills barrel management. Simply stated, a landmark Irish whiskey by all accounts and one of the top one hundred spirits in the world, hands down.

2018 Rating: ★ ★ ★ ★ ★/Highest Recommendation

Bushmills 21 Year Old Rare Finished in Madeira Wood Casks Single Malt Irish Whiskey (Northern Ireland) 40% abv, $125.

Amber, with a hint of core green color; superb purity. I detect old leather, ripe dried fruits (dates, black raisins), dry breakfast cereal in the first inhalations; later whiffs pick up a restrained saltiness and an earthy, soil-like quality that seems to underpin the bouquet. Entry features the Madeira aspect in spades as the taste profile goes fruity, winey, ripe; midpalate echoes the entry to the letter, adding a biscuity/doughy element that nicely rounds out the in-mouth experience, especially in the aftertaste.

2015 Rating: ★ ★ ★ ★/Highly Recommended

Bushmills Black Bush Blended Irish Whiskey (Northern Ireland) 40% abv, $39.

Butterscotch color; perfect clarity. The high percentage of Irish single malt aged in oloroso sherry butts for eight to ten years is immediately evident in the luscious buttermilk biscuit–like, malty, and dried fruit–like opening aroma; second nosing passes after more air contact find a mature, swank, and expressively cereal-like aerated fragrance that is one of the most charming and enthralling in the Irish whiskey category. Entry is zesty, highly spiced (mace, ginger, nutmeg, clove), and hearty in texture as the taste profile reaches for maximum depth of flavor; midpalate echoes the entry, throwing in marzipan, almond paste, and apple butter to boot. Concludes medium long, savory, moderately viscous, and bursting with black raisin and prune parting flavors that leave a mile-deep impression. One of Northern Ireland's most reliably brilliant whiskey ambassadors.

2020 Rating: ★ ★ ★ ★ ★/Highest Recommendation

Connemara 12 Year Old Peat Single Malt Irish Whiskey 40% abv, $75.

Pale straw/lemon-juice color; pristine clarity. While in the "Original" version the peatiness struts its stuff right from the outset, here it is hidden a bit more behind the influence of the oak barrel, and this allows for the malted barley/dry breakfast cereal notes to reign supreme up front, at least; more aeration stimulates the peat-reek but in a spring onion–like manner that's very becoming and vegetal. Entry is velvety smooth texturally and bittersweet in flavor, as the taste profile highlights the wood resin/lipids more than the peated barley; midpalate features a buttery, vegetable cooking oil–like primary flavor around which orbit minor tastes of black peppercorn and bay leaf. Finishes cleanly, moderately long, and just a touch smoky.

2020 Rating: ★ ★ ★/Recommended

Connemara Original Peat Single Malt Irish Whiskey 40% abv, $55.

I like the brightness of the marigold/wheat-field color; perfectly clean and sediment-free.

Immediately clear in the first whiffs is the unmistakable presence of smoky, salted fish peat-reek as it wafts up from the tasting glass; additional inhalations following more air contact encounter deeper fragrances, including salted butter, beef jerky, creosote, sawdust, and lemon curd. Entry is lightly smoked, semisweet, green tobacco–like, clean, and spare; midpalate mirrors the entry, adding nuances of egg white, malted barley, malted milk balls, and toasted bread. Ends on a polite, agile note that's more grainy than smoky. Have always liked this biscuity, well-crafted Irish single malt whiskey.

2020 Rating: ★ ★ ★ ★/Highly Recommended

Dead Rabbit Irish Whiskey 44% abv, $40.

The harvest gold color is shiny and free of sediment. Up-front aromas include tomato vine, new leather, chalk/limestone, and a vivid grain element that's both citrusy and dry; further aeration serves to coax out scents of grain kernel, flaxseed, jasmine, mountain laurel, bay leaf, and roasted malt. Entry highlights the density of the malty graininess in the form of acute dryness and high acidity that keeps the flavor profile razor sharp and crisp; midpalate echoes the entry impressions and adds grain-based depth that brings further richness and gravity to the in-mouth phase. Finishes medium long, toasted, dry, and deeply cereal-like. Delicious and more than adequately complex for a blended whiskey.

2018 Rating: ★ ★ ★ ★/Highly Recommended

Dubliner 10 Year Old Single Malt Irish Whiskey 42% abv, $27.

Pretty golden hue; very good clarity. First, I get a feathery touch of apple peel and banana that then goes more strawberry-like but the entire initial nosing pass is delicate and understated; more time in the glass allows the fruitiness to slightly expand while simultaneously there is evidence of honey and dry breakfast cereal. Entry shows more grain density as the taste profile goes arid and dry, notable for its malty grain aspect; midpalate stays firmly on the dry grain course as the flavor picks up a bit of oak resin and vanillin, which rounds out the graincentric taste focus. A handsome malt of delicacy and elegance.

2018 Rating: ★ ★ ★/Recommended

Dubliner Bourbon Cask Aged Irish Whiskey 40% abv, $29.

Jonquil-yellow color; impeccably clean. The initial nosing passes find an understated aroma that seems clean and neat, but just a bit too inexpressive; more time in the glass allows for increased air contact, which does help to open up the reluctant bouquet in meager waves of dried flowers, pine nut, and sourdough bread. Entry is more animated than the aroma, offering subtle but detectable flavors of nutmeg, pastry dough, baker's yeast, egg yolk, and malted grain; midpalate accelerates the flavor character, adding featherweight touches of oaky vanillin, sweet corn, light caramel, and honey-flavored cereal. Ends up semidry, mildly nutty, and grainy. While there are no glaring flaws that I could point to as deal breakers, I ultimately find this Irish blend too underdeveloped, meek, and uninspiring.

2018 Rating: ★ ★/Not Recommended

Egan's 10 Year Old Single Malt Irish Whiskey 47% abv, $50.

Pale gold/hay color; I see a moderate amount of tendril-like sediment. Opening whiffs detect very pleasant, slightly toasted cereal aromas that are dry and animated; secondary

inhalations after more aeration discover a bigger emphasis on the toastiness of the cereal grain that is now slightly sweet. Entry is welcoming, assertive, sweeter than the bouquet, grainy/cereal-like, generous, and warming; midpalate seems to possess a deeper texture that's creamy but not necessarily oily, and the flavor profile maintains the focus squarely on the dense graininess. It's in the laser beam aftertaste that there's a piney/woody and pear-like aspect that complements the density of the cereal and the elevated abv. A savory and munificent whiskey.
2016 Rating: ★ ★ ★ ★/Highly Recommended

Glendalough Double Barrel Irish Whiskey 42% abv, $36.

Orange-peel color; excellent clarity. Whoa, I like the buttery, Crisco-like, wine-like opening aroma that's soft, piquant, and plush; more air contact stimulates deeper scents, including oak resin, sawdust, oak stave, charcoal, and burnt toast. Entry is richly textured, oloroso sherry sweet, prune-like, creamy, and lightly spiced; midpalate accurately reflects the entry points, adding gingerbread, honeyed breakfast cereal, and ripe melon. Finishes medium long, delicately sweet, and ripe.
2020 Rating: ★ ★ ★ ★/Highly Recommended

Green Spot Chateau Montelena Single Pot Still Irish Whiskey 46% abv, $100.

Finished in Chateau Montelena (California) zinfandel casks for twelve months. Amber/golden wheat-field color; far more infinitesimal sediment than I'd like to see spotted under the examination lamp. Wow, the lovely red wine/zinfandel barrel influence is immediately noticed in delicate waves of bramble-blackberry fragrance; later sniffs pick up slightly spicy scents that remind me most of winter holiday fruitcake or even perhaps mincemeat pies as the fruit/grape element continues to soar. Entry is amazingly toasty, caramelized, nutty, and spiced with cinnamon, allspice, and nutmeg especially; midpalate provides a treasure trove of exceptionally savory flavors, including rum ball, dates, spice cake, praline, cinnamon bun, and chocolate-covered coffee bean. Ends on a high note of expressively earthy and bakery-shop tastes of nougat, sautéed mushrooms, smoked sausage, chocolate fudge, and port. Had the appearance been less problematic, this would have been an easy five star whiskey.
2018 Rating: ★ ★ ★ ★/Highly Recommended

J.J. Corry The Gael Blended Irish Whiskey 46% abv, $75.

Clear, bright flax/yellow color; clean and pure. I like the vivid opening aroma that's mildly salty, menthol/mint-like, floral (honeysuckle, jasmine), and vibrantly herbaceous; further mingling with air brings out orchard fruit aspects, especially yellow pear and nectarine, pear cider, and sour grain notes. Entry is sweet/sour, highly fruited (again, the pear and nectarine), acutely acidic, and therefore fresh and drying on the tongue, and almost like banana hard candy; midpalate features all of the entry impressions, adding nuances of grain kernel and licorice. Finishes ripe in its fruitiness, soft yet razor-edged due to the high degree of acid—clean and refreshing. While neither a complicated nor a profound Irish whiskey, it's one that's entirely enjoyable from start to finish. An amiable pub whiskey.
2018 Rating: ★ ★ ★/Recommended

Jameson Caskmates Stout Edition Blended Irish Whiskey 40% abv, $30.

Aged in craft beer barrels. Brilliant amber/topaz color; impeccable clarity. First sniffs

pick up traces of beer, but also detect rich aromas of grains, wheat field, dry breakfast cereal, unbuttered toast, grain loaf; secondary inhalations unearth rich, lightly spiced tastes of graham cracker, honey wheat bread, bread dough, yeast; a very inviting bouquet. Entry highlights much of the light spices (cinnamon, nutmeg) found in the latter stages of the nosing, plus there's the moderately oily texture that underpins the in-mouth experience with suppleness and sturdiness; midpalate turns unexpectedly fruity, ripe, and delicately sweet as the beer influence takes charge. Finishes smooth, silky in texture, delectably sweet (in a controlled manner), biscuity, bread-like, and very tasty.
2016 Rating: ★★★★/Highly Recommended

Jameson Cooper's Croze Non-Chill Filtered Blended Irish Whiskey 43% abv, $70.
The appearance is highlighted by a golden wheat-field color; I do see some widely dispersed sediment that is not a game changer. The opening nose is gently sweet, grainy, delicately spicy (allspice), and floral; later whiffs detect soft-spoken hints of dry breakfast cereal, malted milk balls, candied apple. Entry is fuller, more assertive than the dainty aroma promises and for that, I'm glad, since now Cooper's Croze evolves into a serious whiskey with expansive flavors of toasted whole grain bread, grain kernel, oak-driven vanilla, maple; midpalate echoes the entry, adding just a light touch of salted caramel. Finish is moderately long as it pleasantly coats the palate and throat with medium-weighted viscosity.
2017 Rating: ★★★★/Highly Recommended

Jameson Gold Reserve Blended Irish Whiskey 40% abv, $68.
Deep-amber color; impeccable purity. The subdued aroma displays genuine depth in the forms of breakfast cereal, malted milk balls, and wet hay; further air contact brings out touches of nougat, chestnut purée, egg cream, and light caramel. Entry flavors are chewy/textured, doughy, fruity, and caramel-like; midpalate is succulent in its fruitiness and yet malty/cereal-like at the same time. Ends on a marzipan/praline note that's medium sweet and pleasant, but not deep.
2015 Rating: ★★★/Recommended

Jameson Limited Reserve 18 Year Old Blended Irish Whiskey 40% abv, $90.
Medium amber hue; spotless clarity. Wow, the dried tropical fruit (pineapple and guava, especially) scent takes command immediately in the initial whiffs; additional time in glass stimulates deeper aromas of pine nut, apricot, pears, honeysuckle, old leather, and orange blossom—a fabulously sensual bouquet. Entry taste is lusciously gripping and honeyed, with earmark flavors of toffee, sweet breakfast cereal, and orange marmalade; midpalate turns nearly profound in terms of depth of flavor, in particular, the long, languid tastes of almond butter and nougat as highlight reel aspects. Finishes dusty dry, astringent, refreshing, and intensely oaky. Serious whiskey drinkers only need apply.
2018 Rating: ★★★★/Highly Recommended

Jameson Select Reserve Black Barrel Blended Irish Whiskey 40% abv, $44.
Beautiful topaz/old gold color; some sediment spotted floating in the core. Out of the gate, the opening aroma is remarkably fruity and biscuity, almost like sugar cookies, yet there's also a yeasty/doughy quality that's fresh and vivid; with aeration, the bouquet turns a

little spicy and toasted, and that adds a pleasing aspect to the fruit and cookie-batter scents. Entry taste is like buttered, toasted wheat bread with cherry preserves and is consequently gently sweet in an old honey manner; the substantial mouthfeel is delightful at midpalate, as are the rich oak and sap tastes that balance the honey element with grace. Concludes bittersweet, bordering on astringent, woody/oaky/toasty, and vividly robust.
2017 Rating: ★★★★/Highly Recommended

Jameson Triple Distilled Blended Irish Whiskey 40% abv, $24.
Mango/amber color; flawlessly clean. Initial sniffs pick up raisiny, caramelized onion, and graham cracker notes that are almost sour in scope; secondary inhalations feature sour apple, egg white, and yeasty notes that are a bit like meringue. Entry is gently sweet and biscuity, very approachable, lightly toasted, and spicy (allspice); midpalate serves up a touch more complexity as the primary flavor becomes more breakfast cereal–like and honeyed. Easy to see why this ubiquitous blended Irish whiskey singlehandedly triggered the revolution and renaissance for Irish distillers in the early 2000s. Excellent value for the money.
2020 Rating: ★★★/Recommended

Kilbeggan Single Grain Irish Whiskey 43% abv, $30.
The saffron color is impeccably clean and free of floating detritus. Right out of the aromatic gate, I pick up mildly faint scents of butcher's wax paper, yeast, and cardboard; later inhalations after more aeration discover a touch more graininess in the form of dry, unsweetened breakfast cereal but nothing of consequence beyond that. Entry is far more vivid than the lackluster bouquet as it offers evolved tastes of unsalted wheat snack crackers, graham crackers, toffee, pipe tobacco, and honey-laced pastry; midpalate reflects the entry, adding textural heft and semisweet tastes of white chocolate, nougat, and cinnamon bun. Aftertaste is bakery shop–like in its controlled, sugary sweetness, and pleasant. The in-mouth stages saved this single grain from Not Recommended status.
2018 Rating: ★★★/Recommended

Kilbeggan Small Batch Rye Whiskey 43% abv, $35.
Old gold/amber color; perfect clarity. The lovely opening fragrance is fruit filled, apple fritter–like, gently grainy, and near ambrosial, exhibiting scents of green apple, pear, and parchment; later sniffs pick up additional aromas of dried violets and leather. Entry is dry, deeply grainy (not necessarily rye, though; just unsweetened breakfast cereal grain), toasted bread–like, and a bit like oatmeal; midpalate displays a narrow focus on the flavor profile that's dry as a bone, lean, and intensely grainy. The aftertaste highlights all the midpalate findings, creating a medium long, baked apple–like taste that's delicious and svelte. Excellent, clean as a whistle.
2019 Rating: ★★★★/Highly Recommended

Kinahan's 10 Year Old Single Malt Irish Whiskey 46% abv, $69.
Gamboge/marigold color; perfect purity. Mildly fruity and a bit reminiscent of bread pudding, the opening aroma here is much grainier than the blend version, which is all fruit and spice; more air contact unleashes an alluring wave of malted milk, barley malt, oaky vanillin, vegetable oil, bacon fat. Entry is measured, grainy sweet, almost more semisweet, beany (cocoa), and caramel-like; midpalate expands on the entry themes as the flavor profile

turns drier, nutty, biscuity, cookie batter–like; of special feature in the midpalate is the satiny texture. Ends on an astringent note that's cleansing, silky smooth, and spicy. A handsome malt that is at its apex of maturity.

2015 Rating: ★ ★ ★ ★/Highly Recommended

Kinahan's Blended Irish Whiskey 46% abv, $40.

Flax/pale gold color; flawless clarity. I like the opening fragrances of crisp red apple, toasted marshmallow, baked pear, cinnamon bun, vanilla bean—I mean, there's a lot happening here aromatically that's both spicy and fruity and terribly charming; further aeration releases minor scents of pipe tobacco and sea salt, but the primary thrust remains the spiced orchard fruits. Entry is crisp, acidic, but refreshing, intensely spiced, toffee-like, and flat-out zesty, which is not a common descriptor for Irish whiskey; midpalate highlights the vanilla and cinnamon bun aspects, as the apple/pear element wanes. Finishes medium long, piquant, peppery, and with a late blooming spirit "kick" that's a pleasing way to end. Really delightful and worth the price tag.

2015 Rating: ★ ★ ★ ★/Highly Recommended

Knappogue Castle 12 Year Old Single Malt Irish Whiskey 43% abv, $46.

Citrine color; perfect clarity. First aromatic impressions are of hard Italian cheese/umami, walnut, paraffin, and parchment; secondary inhalations reinforce the first-pass findings, deepening the umami effect while adding soft scents of tobacco leaf, bay leaf, white rice, and thyme. Entry features delicate, well-structured flavors of peanut butter, toasted marshmallow, cotton candy, and honey; midpalate echoes the entry impressions, throwing in candied almond and dried fig that lengthen the aftertaste.

2019 Rating: ★ ★ ★ ★/Highly Recommended

Knappogue Castle 14 Year Old Single Malt Irish Whiskey 46% abv, $60.

Jonquil/mango color; superbly pure. Opening whiffs pick up defined and sculpted notes of ripe tropical fruits (banana, pineapple, guava) and toasted cereal grains, primarily oats and barley malt; after more aeration, the aroma leaps forward, offering zesty, citrus-peel notes that balance and accentuate the deep woodiness and cereal-grain fragrances. Entry is toasty, dry, integrated, and multilayered; midpalate mirrors the entry stage, adding luscious flavors of caramel, sautéed mushrooms, egg yolk, black raisins, dates, and baking spices, especially bay leaf and parsley. Finishes very extended, toasty, semisweet, and highly complex. Wow.

2019 Rating: ★ ★ ★ ★ ★/Highest Recommendation

Knappogue Castle 16 Year Old Single Malt Irish Whiskey 43% abv, $100.

Harvest gold color; pristine clarity. There is dried bing cherry written all over this opening inhalation initially, then it advances into raisin bran cereal territory all the while maintaining a fresh, vibrant appeal; later sniffs pick up hints of wax paper, candle wax, parchment, apple peel, and furniture polish. Entry is deeply grainy and oaky, even resiny, and maple-like; midpalate offers an array of flavors, including toffee, mincemeat pie, walnut butter, and figs. Aftertaste is long, elegant but powerfully structured, acidic, nearly astringent, yet deeply resiny.

2019 Rating: ★ ★ ★ ★/Highly Recommended

Lambay Single Malt Irish Whiskey 40% abv, $70.

Topaz/amber color; flawless clarity. Immediately, I get charming fruit-salad notes of apricot, kiwi, and tangerine that are ripe and delicately spiced; secondary inhalations pick up more of the spice notes, especially spearmint and thyme; in all, a pleasingly appealing bouquet. Entry maintains the fruitiness I liked in the aroma, but at this point it's more baked than fresh; midpalate displays a mineral-like, earthy aspect that counters the ripeness of the fruit, thereby becoming a more integrated, balanced flavor profile. Finishes brief, sedate, and gently sweet.

2018 Rating: ★★★/Recommended

Lambay Small Batch Blend Irish Whiskey 40% abv, $35.

Color of maize; excellent clarity. This opening nose offers pleasant odors initially of sealing wax, parchment, gum, and glue, then it advances into dry breakfast cereal and dried flowers; secondary inhalations encounter scents of hard cheese, oak resin, shiitake mushroom, and vegetable cooking oil. Entry features a bright, wine-like first flavor that must be a derivative taste of the cognac casks used in finishing; midpalate serves up more of the sweet, malty grain that mingles well with the grapiness, creating a pleasant in-mouth experience that is ripe, mildly grapy, and yet fully grain-driven. Aftertaste is brief, grapy, uncomplicated, and a bit pear-like. Nice idea.

2018 Rating: ★★★/Recommended

Midleton Dair Ghaelach Bluebell Forest Single Pot Still Irish Whiskey 56.2% abv, $280.

Burnt sienna color; to my surprise, I see widely spaced floating tendrils of sediment. Up front, I get ripe peach or even perhaps apricot in the first nosing pass, then the aroma goes gently grainy and cereal-like; second-stage sniffs pick up desirable traces of dry earth, dry stone/granite, and grain kernel/husk. Entry is rich, bittersweet, fudge-like, and caramelized; midpalate is a bit overheated from the cask strength abv, but the overall impression is of heavily toasted grains that are near smoky and a touch resiny. Concludes very bitter, oily, and prickly. The latter stage bouquet and the entry earn the three stars, but the questionable appearance, flat midpalate, and bitter finish prevent any higher rating.

2018 Rating: ★★★/Recommended

Midleton Very Rare 2017 Vintage Release Blended Irish Whiskey 40% abv, $200.

Fulvous/earth-brown color; ideal purity. The softly appealing opening aroma shows equal parts baking spice (allspice, clove), honey, saddle leather, and unsweetened breakfast cereal; later inhalations discover faint hints of sawdust, lanolin, and parchment. Entry is assertive yet graceful on the tip of the tongue as expressive flavors of peanut oil, graham cracker, dried apricot, and allspice make for serious whiskey enjoyment from the first moment; midpalate is the stage where the baking spices take command, in particular, cinnamon, nutmeg, and clove, and they guide the in-mouth experience through to the zesty, bittersweet conclusion, which is extended, savory, grainy, and piquant. While easily a four star Irish blended whiskey, it's not the swoon-making whiskey it's been in the past.

2018 Rating: ★★★★/Highly Recommended

Midleton Very Rare 2018 Vintage Release Blended Irish Whiskey 40% abv, $210.

Marigold/butterscotch color; pristine appearance. First nosings pick up woodsy/

forest-like aromas that are earthy and elemental, calling to mind scents of lichen/moss, wild mushrooms, and steamed white rice; secondary whiffs after more air contact discover strong grain-driven evidence of barley, as well as wheat and graham cracker. Entry is elegant, stately, semisweet, deeply grainy, with background flavors of nut butter, toffee, bear claw pastry, and dried cherry; midpalate echoes the entry stage, adding brown butter, toffee, and mincemeat for depth and complexity. Finishes long, very dry, razor edged due to high acidity, and resiny. Not as heavenly a Very Rare as from several years ago when each release from the mid-1990s through 2010 was a sure-bet five star whiskey.

2019 Rating: ★ ★ ★ ★ /Highly Recommended

Powers Gold Label Blended Irish Whiskey 43.2% abv, $20.

Pale amber color is autumnal/maize-like; impeccable clarity. Opening inhalations feature a bit of spiritiness that is piquant and fruity/grainy simultaneously; subsequent whiffs detect more of a breakfast cereal aspect, which is dry and gently spiced. Entry highlights peppery malt taste while the midpalate stage focuses more on grainy ripeness; medium oily texture. Ends on a grainy/malty sweet note that's pleasant, almondy, and simple. When I evaluated it formally way back in 1993, I didn't like Powers, thinking it too pedestrian. Since then I've become more attuned to its charms. In 2009, I recommended it as a beginner's whiskey for those people who wanted to become acquainted with Irish whiskey. Now, with another reformulation at a higher proof, I think that it's reached its full potential.

2018 Rating: ★ ★ ★ /Recommended

Powers John's Lane Release 12 Year Old Single Pot Still Irish Whiskey 46% abv, $70.

Orange-peel color; immaculately clean and sediment-free appearance. The opening whiffs detect pleasing bakery notes of brown sugar, honey, sugar cookie batter, and almond butter; after more aeration, second passes pick up spice-related fragrances including spice cake, nutmeg, cinnamon bun, and apple-cider donut. Entry features soaring flavors of baked and spiced banana, spiced pear, graham cracker, pistachio, and pumpkin seed; midpalate echoes the entry stage, adding deeply flavorful tastes of fudge, candied walnut, and Madeira. Finishes multilayered, highly complex, and robust.

2019 Rating: ★ ★ ★ ★ ★ /Highest Recommendation

Powers Three Swallow Release Single Pot Still Irish Whiskey 40% abv, $48

Mango color; as clear and clean as is possible. The grain/dry cereal intensity in the first sniffs reminds me most of wild rice, sealing wax, leather, and parchment; secondary inhalations pick up fragrant notes of breakfast cereal with dried fruit, dried apricot, and malted milk ball candy. Entry is toasty, bread crust–like, dry, and nutty; midpalate really opens up the flavor closet as suddenly I'm getting spice notes of mace, allspice, and black pepper, as well as grainy notes of graham cracker, unsalted snack cracker, and oatmeal. Concludes medium long, peppery, a little bit piquant, and oak-like tangy.

2019 Rating: ★ ★ ★ ★ /Highly Recommended

Red Spot 15 Year Old Single Pot Still Irish Whiskey 40% abv, $135.

Harvest gold color; flawless clarity. Up-front inhalations after the pour discover hearty aromas of toasted grain, breakfast cereal with raisins, candied walnut, and leather-bound books; secondary whiffs after more aeration encounter wood-driven aromas, especially coconut, vanilla bean, allspice, and tree bark. Entry is stunningly rich, spicy (nutmeg, clove), cereal-like (Cocoa Puffs), and chocolatey; midpalate mirrors the entry stage impressions, but goes deeper and more complex as supple, honeyed tastes of BBQ sauce, s'mores, dried fruit (dates, raisins), and maple lead into the highly satisfying aftertaste that is fathomlessly long and deep. A single pot still masterpiece.

2019 Rating: ★★★★★/Highest Recommendation

Redbreast 12 Year Old Cask Strength Single Pot Still Irish Whiskey 57.7% abv, $90.

Flax/marigold color; impeccable purity. Smells instantly of dry breakfast cereal in the initial whiffs—the aroma is strikingly dense and stone dry; aeration stimulates the potent abv as it drifts from the glass in waves, but the aromatic properties become biscuity, malty, slightly spiced, and herbal (rosemary). Entry is surprisingly measured, warm on the tongue with the slightest pinpricks of heat and gobs of grainy flavor; midpalate is direct, with highlights of dried orange peel, unsalted snack cracker, and a deft touch of vanilla. Aftertaste is extended, concentrated, and totally dry.

2019 Rating: ★★★★★/Highest Recommendation

Redbreast 21 Year Old Pure Pot Still Irish Whiskey 46% abv, $180.

Topaz color; flawlessly sediment-free. Early smells include oatmeal, dried roses, dried herbs, loose leaf Earl Grey tea, orange blossom; later whiffs detect bigger aromas of malted milk balls, toasted marshmallow, roasted grains, wood plank. Entry is large, candy-shop nutty and bittersweet, oaky; midpalate reveals a long, oily, buttery texture and off-dry, breakfast cereal, snack cracker flavors that are deep, layered, unified. Aftertaste is silky, piquant, spicy, supremely satisfying. True adult drinking.

2018 Rating: ★★★★★/Highest Recommendation

Redbreast Sherry Finish Lustau Edition Single Pot Still Irish Whiskey 46% abv, $75.

Bronze color; excellent purity. Initial nosing passes immediately pick up well-rounded aromas of sponge cake, prune Danish pastry, oloroso sherry, black raisins, and figs in a wonderfully evolved opening aroma; secondary whiffs encounter denser scents, including pineapple upside-down cake, dates, Fig Newtons, and honey. Entry is so lush, plump, dried fruit–like, and raisiny that automatically you want to bestow the highest rating but I press on; midpalate echoes the entry stage, adding deeper flavors of caramel, maple fudge, marzipan, and nougat. Finishes infinitely long, peppery, spicy (heavy dose of clove), chewy in texture, campfire warm, and marshmallow sweet. Another lovely, beautifully crafted Redbreast expression of the highest ranking.

2018 Rating: ★★★★★/Highest Recommendation

Slane Triple Casked Irish Whiskey 40% abv, $30.

Jonquil yellow/gold color; ideal clarity. Opening whiffs pick up robust, nose-tingling aromas of alcohol, peach cobbler, ripe peach, bing cherry, and prickly pear; following more air contact, the aroma morphs into a composed, elegant fruit salad–like bouquet that is heavy on peach and nectarine and light on grain and wood. The grain element comes alive in the entry stage as the taste profile goes drier than I had anticipated, considering the fruitiness of the fragrance; midpalate returns to the heightened fruitiness, but there's also a balancing component of oak that brings the in-mouth stages to a pleasant finish, which is crisp, high in acid, dry, woody, resiny, and gently sweet. Good value here.

2019 Rating: ★ ★ ★/Recommended

Teeling 24 Year Old Vintage Reserve Collection Single Malt Irish Whiskey 46% abv, $499.

Copper/harvest gold color; superb purity. There are curious first aromas in this expensive old malt that remind me of autumn garden, drying leaves, wet cement, damp earth, and clover; secondary inhalations find minerals, sage, bay leaf, textile fiber, and dill. Entry finds that the dill aspect resurfaces as the flavor turns left, going more in the direction now of deep-flavored barley malt; midpalate becomes orchard fruit–like as a baked apple taste takes charge over the malt and the earthiness. Aftertaste highlights the baked apple, cooking spices, oak resin, and dry earth elements as this stage turns into the apex point. I didn't feel it deserved a fourth rating star because I believe that this whisky is on the downside of its life cycle. I would instead buy several bottles of the Teeling Single Malt at $60 a bottle.

2018 Rating: ★ ★ ★/Recommended

Teeling Single Grain Irish Whiskey 46% abv, $50.

The color is goldenrod/harvest gold and the cleanliness factor is ten out of ten. The opening nosing pass is treated to a pungent, deeply earthy aroma that's equal parts forest-like/woodsy, spice shop, and grain silo; secondary inhalations find the aromatics more vivid in their breakdown as fragrances of dry breakfast cereal/oatmeal, parchment, unsalted butter, and raw honey make their case. Entry is delightfully spicy and piquant as vibrant flavors, led by black peppercorn, allspice, and candied pecan, take command; midpalate mirrors the entry but expands the layered textural depth and adds tastes of candied walnut, mincemeat, baked pineapple, and buttered wheat toast. Aftertaste highlights the candied walnut and the wheat toast. A showcase for what single grain whiskey can be.

2018 Rating: ★ ★ ★ ★/Highly Recommended

Teeling Single Malt Irish Whiskey 46% abv, $60.

Aureolin-yellow color; very good clarity. Oooh, I like this opening nose that's tart, citrusy, floral, and deeply grainy; the next whiffs after more aeration detect agile and lean aromas of toasted almond, lemon peel, grain kernel, malted milk, mint, eucalyptus, and a touch of ginger; a seriously compelling bouquet. Entry is deliciously sweet, tobacco-like, green tea–like, and mineral-like in a steely sense; midpalate is savory, mildly spiced with rosemary and tarragon but mostly is all about the sweet, texturally supple and oily maltiness. Ends delectably on lip-smacking, tasty notes of toffee, oak-influenced vanilla, maple syrup, and brown butter. In all, a very nice value.

2018 Rating: ★ ★ ★ ★/Highly Recommended

Teeling Small Batch Irish Whiskey 46% abv, $40.

Citrine/straw color; perfect clarity. The brown sugar, mincemeat, and apple strudel aspects identified immediately in the first inhalation are clearly the alluring result of the half-year of rum cask finishing; second-round sniffing after ten minutes of aeration unearths more layered

aromas, including butterscotch, egg cream, malted milk ball, and lemon curd. Entry is supple and moderately oily in its textural firmness as the flavor menu unfolds in chewy tastes of nougat, almond paste, fudge, and honey; midpalate is where all the taste components converge as they unify into a singular, intensely malty flavor that is biscuit-like, plump, oily, and utterly splendid. Concludes medium long, dusty dry, deeply malty, and pungent.
2018 Rating: ★★★★/Highly Recommended

Temple Bar 10 Year Old Single Malt Irish Whiskey 40% abv, $80.
Saffron color; impeccable purity. The opening aromas are largely reluctant to appear as only a distant graininess emerges; following more air contact, there's barely any more evidence of discernable bouquet, except for soft snack cracker, candle wax, and white grape scents. Entry echoes the delicacy found in the aroma as the flavor profile comes off moderately ripe, off-dry, and grainy; midpalate offers a little more flavor character as tastes of toffee, coffee latte, vanilla bean, and malted milk ball come to the surface. Aftertaste stage is where all the ethereal elements merge into a final taste statement that's quite nice.
2018 Rating: ★★★/Recommended

Tullamore D.E.W. 12 Year Old Special Reserve Irish Whiskey 40% abv, $50.
Golden poppy/jonquil color; flawlessly pure. Initial inhalations pick up traces of parchment, grain kernel, vegetable cooking oil, walnut, and unsalted snack cracker aromas; later sniffs following more aeration detect egg white, meringue, and white flour scents plus a final burst of oak plank/sawdust. Entry is nicely round, supple, honey-like, and grainy, which counters some of the aroma's lack of charm; midpalate features plumper tastes of candied apple, spiced pear, toasted honey wheat bread, nutmeg, and peanut butter. Concludes well and gracefully as the distinct flavors are supported by the viscous, creamy, silky texture.
2019 Rating: ★★★/Recommended

Tullamore D.E.W. Cider Cask Finish Irish Whiskey 40% abv, $55.
Harvest gold color; pristine purity. This mystifying opening aroma reminds me most of cherrywood flavoring, lard, bacon fat, vinegar, and apple peel; secondary whiffs after more aeration discover scents of mace, spring onion, leek, and turnip. Entry is gently sweet, juicy, apple-like, and grainy (sweetened breakfast cereal); midpalate offers deeper layers of bakery spice taste, especially cinnamon bun, Danish pastry, as well as ham studded with clove and pineapple. Finishes bittersweet, with the tart influence of the cider cask mingling with the cereal grain of the base material, but even that doesn't push it into recommendable territory for me. Too simplistic and hollow for its own good.
2019 Rating: ★★/Not Recommended

Tullamore D.E.W. The Legendary Irish Whiskey 40% abv, $24.
A blend of pure pot still, malt, and golden grain whiskeys; triple distilled; matured in both ex-bourbon and oloroso sherry casks. Attractive eighteen-karat-gold color; exceptional purity. Opening inhalations encounter beguiling aromas of ripe fruits, leafy cooking spices like rosemary and thyme, plus baker's wax paper; seven more minutes of air contact accentuate the intense graininess, which is fruity but dry. Entry is delicate yet profoundly grainy and off-dry; midpalate features gently sweet, mildly fruity, and biscuit-like flavors that remind

me of vanilla wafers. Ends on an amiable note of toasted grain cereal, raisins, and honey wheat bread, wherein the oloroso sherry impact becomes abundantly evident.
2017 Rating: ★ ★ ★ ★/Highly Recommended

Tullamore D.E.W. Trilogy 15 Year Old Irish Whiskey 40% abv, $75.

Mango/sunglow color; ideal clarity. First whiffs encounter vivid aromas of peanut shells, sawdust, sawn oak plank, graham cracker, gingerbread, and coffee cake; later inhalations after more air contact identify scents of nougat, almond paste, and toffee. Entry tastes of flan with caramel topping, butterscotch, brown butter, and caramelized onion; midpalate leans more towards the deep graininess that's now turning slightly sweeter and more like maple syrup, creating a formidable taste profile that's round, chewy in texture, peppery (black pepper), and zesty. The character builds long into the finish, which is nutty, spicy, and all about grain.
2019 Rating: ★ ★ ★ ★/Highly Recommended

Tullamore D.E.W. XO Caribbean Rum Cask Finish Irish Whiskey 43% abv, $29.

Orange-peel color; perfect clarity. The opening nose isn't exceptionally vivid, but what is there reminds me of black tea, black peppercorn, and oak resin; later sniffs serve to embellish the black peppercorn without adding much else; one hopes that the mouth stages will pull this one out. Entry is keenly spicy, astringent, and parched; midpalate offers little more in the way of defining flavor characteristics other than a brisk, overly tart harshness that I find objectionable. A rare whiskey dud and miscalculation from the Emerald Isle.
2019 Rating: ★/Not Recommended

Tyrconnell 15 Year Old Madeira Cask Finish Single Malt Irish Whiskey 46% abv, $100.

The jonquil-yellow/gold color is bright and free of sediment. Up front, there are lots of orchard fruit scents, such as Anjou pear, nectarine, and quince, plus background hints of baking spice, notably allspice and clove; secondary inhalations discover deeper fruit notes that now are baked, raisiny, and pastry-like; in all, a highly pleasing bouquet that's obviously affected by the Madeira cask. Entry is supple, chewy in texture, and deeply fruity, with appetizing flavors of stewed pears and prunes, baked apple strudel, and grape preserves; midpalate point is loaded with dried fruits, in particular, black raisins, black plums, and sloes. Finishes long in the throat, waxy, mildly oily, dry as a stone, and flush with raisiny flavor. All systems are GO with this lovely, graceful malt whiskey.
2018 Rating: ★ ★ ★ ★ ★/Highest Recommendation

Tyrconnell 16 Year Old Single Malt Irish Whiskey 46% abv, $100.

Pretty bronze/ochre color; pristine clarity. The first nose impressions are subtle, citrusy, zesty, and slight; later inhalations after further air contact reveal barely discernible scents of pineapple, kiwi, and barley cracker; not a lot of aromatics to grip onto here but what is there is pleasant. Entry is clean, gently sweet (dried pineapple) in a breakfast cereal manner; midpalate is where this whiskey shows its best virtues, featuring estery tastes of apple strudel, pear tart, caramel, crème brûlée, and candy bar. Concludes silky, medium long, brown sugar sweet, and toasted. The superb in-mouth stages made up a lot of ground for this sixteen-year-old Irish malt to reach four stars.
2017 Rating: ★ ★ ★ ★/Highly Recommended

West Cork Glengarriff Series—Bog Oak Charred Cask Single Malt Irish Whiskey 43% abv, $45.

Harvest gold color; ideal purity. Initial whiffs pick up very delicate traces of malted barley, baked banana, and malted milk ball aromas that are harmonious and elegant; second-round inhalations after additional air contact detect more pronounced fruit notes, in particular, pear and plum, as well as subtle wood aspects like sawdust. Entry is creamy in texture, delicately sweet and spiced (cinnamon), and decidedly grainy; midpalate is where all the taste elements come together in a supple, lightly spiced flavor profile that's deliciously ripe and semisweet. Concludes peppery, zesty, malty, and fruity. Terrific value.

2018 Rating: ★ ★ ★ ★/Highly Recommended

West Cork Glengarriff Series—Peat Charred Cask Single Malt Irish Whiskey 43% abv, $45.

Pretty amber/wheat-field gold color; perfect clarity. Right from the first sniff, there is clear evidence of peat-reek in the cigarette ash, smoldering campfire, dill pickle, and creosote scents that are more sweet than dry and totally beguiling; more time in the glass brings out the barley malt crispness that complements the wood smoke peatiness with style; to be clear, the use of peat in this case is judicious and not on the scale of Islay malts. Entry is lusciously smoky, sooty, and more smoked bacon–like than logs in the fireplace, and therefore there's an element of fattiness to it that makes for dazzling consumption; midpalate is round, juicy, plump, and now only mildly smoky as the other flavor components come to the foreground, especially the malted barley, baking spices such as nutmeg and clove, and the oak lipids (fats). Finishes grandly and integrated in plush waves of smoked meat, pipe tobacco–like, and dry cereal flavors that work perfectly in tandem. An Irish whiskey gem that's worthy of a multiple bottle purchase.

2018 Rating: ★ ★ ★ ★ ★/Highest Recommendation

Yellow Spot 12 Year Old Single Pot Still Irish Whiskey 46% abv, $105.

Sandy-brown color; spotless clarity. I like the opening aroma, which is grainy, floral, earthy (woodsy), and green vegetation–leaning; with more aeration, the aroma settles down a bit turning more honey-sweetened breakfast cereal and snack cracker–like as the grain base asserts itself. Entry is honey sweet, toasted, and pleasantly grainy; midpalate mirrors the entry, adding subtle notes of clove, black pepper, and vanilla bean, all of which bring more flavor dimension. Ends up keenly toasted/roasted, bakeshop sweet, and succulent; a winning feature is the silky, moderately oily texture.

2018 Rating: ★ ★ ★ ★/Highly Recommended

WHISKEY–USA

In colonial America before the Revolutionary War (April 1775–September 1783), the colonists' alcoholic beverages of choice were Madeira (the majestic fortified wine from the Atlantic Ocean island of Madeira that lies off Portugal), rum that was produced from sugarcane grown in the Caribbean but distilled and aged in Massachusetts and Rhode Island, applejack (apple brandy) and perry (pear brandy) from the orchards of New York, Virginia, Maryland, and New Jersey, and the locally brewed ales and beers found in taverns and inns.

Whiskey, by comparison, was relegated to lowly status because grains, with the exception of rye, failed to grow abundantly enough throughout the thirteen colonies that abutted each other along the Eastern Seaboard from the Carolinas to New England. Whiskey making, in actuality, didn't occur in the New World to any significant degree until Scots-Irish and German settlers migrated into Pennsylvania and Maryland, places where rye grew relatively well. In those outposts, American whiskey in the spicy form of rye whiskey proliferated.

In post–Revolutionary War America, the government was up to its eyeballs in war debt. After the English were expelled, the fledgling United States owed a gargantuan total of $50 million, virtually all of it borrowed from France and Spain. As these loans were coming due, Alexander Hamilton, the U.S. treasury secretary, and President George Washington decided to stiffly tax distillation and distilled spirits to raise revenue. In a flagrant rebuke, the farmer-distillers of Pennsylvania and Maryland vociferously revolted. In response, Washington sent thirteen thousand militiamen to Pittsburgh to quell the revolt, which they largely did without bloodshed. But, in the meantime, to escape the new lofty taxes on distillation, many hundreds of farmer-distillers packed up and sailed down the nearby Ohio River to the virgin territory of *Kentucke* as the native Americans called it. Then, it was Virginia's westernmost district. We know it now as Kentucky.

What the 1780s settlers discovered was a fertile region where groundwater was pure, the hunting was bountiful, and one grain grew especially well: corn. By 1810, two thousand stills were estimated to be operating in Kentucky, dealing smartly with the bumper crops of maize (corn) by distilling it. The area that experienced the biggest explosion of distilling was Bourbon County, so named in honor of the French aristocracy that helped underwrite the Revolutionary War. The name stuck, as consumers yearned for more "bourbon whiskey."

But the biggest boost to Kentucky bourbon whiskey was when it started being shipped via the Ohio and Mississippi rivers to the bustling port of New Orleans. From there, bourbon traveled north along the East Coast to Philadelphia, New York, and Boston. After the Civil War (1861–1865) reduced stocks, the distilling industries of Kentucky and Tennessee geared up once again, supplying the newly opening territories west of the Mississippi with "red eye" whiskey. Beer and wine didn't travel as well as bourbon did. Consequently, bourbon and Tennessee sour mash whiskey were among the prime lubricants of the Wild West.

Whiskey, thus, became a widely poured potable in the final third of the nineteenth century as it flowed freely in all major USA cities and served as the base of many classic cocktails.

Then, as it did in the British Isles and Canada, the four-headed monster of World War I, Prohibition, the Great Depression, and World War II devastated American whiskey distillers. Distillery closings riddled the industry as sales slumped from 1915 to 1950. The markets rebounded somewhat in the 1950s. Then, whiskey distillers were adversely hit again by the dramatic growth of vodka in the 1960s and 1970s. One positive development from the 1960s was the recognition by the United States Congress of bourbon's importance to America. In 1964, a congressional resolution vaguely implied that bourbon was "America's native spirit," but even that was cold comfort to a once robust industry.

In the late 1980s, prospects picked up once again for American whiskey with the release of high-end, more expensive bottlings made from small lots of barrels (so-called "small batch whiskeys," for instance, Booker's Bourbon) or even more exotic, whiskeys that came from a single barrel, like Blanton's. Today, the American whiskey industry, thanks in large measure to the popularity of small batch, rye, barrel strength, and single barrel whiskeys, is thriving and healthy.

Types of American Whiskey
Straight whiskey
By federal regulation ("standards of identity for distilled spirits"), straight whiskey in the USA means that the "mashbill," or grain recipe, of the whiskey must contain at least 51 percent of one type of grain, i.e., corn, rye, wheat. The grain may be malted or unmalted. Straight whiskey, by law, must also be aged for at least twenty-four months in new, charred barrels at no higher than 62.5 percent alcohol.

Straight bourbon whiskey
While Kentucky is the traditional epicenter of the bourbon industry, in truth and by law, any state in the union can produce bourbon. Virginia and Indiana remain significant distilling centers for bourbon in America. And, scores of craft distillers (producers making forty thousand nine-liter cases or less) are making bourbon in a multitude of states. In order for a whiskey to become properly labeled as a straight bourbon whiskey, it must meet a set of production standards. Those include:

> Straight bourbon's grain mash must be made from at least 51 percent corn.
> Straight bourbon must be matured in new, charred barrels for a minimum of two years.
> Straight bourbon cannot be distilled at higher than 80 percent alcohol by volume, or 160 proof.
> Straight bourbon whiskey can be reduced in alcoholic strength only with distilled water.
> Straight bourbon whiskey must be bottled at least 40 percent alcohol by volume, or 80 proof.
> As a straight whiskey, it is unlawful to add any color or flavor enhancements.

Bourbon distilling usually involves an initial distillation in a column still and a second pass in a pot still-like kettle called a "doubler" or a "thumper" (because of the pounding noises these stills make during distillation). So, America's foremost whiskeys are double distilled, for all intents and purposes.

Unlike Ireland, Canada, and Scotland, bourbon distillers must by law employ new, unused barrels in which to age their whiskeys. Barrels must also be charred on the inside. Charring levels of one to four are the norm, with level four being the deepest. The deeper char levels (three and four) impact the new spirit more than lighter char levels (one and two), imparting smells and tastes of caramel, maple, or vanilla. Bourbon warehouses are known as "rickhouses" and populate North Central Kentucky by the scores. The aging period in Kentucky is generally much shorter than in cooler climates, like those of Ireland and Scotland. Spirits mature much faster in warm, humid conditions than in cool, damp climates and so can be bottled sooner.

Tennessee whiskey

Many Tennessee whiskeys are close in production methods to straight bourbon, except for a filtration process, called the Lincoln County process, in which the whiskey is dripped through maple charcoal chunks housed in huge vats. This happens after distillation and prior to the spirit being placed in new, charred barrels for a minimum of two years. Ten feet deep, the charcoal is so densely packed that it takes each drip many hours to make it to the bottom. The procedure is designed to leach out impurities not stripped away by distillation. The result is a smoky type of whiskey that is reminiscent of campfire smoke.

Because of the inclusion of the Lincoln County process step, law does not allow Tennessee whiskeys to be identified as "bourbon," though currently not all Tennessee distilleries employ this filtration process. This is no hardship for the Tennessee distillers who prefer to be known as makers of fine Tennessee whiskey. For half a century, only two distilleries coexisted in Tennessee: Jack Daniel's and George Dickel. Now, there are small, artisanal distilleries popping up across the state as the regeneration of Tennessee whiskey happens with vigor and purpose.

Rye whiskey

Aside from being America's first important marketable variety of whiskey, rye whiskey was admired among distillers. Once corn-based straight bourbon was crowned "America's whiskey" in the nineteenth century, rye whiskey faded from view. After the repeal of Prohibition in 1933, a handful of rye whiskey brands reappeared, but again the category was overwhelmed by the unstoppable tide of bourbon. By the 1970s and 1980s, rye whiskey was scarcely seen, except for one or two brands.

Then, following the turn of the Third Millennium, more rye whiskeys became available as word spread about this variety's pedigree, historical importance, mixability in classic cocktails, and status within the American distilling industry. At present, there are more straight rye whiskeys in the marketplace than at any time since the early twentieth century as the style has become a bartenders' favorite.

Bottled-in-bond

Prior to 1897, consumers of American whiskey had no governmental protection against fraud. Without any legislation aimed at guaranteeing authenticity, the public was open to having just about anything poured into bottles labeled as "whiskey." Then, a group of influential Kentucky distillers, led by Edmund Haynes Taylor, Jr., roused the United States Congress to pass legislation—the Bottled-in-Bond Act—that would ensure on-site supervision by agents of the Treasury Department in bonded warehouses. The act's standards included that the whiskey identified by the words "bottled-in-bond" had to be matured for a minimum of four years in a federally supervised warehouse, must have been the result of one distillation season (January to June, or July to December) by a single distiller at one location, and be bottled at 100 proof, or 50 percent alcohol by volume. The act was an enormous step forward for the American whiskey industry in the eyes of the consuming public.

North American blended whiskey
After World War II, the North American whiskey category led a genuine revolution in inexpensive blended American and blended Canadian whiskeys, made mostly from neutral grain spirits. Spurred by the legendary Sam Bronfman, CEO of Canada-based drinks giant Joseph E. Seagram & Sons, a pair of Seagram brands—Seagram's 7 Crown from the USA and Seagram's VO from Canada—ruled supreme from the late 1940s through to the mid 1970s. These ubiquitous whiskeys are blends of 20 percent straight whiskey and 80 percent neutral grain spirits. Both are wood aged. While they lack the depth of character, complexity, pedigree, and elegance of straight bourbon, Tennessee sour mash whiskey, and straight rye whiskey, they nonetheless serve a useful purpose as mixers.

Single malt whiskey
This relatively recent American whiskey variety pays homage to the hallmark single malt whiskeys from Ireland and Scotland, while maintaining an American twist. These whiskeys are made from malted grain mash that has been distilled twice in copper pot stills and matured in oak barrels.

> **KSBW = Kentucky Straight Bourbon Whiskey**

1792 12 Year Old Small Batch KSBW 48.3% abv, $50.
Tangerine-orange color; totally free of any floating particles. In the opening whiffs, I pick up scents of sandpaper, dry breakfast cereal (Cheerios, especially), sawdust, oak plank, and drying leaves; later sniffs detect a more pronounced grain/cereal presence that is stone dry and lean. Entry is a tad sharp and edgy initially, but that aggressive aspect gives way to a concentrated graininess that makes the flavor profile more supple and round; midpalate features the sweet corn plushness, as the taste turns bittersweet and coffee bean–like. I find the finish a little too harsh for my personal liking, but the overall impression is recommendable.
2019 Rating: ★ ★ ★/Recommended

1792 Bottled-in-Bond KSBW 50% abv, $36.

Cocoa-brown color; immaculately clean and particle-free. First whiffs detect candy-shop aromas of caramel corn, lightly toasted marshmallow, carob, Ceylon black tea, and walnut; secondary inhalations after more aeration encounter earthier smells, including chalk, limestone, dry sand, and nickel/ore, all of which are backed by a pleasing butterscotch note. Entry showcases a bittersweet, alluringly nutty flavor profile that features candied walnut, praline, nougat, crème brûlée, and caramel corn (Cracker Jack candy); midpalate goes a more bitter route as the taste turns metallic, synthetic, and industrial, turning away from the nice candy-shop direction of the entry. Aftertaste recovers some of that candy-shop/honeyed aspect but retains too much of the earthy, metal coin bitterness of the midpalate. Up until this stage, this whiskey was looking to end up with a three stars/recommended rating, but the disappointing midpalate torpedoed that prospect.
2018 Rating: ★★/Not Recommended

1792 Full Proof KSBW 62.5% abv, $45.

Deep-auburn color; pristine purity. I get straight-at-you gunmetal, metallic, ironworks aromas up front after the pour, plus an oaky polymer, tree-sap odor that's dry and a touch baked; with more aeration, the metallic scent turns into nutshell, acetate, oak-plank aromas that are neither appealing nor unappealing, just there—I detect no graininess or cereal or corn-related fragrances. Entry flashes spirity heat in the first moments but that diminishes rapidly, leaving behind a charming taste profile highlighted by caramel corn and sap-like flavors that are medium bodied and silky in texture; midpalate features flavors of caramel corn, burnt sugar, a deft touch of honey, and then the elevated abv arises again to take command of the midpalate and finish. HINT: Cut two ounces of 1792 with three-quarters of an ounce of mineral water to appreciate this whiskey's full-throttle taste.
2016 Rating: ★★★/Recommended

1792 High Rye Bourbon 47.15% abv, $36.

Very attractive sepia/chestnut-brown color; impeccable purity. First nosing passes pick up muted scents of sandpaper, dry soil, and vegetable cooking oil but not much more; further air contact fails to extract additional aromatic impressions, except for feathery fragrances of breakfast cereal, limestone, and poppy seed that barely register. Entry belies the flimsy bouquet as the initial flavor profile is heartily rich, honeyed, bakery-shop sweet, and reminiscent of cinnamon buns; midpalate is zesty, spicy (peppery, clove-like), tree sap/maple-like, almost fudge-like, and generous. The animation enjoyed in the entry and midpalate continues in the aftertaste as the taste profile turns bittersweet and candied. Too many peaks and valleys for a higher score than three stars.
2017 Rating: ★★★/Recommended

1792 Port Finish KSBW 44.45% abv, $40.

Matured first in American oak for six years, then for two years in ex-port casks. Attractive ruby port/henna color; flawless clarity. To my surprise, the opening inhalations after the pour don't have a lot of aromas to sift through except for butcher's wax paper, floor polish, and paraffin; after more aeration, there are faint traces of loose leaf tobacco, cornmeal, and newly tanned leather, but not much else. Entry is sturdy, animated, completely different than the closed-off bouquet, offering desert-dry tastes of lanolin, vegetable oil, tobacco; mid-palate reaches further in its flavor efforts but an acute bitterness comes to dominate, which I find perplexing since I find no evidence of port whatsoever in any stage of the in-mouth phases. The aftertaste is this whiskey's best moment as finally I unearth a low-key port/wine aspect that mingles well with the corn component, but in my view this happens too late in the game. I see consumers expecting something different being disappointed in this whiskey that never seems to get off the launching pad.

2015 Rating: ★★/Not Recommended

1792 Single Barrel KSBW 49.3% abv, $40.

Rich, new-copper/rust color; excellent clarity. I like the stony, mineral-like, flinty opening aroma that's dry but cornmeal-like and grainy; second passes find that the bouquet has shut down quite a bit, offering only neutral fragrances of sealing wax and corn husk. Entry is juicy, vigorous, caramel corn–like, and sappy, with an underpinning of oak resin and maple; midpalate is similar to entry but adds a keen peppery quality that comes to define it in the final stage before the aftertaste, which is dusty dry, kernel-like, husk-like, and a touch bitter.

2016 Rating: ★★★★/Highly Recommended

1792 Small Batch KSBW 46.85% abv, $30.

Marigold/bronze color; ideal clarity. Immediately in the initial whiffs, I pick up subtle fragrances of marshmallow, dry cement, green tea, and tomato vine; secondary passes after more aeration gather up scents of lead pencil, flint, and dry breakfast cereal; this isn't an expansive bouquet. Entry is pleasantly chewy and bursting with baking spices, namely clove, allspice, and vanilla extract; midpalate is the apex moment, as delightful flavors of orange marmalade, candied almond, honey and biscuits, and honey ham redeem the understated bouquet in spades. Finishes long, viscous, honeyed, and like mincemeat pies.

2019 Rating: ★★★/Recommended

1792 Sweet Wheat KSBW 45.6% abv, $33.

The bright auburn color is dazzling and clear. Opening aroma is heavily weighted towards wheat grain snack cracker (Wheat Thins), tree sap, maple, new leather, black pepper; second sniffs detect more spices than in the first go-round, such as clove, mace, but also cola nut. Entry is large sized, intensely bittersweet, mineral-like (lead pencil, nickel), warming on the palate; midpalate again shows this big-hearted whiskey's core flavor that's now slightly sweeter than the entry but still complex in its complicated minerality and shale-like character. Finishes dry, embers warm, now suddenly prune-like amidst the acute minerality/earthiness. An off-balance whiskey that, in my view, while recommendable, declined in character as the evaluation proceeded and the mineral aspect eclipsed all other elements.

2015 Rating: ★★★/Recommended

Abraham Bowman Limited Edition Coffee Finished Bourbon 67.3% abv, $70.

Bright henna/auburn/russet color; superb clarity. Oy, the coffee bean/espresso influence in the opening inhalations dominates to the point of total supremacy and exclusion, and I'm not so sure that this works in its favor as the whiskey is left at the station; ditto the second whiffs. Entry is properly bittersweet, concentrated, intensely beany and black coffee–like, but

again I can't help but wonder if there is too much of a good thing in this case with such a strong flavor; midpalate mirrors the entry with no restraint whatsoever, and that's where this whiskey loses me. Even though I don't drink coffee, I like the smell of coffee, but this is simply overkill.
2015 Rating: ★★/Not Recommended

Abraham Bowman Limited Edition Gingerbread Cocoa Finished Bourbon 45% abv, $40.
Lovely burnt-orange/copper color; excellent clarity. Up-front smells include dried cherry, gingerbread, cocoa bean, brown butter; with further aeration, the aroma fades a bit too much and too quickly as the bouquet turns grainy and fibrous. Entry is very tasty, mature yet youthfully zesty, peppery, and piquant; midpalate turns on the gingerbread aspect to a higher volume as the corn-influenced whiskey cradles the gingerbread. Concludes nicely with a bittersweet finish that's tangy from the 90 proof, sap-like from the bourbon, and beany from the cocoa.
2017 Rating: ★★★/Recommended

Abraham Bowman Limited Edition High Rye Bourbon 50% abv, $70.
Very pretty rich copper/henna color; flawless purity. Wow, there is no mistaking the emblematic rye content "snap" in the initial whiffs after the pour, and this engaging spiciness is what makes it delectable; second passes, after further aeration, find the rye spice only deepens and broadens as it turns slightly ripe and fruity (boysenberry) sweet, given that the 100-proof strength pushes the rye tanginess forward. Entry is startlingly waxy and oily, perhaps even a tad too much, but the overall flavor impact is powerful and lavish as the fruity highlights stay the course. Midpalate echoes virtually all of the entry characteristics but now the abv turns the experience warmer, toastier, marginally drier, bittersweet, and less ripe as the focus becomes the rye itself. Concludes long, off-dry, intense, complex. Really wanted to bestow a fifth rating star but the furniture wax element at the entry persuaded me otherwise. Still, very tasty indeed.
2015 Rating: ★★★★/Highly Recommended

Abraham Bowman Limited Edition Sequential Series—2nd Use Barrels Bourbon 50% abv, $40/375 ml.
Sinopia-brown color; flawless clarity. This opening nose is All Bourbon/All The Time, offering dense caramel corn highlights, molasses, dark rum, and English toffee notes right off the crack of the bat; secondary impressions include sawn cherrywood, coffee bean, cacao, bittersweet chocolate, and Cocoa Puffs cereal. Entry is deeply roasted, akin to beef off the BBQ, honey slathered, and tasting of caramelized onion and pan-crisped mushrooms; midpalate reinforces the entry findings and pushes the caramel corn aspect to the forefront, which, by extension, dominates the slightly salty, mouth-warming, charred marshmallow/s'mores aftertaste. Get ready for a healthy dose of corn-based sweetness here. I'd have preferred it if the extended oak influence had ratcheted down the corn syrup factor. Lots happening here; much of it positive.
2017 Rating: ★★★/Recommended

Abraham Bowman Limited Edition Sequential Series—4th Use Barrels Bourbon 50% abv, $40/375 ml.
Handsome mahogany color; immaculate purity. This first nosing offers delicate traces

of prune, mincemeat, leather belt, dried apricot, black raisins, and flinty stone; deep and bone-dry secondary inhalations detect subtle fragrances of dried cherry, parchment, lead pencil. Entry features a richly supple texture that underpins the roasted flavors of seared pork ribs, black pepper, grilled peach; midpalate soars to wonderfully lofty flavor heights in the succulent forms of mincemeat pie, holiday fruitcake, toasted scones, marmalade, hot cocoa, and bittersweet chocolate. The finish is where the hint of port seeps through, which serves to close the circle on this tasty experimental whiskey.

2017 Rating: ★ ★ ★ ★/Highly Recommended

Abraham Bowman Limited Edition Vanilla Bean Flavored Whiskey 45% abv, $70.

Attractive burnished-copper color; can see the oils floating in the pristine core; lovely appearance. The first nosings don't get much of anything except for tree bark, faint vanilla bean; later sniffs detect more animated scents of roasted grains, sweetened breakfast cereal, biscuit batter, vanilla wafers. Entry is bittersweet, a touch too raw, but that harshness fades as the taste profile advances into the midpalate, which is angular, austere, intensely woody, and shows just a hint of vanilla. Finish offers more vanilla impact that works with the oak and the grainy/corny whiskey, but the harshness of the entry returns and torpedoes the score.

2015 Rating: ★ ★/Not Recommended

Abraham Bowman Limited Edition Whiskey 53% abv, $70.

Beautiful, brandy-like auburn/sienna color; superb clarity. Wow, there is an intense nut-like quality (walnut, hazelnut) that stops me cold as I sniff the opening aromas due to its fathomless richness; secondary nosing passes detect delectable, mature fragrances, including brown butter, canola cooking oil, old leather-bound books/library, dried flowers, cola nut, and almond paste. Entry is awash with nutty flavors, from candied walnut to winter holiday spice cake to praline to mint to allspice; midpalate reflects the entry, adding subtle notes of buttered popcorn, toasted marshmallow, and honey with biscuits. Aftertaste revisits every facet of the entry and midpalate, wrapped in a light blanket of rum-like brown sugar. A bona fide American whiskey masterpiece.

2018 Rating: ★ ★ ★ ★ ★/Highest Recommendation

Amador Whiskey Co. Double Barrel Finished with Napa Valley Wine Barrels Kentucky Bourbon 43.4% abv, $40.

Rich amber/burnished-orange color; ideal purity. This alluring opening aroma is butter-milk biscuit–like, doughy, nutty, and sap-like—a total delight; further aeration brings out del-icate touches of candied pear, black raisins, pomegranate as the direction of the aroma moves firmly towards fruitiness, which mingles well with the grainy foundation flavor. Entry is supple, bittersweet, chocolatey, fudge-like, and like chocolate-covered walnuts; midpalate is scrump-tiously textured and deeply grainy, with supporting hints of cocoa, berries, vanilla bean. After-taste is medium long, raisiny, plummy, and a bit spicy. Really good job here of flavor marriage.

2016 Rating: ★ ★ ★ ★/Highly Recommended

Amador Whiskey Co. Ten Barrels Straight Hop-Flavored American Whiskey 48% abv, $100.

Topaz color; flawless clarity. Smells of burnt matchsticks and canned walnuts in the

opening whiffs; can't say I love this glaringly awkward aroma even after allowing for more air contact, and I think it all has to do with the hop flavoring (??!!), which simply doesn't work for me aromatically. Entry reflects the bouquet and takes it a step further by making the taste profile seem kernel-like, bean-like, beery, and, most grievously, heavily waxy; midpalate mirrors the entry stage (regrettably) as the intensity of the hops wipes out all other taste possibilities. Aftertaste is as poor as the aroma, entry, and midpalate. A wretched whiskey disaster that never should have been released because it's a bad idea, in my opinion. Horrible.
2016 Rating: ★/Not Recommended

American Born Original Moonshine 51.1% abv, $25.
Clear but with ribbons of oil seen floating in the core. Smells cornmeal-like, grainy, vegetal, mildly fruity, husk-like in the initial inhalations; aeration brings out more customary still house scents of grain mash, yeast, flowery new make spirit (colorless, high proof distillate fresh off the still). Entry shows plenty of giddyup as the abv displays some early fire and heat, but it is clear that there's quality distilling here in the corn bread, caramel corn sweetness; midpalate echoes much of the entry impressions, but the taste profile deepens and lengthens into the tangy aftertaste. One of the better moonshines I've evaluated.
2014 Rating: ★★★★/Highly Recommended

Angel's Envy Cask Strength Finished in Port Barrels KSBW 62.3% abv, $180.
The chestnut-brown color is bright and clear of sediment. First nosings pick up alcohol but not in a searing manner as much as it is sturdy and foundational—there are also other up-front scents, including marzipan, newly tanned leather, sealing wax, cardamom; second phase whiffs detect flaxseed, floor polish, and toasted honey wheat bread. Entry is fiery, waxy, seed-like, beany; midpalate features more of the oak resins and a delicate touch of port alongside tastes of honeyed Cheerios cereal and treacle. Finishes long and hot, with toasted flavors.
2016 Rating: ★★★★/Highly Recommended

Angel's Envy Cask Strength Finished in Port Barrels KSBW 63.95% abv, $170.
Only 7,500 bottles available. Beautiful auburn/bronze color; impeccably clear and free from sediment. Opening nosing passes pick up round, supple aromas of caramel, clove, baked ham, cocoa bean, and marzipan; next round of nosing detects traces of prune, fig, black raisins, and peppery wood. Entry is supported by a sumptuous texture and the campfire warmth of the lofty abv level that both promote the taste profile of dark caramel, dark honey, chocolate-covered cherry without being the least bit sweet; midpalate mirrors the entry findings and adds an oaky intensity that highlights the barrel in a manner that enhances the candy-shop qualities rather than detracts. Finishes long, more bittersweet than sweet, raisiny, and refined. Super delicious.
2016 Rating: ★★★★★/Highest Recommendation

Angel's Envy Cask Strength Finished in Port Barrels/Bottling Year 2017 KSBW 62.25% abv, $200.
The gorgeous color edges towards sienna/henna; flawless purity. I immediately detect deeply embedded fragrances of coffee bean/espresso, pork rind, BBQ sauce, soy sauce, tomato purée, and red wine in the opening round of inhalations; following another eight

minutes of aeration, I pick up toasted grain, Cheerios cereal, multigrain bread, almond, and nougat. Entry is dense in texture, intensely oaky, steeped in black tea and tobacco notes and bittersweet flavors of dark caramel, caramelized mushrooms, treacle, and toasted marshmallow; midpalate features viscous, syrup-like tastes of maple, honey, butterscotch, vanilla extract, and candied walnut. Finishes huge in terms of continuing flavor impact and satiny smooth mouthfeel while the hefty abv stokes a three-alarm fire on the tongue. Incredibly robust bourbon that is not for beginners.

2017 Rating: ★ ★ ★ ★ ★/Highest Recommendation

Angel's Envy Cask Strength Finished in Port Barrels KSBW 60.5% abv, $149.

Immensely pretty bourbon with an eye-catching auburn/henna/old-copper color; impeccable purity. The port aspect comes shining through right from the get-go on this supple, caramel-laden, and pipe tobacco–like opening aroma; additional time in the glass allows for new scents to emerge, in particular, BBQ pork, figs, prunes, candied almonds, and lychees; a blockbuster bouquet that doesn't shy away or try to mask the cask strength. Entry is pruny, raisiny sweet, and ripe, but also roasted and charred, as in BBQ sauce; the midpalate alone is worth the price of the bottle as this praline-sweet taste profile soars to heights that chart new territory for bourbon. The overall impression is of baked bread; pipe tobacco; thick, juicy, lean bacon; all with the magic element of port guiding the way. Concludes long, roasted, meaty, winey, bakery-shop bittersweet, and fudge-like. A masterpiece that will live long in legend after the final bottle is poured; it's the American whiskey equivalent of the rare and iconic Black Bowmore 1964 Sherry Oak Islay Single Malt (see Appendix).

2016 Rating: ★ ★ ★ ★ ★/Highest Recommendation

Angel's Envy Finished in Port Barrels KSBW 43.3% abv, $45.

Old gold/amber color; superb clarity. Starts out with a keen aromatic impression of candle wax, textile fibers, coriander, and hemp plus a nuanced background note of Cheerios/oats cereal; further aeration time in the glass unveils more focused spice notes, especially fennel, sage, and thyme that somehow assimilate into a pleasing, concerted bouquet of flair and depth; 10/10 rocks aromatically. Entry features elements of bacon/pork rind, saltwater taffy, and buttered popcorn; midpalate rises to the standard set by the aroma and taste entry by adding a waxy, moderately oily texture that celebrates the whole package in the solid finish, which is medium dry, toasty, and intensely grainy. Bravo.

2016 Rating: ★ ★ ★ ★ ★/Highest Recommendation

Angel's Envy Rye Whiskey 50% abv, $80.

Corn bread–yellow color; more sediment floating than I like to see. Initial nosing impressions are positive, as understated aromas of black cherry, gum, and lead pencil meld nicely into a fruity/minerally opening bouquet; seven minutes further down the road the bouquet becomes far more animated, juicy, ripe, and only moderately spicy. Entry is surprisingly maple-like, sappy, and resiny, but also oaky sweet; midpalate is succulent, berry ripe, slightly toasty, and tasty. In the aftertaste, resiny oak and tobacco-leaf flavors dominate.

2015 Rating: ★ ★ ★ ★/Highly Recommended

Balcones 1 Texas Single Malt Whisky 53% abv, $70.

Pretty rusty-brown color; shimmering perfection in terms of cleanliness. Owns a luscious opening aroma of malted milk, milk chocolate, peanut butter, and maple fudge; secondary inhalations encounter deeper fragrances, most notably crème brûlée, chocolate-covered orange peel, butter-rich shortbread, toasted almond, corn fritter, and corn syrup; a magnificent bouquet. Entry mirrors the second-stage nosing passes that speak of remarkable richness, density, and depth of character in the succulent, candy-shop forms of nougat, high-cocoa-content dark chocolate, and maple syrup; midpalate provides the drinker with an unparalleled domestic single malt experience as the flavor profile expands to include oak chip, toasted marshmallow, and treacle, all of which last deep into the aftertaste. If not America's foremost single malt whiskey, certainly in the top three.
2018 Rating: ★ ★ ★ ★/Highest Recommendation

Balcones Blue Corn Cask Strength Texas Straight Bourbon 64.6% abv, $80.

Cocoa-brown color; immaculately clean and free of sediment. First inhalations feature fragrant, sweet scents of dark caramel, chocolate-covered almond, distillate, and creamed corn; after more aeration, the aroma turns into a bouquet, as melded odors of dark honey, brown butter, tree sap, molasses, and turbinado sugar treat the olfactory sense. Entry is surprisingly well-behaved, round, succulent, candy-shop sweet, and corn syrup–like; midpalate highlights the dense sweetness of the blue corn while the cask strength abv pushes the flavor profile forward into the long, bittersweet, oaky aftertaste. A serious mouthful only for the most advanced American whiskey aficionados.
2018 Rating: ★ ★ ★ ★/Highly Recommended

Balcones Brimstone Resurrection Second Release Texas Straight Malt Whisky 58.3% abv, $95.

Pretty bronze color; minor sediment seen. This is a dark, toasty, dark bread–like initial bouquet; further aeration brings out textile fiber–like scents, unbuttered popcorn, burlap, Sterno. Entry features aggressively fusel oil–like flavors that seem industrial, furniture polish–like; midpalate stage recovers from the awkward entry, offering tobacco-like tastes of dried leaves, vegetation, and a low degree of cereal graininess. Concludes nicely on a praline note. Came back from the brink.
2015 Rating: ★ ★ ★/Recommended

Balcones Brimstone Scrub Oak Smoked Corn Texas Whisky 53% abv, $60.

Rich sinopia color; flawless clarity. Yes, there is undeniable evidence of grilled meat, smoldering charcoal briquette, mesquite, and wood smoke, but there's also a peculiar alkaline presence that's similar to burning sagebrush, floor polish, and car wax; in the second round of sniffing following more air contact, I detect incongruous, flinty scents of cardboard, chalky soil/limestone, and seashells. Entry offers a strange array of maritime flavors that somehow just don't merge properly as the dense smokiness hovers over the entire first sip that at times is salty and at other times is severely baked and sooty; midpalate is all about the smoke and less about the base material, and that's where it loses me and my already low degree of interest. Awkward, unrewarding, keenly off balance. Pass on it.
2018 Rating: ★/Not Recommended

Balcones Cask Strength Texas Straight Rye Whisky 64.6% abv, $80.
The deep burnt umber/sienna color is dazzlingly tawny port–like; perfect clarity. The initial sniffs detect zesty, snappy, mildly spiced aromas that point directly to the base material—rye; later inhalations pick up unseeded rye bread, rye snack crackers (Ryvita), old leather-bound books, and curiously a last-ditch scent of tropical fruit. Entry is decidedly tangy, even menthol-like, as the flavor profile unfolds quickly on palate in soft waves of cured tobacco, bay leaf, cocoa bean, mint, and marzipan; midpalate stage features sculpted and somewhat incongruous tastes of toasted rye bread, eucalyptus, raisins, prune Danish, and cooking spice (sage, especially). Aftertaste is medium long, moderately toasty, zesty, and piquant.
2018 Rating: ★ ★ ★ ★/Highly Recommended

Balcones Fifth Anniversary Release I Texas Straight Bourbon 64.2% abv, $95.
Rich amber/topaz color; core sediment seen. Sassafras, roots, forest floor, dried leaves, bramble-like fragrances greet the olfactory machinery in the first whiffs; spices/herbs abound in the second sniffs, especially allspice, bay leaf; cask strength abv is not an issue; final inhalations detect egg cream, vanilla extract. Entry is creamy textured, aggressive in attack, with developing flavors of cola nut, road tar, pipe tobacco as the cask strength abv settles down somewhat on the tongue; midpalate is rounder than the entry, more caramel-driven, nutty, slightly smoky, charred. Do yourself a favor and dilute with one ounce of mineral water for each two ounces of whiskey. Bracing, a powerhouse.
2014 Rating: ★ ★ ★ ★/Highly Recommended

Balcones Fifth Anniversary Release II Texas Straight Bourbon 65.7% abv, $95.
Deep mahogany/chestnut-brown color; no sediment. Spirit-forward aromas take command early on as supplemental scents such as soy sauce, hoisin, tar, asphalt, cigar tobacco, ash, praline emerge later when the spirit thrust subsides. Entry is coffee-like, aggressive in the attack, slightly salty, keenly bittersweet, beany, delicious; midpalate stage is quieter than the explosive entry, flashing an Asian-leaning flavor profile that includes soy sauce, black bean sauce, tofu, peanut oil, sesame, oak, grilled hot peppers. Absolutely dilute this monster by a one-to-two ratio, water to whiskey, then sit down and enjoy for hours.
2015 Rating: ★ ★ ★ ★ ★/Highest Recommendation

Balcones Pot Still Texas Bourbon 46% abv, $30.
Pretty, deep sinopia color; flawless purity. Wow, I really like the opening aromas that are reminiscent of cherry pipe tobacco, vine fruit (blueberry, blackcurrant), sherry barrel, boot leather, and black raisins; more aeration brings out rustic scents of toadstool, drying leaves, tree sap, and coffee grounds. Entry is roundly textured, deeply spicy (black pepper, clove, allspice, vanilla bean), and succulent with dried fruits, especially apple and pear; midpalate ups the taste ante now with zesty bittersweet flavors of candied almond, carob, gingerbread, and graham cracker. Concludes long, spicy, piquant, and tobacco-like.
2019 Rating: ★ ★ ★ ★/Highly Recommended

Balcones Rumble Cask Reserve Finish Texas Straight Malt I 57.5% abv, $95.
Racy auburn/brick color; minor sediment. The breakfast cereal opening aroma is pleasantly grainy, dry, nutty, oily; secondary whiffs encounter snack cracker fragrances of

wet soil, mulch, forest floor, unsalted Triscuit, and Ryvita. Entry is maple sweet, earthy, reminiscent of tree sap; midpalate features bittersweet flavors of oak resins, treacle, walnut butter, toasted marshmallow, pork rind. Finishes meaty, BBQ sauce–like, fleshy, moderately caramelized.

2014 Rating: ★ ★ ★ ★/Highly Recommended

Balcones True Blue 100 Proof Straight Corn Whisky 50% abv, $80.

Gorgeous auburn color; impeccably clean appearance. The lushness found in the first nosing passes is appealing, deeply corn-like, candied apple–like, and satisfying; later whiffs detect more settled hints of leather saddle, baked fruits (pineapple, banana), cornmeal, black peppercorn, and sweet corn. Entry is intensely sap- and maple-like, as the flavor profile goes clearly in the sweet direction of the corn base material rather than the wood barrel; at midpalate, however, I do pick up the oak influence, especially in the resiny, oily, creamy texture and the vanilla bean–like taste, which now is more bittersweet than sweet. Finishes rich in texture, bittersweet, mineral-like, and oaky in flavor; long in the throat.

2018 Rating: ★ ★ ★ ★/Highly Recommended

Baller Single Malt Whisky 47% abv, $65.

One hundred percent barley; matured three to four years in ex-bourbon barrels and French oak wine casks; filtered through maple charcoal; finished in casks that held homemade umeshu, a customary Japanese ume fruit liqueur blended with shochu. The bright marigold color is appealing until I closely examine it beneath the examination lamp to find more core sediment than I'd like to see; 99 percent of buyers would not spot this flaw, but, as subscribers know, I'm in the 1 percent category that takes the visuals seriously. First inhalations encounter distinct, fully evolved aromas of burning rubber, dark-roast malted barley, rubber band, raging campfire, but there's also an underlying fruitiness that, while incongruous, pulls the aroma together; additional aeration stimulates the tart fruit aspect a tad more as now the bouquet seems moderately salty and snack cracker–like. Entry is rubbery tasting, astringent, lightly toasty, with an oily background flavor; midpalate is a curious marriage of restrained fruitiness and astringent, resiny woodiness wherein the grain element is lost. Aftertaste is austere, acidic, resiny, sooty. I recommend this not because I particularly like it (there are too many flaws), but because whiskey geeks should take a crack at it due to its singularity, inspired, I believe, by the wood finish of the ume fruit liqueur and the maple charcoal filtering. If it were mine, I'd dispense with the charcoal filtering, which causes too much of the campfire aroma and sooty flavor.

2016 Rating: ★ ★ ★/Recommended

Barrell Whiskey Batch #001 American Whiskey 61.25% abv, $60.

Pleasingly warm, pale amber hue; excellent clarity. Enticing first aromas after the pour tweak my interest, mostly in a toasted walnut, peanut shell, peanut butter–like fashion that's deeply roasted and dry; secondary sniffs pick up alluring traces of maple syrup, rice pudding, cigarette tobacco, and the ever-present peanut shell. Entry is lean, narrowly focused on resiny tree sap, spice tree bark, and vegetable cooking oil flavors that are dry, herbal, and bitter initially, then at the midpalate stage they turn bittersweet, toasty, buttery, and oily. Finishes long, warm, and a little prickly on the tongue, honeyed, and candied. A tasty

whiskey that progresses slowly while in the glass through the entire sensory process, ending up being nearly succulent and caramel candy–like.
2016 Rating: ★ ★ ★ ★/Highly Recommended

Barrell Whiskey Batch #002 American Whiskey 61.9% abv, $60.
Sherry cask finish. Topaz/sepia color; some sediment seen floating in the core. Not as intensely nut-like in the opening aroma as #001 but two shades lighter in nuttiness all the same while also offering smells of burnt parchment, campfire, toasted grain, vanilla bean, and brown rice; second-stage inhalations following more aeration discover scents of linoleum, plastic wrap, charred corn on the cob, seared meat, road tar, and creosote. Entry is delightfully round and supple, clearly influenced by the sherry cask as the flavor profile goes toffee-like, creamy in texture, slightly burnt like toasted marshmallow, and espresso-like; midpalate is succulent like black raisins and prune Danish, with a big, blanket-like texture that coats the tongue in a sugary-sweet taste that's dense and chocolatey. Aftertaste is long, raisiny sweet, robust.
2016 Rating: ★ ★ ★ ★/Highly Recommended

Barrell Whiskey Batch #006 Straight Bourbon 61.45% abv, $60.
Burnt-orange/new-copper color; minuscule bits of sediment seen. I get unusual soup-like first aromas here as the fragrance reminds me of beef bouillon/beef stock, red cabbage, vinegar, and ginger—highly idiosyncratic; second-stage inhalations encounter mild fruitiness, black tea, caramelized onion, sautéed mushroom, and Hunan sauce—a strange one. Entry is different from the bouquet in that it's far more grainy, cereal-like, biscuity, and corn-driven, making it seem almost as though the flavor is from a different whiskey altogether; midpalate is deeply corn syrup–like, caramel corn–like, pleasantly sweet, and honeyed. Aftertaste is like broiled meat, BBQ sauce, tomato paste. I reservedly like it, but it follows no pattern of sensory progression that I've experienced before as I find the bouquet so off the charts that I can't bestow a fourth rating star with confidence.
2016 Rating: ★ ★ ★/Recommended

Barrell Whiskey Batch #007 Straight Bourbon 61.2% abv, $60.
The bronze color is stunningly bright and free of sediment. Opening nosing passes pick up hints of cellophane, plastic lamination, grain kernel, creamed corn, and flaxseed; later whiffs following more air contact pick up brown rice, bay leaf, and not much else. Entry is corny sweet, corn syrup–like, honeyed, sherry-like, toasted, pipe tobacco–like, with background tastes of dried cherry and fig; midpalate features a cacophony of flavors including dried tropical fruits (banana, pineapple), vanilla bean, clove, baked ham, caramelized onion, burnt sugar. Aftertaste is long, sugary, roasted, and tomato-paste sweet. I liked it once it hit the mouth, but I take points off for the lackluster bouquet.
2016 Rating: ★ ★ ★/Recommended

Basil Hayden's 10 Year Old KSBW 40% abv, $60.
Ochre/brown-sugar color; flawlessly clean and bright. I like this up-front nose, as it reminds me of spiced apple and pear, as well as breakfast cereal laced with dried fruits; after more air contact, the aroma expands to include notes of prickly pear, turmeric, orange blossom, wet cement, and marshmallow. Entry is dry, citrusy, acidic, refreshing, and only slightly

woody; midpalate revisits all the entry findings and adds dried pineapple, apple doused with cinnamon, and black tea. Aftertaste is brief to medium long, pleasantly spiced, and tart.
2019 Rating: ★ ★ ★/Recommended

Basil Hayden's 2017 Release Dark Rye Whiskey 40% abv, $40.
A unique blend of Kentucky straight rye and Canadian rye with a dose of port. Red-brown/chestnut color; superb purity. The "dark" designation certainly applies to the initial nosing passes as I encounter deep, dense aromas of dark coffee, carob, porter ale, and heavily roasted grain; more time in the glass stimulates scents of seared marshmallow, burnt tobacco, cocoa, and dark bread/pumpernickel. Entry is toasty, bittersweet, and rife with candied fruit and walnut flavors, but especially dates and figs; midpalate offers a taste profile that resembles prune Danish and rugelach. Aftertaste is akin to semisweet chocolate and espresso. I didn't pick up the port until the finish. Interesting idea in this era of broad experimentation. Would I purchase it? Doubtful. That said, it's well made and I see the potential attraction to some whiskey drinkers.
2018 Rating: ★ ★ ★/Recommended

Basil Hayden's 2017 Release Rye Whiskey 40% abv, $45.
Sports a pretty, brilliant burnt-orange color; very good clarity. There's a highly pleasant, if subtle, opening aroma of dry breakfast cereal, dried apricot, and crushed stone that, while mere nuances, combine to offer a lovely aroma of understatement and elegance; more time in the glass allows for a hint of herbs to emerge, such as parsley and savory; this bouquet requires one's full attention and a degree of patience but is worth the work. Entry is desert-sand dry, notably spicy (now black peppercorn, gentian, and caraway); midpalate displays a supple texture, and for the first time there's an animated kick from the abv that adds a pleasurable zestiness to the in-mouth experience. Aftertaste reverts back to the nuanced style that is the core virtue of this whiskey, which concludes aridly dry but, peculiarly, not astringent. For admirers of rye whiskey, this gentlemanly release shows rye in a graceful, polite light.
2017 Rating: ★ ★ ★ ★/Highly Recommended

Basil Hayden's Caribbean Reserve Rye Limited Release Kentucky Straight Rye Whiskey 40% abv, $45.
Label claims that this is a marriage of Kentucky straight rye and Canadian rye whisky, with a dash of blackstrap rum. The deep coloring on this rye whiskey is mahogany/burnt umber; admirably pure. Initial nosing passes are greeted by peculiar scents, ranging from coffee bean to espresso to plastic mug to burning electrical wires to candle wax; secondary whiffs pick up machine shop aromas of oil, metal tools, and leather. Entry is barely drinkable, as the rye whiskeys seem to be fighting each other over turf and thereby creating awkwardness and disharmony caused by the clumsiness of the rum factor; midpalate introduces a trace of tropical barrel stink that rounds out the already one star rated whiskey of no particular note. Misguided idea gone haywire. Avoid as you would deer ticks.
2019 Rating: ★/Not Recommended

Beach Whiskey 40% abv, $28.
Clear as rainwater; perfectly sediment-free. I like the textbook fresh-off-the-still

fruitiness and the keenly estery initial aromatic burst that's full of peach stone/pit fragrance, grain husk, and apple or pear peel; secondary passes don't reveal much more because there simply isn't more to cover. Entry is generously fruity (peachy/peary), unusually ripe, intensely grainy, and amiably fresh and crisp; midpalate is where the already established fruit presence does its best work as it merges with the mildly smoky graininess and toasted kernel aspect, creating a solidly pleasant grain spirit experience that makes most unflavored vodkas pale by comparison, not to mention the majority of white dog (unaged whiskey) offerings in the marketplace. Can't believe that I'm scoring this four stars since I've reviled quite a few white dogs in the recent past or thought others mediocre. While I still don't see their point of existence, I can't deny that this one is mighty tasty.

2016 Rating: ★ ★ ★ ★/Highly Recommended

Beach Whiskey Bonfire Cinnamon 35% abv, $28.

Clear, limpid, clean appearance. The initial nosing passes unearth the cinnamon additive that is spicy but not aggressive or prickly in the nasal cavity; secondary whiffs confirm the first inhalations as the spicy aspect grows measurably but not outlandishly so. Entry is sweet but more in an artificial way, and that test tube/laboratory quality is a turn off; midpalate doesn't recover at all from the fake flavoring impression and that kills the experience in the mouth. Don't waste your time.

2016 Rating: ★/Not Recommended

Beach Whiskey Island Coconut 26% abv, $28.

Transparent with some sediment seen floating in the pewter-tinted core. Much to my surprise, the aroma doesn't offer much in the way of coconut fragrance as the base spirit is represented by soft waves of corn mash and breakfast cereal notes; even after more air contact, the coconut aspect remains buried in the background. Entry features a subtle (which is far better than over-the-top) touch of sweet, shredded coconut as the graininess of the spirit stays the course of dominance; midpalate turns a bit sweeter and more candied than the entry taste. Finishes politely in a mild coconut manner. This is a good job of cautious, judicious flavoring where the flavor additive isn't aggressive and off balance because of out-of-control sweetness.

2016 Rating: ★ ★ ★/Recommended

Bernheim Original 7 Year Old Small Batch Straight Wheat Whiskey 45% abv, $30.

Pretty tawny/ochre color; flawless purity. I've always liked this opening aroma for its clean, lean, and dry cereal–like freshness and vivacity; later inhalations following more air contact encounter biscuity, snack cracker–like scents that are dry, a touch like vinyl, and deeply grainy. Entry is elegant, wheat cereal–like (Wheaties), mature, stately, and compact, with no loose ends showing; midpalate mirrors the entry findings, adding a bit more woodiness that rounds out the in-mouth stages. Remains the standard for American straight wheat whiskey.

2019 Rating: ★ ★ ★ ★/Highly Recommended

Bib & Tucker Small Batch, Batch 001 White Whiskey 46% abv, $40.

Transparent, colorless; some minuscule sediment seen under the lamp but nothing of concern. The sweet corn base is clearly defined immediately in the first whiffs after the pour

as aromas of corn bread, sealing wax, corn fritter merge into a pleasing frontloaded fragrance; following more air contact, the aromatics remain largely intact from the initial sniffs, boasting unbuttered corn on the cob and cornstarch. Entry is pleasantly corny sweet, acceptably piquant and spicy, as well as being a tad prickly from the abv; midpalate mirrors the entry, except for turning drier, and therefore more intriguing as the alcohol presence becomes more apparent and forceful, which works nicely for me since I like the feral taste of raw, unadulterated alcohol. While, as veteran *SJ* subscribers know, I have never been a staunch advocate of, nor have I ever understood the purpose of, moonshine/white dog/white whiskey (just buy Boyd & Blair Vodka, for chrissake!), this is in the slim recommendable stratum.
2017 Rating: ★ ★ ★/Recommended

Bib & Tucker Small Batch Bourbon 45% abv, $55.

Deep-amber/tarnished-copper color; impeccably pure. Whoa, I detect all sorts of tropical fruits up front, from kiwi to grapefruit to pineapple to papaya, that outweigh all other aromatics in the initial inhalations; with more aeration, the nose turns fruitier (pear, quince), riper, but also far more biscuit- and cookie batter–like in the second passes, making for a bakery-shop character that's pleasing. Entry is lean, focused, tightly wound, bittersweet, sap-like, oaky, and spicy (black peppercorn); midpalate features tastes that mirror the entry but also add in a light honey element that rounds out the spiciness. Concludes medium long, off-dry to bittersweet, toasted, nutty. Lots to talk about here that's positive.
2016 Rating: ★ ★ ★ ★/Highly Recommended

Black Dirt 3 Year Old New York Straight Bourbon Whiskey 45% abv, $32.

Color is gamboge; very clean appearance. First sniffs are all about detecting aromas akin to paraffin and sealing wax, with a side note of grain kernel flaxiness; with more aeration, the grain kernel turns more dry cereal–like, perhaps with a bit of dried fruit, and that's a plus. Entry is round, chewy in texture, semisweet, and tangy; midpalate offers an enjoyably roasted/slightly seared taste of grilled, charred-edge sweet corn. Aftertaste follows through nicely with a finish that's fruity (raisin, prune), sappy/resiny, and bean-like (carob or coffee?). A good craft distiller effort from the state of New York.
2020 Rating: ★ ★ ★/Recommended

Blade and Bow KSBW 45.5% abv, $50.

Bright topaz/umber color; pristine clarity. There's a subtle, supple graininess in the opening sniffs that's partly corn-based but also keenly leathery and bittersweet, and because of these early signs I know good things are coming; secondary inhalations after more aeration unearth traces of butter brickle, lead pencil, corrugated cardboard, parchment, and lima bean—it's a multifaceted bouquet but one that works nicely. Entry is honeyed, more bittersweet than sweet, corny but not overly so, caramel-like, dusty dry; midpalate reflects the entry, adding a bread-like toastiness that's just slightly burnt and smoky. Finishes medium long, elegant, and like deeply grilled corn on the cob.
2017 Rating: ★ ★ ★ ★/Highly Recommended

Blade and Bow Limited Release 22 Year Old KSBW 46% abv, $150.

Deep henna/old-copper color that dazzles in its purity. Holy moly, there's a whole load of nuances here as I detect sweet corn, peanut butter, toasted almond, new leather saddle, and Corn Nuts (snack); after more air contact, the aroma releases enticing but balanced fragrances of rich oakiness, vanilla bean, bay leaf, cola nut. Entry features a streamlined succulence that's reminiscent of candied walnut, candied pineapple, chocolate-covered cherry, honey, with all the variables complementing each other, providing a clinic on how older straight bourbons can run with the great whiskeys of Ireland and Scotland; midpalate is airtight, focused on the sweet corn base, delicately sweet, with subtle hints of baked pear, vanilla bean, and honey. Aftertaste features the toastiness of corn and the richness of the luxurious texture. A fine American whiskey.

2017 Rating: ★ ★ ★ ★ ★/Highest Recommendation

Bomberger's Declaration 2019 Release KSBW 54% abv, $90.

Very pretty ochre/tawny color; impeccable clarity. Initial impressions are noticeable by their soft tones of dark caramel, fresh honey from the hive, and caramel corn; later inhalations detect steady, sturdy aromas of sweetened breakfast cereal, sweet corn, corn syrup, and brown butter. Entry is deep with sweet corn, caramel corn, and brown sugar flavors that are more bittersweet than sweet and provide depth to the taste; midpalate ushers in more voluminous, increasingly bittersweet flavors that include caramelized onion, burnt toast, maple fudge, and chocolate-covered coffee beans. Concludes rather short, but biscuity, brown sugar–like, and oven-baked.

2019 Rating: ★ ★ ★/Recommended

Bonnie Rose Orange Peel Tennessee White Whiskey 35% abv, $19.

Corn whiskey with orange-peel flavoring. Colorless, sediment-free purity. Zesty, mildly juicy orange-peel fragrance is obvious right from the first whiffs after the pour, but at least I'm able to identify the corn whiskey more in this aroma than in the Spiced Apple; further air contact doesn't impact the aroma at all as the orange-peel perfume maintains its status as the core aromatic element. Entry offers some pleasant juiciness as the orange-peel flavoring goes zesty and tart rather than tutti-frutti and cloying; midpalate shows a modicum of freshness and orange-peel tanginess that I could see working as a young person's temporary tipple before they move on to better, more challenging libations. Not my cup of tea but then I passed twenty-one many lifetimes ago.

2015 Rating: ★ ★/Not Recommended

Bonnie Rose Spiced Apple Tennessee White Whiskey 35% abv, $19.

Corn whiskey with spiced apple flavoring. Clear and as limpid as rainwater. As advertised, the opening nosing picks up low-key but evident scents of cinnamon, nutmeg, clove, and, finally after a few minutes, green apple; featured fragrances after further aeration include heightened cinnamon that now dominates the bouquet and clove, but any trace of corn whiskey is absent as clearly the moonshine's purpose is solely as the faceless base. Entry is cloyingly spiced with wide ribbons of cinnamon and clove that don't allow any expression from the corn whiskey, thereby creating a sickly bittersweet flavor that's off balance and crude; midpalate echoes the entry. A really bad tasting "shot" aimed directly at immature

legal-age drinkers whose palate range is as broad as a pinhead. Has no redeeming virtues whatsoever, even as a college bar shot.
2015 Rating: ★/Not Recommended

Booker's 25th Anniversary Batch #2014-01 KSBW 65.4% abv, $100.
Copper color; impeccably clean and sediment-free. Funnily, this opening nosing, while 130 proof, is more sedate than the previous batch, offering more elegant, finesse-driven aromas of baked plum, red cherry preserves, prune Danish pastry; secondary inhalations encounter more of the lofty abv as prickly aromas invade the nasal cavity all the way, offering scents of baked banana bread, cornmeal, cinnamon, allspice, eucalyptus. Entry highlights the corn mash aspect to the hilt, as robust, feisty flavors of grain spirit, caramelized onion, BBQ sauce, and charred meats shine brightly; midpalate with water added is biscuity, vanilla laden, cinnamon-like, peppery, rambunctious, sap-like, maple-like, silky, semisweet, all of which last far into the tobacco-like, smoky-sweet aftertaste. A fitting commemorative to a genuine legend.
2015 Rating: ★ ★ ★ ★ ★/Highest Recommendation

Booker's 30th Anniversary Limited Edition KSBW 62.9% abv, $200.
Gamboge color; excellent purity. The opening aroma punches you in the face with an alcohol fist, but then that impact dissipates quickly leaving behind immensely pleasing, grainy fragrances of cornhusk, caramel corn, sweetened cornflakes, lard, black peppercorn, and bacon fat; later inhalations after more aeration discover an entirely new menu of aromas, including oak sawdust, clove, nutmeg, candy bar, and fudge. Entry, as expected, has an abv bite more than a nibble but the taste profile is expansive, even generous in its exhibition of highly acidic, brazenly tannic, resiny, and coconut-like flavors; midpalate echoes the entry findings, adding traces of praline, marzipan, grilled meat, BBQ sauce, and tomato paste. Finishes long in the throat, robust but not savage, and memorable for the heartiness of its character, which ably reflects the no-holds-barred personality of the late Booker Noe.
2019 Rating: ★ ★ ★ ★ ★/Highest Recommendation

Booker's "Annis' Answer" Batch 2016-02 KSBW 63.35% abv, $60.
Seriously pretty and deep new-copper color; I see oils floating in the core but with Booker's that's natural; otherwise pristine clarity. This Booker's edition starts out with a nutty aroma that's dry yet piquant, slightly toasted yet raw, paper-like, mildly honeyed; more time in the glass allows for some of the spirit to blow off, leaving behind aromas of almond paste, nougat, caramel corn. Entry is warming on the tongue but not in the least fiery, toasted like a seared campfire marshmallow, a little reminiscent of tomato paste, and even grilled melon and pineapple; midpalate is succulent in its sweetness, which is clearly corn-driven rather than oak-driven and like sweet corn and creamed corn at the final midpalate stage before the silky aftertaste. Superlative restraint makes this one of the best Booker's in recent memory.
2016 Rating: ★ ★ ★ ★ ★/Highest Recommendation

Booker's "Backyard BBQ" Batch 2018-02 KSBW 64.40% abv, $80.

The beautiful mahogany color is sediment-free and bright. Typical for Booker's, the first nosing pass gets tweaked by the piquancy and prickliness of the high abv, but that's what you pay for so expressions of shock should go unheeded; later sniffs following more aeration time pick out more settled aromas such as black peppercorn, caramel corn, polenta, cornmeal, and corn tortilla. Entry is zesty, BBQ sauce–like, tomato paste sweet, honeyed, and vanilla bean–like; midpalate is loaded with intriguing tastes of gentian, black licorice, raisins, prunes, sweetened cornflakes, and honey ham. Aftertaste is fathomlessly long and deep, honeyed, and luscious.

2018 Rating: ★★★★★/Highest Recommendation

Booker's Batch 2014-06 KSBW 60.5–65% abv, $55.

Brilliant, eye-catching tawny/henna color; flawless purity. First aromas are a banquet of nuts (candied almonds, walnuts), dried apricot, dried figs, fresh pineapple, sawdust, toasted marshmallow, marzipan, flaxseed oil; secondary nosings repeat the exhilarating first-pass findings and add faint, intriguing, and unexpected touches of sea salt, clamshell, tide pool, black peppercorn. Entry is raisiny sweet, intensely corny (corn syrup), nutty, slightly salty, resiny, sap-like; midpalate reflects all the entry impressions and goes further, adding BBQ sauce, pork rind, bacon fat, tomato paste, peppermint. Finishes infinitely long, roasted, beany, bittersweet, and luscious. Booker would have been proud of this robust bottling.

2015 Rating: ★★★★★/Highest Recommendation

Booker's "Big Man, Small Batch" 2015-01 KSBW 64.35% abv, $55.

Gorgeous auburn/rust color; impeccably sediment-free. First off, I get lots of bacon fat, fried pork rind woodiness in the initial whiffs after the pour, but there's far more going on here than that, as in the second passes I encounter deep fragrances of praline, nougat, marzipan, walnut butter, dates, mincemeat. Entry is seductively understated (at 64.35 percent!!), richly textured, maple sweet, with distinct supporting cast notes of vanilla extract, candied walnuts, figs that underpin the corn syrup, cornmeal core flavor that's chewy, multilayered, creamy, silky, supple, and lush. Aftertaste goes peppery, spicy, tangy, piquant but never overly hot and aggressive. The perfect cask strength bourbon.

2015 Rating: ★★★★★/Highest Recommendation

Booker's "Blue Knights" Batch 2017-2 KSBW 63.7% abv, $75.

Rusty color; flawless purity. This nose is nowhere as aggressive as that of Tommy's Batch 2017-1 and consequently comes off as a politer, more moderate whiskey bouquet of ripe fruits (blackberries, red plums), baker's yeast, and sourdough; with more aeration, the fruit component grows in strength as the fruit turns more jammy and like preserves than merely ripe, plus there's a new element of spice (clove) that rounds out the experience. Entry is rich, creamy yet astringent and bittersweet, sort of like high-cocoa-content dark chocolate and chocolate-covered cherries; midpalate finds the cherry component growing in stature, and the creaminess of the texture turning pleasingly oily and maple-like. Ends up being fiery in the throat (it is Booker's after all) as well as cedar-like, cigar box–like, tobacco-y and fruity. A very different expression of Booker's that many people, I believe, will like.

2017 Rating: ★★★★/Highly Recommended

Booker's "Bluegill Creek" Batch 2016-04 KSBW 64% abv, $60.

The bright burnt-orange/bronze color is beautiful and free of sediment. I immediately smell raisins, dates, figs, and hazelnut in the opening whiffs after the pour, reminding me of a spice cake or even holiday fruitcake; second passes detect deeper aromas of sweet corn, caramel corn, caramelized onion, toasted marshmallow. Entry is ripe, juicy, intensely corny, unabashedly sweet but not syrupy as the taste profile is more maple-like than grainy; midpalate offers loads of toffee, fudge, burnt sugar atop crème brûlée, and now even a little spicy (cinnamon stick)—this is a huge, aggressive taste-a-thon that's driven by the cask strength abv. Aftertaste is prickly, fiery, no nonsense, generous, grainy, and caramel corn sweet. Yeah, I love it because there's something unruly and rowdy about it that reminds me of what bourbon must have been like a century ago. In other words, it's not cleaned up for fashionable nitwits who think that everything they place into their piehole has to be polite, tidy, elegant, and tied in a bow.

2016 Rating: ★ ★ ★ ★ ★/Highest Recommendation

Booker's "Booker's Bluegrass" Batch 2016-01 KSBW 63.95% abv, $60.

The first of six bimonthly Booker's releases for 2016. Attractive amber/ochre color; perfect clarity. Initial whiffs after the pour discover remarkably spicy and corn bread–like aromas that are slightly fat and BBQ sauce–like, even showing a little caramelized onion; second inhalations reinforce the first findings and add notes of toffee and honey. Entry is vigorously spirity, warming on the tongue, and like corn syrup; midpalate features lots of oak resins, woody tannins, and vanilla extract that make the flavor bittersweet and very spicy. Aftertaste leans towards fruitcake, as flavors of dried fruits and candied nuts emerge.

2016 Rating: ★ ★ ★ ★ ★/Highest Recommendation

Booker's "Country Ham" Batch 2019-03 KSBW 62.35% abv, $80.

Note: Full disclosure. I am a longstanding member of the roundtable that chooses the final expression of most Booker's. The mahogany color/appearance is pristinely free of floating particles. Right out of the aromatic gate there are (typically for Booker's) LARGE and animated scents of butterscotch, marble pound cake, black peppercorn, mace, and sweet corn; later whiffs following more aeration pick up wispier and drier fragrances of corn husk, masa/tamale, dried nectarine, chive, and green tea. Entry doesn't flamethrow the tongue, as some other Booker's expressions have in the past, but rather gently, gradually warms the taste buds in a cozy campfire-embers manner; midpalate is alive with vibrant flavors, most notably maple syrup, caramel corn, toasted almond, nut butter, honeyed breakfast cereal, and fudge. Ends on a steely/flinty note that's mineral-like, rich in texture, and deeply resinous.

2019 Rating: ★ ★ ★ ★/Highly Recommended

Booker's "Dot's" Batch 2015-02 KSBW 63.95% abv, $59.

Attractive russet/henna color; pristine purity. The initial inhalations encounter an enormous banquet of bakery-shop spice notes, everything from vanilla bean to clove to nutmeg, but also there are aromatic tidal waves of candied walnut, dried pineapple, cigar box, cedar two-by-four, sweetened cornflakes, honey, marzipan; there's a whole lotta fragrance going on here. Entry is surprisingly dry, astringent, and polite considering the abv level, but then after that first moment, there's a flash of spirit fire that ushers in the midpalate, which is lush in

texture, bittersweet, nicely acidic, raisiny, moderately oaky, and like caramelized onion. After-taste is infinitely long, fig-like, date-like, resiny, with a distant touch of blessed rancio. Wow.
2015 Rating: ★ ★ ★ ★ ★/Highest Recommendation

Booker's "Granny's" Batch 2020-01 KSBW 63.2% abv, $90.
The bronze color seems a shade lighter than some of its earlier siblings; excellent clarity. Opening sniffs pick up reserved aromas of peanut butter, grain kernel, nutshell, nougat, and sautéed almonds; secondary inhalations mirror the first nutty findings, adding subtle notes of buttermilk biscuits, crepes, and egg white. Entry introduces a bigness not apparent in the fragrance as the abv carries the flavor profile forward, offering tastes of gummy bears, hard candy, refined sugar, and berry fruit; midpalate falls into KSB line as the taste menu features tried-and-true impressions of caramel corn, licorice, candied walnut, sweetened breakfast cereal, oak resin, and honey. Ends very long in the throat and campfire embers–warm. A pleasing departure from the usual bare-knuckle Booker's style.
2020 Rating: ★ ★ ★ ★/Highly Recommended

Booker's "Kathleen's" Batch 2018-01 KSBW 63.7% abv, $80.
Deep tawny color; excellent, flawless clarity. The round, supple opening nose is dense in corn fritter–like fragrance but not the least overwhelming even though the abv is 63.7 percent; further aeration brings out lovely aromas of buttered corn bread, nougat, toasted almond, minerals, and slate. Entry is admittedly fiery but is also chockfull of sweet corn, caramel corn flavors that come wrapped in sinewy ribbons of texture; midpalate echoes the entry, adding a piquant taste of ground black peppercorn, which adds an acute zestiness that's highly desirable. Aftertaste is long, gently sweet, supple, and maple-like, and surpris-ingly elegant for the normally rock-and-roll pedigree of Booker's.
2018 Rating: ★ ★ ★ ★/Highly Recommended

Booker's "Kentucky Chew" Batch 2018-03 KSBW 63.35% abv, $75.
Mahogany color; excellent clarity. Up-front aromas include baked pineapple, corn on the cob, plus arboreal notes of bark, sap, and cinnamon; secondary sniffs pick up added scents of caramel corn, black peppercorn, maple, agave nectar, and creosote. Entry is warming on the tongue but not burning, and the flavor profile is rife with corn syrup, molasses, and turbinado sugar; midpalate features an oily texture that is dense and thick, and that gives the base for the menu of bittersweet tastes, including treacle, candied walnut, dark caramel, coffee bean, cacao bean, and licorice. Finishes toasty warm in the throat, deeply bittersweet, tart, and acidic.
2018 Rating: ★ ★ ★ ★/Highly Recommended

Booker's Limited Edition Straight Rye Whiskey 68.1% abv, $299.
The cherrywood/cinnamon-stick color is awesomely beautiful; flawless purity. The first inhalations aren't an assault at all by the 68.1 percent abv—instead, the olfactory mechanism is treated to resinous, bark-like, and grainy aromas that are balanced, measured in spiciness, and keenly woody; secondary whiffs detect deep rye flavor in the forms of rye snack crackers and unseeded rye bread. Entry is sublimely toasty, round and rich in texture, honeyed in a controlled manner, and luscious; midpalate reinforces all the entry impressions, adding spir-ity heat that is appropriate considering the degree of alcohol, and the heat underlines all the

positive attributes in the mouth making this one of the best straight ryes in the marketplace. Aftertaste is surprisingly brief, mellow, intensely grainy. Another Booker's triumph.
2016 Rating: ★ ★ ★ ★ ★/Highest Recommendation

Booker's "Maw Maw's" Batch 2015-05 Straight KSBW 64% abv, $60.

Bronze/burnt sienna color; perfect clarity. I smell fruits right out of the aromatic gate, especially apricot and nectarine, but there's likewise a keen spiciness that's piquant and enticing; second whiffs are treated to deeper levels of corn and rye cereals that respectively are caramelized and tangy, but nicely balanced as the cask strength is never an issue. Entry is succulent and bittersweet and full of toffee and caramel-like flavors that remind me of candy corn, honey, butter brickle; midpalate reflects the entry highlights, adding more spirit impact as the tongue warms with the embers-like abv level. Finishes with a flurry of caramelized onion and roasted tomato tastes that are vivid and zesty.
2015 Rating: ★ ★ ★ ★/Highly Recommended

Booker's "Noe Hard Times" Batch 2016-06 KSBW 63.9% abv, $60.

Deep-bronze/auburn/burnt-orange color; flawless purity. Owns the usual sweet corn, cornmeal, corn biscuit Booker's opening aroma, which belies the lofty cask strength abv as the corn intensity is allowed to shine. After more aeration time, the spirit begins to surface in mild waves of dried flowers (carnations) and pear fruit, and it's at this point that the thumbprint of the classic and elemental Booker's bouquet, promoted by the congenial marriage of corn and oak, takes hold. Entry is every bit the extension of the bouquet, as the honeyed, nutty, roasted-meat flavor profile mirrors the mesmerizing dance between the corn-dominated mashbill and the resiny, spicy oak; midpalate is zesty, pruny, raisiny, creamed corn–like, and peppery. Finishes spectacularly long, tangy, breakfast cereal–like (Honey Nut Cheerios), and tobacco-like. Astonishingly supple, succulent, and luscious.
2017 Rating: ★ ★ ★ ★ ★/Highest Recommendation

Booker's "Noe Secret" Batch 2015-06 KSBW 64.05% abv, $60.

The henna/mahogany color is dazzling; unblemished purity. First nosing passes after the pour aren't in the least assaulted by the cask strength potency but rather politely ushered into the aroma that's chockfull of roasted nut, grain kernel, corn husk, caramel corn scents that are more dry than they are sweet; secondary sniffs after more air contact find a remarkable gentlemanly quality to the aroma that is stunning considering the 64.05 percent abv—this later stage discovers deep-set fragrances of dates, mincemeat, apple strudel, sawn lumber, and delicate touches of sage and parsley. Entry flavors detonate on the tongue in rich waves of dark caramel, dark chocolate, cocoa butter; midpalate reflects the entry findings but also adds maple, wood resins, high acidity that maintains the freshness through to the soaring finish that's warming on the tongue, toasty, tomato paste–like, BBQ sauce–like, and meaty. Fabulous.
2016 Rating: ★ ★ ★ ★ ★/Highest Recommendation

Booker's "Off Your Rocker" Batch 2016-05 KSBW 64.85% abv, $60.

Smashing henna/auburn color that's richly burnt-orange in the core; superb purity. Considering the elevated abv level, this opening aroma is sedate and understated as the fragrance showcases cornmeal and unbuttered corn on the cob first and foremost, then adds

lead pencil, cement, shale, and dry earth; more aeration releases some of the spirit that's now as warm as a smoldering campfire that's toasting marshmallows and bacon; it's in the later nosing passes that the aromatic power becomes apparent. Entry features the high-octane abv that singes the tongue, then takes it on an amazing taste journey through levels of caramel corn sweetness, black peppercorn spiciness, and dense oakiness; the midpalate stage is ablaze with spirit-driven heat and vivid flavors, especially candied nuts (walnut) and fruit (pineapple, pear). Finishes with a furious intensity that's emblematic of Booker's. Like the man himself, this whiskey is uncompromising and not for beginners.
2017 Rating: ★★★★★/Highest Recommendation

Booker's "Shiny Barrel" Batch 2019-02 KSBW 62% abv, $80.
Copper color; pristine purity. Up-front aromas include green tobacco, caramel corn, raisin muffins, prune Danish, and raspberry compote; further aeration stimulates deeper fragrances of sweetened breakfast cereal, grilled nectarine, and dried apricot. Entry is a blockbuster experience, highlighted by the warm campfire embers occupying my palate and the succulence of the dried fruits, such as dates, figs, and raisins, that provide the charm; midpalate features robust, peppery tastes that are reminiscent of cigar tobacco, grilled pork, canola oil, and, strangely, chamomile. Aftertaste is a whole other universe of flavor galaxies that shout out campfire, toasted marshmallow, and toffee. Amazing, as always.
2019 Rating: ★★★★★/Highest Recommendation

Booker's "Sip Awhile" Batch 2017-04 KSBW 64.05% abv, $75.
Tawny color; flawless clarity. Wow, this up-front aroma is all about baked tropical fruits, such as banana and pineapple, plus zesty black tea, dry sand, and loose leaf tobacco; later inhalations after more aeration discover candied fruits, holiday fruitcake, prune Danish, and candied walnut. Entry is surprisingly understated alcoholwise, allowing for massive flavors to dominate, in particular, caramel corn, dark honey, brown sugar, coffee bean, and carob; midpalate features more of the corn-influenced tastes of grilled corn, cornflakes, and tamale. Aftertaste turns up the abv heat, but not enough to inhibit the crisp, toasted corn flavor that's caramelized and semisweet.
2018 Rating: ★★★★/Highly Recommended

Booker's "Teresa's" Batch 2019-01 KSBW 62.95% abv, $80.
Burnt sienna color; ideal clarity. Considering the lofty cask strength, the opening aroma is crisp, clean, and reminiscent of sweet corn on the cob, cornmeal, caramel corn, and sawdust than it is of high-proof alcohol; later sniffs encounter bigger, more substantial fragrances, including margarine, green tea, pine forest, and tobacco leaf. Entry is composed, powerful, concentrated, and warming on the tongue as it offers mature and integrated flavors of caramel corn, gingerbread, and honeyed breakfast cereal; midpalate offers all of the entry impressions and much more, including beef jerky, caramelized onion, BBQ sauce, hoisin, and honey buns. Finishes fathomlessly deep and long, semisweet, and a bit like praline.
2019 Rating: ★★★★★/Highest Recommendation

Booker's "The Center Cut" Batch 2015-03 KSBW 63.3% abv, $60.
Lovely cinnamon color; flawless clarity. First whiffs are prickled by the elevated spirit

level, but not attacked by them—first notes include coffee bean, orange rind, toasted grain, corn syrup, corn bread, applewood smoke; second laps detect tomato paste, BBQ sauce, pipe tobacco, cherry juice, oloroso sherry. Entry is intense, fruity, layered, pruny, red cherry–like, roasted; midpalate finds the spirit prickling all over the tongue as the silky texture supports flavors of candied pear, candied walnut, prunes, dates, tomato paste, grape preserves, sweet sausage. A marvelously attractive finish that's warming, toasted, smoky BBQ sweet, honeyed. Another Booker's gem.

2015 Rating: ★ ★ ★ ★ ★/Highest Recommendation

Booker's "The Center Cut" Batch 2015-04 KSBW 63.5% abv, $60.

The deep-auburn/burnt sienna color is brilliant, sediment-free, and highly appealing visually. Opening fragrances are chockfull of spirit warmth, charcoal briquette, pipe tobacco, praline, citrus, bacon fat, black pepper, this could go on forever; second passes pick up beeswax, dried chrysanthemum, poppy seed. Entry is a powerhouse of corn whiskey sweetness without being overly sweet plus there's a supporting flavor of oak resins that balance out the corniness; midpalate is fiery, peppery, toasty, bittersweet, deeply resiny. Finishes in lengthy fashion as the oiliness creates a creamy, silky texture in the throat that's warming but prickly and resiny. Good, but not as momentous as the 2015-03, 2015-02 or 2015-01 editions, which were all five star whiskeys, due to the spirit assault and the lumberyard scale resins. In the last couple of years, the releases have been coming out bimonthly and this aggressive schedule runs the risk of misfires, as evidenced here.

2015 Rating: ★ ★ ★/Recommended

Booker's "Tommy's" Batch 2017-01 KSBW 64.25% abv, $75.

Sinopia-brown color; impeccably clean. I immediately get strong hints of hazelnut, nougat, almond butter, cassia bark, cinnamon, and clove; secondary whiffs pick up peppery, tree bark–like scents that are earthy and tangy, along with cornmeal and corn bread aromas that balance out the spiciness. Entry is typically Booker's with an unabashed heat that's more campfire than five-alarm warehouse fire in attack; midpalate is all about the sweet corn base that comes off strikingly like grilled corn on the cob, dripping with salted butter—there are also caramelized flavors of mushroom and sweet Vidalia onion that bedazzle the palate. Concludes long, oily, buttery, creamy in texture, with sweet corn, creamed corn flavors that last a country mile. Booker's all the way.

2017 Rating: ★ ★ ★ ★ ★/Highest Recommendation

Booker's "Toogie's Invitation" Batch 2016-03 KSBW 64.5% abv, $60.

The bright bronze color is deep; impeccable purity. There is a huge amount of black peppercorn in the opening sniffs that is simultaneously prickly and piquant in nature and purpose, making this one of the oddest Booker's bouquets to date; later inhalations detect more of the corn base, but also spicy rye. Entry is rich, peppery, intensely corn bread–like, cornmeal-like, and caramelized onion–like; midpalate serves up all the entry impressions in spades, adding a sausage biscuit quality that's touched with maple syrup. Aftertaste is BIG, roasted, BBQ sauce–like, peppery, zesty, and sassy.

2016 Rating: ★ ★ ★ ★ ★/Highest Recommendation

Boondocks 11 Year Old American Whiskey 47.5% abv, $40.

Jonquil/dusty-yellow color; free of sedimentary particles. I like the opening fragrances that include sweet cereal grains, toffee, cinnamon, vanilla, and holiday fruitcake; with more aeration the aroma gets fuller and richer but also a little bit drier than the frontline scent as the wood influence becomes the dominant factor. Entry is pleasantly sweet, but almost a bit too syrupy and is like whiskey-soaked fruit in flavor; midpalate is spicy (nutmeg), spirity but not prickly or harsh, warming on the palate, and pruny. Finishes medium long, moderately deep in texture, with a dried fruit–like sweetness.

2017 Rating: ★★★/Recommended

Boondocks 11 Year Old Cask Strength American Whiskey 63.5% abv, $60.

Eighteen-karat-gold color; impeccable clarity. Even though the abv is a lofty 63.5 percent, the alcohol doesn't singe my nose as I thought it might in the opening sniffs after the pour, and instead I pick up appealing scents of sweetened breakfast cereal and green tobacco leaf; later inhalations encounter light touches of baking spice (vanilla bean, clove) and newly tanned leather. Entry surges forward carried by the high-octane abv, which now turns on its afterburners as it becomes warming to the point of being fiery, but there are pleasing tastes to identify, mostly a deep corniness that is like corn syrup as well as a candied banana flavor that seems out of place but is clearly present. Midpalate mirrors the entry in terms of abv intensity and flavor profile, but by this point the abv becomes an issue that begins to detract from the taste profile. Aftertaste is fierce, feral, toasty, sweet, corn-like.

2017 Rating: ★★★/Recommended

Boot Hill Distillery Batch #6 Red Eye Whiskey 40% abv, $35.

Amber color; inconsequential, fiber-like tendrils, too few to be concerned about, seen floating. I get fruity, pleasantly ripe scents up front, mostly akin to black raisins, prunes, and red plums; later sniffs pick up gentle notes of sweet corn and caramel corn. Entry flavor is definitely on the sweeter side of the scale as robust tastes of caramel corn, cocoa powder, honey, and chocolate-covered cherry make the flavor profile pleasing; midpalate maintains the unabashed, almost candy-like element as wood-driven vanilla bean takes charge, giving off confectionery tastes similar to flan or cream caramel desserts. Concludes medium long, sinewy in texture, moderately oily, and like brown sugar.

2018 Rating: ★★★/Recommended

Boot Hill Distillery Batch #7 White Whiskey 40% abv, $25.

Clear and bright flax/straw-yellow color. The power of the kernel-like graininess is staggering in its bone-dry intensity and depth in the first inhalations; more time in the glass allows the aroma to unfold as the fragrance direction now goes malty, buttermilk biscuit–like, brown gravy–like, floral, and zesty. Entry is off-dry, deeply grainy, and unsweetened breakfast cereal–like, and offers a tantalizing taste of chocolate-covered malted milk ball; midpalate turns candy-shop sweeter, more cocoa-like, and grainy. Finishes medium long, fruity, flowery, and high in acid so that the structure maintains its integrity to the end. One of the finest, if not the best, unaged so-called white whiskeys (white dog, white lightning) going. While I have often lambasted this American subcategory, this offering sets a new tone and standard.

2018 Rating: ★★★★/Highly Recommended

Bowman Brothers Small Batch Virginia Straight Bourbon 45% abv, $30.

Bronze/topaz color; clear and free of sediment. I get bunches of corn-related aromatic notes in the first nosing pass, including caramel corn (Cracker Jack candy), sweet corn on the cob, cornmeal, toffee, and maple; after more time in the glass, the aroma turns a smidgen riper as the fragrance starts to lean towards dried fruits, especially apricot, pear, pineapple, and green apple. Entry is dense, strikingly maple oriented, juicy, succulent, caramel-like, and creamy; midpalate is marginally drier than the entry due primarily to the emergence of the barrel influence as the taste profile turns more resiny/sappy and astringent. Concludes medium long, toasty, off-dry, and woody. The taste entry point is this whiskey's best moment.

2018 Rating: ★ ★ ★/Recommended

Breuckelen 77 Local Rye & Corn Whiskey 45% abv, $45.

Fifteen percent corn/eighty-five percent rye. Attractive topaz/medium-amber color; clean and pure. The natural, inherent zestiness of the rye majority takes charge right from the start, giving off fragrances of rye crackers, seedless rye bread, new leather; secondary whiffs supply a touch of dried grain husk. Entry is pleasantly off-dry to sweet, intensely grainy, satiny in texture, and nicely spirity without being hot; midpalate reinforces the entry impressions while the taste profile turns just a half notch sweeter as the corn element emerges more as the flavor evaluation approaches the finish that's medium long, keenly grainy, modestly oaky. Me like.

2014 Rating: ★ ★ ★ ★/Highly Recommended

Breuckelen 77 New York Wheat Whiskey 45% abv, $45.

One hundred percent wheat from New York State. Bronze/topaz color; impeccable clarity. All I can think of is unsalted Wheat Thins snack crackers as I sniff this whiskey for the first two minutes; minutes later, aeration has opened the scent up a little more, and the desert-dry bouquet turns nutty, slightly peppery. Entry is sweeter, juicier than the aroma stages, giving off flavors of honey, sweetened cereal, biscuit batter; midpalate is gently sweet, deeply grainy, modestly woody, clean, and acidic. Aftertaste is medium long, drier than the midpalate, resiny, woody, dare I say, elegant.

2014 Rating: ★ ★ ★ ★/Highly Recommended

Breuckelen Bottled-in-Bond 4 Year Old Straight Bourbon 50% abv, $100.

This color is bright burnt sienna and free from sediment. On the nose, I encounter aromas of textile fiber/nylon, butcher's wax paper, candle wax, lima bean, fava bean, and digestive biscuits; further air contact unleashes spicy notes of black peppercorn and mace, along with traces of sawdust, cardboard, and rice pudding—an atypical bouquet for straight bourbon. Entry introduces a low degree of corniness, mostly as cornmeal, plus there are background hints of stone fruits, primarily apricot and black cherry; midpalate features a pleasing, sap-like, maple-y taste profile that's more fitting for straight bourbon. The allure of the midpalate bleeds over into the pleasant aftertaste, which is toasty, bacon fat–like, and nutty. It's the fine in-mouth stages of entry, midpalate, and finish that make this whiskey recommendable.

2017 Rating: ★ ★ ★/Recommended

Broadslab Legacy Reserve Hand-Crafted Liquor 45% abv, $26.

Corn. Slightly dull straw-yellow color; no sediment of concern. This aroma isn't as demonstrative as its clear sibling's and that's too bad; there's just a varnish-like fragrance that's all about cleaning fluids, vinyl, and polishing compounds but not a lot in reference to libations. Entry is a dead end of unsavory flavors that are deeply resiny and unpleasantly aggressive; midpalate echoes the entry, reminding me of dirty barrels. I stop there. This is a train wreck that might work in somebody's mind but not in actual execution.

2014 Rating: ★/Not Recommended

Broadslab Legacy Shine Hand-Crafted Carolina White Liquor 45% abv, $24.

Corn. Clear and colorless as springwater. Opening smells are amiable, mildly fruity, floral, with a strong cornhusk quality that's pleasant and fiber-like; subsequent inhalations unearth tightly wound, drier-than-I-expect aromas of cornmeal, Wheaties cereal, feints; it's a genuine trip down Moonshine Lane. Entry is vivaciously spirity, minerally; midpalate is corn-driven, dry, zesty, clean. Ends up crisp, razor-edged, steely. A solidly made, serviceable, recommendable example of unaged corn-based moonshine.

2014 Rating: ★ ★ ★/Recommended

Buffalo Trace Antique Collection 2012 Eagle Rare 17 Year Old KSBW 45% abv, $70.

Lovely burnt-orange/bronze color; superb purity. Smells up front of lead pencil, limestone, and deep roasted grains; after another seven minutes of air contact the aroma expands into a full-fledged bouquet that is dusty dry, ashy, and like sawdust and toasted marshmallow; becomes luscious in the second round of nosing passes. Entry is rich, caramelized, maple-like and honeyed; midpalate focus falls squarely on dried apricot, candied walnut, and beeswax. Concludes long in the throat, silky in texture, measured in abv, and oh so graceful.

2012 Rating: ★ ★ ★ ★ ★/Highest Recommendation

Buffalo Trace Antique Collection 2012 George T. Stagg KSBW 71.4% abv, $70.

Deep-bronze/near–chestnut brown hue; gorgeous appearance. Opening whiffs encounter buttered honey wheat toast, salted butter, prunes and figs; another eight minutes of air contact release confectioner-shop notes of dark caramel, nougat, candied almond, and brown sugar; considering the abv, the spirit is relatively calm and elegant. Entry is enormous, honey sweet, and intensely grainy and concentrated; bittersweet midpalate phase features s'mores, dark chocolate with high cocoa content, cooking oil, and caramel corn. Ends on a spicy/zesty, toasted marshmallow taste that is simultaneously fruit, biscuit, and grainy. Amazing, yet again.

2012 Rating: ★ ★ ★ ★ ★/Highest Recommendation

Buffalo Trace Antique Collection 2012 Sazerac 18 Year Old Kentucky Straight Rye Whiskey 45% abv, $70.

Burnt-orange/amber hue; good clarity. I'm nearly overwhelmed by the pungent smell of old leather/men's club/library books in the initial whiffs; in the second passes, I pick up dried tropical fruits, especially banana, as well as more subtle notes of praline and wax paper. Entry is silky, buttery, and candied almond–like; midpalate features sweet butter notes, along with roasted almonds and cashews. Finishes long, smooth as satin, and spicy/tangy. A perennial winner for rye whiskey.

2012 Rating: ★ ★ ★ ★/Highly Recommended

Buffalo Trace Antique Collection 2012 Thomas H. Handy Sazerac Kentucky Straight Rye Whiskey 66.2% abv, $70.

Deep-topaz color; excellent purity. Ride 'em cowboy, here we go with truckloads of spicy, candied fruits (berries especially), old saddle leather, pork rind, and bacon fat—just in the opening inhalations; another seven minutes of aeration unleash massive yet integrated aromatic waves of pine tar, clove and cinnamon, dates, and pipe tobacco; incredible bouquet. Entry is warming, but not hot, on the tongue, chalky, raisiny and grainy/spicy; midpalate taste profile includes more subtle flavors of chocolate-covered cherries and almonds, brown sugar, honey, and lemongrass. Extraordinary whiskey by any measure.
2012 Rating: ★ ★ ★ ★ ★/Highest Recommendation

Buffalo Trace Antique Collection 2012 William Larue Weller KSBW 61.7% abv, $70.

Mature brownish/copper color; flawless clarity and a visual treat. There are narrowly focused elements of dark caramel, cocoa, and praline in the aggressive opening aroma after the pour; following another seven minutes of aeration, the aroma expands begrudgingly to include tree sap, maple syrup, resin, and black tea. Entry is sensationally explosive and animated once on the tongue, firing off soaring flavors of candied pears, Tupelo honey, English toffee, and pipe tobacco; midpalate tastes focus more on the oak impact and are therefore deeper with baking spice, especially clove, nutmeg, allspice, and cinnamon. Finishes sweetly, but not unctuously, and amazingly composed, stately, and fruity. Yet another textbook on bourbon making by Buffalo Trace. BRAVO!
2012 Rating: ★ ★ ★ ★ ★/Highest Recommendation

Buffalo Trace Antique Collection 2013 Eagle Rare 17 Year Old KSBW 45% abv, $70.

Dullish amber/old-gold color; more floating debris seen than I'd like. Smells of caramel corn, honey, and heavily charred oak barrels in the initial whiffs; secondary inhalations encounter subtle scents of crème brûlée, vanilla custard, corn fritters, and toffee. Entry is oily, peppery, bittersweet, and praline-like; midpalate is viscous, honeyed, brown-sugar sweet, and zesty with a touch of citrus. Aftertaste is silky, long, concentrated, and honeyed. Don't know what to say about the so-so appearance, which knocked off a rating star. Otherwise, luscious as always.
2013 Rating: ★ ★ ★ ★/Highly Recommended

Buffalo Trace Antique Collection 2013 George T. Stagg KSBW 64.1% abv, $70.

Auburn color; sediment-free. Assertive grain spirit aromas are featured in the opening inhalations, along with fragrances of candied walnut, pea soup, old leather, and almond paste; further aeration brings out aromas of bacon/pork, lead pencil, oak resin, and unsweetened breakfast cereal. Entry is incredibly lush, intensely nutty, and acutely spirity (nearly hot, so be sure to add some mineral water); midpalate is buttery/creamy, toffee and dark caramel–like, beef bouillon–like, and dry. Aftertaste echoes the midpalate. Exceptional quality again.
2013 Rating: ★ ★ ★ ★ ★/Highest Recommendation

Buffalo Trace Antique Collection 2013 Sazerac 18 Year Old Kentucky Straight Rye 45% abv, $70.

Beautiful, bright new-copper color; impeccable purity. I get an unusual amount of

fruitiness (blackberry) in the opening nose, which I like but didn't expect, along with a pleasing nougat-like factor; more time in the glass stimulates unseeded rye bread dough, sawdust, cardboard, and lard as the blackberry element slowly fades. Entry is raisiny sweet, breakfast cereal–like, and plummy; midpalate features an oily texture that's satiny with integrated flavors of rye bread, oaky vanilla extract, allspice, and toasted marshmallow. Glorious.
2013 Rating: ★ ★ ★ ★ ★/Highest Recommendation

Buffalo Trace Antique Collection 2013 Thomas H. Handy Sazerac Kentucky Straight Rye 64.2% abv, $70.
Bright amber/topaz color; superb purity. First nosings detect dry aromas of cigar box, loose leaf tobacco, marshmallow, and pear rind; another pass after further aeration picks up bay leaf, thyme, moss, and orchard fruit. Entry is stunningly fruity (highly unusual), grapy/raisiny, and Christmas fruitcake–like; midpalate mirrors the entry as the fruit meter rises, as does the jammy ripeness. Concludes almost ambrosial, dried fruit–like, moderately nutty, and toasted. Lots happening here.
2013 Rating: ★ ★ ★ ★/Highly Recommended

Buffalo Trace Antique Collection 2013 William Larue Weller KSBW 68.1% abv, $70.
Deep chestnut-brown color; pristine clarity. Deep, rich spirit aromas in the initial whiffs of oak plank, tree resins, creosote, and pecans; secondary sniffs encounter parchment, sod/earth, and lanolin. Entry is bittersweet, with gobs of pruny, plummy tastes as well as black raisins and black peppercorn; midpalate tastes include hard cheese, nougat/candy bar, dark toffee, and cola nut. Ends up meaty/beefy, bittersweet, and like buttercream frosting. A monster.
2013 Rating: ★ ★ ★ ★/Highly Recommended

Buffalo Trace Antique Collection 2014 Eagle Rare 17 Year Old KSBW 45% abv, $80.
Brilliant topaz/burnt sienna color; pristine purity. Initial sniffs detect intensely grainy aromas of corn cakes, polenta, cornstarch that are dry to off-dry and crisp with acidity; later inhalations pick up traces of nougat, nutmeg, clove, bay leaf, parsley. Entry flashes a quick sensation of campfire warmth, along with chewing tobacco, honey wheat toast, ginger; midpalate is vividly alive with corn muffin, honey, raisiny tastes that lift the in-mouth experience by a couple of notches. Finishes deeply flavorful, silky in texture, off-dry, slightly maple-like. Always a huge crowd pleaser due primarily to its approachable nature, and this is no exception.
2014 Rating: ★ ★ ★ ★/Highly Recommended

Buffalo Trace Antique Collection 2014 George T. Stagg KSBW 69.05% abv, $80.
Henna/tawny color; impeccable clarity. Considering the loftiness of the barrel strength, the first nosing passes are not blown into infinity but rather are treated to compelling, inviting aromas of spice cake, cardboard/parchment, beeswax, fennel; later sniffs pick up corn muffins, sweetened cornflakes, plus a dash of honey. Entry flavors showcase the elevated spirit, to be sure, but likewise feature semisweet tastes of caramel, English toffee, fudge, toasted hazelnut; midpalate stage echoes the entry impressions, adding butterscotch, dark honey, charred marshmallow, baked pear. Finishes long, campfire warm, toasty, charred almost like seared beef or pork, highly complex, steely.
2014 Rating: ★ ★ ★ ★/Highly Recommended

Buffalo Trace Antique Collection 2014 Sazerac 18 Year Old Kentucky Straight Rye Whiskey 45% abv, $80.

Luminous bronze/cinnamon color is striking in its depth and sediment-free clarity. Wow, I detect early fragrant dried cherry notes that are soon joined by lesser scents of toasted seedless rye bread, salted butter, white peppercorn; later sniffs encounter a ratcheted up rye bread presence, as well as palm oil, black caraway. Entry is gently sweet, even succulent as in dried berries, toffee, almond paste; midpalate is breathtakingly elegant, roasted, more off-dry than sweet, honeyed, concentrated, complex right through the extended, languorous finish. Hits the ball out of the park . . . again.
2014 Rating: ★ ★ ★ ★ ★/Highest Recommendation

Buffalo Trace Antique Collection 2014 Thomas H. Handy Sazerac Kentucky Straight Rye Whiskey 64.6% abv, $80.

Rust/copper/burnished-orange color; flawless purity. First up, I get unusually disparate aromas of gunpowder, nickel, rye bread, hemp/textile, truffle—I mean, what's happening here? Second-level aromatics offer more settled, more melded fragrances of rye snack crackers, bay leaf, dried flowers, candle wax. Entry is sultry, semisweet, roasted, nutty, woody, creamy; midpalate features deeply complex flavors of toasted rye bread, BBQ sauce, tomato paste, brown sugar, vinegar, clove. Concludes very long, sinewy, burnt/charred, semisweet to bittersweet, candied. The entry, midpalate, and finish are fabulously concentrated and rewarding.
2014 Rating: ★ ★ ★ ★/Highly Recommended

Buffalo Trace Antique Collection 2014 William Larue Weller KSBW 70.1% abv, $80.

Auburn/ochre color; exemplary sediment-free clarity. First whiffs detect little in the way of description, except for a pine-like, pruny aroma that is meek; aeration stimulates bigger aroma like pancetta, grilled meats, salted butter, cornmeal, cassia, cayenne. Entry features robust, chewy, oily, bittersweet flavors of dark chocolate fudge, cocoa, dark caramel; midpalate highlights the candy-shop aspects found at entry but adds demerara sugar, maple syrup, mocha tastes. Aftertaste is huge, viscous, roasted, and BBQ sauce–like. It might border on being too sweet for some drinkers.
2014 Rating: ★ ★ ★ ★/Highly Recommended

Buffalo Trace Antique Collection 2015 Eagle Rare 17 Year Old KSBW 45% abv, $80.

Very pretty rust color; flawless purity. First whiffs discover highly refined and pleasant toasted grain aromas that are dusty dry, lightly spiced (clove), and moderately oaky/woody/resiny—this is not now nor ever has been a hearty aroma and is more reliant on finesse than power; following another several minutes of aeration, the aroma transforms into a disarming bouquet that features defined fragrances of buttered popcorn, lychee, candle wax, unsweetened breakfast cereal, toasted English muffin. Entry is pleasingly oily in texture, mildly sweet, maple-like, roasted grain-like, more tannic than usual, and intensely corny; midpalate reflects the entry impressions and adds delicate traces of almond paste/nougat/candy bar that usher in the aftertaste, which is medium long, crisp, toasty, but borders on being too astringent.
2015 Rating: ★ ★ ★/Recommended

Buffalo Trace Antique Collection 2015 George T. Stagg KSBW 69.1% abv, $80.
Stagg has been the flagship marque of the Antique Collection. Attractive new-copper/rust color; flawless purity. Early aromas are harmonious, roasted/grilled, dense, grainy/corny, not spicy at all but more dry and resiny, with underlying scents of dry earth, autumn leaves, parchment; secondary nosings, after more aeration, detect bigger, rounder aromas in the forms of birch beer, vanilla bean (Yes! Suddenly there's spice!), cocoa bean, egg white, baker's yeast, caramel. Entry is warming in the mouth as vibrant flavors of vanilla extract, cocoa butter, dark-chocolate-covered cookies, caramel corn enchant the palate; midpalate is candy-store succulent, with deeply impactful tastes of candied walnut, candied fruit (pear, apple), custard/crème brûlée, caramelized sugar, caramelized onion. Finishes fathomlessly deep and long, bittersweet, concentrated. Another GTS of universal appeal.
2015 Rating: ★★★★★/Highest Recommendation

Buffalo Trace Antique Collection 2015 Sazerac 18 Year Old Kentucky Straight Rye Whiskey 45% abv, $80.
The brilliant cinnamon/russet color sparkles in the glass; impeccable clarity. Wow, the rye-bread-with-caraway-seeds opening aroma is spot on and like roasted grain and toasted marshmallow; later whiffs include aromas of beeswax, bacon fat, and rye snack crackers. Entry is beautifully supple and ribboned with oils while the taste profile offers bittersweet notes of candied almond, brown butter, molasses, holiday spice cake, toffee; midpalate echoes everything found at entry and throws in black tea and loose leaf tobacco in an earthy display of completeness that leads to the lip-smacking finish, which is simultaneously sweet and dry, candied and biscuity, narrowly focused and voluptuous. A seductive straight rye, with lots of secrets and tantalizing layers.
2015 Rating: ★★★★/Highly Recommended

Buffalo Trace Antique Collection 2015 Thomas H. Handy Sazerac Kentucky Straight Rye Whiskey 63.45% abv, $80.
Color is henna/auburn; clarity level is top-notch and flawless. First nosings pick up the high abv in waves of oaky tannins, spirity flowers/esters, and a high degree of oak resins/polymers that are in attack mode; later inhalations find the aroma not at all settled and, as such, the aroma never quite turns into a bouquet, which I find disconcerting considering the superb history of this whiskey—the aroma is simply off, no other way to put it. Entry taste profile offers more charm than the aroma affords, to be sure, featuring warm-in-the-mouth flavors of cherry-bomb chili pepper, rye toast, caramelized sugar; midpalate is even nicer and calmer than the entry as rich, spicy flavors of vanilla bean, clove, cinnamon, and fudge converge at the tail end of the midpalate, leading into the satisfying aftertaste that's subdued, embers-warm, honeyed, brown sugar–like, toasty, mellow. I didn't think this rye would recover from its aromatic funk but it did in the entry, midpalate, and soft finish enough to be recommended. This is hardly reminiscent, though, of previous editions, which have been superb.
2015 Rating: ★★★/Recommended

Buffalo Trace Antique Collection 2015 William Larue Weller KSBW 67.3% abv, $80.
Stunningly beautiful, brandy-like mahogany/chestnut/tawny color; perfect clarity. Initial inhalations pick up a wide array of yummy aromas, most notably, unbuttered corn on

the cob, cornmeal, unsweetened cornflakes, oak resins, black pepper, textile fibers, parchment; another few minutes of air contact unleash biscuit-like, cookie batter aromas that are marginally sweet and spicy and subtle. Entry flavors are wonderfully integrated, more maple sweet than honeyed, spicy/peppery but not hot—grainy, concentrated, multilayered, splendidly luscious. Midpalate reflects the entry and adds savory tastes of black raisins, cocoa butter, charcoal, BBQ sauce, vinegar, bacon fat, pork rind—I mean, man, this could go on for hours. Aftertaste is surprisingly polite, buttery, raisiny sweet, prune-like, satiny textured, warming on the tongue but not fiery; utterly lovely and delicious.

2015 Rating: ★ ★ ★ ★ ★/Highest Recommendation

Buffalo Trace Antique Collection 2016 Eagle Rare 17 Year Old KSBW 45% abv, $90.

The 2015 edition of this whiskey had a bit of a downturn, scoring only three stars after several years of being four and five stars. This year's expression shows a clean, new-copper color and sediment-free clarity, with swirls of oil seen in the core. Aromawise, I pick up immediate traces of matchstick, sulfur, turnip, linseed oil, flax, textile fiber, nutshell (walnut); after more air contact, the nose remains fibrous, elemental, starchy, now only slightly sulfuric, and like electrical cable; what's going on here? Entry is lush in texture, lead pencil dry, keenly resiny, moderately spicy (clove, allspice), and a touch maple-like; midpalate brings in more bourbony attributes, namely caramel corn, vanilla wafer, dried apple, which raise the level of enjoyment and expectation. Finishes medium long, silky, beany, brown-sugar sweet, and approaching caramelization. The midpalate and aftertaste rescued this whiskey from the two star heap, but after two straight years of underachievement, I'm beginning to wonder about it.

2016 Rating: ★ ★ ★/Recommended

Buffalo Trace Antique Collection 2016 George T. Stagg Barrel Proof KSBW 72.05% abv, $90

The henna/auburn color is sensationally breathtaking; unblemished purity. I get early-on faint aromatic hints of bread dough, poppy seed, saddle leather, black peppercorn, and candle wax; second-stage inhalations after more air contact still find the bouquet in an understated, coiled posture, which, considering the lofty abv, is surprising so I move on. Entry is a flavor feast of caramel corn, egg cream, honey, maple syrup, fudge, cocoa bean, dark chocolate, nougat, candied walnut; midpalate continues with the banquet of taste in the forms of all the entry findings plus vanilla bean, oak resin/sap, crème brûlée, black tea, pipe tobacco, lanolin, and cooking oil. The luxurious finish is every bit as profound and as complex as the entry and the midpalate. Is it the equal of the legendary 2012 George T. Stagg? Not quite, but it is very close.

2016 Rating: ★ ★ ★ ★ ★/Highest Recommendation

Buffalo Trace Antique Collection 2016 Sazerac 18 Year Old Kentucky Straight Rye Whiskey 45% abv, $90.

Color is bright topaz, with flawless purity. The opening aromatics are delicate, slightly closed off and what can be discerned early-on is primarily kernel-like, stone dry, earthy, mossy, and mushroomy; more time in the glass finds the fragrance evolving into feinty hints of peanut, wax paper, oilskin parchment, and green tobacco. Entry is delightfully spiced

with cinnamon, clove, and mace, making the case for holiday spice cake filled with dried fruit and candied nuts; midpalate echoes the entry and adds the textural elements of oiliness, fats/lipids, and gravity, which give a solid platform to the buoyant flavors of spice, roasted grain, rye bread, and cake batter. The lovely finish is full-bodied, honey sweet, and mouth filling in the most pleasing aristocratic way.
2016 Rating: ★ ★ ★ ★/Highly Recommended

Buffalo Trace Antique Collection 2016 Thomas H. Handy Sazerac Straight Rye Whiskey 63.1% abv, $90.
Like its stablemate, the Eagle Rare 17, this usually awesome whiskey stumbled last year, scoring only three stars after a string of rave reviews. Its deep amber color bedazzles the eye; impeccable purity. Right from the first whiffs, the aroma is vividly alive with deep cereal scents of cooked mash, bran, Horlicks, pork sausages; later inhalations following more aeration detect notably dry fragrances of stone, minerals, arid desert. Entry is markedly sweeter, spicier, meatier, and oilier than the bouquet suggests, making my perceptions shift gears on the fly as I see the final rating rise; midpalate is robust, acutely spirity but only in a warming sense, not a four-alarm fire, as the oleaginous flavor profile boasts of candied nuts, praline, gingerbread, brown butter, bacon fat that all bleed over into the fat, chewy finish, that concludes with a maple syrup note that's a knockout. Admittedly, I ride the four/five star fence with this edition and pondering it further I believe that four stars is correct.
2016 Rating: ★ ★ ★ ★/Highly Recommended

Buffalo Trace Antique Collection 2016 William Larue Weller KSBW 67.7% abv, $90.
The gorgeous rusty-ochre color is like a shimmering palo cortado sherry; pristine sediment-free clarity. Initial nosing passes discover oily, nutty notes of bacon fat, pork shoulder, cigar tobacco, candied walnut, BBQ sauce, tomato paste, I mean, this could go on forever; with additional aeration, the bouquet turns more corny/grainy and oaky as the wood influence takes the helm. Entry is supple, massively textured, chewy, ripe with dried-fruit flavors of figs, black raisins, prunes, and dates; midpalate is toasty, honeyed, raisiny, and the most succulent of the five 2016 Antique Collection whiskeys. Aftertaste is endless, complex, multilayered with sweet breakfast cereal, caramel corn, and honey flavors that just keep coming at you. Rivals the extraordinary 2012.
2016 Rating: ★ ★ ★ ★ ★/Highest Recommendation

Buffalo Trace Antique Collection 2017 Eagle Rare 17 Year Old KSBW 45%, $90.
This bright color could best be considered tawny; the cleanliness is top-notch. The first nosing discovers generous but soft notes of cornstarch, cornmeal, honey, floral pipe tobacco, brown sugar, and Cocoa Puffs cereal; secondary sniffs pick up earthier, confection-like scents of truffle, chocolate-covered cherry candies, parchment, and caramelized onion. The entry's broad, generous flavors of buttered toast, cinnamon bun, brioche, and unsalted butter along with its creamy texture make for scrumptious in-mouth enjoyment; the midpalate stage refocuses the taste to reflect the mashbill's corn contribution in the lavish mouthfeel and the bountiful flavors of corn bread, cinnamon bun, vanilla extract, oak resins, and dried apricot. The most indulgent Eagle Rare 17 Year Old since the slinky 2013 (four stars). Truly lovely.
2017 Rating: ★ ★ ★ ★/Highly Recommended

Buffalo Trace Antique Collection 2017 George T. Stagg KSBW 64.6% abv, $90.

This color is brilliant mahogany, showing pristine purity. The big-hearted abv plays only a supporting role in the initial whiffs, which early on are devoted much more to raisins, figs, candied fruits, stewed apples, and fruitcake than to grains or wood; it's only after ten additional minutes of aeration that the corn syrup and charred-oak intensity emerges with a hurricane-like fragrance that's dark, rich, oily, and bittersweet. Entry reflects the virtues found in the second inhalations as the taste profile goes bakery shop and confectionery in wave after wave of brown sugar, chocolate cake frosting–like flavors that are pleasingly bittersweet and creamy; midpalate, by contrast, brings back some of the candied fruit, figs, and chocolate-covered raisins of the first whiffs, making the entire experience a glorious circle of enjoyment. Ends on a fathomless note of confectioner richness and corn syrup bitterness. Another five star triumph for GTS—it now rightfully belongs on my short list of America's greatest whiskeys.

2017 Rating: ★ ★ ★ ★ ★/Highest Recommendation

Buffalo Trace Antique Collection 2017 Sazerac 18 Year Old Kentucky Straight Rye Whiskey 45% abv, $90.

Color is fulvous/burnt sienna and impeccably clear. First nosings pick up keenly spicy, nutty, earthy, and floral notes of jasmine, licorice, hay, candied walnut, green leaf tobacco, lichen, and freshly turned soil—I mean, this opening aroma is front-loaded with animated yet elegant fragrances; more aeration brings in cigar box, nutmeg, cinnamon pod, and oaky resin—this part of the analysis can go on for hours. Entry is lush in texture, deeply peppery (black peppercorn), arid, and baking spice–like in the forms of allspice, clove, and cinnamon; midpalate is leaner in texture, biscuity, still peppery, and even a touch waxy. Concludes medium long, more spicy than grainy or woody, and dry as a bone.

2017 Rating: ★ ★ ★ ★/Highly Recommended

Buffalo Trace Antique Collection 2017 Thomas H. Handy Sazerac Straight Rye Whiskey 63.6% abv, $90.

This rye whiskey's color is deep bronze; displays immaculate purity. Even though the abv is stratospheric, it is not an issue in the first whiffs after the pour and serves only as the platform for mature scents of old saddle leather, pine nut, wet cement, damp earth, and split peas; more time in the glass affords the bouquet to deepen and become woodier, resiny, oily (vegetable cooking oil), and grainy (breakfast cereal). Entry is piquant, intense due to the lofty abv but is neither burning nor harsh, nutty, oaky, and oily; midpalate stays the zesty/spicy course as now the alcohol begins to assert itself more in the manner of deepening texture than five-alarm burn, and there's a distinct flavor profile that's rich in woody tannin and lipids. With my lips tingling, the finish is elegant, offering candy-shop hints of nougat, almond butter, dark chocolate, and toffee.

2017 Rating: ★ ★ ★ ★/Highly Recommended

Buffalo Trace Antique Collection 2017 William Larue Weller KSBW 64.1% abv, $90.

Owns a beautiful color space between auburn and burnt umber; ideal clarity. Right off the crack of the aromatic bat, I get bounteous fragrances of nutmeg, clove, cardboard, crème caramel, sponge cake, sandalwood, and allspice; more air contact brings out additional wood-driven scents of lead pencil, ink, bacon fat, pork rind, flint, and black pepper—never is the 64.1 percent abv an issue. Entry is heavenly in its richness and bearing, as sumptuous, no-limits flavors of black tea, crème brûlée, dark honey, oloroso sherry, and marzipan thrill the taste buds; midpalate is every bit as seductive as the boundless entry, as the flavor profile discreetly turns smoky, deeply honeyed, turbinado brown sugar–like, and as rich as dark caramel. Aftertaste is endless, bittersweet, oily rich, toasted, smoky, and cigar-like. Yet another amazing chapter in the enchanting story of William Larue Weller Uncut/Unfiltered. Magnificent.

2017 Rating: ★★★★★/Highest Recommendation

Buffalo Trace Antique Collection 2018 Eagle Rare 17 Year Old KSBW 50.5% abv, $99.
Bronze color; impeccably free of sediment. Right from the first whiffs I like this stone-dry, slightly parched and smoky opening aroma that offers back notes of road tar/asphalt, chicory, and roasted coffee bean; secondary inhalations detect corn husk and silk, espresso, cacao, and high-cocoa-content bittersweet chocolate. Entry is supple in texture, almost plump, as the taste menu includes bacon fat, pork rind, mesquite, dark caramel, corn syrup, and tomato paste; midpalate features fully matured tastes of BBQ ribs, charcoal, tree sap/maple, hoisin, soy sauce, and brown butter in equal measure. Finishes medium long, bittersweet, and chewy. I like the modest elevation in the abv level from 90 proof (45 percent) to 101 proof.

2018 Rating: ★★★★/Highly Recommended

Buffalo Trace Antique Collection 2018 George T. Stagg KSBW 62.45% abv, $99.
Sinopia/rust-like color; flawless clarity. Oh my, this opening aroma is round, evolved, mature, swank, and multilayered from the get-go as an array of aromas are featured, from cornstarch and cornmeal/polenta/tamale to almond paste/nougat to dried orchard fruits (quince, dates, prunes) to mincemeat and Danish pastry; secondary whiffs encounter all of the above as well as maple syrup/tree sap, fudge brownie, and treacle. Entry is succulent, nearly ambrosial, and creamy in texture as the flavor profile highlights the caramel and fudge-like features; midpalate is a cornucopia of delectable flavors, including hot chocolate, espresso, black coffee, cake frosting, candied fruits (pineapple, pear) and nut (walnut especially), and caramel corn. Aftertaste stands as an elegant but hearty and fully integrated monument to this now legendary American whiskey. After so many great editions of this bourbon, I've run out of superlatives to describe its grandeur. All I can say with certainty after thirty years of spirits criticism is this: George T Stagg is one of the world's five greatest whiskeys and one of its ten greatest spirits.

2018 Rating: ★★★★★/Highest Recommendation

Buffalo Trace Antique Collection 2018 Sazerac 18 Year Old Kentucky Straight Rye Whiskey 45% abv, $99.
Marigold/fulvous color; pristine purity. Initially, I pick up razor-edged aromas of unseeded rye bread, toasted oats, Rice Krispies breakfast cereal, steamed brown rice, oyster sauce, and sesame cooking oil; secondary nosing passes encounter more of the unseeded rye bread, with just a glancing touch of marjoram. Entry is lean, edgy, and bread crust–like as

the oiliness of the texture lines the throat; midpalate mirrors the entry phase, as the later impressions deepen this rye's sculpted, lanky texture into a tightly wound mouthfeel that keeps the flavors reined in even through the brief finish that is dry, mineral-like, and flinty. Far from my favorite Sazerac 18 member of the vaunted Antique Collection.

2018 Rating: ★ ★ ★/Recommended

Buffalo Trace Antique Collection 2018 Thomas H. Handy Sazerac Kentucky Straight Rye Whiskey 64.4% abv, $99.

Mahogany color; unblemished clarity. Wow, there's a ton of black peppercorn zestiness in the first whiffs after the pour, then the aroma shifts gears slightly, turning more bready and doughy, as the aromatic profile touts measured fragrances of hops, rye grain kernel, campfire, and oak resins; secondary inhalations encounter scents of apricot stone, Ryvita crackers, and paraffin. Entry takes off like a space launch from Cape Canaveral in a cascade of richly textured flavors, such as butter brickle, caramel, nougat, candy bar, and praline; midpalate reinforces the entry impressions, going deeper with the rye kernel aspect, which brings about a desirable oiliness in the throat that pushes forward the broad dimension of taste. Ends grandly on oily, peppery, grainy terms that promote the core flavor of toasted rye bread. Lovely and hearty.

2018 Rating: ★ ★ ★ ★/Highly Recommended

Buffalo Trace Antique Collection 2018 William Larue Weller 18 Year Old KSBW 62.85% abv, $99.

Cocoa-brown color; excellent purity. I immediately respond to the first vivid yet supple scents of toasted cereal grains, dry breakfast cereal, and unsalted snack cracker; after more aeration, the bouquet enters a spectacular phase of harmony as mature fragrances of caramel corn, unsweetened cornflakes, and English toffee delight my sense of smell. Entry is down-right luscious in its fullness, creamy in texture, raisiny in foundation as the integrated surface tastes of prune Danish, dark honey, and chocolate fudge astound and amaze; midpalate is all about the raisin-like sweet grain, oak-influenced vanilla bean, and honey-flavored cereal tastes that go off the charts of taste pleasure. Aftertaste echoes the midpalate delights, as well as reprising the aromatic aspects of English toffee and caramel corn in full flight.

2018 Rating: ★ ★ ★ ★ ★/Highest Recommendation

Buffalo Trace Antique Collection 2019 Eagle Rare 17 Year Old KSBW 50.5% abv, $99.

Glorious sienna/ochre color; ideal purity. Initial whiffs detect arid landscape dryness that's woody/oaky and flinty, but then the dryness gradually fades, leaving behind more than delicate traces of grain husk and cornmeal; secondary inhalations encounter continued grain husk scents that are dry but deeply cereal- and baked bread–like; this isn't a multilayered bouquet but its directness is appealing. Entry talks big right away, as the alcohol grade, though a mere 45 percent, is pungent and tangy, clearly directing the early flavor profile; midpalate showcases the campfire warmth found in the entry stage, and that element evolves into a bittersweet, intensely woody aftertaste that's supple in texture and moderately candied and nutty (nougat). One of the better Eagle Rares/Antique Collection of recent offerings.

2019 Rating: ★ ★ ★ ★/Highly Recommended

Buffalo Trace Antique Collection 2019 George T. Stagg 15 Year Old KSBW 58.45% abv, $99.

Lovely, impeccably clean, old-copper/rust color. There's immediate, if at first distant evidence of corn syrup, masa/cornmeal, black peppercorn, nougat/candy bar, and demerara sugar; second inhalations after more aeration discover deeper, fuller fragrances of pipe tobacco, ginseng, soy sauce, hoisin, Cracker Jack candy, and cotton candy. Entry is stunningly succulent, honeyed, creamy in texture, caramel-like, and fudgy, all without the elevated proof getting in the way; midpalate mirrors the richness of the entry impressions, adding cigar tobacco, cream caramel, espresso, chocolate fudge, and bear claw pastry to the flavor menu. Ends as sublimely as it began, with utterly luscious layers of corn-fed sweetness and honey-like aromas. Continues as, in my view, America's greatest whiskey.
2019 Rating: ★★★★★/Highest Recommendation

Buffalo Trace Antique Collection 2019 Sazerac 18 Year Old Kentucky Straight Rye Whiskey 45% abv, $99.

Gamboge color; impeccable purity. Opening whiffs pick up deeply layered scents of seedless rye bread, lightly sweetened breakfast cereal, cinnamon stick, and black currant preserves; following more aeration, there's a noticeable advance in butter-like creaminess that's almost akin to cake frosting; in all, an elegant, composed, bakery-shop bouquet. Entry reflects the olfactory findings, adding marginally more impactful dried-fruit tastes, namely dates, black raisins, black currants, and pineapple; midpalate is reassuringly firm in structure, a touch more bittersweet than sweet, woody/oaky/resiny, and tannic. Aftertaste echoes the midpalate, except for a heightening of the resinous aspect that crescendos in a desert-dry finish that leaves the entire palate parched and in need of water.
2019 Rating: ★★★★/Highly Recommended

Buffalo Trace Antique Collection 2019 Thomas H. Handy Sazerac Kentucky Straight Rye Whiskey 62.85% abv, $99.

Sinopia/tawny color; couldn't be any cleaner than it is. Lordy, Lordy, this first nosing pass delivers a laser-like introductory aroma of pine forest/cedar plank/pine cone that's one-pointed and whistle clean; allowing for more air contact, I find additional if supplementary fragrances that include furniture polish, shoe shine wax, wet dish towel, and honeycomb. Entry takes a left turn from the aroma, as the taste profile ignores the pine element in favor of grain husk, dry cereal, hominy, oatmeal/porridge, and molasses; midpalate serves up zesty (the high abv), toasty, grain-based flavors of pancakes, wheat bread toast, Eggo, and corn muffin. I like the finish more than the midpalate since there's a softening of the alcohol, which allows more of the rye character to emerge as it did in the entry phase. Complex.
2019 Rating: ★★★★/Highly Recommended

Buffalo Trace Antique Collection 2019 William Larue Weller 12 Year Old KSBW 64% abv, $99.

Rufous/auburn color; flawless purity. First nosing passes detect subtle aromas of toasted walnut, almond butter, caramel, brown sugar, and fresh, young honey; more air contact stimulates additional scents of rosewood, black cherry, prune Danish, treacle, and cinnamon rolls. Entry is round, compact, highly concentrated, roasted, slightly smoky, and outrageously beguiling in an apple turnover manner, all without any sense of burn or abv heat; midpalate rustles up some campfire embers–like warmth that's more a supplemental aspect than a head-lining characteristic, as the dominant flavors include charred/grilled tomato, brown butter (salted), maple syrup, molasses, flint/mineral, and chocolate-covered coffee bean. Aftertaste seems infinite, if flinty in nature, deeply bittersweet, multilayered, and complex. Bravo, once again, for this annual release that never seems to waver from brilliance.

2019 Rating: ★ ★ ★ ★ ★/Highest Recommendation

Bulleit Barrel Strength Kentucky Straight Rye Whiskey 59.7% abv, $50.

Lovely burnt-orange/bronze color; perfectly pure clarity. The initial whiffs are tight, cornmeal-like, and potent but neither overpowering nor prickly in their approach; second-ary inhalations after more aeration discover a lean, narrowly channeled aroma that's ash-like and focused intently on cornmeal, road tar, and intensely woody/resiny scents that are dry and totally void of any grainy fruitiness. Entry features woody, sap-like tastes of oak resins, acid, and tobacco leaf; midpalate echoes the entry in the wood intensity that's bone-dry and tapered. I find the finish a little lacking in scope and flavor latitude as the wood influence overshadows all other taste possibilities. Recommendable but I prefer the lower strength bottlings of Bulleit bourbons and ryes.

2016 Rating: ★ ★ ★/Recommended

Bulleit Bourbon 10 Year Old KSBW 45.6% abv, $45.

Lovely, deep amber/bronze color; perfect clarity. Smells wonderfully of buttered pop-corn, hay, sawdust, and creamed corn in the initial inhalations after the pour; another seven minutes of air contact unleash slightly sweeter, nutty/nougat-like aromas that fill my office with breakfast cereal fragrance. Entry is sinewy and moderately oily in texture, flashing harmonious flavors of caramel corn, brown butter, sage, and beeswax; midpalate focuses on the elegant but firm texture that's rich and oily/creamy while the taste profile addresses semisweet cereal grains. Finishes nicely in a composed manner that's elegant yet substantial. Hits the mark.

2016 Rating: ★ ★ ★ ★/Highly Recommended

Bulleit Bourbon Frontier Whiskey KSBW 45% abv, $40.

Orange-peel color; I can see oils floating in the core but clean overall. I've always responded favorably to this biscuity, sugar-cookie batter, vanilla wafer–like first aroma; secondary inhalations pick up scents of cornmeal/masa/polenta, allspice, cinnamon, and cornflakes with peaches. Entry is supple, satiny, drier than the bouquet, and therefore more woody/oaky and vanilla bean–like; midpalate is cocoa-like, dense, concentrated, and akin to holiday fruitcake or even rum cake. Ends on a semisweet, cane sugar–like note that's gen-uinely tasty. One of the best mixing bourbons around for classic whiskey cocktails like the Manhattan, Whiskey Sour, or Old-Fashioned. Good value to boot.

2020 Rating: ★ ★ ★ ★/Highly Recommended

Burnside 4 Year Barrel Aged Straight Bourbon 48% abv, $28.

Lovely topaz/amber color; excellent purity. Smells keenly grainy, biscuity, and break-fast cereal–like in the initial whiffs after the pour—nice beginning; six more minutes of air contact ratchet up the grainy sweetness to an appealing degree, but there's also an evolved, sinewy dark caramel aspect that is bittersweet and which closes the aromatic circle. Entry reflects the bittersweet element noted in the final nosing, and the aeration adds a touch of caramel corn flavor; midpalate is medium-long, tasting of brown butter, charred oak, cigarette tobacco, and toffee. Ends toasty and sweeter than the midpalate. I like this no-nonsense whiskey because it surges straight ahead with no pretense or fake moves, and I look forward to more releases from Eastside Distilling, which produces this. Nice job.

2015 Rating: ★ ★ ★ ★/Highly Recommended

Burnside Double Barrel Straight Bourbon 48% abv, $44.

Deeper in color than the sibling 4 Year Barrel Aged, showing an attractive bronze hue that is flawless in its clarity. Opening sniffs encounter generous aromas of caramel, vanilla, sawdust, and baking spices; another six minutes of aeration release added fragrances of old honey, minerals/stone, snack crackers, and honey wheat toast. Entry offers roasted/toasty tastes of grain, toasted bread, charred beef, and honey; midpalate is delightfully caramel-like and tobacco-y, with just enough of a spirit kick to keep it intriguing and genuine. Ends bakery-shop sweet and biscuity, almost like Danish pastry.

2015 Rating: ★ ★ ★ ★/Highly Recommended

Cascade Blonde American Whiskey 40% abv, $20.

Saffron color; pristine purity. Up front, I pick up pleasant, simple notes of sesame seed, corn/maize, and graham cracker; later inhalations detect additional mineral-like scents of limestone, dry soil, and flint. Entry is top-heavy with sweet-leaning grain and breakfast cereal flavors, as well as candied almond and muesli; midpalate mirrors the entry stage, adding only a solitary flavor of tree sap/maple. A no-frills beginner whiskey that's a good value, but nothing beyond that stature.

2019 Rating: ★ ★ ★/Recommended

Catoctin Creek Cask Proof Organic Roundstone Rye Whiskey 56.7% abv, $89.

Gorgeous new-copper/henna appearance; impeccably clean and clear. Initial whiffs encounter sturdy aromas rife with dry rye cereal, black pepper, oak sawdust, lead pencil, newly tanned leather, honey; secondary sniffs detect even richer scents of oak plank, vanillin, egg cream, clove—a vibrant, animated bouquet that pleases. Entry is richly creamy, sap-like, honeyed, almost oloroso sherry–like, and, amazingly, not in the least aggressive with the abv; midpalate is enchantingly spicy/peppery, fruity, ripe, nutty. Aftertaste is focused on the rye and the oaky sappiness, which lends a concluding sweetness that's seriously delicious. This supple, distinctive rye is Catoctin's pinnacle achievement, thus far.

2016 Rating: ★ ★ ★ ★ ★/Highest Recommendation

Catoctin Creek Mosby's Spirit 40% abv, $29.

Colorless appearance; some tendrils seen floating—inconsequential. I really like this white dog first aroma that bursts with pears, bananas, quince, and oatmeal in the first inhalations after the pour; with more aeration, the bouquet becomes a little floral, juicy, and peppery. Entry is lithe, silky, almost grapy, refreshing, and clean; midpalate taste profile highlights the inherent fruitiness, which is deep and enchanting, banana-like and spicy/

zesty. Finishes as clean as any white dog available, with a fruity finale that accentuates the gently sweet cereal grain. Hard to put down. Scrumptious. And this from someone who generally doesn't care for unaged whiskey.

2016 Rating: ★★★★/Highly Recommended

Catoctin Creek Organic Roundstone Rye Whiskey 40% abv, $39.

One hundred percent rye, matured in new Minnesota white oak barrels for just less than two years. Like it seems with all Catoctin spirits, there is a touch of sediment in the core; otherwise pretty sepia/topaz color. It opens aromatically with dry cereal and wax paper scents that are mildly spicy; second sniffs after a few more minutes of air contact detect traces of sawdust, lead pencil, dry earth, and laminate. Entry features sap-like, oaky, tannic flavors that accentuate the rye grain nicely as the flavor profile starts out dry and intensely woody, then proceeds at midpalate to turn more spicy and focused. Finishes medium long, moderately toasty, tannic, and tobacco-like.

2016 Rating: ★★★/Recommended

Catoctin Creek Organic Roundstone Rye Whiskey 46% abv, $52.

Excellent purity; attractive amber/bronze color. This initial aroma is surprisingly sedate and understated, giving off modest scents of new leather pocketbook, elastic, white pepper; secondary sniffs pick up marginally more accentuated aromas of almond butter, leather, cellophane, delicate rye cereal, but little more—c'mon, aroma, give us something to hold on to. Entry is round, creamy, biscuity, bakery shop–like, nougat-like; midpalate offers a buttery texture that's mildly toasted, marshmallow-like, with background flavors of caramelized sugar, honey. Aftertaste is medium long, roasted, grainy, and elegant. Borderline three/four star whiskey. Had the aroma offered more than flaccid fragrance, I'd have given a fourth rating star to honor the positive texture and flavor of the in-mouth stages.

2016 Rating: ★★★/Recommended

Cedar Ridge Iowa Bourbon 40% abv, $39.

Pretty buff/amber color; flawless clarity. I get immediate scents of baked bread, baker's yeast, newly tanned leather, parchment, and dry breakfast cereal in the first inhalations; this surprisingly dry aroma for a corn-based bourbon is nimble, lean, clean, tightly wound, citrus zest–like, and mildly pleasurable in its composed manner. The clenched entry flavor is every bit as savory and compact as the aroma and willing to offer up only taut, narrowly confined tastes of black pepper, black tea, and dried mushrooms; midpalate remains on the dry, dense, grainy course laid out by the entry stage, leading to a brief finish that's flinty dry and spicily grainy. The corn-rye-barley mashbill must be high in rye and barley for this bourbon to end up being this aridly dry.

2017 Rating: ★★★/Recommended

Cedar Ridge Malted Rye Whiskey 43% abv, $42.

Ochre color; superb cleanliness. Initial whiffs encounter mildly pleasant notes of unseeded rye bread, old leather books, Ryvita dark-rye crackers, and bran; later inhalations find additional scents including vegetable cooking oil, flaxseed, pea pods, and pine nuts. Entry is round and silky in texture, nicely spicy (black pepper, clove, ginger), and woody/

resiny; midpalate heightens the entry impressions as the overall flavor goes keenly spicy, dry, yet floral and finally bittersweet and kernel- and pod-like in the aftertaste. I'd actually say that this Cedar Ridge rides the fence between three and four stars and is therefore my favorite of the collection. If it were mine, I'd allow it another six to twelve months in barrel to mellow it further.

2017 Rating: ★ ★ ★/Recommended

Cedar Ridge Single Malt Whiskey 43% abv, $48.

The sandy-brown color is pale and pristine. First out of the aroma box are moderately animated fragrances of oatmeal, dried hops, pork sausage meat, and potato scone; more time in the glass allows the bouquet to stretch out a little, adding brown rice, grain husk, and iron tonic to the aroma menu—if you're expecting this domestic single malt to resemble those from Scotland, put that idea out of your mind before you plunk down your $48. Entry is crackling dry, mildly spicy, yeasty, doughy, metallic, and very much like malted milk; midpalate flavors are a little too stringent and rigid, as this stage mirrors the entry phase especially in the sense of metallic, brittle, iron-like flavor that suddenly turns bean-like in the aftertaste, which almost restores the rating star that this whiskey lost in the flavor phase . . . but it's just not enough to make this anemic, anorexic single malt recommendable.

2017 Rating: ★ ★/Not Recommended

Cedar Ridge Wheat Whiskey 40% abv, $42.

One hundred percent white winter wheat. Chardonnay-like yellow/gold color; excellent purity. First nosings pick up desert-dry grain husk notes that remind me of Wheat Thins crackers, parchment, and peanut shells; secondary whiffs detect marginally greater depth in the forms of potato skins, mashed potato, and boiled pork—frankly, this is an uninspiring wheat whiskey bouquet that has risen to nothing more than mediocrity. Entry flavors are chewy in texture, slightly spiced (freshly ground black peppercorn, saffron, sage in meager amounts), and nicely grainy/breakfast cereal–like; midpalate shows yet a little more in terms of gustatory character, offering dry but substantial tastes of unsalted snack cracker and toasted wheat bread. Finishes medium long, with pleasantly dry flavors that are supported by the solid, creamy texture. All that said, there's not enough quality here for a recommendation. The distillers at Heaven Hill, who produce the lovely Bernheim Original Kentucky Straight Wheat Whiskey (four stars), won't be looking over their shoulders because of this entry. That said, I see unrealized potential here.

2017 Rating: ★ ★/Not Recommended

Charbay Doubled & Twisted Whiskey 45% abv, $50.

This one-of-a-kind whiskey is a blend of 50 percent three-year-old straight malt whiskey, 30 percent seven-year-old stout whiskey, and 20 percent three-year-old pilsner whiskey. Very pretty amber/topaz color; excellent purity level. Opening aromas are intensely beer-like, hoppy, multigrain bread–like, and malty; secondary whiffs after allowing for more air contact pick up the stout and pilsner fragrances at equal degrees of impact, creating a slightly sweet and fruity second-stage bouquet. Entry echoes the bouquet as the taste profile reflects the beer/ale influence that's now quite hoppy and floral tasting; midpalate features

the malted grain aspect in spades as the flavor profile turns suddenly drier and more butter-milk biscuit–like. Finishes fruity, malty, flowery, and intensely ale-like.
2018 Rating: ★ ★ ★/Recommended

Charbay R5 Aged Hop Flavored Whiskey Lot 610A 49.5% abv, $75.
Alembic still/double distilled. Pale gold/amber color; excellent purity. Initial inhalations encounter near-sweet scents of malt, sunflower seed, and leather plus background traces of orange and lemon peel—intriguing to the maximum; another six minutes of aeration unleash round, supple, and intensely grainy notes that are more spirit than beery. Entry is fruity and amazingly citrusy, yet malty and gently sweet; midpalate phase is toasty, mildly oaky, and concentrated in yeast and hoppiness; Aftertaste is medium long, doughier than the Lot 610C, and strikingly ale-like. Liked this version a lot but I loved the Lot 610C.
2014 Rating: ★ ★ ★ ★/Highly Recommended

Charbay R5 Clear Hop Flavored Whiskey Lot 610C 49.5% abv, $52.
Alembic still/double distilled. Pristine crystalline appearance; minor sediment, incon-sequential. Smells delectably beery, yeasty, and hoppy in the first whiffs after the pour and reminds me also of sunflower seeds and India Pale Ale; another seven minutes of air contact release bread-like notes but also malt aromas that are biscuity, leafy/vegetal, and clean. Entry is keenly crisp and razor edged, lovely, concentrated, and floral; midpalate soars into the stratosphere with juicy/citrusy flavors that beautifully accent the hoppy/yeasty/malty base taste and moderately oily texture; it's luscious, in fact. Finishes elegantly, in a subdued way that's all about the hops. Loved it from start to finish, and it's one of my all-time favorite efforts from Master Distiller Marko Karakasevic. Beer lovers take note.
2015 Rating: ★ ★ ★ ★ ★/Highest Recommendation

Chicken Cock 10 Year Old Double Barrel Bourbon 52% abv, $250.
Butterscotch/light caramel color; clean as a whistle. To my delight, the 104 proof doesn't attack the olfactory mechanism as I thought it might and, therefore, the opening nosing passes are treated to cereal grain tanginess and aromas of oak chips and sawdust; secondary passes discover equally alluring and manageable aromas of parchment, tree bark, cinnamon, clove, and hay. Entry shows a bit of heat, but it's completely manageable and warming rather than burning; midpalate opens up the flavor box, offering succulent tastes of baked banana, banana bread, gingerbread, Danish pastry, and candied walnut. Ends on a fine, elegant note of spiced fruit.
2019 Rating: ★ ★ ★ ★/Highly Recommended

Clyde May's Cask Strength 10 Year Old Alabama Style Whiskey 57% abv, $100.
Lovely mahogany color; pure as one expects from a quality distiller such as Conecuh Ridge. Oh my, I get lots of up-front butter brickle, peanut butter, and nougat odors right out of the aromatic gate; secondary nosing passes offer complex scent layers of mincemeat, dried apricot, canvas tarp, textile fiber, and seasoned oak. Entry is maple-like, bittersweet, cocoa bean–like, tasting of praline, apple butter, and almond paste; midpalate is campfire warm in the mouth at 114 proof but not burning and tastes of charred/grilled meats, bacon

fat, caramelized onion, sautéed mushrooms, cigar tobacco, and treacle. A heavyweight class aftertaste that highlights the charred, tobacco-like aspects of the midpalate. Not for everyone, that's for sure, due to its massive structure, which is long on assertiveness and short on nuance.

2018 Rating: ★ ★ ★ ★/Highly Recommended

Clyde May's Cask Strength 8 Year Old Alabama Style Whiskey 58.5% abv, $60.

Similar ginger/cinnamon color to the Straight Bourbon but with a touch more henna/auburn; ideal clarity. I definitely identify the cask strength abv—it would be hard to miss—but in fairness it is not the dominant asset to the first nosing pass—the primary aromatic is the dry-as-a-bone graininess that's like beeswax and textile fiber; later sniffs pick up tar, floor polish, candle wax, mild baking spice. Entry is warm, not fiery, and intensely grainy, spicy, woody, resiny, bittersweet; midpalate features a hearty vanilla bean flavor that's bittersweet, roasted, and akin to vanilla crème brûlée. The finish is smoldering campfire warm, spicy, a bit like fudge or treacle, robust, and generous. I like it a lot.

2017 Rating: ★ ★ ★ ★/Highly Recommended

Clyde May's Straight Bourbon 46% abv, $40.

Seriously pretty brick/cinnamon color; flawless purity. The first inhalations pick up trace amounts of flaxseed, vegetable oil, grassy vegetation, grain kernels; after more time in the glass the aroma stays quite oily and kernel-like but adds a supporting scent of buttermilk biscuit. Entry is heavily toasted, almost burnt, with BBQ flavors of seared brisket, maple, black peppercorn rub, and caramel corn; midpalate is richly textured, complex, more corn-syrup sweet than either honeyed or sugary, and shows a large dose of oakiness, which comes off as vanilla bittersweet. Concludes with the same panache and force of character as at entry phase. Nicely done.

2017 Rating: ★ ★ ★ ★/Highly Recommended

Clyde May's Straight Rye Whiskey 47% abv, $45.

Burnt sienna color; clean and clear of sediment. The rye evidence is clear right from the first whiffs after the pour, as high-toned scents of seedless rye bread and Ryvita snack crackers make their statements; secondary inhalations following more air contact add subtle background fragrances of bread dough, India Pale Ale, and rope/hemp. Entry is front-loaded with savory, spicy, tangy flavors of black pepper, sarsaparilla, root beer, and black tea; midpalate offers hearty, accelerated flavors of barley wine, Ryvita, rye bread, and English breakfast tea. Ends up slightly charred/seared, toasted, and bone-dry.

2019 Rating: ★ ★ ★ ★/Highly Recommended

Collabor&tion Finished in American Brandy Barrels Straight Bourbon 56.5% abv, $125.

Lovely sinopia color; perfect purity. Initial sniffs are confronted with evolved, mature aromas of butter brickle, almond butter, nougat candy-bar filling, butterscotch, and English toffee; secondary inhalations go deeper, picking up scents that are reminiscent of unsalted butter, peanut butter, peanut shells, caramel-covered apples, and apple cider. Entry is aggressive with alcohol, but then it IS 56.5 percent—there are plenty of supporting flavors that

simmer disconnected beneath the alcohol surface, such as corn syrup, brown rice, tree sap, maple, and beef jerky but they remain separate from the alcohol assault; midpalate stage features heavyweight, plodding layers of cooking oil, charred marshmallow, burnt toast, cedar, and brown sugar. Concludes medium long, overly baked/seared/charred, and grainy but not necessarily corny, with a pinch of dark honey. Overbearing, lacking elegance and definition.
2017 Rating: ★/Not Recommended

Collabor&tion Finished in Muscat Mistelle Barrels Straight Bourbon 47% abv, $125.

Lustrous tawny-brown color; minor cloudiness seen but inconsequential. I get immediate, no-fooling scents of coconut, wax paper, pine tar, baked apple/apple strudel, pear skins, and textile fibers in the first whiffs; later inhalations detect direct fragrances of wet cement, cinder block, flint, clay, coins, orange blossoms, and honeysuckle. Entry is tightly wound, lean, highly acidic, crisp, and moderately fruity/grainy as the abv level (47 percent) doesn't shy away, making itself known right from the first sip; the razor-edge, brittle acidity noted in the entry continues into the midpalate phase as the flavor profile turns spicier (cinnamon, clove), grapy, and orchard fruit–like (quince, pear), but nowhere can the grain be found. The finish is zesty, baked, and prickly from both the alcohol and the intense wine-like spiciness. Here are my closing thoughts on this whiskey: Due to the overwhelming power of the muscat mistelle barrel finishing, any sense of straight bourbon falls by the wayside. It'd be better labeled as "American Whiskey" because consumers who know and like the innate corniness of straight bourbon will be disappointed by the muscat mistelle doing all the driving.
2017 Rating: ★★/Not Recommended

Colonel E.H. Taylor Amaranth Grain of the Gods Bottled-in-Bond KSBW 50% abv, $70.

Harvest gold/amber color; exceptionally pure. The curiously expressive first aromas remind me a little of dried cranberry and/or dried red cherry; further air contact stimulates additional wide-ranging scents, including grape preserves, Wheat Thins crackers, sweetened oatmeal, and sour hard candy. Entry is a lean, mean flavor machine, offering not-so-subtle tastes of candied walnut, praline, almond paste, and butterscotch; midpalate echoes the entry stage, adding grainy, dry breakfast cereal flavors that merge nicely with the nuttiness. Intriguing.
2019 Rating: ★★★★/Highly Recommended

Colonel E.H. Taylor Barrel Proof Uncut & Unfiltered KSBW 67.25% abv, $70.

Matured on the sixth floor of Buffalo Trace Distillery's Warehouse C in Frankfort, Kentucky. The extraordinary depth of this auburn/henna color is striking to the eye; ideal clarity. I immediately get roasted Brazil nuts, cola nut, cocoa, and toasted marshmallow in the first tenth of a second of sniffing after the pour; seven more minutes of air contact unleash profound scents of treacle, dark caramel, dark honey, Danish pastry/bear claw, pipe tobacco, and, well, this could go on for an hour. Entry is sappy and maple syrup–like, intensely bittersweet, waxy, and coffee beany; midpalate goes even deeper (you can only imagine) into the spectacular taste profile, adding flavors of balsamic vinegar, caramel corn, baked cherry and blackberry. Incredible aftertaste that isn't hot or raw, but actually caressing and oily. A masterpiece that, in truth, might be too much for inexperienced whiskey devotees. This is a whiskey that one aspires to after a few years of regular tasting. Wow. I diluted it with spring-water down to about 50–51 percent and it's even better.

2015 Rating: ★ ★ ★ ★ ★/Highest Recommendation

Colonel E.H. Taylor Bottled-in-Bond Kentucky Straight Rye Whiskey 50% abv, $70.
Topaz color; impeccably clean and free of sediment. The bone-dry, lightly spiced opening nosing pass could only be straight rye, as gentle aromatic waves that resemble unseeded rye bread, toasted oats, oatmeal/porridge, and Ryvita snack crackers emerge as a unified fragrance; with more air contact, the bouquet turns richer and meatier, gaining along the way a deeper spiciness that highlights vanilla: in all, a characterful bouquet. Entry is lushly textured, acutely spicy (baking spices, cinnamon, clove, and vanilla), and delightfully oily/resiny; midpalate mirrors the entry stage, with the resiny aspect taking the lead and thereby maintaining the squeaky-clean, tannin-driven dryness that carries over into the splendid finish.

2018 Rating: ★ ★ ★ ★/Highly Recommended

Colonel E.H. Taylor Cured Oak Bottled-in-Bond KSBW 50% abv, $70.
Luminous henna/auburn color; flawless purity. There's a high-flying fragrance of but-tered popcorn right out of the gate that turns fruity, damn-near ambrosial as the whiskey aerates; later whiffs detect more subtle, settled notes of white raisins, quince, dried tropical fruits (pineapple), clove, nutmeg, bread dough. Entry is sweet, honey-like, but then sud-denly lean and almost austere as the oak resin/sappiness overtakes the fruit and grain aspects; midpalate echoes the latter phase of the entry as the oak resins rule the day until the after-taste, when the dried fruits reemerge and take back the lead flavor. A roller-coaster ride of taste impressions, which, while intriguing, is the reason why I can't bestow a fifth rating star.

2015 Rating: ★ ★ ★ ★/Highly Recommended

Colonel E.H. Taylor Four Grain Bottled-in-Bond KSBW 50% abv, $70.
Those four grains are, of course, corn, first and foremost, but also wheat, rye, and malted barley. Dazzling burnt sienna color; ideal purity. The initial whiffs unearth nuances of baking spice, mostly clove, vanilla bean, and nutmeg, along with compelling, totally dry smells of textile fiber, new leather, and honey wheat toast; secondary inhalations after more aeration discover hints of cornstarch, baker's yeast, sourdough, nectarine, and green tobacco leaves. Entry is sultry, keenly spicy (black peppercorn, pineapple sage), biscuity, graham cookie–like, and zesty (citrus peel); midpalate is front-loaded with gingerbread, fruitcake, dates, figs, prunes, hazelnut, dried cherry, and root beer–like flavors. Finishes long, lean rather than creamy, astringent, and deliciously ripe and preserves-like.

2017 Rating: ★ ★ ★ ★/Highly Recommended

Colonel E.H. Taylor Seasoned Wood Bottled-in-Bond KSBW 50% abv, $80.
Bright bronze/ginger color; completely sediment-free. First whiffs detect parchment, beeswax, bread crust, and oak resin; following more air contact, the ethereal aroma turns slightly toasted, roasted bean–like, nutty, and bitter. Entry is fuller than the bouquet, featur-ing warming/campfire embers spirit on the tongue plus roasted almond, candied pineapple, bay leaf, sage, and brown sugar; midpalate mirrors the entry, adding more of the comforting

spirit rush, treacle, and marzipan. Finish highlights the toastiness, nuttiness, and herbal leaning of the entry.

2016 Rating: ★ ★ ★ ★/Highly Recommended

Colonel E.H. Taylor Single Barrel Bottled-in-Bond KSBW 50% abv, $60.

Sinopia color; superb clarity. The initial aromatic impressions are reminiscent of crème brûlée, chocolate-covered orange peel, egg white, and sawdust; later sniffs pick up roasted scents of peanuts, walnuts, oak resins, cottage cheese, and paraffin. Entry is succulent in its nutty sweetness and multilayered in its complex texture; midpalate is resiny, maple syrup–like, lusciously creamy, and focused, as the crème brûlée aspect returns to thrill the taste buds all the way deep into the fathomless finish. A clinic on bottled-in-bond straight bourbon that earns every one of its five stars.

2018 Rating: ★ ★ ★ ★ ★/Highest Recommendation

Colonel E.H. Taylor Small Batch Bottled-in-Bond KSBW 50% abv, $60.

Cocoa-brown color; flawless purity. Wow, there's a potent, earthy aromatic streak of black peppercorn in the first whiffs after the pour that I find mesmerizing in its piquant dryness; more time in the glass allows for other fragrances to emerge, namely lead pencil, nickel, granite, and dried pear. Entry highlights the lead pencil, mineral aspect but also showcases subtle scents of grain kernel, sweet corn, crushed violets, and molasses; midpalate is round, full weighted in texture, yet surprisingly agile, peppery, earthy, and focused on the sweet corn. Finishes long, off-dry, piquant, toffee-like, and acceptably prickly. Lovely and composed, from its peppercorn-like start to its English toffee–like aftertaste.

2018 Rating: ★ ★ ★ ★/Highly Recommended

Colonel E.H. Taylor Warehouse C Tornado Surviving Bottled-in Bond KSBW 50% abv, $70.

The story on this release starts on Sunday, April 2, 2006, when a monster springtime storm barreled through central Kentucky, laying waste to several areas, including Buffalo Trace's legendary Warehouse C—legendary because Warehouse C was erected by Colonel Edmund Haynes Taylor, Jr. in 1881, and to this day it houses 24,000+ barrels of maturing spirit. The storm damaged both the roof and the brick north wall. Miraculously, no barrels were affected . . . except that they were exposed to the elements until the repairs were made. Some of the barrels were sampled and thought to be special enough to be blended into one cuvée that was named "Warehouse C Tornado Surviving Bourbon." Tah-dah! Rich burnt-orange color; ideal clarity. All sorts of confectioner aromas abound in the opening sniffs after the pour, including baked apple, brown sugar, dark caramel, and cinnamon; an additional seven minutes introduce elements of dark honey, treacle, marzipan, old leather chair, and burnt marshmallow/s'mores. Entry is lush, thick, succulent, and unabashedly bittersweet; midpalate is remarkably fruity and ripe, especially baked pears, baked apple strudel, and cherry pastry. In the aftertaste, the texture is the main star, as it oozes down the throat like molasses. Utterly decadent and voluptuous.

2014 Rating: ★ ★ ★ ★ ★/Highest Recommendation

Coopers' Craft Barrel Reserve KSBW 50% abv, $31.

Tawny color; pristine clarity. The subtle elegance of the spice cake–like opening aroma is a "tell" that something pleasing is about to follow; after more commingling with air, the aroma unfolds in layers of bittersweet spices (nutmeg, cinnamon), roasted grain, cotton candy, unbuttered popcorn, and masa. Entry explodes on the tongue in stunningly rich and mature flavors of BBQ sauce, tomato paste, brown sugar, and caramel; midpalate reflects all the entry findings, throwing in maple syrup, bark chocolate, pork rind, bacon fat, and hoisin. Ends up deeply bitter, toasted, espresso-like, and grainy.

2019 Rating: ★★★★/Highly Recommended

Coopers' Craft KSBW 41.1% abv, $23.

Caramel color; excellent purity. I like this opening aroma due to its gentle sweetness and savory nut-like nature; secondary sniffs following more aeration discover deeper fragrances, including brown sugar, bear claw pastry, clove, nutmeg, and apple tart. Entry offers tangy flavors of almond paste, dried fruits (dates, figs), mincemeat pie, and corn bread; midpalate features toasted marshmallow, candied walnut, and cigar tobacco. Finishes medium long, drier than the entry and midpalate, and deeply grainy. Good value.

2019 Rating: ★★★/Recommended

Coppersea "Bonticou Crag" Bottled-in-Bond Straight Malt Rye Whiskey 50% abv, $120.

Appealing henna/auburn color; ideal purity. Opening smells are dry and reminiscent of grain husk, laminate, shellac, and candle wax; with more aeration the waxiness blows off leaving behind off-dry and tightly wound scents of seedless rye bread, Ryvita wafers, mincemeat, dried apricot, and walnut butter. Entry is deeply bittersweet at first, offering dense, deeply nutty flavors that are more akin to bakery shop than candy shop, in that the taste profile leans more to pastry with crushed nuts than candy bar or hard candy; midpalate reflects the bittersweet entry impressions, adding a textural heartiness that's equal parts spicy (mace, allspice) and grainy (rye, oats). Finishes gracefully as the taste profile is politely underscored by the oily texture and the power of the 100-proof strength, but the reality is that the abv never eclipses the rye component or the oak spiciness, and that's called balance.

2018 Rating: ★★★★/Highly Recommended

Coppersea "Big Angus" Green Malt Whiskey 48% abv, $90/375 ml.

This unique commemorative bottling honors the legacy of the late Angus MacDonald, Coppersea's founding master distiller. It's comprised of 100 percent un-kilned, "green," two-row barley malt. Brilliant, free of sediment, cocoa-brown appearance. Smells like no other craft whiskey I've evaluated in that there's a mélange of exotic aromas, starting foremost with damp grain, lead pencil, wood shavings, sawdust, vine leaves, and green tomatoes; with more air contact, the cereal grain begins to seep through, along with fragrances of wet wool, plastic rope, green tea, teapot, and nylon/textile fiber. Entry is intensely grainy/barley-like and surprisingly off-dry, resiny, and maple-like; the midpalate stage is this whiskey's finest moment as the taste profile unfolds in alluring waves of digestive biscuit, malted milk ball, and sugar cookie flavors that last deep into the delicious aftertaste.

2017 Rating: ★★★★/Highly Recommended

Coppersea "Excelsior" Bourbon 48% abv, $75.

Bright topaz/bronze color; superbly clean and free of sediment. There's a curious woodsy/forest floor opening aroma that's elemental, mossy, truffle- and mushroom-like initially, then blows off leaving the door open for more expected scents of corn husk and cornmeal/tamale; further air contact works wonders with this atypical but alluring bouquet as the primary aromatic thrust becomes unbuttered corn bread. Entry is pleasantly edgy, showing a bit of sharp-elbowed alcohol that I like, but there's also plenty of corn on the cob, cornstarch, off-dry flavors that lead into the bountiful midpalate stage that's rife with caramel corn, cocoa bean, and bittersweet dark-chocolate tastes. Ends up marginally sweeter than the midpalate as the corn base continues to expand.
2017 Rating: ★ ★ ★/Recommended

Coppersea Aged 7 Months New York Green Malt Rye Whiskey 45% abv, $100.

A 100 percent floor malted, locally grown, Hudson Valley, New York, rye. Pretty new copper/burnished-orange color; flawless, sediment-free purity. Oh my, the baking spice element right off the crack of the aromatic bat is astoundingly animated, as defined yet interwoven aspects of clove, allspice, cinnamon, nutmeg vie for attention; secondary sniffs finally locate the flaxen grain underpinning that supports the banquet of spice notes; a highly unusual aroma of note. Entry echoes the spiciness of the aromatic stages and adds star anise, black tea, quinoa, dried black cherry flavors; midpalate is a symphony of spicy notes that come together in the aftertaste. Unlike any other whiskey I've tasted in many years and immensely pleasing.
2015 Rating: ★ ★ ★ ★/Highly Recommended

Coppersea New York Raw Rye Whiskey 45% abv, $60.

Pot still. Mashbill is 75 percent raw, unmalted rye and 25 percent malted barley. Almost colorless, limpid appearance, with a shade of pewter/silver tint and above-average clarity. Initial whiffs encounter concentrated, intensely grainy aromas that are tart, sour, floral, yeasty, doughy, very early morning bakery–like just as the first batches of sourdough bread are being kneaded; with further air contact, the bouquet turns fruitier, grapier, waxy, textile fiber–like, and almost plastic-like in nature. Entry is wildly grainy, more rye bread-like than the aroma stage, peppery (black peppercorn), off-dry, seed-like (caraway); midpalate is fresh, drier than the entry, nearly astringent, and thereby clean and lean, almost austere, but with an underlying substance that's solid. Finishes clean, crisp, intensely grainy, bread-like. What unaged whiskey/moonshine/white dog can be, but so few are.
2015 Rating: ★ ★ ★ ★/Highly Recommended

Copperworks Release No. 002 American Single Malt Whiskey 53% abv, $60.

Beautiful new-copper color; dazzling clarity. Up-front aromas right after the pour include pencil eraser, electric cables, matchbox, saltwater taffy, cocktail peanuts, candle wax, and salted butter; giving this whiskey a bit more time in the glass, I find that the salted peanut and wax aspects remain pronounced elements even as the cable/matchbox scents fade to the background. Entry is stylishly beer-like (in particular, India Pale Ale), doughy, and yeasty, even a touch hop-like as the dense maltiness blankets the palate; midpalate is pleasantly zesty, malty, totally dry, and deeply cereal-like. Finishes uncannily like an IPA in

the too-fiery mouth. I like this domestic single malt enough to recommend it, but if it were mine, I'd reduce the abv to 45 percent or 46 percent from the 53 percent to allow more of the grain/oak interplay to express itself.
2017 Rating: ★ ★ ★/Recommended

Dancing Goat Limousin Rye Whiskey 46% abv, $40.

Citrine color; some sediment found floating in the core. Owns a pleasing first scent that is delicate, lightly spiced with cinnamon, and keenly bakeshop-like; additional time in the glass brings out fragrances of lanolin, moss on wet stone, and unseeded rye bread. Entry is piquant with black pepper flavor, and therefore bone-dry and zesty; midpalate presents you with a luscious buttermilk biscuit–like flavor that's sprinkled with nutmeg and clove, and that development proves to be the winning aspect for me. Aftertaste is long, deeply grain-like, gently sweet, ripe, and complex. A dandy rye.
2018 Rating: ★ ★ ★ ★/Highly Recommended

Dark Corner Lewis Redmond Carolina Bourbon 43% abv, $65.

Very pretty old gold/medium-amber color; perfect purity. I like the crackling clean and zesty opening aromas that feature creamed corn and sweetened breakfast cereal as the early-on headliners; another seven minutes of air contact release drier, waxy scents that are akin to textile fibers and sarsaparilla. Entry is pleasantly acidic and caramel-like up front, providing a crisp confectioner taste; midpalate features tangy, spicy (black pepper) flavors that culminate in the off-dry and grainy aftertaste. Nice job here, in that this bourbon stays within itself and doesn't make the mistake of trying to be something that it's not, like by being over-oaked or, worse, grainy sweet.
2014 Rating: ★ ★ ★/Recommended

Douglas & Todd Small Batch Bourbon 46.5% abv, $40.

Harvest gold color; superbly clean and sediment-free. Right out of the aromatic gate I get expressive scents of grain husk, lima bean, pea pod, and newly tanned leather; later sniffs after more air contact reveal grain-field fragrances, such as wheat chaff, mown hay, barley, and clay soil. Entry shows a trace of corny sweetness, as well as astringent flavors of black tea, cigarette tobacco, and soy sauce; midpalate is awkward in that the distant sweet corn aspect is overwhelmed by the acidic astringency and top-heavy oakiness, thereby creating an off-balance whiskey. Finishes without a whisper of grain or corn, but with oodles of resiny oak/wood plank. What's missing here is good barrel management.
2019 Rating: ★/Not Recommended

Downslope Double Diamond Whiskey 40% abv, $35.

Pale straw-yellow color; impeccable clarity. Sports a pleasant fruity (dried pineapple) first aroma after the pour that's also sweetly grainy/breakfast cereal–like; the grain picks up the pace in the second passes, and the addition of citric acid (lemon zest) and brown sugar make for moderately enjoyable sniffing. Entry is delicately sweet, strikingly chocolate marshmallow–like and plump; midpalate is more layered than the gangly entry, showing off so-so tastes of light toffee and honey. Finish is simple, undemanding, and grainy. Drinkable, but flimsy, undernourished, and too hollow for a recommendation. Do I note potential? Definitely, yes!

2014 Rating: ★★/Not Recommended

Downslope Limited Edition Cognac French Oak Double Diamond Whiskey 51% abv, $65.

Pale golden marigold color; excellent purity. I encounter a winey, grape-influenced opening aroma plus nutty, caramel corn elements; after another eight minutes in the glass, the bouquet turns a bit butcher's wax paper–like, almost akin to textile fiber—what's lacking aromatically is grain presence. Entry is gently sweet, corny/grainy (thank you), and nutty; midpalate is delightfully sweet/sour, breakfast cereal–like and tangy. Not a landmark whiskey, but certainly good enough for three stars.

2014 Rating: ★★★/Recommended

Downslope Limited Edition Double-Casked French Oak Double Diamond Whiskey 48% abv, $50.

Interesting reddish-brown/henna/tawny color; very minor sediment seen. Out of the gate this aroma smells of soy sauce/hoisin, tree bark, toasted grain, and cooking oil; after another seven minutes of air contact tack on linseed oil, cigar tobacco, and brown sugar. Entry is more defined and refined than the bouquet in that the taste profile highlights resiny oak and brown-butter flavors; midpalate advances the brown butter especially, having it become almost like nougat/buttered almond. Finishes well, bakery-shop sweet and savory.

2014 Rating: ★★★/Recommended

Dry Fly 101 4 Year Old Straight Bourbon 50.5% abv, $50.

Bronze color; excellent purity. Opening whiffs pick up mildly sweet traces of caramel corn, buttermilk biscuit, baker's yeast, and bread dough; secondary inhalations discover broader aromas that include Parmesan cheese, brown rice, snack cracker, and dried orange. Entry offers dry to off-dry tastes of unbuttered biscuits, soybean, carob, and turbinado sugar; midpalate features more of the oak influence in the forms of maple, tree sap, and bark flavors that elevate the taste profile. Aftertaste is medium long, toasted, bittersweet, charred, and mildly oily.

2019 Rating: ★★/Not Recommended

Dry Fly 3 Year Old Cask Strength Straight Wheat Whiskey 60% abv, $50.

Ochre color; flawless clarity. Right from the get-go, there are potent and pleasing Wheat Thins snack cracker–like aromas that are crisp, grainy, and dry, as well as oak-driven scents of resin and pine tar; later whiffs detect more in the way of alcohol as the cask strength status bulls its way forward, eclipsing the oak and grain components. Entry flavors include fiery tastes of cereal grain, BBQ sauce, tomato paste, gum, and toasted marshmallow; midpalate reflects the entry impressions, adding zingy tastes of black peppercorn and fudge. Finishes very long, nearly hot on the tongue, prickly, and fig-like.

2019 Rating: ★★★/Recommended

Dry Fly 3 Year Old Port Barrel Finish Straight Wheat Whiskey 45% abv, $50.

Tawny color; superbly clean. This opening aroma is chockfull of dried fruits, especially

black raisins, prunes, and apricot, as well as a deep graininess that's the perfect foil for the dried fruits; later sniffs pick up fragrances of black tea, chocolate-covered cherries, and Honey Nut Cheerios cereal. Entry is pleasantly winey/port-like right from the first sip, and that sets the table for the late-coming graininess that balances the ambrosial aspect; midpalate echoes the entry as the flavor profile expands slightly, adding cocoa bean and coffee latte elements that provide depth and concentration. Finishes a bit feeble, but the aroma, entry, and midpalate are good enough to warrant the recommendation.
2019 Rating: ★ ★ ★/Recommended

Dry Fly 3 Year Old Straight Triticale Whiskey 45% abv, $40.

Fulvous/old gold color; pristine clarity. The curiously wax- and onionskin paper–like aroma in the opening inhalations doubtless is directly related to the grain choice, called triticale, a hybrid created in nineteenth century Scotland from wheat (triticum) and rye (secale); after more aeration, the unique fragrance reminds me most of legumes, especially pinto beans, soybeans, and lentils. Entry is stunningly bitter, nutty, and beany at first, then as I savor the taste, it becomes more woody, sap-like, and resiny; midpalate serves to reinforce the entry findings as the overall impression of polymers and wax paper just won't make way for any other flavor characteristics to peek through. Finishes intensely bitter and, at least for me, unpleasant. Just didn't work for me.
2019 Rating: ★/Not Recommended

Dry Fly O'Danaghers 5 Year Old Caledonian Single Pot Still/Single Barrel Whiskey 45% abv, $60.

Sandy-brown color; the appearance is disturbingly cloudy with unappealingly large chunks of paper-like sediment seen floating both in the glass and the bottle; not good. The first nosing passes pick up stale, wooden, sawdust-like aromas that are oaky and tanky; secondary inhalations locate more acceptable fragrances, mostly brown rice, newly tanned leather, and library. Entry offers some pleasant graininess that's slightly fruity (nectarine), woody, resiny, and dry; midpalate features a tartness that's crisp and lean, showing off more of the barrel than the grain. Ends up near recommendable, as the latter stage aroma, entry, and midpalate combine to redeem at least some of the visual flaws . . . but not enough.
2019 Rating: ★ ★/Not Recommended

Dry Fly O'Danaghers 5 Year Old Hibernian Triple Distilled Pot Still/Single Barrel Whiskey 45% abv, $60.

Amber/marigold color; excellent purity. Initial whiffs detect deeply malty, snack cracker–like, and toasted scents that are mature and nicely integrated; later inhalations after more aeration discover notes of allspice, mace, graham cracker, and espresso. Entry is pleasantly roasted, nutty, oaky, and somewhat like maple syrup; midpalate offers touches of dried orange rind, almond butter, nougat, candy bar, and honey. Concludes medium long and only moderately intense as the taste profile fades a bit in the finish.
2019 Rating: ★ ★ ★/Recommended

Early Times Bottled-in-Bond KSBW 50% abv, $24.

Burnt sienna color; excellent clarity. Initially, I pick up lots of cooking spice aromas, especially parsley, bay leaf, and basil that morph into oak-driven, sawdust, and oak plank scents over time; more aeration releases toasted grain/whole wheat bread notes that come to underline the entire bouquet experience. Entry is warming on the tongue, caramel-like, bittersweet, and reminiscent of caramel corn; midpalate features charcoal briquette, tomato paste, brown sugar, vinegar, and honey flavors that are supported nicely by the 100-proof alcohol level. While I'd wished for greater complexity, the overall experience is pleasant and bakeshop-like enough to easily warrant a recommendation. That said, if you are expecting multiple layers of depth from this bottled-in-bond whiskey, search elsewhere.

2018 Rating: ★ ★ ★/Recommended

Early Times Kentucky Whiskey 40% abv, $13.

Amber color; completely free of sediment. First off, I pick up pleasant spiced apple notes that highlight cinnamon and clove; the orchard fruit aspect stays vivid well into the second nosing passes as it combines with an ascendant sweet corn graininess to make an altogether acceptable, if simple bouquet. Entry flavors favor the sweet corn grain and marzipan while the baking spice elements remain constant, especially the clove; midpalate is juicy, toffee-like, and totally enjoyable. Can't believe how much better this incarnation is to the flimsy version evaluated fourteen years ago. Excellent value, as long as one understands that this crowd-pleaser won't be as profound or multilayered a whiskey experience as, say, a Woodford Reserve or an Old Forester. But it's become a winner as an everyday great value.

2018 Rating: ★ ★ ★/Recommended

Eight & Sand Blended Bourbon 44% abv, $30.

Pumpkin-orange color; excellent purity. Out of the gate, the aroma is listless and numb, as I get next to nothing of note so I move on; even after more air contact, this aroma remains in need of a transfusion, as the most it can convey is a distant lemon-peel zestiness. Entry is far more animated than the anemic bouquet, offering bittersweet flavors of tree bark, oak resins, maple, and butterscotch; midpalate seems to be searching for a purpose, as the flavor profile can't offer more than a bittersweet, bear claw pastry taste but not much beyond that. This flaccid blended whiskey is drinkable, and perhaps it can be successful in something like a Ward Eight cocktail, but on its own it fails to deliver.

2019 Rating: ★ ★/Not Recommended

Elijah Craig 12 Year Old Small Batch Barrel Proof KSBW 65.7% abv, $65.

Rust/mahogany color; immaculate purity. Opening scents include fragrances reminiscent of orange pekoe tea, brown sugar, dark honey, maple, and vanilla bean; secondary inhalations detect deeply layered, highly complex aromas of cinnamon, clove, chocolate-covered raisins, sawdust, and peanut butter; a bouquet that keeps offering new layers with time. Entry is incredibly rich, oily/buttery in texture, with mature, candy-shop tastes of fudge, cacao, carob, turbinado sugar, dark honey, and candied walnut; midpalate reflects the entry findings, adding further flavors of chocolate cake frosting, espresso, black coffee, and bittersweet dark chocolate. Aftertaste turns a bit too metallic/steely, and that undermines the bittersweet element so lovely in the midpalate.

2018 Rating: ★ ★ ★ ★/Highly Recommended

Elijah Craig 18 Year Old KSBW 45% abv, $120.

The bright new-copper/russet color is dazzling; flawlessly pure and sediment-free. I get cherries, red plum, and cranberry aromas in the very first sniffs after the pour, then the orchard fruits turn more grainy and cereal-like as the fragrance evolves with more air contact; second inhalations following even more aeration turn the bouquet into a bakery banquet, notable for scents of cinnamon, clove, vanilla bean, allspice, cookie dough, baker's yeast. Entry offers narrowly focused mineral-like tastes of totally dry stone, dry earth, and shale that are even a touch baked; midpalate highlights the dryness of the mineral aspect plus now the mashbill elements come clearly into effect as the cornmeal taste comes to dominate along with a touch of spiciness. Finishes medium long, oaky/resiny, peppery, desert dry, grainy.

2015 Rating: ★★★★/Highly Recommended

Elijah Craig 20 Year Old Single Barrel KSBW 45% abv, $130.

Orange/copper color; impeccable clarity. Opening smells like buttered corn on the cob, corn syrup, breakfast cereal, and honey; eight minutes of further aeration bring out scents of uncharred oak plank, tobacco, and pine. Entry is gloriously harmonious and balanced between acidity, grain, and wood in a lithe, agile manner that belies the age; midpalate is nimble, cereal-like, moderately oily/viscous, and almost fruity and spicy. Finishes svelte, focused, and, in my mind, about as luscious as a bourbon can be. I've always admired any Elijah Craig bottling but this edition is mind-blowingly superb.

2015 Rating: ★★★★★/Highest Recommendation

Elijah Craig 23 Year Old Single Barrel KSBW 45% abv, $200.

The brilliant copper/bronze color is stunning visually; perfect clarity. I get BBQ sauce, tomato paste, nut butter, wood smoke, baked banana, totally dry fragrances in the initial inhalations, then in the second round, the aroma expands to include old leather books, parchment, corn bread, oak, vanilla bean; a powerful, multilevel bouquet. Entry is bittersweet, intensely oaky/woody, spicy, tangy, altogether lovely; midpalate soars with dusty-dry flavors of corn bread, buttered popcorn, sesame, vanilla bean. The vanilla bean becomes the dominant taste in the finish. I'm beginning to wonder if we are now approaching or even pushing beyond the realistic aging limits and capabilities of straight bourbon. Are we asking too much?

2015 Rating: ★★★★/Highly Recommended

Elijah Craig Barrel Proof Batch C-917 12 Year Old KSBW 65.5% abv, $65.

Mahogany/sinopia color; perfect purity. I smell the tantalizing aromas found in early morning bakeries when the still-warm pastries are at their freshest and most fragrant, richly aromatic with sugar glaze, fruit preserves, and nut pastes; after another eight minutes of aeration, the aroma turns woodier and more spirity as the oak and alcohol influences begin to overtake the grain base. Entry is deep, dense, succulent, spirity, maple-like, and sugary—in other words, luscious; midpalate is multilayered, deeply honeyed, fruity, raisiny, oaky/resiny, and incredibly delicious. Finishes fiery, yet grainy and semisweet enough to offset much of the barrel-strength heat. There have been so many reliable, take-it-to-the-bank whiskeys released under the Elijah Craig label. Here is perhaps the flagship. Suggestion: add water in a three-to-one ratio in favor of the whiskey for maximum enjoyment.

2018 Rating: ★★★★★/Highest Recommendation

Elijah Craig Barrel Proof Batch-A119 12 Year Old KSBW 67.6% abv, $60.

Sienna color; superb purity. Initial aromatic impressions are a bit hazy and unclear, as I get both mineral and grain that are amorphous and only gently guided by the barrel strength abv; the obscurity found in the first nosing passes continues after more air contact, as now the aroma offers low degrees of wood, forest elements, sawdust, and grain. Entry features more identifiable aspects, including praline, nougat, chocolate candy bar, candied walnuts, and cedar/pine; midpalate branches out, offering powerfully zesty and piquant flavors of butterscotch, cake frosting, cocoa powder, maple syrup, and caramel. The vitality of the taste phase remains strong in the aftertaste, echoing many of the midpalate findings.

2019 Rating: ★ ★ ★ ★/Highly Recommended

Elijah Craig Barrel Proof Batch-A120 KSBW 68.3% abv, $60.

Mahogany color; flawless clarity. The potent abv comes through immediately in the first whiffs as the alcohol sears the nasal passages before blowing off, revealing subtler scents of brown sugar, cake frosting, hot cocoa, and charred corn on the cob on the grill; second passes unearth toastier, more roasted aromas including baked ham, fried bacon, and BBQ sauce. Entry burns the tongue a bit, which overshadows the initial taste sensations; midpalate sees the abv recede a little, and this allows for greater access to the grainy, kernel-like flavors that are deeply sweet corn–like and sugary/corn syrup–like. Finishes four-alarm hot so please add water, as this take-no-prisoners KSBW burns the town to the ground.

2020 Rating: ★ ★ ★/Recommended

Elijah Craig Barrel Proof Batch-B519 12 Year Old KSBW 61.1% abv, $60.

Rust/carnelian color; flawless clarity. Even though this bourbon is barrel strength, the alcohol factor remains relatively hidden in the first whiffs after the pour, but there are notes of jasmine, honeysuckle, whole grain bread, and carob; later sniffs pick up fragrances of honey, sweetened oatmeal, toasted wheat bread, and brown sugar. Entry is surprisingly docile, showing just a whisper of abv heat that actually underscores the flavors of maple syrup, tree bark, cinnamon, clove, and mace; midpalate is all about the cask strength alcohol warmth and bittersweet caramel corn flavor. Aftertaste is fathomlessly long, complex, mineral-like, and concentrated on spice beans/pods (vanilla, cinnamon, nutmeg).

2019 Rating: ★ ★ ★ ★/Highly Recommended

Elijah Craig Barrel Proof Batch-B520 KSBW 63.6% abv, $80.

Vermillion color; excellent clarity. Opening notes are of cardboard, caramelized onion, "red layer," meaning the caramelized sugar of a charred white oak barrel, and creamed corn; later sniffs detect brief encounters with the high abv, but those are softened by the intensity of the corn kernel graininess. Entry is admittedly warm to Arizona hot, as the cask strength bigness turns aggressive, so I suggest that room-temperature mineral water be added before tasting; with mineral water added, the taste profile turns round, chewy, semisweet, prune-like, and deeply corny; midpalate is fat, juicy, with highlights of burnt sugar, honey, caramel, and soy sauce. Finishes very long, chunky, raisiny, and plummy. With dilution, an easy four star rating.

2020 Rating: ★ ★ ★ ★/Highly Recommended

Elijah Craig Barrel Proof Batch-C919 12 Year Old KSBW 68.4% abv, $60.
Caramel/bronze color; completely sediment-free. First sniffs after the pour detect aromas that are reminiscent of grilled meats, roasted corn, and a little bit fruity, mostly in dried vine (blueberry, red currant) and orchard fruits (Anjou pear, tangerine); later inhalations after more air contact pick up scents of lard, bacon fat, foie gras, and oak lipids. Entry is round, chewy in texture, moderately fiery on the tongue, rich in corn-driven sweetness and graininess; midpalate offers a more complex and concentrated flavor profile than the entry, as heavily roasted and toasted tastes of corn bread, maple fudge, nougat/candy bar, and mature honey dominate this stage. Finishes very long, narrowly focused, corn-husk bitter, and a bit unwieldy due to the abv intensity.
2019 Rating: ★★★/Recommended

Elijah Craig Kentucky Straight Rye 47% abv, $60.
Cocoa-brown color; perfect purity. Initial whiffs detect bread-like aromas that are similar to seeded rye bread and buttermilk biscuits; later inhalations pick up deeper, more substantive scents of licorice/anise, toasted marshmallow, and most intriguing of all, bacon fat. Entry is intensely complex, concentrated, dry as a bone, and spicy; midpalate mirrors the entry, adding bean-like tastes of coffee and carob, as well as dried pineapple, tobacco, vinegar, and BBQ sauce. Finishes extra long, desert dry, and just slightly prickly on the tongue. A stunningly delicious entry into the busy straight rye whiskey sweepstakes. WOW!
2020 Rating: ★★★★★/Highest Recommendation

Elijah Craig Small Batch KSBW 47% abv, $33.
Pretty mahogany color; flawlessly free of sediment. The first inhalations after the pour pick up toasted grain notes that are dry, lean, and kernel-like, roasted and snack cracker–like; secondary whiffs encounter peppery scents that are alluringly spicy and piquant, as they delicately accentuate the deep, earthy, and dry graininess. Entry is decidedly sweeter and riper than the austere bouquet, offering a flavor profile that's a bit like BBQ sauce, tomato paste, black peppercorn, and grilled meat; midpalate is the apex moment for this KSBW as the flavor detonates on the tongue, featuring succulent tastes of hoisin, fried rice, toasted marshmallow, praline, caramel corn, cinnamon bun, and honey. The tour de force flavors continue deep into the finish, drawing the ideal close to the entire eye-to-nose-to-mouth experience. The distillers at Heaven Hill continue to provide a master class on how it should be done.
2018 Rating: ★★★★★/Highest Recommendation

Elmer T. Lee Commemorative 1919–2013 Single Barrel KSBW 46.5% abv, $35.
Deep amber color; completely sediment-free. Initial nosings pick up plenty of dried cherry, Danish pastry, figs, dates, vanilla bean scents that have already integrated nicely; secondary sniffs encounter more of the oak impact than the dried fruit–driven grain, mostly in the forms of resin and baking spice, including vanilla and clove; highly sophisticated bouquet. Entry is remarkably sinewy in texture, sweet-corn sweet, toffee-like, spicy; midpalate reflects the entry perfectly, heaping on touches of coffee bean bitterness that balances the

corny sweetness perfectly. Finishes supple, long, gently sweet, maple-like. A fitting liquid tribute to a genuinely great whiskey man and a true pioneer.
2015 Rating: ★ ★ ★ ★ ★/Highest Recommendation

Evan Williams KSBW 43% abv, $14.

Copper color; flawlessly clean. There's no mistaking the corn base of this fragrant opening aroma as vibrant scents of cornmeal, sweetened cornflakes, cinnamon, beeswax, and burning embers enchant all the way to the second passes; following more aeration, the fading bouquet turns slightly fruity and ripe as lean aromas of lemon drop, kiwi, and lychee dance upon the sturdy caramel corn foundational fragrance. Entry is plush, intensely corn syrup–like but not overly sweet as the roundness of the texture leaves deep impressions of charred oak, caramel corn, and toasted almond; midpalate mirrors the entry, adding a degree more heft to the texture. Finishes long in the throat, bittersweet, and elegant, with a final flavor of holiday fruitcake. Excellent value for money.
2018 Rating: ★ ★ ★/Recommended

Evan Williams Master Blend KSBW 45% abv, $60.

A blend of five Heaven Hill Evan Williams brand whiskeys: Evan Williams Black, EW Bottled-in-Bond, EW 1783, EW Single Barrel, and EW 23 Year Old. Caramel/toffee color; spotless purity. Up front, I get gently sweet, sweetened cornflake cereal, brown sugar aromas that are inviting; after more aeration, the aroma turns a bit fruity, but more in the vein of candied fruit (banana, orange) than fresh fruit, and I likewise get scents of fudge brownie and caramel corn; a pleasing bouquet that's easily accessible. Entry is bittersweet, peppery, and now the breakfast cereal is without the fruit, creating a leaner, more acidic impression on the tongue; midpalate stays the course set in the entry stage, relying more on the grain/cereal flavor thrust as the underlying core. Ends medium long, heavily toasted, tobacco-like, and dry.
2019 Rating: ★ ★ ★/Recommended

Evan Williams Red 12 Year Old KSBW 50.5% abv, $130.

Harvest gold/fulvous color; sediment-free purity. Right away, I pick up understated, utterly dry fragrances of saddle leather, library books, cornstarch, sawdust, and dry stone; more time in the glass doesn't stimulate much more in the way of aromatic release, but what's there is pleasant and under the radar. Entry offers significantly more in sensory development as substantial flavors of toffee, fudge, egg cream, vanilla bean, and cola nut make their case; midpalate sees the various flavor elements merge into a singular semisweet taste that's spicy, peppery, grainy, and slightly resiny/woody/tree bark–like. Finishes arid and spicy, with latent flavors of candied almond and graham cracker.
2019 Rating: ★ ★ ★ ★/Highly Recommended

Evan Williams Vintage 2002 Single Barrel KSBW 43.3% abv, $26.

Lovely topaz/deep amber color; flawless purity. Opening aroma is vividly alive with dry grain/breakfast cereal and oak resin notes that are beautifully integrated; additional time in the glass adds delicate scents of wax, pepper, palm oil, and cornstarch. Entry is voluptuously textured, oily/buttery, and bursting with caramel corn flavor—WOW; midpalate is luscious, as

the acid level, wood extract, and corn richness meld to make an extraordinary bourbon experience that's perfectly harmonious. Concludes strong and robust but likewise elegant and classic.
2014 Rating: ★ ★ ★ ★ ★/Highest Recommendation

Evan Williams Vintage 2003 Single Barrel KSBW 43.3% abv, $26.
Old gold hue; showing a little more sediment than I like to see. Opening sniffs pick up delicate aromas of toasted marshmallow, toffee, and ash; secondary inhalations after six minutes of further air contact reveal lovely, integrated scents of brown butter, almond paste, and sawdust/wood plank. Entry is measured, firm, moderately oily, and grainy sweet; midpalate hums along like a fine twelve-valve engine, giving off assured tastes of caramel corn, peanut butter, and oak resin. Composed and integrated in the lush, off-dry aftertaste. An understated edition of quiet strength and presence.
2015 Rating: ★ ★ ★ ★/Highly Recommended

Evan Williams Vintage 2004 Single Barrel KSBW 43.3% abv, $27.
Medium amber/straw color; uncharacteristic sediment seen. First inhalations detect generous, animated aromas of caramel corn, cornmeal, peanut butter, pine needle; later sniffs encounter added scents of black pepper, slate/stone, lemongrass. Entry is sap-like, honeyed, viscous, peppery; midpalate highlights more of the corn aspect, with grainy flavors of buttered popcorn, creamed corn, cooking spice. Ends gracefully, integrated, balanced, off-dry, nutty. Once again depicts why bourbon is one of the hottest spirits categories on the planet and one of the most affordable spiritous pleasures.
2016 Rating: ★ ★ ★ ★/Highly Recommended

FEW Bourbon 46.5% abv, $50.
Tawny/sinopia color; brilliant purity. First aromatic impressions are of steamed brown rice, beeswax/paraffin, toasted rye bread, and spicy oak (lots of vanilla bean); later inhalations after more aeration encounter fragrances of butcher's wax paper, linseed oil, sesame seeds, vegetable cooking oil, and dry breakfast cereal. Entry is supple in texture, spicy/peppery, toasted, off-dry, and pleasantly woody; midpalate finds the taste profile gaining in power as the flavors merge into a single note of oak-driven graininess that is sappy, maple-like, peppery, and semisweet. Concludes medium long in the throat, caramelized, semisweet, and zesty. I like the manner in which its power quotient rises all through the evaluation process.
2018 Rating: ★ ★ ★/Recommended

FEW Rye Whiskey 46.5% abv, $65.
Burnt sienna/bronze color; flawless clarity. This aroma could only be rye as the first fragrances resemble seedless rye bread and rye-based snack crackers, offering just a bit of piquant spiciness; after more air contact, the seductive bouquet features traces of black pepper, unsalted butter, saddle leather, wet cement, and pumpernickel bread. Entry is rich in texture, chocolatey, burnt marshmallow–like, and toffee-like; midpalate soars with splendid, focused flavors of holiday spice cake, cinnamon bun, dark caramel, chocolate-covered orange peel, and clove. Ends on a toasted, roasted coffee bean/espresso note that's long, piquant, and devilishly savory.
2018 Rating: ★ ★ ★ ★/Highly Recommended

FEW Single Malt Whiskey 46.5% abv, $70.

Sandy-brown color; perfect purity. I get pungent, waxy, synthetic-like aromatics of wet wool, damp floor maltings, wort, nylon, and beer yeast in the opening whiffs; later inhalations don't pick up a whole lot of change to the wet wool/damp malt/synthetic with the added aeration so I move onto the tasting phases. Entry reveals a dry, malty taste that's reminiscent of breakfast cereal and toasted multigrain bread, with just a deft touch of orchard fruitiness; midpalate can't shake the damp aspect, but there's an astringent dry cereal flavor that's suddenly spicy and assertive all the way to the aftertaste. Finishes off-dry, deeply cereal-like/grainy and malted milk ball–like.

2018 Rating: ★ ★ ★/Recommended

Fitch's Goat 100% Corn Whiskey 48.5% abv, $36.

Corn. Pale goldenrod/hay-field gold color; minor tendrils of sediment seen. This opening bouquet is more waxy, plastic-like, fibery/textile in nature; further aeration releases stone-dry scents of wheat germ, bay leaf, beeswax, furniture polish. Entry is resiny, woody, a little lacking in graininess as the wood impact eclipses the corn; midpalate falls into the oak barrel trap of aggressive wood, knocking the grain base out of the picture. Out of balance. Needs work.

2014 Rating: ★/Not Recommended

Fitch's Goat Moonshine 43.5% abv, $26.

Corn. Lucent; relatively sediment-free. I favorably respond to this first burst of floral/ flower-shop aroma that's as though the pot still is in my office—clean, crisp, acidic, cereally; later sniffs find the floral aspect turns fruity, as in tropical fruits, banana, pineapple, even quince. Entry is toasty, dense, grainy, off-dry, slightly bitter; midpalate mirrors all the entry findings and adds burnt cereal, caramelized onion, maple. Ends charred, deeply grainy. Superb example of moonshine.

2014 Rating: ★ ★ ★ ★/Highly Recommended

Five Fathers Pure Rye Malt Whiskey 55% abv, $45/375 ml.

Pretty copper/burnt-orange color. Owns a saddle leather, animated textile fiber/hemp opening aroma that's assertive and not a little like walking through a furniture-store showroom; seven more minutes of air contact doesn't stimulate much else in the way of bouquet. Entry is keenly astringent, making my mouth pucker, due primarily to the 110-proof degree of alcohol, but there are some pleasant sideline flavors, in particular, gum, grape, and resin; midpalate features more of the grapiness/jamminess, and that actually works for me since it eclipses the abv. Unmemorable, in the face of the many sensational rye whiskeys available, but nevertheless praiseworthy enough to try for the experience of looking at rye from a different angle.

2015 Rating: ★ ★ ★/Recommended

Four Roses 125th Anniversary Limited Edition Small Batch KSBW 55% abv, $85.

A blend of three Four Roses mashbills: OBSV (eighteen years old), OBSK, and OESK (each thirteen years old). Cocoa-brown; flawlessly pure. The opening fragrances are fully integrated, caramel corn–forward, slightly prickly from the elevated abv but, man oh man, this first nosing is also sublimely ambrosial, showing an array of dried dark fruits, such as prune, cranberry, blackberry, and black plum; secondary aromatic hits pick up bakery-shop fragrances like cinnamon bun, prune Danish, marble bread, and gingerbread—a spectacular bouquet on all fronts. Entry is lush and focused on the grain intensity, primarily sweet corn, but also on the residual tastes of maple, toffee, fudge, walnut butter, and baked apple; mid-palate reinforces the entry findings and adds nougat and butter brickle tastes just to round off the in-mouth experience that goes on forever in the finish.

2018 Rating: ★★★★★/Highest Recommendation

Four Roses 13 Year Old Single Barrel, Barrel Strength KSBW 46.3% abv, $80.

Deep copper color; flawless purity. Corn, sweet corn, cornmeal, and bacon fat aromas round out this grainy/meaty opening fragrance; after another eight minutes of air contact, the aromatic profile leaps forward into territories of brown rice, anise, black pepper, and pipe-tobacco perfume; a tantalizingly luscious bouquet that could only be from the USA. Entry is lead-pencil minerally, clean, textile-like, and dry; midpalate features full-volume, seductive flavors of hazelnut, almond butter, candy bar nougat, and fudge. Concludes on a biscuity, cake-like, minerally note that is semisweet, caramel, egg cream, and vanilla bean. The lead pencil aspect reappears in the finish as the dominant feature, and that dominance keeps at bay the fifth rating star.

2015 Rating: ★★★★/Highly Recommended

Four Roses 2012 Single Barrel KSBW 54.7% abv, $100.

Gorgeous new-copper color. Deliriously luscious scents of corn on the cob, caramel corn, and lychee abound in the opening sniffs after the pour; further air contact brings out sap and maple notes that add to the aromatic complexity. Entry is satiny smooth, delicately corny sweet, and fruity (raisins, prunes); midpalate is profound, multilayered, corn cereal sweet, and honeyed. Aftertaste is long, buttery, and bittersweet. Fabulous.

2014 Rating: ★★★★★/Highest Recommendation

Four Roses 2014 11 Year Old Single Barrel Recipe OESF Barrel Strength KSBW 60% abv, $80.

Burnished-orange color; perfect purity. Opening whiffs pick up toasted marshmallow, dry breakfast cereal, corn fritter fragrances that are harmonious, complex, elegant; the barrel strength power never inhibits the aroma or eclipses the scents as the whiskey aerates; secondary sniffs detect buttercream, cocoa, marzipan. Entry is sublimely supple, satiny in texture, robust without being overpowering, fruity (dried apricot, black raisins), intensely corny; midpalate is sweeping in flavor latitude and depth as deeply woody, grainy, vegetal, spicy tastes of tomato paste, BBQ sauce, molasses, oaky vanilla, caramelized onion, dark choco-late, and espresso vie for dominance through the luxuriant aftertaste. Magnificent whiskey from one of the great whiskey distilleries on the planet. Lip-smacking great.

2015 Rating: ★★★★★/Highest Recommendation

Four Roses 2014 Small Batch Barrel Strength KSBW 60% abv, $80.

Deep copper color; flawless clarity. Wow, this opening nose offers hugely impressive smells of candy shop, nougat, dark caramel, chocolate-covered coffee bean, sweet corn; later sniffs after further air contact reveal baked pear, caramel corn, salted dark chocolate;

a fabulous bouquet of multidimensional depth and elegance. Entry is maple and tree-sap bittersweet, zesty, nutty; midpalate reaffirms entry findings and expands the profile by adding almond butter/paste, sea salt, old dark honey. Incredibly complex and concentrated all through the rewarding, maple-like aftertaste. Another Jim Rutledge classic.
2015 Rating: ★ ★ ★ ★ ★/Highest Recommendation

Four Roses KSBW 40% abv, $20.
Amber/topaz color; clean as a whistle. First nosings after the pour pick up intensely corn-like scents that remind me of Cracker Jack caramel corn candy as well as Danish pastries filled with almond paste; secondary whiffs encounter deeper fragrances of corn husk, new leather, damp hay, and dried flowers. Entry is semi-rich in texture, off-dry to bittersweet in surface taste, and shows a nut-like, moderately oily core flavor that's reminiscent of grain kernel and graham cracker; midpalate adequately reflects the entry, adding tangy baking spice elements of cinnamon and clove. Finishes remarkably long and lip-smacking for a frontline KSBW. Very good value.
2018 Rating: ★ ★ ★/Recommended

Four Roses Single Barrel Warehouse HW/Barrel No. 48-4K KSBW 50% abv, $40.
The pretty bronze color unfortunately has far more floating debris/sediment than I like to see in a forty-dollar whiskey. Initial inhalations detect deep fragrances of dark caramel, sautéed mushrooms, pecan pie, and chocolate-covered orange rind; secondary sniffs are treated to bakery-shop aromas, including prune Danish, sourdough bread, vanilla bean, clove, and custard tart. Entry is round, supple, richly textured, and raisiny bittersweet; midpalate highlights the black raisin and prune aspects, as well as the candied features, which taste of hard candies from Jolly Rancher. Concludes a little briefer than I anticipated, bittersweet, and Dr Pepper–like. Overall, considering the producer, this is a disappointment that leads me to think that this particular barrel was substandard. From the scoring history of previous editions, this whiskey should rate at the minimum four stars.
2018 Rating: ★ ★ ★/Recommended

Four Roses Small Batch Barrel Strength KSBW 54.25% abv, $126.
The henna/new-copper color is sparkling and flawlessly clean. Opening whiffs offer a wide array of harmonious scents, starting with caramel corn, butcher's wax paper, limestone, flint, and yellow grapefruit; secondary inhalations pick up subtle notes of oak/wood, vegetable oil, and toffee—a fully integrated bouquet. Entry is splendidly textured and silky while the flavor profile is bountifully populated with tannic, fresh, intensely grainy/corn-like flavors; midpalate features red cherry compote, vanilla fudge, honey, and is every bit as fruity as it is grainy and woody—remarkable flavor balance throughout. Finishes long, decidedly bittersweet, sumptuous, and simply delicious. How does this distillery keep making such landmark whiskeys?
2016 Rating: ★ ★ ★ ★ ★/Highest Recommendation

Four Roses Small Batch KSBW 45% abv, $35.
Fulvous brown color; superb purity. My initial aromatic impressions are of oak plank flooring, sawdust, lumber yard, and aged rum; later inhalations after more aeration connect

with subtle scents of toasted sourdough bread, egg cream, vanilla soda, and brown sugar; not a terribly expressive bouquet. Entry is keenly piquant, baking spice–like, and peppery right from the first sip that accentuates the deep graininess; midpalate is bittersweet, honey-like, chocolate-covered cherry–like, and resiny/oaky. Aftertaste echoes the midpalate, lasting medium long in the throat.

2018 Rating: ★ ★ ★ ★/Highly Recommended

George Dickel Barrel Select Tennessee Sour Mash Whiskey 43% abv, $39.

Brilliant copper color; unblemished clarity. First sniffs encounter round, supple, corny notes that are more breakfast cereal–like than corn on the cob or canned corn; later whiffs pick up resiny/oaky notes that add complexity and brown-butter fragrance. Entry is toffee-like, with foundational notes of brown sugar, clove; midpalate is resiny/woody, with a twinge of sharpness in the finish.

2016 Rating: ★ ★ ★/Recommended

George Dickel Bottled-in-Bond Tennessee Sour Mash Whiskey 50% abv, $36.

Burnt-orange color; ideal clarity. Up front, I respond favorably to the seed-like, deeply grainy and buttery/fatty aroma that sets the stage nicely; secondary inhalations pick up more bread-like, sourdough crust–like scents as well as oak notes of sawdust, plank, and resin that work well with the bread-like core fragrance. Entry is creamy in texture, slightly piquant, black pepper–like, and even a touch prickly, but I appreciate the vivacious personality of it; midpalate introduces a semisweet, candy shop, caramel flavor, fudgy taste that's disarming and weighty. Aftertaste echoes the palate stage, as the profile turns more bittersweet, charred, and BBQ sauce–like. A handsome bottled-in-bond offering from Tullahoma, Tennessee.

2019 Rating: ★ ★ ★ ★/Highly Recommended

George Dickel No. 1 Foundation Recipe White Corn Whiskey 45.5% abv, $22.

Mineral-water clarity. Toasty, roasted cereal grains, caramel corn, textile fibers, and matchstick aromas explode from the glass in the first whiffs; air contact slowly evolves the toastiness into burnt fiber, burlap, and corn silo smells. Entry is burnt, intensely toasted grain, charred corn on the cob off the grill, sweet like BBQ sauce and tomato paste; midpalate mirrors entry, adding hoisin sauce, soy sauce, molasses. I'm not a white dog fan, but this quirky dog works better than many of them.

2015 Rating: ★ ★ ★/Recommended

George Dickel No. 8 Tennessee Sour Mash Whiskey 43% abv, $39.

Bright amber color; excellent purity. Gentle smells of creamed corn, spice cake, ginger in initial inhalations; later on, I get easy scents of canned pineapple, hazelnut. Entry is delicate, spicy/peppery, semisweet, marshmallow-like; midpalate follows through on all entry tastes, leading to nicely spicy, confectioner's-shop aftertaste.

2017 Rating: ★ ★ ★/Recommended

George Dickel Rye Whisky 45% abv, $25.

Mashbill is 95 percent rye, one of the highest rye content whiskeys available. Bright

topaz/amber color; excellent clarity. The first nosings encounter almost fruity fragrances of figs and nuts, then it turns spicy and peppery in the later sniffs following six minutes of air contact. Entry is succulent, toasty, and moderately spicy; midpalate shows a slightly sweeter side of the taste profile, offering exceedingly pleasant dark caramel, honey, and sweetened breakfast cereal flavors that unite in the satisfying finish.
2014 Rating: ★ ★ ★ ★/Highly Recommended

Golden State California Corn Whiskey 45.4% abv, $39.

One hundred percent California-grown corn. Pot still distillation. Transparent; sediment-free purity. This opening aroma is marginally sweeter and more corn-like than that of this distiller's vodka, which is slightly more reined in; this is intensely corny, husk-like, vegetal, and strikingly like unbuttered, grilled corn on the cob. Entry is corndog all the way, with an interesting buttermilk batter–like underpinning flavor; midpalate is cornfield-in-August thick with fresh corn kernel flavor and little else.
2016 Rating: ★ ★ ★/Recommended

Grand Traverse Islay Straight Rye Whiskey 45% abv, $49.

Butterscotch color/totally sediment-free. First nosing passes after the pour unearth scents akin to textile fiber/rayon, candle wax, furniture polish, oak plank, and sawdust; further inhalations following more air contact encounter the identical menu of aromas as the initial sniffs, with the only addition being a meager trace of dry cereal. Entry reveals a keenly peppery, waxy flavor that's odd and unappealing; midpalate echoes the entry and it's here where I say "enough." Do the words "God-awful" or "nightmarish" mean anything to you?
2019 Rating: ★/Not Recommended

Grand Traverse Ole George Double Barrel Straight Rye Whiskey 46.5% abv, $64.

Tawny color/spotlessly clean. Initial whiffs detect slight, frightfully lean aromas of oak resin, rayon, textile fiber, and grain husk; extra time in the glass doesn't assist one iota as the aromatics offer only faint hints of dry grain, onion peel, and vinyl furniture coverings. Entry is as dismal as the go-nowhere aroma, and that I find ludicrous; midpalate shows a bit more personality in the dry forms of breakfast cereal, seedless rye bread, and puff pastry, but where's the spiciness of rye or the seductive vanilla notes from oak? Finishes as poorly as it smells and tastes. Wretched. Grand Traverse, how could you release this whiskey?
2019 Rating: ★/Not Recommended

Grand Traverse Ole George Straight Rye Whiskey 46.5% abv, $54.

Sinopia color/ideal clarity. I pick up barely perceptible hints of cereal grain that are crowded out by the textile fiber, hemp, new rope-like aromas that are limp; another period of air contact fails to stimulate more than the faint cereal grain. Entry tastes most like lead pencil, metal, nickel, and dry stone, with no evidence of grain or wood to speak of; midpalate has no effect that's positive, and that's what I can't understand about this whiskey from a renowned craft distiller who's been around the block. This awkward whiskey is inexcusably miserable and bleak.
2019 Rating: ★/Not Recommended

Grand Traverse Ole George Whiskey 100% Straight Rye Whiskey 46.5% abv, $54.

Attractive amber color; excellent purity. First nosing finds desert-dry hints of caraway, rye bread, Ryvita crackers, straw, oak; later sniffs unearth additional scents, including camphor, black pepper. Entry is smooth, snappy, peppery, spicy, savory; midpalate highlights the rye bread element as well as the black pepper.

2015 Rating: ★ ★ ★/Recommended

Grand Traverse Straight Bourbon 46% abv, $54.

Ochre color/unblemished clarity. Opening sniffs encounter distant, tanky aromas that are metallic and flinty, showing only hints of cereal grain and oak; secondary inhalations after more aeration fail to detect anything more than butcher's wax paper and oatmeal. Entry improves the experience moderately, as the first evidence of corn appears in the flavor profile, but there's not much else going on here; midpalate brings a touch of oakiness to the dance in the forms of bacon fat and nutmeg. Concludes medium long, sweet corn–like (at last!), sinewy in texture, and baked.

2019 Rating: ★ ★/Not Recommended

Heaven Hill 27 Year Old Small Batch Barrel Proof KSBW 47.35% abv, $399.

Rufous/rust color; impeccably pure. Up front, the tight, narrow aromatic focus is clearly on the charred oak barrel impact, as ligneous fragrances of tobacco ash, soot, cellulose, tree bark, and lipids reign supreme in the arboreal opening inhalations; after another ten minutes of air contact, the bouquet marginally opens the aromatic door to let escape light fragrances of corn husk, polenta, and cornmeal, but that's all. Entry is remarkably buttery/oily, fat and viscous in texture due naturally to the unusually long duration of barrel aging, which stimulates a deep bittersweet flavor profile that's more grainy than fruity but somehow incomplete; midpalate proves to be the apex moment for this elder statesman, but nonetheless, to my taste at least, it has skated well along on the downside of its life cycle, and therefore is more of an over-oaked clunker than a mature jewel.

2018 Rating: ★ ★/Not Recommended

Heaven Hill 7 Year Old Bottled-in-Bond KSBW 50% abv, $40.

Medium brown/old gold color; perfect clarity. I like the first olfactory impressions, which are tight, focused on the mashbill's corn element, and integrated; more air contact lifts the later fragrances into the bakery-shop arena of baked fruits, apple strudel, mincemeat pie, and prune Danish; this is a seriously attractive KSB bouquet. Entry is firmly structured, drier than the aroma, focused tightly on the sweet corn/caramel corn/Cracker Jack character; midpalate is buttery/creamy, seductively round and supple, oaky but neither tannic nor resiny. Finish echoes the midpalate, but turns up the alcohol heat a couple of notches as the sensory experience ends with a soft explosion of corn-syrup flavor.

2019 Rating: ★ ★ ★ ★/Highly Recommended

Heaven's Door The Bootleg Series 2019 American Whiskey 55.75% abv, $500.

Golden/grain-harvest color; pristine clarity. Nose is crisp, grainy, and fruity right from the get-go; later sniffs bring up crème caramel, butterscotch, sawdust, and light honey. Entry

is tight, resiny/woody, toasty, and dry; midpalate owns a sinewy texture that tastes bitter-sweet and a touch smoky. Long, woody, toasted marshmallow–like, and smoky.
2020 Rating: ★ ★ ★ ★/Highly Recommended

High West Double Rye—A Blend of Straight Rye Whiskeys 46% abv, $35.
Sandy-brown/wheat-field color; excellent purity. Up front, I pick up beeswax, parchment, and kiwi-like aromas that are agile and lean; secondary whiffs detect more of the beeswax and now butcher's wax paper and candle wax—whither the grain and/or the oak? Entry is mineral-like (lead pencil), stone dry, and finally grainy, but the overall first taste impression is of wet stone/minerals; midpalate comes to the rescue as the rye aspect at last emerges, offering a mellow clove-like, spice cake flavor that delivers the recommendation. Concludes zesty, oaky, and rye bread–like.
2018 Rating: ★ ★ ★/Recommended

High West Rendezvous Rye—A Blend of Straight Rye Whiskeys 46% abv, $80.
Attractive copper color; perfect clarity. First aromatic impressions orbit around the core scent of toasted rye bread, with the satellite fragrances being cherry-filled pastry, allspice, and brown sugar; after more aeration, the aroma turns bittersweet, spicier than the initial pass, and peppery. Entry is sinewy in texture, piquant, savory, and cooking oil–like; midpalate is lean, black peppercorn–like, resiny, dusty dry, and woody. Finishes medium long, lightly toasted, properly grainy/rye-like, and narrowly focused. If this blended straight rye were mine, I'd add a rye that had a bigger, lusher profile to fill in the vacant spaces.
2018 Rating: ★ ★ ★/Recommended

High West Yippee Ki-Yay—A Blend of Straight Rye Whiskeys 46% abv, $100.
The mahogany color is gorgeously rich and sediment-free; a visually pleasing whiskey. There's an appealing floral/dried-flower aspect to the opening inhalations that is almost perfume-like; that unusual characteristic turns positively fruity/fruit salad–like with more air contact as the aroma transforms into a round bouquet, full of kiwi, apricot fragrances that swell with aeration. Entry is deeply fruity, red cherry–like, with a hint of baked and spiced red apple; midpalate turns a touch like sweetened breakfast cereal with dried fruit and is as sweet as black cherry juice. Finishes sweetly, ripe, herbal, and juicy fruity. A serious departure for a rye whiskey but I like it quite a lot.
2016 Rating: ★ ★ ★ ★/Highly Recommended

Highspire Whiskey 40% abv, $46.
This whiskey is produced from 100 percent heirloom rye and is twice distilled in a pot still. The fresh spirit is then matured for four months in barrels that formerly housed wine. Pretty topaz/new leather–like color; perfect clarity. Opening nosings detect dense, intense, deeply grainy aromas that have traces of paraffin, snack cracker, and dry breakfast cereal; secondary whiffs discover elements of porridge and rye bread. Entry is off-dry, lightly toasted, and the back end of the entry offers a nuance of red wine ripeness that I find appealingly complementary to the potent rye presence; midpalate finds that the winey-ness accelerates quite a bit so that by the time the evaluation is morphing from

midpalate to finish, the grapiness is almost jammy/juicy, which marries deliciously with the rye foundation.

2016 Rating: ★ ★ ★ ★/Highly Recommended

Hillrock Estate Double Cask Rye Whiskey 45% abv, $90.

Bright new-copper/henna color; sediment-free clarity. All sorts of spiciness is going on in the first inhalations, all of which are baking spices—nutmeg, clove; later sniffs detect butterscotch, cooking oil, freshly ground nutmeg, parchment. Entry is oaky sweet, with vanilla and seedless rye bread tastes; midpalate is bread doughy, delicately sweet but more spicy than sweet, especially in the aftertaste, where the flavor detonates on the tongue.

2016 Rating: ★ ★ ★ ★/Highly Recommended

Hillrock Estate Single Malt Whiskey 48.2% abv, $115.

Deep-amber/topaz color; flawless purity. I smell deep and completely dry concentrations of grain kernel, hemp/rope, toasted malt in opening whiffs; later on, I detect old leather, men's club/library, burlap aromas. Entry is dusty dry, intensely grainy to the point of being fruity; midpalate is caramel-like, toasty, slightly smoky, rich, viscous, honeyed—the best part of the experience. Finishes a bit fat, creamy, honey-like.

2016 Rating: ★ ★ ★ ★/Highly Recommended

Hillrock Estate Solera Aged Bourbon 46.3% abv, $80.

Aged in American oak barrels and finished in sherry oak casks. Attractive amber color; excellent clarity. First aromas after the pour call to mind toasty/roasted scents of linseed oil, soybean, tobacco, legumes, and butcher's wax paper—there's a whole slew of intriguing aromatics going on here; following eight minutes of further aeration, the nose turns decidedly bittersweet, oaky, grainy, and dusty dry. Entry is beautifully balanced, toffee sweet, pipe tobacco–like, and honeyed from the sherry influence; midpalate is even nicer as the taste profile goes slightly more toasty and nutty (almond paste, really). Aftertaste is supple in texture, measured in its sweetness, and scrumptiously integrated. Great job by Master Distiller Dave Pickerell. A Hudson Valley, New York, craft whiskey beauty.

2015 Rating: ★ ★ ★ ★ ★/Highest Recommendation

Hirsch Small Batch Reserve Straight Bourbon 46% abv, $40.

Bronze color; very good clarity. This opening aroma is subtle and understated as compared to other Hirsch whiskeys I've reviewed in past years, but the grain core is solid and as dry as a desert; more air contact changes the dynamic of this bouquet as the oxygen rustles up savory aromas of palm oil, pinto bean, wood shavings, and sweet corn. Entry is supple, rich in texture, bittersweet, and tree sap–like; midpalate mixes the sappiness with the corn foundation, getting a sweetened cornflakes cereal base flavor that's the ideal platform for lesser tastes, such as honey, allspice, black peppercorn. Finishes medium long, acutely peppery, and substantial. Really like the powerful finish.

2016 Rating: ★ ★ ★ ★/Highly Recommended

Hochstadter's Vatted Straight Rye Whiskey (USA/Canada) 50% abv, $35.

Topaz/amber color; excellent purity. I favorably respond to the first whiffs that are nicely juicy, moderately spiced with black pepper, thyme, and marjoram, while the graininess keeps the aromatics dry and dusty; following more aeration, the toasted grain component makes a strong case for dominance as the juiciness subsides. Entry is off-dry to bittersweet, intensely grainy, mildly spicy, and moderately dense in texture; midpalate is where the taste profile takes off as generous, crisply acidic, and fresh flavors of dates, figs, mincemeat, and apple crumble come into play. Aftertaste shows some woodiness that pleasingly balances with the fruitiness and bittersweet rye. A welcome, affordable entry into the crowded North American rye whiskey sweepstakes.

2016 Rating: ★ ★ ★ ★/Highly Recommended

Hooker's House Finished in Pinot Noir Barrels Sonoma-Style Bourbon 50% abv, $36.

Wow, this is a stunningly attractive copper-colored whiskey with flawless clarity. The initial whiffs of this whiskey are all about black pepper, assertive but not aggressive spirit, pipe tobacco, and roasted cereals; additional time in glass brings out deeper fragrances of dates, raisins (the wine barrels?), brown sugar, and big-time, zesty nutmeg. Entry is full-on in its spiritiness, but is also baked and caramel-like while not in the least being cloying; midpalate is lip-smacking sweet and toasty and alluringly winey without being juicy or fruity; the grain is never overshadowed by the pinot noir barreling aspect. Aftertaste is tight, bakery-shop bittersweet, toffee-like, and honeyed.

2014 Rating: ★ ★ ★ ★/Highly Recommended

Hooker's House Finished in Zinfandel Barrels Sonoma-Style Rye Whiskey 47% abv, $36.

The amber/flaxen hue is pretty and unblemished by sediment. Oh man, the zinfandel influence is unmistakable in the opening inhalations after the pour—by that I mean that there are obvious scents of raisins, blackberry, and grape seeds; further aeration time stimulates an entrancing grain/grape perfume that's not sweet but ripe and is restrained in its oakiness. Entry is remarkably sap-like, viny, and wine-like, as the zinfandel impact leaves no guessing as to its influence; midpalate is pleasingly rye bread–like but is still a stage for the juicy zinfandel. Finishes nicely as the grain and grape finally integrate into a married impression. There is clear quality here. If it were mine, though, I'd dial back the wine barrel by 33 percent.

2014 Rating: ★ ★ ★/Recommended

Hudson Baby Bourbon 46% abv, $45/375 ml.

Beautiful henna/bronze color; sediment-free. This aroma is all sweet corn and corn syrup in the initial inhalations, along with floral/leafy elements that add freshness; secondary nosings following seven more minutes of air contact discover multilayered aromas that include honey wheat toast, maple syrup, allspice, and loose leaf tobacco. Entry is sweet, like creamed corn, and honey-like; midpalate is far more expansive in the spices, especially vanilla and nutmeg, plus buttered and salted corn on the cob. Finish is sophisticated, layered, medium long, nougaty, and roasted.

2017 Rating: ★ ★ ★ ★/Highly Recommended

Hudson Four Grain Bourbon Oak 46% abv, $45/375 ml.

Pretty topaz/amber color; unblemished purity. This opening bouquet is very complex, dry, and intensely grain-driven more than wood-driven; following another seven minutes of air contact, the aroma expands to become a dry breakfast cereal mélange as well as a dried yellow fruit, biscuit affair. Entry is toasty, grainy, and dusty; midpalate is more animated with flavors of snack crackers, salt, pipe tobacco, and brown sugar. Finish is narrowly focused on the grains, yet the wood influence starts to shine through at last in the distinctive form of vanilla. The rare whiskey that allows these divergent grains to meld into one luscious flavor. Others have tried and failed. This four-grain is superb.

2016 Rating: ★ ★ ★ ★/Highly Recommended

Hudson Manhattan Rye Whiskey 46% abv, $45/375 ml.

Very pretty russet/auburn color; flawless purity. I like the first aromas of this whiskey a lot as they highlight the natural spiciness of rye and the vanilla aspect of the American oak, making for crisp, nicely acidic, and tangy aromas; second round of sniffings after further aeration time finds the aroma more bread-like and pastry-like than in the first inhalations, and there's also a keen spiciness that leans heavily towards coconut. Entry is honeyed, woody, sap-like, and deliciously balanced; midpalate showcases this whiskey's complexity as the bread element turns tobacco- and cigar-like. Aftertaste is medium long, spicy, and moderately oily.

2017 Rating: ★ ★ ★ ★/Highly Recommended

Hudson New York Corn Whiskey 46% abv, $35/375 ml.

Ideally transparent and clear of sediment or debris. Smells immediately of cornflakes, corn on the cob, and beeswax; another six minutes of air contact stimulates other scents, mostly white flour, shale, and beets. Entry is gently sweet and corn syrup–like, then at midpalate the flavor profile turns meatier and bigger in texture and spiciness. BIG CORN, BIG FLAVOR, but there's also a creaminess to it that works in an integrated manner. As white whiskeys go, quite restrained and focused.

2018 Rating: ★ ★ ★/Recommended

Hudson Single Malt Whiskey 46% abv, $45/375 ml.

Amber/honey color; superb clarity. Opening whiffs detect toasted bread and a cedary/cigar box scent that's alluring and totally dry and grainy; another seven minutes of exposure to air introduce an acute old leather fragrance that's reminiscent of entering a library filled with old books. Entry is desert dry, dusty, and cherry preserves–like; midpalate plays up the dried red fruit aspect as the focus shifts back to the grain, which is just a touch smoky. Aftertaste mirrors the midpalate as the profile goes in the direction of the barley malt and away from the oak sap and vanilla. If you're thinking that this is a Scotch single malt knockoff, you'll be disappointed because it is not in the least evocative of Scotch. It is its own creature and a stand-alone whiskey.

2017 Rating: ★ ★ ★/Recommended

I.W. Harper 15 Year Old KSBW 43% abv, $75.

Eye-catching new-copper color; excellent purity. First aromatic burst I get in the inhalations after the pour is an acute nuttiness that's compelling, dry, and toasty; further aeration brings out scents of new leather, butcher's wax paper, nougat (that nuttiness again), sawdust, roasted grains. Entry is sedate, balanced, dry to off-dry, lightly toasted, genteel, elegant, but deeply flavorful—don't be fooled into thinking that there isn't multilayered complexity here because there's a ton of it; midpalate echoes the entry except for a ratcheting up of the sweetness to a toffee-like level that's disarming and harmonious. Finishes roasted, integrated, deliciously dry, and crisp.

2016 Rating: ★ ★ ★ ★ ★/Highest Recommendation

Isaac Bowman Port Finished Small Batch Straight Bourbon 46% abv, $40.

Fetching tawny/honey color; superb clarity. The port barrel finishing is apparent right from the opening sniffs, which are winey, grapy, onion-like, and delicately spiced with faint hints of cinnamon, black peppercorn, and clove; following further aeration, the bouquet turns slightly smoked, meaty (baked ham, especially), roasted grain–like, and biscuity. Entry is delightfully tart, astringent, cereal-like, and spicy (deep tastes of cinnamon stick, clove, allspice); midpalate is where the best action on this whiskey is, as dense flavors of dark caramel, honey, and cocoa bean are accented with the pruny, date-like, nicely bittersweet contribution of the port barrel. Finishes medium long, peppery, piquant, and solid.

2018 Rating: ★ ★ ★ ★/Highly Recommended

J.H. Cutter Whisky 48% abv, $50.

A blend from Hotaling & Co. in San Francisco of 73 percent Kentucky bourbon, 17 percent Old Potrero 18th Century Style, and 10 percent Old Potrero Rye Whiskey Port Barrel Finish. Bronze color; very clean appearance. Evidence of the corn-based bourbon is immediately obvious as the aroma comes across like cornhusk, tamale/cornmeal, slightly sweet, and toffee-like; later sniffs pick up traces of chocolate-covered cherries and prune Danish fragrances. Entry continues the bourbon-induced corniness but there's also a faint hint of the port barrel in the continuance of the prune-like aspect; midpalate goes all out for more significant sweetness, as the corn and prune elements dominate from this point deep into the honeyed, raisiny aftertaste. This whiskey's flavor arc just got better with every stage of development.

2019 Rating: ★ ★ ★ ★/Highly Recommended

J. Henry & Sons Cask Strength Wisconsin Straight Bourbon 60% abv, $75.

Perfectly clean and clear of sediment; deep, henna/auburn color. Grain intensity is pronounced in the first nosing pass as are earthy, soil-like attributes that are dusty dry and almost brittle and leathery; second passes discover corn husk, tamale, cornmeal aromas that are a little spicy, cocoa bean–like, doughy, dried berry–like and waxy. Powerful entry flavors are influenced by the elevated abv and possess sideline tastes of bread dough, yeast, dark chocolate, cinnamon; midpalate stage is where this bourbon soars as the abv settles down, allowing for radiant tastes of corn syrup, creamed corn, caramel, vanilla bean, and burnt sugar to shine. Finishes long, more bittersweet than sweet like burnt sugar, with shades of dark caramel, honey, toasted corn bread, flaxseed oil. A true bourbon heavyweight for seasoned veterans and creative bartenders who'll know what matching ingredients will accentuate its depth of character.

2016 Rating: ★ ★ ★ ★/Highly Recommended

J. Henry & Sons Wisconsin Straight Bourbon 46% abv, $50.

Attractive hazel/topaz color; free of sediment, and I can see oils in the core. Right after

the pour, the strong smell of corn bread, cornmeal, and unbuttered corn on the cob are apparent as the aroma leans to the drier side of the dryness/sweetness scale; additional time in the glass brings out aromas of lead pencil, limestone/chalk, bread dough, black raisins, brown sugar—the final impressions are of new car leather, orange pekoe tea, toasted corn bread. Entry flashes an amazing cereal lift along with alluring flavors of toffee, dry breakfast cereal, nutmeg, allspice, roasted almond, caramel; midpalate features a drier, crisper taste profile than the entry and is slightly more oily. Aftertaste is mineral-like, chalky/stony, with supplemental accents of oak resin/tree sap, maple, and is totally dry. Classy, elegant, focused, and toasty.
2015 Rating: ★ ★ ★ ★/Highly Recommended

J.R. Revelry Handcrafted Small Batch Bourbon 45% abv, $35.

Distilled in Indiana. Attractive, bright amber/topaz color; superb purity. Smells appealingly of pimento, black pepper, red cherry, white raisin, oak; second-stage whiffs find a marginally sweeter aroma complete with peanut butter, huckleberry notes; solid, pleasing bouquet. Entry is a touch sharp, lead pencil–like, lightly toasted, resiny, metallic, bold; midpalate offers a more expansive, less aggressive flavor profile of baking spices (allspice, clove), dried berries, raisins, prune, figs. Ends dry, acutely spicy/peppercorn-like, deeply oaky.
2015 Rating: ★ ★ ★/Recommended

Jack Daniel's Old No. 7 Tennessee Sour Mash Whiskey 40% abv, $30.

Fulvous color; excellent clarity. First nosing passes don't pick up much as the opening aroma is a bit muted, except for a feathery hint of corn bread; additional aeration assists in bolstering the aroma through more animated scents of sawdust, lumberyard, pine nuts, and unsweetened cornflakes—just not a lot happening here in terms of aromatic definition. Entry is sap-like, gently corn syrup–like, mildly spicy, and altogether pleasant if basic; midpalate shows more character as the taste profile turns honey-like, dried fruit–like (pear, apricot, black raisins), and lightly toasted. In all, a decent whiskey quaff that is well made but just a bit too lightweight and lacking in aromatics to be recommended.
2018 Rating: ★ ★/Not Recommended

Jack Daniel's Single Barrel Tennessee Sour Mash Whiskey 67.3% abv, $65.

Color is an eye-catching burnt sienna/deep auburn; superb clarity. Feral opening aromas charge from the glass in semisweet waves of dried chrysanthemum, pomegranate, red cherry, cedar plank; second whiffs detect a pleasing grapiness that's raisiny and woody at the same time as the abv comes more into play. Entry is round, satiny in texture, leafy, vegetal, fiery on the edges of the palate, yet juicy and orchard-fruit ripe; midpalate is oily, creamy, lush, oaky, spicy (vanilla extract), resiny, raisiny, juicy, tobacco-like. Finishes long, ripe, fruity, and medium hot. I've always liked JD Single Barrel bottlings.
2015 Rating: ★ ★ ★ ★/Highest Recommendation

Jack Daniel's Tennessee Rested Straight Rye Whiskey 40% abv, $50.

Mashbill of 70 percent rye; 18 percent corn; 12 percent malted barley. Bright amber color; pristine clarity. Delicate cola nut scent opens up the aromatic stage, followed by a green-apple fragrance that's bolder suddenly than the cola nut; further air contact brings out pear, yellow plum, white raisin odors that are fresh and youthful. Entry accentuates the orchard fruit element as the taste profile goes acidic; midpalate sees the fruit flavors fade quickly, being replaced by an acute graininess that's especially spicy and tangy. Clearly immature, and I can't help but think that another year in oak would nicely and adequately round off the fruit acid edge.

2015 Rating: ★ ★/Not Recommended

Jack Daniel's Unaged Tennessee Rye Mash Whiskey 40% abv, $50.

Flawless purity. Opening smells introduce immediate earthy/mossy punch, with hints of vinyl, rayon fiber, and salty shale/calcareous soil notes; following another seven minutes of aeration, the aroma turns kernel-like/beany, especially pinto and kidney beans. Entry is silky smooth, creamy, and moderately sweet, which I find surprising since it's rye grain; midpalate is even more pleasing than the entry as the taste profile accelerates to high-grade graininess and peppery/spicy flavors that turn succulent and round in the appealing, medium long, and fruity (dried apricot) finish.

2014 Rating: ★ ★ ★/Recommended

Jefferson's Ocean Voyage 15 Aged at Sea Straight Bourbon 45% abv, $100.

Bronze color; totally clean and free from sediment. The opening sniffs detect dry, grainy, snack cracker aromas that are resiny/oaky and sawdust-like; secondary inhalations after more time in the glass encounter slightly spicy aromas that are reminiscent of salted Wheat Thins crackers and light, new honey. Entry is pleasingly dry, fresh, clean, crisp, and tannic; midpalate offers round, supple flavors that are toastier than those found in the entry and oilier (a positive). Finishes long, juicy, elegant, off-dry, and just slightly like creamed corn.

2018 Rating: ★ ★ ★ ★/Highly Recommended

Jefferson's Presidential Select 21 Year Old Straight Bourbon 47% abv, $130.

Gorgeous, brilliant new-copper color; unblemished purity. Wow, the delicately sweet cornmeal and baking spice (cinnamon) rush of aroma in the initial whiffs after the pour is highly compelling and classy; seven more minutes of air contact reveal more depth of character in the forms of nougat, chocolate-covered cherry, and caramelized onion; an epic tour de force bouquet. Entry is stunningly oily (a huge positive), deeply nutty (walnut), buttery/creamy, and simply luscious; midpalate reflects everything discovered in the entry, adding lip-smacking notes of toasted marshmallow and peanut butter. Finishes in a bittersweet manner that's nutty and oaky.

2015 Rating: ★ ★ ★ ★ ★/Highest Recommendation

Jefferson's Reserve Groth Reserve Cask Finish KSBW 45.1% abv, $80.

Finished in French oak barrels that previously aged cabernet sauvignon from the famed Groth Vineyards in Oakville, Napa Valley, California. The color of this whiskey is brilliant orange/ginger/cinnamon; unblemished purity. Initially, I smell paraffin, oaky tannins, wax paper, pear juice, and hints of vanilla, clove; after more time in the glass, I at last unearth soft scents of grapes, grape preserves, amidst the waxy tobacco leaf and leather. Entry is juicy, spicy (baking spices mostly, such as vanilla bean, nutmeg, clove), grapy, yet nicely corny at the same time; in the midpalate, the oak comes to the forefront as the taste profile turns

seriously succulent, candy shop–like, caramelly, fudge-like, buttery, and totally yummy. The finish trails off a bit, but the overall impression is of very good quality.
2015 Rating: ★ ★ ★ ★/Highly Recommended

Jim Beam Bonded KSBW 50% abv, $23.

Bright burnt-orange/sienna color; impeccable clarity. Sweet corn, sweet corn, and more sweet corn in the straightforward but highly pleasurable opening aroma; this is followed by scents of corn syrup, creamed corn, and caramel corn in the later whiffs. Entry is round, warming, toasted, corny, and inviting; midpalate advances all the no-nonsense charm found in the bouquet and entry as the flavor profile turns chewy in texture, honeyed, oaky, vanilla bean–like, roasted. Finishes medium long, embers-warm, nutty, buttery, creamy.
2015 Rating: ★ ★ ★ ★/Highly Recommended

Jim Beam Distiller's Masterpiece Finished in PX Sherry Casks KSBW 50% abv, $200.

The color alone, a beautiful mahogany/chestnut-brown with russet core highlights, tells its own story about the Pedro Ximénez influence; impeccable clarity. Opening aromas are fruity, dried (black raisins, dates), baked, but not in the least sweet or sugary; further air contact brings out a pleasing nuttiness that goes well with the dried fruitiness, which in the second nosing turns tropical. Entry is bittersweet, acidic, clean, fruity, slightly honeyed, nutty/nougat-like; midpalate echoes the entry phase, but offers cigar box, clove, nutmeg, mace, and black pepper aspects that round out the flavor profile, giving it a zestiness that lasts deep into the cocoa-bean finish.
2015 Rating: ★ ★ ★ ★/Highly Recommended

Jim Beam Distiller's Masterpiece KSBW 50% abv, $199.

A whiskey that's been finished in sherry butts that used to age Pedro Ximénez sherry. Dark bronze/burnt-orange color; excellent purity. First nosings detect the PX sherry impact immediately in the form of date- and fig-like aromas that mingle nicely with bourbon's natural corny sweetness; the second passes after eight minutes of aeration encounter lush aromas of prunes, grape jam, and old oak. Entry is thickly textured, silky, succulent, and potent in its spirity warmth; midpalate highlights the pruny/raisiny aspect of the PX while not losing its bourbon core. Ends on a sweet, raisiny note that borders on being overplayed.
2016 Rating: ★ ★ ★ ★/Highly Recommended

Jim Beam Honey KSBW Infused with Natural Flavors 35% abv, $16.

Fourteen-karat-gold color; sediment-free. This nose is a little too closed off at first, giving up only a slight fruitiness; later inhalations discover nothing. Entry is honey sweet, succulent, fruity/grainy; midpalate highlights the engaging honey flavoring, which is more semisweet than flat-out sweet. In-mouth phases redeem the lackluster bouquet.
2014 Rating: ★ ★ ★/Recommended

Jim Beam KSBW 40% abv, $16.

Cocoa-brown color; impeccably pure. In the first nosing passes I pick up faint hints of corn syrup and brown sugar, plus a light touch of butcher's wax paper; more time in the glass allows the bouquet to open up, now featuring deft scents of margarine/cooking oil, sweet corn, and buttered popcorn. Entry is pleasantly spicy (ground black pepper), more bittersweet than flat-out corny sweet, and a touch oaky/resiny and vanilla-like; midpalate highlights the entry findings and throws in comforting flavors of prune Danish, nutmeg, and creamed corn. Aftertaste is this bourbon's best moment as the supple, satin-like finish provides loads of corny, oaky, toasted flavors that are delightful. Remains one of the best values in American whiskey.

2018 Rating: ★ ★ ★/Recommended

Jim Beam Maple KSBW Infused with Natural Flavors 35% abv, $16.

Pale gold color; clean. I get all the maple one could want from a flavored whiskey in the first sniffs; goes butterscotch in later inhalations. Entry is acutely maple-like and within a nanosecond I'm automatically thinking *pancakes*; midpalate is semisweet, not sweet, and judiciously maple-like, not over the top.

2014 Rating: ★ ★ ★/Recommended

Jim Beam Red Stag Hardcore Cider KSBW 40% abv, $35.

Pale topaz color; superb clarity. I like the up-front apple cider aroma, which is tart, zesty, peel-like, and not the least bit sweet. Entry is pleasingly tart, acidic, fresh; midpalate works well as the apple freshness merges nicely with the straight bourbon. Bourbon purists, get over it. Flavored whiskeys, like Red Stag, can be good and appealing to a younger crowd.

2014 Rating: ★ ★ ★/Recommended

Jim Beam Signature Craft 12 Year Old Small Batch KSBW 43% abv, $40.

Lovely bronze/burnished-orange hue; perfect clarity. I like the rich cornmeal, corn on the cob aromas that leap from the sampling copita immediately after the pour, letting you know without hesitation that this spirit could only be one thing—bourbon. Secondary whiffs following seven minutes more of aeration pick up faint traces of allspice, oak plank, and honey; a lusty bouquet that pleases. Entry features more of the spicy oak than the mash-bill grains and is therefore piquant and zesty in nature; midpalate, by contrast, showcases the fruity corn and rye in the formula that eclipse the oak presence, culminating in a satisfying finish that is beautifully balanced and elegant. All parts, from the right abv level to the right age to the superb aftertaste, are working in harmony.

2016 Rating: ★ ★ ★ ★ ★/Highest Recommendation

Jim Beam Signature Craft Quarter Cask Finished Small Batch KSBW 43% abv, $40.

This special Beam KSB has been accentuated with bourbon that was aged in small, newly charred, so-called "quarter casks" for four to eight years. The smaller barrels afford greater contact and absorption between whiskey and wood to the tune of about 30 percent, which increases complexity. Attractive goldenrod color; unblemished clarity. This opening aroma has caramel corn written all over it as well as hints of clove, baked pear, green melon, honey; secondary inhalations turn the corn aspect into more of a buttered corn on the cob presence. Entry is robust, peppery, spicy, more bittersweet than flat-out sweet, densely corn bread–like; midpalate brings out an intense woodiness, which is more oily than resiny. After-taste highlights the charred oak element, reminding me a little of BBQ sauce, tomato paste.

2015 Rating: ★ ★ ★ ★/Highly Recommended

Jim Beam Signature Craft Rare Spanish Brandy Finish Small Batch KSBW 43% abv, $40.

Topaz color; impeccable purity. Holy moly, there's a butterscotch convention happening in the opening nose of this stylized bourbon from Jim Beam; another eight minutes of air contact release an entire new set of aromas, including plums, mincemeat, nutmeg, clove, and cocoa bean. Entry is succulent, nougat-like, nutty, and intensely fruity; midpalate soars into the stratosphere in terms of deep flavor as robust, take-no-prisoners flavors of caramel, honey, plum preserves, figs, and coffee all pull the oars in unison. Finishes chewy, baked fruit sweet, and oily/buttery in texture.

2015 Rating: ★★★★★/Highest Recommendation

Jim Beam Single Barrel KSBW 47.5% abv, $35.

Maize/amber color; ideal clarity. Big, rich, corny notes are abundant in the first sniffs; to my delight, the elevated abv doesn't get in the way of the bouquet, which is pleasingly roasted, sawdust-like, elegant. Entry is lush, viscous, buttery/creamy, vanilla bean–like; midpalate reflects the entry perfectly, adding sweetened breakfast cereal, honey, snack cracker, English toffee. In the wake of the superb Signature Series bottlings, this marque continues Beam's current hot streak.

2016 Rating: ★★★★★/Highest Recommendation

John E. Fitzgerald 12 Year Old Very Special Reserve KSBW 45% abv, $300.

Spectacular tawny port/cinnamon color; impeccably clean. I'm getting all sorts of intense raisiny, plummy, caramel corn scents in the first inhalations that are leathery, deeply grainy, moderately spicy, and woody, but stunningly harmonious, evolved, and supple; second whiffs after more aeration serve to reinforce the first-stage findings and top them off with bakery-shop fragrances, mostly baked orchard fruits, candied nuts, dark caramel, cocoa bean. Entry is sap-like, maple-like, and more bittersweet than flat-out sugar sweet as the taste profile seems a little bit baked and BBQ sauce–like, even with a dollop of tomato paste; midpalate is more compact and focused than the wide-ranging entry as the profile turns biscuity, heavily toasted, and marzipan-like. Concludes dense, bittersweet, beautifully balanced, and at its peak maturity. Truly lovely and hearty, without being overly large.

2017 Rating: ★★★★★/Highest Recommendation

Johnny Drum Private Stock KSBW 50.5% abv, $38.

Bronze color; pristine clarity. Initial whiffs detect the slightest traces of TCA (trichloroanisole) mustiness, but thankfully that blows off in short order, leaving behind a dry, arid aroma that's deeply grainy, concentrated, and waxy; secondary inhalations are treated to a warming, toasty, marshmallow-like set of gently sweet fragrances that remind me most of nougat and my favorite old-time candy bar (Baby Ruth). Entry is bean-like, espresso-like, bitter, and complex; midpalate reaches for flavor in another direction that's separate from the bean-like entry, featuring more of a sweet grain, caramel corn, and marzipan taste that leads into the medium long, toasted marshmallow–like finish.

2020 Rating: ★★★/Recommended

Journeyman Not a King Rye Whiskey 45% abv, $49.

Mashbill is 60 percent rye/40 percent corn. Pretty sepia/cinnamon color; very good clarity. Wow, there's a keen spiciness in the first nosing pass that evolves into seeded (caraway) rye bread and new saddle leather; more aeration helps to develop deeper fragrances of rye snack cracker (Ryvita), rye bread, ground black pepper. Entry is sweeter, more sap-like and resiny than the bouquet and turns stunningly maple-like right before the midpalate stage; midpalate is caramelized, succulent, toasted, maple all over the place, and fabulously tasty. Finishes long, resiny/oaky, rich in texture, a little spiky alcoholwise, but luscious and creamy. A pinnacle achievement for this Michigan distiller.

2016 Rating: ★ ★ ★ ★ ★/Highest Recommendation

King of Kentucky 14 Year Old Single Barrel KSBW 62.5–72.5% abv, $199.

Note: The abv range varies from bottling to bottling from the sixteen dedicated barrels of this rare offering. Rusty-brown/tawny color; excellent clarity. Right off the crack of the aromatic bat I get truckloads of cigar tobacco scent, along with supporting whiffs of menthol, eucalyptus, tomato vine, and coffee grounds. The wildly idiosyncratic nature of this bouquet continues after more air contact as the aromatic compass now points in the direction of wild mushroom, brambles, Parmigiano-Reggiano, chai, green tea, and baker's wax paper; unlike any other straight bourbon bouquet in existence, and I love it. Entry is all bourbon business, all the time, as the flavor profile features stellar, if more predictable, tastes of caramel corn, creamed corn, pipe tobacco, vanilla bean, and maple syrup; midpalate mirrors the entry stage but adds succulent flavors of raisins, prune Danish, nougat, and mincemeat. Finishes in grand fashion as the wood-alcohol-grain-acidity elements merge into a singular flavor that exemplifies how breathtaking distilling and oak maturation in Kentucky can be. An instant classic and one for the ages.

2018 Rating: ★ ★ ★ ★ ★/Highest Recommendation

King of Kentucky 2019 Release KSBW 65.5% abv, $250.

Gorgeous cordovan/burnt umber color; perfect clarity. Holy moly, I detect full-throated aromas of prune Danish, applejack, pork rind, apple butter, milk chocolate, and latte in the opening inhalations; more air contact releases more fragrances, most notably, cola nut, Dr Pepper, bacon fat, lard, bean curd, chickpea, and maple syrup. Entry is soaring in alcohol richness, heat, and splendor while the flavor profile features heavily roasted and BBQ-like tastes of pork ribs, sweetened cereal (Cocoa Puffs?), honey buns, and loads of baking spices, especially allspice, mace, and clove; midpalate is succulent, toasted to the point of charring, tasting of seared meat and baked apple. Aftertaste is warm but neither hot nor burning, plush and creamy in texture, and flat-out luscious.

2019 Rating: ★ ★ ★ ★ ★/Highest Recommendation

Knob Creek 25th Anniversary KSBW 60.9% abv, $130.

Ochre/fulvous color; superb clarity. Considering the abv level of this bourbon, the opening nose is mute, except for a background note of citrus peel; further aeration brings out meatier aspects, primarily corn bread, brown sugar, allspice, and fresh, new honey. Entry reflects many of the aromatic findings, including the citrus peel, but there's also lemongrass, baked/grilled pineapple, sassafras, parsley, and bay leaf; midpalate highlights this whiskey's

corniness, mostly in the form of sweet, creamed corn, but there are likewise pungent tastes of cola, oak resins, bacon fat, watermelon, and lychee. Finishes a bit hot, sinewy in texture, peppery/spicy, toasted, and long. I've been an ardent advocate of Knob Creek since its birth a quarter century ago when Booker Noe introduced it to me in his Bardstown kitchen. For this commemorative edition, I would have liked to see a more bountiful aroma.
2017 Rating: ★ ★ ★ ★/Highly Recommended

KO Bare Knuckle American Rye Whiskey 45% abv, $46.

One hundred percent rye. Burnt sienna color; flawlessly clean. I get all sorts of intriguing scents here in the opening inhalations, including canvas, textile fiber, sesame seed, and seeded rye bread; later sniffs detect cardboard, rye snack crackers, and a delicate touch of citric acid (lemon peel). Entry showcases the rye grain in spades as the flavor profile is dominated by rye bread, honey, poppy seed, and dried apricot flavors; midpalate spiritiness fuels a pleasing, comforting campfire embers–like warmth in the throat as the slightly smoky flavor profile remains steady, moderately viscous, and on course. Finishes medium long, warm, bittersweet, and bakery-shop succulent. No surprises. Just steady-as-she-goes distilling.
2018 Rating: ★ ★ ★/Recommended

KO Bare Knuckle American Wheat Whiskey 45% abv, $36.

Wheat dominant/rye mashbill. Bronze color; perfect clarity. Here, the presence of wheat is unmistakable, as the early aroma displays traces of semolina, unseeded white bread, and dry, unsweetened breakfast cereal; extended air contact doesn't release much of anything new except for an added scent of parchment. Entry is gently bittersweet and a little bit earthy/metallic/coin-like; midpalate features a sharp-edged cereal flavor that's astringent, piquant (black peppercorn), and spirity, but the dominant presence of the wheat maintains the tangy focus of the flavor profile. Concludes medium long, slightly and unexpectedly honeyed, and bittersweet.
2018 Rating: ★ ★ ★/Recommended

KO Bare Knuckle Straight Bourbon 45% abv, $40.

Tawny/sinopia color; excellent purity. I favorably respond to the desert dry, moderately grainy/breakfast cereal scents offered in the initial whiffs in that there's nothing groundbreaking here, but there is a solid, no-nonsense, corn-based quality that is reassuring and proper. Secondary sniffs pick up not so much a deepening of the first-round findings but more of a calm, settled continuance—there's a lot to be said about a straightforward, totally grounded, grown-up bouquet in the current unpredictable world of aromatic theatrics and tricks brought by some artisanal distillers. Entry reflects the sturdy aromatic properties, to be sure, but adds more spirity warmth, creamed corn fullness, and caramel corn zestiness as the flavor profile exhibits greater scope and dexterity than the plow horse–like aroma; midpalate expands the flavor menu with vivid tastes of allspice, mace, roasted ham, maple, brown sugar, and candied almond. Ends on a succulent note, completing the evaluation circle nicely. Rock-solid quality.
2018 Rating: ★ ★ ★ ★/Highly Recommended

Koval Bourbon Single Barrel Whiskey 47% abv, $52.

Pale fourteen-karat-gold color; average purity. Okay, so I'm getting truckloads of

Christmas fruitcake, raisins, candied almond, candied pineapple in the initial sniffs; later whiffs detect harmonious hints of nutmeg, clove, vanilla that add nicely to the cake-nut-fruit fragrance. Entry is all-bakery-all-the-time semisweet and toffee-like, with subtle hints of brown butter and praline; midpalate reflects entry findings. Aftertaste is the big winner, though there's a palpable fieriness that is acceptable.
2016 Rating: ★ ★ ★ ★/Highly Recommended

Koval Lion's Pride Organic Single Barrel Bourbon 47% abv, $52.

Pretty old gold/amber color; pristine appearance. I like the caramel corn/Cracker Jack candy opening aroma a lot; with further aeration time, the bouquet takes on an herbal quality (dried sage, thyme, bay leaf especially) that takes charge of the aroma, bringing a garden freshness to it. Entry is curiously dry/semisweet and candied; midpalate features some spirit-driven warmth and kick to support the herbaceous foundation flavor. Aftertaste is sturdy, semisweet, corny, and caramel-like.
2015 Rating: ★ ★ ★/Recommended

Koval Oat Single Barrel Whiskey 40% abv, $49.

Straw-yellow/amber color; excellent purity. Wow, I encounter toasted breakfast cereal notes that remind me of Honey Nut Cheerios in the opening nosing; the delicate sweetness remains a prominent feature in the second nosing phase. Entry mirrors the toasted grain bouquet; midpalate is silky smooth, creamy in texture, and biscuity and yeasty like cookie dough. Long finish that's a touch saline.
2015 Rating: ★ ★ ★ ★/Highly Recommended

Koval Organic White Rye Whiskey 40% abv, $35.

Mineral-water clear and clean. Opening nose is snappy, grainy, and almost like baked fruit as there is a nuance of charred sweetness underneath the grain intensity; bouquet turns semisweet with aeration and roasted; me like. Entry is fruity, fulfilling the nose impressions, and gently sweet; midpalate highlights the grainy sweetness more than the fruit aspect. Longer than expected finish.
2016 Rating: ★ ★ ★/Recommended

Koval Rye Single Barrel Whiskey 40% abv, $49.

Pretty burnt-orange color; flawless clarity. I get big hits of new saddle leather, glass/sand, baked cherry in first whiffs; later on, glass/sand goes to parchment, but cherry/berry fruit lingers. Entry is resiny, deeply woody/stemmy, bark-like, but delicately sweet; midpalate brings the disparate flavor elements together in a stylish manner that's dry, waxy, toasted. A distinctive, high-quality rye.
2015 Rating: ★ ★ ★ ★/Highly Recommended

Larceny Barrel Proof Batch-B520 KSBW 61.1% abv, $50.

Burnt-orange color; impeccable purity. Up-front aromas are slightly burnt, salty, grainy, and almost white flour biscuit–like; secondary passes pick up scents of caraway seed, vegetable oil, tomato vine, and black peppercorn. Entry features pleasant, throat-warming flavors of semisweet chocolate, cocoa bean, black coffee, and dark caramel; midpalate carries on the candy-shop taste richness and intensity as the abv is never an issue, and this hearty whiskey can therefore be enjoyed straight without the addition of mineral water. Finish is long, chewy, tight, and semisweet.

2020 Rating: ★ ★ ★ ★/Highly Recommended

Larceny Old Fitzgerald Very Special Small Batch KSBW 46% abv, $25.

Pretty, deep-amber color; minor sediment seen under the examination lamp—inconsequential. Toasty, round, intensely grainy, and supple first aromatic notes greet you right after the pour; seven more minutes of air contact release subtle scents of cocoa bean, cigar box and pipe tobacco; a comely bouquet. Entry is hugely chunky, bacon fat–like and honeyed; midpalate focuses tightly on sweetened breakfast cereal (honey-flavored cereal, to be precise), caramel corn, cigarette ash, and tobacco. No wallflower, this attractive, demonstrative whiskey carries forward the marvelous tradition of Old Fitzgerald with panache.

2016 Rating: ★ ★ ★ ★ ★/Highest Recommendation

Legent KSBW 47% abv, $35.

A unique style of KSBW that begins with Beam bourbon and then spends time in both red wine and sherry casks before being blended with more Beam bourbon. Rust-like color; excellent purity. Initial inhalations discover succulent notes of dried black cherry, poached pear, brown sugar, and candied almonds; second passes pick up additional fragrances of tar, cigar tobacco, black tea, maple, and cinnamon. Entry is rife with dried fruits, especially nectarine, blackberry, and peach, flavored tobacco, and toasted raisin bread; midpalate boasts robust flavors of bittersweet chocolate, cocoa powder, and treacle. Finishes long, delicate in its elegance, and dry as a bone. A special collaborative treat from the world-class whiskey men Fred Noe of Jim Beam and Shinji Fukuyo, Suntory's chief blender. A steal for the price.

2019 Rating: ★ ★ ★ ★ ★/Highest Recommendation

Litchfield 8 Year Old Batchers' Double Barreled Bourbon 44% abv, $75.

Attractive deep-henna/tawny color; impeccable clarity. Owns a lush, grainy opening fragrance that's mature and properly resiny/oaky, considering its age; secondary inhalations after more aeration detect a delightful corniness that's somewhere between toasted and caramelized, and it's that element that underscores the bouquet. Entry is succulently sweet, lush, and roasted; midpalate is this whiskey's best moment as the foundational cornmeal flavor supports more animated, headlining tastes of candied apple, cocoa bean, toasted marshmallow, and waffles with maple syrup. Finishes long, roasted, and a bit like tomato paste and BBQ sauce. Classy and elegant.

2016 Rating: ★ ★ ★ ★/Highly Recommended

Litchfield Batchers' Bourbon 43% abv, $45.

Pale topaz color; flawless purity. Smells of candle wax, corn husk right out of the gate as the opening aroma goes totally dry, earthy, and dusty; further air contact releases more of the mashy/beery/yeasty fragrance than I think should be present. Entry is pleasingly corn-like and grainy, but the waxy remnants from the bouquet linger; midpalate sees this whiskey's evolution take a positive turn as the graininess becomes intense as it interplays with the oak

barrel resins/acids, creating a palatable taste profile. Aftertaste is off-dry, just a touch spicy, resiny, and caramel corn–like.
2016 Rating: ★ ★ ★/Recommended

Little Book "The Easy" Blended Straight Whiskey 60.24% abv, $80.
This is a unique blend of four-year-old KSBW, thirteen-year-old corn whiskey, six-year old (roughly) 100 percent malt whiskey, and approximately six-year-old high-rye whiskey. I'd describe this color as midway between fulvous and sandy brown; excellent purity. Right off the crack of the odor bat, I pick up pleasant aromas of toasted honey wheat bread, brewer's yeast, cigar box, and cedar; more time in the glass allows the bouquet to evolve into a metallic, flinty bouquet that's earthy, stony, resiny, and woody. Entry flashes a bit of alcohol two-alarm fire but then that aspect quiets down, affording the sweet corn/caramel corn taste profile to emerge; midpalate highlights the candy-shop element found in the entry, adding delectable notes of lychee, Madeira cake, ginger, and malted milk balls. Concludes throwing off considerable amounts of heat and mildly bittersweet. Pretty good first effort by Freddie Noe—Booker Noe's grandson, Fred Noe's son.
2017 Rating: ★ ★ ★/Recommended

Little Book Chapter No. 2 "Noe Simple Task" Blended Kentucky Straight Rye and Canadian Whiskies 59.4% abv, $100.
Saffron color; excellent clarity. Up front, I smell heavily roasted/seared aromas of seeded (caraway) rye bread, burnt matchstick/sulfur, raging bonfire, carbon, and charred marshmallow; secondary inhalations reinforce the initial impressions as robust, off-the-chart fragrances of creosote, charred embers, mesquite, and forest fire regrettably remain the dominant aromatic factors. Entry is just awful—unbalanced, harsh, raw, and unappetizing—as this whiskey's flavor profile is torpedoed from the first moment; midpalate assaults the taste buds in high degrees of resin oakiness, tree sap gone wild, tannic acid, and an alcohol level that serves only to promote how off-center and lousy this whiskey is. The promise that was seen in the first Little Book (rated three stars) is utterly shot down by this misguided second edition.
2018 Rating: ★/Not Recommended

Longbranch KSBW 43% abv, $40.
A collaboration between Wild Turkey Master Distiller Eddie Russell and actor Matthew McConaughey. Deep-bronze color; impeccable clarity. In the initial nosings after the pour, I pick up soft cherry-like and berry-reminiscent aromas that are fleeting and nuanced, but there's a definite gentle sweetness present that's alluring; with more air contact, the aroma evolves into a bouquet, offering complex fragrances of sweet corn, cherry pie, candied almond, and marshmallow. Entry is deep, mineral-like, earthy, desert dry, and biscuit-like; midpalate highlights the resiny oak along with a smoky toastiness that's both grainy and spicy, and it's clear that this stage is this whiskey's apex moment. Finishes grainy, tight, bittersweet, and mildly honeyed, hitting the right notes all along the way.
2018 Rating: ★ ★ ★ ★/Highly Recommended

Lovell Bros. Georgia Sour Mash Spirits 47.6% abv, $45.
Clean, colorless, and pristine as mountain springwater. Sports a dazzlingly wild

opening aroma of carnations, fruity, fresh-off-the-still spirit that's also grainy, cereal-like, textile fiber–like, PVC pipe–like; later sniffs find a bouquet that hasn't settled down at all; in fact, it seems to have grown in energy and expressiveness. Entry reveals a chalky, deeply grainy flavor that's as semisweet as it is warming on the tongue; midpalate is toasty, grainy/corny, semisweet, maple-like, honeyed, charred. Holy Grandma, what a sublime mouthful of real-deal moonshine.

2015 Rating: ★ ★ ★ ★/Highly Recommended

Lovell Bros. Georgia Sour Mash Whiskey 43% abv, $45.

Bright corn-yellow color; minor sediment seen of inconsequential nature. Opening scents offer subtle notes of quince, under-ripened pear, malted milk balls, baker's yeast, sourdough; secondary aromas include grain husk, Wheat Thins, envelope glue, textile fiber. Entry is smooth, vanilla-like, oaky, semisweet, chewy; midpalate features more toasted grains, dry breakfast cereal, maple flavors that last deep into the compelling aftertaste. While I enjoyed the feral quality of the Sour Mash Spirits more, I see huge potential here for actual whiskey in bottlings to come.

2015 Rating: ★ ★ ★/Recommended

Low Gap 100-Proof Whiskey 50% abv, $75.

Pot still. One hundred percent malted Bavarian hard wheat. Matured two-plus years in three new and used American oak barrels. Jonquil/straw-yellow color; good to very good clarity. First whiffs display dry elements of cardboard, parchment, sand, snack cracker, new leather; secondary sniffs detect a broader grain base that's firm, a touch sawdust-like, bread-like, pleasing. Entry is gently spiced, peppery, oily, vegetal, and quite tasty as the flavor profile ascends the sweetness ladder; midpalate is toasty, off-dry, concentrated, grainy, nicely astringent, and therefore clean and crisp through the aftertaste. The virtues grow with air contact and time in the glass. Shows lots of grip and character.

2015 Rating: ★ ★ ★ ★/Highly Recommended

Low Gap 2 Year Old Blended Whiskey 46% abv, $65.

Pot still. Malted corn and barley grains. Matured in used Pappy Van Winkle barrels. Wheat-field/fourteen-karat-gold color; considerable sediment seen floating about the core. Shows a lovely, composed, stately opening aroma that's biscuity, slightly spiced (mace), stony/metallic/earthy, leathery; later sniffs encounter more of the grain foundation in a dry, minerally scent that's elegant, clean, crisp. Entry is surprisingly sweeter than the dusty aroma and focuses squarely on the corn aspect more than the barley as the flavor profile highlights cornmeal, caramel corn, honey, clove that carry on through the midpalate and deep into the graham cracker–like aftertaste. Unique. Crackling and savory. Had the texture been more viscous, more satiny, richer, however, I'd have bestowed a fifth rating star.

2015 Rating: ★ ★ ★ ★/Highly Recommended

Low Gap 2 Year Old Single Barrel Whiskey 50.2% abv, $75.

Extremely limited release. Old gold color; excellent clarity. I detect superbly integrated early-on scents of leather glove, wax paper, grain husk, and sawdust—while perhaps this doesn't sound too exciting, the fact is this opening aroma is delightful and composed, with no loose ends; another eight minutes of aeration bring out more of the grain aspect, which turns out to be biscuity. Entry is delicately grainy sweet in a measured fashion, but it's also fruity and toffee-like; midpalate features the toffee/caramel-candy element in its most sublime expression while the grainy foundation carries the flavor profile deep in the aftertaste, in which more of the oaky resin shows up to close the flavor circle. Astonishingly luscious.

2015 Rating: ★ ★ ★ ★ ★/Highest Recommendation

Low Gap 2 Year Wheat Whiskey 43.1% abv, $60.

Pretty amber color; flawless purity. First whiffs pick up subtle snack cracker, vinyl aromas that are kernel-like; after more aeration, I get grain kernel/bud, cooking oil, seeds (poppy), sawdust. Entry is long on luxurious texture, dry-as-a-bone grain flavor (Wheat Thins); midpalate features tastes of margarine, dry breakfast cereal, oak, and minerals all wrapped in a voluptuous texture. Finishes long, desert dry, waxy/oily, scrumptious.

2016 Rating: ★ ★ ★ ★/Highly Recommended

Low Gap 4 Year Old Wheat Whiskey 45.5% abv, $75.

Pristine, pale amber color; sediment-free appearance. I get office-supply scents of parchment, Scotch tape, manila envelope in the initial sniffs, then that quickly blows off, leaving room for dry breakfast cereal and flint-like scents that push the aromas forward into the secondary inhalations that exhibit waxy, snack cracker–like, grain kernel fragrances that have an appealing suppleness. Entry is tightly wound, desert dry, astringent, and as flinty as the first-stage bouquet; midpalate is fuller and chewier than the entry as the taste profile significantly expands, now featuring nutty, roasted, grainy, crisply dry, and acidic flavors, with a background touch of oaky vanilla. Complex, sinewy finish.

2016 Rating: ★ ★ ★ ★/Highly Recommended

Low Gap Blended Rye Whiskey 42.7% abv, $100.

Gold/mango color; flawless clarity. Like so many rye whiskeys of late, I pick up a touch of waxiness (sealing wax, this time) in addition to rye husk, unseeded rye bread, and mild orchard-fruit fragrance (pear) in the initial whiffs after the pour; with more air contact, this blended rye shows off deeper aromas including dry, unsweetened breakfast cereal, brown sugar, and honeysuckle. Entry is generous and markedly sweeter than the bouquet, lightly toasted, seed-like (sesame), and a touch like caramelized onion; midpalate mirrors the entry only to a small degree as the taste profile soars with flavors of toasted marshmallow, soy sauce, hoisin, crab apple, and tomato paste. Finishes long, suddenly peppery and piquant, and pleasantly warming in the throat.

2018 Rating: ★ ★ ★ ★/Highly Recommended

Low Gap Clear Rye Whiskey 42.6% abv, $45.

Pristine, limpid appearance. Oh my, I love the out-of-the-gate, off-dry and fruity fragrance of pumpernickel rye bread, grain kernel, Ryvita snack cracker; further air contact helps to integrate the scents into one aromatic thrust that's gently sweet and profoundly cereally. Entry is flax-like, grainy, with a hint of background fruitiness; midpalate captures the attention of all taste buds as waves of medium-weight viscosity/oiliness, seeds, bread yeast carry the taste profile forward elegantly and without diminishment. Finishes as fresh, fruity, grainy, yeasty as the entry. This edition is the equal to that of 2013. Bravo, Jack Crispin Cain, Devin Cain. This is beautiful distillation.

2014 Rating: ★ ★ ★ ★ ★/Highest Recommendation

Low Gap Rye Whiskey 43.7% abv, $75.

Amber/sandy-brown color; completely sediment-free. Holy jeepers, the opening inhalations are treated to radically atypical (for rye whiskey) but wholly intriguing fragrances of butcher's wax paper, cereal husk, polythene, arid landscape, and textile fiber; more time in the sampling glass affords the bouquet the chance to unfold as it now features unusual scents of peanut shell, dry cement, aloe spear, and parchment. Entry throws much of the aromatic impressions straight out the window as the flavor profile takes a sharp left at the corner of Piquant and Sassy Streets, offering unabashedly tangy, deeply flavorful tastes of seedless rye bread, Ryvita crackers, black peppercorn, and oak resins; midpalate largely echoes the findings of the entry. Concludes softer, zestier, but more elegant and calmed than the take-no-prisoners midpalate. This is not five star territory but the sheer audacity of this unbridled rye whiskey makes it one to definitely try.

2018 Rating: ★ ★ ★ ★/Highly Recommended

Low Gap Straight Bourbon 43.2% abv, $75.

Brilliant topaz color; impeccably clean. First nosings pick up alluring notes of unbuttered popcorn, corn husk/silk, clove, and medium-level oak char; secondary inhalations detect the wood resins again and they remind me more of cooking oil than baking spices. Entry is lush in texture, bittersweet, vanilla-like, toasty, and pleasantly dried out, almost like dried tropical fruit; midpalate is like grilled meat rubbed with a tomato paste and brown sugar rub, then it becomes woodier/resiny/maple-like in the multilayered aftertaste. Nice job here of highlighting near-textbook bourbon attributes.

2016 Rating: ★ ★ ★ ★/Highly Recommended

Maker's 46 KSBW 47% abv, $40.

Cocoa-brown color; immaculately clean and free of sediment. The opening aromas are reminiscent of sawdust and oak planks, as well as baker's yeast, egg whites, cornflakes cereal, and new leather; secondary inhalations after more air contact discover sensual aromas of freshly turned earth, buttermilk biscuits, honey ham, and creamed corn. Entry is dazzlingly caramelized, crème brûlée–like, and heavily toasted; midpalate offers a rich, oily texture and piquant tastes of pepper steak, honey, brown sugar, chocolate cake frosting, and pecan pie. Aftertaste is luscious, extended, bittersweet, and nutty.

2018 Rating: ★ ★ ★ ★ ★/Highest Recommendation

Maker's Mark Cask Strength KSBW 55.35% abv, $50.

Copper color; flawless purity. The elevated abv makes the up-front nosings campfire warm and slightly prickly, but there's no denying the unbuttered popcorn–like, toasted marshmallow–like splendor of it as it unfolds into a supple, bittersweet opening aroma; after more time in the glass, I return to sniff added scents of Brazil nut, wood plank, resin, green

tobacco, and black tea; this is a complex bouquet, to say the least. Entry is acutely zesty, peppery, piquant, and tobacco-y; midpalate is where the best virtues of this cask strength whiskey reside, as the taste profile features caramelized onion, sautéed mushrooms, egg yolk, and buttered corn bread flavors. Aftertaste stage is loaded with plenty of alcohol accentuation that carries forward the bittersweet corn bread, sweet corn, and caramel corn flavor.
2018 Rating: ★ ★ ★ ★ ★/Highest Recommendation

Maker's Mark KSBW 45% abv, $25.
    Bronze color; impeccably pure. First nosings following the pour are treated to vivid and alluring aromas of unbuttered popcorn, corn bread, and maple syrup; secondary whiffs encounter deeper aromas, including soy sauce, soybean, butterscotch, and hummus. Entry is stunningly rich and oily in texture, ripe and candy-shop sweet, and delicately spiced (vanilla, nutmeg, especially); midpalate is lush in creamy texture and candied in bakeshop flavors that are absurdly spicy, sweet corn–driven, biscuity, and downright pleasing. Finishes long, bittersweet, honeyed, and cereal-like (Honey Nut Cheerios). Remains one of the greatest American whiskey values of our generation.
2018 Rating: ★ ★ ★ ★/Highly Recommended

Mic.Drop. 8 Year Old Straight Bourbon 56% abv, $100.
    Made at MGP, Indiana. Mashbill is 75 percent corn, 21 percent rye, 4 percent malted barley. This color is full-out tawny brown and is immaculately clean and free of sediment. Aromatically, this straight bourbon offers nicely toasted, baked fruit, candied almond, meringue, and crème caramel fragrances that are composed, mature, and integrated; later sniffs pick up scents of black pepper, nougat, lead pencil, seasoned tobacco leaf, and margarine. Entry is peppery, spicy, tangy, and corny, with shockingly little alcohol push considering the 56 percent level; midpalate is elegant, on the drier side of the dry/sweet scale, and there is ample bittersweet caramel corn/corn-syrup presence that keeps the focus straight, succulent, and narrow. Finishes woody, resiny, earthy, and properly corn-driven. Another MGP gem from America's heartland.
2017 Rating: ★ ★ ★ ★/Highly Recommended

Michter's 10 Year Old Single Barrel KSBW 47.2% abv, $120.
    Rich copper/ochre color; ideal clarity. Right from the first nosing pass it is abundantly obvious that this is top-grade straight bourbon as the corn bread, sweet corn, and caramel corn aromas make the case; later sniffs encounter deeper, more layered fragrances of baking spices (allspice, mace, and clove, especially), sweetened breakfast cereal, toasted marshmallow, and chocolate-covered orange rind. Entry is powerful, more bittersweet than flat-out sweet, praline-like, and dried fruit–like, in particular, prune, black raisins, and cherries; midpalate mirrors the entry, adding a density in the texture that ushers the flavor profile into the luscious aftertaste that's top loaded with pastry treats (chocolate spiral pound cake) and hard candy–like tastes. Yet another whiskey masterpiece from this American whiskey distillery.
2018 Rating: ★ ★ ★ ★ ★/Highest Recommendation

Michter's 10 Year Old Single Barrel Kentucky Straight Rye Whiskey 46.4% abv, $150.
    The cocoa-brown color is lustrous and free of sediment. The initial whiffs after the pour

pick up notable aromas of cherry compote, cinnamon, nutmeg, clove, and bay leaf as the spice quotient here is off the charts; more air contact stimulates more fragrances, including BBQ sauce, tomato paste, boisé (oak extract), flan, and caramelized sugar. Entry is a touch sweet but also deeply grainy (Ryvita crackers) and reminiscent of seedless rye bread; midpalate offers gigantic but fully integrated flavors of breakfast cereal grains, oatmeal, muesli, dried fruits, and nutmeg. Finishes very long, sinewy, and moderately oily in texture, softer than the big-hearted midpalate, and deeply savory. A mature, textbook straight rye that sets the tone as forcefully as any of its peers, reminding me most of the Thomas H. Handy Sazerac (five stars) from the legendary Buffalo Trace Antique Collection of 2012.

2018 Rating: ★★★★★/Highest Recommendation

Michter's 20 Year Old KSBW 57.1% abv, $600.

The rusty-ochre color is dazzling and mahogany-like; perfect purity. It's the acute nutmeg- and mace-like spiciness of the opening aroma that's so riveting and expressive; after more aeration, the aroma calms down on the spice front, which allows the richness of the bouquet to develop as the merging of grain-wood-alcohol-acid reaches its peak performance, aromatically speaking—at this juncture I'm pondering lighting a cigar. Entry is sublimely compact, dense, and complex; midpalate soars into the taste profile stratosphere as the integration of components is at the perfection point—tastes wonderfully of praline, nougat, candy bar, dark caramel, mincemeat, maple-smoked bacon, smoked ham. Aftertaste embellishes all the virtues found and deeply appreciated in the midpalate. Another magnificent whiskey released by the Michter's band of magicians.

2017 Rating: ★★★★★/Highest Recommendation

Michter's 25 Year Old KSBW 58.1% abv, $800.

The depth of auburn/burnt umber/oloroso sherry color is astoundingly attractive; flawless purity, with a sheen of oils floating in the core. First inhalations encounter huge bakery-shop and candy-store aromas of chocolate fudge, peanut butter, praline, hazelnuts, and vanilla bean; with more aeration, the grain element comes alive in the forms of caramel corn, burnt marshmallow, caramelized onions, buttered popcorn, and marzipan—a monster of a bourbon bouquet. Entry is as warming as having hot chocolate with whipped cream on your tongue, but also there are flavors of pipe tobacco, bittersweet chocolate, meringue, and Madeira cake; midpalate stage finds all the various flavors merging into a singular taste of bittersweet caramel corn that is off-the-charts luscious. Aftertaste is fathomless, dense, warming on the tongue, and utterly sensational. Crazy delicious.

2017 Rating: ★★★★★/Highest Recommendation

Michter's Original US*1 Small Batch Sour Mash Whiskey 43% abv, $44.

Bright topaz color; unblemished clarity. Right off the crack of the aromatic bat, there's a high concentration of caramel corn, cornmeal, and breakfast cereal flakes; secondary sniffs encounter subtle notes of dried berries, citrus zest, maple, and vanilla bean. Entry is silky smooth, beany (vanilla, cocoa), and moderately sweet and brown sugar–like; midpalate is creamed-corn sweet, caramel-like and filled with baking spices, mostly allspice, clove, and nutmeg. Finishes long, grainy sweet, and nougat. Another winner from Michter's.

2018 Rating: ★★★★/Highly Recommended

Michter's US*1 Barrel Strength Kentucky Straight Rye Whiskey 55.9% abv, $75.

Chestnut-brown color; pristine purity. First inhalations detect unseeded rye bread, breakfast cereal, Ryvita snack crackers, lead pencil; secondary sniffs detect more of the oak aspect in the forms of tannin and subtle vanilla bean fragrances. Entry is hugely appealing, zesty, BBQ sauce–like, a little like tomato paste, beef bouillon; midpalate flavors offer a silky texture, tangy, grainy, doughy flavors that are never overrun by the elevated abv, which is always cast in the part of a supporting character. Aftertaste is hearty, woody, long, toasted, and opulent. I love the way the cask strength is not an issue. Straight rye at its best.

2018 Rating: ★ ★ ★ ★ ★/Highest Recommendation

Michter's US*1 Single Barrel Kentucky Straight Rye Whiskey 42.4% abv, $48.

Burnt sienna color; immaculate clarity. First sniffs come up against a muted aroma, which begrudgingly gives off feathery scents of seeded rye bread and graham cracker, but little more; after more aeration time, the nose opens up a bit, allowing wispy fragrances of maple syrup, clove, and pancake batter to escape. Entry is far more animated than the aromatics as straightforward, peppery, piquant, and dried-fruit (prune, date) flavors make their case with a good deal of force; midpalate stage features a creamy, moderately oily texture that supports the off-dry tastes of rye bread, dried black fruits, lead pencil, and oak resin. Aftertaste offers bittersweet tastes of grain husk, Ryvita cracker, and turbinado sugar.

2018 Rating: ★ ★ ★ ★/Highly Recommended

Michter's US*1 Small Batch KSBW 45.7% abv, $48.

Ochre color; flawless purity. Instantly in the first sniffs there are corn-driven aromas of buttered corn on the cob, corn bread, cornflakes cereal, and polenta; additional time in the glass affords the bouquet the chance to deepen the existing fragrances, and it does just that as the array of aromas turns moderately sweeter and more buttermilk biscuit–like. Entry is slightly honeyed and praline-like, toasted and a touch smoky, as the flavor profile proves to be expansive as it includes flavors of pipe tobacco, caramel corn, maple, chocolate fudge, and bacon fat; midpalate echoes the impressions, adding hints of brown sugar and blackstrap molasses. Ends on a splendidly animated, bakery-shop pastry note with savory tastes of nougat, almond paste, and brown sugar.

2018 Rating: ★ ★ ★ ★/Highly Recommended

Michter's US*1 Small Batch Unblended American Whiskey 41.7% abv, $48.

Numerous Michter's bottlings have been reviewed by us over the last decade, overwhelmingly to four and five star ratings. Handsome cinnamon/mahogany color; excellent clarity. I get bread yeast, dark caramel, cocoa bean, worn saddle leather aromas in the first inhalations; later whiffs detect deeper grain scents as well as figs, black raisins. Entry is succulent, full weighted in texture, bittersweet, oaky, toasted; midpalate reflects the entry and goes further by adding candied pineapple, chestnut purée, dark chocolate. Aftertaste is extended, rich, brown sugar–like. Another remarkable addition to the world-class Michter's portfolio.

2018 Rating: ★ ★ ★ ★/Highly Recommended

Michter's US*1 Toasted Barrel Finish Kentucky Straight Rye Whiskey 55% abv, $75.

Sinopia/tawny color sparkles beneath the examination lamp; impeccably clean. As with virtually all Michter's US*1 whiskeys, the nose is firmly grain forward in waves of dry break-fast cereal, pork sausages, brown gravy, and just-out-of-the-oven pumpernickel bread; in secondary level nosings the brown bread aspect becomes accentuated as the bouquet turns hop-like, floral (dried carnation petals), chaff, grain kernels, wheat field–like, spicy (sage, parsley), and moderately toasty. Entry flavors are expansive, generous, and animated, remi-niscent of cinnamon buns, bakery shop, vanilla bean, and ham studded with clove; midpal-ate is where the abv level shows off in ripples of campfire warmth that cradle the palate in gentle, almost juicy succulence. The slinky finish is opulent in texture, spicy, arid, and tightly focused in rye flavor. It's the harmony between the judicious wood usage and the richness of the rye that make this whiskey so luscious.

2017 Rating: ★ ★ ★ ★ ★/Highest Recommendation

Michter's US*1 Toasted Barrel KSBW 45.7% abv, $53.

Bright, new-copper/burnt-orange color; flawless purity. Smells alluringly of toasted marshmallow, raisin bran cereal, dried cherry, boysenberry compote, holiday spice cake; it's really not until the second inhalations following more air contact that the first traces of corn appear, and only then as a supporting aroma to the ambrosial fruitiness that forms the core fragrance of this appealing bourbon. Entry is intensely raisiny, fig-like, nougaty, ripe, sweet/sour, even a touch honeyed; midpalate shows the oily, slightly smoky texture nicely as the texture underpins the flavors of cinnamon, Honey Nut Cheerios cereal, loose leaf tobacco, butterscotch. Aftertaste reaches deep, offering moderately oily, buttery, now bitter-sweet tastes that push away from the fruit and get closer to the grains of the mashbill. A bit of a roller-coaster ride, but worth it.

2016 Rating: ★ ★ ★ ★/Highly Recommended

New Richmond Straight Rye Whiskey 45.3% abv, $42.

The rich new-copper color is dazzling and pure. I get an intriguingly broad array of open-ing scents, from humid air to delicate spices (allspice, nutmeg) to cereal grain to parchment to graham crackers; additional time in the glass allows the aroma to transform into a benign bouquet, featuring soft hints of textile fiber, vinyl, and oaky resins. Entry flavors (delicate spice, crackers, cereal) are cradled in a moderately oily texture (love it) that pushes the tastes forward; midpalate shows just a flash of abv warmth that adds to the complexity without being a dom-inant factor. Finishes medium long, a bit fruity, and tangy (sarsaparilla). I have long believed that 45th Parallel Spirits Distillery (the producer) is one of the finest artisanal producers in the nation. This fine effort, sophisticated and sturdy, bolsters that belief.

2017 Rating: ★ ★ ★ ★/Highly Recommended

Noble Oak Small Batch Double Oak Matured Bourbon 45% abv, $35.

Matured for at least twelve months in new, charred, American white oak barrels, then switched to Spanish sherry casks for an unspecified time. Distilled in Indiana. Ochre color; some minor sediment seen beneath the examination lamp. First smells are of caramel corn, oloroso sherry, grape preserves, and red plums; with more air contact, the aroma opens up more, offering vibrant scents of pipe tobacco, menthol, plastic, lemon curd, and nutmeg. Entry is rich, sherry-like, toasty, and creamy in texture; midpalate features deeper corn-related flavors, such as cornmeal, caramel corn, and roasted corn on the cob, to balance out the sherry influence, which was near dominant. Ends on a pleasantly sweet, candied note that's warm and coating in the throat. While long-time *SJ* readers know my fondness for sherry oak maturation in whiskey, I think this whiskey borders on being too heavily sherry influenced. That acknowledged, I still think that there is enough overall quality to merit a recommendation.

2018 Rating: ★★★/Recommended

Old Charter Oak Collection/French Oak KSBW 46% abv, $70.

Burnt sienna color; impeccable clarity. First impressions are muted, as nuances of black pepper, vinyl, saddle leather, and pumpkin seed struggle to make an impression; following more air contact, the aroma makes only small gains aromatically, offering faint hints of waffles, unsweetened breakfast cereal, and biscuit batter. Entry is grainy, dense, and semisweet, with tangy flavors of bear claw pastry, nougat, and almond paste; midpalate maintains the semisweet direction, now highlighting tastes of dried dates, figs, raisins, and mincemeat. Concludes medium long, mildly toasty, and deeply spicy. Recommendable, but the deep-rooted semisweet nature might be too much for some drinkers.

2019 Rating: ★★★/Recommended

Old Elk Blended Straight Bourbon 44% abv, $50.

Topaz color; impeccable clarity. The initial inhalations don't pick up much in the way of aromatics but I keep trying; allowing for more air contact, I make another attempt only to find that aeration hasn't stimulated the molecules enough to constitute a viable aroma, so I move on. Entry offers caramel corn and bittersweet flavors that are assertive and vivid, making me wonder why the bouquet was so anemic; midpalate features the sweetness of creamed corn, toffee, and corn syrup plus the addition of oak tannins, which counterbalance the inherent corn-based sweet-a-thon. Concludes long, languid, and plush in the throat. Definitely displays more than ample in-mouth charm for a recommendation, but the obvious deficiency in the aroma makes me blanch at the overblown price tag, which ultimately kills the recommendation.

2018 Rating: ★★/Not Recommended

Old Fitzgerald 9 Year Old Bottled-in-Bond Fall 2018 Edition KSBW 50% abv, $90.

Pumpkin/burnt-orange color; pristine clarity. Strangely, I don't seem to be able to detect much in the first sniffs other than a featherweight fibrous/linen-like quality that's wafer thin; following more aeration, there's greater aromatic substance at hand in the forms of cornstarch, cornmeal, espresso, and toffee. Entry is deep, dense, honey biscuit–like, buttery, nutty and almost praline-like, and tobacco-y; midpalate features highly appealing flavors of caramel corn, Reese's peanut butter and chocolate candy, bacon fat (from the charred barrel doubtless), toasted marshmallow, and candied walnut. The in-mouth splendor continues into the long, prickly aftertaste as mature, animated, campfire-warm, and bittersweet tastes of candied nuts, dried orchard fruit (apricot), honey, and treacle abound.

2018 Rating: ★★★★/Highly Recommended

Old Fitzgerald Bottled-in-Bond Fall 2019 Edition KSBW 50% abv, $135.

Tawny color; excellent purity. Opening nose without hesitation explodes in clouds of caramel corn, sweetened breakfast cereal, corn muffin, and buttermilk pancake batter aroma

that delight from the start; later sniffs pick up traces of bubble gum, powdered sugar, and dark honey. Entry is rich, silky in texture, and front loaded with succulent tastes of honey, salted butter, dark caramel, and English toffee; midpalate echoes the entry, adding top notes of bean curd, egg white, meringue, red layer from the charred oak, and caramelized onion. Aftertaste is long, zesty, and piquant. Best of this series? May well be.
2020 Rating: ★ ★ ★ ★ ★/Highest Recommendation

Old Fitzgerald Bottled-in-Bond Spring 2018 Edition KSBW 50% abv, $110.
Tawny hue; impeccably clean. First whiffs pick up alluring scents of prune Danish, baking spices like cinnamon, mace, and nutmeg, along with traces of grilled orchard fruits (peach, nectarine), and almond paste; secondary inhalations detect deeper fragrances of sweet corn, paraffin, and sealing wax. Entry offers succulent opening flavors of baked pine-apple, vinegar, black peppercorn, peanut butter, and praline; midpalate is awash in bitter-sweet flavors, including mincemeat, baked apple bathed in cinnamon, dark toffee, and old honey. Aftertaste is sumptuous, richly textured, slightly smoky (great cigar companion, this), spicy, bittersweet, and toasted marshmallow–like. A bottled-in-bond road map on how it should be done. Gloriously delicious.
2018 Rating: ★ ★ ★ ★ ★/Highest Recommendation

Old Fitzgerald Bottled-in-Bond Spring 2019 Edition KSBW 50% abv, $130.
Cocoa-brown color; sediment-free. I encounter round, dense, woody, nutty, lightly spiced, and deeply grainy opening aromas that remind me of bacon fat and baked ham more than anything else; secondary inhalations confirm the first whiff findings, adding deft touches of sarsaparilla, hyssop, peppermint, and pine forest. Entry is succulent, chewy in texture, honeyed, raisiny, pancakes and maple syrup–like, and just flat-out luscious; mid-palate continues the opulence and majesty found at entry, as soaring, bittersweet, candied, nutty, and woody flavors are too numerous and multileveled to expound on in this space.
2019 Rating: ★ ★ ★ ★ ★/Highest Recommendation

Old Forester 100 Proof KSBW 50% abv, $22.
Bronze color; ideally free of detritus. Aromatically, this whiskey is integrated, under-stated, a 6 on the 10-point sweetness meter, cereal-like, grainy, and soy-like in the open-ing whiffs after the pour; secondary inhalations identify all the first-stage impressions and add succulent notes of butterscotch, candied almond, hoisin, and chocolate-covered raisins. Entry features exotic and appealing flavors of soy sauce, candied yam, sautéed scallions, brown rice, and baked ham; midpalate mirrors the entry, throwing in caramel corn, butter-scotch, butter brickle, and toasted marshmallow. The yummy, treat-like finish is balanced, semisweet, cornmeal-like, and elegant. Tremendous value.
2019 Rating: ★ ★ ★ ★/Highly Recommended

Old Forester 1910 Old Fine KSBW 46.5% abv, $55.
Cordovan/auburn color; flawless clarity. Wow, this enticing opening aroma is all about candy-store treats, especially butterscotch, malted milk ball, chocolate-covered raisins, and caramel; later sniffs pick up additional scents including old book leather/library, attic, saw-dust, and oak plank. Entry is richly textured, toasted, piquant, and just a touch prickly with

alcohol heat; midpalate stays the course with the sumptuous texture as well as opulent tastes of butter-cream candies, cocoa powder, chocolate chip cookie, cinnamon bun, and fudge. Finishes medium long, oaky/maple-like, resiny, semisweet, and toasty.
2019 Rating: ★ ★ ★ ★/Highly Recommended

Old Forester Kentucky Rye Whisky 50% abv, $23.
Chestnut-brown color; perfect purity. The first nosing passes detect feathery aromas of delicate baking spice (allspice), sage, red cherries, and kiwi; secondary inhalations after more aeration encounter lithe, ethereal fragrances of nutmeg, seedless rye bread, and pumpkin seed. Entry is delightfully tangy, spicy (now it's cinnamon and clove), tasting of baked ham and BBQ sauce; midpalate reflects the entry-stage findings, adding subtle tastes of brown sugar and caramelized onion that come wrapped in a succulent, viscous texture. Aftertaste is long, semisweet, honeyed, and woody. Great value.
2019 Rating: ★ ★ ★ ★/Highly Recommended

Old Forester KSBW 43% abv, $20.
Caramel/Persian-orange color; immaculate clarity. Opening fragrances are zesty, with scents of fruitcake, dried fruits (apricot, banana), bubble gum, and ginger ale; later whiffs pick up deeper, more evolved fragrances of sweet corn, corn masa/corn tortilla, and polenta. Entry is unabashedly corn-syrup sweet and viscous, with outlier flavors of creamed corn, caramel corn, and demerara sugar; midpalate replays the entry impressions, but with even more concentrated texture that is akin to biscuit batter. Concludes gently sweet, affably polite, and clearly defined as only one variety of American whiskey: straightforward bourbon.
2019 Rating: ★ ★ ★/Recommended

Old Grand-Dad 114 KSBW 57% abv, $29.
Pretty amber color; impeccable clarity. First sniffs encounter appealing aromas of dry breakfast cereal, nutshells, and dried apricot; later whiffs pick up a bit of alcohol, which is no surprise, but the degree is easy to handle. Entry is gently sweet, corn-like, and warming on the palate; midpalate echoes the entry, leading to a polite finish that's a joy to behold. Still one of the greatest values in USA whiskey.
2020 Rating: ★ ★ ★ ★/Highly Recommended

Old Grand-Dad Bottled-in-Bond High Rye Mash Bill KSBW 50% abv, $25.
Attractive orange/copper color; sediment-free clarity. Opening nose is vacant and "little," considering the abv, offering only mild scents of buttered corn on the cob, brown butter, brown sugar; further air contact brings out more of the grain, breakfast-cereal aspect, which is welcome, and then there's a late dash of baked banana that's delightful. Entry is gently sweet, warming on the tongue, sappy/resiny, straightforward, spicy, and unabashedly cornmeal-like; midpalate picks up the flavor impressions, giving off tastes of new honey, light toffee, marzipan, praline, making the finish far more complex than I thought it would be.
2018 Rating: ★ ★ ★ ★/Highly Recommended

Old Potrero 18th Century Style Whiskey 51.2% abv, $70.
Amber in color; pristine clarity. Intriguingly, I smell steamed white rice in the first sniffs

but little more; secondary inhalations introduce nuanced scents of grain husk, oatmeal, and parchment, but little else upon which to grip. Entry is toasted, snack cracker–like, off-dry as a hint of nougat/almond paste lurks in the background; midpalate pushes the nougat/candy bar flavor a bit forward, making this stage a tad more honeyed. Aftertaste integrates the few, faint character elements that were discerned through olfactory and gustatory avenues, putting it across the finish line for a recommendation.

2019 Rating: ★ ★ ★/Recommended

Old Potrero Finished in Port Barrels Straight Malt Whiskey 57.3% abv, $100.

Tawny color; impeccably clean. I like this first nosing pass, as tangy, cereal grain, dried-fruit (raisins, pineapple) aromas come off rich, defined, and integrated; after more air contact, the nose opens up more to include fragrances of baked peaches, prune Danish, bear claw pastry, and mincemeat pie. Entry offers a round, sumptuous texture that supports evolved flavors of BBQ sauce, tomato paste, brown sugar, and candied walnut; midpalate features all of the entry findings and adds succulent touches of braised pork, butterscotch, black raisins, and, yes, ruby port. Finishes long in the throat, plush in texture, and ripe. The best Old Potrero whiskey by a long shot.

2019 Rating: ★ ★ ★ ★/Highly Recommended

Old Potrero Single Malt Hotaling's Whiskey 50% abv, $113.

Gold color; as pure as one would desire. In the opening whiffs I get not-so-subtle scents of butcher's wax, paper, textile fiber/nylon, grain husk, and earthenware/pottery/clay; all of the first identified aromas remain robust in the later nosing passes following more aeration. Entry is briskly clean, dry as the desert, and intensely grainy and husk/kernel-like; midpalate reinforces the entry impressions, heightening perhaps only the husk/kernel aspect. Finishes predictably dry and almost astringent without adding anything new to the discussion. My biggest issue with this pricey whiskey is that it doesn't evolve in the glass, remaining staunchly grainy/husk-like and never expanding beyond that point. Couldn't possibly recommend it.

2019 Rating: ★ ★/Not Recommended

Old Potrero Single Malt Straight Rye Whiskey 48.5% abv, $75.

Tangerine color; flawlessly pure. I get immediate fragrances of steel tank, rye bread, hard cheese rind (Romano), and leather boot; further aeration brings out a waxiness that's more paper-like than candle-like, and there's also a white rice scent buried in the last row of the second balcony. Entry comes off sweeter than the aroma implied it would, setting off frontline flavors of caramel, fudge, dark chocolate, cocoa, and praline; midpalate goes with the sweet theme, adding touches of toasted marshmallow and s'mores. Ends up bittersweet, pleasant, and round in texture.

2019 Rating: ★ ★ ★/Recommended

Old Rip Van Winkle 10 Year Old Handmade Bourbon 53.5% abv, $70.

Burnt-orange/bronze color; flawless purity. Expressive opening aromas include toffee, caramel corn candy, toasted almond, and baked peach; later sniffs following more aeration pick up nuances of tropical fruits, especially baked banana and fresh pineapple. Entry is piquant and spicy (allspice, mace), showing midrange levels of abv heat that make the taste

buds stand at attention; midpalate features a mellower flavor approach that's quite biscuity, graham cracker–like, corn bread–like, and tangy due to the accelerated spiciness. Finishes firmly structured, chewy in texture, semisweet, slightly smoky, and campfire warm in the throat. Hearty and zesty, but neither feral nor aggressive.
2019 Rating: ★ ★ ★ ★/Highly Recommended

Old Rip Van Winkle 12 Year Old Special Reserve Bourbon 45.2% abv, $80.

Butterscotch color; impeccably clear and clean. Early on, I detect earthy, forest-like, and lightly spiced scents that are vegetal, root-like, and a bit muted; further aeration brings out moderately grainy and bean-like aromas that are gently toasted and medium sweet. Entry highlights sweetened breakfast cereal, corn syrup, and mincemeat pie flavors that are more bakery-shop prone than candy-store leaning; midpalate offers a textural richness that was not present in the entry stage, leading to the enjoyment of fresh honey and marmalade tastes that are satisfying, firm in structure, and semisweet. Concludes long in the throat, corn-syrup sweet, and moderately spicy.
2019 Rating: ★ ★ ★ ★/Highly Recommended

Old Rip Van Winkle 13 Year Old Family Reserve Rye 47.8% abv, $120.

Orange-peel color; perfect clarity. This opening aroma is delicate, lightly spiced with traces of nutmeg and dried orange rind, and gently fruity (tangerine, nectarine); secondary whiffs encounter much of the same, except for an elevated citrus-like component that is reminiscent of kumquat and a faint trace of eucalyptus oil. Entry is forward leaning, resiny, oaky, and void of fruit, as the primary flavor elements are clearly oak-driven lipids and acids as well as grain kernel; midpalate is the highlight reel moment, as the flavors harmonize, creating a full-throated, assertive, yet medium-weighted texture that envelops the toasty, green tobacco–like, resiny/sap-like tastes that usher in the medium-long, slightly roasted, and green aftertaste. The memorable midpalate stage makes this rye whiskey worth the hunt.
2019 Rating: ★ ★ ★ ★/Highly Recommended

Orphan Barrel Barterhouse 20 Year Old KSBW 45.1% abv, $75.

Diageo's Orphan Barrel extra-aged whiskeys, including Barterhouse, Old Blowhard, and now Rhetoric, have had tongues wagging due to their age statements. All were matured in barrels for twenty years or more, which flies in the face of conventional American whiskey tradition. A majority of stateside whiskey distillers, mainstream and craft, who ply their trade in warmer climate states such as Tennessee, Virginia, Georgia, Alabama, and Kentucky make the case that American corn-based spirit ages to maturity within the four- to ten-year span in cask. Distilled liquids mature quicker in balmy, humid conditions because alcohol expands as temperatures rise, and when alcohol bloats, it increases the amount of wood contact, thereby accelerating maturation. Longer aging periods are typical for whiskeys produced in the cooler British Isles. That's why twenty-five-year-old Scotches are relatively common. The emergence of a program like Orphan Barrel challenges the customary viewpoint of USA whiskey distillers, and that makes for intriguing reviewing and conversation. To my way of thinking, if the whiskey tastes good, shows balance, and is recommendable to friends, my concerns about aging tenure and conventions diminish. If it is good, it is good, no matter the age. Attractive topaz color; some strands of sediment seen floating. Wow, this first nosing pass detects startling aromas of shale, quarry, wet stone, wet cement, sandy beach on a rainy day; subsequent inhalations add only a beeswax/beehive scent, but no fruit or grain to speak of. Entry is delicately sweet, deeply grainy, almost fruity/jammy, properly woody/oaky, spicy—where was this bourbon splendor in the quarry-like aromatic stages? Midpalate is toasty, caramel-like, bittersweet, maple-like. Aftertaste highlights the oak resins. An intriguing tale of two distinct and laudable whiskey parts: stony/earthy aroma and voluptuous/grainy-sweet bourbon taste.

2015 Rating: ★ ★ ★ ★/Highly Recommended

Orphan Barrel Forged Oak Batch WL-CF-2 KSBW 45.25% abv, $65.

Brilliant, burnished-orange/bronze color; flawless purity. The first whiffs encounter ethereal scents that are underdeveloped at this stage, and therefore amorphous; secondary nosing passes following further air contact just simply do not pick up much more in the way of aromatic presence other than delicate touches of black pepper and creamed corn. Entry offers a taste profile that's far more animated than the tight bouquet as flavors of spice (pepper), cornmeal, snack crackers, unsweetened breakfast cereal, all make an appearance; midpalate goes even further as the flavor landscape expands to include dried tropical fruit (banana, pineapple), vanilla, toasted oak, and soft cheese that last deep into the butterscotch-like finish. Came all the way from two star territory to four star due 100 percent to its flavor and finish appeal.

2015 Rating: ★ ★ ★ ★/Highly Recommended

Orphan Barrel Lost Prophet 22 Year Old KSBW 45.05% abv, $120.

Gorgeous copper color; flawless purity. Exquisite opening aromas include brown butter, bacon fat, oaky vanilla, cocoa, coffee bean, old leather; secondary notes focus more on the grain aspect which is off-dry and toasted. Entry is honeyed, intensely woody but not resiny, like dried fruits, especially dates, figs; midpalate soars with roasted, grainy, sweet corn flavors that are perfectly integrated and aligned. Aftertaste is long, beany, nutty, leathery, immensely satisfying, and complex.

2015 Rating: ★ ★ ★ ★ ★/Highest Recommendation

Orphan Barrel Old Blowhard 26 Year Old KSBW 45.35% abv, $150.

Beautiful, brilliant copper color; inconsequential floating tendrils seen. Opening whiffs encounter wood plank, sawdust, lumber mill, parchment, wax paper; aeration serves only to add minor notes of spiciness and grainy fruit. Entry is narrowly focused on oaky vanilla, with a passing glance at sweetened breakfast grains; midpalate is immensely toasty, bready/doughy, caramel-like, even a little charcoal-like and BBQ sauce reminiscent. Aftertaste features the charcoal/burnt wood, maple sugar, honey, tomato paste. Borders on being over-oaked, but all the same, there's lots of corn-driven pleasure here.

2015 Rating: ★ ★ ★ ★/Highly Recommended

Orphan Barrel Rhetoric 20 Year Old KSBW 45% abv, $85.

Gorgeous, deep-bronze/new-copper color; flawless purity. I get baked cherry notes in the up-front aroma, then it turns very much like breakfast cereal and snack cracker as the fragrance mingles with air; later inhalations encounter hints of maple sap, tree bark,

deep-toasted marshmallow, praline, old library. Entry features intense flavors of corn-meal, tree sap, cocoa, old honey; midpalate is deep, complex, oaky but not resiny, caramel corn–like, balanced, luscious, mature. Finishes long, silky, bittersweet, almost citrusy/zesty.
2015 Rating: ★★★★★/Highest Recommendation

Orphan Barrel Rhetoric 21 Year Old KSBW 45.1% abv, $100.
Copper color; flawless purity. Initially, I pick up earthy, oily scents of creosote, lichen/moss, black tea, and forest floor after rain; secondary passes detect dried and cured tobacco leaf, basalt, limestone, Lapsang souchong tea, and granite fragrances; this is an uncommon bouquet for a corn-based whiskey. Entry is gently sweet, maple syrup–like, succulent, intensely fruity (black plum, blackberry) and ambrosial, and I love it; midpalate stage offers measured and harmonious tastes of oaky vanillin, bacon fat, mincemeat, baked pears, and marshmallow. Ends on a high note that's long in the throat, heavily toasted and roasted, almost BBQ sauce– and tomato paste–like, round and supple. A fine whiskey that has withstood the test of time with grace.
2018 Rating: ★★★★/Highly Recommended

Orphan Barrel Rhetoric 22 Year Old KSBW 45.2% abv, $110.
Cocoa-brown color; excellent clarity. I get ground black peppercorn fragrance right off the crack of the aromatic bat plus lesser scents of lead pencil, minerals, and pea pod; a second round of sniffing following more air contact brings into play aromas of buckwheat, nail polish, grain husk, cornstarch, and soda crackers. Entry is spare and lean, as a flavor profile starts to build in small blocks of caramelized onion, sweet corn, and dark caramel, and there's a flash of musty TCA that bothers me a bit; midpalate is medium weighted in texture, pleasantly corny (no, it's not as corny as Kansas in August, thank you very much), resiny/oily, and a touch narrow in flavor focus. Aftertaste features redeeming flavor factors, especially the acute oiliness that affects the texture to the positive and leads to a cigar tobacco–like final taste.
2018 Rating: ★★★/Recommended

Orphan Barrel Rhetoric 23 Year Old KSBW 45.3% abv, $120.
Darkest of the four Rhetorics, a deep mahogany/chestnut color; superbly clean and free of sediment. Up-front nosings pick up vibrant scents of Jolly Rancher hard candy, peanut butter, and rum-like brown sugar that makes the aroma bittersweet; secondary inhalations encounter mineral/earthy odors of lead pencil, sagebrush, bay leaf, Italian parsley, and dry stone. Entry features lovely, rich flavors that float upon a creamy texture, including marzipan, almond paste, apple butter, maple fudge, and caramel corn; midpalate echoes the entry splendor, adding honey and sweetened breakfast cereal. Finishes long, luxuriously creamy on the palate, sweet-corn sweet, and luscious. The in-mouth stages are spectacular.
2018 Rating: ★★★★/Highly Recommended

Orphan Barrel Rhetoric 24 Year Old KSBW 45.5% abv, $130.
Bronze/sinopia color; impeccably clear. At first, the opening nose is nondescript, but then it slowly opens up, offering nuanced mineral-like scents of arid earth/desert, dry leaves in autumn, and loose leaf tobacco; secondary sniffs after more aeration discover barely

discernable grain, cornstarch, and unsalted snack cracker fragrances. Entry is toasty/roasted, sweet as tomato paste and BBQ sauce, and similar to honey-basted ham; midpalate resembles roasted corn, creamed corn, and caramel. Aftertaste is medium long, maple-like, rich in texture, and honey sweet. Once again, the in-mouth stages come to the rescue.
2018 Rating: ★ ★ ★/Recommended

Orphan Barrel The Gifted Horse American Whiskey 57.5% abv, $50.
Exceedingly pretty and bright new-copper penny color; unblemished clarity. The elevated spirit is immediately prevalent in the initial passes, but it's not so dominant that scents of cereal grain, unsalted snack cracker, and baked pear fail to come through because they most certainly do; further air contact releases toasted grain fragrances along with pear tart, baked pineapple, terra-cotta, and waxed floor. Entry is warming but not fiery, abundant but not lush, baked and toasty, bittersweet and prickly; midpalate is pleasant, offering much of the warm embers–like heat from the entry but somehow this taste profile loses its way as it approaches the aftertaste, turning intensely waxy, resiny, floor polish–like as the grain aspect fades completely from sight, leaving behind only the density of the oak resins.
2016 Rating: ★ ★/Not Recommended

Orphan Barrel Whoop & Holler 28 Year Old American Whiskey 42% abv, $175.
Produced at George Dickel Distillery in Tullahoma, TN. Pretty amber/topaz color; excellent clarity. Lovely, delicate aromas waft up from the sampling glass of peach cobbler, toasted almond, gum, grapefruit marmalade; more aeration stimulates deeper, more assertive scents of honeysuckle, butter brickle, peanut butter; this is a very nice bouquet that's subtle yet commanding. Entry is sprightly in its spiritiness (seems higher than 42 percent), prickly even, but with melded, mature flavors of caramel and honey; midpalate shows a medium chewy texture, and the taste profile suddenly turns drier than the entry, boasting the oak resins and acids more than the grain component. The wood intensity from twenty-eight years eclipses the grains by too wide a margin. That said, there is enough quality here for a recommendation.
2017 Rating: ★ ★ ★/Recommended

Paddleford Creek Small Batch Bourbon 41.5% abv, $21.
Bright eighteen-karat-gold color; flawless purity. First sniffs detect subdued scents that include newly tanned leather, canned corn, and candle wax; another six minutes of air contact don't stimulate much more aromatically, save for distant parchment and sawdust smells. Entry is pleasing as well-developed tastes of dry, unsweetened breakfast cereal and resiny oak take charge; midpalate stays the course mapped out in the entry, adding only a waxy texture. Ends off-dry, uncomplicated, and clean.
2015 Rating: ★ ★ ★/Recommended

Pappy Van Winkle 15 Year Old Family Reserve Bourbon 53.5% abv, $120.
Persimmon color; ideal purity. My first nosings pick up pronounced fragrances of flan topped with caramel, egg cream, oak plank, nutmeg, and brown sugar; further aeration stimulates additional aromas, including sealing wax, grain husk, masa/tamale, and polenta. Entry is texturally rich and comely, with zesty, piquant, and surprisingly dry opening flavors of black peppercorn, toasted marshmallow, and burnt tobacco; midpalate stage reverberates

with lively flavors of cinnamon bun, vanilla extract, maple fudge, graham cracker, and oak resins. The finish is long, semisweet, woody, candied, and concentrated. Extremely yummy.
2019 Rating: ★ ★ ★ ★ ★/Highest Recommendation

Pappy Van Winkle 20 Year Old Family Reserve Bourbon 45.2% abv, $200.
Fulvous color; clean and free of sediment. Initial inhalations pick up toasted almond, butcher's wax, and vinyl notes that are driven by grain husk/corn husk dominance; later sniffs detect multilayered scents of dry breakfast cereal, toasted sourdough bread, and black walnut. Entry flavors of nougat, bear claw pastry, and hominy are supported by a viscous texture that wraps around the tongue like velvet; midpalate stage provides the drinker with a rare experience of complete elemental harmony in which all the moving parts—alcohol level, base material, pH, acidity, and oak—are perfectly synchronized. Aftertaste showcases the oaky lipids (fats) that make this KSB so undeniably brilliant and unique.
2019 Rating: ★ ★ ★ ★ ★/Highest Recommendation

Pappy Van Winkle 23 Year Old Family Reserve Bourbon 47.8% abv, $300.
Ochre color; pristinely clean. Wow, the curious opening aroma is bursting with bean- and curd-like fragrances that are elemental, earthy, almost wet sand–like, and yet is reminiscent of egg white and meringue; second passes uncover legume aromas that also give off flashes of pound cake, cornmeal, and cornstarch . . . mind bending, really. Entry is full in texture, juicy, fruity (dried fruits mostly, like figs, black raisins, dates), and succulent; midpalate hums with vibrancy considering this whiskey's advanced age, as wildcard flavors of raisins, brown sugar, chocolate fudge, cocoa, treacle, and mature rum vie for dominance. Aftertaste is raisiny, tart, and bakery goods–like. A very good KSB, but I prefer the 15 and 20 Pappys.
2019 Rating: ★ ★ ★ ★/Highly Recommended

Parker's Heritage Collection 11 Year Old Single Barrel KSBW 61% abv, $130.
Wow, the deep mahogany/rust color is dazzling and pure. What I detect aromatically right from the start are mesmerizing toasted/roasted smells of sweet corn (like corn on the cob cooking on a grill), dried hops, coffee bean, espresso, grain kernel, and toffee; later sniffs after more aeration discover mature, fully melded scents of oak resin, maple, cigar box, matured tobacco leaf, old leather-bound books, vegetable cooking oil, and unsalted butter—this is an olfactory treat of the first magnitude. Entry is warming in the mouth but neither raw nor aggressively hot, intensely nut-like (candied walnuts), succulent, bittersweet, caramel corn–like, yet composed, elegant, and hearty; midpalate is its zenith moment as the flavors converge into one bittersweet, dense, deeply corn-like taste that's weighty, satiny in texture, leaning more to spicy dryness than corn-syrup sweetness (hence, bittersweet) and perfectly balanced. Concludes nearly fat in the throat, creamy, and fathomlessly long. Easily in my top two or three editions of this masterful annual series. This, my friends, is what American whiskey making is all about at its very finest.
2017 Rating: ★ ★ ★ ★ ★/Highest Recommendation

Parker's Heritage Collection 13 Year Old Cask Strength Kentucky Straight Wheat Whiskey 63.7% abv, $90.
Deep burnished orange/bronze color is gorgeous; flawless purity. First whiffs detect dry,

almost fiber-like aromas of cotton fabric, snack crackers, unsweetened breakfast cereal, sour-dough toast; second-stage inhalations after further air contact detect traces of dark honey, textile fiber, bread dough. Entry is sweeter than the bouquet, offering toasted, roasted, charred flavors of burnt toast, toasted marshmallow; midpalate flavors are riper than those of the entry, plus they are plummy, fruity, baked, honeyed, and all-around tantalizing. Ends on a sap-like note that's resiny, maple syrup–like, deeply spicy (black pepper and vanilla). Exquisitely luscious.

2015 Rating: ★ ★ ★ ★ ★/Highest Recommendation

Parker's Heritage Collection 18 Year Old Kentucky Straight Malt Whiskey 54% abv, $100.

Bronze/saffron color; flawless clarity. I like the initial aromas after the pour as they are powerful yet sedate in their scale—I discover animated scents of honeysuckle, jasmine, new leather, sweetened breakfast cereal; second inhalations encounter a melded, integrated bouquet that highlights toasted marshmallow, baked pear, honey. Entry is off-dry, almost nutty, then flavors of cocoa bean, dark chocolate, fudge, and nougat explode in the midpalate stage, which highlights delectable tastes of roasted nuts, grilled meat, and is chewy and bakery-shop luscious; midpalate reminds me of chocolate croissant, cocoa butter, molasses, chocolate fudge. Aftertaste is long, buttery, oily, sweet, and utterly delicious.

2015 Rating: ★ ★ ★ ★ ★/Highest Recommendation

Parker's Heritage Collection 2016 24 Year Old Bottled-in-Bond KSBW 50% abv, $249.

Deep cinnamon/henna color that bedazzles the eye; perfect clarity. Initial nosing impressions are of a whiskey that's subtle, almost restrained in its potency (it is 50 percent abv after all), slightly nutty, resiny/sappy, more dry than sweet for a straight bourbon, and moderately floral (dried violets); second-round sniffs pick up more animated fragrances, especially parchment, lead pencil, minerals, and stone—a narrowly focused bouquet that seems ready to explode with aroma but just can't seem to get off the launching pad. Entry bursts from its self-imposed aromatic bounds with a mild cascade of dry, slightly biting flavors that mirror, to a degree, the impressions of the nose, namely lead pencil, metal, oak resins, dried flowers; midpalate is where this bourbon does its best work in the flavor profile of caramel corn, bacon fat, smoked sausage meat, and dried cherry. Aftertaste is very tight from the high level of oaky tannic acid, and by this point the taste has pretty much dried out due to, I believe, too much time in barrel. Still enough there to enjoy as a bottled-in-bond bourbon.

2016 Rating: ★ ★ ★/Recommended

Parker's Heritage Collection 7 Year Old Finished in Orange Curaçao Barrels KSBW 55% abv, $90.

Tawny/sinopia-brown color; perfect purity. Wow, this opening aroma has soft, tart hints of dried orange rind that mingle nicely with the cornflakes breakfast cereal scent of bourbon; more time in the glass allows the bouquet to become more expressive as added subtle scents of tangerine, polenta, and cornstarch combine for a unique bouquet. Entry is candy sweet with dried orange-peel zest and oiliness that merge well with the caramel corn and pork rind flavors; midpalate provides the platform for the disparate taste elements to come together into a unified flavor profile, but that doesn't appear to happen as the orange curaçao influence dominates and the alcohol overheats in the throat. This would have worked had the abv's volume been turned down to 45–47 percent. I like the innovative concept, but the high proof got in the way of success.

2018 Rating: ★★/Not Recommended

Parker's Heritage Collection Heavy Char Kentucky Straight Rye Whiskey 52.5% abv, $150.

Cocoa-brown color; flawless purity. Oh my, the immediate effect of the seedless rye bread aroma is stark and definitive, desert dry and piquant, roasted and deeply grain husk–like; further time in the glass brings out traces of sawdust, black peppercorn, coffee bean, and pinto bean fragrances that underscore the rye grain aspect. Entry is sturdy in structure, slightly zesty, round and supple in texture, and campfire embers–warm; midpalate breaks new flavor ground by adding tastes of bacon fat, sausage meat, and maple candy. Concludes long in the throat, more peppery than I anticipated, but that's just fine, and gracefully integrated. Another superb expression from this esteemed American whiskey series from Heaven Hill that honors the legacy of the late Parker Beam.

2019 Rating: ★★★★/Highly Recommended

Parker's Heritage Collection Master Distiller's Blend of Mashbills KSBW 63.5% abv, $80.

Gorgeous deep-topaz/bronze appearance; impeccable clarity. Even though the cask strength abv is lofty, the opening aroma isn't in the least overpowering or hot and is, in fact, concentrated, oaky, dry and oily; after another seven minutes of air contact, the aromatic profile opens further, releasing BIG WOOD scents of oak plank, resin, and char that supports the intense graininess. Entry is incredibly elegant, gamey, pork rind–like, with touches of soy sauce, Worcestershire sauce, and caramelized onion; midpalate offers smoky flavors of BBQ meat, molasses, candied pear, and cigar tobacco. Finishes extra long in the throat and oily/buttery.

2014 Rating: ★★★★★/Highest Recommendation

Peerless Barrel Proof Kentucky Straight Rye Whiskey 54.1% abv, $125.

Clean and clear bronze color. Up front, I smell orchard fruits, candle wax, newly tanned leather, sawdust, oak plank, and unseeded rye bread; later sniffs following more air contact unearth deeper aromas of light honey, mint/menthol, honeysuckle, jasmine, and black tea. Entry is gently sweet, rich in texture, caramel-like, and peppery; midpalate features the rye grain aspect as the taste profile turns drier and more succulent, as well as oily in texture. Finishes medium long, off-dry, slightly nutty, grainy, breakfast cereal–like, and appealingly plush.

2018 Rating: ★★★★/Highly Recommended

Penny Packer KSBW 40% abv, $22.

Pretty bronze/goldenrod color; impeccable clarity. First nosing encounters understated, simplistic aromas that include brown butter and popcorn; further aeration time of seven minutes brings out barely perceptible scents of lacquer, wood resins, and pear. Entry is at least more animated than the indifferent bouquet as pleasant bittersweet tastes of almond paste and butter brickle take the lead; midpalate doesn't deviate much from the entry course, except to add a brown sugar aspect that supplements the candy bar–like primary flavor. Concludes politely on a nutty note.

2014 Rating: ★ ★ ★/Recommended

Pikesville Straight Rye Whiskey 55% abv, $50.

Rich, bronze/ochre color; impeccable clarity. Goodness gracious, this opening bouquet is evolved, intensely nutty, with vegetal underpinnings that remind me of grass, forest floor, but the top-note aromas are delicately floral; second passes highlight the dried flower aspect but also chime in with nuances of clove, nutmeg, black cherry, pomegranate—for a whiskey that's 110 proof, the bouquet is lithe and elegant. Entry offers bigger, meatier sensations than the wispy aroma in the spirit-driven forms of cocoa bean, dark caramel, high-cocoa-content chocolate, caramelized onion; treacle; midpalate reinforces the entry findings but throws in honey and egg cream for laughs. Finishes toffee-like, intensely concentrated, oily, slightly salty, complex, woody/resiny, fruity. A paradoxical rye whose bouquet borders on being delicate before the flavors explode on the palate like TNT.

2015 Rating: ★ ★ ★ ★ ★/Highest Recommendation

Pine Barrens Cherrywood Smoked Malt American Single Malt Whisky 47.5% abv, $45.

Bright, pretty, new-copper color shines under the examination lamp; excellent clarity. Opening nosing passes on this peculiar but curiously alluring single malt remind me of cardboard, flax/textiles, candle wax, sorghum, tofu, oatmeal, and for some reason make me think of "late autumn/early winter"—go figure—actually, maybe not; second inhalations reprise the findings of the initial passes, adding nothing new. Entry is deeply grainy, superficially dry, and acidic, but underneath the surface there's an undercurrent of tree sap/resin that's slightly sweet, tangy, and moderately oily, even marginally fruity that lasts long into the midpalate and aftertaste, making for a unique single malt whiskey experience that is worth the trip. I'm not going to tell you that I loved it because I didn't, but there is a genuine baseline of quality.

2015 Rating: ★ ★ ★/Recommended

Ransom Rye-Barley-Wheat Whiskey 46.7% abv, $59.

The stunningly bright appearance is a ginger/cinnamon color and is flawlessly pure. There exist all sorts of exotic aromatic layers in the opening whiffs, including burnt match, nail polish, grain kernel, vegetable oil, walnut, and oak resin/tree sap; more aeration stimulates deeper scents of onionskin parchment, Italian parsley, bay leaf, chewing tobacco, kidney bean, lentils, and sea salt. Entry is grain forward, beany, and kernel-like, slightly waxy, supple, round, dry, yet also tangy; midpalate is the highlight moment for me as the tastes converge on the palate, making for unforgettable flavors that are dry, lean but not austere, astringent, oily, resiny, and just downright luscious, nutty, and ever unfolding. Aftertaste comes off moderately toasty, dry and grainy, nutty.

2016 Rating: ★ ★ ★ ★ ★/Highest Recommendation

Ransom The Emerald 1865 Straight American Whiskey 43.8% abv, $79.

Malted and unmalted barley, malted rye, rolled oats comprise mashbill. Pot still. Brick/burnt sienna color; sediment-free. Zesty, unique first fragrances have aspects of Cheerios, dry sand/minerals, tarragon, oatmeal, muesli, rice cakes, lager beer, yeast; after more air contact, the bouquet turns vegetal and herbal, almost like fall forest but there's also a fine toastiness to it that I favorably respond to. Entry is sweet in a dried herbs manner that highlights tarragon, mint, parsley, and honey; midpalate goes the honeyed grain (Honey Nut Cheerios?) route as the weirdly grainy flavor underpinning ushers the flavor profile into the aftertaste stage that is subtler and more understated than either the entry or the midpalate. Can't recall tasting any whiskey like this. Somehow, it's very old-fashioned to my taste, but I like it and appreciate its point.

2016 Rating: ★★★/Recommended

Rebecca Creek 4 Year Old Texas Single Malt Whiskey 40% abv, $26.

Gold/gamboge color; very good clarity. In the opening sniffs I detect curiously prominent aromas of butcher's wax paper, paraffin, corrugated cardboard, parchment, and tape adhesive, almost as though this whiskey was lovingly made at Staples; further aeration fails to release much more than a weak-kneed graininess that fizzles in the face of the office-supply-shop bouquet. Entry offers a pleasant malted grain toastiness that somewhat redeems the dismal bouquet, but every time I bring the sample glass back to my lips, I catch another jolting whiff of manila folders and floor wax that diminishes the gains made in the mouth; midpalate flops big-time as the waxiness now takes charge, eclipsing the grain element entirely. This whiskey is an unmitigated mess and should be withdrawn from the marketplace by the distiller to avoid irreparable damage with the buying public, bars, and liquor retailers.

2016 Rating: ★/Not Recommended

Redemption 10 Year Old Straight Rye Whiskey 55.50% abv, $180.

Rusty ochre color; sediment-free. First nosing passes pick up sedate aromas of poppy seed, rye husk, rye cereal, but not much more; secondary passes detect faint elements of dried fruits, lead pencil, minerals, dry stone. Entry belies the lackluster bouquet as vivid flavors of brown sugar, cake frosting, and black pepper vie for dominance; midpalate settles down a bit as the taste profile features more of the grain/rye aspect in a dry but oily manner and adds nuances of plum, black raisins, mincemeat. Aftertaste is medium long, spicier than the midpalate, oily in texture, chewy, tobacco-like, roasted.

2016 Rating: ★★★★/Highly Recommended

Redemption 6 Year Old Straight Rye Whiskey 60.95% abv, $80.

Pretty bronze/russet color; flawless purity. There's a slight juiciness to this opening whiff, mostly grapes and raisins, that float atop the foundational fragrance of rye snack crackers and rye breakfast cereal; later inhalations after more aeration discover the spice and sawdust that I'd been expecting earlier on; the last aromatic stage goes all seedless rye bread on me. Entry is keenly spiced (black pepper, cinnamon) and herbal (thyme, bay leaf); midpalate features a sinewy texture that's delightfully oily, and the desert-dry tannic presence becomes the dominant attribute over the rye and the spice. Aftertaste is oily, tart, mildly bitter, fleshy—very tasty.

2016 Rating: ★★★★/Highly Recommended

Redemption 7 Year Old Straight Rye Whiskey 61% abv, $80.

Deep-copper/sorrel/bay color; pristine clarity. The zesty aroma of black peppercorn is

rampant in the initial inhalations after the pour and maintains its status in subsequent whiffs; secondary sniffs after more aeration find that the pepper has faded but that seedless rye bread scent has filled the void; surprisingly the bouquet is not multilayered. Entry reveals a whole other universe of attributes that the nose never exposed, as the taste profile offers everything from candle wax and furniture polish to dried apricot to candied walnut to poppy seed to loose leaf tobacco; midpalate highlights the chewy/dense texture and the dried fruits (apricot, pineapple) as well as dark caramel, chocolate fudge, and cocoa bean. Finishes long, embers-warm, with toasted marshmallow and s'more-like aftertastes. Had the bouquet offered more substance, it'd easily be a five star rye.
2016 Rating: ★ ★ ★ ★/Highly Recommended

Redemption 8 Year Old Straight Rye Whiskey 61.25% abv, $90.

Old-copper/henna color; unblemished clarity. I get chocolate, cocoa bean, burnt marshmallow, and maple syrup in the up-front aromas; secondary whiffs pick up molasses, brown sugar, honey, cinnamon, black pepper, raisin bread, black plum fragrances. Entry is rich, nearly decadent in texture, and the taste profile offers embers-warm flavors of spiced apple, baked pear, toasted rye bread; midpalate is lush, acutely oily and chewy in texture, pruny, raisiny, bittersweet, date- and fig-like, mincemeat-like, and a touch like holiday fruitcake. Finishes very long, ripe, sweet, roasted, praline-like, nutty/nougaty. A fabulously luxurious rye of giant proportions.
2016 Rating: ★ ★ ★ ★ ★/Highest Recommendation

Redwood Empire American Whiskey 45% abv, $45.

A blend of four-, five-, and eleven-year-old bourbon, and two- and three-year-old rye whiskey. Striking tawny color; excellent clarity. At first, I get somewhat limp aromas of hemp, rope, textile fiber, and green tobacco leaves; following more aeration, the nose turns leathery, upholstery-like, unfrosted yellow cake–like, eggy, hoppy, and chaff-like—I can't say that I liked this whiskey bouquet since it didn't have a clear grain direction. Entry is significantly better than the meandering aroma, as distinctive flavors of cornmeal, caramel corn, unsalted snack cracker, and dry breakfast cereal vie for dominance along with woody flavors of maple and vanilla extract; midpalate is satiny in texture, acutely spicy (black peppercorn, clove, cinnamon), grainy, and oaky/maple-like. Aftertaste is pleasantly off-dry to semisweet, coffee bean–like, and toffee-like. The in-mouth phases, from entry to finish, saved this whiskey since the bouquet was a mirage of hollow fragrances.
2017 Rating: ★ ★ ★/Recommended

Relativity The New American Whiskey 40% abv, $35.

Four-grain mashbill using corn, wheat, rye, and barley. The label reports that this whiskey was "Naturally colored and flavored with American oak wood segments. Aged in oak barrels for a minimum of six months." The producers call their maturation process "compression matured technology," created to simulate the four seasons. Fulvous/topaz color; excellent clarity. Opening nose smells of dry cereal grains, newly tanned leather, sawdust, and grain-based snack cracker; further aeration does little to bring out more aromatics so I move on. Entry is toffee-like, candy-shop sweet, nougat-like, and similar to malted milk balls; midpalate delves deeper into the flavor profile, featuring a nicely layered, biscuity taste

menu that highlights appealing things like salted butter, Walkers Shortbread, chocolate custard, and maple. Finishes sweet, sugar cookie–like, and in the tail end, somewhat like toasted marshmallow. The succulent midpalate and aftertaste are worth the trip.
2018 Rating: ★ ★ ★/Recommended

Remus Repeal Reserve Series III Straight Bourbon 50% abv, $85.

Gorgeous deep-copper color; impeccably clear of sediment. Opening fragrances include toffee, nougat, cornmeal/polenta, and baking spices, such as cinnamon, nutmeg, and allspice; further aeration brings out bigger, more pronounced scents of oak plank, tree bark, cinnamon, caraway seeds, and carob. Entry is succulent, heavily roasted, and charcoal-like, plus it's semisweet and akin to bittersweet chocolate; midpalate echoes the entry impressions and adds taut flavors of coffee bean, corn syrup, and toasted marshmallow. Finishes long, leaner than the midpalate, tart, and crisp, showing dashes of corn-syrup flavor. Seriously tasty and complex.
2019 Rating: ★ ★ ★ ★/Highly Recommended

Remus Volstead Reserve 14 Year Old Bottled-in-Bond Straight Bourbon 50% abv, $200.

Tawny color; totally free of sediment. Up front in the aroma, I get flashing traces of grain, dry breakfast cereal, dried flowers (orange blossom, especially), saddle leather, and limestone; later whiffs after more aeration pick up saltwater taffy, poppy seed, coriander, and chickpea. Entry is stunningly luscious, piquant, lushly textured, and exploding with bakery-shop flavors, in particular, prune Danish, apple strudel, and an entire menu of baking spices, most notably, clove, allspice, and vanilla bean; midpalate stage features all of the entry-stage findings plus sultry flavors of BBQ sauce, tomato paste, cinnamon bun, caramelized onion, and crème brûlée. The spectacular finish is infinitely long, succulent, bittersweet, and peppery. A mesmerizing combination of power and elegance.
2019 Rating: ★ ★ ★ ★ ★/Highest Recommendation

Reservoir Bourbon 50% abv, $42/375 ml.

Mahogany/chestnut color; superbly clean. I like the opening aromas that flash earthy, furniture store–like scents of tomato paste, lacquer, wood polish, oak resin, dates, and figs with equal measure; after more time in the glass the aromatics turn distantly fruity (almost tropical), seed- and grain kernel–like, and foresty/tree bark–like. Entry is a tad too harsh for my liking as the alcohol attacks the palate along with the intense woodiness, thereby losing the modifying grain element; midpalate doesn't improve my impressions from the entry stage, as the overbearing oakiness/resiny/bark-like component won't allow for any other characteristic to emerge. Ditto the aftertaste. Over-wooded once in the mouth.
2019 Rating: ★ ★/Not Recommended

Reservoir Rye Whiskey 50% abv, $42/375 ml.

Rusty/rufous color; spotlessly clean. I pick up moderately spicy rye notes (black peppercorn) in the first inhalations plus feathery traces of witch hazel, beeswax, and burning electrical wire; secondary whiffs detect more settled aromas of seedless rye bread, Ryvita crackers, and cardboard box. Entry offers a slinky, silky texture and dry flavor that are highlighted by graham cracker and candied almond flavors; midpalate shows a whole host of tastes, including dates, marzipan, praline, nougat, Fig Newton, vanilla extract (from the deep oak tones), and prune Danish. Finishes quite well, capping off a recovery from a so-so bouquet.

2019 Rating: ★ ★ ★/Recommended

Reservoir Wheat Whiskey 50% abv, $42/375 ml.

Burnt umber/old tawny port–like color; sediment-free purity. Curiously, I don't get much from the opening inhalations, except for wet cement, wet sand, and parchment; later sniffs pick up distant grain scents, mostly unsalted snack cracker and dry breakfast cereal. Entry is pleasantly animated and grainy, almost candied from the vanilla bean influence of the oak barrel; midpalate treats the taste buds to flavors of sweetened coconut, candied walnut, praline, meringue, and baked apricot. Aftertaste is brief, nutty, and oily.

2019 Rating: ★ ★ ★/Recommended

Rieger's Monogram 2017 Oloroso Bota Whiskey 52% abv, $100.

A blend of nine-year-old corn whiskey and eleven-year-old rye whiskey that was matured in the solera aging system of Williams & Humbert (sherry producers in southern Spain) botas (barrels) that once contained oloroso sherry. Color is bronze; excellent purity. The first nosings are all about powerful, piquant aromas of egg yolk, burnt matches, caramelized onion, meringue, black plums, black raisins, prunes, and mincemeat—there is no holding back as the high abv thrusts the aromas into your face; further aeration time sees the bouquet settle down a little as it now features s'mores, charred marshmallow, sulfur, brown sugar, and dark chocolate. Entry is spiked with lots of alcohol that makes my lips tingle while the flavor profile hits the right notes of oloroso sherry in abundance, all while deep-sixing the cereal aspects of the whiskey; midpalate echoes the entry as the whiskey aspect attempts a comeback amidst the blitz of oloroso sherry flavor. Aftertaste highlights the, you guessed it, oloroso sherry but it's here where the separate characteristics finally begin to merge. I'm recommending it because Rieger's Monogram is a valiant attempt at doing something different. My primary criticism is that less is indeed sometimes more when dealing with powerful flavors, such as oloroso sherry.

2017 Rating: ★ ★ ★/Recommended

Rittenhouse Bottled-in-Bond Straight Rye Whiskey 50% abv, $28.

Auburn color; unblemished clarity. Initial inhalations detect woody fragrances, in particular cherrywood and oak; second nosings pick up slightly sweeter scents of toasted marshmallow and brown sugar. The chewy entry offers buttercream and dark caramel tastes that blanket the tongue; midpalate focuses more on the breakfast cereal element as the flavor profile becomes roasted, nearly fruity, and honeyed. Concludes rich in texture, reminiscent of maple syrup.

2020 Rating: ★ ★ ★ ★/Highly Recommended

Rock Town 3 Year Old Arkansas Straight Bourbon 46% abv, $45.

Tawny color; immaculate clarity. The strange opening aroma is like wax paper and damp earth and not to my liking at all; later sniffs pick up pod-like scents of uncooked green pea and green beans, and that simply doesn't thrill my olfactory sense. Entry offers descriptive flavor aspects (pleasing nuttiness, dry grain, breakfast cereal) that redeem some of the deficiencies of the bouquet; midpalate furthers the positivity via the richness of this whiskey's texture and

the deep tastes of caramel corn, molasses, honey, and brown sugar. Finishes long, semisweet, cocoa-like, and chocolatey. It came from a long way back to be recommended.
2019 Rating: ★ ★ ★/Recommended

Rock Town Arkansas Bourbon 46% abv, $35.
Sinopia color; flawlessly pure and free of sediment. Initial whiffs after the pour pick up grainy, snack cracker–like, unbuttered popcorn–like aromas that are desert dry and waxy; later sniffs pick up leathery scents that remind me of saddle leather or leather-bound books, with the additional presence of candle wax or paraffin. Entry flavors are reminiscent of toasted wheat bread, bread dough, unsalted snack cracker, and coffee bean; midpalate stays the course on the grain intensity but doesn't offer anything else of interest, such as spice or oak. Simple and a one-note song about nondescript grain.
2019 Rating: ★ ★/Not Recommended

Rock Town Arkansas Rye Whiskey 46% abv, $40.
Pretty auburn/russet color; excellent purity. The opening nose is peculiarly elemental in that it reminds me of tile, damp forest floor, fresh water lake, and rain, which is perhaps not so great for rye whiskey; the intense earthiness continues into the second nosing passes as I continue in vain to search for the rye grain. Entry is similar to the earthy bouquet, but at least now I do get some graininess that's tangy and gently spicy; midpalate sees vast improvement as the grain aspect ascends in a spicy spiral that's peppery, mace- and allspice-like, as well as seed-like (sesame). So atypical and erratic that I can't recommend it.
2019 Rating: ★ ★/Not Recommended

Rock Town Four Grain Sour Mash Arkansas Bourbon 46% abv, $40.
Golden brown color; spotless purity. I don't seem to be able to discern much in the way of early aromatics other than a leather boot–like fragrance; with more air contact, I discover light touches of bacon fat, pork rind, ham, and seeded rye bread. Entry is pleasantly spicy (black pepper) and seed-like (poppy), confirming the second nosing pass impressions; midpalate features a nice graininess that's bread- and biscuit-like. Ends bittersweet, taffy-like, fudge-like, and very much like chocolate-covered walnut.
2019 Rating: ★ ★ ★/Recommended

Rossville Union Barrel Proof Straight Rye Whiskey 56.3% abv, $70.
Fulvous color; ideal clarity. Even though the stratospheric abv is slightly above 112 proof, the initial nosing passes are all about the savory rye grain and the barrel and NOT the alcohol, which is a testament to the talented distilling team at MGP; secondary whiffs after more aeration discover comely fragrances of raisins, prunes, dried peach, and Danish pastry. Entry is roasted, grainy, more off-dry than desert dry, and mildly piquant; midpalate features more of the toasted rye grain in flavor bursts of dry breakfast cereal, muesli, oak resins, maple fudge, and dried orchard fruits, as the elevated abv provides the lush texture to carry the flavor profile forward deep into the complex, wholly satisfying aftertaste. Well executed, seriously deft distilling and oak aging here. A definite winner for any admirer of straight rye whiskey.
2018 Rating: ★ ★ ★ ★/Highly Recommended

Rossville Union Straight Rye Whiskey 47% abv, $40.
Peruvian-brown/amber color; flawless purity. First off, I pick up faint hints of orchard fruits (yellow pear, quince) as well as some tropical fruit (mango) that quickly morph into dry wood and sawdust scents, which are accented with baking spices (nutmeg, mace); secondary passes reveal a toasted rye bread with butter-like aroma that's dry, nuanced, and pleasing. Entry is startlingly bittersweet and pungent as the flavor profile takes a sharp left turn away from the sedate, dry bouquet; midpalate highlights candy-shop tastes akin to candied almond, butterscotch, and honey while the texture remains lean and sinewy. Finishes peppery, punctuated, zesty, and agile. An unusual domestic whiskey whose vivid flavor profile is seemingly disconnected from its subtle aromatics, but as a whole package it works.
2018 Rating: ★★★/Recommended

Rough Rider Bull Moose Rye Whiskey 45% abv, $36.
Burnt sienna color; flawless clarity. This opening nose is ripe, fruity, cereal-like, and even a bit like cherry compote; with more aeration, the aroma settles down into a moderately spicy/peppery bouquet that's direct, assertive, vivid, and delicately sweet and ripe. Entry is jam-packed with flavors, including seedless rye bread, toasted marshmallow, sour-grape hard candy; midpalate mirrors the entry, but at this stage it's the silky texture that tells the biggest story. Aftertaste treats the taste buds to a fully rounded-out, supple rye that's quite lovely.
2016 Rating: ★★★★/Highly Recommended

Rough Rider Straight Bourbon 45% abv, $36.
Sepia-brown color; excellent purity. First whiffs capture delicate aromatic notes of corn husk/tamale, corn bread, and toasted cocoa bean; secondary inhalations encounter high-cocoa-content dark chocolate, sweetened breakfast cereal, sealing wax, and oaky resins. Entry is pleasingly rich, sinewy in texture, as bittersweet as it is sweet, chewy, and delectable; midpalate reflects many of the entry findings, adding toffee and caramel corn flavors that usher in and dominate the savory aftertaste.
2016 Rating: ★★★/Recommended

Rough Rider The Big Stick Cask Strength Rye Whisky 60.5% abv, $60.
Lovely bronze/auburn color; ideal, flawless purity. I liked the aroma on this rye from the very start as it clearly points to the base grain in spades through the defining fragrances of salted crackers, prune, new leather, loose leaf tobacco; second passes reveal spicier notes such as sage, sea salt, toffee, saltwater taffy, chalk/limestone. Entry is voluptuously sweet and spicy, with dried-fruit notes of raisin and prune; midpalate soars to flavor profile heights in waves of campfire-warm elevated abv, caramel, candied walnut, fudge. Ends on an embers-warm note that embraces the tongue, wrapping it in oily layers of spice, grain, oak, and brown sugar. One fraction of a step away from being unctuous, but luckily it didn't reach that point, being instead a robust, slightly fiery dram of succulence and dried fruit.
2015 Rating: ★★★★/Highly Recommended

Russell's Reserve 10 Year Old KSBW 45% abv, $37.
Lovely, bright burnt sienna/burnt-orange color; perfectly sediment-free. Wow, the sweet corn element in the opening whiffs is firmly in control of the aroma, and I'm really

glad about that since the fragrance can only point to straight bourbon and nothing else, but it's also the balance of it with the oak, acidity, and alcohol that makes it so becoming—you really want to badly taste it. Second sniffs gather in added scents of vanilla wafer, graham cracker, honey wheat bread. Entry is moderately sweet, maple-like, resiny, sappy, intensely corn-like, toasty, and succulent; midpalate echoes the entire entry experience and adds beany/corn kernel flavors that are slightly drier than the entry, but just as harmonious and luscious. Aftertaste brings all the components together in a classy, nuanced final flavor that is about as enjoyable as I think 90-proof straight bourbon can be. Seriously yummy.
2017 Rating: ★ ★ ★ ★ ★/Highest Recommendation

Russell's Reserve 2002 Barrel Proof KSBW 57.3% abv, $250.

Mahogany/red-brown color; perfectly pure and free of sediment. Immediately after the pour, there are ripe, dark fruit (black cherry, black plum) scents plus baking spices like clove, cinnamon, and vanilla bean that round off the fruitiness; secondary inhalations are treated to raisiny, peppery, bacon fat, cayenne, and BBQ sauce aromas that are full throttle. Entry echoes the bouquet in spades, featuring piquant, pungent flavors of tomato paste, caramel, rum cake, toasted almond, nougat, and candy bar; midpalate goes further into the flavor stratosphere, offering gargantuan tastes of corn spirit, black cherry, prune, and caramel corn, which reach deep into the fathomless aftertaste that turns more bittersweet than sweet, thereby creating the ideal finish. A genuine milestone, I believe, for Wild Turkey's Russell's Reserve program. This is that occasional over-fifteen-year-old straight bourbon that defies all logic, tradition, and explanation, and is just simply a magnificent American whiskey of the highest standard.
2018 Rating: ★ ★ ★ ★ ★/Highest Recommendation

Russell's Reserve 6 Year Old Kentucky Straight Rye Whiskey 45% abv, $42.

Pretty topaz/amber color; unblemished clarity. Opening whiffs detect slightly sweet but spicy aromas that are dusty dry, mineral-like, lead pencil–like, and beautifully understated and elegant; second nosing passes following more aeration discover resiny/oaky scents that accentuate the black pepper, stone-like aspects, making for a bouquet that is more finesse-driven than powerful. Entry flavors are rich, dry, intensely woody, almost cedar-like, with underlying flavors of toasted bread, breakfast cereal; midpalate reinforces all the virtues found at entry and adds supplementary flavors of brown butter, tree sap/maple, cola nut, birch beer. Finishes medium long, very classy and understated, balanced and supple.
2017 Rating: ★ ★ ★ ★/Highly Recommended

Russell's Reserve Single Barrel Non-Chill Filtered KSBW 55% abv, $52.

Gorgeous, shimmering bright, bronze/cinnamon color; impeccable clarity. Initial inhalations pick up traces of corn syrup, cornmeal, black peppercorn, parchment, dry stone; second passes encounter deeper, multilayered fragrances of praline, almond butter, spiced apple, mace, bay leaf. Entry is fully evolved, warming on the tongue, round and supple, bittersweet, caramel corn–like, rich, buttery/creamy; midpalate reflects all the attributes found in the entry and adds tomato paste, BBQ sauce, brown sugar, crème brûlée flavors that extend long into the succulent, totally satisfying, and roasted finish that's a fitting way to conclude this top-of-the-line KSB experience. A complete whiskey.
2016 Rating: ★ ★ ★ ★ ★/Highest Recommendation

Russell's Reserve Single Barrel Non-Chill Filtered Kentucky Straight Rye Whiskey 52% abv, $60.

Attractive ochre/terra-cotta color; flawless purity. First inhalations encounter toasted, roasted aromas that are moderately fruity (dried apricot) and full-on grainy, almost to me like muesli/granola with dried fruits, a compelling fragrance that I find highly appetizing; second sniffs pick up deeper scents of almond, pine nuts, gum, allspice, mace. Entry is tightly wound, focused, dry to off-dry, subtly spicy (mace, allspice again), deeply woody/resiny, tannic, vanilla bean–like, with a background note of bacon fat that's merely a nuance; midpalate is textbook straight rye, offering a medium toastiness, along with melded flavors of honey nut breakfast cereal, vanilla extract, pine nut, soy sauce, black pepper. Concludes silky in texture, totally dry, bacon-like, soy sauce–like, powerful in structure and impact.
2017 Rating: ★ ★ ★ ★/Highly Recommended

Savage & Cooke "Second Glance" American Whiskey 44% abv, $38.

Made at MGP, Indiana. Luminous autumnal earth yellow/amber color; superb clarity. I pick up burnt match and embers/smoldering campfire notes in the initial whiffs, along with subtle undertones of creosote, pine tar, grain husk, and floor wax; more air contact heightens the burnt match/sulfur smells to the point of them morphing into fragrances reminiscent of vinyl, plastic furniture covering, fava bean, soy/tofu, resin, and cordite. Entry is alluringly off-dry, grainy, plus a touch woody/oaky/vanilla-like and beany; midpalate turns acutely bittersweet, shriveled, dried out, raisiny, baked, and spiked with piquant baking-spice notes, especially clove, cinnamon, and allspice. Finishes trim, lithe, but brief. The un-whiskey-like, industrial alcohol bouquet torpedoes this whiskey immediately, leaving too much ground to make up for the in-mouth stages. Take a pass.
2017 Rating: ★ ★/Not Recommended

Savage & Cooke "The Burning Chair" Straight Bourbon 44% abv, $55.

Made at MGP, Indiana. Tawny/mahogany color; sediment-free purity. This opening nose is all about cereal grain, sealing wax, dry breakfast cereal, multigrain bread, and baker's yeast; with more aeration, the bouquet settles on a dry, prickly pear–like scent that reminds me of walking in an arid desert landscape where moisture is scarce and parched, and cracked earth is prevalent. Entry reveals a highly spiced first flavor of nutmeg and mace, with pleasant background tastes of cola nut and black peppercorn; midpalate is grainy and resiny, featuring baked flavors of charred corn on the cob, maple, caramelized onion, and burnt sugar. Concludes medium long, oily, tannic, bitter, and resiny.
2017 Rating: ★ ★ ★/Recommended

Seven Devils Straight Bourbon 45% abv, $30.

Mashbill of corn, rye, malted barley. Pretty amber/ginger color; excellent clarity. Up-front aromas offer scents of wax paper, textile fiber, peanut butter/shell; secondary whiffs encounter more mainstream bourbon-like corn-driven fragrances, including cornmeal and corn on the cob. Entry is firm, clean, crisp, oaky, corn-like; midpalate is more focused on the corn as the oak draws back, allowing the grain to thrive. Nutty finish. The abv is not an issue

until the embers-warm aftertaste. Good beginning here. Well done. I see genuine potential for even better incarnations.
2015 Rating: ★ ★ ★/Recommended

Shenk's 2019 Release Kentucky Sour Mash Whiskey 45.6% abv, $80.
Black tea/burnished-orange color; excellent purity. Up front, I get big citrus, lemon peel, key lime pie fragrances that tap dance up from the glass with subtlety and elan; this fruit-driven bouquet keeps the citrus coming, but with more aeration changes the direction to baked apple, baked pear, orchard fruit presence that's gently ripe and delicately grainy. Entry shows a bit of alcohol heat attack as the abv dominates the first in-mouth impressions, eclipsing the fruit and soft grain aspects; midpalate turns up the grain dial, exposing the oak influences of tannic acid and resin. Ends on a narrowly-focused woody/oaky tenor that's lean and sinewy, making me think of light whiskey.
2019 Rating: ★ ★ ★/Recommended

Smooth Ambler Contradiction A Blend of Straight Bourbon Whiskies 50% abv, $50.
Bright, shimmering bronze/ochre color; flawlessly clear of sediment. This opening aroma is subdued, a little flaxen-like, slightly beany; later inhalations pick up aridly dry notes of cotton fiber, burlap, and split pea. Entry is substantial on the palate, drier than I had anticipated, intensely woody/oaky/resiny; midpalate features more of the candy corn, caramel corn aspects that are true to the genre. Finishes in a flurry of oily texture, toasted corn–based, corn fritter, honey ham flavor.
2017 Rating: ★ ★ ★ ★/Highly Recommended

Smooth Ambler Old Scout American Whiskey 49.5% abv, $35.
Impeccably clean new-copper color. I like the ripe, sweet rose, sweet red cherry–like, entirely atypical opening nose that's friendly and inviting in its deeply fruity, almost ambrosial manner; more time in the glass urges a fragrance hinting of plum pudding and mincemeat to take hold, making the later pastry-like stages pleasant. Entry mirrors the fruitiness of the aroma, adding woody, vanilla bean elements that enhance the cherry/berry components; mid-palate is sound, solidly constructed, medium oily, drier than the fruity bouquet, and seriously grainy. Finish highlights the grain density, spirit impact of the abv, and shift in flavor focus from fruit to oak and grain, making it a compelling ride from bottle opening to aftertaste.
2017 Rating: ★ ★ ★ ★/Highly Recommended

Sonoma County Distilling Company 2nd Chance Wheat Whiskey 47.1% abv, $55.
The mashbill contains unmalted Canadian wheat as the primary grain with malted rye from the UK. Double distilled in pot stills. Attractive fourteen-karat-gold color; superb clarity. The opening flourish of aromas includes salted snack crackers, a bevy of dried herbs such as sage, parsley, cilantro, loose leaf tobacco, and Shredded Wheat cereal; secondary whiffs pick up an astringent dryness that's akin to arid landscape/high desert. Entry mirrors the later stage nose as the acute astringency cleanses the palate first, then allows the biscuity, snack cracker flavor to dominate, with a slightly salty/saline twist that is supple, round, and creamy in texture; midpalate sees the 47.1 percent abv impact mostly in a warming of the palate that's not searing or fiery but more smoldering, and this gives the cereal graininess

a chance to emit just a deft trace of sweetness as the midpalate transitions to the finish. A whiskey that gets better over the duration of the analysis.

2017 Rating: ★ ★ ★/Recommended

Sonoma County Distilling Company Black Truffle Rye Whiskey 50% abv, $80.

You got that right . . . this is rye whiskey flavored with black truffles . . . just go with it. Beautiful auburn/russet color is totally free of sediment. First nosing passes can't help but pick up deeply earthy aromas of forest floor, moss, fungi, and, yes, black truffles that govern the frontline bouquet; later sniffs echo the opening findings, adding slim measures of brine, dill, black pepper, oak plank. Entry reflects the quintessential earthiness of the bouquet but the 50 percent abv pushes forward industrial flavors of truffle, wax, and cooking oil; midpalate reinforces the entry impressions that simply aren't in the least savory or tasty, but rather raw, moldy, soil-like, and bitter. A bold experiment that didn't work. So, my parting thought is . . . don't go with it.

2017 Rating: ★/Not Recommended

Sonoma County Distilling Company Cherrywood Rye Whiskey 47.8% abv, $55.

Creative mashbill is made up of unmalted Canadian rye, unmalted Canadian wheat, cherrywood smoked malted barley from Wyoming. Double distilled in pot stills. Lovely bronze/burnished orange color; pristine purity. Initially, I encounter mildly alluring scents of dried cherry/prune/black raisins that underscore a dry oakiness that's almost roasted/toasted/charred; secondary whiffs encounter traces of seeds, grain kernel, old saddle leather, black peppercorn. Entry is fresh, acidic, dry to off-dry, raisiny, very cherrywood influenced; midpalate adds tasty flavors of sweetened cereal grain (Grape-Nuts especially), maple syrup, saltwater taffy, toasted marshmallow. Aftertaste is creamy, lush, bittersweet. Nice job with this one.

2017 Rating: ★ ★ ★ ★/Highly Recommended

Sonoma County Distilling Company Sonoma Rye Whiskey 48% abv, $55.

One hundred percent rye whiskey, comprised of unmalted Canadian rye and malted UK rye. Double distilled in pot stills. Deep topaz/sepia color; some very minor particle specks seen floating in the core. The opening aroma is a bit featureless and awkward as there is nothing of consequence to grip on to aromatically; secondary sniffs detect traces of black pepper, metals, lead pencil, carbon, burnt pineapple. Entry is pleasantly grainy and cereal-like, with soft hints of sweetness, baking spice (vanilla), and honey; midpalate echoes the entry, adding supplementary tastes of praline, almond paste/nougat. Aftertaste features a surprising bump in textural richness that nearly makes this rye recommendable. But there's too much ground lost in the aromatic stages of the entry for the midpalate and finish to recoup.

2017 Rating: ★ ★/Not Recommended

Sonoma County Distilling Company West of Kentucky No. 1 Bourbon 47.8% abv, $55.

Mashbill of unmalted yellow corn and unmalted Canadian rye, double distilled in pot stills. New-copper color is deep and henna-like; flawless purity. There's a definitive fruitiness to this opening aroma that's similar to dried cherries or dried red plums, and that makes for pleasing sniffing right from the start; later inhalations pick up oodles of baking spice, including allspice, clove, nutmeg in equal measure. Entry is dry at first and a touch inflammatory from the 47.8 percent abv, but the overall impression is of focused flavors of caramel corn, clove, rum ball candy, and baked cherry; midpalate stresses the baked fruit (cherry plus prune), spicy oak, and the orchestra of baking spices. Aftertaste is solid in structure, suddenly more bittersweet than dry, and flat-out tasty.

2017 Rating: ★ ★ ★ ★/Highly Recommended

Sonoma County Distilling Company West of Kentucky No. 2 Bourbon 47.5% abv, $55.

Mashbill of unmalted yellow corn and unmalted Canadian wheat, double distilled in pot stills. Palo cortado sherry–like auburn color is free of sedimentary particles and very attractive. First nosings detect dry to medium dry aromas of parchment, beeswax, peanut, dry, unsweetened breakfast cereal. Secondary inhalations find light touches of wood resins, sawdust, new leather, but little in the way of spice, candy, honey, or corn. Entry taste is such that I figure the wheat content to be sizeable on the mashbill as the initial taste reminds me of the 2nd Chance Wheat Whiskey and is atypical for a bourbon style; midpalate sips offer a bit more corn-based animation as the flavor profile gears up into a slightly sweeter mode that's more fitting for bourbon. Aftertaste owns a harshness that affects the rating downward. I see good things coming in the next generation or two. Recommendable but could be better.

2017 Rating: ★ ★ ★/Recommended

Sonoma County Distilling Company West of Kentucky No. 3 Bourbon 46% abv, $55.

Mashbill of unmalted yellow corn and unmalted Canadian rye, double distilled in pot stills. Dark bronze color; I can see ribbons of oils floating in the core of this unblemished whiskey. I like the initial aromas of this whiskey as they are balanced between oakiness, graininess, and spiciness in somewhat equal proportion; further aeration brings out leathery and tobacco leaf aspects that are earthy, substantial, and tending to dryness. Entry is decidedly sweeter and spikier than either No. 1 or No. 2, giving the front-load flavor personality and intriguing depth of character; midpalate is round, buttery, slightly smoked, toasty, caramel-like, fudge-like, and keenly bittersweet. Finishes long, supple, spicy (cinnamon, allspice), biscuity, even a little bit honeyed.

2017 Rating: ★ ★ ★ ★/Highly Recommended

Spring 44 Single Barrel Bourbon 50% abv, $60.

Bright amber/gamboge color; unacceptably frightful amount of large gray sediment seen—a cosmetic no-no. I pick up traces of cement/wet sidewalk, butcher's wax, dry breakfast cereal in the opening inhalations; later whiffs see spicy and biscuity aromas emerge, but in general, there's a hollowness to this bouquet. Entry is lush, concentrated, caramel-like, bittersweet; midpalate features all the entry aspects plus a honey nut cereal element that raises this whiskey's stock price, but not enough for a third star and a recommendation. Beleaguered by filtration and wood management flaws.

2015 Rating: ★ ★/Not Recommended

Spring 44 Straight Bourbon 45% abv, $40.

Pretty topaz color; excellent clarity. I like the toasty/roasted cereal aspect of the opening aroma, which is likewise moderately fruity/ripe, spicy/peppery, waxy, sawdust-like; later whiffs detect casaba melon, wood plank, nutshell aromas. Entry is savory, baking spice/cake frosting sweet (vanilla extract), viscous, nutty; midpalate is intensely honeyed, maple-like, with touches of brown butter, snack cracker, shortbread. Finishes beautifully, elegantly, composed, full-bodied. Gloriously luscious.

2015 Rating: ★ ★ ★ ★ ★/Highest Recommendation

St. George Spirits Lot No. 14 Single Malt Whiskey 43% abv, $80.

Sunflower-yellow color; excellent purity. Opening scents are all barley malt as well as a touch of plum-like fruitiness that mingles well with the grain intensity; the ripe, dried-fruit fragrances are clearly influenced by the partial maturation in port and sherry barrels all through the second-stage inhalations. Entry is juicy, slightly pruny, nutty, dry yet ripe; midpalate is more grainy/cereal-like than the entry as the malted barley takes charge of the flavor profile, lasting into the off-dry, baked, plummy conclusion. Highly appealing domestic single malt.

2015 Rating: ★ ★ ★ ★/Highly Recommended

St. George Spirits Lot No. 15 Single Malt Whisky 43% abv, $90.

Bright yellow-gold/straw color; good clarity. Much to my surprise and delight, there's an appealing tropical fruitiness to the opening inhalations that talk to me about citrus, pineapple, and banana fragrances as much as they do semisweet barley malt; second passes discover grape jam, raisins, figs, pine flooring, citric acid, pear tart. Entry continues the fruit-a-thon theme just like the bouquet, and that's okay because the tropical and vineyard fruits are underpinned by hearty flavors of oak, malted milk balls, vegetable oil, tobacco; midpalate bursts with juiciness and an acute tree sap taste that nicely balances the ripeness of the prevailing fruit flavors. Aftertaste is ripe, semisweet, juicy, zesty, atypical, and just a touch tannic to make things really intriguing.

2016 Rating: ★ ★ ★ ★/Highly Recommended

St. George Spirits Lot No. 16 Single Malt Whiskey 43% abv, $90.

Wheat-field/straw-yellow color; excellent purity. The opening aroma is a dusty, dry one-note song of malt-malt-malt, with little room left for anything else; secondary whiffs find a little more animation in the aromatic forms of baked potato, potato scone, old saddle leather, and chaff. Entry is nicely off-dry, cleansing, and biscuity, as the taste profile starts to fatten up, becoming more shortbread (Walkers, especially) batter–like, buttery, and tangy/spicy; midpalate highlights the graininess, and the overall effect is of a moderately sophisticated off-dry flavor that's medium bodied, mildly oily, toasted, and cookie-like. Aftertaste features the shortbread aspect, which is pleasant and lithe.

2017 Rating: ★ ★ ★/Recommended

Stagg Jr. KSBW 65.95% abv, $50.

Pretty burnt sienna color; impeccable clarity. Up-front inhalations are treated to earthy, multilayered aromas of wet straw/grass, forest floor, lichen, wild mushrooms, and wild flowers; with more air contact, the aroma shifts gears becoming more waxy, grain kernel–like, and more like a wood plank floor sprinkled with sawdust; surprisingly, at no time is the elevated abv an issue in the bouquet. Entry is megapowerful in its opening thrust of corn syrup, caramel corn, maple syrup, vanilla bean, and crème brûlée crust; midpalate explodes on the palate in a rainbow of majestically vivid flavors, including dark caramel, dark honey, cocoa powder, sweet tea, caramelized onion, and treacle. Aftertaste is infinitely long, richly textured, dark and ripe, sweet and honeyed. A tremendous value.

2018 Rating: ★ ★ ★ ★ ★/Highest Recommendation

Tanner's Creek Blended Bourbon 42.5% abv, $35.

Exceptionally pretty cocoa-brown/bronze color; very good clarity. Initial, nuanced smells are of pumpkin seed, honeysuckle, black tea, and pumpernickel; secondary sniffs following more air contact encounter featherlight scents of peanut butter, damp hay/grass, moss on damp stone, and unsalted grain snack crackers—what this bouquet lacks is a definitive, distinctive character aspect. Entry is deeply oaky/resiny and severely tannic, thereby creating a high degree of astringency that parches the palate to the point of Sahara-like status; midpalate echoes the entry, squeezing out even more moisture from the dry riverbed–like taste buds to the point where I refuse to continue the review process into the finish. Not a good whiskey from MGP, as it is too wildly one-dimensional.

2018 Rating: ★/Not Recommended

Texas Ranger 1823 Blended Whiskey 40% abv, $70.

Burnished-copper color; immaculate purity. Initial aromatic impressions include hazelnut paste, coffee bean, cocoa bean, nougat, brown butter, dark chocolate; secondary passes find that the candy-shop elements have toned down a little, allowing for traces of grain kernel and husk to emerge. Entry is intensely honey-like, toasted marshmallow–like, and so unabashedly sweet that it's nearly a whiskey liqueur; midpalate serves only to bolster the entry impressions as the flavor profile maintains its ultrasweet direction deep into the candy bar aftertaste. This whiskey (liqueur) is cataclysmically out of balance with the clumsy sweetness clobbering any hints of grain, acidity, or wood. Through it all, I see potential here if the sugar dial were to be turned down by two-thirds. As it stands, this whiskey/liqueur will appeal only to consumers with a severe sweet tooth.

2016 Rating: ★ ★/Not Recommended

Trail's End Finished with Oregon Oak KSBW 45% abv, $50.

Pretty burnished-orange/ochre color; ideal purity. This nose jumps out of the glass without any urging and makes its case in no-nonsense aromatic language, offering heady scents of spiced apple, baked pear, dried pineapple, sweetened breakfast cereal, and caramel corn; secondary whiffs reinforce the elegant yet powerful opening fragrances, adding only oaky vanilla to the menu. Entry is satiny smooth, but with a bit of kicky prickliness that's warming on the tongue and decidedly delicious in a corn syrup manner that's more bittersweet than flat-out gummy sweet; midpalate mirrors the entry, as the texture turns huskier and spicy. Finishes extra long, a touch peppery. I felt that this very good whiskey lost a little momentum in the midpalate, but overall this is a superb bourbon.

2016 Rating: ★ ★ ★ ★/Highly Recommended

Traverse City Whiskey Co. American Cherry Edition Flavored Bourbon 35% abv, $30.

Color is rust; cleanliness factor is perfect. First nosing is all sour yellow cherries, with

nuances of cherry compote; the bouquet is so unabashedly dominated by the cherry fragrance that there's no point in further inhalations. Entry is appealingly sour cherry–like, intensely ripe, and succulent—the strength of this flavor is that it's not at all sweet or unctuous; midpalate echoes the entry as the cherry density fades a little, leaving enough space for the bourbon to shine through, and that element alone makes it worth recommending for people who like flavored whiskeys. But the fact that this flavored whiskey never once goes the overly sweet, jammy route is a testament to the distilling and blending skill of the Traverse City team. Well done.
2017 Rating: ★ ★ ★ ★/Highly Recommended

Traverse City Whiskey Co. North Coast Rye Whiskey 45% abv, $40.

Brilliant, light-catching copper/burnt sienna color; impeccable clarity. The dry opening nose is clearly spicy rye, with high-toned breakfast cereal likenesses and toasted grain aromas that remind me of seedless rye bread and unsalted snack crackers; secondary sniffs pick up added earthy aromas of chaff, grain husk, cardboard, butcher's wax paper, and brown gravy. Entry is aridly dry, nicely spiced with cinnamon and allspice notes, nimble and lean; midpalate is zesty, tangy, deeply dry cereal–like, and just deftly bittersweet, reminiscent of high-cocoa-content dark chocolate. Concludes as a mirror image of the midpalate, in particular, the bittersweet chocolate aspect, but the abv turns a bit aggressive in the heat department.
2017 Rating: ★ ★ ★/Recommended

Traverse City Whiskey Co. Stillhouse Edition Port Barrel Finish Straight Bourbon 43% abv, $40.

Bronze/ochre color; flawless purity. Ohhh yeah, I like this biscuity, raisin bread–like, Danish pastry aroma right from the first whiff as the baked fruit aspect actually heightens the grain/sweet corn intensity by providing a parallel aroma; wow, this aroma knows no bounds as with aeration it fills out, offering piquant scents of black peppercorn, pipe tobacco, apple strudel, winter holiday fruitcake, candied almonds, and mince pie—it's a dazzler of a bouquet. Entry is peppery, fruity (dates, black raisins), spicy (clove, nutmeg), and orange marmalade–like; midpalate is silky in texture, a bit hot all of a sudden, which surprises me since 45 percent abv isn't that high, and is citrusy ripe and baked orchard fruit (apricot especially) sweet. Finishes a little short of the mark in terms of length, but the flavor profile remains agreeably fruit laden, round, and juicy.
2017 Rating: ★ ★ ★ ★/Highly Recommended

Traverse City Whiskey Co. XXX Straight Bourbon 43% abv, $33.

Bright fulvous/sandy-brown color; pristine clarity. Right from the first sniff, I get lots of baked corn bread, masa (the dough for tamales that is a starchy mixture of lard and corn hominy), cedar, cigar box, and potato scone notes, all of which point to bourbon; secondary inhalations encounter more settled, integrated aromas, such as loose leaf tobacco, black tea leaves, corn bread with butter, corn on the cob, and cornflakes. Entry is delightfully crisp, yet corn-syrup sweet and lush; midpalate features layers of baking spice flavors, mostly clove, cinnamon, and vanilla bean, that push forward the sweet corn foundational flavor—the label says that this whiskey was matured in new white oak barrels for "two years or more," and I think that it would have benefited from more of the "more" to round off some of the

brittle edge of the new oak. Finishes fresh, medium long, and entirely proper for a bourbon youngster. My instincts tell me that this whiskey will be even better in the next edition.
2017 Rating: ★ ★ ★/Recommended

Treaty Oak Ghost Hill Bourbon 47.5% abv, $50.

Tawny/copper color; superb clarity. I pick up a similar beeswax-like opening aroma that's strongly associated with textile fibers, paraffin, and cornhusk; secondary inhalations after more air contact introduce a bigger grain/corn presence, mostly in the forms of polenta, unsweetened cornflakes, and cornmeal. Entry owns a richness that's obviously corn-driven as the taste profile goes semisweet, cocoa- and fudge-like, and the texture features a buttery/oily feel that's pleasant; midpalate combines the various flavor aspects, the oily texture, the strong acidity, the oaky vanillin, and the heightened corn taste, creating a satisfying bourbon experience that runs deep into the finish. A Texas bourbon worth the price tag.
2018 Rating: ★ ★ ★ ★/Highly Recommended

Treaty Oak Red Handed 10 Year Old Rye Whiskey 50% abv, $65.

Flax/jasmine color; impeccable clarity. The up-front nosing passes detect traces of unseeded rye bread, toasted oats, and unsalted butter; secondary sniffs after more air contact encounter soft, unevolved scents of lard, pine, and dried flowers (violets). Entry features a slender, fibrous texture that supports simple flavors of baked honey wheat bread, Ryvita crackers, and black peppercorn; midpalate echoes the entry impressions, deepening only on the rye grain front and not the texture. Finishes too limp and undeveloped for a rye that spent a decade in oak. What gives here? I don't expect every rye whiskey I evaluate to be on the level of Thomas H. Handy, or Michter's US*1, but this one simply lacks the rye character that's necessary for a recommendation.
2018 Rating: ★ ★/Not Recommended

Treaty Oak Red Handed Bourbon 47.5% abv, $40.

Bronze color; flawlessly pure. Initial whiffs encounter strong scents of resin, beeswax, paraffin, grain husk, and grain kernels; later inhalations following more aeration detect additional fragrances reminiscent of steamed brown rice, wheat germ, oats, and vinyl. Entry leads off with vivid, lean, and bone-dry tastes of unbuttered corn on the cob, mace, grain kernel, grain husk, and black tea; midpalate stays the spare, no-fat course as the taste profile offers a svelte texture that's low on oiliness and flavors that are contained and moderately complex. Aftertaste stage is where there is more animation as the flavor menu fills out a bit, offering bittersweet cornmeal, candy bar, and corn bread tastes that accent the slender body. Good, but could be improved by adding more textural substance.
2018 Rating: ★ ★ ★/Recommended

Triple Crown North American Blended Whiskey 40% abv, $20.

Eighty percent neutral grain spirits, 20 percent straight bourbon. Goldenrod/old gold color; impeccable clarity. Very grainy in the initial whiffs, which, given the nature of it, one would expect; aroma falls down a bit with aeration since there's just not enough straight whiskey to hold the bouquet together for long. Entry is sweeter than I thought, then at midpalate it turns overly oily and resiny. Pedestrian. I wanted to like it more because I didn't want to be dismissive, knowing its makeup. That said, it simply isn't tasty at all and features no redeeming virtues.

2016 Rating: ★/Not Recommended

TX Texas Strength Bourbon 45% abv, $50.

Copper/tawny color; completely pure and free from sediment. The first whiffs encounter scents of plastic, vinyl, leather, and hemp; later inhalations following more air contact offer mildly pleasing aromas of textile fiber, cornhusk, cornstarch, and grain kernel. Entry is sweetly nuanced, grainy and breakfast cereal–like, lightly honeyed, and nutty; midpalate features most of the entry impressions, adding a bit of abv heat that envelops the tongue. Ends tasting like charred meat, smoked sausage, and molasses.

2019 Rating: ★ ★ ★/Recommended

Union Horse Legacy Series Company Reserve Straight Bourbon 46% abv, $38.

Brilliant new-copper color; sediment-free. Uh-oh, what I get up front aromatically are whiffs of nail polish, floor wax, parchment, and beeswax, but scant evidence of grain or oak impact; more aeration helps out as the bouquet becomes more grainy/corny and less waxy in later stages, but there's a resiny quality that lingers a bit too long as it masks the corn. Entry features some nice flavors of cornmeal, corn bread, and buttermilk biscuits, but the residue of resiny waxiness remains, even if subdued; midpalate improves as lean tastes of corn husk, toffee, maple, and black pepper rise to the top and lead into a medium-long, austere, oaky finish.

2016 Rating: ★ ★ ★/Recommended

Union Horse Legacy Series Reunion Straight Rye Whiskey 46.5% abv, $41.

Burnt sienna/bronze color; completely free of any sediment. I like this millhouse/grainery first aroma that's both bakery-like and fruity (dried cranberry); second passes pick up fragrances of honey wheat toast, raisin bread, cinnamon. Entry is full of baking spices, especially allspice, nutmeg, as well as bigger, meatier, oakier tastes of vanilla bean and maple; midpalate is oily, spicy, fruity, caramel-like. Long finish is rife with almond paste, dried apricot flavors. Nice.

2016 Rating: ★ ★ ★ ★/Highly Recommended

Very Old Barton KSBW 45% abv, $14.

Saffron/harvest gold color; perfect purity. Linear opening aroma is earthy, parched, and a touch prickly, showing dry-as-a-bone notes of cooking spices (bay leaf, parsley, coriander) and dry cereal; secondary passes following more air contact reveal marginally deeper and denser scents, including oak sap/resin, savory, and black pepper. Entry offers a straight line of flavor, similar to the bouquet, that's woody, bark-like, and root beer–like; midpalate highlights the tightness of the resiny flavor profile that skims along the surface without ever diving deeply. Aftertaste reflects back all the findings in the bouquet and in-mouth stages. Just doesn't exhibit enough bourbon depth or complexity for me to bestow a recommendation. In other words, you get what you pay for: a cleanly made, superficial whiskey.

2019 Rating: ★ ★/Not Recommended

W.L. Weller C.Y.P.B. KSBW 47.5% abv, $40.

Cocoa-brown color; free of sediment. With this opening aroma, I have to dig deep to find any appreciable fragrance, but when I finally do, I encounter pleasing scents of cigar tobacco, dried violets, dry stone, and nougat/almond paste; later whiffs unearth deeper, more substantial yet subtle fragrances including peanut butter, toasted wheat bread, caraway seed, and cake batter. Entry is succulent, semisweet, and rife with dried fruits, in particular, raisins, figs, and dates; the midpalate stage is the apex moment wherein the taste profile unfolds completely, offering stately, integrated flavors of candied almond, black pepper, honey, praline, cola nut, bacon fat, and molasses. Finishes long, semisweet, toasted, and fudge-like.
2019 Rating: ★ ★ ★ ★/Highly Recommended

W.L. Weller Full Proof KSBW 57% abv, $50.

Bronze/brown leather color; immaculately pure. Right from the initial whiffs I like this opening nose for its harmony, elegance, and fruit-filled personality, plus there's absolutely no hint of abv burn, even at 114 proof, which is always a great sign of things to come; and I can report that those aromatic things to come are astonishingly lovely, seductive without being decadent as the primary fragrances include orange marmalade on toast, cornmeal (masa), dried figs and dates, black raisins, and chocolate-covered cherries. Entry reflects many of the aromatic attributes while adding the zest of the elevated alcohol that underpins the entire flavor impression; midpalate offers a taste banquet that's brimming with toasted almond, nougat candy bar, cashews, toasted wheat bread, and salted pork. Finishes long, peppery, piquant, manageably fiery, and damn near succulent.
2019 Rating: ★ ★ ★ ★/Highly Recommended

W.L. Weller Old Weller Antique 107 KSBW 53.5% abv, $20.

Ochre color; spotless purity. The elevated abv is only slightly evident as the aromatic fumes prickle inside the nasal cavity but don't singe it—otherwise, there are lots of early aromatic nuances here, in particular, charred oak, berry fruit, bacon fat, and honey; secondary passes detect latent scents of black peppercorn, black tea leaf, walnut, and mace. Entry is rich and lush in texture (thank you, lofty abv), honeyed and toffee-like in flavor; midpalate highlights are the depth of the texture, the bittersweet character of the honeyed breakfast cereal, and the roasted nuttiness, all of which last long into the campfire-warm, slightly smoky aftertaste. I was very close to bestowing a fourth rating star until the fieriness of the abv lashed out in the final in-mouth phase.
2018 Rating: ★ ★ ★/Recommended

W.L. Weller Single Barrel KSBW 48.5% abv, $50.

Color is carrot/tangerine; impeccably pure. Opening inhalations encounter scents of tart orchard fruits (pear and quince, especially), grain kernel, corn husk, and snack cracker; secondary whiffs after more air contact welcome the caramel corn, caramelized sugar, and cocoa powder scents that accentuate the core fruitiness. Entry explodes on the tongue in a rainbow of flavor colors that include carob, Nutella, roasted walnut, candied banana, and chocolate brownie; midpalate mirrors the entry findings, adding a lush, velvet-like texture that ushers in the long, languid, flinty/metallic, and dry-as-a-bone aftertaste. Superb price/quality ratio.
2020 Rating: ★ ★ ★ ★/Highly Recommended

W.L. Weller Special Reserve KSBW 45% abv, $18.

Pretty cocoa-brown color; flawless cleanliness. Opening nose is chockfull of bakery treats, in particular, dark caramel, fudge, brown sugar, and almond paste (like a classic bear claw pastry); in the secondary passes more tightly wound bakeshop aromas are featured, especially prune Danish, cinnamon bun, and apple fritter. Entry is bittersweet and toasted, offering BBQ-like flavors of tomato paste, paprika, and black pepper; midpalate offers roasted grain flavors of unbuttered popcorn, unsweetened dry breakfast cereal, and caramel corn. Finishes bittersweet, mineral-like, earthy, and lightly toasted. A solid, buy-three-bottles value.

2018 Rating: ★ ★ ★/Recommended

Westland 5th Annual Peat Week American Single Malt Whiskey 50% abv, $100.

Jasmine/flax color; flawlessly clean. Yes, indeed, form confirms name, as the gently sweet fragrance of campfire smoke, toasted marshmallow, pipe tobacco, and seaweed point directly to the undeniable presence of peat; after more aeration, the peatiness turns spicier and more black-pepper piquant, and this development allows the barley to emerge. Entry is tangy, honey sweet, and smoky; midpalate provides the pinnacle moment, as the roasted grain aspect builds in density and intensity, leading to a finish that's bold, hearty, deeply grainy/malty, and positively delicious in its light-handed smokiness.

2019 Rating: ★ ★ ★ ★/Highly Recommended

Westland American Oak American Single Malt Whiskey 46% abv, $70.

Harvest gold/fulvous color; flawlessly clean. Initial nosing passes pick up toasted, nutty, breakfast cereal notes that are dry and settled; secondary whiffs detect bigger notes of malted grain and almond butter. Entry is acidic, dry, cleansing, and grainy; midpalate features deeper layers of grain tastes that accentuate the oak influence by turning the flavor profile in a sweeter, slightly oilier direction. Very pleasant in the aftertaste, which highlights the cereal rather than the oak.

2019 Rating: ★ ★ ★/Recommended

Westland Garryana 2018 Edition 3|1 American Single Malt Whiskey 56% abv, $150.

Cocoa-brown color; pristine clarity. Intriguingly, there's a clearly defined woodiness in the initial inhalations that's reminiscent of cherrywood and/or rosewood in its nuanced fruitiness; secondary sniffs pick up more of the malted barley foundation element that comes out from behind the curtain of oaky astringency. Entry is tart, zesty, resiny from the 112 proof, but neither hot nor harsh; midpalate is where the action starts as the parading flavors march in lockstep, especially the tastes of sweetened breakfast cereal, honey buns, puff pastry, bear claw pastry, and mocha. Concludes long, leisurely, praline-like, and nougaty. My favorite Westland offering? Yes.

2019 Rating: ★ ★ ★ ★ ★/Highest Recommendation

Westland Peated American Single Malt Whiskey 46% abv, $70.

Mango/amber color; very good clarity. Shows a round, slightly oily opening aroma that's moderately smoky, being more cigar ash–like and chimney sooty than iodine-, creosote-like, or medicinal in its slender peatiness; more aeration allows for the malty grain to emerge from behind the see-through veil of smoke, and that development brings with it a dash of caramel sweetness; I like this well-behaved bouquet. Entry more than adequately reflects the olfactory impressions, with the graininess now being more expressive, thereby creating an astringency that's refreshing; midpalate says all the right things as the taste profile turns biscuity, gingerbread-like, and spicy in equal parts, and that leads into the elegant aftertaste that's zesty, grainy/malty, gently smoky, and pipe-tobacco sweet. Lovely.

2019 Rating: ★ ★ ★ ★/Highly Recommended

Westland Reverie American Single Malt Whiskey 50% abv, $135.
Ochre color; completely free of sediment or haze. I like the deeply grainy/malty, malted milk ball–like opening aroma that's dry and sawdust-like; secondary inhalations after more air contact discover traces of dried fruits, mostly raisins, dates, and nectarine, along with subtler hints of pine, mint, and eucalyptus. Entry is balanced, delicately sweet, honeyed, and spiced with baking spices such as allspice and mace; midpalate is loaded with nut-like tastes, including nougat, almond paste, and candied walnut. Finishes long in the throat, gently sweet, maple-like, and fudgy.

2019 Rating: ★ ★ ★ ★/Highly Recommended

Westland Sherry Wood American Single Malt Whiskey 46% abv, $70.
Goldenrod color; ideal purity. The sherry wood impact is immediately evident in the first whiffs, offering languid, raisiny, plum-like, and grilled pineapple scents that work in harmony; secondary inhalations discover more layered scents, including chocolate-covered raisins, sweetened coconut, baked banana doused with nutmeg, and sweet malt. Entry is elegant, polite, and fruity in a baked manner that says more orchard fruit than tropical; midpalate merges the malt, raisiny sherry wood, and the moderate acidity, thereby creating a solid, mildly ambrosial, moderately woody/oaky/vanilla-like taste profile that displays a ton of sophistication. Cruises through the malty finish with style.

2019 Rating: ★ ★ ★ ★/Highly Recommended

Westward American Single Malt Whiskey 45% abv, $70.
Marigold color; flawless purity. The first whiffs pick up a decidedly grainy/dry breakfast cereal/snack cracker aroma that's dry, leathery, and just a touch salty; later inhalations after more aeration encounter fragrances of saddle leather, walnut butter, and peanut shells. Entry flavors (malted milk balls, cocoa powder, candy bar with nougat) come wrapped in a supple, round, and chewy texture that's satiny and full weighted; midpalate features an intensely honey-nut aspect that eclipses all other taste factors, but it somehow works considering the voluptuous nature of the texture. Ends medium long, zesty, and caramel-like.

2019 Rating: ★ ★ ★ ★/Highly Recommended

Westward Cask Strength American Single Malt Whiskey 62.5% abv, $119.
Burnt sienna color; 100 percent free of sediment. This opening aroma is full-bodied, hearty, zesty with alcohol, and a little like coffee latte; later inhalations following more aeration pick up traces of roasted pork, grilled meats, roasted barley malt, and chocolate-covered raisins. Entry is succulent with candied fruits (orange peel especially), candied almonds, marshmallow, cake frosting, and malted milk balls; midpalate turns the abv heat up a notch,

as the flavor profile warms the throat with semisweet tastes of honeyed oats, grilled vegetables, pork rind, and BBQ sauce. Ends semisweet and piquant.
2019 Rating: ★ ★ ★ ★/Highly Recommended

Westward Oregon Pinot Noir Cask American Single Malt Whiskey 45% abv, $65.
Tawny/rust color; excellent clarity. Initial fragrances are a bit muted, offering only nuances of black raisins and roasted barley malt; secondary inhalations after more air contact pick up only scraps of aroma left over from the first sniffs. Entry is semisweet, ripe with grapy fruit, astringent from the acidity and the oak presence, and grainy from the malted barley, but disjointed somehow; midpalate strives to merge the disparate flavor components and succeeds to some extent, particularly in the pleasant aftertaste.
2019 Rating: ★ ★ ★/Recommended

Westward Oregon Stout Cask American Single Malt Whiskey 45% abv, $90.
Gamboge color; perfect clarity. I get first aromas of grain husk, patent leather, grain field at harvest, vinyl, and toasted wheat bread; secondary whiffs pick up all of the first round impressions plus small bits of rayon/textile fiber, steamed peas, and polenta. Entry is sweeter, more yeasty, and far more beer-y than either stage of the bouquet; dry to bittersweet midpalate flavors range from hops to ale to hoisin to soy sauce to yeast to malted barley cereal. Interesting idea that's nicely accomplished.
2019 Rating: ★ ★ ★ ★/Highly Recommended

Wild Turkey 101 KSBW 50.5% abv, $32.
Color is burnt sienna; appearance is spotlessly clear of sediment. The suppleness, bacon fat, and corny/corn bread sweetness of the opening fragrance make it clear this KSBW means business; later whiffs pick up an entire roster of delicious scents, including cinnamon bun, nutmeg, spice cake, rum raisin, dark chocolate, and honey. Entry flavor reflects many of the aromatic impressions, in particular, the rum raisin and spice cake characteristics; midpalate is chockfull of charm, starting with the oily texture that underpins the taste profile that itself is like buttered sweet corn, maple sugar, and red layer tanginess from the char level 4 barrel. Finishes medium long, warm, but neither hot nor raw in the throat. Tremendous value for the money.
2020 Rating: ★ ★ ★ ★/Highly Recommended

Wild Turkey 81 Kentucky Straight Rye Whiskey 40.5% abv, $20.
Pale amber/marigold color; minor, inconsequential sediment seen. Smells up front of green vegetation, mown grass, damp earth, and new leather; another seven minutes of air contact brings out a kernel-like aroma that's dry and beany/grainy; very little spiciness to speak of. Entry is marginally on the sweeter side of the dry/sweet scale and is keenly grainy/biscuit; midpalate turns up the sweetness and spice dials, offering piquant and fruity flavors of cinnamon, cherry, and baked apple. Finish is long, sinewy, and pleasingly spicy. This is a solid rye that goes well in cocktails.
2015 Rating: ★ ★ ★/Recommended

Wild Turkey Kentucky Spirit Single Barrel, Barrel #224/Warehouse A/Rick #2, KSBW 50.5% abv, $57.

Ochre/fulvous color; flawless purity. The first nosing passes don't pick up much in the way of expressive aromas, so I back off to allow it to aerate for five minutes; the second inhalations offer only amorphous fragrances of oak barrel, distant cinnamon, wax candle, and wheat germ; I expected more aroma from this whiskey. Entry picks up the pace a little as the flavor profile features semisweet tastes of brown sugar, English toffee, prunes, and sweetened breakfast cereal with dried fruit; midpalate echoes the entry impressions, adding espresso, coffee bean bitterness, which counters some of the sweet intensity. Concludes surprisingly brief, compact, but pleasantly honeyed. An uneven KSBW experience. I've evaluated other expressions of this KSBW with greater success. This barrel, not so much.
2020 Rating: ★★★/Recommended

Wild Turkey Master's Keep 17 Year Old KSBW 43.4% abv, $150.

Remarkably bright orange/henna color that's gorgeous; excellent clarity, unfettered by debris. In the initial sniffs, I pick up delicate, if peculiar, aromatic features such as new baseball-glove leather, parchment, sawdust, pine, textile fiber, flaxseed oil, apple peel; second passes after more time in the glass bring out gentle spices as well as paper cup, rye bread, cornmeal, cornstarch; this is a highly unusual bouquet that's likable. Entry is succulent yet narrowly defined and contained within the tight bounds of creamed corn, corn syrup, caramel corn; midpalate echoes the entry, going deeper into the grain kernel core flavors that make this bourbon, along with superb acidity, the benchmark that it is since it is at once spicy, zesty, fruity, grainy, oaky, sap-like, candied, bittersweet, fathomlessly luscious long into the finish. Bravo, Eddie Russell. This is distilling brilliance at its American best.
2017 Rating: ★★★★★/Highest Recommendation

Woodford Reserve 2013 Master's Collection Classic Malt Whiskey 45.2% abv, $100.

Oyster shell/dusty yellow color; minor floating debris. Assertive fibrous, flaxen/textile, kernel-like opening aroma that highlights wax paper, grass seed head; later sniffs detect desert dry scents that do not deviate from first impressions. Better in mouth than in nose, this oddball whiskey offers a biscuity entry, then features ungainly flax/textile notes that are harsh and unpleasant. A messed up experiment that shouldn't have been released to the public.
2015 Rating: ★/Not Recommended

Woodford Reserve 2013 Master's Collection Straight Malt Whiskey 45.2% abv, $100.

Sunset-orange/pale amber color; pristine clarity. I detect a subtle nuttiness that is dry yet slightly spiced in the initial whiffs; later on, there are distinctive notes of wheat germ, oak plank and resin, dried legumes. Entry is awkwardly raw, overly wooded, and like drinking paint remover; midpalate is worse than the horrible entry. A disastrous release that tarnishes the Woodford Reserve reputation.
2015 Rating: ★/Not Recommended

Woodford Reserve Distillery Series Double Double Oaked KSBW 45.2% abv, $49/375 ml.

This color can only be described as cherry-juice red/prune; flawless clarity. The nose isn't as animated as that of the Sweet Mash Redux, but it offers its own set of charming attributes, mostly wood influenced and maple-like in the first nosings after the pour; second whiffs pick up subtle notes of cornmeal, sweetened cornflakes, corn fritters, caramel corn—in other words, CORN. Entry is honey sweet, maple-like, with underlying touches of dark toffee, brown sugar, nougat; midpalate echoes the findings of the entry and adds cocoa butter, dark chocolate, and fudge that all last deep into the expansive, candy-shop aftertaste that's a treat. A fantastic whiskey!

2016 Rating: ★★★★★/Highest Recommendation

Woodford Reserve Distillery Series Sweet Mash Redux KSBW 45.2% abv, $49/375 ml.

The stunning appearance is highlighted by its remarkable henna/mahogany color and unblemished purity—dazzling! First nosing passes reveal deep-seated aromas of piquant grains, primarily buttered popcorn, and sweetened breakfast cereal; second inhalations following more aeration pick up toasted scents, like s'mores, as well as old leather book, textile fiber, palm oil, black pepper, toasted honey wheat bread. Entry offers a veritable symphony of flavors, everything from raisins to BBQ sauce to pork rind to tomato paste to caramel to holiday spice cake to honey; midpalate is succulent, bittersweet, toasty, resiny, maple-like. Finish reflects the midpalate in languid waves of campfire-warm, dried fruit, concentrated tastes. A milestone for Woodford Reserve.

2015 Rating: ★★★★★/Highest Recommendation

Woodford Reserve Kentucky Straight Malt Whiskey 45.2% abv, $35.

Bronze color; spotlessly free of sediment as one would expect from this distillery. As with so many Woodfords, this opening aroma is biscuity, supple, buttery, and creamy at first, then it trails off into the forest, offering mossy, woodsy, and leafy notes that are beguiling, earthy, and elemental; second whiffs after allowing for more aeration discover deft touches of paraffin, parchment, and cooking oil. Entry is round, chewy, and loaded with nut-like flavors that are slightly bitter, nougat-like, and totally yummy; midpalate stage offers slightly smoky tastes of toasted marshmallow, grilled meat, BBQ sauce, and tomato paste. Finishes dry, roasted, deeply grain kernel–like, and pungent without being aggressive. Really nice effort here.

2018 Rating: ★★★★/Highly Recommended

Woody Creek Colorado Straight Rye Whiskey 45% abv, $45.

The straw/dusty-gold appearance is old sauternes–like and free of sediment. The first inhalations pick up assertive scents of unseeded rye bread, dried orchard fruits, especially pear, and nuances of baking spice, primarily allspice and clove; secondary whiffs detect bigger hits of baking spices as the bread recedes and the fruits vanish altogether as the bouquet goes super tangy. Entry is a touch more level than the spiky latter nosings as the flavor profile includes elements of zesty rye grain, spice cookies, graham cracker, roasted almond; midpalate features the rye grain now in the form of controlled spiciness, but there's also a sudden medium-range succulence that's savory, tight, and tasty. Finishes medium long, with once again a heightened baking spice aspect that leads the taste parade. Little bit of an

up-and-down flavor ride after a spice-driven bouquet that kept it from a fourth rating star. Otherwise, a capable straight rye with excellent cocktail prospects.
2016 Rating: ★ ★ ★/Recommended

Wyoming Whiskey Outryder Bottled-in-Bond Straight American Whiskey 50% abv, $55.
Produced from Wyoming corn, rye, and malted barley; a marriage of two mashbills distilled in November 2011; all grains are non-GMO. Beautiful sepia/chestnut color; unblemished purity. Wow, I like this up-front, atypical aroma that's a bit parchment-like, but it's also grainy, oaky, stony/flinty, earthy, and mushroomy; secondary whiffs pick up expanded scents of cedar plank, cigar box, pencils. Entry is delicately yet compellingly spicy as the rye component really stands out in the early taste profile; midpalate flavor impact of the rye drops off as suddenly the stony/flinty aspect unearthed in the bouquet comes to dominate the flavor profile. Finishes breakfast cereal sweet and grainy once again. A bit of a roller-coaster ride and it's that up-and-down feature that keeps it at three stars. That said, I see potential here.
2017 Rating: ★ ★ ★/Recommended

Wyoming Whiskey Single Barrel Bourbon 44% abv, $60.
Pretty cocoa-brown color; excellent clarity. In the opening nose I get seemingly incompatible fragrances of toasted bagel, Rice Chex cereal, India ink, parchment, poppy seed, seaweed, and vinyl—what the @&*^!; secondary whiffs following six to seven minutes of more air contact only rattle my brain even more as the aroma turns glue-like, a little stinky/musty, and heavily oaky/resiny, all of which overshadow any sense of cereal grains. Entry appears to regain some semblance of order as the initial tastes are dry, grainy, sap-like, and composed, yet there remains a lingering mustiness that, while less than in the aroma, torpedoes the in-mouth experience; midpalate regains some virtue as the fusty/barrel taint aspect fades somewhat. Aftertaste is the best stage as the corn element comes to the forefront. All that said, after the four star Wyoming Whiskey Bourbon tasted and admired in 2016, this single barrel offering is a disappointment.
2017 Rating: ★ ★/Not Recommended

Wyoming Whiskey Small Batch Bourbon 44% abv, $50.
Attractive amber/honey color; excellent purity. Up front, the aroma is crisply acidic, and therefore very fresh, with side notes of cigar box, caramel corn, toasted cereal grain, oak resin, raisin; secondary inhalations following more time in the glass find appealing nuances of dried cherry, prune, brown butter, caramelized onion. Entry is lean, almost austere in its narrow grain focus, and dry on the tongue; midpalate expands the taste landscape by adding praline, candied walnut, roasted almond, pecan pie. Aftertaste is tightly wound, desert dry, toasted to almost char level, maple-like, and completely intriguing. A whiskey distiller to watch.
2016 Rating: ★ ★ ★ ★/Highly Recommended

Yellow Rose Blended Whiskey 40% abv, $32.
Attractive fourteen-karat-gold color; very good purity. I find a mineral/chalky aroma

in the first burst, but then that blows off, leaving behind mildly pleasant praline and toffee notes; aeration time of another six minutes allows for a chocolate-covered cherry scent to develop. Entry is caramel/confectioner sweet and oaky; midpalate maintains the candy-shop sweetness that evolves more into a nougat-like flavor that might be too sweet and clunky for some veteran whiskey imbibers, including me. Aftertaste reflects the off-balance entry and midpalate to a tee. A stylistic endeavor, but it swings too dangerously far to the sweet side of the dry/sweet meter.

2015 Rating: ★ ★/Not Recommended

Yellow Rose Outlaw Bourbon 40% abv, $65.

Bright copper/bronze color; perfect clarity. Offers a fundamentally sound grainy/cereal aroma in the opening whiffs following the pour plus a bit of candle wax; after seven more minutes in glass, the bouquet rounds out with textile fiber and worn leather fragrances; a respectable, workman-like bourbon bouquet. Entry shows an equal measure of breakfast cereal and wood resin; midpalate comes off simplistic with a hollow flavor core that's moderately sweet from the grain but also features a high degree of wood resin, which eventually breaks down the grain component by the finish, which is its nadir. Needs work.

2015 Rating: ★ ★/Not Recommended

WHISKY—CANADA

Canada's first licensed distillery opened in 1769. Large numbers of Scottish and Irish immigrants who then entered Canada in the nineteenth century brought with them a natural thirst and skill for producing good whisky. In the 1840s, some reports claim that over two hundred distilleries were making whisky, primarily in Ontario and Quebec. Column still distillation is used for base whiskies and pot stills are utilized for what Canadian distillers term their "flavoring whiskies." In the majority of instances, the two whisky styles are married to create a rich, delectable blend. The acknowledged thumbprint character of almost all Canadian whiskies is their delightful drinkability. Canadian whiskies are designed, first and foremost, to be smooth and approachable. In light of the 200+ million bottles that are produced each year, one would have to draw the conclusion that this approach has worked out.

Canadian whiskies are typically made from a majority of corn and lesser portions of rye and barley. Canadian whiskies are matured in barrels, often used barrels, for a legal minimum of three years. Interestingly, as opposed to the rigors of governmentally imposed production regulations south of the border in the USA, Canada's whisky industry is largely self-regulated and is thus a significant departure from other whiskey-making nations, except for Japan. This liberal system allows for the addition of whiskeys from other nations as well as flavoring agents such as sherry. This approach has triumphed for more than a century and a half, as Canadian whiskies have flourished globally and have come to be viewed as reliable and welcome libations. On top of having first-class entrée on an international scale, the gentle, mildly sweet nature of Canadian whiskies makes them prime ingredients in scores of whiskey cocktails.

Two pivotal companies, Hiram Walker & Sons and Joseph E. Seagram & Sons, led the charge in the nineteenth century, and some of their brands still resonate to this day. In recent years, however, smaller distilleries, like Forty Creek in Ontario, Glenora in Nova Scotia, and Urban, The Liberty, and Okanagan in British Columbia, have raised the bar in terms of offering more idiosyncratic, limited-production whiskies that reflect their region. Whisky now represents 25 percent of all spirits produced in Canada, originating in over twenty distilleries sprinkled around the vast Canadian nation from Nova Scotia to British Columbia. Whisky is the only Canadian spirits category that has an "appellation protected" status, meaning that Canadian whisky can only be produced in Canada.

Alberta Premium Dark Batch Canadian Rye Whisky 45% abv, $30.

Beautifully lustrous old-copper-kettle color; superb, sediment-free purity. This opening aroma is mature, evolved, a little kernel-like/beany in nature, but there's likewise a compelling black tea with bergamot element that I like a lot; later sniffs pick up more wood chip/sawdust, oak resins/tannins, new leather scents that add depth and density to the black tea component. Entry dispenses with the black tea and comes on strong with oaky notes that are both spicy (cinnamon, clove) and raisiny; midpalate is more maple-like, sugary but not overly sweet, toasted, grainy, even a little honeyed. Finishes gracefully elegant, more bittersweet (dark chocolate) than sweet, nutty, woody, sap-like, and splendid. A seriously tasty whisky.

2016 Rating: ★ ★ ★ ★/Highly Recommended

Alberta Premium Rye Canadian Whisky 40% abv, $30.

Bright amber/old gold color; ideal clarity. I get all sorts of pleasant candied fruitiness in the initial sniffs after the pour, including spiced pear, cinnamon apple, guava; the later whiffs fade in intensity, but there remains a solid grain core that's basically dry but with a hint of brown-sugar bitterness. Entry is roasted, baked, caramelized, sautéed mushroom–like; midpalate carries forward the roasted aspect of the entry to the point of it resembling BBQ sauce or a rub. Finishes medium long, bittersweet, heavily baked.

2016 Rating: ★ ★ ★/Recommended

Canadian Club 100% Rye Whisky 40% abv, $20.

Bright new-copper/burnt-orange color; flawless purity. I favorably respond to the delicately spicy, snack cracker–like opening aroma that is neither aggressive nor timid; secondary whiffs after more aeration find deeper fruit elements (both tropical and orchard stone fruits) and also a fine-tuned biscuity quality that's savory. Entry is chewy, fruity, oaky, grainy, and a little like seedless rye bread; midpalate is described more as off-dry than dry or sweet and offers multiple layers of tree sap, maple, nougat, candy bar. Aftertaste is like caramel, toffee, marzipan. A handsome rye whisky that would be better served with a 43–44 percent abv rather than the lackluster 40 percent.

2016 Rating: ★ ★ ★/Recommended

Canadian Club 1858 Canadian Blended Whisky 40% abv, $15.

Pretty sepia/topaz color; excellent clarity. The first nosing passes don't pick up much in aroma other than a distant dried-fruit scent that's almost like candied fruit; secondary inhalations are a bit juicier but still rather hollow. Entry exhibits a touch more character as the flavor profile emerges, being led by Juicy Fruit gum, white refined sugar, and just a mere dash of nutmeg; midpalate shows more in the way of depth and core as the taste turns in the direction of sweetened breakfast cereal and toasted honey wheat bread. Finish is brief, quite neutral. Though impressed by the recovery made by the entry and midpalate, I just don't feel that there's enough to drag this potentially good whisky into recommended territory. Having it fade in the aftertaste didn't help.

2016 Rating: ★ ★/Not Recommended

Canadian Club Classic 12 Year Old Small Batch Canadian Whisky 40% abv, $22.

Deep auburn/henna color, almost chestnut; unblemished clarity. I have always appreciated the grain density, elegance, and depth of quality of this whisky's bouquet and this trip is no different; later sniffs discover acres of pine tar, tree sap, maple candy, fudge-like aromas that are round and supple. Entry highlights luscious flavors of dark caramel, candied cereal, cinnamon bun, almond paste, brown sugar; midpalate features many of the entry virtues plus a deepening of the oak resin and breakfast cereal that lasts long into the chewy, buttery finish. A beauty of Canadian whisky making.

2016 Rating: ★ ★ ★ ★/Highly Recommended

Canadian Club Dock No. 57 Blackberry Whisky 40% abv, $16.

Pretty topaz color; excellent purity. Comes right out of the aromatic gate with high-flying blackberry fragrance that dominates throughout the entire first nosing; with further aeration, the blackberry scent turns preserves-like and alluringly jammy, but not necessarily overpowering. Entry is delicately fruity and ripe; midpalate features an unmistakable blackberry flavor but it's tightly controlled and more ripe than sweet. Aftertaste is medium long, berry-like, and delicately jammy.

2015 Rating: ★ ★ ★/Recommended

Canadian Mist Blended Canadian Whisky 40% abv, $9.

Pleasant earth yellow/wheat-field color; spotless purity. Initially, I pick up stale, kernel-like aromas that seem heavy, flaxen, waxy, and woody; later inhalations following more aeration detect the same chunky scents that are laden with candle wax and flax/textile fiber aromas. Entry flavor redeems some of the aromatic staleness with gently sweet, caramel corn–like tastes that seem fresher than the dulled-out bouquet; midpalate stays the course with the headlining corniness, as the flavor profile resembles sweetened breakfast cereal and/or marmalade on toast. Simple, uncomplicated, and while it has no deal-breaking flaws, it's a solid two star whisky.

2018 Rating: ★ ★/Not Recommended

Collingwood Rye 21 Year Old Whisky 40% abv, $70.

Deep amber tone; pure and sediment-free. I detect orchard fruits up front, mostly pears, quince, and apple fragrances that are highly appealing; later sniffs get spiced apple, citric acid, white grapes—an intriguing bouquet. Entry is rich, satiny in texture, ripe, fruity sweet, yet with enough acidity to remain fresh; midpalate features baked apple, spiced pear flavors that are delicious. Tight finish. A Canadian whisky that delivers big-time.

2015 Rating: ★ ★ ★ ★/Highly Recommended

Crown Royal Cornerstone Blend, Noble Collection 40.3% abv, $60.

Deep-amber/topaz hue; excellent clarity. I get a considerable amount of dried fruits in the opening round of sniffing, mostly orchard fruits (cherry, plum) rather than tropical or citrus, plus there's a phantom trace of woody resins; later whiffs detect more in the way of minerals, dry stone/granite, and nickel rather than fruit, all of which brings a pleasing dusty dryness to the latter aromatic stages, which are highly pleasant. Entry is oily, resiny, deeply

woody, and dry, even a touch spicy (nutmeg, cinnamon); midpalate highlights the baking spices and the now sweet oak as the fruit aspects fall away entirely in favor of the acids and fats of the oak. Aftertaste is medium long, bittersweet, tightly wound, and very pleasing.
2016 Rating: ★ ★ ★ ★/Highly Recommended

Crown Royal Fine Deluxe Blended Canadian Whisky 40% abv, $25.

Pretty topaz/amber color; excellent clarity. Up front, I get grainy, ripe, and raisiny aromas that are mature, ambrosial, and keenly pleasant; further aeration unleashes woodier aromas, including vanillin, bacon fat from the oak lipids, and dried flowers that work in harmony with the juiciness. Entry is bakery-shop sweet (refined white sugar), spicy (clove, allspice), and nutty (candied walnut), all making for an alluring no-nonsense flavor profile that is easy and quaffable; midpalate echoes the entry, adding nothing new of consequence. Aftertaste is rock steady, delicately sweet, spicy, and charming. The overall experience, while neither profound nor complex, is so utterly pleasing that it's no wonder to me why Crown Royal accounts for nearly eight million case sales per year. Excellent value.
2018 Rating: ★ ★ ★/Recommended

Crown Royal Hand Selected Barrel Canadian Whisky 51.5% abv, $55.

Brilliant bronze color is sediment-free and pure. Opening whiffs pick up a medium toastiness, along with newly tanned leather, sawdust, clove, baked pineapple. Second passes discover deeper fragrances, especially Christmas holiday cake, complete with candied walnut, dried apricot and pineapple; cinnamon, and nutmeg—considering the 103 proof, the spirit never assaults the olfactory mechanism, allowing the natural aromas to abide. Entry flavors are campfire-embers warm, compellingly toasty, woody/resiny, mildly honeyed, marshmallow-like, cocoa bean–like; midpalate is where this whisky soars as the mélange of flavors suddenly meld with the abv level, creating a stylized whisky of extraordinary pleasure and culture whose refined attributes last long into the lovely, robust aftertaste.
2016 Rating: ★ ★ ★ ★ ★/Highest Recommendation

Crown Royal Maple Finished Fine Deluxe Maple Flavored Whisky 40% abv, $25.

Attractive amber color; flawless clarity. The first aromatic impression is definitely of maple but there's also more than a hint of corn whisky; following another six minutes of air contact, the aroma expands to include oak, creamed corn, and allspice. Entry is firm, more off-dry than sweet, slightly bitter from the sappy maple, and pleasing overall; midpalate is supple, intensely grainy, and therefore more whisky-like than liqueur-like, but with a maple twist that does work well. Finishes clean, long, and sap-like. Pancakes, anyone?
2015 Rating: ★ ★ ★ ★/Highly Recommended

Crown Royal Noble Collection Wine Barrel Finished Canadian Blended Whisky 40.5% abv, $60.

Attractive copper-kettle/auburn color; excellent purity. There are soft first aromas up front that remind me of Anjou pear, clove, and fruit pastry in the most delightful, if nuanced, manner; ten additional minutes of air contact unleash more generous scents of cinnamon, allspice, nectarine, and walnut butter. Entry is gently sweet, delectably oily in texture, slightly toasted/roasted, deeply cereal-like, and sappy/resiny; midpalate features a

deft touch of red wine grapiness that merges well with the semisweet, breakfast cereal–like graininess of the foundational material. The emergence of an abv-driven campfire warmth in the finish brings the experience to a pleasingly comfortable and cozy close.
2017 Rating: ★ ★ ★ ★/Highly Recommended

Crown Royal Northern Harvest Rye Whisky 45% abv, $30.

Pretty new-copper/burnt-orange color; flawless clarity. I like the early fragrance, which is simultaneously fruity (quince, Anjou pear) and spicy (nutmeg, allspice) with the 90-proof spirit never getting in the way; second sniffs after additional air contact find the fruit aspect turning more cherry-like than pear-y and the rye spirit coming alive as the baking spice intensity grows; highly sophisticated bouquet. Entry flavors are evolved, mature yet vividly fresh and acidic as the oak influence fades slightly, leaving the door ajar for the grainy fruit to reemerge. Finishes medium long, spirity, balanced, nearly succulent in its ambrosial third act, and satisfying. Another excellent, fairly priced, timely expression of Crown Royal.
2017 Rating: ★ ★ ★ ★/Highly Recommended

Crown Royal Single Barrel Canadian Whisky 51.5% abv, $55.

This offering is an interesting snapshot of one of the top-shelf whisky components—Coffey Rye—that makes up the Crown Royal Deluxe blend. Eye-catching topaz/sepia color; unblemished clarity. First and second nosings detect remarkably complex toasted grain, seeded rye bread aromas along with sideline scents of almond paste/nougat, baked pear, roasted walnut; a lovely, even stately bouquet of balance and depth. Entry flavor is maple-like, sap-like, sweet but austere and minerally, doughy yet spicy; midpalate tastes surge forward featuring bakery spices, especially allspice, vanilla bean, nutmeg, and clove that accentuate the rye element. Then in the finish there's an unexpected dried orange peel flourish that caps off a satisfying experience of the first rank.
2016 Rating: ★ ★ ★ ★ ★/Highest Recommendation

Crown Royal Vanilla Flavored Whisky 35% abv, $25.

Pleasant topaz/amber color; perfectly clean appearance. Vanilla bean is apparent right off the crack of the aromatic bat, leaving little room for any other fragrance; secondary inhalations following more aeration finds that the vanilla bean dominance doesn't waver; I move on. Entry is very sweet as there is no mistaking what flavor profile it is—vanilla bean; midpalate is heavy on vanilla, more like cake frosting intense than anything else. Finish ditto. The lack of subtlety kills it. After all the great work the Crown Royal team has done, they should know better.
2017 Rating: ★/Not Recommended

Crown Royal XO Cognac Cask Finished Blended Canadian Whisky 40% abv, $50.

Sandy-brown color; impeccably clean. Here is where the barrel influence, at least aromatically, is highly noticeable right from the initial whiffs, as there is a resiny, earthy, dusty-dry, Parmesan-like fragrance that is alluring and subtle; further air contact sees the earthiness fade while a grainy, cornstarch-, cornmeal-like scent ascends along with a raisin-like back note. Entry is delicately sweet and caramelized, exposing sweet corn, honey,

and toffee elements; midpalate is the apex moment in which a latent grapiness/wine-like aspect combines admirably with the graininess in a fine marriage of grape and grain that unfolds deep into the aftertaste. Masterful blending, here.
2018 Rating: ★ ★ ★ ★/Highly Recommended

Crown Royal XR Blended Canadian Whisky 40% abv, $130.
Ochre/burnt-orange color; flawless purity. The opening sniffs pick up an intriguing and compelling mixture of feathery aromas, including scallion, mace, brown butter, raw sugar-cane, and sawdust; further air contact reveals deeper scents, such as newly tanned leather, vegetable cooking oil, lightly toasted wheat bread, and paraffin. Entry is a sensational explosion of integrated flavors, including corn bread, nutmeg, clove, cinnamon, honey, caramel, and egg cream; midpalate builds upon the wonderful entry as deeper, more complex tastes like marmalade, mincemeat, baked pear, spiced apple, and prune Danish lavish the palate with full-throated yet elegant flavors that seem to be infinite in the throat. Nothing short of a masterwork and one of the world's top fifty whiskies.
2018 Rating: ★ ★ ★ ★ ★/Highest Recommendation

Ellington Blended Canadian Whisky 40% abv, $11.
Goldenrod color; excellent clarity. Straightforward up-front aromas are of corn syrup and unbuttered popcorn, with delicate hints of honey; secondary inhalations bring out a little bit of sharpness in the bouquet but not enough for concern. Entry is sweet, mildly corny, and a bit harsh on the tongue; midpalate highlights grain distillate more than corn spirit or wood and as a result disappoints; even though there isn't a major flaw, I find the core of this whisky to be hollow and superficial. Drinkable, but not recommendable.
2014 Rating: ★ ★/Not Recommended

Ellington Reserve Canadian Whisky 8 Year Old 40% abv, $15.
Pretty topaz/amber color; flawless purity. I detect early aromas of sawdust and wood plank plus a dollop of ripe fruit in the first aromatic go-round; further aeration heightens the fruit aspect in the bouquet. Entry is delicately sweet, grainy, and moderately resiny/woody; midpalate is intensely grainy, acidic, and oaky, but not necessarily in equal proportion, and I therefore find the in-mouth stage a little off balance. Aftertaste features a caramel accent that levels off the imbalance to a degree but, as much as I want to, I still have trouble thinking of this as a recommendable whisky. Again, no glaring flaws, but just a lack of bona fide depth.
2014 Rating: ★ ★/Not Recommended

Gibson's Finest 12 Year Old Canadian Whisky 40% abv, $25.
Medium amber color. Initial whiffs encounter grainy sweet aromas of sugary breakfast cereal and Pop-Tarts; secondary passes detect toasted marshmallow and nougat. Entry is unabashedly sweet, maple- and sap-like; midpalate maintains the grainy sweetness but doesn't go overboard with it, and that's the saving grace. Aftertaste is chewy, round, and praline bittersweet.
2015 Rating: ★ ★ ★/Recommended

High River Blended Canadian Whisky 40% abv, CAD$35.
Bright amber color; minor sediment seen but inconsequential. The first nosing passes pick up flattened-out, slightly stale, grain kernel, old silo–like aromas of flaxseed, sealing wax, and old leather/library; additional aeration does provide some assistance as the staleness blows off a bit, leaving space for fragrances of corn bread, English muffin, and toasted white bread. Entry shows off pleasant tastes of graham cracker, toasted marshmallow, and caramel corn; midpalate is raisin-like, pruny, and brown-sugar sweet. Finish is brief, corny. Overall, a ho-hum Canadian blend that's short on aromatic charm, moderately pleasing in the mouth, and quick finishing.
2018 Rating: ★★/Not Recommended

J.P. Wiser's 18 Year Old Limited Release Canadian Whisky 40% abv, CAD$65.
Old gold/bronze/topaz color. Notes of old leather, men's club/library mix with grainy scents in the first sniffs after the pour; later inhalations encounter butterscotch, toffee, and treacle fragrances. Entry is caramel sweet and maple-like; midpalate is round, supple, and grainy/corny. Aftertaste features corn syrup, marshmallow, toasted honey wheat bread, and brown sugar. Nicely complex.
2015 Rating: ★★★★/Highly Recommended

J.P. Wiser's DeLuxe Canadian Whisky 40% abv, CAD$26.
The deep amber tone is almost a bronze color. Very corn-driven opening aroma that focuses on corn syrup and caramel corn scents; additional air contact enhances the corn influence as the bouquet turns sweet and almost but not quite syrupy. Entry is slightly spicy (nutmeg) and cornmeal, corn bread, and corn-syrup sweet; midpalate is grainy/corny sweet. There's an appealing side to this sweet, toffee-like whisky that I respond to.
2015 Rating: ★★★/Recommended

J.P. Wiser's Legacy Canadian Whisky Pinnacle Rye Blend Pot Still Rye Whisky 45% abv, CAD$50.
The bright copper color is attractive. There's a floral aspect to the aroma in the first nosing pass that's pleasing and garden fresh (jasmine, honeysuckle come to mind); aeration stimulates more complexity as the aromatic direction turns more grainy and herbal. Entry reflects that herbaceous aspect yet is equally grainy and breakfast cereal–like; midpalate is long, deep, bittersweet, herbal, fruity, and oaky. Finishes elegantly, firm, spicy, and with grip.
2015 Rating: ★★★★/Highly Recommended

J.P. Wiser's Small Batch Canadian Whisky 43.4% abv, CAD$30.
Lovely bronze hue. This opening aroma is not as sweet as that of the Wiser's DeLuxe and is actually more nut-like and resiny; further aeration brings out the oak resins/sap aspects more and also a sesame seed quality as the grain base remains beneath the surface. Entry is dry, intensely resiny to the point of astringent yet is moderately complex; midpalate features the grain element more and a silky texture. The finish goes a bit harsh in the throat, which prevents a fourth rating star.
2015 Rating: ★★★/Recommended

Masterson's 10 Year Old Straight Rye Whiskey 45% abv, $79.

Saffron color is attractive and pristine. First inhalations detect candle wax, grain husk, and a highly pleasant, slightly spiced (cinnamon) fruitiness that's squarely focused on orchard fruits, in particular, nectarine and pear; the genteel nature of the bouquet is accentuated in the second passes after further aeration as the bouquet turns bakery shop–like, in that the aroma becomes spiced, doughy, and biscuity, almost like sugar cookies with vanilla frosting. Entry is delicately sweet, keenly spicy (cinnamon again plus vanilla bean), mildly spirity, with the orchard fruit now completely faded; midpalate is all spice all the time with a dollop of sweet, tangy oakiness, and a parting shot of vanilla-extract bitterness that ushers in the toasted marshmallow aftertaste. Nice job here as Masterson's once again comes up with a dandy whiskey.

2015 Rating: ★ ★ ★ ★/Highly Recommended

Mister Sam Tribute Blended Whiskey 66.9% abv, $250.

A happy marriage of Canadian and American whiskeys. Deep mahogany color; impeccable clarity. Nose of cigar box, pipe tobacco, Madeira cake, and toffee in that order of ascent, then there's a rush of oaky vanilla, limestone, flint, and sweetened breakfast cereal; elegant, grainy, woody. Entry provides a bona fide "WOW!" moment that is scintillating, fiery, and lush; midpalate provides deep tastes of prunes, raisins, mince pie, candied walnut, toasted marshmallow, pecan pie, and chocolate covered cherry. The full-bodied, oily aftertaste is a hugely satisfying grand finale.

2020 Rating: ★ ★ ★ ★ ★/Highest Recommendation

Okanagan Laird of Fintry Single Malt Whisky 42% abv, $70.

Topaz color; flawless clarity. I smell ample dried cereal, barley malt, malted milk ball notes in the first sniffs; later whiffs feature cherry pit, anise, grape jam, mint, dried herbs (thyme), fennel aromas. Entry is deeply breakfast cereal–like, dry as a bone, pleasantly acidic, grainy/malty; midpalate highlights deft, astringent touches of malt, toffee, nougat, almond butter. Concludes long, toasty, slightly saline, savory.

2015 Rating: ★ ★ ★ ★/Highly Recommended

Orphan Barrel Entrapment 25 Year Old Canadian Whisky 41% abv, $150.

Mashbill is 97 percent corn and 3 percent malted barley. Distilled and matured at Crown Royal Distillery in Gimli, Manitoba, Canada, and bottled in Tullahoma, Tennessee. Color is chestnut/cocoa brown; purity is immaculate and particle-free. First whiffs pick up waxy, taper candle–like aromas that remind me of cardboard, parchment, and textile fiber (nylon, perhaps?); after more time in the glass, the aroma stretches out a bit more, offering grain husk, cornmeal/tamale, and gently spiced (nutmeg) aromas that are mildly pleasing and expressive. Entry at least shows far more vibrancy than the desultory bouquet, as zesty flavors of black pepper, cinnamon, gingerbread, and cornmeal reach for the heights; midpalate echoes the entry impressions, adding substance-enhancing flavors of oak-driven lipids (fats), wood resins, maple, honey, and custard. Finishes gracefully long, tangy, and semisweet. Frankly, the lackluster casualness of the aroma held this otherwise excellent whisky back from earning a fifth rating star.

2018 Rating: ★ ★ ★ ★/Highly Recommended

Pike Creek Canadian Whisky Finished in Vintage Port Barrels 40% abv, $32.

Pretty burnt-orange/copper color; superb purity. Right from the first pour, I detect none-too-subtle aromas of port, black coffee, and minerals/limestone; following another seven minutes of air contact, the aroma turns fruity, ripe, especially dried Mediterranean fruits such as dates or figs. Entry taste is intensely ripe and unabashedly fruity, and the semi-sweet aspect reminds me of pipe tobacco and clove; midpalate flashes flavors of black tea, cinnamon, orange peel, and toffee, all the while maintaining its focus on the fortified wine aspect, which is indelible. Aftertaste is ripe, piney, fruity, and medium long. Damn near a flavored whisky, so evident is the port presence.

2016 Rating: ★ ★ ★ ★/Highly Recommended

Royal Canadian Small Batch Blended Canadian Whisky 40% abv, $20.

Bronze color; impeccably clear and clean. I immediately get gentle, lapping waves of cornmeal and cornflake aromas that are alluring, dry, and substantial; more air contact broadens the aromatic scope, adding scents of pipe tobacco, black tea, toasted almond, and bacon fat. Entry is spicy (cinnamon), zesty, bakery shop–like, and lightly toasted; midpalate is lean yet firmly structured and delicately sweet. The aftertaste provides the highlight reel as the flavors merge into a harmonious taste of marzipan and cocoa powder that makes the difference.

2018 Rating: ★ ★ ★/Recommended

Tap 357 Canadian Maple Rye Whisky Blended Canadian Rye Whisky with Natural Flavors and Caramel Colors 40.5% abv, $30.

Yellow/pale gold color; superb clarity. Smells, not surprisingly, like maple syrup and very dry breakfast cereal in the first sniffs after the pour; maple fragrance remains the primary aromatic focus well into the secondary passes following seven minutes of additional air contact. Entry is intensely maple-like, biscuity, and bittersweet; midpalate features a continuation of the maple dominance. Concludes pleasantly enough, with a toned-down maple aspect. I wanted to like this more than I did, but the limitations include the fact that unless the imbiber really enjoys maple, chances are they won't drink this pseudo-whisky, which is more liqueur-like, in truth.

2015 Rating: ★ ★/Not Recommended

Tap 8 Sherry Finished Aged 8 Years Canadian Rye Whisky 41.5% abv, $40.

Pale-amber/topaz color; excellent clarity. Opening nosing passes detect pleasing aromas of bacon fat, lard, charred meat, candle wax; secondary sniffs encounter rounder scents of rye snack crackers, seeded rye bread, old leather, oak. Entry is supple texturewise, honey sweet, tree sap–like, a touch maple-like, grapy, winey, simple, and straightforward. Finishes well with a woody/oaky flurry of taste that's slightly astringent. I like this substantially more than its sibling, Tap 357.

2016 Rating: ★ ★ ★/Recommended

WhistlePig Old World Series Madeira Finish Straight Rye Whiskey 45% abv, $118.

Rich burnished-orange/rust color; flawless clarity. I detect quite a bit of woodiness up front in the opening whiffs, so much so that I'd describe this best as sappy/resiny, almost bark-like; secondary passes reveal little more in terms of aromatic expansion with a dearth of fruit, spice, nuts, grain, dough/yeast, etc. Entry improves the experience as the taste profile offers hints of sautéed mushroom, dates, dried flowers/leaves, toasted grain; the midpalate stage is this plodding whiskey's best moment as off-dry flavors include ripe grapes, grape jam, and candied walnut that highlight the experience and lead to the tart but juicy finish. Takes this whiskey a while to get up and running by the midpalate stage, and some more persnickety folk might not like that aspect. Again, the price tag works against this whiskey because of high expectations.

2015 Rating: ★ ★ ★/Recommended

WhistlePig Old World Series Port Finish Straight Rye Whiskey 45% abv, $118.

Very pretty bronze/chestnut color; perfect clarity. I get huge, appealing hits of dried black fruit aroma, especially plums, figs (almost like Fig Newton cookies), raisins, but also there are supplemental scents of new leather, tar/asphalt, sweet oak, old dark honey; secondary passes pick up more nuttiness than detected in the opening nosing, but there's a continuance of the dried-fruit/mincemeat component that melds well with the nut aspect; an alluring bouquet. Entry is unabashedly sweet, intensely ripe, grapy; midpalate features an opulent texture that supports the raisiny flavors, which are now totally dried out, angular, even lean as they advance into the austere, earthy, minerally finish. The appearance, luxuriant bouquet, and entry stages are so pleasant that I recommend this straight rye for those highlights, even though at midpalate the flavor dries out, leaving the aftertaste dangling and directionless. Is the price tag too dear for a three star whiskey? Only your financial advisor can decide.

2015 Rating: ★ ★ ★/Recommended

WhistlePig Old World Series Sauternes Finish Straight Rye Whiskey 45% abv, $118.

New-copper/palo cortado color; impeccable purity. There's an obvious element of brown butter at the aromatic beginning that morphs into buttered popcorn, toasted grain, burnt log, fading campfire, old leather wallet; after another few minutes of air contact, the bouquet dispenses with the toastiness/smokiness and launches a full-court press of dried fruits, roasted almond, black peppercorn, light honey scents that work. Entry is concentrated, grapy, resiny, gently sweet; midpalate is long, ropy, chewy, more bittersweet than sweet, and therefore more intriguing. Aftertaste echoes a touch of the early toasted aspect, closing the circle on this pleasing rye.

2015 Rating: ★ ★ ★ ★/Highly Recommended

WhistlePig Straight Rye Whiskey 45% abv, $118.

The henna/auburn color is spoiled a bit by a haze in the core that's not sediment or floating debris, but just a mild turbidity that shouldn't be there. I like the roasted nut (walnut) opening aroma as it stretches out with more air contact to become spicy (sage), minty, and floral (jasmine) into the second passes. Entry is pear-like, juicy, floral, toffee-like, honeyed, zesty, citrusy; midpalate highlights all the entry features plus a sweet graininess that's like sweetened breakfast cereal. Ends on high notes of oily richness and sherry-like sweetness.

2015 Rating: ★ ★ ★ ★/Highly Recommended

WhistlePig The Boss Hog 2014 "Spirit of Mortimer" Straight Rye Whiskey 59–62% abv, $189.

Pretty tawny/henna/auburn color is ruined by masses of floating particles that look unsightly—a visual disaster by any measure. Opening aroma offers sour fruits, wet dog, wet pavement, minerals, some graininess, and some wood; secondary inhalations after further aeration feature more pleasant aspects such as loose leaf tobacco, unseeded rye bread, rye snack crackers, subtle spiritiness, considering the elevated abv. Entry is fiery, caramel-like, fruity, with lesser flavors of marzipan, sour cherry; midpalate is sweeter than the entry, offering succulent tropical notes of pink grapefruit, passion fruit, sweetened breakfast cereal, honey wheat toast, all of which reach deep into the finish. The in-mouth phases of entry, midpalate, finish, where the flavor impact expands by stage, nearly save this whisky from the trash heap. Charging $189 for this flawed whisky is unwarranted. Skip this and plunk down $55 for the Crown Royal Single Barrel if hankering for dazzling Canadian rye whisky. **2015 Rating: ★★/Not Recommended**

WhistlePig The Boss Hog 2016 "The Independent" Straight Rye Whiskey 60.3% abv, $300.

Produced in Alberta, Canada. Gorgeous appearance of bright bronze/brick color and sterling purity. The opening nose is a banquet of luscious aromas, from butterscotch to toffee to cocoa bean to sweetened breakfast cereal; secondary inhalations after more air contact discover a complex, intertwined network of aromas, including woody vanilla, nutmeg, clove, sawdust, holiday fruitcake, and dried tropical fruits, that stimulate and compel the drinker to sniff some more; a lovely bouquet of the first rank. Entry is spiky, prickly, warming, and a bit fiery as the elevated abv takes charge of the early stage; at midpalate, the flavor settles down into a comforting, zesty, deeply grainy and spicy (cardamom, black pepper), steely, and powerful taste that lasts long into the mellow aftertaste that's more bitter than sweet. This whisky, while overpriced, showcases how wonderfully accentuated rye can be when handled with care and precision. **2017 Rating: ★★★★/Highly Recommended**

WHISKY–JAPAN, TAIWAN, FRANCE, INDIA, AND MORE

Two large and ambitious firms dominate the Japanese whisky trade, Suntory and Nikka. In terms of style, Japanese whiskies tend to resemble those produced in Scotland due to their dryness and the use of malted barley. That said, they have developed a style of their own that is currently recognized as classical and elegant.

Production of whisky on a small, local scale began in Japan in the 1870s, but the first commercial distillery proved to be Yamazaki, which opened in 1924. The guiding light of Yamazaki was a visionary named Shinjiro Torii, a pharmaceutical wholesaler, who later founded Kotobukiya. Torii's company would later evolve into the beverage giant Suntory.

Torii had a favorite employee, Masataka Taketsuru, who with gusto took on the study of whisky by traveling to Scotland after World War I. He returned to Japan and helped Torii to establish Yamazaki. Ten years later, in March 1934, he left Yamazaki to start his own company in Hokkaido, which he called Dai Nippon Kaju K.K. and later became Nikka, Yamazaki's main rival. Today, there are between ten to twenty whisky distilleries, including Yamazaki, Chita, and Hakushu (Suntory), Yoichi and Miyagiko (Nikka), Fuji Gotemba (Kirin), Chichibu and Shinshu (Hombo), Eigashima, and White Oak.

Japanese whiskies, comprised of malted barley, are distilled twice in pot stills. To distinguish their whiskies from those of Scotland, to which they are often compared, the Japanese sometimes utilize indigenous oaks, such as *mizunara* that is high in vanillins. Mizunara oak imparts unique flavors that cannot be duplicated elsewhere.

While single malt whiskies, like Yoichi and Yamazaki, are the primary calling card of Japanese distilleries, blended whiskys, such as Hibiki, are becoming more prevalent and admired by discerning whisky lovers.

Yet, there exists no small degree of controversy about the provenance of some Japanese blended whiskies due to Japan's elastic liquor laws, which unfortunately permit a wide range of whiskies to be included in a bottle labeled as "Japanese whisky," even ones produced outside of Japan. This type of legal laxity does not belong in a modern world where guarantees of authenticity are viewed as standard operating procedure for national industries that enjoy global audiences.

As for the other whiskey-making nations included in this chapter—France, Wales, Taiwan, Australia, India, Sweden, South Africa, Spain, and Finland—it is safe to say that huge strides are being made around the world in the effort of making world-class whiskey.

Armorik Armagnac Cask Finish Single Malt Whisky (France) 46% abv, $90.

Buff/amber color; impeccably clean and free of sediment. First nosings offer traces of tobacco leaf, geranium, dried leaves, lead pencil, and malted milk ball candy; later sniffs pick up pleasantly toasted aromas of breakfast cereal, crumpets, and multigrain bread. Entry is delicately sweet and maple-like—the sweetness comes from an irrepressibly fruity ripeness that reminds me most of blackberry jam; midpalate is balanced, grainy, estery, and slightly peppery—in all, a well-knit flavor profile that extends into the satisfying finish as the taste turns drier, leaner, and nutty. Lovely.

2017 Rating: ★ ★ ★ ★/Highly Recommended

Armorik Classic Breton Single Malt Whisky (France) 46% abv, $120.

Citrine color; absolute purity. First off, I get aromatic waves of maltiness and graininess that are pleasing and totally dry; with more aeration the aroma turns down the malt/grain volume, allowing other fragrances to emerge, including saltine cracker, lead pencil, pretzel dough, and baked ham. Entry is zesty, piquant, slightly tannic, but dry and appreciably oily in texture; midpalate turns even drier as the oak impact takes charge of the taste profile in a peppery, tangy manner that lasts long into the agile, tinder-dry aftertaste.

2019 Rating: ★ ★ ★/Recommended

Armorik Double Maturation Breton Single Malt Whisky (France) 46% abv, $120.

Mustard color; flawless clarity. To my disappointment, I don't get much in the way of aroma at all in the initial whiffs except for a citrusy note; more air contact can pry open only a whisper of malted milk ball scent, so I move on. Entry is desert dry, pleasantly grainy/ malty, and a bit metallic and flinty; midpalate is stone dry, but more grainy/malty than the entry, and therefore shows more grip and core substance that leads into the mildly sooty, peppery, tangy, unsweetened breakfast cereal–like aftertaste. There is enough in-mouth recovery to warrant a recommendation.

2019 Rating: ★ ★ ★/Recommended

Armorik Sherry Finish Breton Single Malt Whisky (France) 46% abv, $120.

Harvest gold color; this whisky couldn't be purer than it is. Oh my, I can immediately pick out the raisiny, burnt match–like, baked plum, and figgy fragrance of the sherry wood finish in the opening whiffs; once the whisky aerates a bit more, the malted barley notes make their way to the top of the glass, providing supple, round, biscuity aromas that nicely complement the dried-fruit aspect of the sherry wood finish. Entry flavors are all about the harmony between the dried fruit of the finishing oak and the base material; midpalate features the moderately oily texture that adds yet another pleasing dimension to this sophisticated single malt whisky that lasts deep into the cigar box–like finish. Really lovely from start to end.

2019 Rating: ★ ★ ★ ★/Highly Recommended

Armorik Triagoz Breton Single Malt Whisky (France) 46% abv, $120.

Flax color; not a speck of sediment seen. I like the first sniffs that discover stone-like, flinty scents that are dry and earthy yet show a piquant tanginess that's peppery; second nosing passes after allowing for more aeration find soft notes of unsalted grain cracker, malted barley, sawdust, and oak plank. Entry is firmer in texture than I had anticipated, offering a pleasant oiliness that coats the palate and makes the flavor profile sweeter, more sugar cookie–like than I thought it would be; midpalate is dense, satiny, almost creamy in texture and zesty, tangy, peppery, and resiny in flavor and, frankly, the whole package is delightful. Ends warm in the throat, buttery on the tongue, and just plain tasty.

2019 Rating: ★ ★ ★ ★/Highly Recommended

Armorik Vintage 2002 Breton Single Malt Whisky (France) 56.3% abv, $120.

Gamboge color; unblemished purity. I immediately get curious aromatic notes of cardboard and parchment plus a sideline scent of sealing wax that perplexes me; secondary inhalations after about a dozen more minutes of aeration find unusual fragrances of linen, flannel, and burlap mixed in with dried flowers and apple peel. Entry is texturally round, quite oily, and full as the abv makes itself known in the form of campfire-embers warmth, marshmallow sweetness, and honey; midpalate takes a slightly different road than the entry as the flavor profile turns woodier, more vanilla-like, nutty, and malty. Finishes very long, pleasantly warming, and caramel-like. This malt whisky grew on me as the evaluation progressed.

2019 Rating: ★ ★ ★ ★/Highly Recommended

Bain's Cape Mountain Whisky Single Grain Whisky (South Africa) 43% abv, $39.

Attractive marigold/amber color; perfect purity, showing no sediment. First whiffs detect dry, unsweetened breakfast cereal and snack-cracker aromas that are alluring and moderately spicy; later sniffs after more air contact discover deeper scents of new leather, textile fiber/hemp, parchment, and harvest-time wheat field. Entry is gentle yet sturdy, slightly sweet, and honeyed, with background notes of clove, mincemeat, caramelized onion; midpalate acknowledges all of the entry findings and adds black pepper and citrus zest. Finishes medium long, astringent, with a youthful vigor.

2015 Rating: ★ ★ ★/Recommended

Bastille 1789 Blended Whisky (France) 40% abv, $37.

Goldenrod/harvest gold color; excellent purity. Initial fragrances include graham cracker, peanut butter, Honey Nut Cheerios breakfast cereal, and toasted oats; secondary sniffs pick up further aromas, including unsalted snack cracker, grain kernel, and sawdust. Entry flavors are vivid, slightly smoky, tannic, and therefore very dry, woody/oaky/resiny, and deeply grainy; midpalate features sculpted tastes of oak resin, flaxseed oil, light caramel, and sweetened breakfast cereal. Finishes medium long, pleasantly oily in texture, off-dry, and mildly honeyed.

2018 Rating: ★ ★ ★/Recommended

Bastille 1789 Single Malt Whisky (France) 43% abv, $70.

Wheat-field gold/saffron color; superb purity. The opening aromas are opulent, toasty, grainy, malty, and ripe and, frankly, much nicer than when I evaluated it in 2011; second-stage nosing passes detect delicately spiced fruit-like scents, especially spiced pear, as well as elegant, supplemental fragrances of toffee, cinnamon, allspice, and honeysuckle. Entry carries through on the spiced pear aspect while also featuring ginger snap cookies,

vanilla wafers, and chocolate-covered malted milk ball candies; midpalate echoes the entry, adding more substantial texture elements and acidity that push the spiced fruit and toasted grain flavors forward into the delectable, savory, and medium-long aftertaste.
2018 Rating: ★ ★ ★ ★/Highly Recommended

Berentzen Bushel & Barrel Flavored Straight Bourbon Whiskey (Germany) 30% abv, $23.

Attractive burnt-orange color; superb clarity. Immediately, there's a waxy, slightly spiced apple-peel rush in the opening inhalations that remains potent well into the second nosing passes where little else is discernible; a one-note bouquet that, by all rights, should have offered more scope. Entry is sweet apple-like, with a timid supporting flavor of whiskey, but so dominant is the apple that the whiskey is like a mouse under a steamroller; midpalate echoes all the entry findings, offering no further elements of note. This flavored whiskey isn't at all terrible tasting, but it would be recommendable had the blender mustered any sense of balance by toning down the apple flavoring and thereby allowing the whiskey character to have a chance at contributing something worthwhile.
2015 Rating: ★ ★/Not Recommended

Brenne 10 Year Old Finished in Cognac Casks Single Malt Whisky (France) 48% abv, $100.

Maize color; free of sediment clarity. First aromas here remind me of forest/woods, mushrooms, moss, damp straw, and loose-leaf, uncured tobacco; later inhalations pick up more of grain/malted barley definition, which is aided in large measure by the 96 proof. Entry offers a creamy, oily texture, which I like, as it pushes forward the off-dry maltiness that remains woodsy, earthy, mineral-like, and elemental; midpalate sees the flavor profile fade just a bit in the grain intensity department, as the alcohol takes charge leading to a crisp, clean, medium-long finish.
2018 Rating: ★ ★ ★/Recommended

Brenne Estate Cask Finished in Cognac Casks Single Malt Whisky (France) 40% abv, $60.

Jasmine/flax color; flawless clarity. Wow, there's a dash of baked pineapple fragrance here that's tropical fruit–like and, zesty, all at the same time; with more aeration, the tropical fruit element retains its pineapple-like presence as the bouquet turns plumper and sweeter. Entry is fat, oily, and very ripe as flavors of banana cream pie, unsalted butter, and sweetened breakfast cereal make impressions; midpalate mirrors the entry, adding a touch more acidity that reduces some of the grain kernel–like fatness for the better. Finishes brief, oily, a touch piquant, and simple. Nothing flashy or profound here, but enough fundamental single malt quality for a recommendation.
2018 Rating: ★ ★ ★/Recommended

Brenne Single Malt Whisky (France) 40% abv, $67.

Attractive bronze color; no sediment to be found. Smells damp-grain sweet, earthy, chalky/limestone, spicy in the initial whiffs, then turns floral, summer garden–like, mildly tobacco-like, moderately waxy in the secondary inhalations, bringing to mind unlit candles and carrot cake. Entry reflects the grain-driven sweetness in the bouquet, but then the mid-palate makes the case for stony dryness as the grain is eclipsed by earthiness and by the final taste of dates/figs in the finish. Didn't love it because it wanders all over the flavor map, in particular, but there's also an elemental appeal to it. Different, savory.

2015 Rating: ★ ★ ★/Recommended

Fukano 2017 Edition Whisky (Japan) 42.8% abv, $80.

Made from malted and un-malted rice in a pot still by fifth-generation distillers, located on the Japanese island of Kyushu. Pretty marigold/yellow; superb clarity. Out of the gate, I pick up very clean, green tea, geranium-like aromas that are dry, slightly toasted, and earthy (tilled soil); secondary sniffs after more air contact reveal deeper though still aridly dry scents akin to mineral/stone quarry, orchard fruit pit, and soybean. Entry is spirity warm on the tongue and front-loaded with tangy and dry snack cracker flavors; midpalate goes deeper into the flavor profile, offering unsweetened breakfast cereal, dried hops, and astringent oak resin tastes that are razor edged and brittle. Finishes brief to medium long, arid, slightly toasted, and cleansing. Differently tasty for those whiskey lovers who prefer cruiser-weight agility and a tightly wound, astringent style.

2017 Rating: ★ ★ ★ ★/Highly Recommended

Hakushu 12 Year Old Single Malt Whisky (Japan) 43% abv, $45.

Straw-yellow color; flawless clarity. Offers heightened aromas of seed pod/kernel, sealing wax, and multigrain bread in the initial inhalations after the pour; the waxiness develops into a dry, astringent maltiness/breakfast cereal bouquet that is vivid and appealing. Entry taste shows traces of smoke and iodine, but is not a peat bomb, as the subtle smokiness weaves its way into the malty grainy element with style; midpalate is delicious, integrated, poised, gently sweet, and almost sugary. Finishes medium long in the throat, medium oily in texture, and charmingly sweet and succulent.

2015 Rating: ★ ★ ★ ★/Highly Recommended

Hibiki 12 Year Old Blended Whisky (Japan) 43% abv, $60.

Light-amber/marigold color; excellent purity. Smells of sawdust and pecans in the opening sniffs, plus a bit of summer flower garden (carnation) and spice (nutmeg); there's an acute nuttiness to the aerated bouquet that becomes more like candle wax with further exposure to air; intriguing and unique. Entry taste is cocoa-like, bittersweet, and nicely textured, almost oily (a plus); midpalate stage reveals an intensely grainy core flavor that's both astringent, slightly sweet, and caramel-like. Concludes in a stately manner that's bittersweet, honeyed, and refreshing. A superb blended whisky.

2018 Rating: ★ ★ ★ ★/Highly Recommended

Hibiki Harmony Blended Whisky (Japan) 43% abv, $65.

Amber/topaz color; impeccable clarity. First inhalations are vibrantly spicy, with piquant baking spices emanating from every molecule, especially nutmeg, clove, mace, along with delicate touches of oaky resins/tree sap; second passes encounter more breakfast cereal grains, most notably barley malt, that marry nicely with the still-evident spices and wood notes; a lovely, integrated bouquet. Entry has a smokiness right out of the gate that's unexpected and cigar tobacco–like; midpalate is balanced, with a razor's edge of acidity that maintains the freshness while supporting the bakery-shop surface flavors. Ends with a quiet burst of resiny woodiness that subdues the spiciness but accentuates the dry grain. Highly sophisticated and complex.

2018 Rating: ★ ★ ★ ★/Highly Recommended

Kavalan Concert Master Matured in Port Casks Single Malt Whisky (Taiwan) 40% abv, $90.

Very pretty henna/auburn color; impeccable clarity. Opening nasal impressions include brown sugar, caramel, and deeply toasted grain; the grapy, spicy port pipe (cask) influence accelerates in the second passes after further air contact, making for compelling sniffing. Entry is pruny, almost more Madeira-like than port-like, and candied and caramel-like; midpalate features a more reined-in fruitiness that allows for some evidence of the malt, which is toasty and dry. Ends on a baked fruit note that is a touch bittersweet. Intriguing.

2015 Rating: ★ ★ ★/Recommended

Kavalan Single Malt Whisky (Taiwan) 40% abv, $120.

Amber color; superb purity. In the initial whiffs I detect soft tannins, candle wax, grain husk, and wood plank scents in abundance; after another seven minutes of air contact, the core fragrance remains focused on the grain husk, but satellite scents emerge, including baked plum, fruit pastry, and black pepper. Entry is gently sweet, grainy/malty, and roasted; midpalate is pleasingly satiny, fruitier than the entry, and slightly honeyed. Finishes long in the throat, more honeyed than the midpalate stage, and very much like baked fruit. Comes on strong enough in the midpalate and the finish to pull out the fourth rating star.

2016 Rating: ★ ★ ★ ★/Highly Recommended

Kavalan Solist Matured in Bourbon Casks Cask Strength Single Malt Whisky (Taiwan) 58.2% abv, $175.

Light-amber/old gold/hay-yellow color; sediment-free purity. First nosing passes encounter vigorous, spirity fragrances that are husk-like and waxy and off-dry; following another eight minutes of air contact, the bouquet turns sweetened cereal–like and even a bit candied and reminiscent of a confectioner shop. Entry is warm from the cask strength abv but is not abusive to the palate, and the taste profile is strikingly like trail mix, meaning dry cereal combined with dried fruit and nuts; midpalate reflects much of the entry aspects, adding a bit of dried, sweetened coconut. Concludes very nicely in a sweetened breakfast cereal manner that's oily in texture and keenly grainy/malty.

2016 Rating: ★ ★ ★/Recommended

Kavalan Solist Matured in Vinho Barriques Cask Strength Single Malt Whisky (Taiwan) 57% abv, $175.

Lovely chestnut color; excellent clarity. Whoa, very heady/spirity from the cask strength as assertive vapors rise from the glass and attack the olfactory bulb; to my delight, the abv aspect settles down with further aeration, and the bouquet now offers a mélange of aromas including pork rind, toasted marshmallow, toasted grain, soy sauce, and red-wine vinegar. Entry is sweet, winey, grapy, and chockfull of dark caramel, Raisinets, and dark honey flavors, which overshadow the grain/malt; midpalate is pleasantly toasted and sweet, reminding me of charred marshmallows over a campfire. Finishes long, intensely charred, sap-like sweet, and smoky. Simply too toasted, sappy, and charred for my liking. Lacks any notion of subtlety or nuance.

2015 Rating: ★★/Not Recommended

Kikori Whiskey (Japan) 41% abv, $47.

Canary yellow color; excellent purity. I would have loved it if the aroma had offered me more in the first inhalations other than meek whiffs of candle wax and stone/granite; in the second passes, I encounter faint seed-like scents such as sunflower seed and pumpkin seed, but beyond those it is vacant. Entry offers slightly more character than the anemic bouquet in the bittersweet forms of toffee, coffee latte, cocoa bean, and brown butter; midpalate echoes the entry and doesn't add much in the way of new flavors other than an oiliness that affects the texture. Concludes brief, suddenly grainy, cereal-like, and sappy. Waits too long to start its engine.

2018 Rating: ★★/Not Recommended

Nikka Coffey Grain Whisky (Japan) 45% abv, $70.

Maize/eighteen-karat-gold color; inconsequential sediment seen—not a problem. First sniffs detect spice cake, leafy/twiggy/forest vegetation scents; later whiffs pick up traces of toasted grains, kernel/bean, parchment; a delicate aromatic profile that's dry, grainy. Entry is sweeter than expected, resiny/oaky, honeyed; midpalate features more of the resiny oak influence, vanilla wafer, deep-roasted grains. Ends dry to off-dry, tight, viscous.

2019 Rating: ★★★★/Highly Recommended

Nikka From the Barrel Blended Whisky (Japan) 51.4% abv, $65.

Harvest gold color; ideal purity. Up-front inhalations pick up a varied menu of highly complex fragrances, starting with seeds, including poppy and caraway, and then leading to roasted grains, Lapsang souchong tea, furniture polish, aged leather, and cigar ashes; with more air contact, scents of roasted asparagus, gentian, sautéed mushroom, freeze-dried coffee, and Carnation evaporated milk get added to the long aromatic roster; a stunningly unusual yet beguiling whisky bouquet. Entry tastes like charred meats and roasted grains, but then at midpalate it suddenly turns bittersweet, also like sap, maple, pipe tobacco, toasted marshmallow, pine nut, and brown butter, returning in the aftertaste a bit to the seed-like beginning, especially toasted sesame. I can't think of a whisky from anywhere in the world that is remotely similar to this wonderful Japanese virtuoso.

2019 Rating: ★★★★★/Highest Recommendation

Nikka Miyagikyo Single Malt Whisky (Japan) 45% abv, $80.

Marigold/deep-straw color; superb purity. Immediate smells after the pour are grainy, malty, and like brown rice, with background touches of baking spices (allspice, mace), tofu, and soy sauce; secondary inhalations encounter "greener," more vegetal aromas that eclipse the baking spices. Entry is subtle, keenly spicy (the baking spices make a big return), desert dry, and moderately malty; midpalate features a delightful and satisfying crisp flavor profile that borders on being astringent and edgy as the maltiness merges nicely with the resiny oak,

providing a tightly focused taste experience that's clean and intensely grainy. Finishes a little too short, deeply malty, and even now a touch peppery. Had the aftertaste not dropped off too abruptly, I'd have given this single malt a fifth rating star. It has a lot going for it.
2017 Rating: ★ ★ ★ ★/Highly Recommended

Nikka Taketsuru 12 Year Old Pure Malt Whisky (Japan) 40% abv, $70.
Jonquil/gold color; superb clarity. I encounter faint traces of ripe apple/pear, new leather, candle wax in the opening whiffs; later inhalations pick up more cereal-driven fragrances, especially malt and oatmeal. Entry is honeyed, like Honey Nut Cheerios; midpalate is oily, rich in texture, nutty, candied, with tastes of caramel, nougat. Concludes woody/oaky, semisweet. A delicate whisky of nuance and subtle complexity.
2016 Rating: ★ ★ ★ ★/Highly Recommended

Nikka Taketsuru 17 Year Old Pure Malt Whisky (Japan) 43% abv, $150.
Bright topaz/amber color; excellent purity. Up front, I detect warming, multilayered, roasted cereal notes that are off-dry, kernel-like, even a touch salty; later inhalations pick up steamed brown rice, soybean, butcher's wax, poppy seed. Entry is fruity, snack cracker–like, buttery/creamy; midpalate features candy bar, vanilla bean, clove flavors. Finishes buttery, toasty, elegant, long in the throat.
2017 Rating: ★ ★ ★ ★/Highly Recommended

Nikka Taketsuru 21 Year Old Pure Malt Whisky (Japan) 43% abv, $150.
Bronze color; flawless clarity. I notice that this opening aroma is less concentrated than that of the 17 year old, but still has a measure of kernel-like intensity left; later sniffs pick up lemongrass, citrus peel, black pepper. Entry is soft, buttery, gently sweet, lightly spiced; midpalate is really luscious, deep, confectioner shop–like, biscuit batter–like, honeyed. Aftertaste is lovely, complex. This malt came back strong in the entry and midpalate stages.
2016 Rating: ★ ★ ★ ★/Highly Recommended

Nikka Yoichi Single Malt Whisky (Japan) 45% abv, $80.
Gamboge/flax/chardonnay color; unblemished clarity. In the first nosing passes I pick up all sorts of malty scents, from nougat to candied almond to malted milk balls to milk chocolate to maple; secondary whiffs after more aeration discover salted butter and lightly smoked, toasty aromas that are basically dry, but also nicely rounded and supple. Entry is savory, bittersweet, grainy, toasted bread–like, nutty; midpalate features a medium-full texture that caresses the palate while the dry-leaning flavor profile highlights the malty grain and wood resins, especially the tannic acid, which dries out the flavor so that by the finish it's squeaky-clean and tight. A really tasty, well-made malt.
2017 Rating: ★ ★ ★ ★/Highly Recommended

Nomad Outland Whisky (Spain) 41.3% abv, $39.
Ochre/fulvous color; flawless clarity. Immediately in the first inhalations I pick up the round, raisiny quality of olosoro sherry as well as lighter touches of allspice, cranberry, and malted milk; secondary passes detect deeper fragrances of salted butter, bacon fat, and honey. Entry flavors include maple, prune, black raisins, and dried orange peel; midpalate

deepens the entry impressions and piles on ambrosial tastes of dried orchard fruits, winter holiday fruitcake, mincemeat, and spice cake. Aftertaste is gently sweet, a little like maple syrup, reminiscent of pipe tobacco, and toasty. Very seductive.

2018 Rating: ★ ★ ★ ★/Highly Recommended

Ohishi Brandy Cask Whisky (Japan) 41.6% abv, $75.

Gamboge/fourteen-karat-gold color; superb clarity. Smells gently of honeysuckle flowers, coconut, lavender, damp earth, and mown hay in the opening sniffs after the pour; with additional time in the glass, the aroma shifts its focus more to the dry grain/grain kernel and away from the florist shop as the bouquet offers fragrances of dried hops and potato scone. Entry shows a winey, grapy, nearly ambrosial taste profile that flies in the face of the grainy/flowery aroma, yet somehow works; midpalate features tight flavors of dried fruit, especially figs, raisins, orange that last deep into the pleasing aftertaste. What I enjoyed about this whisky is its gradual evolution to its crescendo moment at midpalate and finish.

2017 Rating: ★ ★ ★ ★/Highly Recommended

Ohishi Sherry Cask Whisky (Japan) 41.9% abv, $75.

Bay/sepia color; completely sediment-free. Initial whiffs pick up heavily toasted grain, campfire aromas of toasted marshmallow, seared pork, bacon fat, tomato paste, asphalt; with more air contact the bouquet expands to include old leather, library, cigar ashes, and Lapsang suchong tea. Entry offers a faint touch of wine/sherry that fades quickly as the richness of the buttery oak takes charge; in midpalate, the flavor profile changes over to a mild smokiness that's strikingly like black tea with honey as the sherry influence returns, leading into a pruny/raisiny aftertaste that's robust, clean, bittersweet, and oaky.

2017 Rating: ★ ★ ★/Recommended

Ohishi Tokubetsu Reserve Whisky (Japan) 40.5% abv, $250.

Made with a combination of their own organic gohyakumanishi rice and mocha rice from Kumamoto Prefecture, then matured in sherry casks. Earth yellow/ochre color; flawless purity. First whiffs are dominated by sherry cask–influenced raisin bran cereal, prune Danish, and crème caramel dessert; later aromas following more aeration carry the sherry cask aspect forward, adding soft touches of burnt matches, sulfur, and Assam tea. Entry picks up right where the second nosing left off with the sherry bomb impact as it throws off heavily baked tastes of oloroso sherry, winter holiday fruitcake, mincemeat pie, and stewed prune; midpalate is yet another figs/dates/raisins flavorfest that is far more bittersweet than sweet and even a little cocoa bean–like or, even better, espresso-like as heavy-hitting spices such as clove, nutmeg, and cinnamon vie for dominance all the way through the generous but not fat aftertaste.

2017 Rating: ★ ★ ★ ★/Highly Recommended

Paul John Brilliance Single Malt Whisky (India) 46% abv, $60.

Bright amber/old-gold color; flawless purity. Starts out aromatically showing ample dry breakfast cereal and waxy fruit aromas, especially apple, pear; in the second passes, the aroma expands meagerly to include sealing wax, parchment, cellophane—I wouldn't call this a demonstrative bouquet, but it is adequately appealing. Entry is alluringly grainy/malty, a

touch sweet and ripe, and reminiscent of muesli; midpalate is zesty, vibrant, slightly prickly on the tongue, and sappy. Aftertaste features both the malted barley and plenty of oak polymers and acids that together make for a balanced, youthful dram.
2016 Rating: ★ ★ ★/Recommended

Paul John Edited Single Malt Whisky (India) 46% abv, $65.
Topaz color; unblemished clarity. This opening burst of aromatics features a dry cereal, snack-cracker aroma that's dry and grainy; secondary inhalations following more air contact discover a malted milk ball scent that speaks well of the malted barley, if in an understated manner. Entry features narrowly focused flavors, mostly slightly sweet barley malt cereal, oatmeal, and candied fruits, predominantly pineapple; midpalate is properly grainy/malty, a little bit astringent as a black pepper taste ascends to complement the malted barley and sap-like oak. Finishes medium long, intensely woody, a touch bitter.
2016 Rating: ★ ★ ★/Recommended

Paul John Select Cask Classic Single Malt Whisky (India) 55.2% abv, $95.
Appealing ginger color; perfect purity. First whiffs pick up some reluctant spices, notably parsley, bay leaf, as well as acute notes of wax paper, beeswax, and linseed oil; later sniffs unearth vegetal hints of runner peas, snow pea, and asparagus that lie beneath the topical graininess. Entry is richer than either the Brilliance or the Edited whiskies, featuring nicely melded tastes of light toffee, cocoa butter, the omnipresent black pepper, grain husk oils; midpalate reflects the entry impressions to a tee, adding honeyed breakfast cereal, toasted almond, marshmallow, caramel. Aftertaste is long, grainy, caramel-like. The elevated abv is never an issue.
2016 Rating: ★ ★ ★ ★/Highly Recommended

Paul John Select Cask Peated Single Malt Whisky (India) 55.5% abv, $100.
Darkest of the four Paul Johns, a deep bronze/auburn color; impeccable purity. The smoky astringency highlighted in the initial inhalations narrowly focuses on one element only—peat-reek; later whiffs detect more graininess, almost a kernel-like oiliness that mingles well with the tobacco smokiness. Entry is supple, creamy in texture, and top-loaded with peat-reek smokiness, campfire smoke, toasted marshmallow, BBQ sauce, cigar box; midpalate echoes the entry aspects, adding a pruny sweetness that mingles nicely with the lofty alcohol, carrying forward the taste profile into the finish with aplomb and style. A peaty single malt that displays the kind of balance necessary to compete with those of maritime Scotland.
2016 Rating: ★ ★ ★ ★/Highly Recommended

Penderyn Aur Cymru Madeira Single Malt Whisky (Wales) 46% abv, $70.
Very pale flaxen color; excellent purity. Offers plenty of grainy/malty fragrance in the initial inhalations after the pour, plus there is a fortified wine pruniness that is gentle, ripe, and mature; following another eight minutes of air contact, the bouquet expands marginally to include citrus fruits. Entry is sweet, sap-like, and honeyed in a sweetened breakfast cereal manner; midpalate highlights the Madeira wood aspect by turning raisiny sweet and concentrated. Ends on a sweet, sugary note that showcases the Madeira wood nicely.
2016 Rating: ★ ★ ★/Recommended

Rozelieures Fumé Collection Single Malt Whisky (France) 46% abv, $80.

Six to eight years old. Matured in 100 percent first-fill fino and oloroso sherry casks. Pretty sepia color that displays a mass of bubbles at the bottom of the glass. Oh my, the honeyed sherry richness is apparent right from the opening inhalation and that's the hook for me; added time in the glass serves to stimulate round, supple, buttery aromas of black raisin, prune, and clove that make this like an aromatic trip to a bakery shop. Entry reinforces the deep sherry aspect in the forms of spice cake (nutmeg, clove), brown sugar, caramelized sugar, candied walnut, dried tropical fruit flavors like banana, pineapple; midpalate echoes the entry but goes a half-notch deeper as the sherry underpinning shines at the point of convergence with the suddenly astringent, bittersweet, coffee bean-/espresso-like finish (where did that come from?). Intriguing, complex, but still a youngish whisky that might be served well by another two years in barrel.

2016 Rating: ★ ★ ★/Recommended

Rozelieures Origine Collection Single Malt Whisky (France) 46% abv, $50.

Minimum of four years old; matured in used sherry and cognac barrels. Brilliant burnt sienna color; oddly showing a rash of bubbles that cling to the inside wall of the sampling glass. First sniffs detect pleasing scents of ripe tropical fruits, damp cereal, freshly chopped parsley, wet stone, and gunmetal; secondary whiffs encounter an immature, banana-like, almost lemon/citrus tartness that must be the barley influence as the bouquet takes a right turn down Sour Street. Entry highlights the grain kernel since there's an oiliness that rules the opening flavor profile with a firm hand; midpalate offers a meager juiciness/ripeness that tries to make an inroad but ultimately fails in the face of the grain oil density that lasts deep into the astringent finish. A gawky young whisky that hasn't been allowed to shed some of its awkwardness, namely the barley-driven harshness that would, with more time, smooth out. Began well in the nose, then stumbled throughout the in-mouth stages. Pass on it.

2016 Rating: ★ ★/Not Recommended

Rozelieures Rare Collection Single Malt Whisky (France) 40% abv, $64.

Minimum of five years old. Lightly peated malt that is barreled in used sherry and cognac casks, then finished in ex-sauternes. Ochre color; again, I see wall-clinging bubbles under the examination lamp—curious. Here is a nicely sour malted barley aroma that's youthful, intensely grainy, dry cereal-like, and minerally; with further aeration, the aroma transforms into a bouquet as the primary fragrance remains the barley, but the supporting scents—black pepper, jerk rub, toasted bread, lead pencil—converge to create an elegant aroma that's totally dry. Entry offers a sap-like first flavor that lays the foundation for subsequent tastes of caramel, white raisin, quince, and white pepper; midpalate underlines the raisin/quince element, but then advances a nearly mint-like spiciness that plays well off the dried-fruit components, setting the stage for the medium long, candied aftertaste.

2016 Rating: ★ ★ ★/Recommended

Rozelieures Tourbé Collection Single Malt Whisky (France) 46% abv, $90.

Minimum of eight years old. Aged in first-fill used bourbon casks and new barrels made from Lorraine forest oak. Thirty ppm of peatiness. Oldest of the four Rozelieures but the lightest in color, featuring a topaz/straw-yellow shade in which rest a few bubbles. This lightly phenolic aroma shows early signs of ashtray, loose cigarette tobacco, and iodine but very little barley malt cereal; further air contact only stirs up more phenols as the dry bouquet now turns into a smoke-filled room that's littered with cigarette butts. Entry is pleasingly cigar-tobacco sweet and sappy, with sideline flavors of mincemeat, chocolate-covered walnut, marshmallow, light toffee; midpalate mirrors the entry, adding honey and dried flowers. By a long shot, the best of the four Rozelieures, not because of the added peatiness but because of the longer period in barrel, which has smoothed out much of the youthful clumsiness seen in the other three.

2016 Rating: ★ ★ ★ ★/Highly Recommended

Spirit of Hven Backafallsbyn Tycho's Star Single Malt Whisky (Sweden) 41.8% abv, $130.

The fulvous/tawny-brown color is eye-catching and brilliant; sediment-free. I like this deeply malty, malted milk ball–like, and brown bread/pumpernickel–reminiscent initial aroma that's fresh, a touch smoky, robust, off-dry, and strikingly eastern Speyside Scotland–like, in particular, similar to malts from great distilleries such as Glendronach and Glen Garioch; secondary inhalations substantiate the first BIG MALT impressions, adding oak impact-linked fragrances of bacon fat, fatty acids (lipids), resin, and vanillin. Entry is delectably smoky (more like campfire embers than three-alarm fire), tannic, and therefore dry, woody, cheese-like, black tea–like, orangey, and full-bodied; midpalate plays off the entry findings, highlighting the smokiness of the malted barley and bringing my Mental Library of Whiskey Impressions back once again to Speyside's eastern reaches, where the single malts are hearty, earthy, malty, and deeply flavored. Seriously nice job here of emulation.

2017 Rating: ★ ★ ★ ★/Highly Recommended

Sullivan's Cove Rare Small Batch French Oak Cask Malt Whisky (Australia) 47.5% abv, $165.

Deep-amber/old gold color; sediment-free. I relish the off-beat, chewy, robust, almost combustible opening fragrance, which offers potent, no-nonsense hints of sulphur/burnt match, charred oak, toasted grains, and scrambled egg; after another eight minutes of air contact, the nose goes deeply into oak resins, baked pineapple, sulphur, egg cream, and brewer's yeast. Entry is supple, surprisingly sweet, with none of the burnt match element at all; midpalate is a banquet of flavors, including buttered toast, honey wheat bread, honey, red wine, raisins, and figs—wow. Concludes toasty, oaky, viscous, date-like in its sweetness, and decidedly yummy.

2015 Rating: ★ ★ ★ ★/Highly Recommended

Suntory Toki Whisky (Japan) 43% abv, $40.

A blend of Hakushu Distillery malt whisky and Chita Distillery grain whisky. Strikingly bright chardonnay-like gold color; impeccably pure, as all Japanese whiskies are. First nosings detect cooking spices, like bay leaf, parsley, and gentian that push forward the cereal grain back notes after the pour; secondary inhalations discover painfully subtle aromas of dry stone/gravel, silicon, textile fiber. Entry is pleasantly grainy sweet and tidy, cleansing and acidic, and now a touch tingly on the tongue; midpalate finds the various components—spices, grains, acids, oak—merging into a unified taste profile that's tight, grainy sweet, slightly resiny/sappy, and generally pleasing in its simplicity. While nowhere near the stately complexity of Suntory's legendary Yamazaki and Hakushu single malts, Toki is meant to show a more nimble, versatile and entry-level side of this great company that's wholly contemporary. For me, job well done.

2016 Rating: ★ ★ ★/Recommended

Teerenpeli Kaski Single Malt Whisky (Finland) 43% abv, $110.

Cocoa-brown/mahogany color; overall good purity. First whiffs pick up pronounced elements of smoldering campfire, wood resin, sawdust, and cigarette tobacco; secondary passes encounter leathery, old book–like scents that are dry, attic-like, dusty, and clunky. Entry is slightly sweet, heavily roasted, and oloroso sherry–like ripe, with side notes of baked grain and baked fruits; midpalate flattens out in terms of sweetness, as the taste profile turns bittersweet. The aftertaste is the apex moment for this malt, as the roasted quality turns into flavors of mincemeat, spice cake, baked Alaska that won me over enough to bestow a third star and a recommendation.

2018 Rating: ★ ★ ★/Recommended

Yamazaki 12 Year Old Single Malt Whisky (Japan) 43% abv, $85.

Goldenrod color; superb purity. Up front, I pick up just-ripe but acidic yellow fruits (pear, banana, quince), as well as cellophane, dill, oak plank, and lanolin; secondary nosing passes detect parchment, vegetable cooking oil, and almond. Entry is deeply malty, unsweetened breakfast-cereal dry, and roasted/toasty; midpalate is this whisky's high-point moment as elegant but substantial breakfast cereal, toasted bread, and bakeshop tastes abound, creating a comforting, amiable profile that's moderately oily, roasted, and dense. Aftertaste follows through well on the midpalate, offering long, deep, and sinewy flavors and feels that are resiny, off-dry, and cocoa-like. A lovely twelve-year-old malt of superior sophistication.

2018 Rating: ★ ★ ★ ★/Highly Recommended

Yamazaki Sherry Cask 2016 Edition Single Malt Whisky (Japan) 48% abv, $300.

The black tea/chestnut/old oak color is as deep as any whisky color I've seen in years; impeccably pure, though nearly opaque. Initial whiffs detect off-dry fragrances of pipe tobacco, chocolate-covered orange peel, old leather saddle, sweet grass, asphalt; secondary inhalations pick up black raisins and black plums, but the latter bouquet is neither sweet nor ripe as the malted barley is clearly present, making for a balanced aroma that is more delicate and elegant than pronounced or burly. Entry maintains the lovely delicacy found and appreciated in the bouquet—the malted barley exists in harmony with the sherried oak in a manner that's classy and balanced as one aspect seamlessly promotes the other; midpalate is where the silky texture comes into play, and the flavor profile turns fruitier and riper than the entry. Aftertaste is loaded with compelling taste attributes, including chocolate-covered raisins, cocoa butter, oloroso sherry, prunes, and dates. A masterfully crafted whisky that is world-class all the way.

2016 Rating: ★ ★ ★ ★ ★/Highest Recommendation

Yamazaki Single Malt 25 Year Old Whisky (Japan) 43% abv, $1,600.

Orange/copper color; superb clarity. First whiffs pick up hazelnut, brown sugar, nougat aromas; later inhalations encounter old leather, cinnamon, brown sugar, honey, toffee. Entry is buttery, viscous, honey sweet, malty; midpalate is luscious, succulent, profoundly grainy/malty, graham cracker–like. Finishes very long, oily, silky, honeyed/sherried. Fabulous.

2016 Rating: ★ ★ ★ ★ ★/Highest Recommendation

THE WORLD'S
BRANDIES

Before we proceed into the complex realm of brandy, please recognize one important factor: brandy making is an ancient industry, practiced for centuries wherever grapes and fruit have been cultivated and wine has been made. In many societies brandy has been an integral, revered lubricant of social and cultural histories.

Most historians now agree that the first formalization of distilling practice and institutional instruction in Europe came in the twelfth century via the Salerno School of Medicine, located in the Italian port city of Salerno. The thirteenth and fourteenth centuries witnessed a steady expansion of European distilling expertise and application as the Roman Catholic Church's clergy and city-state aristocracy glommed onto the distilling concept, initially for medicinal and mystical purposes, then later for recreational reasons.

According to findings from *Scientific American*, many historical records point to brandy in the form of unaged, clear distillate being made in France as early as the late 1200s, most probably by Raymond Lully, an assistant of the noted physician of the era, Arnaldus de Villa Nova. Reportedly, Villa Nova first dabbled in distilling grain- and fruit-based spirits at the end of the 1200s, creating *aqua ardens*, or burning water, even treating Pope Clement V in 1299 with distilled grape wine. (Sources: *A General View of the Writings of Linnaeus* by Richard Pulteney, Cambridge Library Collection, 1805, and *Brandy: A Global History* by Becky Sue Epstein, Reaktion Books, 2014.)

Another report in *The SAGE Encyclopedia of Alcohol: Social, Cultural, and Historical Perspectives* (Martin, ed., 2014) has religiously fervent Lully believing that brandy was a gift from God. He wouldn't be alone in thinking that. In that pivotal era, the years from 1300–1350, for the development of distillation in Europe, Villa Nova and Lully called their distillates *eau-de-vie*, French for "water of life." Other period experimenters, most often Christian clergy in abbeys and monasteries, likewise referred to their distillates in the Latin version of "water of life," *aqua vitae*.

The English word "brandy" didn't appear in the lexicon until later. *Brandy* is derived from two mid-1600s Middle Dutch words for "burnt wine," *branden* (burn, distill) and *wijn* (wine). They evolved into *brandiwijn*, which was derived from the earlier Dutch terms *gebrande wijn*. Brandy, the term, is employed to describe any potable alcoholic liquid that is distilled either from fermented fruit juice (wine), most specifically grapes, plums, berries, pears, apples, pineapples, and cherries, or grape pomace, meaning the leftover skins, seeds, and pulp from the vinification (winemaking) process.

The sixteenth-century Dutch connection dawned due to the commercial enterprises centered in Holland that shipped wine primarily from southwestern France to European, colonial, and British ports of call. The barreled wine had been fortified with distilled spirits in order to preserve its quality during the rigors of oceanic transport. The idea was to dilute the mixture with water back to ordinary wine levels of alcohol when it arrived at the designated port. What the shipment receivers kept discovering was that the wines fortified with spirits were even more scrumptious than the wine itself. This accidental development gave rapid and sustained rise to the brandy industry, particularly in France's Gascony and Cognac regions.

As a distilled spirit category, brandy encompasses some of the most illustrious and historically important distillates civilization has ever created, among them cognac, calvados, Armagnac, pisco, grappa, stravecchio, brandy de Jerez, applejack, barack palinka, tuica, macieira, kirschwasser, slivovitz, marc, and scores of other fruit brandies/eaux-de-vie. Virtually every wine- and fruit-producing region the world over makes some form of brandy.

COGNAC-FRANCE

Cognac originates in France's southwest district known as Poitou-Charentes. This enthralling region includes the Atlantic coast, highlighted by the Bay of Biscay and the coastal city of La Rochelle, and the demarcated brandy-making district, Cognac. Poitou-Charentes rests south of the Loire Valley, west of Nouvelle-Aquitaine (formerly Limousin), which is famous for its oak forests that provide much of the wood for French barrel making, and north of Aquitaine, a gateway to northern Spain and the home of the hallowed wine mecca, Bordeaux.

Cognac's Demarcated Districts

The Poitou-Charentes's main topographical feature is the meandering river Charente, which crisscrosses the area flowing southeast to northwest from Angoulême to the North Atlantic. The Charente is fed by the Né, Antenne, and Seugne rivers. The Charente-Maritime and the majority of the Charente *départements*, along with areas of the Dordogne and Deux-Sèvres départements participate in the brandy zones. The maritime-influenced climate affords warm, humid summers and mild, damp winters. The total officially demarcated region is comprised of just over one million hectares, or about 2,471,000 acres (1 hectare = 2.47105 acres). The actual space of this large area that is devoted to vineyards is only 79,636 hectares (196,785 acres). This swath of illustrious real estate is divided into six distinct grape-growing areas, known as "crus." Fully 95 percent of the 79,636 hectares are devoted to the production of white wine for cognac. Primary grape varieties are ugni blanc, colombard, and folle blanche.

These half-dozen growing areas were defined initially by soil types in 1860 by geologist Henri Coquand and then, in 1938, were delimited and ratified by decree.

> **Grande Champagne:** Approximately 13,150 hectares of thin but sponge-like, chalky (calcareous) soil that rests upon Montmorillonite clay, which captures, then retains moisture. The Grande Champagne cru surrounds the town of Segonzac. It produces an exquisitely fine, high-quality, long-lived cognac. It is known as the Premier Cru du Cognac.

> **Petite Champagne:** Some 15,246 hectares of clay and compact chalky soils. Petite Champagne's soil is much of the same quality of Grande Champagne, but a touch lighter, as are its eaux-de-vie. Its vineyards cradle Grande Champagne, lying to the southwest and southeast.

> **Borderies:** Only 3,987 hectares of unique flinty soil on a plateau above the Charente river. The eau-de-vie has a slight nutty taste. Borderies, which wraps around

the town of Burie (northwest of city of Cognac), is the smallest of the crus in terms of acreage. Eaux-de-vie from Borderies mature faster than those from the Champagnes and have rich, flowery (violets), frequently nut-like aromas.

Fins Bois: The 31,000 hectares of clay/chalky soils that are known as "groies" are similar to those of the Champagne crus, except for their reddish hue and hard stones from the Jurassic era. A subtle flowery bouquet characterizes this eau-de-vie. The largest cru, Fins Bois, is a low-lying area that encircles the Champagnes and Borderies. It lies, approximately, in the triangle between the towns of Rouillac, Matha, and Pons. Its eau-de-vie has round, hearty, powerful aromas with a salty touch of the maritime influence.

Bons Bois: Less chalky but more sandy, coastal soil of 9,308 hectares that is well-reflected in the eaux-de-vie. Bons Bois vineyards, encased by pine and chestnut forests, feature more widely dispersed vine plantings that are often intermingled with other crops. This region is not a major player in top-tier cognac production.

Bois à Terroirs or **Bois Ordinaires:** The 1,101 hectares of soil devoted to grapes for cognac are influenced by the Atlantic climate. The Île de Ré, an island off the coast, is considered in Bois à Terroir and is famous for its salt-air tanginess (think: Camus). Bons Bois and Bois Ordinaires are the exterior crus heavily influenced by the climate of the Atlantic Ocean, providing quick-maturing eaux-de-vie. They contribute less and less to the overall production of cognac but are, nevertheless, known to produce some interesting cognacs.

Fine Champagne: This special label designation is NOT a demarcation but rather is the blending of Grande and Petite Champagne eaux-de-vie, with a minimum of 50 percent of Grande Champagne. The House of Rémy Martin is the leading producer of Fine Champagne.

Labeling Laws

All grape-growing parcels must be registered with the Bureau National Interprofessionnel du Cognac (BNIC). The BNIC has the legal authority to monitor and certify any cognac's official age, starting with "Compte 00" for eau-de-vie that was distilled after April 1 of a given year. Compte 1 eau-de-vie is aging cognac that has gone past its second April 1 but is not yet legally mature. Compte 2 is basically VS-level cognac, meaning that it's spent a minimum of twenty-four months in French white oak barrels. The legal definitions are:

VS (Very Special) and **Three Star** cognacs (Compte 2) contain eau-de-vie that spent at least two years/twenty-four months in white oak barrels.

VSOP (Very Superior Old Pale) and **Réserve** cognacs (Compte 4) contain eau-de-vie that spent at least four years/forty-eight months in white oak barrels.

Napoléon cognacs (Compte 6) contain eau-de-vie that spent at least six years/ seventy-two months in white oak barrels.

Hors d'Age, XO, and **Extra** cognacs (Compte 10) contain eau-de-vie that spent at least ten years/120 months in white oak barrels, as of the regulation change that went into effect in 2018.

Vintage cognacs are rare single-harvest brandies. So then, 1999 Vintage XO must be produced from 100 percent grapes harvested in the autumn of 1999.

Augier L'Océanique Île d'Oléron Cognac 41.7% abv, $69.

Ugni blanc from the Bois Ordinaires district. Lightest in color of the three Augiers, this appearance is sediment-free and the flax/yellow color of brut champagne. This initial nosing pass unearths subtle aromatic traces of tree bark, white raisins, quince, and even a barely perceptible hint of sea breeze; following more time in the glass, the aroma turns riper and fruitier, more biscuity and layered, and therefore complex. Entry is soft yet sturdy and dry, acidic enough to thicken the texture, spicy enough to add a pleasing zestiness and, overall, very nice; midpalate is round, deeply spicy (nutmeg, cinnamon, vanilla bean), raisiny sweet (in fact, the sweetest of the three Augiers), and plushly textured. The raisiny aftertaste begs for a cigar accompaniment or, better, a crème brûlée.
2016 Rating: ★ ★ ★ ★/Highly Recommended

Augier Le Sauvage Petite Champagne Cognac 40.8% abv, $69.

Ugni blanc. Impeccably clean; the eighteen-karat-gold color is dazzling. I really like this opening nose due to its generous fragrances of red apple, red grapes, and red plums—the fruitiness is undeniably charming; further inhalations after more air contact serve to enhance the richness and ripeness of the fruit while adding nuances of cinnamon and clove—a comely, fruit-driven bouquet that's almost impossible not to like. Entry is ripe, gently sweet, keenly spicy (cinnamon apple), and wrapped in a satiny texture that adds gravitas to the flavor profile; midpalate is nimble, dry, but not austere, and delightfully juicy/grapy and pastry-like (apple strudel). Concludes in cascading waves of dried-fruit tastes that are lightly spiced. One of the finest 100 percent Petite Champagnes.
2016 Rating: ★ ★ ★ ★ ★/Highest Recommendation

Augier Le Singulier Fine Champagne Cognac 40.8% abv, $69.

Folle blanche. Pretty amber/topaz color; a slight bit of minuscule sediment seen under the examination lamp. First sniffs discover delicate aromas of white raisins, quince, limestone, chalk, flinty minerals; second nosing passes after more aeration encounter tart fragrances of orchard fruits, primarily green apple and pear, that mingle nicely with the grapiness and

light spice. Entry is crisply razor edged in acidity, nearly astringent, dry and lean, with an underlying nuttiness that brings a little oiliness to the texture; midpalate reflects the entry impressions to a tee, adding only a deft touch of oak resins that add to the mouthfeel. After-taste is medium long, sap-like in its mouth-parching dryness, grapy, sinewy.
2016 Rating: ★★★★/Highly Recommended

Bache Gabrielsen American Oak Cognac 40% abv, $40.

Aged in Tennessee oak barrels for a minimum of six months after at least three years in French limousin oak; 100 percent ugni blanc grapes, mostly from the Fins Bois district. Very attractive bronze/chestnut color; flawless purity. Immediately after the pour, I pick up fruity/orchard-like aromas of nectarine and red plum that are supple, ripe, and downright succulent; more air contact loosens up fragrances of green tobacco, beeswax, cellophane, parchment, and under-ripe pears in the second-stage inhalations. Entry is astringent, cleansing, intensely woody, toasted, and sap-like; midpalate features more fruit than in the entry, but the fruit is baked and slightly caramelized. Aftertaste is medium long, waxy, and drier than the midpalate.
2017 Rating: ★★★/Recommended

Bache Gabrielsen Sérénité Extra Grande Champagne Cognac 40% abv, $190.

Deep auburn/burnt sienna color; flawless purity. In the initial whiffs, I pick up earthy/woodsy traces of truffle, wet leaves, clove, tree bark, cinnamon, and oak moss; later sniffs detect dried fruits (apple, banana), toffee, cocoa, saffron, and dried fig; there is a lot happening here aromatically, and as the bouquet evolves it gets better and better. Entry is nicely balanced between acidity, nutty and spicy oak influence, fruit presence, and alcohol; the midpalate stage features more of the fruit aspect as the taste profile evens out in the finish. Very nice mature cognac from Grande Champagne.
2017 Rating: ★★★★/Highly Recommended

Bisquit & Dubouché VS Cognac 40% abv, $35.

Old gold color; superbly clean. I like the freshness of the opening aroma, which is reminiscent of cinnamon spice cake, baked bananas, and stewed prunes; secondary whiffs detect more grape and yellow-raisin character, and that's a welcome development. Entry reflects the first nosing, as the primary taste is one of baking spices, mainly cinnamon, clove, and nutmeg; midpalate is tart, a touch baked, with perhaps a bit too much char in the finish. That said, a good value nonetheless.
2020 Rating: ★★★/Recommended

Camus Borderies Single Estate Family Réserve XO Cognac 40% abv, $199.

Cherry/vermilion color; flawless clarity. The initial inhalations detect under-the-radar scents of baked cherry pie, black currant, toasted walnut, and soy sauce; more time in the glass unleashes more pronounced scents of pipe tobacco, lychee, sarsaparilla, and guignolet (the French cherry liqueur). Entry is densely textured, spiced with flavors reminiscent of black peppercorn, date bread, black raisins, prunes, and cherry turnover; midpalate reinforces the entry findings adding cassis, crème brûlée, and tart cherry tastes that multiply the complexity. Concludes long, satiny, meaty, and baked in the finish, as exotic and unexpected

flavors of BBQ sauce, tomato paste, and Worcestershire sauce make cameo appearances. An extremely intricate and characterful XO Borderies of the highest grade.
2018 Rating: ★ ★ ★ ★ ★/Highest Recommendation

Camus Borderies VSOP Cognac 40% abv, $55.

Visually appealing chestnut-brown/sepia color; flawlessly pure. The generous opening aromas offer alluring fragrances of candied walnut, dried pineapple, white raisins, quince, egg white, and meringue; later sniffs detect lemon zest/citric acid, burnt match, flinty dry earth, and limestone; a highly sophisticated VSOP aroma that rises above most others. Entry is richly textured, holiday fruitcake sweet, and deep in stone-fruit flavor; midpalate largely echoes the focused entry phase attributes, adding pine, pipe tobacco, dates, and cherry preserve. Finishes medium long, elegant, nutty, ripe, and sweet, but neither unctuous nor buttery. A dynamite VSOP that could easily be mistaken for an XO. Superb.
2017 Rating: ★ ★ ★ ★/Highly Recommended

Camus Borderies XO Cognac 40% abv, $180.

Lovely auburn/burnt-orange color; unblemished clarity. Wow, the depth of this initial aroma is fathomless and multilayered in the finest sense as mature fragrances of cigar box, cedar, mince pie, and allspice carry the day; later inhalations discover wood-influenced scents of rice pudding, nutmeg, sponge cake; a remarkably complex bouquet. Entry is resinous in texture, creamy, moderately oily, acutely peppery, and clearly on the dry side of the dry/sweet scale; midpalate reveals a deep nut-like flavor profile (walnut, almond) that is accented by tastes of dried flowers, black raisins, figs, and oak-derived tannins, hence the mouth-parching dryness. Aftertaste is intensely woody/resiny and astringent.
2017 Rating: ★ ★ ★ ★/Highly Recommended

Camus Cognac Île de Ré Fine Island Cliffside Cellar Cognac 40% abv, $95.

Topaz/deep amber color; pristine clarity. The aromatic spikes in the first sniffs are higher in intensity in this version as the maritime influence hits its apex in the mildly salty/saline fragrance that's also deep in dried fruits and nuts; following seven more minutes of air contact, I pick up noticeable smells of seaweed, baking spice (nutmeg), and ripe grapes. Entry is zesty, salty, resiny/woody, and off-dry to bittersweet; midpalate features mildly astringent, complex flavors of oak, saltwater taffy, light caramel, and soy sauce. Finish is lovely, elegant, tangy, and off-dry.
2018 Rating: ★ ★ ★ ★/Highly Recommended

Camus Cognac Île de Ré Fine Island Cognac 40% abv, $47.

Attractive golden hue; flawless clarity. Highly aromatic first nosings after the pour offer toasted/roasted scents of burnt toast, marmalade, and English toffee, along with a low-grade fruitiness; further air contact extracts the fruit in the forms of baked pears, ripe banana, and even kiwi; a desirable cognac bouquet that's assertive and sprightly. Entry is salty in a subtle way and off-dry, piney/woody, and resiny; midpalate features the wood plank/resin aspect, with sassy background notes of sarsaparilla and roots. Finish is expressively earthy/rooty/woodsy.
2018 Rating: ★ ★ ★/Recommended

Camus Cognac Île de Ré Fine Island Double Matured Cognac 40% abv, $65.
Rich topaz color; totally debris-free. Owns a similar opening aroma to the Fine Island's, in that there is a toasted quality to it as well as a trace of marmalade, but this seems more refined and delicate; I definitely encounter peaches and pears in this aerated bouquet that's more fruity and ripe than the edgy Fine Island; me like very much. Entry is juicy, toffee-like, caramel-like, and gently sweet; midpalate is lush, succulent, and rich in butter candy–like flavors. Aftertaste is silky, dried fruit–like, biscuity, and elegant, without being wimpy.
2018 Rating: ★★★★/Highly Recommended

Camus Very Special Cognac 40% abv, $35.
Burnt sienna color; immaculately clear. I immediately get an entire range of start-up aromas, including espresso, Earl Grey tea/bergamot, pineapple juice, and sour apple candy; later sniffs pick up a refreshing tartness that's slightly toasty but clean all the way. Entry is pleasantly juicy, dry, and fruity, with the taste emphasis on white raisins and yellow plum; midpalate offers a broader scope of flavors that include black pepper, black tea, minerals, and toasted oak. Ends parched, mineral- and stone-like, and toasty. Good value.
2019 Rating: ★★★/Recommended

Camus VS Elegance Cognac 40% abv, $31.
Pretty harvest gold; minor sediment. Ripe grapes and pine sawdust are the early aromatic features that grab my attention; then baked banana, nutmeg, oak plank, black pepper. Entry is focused squarely on the concentrated grapiness/jamminess; midpalate flavors include marmalade, fruitcake, grape jam. Finishes crisply, fruity, intense, and supple. A milestone VS that bedazzles me.
2014 Rating: ★★★★/Highly Recommended

Camus VSOP Elegance Cognac 40% abv, $45.
Topaz color; flawless clarity. I get notes of beeswax, parchment, delicate fruit in first whiffs; later, aroma fades a bit, but offers gum, allspice, and clove. Entry is buttery, toffee-like, with a pleasing almond paste taste; midpalate is leaner than the VS, earthy/chalky, mineral-like, and oaky. Aftertaste is medium long.
2014 Rating: ★★★/Recommended

Camus XO Elegance Cognac 40% abv, $139.
New-copper/burnt-orange color; impeccable purity. I smell new leather saddle, toasted walnut, marzipan, nougat in the first sniffs; baked tropical fruit notes emerge with aeration, including guava, banana, along with toasted marshmallow. Entry is buttery, semisweet, pruny, fig-like; midpalate features toffee, pralines, cooking oil, dried fruits, nutmeg. Luscious, rich, satiny.
2014 Rating: ★★★★/Highly Recommended

Camus VSOP Cognac 40% abv, $55.
Ochre color; superb clarity. First whiffs detect evolved, mature scents that are dry yet round and moderately fruity, with background notes of geranium, carob, and cola nut; after more air contact, the aroma takes on a fruitier mode as the carob merges with red apple,

black raisins, and figs. Entry is seamlessly round in texture, succulent, and gently spicy and reminds me of apple tart spiced with cinnamon and nutmeg; midpalate is lush, spicy to the point of nearly being piquant, with defining flavors of toasted marshmallow, English toffee, and butterscotch. Finishes with yummy candy-shop tastes that come wrapped in a supple texture. Superior VSOP offering from this fabled house.
2019 Rating: ★ ★ ★ ★/Highly Recommended

Camus XO Cognac 40% abv, $185.
Mahogany color; totally free of sediment. Wow, this opening nose features distinctive fragrances of prune Danish, pear tart, clove, nutmeg, and bakery shop; following more aeration, the bouquet turns fruitier, more ambrosial but without being sweet or ripe, just zesty, fresh, and peel-like. Entry is succulent, bittersweet, fruity, and toffee-like; midpalate is where the taste profile really gets purring, as mature flavors of brown butter, turbinado sugar, honey, buttery puff pastry, and spiced orchard fruits have my taste buds singing the arias of *La Bohème*. Finishes long, toasty, buttery, and sleek. Wow.
2019 Rating: ★ ★ ★ ★ ★/Highest Recommendation

Château de Montifaud Napoléon Fine Petite Champagne Cognac 40% abv, $113.
Copper color; impeccably pure. I can tell from the aromatic outset that this cognac's maturity (fifteen to eighteen years) is the driving force behind the balanced, integrated opening fragrance that's equal parts oak/wood and raisiny, dried, prune-like fruit; after more air contact, the aroma shows off its regal harmony in a bouquet that's subtle, mildly spicy and zesty, a touch citrusy, and leathery. Entry is dry, high in acid, and therefore clean as a whistle, coconut- and vanilla bean–like from the French oak, and deeply plummy and raisiny; midpalate flashes more of the oak presence as the taste profile turns tarter and slightly bittersweet, but all the while this racy cognac delivers on the palate with grace and power. Aftertaste is supple, chewy in texture, pipe tobacco–like in flavor, and fig-like.
2019 Rating: ★ ★ ★ ★/Highly Recommended

Château de Montifaud Selection Fine Petite Champagne Cognac 40% abv, $98.
Gamboge/harvest gold color; spotlessly clean. Initially, I pick up faint hints of nectarine and quince in the first whiffs after the pour, then those recede, leaving the door open for white raisin, kiwi, and green melon fragrances; aeration helps with the emergence of bakery-shop aromas, especially lemon curd, pear crumble, and allspice. Entry is tart, astringent, highly acidic, and therefore fresh and cleansing; midpalate offers pleasing, youthful (four to five years) flavors of dried apricot, white raisins, and grilled pineapple; the flavor profile is all about vivid fruit presence. Finishes long, dry, mineral-like, and tart from the various dried-fruit aspects.
2019 Rating: ★ ★ ★/Recommended

Château de Montifaud XO Silver Petite Champagne Cognac 40% abv, $122.
Burnt-orange color; clear and clean. This first nosing pass finds surprisingly muted aromas that are vaguely fruity but I simply don't get more than that; second passes after more than ten minutes of aeration fail to expand the aromatic profile to any discernable degree so I move forward. Entry is round, bountiful, buttery/creamy, and quite luscious with baked

pear, baked apple, and baking spice (nutmeg, clove) attractions; midpalate is delightfully elegant and robust simultaneously as the oak and baked fruit elements merge into a delicious, harmonious, potent, and spicy flavor that's mature (twenty-two to twenty-three years) and richly rewarding. Ends a touch semisweet, succulent, ambrosial, and maple-like. Had the bouquet offered more, I'd have easily bestowed a fifth rating star.

2019 Rating: ★ ★ ★ ★/Highly Recommended

Château de Triac Single Vineyard Fins Bois Cognac 40% abv, $55.

Burnt sienna color; excellent purity. Up front, I pick up toasted, nut butter–like aromas that are gently sweet, fruity (pear, white grape), and spicy; secondary whiffs encounter traces of sawdust/wood plank, along with stone-dry fruit notes. Entry is pleasingly juicy, lush in texture, and dried-fruit dry (raisins, figs, apricot) but tangy and resiny; midpalate stage features a melding of the dried fruit with the sap-like oakiness, thereby creating a round, supple, sugar maple–like taste profile that lasts moderately long into the bittersweet, slightly smoky, and roasted finish. Evidence that eaux-de-vie from the Fins Bois demarcated district can run with the big boys of Grande Champagne, Petite Champagne, and Borderies.

2018 Rating: ★ ★ ★ ★/Highly Recommended

Courvoisier Initiale Extra Cognac 40% abv, $500.

Blend of Grande Champagne and Borderies eaux-de-vie of between thirty and fifty years old. Rust/tawny color; flawlessly clean and pure. The initial impressions from the nose are gloriously raisiny and forest-like, complete with succulent notes of mincemeat, prune Danish, and sautéed mushroom from the clearly evident sign of grape eau-de-vie supermaturity: rancio; this is one bouquet that I could easily sniff all day long, as the primary message here is great maturity, wonderful complexity, and impeccable blending; cognac fragrance just doesn't get better than this, period. Entry is ambrosial, with baked apple and baked pear flavors that come off gently spiced (clove, mainly), piquant, tangy, and sublimely creamy in texture; midpalate is a clinic on how beautifully mature eau-de-vie can be when properly managed and guided through the maturation process with skill as every aspect of the flavor profile whispers about harmony, grace, and integration. A perfect aged grape distillate of the top rank and one of the best cognacs produced right now.

2019 Rating: ★ ★ ★ ★ ★/Highest Recommendation

Courvoisier VS Cognac 40% abv, $25.

Seriously pretty appearance of bright copper/henna color, and unblemished, sediment-free clarity. First nosing passes detect delicate aromas of ripe grapes, bacon fat, grilled pineapple, and roasted almond—a good start; further air contact of several minutes does little service to this bouquet as all the fruit aspects fade into oblivion, leaving behind only a waxy scent. Entry picks up the pace a bit from the late-stage aroma as a smidgen of dried fruits (white raisin, pear) reappears amidst larger flavors of oak resins, tree sap, and maple; midpalate sees the flavor profile calm down a little as it features holiday spice cake, dried fruit, candied nuts in equal measure, but please note that the tail end of the midpalate and the entire aftertaste are candy-shop sweet. While it is not a style that I like or believe to be contemporary, I see where adults who hanker for unctuous beverages would seek it out.

2015 Rating: ★ ★/Not Recommended

Courvoisier VSOP Cognac 40% abv, $35.

Rich auburn/burnt-orange color; ideal purity. Shows pleasing old leather, men's club, cigar tobacco notes along with subtler scents of dried apricot and paraffin in the initial inhalations after the pour; second sniffs reveal fading aromas on all fronts as the underlying sweetness takes charge of the bouquet. Entry features pleasant flavors of marzipan, dark caramel, maple, and soy sauce; midpalate mirrors the entry, adding nuances of oaky vanilla and tobacco, but the overriding character is the unabashed syrupy sweetness so that even the texture seems frontloaded with sugar. Ends on a concentrated note of refined sugar. While I found the aroma and the entry acceptable, as a whole there is little sense of harmony, little indication of integration. It is an antiquated style that is top-heavy with sugary sweetness.
2015 Rating: ★★/Not Recommended

Courvoisier XO Cognac 40% abv, $150.

Eaux-de-vie from Grande Champagne, Petite Champagne, and Borderies, aged between eleven and twenty-five years. Color is deep auburn; clarity is ideal. First whiffs pick up lush aromas of caramel, apple butter, walnut, and black tea; later inhalations encounter zestier, fruitier aromas, as refined scents of citrus peel, apple peel, kiwi, and date flourish. Entry is stunningly luscious, tobacco-like, raisiny, and caramel-like; midpalate features all the entry notes plus deft touches of carbon/woodsmoke, minerals, and black peppercorn. Aftertaste is lip-smacking delicious, bittersweet, a bit chunky, but overall lovely and hearty.
2019 Rating: ★★★★/Highly Recommended

Courvoisier XO Imperial Cognac 40% abv, $120.

Russet/cinnamon color; flawless purity. There are traces of prune Danish, mincemeat, dried pineapple, nectarine, and pipe tobacco in the opening whiffs after the pour—this is hardly an animated aroma, but I note some elemental, understated quality; the second passes unearth a mild ambrosial aspect that is delicately sweet and ripe. Entry is sweet, even pruny, but not as rousingly unctuous as the VS and VSOP and for that I'm grateful; midpalate sees the sweetness settle down, allowing for elements of oak, vanilla bean, toffee, and candied almond to emerge and merge as the midpalate evolves into the pleasing aftertaste. Finishes long, more bittersweet than sweet, somewhat maple-like.
2015 Rating: ★★★/Recommended

Croizet Black Legend Grande Champagne Cognac 40% abv, $75.

Sandy-brown/harvest gold color; about as immaculate as is possible. Initial sniffs pick up fading aromas of apple peel, grape jam, mincemeat, and figs; whereas in the first whiffs the fruit is accentuated, secondary inhalations discover earthy, more woodsy/floral, and mineral-like scents, including flint, honeysuckle, lilac, and lavender. Entry is velvety in texture, semisweet, intensely grapy/prune-like, and a bit spicy with allspice and clove tastes; midpalate features a luxurious texture that's lush without being fat, as there is enough acidity to maintain freshness. Ends on a jammy note that's grapy and pomegranate-like.
2019 Rating: ★★★★/Highly Recommended

Croizet VS Cognac 40% abv, $45.

Sunglow/mikado yellow color; superb purity. Oh my, this opening nose is rife with

buttery, cream cheese aromas that turn spicy (sea salt), earthy/smoky (stone, campfire embers), leathery (old books), and woodsy (eucalyptus) quite early on; after additional air contact, the bouquet features more of the earth/stone aspect than anything else as it turns dry and paraffin-like. Entry features a mild fruitiness that's a bit baked and toasted; what is clear at midpalate is how young, vital, and fresh this VS is, as depicted in the flavor highlights that resemble baked banana, cinnamon bun, and apple strudel. Concludes nimble, fruitier than at any previous stage, and irrepressibly delicious, clean, and ambrosial. One of Cognac's foremost VSs. Lovely.
2019 Rating: ★★★★/Highly Recommended

Croizet VSOP Grande Champagne Cognac 40% abv, $65.

Golden poppy color; pristine clarity. This opening aroma plays things coyly as I search for a grippable fragrance that's a little more expressive than the low-degree burnt match odor; secondary whiffs following more aeration pick up amorphous aromas akin to scrambled eggs, rubber pencil eraser, and grape preserves. Entry offers more animation, as the flavor profile features dried fruit (raisins, dates), nut butter, baked pear, and brown sugar; midpalate pretty much mirrors the entry, adding traces of oaky resins, bacon fat, and savory. Finishes medium long, more woody than fruity, and semisweet.
2019 Rating: ★★★/Recommended

Croizet XO Grande Champagne Cognac 40% abv, $139.

Sienna/rust color; small bits of sediment (cork?) seen under the examination lamp, but inconsequential. Opening whiffs have to search for serviceable aromas, which I find disappointing for an XO-level cognac; after allowing for much more aeration, secondary inhalations pick up only featherlight scents of parchment, candle wax, and thyme. Entry takes a far different tack, as the opening flavors are rich, oak-driven, and therefore resiny and lean, as well as caramel-like, candied, and fudgy; midpalate accentuates the sumptuous entry impressions, adding luscious tastes of honey, oloroso sherry, maple, and marshmallow. Aftertaste is extended, sweet, fresh, candied, and cocoa-like. The abrupt change (and total redemption) in sensory impressions from bouquet to flavor is astounding to me.
2019 Rating: ★★★★/Highly Recommended

D'USSÉ VSOP Cognac 40% abv, $45.

Very pretty deep-topaz/new-copper color; pristine purity. I like the richness of the opening aroma after the pour due primarily to its fruitcake quality, which includes dried tropical fruit, nuts, and light spice; six more minutes in the glass reveal a deeper, meatier aspect that I can only describe as old leather in a library. Entry is solid, firm, oaky sweet, and nicely viscous; midpalate features dark toffee, honey, maple, and dried fruit, especially raisins and prunes. Finish is long, off-dry, and piquant. A VSOP with the substance of an XO. Nice job here. Excellent value.
2017 Rating: ★★★★/Highly Recommended

D'USSÉ XO Cognac 40% abv, $230.

Gorgeous henna/auburn/tawny color; superb clarity. Opening aromas offer baked banana, tropical fruits, old leather books, black raisins, black plums; secondary inhalations

showcase praline, nougat, marzipan fragrances that are candy store–like, more than bakery-like in their dried fruit, holiday cake profile. Entry is big-hearted, robust, with top-shelf flavors of dark caramel, dried apricot, dried cherry; midpalate features the dried fruit (prune), along with hazelnut, cocoa, chocolate-covered coffee bean. Aftertaste is solid in its core, woody, vanilla-like, almost PX sherry. If your cognac leanings are for heartier styles, where the fruit and wood are expressive, then glom on to this big-hearted, chewy XO.
2019 Rating: ★ ★ ★ ★/Highly Recommended

Delamain Extra XO Grande Champagne Cognac 40% abv, $320.

Blend of thirty-five- to forty-year-old Grande Champagne cognacs. Sinopia/bronze color; pristine clarity. The first nosings collect mature, fully integrated, and deceptively concentrated aromas of buttercream, bacon fat, and lichen/moss/porcini mushroom that take a few deep inhalations to locate, but once located, they are sublime; the second passes are much more open as round, succulent fragrances of old oak, cedar wood, pipe tobacco, and Parmesan cheese make for seductive sniffing. Entry taste profile is a textbook on how older cognacs should both feel and taste as oily, buttery, slightly oaky flavors thrill the gustatory sense with gently spiced (vanilla, nutmeg), dried fruit–like (raisins, dates), and toasted tastes that along with the midpalate impressions are the defining moment for this very mature cognac. Finishes as elegantly and stately as the midpalate, but perhaps even showing a trace more richness and baking spice. A showcase for the majesty of cognac at its most memorable and classic.
2017 Rating: ★ ★ ★ ★ ★/Highest Recommendation

Delamain l'Aigle XO Grande Champagne Cognac 40% abv, $180.

Tawny/topaz color; flawless clarity. There's an initial, engaging, baked juiciness to this aroma that's youthful and vivid, as it resembles dried apricot, dried fig, saffron, and mince pie and then, just as quickly, dry stone/granite and dry earth; with more air contact, the bouquet becomes nicely integrated and fruit pastry–like, with marginal traces of sandalwood and green tea. Entry is seductively juicy, floral, bakery-shop spicy (vanilla, clove, nutmeg), with vivid flavors of grilled orchard fruits and Danish pastries; midpalate offers languid tastes of guava, cherry strudel, and cinnamon bun. Aftertaste features a long, keenly peppery flavor that's piquant, dry, and mineral-like.
2017 Rating: ★ ★ ★ ★/Highly Recommended

Delamain Pale & Dry XO Grande Champagne Cognac 40% abv, $120.

Blend of twenty- to twenty-five-year-old Grande Champagne cognacs. Earth yellow/sandy-brown color; perfect purity. I like the melon-y opening scents that are zesty and fresh, but it's after more air contact that this deceptively complex bouquet shows its best virtues in the forms of cigar box, pipe tobacco, violet, and honeysuckle. Entry is intensely bean-like, peppery, yeasty, and dried fruit–like; midpalate is toasty, seductively pruny, and raisiny, with background notes of cocoa and dried fig. Finishes creamy yet streamlined texturally, with long-in-the-throat flavors of marmalade and prune.
2017 Rating: ★ ★ ★ ★ ★/Highest Recommendation

Delamain Vesper XO Grande Champagne Cognac 40% abv, $150.

Blend of thirty- to thirty-five-year-old Grande Champagne cognacs. Cinnamon/

mahogany color; impeccably pure. On the immediate side, I pick up slightly smoked fragrances of smoking campfire embers, cherry compote, damp soil, and tobacco; a complex, intricate aroma turns even more so after additional aeration as scents of mushrooms, moss, forest vegetation, and walnut converge into a single point. Entry is keenly spicy/peppery, oaky, vanilla-like, and semisweet; the drier midpalate stage adds candied almond, walnuts, nougat, and allspice flavors that add up to a satiny aftertaste where its highlight flavors include black peppercorn, oaky resins, and cocoa bean.

2017 Rating: ★★★★/Highly Recommended

Delpech Fougerat VS Cognac 40% abv, $44.

Amber/topaz color; fastidiously clean. First nosing passes discover a surprisingly zesty, tangy aroma that's animated and delightfully spicy, with the focus on slightly under-ripened grapes, which is what makes it so clean and fresh aromatically; second passes add more complexity as the mingling with air settles down the grapiness, allowing for a light woodiness to emerge. Entry is fresh, clean, vivaciously grapy/fruity, ripe, and vanilla-like; midpalate accentuates the acute grapy quality, but finally the oak intervenes and adds complementary notes of nutmeg, clove, and tree sap that give luster and length to the aftertaste. I see big potential here for cocktail inclusion, especially the great Sidecar cocktail.

2016 Rating: ★★★/Recommended

Delpech Fougerat VSOP Cognac 40% abv, $49.

Pretty hazel-brown color; flawless purity. This opening aroma offers mature notes in the forms of toffee, candied nuts (walnuts), nougat, and fig; second inhalations pick up deeper scents of palm oil, brown rice, black tea leaves, allspice. Entry features layers of bittersweet complexity, mostly in the forms of clove, black pepper, light caramel, honey, roasted chestnut; midpalate reflects the entry impressions perfectly, adding a textural chewiness that's quite substantial, spicy, and sensuous. Aftertaste closes the circle by highlighting flavors of toffee, candy bar/nougat, and fig. Very nice VSOP of genuine gravitas.

2016 Rating: ★★★★/Highly Recommended

Delpech Fougerat XO Cognac 40% abv, $83.

Lovely ginger/henna color; impeccable purity. Initial nosings detect a quiet spiciness that's seductive and round, plus wood/oak elements of vanilla extract, carbon, tobacco leaf; second inhalations dig a bit deeper and find candle wax, parchment, grape jam, toasted almond fragrances that are very subtle. Entry is lush in texture, rich and creamy, unabashedly sweet and ripe, grapy, and resiny, all at the same time and at the same volume; midpalate is highly complex, spirity warm, toasted, nutty, oaky sweet, and full of vanilla notes. Finishes very long, sweet but not syrupy, grapy, raisiny, pruny, and caramelized. A beauty that's stunningly affordable for the level of quality involved.

2016 Rating: ★★★★★/Highest Recommendation

Distillerie du Peyrat Organic Selection Fins Bois Cognac 40% abv, $35.

Citron color; ideal clarity. Up front, I pick up immediate aromas of brown butter, leather razor strap, black peppercorn, and popcorn; further aeration stimulates traces of green tobacco, dried apricot and dried peach, and apple peel. The intense fruit notes, most prominently white raisin and white peach, take command instantaneously as the flinty texture shines through the entry stage due to heightened acidity; midpalate features more of the oak impact as the flavor profile turns lean, crisp, and slightly resiny/nutty. Concludes medium long, vegetal, completely dry, woody, and vibrant.

2018 Rating: ★ ★ ★/Recommended

Distillerie du Peyrat Rare Single Distillery Certified Organic Cognac 40% abv, $60.
Topaz color; immaculate purity. This opening aroma is a little waxy, estery, and candle-like, without offering much in the way of fresh or baked or preserved fruit—but this can change with aeration; after allowing another twelve to thirteen minutes of air contact, the fragrance does fill out with more fruit participation, mostly in the form of black raisin and dates; overall, I'd say that the bouquet is acceptable, even if it took a while to evolve, because there's a nice harmony between the dried black fruit and the buttery, bacon fat–like oak element. Entry is keenly dry, almost astringent, as the high level of acidity maintains the sturdy structure, allowing the fruit and oak to merge into a tasty flavor profile that's nearly smoky in its ripeness. Midpalate shows maturity, elegance, and a supple, creamery butter–like roundness that reaches deep into the aftertaste.

2017 Rating: ★ ★ ★ ★/Highly Recommended

Distillerie du Peyrat XO Organic Cognac 40% abv, $90.
Tawny/ochre color; impeccably clean. Initial whiffs detect dry but charred aromas of braised meat, brown sugar, honey-glazed ham, and rum barrel; secondary inhalations following more aeration encounter equally deep fragrances of cherrywood, pipe tobacco, and meringue. Entry is supple in texture, more bittersweet than dry, and reminiscent of dried figs and/or dates; midpalate accentuates the acute bittersweet aspect via the flavors of nougat, candied walnut, dates, chamomile, and dark caramel candy. Finishes long, intensely bittersweet, peppery/spicy, and toasted.

2018 Rating: ★ ★ ★ ★/Highly Recommended

Ferrand 10 Générations Grande Champagne Cognac 46% abv, $61/500ml.
Jonquil color; perfect purity. Even though the abv is elevated at 92 proof, at no point in the first inhalation does that pose an issue as the deep tropical fruit and nougat scents charm me; more aeration stimulates bigger aromas, especially stewed apple, dried apricot, and fruit tart. Entry is richly textured, almost smoky and tobacco-like, with background notes of toffee, brown sugar, and chocolate-covered raisins; midpalate offers more acidity, as the flavor profile includes a touch of lemon zest, grape skin, and cocoa powder. Aftertaste, which is long, sinewy in texture, spicy, and semisweet, is perhaps the highlight moment of this Grande Champagne.

2019 Rating: ★ ★ ★ ★/Highly Recommended

Ferrand 1840 Grande Champagne Cognac 45% abv, $43.
Modeled after pre-phylloxera-era cognacs from the mid-nineteenth century. Pretty saffron/sunflower-gold color; flawless clarity. I favorably respond to the toasted nuttiness found in the initial whiffs that likewise offer touches of brown butter, dried stone fruits (apricot, nectarine), campfire; second-stage sniffs unearth a slight sulfuric/burnt match aspect as well

as a waxiness that's pleasant. Entry is where this cognac shows its best stuff as the introductory flavors of baked apricot, brown butter, hazelnut, brown sugar all form a creamy, substantive texture that carries the taste profile forward into the ripe, fruity aftertaste.
2018 Rating: ★ ★ ★ ★/Highly Recommended

Ferrand Abel Cognac 40% abv, $450.
Unfortunately, I see quite a bit of unsightly sediment in this bottling of Abel; copper color. The first nosing passes find alluring fragrances of dried fruits (prunes, dates), holiday spices (clove, nutmeg), candied nuts, dark cake batter, brown sugar; second-stage whiffs echo the initial stage's biscuity bouquet accurately. Entry is intense, baked, and nutty; midpalate is peppery, smoked, burnt, and fruity in the core and oaky/resiny superficially. Completes its journey in relative style and grace though I don't believe that it's as lush and wonderous as it was when I first rated it five stars. Solid, sturdy, earthy enough for four stars still, even with the sediment issue, which is unflattering.
2018 Rating: ★ ★ ★ ★/Highly Recommended

Ferrand Ambre Grande Champagne Cognac 40% abv, $45.
Bronze color; flawless purity. Up front in the aroma, I get animated scents of nectarine/peach, allspice, lemon zest, and white grapes; later inhalations following more aeration encounter woodier, more leathery, black tea fragrances that accentuate the orchard fruit elements. Entry is smooth and silky, complex yet straightforward in its raisiny aspect, ripe and bittersweet; at midpalate, there's a seductive toastiness that's brought on by the resiny quality of the oak barrel, and that component alone deepens the in-mouth experience. Aftertaste echoes the midpalate in particular, in which the toasted oak/black tea complexity of this eau-de-vie abounds.
2018 Rating: ★ ★ ★ ★/Highly Recommended

Ferrand Ancestrale Grande Champagne Cognac 40% abv, $800.
Gorgeous auburn/burnished-orange color; pristine purity. Initially, I encounter provocative smells of bacon fat, pork rind, lard that form the foundational scent, then in later stages I discover baked orchard fruits, roasted walnut, rancio, soft cheese, mushrooms, Parmesan. Entry is powerful and deeply concentrated with dried fruits and nuts; midpalate offers an oily, creamy texture that underpins a fabulous flavor integration that is marvelously tight. Concludes dry, toasty, tobacco-like, pruny. Still the finest Pierre Ferrand expression.
2018 Rating: ★ ★ ★ ★ ★/Highest Recommendation

Ferrand Renegade Barrel 2017 Edition Eau-de-Vie Double Maturation Artisanal Brandy (France) 47.1% abv, $90.
Pierre Ferrand cognac that is double matured first in a standard 350-liter oak barrel, then finished in a 225-liter barrel made from chestnut, a variety of wood barrel that was occasionally used in Cognac prior to World War II. Ochre/copper color; lustrous purity. First aromas are abundant and rippling with ripe banana and pineapple fragrance, as the vivid tropical fruit component runs away with the early inhalations; secondary whiffs find enhanced fruitiness by the interaction of baking spice elements, mostly clove and nutmeg, thereby creating a firm, sturdy bouquet that's atypical and delightfully pleasant. Entry is

rich and mellow in texture, round and chewy in flavor, and deeply bittersweet and luscious; midpalate echoes the entry, throwing in almond paste/walnut butter for kicks as the fruit recedes slightly, allowing the wood influence to dictate the flavor direction through the long, lush aftertaste that's begging for a Cuban cigar. Unique, inventive, and delicious.

2018 Rating: ★ ★ ★ ★/Highly Recommended

Ferrand Réserve Double Cask Cognac 42.3% abv, $80.

Sepia/amber color; pristine clarity. My, my, the fruit component in the initial inhalations knocks me out with its freshness, ripeness, and purity, which isn't to imply that it's sweet because it isn't—just delightfully ripe and ambrosial right from the first whiff; later nosings add elements of baking spices (cinnamon, clove, nutmeg) that balance out the fruit intensity, creating a lovely, evolved, yet youthful bouquet of the top rank. Entry is toasty, roasted, and an awful lot like baked orchard fruits, in particular, pears and apricots and, by this juncture, I've got fruit tart/fruit pastry in my mind's eye; midpalate is leaner, more focused, acidic, and astringent than the entry phase, and it's here where the oak makes its play in the forms of resin, maple, vanilla, and cocoa butter. Aftertaste is medium long, apricot-like, and a bit like quince in the finale.

2017 Rating: ★ ★ ★ ★/Highly Recommended

Ferrand Réserve Grande Champagne Cognac 40% abv, $70.

Eye-catching topaz/burnished-orange color; superb purity. Opening whiffs detect winter holiday spice cake attributes that feature pleasing fragrances of dried apricot, cake batter, cinnamon, allspice, candied nuts; second-stage nosings echo the first stage to a tee. Entry is medium-rich, nutty, oily, and raisiny/plummy ripe; midpalate focuses on plums/prunes and a maple-like underpinning flavor that is delicious. Ends on sturdy notes of dark caramel and sweet candied orange. Still a lovely, sophisticated example of Grande Champagne complexity.

2015 Rating: ★ ★ ★ ★/Highly Recommended

Ferrand Sélection des Anges Grande Champagne Cognac 40% abv, $150.

Bright bronze/amber color; sediment-free clarity. Bouquet is lively, animated, and deeper in the second stage than when I reviewed it in 2009. Entry is complex, concentrated, offering ambrosial flavors of candied walnuts, chocolate-covered cherries, and marshmallow; midpalate hits the balance between sweetness/acidity perfectly as the taste profile is rich, mellow, sappy, pruny, nutty, honeyed. Still reminds me a little bit of cream sherry. After almost a quarter century, this Grande Champagne has at last convinced me to bestow a fifth rating star.

2019 Rating: ★ ★ ★ ★ ★/Highest Recommendation

François Voyer Extra Grande Champagne Cognac 42% abv, $n/a.

Mahogany color; pristine clarity. In the initial nosing passes, I pick up faint garden-like hints of prickly pear, geranium, violet, and bramble; secondary sniffs following more aeration detect deeper scents of black pepper, oak, and dried fruits (white raisins and apricot especially). Entry is multilayered, piquant, and dry, as tightly wound flavors of Fig Newton cookies, bacon fat, tobacco leaf, and praline jump out at me; midpalate features all the noted entry flavors plus traces of cola nut and toffee. Ends on a semisweet note of dark chocolate, toasted marshmallow, and caramel.

2019 Rating: ★★★★★/Highest Recommendation

François Voyer XO Gold Grande Champagne Cognac 40% abv, $n/a.

Cocoa-brown color; superb clarity. I note an earthy, nuanced opening aroma that smells a bit like baked brown bread and even a touch like pipe tobacco; later sniffs encounter more expressive fragrances of brown sugar, cocoa, espresso, and dates. Entry is delicately fruity (quince, white grape) first and foremost, with supplementary flavors of lychee, Nutella, and bay laurel; midpalate is vividly spicy (cinnamon, nutmeg), toasty/earthy (tobacco leaf), and caramel-like. Finishes long, toasted, date-like, and slightly smoky.

2019 Rating: ★★★★/Highly Recommended

Frapin 1270 Single Family Estate 1er Cru Grande Champagne Cognac 40% abv, $55.

Marigold color/gamboge color; textbook purity. I like this grapy/raisiny and radiantly fresh opening aroma because it could be nothing other than high-ranking grape brandy from Cognac; the ambrosial aspect continues on after more aeration, and my brain's love meter keeps ascending. Entry is vividly tasty, with robust flavors of caramel, fudge brownie, chocolate-covered cherry, and black raisin leading the taste parade; midpalate goes all-in on the heartiness of the flavor profile, as pronounced tastes of mincemeat, holiday fruit-cake, cinnamon bun, and bear claw pastry leave deep impressions. Aftertaste maintains the momentum found in the entry and midpalate stages. A dynamic cognac from the masterful talents of the Frapin team.

2019 Rating: ★★★★/Highly Recommended

Frapin Château Fontpinot XO Grande Champagne Cognac 41% abv, $159.

Wheat-field gold color; pristine purity. Smells of dried fruits up front, in particular, white raisins, yellow plum, and pineapple; after more contact, the fragrance turns a bit more toasty/roasted and orange marmalade–like. Entry features a foundational flavor of ripe white grapes, fresh honey, and oak resin; the midpalate stage features an extended, satiny, honey-sweet taste, as well as a keen astringency that maintains this cognac's vivid freshness. Ends roasted, bittersweet, and mildly spiced (clove, cinnamon). Still, in my view, one of the finest Grande Champagne cognacs money could buy.

2019 Rating: ★★★★★/Highest Recommendation

Frapin Extra Grande Champagne Cognac 40% abv, $599.

Cocoa-brown color; completely sediment-free. Initial whiffs detect mature, oaky, rancio-driven aromas of mushrooms, old leather books, walnut butter, Parmigiano Reggiano, milk chocolate, and carob; secondary inhalations discover deeper scents of black raisins, dates, figs, and candied almond. Entry impressions are highlighted by the creamy texture that supports the integrated flavors of dried fruits, nuts, clove, nutmeg, and quince; midpalate mirrors the entry, featuring deeper, more ponderous flavors of baked ham, jasmine, cake batter, gingerbread, and berry compote. Concludes lengthy, silky, and a touch smoky. Magnificent.

2019 Rating: ★★★★★/Highest Recommendation

Frapin VSOP Grande Champagne Cognac 40% abv, $69.

Burnt sienna color; unblemished clarity. Up front, I pick up traces of baked fruits, especially peach and pear, plus a touch of baking spice, in particular, mace; more air contact stimulates deeper fragrances of vanilla bean, dried apricot, and old leather. Entry is juicy and ripe, toasty, and honeyed; midpalate accentuates the dried fruit that comes off as being a little more tropical (guava, especially) in nature than orchard-like. Concludes silky in texture, mildly honeyed, and elegant. A classy VSOP that beams with Grande Champagne elegance and depth.
2019 Rating: ★★★★/Highly Recommended

Frapin XO VIP Grande Champagne Cognac 40% abv, $175.

Attractive auburn color; flawless purity. First inhalations connect with substantial, woody, mature, and intensely grapy aromas that shine with vibrant freshness and acidity; more time in the glass allows for harmonious fragrances of toasted almond, marmalade, bear claw pastry, and moss/earth. Entry is texturally oily and satiny while the taste profile overflows with fruity, zesty, tobacco-like and mature tastes; midpalate features vanilla, fudge, coffee bean/espresso, and dark caramel. Ends on a graceful note, with racy flavors of dried banana, dried nectarine, and vanilla. Sensational.
2019 Rating: ★★★★★/Highest Recommendation

Gilles Brisson VS Grande Champagne Cognac 40% abv, $35.

Bronze color; flawlessly clean. Oh man, there are grapy, juicy, tropical fruit (banana especially) aromas flying all over the place in this first whiff; with more air contact, the aromatics expand to include walnut, sawdust, pear, nectarine, and gum. Entry is supple, round, and medium weighted, but to my dismay I pick up a faint hint of the beginnings of TCA/cork taint (trichloroanisole), which gives off a barely perceptible mustiness; in the midpalate stage, the TCA becomes woefully apparent, as it interferes with the otherwise pleasant pear/tropical fruit layers. Aftertaste is mushroom-like, rustic, moldy, and painfully tainted yet still fruity; but the damage has been done. I hate like hell to experience this because all the hard work that goes into making a fine brandy from a top-drawer district is thrown out the window due to faulty corks.
2018 Rating: ★/Not Recommended

Gilles Brisson VSOP Grande Champagne Cognac 40% abv, $44.

Rich ochre/tawny color; immaculate purity. First off, I pick up mildly toasted, bakery-like aromas of prune Danish, flaky pastry, white raisins, and dates; secondary passes detect dry-as-a-bone fragrances of oaky lipids (fats) and resins along with juicier notes of figs and white raisins. Entry is nicely supple in texture, plump even, with juicy, compote-like notes of dried apricot and white raisins; midpalate echoes the entry impressions, adding delicate touches of pineapple, black pepper, and orange rind. Finishes medium long in the throat, more off-dry than dry, and pleasantly fruity/juicy.
2018 Rating: ★★★/Recommended

H by Hine VSOP Fine Champagne Cognac 40% abv, $50.

Medium amber color; excellent purity. I smell all sorts of dried yellow fruits in the opening nosings after the pour, including pineapple, pears, figs, and dates; another eight minutes of air contact bring out deft traces of light caramel, white grapes, and marmalade; a very pleasant bouquet. Entry reflects the aroma in that, while not ambrosial or deep, the first taste impressions are of dried fruits, with a touch of nuttiness thrown in; midpalate is clean, tangy, and totally integrated in a medium-bodied manner. Nimble in the aftertaste, as the fruit element remains firmly in charge. My concern was the depth aspect, in particular, because of Hine's profound pedigree, but beyond that it is recommendable.

2017 Rating: ★ ★ ★/Recommended

Hardy Legend 1863 Cognac 40% abv, $60.

Primarily Petite Champagne eaux-de-vie with a measure of Borderies; aged for "up to 12 years," according to the data sheet. The cocoa-brown color is dazzling; impeccably clean. Oh my, I like the understated chocolate-covered coffee bean–like first aroma that's bitter-sweet and tangy; after more air contact, the mesmerizing perfume turns to cigar box, leather, hazelnut, even orange zest. Entry bathes the tongue in oily bittersweet flavors reminiscent of English toffee, tobacco, lychee, and candied fruits; midpalate stays the course laid down at entry, adding only a modifying flavor of toasted oak that adds a touch of tannic bitterness. Concludes medium long, slightly spicy, raisiny, and piquant.

2017 Rating: ★ ★ ★ ★/Highly Recommended

Hardy Noces d'Argent Fine Champagne Cognac 40% abv, $360.

Deep mahogany/chestnut color; perfect clarity. I get harmonious aromas of candied walnut, dried pineapple, old library, marzipan, nougat in the first inhalations after the pour; with further aeration, the bouquet turns sweeter, more honey-like, tannic, fig-like, plus there's a lurking scent of soft cheese/rancio that underpins the second-stage whiffs. Entry features dried berries (cranberry, blackberry), crème caramel topping/caramelized sugar, egg cream, custard; midpalate soars into the taste satisfaction stratosphere as the honey sweetness lays the foundation for more superficial flavors, like brown sugar, toasted marshmallow, milk chocolate, maple, oaky vanilla. Finishes medium long, velvety in texture, succulent, ripe, intensely grapy, and sweet. A cognac masterpiece.

2015 Rating: ★ ★ ★ ★ ★/Highest Recommendation

Hardy Noces de Perle Grande Champagne Cognac 40% abv, $1,000.

Blend of ten Grande Champagne cognacs, aged for at least thirty years. Bright new-copper/bronze color; excellent clarity. First inhalations unearth dusty dry, earthy aromas of tobacco leaf, black tea, black pepper; second nosing passes after more aeration time encounter grapier, fruitier aromas that are more tropical than temperate zone in nature and slightly candied; this is a subdued aroma that carries a subtle power. Entry starts to exhibit this cognac's true succulent nature, which is best defined by the flavor aspect more than the aromatics; midpalate is vividly alive with a banquet of tastes, including grape preserves, candied apple, pipe tobacco, black pepper, caramel, chocolate fudge, raisin bread. Aftertaste echoes the midpalate and is satiny in texture, delicately sweet, and fruity.

2015 Rating: ★ ★ ★ ★/Highly Recommended

Hardy VSOP Fine Champagne Cognac 40% abv, $46.

Grande Champagne and Petite Champagne, matured for at least eight years. Gorgeous auburn/henna color; superb purity. Opening whiffs detect powerful aromas of praline, candy bar, nougat, new leather, black tea; second inhalations following further air contact reveal hints of tomato paste, BBQ sauce, caramelized sugar, caramelized onion, chocolate-covered raisins. Entry is soft, bittersweet, bean-like, nearly fudge-like, roasted, with hints of bacon fat and coffee; midpalate features the coffee bean aspect as well as the BBQ sauce flavor that's concentrated and focused on dried fruits, mostly berries. Aftertaste is extended, chewy, drier than the midpalate, and resiny/maple-like.

2015 Rating: ★ ★ ★ ★/Highly Recommended

Hennessy Master Blender's Selection No. 1 Cognac 43% abv, $80.

Color is cinnamon/copper; impeccably clean and clear of any sediment; awesomely beautiful. Frontline nosings immediately after the pour find mature, integrated, and pleasantly spicy aromas that highlight brown butter, cooking oil, old leather, oilskin, green tobacco; secondary whiffs following more air contact identify a subtle prickliness due to the 43 percent abv that I like, and it's this alcohol boost that then accentuates the dried-fruit aspect (raisins, prune) that make the bouquet substantial. Entry showcases the more mature eaux-de-vie that contributed to this blend in the flavors of oloroso sherry, honey, dark caramel, milk chocolate; midpalate pushes the maturity factor along even more as now the taste profile displays a creamy opulence of texture that obviously is oak-driven. Aftertaste closes the circle in style as the flavor turns maple-like, tobacco-y, and marmalade-like.

2017 Rating: ★ ★ ★ ★ ★/Highest Recommendation

Hennessy Master Blender's Selection No. 3 Cognac 43% abv, $110.

Auburn color; impeccable clarity. First inhalations after the pour identify bright, vivid aromas of sultana, red plum, hazelnut, melon, and baking spices, in particular, clove and allspice; secondary whiffs pick up added scents of winter holiday fruitcake, candied almond, peach cobbler, dried apricot, and dark caramel. Entry features raisiny, pruny, dried-fruit tastes that are semisweet, crisp, and oaky in a vanilla-like manner; midpalate highlights the dried fruits and spice cake aspects, adding a medium weight texture that's nicely oily and lean. Ends with a flurry of succulent, tightly wound flavors that are bittersweet and tangy.

2018 Rating: ★ ★ ★ ★/Highly Recommended

Hennessy Paradis Imperial Cognac 40% abv, $2,600.

The eaux-de-vie range from thirty to 130 years in this highly palatable cognac that is amber in color and clean as a whistle. First inhalations pick up peanut butter, peanut oil fragrances that set the stage for deeper scents of dried apricot, lychee, pear drop; secondary whiffs pick up background notes of new leather, oak, mace, allspice. Entry features dusty, dry tastes of prunes, black raisins, black cherry compote, toffee; midpalate reinforces all the entry impressions and adds a curious but fitting note of tobacco. Finishes long, chewy, subtle, balanced, with dashes of rancio and black pepper. Delicious.

2016 Rating: ★ ★ ★ ★/Highly Recommended

Hennessy Privilege VSOP Cognac 40% abv, $60.

I've always liked the rusty/sorrel color of this handsome cognac; sediment-free clarity. Opening aroma is laid-back, showing only nuances of green melon, sweet oak, vines; further

air contact sees the emergence of toasted marshmallow, banana bread but little else; the lightweight (read: flimsy) nature of the bouquet has since 1995 disappointed me. Entry is sweet, sap-like, maple-like, quasi-complex; it's in the midpalate stage where this cognac at last gets its mojo working as roasted flavors of coffee, almond paste, maple come together in a harmonious manner, but in the finish there's a fading of the taste gains made in the midpalate that brings a possible three-star cognac back down to two stars and harsh reality.
2016 Rating: ★★/Not Recommended

Hennessy VS Cognac 40% abv, $33.
Attractive cinnamon-brown color; flawless purity. Engagingly fruity (pears, bananas) in the first inhalations followed by notes of chocolate-covered cherries, black raisins in the second passes. Entry is toasty, mildly sweet, grapy, ripe, simple, direct; midpalate maintains the fruity posture established in the aroma and entry but comes off as having little true distinction or "core." Easy drinking, for certain, but lacks genuine depth of character.
2016 Rating: ★★/Not Recommended

Hennessy XO Cognac 40% abv, $325.
The deep bronze color is attractive and flawlessly pure. Initial whiffs pick up scents of dried grapes, figs, dates, prunes; further aeration releases delicate fragrances of spice (vanilla), peanut oil. Entry remains aggressive, woody, candy-shop sweet; midpalate is front-loaded with vanilla cream, nougat, caramel, and a bittersweet flavor that lasts deep into the aftertaste that's broad-shouldered, beefy, and reminiscent of cake frosting. If you're looking for a virile, strapping brandy of genuine depth and sweet-leaning flavors, your search is over. Hennessy XO was in fact the very first XO. Cool.
2016 Rating: ★★★/Recommended

Hine Antique XO Premier Cru Grande Champagne Cognac 40% abv, $209.
Lovely, deep-mahogany/burnt sienna–brown color; flawless clarity. Initial whiffs detect fruity, nutty opening aromas that remind me pleasantly of winter holiday fruitcake (dried pineapple, white raisins, candied walnut) and roasted chestnuts; second nosing passes following more air contact bring in snappy, zesty aromas of baked ham with pineapple, clove, and mace; in all, an evocative bouquet of the early winter season. Entry features a steely, mineral-like taste that's more earthy/elemental than fruity/nutty; midpalate reinstates the dried fruit and candied walnut components that were so prominent in the nosing stages, and it is here where the richness of the oily texture becomes evident. Ends on a flinty, stone-like, dry as a bone, mineral-like aftertaste.
2018 Rating: ★★★★/Highly Recommended

Hine Homage to Thomas Hine Grande Champagne Cognac 40% abv, $153.
Marigold color; spotless purity. First inhalations encounter pleasingly juicy and tart aromas of white grape, Anjou pear, and nectarine that are supported by background notes of egg white, meringue, and sourdough bread; secondary whiffs detect traces of lemon peel, key lime pie, and custard; a yummy, fruit-forward bouquet. Entry reflects the fruit-filled nose only for a flashing second or two, then quickly shifts into fruit/wood mode, as the ambrosial aspect turns baked, resiny, sap-like, honeyed, and toasted; like the entry, the midpalate

stage flaunts the fruit/wood partnership that comes gift wrapped in a silky, creamy texture. Ends drier, chewier, and more astringent than the entry and midpalate stages, reflecting the ascendency of the oak impact.

2019 Rating: ★ ★ ★ ★/Highly Recommended

Hine Rare VSOP Fine Champagne Cognac 40% abv, $60.

Topaz/light brown color; impeccable clarity. This opening aroma is far more complex, nutty, woody, and resiny than that of the H, which was breezy and fruity; after another eight minutes of aeration, the wood aspect takes a dominating stance as the depth of character seems almost more XO-like than VSOP. Entry flashes succulent tastes of coffee, toffee, dried red fruits, and oaky vanilla; midpalate features the silky texture, caramel, prunes, dates, and raisins in abundance. Finishes long, satiny, and cleanly tart. This expression owns a classic Hine personality. Interestingly, I rated this cognac a mere two stars in 2004. Either the cognac or I have vastly improved.

2017 Rating: ★ ★ ★ ★/Highly Recommended

Jean Fillioux Cep d'Or XO Selection Vieux Grande Champagne Cognac 40% abv, $90.

Twelve years old minimum. Seriously attractive bronze/bright old gold color; inconsequential sediment spotted. First whiffs encounter ripe, substantial aromas of beeswax, parchment, faint baked banana, and minerals; secondary nosings after further aeration come out slightly toasted, grapy-ripe, earthy/stony, and clean as a whistle. Entry is delightfully sweet and grapy in a jammy, compote way, and the texture is like fine silk—man, this is savory; midpalate is medium long, subtle, integrated, and sound. Ends on perhaps its best moment of the evaluation as the supple viscosity, deep richness of the oak, and the crispness of the fruit converge in a glorious moment of triumph.

2017 Rating: ★ ★ ★ ★ ★/Highest Recommendation

Jean Fillioux Cigar Club Grande Champagne Cognac 40% abv, $170.

Beautiful mahogany/sinopia-brown color; unblemished purity. This opening aroma is muted and reluctant so I back off for ten minutes; following more aeration, the aroma comes alive in the exotic forms of baked banana, roasted meat, BBQ sauce, fish oil, cocoa bean, and soy sauce. Entry bursts with soy sauce, Asian cooking spice–like flavors that are elemental, bitter, vegetal, and spicy; midpalate takes an unexpected left turn as it highlights desert-dry flavors of black tea/orange pekoe, bean curd, and green vegetable that mingle with the dried apricot and raisiny fruits; there is a massive amount of taste explosion here. Finishes long, bittersweet, caramelized onion–like, toasted marshmallow–like, and utterly luscious. A wonderfully weird, deeply flavorful cognac that takes a couple of bizarre turns to produce delightful results.

2018 Rating: ★ ★ ★ ★/Highly Recommended

Jean Fillioux COQ Grande Champagne Cognac 40% abv, $52.

Five years old minimum. Straw-yellow color; to my dismay, lots of tendril-like sediment seen under the examination lamp. Visual issues aside, the initial whiffs encounter lovely, melded scents of spiced pear, cardamom, and ripe white grapes; after allowing this cognac to sit undisturbed for seven more minutes, the second round of inhalations produces juicy, luscious, and fruity aromas that are in harmony; Grande Champagne cognac at its fruity, seductive aromatic best. Entry is intensely grapy, semisweet, ripe, and supple; midpalate reinforces the entry juiciness and youthful vigor. Finishes long, silky, tarter than I expected, and delicious.

2017 Rating: ★ ★ ★ ★/Highly Recommended

Jean Fillioux La Pouyade Vieille Grande Champagne Cognac 42% abv, $70.

Eight years old minimum. Pretty, light-amber/old gold color; inconsequential, widely spaced sediment seen floating—a non-issue. Like the elegant COQ, the opening sniffs detect significant vine and orchard fruits, especially white grapes, quince, and kiwi; secondary inhalations after another seven minutes of air contact find delicate traces of oak, sawdust, and pine plank that nicely underscore the fruit presence. Entry is semisweet but simultaneously tart and clean, as the acid level is clearly high; midpalate features grape preserves, toffee, nougat, and wood resins. Aftertaste shines for its baked fruit aspect, which provides an alluring accompaniment to the evident oak presence.

2017 Rating: ★ ★ ★ ★/Highly Recommended

Jean Fillioux Réserve Familiale Très Vieille Grande Champagne Cognac 40% abv, $330.

Fifty years old minimum. Gorgeous old-copper/bronze color; impeccable purity. Starts out aromatically quite subtle and understated in the first sniffs after the pour, then after another seven minutes of air contact, the bouquet detonates, offering deep, profound fragrances of green melon, cantaloupe, sherry, old oak resin, mushrooms, forest floor, and moss; a giant dose of rancio is the key. Entry is tart, densely fruity, startlingly fresh for its age, and acutely resiny; midpalate is multilayered, cheese-like, woodsy, herbal, honeyed, and rich. Crazy delicious.

2017 Rating: ★ ★ ★ ★ ★/Highest Recommendation

Jean Fillioux Single Cask #96 XO Grande Champagne Cognac 45% abv, $135.

Pretty copper color; flawless clarity. The aroma right from the very first sniff conveys gracefulness, integration, and power through expressive aromas of spiced pear, chocolate-covered raisins, and cherry blossom; later whiffs pick up earthy, oak-impacted traces of hard cheese, sawdust, marzipan, and almond butter. Entry features the oak influence, in particular, in the sap-like, honeyed opening flavor that's succulent, acidic, and therefore fresh, and peppery/piquant; midpalate brings all the taste aspects together for an illustrative exhibition of Grande Champagne wallop and charm as the flavor profile goes orchard fruit–like, intensely oaky and resiny, honeyed, spicy, and espresso-like. Ends long, oily, toasted, toffee-like, and buttery in texture. Loved it.

2018 Rating: ★ ★ ★ ★ ★/Highest Recommendation

Jean Fillioux Très Vieux Très Vieille Grande Champagne Cognac 40% abv, $120.

Twenty-five years old minimum. Eye-catching copper color; substantial amounts of wispy sediment seen. I get lots of streamlined scents of nougat, banana in brown sugar syrup, some maple, and clove in the initial inhalations after the pour; secondary sniffs detect butter, Christmas cake spices (clove, cinnamon), and dried yellow fruit, including pear, pineapple, and kiwi. Entry is deep, acidic, resiny, and even a tad chewy; midpalate is tobacco-like,

cheese-like, eggy, bacon-like, and toasty. Finishes satiny in texture, cigar tobacco–like, resiny/oaky, meaty, clean, and oh, so sensuous.
2017 Rating: ★ ★ ★ ★ ★/Highest Recommendation

Jean Fillioux XO Grande Réserve Grande Champagne Cognac 44% abv, $130.
Thirty-two years old minimum. Dazzling bronze/burnished-orange color; trivial amount of minor sediment. Smells magically of cocoa, nougat, buttered almonds, and red fruit compote in the incredible opening whiffs after the pour; secondary sniffs discover fragrances of prune, black raisins, honey, and vanilla wafer. Entry is succulent, semisweet, honeyed, and almost sherry-like; midpalate caresses the palate in a satiny robe of texture and tastes of raisins, figs, dates, and prune Danish. Concludes with a swift rush of acidity and the resiny oak kiss-off that's a flavor to behold. Wow.
2017 Rating: ★ ★ ★ ★ ★/Highest Recommendation

Jean Fillioux XO So Elegantissime Vieille Grande Champagne Cognac 41% abv, $190.
Twenty years old minimum. Bright amber/topaz hue; perfect, sediment-free clarity. I encounter integrated scents of beeswax, forest floor, cocoa bean, and sawdust in the initial nosings after the pour—lovely and composed bouquet from the start; multilayered aromas of toasted walnut, nougat/candy bar, and hard cheese (Parmesan/umami) are featured in the second round of nosings. Entry is spicier than the aroma, highlighting nutmeg and allspice, with a background trace of thyme; midpalate is sinewy in texture, grapy, raisiny, and date-like. Finishes in the fruity/raisiny vein started in the midpalate and expands from there, finally exploding with dried red fruit in the throat. Just keeps building to the aftertaste crescendo.
2016 Rating: ★ ★ ★ ★ ★/Highest Recommendation

Léopold Raffin VSOP Cognac 40% abv, $50.
Pretty tawny/henna color; unblemished purity. Sports an emphatically fruity opening aromatic burst that reminds me of Christmas fruitcake, loaded with dried apricot, pineapple, spice, and nuts; the second phase of nosing finds more woodiness and an earthy/mossy quality that is appealing and different. Entry is deep with dark caramel and nougat headlining flavors that eclipse the dried-fruit aspects; midpalate is toasty, marshmallowy, charmingly sweet, and oaky. Concludes with broad flavor strokes of toffee and brown sugar. I like this traditional, big-shouldered style but some imbibers who prefer more agility might not.
2015 Rating: ★ ★ ★ ★/Highly Recommended

Lhéraud 1975 Grande Champagne Cognac 49% abv, $1,042.
Stunningly gorgeous deep, dark auburn/henna/deep-copper color; ideal clarity. Right out of the gate I get nuances of mature oak, dried orchard fruits (pears, apricots), paraffin, cigar tobacco/cigar box; second passes unearth impossibly subtle and delectable scents of dried citrus peel, black pepper, prune. Entry is clean, mature, and tightly wound around bittersweet flavors of prune juice, dates, figs, candied almond; midpalate shows a flash of spirity heat but that fades quickly, leaving the door open for an intense oak-a-thon that quashes the dried fruits and roasted nuts, lasting long into the vanilla-filled aftertaste. An appealing relic that has lost some of its vigor, but still shows remarkable stamina and presence.
2015 Rating: ★ ★ ★ ★/Highly Recommended

Lhéraud Cuvée 10 Petite Champagne Cognac 42% abv, $137.
Attractive copper-kettle color; flawless purity. This voluminous aroma is layered with ripe tropical fruits (guava, banana, tangerine, lemon), fresh spring garden delights (jasmine), and enough subtle baking spices to fill a shop space (vanilla, allspice, clove); second passes detect succulent scents of lemon-drop candy, gooseberry, candied walnut, dried apricot. Entry is sap-like, maple sweet, and chewy/creamy to the feel as the taste profile soars and bulls its way into the complex midpalate that's bordering on being fat and BBQ sauce–like, so robust is it. Aftertaste echoes the midpalate in terms of the fleshy texture and sweet cream core taste. A serious handful of hearty PC cognac, and by that I do not mean politically correct. Big-hearted, straightforward, grape brandy pleasure.
2015 Rating: ★ ★ ★ ★/Highly Recommended

Lhéraud Cuvée 20 Petite Champagne Cognac 43% abv, $196.
The deep amber/saffron color is dazzling and clear of sediment. Like that of its younger sibling the Cuvée 10, this is a hearty, multilayered initial aroma that's simultaneously spicy (cinnamon, vanilla bean), fruity (star anise, grapefruit, bitter orange), nutty, and raisiny—lots happening all at once; following more aeration, the bouquet turns leathery, dusty, sap-like, resiny, maple-like, honeyed, and appealingly intense. Entry is peppery, piquant, almost prickly on the tongue but also sweet, sappy, oaky, spicy (vanilla is vociferous); midpalate shows a more elegant side in which the taste elements have settled down and integrated, forming a harmonious, measured, stately flavor profile that has a trace of rancio in the tobacco-like, toasty finish. One of the best, most classical PC cognacs.
2015 Rating: ★ ★ ★ ★ ★/Highest Recommendation

Lhéraud VSOP Petite Champagne Cognac 40% abv, $92.
Bronze/ochre color; superb purity. Oh my, the ambrosial up-front aroma is all about casaba melon, kiwi, banana, and baking spices, in particular nutmeg, along with sawdust, oak plank, brown butter, light honey, raisins—I mean, there's so much happening here I can hardly keep up keying in all the aromas; further aeration sees the white grape/white raisin aspect get accentuated with air contact—a sensuous bouquet whose hallmark is ripe tropical fruit. Entry is succulent (big surprise!), jammy, moderately oily in texture, resiny/woody, and almost a little like cocoa butter or even apple butter; midpalate relies more on the oak component to push forward the ripe fruit and grape jam in round, creamy waves of flavor that last deep into the honey-like finish. Classy and still youthfully fresh and vibrant.
2015 Rating: ★ ★ ★ ★/Highly Recommended

Lhéraud XO Charles VII Petite Champagne Cognac 44% abv, $595.
Brilliant, light-catching auburn/tarnished-chestnut color; sediment-free purity. Here's an opening bouquet that's very oak-driven and almost hard cheese–like rather than grapy/fruity; with more time in the glass, the aroma turns mildly nutty, leathery, waxy, and cigar box–like; this aroma has a high degree of oak polymers and hemicellulose aspects that drive up the complexity. Entry is chewy, cocoa bean–like, intensely oaky, sap- and maple-like, honeyed, with a dash of earthiness; midpalate features the mélange of dried fruit, nut, spice, bean, and wood flavors as they fuse into an integrated flavor profile that exhibits iconic Petite

Champagne power and finesse. It's a beautifully articulate argument for the little-appreciated cause of Petite Champagne cognac.

2015 Rating: ★ ★ ★ ★ ★/Highest Recommendation

Louis Royer XO Fine Champagne Cognac 40% abv, $135.
Gorgeously attractive deep henna/auburn color; perfect clarity. I encounter deeply nutty aromas here that are evocative and elegant in the first nosings; seven more minutes of air contact stimulate more subtle aromatics, including leather, baking spices (clove, vanilla), sawdust, tea, and oak plank; a deceptively serious bouquet. Entry is richly rewarding in its suppleness and caramel-like flavor; midpalate highlights aspects of honey, cocoa, and chocolate orange. Aftertaste is luscious, honeyed, and profoundly deep.

2018 Rating: ★ ★ ★ ★ ★/Highest Recommendation

Maison Gautier VS Cognac 40% abv, $20.
Topaz/amber color; sediment-free purity. First aromatic impressions are all about white grapes and raisins, plus a bit of pineapple scent due to the keen acidity; second-stage inhalations following more air contact bring out deft touches of baking spices, primarily cinnamon, nutmeg, and clove that accentuate the fruitiness. Entry stays the ambrosial course as the grapy/tropical-fruit flavor layers dominate the initial taste samplings, giving way at the later midpalate phase to a resiny woodiness that adds textural volume to the in-mouth experience. Concludes medium long, dry as an arid landscape, and mildly baked.

2018 Rating: ★ ★ ★/Recommended

Maison Gautier VSOP Cognac 40% abv, $30.
Cocoa-brown color; superb clarity. Strangely, as opposed to the animated bouquet of the VS, I don't encounter much in the way of brandy aromatics in the opening whiffs with this VSOP other than a distant woodiness/sawdust quality that's in a fragrance galaxy far, far away; allowing for more aeration over the extended span of ten minutes, I at last discern delicate scents of buttercream, light honey, walnut, fig, dried fruits, such as white raisins and prune. Entry is zesty, dry as a bone, slightly caramelized, spicy, and piquant; at midpalate the flavor profile turns nutty, moderately oaky, and vanilla-like. Finish comes off lightly toasted, as in toasted marshmallow.

2018 Rating: ★ ★ ★/Recommended

Maison Surrenne Distillerie Galtauld 100% Borderies Cognac 40.5% abv, $100.
Attractive bronze/burnt-orange color; very minor floating debris seen—inconsequential. Opening sniffs detect ambrosial, bakery-like notes of gingerbread, mincemeat, raisins, dried pineapple, dried apricot; further aeration time sees the fruit element dissipate, leaving the door open for oak and nut scents. Entry is sinuous, oily, fruity, oaky, resiny, cheese-like, mushroomy; midpalate mirrors everything going on in the entry, adding dark caramel, toasted marshmallow. Finishes long, narrowly focused on caramel. Flat-out luscious.

2014 Rating: ★ ★ ★ ★ ★/Highest Recommendation

Maison Surrenne Heritage No. 2 Cognac 40% abv, $1,200.
Bay/topaz color; flawless purity. This opening aroma is diametrically opposed to both

the 100 percent Borderies and Lot David Picoron because it is metallic, stony, steely, yet compellingly earthy, mineral-like; additional aeration doesn't significantly alter the aromatic profile except for the introduction of nectarine as the bouquet stays the mineral, dusty-dry, quartz-like path. Entry is fruity sweet, ripe, tannic, astringent, elegant; midpalate goes more for the oak intensity, which nicely accentuates the understated fruit. Ends medium long, minerally, medium sweet.

2014 Rating: ★ ★ ★ ★/Highly Recommended

Maison Surrenne Lot David Picoron Single Vineyard 1975 Cognac 40% abv, $275.

Brilliant copper color; superb clarity. First sniffs detect subtle nuances of vines, vegetation, damp earth, baking spices (clove, nutmeg); later inhalations encounter baked pear, white raisins, quince. Entry is dusty, vanilla-bittersweet, toasted, toffee-like, gently grapy, bread dough; midpalate echoes all the entry impressions and magnifies the grapiness. Concludes woody, resiny, maple-like, toasty.

2014 Rating: ★ ★ ★ ★/Highly Recommended

Martell Blue Swift Eau-de-Vie de Vin Finished in Bourbon Casks VSOP Cognac 40% abv, $45.

Mahogany/auburn color; flawlessly pure. The first inhalations pick up brown butter–like aromas that are toasty, plush, and bakery-shop bittersweet; later whiffs detect notes of lead pencil, shale, lanolin, and vanilla-flavored custard/flan. Entry is intensely oaky/woody, as well as tight, bean-like (cacao especially), and deeply raisiny and prune-like; midpalate largely echoes the entry, adding more volume to the creamy texture, as well as more developed baking spices, namely clove, mace, and cinnamon. Aftertaste is firm in structure, resiny/oily, densely spiced (now vanilla and clove), and attractively bittersweet. Good idea for a twist on cognac and it's pulled off well.

2018 Rating: ★ ★ ★ ★/Highly Recommended

Martell Caractère Cognac 40% abv, $35.

No age designation (VS, VSOP, XO). Light topaz/amber color; flawless purity. Opening aromas are delicate, somewhat laid-back, and include lightly toasted marshmallow, white raisins, dates, almond paste; later whiffs after more air contact encounter lacy, slowly fading traces of oak, pineapple, guava, pine nut. Entry is warming, honey sweet, creamy in texture, if a bit homogenized; midpalate features fleeting flavors of vanilla, nutmeg, white raisins, but not a lot of depth. This is Cognac 101 in the truest sense that highlights cognac's easy drinkability more than its core substance. Entry level, but good enough to be recommended as such.

2015 Rating: ★ ★ ★/Recommended

Martell Cordon Bleu Grand Classic Cognac 40% abv, $175.

Topaz/burnished-orange; impeccable purity. First whiffs give me walnuts, dried flowers—a sophisticated, mature scent; later sniffs detect dried pears, white raisins, maple, old leather; the bouquet is vibrant, expressive, and a feast for the olfactory sense. Palate entry is dense, languid, oily/buttery, semisweet, and decadently rich; midpalate sings with prune/raisin flavor that's silky and rich, never hot or the slightest bit rough; exhibits complete taste

integration that is wrapped in a creamy textural robe. Finishes extended, smooth as silk, medium weighted, and a bit caramel-like. As good an XO-level cognac from a "Big Four" producer (Martell, Hennessy, Rémy Martin, Courvoisier) that exists.
2018 Rating: ★ ★ ★ ★ ★/Highest Recommendation

Martell VS Fine Cognac 40% abv, $35.

Medium amber/burnished-orange color; unblemished purity. Initial whiffs detect lithe scents of white grapes, candied nuts, and oaky vanilla; later sniffs after another seven minutes in the glass pick up delicately sweet and almost floral fragrances of honeysuckle, fudge, and trail-mix dried fruit (especially apricots); terrific bouquet. Palate entry is supple, semisweet, and caramel-like; midpalate displays tons of elegance and harmony in both texture and pruny/figgy flavor that's accented by baking spices (mace, allspice) and candied almonds. Finishes with all the grace of the entry and midpalate.
2018 Rating: ★ ★ ★/Recommended

Martell VS Single Distillery Cognac 40% abv, $33.

Sandy-brown color; superb clarity. I like the opening aroma, which is tart yet ripe and engagingly fruity with perfumed scents of kiwi, pomelo, and white grapefruit; further air contact heightens the tartness as the fruit layer leans more towards white grapes and grape-fruit now, remaining fresh and vigorous for the entire second stage of inhalation. Entry is dry and toffee-like at the same time, giving off a menu of flavors that includes oak resins, white raisins, candied walnut, and apple rind; midpalate takes a slightly different direction as the taste profile turns orchard-fruit-peel bitter and squeaky-clean astringent. Finishes tightly wound, lean, tart but not sour, and razor-edged.
2018 Rating: ★ ★ ★/Recommended

Martell VSOP Cognac 40% abv, $40.

Stunningly gorgeous and brilliant copper color; good clarity. The first nosings fall a little flat as the aroma never gets off the ground, aside from a soft caramel candy scent; an additional seven minutes of exposure to air accomplishes little, if anything, in terms of coaxing out more in the way of expressive bouquet, resulting in a meek candy/light honey smell and that's all. Palate entry is slightly bitter in a resiny manner and is therefore a tad awkward; midpalate is better as the modest taste profile settles in, offering sweet tastes of honey, toffee, and candied nuts. Low-impact finish. Surely drinkable, but it's surprisingly a lackluster VSOP when compared to the VS, considering the skill of the producer.
2018 Rating: ★ ★/Not Recommended

Martell XO Extra Old Cognac 40% abv, $225.

Pretty chestnut color shows traces of sediment. Up front, I get pears, grapes, oily/buttery, mature scents in the opening whiffs that still own the promise of youthful vitality; the spirit is pleasantly prickly in the second whiffs and I like that; loads of nutty (almond), fruity (white raisins, apricot), and floral (honeysuckle, violets) character. Palate entry is sweeter and more ambrosial than its sibling, the Cordon Bleu; it is round, luxurious, and slightly coffee-like in its bittersweet approach at midpalate. Ends with a little numbing, prickly sensation.
2018 Rating: ★ ★ ★ ★/Highly Recommended

Merlet Brothers Blend Cognac 40% abv, $46.
Color of hay/old, yellowed parchment; excellent purity. The opening aromas are muted, except for a distant fruitiness; later inhalations after seven minutes of additional aeration provide only a meager amount more in terms of bouquet, in particular, a mildly pleasing grapiness. Entry is delightfully zesty and spicy and peppery; midpalate features the tastes of ripe grapes, oak, and almond paste. Aftertaste doesn't add anything new to the flavor profile, but it does bring the elements together in a pleasing finish that isn't profound or flashy, just pleasant.
2015 Rating: ★★★/Recommended

Merlet Sélection Saint-Sauvant Cognac 45.2% abv, $130.
Lovely new-copper/burnished-orange color is pristine and bright. Initial inhalations encounter wonderfully ripe grape and baked pear fragrances that are pushed forward by the higher abv; after more time in the glass, the aromatics turn bakery spice–like (especially clove, nutmeg), biscuity, and a bit lead pencil–like. Entry is lean, almost austere at first, then the taste turns nutty, viny/vegetal, oaky; midpalate highlights the metallic/lead pencil aspect prior to returning to the baked orchard fruit. Finish is moderately long, medium bodied, chiseled, lean. I like this recommendable cognac but its austere character in the mouth prevented me from bestowing a fourth rating star.
2015 Rating: ★★★/Recommended

Monnet VS Cognac 40% abv, $30.
Attractive golden-yellow/amber color; spotless purity. Offers strong scents of white grapes and green melon in the initial inhalations after the pour; the second passes following further aeration time feature fresh, vivid grape spirit, oaky spice, new leather, and dried herbs (bay leaf). Entry is pleasingly directed towards the oak (limousin, by the vanilla aspect), which comes off in tastes of clove, vanilla, and nutmeg; midpalate is fruitier/grapier than the entry stage. Finishes a touch smoky/toasted and caramel-like, both of which meld well with the heightened fruit.
2014 Rating: ★★★/Recommended

Monnet VSOP Cognac 40% abv, $52.
Bronze/old gold color; flawless clarity. I encounter traces of dark fudge, caramel, raisins, and brown sugar in the opening whiffs after the pour; following another seven minutes of aeration, the bouquet goes from confections to fruits, in particular, baked fruits, such as banana and pears, and also resinous oak. Entry is firm, acidic/astringent, semisweet, and like chocolate-covered banana; midpalate is more pear-like than like tropical fruit and is spicy (clove, allspice). Concludes long in the throat, narrow in focus, and directed at the baked fruit and wood. A classy VSOP to reckon with.
2014 Rating: ★★★★/Highly Recommended

Naud VS Cognac 40% abv, $50.
Bronze color; impeccably clean. In the opening sniffs I pick up featherlight scents of pear, white grape, leather-bound books/library, and milk chocolate; later whiffs encounter lightly spiced aromas of nutmeg, mace, and oak plank. Entry offers a medium-weighted,

mildly buttery texture that underpins the flavor profile, which includes brown sugar, praline, and candied almond; midpalate stage features dried fruit, especially dates, plus tangy notes of black pepper and dark honey. Aftertaste is medium long, dry, and piquant.

2018 Rating: ★ ★ ★/Recommended

Normandin-Mercier 1976 40 Year Old Petite Champagne Cognac 41.4% abv, $350.
Bottled in 2016. Sandy-brown color; pristine purity. First inhalations detect mature, old leather–like, fruit (red cherry) compote–like aromas that are supported by lesser scents of crème caramel/flan, English toffee, and turbinado sugar; secondary whiffs pick up additional fragrances of gingerbread, spice cake, dried orange peel, bergamot, and cinnamon bun; an exceptional bouquet. Entry is off-dry to semisweet, tasting of toasted marshmallow, candied walnut, bacon fat, and marzipan; midpalate features stately, mature tastes of dried figs, brown sugar, prune Danish, mincemeat pie, and cinnamon bun. Ends on a honeyed note that is nuanced rather than aggressive. A fabulously enchanting cognac of regal stature.

2019 Rating: ★ ★ ★ ★ ★/Highest Recommendation

Normandin-Mercier Christmas Petite Champagne Cognac 45% abv, $136.
A seasonal, one barrel release. Burnt sienna color; impeccable clarity. Right out of the aromatic gate I get vivid fragrances of Fig Newtons, dates, mincemeat pie, and spiced (allspice, mace) and baked banana; secondary passes detect more fruit-driven scents, including black raisins, black plum, gooseberry, and gentian. Entry is round and supple in texture, toffee-like, with supplemental flavors of spiced pear tart, nutmeg, mace, and brown sugar; midpalate echoes the entry stage, adding a deft touch of oakiness that comes off as vanilla extract, which marries nicely to the orchard-fruit aspect. Finishes elegantly, long in the throat, sinewy, and bittersweet.

2019 Rating: ★ ★ ★ ★/Highly Recommended

Normandin-Mercier La Péraudière Cask Strength Grande Champagne Cognac 45% abv, $250.
Ochre color; lovely, rich, pure core appearance. Opening sniffs pick up radiant aromas of earthy limestone/chalk, dates, figs, kiwi, saddle leather, and violets; secondary inhalations are of roasted meat, dried orange peel, dark chocolate, fudge, and oaky vanilla; midpalate is the pinnacle moment as the flavor profile features a rich, viscous texture that supports integrated, old rum–like tastes of dried fruits (prune, black raisins), winter holiday fruitcake, nutmeg, baked ham with clove, and nut butter/Nutella. Finishes long, almond paste–like, lusciously creamy, and oaky sweet. A sterling, top-rank Grande Champagne cognac superstar from the 1992 harvest.

2019 Rating: ★ ★ ★ ★ ★/Highest Recommendation

Normandin-Mercier Prestige Fine Champagne Cognac 40% abv, $100.
Caramel color; bright, pristine appearance. "Subtle" is the operative term for the initial inhalations, as the first sniffs pick up very little fragrance other than egg white, meringue, and candle wax; secondary whiffs pick up latent scents of distant caramel, dried red fruits, and limestone. Entry is toasty, roasted, oaky, and sap-like, with faint touches of vanilla

bean and black plum; midpalate shows more integration as the taste profile beefs up a bit, texture-wise, exposing a slight measure more of baked banana and gingerbread. Finishes woody, dry, and elegant.

2019 Rating: ★ ★ ★/Recommended

Normandin-Mercier VSOP Petite Champagne Cognac 40% abv, $70.

Citron/satin-sheen gold color; superbly clear. Up-front aromas include cherry pie, black raisins, dates, and most of all, prune Danish; aeration finds the aromatics building in power and assertiveness as the primary fragrance of red fruit gives way slightly to more tropical fruit perfume, namely pineapple and guava; a lovely ambrosial bouquet. Entry is significantly drier than the nose implies it would be, as the oak influence takes charge, causing the flavor profile to go tart, tight, deeply resiny, and astringent; midpalate is squeaky clean and tightly wound, as the oak eliminates the fruit component, thereby making this stage all about tree sap, resin, and, in my view, off-kilter. This evaluation is a tale of two distinct impressions: one, the fruity, pleasing aroma and, two, the overly wooded flavor. The problem is that they do not meet in the middle.

2019 Rating: ★ ★/Not Recommended

Normandin-Mercier XO Grande Champagne Cognac 40% abv, $165.

Beautiful mahogany color; flawless clarity. First aromatic impressions are of old books/library, hard cheese, moss, and shiitake mushroom, which leads me to think "rancio"; secondary whiffs offer traces of lead pencil, flint, caramel custard/flan, egg white, baked apricot, and toffee. Entry is mineral-like and earthy dry at first, then the flavors open up by midpalate, going more towards breakfast cereal with dried fruit, pipe tobacco, and nutmeg. Concludes medium long in the throat, biscuity, toffee-like, and gently ripe and sweet.

2019 Rating: ★ ★ ★ ★/Highly Recommended

Pierre Croizet VS Cognac 40% abv, $30.

Pale ochre color; excellent purity. First nosings offer youthful vitality and fresh, grapy scents that are mildly sweet and ripe while being engaging and simple—no ponderous, hour-eating complexity here; following more aeration, the grapiness deepens, becoming much riper and jammier than previously—in fact, for a brandy youngster, it's a delightful bouquet that requires no effort. Entry is sweet, unapologetically grapy, easy, vibrant, and straightforward; midpalate echoes all the findings in the entry. Finishes amiable, uncomplicated, intensely grapy/fruity, properly acidic, and therefore fresh and clean. Nice job on this entry-level brandy.

2016 Rating: ★ ★ ★/Recommended

Rémy Martin 1738 Accord Royal Fine Champagne Cognac 40% abv, $59.

Bright new-copper/topaz color; unblemished clarity. Opening whiffs detect pleasantly pruny/raisiny notes that leave little room for anything else; another seven minutes of aeration bring out deeper layers of sawdust, cedar plank, cinnamon/nutmeg, and nougat. Entry offers mature but vividly fresh tastes of dark caramel, toffee, oaky vanilla, and honey; midpalate reinforces all of the entry flavors and adds tastes of butter brickle and brown butter.

Concludes long, focused on the soft candy and honey flavors; chewy in the aftertaste, and slightly toasted/smoky.

2019 Rating: ★ ★ ★/Recommended

Rémy Martin VSOP Fine Champagne Cognac 40% abv, $47.

Shimmering amber/honey color; unblemished clarity. In the first sniffs after the pour, I pick up evidence of fresh, raisiny grape spirit, baked yellow fruit (pears, quince), and caramel; more time in the glass unleashes roasted scents of chestnut purée, pine, palm oil, and sautéed butter. Entry goes in the direction of raisiny, nearly over-the-top sweetness, but at midpalate the flavor profile gets its footing back as the semisweet taste profile becomes more focused on the grape spirits and oak and less on the concentrated caramel. Is it better than in 1992 when I first evaluated it? Yes. Would I buy it today? Probably not, especially if I could find more elegant VSOPs, such as Camus, Hardy, or Frapin.

2019 Rating: ★ ★/Not Recommended

Rémy Martin XO Fine Champagne Cognac 40% abv, $225.

Tarnished-copper/henna color that's appealing; bright purity. First inhalations discover nuanced traces of dried fruit (especially apricot, peach), black pepper, saddle leather, and oak; aeration brings out more potent but off-dry scents of spirits, oak, spice (nutmeg), and marzipan. Entry is elegant and integrated on all levels; midpalate builds on the finesse-driven entry, as the taste profile turns far more focused, especially on the resiny, coconut-like oak, and dried fruit. Concludes in the mouth gracefully, chewy, and as harmonious as it starts. While this is not what I consider to be an overly complex XO, it nonetheless shows a wealth of charm. The midpalate and finish are particularly savory and elegant.

2019 Rating: ★ ★ ★ ★/Highly Recommended

Richard Hennessy Cognac 40% abv, $3,200.

Deep topaz/auburn color, with cocoa core; impeccable clarity. Initial inhalations pick up soft aromas of cardamom, nutmeg, chocolate-covered cherries, licorice; secondary sniffs encounter deeper cocoa aspects that turn into dark chocolate, tree sap, oak, hard cheese, nut-like damp-earth scents. Entry is chewy, rich, mature, oaky but not resiny; midpalate echoes the entry, adding blueberry muffin and, akin to the Paradis Imperial, a touch of pipe tobacco. Concludes long, succulent, raisiny, pruny, bittersweet. Simply, still the finest, most majestic expression of Hennessy.

2014 Rating: ★ ★ ★ ★ ★/Highest Recommendation

Tesseron Extreme Grande Champagne Cognac 40% abv, $5,500.

Only three hundred bottles produced annually for the world. Bright burnt sienna/bronze color; impeccable clarity. This aroma after the pour is diametrically opposed to that of the Trésor, in that, while not a bit fruity at first, it leans more to tobacco, sea salt, chalky soil, minerals, slate; later inhalations detect an undercurrent of white grape preserves, apple butter, almond paste, nougat that fly under the radar as the damp earth/wet soil aromas dominate deep into the bouquet phase. Entry is oaky/resiny, earthy/mushroom-like, vanilla bean–like, toasted marshmallowy, meaty, with underpinning flavors of tomato paste, bacon fat; midpalate echoes the entire entry-stage experience, adding succulent flavors of pear or apple tart, cigar tobacco, and dark caramel/fudge. Finishes fathomlessly long and deep, bittersweet, spicy, luxuriously mature, and integrated.

2015 Rating: ★ ★ ★ ★ ★/Highest Recommendation

Tesseron Lot No. 29 XO Exception Grande Champagne Cognac 40% abv, $700.
Flawless clarity; topaz color. Roasted/toasty aromas in first whiffs highlight quince, lemongrass; later scents include citrus, wheat bread toast with marmalade, tangerine. Entry features citrus fruits, fruitcake, caramel, saltwater taffy; midpalate is confectioner shop semisweet, satiny in texture, and nutty. Delicious aftertaste of dark chocolate candies with nuts.

2014 Rating: ★ ★ ★ ★/Highly Recommended

Tesseron Lot No. 53 XO Perfection Grande Champagne Cognac 40% abv, $315.
Old gold/nut-brown color; impeccable purity. I detect nuanced aromas of bacon, pork rind, brown sugar in initial inhalations; later, aspects of clove, vanilla bean, cocoa bean, black raisins dominate. Entry is sultry, silky, rich, sweet but not cloying; midpalate flavors include chocolate-covered raisins, peanuts, orange rind, allspice, pineapple. Finishes extra long, honey sweet, dried fruit–like, complex, harmonious, classic.

2014 Rating: ★ ★ ★ ★ ★/Highest Recommendation

Tesseron Lot No. 76 XO Tradition Grande Champagne Cognac 40% abv, $135.
Sediment-free; sepia/brown color; shades lighter than No. 53. Subtlety rules the aromatic day as restrained scents of nutmeg, old leather, carnations highlight the first nosing; honey wheat bread, lemon curd, citrus zest, dried pineapple abound in later sniffs. Entry is brown-sugar sweet, toasted marshmallow–like, highly spiced; midpalate is long, silky, delicately sweet and spiced, fruity, yet dusty dry. Concludes understated, bakeshop sweet, spicy, and utterly luscious.

2014 Rating: ★ ★ ★ ★ ★/Highest Recommendation

Tesseron Lot No. 90 XO Selection Grande Champagne Cognac 40% abv, $75.
Topaz color; unblemished clarity. I get toned-down fruit notes, especially white grapes, kiwi, plus background baking spices (cinnamon, nutmeg) in the first whiffs; later on, more developed aromas of vanilla cream, cake frosting, pipe tobacco occur. Entry is sweet, succulent, raisiny; midpalate offers sap-like, heightened sweet tastes of honey, maple sugar, and granulated sugar. Recommendable but the overpowering sweetness negatively affects the balance.

2014 Rating: ★ ★ ★/Recommended

Tesseron Royal Blend Grande Champagne Cognac 40% abv, $1,500.
Sediment-free; umber/chestnut color. Yellow plums, white grapes, kiwi, and pineapple all show up in the initial whiffs; the slightly sour fruit aspect continues in later inhalations. Entry is expressive, toasty, intensely grapy and oaky, peppery and spicy; midpalate reinforces all the entry flavors, adding notes of paraffin, old honey, dried pineapple. Lots going for it, but, for me, I prefer No. 53 and No. 76, in particular the No. 53.

2014 Rating: ★ ★ ★ ★/Highly Recommended

Tesseron Trésor Grande Champagne Cognac 40% abv, $1,200.
One thousand bottles per year for the world. Deep mahogany/tawny port–brown color; owns a slight haziness. Oh my, the ambrosial presence of vine and orchard fruit (white grape, pear, yellow apple) is startling in its succulence and conviction in the initial inhalations; second passes encounter heftier elements of spice (allspice, cinnamon, clove), caramelized sugar, crème brûlée, toasted honey wheat bread, sautéed mushrooms; a superlative bouquet that's long on fruitiness and earthiness. Entry mirrors the bouquet, especially in the earthy aspect that's clearly rancio-driven as flavors of pine/cedar, honey, mushroom paté are made piquant by the baking spices; midpalate is gloriously lush but defined, as narrowly focused tastes of baking spice, dried and baked fruits, and gently sweet pipe tobacco drive the flavor profile forward into a languid, lavish aftertaste that can only be described as sublime.
2015 Rating: ★★★★★/Highest Recommendation

The Forgotten Casks 16-2 Cognac 40% abv, $112.
Blended by French master blender extraordinaire Alain Royer. Color is a sturdy amber/golden wheat field; I can see wisps of oils floating in the pristine core. Opening sniffs identify orchard fruit–like scents, in particular, quince and yellow pear that float atop deeper aromas of white raisins, sawdust, oak plank, and gooseberry; later inhalations come across as drier, woodier scents that overshadow the fruit aspects. Entry is softly fruity/grapy, oaky, and a touch spicy (nutmeg, clove), but the big splash is found in the midpalate, which is creamy in texture, piquant, and spicy in flavor profile, and just all-around yummy. Aftertaste narrows down the flavor function to a tightly wound piquancy.
2016 Rating: ★★★★/Highly Recommended

Through The Grapevine Conte Filles Aged 18 Years Cask #63 Petite Champagne Cognac 47% abv, $97.
Tawny/rusty color; flawlessly pure; really pretty appearance. First sniffs detect pungent notes of BBQ sauce, oak char, woodsmoke, charcoal briquettes, and creosote; secondary inhalations following more air contact find distinct echoes of the initial aromatic impressions, as well as notes of lanolin, vegetable oil, flaxseed oil, and lard. Entry is highly caramelized, bittersweet, candied in a praline manner, and dense with nut-like flavor; midpalate highlights the intense nuttiness, leaving no room for any faint likeness of grapes and that, for me, is this cognac's downfall. Any grapiness, which must be evident in any recommendable top-tier Petite Champagne cognac, is overshadowed by over-the-top waxy, resiny oak presence. Unacceptable.
2018 Rating: ★★/Not Recommended

Through The Grapevine Fanny Fougerat Single Cask 1994 Borderies Cognac 52.8% abv, $151.
Earth yellow/sandy-brown color; ideal clarity. In the opening inhalations, I pick up traces of vinyl, plastic, and textile fiber, as well as baked fruits, especially banana, green melon, and apricot; secondary whiffs detect discernable hints of dark caramel, cigar tobacco, chocolate-covered raisins, and marshmallow. Entry is pleasantly nutty, floral, bittersweet, and fruity while the texture is round, supple, and creamy; midpalate echoes the entry findings,

focusing mostly on the candied fruits and almonds. The elevated alcohol by volume isn't a noticeable factor as it is easily integrated into the final aftertaste impressions of roasted and candied nuts, candied fruits, oaky vanillin, and toffee.

2018 Rating: ★ ★ ★/Recommended

Through The Grapevine François Voyer Lot 93 Grande Champagne Cognac 45.9% abv, $170.

Burnt sienna color; some inconsequential tendrils of sediment seen. Opening whiffs pick up scents of sealing wax, paraffin, and textile fibers; after more air contact, the aroma blossoms into a cascade of fragrances, ranging from oak resin to candle wax to waxy fruits to dried pineapple to flax. Entry is robust in its dried-fruit base flavors, which are reminiscent of roasted pork tenderloin, grilled pineapple, and grilled apricot; midpalate is roasted, dry, earthy, flinty, stone-like, and intensely woody/resiny to the point of fruit/grape exclusion. Ends up tasting like a pinewood two-by-four. In the end, it's this severe eclipsing of the grape element in favor of the resiny/sappy oak barrel that doesn't make it recommendable. Very disappointing. A far cry from what I expect from Grande Champagne.

2018 Rating: ★ ★/Not Recommended

Through The Grapevine Rémi Landier Lot 73 Fins Bois Cognac 47.8% abv, $200.

Beautiful cocoa-brown color; some minor sediment seen. Immediately in the opening sniffs I pick up succulent notes of grilled pineapple and red plum, plus supporting aromas of dark caramel, parchment, pipe tobacco, and lima bean; after more time in the glass, secondary inhalations encounter vibrant and dense fragrances of pipe tobacco, figs, dates, sautéed mushrooms, and rancio. Entry shows off its massive flavor profile that includes toasted marshmallow, BBQ sauce, tomato paste, candied walnut, pine nut, high-cocoa-content dark chocolate, candied orange rind, black raisins, dates, and treacle; midpalate reprises the entry impressions, adding brown butter and honey that usher in the aftertaste with penetrating style and density. A superbly rendered Fins Bois cognac that distinctly demonstrates what this demarcated district can produce when given the chance and the right producer. An awesome display of elegance and sheer power.

2018 Rating: ★ ★ ★ ★ ★/Highest Recommendation

Through The Grapevine Vallein Tercinier Single Cask 1988 Fins Bois Cognac 58.3% abv, $169.

Topaz color; spotlessly pure. This cask strength aroma takes no prisoners in the opening inhalations as the robust alcohol prickles in the nasal cavity in pungent waves of waxy oak, dried fruits, and pine cone zestiness; secondary whiffs after more aeration discover pleasant aromas of toasted oak, baked pears, candied apples, and jasmine fragrance. Entry provides plenty of flavor impact that's driven by the high abv as the taste profile includes grilled pears and plums, light caramel, fudge, and honey; midpalate features all of the entry impressions plus a zesty spiciness that underscores the grilled fruits especially. Aftertaste is long, languid, moderately oily and woody/fatty, and keenly bittersweet. If this cognac were mine, I'd bring the abv down to perhaps 47/48 percent to bring out more of the lovely fruit element. You can do that yourself by adding a touch of mineral water, if you care to.

2018 Rating: ★ ★ ★ ★/Highly Recommended

ARMAGNAC—FRANCE

While cognac has since its inception been produced mostly as an export spirit, influenced by seventeenth-century Dutch merchants for foreign markets, armagnac is considered by the French public as THE grape brandy of France. Regrettably, armagnac is sometimes erroneously perceived to be a kind of cognac. While made from grapes like cognac, armagnac owns a different set of characteristics and criteria.

Armagnac's Demarcated Districts

Armagnac boasts three demarcated districts, as officially declared in 1909. Each gained AOC (appellation d'origine contrôlée) status in 1936.

Bas-Armagnac: Bas-Armagnac's capital is the bustling town of Eauze and is the westernmost district; it constitutes approximately 57 percent of total armagnac brandy production. The character of Bas-Armagnac brandies is closely associated with its sandy/silty soils and stony ground dotted with sand dune–like formations and rusty iron colors. Interestingly, the region's argillaceous soils tend to produce grapes that live on the edge. The grapes from this area produce hearty eaux-de-vie that are fruity, round, and with raisiny notes that can mature for decades. But they can simultaneously exhibit zestily sour notes, reminiscent of lemon peel.

Ténarèze-Armagnac: This district lies in the center and has the town of Condom as its hub. Ténarèze accounts for nearly 40 percent of Armagnac's brandy output. Its clay/limestone/sand soils are similar to some of Cognac's choicest soil types. Thus, Ténarèze brandies tend to be very full-bodied, lush in texture, spicy, potent tasting, and long-lasting. While the brandies from Bas-Armagnac dominate the conversation, those hailing from Ténarèze are just as seductive.

Haut-Armagnac: This area is called "White Armagnac" due to the abundance of limestone. It is the area's largest district, cradling both Bas-Armagnac and Ténarèze, but it contributes a mere 3 percent of Armagnac's total eau-de-vie output. Aside from making succulent eau-de-vie, Haut-Armagnac is best known for its inexpensive, highly acidic, and crisp white wines grown on chalky, clay soils.

By law, ten grape varieties are permitted for the production of armagnac. The four dominant grapes are baco 22A and, just as in Cognac, ugni blanc, folle blanche, and colombard. The secondary grapes that are allowed but infrequently utilized are mauzac blanc, mauzac rosé, plant de graisse, meslier St. François, jurançon blanc, and clairette de gascogne.

Some producers occasionally offer single-variety armagnacs. The Armagnac region's fifteen thousand hectares also account for vin de pays Côtes de Gascogne (table wines) and floc de Gascogne, Armagnac's lovely aperitif. Floc de Gascogne is a vin mistelle, or a blend of unfermented grape juice mixed with armagnac, made in the style of Cognac's pineau des charentes.

Currently, there are about four thousand grape growers in Gascony, of which approximately 250 produce and bottle armagnac. There are also around forty négociants, or brandy entrepreneurs, who buy already-barreled armagnac from grower/distillers and age and bottle armagnac under their own label. Francis Darroze is the most renowned of these houses.

Labeling Laws

Armagnacs are aged in oak. Once the eau-de-vie comes off the Alambic Armagnaçais (the region's distinctive distilling apparatus), the virgin spirit is quickly pumped into new 400- to 420-liter oak barrels (*pièces* in French) for from six months to two years. Most are then pumped into older barrels for longer periods of slow maturation. Black oak from the forest of Monlezun is the customary choice, but oak from the forests of Nouvelle-Aquitaine, Tronçais, or Allier is also utilized today. In warm, sunny, and temperate Gascony, the loss of spirit to evaporation (the infamous *angel's share*) usually happens at an annual rate of between 2 percent and 5 percent.

Regardless of the source of the oak, armagnac must be aged in oak for a minimum of two years, with other minimums required for particular designations.

VS (Very Special; a.k.a. **Three Star**) armagnacs are aged in French oak casks for at least one year but no more than three.

VSOP (Very Superior Old Pale) armagnacs are by law aged in French oak casks for at least four years but no more than nine.

Napoléon armagnacs are by law aged in French oak casks for at least six years but not more than nine.

Hors d'Age and XO (Extra Old) armagnacs, since 2015, can't by law be sold before they are aged in barrels for a minimum of ten years.

Vintage armagnacs must be made from grapes that were harvested from only a single vintage year (1999, 2009, et cetera).

Other armagnac bottlings may cite specific ages, such as 15 Ans (15 years old), 20 Ans, et cetera. Vintage armagnac is far more common than the rather rare vintage cognac. Every harvest season, approximately nine to ten million bottles of armagnac are produced in Gascony. No less than 65 percent of armagnac is sold within France, while the balance of 35 percent is exported to over 130 nations.

Blanche Armagnac is unaged armagnac, a kind of moonshine brandy.

Artez 22 Year Old Vintage 1995 Single Cask Bas-Armagnac 46% abv, $115.
Chestnut/deep brown color; immaculately clean and pure. I like the opening aroma right away as it features rich grapy/white raisin, yellow plum, and baking spice (clove, cinnamon) fragrances in equal measure; more time in the glass allows the aroma to expand to include scents of baked banana, cherry strudel, and crème caramel dessert. Entry is tightly wound, lean, and acidic without an ounce of oaky lipids (fats) or resins showing as the baked fruit aspects ascends, becoming even more accentuated than in the bouquet; midpalate echoes the entry-stage findings, adding a heightened nuttiness that's more paste- and butter-like than candied. The deep-seated nuttiness lasts long into the finish, providing a silky texture and a razor-edged crispness that are beguiling and sensual. Even at twenty-two years and counting, it is clear that this bas-armagnac has lots of vibrancy to spare.
2018 Rating: ★ ★ ★ ★/Highly Recommended

Artez Napoleon Baco Bas-Armagnac 40% abv, $40.
Stunning henna/cinnamon color; perfect clarity. I first get some sturdy fragrances of peanut butter, cocoa butter, brown sugar, and chocolate-covered raisins; with more air contact, the aroma goes buttery, nutty, oaky, and slightly spiced—all in all, a beefy, robust, assertive bouquet. Entry is, like the aroma, round, dry, deeply woody, and bitter in flavor; midpalate offers a bit more in the way of variety as the woodiness becomes oily/sap-like, but there is at last evidence of dried red fruits/raisin that add a nice dimension. Finishes long, sap-like, intensely oaky, bitter, and dry.
2016 Rating: ★ ★ ★/Recommended

Artez Napoleon Folle Blanche Bas-Armagnac 40% abv, $40.
Topaz/auburn color; impeccable purity, with oils seen floating in the core. Initial whiffs find a more elegant opening aroma than the burly baco as the first impressions are of ripe grapes, holiday spice cake, dried tropical fruits (pineapple, banana), oaky tannins, sawdust, and brown butter; secondary inhalations encounter a more streamlined, integrated bouquet of gravitas and harmony where the fruit and wood marry seamlessly. Entry is elegant, dry, mildly oaky, a touch toasty, and velvety in texture; midpalate reaffirms the splendid flavors found in the entry, being more woody than I recall, but still the flavor integration is what makes this brandy so delectable. Finishes medium long, with savory tastes of toffee, crème brûlée, vanilla bean.
2016 Rating: ★ ★ ★ ★/Highly Recommended

Artez Napoleon Ugni Blanc Bas-Armagnac 40% abv, $40.
Pretty, brilliant copper color; unblemished purity. There's a curious aroma in the up-front stage that I can't pinpoint, but it reminds me of lead pencil, dry stone (limestone), and uncured tobacco leaf; with more aeration the aroma stays the mineral-laden course that blocks anything resembling fruit/grape from participating. Entry is bitter, too woody for me, peppery/spicy, dry as a bone, and overly mineral-like; midpalate is keenly peppery, bitter, metallic, and like licking a dry stone. Concludes well enough in flavor (salted caramel) to restore a rating star. No doubt about it: reach for the lovely folle blanche.
2016 Rating: ★ ★/Not Recommended

Baron de Lustrac 25 Year Old XO Brut de Fût Limited Edition Bas-Armagnac 42.4% abv, $95.

Brilliant, light-catching sepia/russet color; pristine clarity. I'm getting all sorts of splendid aromas in the opening whiffs, from cinnamon to nutmeg to baked pear to dried fruits to candied almond to toffee; secondary inhalations offer succulent, bittersweet fragrances of dried flowers, brown butter, bacon fat, sautéed mushrooms, dark caramel—this bouquet just keeps unfolding. Entry captures all the magic of the bouquet and adds a silky texture to the equation that's moderately oily and viscous and not the least bit syrupy or ropy; midpalate features all the charms found in the nose and entry, but it's here that the oak makes itself known in a toasted manner that's mildly resiny and vanilla-like. Finishes long, satiny, spicy, zesty, mature. A brandy at its peak.

2016 Rating: ★ ★ ★ ★ ★/Highest Recommendation

Baron de Lustrac 8 Year Old Bas-Armagnac 40% abv, $54.

Burnt-orange/sandy-brown color; shimmering, spotlessly clear of sediment. First sniffs pick up earthy fragrances of sand and cement, then those quickly morph into more suitable grape brandy scents of baking spices (cinnamon, nutmeg) and dried fruits, mostly dates, mincemeat, and plums; allowing for more aeration time, I pick up even deeper dried-fruit aspects, primarily of mincemeat and now pears as the bouquet rounds out. Entry is squeaky clean and crisp, showing plenty of mouth-cleansing acidity, as well as vanilla bean, pistachio, brown butter, and oil; midpalate echoes the entry impressions as I find the youthful vigor and elegant suppleness of this stage very satisfactory. Aftertaste goes in the taste direction of cigar tobacco, brown butter, chutney, and white raisins.

2018 Rating: ★ ★ ★ ★/Highly Recommended

Baron de Lustrac Distilled 1989 Bottled 2017 Folle Blanche Bas-Armagnac 42% abv, $99.

Burnt umber color; excellent clarity. Up-front nosings encounter intriguing opening aromas of bacon fat, lard, grilled pork tenderloin, black peppercorn, and cardboard before turning more tobacco-like, even black tea–like; after more aeration, the bouquet reprises the bacon fat, lard aspects becoming more like vegetable cooking oil as I begin to wonder if any traces of fruit will emerge. Entry flavors definitely reflect the oiliness found in the nose, but there is far more evidence here of baked and dried fruits, especially white raisins, yellow plums (quince), and mango; midpalate takes on the task of organizing the various aspects into a unified flavor that highlights the bacon fat, baked fruits, and the oaky vanillin, which now is coming off as coconut. Aftertaste is medium long, dense with the fatty element in the texture, spicy, and fruity and altogether complex and concentrated.

2018 Rating: ★ ★ ★ ★/Highly Recommended

Baron de Lustrac XO 15 Year Old Bas-Armagnac 40% abv, $65.

Cocoa-brown color; flawless purity. Similar to the spry eight-year-old sibling, I immediately get earthy/elemental scents of wet pavement, sand, and drying cement that linger a bit longer before giving way to subtle, low-volume bakery-shop fragrances of allspice, mace, bear claw pastry, and baked tropical fruits (pineapple, banana); later inhalations after an allowance for more air contact detect deeply layered aromas of puff pastry, cinnamon bun, grape juice, powdered sugar, and prunes. Entry flavors, which are delightfully savory, echo the latter stage aromatics to a tee, making it very "more-ish"; midpalate reflects the entry impressions but deepens the entire taste profile as the additional maturity takes hold. Ends up more acidic than I'd have thought, and therefore comes off crisp and lean as the dried-fruit elements turn up their volume.

2018 Rating: ★★★★/Highly Recommended

Baron Gaston Legrand 1965 Bas-Armagnac 40% abv, $337.

The deep henna/auburn color is striking and perfectly clean. Opening nosing passes detect waxy, cooking oil–like aromas that are oaky, oily, tobacco-like, vegetal, leafy, walnut-like; second inhalations after more aeration discover notes of caramel, dark toffee, brown butter, dark honey. Entry is rich, honeyed, almost sherry-like, grapy, winey, juicy, and ripe; midpalate offers roasted, BBQ sauce–like, tomato paste, toasted marshmallow flavors that accentuate the oak intensity and make the abv seem higher than 40 percent. Aftertaste is deep, robust, chewy, creamy, smoky, roasted, and delicious. Hard to believe that this animated brandy is fifty years old, considering how vivid it is. Glorious.

2015 Rating: ★★★★★/Highest Recommendation

Castarède VSOP Bas-Armagnac 40% abv, $59.

Burnt sienna color; pristine clarity. First sniffs pick up baked and candied banana, mincemeat, spiced pear (nutmeg), and white raisin fragrances that are all firm, hearty, and vivid; secondary inhalations encounter succulent aromas of dates, figs, sugar cookie batter, egg whites, and Danish pastry; a superb aroma that's loaded with fruit, nuts, and spice. Entry is chockfull of baked fruit flavors, especially pear, banana, and sultana, plus pastry shop tastes of mincemeat pie, pecan pie, hazelnut, black tea, and sugar beet; midpalate offers a mélange of flavors that mirrors the entry phase, adding cola nut, yuzu, and cinnamon to boot. Finishes long, tangy, spicy, bittersweet, and just flat-out delicious.

2018 Rating: ★★★★/Highly Recommended

Castarède XO 10 Year Old Bas-Armagnac 40% abv, $110.

Very pretty copper/tawny color; unblemished clarity. The opening smells are exotic and understated, offering fragrant and mature scents of old library books, worn leather saddle, peach cobbler, and autumn forest; more aeration stimulates aromas of chocolate-covered raisins, prunes, baked Alaska, baked and spiced banana, and chicory. Entry is a bountiful feast of flavors, ranging from prune Danish to grilled peach to banana bread to winter holiday fruitcake; midpalate phase echoes the entry impressions, adding succulent and ambrosial baked fruits, such as dates, pears, and nectarine plus baking spices like clove, cinnamon, and allspice, thereby creating a tour-de-force flavor profile that is as dazzling, complex, and sturdy as any other from Bas-Armagnac. Aftertaste is fathomlessly long, silky in the throat, and supple.

2018 Rating: ★★★★★/Highest Recommendation

Château Arton Fine Blanche Armagnac 45% abv, $35.

Void of color; spotlessly clean and sediment-free. Up front, I get seductive, vivid aromas of spiced mincemeat (cinnamon, vanilla, and clove, with apples and pears), sultanas, figs,

parsley, sage, and grape jam; secondary inhalations are ripe, intensely fruity and jammy, leafy and vegetal, yet exhibit a gentility and reserve that makes the olfactory stages keenly pleasant and memorable. Entry explodes on the tongue in a tsunami of spirit-driven flavor that highlights the pear and white raisin aspects; midpalate turns softer, as the taste profile turns incredibly ripe, peel-like, seed-like, bitter, and yet dense with grapiness. Aftertaste is long and sculpted, tannic, and therefore desert dry. I liked this blanche armagnac a lot until the midpalate when it turned narrow in scope and stingy in flavor. Was on the path to four stars until then.
2017 Rating: ★★★/Recommended

Château Arton La Réserve Haut-Armagnac 45% abv, $80.
The deep mahogany color is very attractive and free from any form of residue. First whiffs pick up deeply woody aromas, as in resin, floor polish, and pine tar, plus old leather-bound books, worn saddle, and butter brickle; secondary sniffs encounter no fruit to speak of, but add scents of parchment, butcher's wax paper, toffee, and treacle. Entry is thick with bittersweet flavors of caramel, toasted almond, candy bar, nougat, and walnut; midpalate goes a bit too bitter and fruit deficient, but it does offer a modicum of candy-shop flavors that deliver pungent and off-dry tastes of roasted nuts, cocoa, and espresso. Finishes medium long, chocolatey, toasted, and pleasant.
2017 Rating: ★★★/Recommended

Château de Lacquy Hors d'Age Bas-Armagnac 41% abv, $80.
Saffron color; impeccable clarity. Ooooh, I like this biscuity, buttermilk pancake batter–like opening aroma that shows just a teasing whisper of baking spice (vanilla bean); with more air contact, the bouquet turns into an early morning visit to the bakery shop when all the cakes, pastries, and fruit turnovers are fresh and hot; a Bas-Armagnac dazzling aroma. Entry is drier than the aroma promised, as the taste profile offers oaky/resiny flavors that underscore the grapiness; midpalate echoes the entry in its bittersweet approach and adds light touches of cinnamon stick, sugar glaze, and almond paste for kicks. Concludes long, medium weighted in texture, balanced, and keenly tart.
2020 Rating: ★★★★/Highly Recommended

Château de Lacquy Reference Bas-Armagnac 40.5% abv, $45.
Ochre color; excellent purity. Up front in the first sniffs, I pick up an earthy, soil-like scent that's dry and mineral-like, but there are also traces of orchard fruit peel that lurk in the background; with more aeration, I pick up aromas of unsalted butter, wood pile, pipe tobacco, and lychee. Entry is similar to ripe grapes, fruit salad, and barely discernible caramel flavor; midpalate carries over the caramel aspect but then adds faint hints of mace, pear rind, and flint that all add up to a dry, mineral-like finish.
2020 Rating: ★★★/Recommended

Château de Lacquy VSOP Bas-Armagnac 40% abv, $65.
In an interesting development, I find the appearance of the Lacquy VSOP significantly darker than that of the sibling XO; this color is henna/brick and immaculately pure. Nosewise, there are appealing elements of flint, limestone, dry earth, chalk, and almond in

the opening whiffs; further air contact unleashes sturdy, solid aromas of butcher's wax paper, dried violets, honeysuckle, and a deft touch of orange zest. Entry is oily, satiny in texture, with tobacco-like, leafy flavors that underscore the dried-fruit (figs) and nut-butter aspects nicely; midpalate highlights a flavor of lanolin, which helps to explain the oily, resiny texture. In the finish, the taste profile of concentrated oak resin stays the course deep into the aftertaste.

2017 Rating: ★★★/Recommended

Château de Lacquy XO Bas-Armagnac 43.5% abv, $102.

Color is bright burnt-orange/bronze; clarity is ideal. First aromatic impressions include toasted multigrain bread, scone, and buckwheat that are superficial since deeper still are scents of cigar box, pipe tobacco, and lichen/moss; secondary inhalations detect toffee, butter brickle, almond paste, and cocoa bean. Entry flavors are zesty, moderately oily, and robust in the forms of black pepper, caramel, brown butter, and sautéed mushroom; midpalate offers delightfully tangy and piquant tastes of toasted marshmallow, chocolate-covered cherries, and stewed dates. Aftertaste is languid, medium long, silky. The higher abv helps the process by pushing the flavors forward with verve.

2017 Rating: ★★★★/Highly Recommended

Château de Laubade 12 Year Old Bas-Armagnac 40% abv, $70.

Golden poppy color; impeccably clean and clear of sediment. I immediately like the dry-as-stone opening aroma, which reminds me a little of espresso, coffee bean, and carob right out of the starting block; secondary sniffs after more aeration discover latent dried-fruit fragrances, mostly dates, fig, and lychee. Entry is deeply flavorful, with succulent tastes of dark fruits (black plum, black raisin), molasses, and mace; midpalate highlights the bittersweet jammy and old oak flavors and the lush texture. The aftertaste is perhaps this brandy's best moment as the savory, now pipe tobacco–like, dried fruit, and nutty flavor thrills the taste buds.

2019 Rating: ★★★★/Highly Recommended

Château de Laubade 1975 Barrique No. 74045 Bas-Armagnac 44.2% abv, $350.

Armagnac from one barrel (barrique). Baco, ugni blanc grapes. Drop-dead gorgeous, rich henna/copper color; superb purity. Opening aromas are ethereal, ghostlike in their subtlety, but there's enough expression to notice muesli/trail mix, dried pear/apricot, peanut, whey; secondary whiffs aren't offered much more in the way of aromatic tangibles so I move on to entry. Entry is gently sweet, honeyed, opulent yet finely acidic, and therefore fresh, even razor edged; midpalate is fruity, dry, honeyed, almost sherry-like, spiced with vanilla, clove, nutmeg. Finishes medium long, bittersweet, mildly toasted, keenly oaky, grapy.

2014 Rating: ★★★★/Highly Recommended

Château de Laubade 1976 Barrique No. 74043 Bas-Armagnac 44.8% abv, $342.

Baco, ugni blanc grapes. Moderately dark amber/copper color; good purity, except for chunks of black wax from the irritating seal. Early on, I detect linseed oil, flax, textile fiber, saltine cracker, salted butter that's being sautéed; second passes following additional time in the glass don't pick up much different except for a touch of limestone/chalk. Entry is sinewy in texture, more bittersweet than sweet, like toasted marshmallow, nougat; midpalate offers grilled fruit (pineapple, apricot), treacle, marzipan, praline flavors that run long into the bittersweet aftertaste.

2014 Rating: ★ ★ ★/Recommended

Château de Laubade 1978 Barrique No. 74104 Bas-Armagnac 45.8% abv, $326.

Baco, ugni blanc grapes. The attractive auburn/henna color is hampered by the unavoidable intrusion of black wax from the hardened wax seal—these absurdly outdated seals might look "traditional" and pretty to most people, but they are nothing but a royal pain in the ass to crack open, and when you do, pieces invariably tumble into the glass. I pick up resiny, piney, sawdust notes in the initial whiffs after the pour but no fruit or spice to speak of; further aeration allows for some fruitiness to emerge as well as a candied nut aspect (walnut) that's alluring. Entry is taut, peppery, raisiny, and like candied walnuts (that carries forward from the bouquet); midpalate is bittersweet, pruny, oaky, drier than the entry, acidic, highly tannic, and therefore astringent. Aftertaste is narrowly focused on oak resins, tannin.

2014 Rating: ★ ★ ★/Recommended

Château de Laubade 1979 Barrique No. 74105 Bas-Armagnac 46.2% abv, $290.

Baco, ugni blanc grapes. Deep, dark chestnut/bronze color; excellent clarity. Here I smell caraway, cardamom, road tar, dried plums, lead pencil, metals in an amazing menu of seemingly divergent aromas that actually work well in the opening whiffs; secondary inhalations find candle wax, flaxseed, parchment aromas. Entry is significantly sweeter than the bouquet alluded to and is candy-shop sweet, succulent, nutty, and filled with dried orchard fruits, especially nectarine, with pear taking the lead; midpalate is toastier than the entry, even baked as the taste profile takes another turn bringing out flavors of buttered rum, nougat, candied almonds, egg cream, biscuit batter, honey. Finishes long, bittersweet, toasty, oaky, satisfyingly supple, and round. At the sweet spot of its life cycle.

2014 Rating: ★ ★ ★ ★ ★/Highest Recommendation

Château de Laubade 1980 Barrique No. 74044 Bas-Armagnac 46.7% abv, $287.

Baco, ugni blanc grapes. Pretty, bright new-copper color; flawless purity. Holy moly, the butterscotch aspect comes leaping from the glass, filling my office with bakery and candy-store aromas that I find highly appealing; deeper inhalations after more air contact bring out a wide array of charming aromas including English toffee, saltwater taffy, brown butter, toasted raisin bread. Entry is satin smooth, gently sweet, raisiny/pruny, almost custard-like; midpalate is rich, honey sweet, pleasantly acidic, delicate almost, citrusy (orange peel), gloriously juicy, and harmonious. Aftertaste is chewy texturewise, alluringly bakeshop-like, toasted, honeyed, vanilla-like, spicy. Scrumptious.

2014 Rating: ★ ★ ★ ★ ★/Highest Recommendation

Château de Laubade 1982 Barrique No. 74094 Bas-Armagnac 47.6% abv, $284.

Baco, ugni blanc, and colombard grapes. Deep, dark auburn color; sediment from black wax closure. This unusual nose is slightly salty, oaky/resiny, flaxseed-like, waxy, intriguingly nuanced, and coy; following further aeration, the bouquet offers deeper, more assertive aromas of black peppercorn, caraway seed, poppy seed, sawdust, oak plank. Entry is startlingly sweeter than the bouquet and deeper and more raisiny/pruny; midpalate phase is alive with dried fruits of various types, including apricot, pineapple, plus a subtle element of lychee—lots going on here at this stage. Finishes long, silky in texture, nutty, oily, biscuity, buttery. Seriously delicious, complex, full of character.

2014 Rating: ★ ★ ★ ★ ★/Highest Recommendation

Château de Laubade 1983 Barrique No. 74091 Bas-Armagnac 48.1% abv, $250.

Baco, ugni blanc grapes. Deep-bronze/copper color; superb clarity—sediment-free. Right up front, I smell butterscotch, plum pudding, raisins, crème brulée, brown sugar in an engaging aroma that's more bakery-like than anything else; secondary inhalations detect lots of demonstrative, peppery/spicy aromas that balance nicely with the pastry/fruit strudel aspect noted in the opening whiffs—there's an amiable substance here that's very pleasant. Entry is clean, bittersweet, meaty, oily, a touch honeyed, tangy; midpalate echoes everything noted in the entry and adds sweet oak, vanilla extract, dark caramel that all go the distance deep into the sinewy aftertaste.

2014 Rating: ★ ★ ★ ★/Highly Recommended

Château de Laubade 1986 Barrique No. 84010 Bas-Armagnac 48.5% abv, $241.

Baco, ugni blanc grapes. Brilliant ochre/dark amber color; inconsequential sediment seen. First aromatic impressions are soft, elegant, understated, slightly toasted, almost muesli-like; secondary inhalations encounter subtle spices (nutmeg, clove), dried fruits (apricots, bananas), nuts. Entry is smooth, oily, toasted marshmallow–like, candied; midpalate is pleasantly acidic, baked, dried fruit–like, nutty. Concludes long, mildly resiny in a comforting manner, buttery, appealing, sturdy. A pleasing balance of maturity and freshness.

2014 Rating: ★ ★ ★ ★/Highly Recommended

Château de Laubade 1989 Barrique No. 77048 Bas-Armagnac 49.2% abv, $233.

Baco, ugni blanc, and colombard grapes. Slightly dullish burnt-orange color; sediment spotted partly from hardened black wax at stopper and partly gray tendrils unassociated with cork stopper. Muted aromas greet my olfactory machine, and with the exception of black peppercorns and mace, I don't pick up much more; secondary sniffs detect subtle nuances of sulfur, salted butter, egg yolk, sawdust, but not in any great splash of exhibition. Entry is deeply grapy, baked pear–like, raisiny, pruny, roasted; midpalate mirrors the entry as all fruit impressions are registered once again but more in a baked manner. Finish is slightly honeyed, brown-sugar sweet, oaky/woody.

2014 Rating: ★ ★ ★/Recommended

Château de Laubade 1990 Barrique No. 83034 Bas-Armagnac 50.5% abv, $223.

Baco, ugni blanc, and colombard grapes. Lovely, bright bronze color; no sediment seen. Offers grapy, fruit salad–like aromas up front that are both tannic and toasted as the aroma sports a youthful, vigorous first impression; by the time of the second nosing passes, the bouquet has evolved, adding nuttiness, brown butter, vegetable oil, dry earth. Entry is acutely resiny, toasty, significantly drier than the bouquet, and chalky/limestone-like; midpalate goes brittle, dusty dry, deeply woody, in fact, so woody that I wonder what type of barrel this was matured in—the impression is that the barrel was flawed. The attacking taste profile

in both the midpalate and aftertaste kill any chance for a recommendation. Rarely does an armagnac from this esteemed producer disappoint as boldly like this one.
2014 Rating: ★★/Not Recommended

Château de Laubade Extra Single Estate Bas-Armagnac 40% abv, $260.

Gorgeous copper color; ideal clarity. Initially, I detect low-impulse scents of tree bark, oak sap, maple, and wet sand, but little more that's grippable; secondary inhalations encounter only slightly more animated fragrances of dry autumn leaves, marzipan, almond butter, and nougat, but zero fruit. Entry explodes on the tip of the tongue in fathomless flavors of pecan pie, walnut butter, nougat, candy bar, dark chocolate, and toasted marshmallow; the extra-large confectioner's flavor profile continues in the midpalate stage, offering titanic, decadent tastes of fresh dark honey, brown sugar, cake frosting, carob, and mincemeat pie. Finishes extra long, silky to the touch, round, supple, and succulent.
2019 Rating: ★★★★★/Highest Recommendation

Château de Laubade L'Unique Single Cask Bas-Armagnac 48.7% abv, $60.

This unusual single cask offering from Château de Laubade is 100 percent colombard grape variety (not ugni blanc!) that was first matured for six years in customary Gascon oak, then finished for six months in a French oak cask that previously had aged French single malt whisky. Pretty marigold color; superb clarity. Smells up front of slightly overripe grapes and oak cask in equal measure; second passes highlight nuanced aromas of raisins, blackberry, and black currant along with deft touches of honey, malted milk balls, and camphor. Entry is zesty, piquant, peppery, and spicy, with sideline flavors of malted milk and candied walnut; midpalate echoes the entry, adding a buttery, creamy texture that underpins the entire midpalate experience. Concludes more grapy and raisiny than anything else. Great idea.
2020 Rating: ★★★★/Highly Recommended

Château de Laubade VSOP Bas-Armagnac 40% abv, $40.

Very pretty gamboge/golden wheat-field color; excellent purity. I get immediate, if sedate, scents of old saddle leather, library books, nutmeg, allspice, and baked apricot in the initial sniffs after the pour; further aeration unleashes just-below-the-surface fragrances of sweetened black tea, lemon zest, and cardamom; this elusive bouquet always seems just an arm's-length away. Entry is more pronounced than the aroma as appealingly pungent flavors of honey, grilled apricot, gingerbread, and chamomile vie for dominance; midpalate stage is where this armagnac offers its best virtues in the forms of bittersweet flavors of English toffee, buttered toast, charcoal, and toasted marshmallow. Finishes briefly and with a bittersweet taste of fruit stone.
2017 Rating: ★★★/Recommended

Château du Tariquet 12 Year Old 100% Folle Blanche Cask Strength Bas-Armagnac 47.2% abv, $76.

Ochre/tawny color; immaculately clean. This first nosing pass encounters a woody, mature, and mildly fruity aroma that features elements of tree sap, sawdust, and dried fruits, in particular, apricot and pear; allowing for more aeration time, I then pick up more

elemental scents such as slate/flint, dry earth, and textile fiber. Entry goes in a different direction from the second inhalation stage by offering succulent dried-fruit tastes, like guava, kiwi, white grape, and white peach; midpalate highlights the pleasant fruitiness found in the entry stage, adding cat-feet touches of unsalted butter, brown sugar, cacao, and dark caramel. Aftertaste is medium long, bittersweet, mildly honeyed, and crisp from the high acidity.
2018 Rating: ★ ★ ★ ★/Highly Recommended

Château du Tariquet 15 Year Old 100% Folle Blanche Cask Strength Bas-Armagnac 50.5% abv, $58.
    Mahogany/cocoa-brown color; impeccably clear. Right out of the aromatic gate, this nose is dashing for the roses, as finely chiseled and defined aromas of prune Danish, mincemeat pie, cherry strudel, and raspberry jam thrill the olfactory sense; secondary inhalations after more air contact pick up right where the first impressions left off, offering succulent, pastry-like, mildly spicy (vanilla, clove), and gently sweet fragrances that are immensely charming. Entry accentuates every high point found in the bouquet by making each one subtle, clean, crisp, and seamlessly integrated into the creamy texture; midpalate provides a flavor extravaganza of the highest degree as the perfectly melded tastes float on the tongue in supple waves of now bittersweet, honeyed, baked, and dried-fruit flavors. Finishes long, succulent, and sublimely luscious. Not once does the cask strength abv do anything but provide the most complimentary vehicle for this outstanding, in its prime, bas-armagnac.
2018 Rating: ★ ★ ★ ★ ★/Highest Recommendation

Château du Tariquet 1993 Bas-Armagnac 45.2% abv, $90.
    Dazzling russet/ochre color; sediment-free and pure. Offers up seductive, semisweet opening fragrances of candied almond, BBQ sauce, caramelized onion, tomato paste; later whiffs pick up even more animated scents of chutney, ripe tomato, brown sugar, bakery. Entry is chockfull of ripe fruit flavors, including grape, plum, and pear, as well as marshmallow, sweet oak, caramel; midpalate features the candy-shop sweetness along with resiny oak, honey, molasses, treacle. Finishes very long, silky, bittersweet, cocoa-like, dark chocolate–like, raisiny, and pruny.
2015 Rating: ★ ★ ★ ★/Highly Recommended

Château du Tariquet 8 Year Old 100% Folle Blanche Cask Strength Bas-Armagnac 50.5% abv, $58.
    Fulvous brown color; perfect purity. There are immediate aromas of black raisins, prunes, and dates in the opening inhalations plus a bit of rum barrel–like spiciness that I like a lot even though I know that French oak barrels were used for maturation; further sniffs pick up pleasing scents of cherry compote, blackberry jam, and mincemeat. Entry is surprisingly rich and thickly textured for such a young brandy, but, hey, I'll take it, as I will the sharp-ish back note baking spice aromas of cinnamon, allspice, and clove; midpalate features much of the spiciness of the entry as well as biscuity flavors of banana bread, cinnamon bun, and prune Danish. Finishes medium long, a touch sharp from the cask strength abv, and moderately nutty. While admittedly I didn't swoon over this brazen, obviously immature brandy, I did like its appealing spiciness and bakery-shop fruitiness.
2018 Rating: ★ ★ ★/Recommended

Château du Tariquet Blanche Armagnac 46% abv, $45.
Crystal clear and sediment-free, colorless appearance. Intensely grapy opening nosing with hints of honeysuckle and orange blossom fragrances that are being pushed forward by the 46 percent abv level; with more air contact, the orange blossom wanes while the grapiness deepens and becomes raisiny and overripe, but not cloying. Semisweet entry tastes include white raisins, ripe Anjou pear, walnut butter, beeswax; midpalate is fruity, juicy, tart, peel-like, zesty. Concludes medium long, concentrated, purifying, not succulent or ambrosial but fruity.
2015 Rating: ★ ★ ★ ★/Highly Recommended

Château du Tariquet Hors d'Age 52 Cask Strength Bas-Armagnac 52% abv, $150.
Rust color; pristine clarity. Oh my, the pipe tobacco–like, smoke-shop opening aroma just blows me away with its uniqueness and complexity; further down the aeration path, the aroma expands to include hints of inner tube, dry stone, arid landscape, pine cone, and pine nut. Entry offers BIG flavors of buttermilk biscuit, praline, almond butter, honey, and stewed fruits; midpalate echoes the entry, adding tastes of oak-driven oils (lanolin, bacon fat, lard) that form the texture, making it thick and silky as the flavor profile turns tannic and earthily bitter. Aftertaste is long, dry, bitter, piquant, cocoa bean–like, and coffee cake–like. A highly complex bas-armagnac that's worth the search.
2018 Rating: ★ ★ ★ ★/Highly Recommended

Château du Tariquet VS Classique Bas-Armagnac 40% abv, $35.
Pretty topaz color; unblemished clarity. First inhalations are subtle, delicate in strength, offering nuances of smoked almond, margarine, streaky bacon; second whiffs encounter an integrated bouquet that's round, quietly grapy, and moderately oily/buttery. Entry is wonderfully oily in texture, almost creamy, with large flavors of toffee—nutty and semisweet; midpalate focuses on the acute, ripe grapiness of the flavor profile, with mere hints of oak resins, vanilla bean, roasted almond, light caramel. Concludes medium long, sweeter than the midpalate, nougat-like, toasty.
2015 Rating: ★ ★ ★/Recommended

Château du Tariquet VSOP Bas-Armagnac 40% abv, $45.
Bright copper color; sediment-free purity. Initial inhalations detect subdued, polite aromas that lean more towards woodiness than fruit/grape, and are therefore stone dry, even dusty; later sniffs encounter undercurrents of baking spices (nutmeg, clove) and nuts as the oaky/sawdust primary fragrance stays the course. Entry explodes on the tongue with vivid and melded flavors of raisins, prunes, butterscotch, toffee, linseed; midpalate highlights the oakiness, which has now turned moderately sweet and chewy in texture. Finish is extended, embers warm, semisweet, intensely grapy/raisiny, pruny, and wholly satisfying.
2015 Rating: ★ ★ ★ ★/Highly Recommended

Château du Tariquet XO Bas-Armagnac 40% abv, $60.
Gorgeous, bright, bronze/burnt sienna color; perfect purity. First inhalations are nuttier than I recall and mildly fruity/grapy, with faint background aromas of beeswax and paraffin; second passes don't pick up anything more of substance as the nut factor remains in charge

aromatically. Entry is beautifully textured in creamy levels of nut-driven semisweetness; midpalate is the star of the sensory experience as the stunning flavor profile greatly expands into dried fruits (pineapple), nut paste, candy bar, cocoa butter, brown sugar; toasted marshmallow that all last long into the savory aftertaste. I like the sheer splendor and opulence of the entry, midpalate, and finish. The in-mouth stages are seriously luscious.

2015 Rating: ★ ★ ★ ★/Highly Recommended

Comte de Lauvia Millésime 1972 47 Year Old Armagnac 43.8% abv, $n/a/700 ml.

Very pretty chestnut/mahogany color; perfect clarity. Considering the maturity of this armagnac, the first nosings pick up ample hints of toasted oak, candy bar with nuts, brown butter, and toasted almond; after more air contact, the aroma profile turns more animated, featuring fragrances of leather-bound book/old library, spice cake, cinnamon, and bear claw pastry. Entry is astonishingly luscious, bittersweet, toasted, and driven by baked and spiced fruit elements, primarily spiced apple and pear; midpalate includes all the entry findings plus an assertive taste of cocoa butter/cake frosting that comes to define the entire taste profile. Finishes fathomlessly long, bittersweet, and cocoa-like. Outstanding.

2019 Rating: ★ ★ ★ ★ ★/Highest Recommendation

Dartigalongue 1984 30 Year Old Barrel Strength Bas-Armagnac 43% abv, $135.

Dark-bronze/chestnut color is pretty and pure. I'm picking up all sorts of dried fruits, especially raisins, dates, prunes, and dried cherry in the initial nosing passes, and there are also barely perceptible nuances of kiwi and loose leaf cigarette tobacco; second-stage nosings detect dried apricot, quince, and pineapple plus newly tanned leather. Entry is wonderfully ambrosial, ripe with orchard fruits, hefty in texture, ribboned with tangy flavors of cinnamon, clove; midpalate is a textbook on bas-armagnac glory as the entry findings are solidified by the velvety texture that supports the luscious honey-nut, dried-fruit flavors through to the end of the succulent aftertaste. A B-A in perfect harmony.

2015 Rating: ★ ★ ★ ★ ★/Highest Recommendation

Dartigalongue 1985 33 Year Old Bas-Armagnac 43% abv, $132.

Cocoa-brown color; flawlessly pure. Initial whiffs pick up faint hints of peach cobbler, nectarine peel, and citrus zest; allowing for more aeration, later inhalations detect greater aromas that include egg white, meringue, cotton candy, refined sugar, and caramel candy. Entry is incredibly sumptuous, languid, and piquant, as the lush, velvety texture provides the perfect platform for the mature, baked fruit flavors that deeply impress; midpalate stage is, I believe, the apex moment that integrates the various components into a unified flavor that is harmonious, sensuous, and deeply honeyed. Finishes as lovely as it began, with intensity, harmony, length, and grace. Stupendously luscious and worth every cent.

2019 Rating: ★ ★ ★ ★ ★/Highest Recommendation

Dartigalongue 40 Year Old 1980 Bas-Armagnac 42% abv, $200.

Gorgeously deep chestnut color; flawless purity. An opening aroma to die for, as the aromatics offer a stunning menu of succulent fragrances, from baked pineapple to buttered croissant to chocolate fudge to espresso to . . . well, this could go on forever; secondary whiffs unearth baked orchard fruits, tar, cigar tobacco, and pumpernickel bread. Entry is even

more majestic and divine than the sensational bouquet, as the balance between oaky sweetness, mineral earthiness, treacle, and baked fruit make for beautiful flavor music; midpalate is a softer reflection of the entry, and that leads to a bittersweet aftertaste that's endlessly long, compact, and luscious without being opulent or fat.
2020 Rating: ★ ★ ★ ★ ★/Highest Recommendation

Dartigalongue Cuvée Louis Philippe Bas-Armagnac 42% abv, $200.

Comprised of 70 percent 1974 and 30 percent 1976 bas-armagnacs. Brilliant bronze color; flawless clarity; a beauty to behold visually. Enticing first nosings detect smoky, burnt, textile scents; then after another eight minutes of air contact, the aroma opens wider, highlighting the toasty/burnt aspect as well as tangy notes of dates and figs. Entry is lusciously buttery/creamy in texture, intensely woody and dried fruit–like; midpalate follows through well with the dried fruit, adding toasted hazelnut, anise, and chocolate fudge near the aftertaste. Concludes richly, deeply, and very cocoa-like. This is not Armagnac 101, but a B-A to aspire to when your palate is ready to deal with masses of flavor and complex layering.
2015 Rating: ★ ★ ★ ★ ★/Highest Recommendation

Dartigalongue Grande Eau-de-Vie Bas-Armagnac 40% abv, $120.

The dense copper color is dazzling and free from sediment. First sniffs detect old leather-bound books, library, coffee grounds, saddle leather, and cedar; more time in the glass releases bakery-like aromas of mincemeat pie, pear tart, nutmeg, allspice, and biscuit batter. Entry is seductively succulent, as in dried apricot, white raisins, and prune, as well as piquant with freshly ground black pepper; midpalate highlights the dried fruits and adds astringent flavors such as citrus peel, nutmeg, flaxseed oil, and lychee. Finishes gracefully and medium long, with a charming ending flurry of oak resin/maple. Very nice indeed.
2017 Rating: ★ ★ ★ ★ ★/Highest Recommendation

Dartigalongue Hors d'Age Bas-Armagnac 40% abv, $62.

Cocoa-brown color; flawless purity. First off, I pick up succulent aromas of brown butter, bacon fat, dried flowers, and muesli; secondary whiffs detect deeper aromas, namely honey, ginger, toasted oak, saltine cracker, and dried apricot. Entry features immediate impact tastes of dark honey, baked fruits (apricot, banana), baking spices (clove, cinnamon, vanilla), and toasted marshmallow; midpalate turns prune-like and raisiny as the taste profile shifts to a ripe and baked fruit posture that's sweet and succulent. Finishes long, prune Danish–like, full in the mouth, and peppery. Refined, mature, and ambrosial. Absolutely must be on your brandy wish list.
2018 Rating: ★ ★ ★ ★ ★/Highest Recommendation

Dartigalongue XO Bas-Armagnac 40% abv, $53.

Lovely mahogany color; flawless clarity. First nosings encounter ambrosial, wonderfully vibrant scents of ripe nectarines and pears, as well as spiced pear torte; secondary sniffs pick up more mature, wood-influenced notes of oak sap, sawdust, pine two-by-four, mushrooms, and cinnamon. Entry is nicely acidic so the first taste is fresh, clean, and crisp, and this is followed by dried-fruit flavors, namely dates, black raisins, and figs; the midpalate is the sweet spot, in which the various aromatic and gustatory aspects merge into a singular flavor

that's mature, bittersweet, tinged with baking spice, moderately oily/fatty, and harmonious. Toasty, sap- and maple-like, and a bit bitter on the finish as the taste profile retreats slightly from the full-out experience of the midpalate.
2018 Rating: ★★★★/Highly Recommended

Delord 25 Year Old Bas-Armagnac 40% abv, $78.

Mahogany color; superb clarity. I get buttery notes up front that give way to bigger fragrances of citrus peel, meringue, egg white, and black tea; secondary inhalations after more aeration discover subtle notes of lime/citrus, black tea, and white raisins. Entry is sensationally clean, zesty, and defined by the notable presence of citrus rind, white raisins, kiwi, nutmeg, clove, and oak nuances; midpalate continues the subtlety found in the entry stage as the quiet merging of the fruit, acid, baking spice, and fatty oak elements creates a sophisticated and integrated core flavor that's about as sublime as mature bas-armagnac can get. The finish is a savory masterpiece of grape brandy balance, elegance, subtle strength, and integration. This bas-armagnac could have no other score but five stars.
2018 Rating: ★★★★★/Highest Recommendation

Delord l'Authentique Bas-Armagnac 45.9% abv, $105.

Tawny/bronze color; superb purity. First nosing passes present me with oodles of baked fruits, in particular, pears and pineapple, as well as earthier scents of cooking oil, oak two-by-four, mace, and lead pencil; further aeration stimulates deeper, wood-tinged fragrances of maple fudge, resin, and unsalted brown butter. Entry soars with roasted/toasted oak and fruit flavors, especially baked pear, and presents a focused taste profile that's rich in texture and almost rum-like in flavor intensity; midpalate is this brandy's pinnacle moment as the aspects identified in the latter bouquet stage and the entry merge into a singular flavor that's baked, fruity, bittersweet, caramelized, peppery, and sinewy in texture. Concludes extra long in the throat, honeyed, raisiny, and perfectly proportioned. A Delord touchstone moment.
2018 Rating: ★★★★★/Highest Recommendation

Delord Napoléon 10 Year Old Bas-Armagnac 40% abv, $42.

Cocoa-brown color; absolute purity. The up-front aroma is all white raisin and nothing but for the first couple of minutes; more time in the glass, however, brings about additional fruity scents, namely delicate hints of kiwi, guava, and citrus peel. Entry reflects the fruitiness of the latter bouquet stage, but there's also a tangy wood note that's bittersweet yet honeyed and lush at the same time; midpalate features the nutty, honeyed, maple-oak notes, adding candied cherry, chocolate-covered raisins, and cocoa bean. Aftertaste assembles the various elements into a cohesive, pleasing, bittersweet, and striking finish.
2018 Rating: ★★★/Recommended

Delord Napoléon 30 Year Old Vintage 1981 Bas-Armagnac 40% abv, $100.

Bottled in 2011. Auburn/henna color; impeccable purity. On the immediate side of the first whiffs I get faint scents of parchment, wax paper, and soybean that slowly unfold, exposing the wax-like polymers of white oak; later sniffs after more air contact pick up hints of unsalted butter, vegetable cooking oil, and oak lumber. Entry is dry to off-dry, waxy in

texture, and with back-note flavors in which the oak eclipses the fruitiness; midpalate is tangy with zesty oak-driven spices and black tea flavors that are lacking in fruit presence. Ends up moderately pleasurable in that its oak element is succulent, but I also find its fruit deficit to be concerning. Knowing all this, home in on the Delord twenty-five-year-old.
2018 Rating: ★ ★ ★/Recommended

Delord XO 15 Year Old Bas-Armagnac 40% abv, $58.

Sandy-brown/topaz color; immaculately clean. I like this opening aroma as I encounter floral/garden-like scents of jasmine, honeysuckle, and green vegetation, along with latent orchard fruit aromas; after more aeration, the bouquet turns a bit like textile fibers, linen, and cotton fiber before becoming mildly nut-like. Entry is engagingly sweet, caramel-like, brown sugar–like, and chewy in texture; at midpalate, more fruit aspects emerge in the forms of black raisins, prunes, and dates. Concludes appealingly long in the throat, moderately lush in texture, medium oily, and peppery. The progressive nature of the innate quality of the bas-armagnac is obvious, in particular, from entry to the alluring finish.
2018 Rating: ★ ★ ★ ★/Highly Recommended

Domaine de Charron 1986 Bas-Armagnac 46.4% abv, $242.

The definition of henna color in brandy; immaculate purity. First inhalations are all about unstained wooden fence post in the initial sniffs, but then the aroma diverts down a different path, offering toasted almond, baked pineapple, and pipe tobacco that underscore the oakiness; I find the secondary nosings to be more fulfilling than the opening ones, as the aromatic profile fills out with supple scents of sesame seed, mace, nutmeg, black peppercorn, vanilla bean, and meringue. Entry is lush, deeply candied, and like chocolate-covered raisins; midpalate features a dense succulence that's bacon fat–like, chewy in texture, woody/maple-like, and like apple crumble or pear tart. Finishes long, silky, astringent, going from pastry-like to mincemeat pie–like. A satisfying older B-A of balance and depth.
2017 Rating: ★ ★ ★ ★/Highly Recommended

Domaine de Charron 1987 Bas-Armagnac 46.6% abv, $222.

Stunningly pretty russet/cinnamon-stick color; perfect clarity. I get all sorts of forest-y, wood-related fragrances in the first whiffs, including sawdust, cedar bark, tree sap, two-by-fours, and resiny plastic that underpin the more superficial earthy scents of tobacco leaf, cigar box, and coffee grounds; by the time I go back for a second round of inhalation, the bouquet has changed a tiny bit, turning more candy shop–like and nutty, especially by offering faint hints of nougat, crunchy peanut butter, and nut-filled candy bar. Entry is alluringly astringent, acceptably bitter, nut-like, resiny/sappy, mature, and black pepper–like; midpalate offers healthy doses of oak char, black raisin, dried fig, and tannin that together maintain the edgy, brittle taste profile all the way through to the crackling pork rind–like aftertaste. It's as though you can taste each of the thirty years of maturation in this ponderous B-A. Ultimately, I come away thinking that the ferocious wood aspect has become too dominant. That said, as a museum piece for the most ardent bas-armagnac freaks, it's probably a worthwhile purchase, hence the three stars. The three Charron offerings from the 1990s are, pure and simple, more enjoyable and harmonious.
2017 Rating: ★ ★ ★/Recommended

Domaine de Charron 1989 Bas-Armagnac 46.8% abv, $215.
One hundred percent baco. Deep brick/cinnamon color; ideal clarity. Leather-bound books, men's club/library, cigar box, and oak tannin aromas abound in the opening inhalations; later sniffs detect more leather (saddle leather this time), dried fruits, unopened attic, and furniture polish. Entry is (to my admitted shock) fruitier than either the 2003 or 1995 at this point and is likewise a touch like soy sauce/Szechuan sauce (a plus for me); midpalate is totally different from the entry as the flavor profile turns creamy, cocoa-like, brown butter–like, a little smoky, even a touch pipe tobacco–like but, boy, do the flavors come together at this juncture, leading into a graceful, decadent finish that's rich to the point of being borderline unctuous, caramelized, and luscious.
2016 Rating: ★ ★ ★ ★ ★/Highest Recommendation

Domaine de Charron 1990 Bas-Armagnac 47.1% abv, $207.
The deep, aged, tawny port-like color is dazzling and dense; impeccable purity. I pick up various sorts of intriguing, arid scents in the opening inhalations, most notably, custard, walnut oil, dark caramel, and oak chips; more time in the glass allows for further accentuation, with the lead fragrances being dark honey, vegetable cooking oil, and high-cocoa-content dark chocolate. Entry is delightfully beany, cocoa-like, almost dark coffee–like as well, bittersweet, and concentrated; midpalate is densely flavored, with big scoops of marzipan, dark chocolate cake frosting, bittersweet chocolate, and treacle—the 47.1 percent abv is simply the subtle foundation that supports the entire classy effort. Nice, mature, and deeply flavored.
2017 Rating: ★ ★ ★ ★/Highly Recommended

Domaine de Charron 1994 Bas-Armagnac 48.7% abv, $185.
Gorgeous appearance that's redbrick/ginger in color; some minor tendrils of sediment seen in the core—inconsequential. This nose is mostly closed off in the first whiffs after the pour, so I do it the courtesy of backing off for ten minutes; even after further air contact, the aroma refuses to offer much animation, so I move on to the gustatory phase. Entry is rich, remarkably chewy, slightly smoky (spent charcoal from the BBQ), tobacco-like (Havana cigar), earthy (mossy, leafy), oaky (resiny, maple-like), spicy (cinnamon, big-time), and bacon fat–like—other than that tantalizing menu for distinctive flavors, not much happening; midpalate echoes the entry, dialing up the oak-o-meter by quite a significant measure, leading to an astringent, desert-dry, bacon-y finish that's sublime and meant only for veteran brandy lovers. Had the bouquet shown up for work, I'd have likely bestowed a fifth rating star on this Hulk Hoganesque B-A.
2017 Rating: ★ ★ ★ ★/Highly Recommended

Domaine de Charron 1995 Bas-Armagnac 48.8% abv, $170.
One hundred percent baco. Bronze color; unblemished clarity. Wow, this initial aromatic burst is acutely peppery, sawdust-like, almost a touch mossy, but nonetheless is totally dry and dusty; secondary sniffs pick up deeper scents of dried fruit (prune, quince) and roasted nuts, but there's also a pronounced prickliness of spirit that takes time to rev up, but once it does the fireworks begin in the olfactory mechanism. Entry is opulent in texture, honeyed, intensely spicy, perhaps a little too metallic, but is very good all the same;

midpalate features gargantuan flavors that mesh into one towering taste that's bittersweet and toasted. Aftertaste highlights the honeyed spiciness.
2016 Rating: ★ ★ ★ ★/Highly Recommended

Domaine de Charron 1999 Bas-Armagnac 49.1% abv, $150.

Deep bronze color; pristine clarity. Curiously, this opening aroma has far more spirity giddyup than either the 2004 or 2001 expressions, which were each slightly higher in alcohol—not a criticism from me because I like the prickly tingle of alcohol in aroma (why else would I subject myself to this morning ritual?), and this B-A definitely provides kick; following more time in the glass, the bouquet takes a left turn by suddenly providing fully ripe aromas of orange marmalade, fruitcake, berry pastry (berry scone), and blueberry muffin. Entry is composed, integrated, deliciously harmonious, subtle in impact, and silky in texture; the midpalate stage confirms all the splendors noted in the sublime entry and leads into the superlative, scrumptious aftertaste that's a little smoky and tobacco-like, which adds to the ripe fruit and toasty oak aspects. An easy five star rating for a brandy that showcases how marvelous bas-armagnac can be when all systems are humming.
2017 Rating: ★ ★ ★ ★ ★/Highest Recommendation

Domaine de Charron 2001 Bas-Armagnac 50.6% abv, $142.

Pretty henna/auburn color; immaculate purity. I smell dried honeysuckle, jasmine, and carnation in the initial nosings that all float atop the deeper fragrances of pipe tobacco, hardwood flooring, sarsaparilla, and campfire embers; more aeration allows the aroma the chance to develop more fully in the forms of black cherry candy, black raisins, black plums, and brown sugar. Entry discovers a lush, satin-like texture that upholds the taste profile, which is unabashedly spirity, warm in the throat, resiny, a bit maple-like, and spicy (clove, allspice); midpalate stage is notable for its convergence of flavors, especially as the dried fruit merges with the lipids and acids (tannin and lignin, especially) of the oak, creating a satisfying grape brandy experience that lasts deep into the dusty, dry, mouth-puckering, astringent (for those curious geeks, that's your tannin) finish.
2017 Rating: ★ ★ ★ ★/Highly Recommended

Domaine de Charron 2003 Bas-Armagnac 50.5% abv, $128.

One hundred percent baco. Brilliant new-copper/russet color; flawless purity. I smell delicate oak-influenced spice, dried red fruits (plums, cherry), raisins, and palm oil in the opening whiffs after the pour; with more aeration the aroma blossoms into a supple, focused bouquet of dry spiciness (almost like jerk rub), tomato paste, porcini mushroom. Entry is intensely bittersweet, caramelized onion–like, caramelized mushroom–like, elemental, woodsy, yet altogether integrated, candied, and luscious; midpalate is lavishly textured, pinpointed in its pepperiness/spiciness, cocoa butter–like, and flat-out luscious through the lingering finish that keeps unfolding for many minutes. The 101 proof isn't an issue at any moment. For me, a bas-armagnac that's in its prime.
2016 Rating: ★ ★ ★ ★ ★/Highest Recommendation

Domaine de Charron 2004 Bas-Armagnac 51.1% abv, $112.

Brilliant new-copper color glow; sediment-free clarity. Right from the first sniffs I get

peanut butter, burnt marshmallow, cedar, red plum, and slight sulfur/burnt match scents that are vigorous and animated; secondary inhalations find Madeira cake, crème caramel, and meringue. Entry is punchy, pungent, nicely baked, spirity, and toasted, with foundational flavors of baked red plum, blackberry jam, and black raisins leading the gustatory parade; midpalate shows off all the appreciated entry impressions as the fruit density dominates the wood influence to the point of eclipse. Aftertaste is juicy, jammy, lusciously ripe, and it's the elevated but unobtrusive abv level that carries the fruit-salad flavors forward. Still young and, if purchased, I'd cellar it for another five to eight years for further wood/fruit integration and taste layering. This B-A has four star potential if allowed the opportunity to mature.
2017 Rating: ★ ★ ★/Recommended

Domaine Loujan Vintage 2000 Bas-Armagnac 46.5% abv, $80.
Ginger/sorrel color; immaculate purity. Wow, there's a whole lot of sophisticated aromatic action taking place in the initial sniffs after the pour—walnut, beeswax, honey nut cereal, chocolate-covered cherry, fig; second inhalations unearth vanilla bean, sawdust, wood plank, black pepper. Entry displays an abv warmth on the tongue that's pleasing but neither hot nor aggressive, along with toasted, roasted flavors of BBQ sauce, pork rind, grape preserves; midpalate echoes the entry and adds a nice touch of cocoa and dark chocolate that mingles well with the dried-fruit aspect. Concludes long, peppery, totally dry, almost bittersweet, and chewy in texture. What's so pleasant about this bas-armagnac right now is the blend of youthful intensity and mature assurance and poise. Buy and lay down for another eight to ten years in cellar conditions. Further integration will, I bet, make it a five star brandy. Consider this one an investment.
2016 Rating: ★ ★ ★ ★/Highly Recommended

Francis Darroze Château de Gaube 1966 Bas-Armagnac 49.6% abv, $85.
One hundred percent baco. Over the years, I've favored Château de Gaube Bas-Armagnacs, like the jaw-dropping 1956 (five stars), 1959, and 1970 (both four stars). Shimmering topaz/amber color; superb clarity. I smell plums, pears, and peaches up front in this ambrosial, orchard-fruit aroma that's remarkably vivid and animated considering its age; following more aeration, the aroma turns woodier, more spicy, and resiny, with subtle hints of sliced mushroom, green tea, old leather, Parmesan cheese—this is a truly wonderful bouquet that's mature yet vivacious. Entry is acutely dry, stony, minerally at first, then it goes fruity, as in dried fruits, mostly grape, prune, date; midpalate turns toasty, baked fruit–like (apricot, nectarine), tobacco-like, raisiny, oaky, and vanilla bean–like. Aftertaste tells me there is evidence of rancio here due to the high degree of mushroom and Parmesan cheese presence. Yee-hah. Ride 'em, cowboy!
2015 Rating: ★ ★ ★ ★ ★/Highest Recommendation

Francis Darroze Domaine Couzard Lassalle 1996 Bas-Armagnac 48.5% abv, $97.
One hundred percent folle blanche. Bronze/ochre color; sediment-free purity. I smell faint hints of dried cranberry, dates, loose leaf tobacco in the opening inhalations after the pour—it's not a massive aroma, by any means; secondary sniffs encounter nuances of black tea, dried flowers (honeysuckle?), new leather. Entry is pleasantly grapy, almost jammy in its density, silky textured, maple sweet; midpalate highlights the maple-like aspect, which

is earthy, sappy, delicately sweet, tangy, elemental. Aftertaste features a pleasing cocoa quality that's really nice and beany. I liked this older Couzard Lassalle more than the gawky 2004 because the extra eight years of maturation clearly helped with its composition and disposition.

2015 Rating: ★ ★ ★/Recommended

Francis Darroze Domaine Couzard Lassalle 2004 Bas-Armagnac 49.6% abv, $85.

One hundred percent folle blanche. Bright new-copper color; flawless purity. This curiously brine-like aroma offers frontline smells of lead pencil, dry stone, nickel, minerals in the initial go-round after the pour; after more time in the glass, the aroma becomes more smoky and toasty, with a strange deficit of fruit. Entry is spare, dusty dry, bitter, acidic, and astringent, densely woody, but again lacking in fruit or spice; midpalate features more in the way of cooking spice (dill), but nothing in the way of grapes/orchard fruits. It doesn't taste bad. It is just off balance to me due to the missing element of fruit. Not my cup of tea and a rare Darroze misstep. Too young, and therefore gangly and awkward.

2015 Rating: ★ ★/Not Recommended

Francis Darroze Domaine de la Post 1980 Ténarèze-Armagnac 48.5% abv, $150.

One hundred percent ugni blanc. Saffron/straw-gold color; sediment-free clarity. Holy smokes, this initial aroma is vibrant, fruity, oaky, spicy, and tangy, with loads of pipe tobacco, citrus, toffee, coffee, limestone/chalk, pear; second inhalations discover saddle leather, candle wax, butcher's wax paper, sausage meat, marjoram, jasmine, orange blossom—where does it all end? Entry flavors are a veritable banquet of dried fruits (peach, nectarine), flowers (jasmine), spices (nutmeg, allspice, mace), nuts (walnut), and wood (sweet oak, vanilla); midpalate echoes the sublime tastes of the entry and deepens them as the density level crashes through the ceiling—this is a lush, oily, bittersweet midpalate. Aftertaste is slightly smoky, intensely fruity, perfectly mature, and succulent. Displays the underappreciated virtues of Ténarèze with flair and class.

2015 Rating: ★ ★ ★ ★ ★/Highest Recommendation

Francis Darroze Domaine de Lamarquette 1985 Bas-Armagnac 48.5% abv, $130.

One hundred percent baco. Brilliant sepia/topaz color; impeccable purity. I like the opening aroma due to its savory spiciness, which highlights tarragon and black pepper, but also its leathery/old book fragrance that's simultaneously stately and mature; second inhalations after more air contact bring out the dried apricot, dried pineapple scents that mingle well with hints of black tea—there's nothing hurried about this bouquet. Entry offers candy-shop flavors of caramel, cocoa butter, chocolate-covered orange peel, toasted marshmallow, saltwater taffy; midpalate maintains the bittersweet-to-sweet focus as the taste advances into more of an oily, buttercream, cake frosting state that is luscious and satiny. Finishes long, toasty, baked, bittersweet, candy bar–like. A robust bas-armagnac at its maturity apex.

2015 Rating: ★ ★ ★ ★/Highly Recommended

Francis Darroze Domaine de Monturon 2003 Bas-Armagnac 49.5% abv, $87.

One hundred percent baco. Pale amber color; flawless clarity. This aroma is a little subdued up front, as I pick up faint hints of oak, sawdust, and not much more in the first sniffs;

more air contact releases a bit more aroma, mostly vegetation, forest floor, drying leaves, but nothing in the way of fruit or spice. Entry is delightfully dry, slightly tannic, and therefore a touch astringent and fresh, but there is a solid core of fruit presence (gooseberry, kiwi, white raisins) that underpins the early flavor profile; midpalate continues with the bitterness as it now becomes more oaky/resiny, but the fruit aspect deepens as the taste of baked tropical fruits takes charge, lasting long into the roasted, baked aftertaste.

2015 Rating: ★ ★ ★/Recommended

Francis Darroze Domaine de Pounon 1990 Bas-Armagnac 50% abv, $115.
   One hundred percent baco. Lovely henna/auburn color; ideal clarity. There are lots of earthy, woodsy, tobacco-like smells here in the initial whiffs, including cigar tobacco, tree bark, moss, driftwood, pine/cedar sawdust, plus a small dose of baking spice (clove); secondary sniffs find hard cheese/Romano cheese and old leather notes that accent the baking spice. The elevated abv creates noticeable heat on the tongue at entry, not a burning sensation, but an embers-like warmth that's comforting, and this is alongside a taste profile that's mature, evolved, and dense with jam-packed flavors of dried flowers, holiday spice cake, graham cracker, candied pecan, praline, black raisins, prunes; midpalate reprises many of the aspects found at entry, adding a touch of caramelized sugar. The aftertaste is every bit as decadent as the entry and midpalate, lasting long in the throat. More akin to the sublime 1989 that earned five stars than any other Pounon I've had. Majestic, stately, complete.

2015 Rating: ★ ★ ★ ★ ★/Highest Recommendation

Francis Darroze Domaine de Rieston 1995 Bas-Armagnac 48.8% abv, $105.
   One hundred percent baco. Pretty topaz/ginger color; excellent purity. The spiky alcohol is zesty in the nose, almost citrusy in its character, in the opening inhalations, and there are traces of green melon, slate, and parchment; secondary whiffs detect green tea, green vegetable, oak plank. Entry offers dry to off-dry tastes of candied stone fruits (cherry?), caramel, brown sugar, vanilla bean; midpalate goes deeper into the caramel, brown sugar attributes as the flavor profile turns candy-shop bittersweet. Finish is tightly wound, intensely honeyed, quite lush and sweet. I have this sitting atop the three star/four star fence so I'm giving it three stars due to my concerns about the high degree of candied sweetness, which might be appealing to a lot of people, just not me because I feel that it's slightly off balance. That said, it does have some admirable virtues.

2015 Rating: ★ ★ ★/Recommended

Francis Darroze Domaine de Tillet 1975 Bas-Armagnac 40.5% abv, $162.
   One hundred percent baco. Bronze/burnt sienna color; unblemished purity. The first nosings don't pick up a great deal of aromatics (its age?), except for traces of coffee bean, chocolate cake, mocha; later sniffs detect more in the way of dried fruits (raisins, apricot), baking spice (cinnamon, clove), leather (book jacket), and honey. Entry is firm, sturdy, mature, more focused on oak than either fruit or spice, dusty dry; midpalate echoes the entry to a tee, but adds nothing. Aftertaste is very dry, ethereal almost, more woody than anything else, and in my mind, tired and over-the-hill. Maybe a decade ago this brandy would have been recommendable but not now.

2015 Rating: ★ ★/Not Recommended

Marie Duffau 1979 Bas-Armagnac 45.5% abv, $110.
Chestnut-brown color; ideal clarity. There's a delightful pastry-like juiciness, similar to apple strudel, to this opening aroma that's fetching and deeply satisfying; secondary inhalations reach a more defined point as the aroma opens up with more air contact, exposing fragrances of peanut butter, candied almond, and baked pear. Entry is richly textured, brown-sugar sweet, and loaded with oak notes, namely, vanilla bean, astringent tannins, and vegetable cooking oil; midpalate is tight as a drum, narrowly focused on the baked fruits and baking spices (allspice, mace), as well as the oak-impact elements such as vanilla extract, oyster sauce, and charred meats. Concludes long, dense with oak impressions, and heavily toasted. Lovely all around.
2018 Rating: ★ ★ ★ ★/Highly Recommended

Marie Duffau Hors d'Age 12 Year Old Bas-Armagnac 40% abv, $52.
Sienna color; ideal purity. Initial whiffs pick up BBQ sauce, tomato paste, red cherry compote, white raisins, and black peppercorn; secondary inhalations find an oakier bouquet, one that's piquant with baking spices (allspice, nutmeg) and dried fruits (dates especially). Entry is supple in texture, zesty from the peppercorn aspect, nicely woody/sap-like, and akin to holiday fruitcake elements, especially the candied nuts and dried pineapple; midpalate echoes the entry impressions while adding a touch of cola nut for balance. Aftertaste highlights the cola nut, Dr Pepper aspects, turning semisweet. This bas-armagnac has lots of moving parts that get into sync in the finish.
2018 Rating: ★ ★ ★ ★/Highly Recommended

Marie Duffau Napoléon Bas-Armagnac 40% abv, $36.
Topaz/chestnut color; impeccably free of any sediment or haze. Up front, there's a slight medicinal property that blows off rapidly, leaving behind trace scents of wax paper, parchment, textile fiber, and latent orchard fruit (quince); regrettably, more air contact doesn't stimulate more in the way of definable aromatic presence, so I move on. Entry is viscous, round, biscuit-like, doughy, semisweet, and tangy; midpalate features the stellar texture that's supple and creamy, as much as the baked fruit tastes of banana and plum that go tangy and zesty with time. Finishes long, buttery to the taste, oaky-spicy, honeyed, and lush. Had the bouquet been more evolved and expressive, a fourth rating star would have been bestowed.
2018 Rating: ★ ★ ★/Recommended

Marquis de Montesquiou Extra Armagnac 43% abv, $70.
Copper color; free of sediment and bright clarity. This opening bouquet is oaky, mature, and settled, offering bright aromas of toasted marshmallow, cocoa powder, butterscotch, graham cracker, and spice cake; later inhalations after more aeration encounter deeper fragrances of chocolate-covered orange peel, dried fig, and allspice. Entry is slinky and sleek in texture, all the while big flavors abound, including chocolate fudge, latte, honey, and saltwater taffy; midpalate features the comely, creamily viscous texture that moves the taste profile forward like a pulsing river.
2019 Rating: ★ ★ ★ ★/Highly Recommended

Marquis de Montesquiou Fine Armagnac 40% abv, $30.
Goldenrod color; impeccable clarity. I immediately pick up in the first whiffs assertive and likable scents of ground black pepper, cayenne, malted milk ball, and espresso; more aeration brings out zestier, bakeshop fragrances of dried apricot, nutmeg, cinnamon bun, and spiced pear. Entry is dry, astringent, high in acidity, and crisp tasting in a spicy manner; midpalate turns spicier and more like praline and almond paste; texture is medium in viscosity. Aftertaste is pleasant but heavy on the oak-influenced spiciness, which might be too much for people searching for more fruit. Quite stylistic.
2019 Rating: ★★★/Recommended

Marquis de Montesquiou Reserve Armagnac 43% abv, $45.
Bronze/harvest gold color; flawless purity. Up front, I get light whispers of caramel, toffee, and fudge aromas that are amorphous in the first nosing passes; later inhalations after more air contact bring out more substantial scents of bacon fat, BBQ sauce, vanilla bean, crème brûlée, and candied orange. Entry introduces jammy, orchard-fruit-like preserves, mostly pear and nectarine; midpalate brings the baked fruit and caramel aspects together in a charming taste profile that's mature, sophisticated, and bakeshop-like. In the aftertaste, it's clear that the 86 proof is the key to this armagnac's appeal, as it serves as the catalyst in pushing the flavor elements forward while providing the firm core. Really tasty.
2019 Rating: ★★★★/Highly Recommended

Marquis de Montesquiou VSOP Armagnac 40% abv, $55.
Fetching appearance of auburn/rust color; superb purity. The opening nose is intensely ripe and candy-shop sweet, flashing succulent aromas of honey buns, maple syrup, sautéed mushrooms, and treacle; further aeration brings out scents of bacon fat, pork rind, BBQ sauce, vinegar, sawdust, oak plank. Entry continues the husky, brown-sugar sweetness in spades as the taste profile sports a full-bodied texture and plenty of unabashed caramel candy sweetness; midpalate mirrors the entry in all aspects as the flavor maintains its toffee-like posture that favors super-ripe grapes affected by oaky richness. Finishes with the same sweet, candy-like bigness and heartiness found in the bouquet and midpalate. Likely too sweet and syrupy for veteran armagnac aficionados, but a sound entry-level Gascon brandy that holds nothing back.
2017 Rating: ★★★/Recommended

Marquis de Montesquiou XO Imperial Armagnac 40% abv, $125.
Peculiar in that it's a shade lighter than the VSOP and is nut brown/amber in color; impeccably clean and free of sediment. Smells similar to its younger sibling but with less sugar impact as the oak tannins contribute to a drier fragrance that offers scents of cigar tobacco, old library, old leather, baked multigrain bread, and black peppercorn; secondary whiffs encounter notes of mead, figs, stewed prunes, mince pie. Entry is far more reined in and sophisticated in its bearing than the runaway VSOP, as integrated flavors of sweet oak, vanilla bean, dark honey, molasses, and cake frosting make for enjoyable early quaffing; midpalate accentuates the woodiness of the flavor profile as a keenly resiny taste keeps the in-mouth phase on the drier, astringent side of the dry/sweet scale. Concludes long,

bittersweet, sinewy in texture, a little austere, astringent, and nutty. The in-mouth stages are what make this a four star brandy.

2017 Rating: ★ ★ ★ ★/Highly Recommended

Saint-Vivant VS Armagnac 40% abv, $33.

Pretty amber color; superb purity. This opening nose is strikingly juicy, fruity, grapy, and fresh, even a touch ripened and prune-like, with no hint of oak/tree sap/resin whatsoever; secondary whiffs encounter more spice aspects, particularly cinnamon, clove, in what now has morphed into a winter holiday fruitcake aroma as the fruit, spice, and candied-nut elements create a lasting aromatic thumbprint. Entry mirrors the fruit-bomb bouquet with lip-smackingly ripe tastes of black raisin, prune, dates, candied almond, and brown sugar; midpalate continues the fruitcake-a-thon as finally there's a trace of oak in the fleeting form of vanilla bean, but basically through the finish, this armagnac is all about the grapes/fruit. While it lacks a certain complexity and maturity that extended time in oak brings to older brandies, its youthful vivacity deserves recognition. An entry-level armagnac with discernible charms.

2016 Rating: ★ ★ ★/Recommended

CALVADOS–FRANCE

Without question, calvados is the world's finest apple and pear brandy. It hails from Normandy in France's northwest corner, which has the perfect climate, precipitation level, soil type, and topography for orchards. Calvados is defined as a distilled spirit made either from cider apples or a marriage of cider apples and perry (pear cider) pears. After harvesting in the autumn, apples are pressed and the juice is fermented into cider. The cider is then distilled, and the resultant crystal clear spirits are placed in oak barrels ranging in size from 220 to 400 liters (50 to 105 gallons) or huge vats that can hold up to 6,000 liters (1,500 gallons).

Calvados's Demarcated Districts

Calvados AOC: The largest demarcated region (70 percent of total annual calvados production) is designated as "Calvados AOC" in which the apple and pear ciders are distilled in column stills using but one distillation. The apple and pear cider brandies labeled under this classification are generally good, but lacking in distinction. They must by law be aged in oak barrels for two years. Calvados AOC includes the départements of Calvados, Orne, Manche, and sections of Mayenne, Sarthe, Eure-et-Loir, and Eure.

Calvados Pays d'Auge AOC: Brandies from the more tightly regulated "Calvados Pays d'Auge" district, on the other hand, are to calvados what Grande Champagne, Petite Champagne, and Borderies brandies are to cognac. In other words, they are the best of the best. These frequently exquisite and delicate brandies are double distilled in copper pot stills and, consequently, offer far more depth of character and the chance of long life than those labeled only as Calvados AOC. A slow six-week fermentation period of the cider is required. Minimum aging in oak barrels or vats is two years. This exclusive area includes only the easternmost reaches of Calvados and a tiny scattering of other adjoining départements.

Domfrontais AOC: The third district is Domfrontais, an official designation that was created only a decade ago. As opposed to Calvados and Calvados Pays d'Auge, at least 30 percent of the juice must come from pears. Column still distillation. The combination of apple and pear makes Domfrontais brandies concentrated and fruitier than those from the apple-dominant districts. Minimum maturation in oak for Domfrontais is three years.

Fermier Calvados: These are considered as "farm made" calvados that are produced totally from one estate's orchards, both inside and outside of Pays d'Auge.

Labeling Laws

The varying legal label designations for Calvados run as follows:

Fine/Three Stars: Two-year minimum in French oak barrels

Vieux/Réserve: Three-year minimum in French oak barrels

VO/Vieille Réserve: Four-year minimum in French oak barrels

VSOP: Five-year minimum in French oak barrels

Extra/XO/Napoléon/Hors d'Age/Age Inconnu: Six-year minimum in French oak barrels

The rules of Calvados are less strict than those enforced in France's other two great brandy regions: Cognac and Armagnac. Caramel is used to maintain color; boisé, or wood extract, is allowed in all classes of calvados for flavor adjustment; and sugar is a legally allowed flavor enhancement, though no one is allowed to sell calvados with more than 2 percent residual sugar.

Boulard Extra Pays d'Auge Calvados 40% abv, $460.
Caramel-brown color; shimmering, unblemished clarity. First inhalations pick up subtle aromatic nuances of apple pastry, especially apple crumble, baked pear, flaxseed, cinnamon, nutmeg, and dried apple; secondary whiffs detect deeper scents of sour apple candy, apple pie, and apple peel; I feel slightly let down with this desultory bouquet. Entry flavors show the vibrancy that was missing in the latter stages of the aroma as lusciously tart, off-dry, candied apple, and pear tart tastes vie for dominance; midpalate is rife with desirably succulent flavors that include maple, oaky vanillin, baked red apple, chamomile, and candied apple. Aftertaste is long, intensely apple-like, tart, and crisp. This pays d'auge turned a corner once in the mouth.
2018 Rating: ★ ★ ★ ★/Highly Recommended

Boulard VSOP Pays d'Auge Calvados 40% abv, $50.
Bronze color; pristine clarity. The fresh-picked, slightly sour, green apple aroma in the initial whiffs is pleasing and accurate; further aeration brings out layers of apple pulp and peel, as well as smatterings of clove and mace baking spices that impart a bakery-shop aura to the aromatic stages. Entry is properly tart, acidic, razor edged, and piquant, all at the same time, presenting the palate with a no-nonsense, totally serious apple-based flavor profile that bears no Jolly Rancher sour candy resemblance; midpalate maintains the tart core taste but, here, the oak barrel influence is noticed mostly due to the oily, resiny texture, which

for me is a plus as it supports the freshness of the apple pulp juiciness. Finishes on the sour side, tightly wound, lean, agile, and apple-like. It's possible that this fine VSOP might be perceived as being too severe for calvados newbies, but I suggest that it is, in fact, a worthy and instructive starting point due primarily to its stripped-down personality in which the apple base is allowed to shine.

2018 Rating: ★★★/Recommended

Boulard XO Pays d'Auge Calvados 40% abv, $90.

Cinnamon color; sediment-free purity. This opening nose is fuller and significantly richer than that of the spartan VSOP, as it exhibits more buttery oak influence and a dose of dark caramel; secondary inhalations introduce holiday spice cake aromas of candied walnut, dried pineapple, green apple, lemon, and apricot, in addition to clove and mace spices. Entry is lush, clean, and deeply spiced apple–like as the flavor profile goes for a bittersweet profile that surfs upon the creamy, oak-laden texture; midpalate stage echoes the entry findings, and indeed I discover that the taste layers dive deeper, becoming more profound with each sip. Finishes elegantly in blankets of bittersweet, caramel-like flavors that are succulent and multilayered.

2018 Rating: ★★★★/Highly Recommended

Chauffe Coeur Hors d'Age Calvados 43% abv, $65.

Old gold/amber color; pristine purity. I get early aromatic rushes of brown butter, oatmeal, bacon fat, crème caramel, flan, and brown sugar; secondary whiffs detect textile-like scents of nylon, synthetic fibers, burnt match, saltine cracker, and baked apple. Entry shows more of the wood impact than that of the apple base material, which I find perplexing; midpalate flexes some textural muscle as the flavor profile turns baked, slightly candied, moderately spicy (clove, nutmeg), and vanilla extract–like. Concludes medium long, intensely spicy (nutmeg, mace, vanilla bean), and mildly apple-like. I prefer the VSOP.

2019 Rating: ★★★/Recommended

Chauffe Coeur VSOP Calvados 43% abv, $50.

Gamboge color; excellent purity. Up front, there's a stunning array of ambrosial scents, including baked apple strudel, clove, cinnamon, apple peel, and unsweetened apple juice; later sniffs pick up riper, earthier fragrances, such as cigar box, pipe tobacco, brambles, tomato vine, black tea, and tree bark. Entry is stone dry, tart, astringent, and only mildly apple-like, but more than anything it's the mouth-puckering tartness that rules the day; midpalate suddenly turns richer and spicier as the taste profile at this point doesn't wholly reflect the entry stage, and that's fine by me as the flavor becomes intensely orchard fruit–like and zesty. Finishes long, ripe, spicy (allspice now), and bittersweet.

2019 Rating: ★★★★/Highly Recommended

Christian Drouin 1962 Calvados 42% abv, $450.

Dark chestnut-brown color; ideal clarity. Wow, this opening aroma is all about luscious apple butter; the buttery/creamy aspect stays the course through the secondary inhalations after an additional eight minutes of air exposure. Entry is nicely acidic (malic acid) and resiny/sap-like; midpalate is tasty, but it falters a little in the apple flavor department as perhaps too much of the oak influence takes hold. Interesting and recommendable for the most extreme aficionados, but not for the casual drinker.

2015 Rating: ★ ★ ★/Recommended

Christian Drouin 1976 Pays d'Auge Calvados 42% abv, $320.

Mahogany/chestnut-brown color resembles cream sherry; very good purity. First sniffs don't pick up much aroma, except for an elusive orchard fruitiness that's more like pear than apple; secondary inhalations fall flat in discovery as the aroma, scant as it is already, fades even more. Entry is awkwardly over-oaked, sappy, resiny, and severely over-the-hill; midpalate can't find any redemptive flavors to rescue this obviously dated brandy. Should have been retired long ago.

2016 Rating: ★/Not Recommended

Christian Drouin 1982 Pays d'Auge Calvados 42% abv, $250.

Excellent sediment-free clarity; topaz color. First nosing passes detect subtle notes of old leather, unspiced apple pie/turnover with flaky crust; further aeration brings on a bit of old library mustiness that's not a negative at all but points to the maturation cellar because there is a high degree of oakiness. Entry is peppery, bittersweet, a touch mature in its roundness, and clean; midpalate maintains the tangy spice as well as the old oak as the apple center comes more alive, especially in the finish where it's deeply apparent and waxy. Deliciously integrated from start to finish.

2015 Rating: ★ ★ ★ ★ ★/Highest Recommendation

Christian Drouin 1986 Pays d'Auge Calvados 42% abv, $230.

Surprisingly light, topaz/burnt sienna color considering its age; impeccable purity. The first aromatic impressions are of a subtle, understated aroma that's just barely fruity/apple-like and a touch waxy; secondary whiffs after more time in the glass discover deeper scents, especially pear tart, apple fritter, spiced apple, sorghum, beeswax, and lanolin. Entry carries over in the taste profile much from the aromatics, in particular, the pear tart, apple fritter, and spiced apple elements; midpalate is where the creamy, thick texture comes into play as the flavors dance upon the viscous texture, making for sumptuous drinking. Finishes very long in the throat, sweet, almost honeyed, heavily baked. A BIG FLAVOR pays d'auge.

2016 Rating: ★ ★ ★ ★/Highly Recommended

Christian Drouin 1992 Pays d'Auge Calvados 42% abv, $180.

Attractive amber/old gold color; perfect purity. Smells vividly of spiced apple pastry in the opening whiffs following the pour, but tart, not sweet; another seven minutes of air contact release nicely acidic scents of apple peel and apple pip. Entry is perfectly astringent, cleansing, and mouth puckering, with just the right amounts of nutmeg and cinnamon; midpalate is crisply apple-like and even a touch pear-like, but the entire stage is pleasingly tart and fresh. Ends on an acidic note that wraps up the experience with class. I love this angular pays d'auge and consider it a vintage benchmark. Hits the sweet spot.

2015 Rating: ★ ★ ★ ★ ★/Highest Recommendation

Christian Drouin 1996 Pays d'Auge Calvados 42% abv, $160.

Beautiful, henna/auburn color; unblemished clarity. This twenty-year-old aroma is vivid and lively in the opening sniffs, offering traces of tropical fruits initially, in particular, guava, before it comes around to apple skin, apple juice, cigar tobacco, and pear skin; later inhalations dig up heftier aromas such as pine, pencil eraser/rubber, oaky resins, cigar tobacco, and baked apple pie. Entry is lush, buttery, acidic, so very fresh, deeply apple-like, pleasantly spiced by clove and nutmeg. Midpalate impressions are as vibrant as those in the entry, featuring zesty, leafy cigar tobacco; vanilla wafer; spiced apple (now cinnamon); and apple strudel. Finishes a little like holiday spice cake that has dried apple and apricot embedded in the dough.

2016 Rating: ★ ★ ★ ★/Highly Recommended

Christian Drouin 1997 Pays d'Auge Calvados 42% abv, $140.

Cocoa-brown/peru color; impeccable clarity. Right off the crack of the aromatic bat there are mesmerizing aromas of apple pie, apple strudel, baked apple, with supplemental notes of cinnamon, Anjou pear, and apple cider thrown in for good measure; after more aeration, there's a surge in the apple cider aspect that turns brown sugar–like and dense with more time in the glass. Entry is zesty, crackling, bittersweet, juicy, and intensely like cinnamon-doused baked apple; midpalate turns spicy (cinnamon, clove, mace) and piquant as the apple base goes narrowly focused and dry, yet rich in texture, peppery, and high in acidity, almost turning prickly and pungent in the process. Aftertaste is long, spiced apple–like, and for the first time, oaky/woody/resiny. A twenty-year-old calvados of tight structure and delectably pleasing apple strudel flavors.

2017 Rating: ★ ★ ★ ★/Highly Recommended

Christian Drouin 25 Year Old Pays d'Auge Calvados 42% abv, $195.

Deep beige/toast color; pristine clarity. This delicate aroma is evolved, integrated, understated in its bearing, offering soft flavors of pear peel, baked apple, applesauce; secondary whiffs don't unearth anything new as the bouquet stays the subtle and safe course. Entry reminds me how buttery this texture is, and the impression of it is lasting and sublime, as are the lightly toasted and oaky flavors of baked apple, baked pear, apple pastry. Midpalate includes all the entry flavors, embellishing the baked apple aspect especially, as the mellow, rich ocean of texture carries the taste profile along without any strain into the big-hearted, spicy finish.

2016 Rating: ★ ★ ★ ★/Highly Recommended

Christian Drouin Hors d'Age Pays d'Auge Calvados 42% abv, $150.

Sepia/topaz in color; sediment-free and visually appealing. This initial aroma features a mildly toasted fragrance that's bakery-like, doughy, and even pastry-like in its stately bearing; more aeration brings out tightly knit scents of nutmeg, lightly toasted marshmallow, spiced apple fritter, pear peel. Entry offers stunningly opulent flavor assets, including spiced apple, apple pie and pastry (strudel), red apple peel, loose leaf and unsmoked pipe tobacco; midpalate echoes the entry perfectly but turns a little bit drier as the apple/fruit recede slightly, leaving an opening for spices like vanilla, allspice, and cinnamon to jump in and fill the minor void majestically. Aftertaste seems fathomless and endless as the taste profile goes more delicate and spiced while the texture grows in creamy stature.

2016 Rating: ★ ★ ★ ★ ★/Highest Recommendation

Christian Drouin Pale & Dry Pays d'Auge Calvados 40% abv, $60.

Attractive golden-yellow/chardonnay color; impeccable purity. I get all sorts of spices in the opening whiffs after the pour, including cinnamon, nutmeg, and clove, that mingle well with the apple butter base scent; with aeration, the nose becomes slightly viny/leafy/vegetal but no less charming. Entry is tart, apple peel–like, and just a touch caramel-like; midpalate is spicy (vanilla), apple strudel–like, toasty, buttery, and luscious. Ends on a cinnamon note.
2015 Rating: ★ ★ ★ ★/Highly Recommended

Christian Drouin Réserve des Fiefs Pays d'Auge Calvados 40% abv, $72.

Gamboge color; flawless clarity. Initial nosings detect poised baked apple, apple fritter, apple peel aromas that are slightly spiced with nutmeg, clove, and cinnamon; more aeration stimulates additional scents of applesauce and apple hard candy. Entry is lightly toasted, crisp, even brittle with acidity, and loaded with nougat/almond butter background flavors; midpalate echoes the entry, adding more of the baking spices, especially mace, as well as deft touches of green tea, gingerbread, and apple rind. Finishes gloriously long, tight, lean, and apple strudel–like.
2019 Rating: ★ ★ ★ ★/Highly Recommended

Christian Drouin Selection Pays d'Auge Calvados 40% abv, $38.

Buff/citron color; superb clarity. Right from the crack of the aromatic bat there is no mistaking the sour green-apple presence as the nose abounds in tart orchard-fruit juiciness; more time in the glass allows for the bouquet to expand, now including apple fritter, apple strudel, lemon peel, and nutmeg. Entry is gracefully layered with apple tart, apple slices, lemon peel, and pastry; midpalate is long, tart, juicy, pleasantly acidic, and slightly piquant. Aftertaste highlights the innate tartness of green apple as the finish cleanses the palate as nicely as the entry did. A lovely, balanced, sophisticated pays d'auge.
2018 Rating: ★ ★ ★ ★/Highly Recommended

Christian Drouin VSOP Pays d'Auge Calvados 40% abv, $88.

Wheat-field gold; flawlessly clear. I like the opening aroma of apple butter, nougat, fried egg in butter, and black peppercorn; secondary inhalations discover slightly meatier, more buttery fragrances that are round, supple, and integrated, reflecting very ripe, bittersweet apples. Entry is dense in texture, woody, sap-like, dry, tart, and acidic; midpalate phase is where this calvados shines brightest, as all the entry findings are buttressed by additional tastes of butterscotch, toffee, orange marmalade, tangerine, orange pekoe tea, and a delicate touch of salinity. Ends on a high note of tartness, dryness, and tangy astringency. Delicious.
2019 Rating: ★ ★ ★ ★ ★/Highest Recommendation

Christian Drouin XO Pays d'Auge Calvados 40% abv, $90.

Very pretty and bright amber color that is flawlessly pure. The intensely ripe green-apple opening scent is seductive and slightly spicy; with more air contact, the aroma opens up more, offering succulent outdoorsy fragrances of summer flower garden, orchard in August, apple pie/apple tart. Entry is velvety in texture, spicy to the point of being mildly piquant, even

peppery; midpalate pretty much mimics the entry flavor profile, adding mace, clove, vanilla bean, brown butter, egg cream. Finishes long, piquant, zesty, and delectable.
2016 Rating: ★★★★/Highly Recommended

Claque-Pepin 20 Year Old Calvados 40% abv, $120.
Sinopia color; textbook clarity. Wow, I pick up intriguing fragrances of old library, leather-bound books, sawdust, toasted almond, and maple syrup, each in abundance, each nicely melded to each other; here, after more aeration, the totality of the bouquet becomes apparent in the impressions of dried flowers, cane sugar, nougat, candy bar, and spiced apple. Entry is buttery; creamy in texture; toasted; charcoal-like; spiced, baked apple–like; baked pear–like; nutty; and flinty dry. Midpalate echoes all the entry impressions adding apple peel, toasted marshmallow, candied apple, and tree bark. Concludes medium long, dry, tangy. Lost a bit of momentum by the midpalate perhaps due to its age but it's still delightful.
2019 Rating: ★★★★/Highly Recommended

Claque-Pepin Fine Calvados 40% abv, $30.
Goldenrod color; superbly free of sediment. I like the zesty first nosing passes as the richness of baked apple pastry that's slightly spiced with cinnamon makes its case with conviction; with aeration, the juiciness of the apple becomes apparent, and it's this development that makes this aroma so pleasing. Entry is tangy, apple- and pear-like, baked, spicy (now more mace and nutmeg than cinnamon), but it's the richness of the velvety texture that rings my chimes; midpalate is chunky, silky in mouthfeel, and vividly tart and apple peel–like, and it's the acidity that balances the buttery texture, thereby creating a solid four star experience. Ends up gently sweet, juicy, ripe, and amazingly fresh.
2019 Rating: ★★★★/Highly Recommended

Claque-Pepin Hors d'Age Calvados 40% abv, $60.
Copper color; flawless clarity. Whoa, this opening nose is weirdly appealing even though it crackles with earthy, forest-like fragrances that are reminiscent of brambles, vines, and bark; later sniffs after more air contact pick up nutty and fiber-like scents that are peppery, plastic-like, waxy, and just barely fruity and apple-like. Entry defies the olfactory findings as the taste profile offers highly acidic and therefore tangy flavors of unsweetened apple juice, apple peel, apple strudel, and nutmeg; midpalate builds upon the entry impressions by making the wood influence stronger, which brings with it a buttery, silky texture. Finishes medium long, toasty, lightly spiced (clove, salt, cinnamon), and tobacco-like. The lustrous nature of the flavor profile redeems some of the softness of the aroma.
2019 Rating: ★★★★/Highly Recommended

Claque-Pepin Vieille Reserve Certified Organic Calvados 40% abv, $44.
Marigold/hay-field yellow color; minor tendrils of sediment seen under the examination lamp but nothing of consequence. Smells predictably of tart apples and Jolly Rancher sour apple in the first inhalations after the pour; with more aeration, the bouquet fills out nicely, featuring deft touches of cinnamon, clove, allspice, and candle wax. Entry offers an apple-cider juiciness that's brittle and hard-edged on the tongue, but this dissipates in

the midpalate as the baking spices return to underpin the tart-apple core flavor. Short- to medium-length finish, tart, acidic, and mildly clove-like. A pleasant, middle-of-the-road calvados of juicy charm.

2017 Rating: ★★★/Recommended

Coquerel Fine Calvados 40% abv, $27.

Harvest gold color; attractive, sediment-free appearance. First whiffs are treated to a fresh, just-picked red apple aroma that's properly tart, zesty, lightly spiced (cinnamon), and peel-like; later inhalations after more aeration stay the pleasant course set in the opening sniffs, perhaps leaning a bit more towards applesauce than apple peel. Entry is peculiarly metallic/steely and unpleasantly bitter; don't know what's happened here in this starkly unappealing, cleaning fluid–like flavor profile that doesn't at all echo the nicely tangy bouquet; midpalate is as pleasant a moment as finding out you have to have oral surgery . . . right now. Finish is an unmitigated travesty that rudely assaults the taste buds. Hands down, one of the top five worst spirits I've reviewed recently.

2018 Rating: ★/Not Recommended

Coquerel VSOP Calvados 40% abv, $45.

Sandy-brown color; superb clarity. This opening aroma shows an off-dry menu of fragrances that includes baking spices (nutmeg, vanilla), slightly tart red apple, apple peel, and baked apple; secondary sniffs unearth pleasant but slightly fading scents of parchment, apple butter, and nutmeg. Entry offers cooked tastes of apple peel, spiced apple hard candy, and apple strudel, but there's an obvious hollowness in the core flavor that's mineral-like and flinty; midpalate features some apple peel and spiced apple juiciness, but hardly enough to perceive this as anything other than under par for the category. Aftertaste is meek, dull, showing just a trace of elegance. A fat and flabby disappointment.

2018 Rating: ★/Not Recommended

Manoir d'Apreval 1980 Pays d'Auge Calvados 42% abv, $230.

Chestnut-brown color, with orange core highlights; sediment-free. I detect all sorts of bakery-shop aromas, everything from apple strudel/galette to apple butter to allspice and clove to almond paste; later inhalations pick up apple juice elements that are tart and fully evolved. Entry is clean, moderately toasted/baked, tart, acidic (thereby refreshing), and not so much spicy as woody/resiny; midpalate echoes much of the entry assets, but it's the tangy, silky, apple butter texture at this point that wins the day and my unswerving attention. Classic pays d'auge splendor.

2014 Rating: ★★★★★/Highest Recommendation

Manoir d'Apreval Blanche Calvados 40% abv, $55.

Three+ years old. Oyster-shell/tarnished-silver color; very good purity. The keenly tart apple freshness discovered in the first aromatic burst is evocative and compelling; later on, I detect subtle traces of baking spice (cinnamon), green leaf, green tea, vegetation scents. Entry is piquant, moderately spicy, apple peel–like; midpalate reflects the entry perfectly, adding a mineral/stone aspect that's astringent and cleansing.

2014 Rating: ★★★/Recommended

Manoir d'Apreval Cuvée Gustave Pays d'Auge Calvados 41% abv, $356.

Forty+ years old. Deep topaz color; sediment-free purity. I get a fruity toastiness that's nice but obviously mature; later inhalations encounter hard cheese, mushroom, forest floor, apple hard candy, leather. Entry features the cheese aspect to the hilt, leaving just enough taste space for tart red apple, cider, oaky vanilla; midpalate is toasty, maple-like, viscous, nutty as well as fruity, and creamy in texture. Awe inspiring.

2014 Rating: ★ ★ ★ ★ ★/Highest Recommendation

Manoir d'Apreval Cuvée Victor Pays d'Auge Calvados 41% abv, $283.

Thirty+ years old. Ochre/deep amber color; pure and oily. Opening sniffs encounter old leather books/library, pipe tobacco, herbal tea, distant spiced apple; later whiffs detect beeswax, deeper herbal tea aspects, tart apple peel, sawdust. Entry flashes subtle tastes of very ripe apple, apple compote, fruit salad, oak, apple butter; midpalate reflects all entry attributes and goes the extra mile in viscosity, but compared to the crackling 1980, I detect a little weariness amidst the many virtues.

2014 Rating: ★ ★ ★ ★/Highly Recommended

Manoir d'Apreval Grande Réserve Pays d'Auge Calvados 42% abv, $92.

Eighteen-karat-gold/hay color; unblemished purity. I encounter truckloads of apple pastry scents in the first inhalations that are more like the bakery than the candy shop; secondary whiffs include slightly toasted fragrances of baked apple, baked pear, lemongrass. Entry is zesty, pleasantly spicy, fruity, tart; midpalate highlights the piquancy of the spiced, baked apple, with a waxy texture. Ends woodier, more resiny than the Réserve.

2014 Rating: ★ ★ ★ ★/Highly Recommended

Manoir d'Apreval Réserve Pays d'Auge Calvados 42% abv, $67.

Five+ years old. Ecru/electrum color; impeccable clarity. I get lots more apple pulp/meat, baked fruit, and baking spice complexity (clove, allspice) in the first whiffs than with the Blanche; later sniffs pick up faint evidence of vanilla, oak, wood plank, burlap. Entry highlights the spiced, baked apple element and a silky texture; midpalate features apple butter, brown sugar, bakery-shop flavors of pastry, apple strudel. Ends long, with spicy, astringent flavors that highlight the cleanness of the apple spirit.

2014 Rating: ★ ★ ★ ★/Highly Recommended

Manoir d'Apreval XO Pays d'Auge Calvados 42% abv, $134.

Topaz/burnished-orange color; flawless clarity. Oh my, the rich fragrance of ripe apple meat, apple compote is stunning in the opening sniffs; with aeration, baking spices emerge, especially nutmeg, cinnamon, as well as old leather, old oak aromas. Entry is sweet yet simultaneously tart and intensely spicy; midpalate is tangy, savory, succulent, like ripe red apples, satiny in texture. Concludes a touch rancio-like, earthy/mushroomy, black tea–like. Highly complex.

2014 Rating: ★ ★ ★ ★/Highly Recommended

Morice Pays d'Auge Calvados 42% abv, $41.

Fawn color; excellent clarity. Wow, this is a very different first aroma that is startlingly

juicy, apple-like, pear-like, and spiced (mace) to the point where I can't put the glass down because I want to discover more orchard-related fragrances; aeration serves to heighten the ambrosial nature of the bouquet as it turns even juicier than in the initial sniffs. Entry is succulent, rich, slightly prickly, tarter than the bouquet, and keenly like spiced apple; midpalate enthralls the taste buds as the flavor profile adds a touch of oaky texture that underscores the density of the apple character. Finishes quite tart, a bit too metallic-bitter, but overall very nicely. Until the slight slipup in the aftertaste, this pays d'auge was en route to five star status.
2018 Rating: ★★★★/Highly Recommended

Noble-Dame Calvados 40% abv, $32.

Earth yellow color; minor, inconsequential sediment spotted. At first, what I get aromatically are rubber bands, stucco, vegetable cooking oil, and very faint orchard fruit (apple? pear? nectarine?) that is nondescript; further aeration time of twelve minutes doesn't shake free much more in the way of fragrance other than earthy notes, like dry sand, cement, flint; a disappointing bouquet that doesn't say "apple." Entry taste makes something of a recovery for this calvados as the spiced-apple surface flavor is strong, unequivocal, and vibrant; midpalate is slightly toasty, keenly apple-like, a touch baked, and moderately spiced (cinnamon, vanilla). Ends up like baked apple, a little too metallic for my taste, and waxy in texture. For me, just not enough there to justify the price.
2018 Rating: ★★/Not Recommended

Roger Groult 8 Year Old Pays d'Auge Calvados 41% abv, $64.

Harvest gold color; ideal purity. The delicacy of the opening aroma is deceiving in that once you go deeper, there are layers of fragrance that could easily be overlooked if you hurry, aromas such as apple butter, apple peel, and lightly spiced applesauce; secondary inhalations discover scents of apple strudel, puff pastry, pear juice, and allspice. Entry is pleasingly tart and fresh, zesty, and modestly piquant; midpalate provides a wider spectrum of flavors, including waxy apple peel, apple pastry, and apple turnovers. Finish is medium long, nicely apple-like, and fresh.
2018 Rating: ★★★/Recommended

Roger Groult 12 Year Old Pays d'Auge Calvados 41% abv, $90.

Goldenrod/saffron color; impeccable clarity. There's a foxy leaning to this opening aroma that's quite vegetal, sweaty, and vinous, so I'm hoping that more air contact will rectify the situation; secondary whiffs discover a whole new aromatic profile as whatever was bedeviling it initially now has blown off, leaving behind a chunky, assertive bouquet that's akin to apple tart and apple strudel more than fresh, ripened apples. Entry is satiny in texture, mildly piquant in spice level, and pleasing baked apple–like; midpalate reflects the entry impressions very well, leading to a fulfilling aftertaste that's keenly spicy, a touch prickly, and overall quite yummy.
2018 Rating: ★★★/Recommended

Roger Groult 18 Year Old Pays d'Auge Calvados 41% abv, $110.

Saffron/sandy-brown color; immaculate clarity. Up front, I pick up solid, straight-ahead, mature fragrances of spiced apple, pastry crust, apple rind, pear juice, and cinnamon; it isn't until after further aeration that the oak aspect enters the aromatic picture, giving off subtle nuances of vanilla bean and coconut that beautifully underscore the ripe apple perfume. Entry is supple and slightly fat in texture while the primary flavors are spiced apple, apple strudel, baked apple, and bacon fat; midpalate focuses more on the structure as the texture turns buttery and sinewy, all of which accentuate the apple pastry aspect, making the mid-palate worth the price of admission. Aftertaste is long, suddenly quite spicy, buttery, and baked/toasty. Delicious.

2018 Rating: ★ ★ ★ ★/Highly Recommended

Roger Groult 25 Year Old Pays d'Auge Calvados 41% abv, $182.

Cocoa-brown color; very minor sediment seen, inconsequential. Yes, I get odors of old oak/sawdust right away as I do a full measure of baked apple, but once again as with the twelve-year-old, there's a lurking presence of sweatiness that concerns me; like the twelve-year-old, with more air contact the sweat issue recedes, leaving the aromatic door open for deft, mature fragrances of black pepper, oak plank, apple butter, and spiced, baked apple. Entry is lusciously sweet and apple ripe and buttery/creamy, and I can't help but wonder how this entry transformed my impressions from cautionary amber to full-tilt green light. Midpalate exhibits all the mature attributes of an older calvados, meaning sublime apple strudel taste, slight piquancy from the touch of baking spice (nutmeg mostly), the underscoring influence of oak-impacted lipids (fats) that make the texture rich and creamy, and just an overall apple brandy splendor right through the languid, leisurely aftertaste that begs for a cigar. So here's my critic's dilemma: Do I score it five stars due primarily to the sensational in-mouth stages or do I render only four stars because of my concern about the sweaty early aroma? Guess . . .

2018 Rating: ★ ★ ★ ★/Highly Recommended

Roger Groult Doyen d'Age Pays d'Auge Calvados 41% abv, $220.

Very old calvados of forty years minimum. Fulvous/wheat-field color; superb purity. I don't get all that much in the opening inhalations so I allow it to sit for ten minutes to aerate; regrettably, after more air contact there still is no appreciable aromatics rising from the glass so I move on. Entry is stupendously dull, overmature, too oaky, and off balance; midpalate mirrors the entry. This inexplicably pricey calvados is DOA, and I question the wisdom of its release.

2019 Rating: ★/Not Recommended

Roger Groult Réserve Pays d'Auge Calvados 40% abv, $42.

Sunflower-yellow color; excellent clarity. The nimble lightness of this opening aroma carries the intense fruitiness a long way forward as the apple fragrance is tinted with distant traces of pear fragrance; with more aeration, the crisp apple scent takes charge as the acidity level maintains the astringency. Entry is very tart, squeaky clean, acidic, and deeply apple-like in a razor-edged manner; midpalate carries the entry findings forward as the apple intensity deepens with the blanketing of the palate. It's keenly fresh, edgy, and astringent in the aftertaste. Everything you want in a youthful calvados is presented here.

2019 Rating: ★ ★ ★ ★/Highly Recommended

BRANDY—USA AND WORLD

United States

The saga of New World brandy began five centuries ago. Just recall from where the first immigrants to the Americas came . . . Spain, with an ancient résumé of brandy making; France, where the distillation of wine had been established in Armagnac by the middle 1300s and in neighboring Cognac by the late 1500s, not to mention the distillation of apple cider in Normandy that dates back at least to the mid-sixteenth century; Germany, where distillers created *schnapps* and fruit brandies made from cherries and plums as early as the thirteenth century; Italy, where the centuries-old grape-must spirit known as *grappa* was made in every wine-producing region from unknown periods; and Holland, whose merchants sold and shipped the grape brandies of southwestern France from as far back as the sixteenth century, and who were adept at distillation at the same time.

Brandy making became a staple activity in the colonies. In 1621, town elder Sir Francis Wyatt instructed his citizens in Virginia to "withdraw attention from tobacco and direct it . . . to the making of oil of walnuts and employing the apothecaries of distillation . . ." In the meantime, as the Germans, British, French, and Dutch were consuming large amounts of alembic (traditional pot still) fruit brandies in the east, Spanish settlers from western Texas to southern California were creating their own regional wines and distillates.

In the late eighteenth century, Franciscan priest Junipero Serra established vineyards in all nine of the missions he founded in California. The California mission system produced twenty-one Catholic missions from 1769 to 1833. The majority had thriving vineyards. Many wine historians agree that perhaps the most successful mission in terms of winemaking and distillation was the Mission San Gabriel Arcángel near Los Angeles. It was established in 1771. The padres kept an inventory of their wines and brandies, and in 1829 the records boast of a robust stock of six hundred barrels of wine and two hundred barrels of brandy.

The next boon for California brandy came in the mid-nineteenth century after gold was discovered first in 1842 in the San Fernando Valley and then six years later in 1848 near Sutter's Mill. By 1849, the California Gold Rush was in full swing, in particular in foothills of the Sierra Nevada mountains. San Francisco naturally attracted many of the nouveau riche and thus became home to the wealthiest miners.

With the historic joining of the Union Pacific and Central Pacific railroads in May of 1869, some of the wealthiest miners started to return to their eastern cities throughout the 1870s. With the intercontinental railroad operating, the transport of California brandy to the affluent eastern markets of Chicago, New York, Boston, Washington, St. Louis, Pittsburgh, and Philadelphia was made significantly easier.

In the years following the American Civil War, California brandy's reach and reputation continued to grow as commerce expanded and international natural events took hold. One of those events was the devastation of Europe's vineyards by a rapacious beetle, *phylloxera vastatrix*, a pest that originated in North America. With the European production of wine and brandies decimated for nearly three decades, California's brandy producers ramped up their production and, in the process, gained even more attention as America's favorite domestic brandies.

Simultaneously, another nineteenth-century phenomenon was occurring in America's taverns, pubs, sporting clubs, and metropolitan hotel bars . . . the mixing of spirits with other ingredients, such as fruit juices, bitters, and sugar. Of course, I'm referring to the cocktail. Little known is the fact that until the twentieth century, the United States government classified brandy as medicinal. A bottle of brandy, made in pot stills, was common in most domiciles throughout the nineteenth and early twentieth centuries.

Two world wars and the Korean conflict, the Great Depression, and, most devastating of all, national Prohibition would throw roadblocks in the highway for all beverage alcohol. Distilleries and wineries closed, many permanently during the forty-year span of 1915 to 1955. By the time the world and America began to recover from the half century of crises, the landscape for brandy, in general, had been dramatically altered. Whiskey and beer became the reigning king and queen of beverage alcohol in the 1950s and 1960s, soon to be followed by vodka in the 1970s and 1980s. Brandy became an afterthought.

But during the pivotal 1970s, the first stirrings of resurgence occurred for California brandy in the labels of E&J (Gallo), Christian Brothers, Paul Masson, Italian Swiss Colony, Almaden, and Korbel. These were for the most part column still, high-volume brandies made from Thompson Seedless grapes grown in California's fertile Central Valley. Suddenly, brandy that most any American household could afford was being made at a relatively high level of quality.

The 1980s and 1990s saw a parallel and equally historic occurrence with the dawn of the artisanal brandy movement. Germain-Robin, Jepson, RMS Carneros, St. George Spirits, Osocalis, and Charbay in California and Clear Creek in Oregon came onto the scene. These were the pioneers of contemporary alembic brandy in North America. In the 2000s, other craft brandy producers like Gallo's McCall Distillery, Copper & Kings, Koval, Rhine Hall, and Starlight, just to name a few, spearheaded the next generation of potentially great domestic brandy producers.

United States Labeling Laws

Brandy regulations in the United States are notoriously open-ended, which therefore allows for a broad variety of interpretation. Many producers applaud this status since they feel it allows them wide latitude for ingredients, while other producers decry this loose situation, claiming that a lack of regulation works against the quality aura of American brandy. I agree with the latter.

In the Home of the Brave, brandy that has been produced from other than grape wine must be labeled with a clarifying description of the type of brandy production such as "peach brandy," "fruit brandy," "dried fruit brandy," or "pomace brandy," and brandy that has not been aged in oak for at least two years must be labeled as "immature."

Spanish Brandy

The making of distilled spirits in Spain is inextricably linked with the occupation of the Iberian Peninsula from 711–1492 CE by the Islamic Moors. Likely introduced by the Romans, wine had been made in many of Spain's regions for hundreds of years before the eighth century Moorish invasion from northern Africa. The historical reasoning is this: Assuming that wine had already long existed in Spain, it is highly probable that the scientifically sophisticated Moors dabbled, perhaps extensively, in wine distillation. While in adherence to their Islamic beliefs of abstinence from alcoholic beverages, the Moors did, however, utilize their distilling acumen by making wine for the creation of medicines and cosmetics. The Moors were eventually driven from Spain after 781 years by Christian Spain, following the marriage of Ferdinand II of Aragon and Isabella I of Castile, the so-called "Catholic Monarchs."

The most famous Spanish brandy of all is *Brandy de Jerez*. Spanish law dictates that Brandy de Jerez must be matured in sherry barrels in the demarcated sherry-making district, a.k.a. the "Sherry Triangle," bounded by the cities of Jerez de la Frontera, El Puerto de Santa Maria, and Sanlúcar de Barrameda, located in Andalusia in the south of Spain. The majority of Brandy de Jerez brandies are created out of low-acid white wines made from Airén grapes cultivated in the expansive vineyards of central Spain's massive Denominación de Origen (DO) Castilla-La Mancha district. Wines are produced locally in the city of Tomelloso, which is likewise home to numerous distilleries for brandy production. Blending and aging of eaux-de-vie for the making of Brandy de Jerez happens farther south in Andalusia.

As a matter of routine and custom, they are aged in an ingenious maturation system that mirrors the process utilized for aging sherry: *the solera system*. The solera system can be thought of as a pyramid concept, in which the ground-floor row of barrels contains the oldest brandies and the next row above the ground-floor row is a little younger and so on. The ground-floor row is called the *solera* while the upper rows are known as *criaderas*. When producers need to bottle more supply, they dip into the oldest, mellowest brandies from the solera, but no more than one-third of the barrel's content. Younger brandy from the row of barrels directly (criadera) above replaces the older brandy from the ground floor and so on and so on up the pyramid. The inherent beauty of the solera system is that you are always marrying older brandies with newer, fresher ones. The older brandies lend depth to the younger ones, and the younger ones bring vigor to the older ones.

Brandy de Jerez Labeling Laws

Brandy de Jerez Solera is the fruitiest style because it is the youngest style by law. It must be aged in barrels for at the minimum one year.

Brandy de Jerez Solera Reserva must legally have endured a maturation period in barrel of no less than three years.

Brandy de Jerez Solera Gran Reserva indicates the longest aging period, one of at least ten years before bottling.

In addition to Brandy de Jerez, there are several world-class brandies made in the Catalonian wine regions that surround Barcelona by famed producers like Torres and Bodega Mascaró. Penedès, Spain's home base to its beloved sparkling wine, cava, is the hub of brandy making in Spain's northeast quadrant that borders France. The primary grape types used for the stylish Catalonian brandies are *parellada*, *xarel-lo*, and *macabeo*. Virtually all Catalonian brandies are double distilled in copper pot stills. Being so close to southern France, it is little wonder that the Penedès brandies resemble their French counterparts.

Rest of World

North-central Europe and the area of Eastern Europe known as the Caucasus have for centuries been hotbeds of brandy production. While there is some speculation that the distillation of grapes was occurring in the region of what is now Turkey around 1000 CE, there is scant evidence to support the claim. There is, however, substantial historical record that the nations of Germany, Russia, Ukraine, Georgia, Armenia, Turkey, and Greece have distilled local wines since the eighteenth century, with some producers (Germany's Dujardin, for instance) even importing grapes from France's Charente.

Germany is the primary brandy-producing country in north-central Europe, boasting renowned companies such as Underberg AG's Asbach Uralt (founded in 1892), Dujardin (1743), and Wilthener (1700) as headliners. Prior to World War I, German brandies were known as "cognacs," but then with the implementation of the Treaty of Versailles after the war, that designation was forbidden. Hugo Asbach then coined the word *Weinbrand*, which in 1923 became Germany's official brandy classification.

In Greece, there is Metaxa (1888), a brandy-like elixir that begins life as a brandy, then has muscat grape wine blended into it from the Aegean islands of Samos and Lemnos. While not technically a brandy, it is widely perceived as Greece's hallmark spirit as it is available in sixty-plus countries.

Moving further into the Caucasus Mountain region, in particular, Georgia, Armenia, and Azerbaijan, brandies have been produced there since at least the nineteenth century. Many of the brandies from Caucasus are made in cognac's Charentais tradition of double distillation in alembic stills and long maturation in small oak barrels. During the era of the Soviet Union, Armenian brandy, the majority made by Yerevan Brandy Company (1887), was the dominant spirit from the Caucasus to the far reaches of the Siberian frontier. The dismantling of the Soviet Union brought disaster to Armenia's spirit producers, who are still in a rebuilding stage. Ararat is now the major Armenian brandy and is made from thirteen indigenous grape types, the main three being *voskehat*, *garan dmak*, and *kangun*.

In Ukraine, a huge country that borders the Caucasus, brandy production is turning into a major industry, with companies such as Global Spirits' Shustov Distillery taking the lead. Established in 1863, Shustov, which currently produces Odessa brandy, makes brandy in the cognac tradition, utilizing white grapes like *aligoté*, *pinot*, and *rkatsiteli* that are fermented then double distilled in pot stills.

I would be remiss if Southern Hemisphere nations like Australia and South Africa were not cited as being significant brandy producers. Australian grape growers have been making brandy since the mid-to-late nineteenth century. Château Tanunda of the Barossa Valley (1860s), Hardy's (1853) Black Bottle, and Angove's (1855) St. Agnes are standouts.

In South Africa, legend has it that the initial brandy was created on board a Dutch merchant ship, the De Pijl, while anchored offshore in May 1672. Like with cognac, to whose invention the Dutch contributed, early South African brandies, such as Van Ryn's (1845) and F.C. Collison (1833), used Charentais-style pot stills in which to distill their chenin blanc and colombard white wines. Today's South African brandy scene is dominated by KWV (Koöperatieve Wijnbouwers Vereniging van Zuid-Afrika). And as opposed to most other brandy-producing nations listed here, South African brandies do have strict regulations. With the founding of the South African Brandy Foundation in 1984, the nation's brandy industry became regulated, standardizing four levels of brandy production.

South African Labeling Laws

Blended Brandy is made from at least 30 percent pot still brandy (the balance can legally be comprised of unaged neutral spirit) and matures in oak barrels for a minimum of three years.

Vintage Brandy is made from at least 30 percent pot still brandy with up to 60 percent column still spirit that is aged for at least eight years and up to but not more than 10 percent virgin wine spirits.

Pot Still Brandy must legally contain a minimum of 90 percent pot still brandy and at most 10 percent unaged neutral spirit.

Estate Brandy must by law be entirely produced, matured, and bottled on a single estate.

While label designations like VS and VSOP may be used, they have no bearing on quality.

Argonaut Fat Thumb Premium California Brandy (USA) 43% abv, $53.
A blend of alembic pot still and Coffey still brandies. Mango/jonquil color; very good clarity. This comely opening aroma is rife with caramel, spice (clove, allspice), peanut butter, and dried-fruit (fig, date) notes that have gracefully come together; after more aeration, this stupendously charming bouquet highlights the dried-fruit aspect, as well as subtle hints of tree bark, cassia, dried cherry, honeysuckle, pipe tobacco, and flint; just a superb bouquet, period. Entry is measured, just slightly sweet and grapy ripe, but there's also more than ample acidity to keep the flavor razor edged and keenly fresh; midpalate echoes all the entry-stage findings, adding dried apricot and pear. Finishes long, subtle, richly textured, and deep in dried-fruit aftertastes. Glorious.
2019 Rating: ★ ★ ★ ★ ★/Highest Recommendation

Argonaut Saloon Strength California Brandy (USA) 45.5% abv, $29/liter.
A blend of Coffey still California brandies. Gold/mustard color; pristine clarity. Right from the very first nosing, the clear evidence of piquant alcohol is obvious but then it quickly fades, leaving behind rounder scents of kiwi, candle wax/paraffin, and jasmine; secondary whiffs discover fruitier aromas, especially white grapes, quince, and white peach. Entry is

zesty, vibrant, and crisp due mainly to the clean fruit and the high degree of acidity; midpalate maintains the fruit zest and adds more fruit pulp that deepens the texture. Concludes a bit short on the finish, but the alcohol once again ascends in potency.
2019 Rating: ★ ★ ★/Recommended

Argonaut Speculator Premium California Brandy (USA) 43% abv, $38.
Butterscotch color; sediment-free purity. Opening nosing passes pick up scents of dried flower petals (violet, carnation) and fresh tropical fruits, most notably banana and papaya; later inhalations after more air contact find that the initial impressions are reenforced with fragrances of ginger, grilled peach, and cherry blossom. Entry is firm in structure, relatively high in acid, and therefore dry and near-astringent; midpalate displays an opulence of texture as the fruit-driven acids maintain the crispness appreciated both in the bouquet and the palate entry. Ends on a fruity note that's more orchard-like and peachy than vineyard related.
2019 Rating: ★ ★ ★ ★/Highly Recommended

Argonaut The Claim Premium California Brandy (USA) 42% abv, $200.
One hundred percent Coffey still eaux-de-vie, the majority of which are over twenty years old. Golden poppy/sunglow color; impeccably pure. Initial inhalations pick up juicy fragrances of white grapes/white raisins, pineapple, and kiwi in equal measure; after more air contact, the nose unfolds in layers, as first the juiciness of the tropical fruit comes alive followed by citrus peel/zest, succeeded by notes of guava and star fruit; this bouquet offers an ambrosial experience that's breathtaking. Entry is crisp, clean, acidic, and fruity and juicy; midpalate mirrors the entry stage, throwing in delicate flavors of mango and white chocolate. Aftertaste is extended, mature, rich in texture, and stately.
2019 Rating: ★ ★ ★ ★ ★/Highest Recommendation

Asbach 15 Year Old Spezial-Brand Brandy (Germany) 40% abv, $95.
Rust/cordovan color; immaculate clarity. The initial inhalations offer subtle aromas of tree bark, sap, orange pekoe tea, and oak resins that nicely underpin the dried-fruit fragrance of dates and figs; more air contact opens up a fruity side of the bouquet that's nimble and pear-like. Entry is intensely woody and dried fruit–like; midpalate is the apex moment in which all the components, the oak, fruit, acidity, and forest/earthiness commingle nicely. Aftertaste is nuanced, dry, resiny/oaky, and tobacco-like.
2019 Rating: ★ ★ ★ ★/Highly Recommended

Asbach 1952 Goethe Cask #1 Brandy (Germany) 41.8% abv, $3,000.
Only nine hundred bottles available worldwide/a scant thirteen for the USA. Color is deep chestnut/bronze, bordering on henna; superb clarity. Opening nose offers choice, mature aromas of old leather, men's club, dried peach, cigar box, dried pineapple, candied walnuts, soft cheese, mushroom paté; second inhalations encounter deeper tobacco scents plus a mélange of spice elements, including mace, allspice, sesame seed; a remarkably fresh and animated bouquet for a grape brandy that's so old. Entry is serenely composed, integrated, harmonious, gently sweet but neither cloying nor unctuous; midpalate comes alive

with concentrated grapy/raisiny flavors and underpinning tastes of marzipan, dried tropical fruits that last long into the satisfying finish, which shows dashes of rancio. One of a kind and one of the best grape brandies I've ever evaluated.
2015 Rating: ★ ★ ★ ★ ★/Highest Recommendation

Asbach 8 Year Old Privat-Brand Brandy (Germany) 40% abv, $50.

Ochre/tawny color; perfect purity. First sniffs pick up traces of sliced pineapple, white grape, and quince aromas that are fresh and vibrant; secondary nosing passes succeed in promoting biscuity, maple-like scents that complement the fruit aspects. Entry is clean, svelte, and semidry, with tons of baked fruit flavors that are almost like a nut and fruit tart; midpalate boasts a clean-as-a-whistle flavor profile where the wood starts to impact the acidic fruit element, thereby creating a sophisticated impression of dryness that's prominent all through the midrange finish.
2019 Rating: ★ ★ ★/Recommended

Cardenal Mendoza Carta Real Solera Gran Reserva Brandy de Jerez (Spain) 40% abv, $100.

Color is seal-brown/cocoa bean; superbly clean. Vivid scents of raisins, figs, dates, and more raisins are evident in the first nosing passes after the pour; as this brandy aerates, the bouquet grows stately, composed, and deep in dried fruits, in particular, prunes and dates, yet it never loses the trademark grapiness that you want in great brandy de Jerez. Entry is gracefully sweet/sour and even a tad spicy/peppery; midpalate is raisiny, pruny, one-pointed on the dried fruit, and even a bit treacle-like. Concludes on a spicy, succulent note that's different from its sibling. Decadent and lovely.
2018 Rating: ★ ★ ★ ★ ★/Highest Recommendation

Cardenal Mendoza Solera Gran Reserva Brandy de Jerez (Spain) 40% abv, $50.

The sepia/sienna color is perfectly sediment-free. Initial nosing passes pick up mature, caramelized onion scents that are supported by dried-fruit fragrances, especially dried pear, black raisins, and prune; secondary fragrance impressions include espresso bean, hot cocoa, treacle, marzipan, and chocolate-covered coffee bean. Entry is savory, rich in texture but not syrupy, and bathed in raisiny dried-fruit flavor; midpalate is dense, complex, and deeply pruny. Aftertaste is long in the throat, toasted, bittersweet, and earthy.
2018 Rating: ★ ★ ★ ★/Highly Recommended

Catoctin Creek 1757 Virginia Brandy (USA) 40% abv, $49.

Made from Virginia grapes and aged in French Bordeaux barrels for a minimum of two years. I can see some infinitesimal sediment in the core; pretty copper/burnt-orange color. Initial inhalations pick up pruny, black raisin aromas that are pleasingly fruity and dried, almost like prune Danish, as there is likewise a touch of pastry scent; secondary whiffs detect bigger, riper, more candied fragrances of fruit compote, nougat, cherry preserves, oak plank. Entry features round, chewy, butterscotch and toffee flavors that coat the tongue generously; midpalate flavors turn more almond paste and dried tropical fruit–like (pineapple, in particular) as the dryness/sweetness scale inches more into sweet/bittersweet territory. Aftertaste

is sap-like, densely oaky, and, for me, too aggressively woody, as the dried-fruit (prunes, pineapple, raisins) elements are swamped by the oak polymer tsunami.
2016 Rating: ★ ★/Not Recommended

Charbay No. 89 Aged 24 Years/Distilled in 1989 Brandy (USA) 46% abv, $230.
Matured in limousin oak barrels. Pale-gold/hay-field color; superb clarity. First nosings discover understated aromas of butterscotch, vanilla bean, cocoa bean, lightly toasted marshmallow, steamed peas; secondary inhalations following further aeration encounter coconut, dried violets, dried nectarine, cashews, brown rice. Entry gracefully charms the front palate with lightly toasted flavors of caramelized sugar, brown butter, dried coconut, dried banana; midpalate is slightly citrusy/orangey at first, then the zestiness fades, leaving behind drizzle-like tastes of honey, nutmeg, clove, vanilla bean, fudge, caramelized sugar that all last deep into the balanced, harmonious aftertaste.
2015 Rating: ★ ★ ★ ★/Highly Recommended

Christian Brothers Sacred Bond Aged 4 Years in Bourbon Barrels Bottled-in-Bond Brandy (USA) 50% abv, $26.
Pot still distillation. Pretty burnt sienna color; impeccably clear and clean. Opening nosings detect very delicate, almost ghostlike aromas of white grapes and stony dry soil; after several more minutes of air contact, the aroma simply doesn't open up any more than it did in the initial passes, so I move on. Entry is keenly fruity/plummy and a touch warm from the 50 percent abv but not for a nanosecond hot or fiery; midpalate shoulders much of the quality load as it offers floral/dried violet, baked pineapple, white raisin, and quince flavors that dive deep into the velvety, silky finish, which features taste aspects of toasted marshmallow, plums, and vanilla bean—from the bourbon barrel, no doubt.
2017 Rating: ★ ★ ★/Recommended

Clear Creek Distillery Blue Plum Brandy/Slivovitz (USA) 40% abv, $45.
European brandies made from Italian blue plums like this edition from Clear Creek are labeled as *quetsch* in France (a good one is F. Meyer), *zwetschgenwasser* in Germany, and *slivovitz* in Eastern Europe. Transparent, with the familiar clinging bubbles. Early aromatics are alive with ripe, fruity, ambrosial blue-plum freshness and vivacity; more time in the glass allows a waxy, peppery quality to emerge and take charge. Entry is silky, satiny, vibrant with plummy flavors that are equally ripe, acidic, tannic, tart, and true; midpalate is the mirror image of the entry. Finishes succulent, deeply plummy.
2014 Rating: ★ ★ ★ ★/Highly Recommended

Clear Creek Distillery Eau-de-Vie of Douglas Fir (USA) 47.73% abv, $22/375 ml.
The greenish/yellow/chartreuse color of lime popsicles; absolute clarity—when last I evaluated it, it was a touch hazy, but this time flawlessly clear. This unique aroma is a combination of pine/cedar forest and green apple/pineapple and is remarkably crisp and tight; secondary sniffs find that the fruit is ascending while the pineyness is fading slightly. Entry is keenly piney, resiny, sappy; midpalate is astringent, dry, clean. Finishes a little like pine cleaner, but is curiously appealing.
2014 Rating: ★ ★ ★/Recommended

Clear Creek Distillery Kirschwasser (USA) 40% abv, $45.

Clear as rainwater but with minuscule bubbles hugging the inside of the glass. First nosings detect scents of burnt matches, cherry peel, cherry pit, cherry compote; second-stage sniffings pick up more of the same except that now the cherry aspect has gone over to cherry pie. Entry is medium rich, texturally sound and creamy, moderately fruity, ripe; midpalate reflects all the entry findings and bolsters them with a shot of spirit that carries the message deep into the aftertaste. Sophisticated distilling.

2014 Rating: ★ ★ ★ ★/Highly Recommended

Clear Creek Distillery Mirabelle Plum Brandy (USA) 40% abv, $30/375 ml.

Pristine; colorless; small bubbles are attached to the glass; immaculate purity. Initial aromas focus tightly on the whispery fragrance of plums that are, at once, dry and waxy; further aeration doesn't unleash anything more in terms of bouquet. Entry is pleasingly ripe, juicy, off-dry, plummy; midpalate reinforces all the entry impressions except that the flavor profile is drier at this stage, then turns dusty dry in the highly appealing finish. Composed, so acidic that the freshness level soars. A sublime North American plum brandy.

2014 Rating: ★ ★ ★ ★/Highly Recommended

Clear Creek Distillery Williams Pear Brandy (USA) 40% abv, $45.

The opening aroma is so remarkably spot-on to Williams pear that it's uncanny; fruity, delicate, crisp, softly ripe, and juicy but not a whisper of sweetness; it is just plain pear-like. Entry is acidic, cleansing, fruity, pear-like, a touch minerally/earthy; midpalate echoes all the wonderful findings of the entry stage, adding a bit of pepperiness that contributes a little spiciness. A perfect eau-de-vie that just gets better and truer to the fruit source.

2014 Rating: ★ ★ ★ ★ ★/Highest Recommendation

Coppersea New York Cherry Eau-de-Vie (USA) 45% abv, $60.

Colorless, slightly cloudy appearance, with too many tendrils and particles of sediment evident immediately after the pour; the sediment settles after a few minutes, but the unsightly haze remains. First sniffs pick up scents more of vinyl than of cherries and that's worrisome; with air contact a mild cherry scent is noticed but not enough to overcome the plastic/vinyl aroma that dominates. Entry shows some cherry fruit, which is as ripe as it is tart; midpalate builds upon the cherry entry and offers a good deal of red cherry preserves by the time the midpalate is evolving into the aftertaste, which is lithe, tart, gently sweet, and juicy. Not enough positives, though, to earn a recommendation. Visuals are a major flaw as is the early stage of the bouquet.

2015 Rating: ★ ★/Not Recommended

Coppersea New York Peach Eau-de-Vie (USA) 45% abv, $60.

Murky, hazy appearance; way too much sediment seen floating in the core right after the pour. The opening nosings pick up little aromatic resemblance to peach, just detecting a waxiness that's flax-like; further air contact fails to conjure up anything remotely peach-like, and by this time it's clear that there's a problem here between the cloudy appearance and the

lack of source fragrance. Entry shows a faint glimmer of peach, but by this time the taste profile reveals only a severe production flaw and no realistic hope for recovery.
2015 Rating: ★/Not Recommended

Coppersea New York Pear Eau-de-Vie (USA) 45% abv, $60.
Brilliant transparency; sediment-free purity. Smells of freshly picked yellow pear, gently ripe, sweet, and slightly spicy and peel-like in the opening whiffs after the pour; secondary inhalations echo the first nosing passes as the fruit is cleanly and accurately represented. Entry features a pleasantly astringent flavor that's true to the fruit, properly acidic, alluringly ripe, juicy, and sweet; midpalate is more pear peel–like than pulp-like but retains its juicy character deep into the politely fruity, clean, and tart, if superficial, aftertaste.
2015 Rating: ★ ★ ★/Recommended

Coppersea New York Plum Eau-de-Vie (USA) 45% abv, $60.
Unsightly appearance as clouds of unappetizing sediment are seen clogging up the core; even after another ten minutes, the appearance remains as cloudy as a fish tank. I like the first sniffs that unearth a mildly pleasing and relatively true scent of dark plum along with added fragrances of plastic, candlewax, and linseed oil; second whiffs fall flat as the fruit aspect loses momentum, revealing the industrial core bouquet. Entry offers some plumminess that's ripe and sweet, but ultimately lackluster and superficial; midpalate mirrors the entry but, in fairness, is juicier than the entry, and therefore quite pleasing as the taste profile enters the finish stage on a positive note.
2015 Rating: ★ ★/Not Recommended

Cornelius Apple Jack (USA) 40% abv, $33/375 ml.
Pristine clarity; attractive, bright, pale-yellow/ecru color. I fail to pick up aromatics of distinction in the opening whiffs; later on, after more air contact, there's a faint trace of wax paper, but nothing markable in the way of apple/fruit. Entry is nicely tart, acidic, and therefore fresh, but lacking in apple aspect; midpalate ups the flavor profile ante by featuring tart green-apple pulp and peel. Finishes apple-like, spicy (clove), and biscuity. Improved substantially from fey bouquet to animated aftertaste. But not enough to be recommended for anyone who understands apple brandy or calvados.
2014 Rating: ★ ★/Not Recommended

Cornelius Peach Flavored Brandy (USA) 30% abv, $30/375 ml.
Hazy/turbid, orange/fulvous appearance. Smells remotely of peaches/nectarines, hard candy, old warehouse, grandpa's attic; later sniffs encounter mushrooms, moss aromas that don't add positives to the aromatic ledger; I move on. Entry is regrettably unpleasant, off-balance between fruit/abv/acidity; midpalate echoes all the flaws of the entry. Another sorry case of "If it's 'craft,' it's gotta be great." Woefully awful and I see no potential here whatsoever.
2014 Rating: ★/Not Recommended

Dujardin Fine VSOP Brandy (Germany) 40% abv, $25.
Burnt-orange/rust color; ideal clarity for a pleasing appearance. Opening sniffs detect a truckload of candied fruit sweetness (pineapple, apricot, and raisin, especially) that doesn't

allow for any other fragrance except for marshmallow; second passes detect only the hard candy fruitiness that was so dominant in the initial nosing passes. Entry mirrors the conspicuous ambrosial bouquet in the overstuffed taste profile, which could use a bit of paring down and more acidity to tame the sugary aspect; midpalate shows no mercy on the sweetness scale. I think that there's an amiable brandy here somewhere beneath all the unctuous sweetness. It's not terrible, hence the second star, but it's almost a liqueur more than a brandy.
2015 Rating: ★★/Not Recommended

Dujardin Imperial VSOP Brandy (Germany) 40% abv, $24.

Bright, impeccably clear appearance; medium amber/topaz hue. First nosings offer a rounded, supple purity of fruit that is engaging, slightly like burnt match, and woody—I like it; after another seven minutes of air contact, the bouquet turns more cheese- and nougat-like, while maintaining the burnt match and oak resin background notes. Entry is simple, woody, soft cheese–like, grapy/fruity, and tart; midpalate is toasty and like baked fruits. Concludes brief in the throat, nicely acidic, and therefore fresh and woodier than in either the entry or the midpalate.
2015 Rating: ★★★/Recommended

E&J XO Brandy (USA) 40% abv, $15.

Brilliant copper color; excellent clarity. This first aroma emits pleasurable scents of spiced fruits (pear especially), old leather/men's club, allspice, tobacco; later hits feature oaky vanilla, sawdust. Entry is delicately sweet, fruity, ripe, zesty, spicy; midpalate mirrors all the attributes of the entry and piles on caramel, nougat, almond paste, vanilla bean, cake frosting. Lots happening here and a terrific price/quality ratio brandy that's always been good and ten years down the road is improving to the point where it's now riding the three star/four star fence.
2014 Rating: ★★★/Recommended

E&J VS Brandy (USA) 40% abv, $11.

Pretty, bright topaz color; spotless purity. Out of the box I smell citrus, white grapes, candle wax; later sniffs pick up oak resin, old leather, caramel. Entry is fruity, ripe, delicately sweet, grapy; midpalate echoes all the entry aspects and adds a nutty element. Aftertaste is clean, uncomplicated, balanced, tasty.
2014 Rating: ★★★/Recommended

E&J VSOP Brandy (USA) 40% abv, $13.

Burnished orange color; totally sediment-free. I detect a somewhat closed aromatic profile up front and decide to give it more aeration time; later whiffs pick up distant, indistinct baking spices, some fruitiness. Entry is confectioner-shop sweet, sugary, mildly pleasant; midpalate features a bit of harshness that's metallic, and therefore cancels out the gently sweet opening taste. Perfectly drinkable in its averageness, but that midpalate rawness shoots this one down for me every time.
2014 Rating: ★★/Not Recommended

Germain-Robin Heirloom Apple Brandy (USA) 40% abv, $65.

Brilliant amber color; spotless purity. Initial whiffs encounter crisp aromas of red apple peel, cinnamon, allspice, candle wax, apple butter; later inhalations detect oak sawdust, oak plank, black pepper notes that do not overshadow the fruitiness. Entry is nicely astringent, tart, resiny; midpalate offers dark toffee, cocoa bean, maple. Finish is narrowly focused on the astringency of the apple.

2015 Rating: ★ ★ ★/Recommended

Germain-Robin Select Barrel XO Alambic Brandy (USA) 40% abv, $120.

Bronze/cinnamon color; spotless purity. Initially, I detect nuances of yeast, bread dough, honey wheat toast, English muffin, thyme; next sniffing round I pick up prune Danish, bear claw pastry, brown sugar, hazelnut scents that are delightful. Entry is round, supple, gently sweet, oily/buttery in texture; midpalate is where the grapiness emerges in a dried, raisiny manner that's both tart and succulent. Aftertaste carries with it the depth and character of pot still brandy. Still shines brightly as the guiding North Star of the American distilling night sky.

2020 Rating: ★ ★ ★ ★/Highly Recommended

Germain-Robin Single Barrel V384 Muscat Alambic Brandy (USA) 44% abv, $150.

Bright topaz color; flawless clarity. Smells heartily and succulently of orange blossom, tangerine, bergamot, lemongrass; further aeration brings out tannic fragrances of black tea, black pepper, lanolin; an aromatic, ambrosial feast. Entry is intensely grapy, moderately citrusy, tart, slightly mineral-like; midpalate soars into the flavor stratosphere with toasty, resiny, doughy tastes that underline the grapy, citrusy fruitiness. Finishes chewy, satiny, more oaky than fruity, satisfying. Kept reminding me of Earl Grey tea.

2015 Rating: ★ ★ ★ ★/Highly Recommended

Germain-Robin Small Blend No. 1 Alambic Brandy (USA) 41.8% abv, $245.

A mere 220 bottles. Pinot noir (1990) and French colombard (1983) grapes. Pretty saffron/amber color; impeccable purity. There are distant perfumes of ripe grapes, old saddle leather, old library, pipe tobacco, sweet peas in this understated, mature aroma; secondary whiffs discover evidence of rancio (rare for domestic brandy), old oak, mushrooms, truffle oil, dates. Entry is fig-like, sweet, pruny, earthy; midpalate soars to lofty heights of alembic brandy perfection in delicate waves of dried fruits (banana, plums, grapes), cigar tobacco, brown butter, oaky vanilla. Finishes stately, long, loaded with oak and dried tropical fruits. Newcomers to craft distilling: take heed of this for this is where you want to go in time. Dazzling, complete integration.

2016 Rating: ★ ★ ★ ★ ★/Highest Recommendation

Gran Duque de Alba Oro Solera Gran Reserva Brandy de Jerez (Spain) 40% abv, $150.

Bole/burnt umber color; pristine purity. Opening aroma is ripe, grapy, prune-like, gentian-like, and a bit caramelized; secondary inhalations encounter more dried fruits, including apricot and banana plus a back note of high-cocoa-content dark chocolate. Entry is chockfull of bakery and coffee-shop flavors and spices, including coffee bean, espresso, cacao, gentian, mace, and candied walnut; midpalate reflects the entry impressions perfectly, adding only a touch of wormwood-like taste. Aftertaste is long, bright, and fig-like.

2018 Rating: ★ ★ ★ ★/Highly Recommended

Gran Duque de Alba Solera Gran Reserva Brandy de Jerez (Spain) 40% abv, $46.

Umber/sienna color; flawless purity. Immediately, I pick up deeply honey-like scents that are fruity (dates, figs), succulent, and intensely ripe; secondary inhalations detect dark chocolate and caramel notes that accentuate the dried fruits. Entry is elegant, juicy, plummy, and only moderately sweet; midpalate is more pruny and raisiny than plummy and loaded with other tastes such as pipe tobacco, BBQ sauce, charred meat (pork or beef brisket), and cocoa butter. Aftertaste is memorable for its length and depth and succulence. This brandy took off at midpalate to crescendo in the finish.
2018 Rating: ★ ★ ★ ★/Highly Recommended

Gran Duque de Alba XO Solera Gran Reserva Brandy de Jerez (Spain) 40% abv, $46.

Espresso-brown color; flawless clarity. First nosings detect intensely bittersweet aromas that are reminiscent of citrus curd, slate/flint, chewing tobacco, dried pineapple, and figs; secondary whiffs unearth deeper layers of black raisin, dates, and charcoal. Entry is densely textured, the definition of "bittersweet," very pruny, and black tea–like; midpalate impressions mirror those of the entry, adding layers of nuttiness and coffee bean–like waxiness. Finishes long, bitter, bean-like, with the final taste impressions having no fruit aspect at all and that loses it one rating star.
2018 Rating: ★ ★ ★/Recommended

Hector Legrand XO Brandy (France) 40% abv, $38.

The fetching color is mahogany and suggestive of tawny port of at least twenty years old. First aromas include dried fig, mushroom, clove, and dried tobacco leaf; allowing it to have another seven to eight minutes of aeration, the bouquet adds considerable depth in the forms of prune, mincemeat, old library, leather chair, cigar box, and lychee; this is an animated bouquet that's delightfully bittersweet and baked. Entry shows as much baked pear and nectarine as it does black raisins and prunes to make for satisfying early-on tasting; midpalate exposes more of the wood component, mostly as baking spices, especially vanilla, mace, and clove, that meld well with the baked fruits. Finish is between medium and long in length and offers a pastry-like, mince pie–like finale that's intensely sweet. Had the aftertaste held back on the sugar rush, I'd have given it a fourth rating star. Lots of early stage quality here that gets a bit compromised by the density of the final-act super sweetness.
2017 Rating: ★ ★ ★/Recommended

Ivy Mountain Peach Brandy (USA) 40% abv, $60.

Flax color isn't spotlessly pure, but close enough not to cause ordinary visual concern. First nasal passes pick up delectable, snappy fragrances of just-ripened white peach, peach peel, and peach compote—suffice it to say that it carries off the peach presence more than adequately; second passes find that the peachiness turns slightly riper and more concentrated. Entry is nicely tart and acidic, giving off a fresh, crisp flavor that's true to the source; midpalate is complex and more like peach jam or, better, peach hard candy. Finishes lean, crisp, alluring, tart. Rather than being sweet, fat, liqueur-like and/or unctuous, Ivy Mountain is austere, acidic, fresh, and genuine.
2015 Rating: ★ ★ ★ ★/Highly Recommended

Laird's 86 Straight Applejack (USA) 43% abv, $25.

Harvest gold/wheat-field color; impeccably pure. I like this nuanced opening fragrance that's crisply apple-like, juicy, and round, with delicate hints of allspice and clove; secondary passes after more aeration discover sleek, lithe aromas of bakery spice (now it's clove only) and baked apple/apple turnover. Entry reflects the lithe character of the bouquet as the texture features a wafer-thin oiliness that lends a bit of structure to the apple turnover taste; midpalate remains delicate in its flavor approach as the foundational off-dry taste of baked apple is supported by the medium-weight texture. Nice job.

2018 Rating: ★ ★ ★/Recommended

Laird's Applejack (USA) 40% abv, $22.

Thirty-five percent apple brandy and sixty-five percent neutral grain spirits (NGS). Pretty sandy-brown color; excellent clarity. Initial whiffs come across as a little bit spicy and fruity but almost like waxed fruit, and there's a subtle caramel quality that sneaks up on you; secondary inhalations after more air contact offer a buttermilk biscuit–like aroma that's doughy and yeasty, with just a smidgen of tropical fruit (ripe banana mostly). Entry is harsh, mineral-like, and tanky, there're no other words for the first flavors, and those impressions for me are damning; midpalate exhibits a little more taste enhancement, but there's the underlying raw spirit harshness that dominates through the aftertaste. The aroma is somewhat doable, but the in-mouth stages are sorely lacking, rough, and raw.

2018 Rating: ★/Not Recommended

Laird's Bottled-in-Bond Straight Apple Brandy (USA) 50% abv, $32.

Sinopia color; flawlessly pure. The spice elements (nutmeg, clove) in the initial whiffs are understated but firmly in place as they accentuate the ripeness of the red-apple base aroma; secondary sniffs pick up deeper scents, especially vanilla/vanillin (from oak?), lead pencil/minerals, and apple peel. Entry is sweeter than the nose implies and toasty, ripe, toffee-like, and juicy; midpalate shows flashes of buttery texture that underlines the apple pastry–like flavor profile that's now tart, piquant, and pleasantly astringent. Ends up a touch more astringent than it needs to be in the aftertaste, and that knocks off a rating star. Still recommendable, however, on the strength of the bouquet, entry, and midpalate.

2018 Rating: ★ ★ ★/Recommended

Laird's Jersey Lightning Apple Brandy (USA) 50% abv, $24.

Clear as rainwater, sediment-free appearance. I like the up-front aroma, which is neither fancy nor elegant but rather nicely apple-like, maybe even a bit pear-like, and straightforward; the no-frills bouquet opens up more in the secondary nosings, as the waxy apple scent grows in potency. Entry is sweeter, riper than I thought it would be, and that brings along a bigger baked apple presence that's quite pleasing; midpalate point finds the abv getting into the act as the alcohol starts to prickle on the tongue and warm in the throat, creating a nice sensation that buttresses the apple flavor. Finishes very ripe, fresh, a little raw, but that's okay considering its status. A pleasing alternative to white dog whiskey.

2018 Rating: ★ ★ ★/Recommended

Laird's Old 7½ Year Old Apple Brandy (USA) 40% abv, $40.

Topaz/sandy-brown color; immaculate purity. Up-front aromas include toasted wheat bread, toasted marshmallow, baked apple that's been spiced with cinnamon, and apple butter; secondary inhalations mirror the first passes, adding only a hint of black pepper. Entry seems drier than the aroma, as the frontline flavor is baked apple, but the underlying tastes of nutmeg, peanut, and candied tropical fruits add a luster to the whole experience; midpalate finds the various components merging into a single flavor that's tart, slightly caramel-like, toasted, and akin to dried apple. Finishes long, roasted, and a lot like apple butter. A yummy, perfectly matured American apple brandy.

2018 Rating: ★ ★ ★ ★/Highly Recommended

Laird's Rare 12 Year Old Apple Brandy (USA) 54% abv, $75.

Gorgeous auburn/henna color; pristinely clean. Initial aromatic impressions include tight, earthy, elemental aromas of tree bark, cinnamon, toffee, coffee bean, lead pencil, and distant apple; later inhalations after more aeration unearth scents of oaky resins, tree sap, burnt apple, apple peel, and pear. Entry is heavily toasted, marshmallow-like, bread-like, and intensely woody; midpalate at last introduces the apple aspect, but it's rather burnt and roasted, and as such I feel it's a bit lost amidst the char. Finishes cleanly, astringent, and baked apple–like.

2018 Rating: ★ ★ ★/Recommended

Lepanto OV Solera Gran Reserva Oloroso Viejo Brandy de Jerez (Spain) 40% abv, $70.

Burnt umber color; superb purity. Up front, I get delicately spiced aromas of marzipan, praline, chocolate custard, and chocolate cream pie; later whiffs pick up toasted bread, prunes, caramelized orchard fruits, black cherry, and fudge. Entry is dry, toasty, and akin to caramelized onion and/or deeply sautéed mushroom, but the fact is this taste profile never strays far from prunes/black plums; midpalate has a flint-like stoniness that keeps the primary flavor very dry and acidic, making my mouth pucker a bit. Aftertaste is pipe tobacco–like, earthy, and vegetal without ever losing the bone-dry core flavor; and is very extended. A significant departure from the frontline Lepanto, which is ambrosial.

2018 Rating: ★ ★ ★ ★/Highly Recommended

Lepanto P.X. Solera Gran Reserva Pedro Ximénez Brandy de Jerez (Spain) 40% abv, $70.

Maroon/henna color; pristine clarity. Owns a gentle, elegant opening aroma of holiday fruitcake, nuanced baking spices (cinnamon, clove), candied nuts, and dried fruits (prunes, pears); secondary inhalations detect a broader aromatic spectrum, including notes of honeysuckle, green tobacco, beeswax, and oak sap. Entry is drier, leaner than I thought it would be considering the PX factor, and there's a chewy aspect to the texture that's pleasing; midpalate stays the off-dry to bittersweet course that allows the pruny fruit to remain front and center. Aftertaste is medium long, grapy, semisweet, and keenly peppery/spicy.

2018 Rating: ★ ★ ★ ★/Highly Recommended

Lepanto Solera Gran Reserva Brandy de Jerez (Spain) 40% abv, $55.
Sienna color; pure and as sediment-free as possible. The opening aroma menu is staggering, as it includes everything from dates, figs, nougat, almond paste, mincemeat pie, candied walnut, and an entire array of baking spices, from vanilla bean to cinnamon to clove and mace; more aeration unleashes black raisins, dark toffee, honey, and cream sherry notes. Entry is heavily roasted/toasty, succulent, pruny, and brown-sugar bittersweet; midpalate is where the creamy texture and charred marshmallow aspects take flight. The finish is infinitely long, deeply bittersweet, prune-like, and satisfying.
2018 Rating: ★ ★ ★ ★/Highly Recommended

Lustau Solera Gran Reserva Brandy de Jerez (Spain) 40% abv, $38.
Chestnut/coffee color; superb clarity. Wow, the sultry smell of dates, figs, sea salt, chocolate, and brown butter scintillate the olfactory mechanism; later inhalations following more air contact detect a deep nuttiness that's almost like creamy peanut butter, plus lesser scents of pipe tobacco, tomato paste, BBQ sauce, and hoisin. Entry is semisweet, grapy, caramel- and fudge-like, viscous in texture, and like cake frosting; midpalate features the deep semisweet flavors of crème caramel/flan, toasted nuts, figs, dates, and black raisins. Ends very long, dense in structure, creamy, semisweet, grapy, and tight. An affordable beauty of an SGR BdJ.
2018 Rating: ★ ★ ★ ★/Highly Recommended

Lustau Solera Gran Reserva Finest Selection Brandy de Jerez (Spain) 40% abv, $50.
Maroon/sienna color; pristine clarity. The roundness of the opening aroma is fetching and addictive in its grape intensity, round in texture, more bittersweet than semisweet, doughy, and smelling strikingly reminiscent of Fig Newtons; mature, woody, and caramelized aromas abound in the second round of sniffing after more aeration time. Entry is lush, oily, deep in blankets of texture and semisweet flavors of figs, dates, candied almond, chocolate-covered coffee beans, toasted marshmallow, and dark chocolate; midpalate is a glorious example of masterful production as the taste profile offers more subtlety of flavor than seems reasonably possible, everything from crème brûlée to caramelized onion to sautéed mushrooms to dark cocoa to chocolate-covered cherries. This is not just a brandy but more of a feast for the senses. I can't imagine tasting a better Solera Gran Reserva Brandy de Jerez.
2018 Rating: ★ ★ ★ ★ ★/Highest Recommendation

Lustau Solera Reserva Brandy de Jerez (Spain) 40% abv, $25.
Tawny color; flawless clarity. Oh my, this first nosing pass discovers heavenly, multi-layered aromas of espresso, black coffee, chocolate-covered cherry, cherry cola, and roasted walnut; secondary whiffs after more air contact pick up stony/flinty aromas along with earthy scents of cherry pit, kiwi, star anise, and guava; this is a dense aroma fit for a solera gran reserva. Entry is incredibly buttery, oily, sinewy, and chewy in texture while the flavor profile boasts dynamic tastes of almond butter, dark caramel, roasted walnut, candied dried fruits (pineapple, pear), and honey; midpalate is frontloaded with fudge, dark caramel, butter brickle, and peanut oil flavors. Finishes long, creamy, viscous, semisweet, acidic, and tobacco-like. This brandy peaks in the latter aromatic phase and entry stage, then begins to

incrementally fade by midpalate, becoming quite restrained by the finish. Still, a good value for the low price.

2018 Rating: ★ ★ ★/Recommended

Maraska Sljivovica Slivovitz Old Plum Brandy (Croatia) 40% abv, $23.

The oyster color is so pale that it hardly is discernable; unblemished clarity. Initial whiffs detect pleasingly sour and peel-like scents of plum, with side fragrances of cooking spice (parsley); second passes reinforce the first impressions of moderately deep plumminess. Entry is light bodied, astringent, austere, yet properly plummy/orchard fruit–like in its tartness; midpalate mirrors the entry, adding a rounder touch in the texture that seems to make the taste profile riper and less lean, which leads to the satisfying, if brief, aftertaste.

2015 Rating: ★ ★ ★/Recommended

Mavem Grape Brandy (Portugal) 41% abv, $70.

Copper/burnt umber color; impeccably clean and clear. Initial nosing passes detect nut-like aromas, especially walnut as well as butter brickle and pistachio; secondary whiffs pick up notes of saddle leather, sawdust, and pine cone. Entry features a deeply grapy/raisiny flavor that's slightly burnt and caramelized; midpalate highlights the bittersweet character of the dried-fruit element that carries over into the pleasing aftertaste.

2018 Rating: ★ ★ ★/Recommended

Monteru Single Grape Chardonnay Brandy (France) 41.3% abv, $35.

Citrine/straw-yellow color; excellent clarity. I like the buttermilk biscuit–like initial aroma that's buttery and suggests flavors of cooking oil and pie crust; secondary inhalations reinforce the first whiffs by actually doubling down on the bakery dough aspect and the creamery butter while introducing a beeswax quality that's ripe and fruity. Entry features a waxy, oily texture that supports the dried-fruit/white-raisin core flavor; midpalate merges the various aspects into a singular flavor that's ripe, succulent, and grape- and quince-like. Ends on a deeply ripe and grapy note.

2018 Rating: ★ ★ ★/Recommended

Osocalis Apple Brandy (USA) 49% abv, $83.

Topaz/amber color; impeccable purity. I smell baked apple, apple strudel, yellow-apple fragrance in the initial inhalations; secondary nosings after more air contact reveal deeper, more apple peel–like astringency/zest and a just-picked freshness that's appealing. Entry is toasted, bittersweet, acidic, clean, crisp; midpalate mirrors the entry, adding a light touch of cinnamon spice. Finishes medium long, spicy, velvety, astringent, clean, lightly biting.

2015 Rating: ★ ★ ★/Recommended

Osocalis Rare Alambic Brandy (USA) 40% abv, $42.

Pretty amber/straw-yellow color; excellent clarity. This opening aroma is alive with vibrant dried-fruit aromas, including fig, dates, and black raisins; secondary whiffs pick up tantalizing scents of fruit salad, honey, English toffee, mincemeat. Entry is chockfull of ambrosial, bakery-shop flavors, most notably, baked pear, chocolate-covered raisins, clove, dried apricot, dried pineapple; midpalate reinforces the virtues of the entry by adding citrus zest, white pepper, cocoa bean, cake frosting. Deliciousness continues deep into the chewy finish. One of my favorite domestic pot still grape brandies.

2015 Rating: ★ ★ ★ ★/Highly Recommended

Osocalis XO Alambic Brandy (USA) 40% abv, $118.

Bright saffron/sepia color; flawless purity. There are awesome, atypical opening aromas of buttery oak, brown butter, treacle, saltwater taffy that, though seemingly incongruous, work in harmony for a unique brandy fragrance; later sniffs add traces of clove, cinnamon, candied apple to the aromatic mix. Entry is lusciously textured, intensely grapy, fruity sweet, toasty, oaky; midpalate features more of the fruit than spice as the candied apple, peach, plum, and dark grape vie for dominance. Concludes elegantly, buttery/creamy, toasted, woody, and succulent. A really handsome, mature domestic brandy that deserves a large, appreciative audience.

2015 Rating: ★ ★ ★ ★/Highly Recommended

Privateer International Distiller's Drawer Single Orchard Peach Brandy (USA) 42% abv, $48.

Attractive nine-karat-gold color; good-to-very good clarity. Opening nosings don't pick up much in the way of expected peach fragrance—in fact, there are only faint, incongruous hints of malted milk, steel tank, butcher's wax paper, and cotton fiber; allowing for more air contact, I let this sample rest for ten more minutes, but even that grace period can't jump-start the aroma, so I move on. Entry is only mildly orchard fruit–like as the flavor profile features more waxiness and fruit peel than actual pulp/meat; midpalate does highlight some pleasant fruit but not enough to make the $48 seem worthwhile. Finishes as modestly and nondescript as it begins. There's no major production flaw in this peach-based attempt other than it's merely a lackluster, vacant, rather hollow fruit brandy with some vague appeal.

2017 Rating: ★ ★/Not Recommended

Psenner Slivovitz Brandy (Italy) 40% abv, $39.

Silvery clear; sediment-free. The opening aroma is alive and vibrant with purple plum fragrance that's more juicy than either dried or ripe; secondary scents include plum peel, dry soil/arid desert, prickly pear, and a gentle plum meat freshness that's a joy to behold. Entry is fresh, pleasantly acidic, and therefore cleansing, tart yet just a deft touch sweet simultaneously; midpalate echoes the entry as the taste profile accelerates in the acidity department, making the flavor profile squeaky clean, slightly sour, yet curiously ripe and utterly tasty. Aftertaste is clean as a whistle and zesty/tangy. A winner, this one.

2016 Rating: ★ ★ ★ ★/Highly Recommended

Psenner Wild Raspberry Brandy (Italy) 40% abv, $39.

Transparent, colorless; impeccably clear. First inhalations after the pour are treated to deeply ripe fragrances of raspberry and blackberry in an almost seed-like manner that's more bittersweet than flat-out sweet—I like this first fragrance because it highlights the bitter tanginess of real raspberry; second whiffs detect even riper, more jammy aromas that are now sweeter than in the initial nosings but succulent and fresh. Entry is sweet,

intensely raspberry-like, juicy, jammy, properly tart, and genuine; midpalate is even more preserves-like than in the entry, and that deepens the flavor concentration. Aftertaste echoes the midpalate and is very long for a fruit brandy.
2016 Rating: ★ ★ ★ ★/Highly Recommended

Psenner Williams Pear Brandy (Italy) 40% abv, $39.
Pewter tint; perfect purity. First nosing passes are delicately pear-like, as the major aromatic thrust is on the pear meat/pulp rather than the skin, and is therefore pleasantly spicy and tart; secondary sniffs pick up more intensity on the pear pulp/meat, which makes this stage juicy and almost floral. Entry is ripe, patently pear-like, delightfully juicy, but not at all sweet as it is, in fact, more tangy and tart and mineral-like; midpalate mirrors the entry as the peariness turns densely juicy and sweeter than the entry, then the midpalate evolves into the finish which is sap-like, a bit flinty, but wholly delicious.
2016 Rating: ★ ★ ★ ★/Highly Recommended

Rochelt Wachauer Marille Aged 6 Years Apricot Brandy (Austria) 50% abv, $325/375 ml.
As clear and pristine as springwater. The opening nosings pick up vibrant fragrances of apricot skin, fruit salad, winter holiday fruitcake, slate, and apricot preserves; following more aeration, the bouquet sustains the high degree of piquancy, offering tangy aromas of apricot-filled pastry, green leaf tea, vine leaves, minerals, and limestone/flint. Entry taste is dry, acidic, and therefore cleansing, just a touch fiery as the 100 proof serves notice, and top loaded with ripe apricot flavor. Midpalate stage turns minerally, green tea–like, and stone-like, as the taste profile turns squeaky dry and metal-like, eschewing the apricot core in favor of fruit stone and green tea bitterness. Concludes medium long, stony, and totally dry. Had the midpalate and finish not turned away from the apricot foundation, this eau-de-vie might have gotten a fifth rating star.
2017 Rating: ★ ★ ★ ★/Highly Recommended

Sainte Louise Pale and Old Brandy (France) 43% abv, $20.
Blended, aged, and bottled in France. One hundred percent pot still distillation of a high majority of French eaux-de-vie that are supplemented with eaux-de-vie from Italy and Spain. Rich, burnt-orange/mahogany color; excellent purity. First inhalations pick up plenty of vibrant grape jam, baked nectarine, kiwi, baked peach, and Danish pastry fragrances that are assertive without being aggressive; allowing for another few minutes of air contact, the aroma opens up even more, offering tantalizing, off-dry scents of lemon drop, orange blossom, almond, and clove. Entry is supple, silky, gently sweet, and fruit-salad ripe, with tangy background flavors of caramel and fresh honey from the hive; midpalate mirrors the entry phase, featuring now a toasted orchard-fruit flavor that's baked, delicately spiced, and caramelized. Finishes long, ripe, balanced, and deeply satisfying. Applications in abundance for neat service in a tulip-shaped wine glass or in a classic brandy cocktail, like the Sidecar or Vieux Carré. A phenomenal value that outshines more than a few young VS and even VSOP cognacs and armagnacs.
2017 Rating: ★ ★ ★ ★/Highly Recommended

Schladerer Himbeergeist Raspberry Brandy (Germany) 42% abv, $36.

Attractive limpid/colorless appearance; there is sediment seen under the lamp. Opening nose is pleasingly viny and bramble-like and leafy more than fruity or berry-like, and that's what I like about it so much; aeration stimulates more in the way of real, barely ripe raspberry fragrance. Entry is lean, fruity, but hardly sweet, and is really more ripe than sweet or compote-like; midpalate surges ahead with real-deal raspberry flavor that's acidic, tart, ripe, and fresh. Finishes gracefully, gently, and brief. Delicate doesn't begin to tell the story.

2015 Rating: ★★★★/Highly Recommended

Schladerer Kirschwasser Cherry Brandy (Germany) 42% abv, $42.

Translucent appearance; sediment-free. Again, as with the Himbeergeist, I encounter vegetation, leaves, vines, tree limbs, and only mildly cherry fruit in the opening round of sniffing; secondary whiffs detect much more in the way of cherry fruit. Entry is tart, lean, acidic, clean, crisp, and nicely cherry-like, but not overly so; midpalate is delicate, ripe, fruity, and beautifully balanced. Finishes medium long, moderately juicy, tart, and astringent. It's all about the understatement and underlying foundation of clean spirit.

2015 Rating: ★★★★/Highly Recommended

Seven Tails XO Brandy (France) 41.8% abv, $40.

Pumpkin-orange color; ideal clarity. Right from the first whiffs, I pick up faint suggestions of baking spices, mostly clove and allspice, that underpin the grape-skin core fragrance; aeration doesn't open up a great deal more of aroma. As opposed to the stingy bouquet, the entry flavors are generous, round, very near rich, and semidry; midpalate lifts the flavor profile to pleasant heights, as the tastes run a narrow pathway that includes baked pear, clove, marshmallow, and brown sugar. Finishes quite long, dry as lead pencil, and tangy with clove flavor.

2019 Rating: ★★★/Recommended

St. George Pear Brandy (USA) 40% abv, $40.

Impeccably pure; translucent. Ripe, but dry pear fragrance doesn't necessarily charge from the glass as much as it gently wafts in succulent waves that are zesty/peel-like in the initial inhalations; later sniffs are juicier, plumper. Entry is unbelievably authentic, like spiced pear and true to source; midpalate is lean, tangy (cinnamon), intense, concentrated solely on pear essence. Magnificent. A definitive domestic, world-class pear eau-de-vie.

2014 Rating: ★★★★★/Highest Recommendation

St. George Raspberry Brandy (USA) 40% abv, $40.

Pristine; pure. Sweet, ripe, brambly, genuine raspberry scent in the opening whiffs; later on, the leafy/brambly fragrance emerges as the dominant aroma, which makes it all the more lovely. Entry is dry, narrowly focused on the raspberry, juicy; midpalate echoes the entry. Aftertaste is long, substantial in texture but neither oily nor fat, fresh, keenly raspberry-like. Another distilling classic from the laudable wizards at St. George, to whom all lovers of quality spirits are indebted.

2014 Rating: ★★★★★/Highest Recommendation

St. Rémy XO French Brandy (France) 40% abv, $20.

Sinopia/mahogany color; superb clarity. Up front, I pick up distinctive notes of caramel, Fig Newton, mincemeat, and nougat; secondary whiffs detect bakery-like fragrances of dried dates, dark chocolate, carob, and fudge brownie. Entry is sweet, prune-like, cocoa-like, and clean; midpalate features flavors that echo the entry phase, adding traces of oloroso sherry and maple. Ends up medium long, semisweet, and pleasant overall. Good value for money, but don't mistake this for either a cognac or armagnac just because of its French origin.
2019 Rating: ★ ★ ★/Recommended

The Witch of Agnesi 1799 Small Batch 5 Year Old American Brandy (USA) 40% abv, $59.

A domestic brandy produced by the company owned by Francis Ford Coppola. Gamboge color; there's a slight dullness, a trace of haze in the appearance. I like the first nosing impression, which is biscuity, a touch graham cracker–like, a little spicy (caraway), and citrus fruit tart; following more air contact, the fruit (lemon, white raisins) element accelerates, becoming the dominant scent. Entry is highly acidic, meaning that the fresh fruit aspect suffers under the astringent weight of the acute acidity; midpalate offers only minor fruit that is lost within the acidic storm. Deteriorates from phase to phase, making rotgut look appealing.
2019 Rating: ★/Not Recommended

Torres 10 Imperial Gran Reserva Brandy (Spain) 40% abv, $20.

Spanish brandy Cataluña style. Maroon color; pristine clarity. Big-hearted, opulent aromas of walnut, nougat, almond paste, green tobacco leaves, and dates welcome the olfactory sense in the initial inhalations; later whiffs pick up truckloads of bakery aromas, including Danish pastry, cinnamon bun, holiday fruitcake, dried apricot, candied almond, and baked pear; there is no shortage of aromas here. Entry is chockfull of roasted nut flavors, as well as black tea, pipe tobacco, vanilla bean, coffee bean/espresso; midpalate picks up where the entry left off, featuring toasty, roasted, raisiny, prune-like flavors that come wrapped in a thick coat of texture. Aftertaste is slightly smoky, heavily oaked, more bittersweet than ripe or sweet, and unabashedly delicious and brawny. Wow.
2017 Rating: ★ ★ ★ ★/Highly Recommended

Torres 15 Imperial Reserva Privada Brandy (Spain) 40% abv, $33.

Rusty sienna color; flawless purity. This opening nose is sedate when compared to that of the robust, in-your-face Torres 10, offering melded, understated scents of black raisin, dates, figs, and sawdust—where the 10 is bakery-shop hearty, the 15 is deft, elegant, yet substantial in its potency, using a softer voice; later inhalations discover integrated fragrances of dates, nutmeg, allspice, oak plank, and hard cheese. Entry is stunningly elegant, harmonious, and honeyed, giving the clear impression of superior distillation and wood management; midpalate highlights dense yet nimble flavors of coffee bean, dark chocolate, caramel, marzipan, meringue, and chocolate-covered cherries. Concludes long, sophisticated, opulent, and utterly luscious from start to finish. Scrumptious.
2017 Rating: ★ ★ ★ ★ ★/Highest Recommendation

POMACE BRANDIES–WORLD

Some famous grape brandies made in Europe, most notably in Italy and France, are considered "pomace brandies." Pomace is comprised of vinicultural leftovers, meaning the grape seeds, stems, and skins from winemaking. Pomace brandies, made around the world, have existed for many centuries. The French refer to them as *marc,* Bolivians call them *singani,* Chileans *aguardiente,* Portuguese *aguardente,* Spanish *orujo,* Iranians *araq,* Romanians *tescovina,* Greeks *tsipouro,* and Italians *grappa.* In centuries past these local spirits were held in low esteem by outsiders due to their rustic nature. Today, more than a few of these are viewed as delicacies, with grappa and marc especially considered world-class spirits.

Grappa–Italy

Grappa started out as a rural alcoholic beverage, produced in the late autumn after Italy's grape harvest and the making of regional wine. Though there exist some vague accounts of grappa being made by a physician in Padua in the fifteenth century CE, the initial producer of renown was Bartolo Nardini in the late 1700s. Winemakers took the partially fermented by-product of wine production, the leftover juicy grape pulp, seeds, and skins, known as "pomace," mixed it with water, and sold it to traveling distillers who boiled the pomace in small, mobile copper pot stills.

Long the abrasive tipple of the peasant population that farmed Italy's countryside, its creators fancied grappa in any number of applications: as a relaxing, mood-altering elixir to soothe the ills of their rigorous agricultural lifestyle; as a heating fuel; as a vitamin supplement; a restorative for weary pilgrims; a cure for impotence; and even as a medicine for the frail and infirm. Around 1813, a Florentine distiller named Baglioni added metal plates to his still to create a column still that sped up the process.

Gulping down old-fashioned, pedal-to-the-metal grappa, though, was reason enough to stay hale and hearty. At 50 to 60 percent alcohol, the likely strength for many locally made grappas, all except the most robust country dwellers would be easily and rapidly anesthetized, despite the terrible taste. Flavorings, like honey, flowers, and herbs, were commonly added to primitive grappas to help mitigate their oily, harsh flavor. Sometimes water was added to lessen the impact of the elevated degrees of alcohol. By the eighteenth century, grappa was being produced in most provinces on the Italian peninsula.

Realizing that the only way to combat grappa's rowdy image was to modernize and change customary production methods, a handful of Italy's foremost master distillers and wine producers, led by the Nonino family (Friuli), the Bocchino family (Piedmont), Angelo Gaja (Piedmont), and Jacopo Poli (Veneto), decided to place greater emphasis on quality. Their goal, independent of each other, was to alter the international perception of their native distillate by making grappa less provincial and more cosmopolitan.

By the twentieth century, double distillation was reinstated in many grappa distilleries. The Nonino family was the first to introduce single-grape-variety grappas, refered to as *monovitigno*, a practice that has gained other proponents. Distilling the pomace of individual grape types separately rather than mixing those of multiple grape varieties together was one of the most critical in a string of innovations in the last century.

Sublimely complex yet approachable, contemporary Italian grappas typically range in strength from 40 to 45 percent alcohol. The best are produced from single grapes cultivated on single estates. A growing number are matured in wood barrels made of oak, juniper, birch, ash, cherry, or acacia. Some are flavored with natural flavorings such as chamomile, rue leaves, quinine, anise, pine nuts, rhubarb, almonds, cinnamon, mint, cloves, juniper, and caraway seeds.

No longer the favored spirit of only alpine northern Italy (Friuli-Venezia Giulia, Trentino-Alto Adige, Veneto, and Piedmont), fine grappas hail from such central and southern provinces as Tuscany, Umbria, Campania, Sardinia, Sicily, Basilicata, and The Marches.

There also exist more than a few oak-aged grape brandies hailing from Italy. Among the most famous include Fratelli Branca Stravecchio (also makes Fernet-Branca), which was first introduced in 1888, and Francoli Oak-Aged Grappa. Many of the established grappa producers in Italy's north also oak age a share of their grappas.

Marc de Bourgogne–France

Marc de Bourgogne is the pomace brandy produced in France's Burgundy region from the leftovers of vinification, namely the seeds, skins, stems, and pulp. Marc de Bourgogne has an official AOC designation. Marc has label designations, but all marcs must be oak aged for at least two years. More mature varieties are:

Vieille: aged at least four years

Très Vieille: minimum six years

Hors d'Age: minimum ten years

Singani–Bolivia

Singani is the national drink of Bolivia. A pomace brandy, singani, which now has its own Denomination of Origin, is made exclusively from the seductively aromatic muscat of Alexandria grape, grown in high-elevation vineyards. The legend says that it was first made circa 1530 in the Andes Mountains.

Alexander Cabernet Grappa (Italy) 40% abv, $40.

Silvery clean and pristine; colorless. Wow, this opening nose is bountiful, buoyant, and crackling with red-grape acidity and ripeness, along with a type of waxiness that's very grape skin–like; secondary inhalations after more aeration encounter foxy, grape must–like aromas that remind me of Crayola crayon wax, wormwood, cypress, and gentian. Entry is keenly ripe, juicy, firm in texture, and altogether delicious; midpalate echoes the entry phase, adding small bits of black pepper, grape pulp, and black plum flavors. Ends on a high note of zesty acidity that's cleansing, semisweet, and tight.

2018 Rating: ★ ★ ★ ★/Highly Recommended

Alexander Grappolo (Italy) 40% abv, $100.

Void of color; spotless purity. I immediately like the deep, intense grape must/grape skin perfume that's tannic, damp soil–like, waxy, and desert dry; more air contact releases scents of pear skin, vines, and parchment. Entry is delicate, arid, dry yet ripe, with red-grape intensity that crescendos in the midpalate stage that's juicy, tart, highly acidic, astringent, tannic, cleansing, and plummy/date-like. Ends dry and stony. An all-around winner in large measure for its deep grape character and the pristine freshness brought by the distillation.

2018 Rating: ★ ★ ★ ★/Highly Recommended

Alma Toscana Brunello Montalcino Grappa (Italy) 43% abv, $43.

Silvery colorless and perfectly clean. I smell the lovely, spartan essence of brunello grapes at the height of purity—this is a bouquet of flinty/stony beauty and simplicity; later inhalations pick up deeper acidity and grape-skin bitterness that make the aromatics even lovelier; a textbook Tuscan grappa bouquet. Entry is straightforward yet complex in its intricacy of flavor as levels of taste present themselves in thrilling order of potency, first ripe grapes, then grape skins, then juicy freshness, then acute acidity that holds it all together—oh my, what a beauty; midpalate reflects the majesty of the entry, adding mineral texture and oils. Finishes long, floral, off-dry, clean as a whistle, regal, and beguiling. A clinic of distillation skill.

2016 Rating: ★ ★ ★ ★ ★/Highest Recommendation

Alma Toscana Chianti Classico Riserva Grappa (Italy) 43% abv, $43.

Gamboge/old gold color; pristine, sediment-free clarity. I like the opening aroma because it has a dense grapiness that mingles nicely with the light touches of oaky resin and viny sap; later sniffs reveal an earthy, woodsy fragrance that underscores the grapes and light woodiness. Entry features a resiny/oily texture that's totally dry as the grape/fruit is eclipsed by the wood resins; midpalate is slightly riper and juicier, but only marginally. The quality of distillation is present but, while recommendable, I don't find this grappa as rewarding and inspiring as the great Brunello, or the wonderful Morellino di Scansano, or Vin Santo.

2016 Rating: ★ ★ ★/Recommended

Alma Toscana Morellino di Scansano Grappa (Italy) 40% abv, $39.

Impeccable purity; colorless transparency. This aroma plays the game close to its figurative vest as the initial inhalations don't pick up much scent other than beeswax and dry soil; secondary whiffs add nuances of parchment, sesame seed, palm oil, vegetable oil. Entry is far more animated than the aroma as grapy, fruity, plummy tastes throw a surprise banquet for the taste buds; midpalate is lush, raisiny, grapy, gently sweet but neither syrupy nor oily.

Aftertaste provides a moment of grapy splendor that almost pushes this grappa into five star territory. If the aroma had been more vigorous and generous, a fifth star would have been bestowed. As it is, four stars are fair.
2016 Rating: ★ ★ ★ ★/Highly Recommended

Alma Toscana Moscato Grappa (Italy) 40% abv, $39.

Crystalline clarity and colorless. Owns a light-fingered touch of orange blossom fragrance in the opening sniffs that is more dewy than citrusy; more air contact releases scents of fresh spring garden, candle wax, and parchment. Entry is pleasingly ripe and orangey in that particularly moscato manner; midpalate honors the entry findings by staying the moscato/fruit salad course all the way into the juicy aftertaste. Good and clean, but not nearly as complex as the Brunello or Morellino di Scansano. This I say with a note of disappointment as a true devotee of moscato.
2016 Rating: ★ ★ ★/Recommended

Alma Toscana Vin Santo Grappa (Italy) 40% abv, $43.

Flawlessly clean and pure; colorless. There's a keen waxiness to this opening aroma that's very grape skin–like and nearly seed-like; later sniffs detect more grapes and ripeness than in the first inhalations. Entry is compellingly rich, textured, off-dry, and chewy; midpalate offers a sense of intensely ripe grapiness that's really pleasant and sensuous. Aftertaste is medium long, fruity, grapy, ripe, floral.
2016 Rating: ★ ★ ★ ★/Highly Recommended

Bocchino Carlo Bocchino Riserva Grappa (Italy) 43% abv, $n/a.

Saffron/cocoa-brown color; superb clarity. Up front, I pick up notes of chalk, calcareous soil, limestone aromas; more aeration doesn't pry open the magic box of aromatics by much so I move on to the in-mouth stages. Entry is sour, more pear-like than grapy at first, but then the taste profile shifts gears turning grapier in the midpalate, as well as ripe, fibrous, green tobacco–like, and vegetal/vinous/bramble-like by the time the aftertaste starts. Finishes intensely woody, medium-degree tannic, astringent, vinous, and bitter.
2018 Rating: ★ ★ ★/Recommended

Bocchino della Cantina Privata Grappa Moscato Sauternes Cask Finish Grappa (Italy) 42% abv, $n/a.

Marigold/earth yellow color; as pure as it can possibly be. This opening nose is so different from all other grappas I've recently evaluated, as it evokes subtle fragrances of pear peel, dried orange rind, honey, and jasmine; more aeration time stimulates further fragrances, such as kiwi, prickly pear, and pomelo. Entry is herbal (chamomile, orange pekoe tea), semi-sweet, spicy (black pepper, mainly), and acidic; midpalate goes even sweeter as the dense grapiness comes to the surface, buoyed in part by the tannic oakiness that is an undercurrent presence. Aftertaste is bittersweet, oaky, astringent, and highly complex.
2018 Rating: ★ ★ ★ ★/Highly Recommended

Clear Creek Distillery Cavatappi Nebbiolo Grappa (USA) 40% abv, $45.

Silvery colorless; impeccable purity. Wow, I like this delicately sweet first aroma of ripe fruit, especially grapes but also red plums; secondary inhalations pick up various supplementary aromas such as grape skins, dried violets, leather. Entry is sophisticated, deeply grapy, nearly jammy in that regard; midpalate is round, supple, raisiny, pruny, deliciously dry all through the aftertaste. Echoes Italian grappas in its rusticity.

2014 Rating: ★ ★ ★ ★/Highly Recommended

Clear Creek Distillery Orange Muscat Grappa (USA) 40% abv, $45.

This grappa shows a slight pewter shade to it that's pretty; flawless in terms of purity. Offers a scrumptious, fully evolved opening fragrance, rich and floral (orange blossom), slightly tangy and spiced (most like mace), and entirely appealing; secondary flinty scents include brambles/leaves, green vegetation—a gorgeous, graceful bouquet of the first rank. Entry owns a silky texture; gentle, high acid, and therefore refreshing surface flavor; but this is buttressed throughout the midpalate stage by a firm, creamy ripeness that's moderately orangey, flowery, succulent. Finishes extended, zesty, slightly metallic.

2014 Rating: ★ ★ ★ ★/Highly Recommended

Clear Creek Distillery Pinot Noir Grappa (USA) 40% abv, $45.

Clear and pristine as mountain springwater; colorless with accompanying, widely dispersed clingy bubbles. Smells up front of grape must, grape skins and seeds, in general, grape pulp, and is totally dry and husk-like; in second whiffs, the spirit emerges in fiber-like scents such as cardboard, cotton fiber, parchment. Entry is completely sandy dry, dry to the palate, metallic, coin-like, flinty; midpalate mirrors the entry to a tee as it dries out the palate completely. Ends on an acidic, highly tart note. Felt that this grappa was kind of tired and washed out.

2014 Rating: ★ ★/Not Recommended

Germain-Robin Viognier Grappa (USA) 43.2% abv, $85.

Clear and clean as rainwater. This opening aroma is steely, flinty, slightly baked, beany, and a little bit sulfur-like; not terribly grapy in the second pass either, the aromatic focus is more on burnt matches, dusty soil, vines, leaves, vegetation after additional air contact. Entry is engagingly fruity, almost peach-like, astringent, tart; midpalate reflects the entry, adding a more demonstrative aspect of orchard fruit that lasts deep into the savory aftertaste that's dry and moderately oily. If you are stuck in neutral about grappa in general, try this domestic grappa and you'll become a fan.

2014 Rating: ★ ★ ★ ★/Highly Recommended

Il Grigio da San Felice del Chianti Classico Affinata in Barriques Grappa (Italy) 42% abv, $55.

The straw-yellow/citrine color is pretty and pristine. The first nosing pass picks up oodles of pomace and grape-must funkiness that are brazenly earthy, stemmy, astringent, and grape skin–like—this pungent, grape harvest odor time warps me back to my days working for Sonoma County, California, winemaker Rodney Strong in the 1970s. Entry is elegant, viscous in texture, slightly oaky and spicy, a smidgen smoky, and a whole lot like just-picked ripe grapes; midpalate highlights the crispness of the grape acidity, which

maintains the razor-edged freshness through to the fruity, jammy, medium-short aftertaste. Excellent balance keeps this grappa nimble and stately.
2018 Rating: ★ ★ ★ ★/Highly Recommended

Joseph Cartron 15 Years Marc de Bourgogne (France) 45% abv, $60.
Distilled from the musty red wine pomace of the Volnay, Vosne-Romanée, and Chambolle-Musigny districts in France's Burgundy wine region. The color is a greenish/amber/ khaki, and the clarity is immaculate. Opening smells include pungent aromas of grape skin, beeswax, grape seed oil, and freshly tilled soil; secondary fragrances are mineral-like, flinty, and chalky, with background notes of rubber tire, thyme, rosemary, and wet wool. Entry taste soars in deeply wine-like, off-dry, and spicy flavors of grape preserves, grape seed, and raisins; midpalate is where the 90-proof spirit comes alive, dictating the course for the flavor profile as the taste turns silky smooth, campfire warm, and almost a bit like tropical fruit. Finishes fathomless, long, dense, and grapy. A clinic on how marc should smell, taste, and feel.
2017 Rating: ★ ★ ★ ★/Highly Recommended

Marolo 12 Year Old Barolo Grappa (Italy) 50% abv, $100.
Copper/burnt sienna color; superbly clean. Initial inhalations catch clean, grape must–like, grape skin aromas that are accentuated by light touches of oaky vanilla, sawdust, oak plank, and paraffin; secondary whiffs after further air contact pick up fully integrated aromas of cooking spices (bay leaf, parsley, dill), honey, new leather, and ripe grapes, with never a hint of the 100-proof spirit that is the foundation. Entry is posh, fruity/grapy, tart, almost sour, but weighty in texture; midpalate phase shines brightest for all the various parts merge into a serene, substantial, balanced taste profile that lasts deep into the elegant after-taste. The pinnacle achievement of the Marolo Grappas.
2015 Rating: ★ ★ ★ ★ ★/Highest Recommendation

Marolo 15 Year Old Barolo Grappa (Italy) 50% abv, $50/200 ml.
Bronze color; unblemished clarity. I get notes of black pepper, tobacco leaf, old leather, grape must, oak resin, baker's yeast in the initial inhalations; second passes reveal traces of bacon fat, linseed oil, vegetable oil. Entry is spicy, grapy, ripe, but also oak influenced in terms of the buttery feel and the nutty foundational taste; midpalate is pleasingly integrated, almost toffee-like, and slightly smoky/roasted. Concludes alluringly long, toasty/roasted, nutty, almost more grainy than fruity.
2015 Rating: ★ ★ ★/Recommended

Marolo 20 Year Old Barolo Grappa (Italy) 50% abv, $57/200 ml.
Russet/sorrel color; flawless purity. I smell burnt popcorn at the bottom of a saucepan, and I get unappealing odors of textile fibers, flaxseed, floor polish, and lots and lots of wood-influenced polymers/glues, which I do not want in my grappa; second passes echo the first. Entry displays some semblance of grape/raisins but also lots of resiny flavors that overpower those of grapes; midpalate reflects the entry flavors, but I unearth a little more in the way of grapiness that actually comes off as being cocoa-like and caramelized, which against all odds works. Not an example of how well grappa matures for extended periods in

wood barrels. Can't give it a one star rating because there is clearly an aspect of underpinning quality here. That quality, however, has been stampeded by the wood polymers.
2015 Rating: ★★/Not Recommended

Marolo 5 Après di Moscato Grappa (Italy) 42% abv, $45/375 ml.
Aged for five years in Sicilian barriques that matured moscato di pantelleria. Bright yellow-straw/marigold color; unblemished clarity. I smell appealing aspects of saltwater taffy, salted caramel, caraway seed, poppy seed, bread dough in the opening inhalations; later sniffs encounter deft touches of wood, vanilla, allspice. Entry is sterling, chewy, and alluringly woody, even slightly fat from the polymers and acids of the oak barrique; midpalate echoes the entry, keeping the fruit/grape component low on the radar screen as the buttery oak resins dominate deep into the languid finish.
2015 Rating: ★★★/Recommended

Marolo 9 Year Old Barolo Grappa (Italy) 50% abv, $40/200 ml.
Burnt-orange/topaz color; slight sediment seen under the examination lamp. Wow, the fragrance after pouring is radiant with popcorn, hazelnut, praline, and oak resin scents that aren't as fruity as I'd expected but wonderful in a different manner; further aeration helps to settle down the bouquet a little, and that assists in bringing out more of the grapiness in a pruny/plummy way. Entry is oily to the touch, deeply woody and resiny to the taste, and markedly bittersweet; midpalate is long, buttery/creamy, oaky, and beany.
2015 Rating: ★★★★/Highly Recommended

Marolo Amarone Grappa (Italy) 42% abv, $70.
Old gold/saffron color; sediment-free appearance. I get lots of hot wax, candle wax aromas in the first passes after pouring, plus notes of new leather, tobacco; second nosings encounter more tropical fruit and grape fragrances that are dry and slightly saline. Entry is tightly wound, dusty dry, grapy, musty, yeasty; midpalate goes more for ripe grapes than anything else and is slightly bittersweet. Finishes medium long, moderately grapy, but stone dry and mineral-like. Very nice, but I'd hoped for more grape thrust and presence considering the source.
2015 Rating: ★★★/Recommended

Marolo Barolo Grappa (Italy) 42% abv, $60.
Tint of flax/yellow color; impeccable clarity. Right out of the aromatic gate I get slightly briny, salty aromas that are as resiny as they are raisiny and as waxy as they are peppery/spicy; second passes pick up butcher's wax paper, grape skins, salted bread dough, paraffin. Entry is intensely grapy-ripe, raisiny, not fruity enough to be considered succulent but firmly fruity and almost heady; midpalate is zesty, beautifully textured, waxy, fat, really pleasing in the mouth. Finish is buttery, creamy, nutty. Delicious.
2015 Rating: ★★★★/Highly Recommended

Marolo di Moscato Grappa (Italy) 42% abv, $60.
Clear and color-free; flawless purity. The gently floral, fresh spring garden aromas are delicate, lovely, integrated, mossy, vegetal, with only a slightly musty underpinning; second

whiffs pick up stony, mineral-like, dry scents plus dried-fruit aspects like pineapple, guava; maybe the only element missing is that typical orange blossom scent of moscato. Entry is warming, toasty, waxy, fruity; midpalate highlights the waxiness of the texture and the sprightliness of the dried fruits all the way into the moderately long aftertaste.

2015 Rating: ★ ★ ★/Recommended

Marolo Gewürztraminer Grappa (Italy) 42% abv, $67.

Crystalline as springwater; colorless; sediment-free splendor. The amazing, tropical fruit–like gewürz spice wafts up from the tasting glass, filling my office with radiant floral fragrance and perfume—love it; secondary sniffs get down to brass tacks as the aroma turns into a full-fledged bouquet, offering crisply acidic scents of grape must, yeasts, sweet pea, violets that are transcendent and sublime. Entry is deliciously mineral-like, softly floral, keenly acidic, and therefore fresh and vivid; midpalate is richer, a touch more textured, and oilier than the entry, making the overall late in-mouth impression more robust. Finishes intensely grapy, rustic, concentrated fully on the grape must. "Savage" enough to rate as an old-time grappa; elegant enough to be considered contemporary.

2015 Rating: ★ ★ ★ ★/Highly Recommended

Marolo Sangiovese de Brunello di Montalcino Grappa (Italy) 42% abv, $60.

Void of color; I can see oils floating in the sediment-free core. I like the initial grapiness found in the opening aromatic salvo, but there's likewise a butcher's wax paper scent that's fibrous and paraffin-like simultaneously; second inhalations highlight the estery aspect of the spirit, which is floral and fruity (tropical). Entry is much richer and textured than I thought it would be, and I'm pleasantly surprised by the fullness and grip of the early flavor profile; midpalate offers dusty, dry tastes of white raisins, dried apricot, almond. Concludes dry, moderately fruity/grapy, medium intensity.

2015 Rating: ★ ★ ★/Recommended

Nonino il Moscato di Grappa (Italy) 41% abv, $79.

Clear and pristine as rainwater appearance. First inhalations pick up delicate notes of orange blossom, tangerine, orange peel, and gentle spice (star anise); secondary whiffs after further aeration encounter a more pronounced citrus/mandarin orange fragrance that draws me in, and I find myself inhaling for a long period due to its seductiveness. Entry is firmly structured around a creamy texture upon which float the primary flavors of orange blossom, white grapes/raisins, and quince; midpalate features much of what made the entry pleasant and adds a judicious dose of earthy astringency that balances the near-plumpness of the moscato presence. Finishes as clean as can possibly be, moderately chewy, ripe, acidic, fresh, and totally enthralling and sophisticated.

2018 Rating: ★ ★ ★ ★ ★/Highest Recommendation

Nonino Riserva Vendemmia Aged 18 Months in Barriques and Small Casks Grappa (Italy) 41% abv, $50.

Citrine color; superb appearance. I favorably respond to the opening fragrance as it reminds me of quince/yellow plum, birch leaves, and lichen; secondary sniffs after more air contact encounter woodsy scents of green vegetation and vines, as well as parchment and sawdust. Entry is ripe, peppery, mildly honeyed with oak resins and vanillin; midpalate features lightly toasted flavors of marshmallow, Danish pastry, nougat, and fig. Aftertaste is medium long and creamy, with flavors of buttered whole wheat toast, graham cracker, and honey.

2018 Rating: ★ ★ ★ ★/Highly Recommended

Nonino Vendemmia Grappa (Italy) 41% abv, $45.

Colorless; sediment-free appearance. I like the herbaceous piquancy and economy in the opening nose of this lean, svelte grappa, meaning that the aroma is focused and tight; secondary inhalations discover woodsy notes of forest vegetation (ferns, lichen, vines, mushroom) and a back note of grapiness that underpins the whole aromatic stage. Entry is delightfully crisp, clean, and acidic without being astringent or earthy; midpalate highlights the keen grapiness, which is tart, acidic, and semisweet. Aftertaste is long, chewy in texture, tight, and chiseled. Not an ounce of fat on this refreshing, gripping grappa.

2018 Rating: ★ ★ ★ ★/Highly Recommended

Psenner Adorata Barrique Grappa (Italy) 40% abv, $43.

Pale amber color; unblemished clarity. There's a real acetate quality to this aroma in the first whiffs that's polish-like, wax paper–like, and fatty; later inhalations discover a toasty quality that's slightly roasted and seared; what this bouquet lacks is fruit. Entry is ripe and thankfully fruity, off-dry, and a touch spicy; midpalate echoes the entry and becomes juicier and waxier in texture. Finish is medium long and drier than the midpalate because the acidity suddenly takes charge.

2016 Rating: ★ ★ ★/Recommended

Psenner Gewürztraminer Grappa (Italy) 40% abv, $43.

Flawless purity; colorless. First nosing passes are treated to vibrant, properly spicy, and zesty fragrances that are true to the flowery/fruity aromatic DNA of gewürztraminer—it's hard not to continue sniffing it; after more air contact, the bouquet seems to pick up strength as the flower blossom intensity grows, becoming slightly waxy and oily; an intriguing bouquet that's infectiously pleasing. Entry mirrors the tangy quality appreciated in the aroma and adds a touch more citrus-peel aspect that's keenly acidic, tart, and fresh; midpalate remains delightfully tart, squeaky clean, intensely grapy, and austere (in the positive sense). Finish is lean, dry to off-dry, and surprisingly long. Couldn't find any fault with this animated grappa.

2016 Rating: ★ ★ ★ ★ ★/Highest Recommendation

Psenner Sauvignon Grappa (Italy) 40% abv, $43.

Springwater clear; impeccable clarity. Grapy notes are evident right out of the gate and the focus is more on grape peel and seed than juice or pulp; with more aeration, the aroma turns subtler and more nuanced, as the aroma becomes more leafy, rubbery, and viny. Entry is subtle, alluringly grapy, tart, acidic, dry but not sour; midpalate echoes the entry, as the taste profile remains steely, a touch flinty, but wholly enjoyable as the fruit essence is clearly seen. Aftertaste is dusty dry, flinty/stony.

2016 Rating: ★ ★ ★ ★/Highly Recommended

Singani 63 Muscat of Alexandria Brandy (Bolivia) 40% abv, $30.

Silvery pure and void of color. Initial nosing pass picks up faint hints of orange blossom, orange rind, and red plum fragrances; later sniffs following further air contact detect more assertive aromas of baking spices (clove, nutmeg, mace) as well as ripe grape and plum fragrance. Entry is ripe, off-dry, clean, pleasantly acidic, adequately fruity/grapy, and orange-like; midpalate is this spirit's apex moment as the fruit-salad flavors merge with the floral aspects, creating an overall in-mouth experience that's tight, lean, and moderately bountiful.

2018 Rating: ★★★/Recommended

PISCO–PERU AND CHILE

South America boasts a host of significant grape-based brandies, including Argentina's awkwardly named *coñac*, Bolivia's *singani*, and the most fabled of all, *pisco* from both Peru and Chile. Because of the marketplace impact of pisco, in particular, a breakdown of Chilean and Peruvian production standards is in order.

Labeling Laws for Chilean and Peruvian Piscos

Peru—Pisco can be produced by law solely in the Locumba, Sama, and Caplina valleys in Tacna and in the Departments of Lima, Ica (Ica, Chincha, Pisco), Moquegua, and Arequipa.

Chile—The denominación de origen (DO) was officially made law in 1931. The Chilean DO covers the areas of Coquimbo and Atacama.

Peruvian Grape Varieties/Classifications

Non-aromatic class: *mollar*; negra *corriente*; *quebranta*; *uvina*

Aromatic class: albilla *moscatel de alejandria*, or italia; *moscatel rosada*; torontel

Chilean Grape Varieties/Classifications

Nonaromatic class: torontel; Pedro Jiménez; moscatel de austria

Aromatic class: *moscatel de alejandría* (italia); *moscatel rosada*

Author's note: **Please note that Peru classifies torontel as aromatic while Chile does not. Go figure.**

Peruvian Varieties of Pisco

Puro: a pisco made from a single variety of grape

Acholado: a blend of varietals, usually a mix of aromatic and non-aromatic

Mosto Verde ("green must"): pisco distilled from an incompletely fermented must

Chilean Varieties of Pisco

Unaged: can be aromatic or nonaromatic varieties

Lightly aged (a.k.a. *guarda*): piscos have been matured for at least six but not more than twelve months in oak barrels

Aged (a.k.a. *envejecido*): piscos have been aged a minimum of twelve months in small oak barrels

Artisanal: customary method that spend at least two years in large rauli-wood tanks, often longer (rauli is a Chilean variety of wood especially good for cooperage)

Alto del Carmen Reservado Pisco (Chile) 40% abv, $18.
Maize yellow color; impeccably pure. Early on, I smell faint traces of newly tanned leather, cardboard, parchment (onionskin), egg white, meringue, and lima bean; with more aeration, the egginess grows in stature as does a pencil eraser–like rubberiness that seems incongruous. Entry is flaccid, a bit too limp in acidity, which is why it doesn't seem fresh; midpalate finds the introduction of wood resins and lipids that in tandem defeat any chance for the natural fruitiness to reemerge. Finish is mildly pleasant as the taste profile makes a small comeback by reestablishing the fruit/grape/pear element. All the same, take a pass on this one.
2018 Rating: ★★/Not Recommended

Alto del Carmen The Essence of Muscat Pisco (Chile) 40% abv, $35.
Silvery clarity and void of color. The unmistakable presence of the muscatel of alexandria grape variety is indelibly etched into the first nosing pass as the ambrosial fragrance of orange blossom, orange peel, and quince delight the olfactory sense; with more air contact, the orange-y-ness continues but turns noticeably more zest-like, earthy, and acidic, creating another level of aromatics that push the grape variety forward. Entry is supple, creamy in

texture, and deep in orange zest flavor that turns more like citron by the midpalate stage as the acid level grows in intensity, keeping the in-mouth experience fresh, razor edged, and crisp. Aftertaste is half a notch drier than the midpalate and therefore squeaky clean and mouth puckering.

2018 Rating: ★ ★ ★ ★/Highly Recommended

BarSol Primero Quebranta Pisco (Peru) 41.3% abv, $29.

Void of any color; pristinely clean. First nosing passes pick up tannic scents of grape peel and seed that overlay foundational fragrances of orange blossom, spice cake, and grape preserves; more air contact stimulates deeper fruit and floral aromas, especially grape pulp and juice, as well as jasmine and geranium. Entry is mineral-like, earthy, flinty, and stone dry; midpalate features more wide-ranging tastes, including grape seed, black plum, and coffee bean. Aftertaste is desert dry, astringent from the high tannin level, and lean.

2019 Rating: ★ ★ ★/Recommended

BarSol Selecto Acholado Pisco (Peru) 41.3% abv, $32.

Clear as rainwater; excellent purity. I like the lean opening aromas that are tightly wound, focused, and more akin to grape peels and pulp than juice; additional aeration brings out nuances of patent leather, quince, lead pencil, and damp cement/wet sand. Entry is as tight as a drum, high in acidity, razor edged, and therefore crisp and tart; midpalate exhibits a bit more fleshiness as the grape juice element becomes more apparent along with hints of minerals. Finishes cleanly, with medium length, and maximum grapiness.

2019 Rating: ★ ★ ★/Recommended

BarSol Selecto Italia Pisco (Peru) 41.3% abv, $38.

Crystalline, colorless, and impeccably clean. At first blush, there is a subtlety about the grapiness of the aroma that makes the fragrance come off as being coy, but with persistent sniffing I find deeper levels of chalk, kiwi, red plum, and green tea; with additional air contact, the fragrances open up a little more, revealing scents of ripe red cherry and mincemeat. Entry is taut, raisiny, crisp, ripe, and tannic; midpalate features deeper, more refined flavors of fresh kiwi, guava, green melon, and orange peel. Aftertaste highlights the fruit density in the flavor form of mincemeat pie and almond paste. Fruity, nutty, and totally lovely.

2019 Rating: ★ ★ ★ ★/Highly Recommended

BarSol Selecto Torontel Pisco (Peru) 41.3% abv, $39.

Clean and ideally sediment-free. This lovely opening aroma is all about fresh, spring flower garden featuring highlights of rose petal, honeysuckle, savory, and lemongrass; secondary inhalations pick up a whole other waft of fruit-driven fragrances like grapefruit, red currant, and lavender; a wonderfully inviting bouquet. While the aroma is floral and fruity, the entry flavor is earthier, more metallic, and lead pencil–like as the taste profile lacks the appeal found in the nose; midpalate stays the earthy/elemental/steely course and is disconnected from the bouquet. Finishes short, dry, flinty, and nowhere near as charming as the aroma implied it would be. Disappointing.

2019 Rating: ★ ★/Not Recommended

BarSol Supremo Mosto Verde Italia Pisco (Peru) 41.8% abv, $44.

Flawless clarity; colorless. This opening nose is viny, bramble-like, woodsy, mushroom-like, and mossy; after more time in the glass, the aroma remains in the mossy, grassy, foresty, vine-like mode, and it's this one-dimensional approach that I find uninteresting. At the entry stage, I note a slight improvement in that there is faint evidence of grape juice present, and for that I'm happy; midpalate offers more flavor expansion that features low-grade spiciness (allspice, mace), quince, and lemongrass tastes that work in harmony deep into the pleasing aftertaste. The recovery during the entry, midpalate, and finish from a lackluster bouquet saved the bacon of this pisco. I've tasted this pisco several times in previous years, and I think the quality has slipped from four stars to three.

2019 Rating: ★ ★ ★/Recommended

Capel Premium Pisco (Chile) 40% abv, $17.

Clear and clean-as-rainwater appearance. I like the opening fragrance that's delicate, floral (honeysuckle, especially), and keenly fruity (orange rind, white grape, citron), showing integration and elegance; with further aeration, a clear perfume of smokiness develops, leading to a distinct scent of burnt match and smoldering campfire that consumes the gentle fruit and floral aspects. Entry is off-dry, crisp with acidity, and fresh with grape skins, tannic flavor; midpalate echoes the entry as the grapy, raisiny fruit component makes a big play for dominance and wins. Finishes medium long, raisiny, and mildly earthy, vinous.

2018 Rating: ★ ★ ★/Recommended

Caravedo Quebranta Pisco (Peru) 40% abv, $25.

Translucent, colorless, perfect purity. Smells, sans aeration, immediately and generously of orange blossom, cherry blossom, white raisins, quince, gooseberry jam, and citrus peel; following another few minutes in the glass the flower shop aromas hit their apex, offering cascades of jasmine, rose petal, as well as nimble spices (cinnamon, clove); a tour de force bouquet that's beguiling and fresh. Entry is as fresh as the aroma, but with a much sharper edge of acidity that establishes a bittersweet, astringent core taste; midpalate remains agile and crisp as the flavor profile advances towards the medium-long, slightly cutting aftertaste. The bouquet's ambrosial virtues got bushwhacked a bit by the high degree of acidity in the flavor, thereby deflating some of the aroma's sublime gains. That said, I like the overall impression even if my early expectations weren't realized by midpalate and finish.

2015 Rating: ★ ★ ★/Recommended

Caravedo Torontel Pisco Puro (Peru) 40% abv, $30.

Pristine clarity; pewter tint. The alluring grape/nectarine-like aromatic impact is immediate, dramatic, and full frontal; secondary whiffs encounter more supple fragrances of grape pulp/must, nectarine skin, hazelnut, bay laurel, eucalyptus, and chive. Entry is pure, fresh, and vibrant with ample acidity, dense with grape skin and quince flavor; midpalate soars to new grape-driven flavor heights as the roundness of the creamy texture supports and pushes forward the fruit intensity, vinosity, and crispness. Aftertaste is brief in duration, cleansing, slightly chalky, and delicious.

2018 Rating: ★ ★ ★ ★ ★/Highest Recommendation

Kappa Elqui Pisco (Chile) 42.5% abv, $34.

Impeccable clarity. The lovely, flowery opening fragrance is like orange blossoms and honeysuckle and all the while is grapy, compelling, graceful, and ripe; with aeration, the orange blossom/orange peel aspect builds into a succulent bouquet that's easily in the first ranks of Pisco aromas. Entry is gently sweet and grapy ripe, yet there's a mineral/earthy vein running down the taste profile's spine that maintains the structure beautifully along with the tightly wound acidity; midpalate is gloriously luscious and fruity, with a low-key oiliness that makes for sumptuous drinking. Ends elegantly and firmly on a strong note of acidity and freshness.

2014 Rating: ★★★★★/Highest Recommendation

Payet Acholado Pisco (Peru) 40% abv, $35.

Ideally pristine, colorless. Lovely, elegant, juicy initial aroma is highlighted by scents of berries, red cherry, nectarine, lychee, quince; secondary sniffs encounter light traces of baking spices (nutmeg, allspice), textile fiber, candle wax. Entry is off-dry, complex, grapy with a little orchard fruit thrown in; midpalate is compellingly fruity, ripe but not sweet, mildly tannic, bakery-shop spicy, slightly herbal, very tasty. Aftertaste showcases the grape skins and spice in perfect measure. Savory.

2014 Rating: ★★★★/Highly Recommended

Payet Quebranta Pisco (Peru) 40% abv, $35.

Clean-as-rainwater appearance; flawless purity. First aromatic rush is reminiscent of red cherry, red plum, bubble gum, damp rain forest, with side notes of gunpowder, nickel; the ambrosial aspect remains in the secondary whiffs, which is supplemented with scents of fruit mash, yeast, sour mash, new spirit, and compost-like barnyard aromas. Entry reminds me of fresh spirit off the still in its fruity/floral demeanor, then the taste profile goes south with a touch of rot/decay that guts the in-mouth stage. Viny, bramble-like, horse barn aftertaste is more pleasant than the midpalate. Pass on it.

2014 Rating: ★★/Not Recommended

Payet Torontel Pisco (Peru) 40% abv, $35.

Perfect transparency; sediment-free. Opening aroma is juicy, grapy, citrusy, yellow plum–like, clean as a whistle; deep grapiness stays the course in the second passes while suddenly offering a touch of lychee. Entry is acutely fruity, ripe yet dry, with background flavors of grape peel, pulp, vines; midpalate reflects all the findings of the entry and goes further as the juiciness turns into jamminess. Finishes bittersweet, pithy, tannic, showing elegance all the way.

2014 Rating: ★★★★/Highly Recommended

Portón Acholado Pisco (Peru) 40% abv, $40.

Clear as springwater; colorless. This lovely opening nose is more about fatty lipids, especially pork fat, bacon fat, and unsalted butter, than about grapes/fruits or acidity at this early point. Additional aeration time brings out the fruit and acid but more in the manner of skins/peels, in particular of grapes, plums, and kiwi, more than fruit pulp or juice. Entry is lush in texture, ripe in fruitiness (kiwi especially), and expanding in acidity; midpalate brings the various elements together in an off-dry union of kiwi/prickly pear–like fruitiness that's high in acid and therefore freshness. Ends up being pleasantly ambrosial, a touch sharp, and clean. Very nice indeed.

2018 Rating: ★ ★ ★ ★/**Highly Recommended**

THE WORLD'S
OTHER SPIRITS

RUM/RHUM/RON, ARRACK, AND CACHAÇA—WORLD

Even after centuries of production, rum in our lifetime remains largely misunderstood and, to some degree, abused. I call it the Rodney Dangerfield of Spirits since it gets such scant respect. The problem, however, is this vast, global category's own fault. Unfortunately, rum's lingering image of being a low-grade distillate (a.k.a. pirate juice) has been enforced by numbingly sweet and fruity cocktails. But the fact is that rum is so much more versatile, so much more majestic than that well-worn cliché. Indeed, when rum's full story is digested by those devotees willing to dig for it, the truth points to it being a sophisticated libation of style, substance, socioeconomic, and historical importance that deserves greater respect, proper utilization, and even admiration.

What plays heavily against rum's image more than anything, however, is the lack of an international regulatory board, one that can initially set uniform production standards of quality and labeling and then oversee those standards. As it stands now, each rum-producing nation, of which there are currently over seventy, plays by its own set of loosely adhered-to rules. The lack of authorized supervision frequently leads to dubious, if unguarded, practices, such as adding ingredients that consumers would rather not know about or not being truthful about age statements.

Brash, misguided marketing departments of many rum-producing companies continue to cultivate rum's rustic, ribald image. Today's serious spirits drinkers, by contrast, are often turned off by it. As such, rum's relegation to the spirits category's lower echelons continues, even in light of the fact that there are rums that compete with the world's foremost whiskeys and brandies. The trick is finding those gems born of sugarcane juice or molasses. Hopefully, this little compilation will assist you with that endeavor.

In 2021, the two most important distinctions concerning sugarcane-based spirits come in the forms of *rum*, or those spirits made worldwide from molasses, and *rhum agricole*, or those spirits produced from fresh sugarcane juice mainly in French-speaking Caribbean nations, such as Martinique, Guadeloupe, and Marie-Galant. Rhum agricoles must follow the French government's regulations known as *appellation d'origine contrôlée (AOC)*.

Cachaça is Brazil's national spirit, made from sugarcane juice, and it resembles rum.

Arrack, which originates in Southeast Asia, is a potent spirit produced from diverse base materials, including sugarcane juice and coconut flowers, and is sometimes flavored with red rice.

Clairin is an unregulated variety of traditional rum made in the rural, sugarcane growing regions of Haiti. There are over five hundred small, artisanal rum distilleries, known as *guildives*, on the island. Clairin is made from sugarcane juice or sugarcane syrup and is roughly similar to Brazil's cachaça and the rhum agricoles produced in French territorial islands of the Caribbean. A growing number of rum enthusiasts believe that clairin will be the next "big thing" in distilled spirits.

Author's note: The term "hogo" is a rum-industry descriptor that depicts a smell and flavor quality that's barnyard-like, musty, mushroomy, sulfurous, almost like rotting vegetation.

A. Smith Bowman Virginia Rum (USA) 57% abv, $35/375 ml.

Clear and sediment-free citron/canary yellow appearance. Ooh, I like this biscuity, cookie batter–like, vibrant opening aroma that's doughy, spicy, and a bit grassy/vegetal in equal measure; secondary whiffs after more air contact detect pronounced fragrances of ripe pineapple, citrus rind, marshmallow, and orange blossom. Entry is zesty and prickly with alcohol that dries out the palate on contact, leaving behind an assertive taste profile that's high on green vegetation/grass/hay and candle wax; midpalate accentuates the waxiness that's prevalent in the entry as well as the high-octane alcohol that ratchets up in intensity, thereby overshadowing portions of the flavor profile except for the sugarcane grassiness. Ends up tasting cane-y, bean-like, vegetal, and bone-dry.

2018 Rating: ★ ★ ★/Recommended

Admiral Nelson's Premium Spiced Rum (USA) 35% abv, $9.

Wheat/fallow field color; excellent purity. First aromas are sweet, juicy, fruity, lightly spiced; follow-up inhalations unearth simple brown sugar, cake-frosting scents that are at once lackadaisical and nondescript. Entry is more likable than the anemic bouquet as the taste profile at least makes an effort to please with robust sugar flavors; midpalate shows the spice more than the entry, and that adds some zestiness that is welcome. Inoffensive, drinkable, but hollow.

2016 Rating: ★ ★/Not Recommended

Alander Spiced Rum (USA) 43% abv, $33.

Louisiana sugarcane. Sepia color; unblemished clarity. Opening sniffs uncover wheelbarrows of blatant spicy, fruity, herbal fragrances, including vanilla bean, nutmeg, baked pineapple, clove, huckleberry, allspice, orange peel, brown sugar, egg cream; later inhalations detect rounder, spicier, mellower aromas, especially of the vanilla/clove marriage with cola nut, brown sugar, cranberry muffin; a genuinely original spiced rum bouquet that's intricate, integrated, and altogether lovely. Entry is an expansive, richly woven network of flavors that intersect at all the right points, featuring mostly the spice base of vanilla/clove but also the holiday cake fruitiness of dried pineapple and apricot, along with candied walnut. Midpalate offers exotic flavors of praline, baked banana, cinnamon bun, dates, figs, mincemeat that all mingle for a bang-up finish that's meaty, chewy, densely spicy, gloriously luscious, yet composed. A savory, tangy spiced rum from that traditional hotbed of rum production: Minnesota.

2015 Rating: ★★★★/Highly Recommended

Angostura 1919 Caribbean Rum (Trinidad and Tobago) 40% abv, $38.

Lovely, bright amber color; very good clarity. The opening aroma is filled with notes of berries, flowers, toffee, and tobacco; following another seven minutes of air contact, the bouquet expands to include subtle traces of cherry cobbler, honey wheat toast, toasted marshmallow, toffee, and sautéed almonds. Entry is lean, off-dry and grassy; midpalate is a touch more bountiful than the entry, offering integrated flavors of fruit juice, cigar tobacco, parsley, and oak. Aftertaste highlights the toffee and honey. A grown-up's rum.

2016 Rating: ★★★★/Highly Recommended

Angostura 5 Year Old Caribbean Rum (Trinidad and Tobago) 40% abv, $18.

Pale, old gold color that is hazy and visually unbecoming. Starts out without any distinctive aromas in the opening passes other than bubble gum; further aeration doesn't appear to stimulate many more aromatic possibilities other than more bubble gum and perhaps a smidgen of green tobacco and pear; this is five years old? Entry exhibits a low degree of flavor profile that includes deft touches of nutmeg, malted milk ball, cinnamon bun, and cola; midpalate merely echoes the entry while not bothering to expand on that tired theme. A junk, dumpster-worthy rum.

2020 Rating: ★/Not Recommended

Angostura 7 Year Old Caribbean Rum (Trinidad and Tobago) 40% abv, $23.

Pretty saffron color; very good clarity. This aroma doesn't show much more in terms of aromatic character than that of the appalling five-year-old; I mean really, how can a rum whose label says that it's seven years old show so little in the fragrance? Entry offers a short menu of off-dry tastes, including lead pencil, minerals, brown sugar, cinnamon bun, and bear claw pastry; midpalate, by contrast, does introduce a fair amount of drinking pleasure by making this flavor profile at least a little rum-like. Overall, just forget it. Nowhere near recommendable.

2020 Rating: ★★/Not Recommended

Appleton Estate 21 Year Old Rum (Jamaica) 43% abv, $140.

Mahogany color; unblemished purity. Up front, the tantalizing aromas are integrated, leathery, old library book–like, slightly peppery, and a great deal like dried fruits, in particular, apricot and pineapple; secondary nosing passes after more aeration discover even richer, more substantial fragrances that are at once stately and slightly feral. Entry flavors are textbook aged, pot still rum classics, such as spice cake, caramelized onions, sautéed mushrooms, and black tea; midpalate is this rum's pinnacle moment as the various flavor elements merge into a singular taste that can only be described as being potent, graceful, bittersweet, grassy,

and satiny in texture. I have to consider this a clinic on pot still rum, and one of the top ten rums in the world.
2019 Rating: ★ ★ ★ ★ ★/Highest Recommendation

Appleton Estate Rare Blend 12 Year Old Rum (Jamaica) 43% abv, $43.
Copper color; flawless clarity. The first sniffs have me thinking *decadent dessert*, something like Baked Alaska or vanilla crème brûlée that, while nearly over-the-top, is really just succulent and cocoa butter sweet; more time in the glass sees the übersweetness fade with additional air contact, releasing more of the earthy funkiness of pot still distillation. Entry explodes on the tongue with exuberant flavors of coffee bean, espresso, toasted marshmallow, praline, and candied almond; midpalate turns softer, more delicate in its taste profile, turning spicier and more pastry- and cake-like. Finishes velvety in texture, bittersweet, and dark chocolate–like. Really high on the Yummy Meter.
2019 Rating: ★ ★ ★ ★/Highly Recommended

Appleton Estate Reserve Blend Rum (Jamaica) 40% abv, $27.
Pretty bronze color; impeccably clean and free of sediment. Initial nosing passes pick up subtle traces of dried orchard fruits, mostly nectarine and pear, plus nuances of nutmeg and mace; later inhalations after more aeration encounter heartier aromas, especially sarsaparilla-like barrel funk, mushroom, wet earth, and toffee. Entry offers a dizzying array of tastes, including bear claw pastry, prune Danish, turbinado sugar, dried and candied orange peel, and burnt toast; midpalate advances all the entry impressions, adding toasted marshmallow. Aftertaste is long, viscous in the throat, and bittersweet. Excellent value.
2019 Rating: ★ ★ ★ ★/Highly Recommended

Appleton Estate Signature Blend Rum (Jamaica) 40% abv, $22.
Amber/marigold color; perfectly clean and clear of sediment. The zesty, bakery-like opening aroma is fully loaded with fragrances of brown sugar, cocoa powder, cinnamon bun, and praline; later sniffs after more air contact pick up mellow, integrated scents of black tea, egg cream, vanilla soda, and honey. Entry highlights the bakeshop aspects, providing a rich, peppery, and slightly funky first taste that's far more bittersweet than sugary sweet; midpalate highlights the funky side of this rum by featuring a highly vegetal core flavor that veers away from the bakeshop spiciness, heading more towards a woodsy, tree bark–like character that offers plenty of personality and grace as well as a gentle kick in the head. Great value for the money.
2019 Rating: ★ ★ ★ ★/Highly Recommended

Arôme 28 Year Old True Rum (Panama) 40% abv, $595.
Gloriously bright bronze/henna color; perfectly pure. First aromas are reminiscent of old leather-bound books/library, brown sugar, burning leaves, cinnamon bun, and pound cake; later inhalations detect deeper fragrances of oak plank, maple, oak resins, vanilla bean, sawdust, lanolin, fried pork rind, sesame seed oil, and hoisin sauce. Entry flavors are graceful, balanced, calming, and harmonious without being too heavily oaked or intensely sweet; at midpalate, there's a gently sweet, honey-like taste that's more fruit leaning than grassy or herbal, and it has a controlled spiciness that is reminiscent of clove and cinnamon. Aftertaste

is long, elegant, composed, and mature. I think that this is a very good, well above average rum that still shows plenty of character, considering its age. It is not over-wooded, which is laudable. But, frankly, is it worth almost $600? No.

2017 Rating: ★★★★/Highly Recommended

Avuá Amburana Cachaça (Brazil) 40% abv, $45.
Matured for up to two years in indigenous amburana wood barrels. Pretty pale-green tint; unblemished purity. Initial inhalations are startlingly and pleasingly herbaceous and almost like a grocery store since I detect hints of mint, marzipan, dried flowers, malted milk, and chili peppers that, while disparate, magically work together; second passes heighten the malted milk and mint-like vegetation. Entry is unusual, herbal (dried thyme), grassy, vegetal and viny/woodsy/forest-like; midpalate is grassier to me than anything else, but the grassiness is accentuated by the nuances of delicate sweetness that must be from the sugarcane. Finishes intensely herbal, off-dry, sappy, and slightly minerally. The taste obviously reflects the indigenous wood.

2015 Rating: ★★★★/Highly Recommended

Avuá Prata Cachaça (Brazil) 42% abv, $35.
Unaged. Crystalline appearance that is impeccably clean. First whiffs detect grassy, vegetal (asparagus, brussels sprouts) aromas that are stone dry and earthy in a vegetable garden way; after another seven minutes of aeration, an agave-like saltiness develops that is delightful and clean and is almost akin to soup stock. Entry is surprisingly sweet yet is agile enough due to acidity that the taste profile is fresh and compelling; sweetness dries out in the midpalate as the flavor turns more biscuity/doughy and is accented by spice, especially coriander. Aftertaste is dry, acidic/astringent, vegetal, and very savory. A welcome addition to the slowly growing cachaça category in the USA marketplace. Prime Caipirinha cocktail base.

2015 Rating: ★★★★/Highly Recommended

Bacardí Añejo 4 Year Old Rum (Puerto Rico) 40% abv, $20.
Amber color; pristine clarity. Initial whiffs encounter fat, lipid-like scents of lard, sweet cream, almond paste, and white raisins; secondary sniffs pick up slightly deeper fragrances, including caramel, nutmeg, clove, and citrus rind. Entry is round in texture, drier than I had anticipated it would be, roasted, brown sugar–like, and chewy; midpalate is peppery, spicy, mildly sweet, and a touch honeyed. Concludes on a flat, brief note that's too sugary.

2020 Rating: ★★/Not Recommended

Bacardí Gran Reserva Maestro de Ron (Puerto Rico) 40% abv, $25.
There is the palest of bisque/pewter tint to this rum; superb clarity. For a 40 percent abv rum, the aromatics are potent, assertive, and brimming with grassy, vegetal, off-dry scents that run the gamut from cane to brown sugar to dried flowers to sage and rosemary—the most dramatic and expressive bouquet from Bacardi ever, in my view; second passes find that the toasty bouquet hasn't lost a beat with aeration as it continues to dazzle and delight. Entry tastes include dried pineapple, raw cane, vanilla bean; midpalate is chewy in texture, meaty, as robust as the aroma and entry phases, and gently bittersweet. Aftertaste is where there's a noticeable diminishment of character, but the fact is Maestro de Ron is a real deal. Try this

beauty in a Daiquiri (rum, fresh squeezed lime juice, dash of simple syrup) for maximum pleasure.
2015 Rating: ★ ★ ★ ★/Highly Recommended

Bacardí Reserva Superior 8 Year Old Rum (Puerto Rico) 40% abv, $24.
Attractive ochre color; superb clarity. Opening inhalations detect robust aromas of cinnamon, vanilla bean, and espresso; later sniffs pick up deeper, more concentrated scents of baked tropical fruits (pineapple, banana, especially), pipe tobacco, and gingerbread. Entry is savory, semisweet, and reminiscent of dark chocolate and carob; midpalate is this rum's best moment as the flavors meld into a singular taste that's roasted and bittersweet. Finishes medium long, dry, and a huge leap forward from the four-year-old Anejo.
2020 Rating: ★ ★ ★ ★/Highly Recommended

Bacardí Superior Carta Blanca Rum (Puerto Rico) 40% abv, $17.
Excellent purity; slight pewter-like tint. Not a great deal to grip on to, aromawise, in the first nosings, except for alcohol fumes; this is just a neutered fragrance that offers nothing of note even after additional aeration. Entry is more vodka-like than rum-like and that, to me, is just unforgivable; midpalate is, well, nowhere, as the taste profile is skimpy and mineral-like in its best moment. It's a shame that this otherwise good producer can't raise the level of its bread-and-butter marque. Horribly vacant and undrinkable.
2020 Rating: ★/Not Recommended

Balcones Special Release Texas Rum (USA) 58.5% abv, $70.
Gorgeous auburn/rusty color; perfect clarity. There's a whole lotta early aroma shakin' goin' on here in the forms of prune juice, black raisins, chocolate cake frosting, powdered cocoa; what is surprising is how the abv is reserved and unobtrusive; later inhalations detect almond paste, nougat, dates, Danish pastry. Entry leans towards being bittersweet and pruny, then it turns deeply beany; midpalate echoes the entry but adds a huge dollop of butteriness that affects the texture to the positive. Aftertaste is a trace smoky, pruny, ripe, absolutely spectacular. Abv level might be a problem for the less-seasoned drinker, but level it off with fruit juice or mineral water.
2016 Rating: ★ ★ ★ ★ ★/Highest Recommendation

Banks 5 Island Blend Rum (Multiple Nations) 43% abv, $34.
Crystalline, silvery appearance; unblemished purity. Smells up front of tarmac, sugarcane, baker's yeast, tree bark, funky vegetation, and burning hemp/fiber; another seven minutes of air contact bring out more supple, less edgy aromas of marshmallow, vanilla bean, textile fiber, cocoa, and hard cheese. Entry is willowy in texture, gently sweet, and lusciously oily; midpalate taste profile mirrors the entry but adds an egg cream–like quality that's positively stupendous. Concludes medium long, more bittersweet than sweet, plump, crisp, and infectiously funky and grassy. An A-list distillate and, without doubt, my "desert island" rum. Make no mistake, Banks 5 Island's (Jamaica, Trinidad/Tobago, Barbados, Guyana, and Indonesia) innate funkiness might not be for everyone, but my take is that it is one of the finest, most skillfully blended spirits in the world, at present.
2019 Rating: ★ ★ ★ ★ ★/Highest Recommendation

Banks 7 Golden Age Rum (Multiple Nations) 43% abv, $41.

The seven rum-producing nations included in this superlative and exotic blend are Jamaica, Guyana, Indonesia, Trinidad/Tobago, Barbados, Guatemala, and Panama. Cocoa-brown color; impeccably clean. First nosing passes after the pour encounter deeply spiced aromas, most notably mace, allspice, and clove, that provide a highlight reel of fragrance; secondary inhalations turn in a more herbal, forest-like direction, as vivid aromas of tree bark, cinnamon, root beer, sarsaparilla, peppermint, and Douglas fir impress. Entry is deeply pine-like/cedary, and pipe tobacco–like, and grilled pork–like; midpalate leans in the bitter manner of Lapsang souchong tea, amaro, bitters, and caramelized onion. Finishes bitter, crisply acidic, fresh, and vegetal. While I prefer the Banks 5 Island, this edition is no crash test dummy.

2019 Rating: ★★★★/Highly Recommended

Banks The Endeavour Limited Edition No. 1 Rum (West Indies) 43% abv, $699.

Amber color; better than average purity. Wow! This opening aroma is all about wild forest (moss, lichen), herbal, and earthy (mushroom) notes in the first whiffs following the pour, almost too much to catalog; later sniffs confirm all the botanical woodland findings and then add slate, concrete, wet sand, and anise. Entry is elegant, nearly delicate in its exposition of subtle flavors; midpalate is tangy, herbal, and composed, with moderately sweet tastes of brown sugar, sage, and chocolate cake frosting. Finish is delicious and lush. Superbly satisfying.

2015 Rating: ★★★★★/Highest Recommendation

Barbancourt Reserve Speciale 8 Year Old Rhum (Haiti) 43% abv, $27.

Old gold color; excellent clarity. Opening nose is surprisingly mute and closed off except for faint traces of cigarette tobacco and refined sugar; the next nosing phase turns a bit cane-like, grassy, and forest floor–like. Entry explodes on the tongue in flavors that overwhelm the taste buds in whitewater, level-five rapids fashion, led by chunky tastes of demerara sugar, honey, sugar maple, and Cocoa Puffs breakfast cereal; midpalate builds upon the entry's taste rush in the forms of bittersweet dark chocolate, toasted marshmallow, and hot chocolate. Concludes long in the throat, chewy in texture, zesty, and peppery.

2020 Rating: ★★★★/Highly Recommended

Barbancourt Three Star 4 Year Old Rhum (Haiti) 43% abv, $22.

Golden wheat-field color; impeccable purity. I like the first scents that remind me of cotton candy, nougat, candy bar, lumberyard, and treacle; next nosing passes detect elegant aromas that resemble candied and dried fruits, especially nectarine and apricot. Entry is dense with bittersweet sugarcane, vanilla bean, and mineral flavors; midpalate mirrors the entry, adding tangy flavors of crème brûlée, toasted wheat bread, and raisin bread. Ends firm and meaty in texture, deeply bittersweet, and cocoa-like.

2020 Rating: ★★★/Recommended

Barceló Imperial Rum (Dominican Republic) 40% abv, $30.

Beautiful mahogany color; unblemished clarity. First inhalations after the pour detect savory scents of black tea, minerals, black pepper, brown sugar, and puff pastry; later whiffs after more aeration discover desert-dry, slightly smoky fragrances of potash, campfire embers, grilled meats, and espresso. Entry diverts slightly from the bouquet findings, as the taste profile goes all-out bitter, tasting of minerals/nickel, lead pencil, grilled asparagus, and oak plank; midpalate is more pleasing than the mineral-prone entry stage, as the flavor now offers greater impact from brown sugar, praline, nougat, and molasses. Ends on a friendly, woody note.

2019 Rating: ★ ★ ★/Recommended

Batiste Ecoiste 2014 Rhum Agricole (Marie-Galante) 45% abv, $40.

Transparent, crystalline appearance; minor sediment. Owns the appropriately grassy, wet-straw, green vegetable opening aroma that could only be rhum agricole and not molasses-based spirit; keenly acidic, fresh, herbaceous in the second passes after further air contact, and shows deeper layers of black pepper, turpentine, flaxseed oil, salt, dried rosemary. Entry is zesty, acutely vegetal, intensely grassy, dry; midpalate mirrors the entry perfectly but is more complex and minerally/earthy. Finishes long, concentrated on the earthiness/soil, and fittingly piquant, herbal.

2015 Rating: ★ ★ ★ ★/Highly Recommended

Bayou L'Esprit de la Louisiane Spiced Rum (USA) 40% abv, $22.

Pretty, topaz/bronze color; ideal purity. First whiffs encounter controlled aromas of butterscotch, brown butter, nougat; secondary inhalations pick up bigger traces of baking spices, most notably nutmeg but also clove, sweetened coconut, cinnamon, black cherry. Entry is maple sweet, honeyed, rich, lip-smacking tasty; midpalate reflects all the entry findings and remains firm, substantial, delicious. A serious spiced rum that offers lots of flavor impact due primarily to its 80-proof strength. Prefer it when rum producers don't flinch on the abv with their spiced rums. Yummy.

2018 Rating: ★ ★ ★ ★/Highly Recommended

Bayou L'Esprit de la Louisiane Select Rum (USA) 40% abv, $30.

Pot still distillation. Cocoa-brown/peru color; sediment-free clarity. Initial impressions offer scents of caramel, grass, cane that's been burnt, and a slight welcome funkiness that gives it personality; secondary inhalations following more aeration encounter aromatic traces of wet cement, damp sand, wet leaves, spring shower, brown sugar, and honey. Entry reflects the latter bouquet as the flavor profile goes bittersweet, brown sugar–like, and roasted bean–like; midpalate is chockfull of sugar cookie tastes that focus more on the richness of the sugarcane than any sense of wood barrel, and that's where the strength lies in the in-mouth phase. Concludes satiny smooth, elegant, integrated, and bittersweet.

2018 Rating: ★ ★ ★ ★/Highly Recommended

Bayou L'Esprit de la Louisiane Silver Rum (USA) 40% abv, $20.

Pot still distillation. Totally void of color; superb purity. The first nosings pick up pleasing but intense smells of grass, cane sugar, mown hay, and vanilla cake frosting; after more air contact, the aroma turns more spirity, estery, yeasty, and metallic/earthy. Entry is off-dry, moderately sugary, bitter, and hefty in texture; it's in the midpalate stage where the dense

grassiness soars, leaving in its wake cotton-candy flavors of refined white sugar and cookie batter. Finishes medium long, bittersweet, and caney.
2018 Rating: ★★★/Recommended

Blackheart Premium Spiced Rum (USA) 46.5% abv, $17.
Pretty copper/burnt sienna color; impeccable purity. I detect an entire banquet of spices here, including allspice, clove, cinnamon, and vanilla, that merge well with orange rind, citrusy fragrances in the first whiffs; secondary sniffs encounter enhanced citrus and cherry scents. Entry is at once semisweet, spicy, and fruity; midpalate is pleasingly tangy, citrusy, cherry-like, prickly. I appreciate the fine balance among the various taste attributes, especially citrus, baking spices, orchard fruits, and abv level.
2014 Rating: ★★★/Recommended

Blackwell Fine Jamaican Rum (Jamaica) 40% abv, $30.
Lovely, deep henna/auburn/mahogany color. Oh, Nellie, this opening aroma bursts into tsunami waves of blackstrap, cocoa, brown sugar, and dark caramel; another seven minutes of aeration highlight the cocoa/dark chocolate aspect to the hilt. Entry is sweet, slightly toasted (caramelized onion), marshmallow-like, leathery, and sugary; midpalate is wall-to-wall bittersweet dark chocolate, coffee bean, espresso, molasses, and dark honey flavors. Finishes as deeply as it began—long, bittersweet, and sublime. A superlative and seductive dark rum.
2016 Rating: ★★★★★/Highest Recommendation

Blue Chair Bay Coconut Rum (Barbados) 26.5% abv, $18.
Shimmering clear and pure. Up front, it smells engagingly and expectedly of sweetened coconut; later whiffs following more air contact introduce a trace of baking spice, mostly a dollop of vanilla. Entry is clean, true to the coconut, and bittersweet; midpalate mirrors the entry, offering a firm coconut thrust that lasts long into the finish.
2014 Rating: ★★/Not Recommended

Blue Chair Bay White Rum (Barbados) 40% abv, $18.
Pewter/silver tint; pure and sediment-free. I like the dry, beany/earthy, tropical fruit–like, slightly baked opening aroma, which is assertive, spicy (allspice, clove), yet elegant; secondary inhalations detect more candy-shop/confectioner sweetness in the forms of marshmallow, vanilla, brown sugar, old honey. Entry is sweeter than bouquet, substantial, slightly fruity (banana? guava?); midpalate features a quick blast of molasses, then it turns savory, understated, extended, and oily in the throat, good acidity that maintains the crispness. Mixes well in a bevy of rum cocktails, especially Mojitos, Cuba Libres.
2014 Rating: ★★★/Recommended

BLY Silver Rum (USA) 40% abv, $22.
Pristine, flawlessly pure appearance. Wow, the first sniffs detect abundant and assertive ambrosial scents of tropical and orchard fruits, such as pineapple, banana, pear, and guava, but there's likewise a mineral/flinty undercurrent of aroma that balances the intense ripeness of the fruit, creating a bouquet of memorable proportions; secondary sniffs find touches of

mown grass, lemon zest, marshmallow, and chalk that somehow all work together in harmony. Entry is richly textured, sumptuous without being flabby, deeply marshmallow-like without being sweet, and just plain delicious; midpalate echoes the entry, adding a mineral-like earthiness that balances the fruit density to the point where I believe this to be one of the best white rums I've ever reviewed. Phenomenal value.

2018 Rating: ★ ★ ★ ★ ★/Highest Recommendation

Botran 12 Year Old Rum (Guatemala) 40% abv, $20.

Bronze color; excellent clarity. Opening scents are bakeshop, winter holiday season, and spicy in nature, featuring third-gear aromas of cinnamon-spiced apple strudel, pineapple slices and clove studs on baked ham, spice cake, and sarsaparilla; secondary whiffs detect moderately deep fragrances of baked peach, baked nectarine, mace, and allspice. Entry is toasted marshmallow–like, more bittersweet than flat-out sugar sweet, with burnt/charred notes of grilled fruits; midpalate features grassy, cane-like, vegetal tastes that are clean and mineral-like. Aftertaste is medium in length and depth, toasty, and burnt.

2019 Rating: ★ ★ ★/Recommended

Botran 15 Year Old Rum (Guatemala) 40% abv, $35.

Ochre/sinopia color; flawless purity. Initial nosing passes detect grassy, cane-like scents that are delicate and understated; later sniffs pick up more tobacco-like fragrances that are toasted and slightly charred but not burnt. Entry is deliciously plump and rich, honeyed, and a little like bacon fat; midpalate builds upon the gains found in the entry stage, offering big-hearted flavors of honey ham, smoked bacon, BBQ sauce, tomato paste, and vinegar. Concludes long in the throat, viscous, robust, yet elegant.

2019 Rating: ★ ★ ★ ★/Highly Recommended

Botran 18 Year Old Rum (Guatemala) 40% abv, $40.

Beautiful mahogany color; very minor, inconsequential sediment spotted. Up-front aroma is chockfull of toasted almond, candied walnut, dried fruit, and winter holiday spice cake scents that are very pleasant; later inhalations pick up baked apricot, vanilla bean, espresso, coffee bean, and carob fragrances. Entry features mature flavors of oak-driven resins/sap, honey, rancio, hard cheese, umami, and sautéed mushrooms. Entry is hearty, honey sweet, with tastes similar to sap, tree bark, and cinnamon, and dense with myriad baking spices; midpalate features the baking spice allure and robustness that sidelines the beaniness and the honey aspect. Ends bittersweet, thick in texture, a bit like BBQ sauce and tomato paste. Very yummy.

2019 Rating: ★ ★ ★ ★/Highly Recommended

Brugal 1888 Doblemente Añejado Gran Reserva Rum (Dominican Republic) 40% abv, $40.

Burnt-orange/vermilion/cinnabar color; flawless clarity. The opening aromatic impressions are made up of brown sugar, dark honey, molasses, coffee bean, and winter holiday gingerbread, with a trace of funkiness; second passes encounter hints of lemon peel, candied fruits (apricot?), wet towel, damp leaves/rain forest, mildew, ore. Entry offers more of the musty old barrel/damp fabric funkiness noticed in the first sniffs, and that regrettably

undercuts any chance of fully enjoying the taste profile—what has happened to this once lovely rum, I wonder? Midpalate shows more bittersweet molasses, dark-chocolate flavor that marginally counters the moldy barrel aspect; finishes moldy, dank, and unacceptably stale and smelly. *Author's note*: This review is of a second bottle that I requested due to the first review bottle being tainted by what I suspected to be bacterial issues. After enthusiastically recommending this rum just seven years ago, it disturbs me greatly to see it crash and burn due I suspect possibly to poor barrel management (read: not replacing old worn-out barrels soon enough). I take no comfort in this review as I've been to the Brugal distillery twice and hold them in esteem. But to give this flawed rum anything higher than one star would be a disservice to *SJ* subscribers/readers . . . and to Brugal.
2018 Rating: ★/Not Recommended

Brugal Añejo Rum (Dominican Republic) 40% abv, $37.
Lovely warm amber hue; flawless purity. Opening aromatic waves include moss, moist earth, autumn forest floor, and grain husk; a welcome spiciness develops in the second passes as fragrances of brown butter and oak enter the picture—an unusual bouquet that's more earthy to me than anything else. Entry is acutely earthy/mossy, bramble-like and forest floor–like in its taste approach; the quirky, tea leaf–like earthiness abates slightly in midpalate, leaving the door open a crack for the molasses intensity to fill the void, and it does so immediately. This rum's mossy/mushroomy/green tea–like style might put off some rum purists, but it works in carefully selected cocktails.
2020 Rating: ★★★/Recommended

Brugal Especial Extra Dry Blanco Rum (Dominican Republic) 40% abv, $23.
As clear and clean as rainwater. Initial nosings detect hints of marshmallow, burnt match, and sap; later whiffs after further aeration find traces of rubber pencil eraser, coconut oil, and burning leaves; an intriguing, atypical molasses-based rum bouquet. Entry is keenly sweet, but not cloying, and focused entirely on molasses and coffee bean tastes that are vivid and pleasing; midpalate features moderately oily flavors of coffee bean, cocoa butter, peanut butter, and vanilla wafer. Ends on a high note of vanilla bean that's delightful. I first reviewed this rum in the mid-1990s and gave it three stars. Time for an upgrade. It has held on to its charm and remains a stellar white rum that's ideal for cocktails that call for light rums.
2020 Rating: ★★★★/Highly Recommended

Brugal Extra Viejo Rum (Dominican Republic) 40% abv, $33.
Topaz/bronze color; unblemished clarity. There's a pleasing plumpness to this aroma in the initial stages that comes off as dried fruit and baking spices (cinnamon); following more time for air contact, the fragrance starts to display a low degree of molasses/brown sugar. Entry is invitingly sweet, honeyed, and spicy; midpalate—no surprise—is far more expansive than the entry, as multiple levels of flavor take possession of the taste buds to show them evolved, integrated, and supple tastes of clove, nutmeg, honey, oloroso sherry, Christmas pudding, toffee, and marzipan. Very nutty and oily in the finish. A rocking oak-aged rum of note.
2020 Rating: ★★★★/Highly Recommended

By The Dutch Batavia Arrack (Indonesia) 48% abv, $65.
  Straw-yellow/gamboge color; very good clarity. Opening nosing passes encounter deeply earthy, schist-like aromas that speak of arid landscape, dusty-dry soil, hemp, textile fiber, ink; later inhalations discover more herbal aromas that link directly to sugarcane, grass, green vegetation—the bouquet is, to me at least, kind of halfway between rhum agricole and bison grass–flavored vodka. Entry is dry and slightly bitter, then it goes dense and earthy, vegetal, herbal, and peppery—I like this; midpalate is bone-dry, acidic, woodsy, bark-like, peppery, sappy, and clean. Finishes very long, deeply herbal but not floral or fruity; more earthy and mossy/mushroom-like. Something different and worthwhile for spirits lovers of all categories, especially rum.
2016 Rating: ★ ★ ★ ★/Highly Recommended

Caliche Rum (Puerto Rico) 40% abv, $25.
  Crystal clear and sediment-free. I find intriguing fruity notes in the fragrance right after the pour that turn floral in the second nosing passes following further aeration; a delicate bouquet of grace and elegance. Entry is gently sweet, moderately spicy, and pleasingly floral/herbal; midpalate is medium oily/viscous, cane sweet, and grassy. Finishes medium long and with good viscosity. Tasty when served on its own, but in my view its true purpose is as the base in a classic Daiquiri cocktail in which it shines like a beacon. Judged as the main Daiquiri ingredient, its score goes up to four stars.
2015 Rating: ★ ★ ★/Recommended

Canne Brûlées Banana Flavored Rum (Grenada) 40% abv, $25.
  Pewter tone; absolute clarity. First whiffs detect pleasingly understated scents of banana peel; not much to report about later aromatics other than they are carbon copies of the scanty opening fragrance. Entry is surprisingly dry to off-dry, with barely detectable banana flavor, texture is lean; midpalate is beany/kernel-like rather than banana-like, and it's here where I lose confidence in this rum. The banana flavor is not apparent enough for my liking. While I rail against many flavored spirits for overkill with flavoring, this flavored spirit could, in my view, improve with a greater injection of banana flavor.
2014 Rating: ★ ★/Not Recommended

Canne Brûlées Classic Dark Rum (Grenada) 40% abv, $40.
  Flax/silver-yellow color; very good clarity. Pleasing, zesty aromas of toasted honey wheat bread, vanilla, and brown sugar open up the aromatic proceedings; with aeration, the baking spice element takes command as tangy scents of vanilla bean, clove, gum, allspice integrate well. Entry is deeply grassy, elemental, dry yet bittersweet, brown sugar–like, caney; midpalate is where this rum shines brightest as the entire flavor profile leaps off the charts in waves of molasses, bread dough, yeast, allspice, clove, tobacco. Finishes long, nutty/nougat-like, grassy, brown sugar–like. Classy in a rustic manner.
2014 Rating: ★ ★ ★ ★/Highly Recommended

Canne Brûlées Classic White Rum (Grenada) 40% abv, $25.
  Slightest hint of pewter color; flawless clarity. Subtle earthiness, gum, cake frosting aromas in the initial sniffs; later whiffs pick up slate, granite, butcher's wax paper, parchment

scents that are stone dry. Entry is slightly toasty, dry overall, grassy, leaf-like, vegetal (asparagus, kale); midpalate mirrors the entry to a tee, in particular, the vegetal aspect. Aftertaste treats the taste buds to a toastiness that's almost tobacco-like and very grassy, earthy, soil-like.
2014 Rating: ★ ★ ★/Recommended

Canne Royale Extra Old Rum (Grenada) 40% abv, $40.

Maize/pale-gold/chardonnay color; unblemished purity. Leafy, mossy/lichen, forest floor/mushroom scents initiate the aroma rounds along with nuances of honey and toasted almond; later sniffs detect sand, cement, stone, earthenware aromas that give weight to the experience. Entry is dry, elegant, spicy (peppery), mildly resiny; midpalate mirrors the entry but adds really pleasing, subtle notes of French toast, maple, cinnamon, savory. Aftertaste is lean, acutely spicy, medium long. Not massively built, but effective in its narrow focus.
2014 Rating: ★ ★ ★ ★/Highly Recommended

Captain Morgan 100 Proof Spiced Rum (USA) 50% abv, $29.

Sandy-brown color; excellent purity level. This Captain Morgan opening aroma is far more focused than the Original as the extra 15 percent abv funnels the molasses/dark-honey scent through a narrow corridor that's semisweet, lightly toasted, and very pleasant; later sniffs pick up traces of nutmeg, clove, vanilla bean, and cinnamon that expand the bouquet's horizons markedly. Entry is warm on the tongue like campfire embers and is intensely spicy as the clove especially makes the case for dominance; midpalate offers sap-like, resiny, maple syrup notes that I find satisfying and not overly laden with sweetness. Concludes long, densely maple-like, and very tasty. It's the grown-up Captain Morgan.
2018 Rating: ★ ★ ★ ★/Highly Recommended

Captain Morgan Original Spiced Rum (USA) 35% abv, $23.

Marigold color; perfect clarity. Up front on the nose, there's more than ample candy-shop/bakery fragrances, ranging from brown sugar to fudge to chocolate cake frosting to cocoa bean and malted milk; with more air contact, the aroma deepens while adding spice-oriented scents of cinnamon, allspice, clove, and mace. Entry is full weighted, creamy, and unabashedly sweet, but it's the presence of the baking spices that nicely counters the sugary sweetness, making the flavor profile pleasing and sassy; midpalate mirrors the entry stage to a tee without deviating from the formula. Concludes tangy, spicy, alluringly sweet but neither cloying nor unctuous. Easy to understand its broad-based popularity.
2018 Rating: ★ ★ ★/Recommended

Captain Morgan White Rum (St. Croix) 40% abv, $16.

Void of color; sediment-free. Gently sweet, refined sugar–like, modestly fruity (sugar plums) aromas in the opening inhalations; secondary whiffs discover a basic, white, molasses-based rum 101 bouquet that's neither inspiring nor demanding; simple, straightforward bouquet of little consequence or concentration. Entry is lightweight in texture, lean, mildly sweet, with good acidity; midpalate is pleasantly bittersweet, easy. Finish is brief. No glaring flaws are detected but neither is any sense of defining character, and that's where I cannot go the extra mile by giving a third rating star and a recommendation. Just too bare bones.
2014 Rating: ★ ★/Not Recommended

Carolina Coast Spiced Rum (USA) 40% abv, $25.

Beautiful copper/russet color; impeccable clarity. A different breed of spiced rum, this fragrant rum offers a mélange of fruit and spice notes in the opening whiffs, including cinnamon, baked banana, pineapple, chestnut, baked beans with maple; secondary inhalations detect greater presence from the baking spices, especially cinnamon, clove. Entry is juicy, a bit lean, which is surprising since it is 80 proof; midpalate focused tightly on the baking spices, even ginger. Aftertaste is herbaceous, delicately sweet, tangy.
2014 Rating: ★ ★ ★/Recommended

Caroni 2000 Rum (Trinidad) 55% abv, $215.

Tawny/ochre color; flawless purity. First nosing passes pick up intriguing flinty, metallic scents of steel wool, carbon, steel cable, arid landscape/dry soil, and matches; extra aeration time stimulates fragrances of orchard-fruit pits/stones, waxy apple peel, paraffin, lint, and textile fiber. Entry is desert dry, lean and angular, narrow in bitter flavor focus, compact and self-contained, showing just a glimpse of sugarcane juice right before midpalate stage; here, the taste profile expands somewhat as it turns bittersweet, slightly like cherry juice, peppery (black peppercorn, especially), stony/metallic, and extra lean. Finishes medium long, nimble, keenly black pepper–like, even a touch smoky, bean-like, vegetal, and piquant from the 110 proof. This is Caribbean rum at its most essential, sculpted, clean, with no extra weight, character frills, or fat showing, and that's what makes it so compelling. You get a remarkable impression of sugarcane at its most natural beverage alcohol level. Frankly, I wasn't sure at first whether I could recommend it. Then by the midpalate stage, I was thinking, *You kidding? This is rum at its purest.*
2018 Rating: ★ ★ ★ ★/Highly Recommended

Casa D'Aristi Caribe Silver Rum (Mexico) 40% abv, $20.

D'Aristi rums from Mexico have not fared well with me in the past, ranging in the one and two star spheres in 2001 when last reviewed. Colorless; sediment-free appearance. First nosings pick up fruity aspects (banana) that are vivid and ripe, along with scents of white sugar and plain yogurt; further aeration rounds out the aroma as a grassiness enters the bouquet, making for moderately pleasing sniffing. Entry is a bit stark and biting, but the overall initial impression is clean and crisp; midpalate strangely turns even less flavorful and comes off as being leaden/metallic/tanky. The awkward midpalate advances into the aftertaste in a deeper fit of tinny flavor that kills the nice attributes found in the bouquet and entry. Just can't seem to get it together even after fifteen years. Avoid.
2016 Rating: ★/Not Recommended

Casimir Clairin Rum (Haiti) 48.3% abv, $40.

Pewter color; superb clarity. I immediately like the opening aroma as it reminds me of just-harvested sugarcane in all its vegetal/grassy/elemental glory; with more air contact, the aroma expands to include scents of egg white, sour candy, guava, lemon curd, soybean, and tofu. Entry is delicately bittersweet initially, reminiscent of soy sauce and Hunan seasonings, elemental in its grassiness, but then it turns up the sweetness dial in the midpalate as the flavor profile morphs into a deeply flavorful, sugary, bittersweet mode that's like caramelized onion and pan-seared mushrooms. Aftertaste returns to the caney sweet, brown sugar, light honey, vegetable cooking oil, and grassy place providing a pleasing way to close out the experience.

2018 Rating: ★ ★ ★ ★/Highly Recommended

Chairman's Reserve Original Rum (St. Lucia) 40% abv, $28.

Blend of pot and column still rums from Saint Lucia. Very pretty tawny color; impeccable purity. First nosing passes pick up appealing notes of molasses, tree sap/maple, clove, custard, and meringue; after allowing the aroma to open up through seven more minutes of more air contact, I now detect a meaty fragrance, especially roasted honey ham with pineapple and clove, and maple-cured bacon. Entry is engagingly sweet, roasted, almost charred as in the burnt sugar topping on crème brûlée; at midpalate, there's a pleasant fruitiness (spiced pear, spiced apple with nutmeg) that eclipses the sugary dessert aspect. Finishes medium long, more tangy and bittersweet than flat-out sweet. An English-style sipping rum that's elegant and balanced.

2017 Rating: ★ ★ ★ ★/Highly Recommended

Chairman's Reserve Spiced Rum (St. Lucia) 40% abv, $28.

Mahogany color; flawless clarity. The rush of citrus fruit fragrance from the get-go is fresh, appealing, and zesty—thankfully, it's the piquant nature of the citrus peel that keeps the aroma herbal and spicy; more aeration accentuates the tart lemony fruitiness as well as the tree bark spices of cinnamon and vanilla, plus there's a pinch of clove. Entry highlights the lemon zest as the texture turns creamy, but the core taste relies on the trifecta of clove-vanilla-cinnamon to push the flavor forward; midpalate offers equal parts baking spices and citrus peel to keep the palate engaged, and in the tail end there's a root beer–like taste that leads into the aftertaste, which is bittersweet, cushiony textured, and zesty.

2017 Rating: ★ ★ ★/Recommended

Charbay Rum (USA) 68.5% abv, $450.

Very limited production. Base material is Maui cane syrup that's been aged for five years in stainless steel, then for three years in French oak barrels; bottled uncut and unfiltered. Gorgeous, bright henna/auburn color; perfectly sediment-free. Considering the cask strength, the initial nosing passes are more about the cane syrup than the high abv; secondary sniffs detect more of the spirit presence, but it remains only a support player as the cane syrup sweetness dominates the bouquet. Entry is warming, only slightly prickly with spirity needles, and is remarkably robust, potent, toasty, chewy in texture, and spicy/zesty; midpalate vibrates with cane-y sweetness and oiliness. Finishes extremely long in the throat that's tingling with the spirit, but in the nicest way of campfire warmth. Nice work!

2016 Rating: ★ ★ ★ ★ ★/Highest Recommendation

Chauffe-Coeur Blanc Rhum Agricole (Martinique) 54% abv, $37.

There's a slight silvery/pewter-like tint to this rhum; perfectly pure. Wow, now here is rhum agricole at its aromatic best as the first nosing passes leap from the copita in aggressive waves of bittersweet cane syrup and sugary scents. I mean there's no mistaking what rum category this is; more air contact stimulates deeper, earthier, mossier fragrances, especially forest floor, flinty soil, limestone, chalk, and distant fruit aromas, such as baked pear, grilled nectarine; a glorious bouquet. Entry is supple, round, with zesty flavors of lead pencil, black pepper, cacao, baker's yeast, white flour, and candied almond; midpalate goes ape shit with dusty flavors of dry soil, sugarcane node, malted milk, rose petal, and geranium. Finishes long, round, mushroom-like, and earthy.

2019 Rating: ★ ★ ★ ★/Highly Recommended

Clément Canne Bleue Rhum Agricole (Martinique) 50% abv, $55.

Crystalline appearance, totally limpid; sediment-free. All sorts of grassiness, earthiness, melons, unsweetened pineapple juice, kiwi, vivid aromas come at you with abandon in the initial inhalations; the vegetal, grassy element takes charge after more air contact, brushing aside the fruitiness and focusing the bouquet tightly on the vegetation aspect, leaving no doubt whatsoever about its rhum agricole pedigree. Entry is sleek, silky, intensely grassy/vegetal, almost onion-like as the 100-proof foundation gracefully supports the flavor profile; midpalate is warming, slightly toasted, mossy, earthy, undeniably sensational. Aftertaste teases the palate with hints of tropical fruit that play with the firm, sturdy grassy base flavor.

2015 Rating: ★ ★ ★ ★ ★/Highest Recommendation

Clément Select Barrel Rhum Agricole (Martinique) 40% abv, $30.

Lovely sepia/burnt sienna color; unblemished purity. Opening sniffs encounter elusive scents of old leather, metal/copper, textile fiber, linens; further aeration brings out oaky vanilla, grass/sugarcane, light toffee. Entry is candy-store luscious, caramel toffee–like, and nougat-y; midpalate offers a trace of grassiness amidst the candy store layering of brown sugar, nougat, almond paste. Lip-smacking finish is full-bodied, buttery in texture.

2016 Rating: ★ ★ ★ ★/Highly Recommended

Cockspur 12 Bajan Crafted Rum (Barbados) 40% abv, $30.

Burnished-orange/copper-kettle color; too many floating particles seen for my comfort level. The first sniffs detect lots of yeasty/dusty aromas that remind me of a just-opened bakery; another seven minutes bring out scents of sawdust, lanolin, molasses, brown sugar, and candied nuts, especially walnuts. Entry is chewy, brown-sugar sweet, with a welcome twist of bitterness; midpalate is near-syrupy, intensely sweet and toasted, and more like burnt toast than lightly toasted bread. Finishes medium long, a touch like dried fruit, and spicy, especially clove and nutmeg.

2014 Rating: ★ ★ ★/Recommended

Cockspur 130 Overproof Rum (Barbados) 65% abv, $22.

Clear as springwater; flawless purity. Yikes, I get heaps of molasses and refined sugar in the initial nosing stages, then the aroma turns disarmingly fruity (white grapes, pineapple, kiwi) and ripe in the secondary passes; while the elevated abv is present, it doesn't attack the olfactory sense like some other overproof rums do. Entry is restrained, chewy in texture, bittersweet, beany, spicy, fruity; midpalate takes the abv to richer, tangier heights all the way through the finish, but never for a second obstructs the aroma or flavor profiles.

2014 Rating: ★ ★ ★ ★/Highly Recommended

Cockspur Fine Rum (Barbados) 40% abv, $18.

Pretty amber color; ideal clarity. Exhibits a mildly toasty and smoky opening aroma that's more cocoa-like than sugary/confection-like—nice start; after another seven minutes in the glass, the aroma becomes pleasingly baked and burnt, almost akin to s'mores and toasted marshmallows as the bouquet veers away from sweetness, choosing instead a toasted honey wheat bread note that's agreeable. Entry to palate is baked bread–like, sweeter than the aroma in a biscuity/cookie batter manner and is just generally pleasant; midpalate stage displays the molasses in spades for the first time, and that's fine because now I'm ready for a touch of sweetness that's more bittersweet than sugar sweet.

2014 Rating: ★★★/Recommended

Cruzan Estate Diamond Dark Rum (St. Croix) 40% abv, $20.

A blend of five-year and older rums. Old gold/light amber color; sediment-free, flawless clarity. Owns a woody, toasty initial aroma that's backed up by vanilla bean and allspice underpinning scents; the latter nosing offers enticing aromas of vanilla wafer cookies, Christmas cake, and tobacco leaf. Entry is more channeled than the easy Diamond Light, in that the taste profile is more clearly defined immediately as the resinous oak is apparent right from the start; midpalate is oaky, vanilla-accented, and bacon fat–like. Lots of sophisticated things happening here that I like.

2015 Rating: ★★★★/Highly Recommended

Cruzan Estate Diamond Light Rum (St. Croix) 40% abv, $20.

A blend of five-year and older rums. Pretty pewter/pale straw-green/yellow color; superb purity. Up-front aromas include toasted bread, buttercream candy, and marshmallow; molasses and cocoa bean aspects come alive in the second inhalations following further air contact. Entry is smooth as silk, sweet, and spicy (nutmeg, clove); midpalate is beany, comfortably sweet, tangy, and satiny textured. Finish carries with it a spicy twang that's appealing. Classy, well crafted.

2015 Rating: ★★★★/Highly Recommended

Cruzan Single Barrel Premium Extra Aged Rum (St. Croix) 40% abv, $30.

This rum's burnt sienna color is dazzling and free of sediment. I immediately like the highly complex and intricate opening aromas, in which cooking spices like bay leaf, parsley, and basil mingle with delicate brown sugar, hard cheese (Parmesan), and dried flower (violets) scents; after more aeration, I pick up well-integrated fragrances of fresh honey, toffee, clove, and nutmeg. Entry is pleasantly toasty, almost smoky, and charred, with background flavors of savory, sage, black pepper, and caramelized onion; midpalate impressions are dense, caramel/toffee-like, creamy in texture, and bittersweet. Finishes long, keenly spicy (more baking spices now than cooking spices), and complex. I'm happy to go out on a limb and state for the record that this expression is Cruzan's finest rum to date.

2018 Rating: ★★★★★/Highest Recommendation

Denizen 3 Year Old White Rum (Trinidad & Jamaica) 40% abv, $18.

Colorless, except for a bit of pewter tint; clean as rainwater. Up-front aromas include vanilla cream, cake frosting, a hint of lemon peel, and Juicy Fruit gum; later sniffs detect

ambrosial nuances of grassiness, cane, spearmint, and fruit salad, highlighted by watermelon and casaba. Entry is much drier than the bouquet implies it would be, and this sets the stage for a whole menu of varied flavors, including tree bark, cinnamon, allspice, candied almond, and orchard fruit flavored with brown sugar; midpalate is zesty, semisweet, deeply cane-like, slightly roasted, and showing a deft touch of rum funk. Ends up semisweet, acutely cane-like and grassy, earthy and elemental, with a hint of flintiness.
2019 Rating: ★ ★ ★/Recommended

Denizen Merchant's Reserve 8 Year Old Dark Rum (Jamaica & Martinique) 43% abv, $30.

Pretty amber/bronze color; superb clarity. Whoa, this initial nosing pass conjures up all sorts of Caribbean-related images, such as cigar tobacco, oven-baked plantains, sugarcane fields, baked pineapple, rum funk/mushrooms/fungi, and vinegar; secondary inhalations encounter aromas that are just as hearty as the first whiffs, highlighting the mushroom/fungi aspect the most. Entry is intensely nutty, pecan pie–like, roasted, and bittersweet; midpalate offers additional flavors, including toasted wheat bread, praline, nougat, candied walnut, and spice cake. Finishes long, pipe tobacco–like, gently sweet, and spicy like spice cake. A thoughtful mixture of divergent rum styles.
2019 Rating: ★ ★ ★/Recommended

Denizen Vatted Dark Rum (Guyana & Martinique) 50% abv, $30.

Gorgeous chestnut-brown/auburn color; flawlessly pure. I immediately respond to the winter holiday fruitcake aromas of candied walnut, and dried fruits (apricot, pineapple especially), which points directly at the Guyana rums; later inhalations pick up dense aromas of dark honey, nougat-middle candy bar, BBQ sauce, soy sauce, vinegar, brown sugar, jerk, and tomato paste. Entry mirrors all the second-level aromas, in particular, the tomato paste, jerk, and BBQ sauce; midpalate goes all out on summertime BBQ tastes, especially spicy pork ribs, grilled pineapple, and sweet tomato sauce. Concludes chunky, honeyed, vanilla extract–like, and very, very tangy.
2019 Rating: ★ ★ ★ ★/Highly Recommended

Dictador 20 Year Old Rum (Colombia) 40% abv, $60.

Tawny/copper color; flawlessly pure. I was expecting more aromatic impact, considering the age factor, but I only recognize a painfully few amorphous scents, specifically, gunmetal, nickel, and dry sand in the first inhalations; more aeration unleashes whispery traces of carob, pinto bean, and peanut, but that's about all. Entry shows flashes of mustiness, old attic flavors that then morph into more appropriate old rum flavors of brown sugar, hot cocoa, maple syrup, and tree sap; midpalate seems incapable of expanding on the entry findings, so my last impression is that this rum is over-the-hill and, while there are some mildly pleasant tastes, the spending of sixty dollars should be avoided.
2019 Rating: ★ ★/Not Recommended

Dictador 12 Year Old Rum (Colombia) 40% abv, $40.

Caramel-brown color; unblemished purity. Up-front aromas on this aged rum include cigar tobacco, toasted wheat bread, and pine resin; later inhalations after more aeration discover a touch of rum funk that's earthy, woodsy, mushroom-like, and mossy as well as vegetal, especially brussels sprouts. Entry is dense in texture, with flavors of dark caramel, dark chocolate, and cocoa bean; midpalate finds a nice equilibrium in the taste profile as the acidity becomes more apparent, which benefits the sweetness by mitigating it to an acceptable degree. Finishes nicely, if a touch brief.

2019 Rating: ★ ★ ★/Recommended

Dictador Amber Aged 100 Months Rum (Colombia) 40% abv, $30.

Harvest gold color; spotless purity. Akin to the Claro, this Dictador reveals scant evidence of aroma in the opening sniffs, and I suspect, though I may be wrong, that this is simply the Claro with caramel coloring; same result as the Claro. Entry isn't as cloying and numbing as the Claro, offering flavor elements of toasted marshmallow, nougat, and candied walnut; midpalate tastes include espresso, coffee bean, cacao, and fudge. Ends briefly, too sweet, and simple.

2019 Rating: ★ ★/Not Recommended

Dictador Claro Rum (Colombia) 40% abv, $30.

Cream soda color; superb clarity. The initial nosing passes don't pick up much in the way of aromatics, except for faint echoes of vanilla cream; additional time in the glass fails to stimulate more aromas so I move on. Entry is extremely sweet, cloying, and lacking a sense of balance, which causes it major analytical injury; midpalate mitigates a little of the sweet intensity, offering tastes of white sugar, vanilla cake frosting, and egg white. Concludes deeply bittersweet. It hurt my teeth.

2019 Rating: ★/Not Recommended

Dictador XO Insolent Solera System Rum (Colombia) 40% abv, $100.

Sinopia color; sediment-free appearance. This opening bouquet is round, floral (honeysuckle), bakery shop–like (cherry pie), and fruity in equal measure, and I like it immediately; second passes pick up additional scents, namely, chocolate cake frosting, marzipan, chocolate-covered cherry, Raisinets candy, carob, brownies, and cocoa. Entry is lusciously hot cocoa–like, caramel- and fudge-like, deeply buttery, and beany; midpalate echoes all the entry findings and adds subtle tastes of black peppercorn, treacle, and black raisin to the mix. Ends medium long, succulent, chocolatey, and luscious. A far cry from the mediocrity of the XO Perpetual.

2019 Rating: ★ ★ ★ ★/Highly Recommended

Dictador XO Perpetual Solera System Rum (Colombia) 40% abv, $100.

Pretty tawny/rust color; pristine clarity. In the initial whiffs I pick up distant aromas related to dried fruits, in particular, prune, black raisins, and dates, but little else; secondary inhalations strain to pick up anything more than the dried fruits, but I do manage to detect faint traces of gum, carnation, and dry leaves. Entry is chockfull of sap-like flavors (cinnamon, tree bark, maple) that are more bittersweet than flat-out sweet or honeyed; midpalate is buttery in texture, toffee-like in flavor, and pleasing overall as it leads into the pipe tobacco–like, savory finish, which is comely, but just a little bit hollow. This rum isn't worth its unreasonably lofty price tag when you consider other rums, all highly recommendable, in

the price range of $25–$100, like Plantation Xaymaca, Mount Gay XO, Facundo Exquisito, or El Dorado 21 Year Old.
2019 Rating: ★★/Not Recommended

Diplomatico 2000 Single Vintage Rum (Venezuela) 43% abv, $120.
Brilliant auburn/henna/russet color; immaculate purity. Holy cow, this first aroma is all about holiday fruitcake, dried tropical fruits (banana, pineapple), honey, brown sugar, cola nut, chocolate-covered orange rind, black raisins, dates; secondary whiffs confirm all the first-pass impressions and add succulent notes of dried apricot, nectarine—sensational bouquet. Entry is rich, bittersweet, cola-like, coffee-like, roasted, toasty, charred marshmallow; midpalate is front-loaded with candied fruits, but underneath lies the concentrated underpinning of molasses, dark honey, treacle. Aftertaste is long, languid, silky, intense, complex, majestic. Easily runs with the benchmark Diplomatico Reserva Exclusiva.
2015 Rating: ★★★★★/Highest Recommendation

Diplomatico Distillery Collection No. 1 Batch Kettle Rum (Venezuela) 47% abv, $80.
Beautiful cocoa-brown color; flawlessly pure. In the first sniffs after the pour I detect subtle bittersweet fragrances of toasted marshmallow, brown sugar, crème brûlée, tomato paste, and pralines; allowing for more aeration, the second set of nosings encounters scents of vinyl, sawdust, white raisins, and yellow plum. Entry is a finely tuned taste machine that offers narrowly focused flavors of dark honey, butterscotch, chocolate cake frosting, and cooking oils; midpalate turns bittersweet, oily, sinewy in texture rather than plump or creamy, and it's spicy, mostly like freshly ground peppercorn. Finishes very long, astringent, peppery, lean, yet concentrated.
2018 Rating: ★★★★/Highly Recommended

Diplomatico Distillery Collection No. 2 Barbet Rum (Venezuela) 47% abv, $80.
Dazzling burnt sienna/bronze color; immaculately clean and free of sediment. Initial inhalations offer succulent, dried-fruit scents that lean more towards candy-shop (caramels) and bakery aromas (prune Danish) that are stuffed with brown sugar, praline, plus nougat smells that completely charm the olfactory sense; secondary whiffs following more air contact come across chocolate-covered cherry and rum cake fragrances that bedazzle me. Entry is stunningly luscious, bittersweet, honeyed, with a savory taste of toasted marshmallow; midpalate shows a flash of dried fruits, especially black raisins and prunes, but the overall impression is of that rare variety of aged rum that highlights fathomless depth and complexity. Aftertaste is endless, bittersweet, honeyed, and dessert-like in its bearing. A bona fide classic from this esteemed distillery.
2018 Rating: ★★★★★/Highest Recommendation

Diplomatico Mantuano Rum (Venezuela) 40% abv, $24.
Deep tawny port–like, mahogany color is sediment-free and very attractive. Oh my, this first nosing pass explodes in the nasal cavity in small detonations reminiscent of English toffee, butterscotch, Snickers candy bar, fudge brownie, and butter brickle; after more aeration time, the secondary whiffs detect traces of gooey caramel, chocolate-covered coffee beans, and molasses; a monumental bouquet of icky-sticky splendor. Entry is tamer, more

restrained than the in-yer-face aroma as nuanced tastes of espresso, milk chocolate, and candied almond make for pleasant tasting; midpalate features more of the molasses aspect, which is earthy and mineral-like, moving away from the heightened sweetness, thereby providing a pleasing balance to the in-mouth experience. Ends up bittersweet, bean- and legume-like, and tart.
2018 Rating: ★ ★ ★ ★/Highly Recommended

Diplomatico Planas Rum (Venezuela) 47% abv, $29.
Pewter/tarnished-silver tint; clean-as-a-whistle appearance. I like the earthy, limestone- and dry soil–like opening aroma that calls to mind scents of lead pencil, shale, crystals, and minerals, but beneath all the elemental surface fragrance lies, at its heart, deeply grass-like, dry-as-stone sugarcane; secondary inhalations after more air contact reveal a deeper layer of bittersweet smells, led by molasses and bean curd. Entry is bittersweet, cocoa- and dark chocolate–like, with no other layers to cite; this taste profile is no-nonsense and straight- forward; midpalate echoes the entry and goes a touch mineral-like and even metallic as the foundational flavor goes eggy and vanilla beany. Finishes medium long, deeply bittersweet, bean-like, and flaxen. A gem that oozes minerality.
2018 Rating: ★ ★ ★ ★/Highly Recommended

Diplomatico Reserva Exclusiva Rum (Venezuela) 40% abv, $40.
Color is earth brown; superbly clean. Initial aromatic impressions include mesmerizing scents of walnut butter, brown sugar, prune, black raisins, and cacao bean; secondary passes discover elements of honey, chocolate-covered orange peel, roasted hazelnut, and chalk/ limestone. Entry is sweet but neither bitter nor bean-like and more like nut paste/nougat; midpalate soars to flavor heights that highlight brown sugar, fresh honey, cane juice, citrus rind, maple, and a silky viscosity that coats the entire palate. Finishes long, gently sweet, compact, and almost brandy-like. I can only confess to a possible LSD-flashback episode that in *Kindred Spirits 2* I somehow rated this classic rum only three stars. That is now corrected.
2020 Rating: ★ ★ ★ ★ ★/Highest Recommendation

Don Q 151 Rum (Puerto Rico) 75.5% abv, $25.
Pretty topaz/amber color; excellent clarity. Much to my surprise, the anticipated white-hot abv is anything but white hot in the nose and is, in fact, remarkably delicate, juicy, semisweet, fruity; second pass reveals little more except for a delightful piquancy. Entry is pleasingly warm, like a campfire, and is chewy, mildly peppery, delicately sweet, spicy (vanilla, clove); midpalate is toasty, gently sweet, shockingly approachable, and easy to sip. The heat factor picks up in the aftertaste and deservedly so since it is a 151, but the overall impression is one of superb balance, masterful distillation, and aging.
2015 Rating: ★ ★ ★ ★/Highly Recommended

Don Q 2005 Signature Release Single Barrel Rum (Puerto Rico) 40% abv, $40.
Pale amber color; impeccable purity. First nosing passes pick up delicate aromas of dried tropical fruits (banana and guava, especially), brown sugar, and cinnamon bun; later inhala- tions following more aeration encounter deeper scents of newly tanned leather, marshmallow,

and cotton candy. Entry is smooth as silk, yet there's a barrage of toasted flavors that resemble pastry-shop treats that are spiced with cinnamon, vanilla bean, and caramelized sugar; midpalate echoes the entry as the baking spice elements remain in the ascendency. Aftertaste is medium long, with a delightful taste of lightly toasted marshmallow. Puerto Rican rum at its elegant, highly sophisticated best.

2016 Rating: ★ ★ ★ ★/Highly Recommended

Don Q Double Aged Vermouth Cask Finish Rum (Puerto Rico) 40% abv, $50.

Rums aged five to eight years in American white oak casks, then finished in vermouth barrels. Sandy-brown color; perfectly clean appearance. First nosing passes pick up traces of cacao, grass, caramelized onion, and wine barrel; secondary whiffs find that the wine barrel/white wine aspect has grown in intensity while not altogether eclipsing the grassy, light, honey character. Entry is rife with white wine/white grape flavor that does slightly overtake the natural cane-like flavor of the rum, which I doubt was the strategy of the producer; midpalate sees the taste profile turn mineral-like, flinty, pleasingly dry, and at last firmly rum-like. Aftertaste flourishes with sugarcane/honey-like rum flavors that reassert themselves, and it's this recovery to the base material that makes it recommendable.

2018 Rating: ★ ★ ★/Recommended

Don Q Oak Barrel Spiced Rum (Puerto Rico) 45% abv, $30.

Topaz/amber hue; flawless clarity. There are vividly spicy elements (baking spices, mostly, like clove, allspice, cinnamon) that take the lead in the opening inhalations after the pour, but there are additional fragrances as well, including parchment, sassafras, root beer, carob, and cocoa bean; secondary nosings pick up a settled, integrated bouquet that's moderately spicy without any loss of the rum/molasses element. Entry is dry at first, then moderately fruity and ripe before turning mildly spiced and like baked apple or baked banana; midpalate is nicely bittersweet and beany, fruity, and jammy, with sideline flavors of berry tart, cinnamon apple, and honey. Concludes medium long, gently spiced, elegant, and delicious enough just to have on its own with a slice of orange.

2017 Rating: ★ ★ ★ ★/Highly Recommended

Don Q Signature Release Single Barrel 2007 Rum (Puerto Rico) 45% abv, $40.

Mahogany color; pristine purity. Right from the first sniff I get compelling woody smells, mostly resin and maple, along with tight, dry aromas of caramel-cream chocolates, nougat, and coconut; more time in the glass releases scents of molasses, winter holiday fruitcake, candied walnut, and dried pineapple. Entry is firm, sturdy, buttery, vanilla-like, and oaky; midpalate is the highlight point of the evaluation as all the various components merge into a unified flavor profile that's warm, lightly toasted, buttermilk biscuit–like, maple-like, and tangy. Finishes long, silky in texture, bittersweet, honeyed, and very, very yummy.

2017 Rating: ★ ★ ★ ★/Highly Recommended

Doorly's Fine Old 5 Year Old Rum (Barbados) 40% abv, $12.

Pretty burnished-orange color; impeccable clarity. I smell white raisins and quince in the opening sniffs; additional time in the glass brings out brown sugar/light honey aspects, which are gently spiced with integrated baking spices such as clove, allspice, and vanilla.

Entry is delicately spiced, biscuity, sugary, and delectably more bittersweet than sweet; mid-palate flavor profile offers tastes of Christmas fruitcake, with candied walnuts and dried yellow fruits, like pineapple, apricot, and banana. Finishes lean, focused, and gently spicy.
2014 Rating: ★★★/Recommended

Doorly's XO Fine Old Rum (Barbados) 40% abv, $17.

Maturation finished in old oloroso sherry butts. Gorgeous new copper/tawny/auburn color; superb purity; one of the most attractive rums in the marketplace. The first whiffs encounter a dazzling fruit basket of aromas, from red cherries to guava to kiwi to white grapes; following further air contact, the aroma expands to include pipe tobacco, sherry, new leather, tree sap/maple, and honey. Entry is leaner than I remembered, but likewise shows considerable length and brown-sugar pizazz; midpalate is cocoa-like, chocolatey, and has a good dose of vanilla extract, egg cream, and white raisins.
2014 Rating: ★★★★/Highly Recommended

Dos Maderas 5+3 Double Aged Rum (Caribbean/Spain) 40% abv, $34.

Cocoa-brown/topaz color; excellent, sediment-free clarity. Pleasingly grapy/fruity in the opening aroma, and by fruity, I mean specifically raspberry, black cherry, and black raisin; the ambrosial nose settles down a bit after additional air contact, but the ripeness enjoyed in the initial sniffs remains true and delectable. Entry is fruity/grapy, semisweet, sap-like, and lithe yet concentrated texturally; midpalate is medium sweet, gently spicy (cinnamon, clove), more like nutty pastry filling (almond paste, nougat) than fruit. Finishes composed, tannic, astringent, and woody/resiny. I reviewed this rum in 2008 and liked it much more than the current incarnation, which seems stripped down from the earlier, more sumptuous version.
2018 Rating: ★★★/Recommended

Dos Maderas 5+5 Triple Aged Rum (Caribbean/Spain) 40% abv, $45.

Mahogany/chestnut-brown color; flawless clarity. I pick up early aromatic traces of old book leather, dusty library, graham cracker, treacle, and Mexican mole sauce; secondary nosing passes after more air contact find the nose diminished slightly as I hunt for definable scents other than what I've already discerned in the initial whiffs, but that fails so I move on. Entry is acutely bittersweet, heavily roasted, toffee-like, fudge-like, and dense; midpalate shows a bit more brightness with the introduction of black raisin and date flavors mingling with the chocolate aspects and the sweet oakiness. Ends up being bittersweet, dark chocolate–like, and intensely tannic and woody.
2018 Rating: ★★★/Recommended

El Dorado 12 Year Old Demerara Rum (Guyana) 40% abv, $29.

Rich bronze/saffron color; ideal, sediment-free clarity. I encounter lovely, dry-leaning aromas of dried orchard and berry fruits, in particular, raisins and apricots, plus black pepper spice in the opening inhalations; then after some aeration, subtle hints of tobacco leaf, spiced and baked pear, new leather emerge and take command. Entry is sublimely elegant, harmonious, brown-sugar sweet yet slightly bitter; midpalate soars to one of the greatest heights known to rum as the demerara influence shines brightly in the form of a perfectly balanced

flavor profile of ideal acidity, abv level, sugar intensity, oak impact. Finishes moderately toasted, fruity (dried/baked), velvety in texture, stately, elegant. A perfect molasses-based rum.
2015 Rating: ★ ★ ★ ★ ★/Highest Recommendation

El Dorado 15 Year Old Special Reserve Demerara Rum (Guyana) 40% abv, $44.
Attractive copper/deep auburn color; impeccable purity. Displays similar opening aromatic impressions of dried fruits as the sibling twelve-year-old, but likewise shows a developed trace of paraffin; later sniffs detect dried herbs, especially bay leaf, as well as nuances of old dark honey, walnut, and pineapple. Entry showcases the fruit aspect (baked pineapple, banana) and silky texture; midpalate features deeply flavored brown sugar, cocoa bean, vanilla, black pepper, dates, raisins. Aftertaste is bittersweet, earthy, silky, and just one notch thinner than the majestic twelve-year-old.
2015 Rating: ★ ★ ★ ★/Highly Recommended

El Dorado 21 Year Old Special Reserve Demerara Rum (Guyana) 40% abv, $99.
Gorgeous tawny/henna/chestnut color; sediment-free. First whiffs are all about beeswax/paraffin and butcher's wax paper plus oak resin/tree sap; secondary inhalations pick up toasted nuts, creosote, palm oil, and dates. Entry is sweet, oily, resiny, raisiny, cheese-like; midpalate goes nutty, dense, honeyed, intensely brown sugar–like, silky in texture, slightly metallic. Concludes deeply flavorful, bigger than the fifteen-year-old sibling, idiosyncratic, coin-like/nickel-like, tree sap, nutty.
2015 Rating: ★ ★ ★ ★/Highly Recommended

El Dorado 3 Year Old Demerara Rum (Guyana) 40% abv, $16.
Transparent; not a single speck of floating debris. I find the opening aroma to be inexplicably neutral, except for a minimal fruitiness that lurks in the background; later whiffs echo the initial inhalations—I am puzzled because there are neither sugar nor bean aspects. Entry is drier than the Superior White, almost dusty; midpalate at last displays some demerara character in a kernel-like impression that spins off some minor cocoa bean flavor. Finishes well, elegant, but not animated at all.
2015 Rating: ★ ★ ★/Recommended

El Dorado 5 Year Old Demerara Rum (Guyana) 40% abv, $20.
Lovely topaz color; remarkable clarity. I get buttered rum fragrance in the opening sniffs as well as beeswax and paraffin; further air contact stimulates scents of roasted almond, walnuts, orchard fruit stone. Entry is chockfull of roasted nuts, candy bar, cake frosting flavors that are more bittersweet than sweet; midpalate is oily, brown butter–like, honeyed, almost palo cortado–like. Ends on fascinating notes of pipe tobacco and candied prune.
2015 Rating: ★ ★ ★ ★/Highly Recommended

El Dorado 8 Year Old Demerara Rum (Guyana) 40% abv, $23.
Attractive amber/copper color; impeccable purity. Delicate scents of demerara sugar, paraffin, new leather highlight the early aroma; secondary whiffs encounter canola oil, parchment, toasted almond. Entry is divinely sweet, raisiny, slightly ash-like, resiny/oaky;

midpalate mirrors the entry to a tee, adding toasted marshmallow, marzipan, brown sugar; medium-weight viscosity. Concludes long in the throat, perfectly integrated, sweet but not cloying, and satiny.

2015 Rating: ★★★★★/Highest Recommendation

El Dorado Original Dark Demerara Rum (Guyana) 40% abv, $12.

Very pretty burnt sienna/tawny color; flawless clarity. Surprisingly, this initial aromatic thrust is restrained, almost a touch juicy, with a low degree of dark chocolate/cocoa compared to the Superior White aroma, which is more animated; with more aeration, the bouquet shows flashes of brown sugar, cocoa, coffee latte. Entry is sweeter than the Superior White to the point of becoming bittersweet; midpalate is keenly bittersweet, profoundly cocoa-like, slightly toasted/roasted. Aftertaste features the demerara sugar that is, after all, the core.

2015 Rating: ★★★★/Highly Recommended

El Dorado Spiced Demerara Rum (Guyana) 40% abv, $16.

Bright topaz color; pristine clarity. Interestingly, there isn't the usual baking spice aromatic thrust in the opening inhalations, but rather a baked fruit aspect that is more a nuance than a deep-impact component; secondary passes following further air contact reveal deep-seated fragrances of brown sugar, dry stone, dry earth, vegetation, molasses. Entry is pleasing, tangy, chocolatey, modestly sweet; midpalate is the spiciest stage and the most evolved as a refined flavor of vanilla-laced honey comes to the forefront. Finishes zesty, firm, mildly spiced.

2015 Rating: ★★★/Recommended

Diamond Reserve 151° Overproof Rum (Guyana) 75.5% abv, $20.

Author's note: This wonderful rum was formerly known as El Dorado Superior Overproof Demerara Rum. Pale oyster/bisque tint; ideal clarity. Smells, not surprisingly, of demerara sugar, molasses, cocoa bean, dark chocolate in the first sniffs; I like how the elevated abv not for a moment obstructs or overshadows any other element in the succulent bouquet. Entry is smooth, a bit warm, toasty, marshmallow-like, bittersweet; midpalate is harmonious, lusciously chocolatey, velvety on the palate. Aftertaste is endless, warming like campfire embers, rich.

2015 Rating: ★★★★★/Highest Recommendation

El Dorado Superior White Demerara Rum (Guyana) 40% abv, $12.

Pewter/ecru hint of color; unblemished purity. Lovely toasted honey wheat cereal notes in the opening whiffs that are bolstered by secondary aromas of s'mores, cigarette ash, caramelized onion in later inhalations. Entry is buttery sweet, cocoa-like, oily; midpalate leans more towards cocoa powder, cooking oil, sweet creamery butter; medium density. Finishes slightly smoky, oily. When they say "Superior White," they aren't kidding.

2015 Rating: ★★★★/Highly Recommended

English Harbour 10 Year Old Reserve Rum (Antigua) 40% abv, $75.

The amber color is a tad dull, but the clarity is flawless and sediment-free. Zesty

aromatic notes of white pepper, cinnamon, shrub leaf, honeysuckle, and nutmeg leap to the foreground in the initial blast of fragrance; the spiciness fades with aeration, but the herbal/vegetal quality remains, now being complemented by the sturdy sweetness of molasses; a composed, elegant bouquet. Palate entry is succulent, gently sweet, plump, and moderately textured; midpalate is elegant, stately, and refined with long, roasted flavors of pipe tobacco, fruitcake, candied walnut, and brown sugar. A wonder to behold.
2020 Rating: ★ ★ ★ ★ ★/Highest Recommendation

English Harbour 25 Year Old Reserve Rum (Antigua) 40% abv, $450.

Brilliant and bright under the examination lamp, this copper/deep amber jewel sparkles under the lamp; superb purity. First whiffs detect lively, vivid scents of vanilla cake frosting, brown sugar, honey, and fresh orange blossom; further air contact integrates all the components into a unified, mildly sweet rum bouquet of grace and depth; holy moly, what a gorgeous and classical rum aroma. Palate entry is fruity sweet and ripe as much as it is confectionery; midpalate features harmonious and multilayered tastes of candied plums, Raisinets, candied yellow fruit, ripe peach, honey, and gentle sweetness that come wrapped in a subtle texture. Perhaps my favorite aged, molasses-based rum of all time. A masterpiece.
2020 Rating: ★ ★ ★ ★ ★/Highest Recommendation

Facundo Eximo Diez Años Rum (Bahamas) 40% abv, $60.

Marriage of ten- to twelve-year-old rums. Pretty pale-amber/topaz color; flawless clarity. I get roasted chestnut, baked banana, allspice in the opening inhalations; later sniffs detect dried rose petal, baked pineapple, clove, nutmeg, broiled pork. Entry is silky in texture, delicately sweet and maple-like; midpalate is harmonious, toffee-like, honeyed/sherried, nutty. Concludes creamy, with deep flavors of dark caramel, brown butter, egg cream. A superlative aged rum at its peak of aroma, taste, and texture. I'm all in on this one.
2014 Rating: ★ ★ ★ ★ ★/Highest Recommendation

Facundo Exquisito Rum (Bahamas) 40% abv, $90.

Blend of seven- to twenty-three-year-old rums. Ochre/deep amber color; superb clarity. First nosings are understated, gentle, showing wisps of brown sugar, nougat aromas, and little more; later inhalations after more air contact find fresh nuts, textile fiber, parchment. Entry showcases the intensity of the oak barrels in the forms of sugar maple, tree sap, charred marshmallow; midpalate is oily in texture (a huge plus), hard cheese–like, earthy, with an actual trace of rancio. Finishes long, succulent, round, concentrated, maple-like. Splendid. At its pinnacle of development.
2014 Rating: ★ ★ ★ ★ ★/Highest Recommendation

Facundo Neo Silver Rum (Bahamas) 40% abv, $45.

Author's note: Bacardí's Facundo collection is their premium line of rums named in honor of the company's founder. Blend of rums aged one to eight years. Clean, colorless, and clear as springwater. I like the out-of-the-gate aromas of slate, dry stone, damp earth, matchstick, which are unusual and compelling; later inhalations discover caramelized onion, soy sauce, hoisin, chalk scents. Entry is sleek, honeyed, viscous, buttery, smoky; midpalate features an herbal quality that brings a dryness that's balanced, acidic, peppery, delicious,

earthy, atypical. Ends stony/minerally, dry, full weighted, complex. Like no other white/silver rum I know of and far more complex than virtually all of them. Caveat: something indefinable that I detected in midpalate keeps me from bestowing a fifth rating star.
2014 Rating: ★ ★ ★ ★/Highly Recommended

Facundo Paraíso XA Rum (Bahamas) 40% abv, $250.
Blend of rums up to twenty-three years old. Stunning auburn/henna color; unblemished purity. Opening whiffs can't help but pick up truckloads of dried fruit, mostly black raisins, prunes, cherries, along with scents of pipe tobacco; later aromas include black tea, bergamot, candied walnuts, cocoa butter, agave syrup. Entry is thick in viscosity, caramel-like, beany (cocoa); midpalate features the candy-shop taste of the entry stage, along with potent oloroso sherry, chocolate-covered cherry, treacle flavors that overwhelm the taste buds prior to finish. Aftertaste is nougaty, almond paste–like, gooey. This rum pushes the limit for me as it begs asking, "When does rum become brandy?" It's very good, make no mistake, but there are aspects of it that are too much for me.
2014 Rating: ★ ★ ★ ★/Highly Recommended

Flor de Caña Centenario 12 Year Old Single Estate Rum (Nicaragua) 40% abv, $36.
Chestnut-brown color; perfect purity. First nosing passes pick up succulent notes of dried banana, dried apricot, and white grapes, along with subtler notes of clove, allspice, hazelnut, and pipe tobacco; secondary whiffs detect deeper aromas, especially walnuts, pecans, and confectioners' sugar. Entry blows away the taste buds in waves of dried fruit, mincemeat flavors that are relatively but not overly spicy; midpalate features deep flavors of brown sugar, chocolate cake frosting, carob, espresso, and caramelized onion. Ends on a pipe-tobacco note that's just fruity enough to be ambrosial.
2019 Rating: ★ ★ ★ ★/Highly Recommended

Flor de Caña Centenario 18 Year Old Single Estate Rum (Nicaragua) 40% abv, $50.
Gorgeous cocoa-brown color; spotlessly clean. Up front aromatically, I get traces of saddle leather, marshmallow, buttermilk, and meringue; later sniffs after more air contact pick up juicier aromas of citrus (lemon or lime, can't decide), cola nut, and lychee. Entry comes off a bit cola-like but strangely flat and uninteresting, much to my surprise; midpalate shows only nominal woodiness but lots of vegetal elements that I find curious and distracting. Finishes short, root beer–like, and beany. Deeply disappointing in view of the seven-, twelve-, and twenty-five-year old editions.
2019 Rating: ★ ★/Not Recommended

Flor de Caña Centenario 25 Year Old Single Estate Rum (Nicaragua) 40% abv, $150.
Copper/mahogany color; flawless purity. There are tantalizing hints of raisins, bacon fat, brown sugar, and mincemeat in the initial whiffs following the pour; secondary passes pick up deeper aromas of pipe tobacco, cane, cola nut, cocoa powder, and dark bittersweet chocolate. Entry is bittersweet, piquant, nutty (like candied walnut), praline-like, and toasted; midpalate goes lean and mean, offering dry-as-a-bone flavors of toasted wheat bread, breakfast cereal with honey, and fudge. Ends up toasted, roasted, dry, and bean-like.
2019 Rating: ★ ★ ★ ★/Highly Recommended

Flor de Caña Gran Reserva 7 Year Old Rum (Nicaragua) 40% abv, $25.

Golden-harvest color; clean and free of sediment. Opening whiffs detect roasted walnut, nougat, almond butter notes that mingle with bittersweet turbinado sugar scents; secondary inhalations identify dense candy-shop aromas, especially praline, candy bar, candied walnut, and caramel. Entry is supple in texture, spicy/peppery, and intensely honeyed; midpalate brings home the bacon by offering a bacon fat–like taste that's meaty. Aftertaste mirrors the midpalate stage, but turns sweeter and more sugar cookie–like.

2019 Rating: ★ ★ ★/Recommended

Grander 8 Year Old Rum (Panama) 45% abv, $38.

Attractive, bright gamboge color; unblemished, sediment-free purity. First nosings meet up with oaky, spicy fragrances that are rife with vanilla bean, clove, and honeysuckle; secondary inhalations after additional aeration discover deeper layers of vanilla and honey but now with a touch of bittersweet scent that's derived, I have to think, from the oak—a likable bouquet. Entry is supercharged with prickly spirit that gently stings the tongue, then cools off in midpalate, where the flavor profile turns oily in texture and buttery in taste (brown butter). Concludes biscuity, cake frosting–like, bittersweet, suddenly toasted, candied to a lesser degree, and marshmallowy. A bit of a sensory roller coaster that features compelling highs but likewise a slightly hollow core that gets exposed in the mouth. I like the elevated abv but I was surprised by the relatively lightweight character. My guess is that this is a good cocktail rum.

2015 Rating: ★ ★ ★/Recommended

Habitation Saint-Etienne HSE Blanc Rhum Agricole (Martinique) 40% abv, $22.

Void of color; pristinely pure. The grassy/earthy/sour pineapple intensity hits you between the eyes in the initial inhalations, making it crystal clear that this could not be anything but rhum agricole; with more time in the glass, the aroma turns acutely mineral-like, flinty, soy sauce–like, and sour apple–like (Jolly Rancher style). Entry is vegetal, stunningly cane-like, grassy, herbal, and tongue-on-stone dry; midpalate stays the parched course as the flavor profile turns marginally oily in texture, peppery, coffee bean–like, and properly bitter. Aftertaste is medium long, oilier than the midpalate, aggressive, and deeply spicy/peppery/piquant.

2017 Rating: ★ ★ ★/Recommended

Habitation Saint-Etienne HSE Grande Reserve XO Rhum Agricole (Martinique) 43% abv, $70.

Deep color is sienna/rust; purity level is excellent. The opening inhalations detect heavy doses of oak influence, in particular, potent fragrances of roasted coffee bean, cola nut, vanilla bean, toffee, and maple that eclipse any sense of the natural grassiness of rhum agricole; further air contact sustains the all-encompassing oak dominance, turning vegetable cooking oil–like; the thickness of the oak impact has made this rhum agricole more brandy-like than Martinique rhum–like, and that could be a serious issue for rhum agricole admirers. Entry is zesty, bean-like, spicy, and marginally grassy as finally I get some rhum agricole personality shining through the drapes of oak; midpalate goes nutty, nougat- and candy bar–like, and while I appreciate the flavor profile overall, I fear that more fervent rhum agricole enthusiasts might consider this rhum as being top-heavy with oak maturation and lacking the vegetal funk of lighter, nimbler styles, such as the HSE Blanc. That said, the aftertaste is lovely, dense, rich, cocoa-like, and velvety. A delicious rhum with caveats.

2017 Rating: ★ ★ ★ ★/Highly Recommended

Habitation Saint-Etienne HSE VSOP Rhum Agricole (Martinique) 45% abv, $40.

Tawny/ochre color; impeccable clarity. I get only subtle traces of coffee bean/espresso, cocoa bean, lead pencil, and cedar cigar box in the opening inhalations; more aeration doesn't stimulate much in the way of aromatic assertiveness, as the bouquet remains understatedly earthy, grassy, cane-y, and mineral-like. Entry is wonderfully succulent, juicy, bittersweet, cocoa-like, and smooth as silk; midpalate provides deeply flavorful aspects of dark chocolate, treacle, butterscotch, and dark honey that last into the tightly focused, bittersweet aftertaste that is medium long, ashy, earthy, and restrained. One has to do a lot of the work unearthing the aromatic and gustatory elements, but make no mistake, it's worth the effort.

2017 Rating: ★ ★ ★ ★/Highly Recommended

Habitation Saint-Etienne HSE World Cask Finishes Extra Highland Cask Rhum Agricole (Martinique) 44% abv, $90.

Attractive tawny/mahogany color; superb clarity. There's a deficit here in the initial whiffs of the expected and desired rhum agricole grassiness as the dry, grainy opening aromas lean in favor of whiskey rather than earthy, elemental rhum; secondary sniffs following more air contact serve up echoes of the first inhalations, not adding anything new, so I move on. Entry is off-dry and heavily roasted and grainy; midpalate stays the whisky-like, grainy course as the pleasing innate grassiness of rhum agricole is stuffed below deck. Aftertaste reflects the entry and midpalate, and while the spirit composition itself is mildly tasty, appealing, and therefore recommendable, I question the production judgment of why the natural charm of Martinique rhum agricole is masked by the maturation regime that, to me, seems totally out of character. If you want an official AOC French spirit that tastes like this, why not just buy armagnac? Why introduce confusion to the rhum agricole category?

2017 Rating: ★ ★ ★/Recommended

Habitation Velier Forsyths 2005 Single Rum (Jamaica) 57.8% abv, $85.

Earth yellow/sandy-brown color; excellent clarity. This narrowly focused aroma features tightly-wound fragrances of new leather, unsalted butter, oak plank, ink, and cigar tobacco; secondary whiffs after more aeration encounter subtle odors of sawdust, butcher's wax paper, lanolin, and onionskin parchment. Entry offers low-flying flavors of maple/tree sap, oak resins, chewing tobacco, and honey flavored cereal; midpalate makes an attempt at featuring a genuine rum tasting experience via a waxy texture and flavors that are spicy (allspice, marjoram), lightly honeyed, toasted grain–like, and slightly prickly from the high abv. Concludes surprisingly brief in the throat, peppery, and oily. I wanted to like this Jamaican rum enough for a third rating star and recommendation but it simply fell short. It's too vague and opaque in terms of drinking enjoyment.

2018 Rating: ★ ★/Not Recommended

Habitation Velier Forsyths WP 502 Single White Rum (Jamaica) 57% abv, $51.

A touch hazy; white smoke color. Opening nosing passes detect aggressive and some-what disparate scents of joss stick, burnt sugarcane, talc, chalky soil, burnt brussels sprouts, and legumes; following more air contact, the aroma now offers curious fragrances of tar, nicotine, plastic, Naugahyde, paint, and decomposing forest vegetation, plus all the findings in the first inhalations. Entry echoes all of the bouquet impressions, which I didn't care for or appreciate the significance of; midpalate maintains the nasty sensory assault. Sorry, but I'm missing the point of this unappealing rum that smells like a discount furniture store.

2018 Rating: ★/Not Recommended

Habitation Velier Foursquare 2013 Single Rum (Barbados) 64% abv, $69.

Fawn/earth yellow color; superb clarity. I like this first nose that is biscuity, cereal-like, slightly sweet, graham cracker–like, and gently spiced with fragrances akin to cola nut, clove, and nutmeg; secondary inhalations encounter deeper scents, including cigar tobacco, cara-mel, brown sugar, and lead pencil. Entry is vibrant and prickly from the cask strength, but not so overpowering that you lose the honey wheat, brown sugar, and toffee flavors; mid-palate reflects the entry impressions, adding a buttery/creamy texture that underscores the semisweet flavor profile. Finishes very long, prickly, warming, and semisweet. I suggest that you add mineral water at a ratio of four parts rum/one part water to bring out the richness of the flavor.

2018 Rating: ★ ★ ★ ★/Highly Recommended

Author's note: The next four rum reviews are all labeled as "Havana Club." The first two are from Cuba, where the brand was born. And, the last two are made by Bacardi in Puerto Rico. Rights to the name are being contested in a long court battle between Bacardi and Pernod Ricard, which owns the Cuban brand.

Havana Club Añejo Reserva Rum (Cuba; Not available in the US) 40% abv, $n/a.

Attractive topaz/amber color; ideal purity. The opening inhalations pick up candy-shop aromas of honey, brown sugar, ripe tropical fruits such as guava and banana; secondary nosings detect more of the grassy character of the sugarcane as the bouquet turns drier, narrowing its focus on the vegetation quality of the cane. Entry is succulent, sweet, a touch peppery, and zesty; midpalate is longer, more bittersweet than sweet, and a little bean-like, especially cacao. Finishes medium long, toasted, crisp, and fresh.

2016 Rating: ★ ★ ★/Recommended

Havana Club Añejo 7 Year Old Rum (Cuba; Not available in the US) 40% abv, $n/a.

Created from rums that are at least seven years old and with some that range up to fourteen years. Richer color than the Reserva, more a new-copper/burnished-orange hue; very good clarity. First whiffs encounter substantial, sturdy, serious aromas of nutmeg, clove, walnut, spice cake; secondary nosing passes discover crème brûlèe, orange zest, pipe tobacco, chocolate-covered orange peel—this is a big-league rum bouquet. Entry is tight, lush, and

oily in texture, bittersweet, nutty, slightly funky; midpalate offers coffee bean, vanilla, and a smooth, supple texture. Aftertaste highlights the bittersweet aspect and is therefore crisp, clean, and delicious; finish lingers for a long time—in this case, a welcome development.
2016 Rating: ★ ★ ★ ★/Highly Recommended

Havana Club Añejo Blanco Rum (Puerto Rico) 40% abv, $18.

USA-made Havana Club. The appearance shows a pewter-, vanilla-like tint and blemish-free clarity. First nosing passes pick up alluring fruit and nut notes that remind me initially of guava and hazelnut, then with more air contact seem reminiscent of breadfruit, white rice, and nutmeg. Entry is off-dry, slightly bittersweet at first, and then the taste profile turns more honeyed and bean-like; midpalate shows a bit of sugary fatness that affects the texture, which regrettably goes flabby due to a seeming deficit of acidity. Finishes sweeter than the midpalate, as the honey, brown sugar aspects accelerate in power and influence. While drinkable, I wish it were crisper, more agile, edgier, and less soft in the middle. Can't possibly recommend it.
2018 Rating: ★ ★/Not Recommended

Havana Club Añejo Classico Rum (Puerto Rico) 40% abv, $20.

USA-made Havana Club. Amber color; excellent purity. I like this opening fragrance, which abounds with similar fruitiness and nut-like attributes like the Añejo Blanco; with more aeration the aromatic profile turns more spice-driven as notes of allspice, clove, and mace take charge bringing about a piquancy that is charming. Entry is moderately rich in texture, honey, and brown sugar sweet, but there's more of a woody edge to it than the Blanco version, which gives it a black pepper quality that's mildly appealing; midpalate turns woodier, more resiny, and therefore drier than the entry phase. Aftertaste is brief, a little too nondescript for comfort, and ultimately unsatisfying. I feel there was potential here, but the lack of character in both expressions works against any recommendation.
2018 Rating: ★ ★/Not Recommended

Kirk and Sweeney 18 Year Old Rum (Dominican Republic) 40% abv, $49.

Tawny/old-copper color; excellent clarity. Wow, there's an entire symphony of aromas happening here, everything from cocoa butter to candied almond to pipe tobacco to old leather books to vanilla extract to cake frosting, and that's just for starters; second passes mirror the first whiffs, adding dark chocolate, toasted bread, toasted marshmallow; an amazing bouquet. Entry is succulent, marginally more bittersweet than flat-out sweet, honeyed, almost sherry-like, deeply characterful; midpalate maintains the entry aspects, but the textural difference is what makes this stage so delectable as the body goes silky smooth and oily. Finishes long, honeyed, spicy, fabulously tasty.
2015 Rating: ★ ★ ★ ★ ★/Highest Recommendation

Kirk and Sweeney 23 Year Old Rum (Dominican Republic) 40% abv, $59.

Auburn/henna color; unblemished, sediment-free purity. I pick up more woodiness in this opening aroma than the eighteen-year-old, which was much more candied, but I also detect deep molasses fragrance here, as well; second inhalations after further aeration uncover hints of saddle leather, cooking oil, charred wood, campfire embers; this bouquet

is nowhere near as assertive as the eighteen. Entry is succulent, unabashedly sweet but not cloying, chewy in texture, oaky, sap-like, maple-like; midpalate features more of the oak polymers in the forms of acidity and sap, but the overall taste impression is of elegance, grace, depth of character. I preferred the eighteen due to its wildly long menu of attributes and its verve, but this is a stately rum of genuine class.
2015 Rating: ★ ★ ★ ★/Highly Recommended

Kirk and Sweeney 12 Year Old Rum (Dominican Republic) 40% abv, $35.

Auburn color; good purity, but some minor sediment seen. Offers alluring marshmallow, nutmeg, and candied almond scents in the first whiffs after the pour; after seven more minutes of aeration, I was hoping that the bouquet would expand or deepen, but it didn't, remaining pleasant, to be sure, but for twelve years old, I want and expect more aromatic complexity. Entry is semisweet, brown sugar–like, and quite delicious; midpalate stage shows off plenty of brown sugar, candied nuts, and vanilla bean flavors that make up for the slightly hollow aroma. Aftertaste is tangy, drier than the midpalate, and nicely biscuit batter–like.
2013 Rating: ★ ★ ★ ★/Highly Recommended

La Hechicera Reserva Familia Solera 21 Rum (Colombia) 40% abv, $40.

Brandy-like cocoa-brown color; excellent purity. Up front, I pick up bittersweet aromas that are very bakery- and candy shop–like initially, then the aroma turns pleasantly fruity (peach, pear) with more air contact; secondary inhalations detect more fruit aspects, as the bouquet turns grapy and berry-like more than orchard fruit–like. Entry is deeply oaky/woody, complex, and honey-like; midpalate features traces of cola nut, maple, BBQ sauce, and baking spices, especially vanilla, cinnamon, and clove. Aftertaste is very alluring, tobacco-like, and oaky without being resiny. A great cigar accompaniment, I suspect.
2018 Rating: ★ ★ ★ ★/Highly Recommended

Lemon Hart Navy Spiced Demerara Rum (Guyana) 43% abv, $30.

Mahogany/tawny/henna color; flawless purity. This aroma speaks volumes of cola nut, black cherry jam, marzipan, praline, nougat, and chocolate-covered cherries, and consequently is a tour de force aroma; aeration stimulates multiple layers of soft cheese, Pedro Ximénez sherry (PX), ripe muscatel grapes, demerara sugar, treacle, and beeswax; an incredible experience aromatically. Entry is viscous, toasted, roasted, bittersweet, fig-like, date-like, and oh so luscious; midpalate is extra long and deep, stunningly complex, grapy/raisiny, plummy, pruny, and sensationally tasty and savory. In my top rank of spiced rums.
2016 Rating: ★ ★ ★ ★ ★/Highest Recommendation

Lemon Hart Original 1804 Rum (Guyana) 40% abv, $19.

Deep brown/chestnut color; flawless purity. Smells incredibly enticing and meaty and fatty and smoky and woody and tobacco-like in the opening whiffs . . . WOW; in the second passes, there is a woodsy/leafy/vegetal funkiness to this rhum/rum that is strikingly tobacco-like, especially cigar tobacco, but there is also trace evidence of carob, mushrooms, and esters. Entry is oaky, bordering on earthy/mushroomy, and is wildly different and

expressive; midpalate has elements of cocoa, carob, brown sugar, and seedpod, plus marsh-mallow and dark honey. Like no rum you've ever tasted.
2019 Rating: ★★★★/Highly Recommended

Maggie's Farm La Revuelta Dark Rum (USA) 40% abv, $35.

A dark rum blend of 50 percent USA pot still cane rum and 50 percent column still molasses rum from Trinidad. The chestnut/black-tea color is sediment-free. The initial inha-lations detect understated aromas of latent power and flying-under-the-radar grassiness that are eclipsed in this early stage by fat-laden top notes of brown butter, hickory-smoked bacon, nougat, and Milk Duds candy; later sniffs pick up milk chocolate and brown-sugar scents that are scrumptious and semisweet. Entry discovers a complex taste profile that is ripe, generously textured, dense, deeply toasted, and vivid in its liveliness and honey-like flavor; midpalate uncovers additional beany and herbal flavors of carob, sassafras, root beer, gentian, fennel, and angelica. Finishes medium long, drier than the entry, grassy, earthy, mossy, and woodsy-rustic.
2017 Rating: ★★★/Recommended

Maggie's Farm Queen's Share Rum (USA) 55% abv, $35.

The color is brilliant burnt-orange/ochre; appearance is clean. This opening nose is compellingly ripe, fruity, grassy, bakery-like (like hot cross buns), leathery, and nutty; fur-ther air contact stimulates fragrances of newly tanned leather, cigar box, pipe tobacco, all-spice, and sugar cookies. Entry is gently sweet, warming from the alcohol level but not for a moment hot, harsh, or fiery, and intensely honeyed; midpalate offers a soothing embers-like warmth in the throat, with highlight tastes of bakery treats such as sugar cookies, Danish pastry, fruit tarts, and marshmallow. Aftertaste is medium long, chewing gum–like, sugary, and savory. Well-made overproof rum whose abv level enhances rather than dominates the in-mouth experience. Really good job of balancing the components.
2017 Rating: ★★★★/Highly Recommended

Maggie's Farm Spiced Rum (USA) 40% abv, $30.

Made from turbinado sugarcane sourced from Louisiana, eight spices, and distilled in a copper pot still. Gorgeous color is mahogany leaning to tawny; pristine purity. I like the herb garden–like, foresty, rustic opening fragrance which is a pleasing departure from most spiced rum aromas that are frequently over-the-top on vanilla/cinnamon sweetness; further aeration brings out dashes of lemon peel, anise, blood orange, and nutmeg. Entry features an entire symphony of flavors, from rum to cardamom to ginger to eucalyptus to root beer; midpalate brings all the various characteristics together in a graceful flavor profile that's bittersweet, deeply herbal/floral, and almost more akin to vermouth or bitters than what is regrettably perceived nowadays as "spiced" rum, and for that I applaud it. Maggie's Farm presents a whole new style of spiced rum that is long overdue.
2017 Rating: ★★★★/Highly Recommended

Maggie's Farm White Rum (USA) 40% abv, $28.

Made from turbinado sugarcane sourced from Louisiana and distilled in a copper pot still. Impeccably clean appearance that is as transparent as springwater. The first whiffs after the pour encounter fruity (pear, melon, kiwi, raspberry) and floral (jasmine, berry vines/brambles) aromas that have "new pot still spirit" written all over them; additional aeration releases bakery-like fragrances of bread yeast, sourdough, bread crust, and flaky pastry that merge beautifully with the fruit salad and flowers; this is a delightful, vigorous bouquet from start to finish. Entry is fresh, clean, herbal, and acidic, with the highlights provided by the compelling fruitiness that's mesmerizing in its scope and balance; midpalate features the merging of the fruit basket flavors with the floral hints, alcohol, and acids, forming an overall sense of delicately sweet pleasure that's rare in white rums nowadays. In the aftertaste there's a slight nip from the abv, and the taste profile flattens out a bit too quickly for me as I expected greater finishing length, but nonetheless the final impression is "Highly Recommended."

2017 Rating: ★★★★/Highly Recommended

Malahat Spirits Co. Spiced Rum (USA) 40% abv, $45.

Reddish/brick color; flawless purity. Wow, the spice-shop aromatics fill my office at *Spirit Journal* HQ with wafting fragrances of egg cream, egg white, custard, lemon curd, clove, cinnamon, nutmeg, paprika, blood orange peel; second inhalations after further aeration discover floral scents (jasmine, hibiscus), cedar box, tree bark, root beer, deviled egg, cornstarch. Entry is pleasingly spicy, without being cloying or hot, and there's a juiciness to the profile that's more fresh than dried or baked; midpalate is bright, animated, tasty, savory, full-throttle spicy, and fruity. Finishes long, peppery, heavily clove-like, dry, lip-smacking. For me, if the spices were throttled down a notch, I believe this rum would have a strong chance at four stars.

2015 Rating: ★★★/Recommended

Martí Dorado 3 Year Old Rum (Panama) 40% abv, $19.

Amber color; blemish-free. This opening fragrance is considerably more serious, woody, brown sugar–like, honeyed, and gripping than that of its sibling, the Plata; secondary inhalations encounter melded aromas that talk of egg cream, hazelnut, graham cracker, and gingerbread. Entry is sturdy in texture to the point of being moderately oily, while the taste profile includes delectable flavors of brown butter, hazelnut, honey, nutmeg, and clove; midpalate stage echoes all of the entry impressions, adding savory flavor hints of bay leaf, thyme, and baked pineapple. Concludes medium long in the throat and bittersweet. A superb value.

2018 Rating: ★★★★/Highly Recommended

Martí Estate Strength Rum (Panama) 53.8% abv, $48.

Bright harvest gold/fulvous color; impeccably clean. Considering the high degree of alcohol, the first nosing passes are neither hot nor prickly, as instead they feature delicate aromas of cinnamon, tree bark, clove, and brown sugar; following more air contact, the bouquet turns a bit like candied almond and chocolate-covered orange rind, all the while keeping the abv at bay. Entry is warming, sugar-like, honeyed, and a touch coffee bean–like as the alcohol slowly uncoils, growing in strength by the second; midpalate exhibits a heightened alcohol presence that underscores the deeply bittersweet flavors of molasses, nougat, walnut butter, and dark honey but never gets piercing or hot. Ends on

pleasing notes of butterscotch and light toffee, as the abv becomes like dying embers, warming but not fierce.
2018 Rating: ★ ★ ★ ★/Highly Recommended

Martí Plata 3 Year Old Rum (Panama) 40% abv, $19.
Tarnished-silver/oyster/champagne color is sediment-free. The first nosing passes pick up faint hints of molasses, old honey, and brown sugar as the initial impressions point to a delicate light rum; secondary whiffs detect limestone, refined sugar, and vanilla bean. Entry is fleet with subtle hints of cake frosting, primarily vanilla bean; midpalate is buoyant, nimble, nearly ethereal, yet is crisp, alluring, and tasty. Finishes briefly and airily, with a whisper of brown sugar and light honey.
2018 Rating: ★ ★ ★/Recommended

Mezan XO Extra Old Rum (Jamaica) 40% abv, $37.
The straw-yellow color is very pretty; flawless clarity. First whiffs detect pleasing grassy, fibrous, candle wax notes that suppress the molasses, giving the chance for other aromas to emerge, in particular, baking spices like allspice, nutmeg, cinnamon, and clove; additional air contact releases further fragrances, including pipe tobacco, mace, newly tanned leather; this is an intriguing, slightly funky bouquet that's anything but by the numbers. Entry profile is acutely dry, really dusty dry, and loaded with bittersweet molasses and brown sugar tastes; midpalate offers more thought-provoking flavors, especially cola nut, candied walnut, butterscotch, praline. Aftertaste is medium long, biscuity, toasted, elegant.
2015 Rating: ★ ★ ★ ★/Highly Recommended

Mount Gay 1703 Master Select Rum (Barbados) 43% abv, $150.
Bronze/auburn color; flawless clarity. Wow, this opening aroma is mature, old library–like, leathery, slightly ash- and soot-like, with a cotton flannel aspect that's intriguing; secondary inhalations discover latent citrus rind and orchard-fruit scents that are ripe but not necessarily sweet; in all, this is one of the most sophisticated Barbados rum bouquets you will ever find because each time you inhale it, another fascinating characteristic pops up. Entry is lip-smacking delicious, bittersweet, and doused with cinnamon, vanilla bean, and allspice; midpalate is multilayered with cocoa, espresso, and coffee bean flavors, as well as dark chocolate, old honey, and maple. Aftertaste sees all the various components merge into a singular flavor profile that's potent, expressive, bitter, and at best off-dry.
2018 Rating: ★ ★ ★ ★ ★/Highest Recommendation

Mount Gay Black Barrel Rum (Barbados) 43% abv, $30.
Pretty topaz/amber color; unblemished clarity. Owns a decidedly oak-driven, tobacco-y frontline aroma that is delightfully, if gently, sweet and toasty; secondary inhalations discover deeper aspects, in particular, a Christmas cake spiciness that is charming, to say the least. Entry is cocoa-bean bittersweet and therefore pleasing as hell to me; midpalate stage highlights the cocoa bean, vanilla, nutmeg, and molasses. Aftertaste is medium long, semisweet, and beany. A rum of substance and grace.
2016 Rating: ★ ★ ★ ★/Highly Recommended

Mount Gay Eclipse Rum (Barbados) 40% abv, $21.
Marigold/harvest gold color; ideally sediment-free and clean. First nosing passes pick up pleasingly animated scents of cocoa bean, confectioners' sugar, and sweet tea as served in the southern US; secondary sniffs encounter grass, flint/dry stone, and low-key marjoram cooking spice. Entry is as bone-dry and bittersweet as dark, high-cocoa-content baker's chocolate; midpalate sparkles with crisp, beany, cocoa flavors that retain a high degree of acidity that overlaps deep into the flinty aftertaste. I continue to perceive MG Eclipse as a tremendous, "never lets you down" value.
2018 Rating: ★ ★ ★/Recommended

Mount Gay The Master Blender Collection Pot Still Rum (Barbados) 48% abv, $170.
Only 4,920 bottles available worldwide, 1,002 for the USA. Marigold/fulvous color; ideal clarity. First nosing passes encounter assertive aromas of black tea, candied orchard fruits (apricot, in particular), rum ball candy, brown sugar, and nutmeg; secondary inhalations after additional air contact discover aromas that are more baked and bakery-like than those of the first aromatic salvos, featuring seductive, spice island fragrances of nutmeg, vanilla bean, cinnamon, and mace. Entry is dazzlingly piquant, bitter, desert dry, and now as nutty as it is spicy; midpalate is where the pot still impact and barrel influence make themselves known in spades, as the taste profile goes lush and sinewy in texture and concentrated in maple fudge–like flavor. Aftertaste reflects the midpalate stage admirably, never losing the taste momentum, as the flavor profile remains solidly structured, stone dry, and strikingly complex. As a longtime fan of Mount Gay rums, I place this expression right in the running with the savory 1703.
2019 Rating: ★ ★ ★ ★ ★/Highest Recommendation

Mount Gay XO Extra Old Rum (Barbados) 43% abv, $48.
Sinopia color; impeccably pure. The amount of baking spice that I detect in this opening inhalation is startling as subtle hints of clove, mace, allspice, and cinnamon are present and accounted for, along with a back-note fragrance of candied fruits; after more aeration, the bouquet turns gently, delicately sweet more in a honeyed manner than molasses or brown sugar, and the result is dazzling. Entry is drier than I expected it to be and lean in sinewy texture; the midpalate provides all the mature molasses-based rum pleasure one desires via its resiny oakiness, bittersweet chocolate flavors, and swank, svelte texture. Ends up medium long in the throat, more bitter than bittersweet, and tobacco- and mincemeat-like in taste. Splendid.
2018 Rating: ★ ★ ★ ★/Highly Recommended

Myers's Original Dark Rum (Jamaica) 40% abv, $33.
Dark coffee-brown; through the near-opacity it appears clean. First inhalations detect heavily roasted/toasted aromas of pumpernickel bread, molasses, treacle, and bacon fat; in the next nosing passes there's a deep-seated grassiness that's far more bittersweet than all-out sweet, reminding me somewhat of brown sugar. Entry is bittersweet, bean-like, and keenly smoky; midpalate is drier, more astringent than the entry, going vegetal and deeply molasses-like. Ends up clean, acidic, charcoal-like, and smoky.
2018 Rating: ★ ★ ★/Recommended

Naked Turtle White Rum (US Virgin Islands) 40% abv, $13.
Clean and clear in transparent appearance. I enjoy the rummy, affably friendly, white refined sugar–like opening scent, which is not complex by any means but is still easily likable as a simple white rum; no aromatic changes in the second nosing passes after more air contact. Entry is very sweet, overly so to be truthful, and that aspect alone torpedoes the remainder of the tasting phases as no virtues of note can fight their way through the jungle of marshmallow, gooey sweetness; midpalate is all vanilla cake frosting. It's too bad that the in-mouth experiences undercut the mildly pleasant aroma, but that's what happens when any sense of balance is derailed by too much sugar. Some people might like this sugar bomb. I'm not one of them.
2018 Rating: ★/Not Recommended

Novo Fogo Graciosa Cachaça (Brazil) 42% abv, $40.
Mustard-seed color; excellent clarity. Opening scents are reminiscent of sawdust, oak plank, car wax, and freshly harvested sugarcane; secondary fragrances following more air contact offer nougat-like aromas that are buttery, candy shop–like, and delicate. Entry taste explodes on the tongue in waves of oak chip, fresh honey from the hive, eucalyptus, orange pekoe tea, and brown butter; midpalate stage echoes the entry findings and adds a touch of sea salt–doused caramel. Aftertaste is deliciously bittersweet, medium long in the throat, and pleasantly nougat-like. Very nice, especially in the mouth at entry.
2018 Rating: ★★★★/Highly Recommended

Novo Fogo Tanager Cachaça (Brazil) 42% abv, $40.
Deep carrot-orange color; flawless purity. Wow, I immediately encounter a zesty, salty, and resiny/sap-like scent that's all-rainforest-all-the-time, piquant, and evocative; secondary inhalations after more aeration come across deep, raw, natural aromas of sugarcane and sugarcane juice. Entry is rich, peppery, intensely oaky/woody/tree bark–like, and spicy (cinnamon, clove in abundance); midpalate highlights all the entry impressions and adds underscoring traces of bacon fat and lard that bring a richness to the texture. Aftertaste is long, focused on the lean woodiness of the barrel and the earthy, soil-like flavor of the sugarcane. Really wonderful.
2018 Rating: ★★★★/Highly Recommended

Old Ipswich Greenhead Spiced Rum (USA) 40% abv, $27.
Nine-karat gold/flax color; unblemished. Being an avid tea lover, I detect notes of tea leaves, tea oil, citrus zest, candle wax, parchment in the initial inhalations, plus an herbaceous aspect that's vastly different than mainstream spiced rums. Entry is delicate, leafy/woodsy, citrusy, herbal; midpalate is richer than the entry, cocoa-like, herbal/botanical, quite delicious. Distinctive, compelling, tasty, savory.
2015 Rating: ★★★★/Highly Recommended

Old Ipswich Tavern Style Rum (USA) 40% abv, $27.
Bright amber/jonquil color; sediment-free. Smells up front of light, fresh honey, dry earth, stone/minerals, dry cement; later on, I get mild spiciness (vanilla bean), yeast, bread dough, spice cake. Entry is gently sweet, honeyed, brown sugar–like, uncomplicated;

midpalate shows more baking spices, especially clove, allspice, and is slightly gamey. Concludes well, medium long in throat, piquant.
2015 Rating: ★ ★ ★/Recommended

Old Ipswich White Cap Rum (USA) 40% abv, $25.

Impeccably translucent and clean. Baked cherries, toasted marshmallow, egg cream, molasses abound in first nosing; aeration accentuates the deep black-cherry/plummy fruitiness. Entry is semisweet, as fruity as the aroma, and sap-like, elemental, grassy/caney; midpalate is slightly herbaceous, bittersweet, grassy/earthy. Ends ripe, fruity, simple, pleasing.
2015 Rating: ★ ★ ★/Recommended

Owney's Original New York City Rum (USA) 40% abv, $35.

The colorless appearance sparkles in the examination light; springwater clarity. First aromatic notes are dry, mineral-like, stony, earthy, then, in the advanced second passes, a bittersweet molasses/brown-sugar fragrance takes hold and doesn't let go all the way to the final whiff, which offers a touch of flowery esters. Entry is dusty dry, elemental, slightly toasted, waxy; midpalate is deep, concentrated, multilayered, moderately oily, sturdy in its core. Finishes medium long, bittersweet. Whoever tells you that white rum can't have character should taste Owney's for a genuine revelation. Seriously savory and delicious.
2015 Rating: ★ ★ ★ ★/Highly Recommended

Pampero Aniversario Extra Añejo Rum (Venezuela) 40% abv, $30.

Russet/mahogany color; flawless purity. Opening nosing passes offer potent, bean-like aromas of BBQ sauce, seared meat, honey, treacle; secondary whiffs pick up candied walnut, marzipan, nougat, demerara sugar. Entry is awash in bittersweet, espresso notes, and complex brown sugar/honey flavors that are more savory than sweet; midpalate is succulent, bittersweet, candied, round, supple, luscious all the way through the languid aftertaste that's sap-like and intensely woody.
2016 Rating: ★ ★ ★ ★/Highly Recommended

Papa's Pilar 3 Year Old Blonde Rum (Caribbean/Central America/USA) 42% abv, $30.

Pretty lemon-juice yellow/green-edged color; perfect clarity. In the first inhalations after the pour, I encounter considerable amounts of candied fruits, mostly tropical, such as banana, pineapple, and mango—it's exotic, to be sure; in the next round of sniffing, there's a more clear-cut presence of bakery spices (nutmeg, clove) and refined sugar. Entry is zesty, somewhat fat in texture, and loaded with vanilla bean flavor; midpalate ups the sweetness ante, as the vanilla bean turns to vanilla extract and egg cream tastes, which are admittedly yummy. Finish is long, semisweet, a bit honeyed, and very, very laden with vanilla. I like this rum and recommend it, but it borders on being viewed as a flavored rum, so expressive and dominant is the vanilla aspect, and that brings concern for its usage.
2017 Rating: ★ ★ ★/Recommended

Papa's Pilar Platinum Blonde Limited Edition Rum (Multiple Nations) 46% abv, $38.

Citron color; perfect purity. First inhalations pick up lovely, elegant aromas of bakery-shop spices (nutmeg, clove, cinnamon), molasses, brown sugar, and pastry filled with dried fruit; secondary whiffs encounter walnut, nougat, wet sand, and soybean. Entry is sweet, a bit fat, and chewy in texture, nutty to the point of almost being nut butter–like, and piquant; midpalate offers a supple, creamy texture that supports the zesty flavors that are spicy and even a touch prickly. Ends long in the throat, buttery, metallic, and bitter. The disappointing aftertaste knocked a rating star off the final assessment.

2018 Rating: ★★★/Recommended

Papa's Pilar Spanish Sherry Cask Finished Dark Rum (Multiple Nations) 43% abv, $47.
    A blend of rums sourced from Barbados, Panama, Dominican Republic, and the USA. Coffee/burnt umber color; impeccably clean. There're all sorts of delectable bakery-shop aromas emanating from the tasting glass, including nougat, prune Danish, espresso, coffee bean, and carob; secondary whiffs confirm the first-stage findings, adding scrumptious scents of walnut paste, black raisins, dates, and brown sugar; a seriously yummy bouquet. Entry showcases the sherry influence as the initial tastes resemble mincemeat, baked pears, honey, holiday fruitcake, spice cake, and glazed donut; midpalate is more cane driven, in that there's a greater sense of grass, molasses, and yeast as the flavor profile turns deliciously like rum cake. Finishes winey, sherry-like, and intensely bittersweet. Extremely intense, which might be too much for some less serious rum lovers. This is a whiskey-like or, better, brandy-like rum with a big constitution.

2018 Rating: ★★★★/Highly Recommended

Papagayo Organic White Rum (Paraguay) 40% abv, $32
    Crystalline and pure in appearance. Opening aroma smells fruity (guava, banana) and minerally/earthy; aeration heightens the tropical fruit aspect and introduces orchard fruit as well, in particular, nectarine and pear; this bouquet is the antithesis of what one thinks rum is all about, and yet it's pleasantly different and unique due mainly to its ambrosial freshness. Palate entry is crisp, bittersweet, and brief in staying power; midpalate tastes include baked pear, brown sugar, molasses, and cake frosting. What this rum lacks in heft and texture it more than makes up for in keen freshness, a light touch, and juiciness. Love it. Bravo.

2020 Rating: ★★★★/Highly Recommended

Paranubes Aguardiente de Caña Agricole Rum (Mexico) 54% abv, $40/liter.
    Colorless appearance, free of sediment. Up front, the first aroma is of pine-like cleaning fluid, car wax, glue, cleaning solvent, and creosote; more aeration only solidifies the cleaning fluid–like bouquet, which never lets up and evolves into a more alluring fragrance. Entry taste is slightly less abrasive than the bouquet and that's a start; midpalate does show a smattering of sugarcane likeness but that's short-lived, as the chlorine- and Mr. Clean–like aspects rear their unpleasant heads, lasting deep into the aftertaste. Unlike mezcal, the chances of this fearsome sugarcane distillate from Oaxaca finding an American audience are the same as dial phones making a comeback.

2018 Rating: ★/Not Recommended

Pirassununga 21 Cachaça (Brazil) 40% abv, $15.
    Clear as rainwater. Smells intensely of cane, grass, earth/soil, olive brine, and white pepper right out of the sniffing gate; further aeration time allows many of the aggressive odors to

settle in and round off, leaving behind more graceful scents of herbs (sage, especially), chalk/limestone, and rubbing alcohol. Palate entry is surprisingly sweet (there was hardly any sweetness in the bouquet) and sugary; midpalate features dried herbs, cooking spice (mace, allspice), tree bark, pine, and fresh sugarcane. Clean, medium weighted, oily, concentrated, and mildly sweet in the finish.

2020 Rating: ★ ★ ★/Recommended

Plantation 2005 Rum (Guyana) 45% abv, $40.

Goldenrod/amber color; superb clarity. I like the toastiness of the initial aroma as well as the saline quality of it; secondary whiffs get traces of dried sage, new leather, dried flowers, sea salt, dark caramel. Entry is lusciously sweet, honeyed, brown sugar–like, intense; midpalate turns spicy, tangy, rich in texture, more bittersweet than sweet, beany (cocoa). Extra long finish, a touch grapy, dark chocolate–like. Also has the ideal abv for dark rum.

2014 Rating: ★ ★ ★ ★ ★/Highest Recommendation

Plantation 3 Stars White Rum (Jamaica/Barbados/Trinidad) 41.2% abv, $25.

Pale green color; flawless purity. Opening aroma offers delicate scents of brown sugar, honey, and cocoa bean; later whiffs following further aeration encounter baking spices, especially vanilla and clove; a bouquet of delicacy. Entry is pleasingly biscuity yet is bittersweet and light bodied; midpalate features round, supple flavors of dark chocolate, root beer, toasted marshmallow, and egg cream. Finishes brief, refined, and almost fragile.

2015 Rating: ★ ★ ★ ★/Highly Recommended

Plantation Extrême No. 3 Collection Long Pond Distillery HJC 1996 Rum (Jamaica) 56.2% abv, $250.

Distilled in Jamaica's legendary John Dore pot still, then aged for twenty-one years in ex-bourbon barrels and finished in Ferrand casks for one year. Sinopia/tawny color; textbook purity. There's a potent aroma of bittersweet alcohol right up front that I find appealing that neither burns nor attacks but, instead, charms me with its cinnamon stick, vanilla bean, carob brownie, and chocolate-covered banana fragrances; later whiffs detect drier, more settled aromas, such as birch bark, root beer, candle wax, and cigar tobacco. Entry is piquant, prickly, and dynamically spirity right from the first sip, offering animated flavors of fruit pit, brown sugar, s'mores, and cocoa butter; midpalate mirrors the entry stage, highlighting the cocoa aspects, in particular, as the texture's creamy viscosity supports the flavor profile. Extended aftertaste features bakery-shop/carob-brownie sweetness and chocolate-caramel tastes.

2019 Rating: ★ ★ ★ ★ ★/Highest Recommendation

Plantation Extrême No. 3 Collection Long Pond Distillery ITP 1996 Rum (Jamaica) 54.8% abv, $250.

Distilled in Jamaica's legendary John Dore pot still, then aged for twenty-one years in ex-bourbon barrels and finished in Ferrand casks for one year. Lustrous cocoa-brown color; perfect clarity. This first nosing offers scents that are slightly saline, resiny/sap-like, and matchstick-like; second passes pick up understated fragrances of limestone, lead pencil, minerals, dry soil, and cardboard. Entry is sublimely spicy and zesty yet mature and largely

understated, as buttercream-like, candy-shop flavors dazzle the taste buds; midpalate stage highlights the density of the wood influence via tastes of sweetened coconut, caramel candies, and bittersweet, high-cocoa-content dark chocolate. Ends briefer than I expected on savory notes of Cocoa Puffs cereal and crème caramel flan.
2019 Rating: ★ ★ ★ ★/Highly Recommended

Plantation Grande Reserve 5 Year Old Rum (Barbados) 40% abv, $22.
   Bright amber color; flawless clarity. The opening nosing round is all about baking-shop fragrances, in particular, brown sugar, honey, dark caramel, candied almonds, but also pipe tobacco, toasted marshmallow; secondary whiffs after further aeration discover bacon fat, lard, black raisin, prune—lots of aromatic activity here. Entry is bittersweet, caramelized onion–like, baked, biscuity, roasted; midpalate is engagingly toasty, nearly fruity, as in baked orchard fruits, and resiny. Finishes medium long, bittersweet, chocolatey.
2014 Rating: ★ ★ ★ ★/Highly Recommended

Plantation OFTD Overproof Rum (Jamaica/Guyana/Barbados) 69% abv, $32/liter.
   Mahogany/henna color; excellent purity. The first nosings encounter aggressive, huge tsunamis of maple syrup/tree sap aromas that are dense and intensely bakery spice–like, flashing scents of clove, allspice, and vanilla bean that complement the dried tropical fruits, especially the pineapple fragrance; following more aeration, the aroma becomes a bouquet that features dark caramel, tomato paste, BBQ sauce, almond paste, and prune Danish fragrances. Entry is lip-smacking bittersweet, only mildly hot from the abv level, reminiscent of treacle, caramelized sugar topping on crème brûlée, and deeply cocoa bean–like; midpalate echoes the findings of the entry phase, adding high-cocoa-content dark chocolate, molasses, demerara sugar, as the flavor profile turns strikingly like Spanish brandy. As the midpalate leads into the finish, the warming sensation in the throat is very pleasant and calming, if bittersweet and cinnamon bun–like.
2016 Rating: ★ ★ ★ ★ ★/Highest Recommendation

Plantation Old Reserve 2002 Rum (Jamaica) 42% abv, $45.
   The amber/wheat-field color is pure and sediment-free. The opening aromas are rife with baked coconut, almond paste, baked banana, and green tobacco; secondary inhalations discover nimble, slightly citrusy and peppery fragrances that are gently sweet and piquant with baking spices, especially clove, allspice, and nutmeg. Entry is elegant, substantial, and laden with sugarcane zestiness that's delicate, moderately oily, and flat-out delicious; midpalate captures the essence of the entry stage but adds the crispness of heightened acidity that maintains the tropical fruit structure as it accents the richness of the molasses base. Aftertaste is long, lean, agile, and crisp. Another rum gem from Alexandre Gabriel's Plantation team. Bravo.
2018 Rating: ★ ★ ★ ★ ★/Highest Recommendation

Plantation Original Dark Overproof Rum (Trinidad and Tobago) 73% abv, $28/liter.
   Copper color; superb clarity. First inhalations are not attacked by the stratospheric alcohol degree, but rather are engaged by supple, off-dry scents of brown sugar and gentle spices, clove, nutmeg, mace; further time in the glass allows for the spices to develop, especially

the nutmeg, but now also cinnamon and vanilla bean are evident. Entry is moderate in abv intensity, and this lets the honey, caramel, and grain tastes emerge; midpalate offers greater abv bite and obvious heat, but all the while the honey and spice aspects remain true and steady. Concludes extended, rich, fiery, nutty, fresh, and spicy.
2015 Rating: ★ ★ ★ ★/Highly Recommended

Plantation Original Dark Rum (Trinidad and Tobago) 40% abv, $18.

Burnt-orange color; impeccable purity. Dynamic aromatic activity going on here in the opening fragrance, which includes hints of black peppercorn, clove, cinnamon, baked cherry, prune Danish, molasses; later sniffs encounter vegetation/forest, leaves, black tea, dry stone/slate. Entry is fruity with white raisins, dried pineapple, and is off-dry, brown sugar–like; midpalate is spicy/peppery, piquant, minerally, and significantly drier than the entry stage. Ends fruity, spicy, charming.
2016 Rating: ★ ★ ★ ★/Highly Recommended

Plantation Stiggins Pineapple Rum (France) 40% abv, $30

Original Dark Rum infused with Victorian pineapple. The full-out russet/henna color is dazzling; excellent purity. First nosings pick up pleasing scents of sweetened pineapple, brown sugar, grilled pineapple, but by the second passes the rum aroma component has been discreetly ushered out of the room as the pineapple presence takes full, if slightly sour charge. Entry is amiably soft, mildly ambrosial, and tart enough to maintain the pineapple/citrus focus; midpalate is the stage where this rum shows its best side as the pineapple/rum marriage appears to be fully consummated. Finishes long, more fruity than rummy. Isn't necessarily my cup of tea but I admire its adventurousness.
2017 Rating: ★ ★ ★/Recommended

Plantation Single Cask 1998 Rum (Guyana) 44.8% abv, $150.

Earth yellow/metallic-gold color; perfectly clean and clear of sediment. Up front, I pick up baked cherry, cherry strudel, fig, and dried date aromas, as the initial scent infusions are brimming with red and black fruits; secondary inhalations detect broader fragrances of raisin bread, blue cheese, long-cured cigar tobacco, and chocolate-covered coffee beans. Entry flavors cascade onto the tongue in hearty waves of bittersweet chocolate, cocoa powder, maple syrup, brown sugar, and roasted walnut; midpalate impressions bolster the entry findings, but go significantly deeper and more bitter from (I suspect) the saturation influence of seventeen years in an old bourbon cask (matured in the tropics) and two years in a Ferrand cask (aged in Cognac). Finish is unexpectedly medium brief, as dried fruit becomes the main characteristic. Unlike any rum you'll ever taste.
2019 Rating: ★ ★ ★ ★/Highly Recommended

Plantation Xaymaca Special Dry 100% Pot Still Jamaican Rum (Jamaica) 43% abv, $25.

Golden wheat-field color; pristine clarity. This sterling opening aroma gets right to the point of what pot still distillation does for rum in that there is, first and foremost, a screaming funkiness that is reminiscent of hay fields, sugar cubes, tropical fruits (banana, guava, in particular), leather-bound books, textile fiber, and coffee grounds; next up after ten minutes

of further air contact comes the exotic fragrance of spiced apple and baked banana doused with nutmeg. Entry doesn't shy away from the pot still reek as the flavor profile, in fact, embraces it, causing the initial taste impressions to make you ask "How good is this rum going to get?" as the tidal wave of damp earth, rain forest, and sea salt accelerates. Midpalate sees all the disparate components merge into a delicately honeyed, slightly salty taste that's resiny, lean, and bittersweet. Finishes shorter than I expected, delicately bittersweet, understated, and lovely.
2018 Rating: ★ ★ ★ ★ ★/Highest Recommendation

Plantation XO 20th Anniversary Rum (Barbados) 40% abv, $45.
Attractive bronze color; flawless clarity. The stunning floral/fruity opening aroma is transcendent, ethereal, and intensely marshmallow-like; an additional eight minutes in the sampling glass releases additional fragrances of vanilla, cocoa, and milk chocolate. Entry is cinnamon-like and gently sweet, as the sugary molasses taste turns very soft and chewy; midpalate taste profile reminds me of holiday spice cake, rum-flavored chocolates, and sugar cookies. Concludes medium long, delicate, and only mildly sweet.
2014 Rating: ★ ★ ★ ★/Highly Recommended

Privateer True American Amber Reserve Rum (USA) 50% abv, $27.
Dark straw-yellow/flax color; flawless purity. There's a smokiness to this opening aroma that's pipe tobacco–like, nutty, leafy/vegetal, and candied all at the same time in equal strengths; another six minutes of air contact introduce a parchment quality that mysteriously adds to the bouquet, even though it seems incongruous. Entry is peppery, surprisingly dry, slightly bittersweet, and even slightly sherried; midpalate is delicate, honeyed, gently sweet, spicy, cocoa-like, and polite. Finishes medium-long, spicy, biscuity (vanilla wafer cookies), and cake-like.
2016 Rating: ★ ★ ★ ★/Highly Recommended

Puerto Angel Amber Rum (Mexico) 40% abv, $30.
Oaxacan rum. Gamboge/white burgundy yellow color; flawlessly clear. This aroma is marginally sweeter than the Blanco's but like its sibling is aridly dry, vegetal, though a touch more floral, with delicate traces of cigarette tobacco, marshmallow, baked apple, white raisins; the next aromatic stage offers a rich grassiness that's sappy and estery, with a last-minute touch of bacon fat. Entry is lush, ripe, maple- and vanilla bean–like; midpalate highlights scents of honeydew melon, brown sugar, thyme, and black pepper that are all underpinned by a thick viscosity. Concludes a little toasty, earthy, floral, spicy. Dazzling.
2015 Rating: ★ ★ ★ ★ ★/Highest Recommendation

Puerto Angel Blanco Rum (Mexico) 40% abv, $28.
Oaxacan rum. Lovely tarnished-silver color; pristine purity. First sniffs detect loads of lead pencil, limestone, mineral notes that are supported by dusty, dry scents of hemp/rope, flaxseed, wax paper; later inhalations encounter more nuanced fragrances of dill, sage, hay/straw, burnt paper, black peppercorn, grassy springtime vegetation that remind me of rhum agricole. Entry taste is bittersweet and intensely grassy; midpalate shows a more succulent side as the flavor profile remains juicy, concentrated, and more cedary/

piney than fruity or ripe. Finishes medium long, spicy, compact, bittersweet. Exotic, superbly satisfying.

2015 Rating: ★ ★ ★ ★ ★/Highest Recommendation

Pusser's British Navy 15 Year Old Rum (Guyana) 40% abv, $75.

Lovely chestnut-brown color; impeccably clean. First inhalations detect potent aromas of saddle leather/tack, suede, furniture polish, vinyl, sealing wax, and butcher's wax paper; later sniffs following more aeration detect more vegetation-like fragrances, including soybean, lima bean, and autumn forest. Entry flavors focus on root beer, sarsaparilla, nut butter, cigar tobacco, and black tea tastes that are vividly bitter and desert dry; midpalate highlights the tobacco aspects, buttressed by the bitterness of the black tea and oak resin flavors that underpin the entire taste stage. Aftertaste is very long, lean, nimble, and nutty. A serious rum for veteran aficionados only. No rum beginners allowed.

2019 Rating: ★ ★ ★ ★/Highly Recommended

Pyrat Cask 1623 Rum (Caribbean region) 40% abv, $290.

Attractive henna/tawny color; unblemished purity. Similar to the XO Reserve in its fruity/berry-like opening aroma, but this fragrance has a touch of quinine that makes it herbaceous; secondary sniffs detect a heightening of the quinine/cinchona bark aspect as the bouquet becomes apothecary-like/medicinal and almost akin to bitters. Entry echoes the bouquet as the bitters element gains in strength and becomes succulent in the process; midpalate goes for streamlined fruity, juicy, prune-like ripeness. Aftertaste is tobacco-like, vegetal, bitter, yet enormously satisfying.

2015 Rating: ★ ★ ★ ★/Highly Recommended

Pyrat XO Reserve Rum (Caribbean region) 40% abv, $25.

Pretty topaz/amber color; good clarity. I get tantalizing aromas of caramelized onion, buttered almonds, saltwater taffy in the opening sniffs; later inhalations detect quieter, still salty scents of oak resin, hard cheese, molasses, holiday fruitcake. Entry is ripe, fruity, delicately sweet; midpalate stays as fruit-driven as the entry, adding a pleasing acidity that keeps it fresh and refreshing. Finishes oaky/woody/resiny and nicely sweet.

2015 Rating: ★ ★ ★ ★/Highly Recommended

Real McCoy 12 Year Old Rum (Barbados) 40% abv, $46.

Attractive, bright, new-copper color; flawless, sediment-free purity. First inhalations detect worn leather saddle, dried fruits (cherry, berries), fruit compote; later whiffs pick up on maple, toffee, candied nut aromas. Entry is intensely beany (coffee beans), resiny, oily; midpalate features brown sugar, honey, vanilla bean, English toffee. Concludes medium long, buttery in texture, piquant, bittersweet.

2014 Rating: ★ ★ ★ ★/Highly Recommended

Real McCoy 3 Year Old Rum (Barbados) 40% abv, $20.

Clean and clear as rainwater. Up front, I smell hemp/rope, grass, molasses, brown sugar; later sniffs encounter mild baking spices, tile, dried flowers. Entry is firm, off-dry, sugary but neither cloying nor fat; midpalate is chewy, oily, continues off-dry, moderately bitter, grassy,

multilayered. Ends on a bittersweet, complex note. A serious white rum of consequence and character.
2014 Rating: ★ ★ ★ ★/Highly Recommended

Real McCoy Prohibition Tradition 5 Year Old Rum (Barbados) 40% abv, $29.
Attractive and luminous burnt-orange/bronze color; unblemished purity. I note a pleasing spiciness in the first sniffs that are fruity and ripe more than woody or sugary; another seven minutes of air contact allow for nuances of spice to work their way through, mostly carob. Entry is toasty, rich, bacony, and pastry-like; midpalate is long, toasty, brown sugar–like, and creamy. Finishes vibrant and like dried fruits, especially pears and pineapple. A handsome rum of authentic depth.
2014 Rating: ★ ★ ★ ★/Highly Recommended

Ron Centenario 7 Años Añejo Rum (Costa Rica) 40% abv, $20.
Bronze color; impeccable clarity. First whiffs pick up toasty brown sugar, chocolate custard–like notes that are fresh, sugary, and bright; additional aeration brings out subtle hints of candied fruits, primarily banana and pineapple, that pair up nicely with the bakery-shop sweetness. Entry is very sweet, which causes me a little concern, but then settles down offering grassy, vegetal, cane-like flavors that grow intensely bittersweet; midpalate highlights the cane aspect as the grassiness accelerates into a full-blown sugary sweetness. By the finish, the flavor profile is all about sugarcane dominance as it becomes top-heavy with brown sugar, cake-frosting sweetness, which is way too much. The intense, off-balance sweetness made my teeth hurt.
2018 Rating: ★ ★/Not Recommended

Ron Centenario 9 Años Conmemorativo Rum (Costa Rica) 40% abv, $25.
Fulvous brown color; 100 percent sediment-free. This nose at opening is mute and elusive, giving off barely anything aromawise; more time in the glass stimulates a little bit more of bouquet impressions, mostly granulated white sugar and a trace of baking spice (clove, allspice). Entry features a low-key, understated taste profile that's delicately sweet, honeyed, cane-like, moderately grassy, and bittersweet; midpalate displays a touch more assertiveness as the baking spice introduces vanilla bean that adds some panache and layering. Finishes medium long in the throat, with a medium-range degree of brown-sugar sweetness. Slightly more complex than the 7 Años, but still is an underperformer, in my view.
2018 Rating: ★ ★/Not Recommended

Ron Centenario 12 Años Gran Legado Rum (Costa Rica) 40% abv, $35.
Cocoa-brown/topaz color; flawless purity. Okay, now with this 12 Años I'm beginning to see more character concentration in the initial inhalations after the pour as fruity, candied, bittersweet aromas gently waft up from the sample glass; more time in the glass affords more settling, and this brings about layered scents of honey, maple syrup, pine tar, and brown sugar. Entry features tangy, mildly spicy (black peppercorn, clove) flavors that are medium rich in texture; midpalate goes slightly smoky and ash-like as cigar tobacco and spiced fruit flavors take charge. Aftertaste is spicy, zesty, a bit citrusy, and pleasant. Clearly

to me, this is a rum style that requires more time in oak maturation before it develops into a sophisticated, bankable spirit.
2018 Rating: ★ ★ ★/Recommended

Ron Centenario 20 Años Fundación Rum (Costa Rica) 40% abv, $50.

The sinopia color is bright and deep; perfect clarity. Up front, I detect tobacco leaf and black tea notes that are dry, mildly tangy, and herbal; more aeration brings out sweeter, bakery-shop scents of spice cake, gingerbread, carob, cocoa bean, and allspice. Entry is plump, almost fat in texture, honeyed, maple-like, and pretty damn luscious; midpalate highlights mature, roasted flavors of toasted marshmallow, pipe tobacco, turbinado sugar, brown rice, and oloroso sherry. Finishes long in the throat, mature, opulent, and, to its credit, not overly sweet or cloying. This edition of Ron Centenario just might be its Goldilocks sweet spot.
2018 Rating: ★ ★ ★ ★/Highly Recommended

Ron Centenario 25 Años Gran Reserva Rum (Costa Rica) 40% abv, $75.

Mahogany/rust color is dazzlingly pretty; sediment-free. The intriguing opening scents include brown sugar, cocoa powder, Ceylon black tea, clay/dry earth, and cinnamon; secondary inhalations encounter an amalgamated bouquet that goes bittersweet, medium intense, and mildly honeyed. Entry is sugary sweet, but with an almost citrus-like acidity that maintains the dryness/sweetness equilibrium well; midpalate sees the taste profile turn bittersweet, earthy, almost metallic or stone-like, and that development is a surprise for me. Aftertaste stays the crisp, tangy course as the sweetness never eclipses the earthiness or the black tea aspect, thereby displaying a sense of balance and concentration.
2018 Rating: ★ ★ ★ ★/Highly Recommended

Ron Centenario 30 Años Edición Limitada Rum (Costa Rica) 40% abv, $150.

Sienna/burnt umber color; ideal clarity. I keep trying to locate some up-front aromas after the pour, but there's simply not much to grip on to other than a dry sand odor; secondary inhalations following more air contact also fail to unearth much in the way of mature rum bouquet. Entry is fat, buttery, creamy in texture, and cocoa-powder sweet but not very concentrated; midpalate is, well, sweet and sugary, with a touch of oak resin that makes the maturity statement but doesn't provide genuine quality or depth of character. If this were my rum brand, I'd immediately eliminate this over-the-hill, last gasp of a rum as well as the underdeveloped 7 and the mediocre 9, and run to the finish line with the 12, 20, and 25.
2018 Rating: ★ ★/Not Recommended

Ron Cihuatan 12 Year Old Rum (El Salvador) 40% abv, $38.

Cocoa-brown color; unblemished appearance. I immediately like the biscuity, bakery-shop first aromas that speak of bittersweet dark chocolate, cocoa, and sugar cookie batter; secondary inhalations are admittedly sweet but also show traces of oak, sawdust, plank, dark honey, and resin. Entry tastes include buttercream chocolate candies, honey, and molasses; midpalate is very sweet, almost to the point of being bittersweet, and that, for me, is its saving grace for a recommendation. Concludes long, sweet, toasty, and mildly peppery. Might be too much sweetness for some, I agree, but the reason I'm recommending it is due to its high acidity level, which does maintain the structure.

2018 Rating: ★ ★ ★/Recommended

Ron Zacapa Centenario Sistema 23 Solera Gran Reserva Rum (Guatemala) 40% abv, $48.

A blend of rums from six to twenty-three years old. Mahogany/tawny port–like color; superb clarity. Initial sniffs pick up highly complex and concentrated aromas of prunes, white raisins, green tobacco, mincemeat pie, and jerky; next round of inhalations picks up further fragrances, in particular, dried flowers, hazelnut, dried apricot, cream sherry, and a faint touch of TCA mustiness. Entry is lively, coffee-like, prune-like, raisiny, and sherried; midpalate features expressive tastes of maple syrup, honey wheat breakfast cereal, toasted oats, candied walnut, and winter holiday fruitcake. Finishes long, semisweet, and prune-like. Had I not detected a slight amount of TCA from the cork closure, I'd have bestowed a fifth rating star.

2020 Rating: ★ ★ ★ ★/Highly Recommended

Rumson's Gold Rum (Trinidad) 40% abv, $25.

Marigold color; clear and clean. Right off the crack of the bat there's a nutty, grassy, earthy scent that's manufactured and banal; further aeration fails to raise the level of quality to anything past shoe leather. Entry is metallic, lumbering, flinty, and awkward; midpalate can't seem to up this rum's game as prickly flavors of limestone, shale, and stone provide the dim highlights. A dullard's delight.

2019 Rating: ★/Not Recommended

Rumson's Grand Reserve Rum (Trinidad) 40% abv, $45.

Harvest gold color; impeccably clean. This opening aroma, in keen opposition to the Gold edition, is vividly spicy (nutmeg, clove), pastry-like (bear claw), nutty, and confectioners' sugar–like; later whiffs pick up additional scents of toffee, brown sugar, BBQ sauce, tomato paste, and vinegar. Entry echoes the second-stage aromatics, offering the identical sensory aspects but in gustatory form; midpalate is creamy in texture, round, supple, and honeyed. Ends medium long, buttercream-like, and a touch spicy.

2019 Rating: ★ ★ ★/Recommended

Sailor Jerry Spiced Rum (USA) 46% abv, $25.

Burnt sienna color; sediment-free and pure. I can't find the aromatic handle in the first inhalations after the pour, as the nose offers little more than faint odors of marshmallow and baked tropical fruits; after allowing for more air contact, I still have trouble gripping on to aromas of substance that are more than ghostlike whispers of marshmallow, candied orange, and refined sugar, so I move on. Entry is flat tasting, industrial, and lacking in spice definition; midpalate merely echoes the anemic entry stage as the flabby, flat-as-a-pancake flavor profile goes nowhere fast. Finishes insipidly and vacant.

2018 Rating: ★/Not Recommended

Saint James Imperial Blanc Rhum Agricole (Martinique) 40% abv, $32.

Crystalline appearance; colorless. The barnyard opening aromas are all about rain forest

dampness, wet cement, mown grass, and lima beans; secondary whiffs after more air contact bring out scents of vines, brambles, wet leaves, burnt match, and dampened campfire. Entry is deeply vegetal, bitter, and bean-like, with a creamy texture that's silky; midpalate is the best stage for unbridled enjoyment as the elemental, earthy, grassy, cane-like taste profile is supported by the buttery texture relatively deep into the aftertaste. I believe that a higher abv level of, say, 48–50 percent would make this rhum agricole significantly better and more memorable.
2019 Rating: ★ ★ ★/Recommended

Sajous Clairin Rum (Haiti) 54.3% abv, $40.
Corn-silk color; pristine clarity. First aromatic impressions are of nail polish, varnish, oak resin, lard, and crisped pork rind; additional aeration time allows for the more elemental aspects of wet earth, damp grass, bamboo, sugarcane, orchard fruit pit/stone, and shale to emerge. Entry is semisweet, deeply earthy/vegetal, grassy, gentle on the throat, and nearly creamy/oily in texture; midpalate turns succulent, buttery, vegetable cooking oil–like, brown sugar–like, and zesty from a ground black pepper quality that's piquant and alluring. Concludes medium long, keenly peppery, resiny/sappy, tobacco-like, and cane-y.
2018 Rating: ★ ★ ★ ★/Highly Recommended

Stolen Overproof Rum (Jamaica) 61.5% abv, $20.
Aged six years. Pot still distillation. Amber color is akin to amontillado sherry; excellent clarity. Now this opening aroma I really like, as the depth of the sugarcane grassiness could be nothing else but rum, and the spirity face slap could only be overproof so round 'em up, cowboy; second whiffs after more air contact discover, to my surprise, tropical fruit elements that are banana- and pineapple-like as well as not-so-subtle hints of hemp/rope, mown hay, hogo (natural rum funkiness), and beeswax. Entry is remarkably savory, lusciously oily, and only moderately fiery considering the abv level and that, to me, is a positive sign of excellent distillation; midpalate highlights the grassy nature of this rum, framed by flavors of cigar tobacco, mace, brown sugar, toasted marshmallow, and gum. Finishes long, sinewy in the mouth, tobacco-like, resiny, maple-like.
2016 Rating: ★ ★ ★ ★/Highly Recommended

Stolen Smoked Rum (Caribbean) 42% abv, $25.
Very pretty appearance—chestnut/mahogany-brown color and perfect purity. Yes, I get an element of charcoal smokiness up front, but I likewise pick up an espresso-like fragrance that's just as vibrant; secondary inhalations encounter sooty, chimney-like aromas that are now turning bitter and bacon-like as the bouquet moves in the direction of genuine beaniness. Entry is like licking a just-dumped ashtray as the smoke-a-thon reaches a high level and thereby loses its way as a rum and borders on being a liqueur without any sweetness; midpalate mirrors the entry, and by now I just don't see the point of this, even though I did find some quality in the aroma. Tastewise, this rum fails to impress me. For some reason beyond me, being smoked simply doesn't work in this instance. Perhaps some clever bartender will create a dynamite cocktail that will trigger sales, but even there I feel it'll be an uphill journey.
2016 Rating: ★ ★/Not Recommended

Stonewall American Rum (USA) 42% abv, $28.
Jonquil/maize color is bright and pure. First aromatic impressions are of hot-button molasses-based rum fragrances like brown sugar, vanilla extract, marshmallow, graham cracker, and new honey; second-stage aromatics turn fruitier than the bakery-shop-like first stage, offering pleasing scents of tropical fruits (banana, guava), kiwi, gum. Entry is vegetal, earthy, woodsy, rustic, moderately sweet and ripe; midpalate features many of the entry aspects, adding vanilla bean. Finishes fruity, gently sweet, plummy, and a touch fiery.
2015 Rating: ★ ★ ★/Recommended

Stroh 160 Original Spiced Rum (Austria) 80% abv, $33.
The port-like reddish-brown color is pure and bright beneath the examination lamp. The 80 percent abv comes reaching out of the glass and pulls me in and there's no escape, but I have to say that I like the robust quality of this aroma, which is pleasantly spiced with citrus peels, herbs (cola nut, sarsaparilla, coriander, allspice, mace, cubeb, and more); the second nosing pass finds the abv settled down a little, leaving the door open for earthy fragrances of wet soil, wet stone, rain forest. Entry is keenly fruity, spicy, and, yes, fiery, but in a manner that's acceptable, even delectable; midpalate is where the flavorings shine brightest, especially the citrus, cranberry, cinnamon, tree bark, plum, cracked black pepper, paprika. Aftertaste brims with spicy and bright fruity flavors. A unique rum that's a standout.
2015 Rating: ★ ★ ★ ★/Highly Recommended

Sugar Skull Mystic Vanilla with Natural Flavor Caribbean Rum (USA) 40% abv, $28.
Transparent, clean, pure, slight pewter/tarnished-silver tint. Up-front aromas focus on vanilla bean and even a touch of vanilla extract as the concentration stays narrowly fixed; ditto the second inhalations—nothing new here so I move on. Entry is vanilla-bean fixated, and while it is sweet, to its credit, it's not overly sweet like the Tribal Silver; midpalate is properly beany, spicy, cake frosting–like, narrow in scope. Nothing to discuss about the finish. Vanilla bean. Over and out.
2015 Rating: ★ ★/Not Recommended

Sugar Skull Native Coconut Blend with Natural Flavor Caribbean Rum (USA) 21% abv, $28.
Pewter appearance; limpid and impeccably pure. Offers a Candy Cane Lane fragrance of heavily sweetened coconut and little else; the softness of the bouquet is mildly pleasant, but there's a hollowness that's obvious. Entry flavor is actually fine, in that it's simple and uncomplicatedly sweet and coconut-like; midpalate echoes the entry, offering little grip or true substance. This liquid is merely a trifle, a cavalier plaything for young (one hopes) consumers who eventually will get their adult beverage game together with maturity (again, one hopes and this time prays).
2015 Rating: ★ ★/Not Recommended

Sugar Skull Tribal Silver with Natural Flavor Caribbean Rum (USA) 40% abv, $28.
Totally pristine, colorless; sediment-free and pure. First nosings after the pour detect soft, earthy scents of dry stone, limestone, arid desert, metals; later sniffs pick up low-flying

fragrances of dried leaves, linen, barely perceptible hints of sugarcane. Entry, by stark contrast, is way too sugary sweet, as the opening flavor almost makes my teeth hurt from the high degree of sugar; midpalate is the same, with no redeeming values or attributes and, worst of all, bears little resemblance to good light rum (Banks 5 Island, Caliche, Blue Chair Bay) because it's an unrelenting sugar bomb and nothing else of substance. Avoid like Lyme-bearing ticks.
2015 Rating: ★/Not Recommended

The Baron Samedi Spiced Rum (Caribbean) 45% abv, $22.

Gorgeous henna/rust/cinnamon color; flawless clarity. I pick up very pleasant aromas of cacao, dark chocolate, baked ham studded with cloves, vanilla bean in the first nosing round after the pour; secondary passes detect subtler scents of dried cherry, dried cranberry, new leather, and citrus peel. Entry is bittersweet, intensely beany/kernel-like, spicy (cinnamon, clove, vanilla), and pruny; midpalate echoes the entry, adding only a hint of spiritiness that brightens up the in-mouth phase. I have real issues with the majority of spiced rums because of a usually heavy-handed use of flavorings, but Baron Samedi offers a balanced taste that's buttressed and given structure by the 45 percent abv. Nice job here.
2016 Rating: ★★★/Recommended

Transcontinental Rum Line 2004 Rum (Guyana) 56.5% abv, $103.

Flax color; completely sediment-free. This opening aroma reminds me immediately of Cracker Jack candy, leather saddle, herb garden, and meringue/egg whites; further aeration brings out aloe, flaxseed oil, vinyl, and razor-strap leather. Entry is plump in texture (due, I suspect, to the elevated abv) and rich in sugarcane flavors, namely grass, turbinado sugar, cocoa powder, and white chocolate; midpalate offers a harmonious display of prickly flavors in the forms of salted butter, egg cream, and cola nut. Concludes long in the throat, exuding campfire warmth and bittersweet tastes of cocoa and dark-chocolate cake frosting. A serious rum fit for veterans only.
2018 Rating: ★★★★/Highly Recommended

Transcontinental Rum Line 2011 Rum (Panama) 43% abv, $50.

Saffron color; immaculate purity. Up-front aromas offer a full array of succulent, ripe fruit (marula, prickly pear, fig), and spice-related (clove, vanilla bean, cola nut) fragrances that shine brightly; secondary whiffs pick up additional scents of caramel, cocoa powder, and honey. Entry tastes include cola, chocolate-covered coffee bean, and malted milk; midpalate echoes the entry impressions, adding caramel, nougat, candy bar, and treacle. Ends on a sweet, pruny note that lasts deep into the aftertaste.
2018 Rating: ★★★★/Highly Recommended

Transcontinental Rum Line 2012 Rum (Jamaica) 57.18% abv, $55.

Mustard color; impeccably clear. I like this opening aroma as it offers no-nonsense, off-dry fragrances of cocoa powder, egg cream, vanilla bean, sarsaparilla, and BBQ sauce; allowing for more aeration, I find pleasantly zesty aromas abounding in the latter-stage inhalations that feature succulent scents of candied almond, honey, baked banana coated with brown sugar, and bacon fat. Entry follows through nicely in reinforcing the aromatic impressions in the taste profile that is delightfully bittersweet, tangy, mildly piquant, and dark chocolate–like; midpalate mirrors the entry stage, adding a smidgen of nut butter flavor that makes the texture suppler. Aftertaste is long, more sweet than bittersweet, cocoa-like, and earthy/herbal. The high abv isn't a factor at all as it, without calling attention to itself, supports the menu of flavors. Lovely and elegant from start to finish.

2018 Rating: ★ ★ ★ ★ ★/Highest Recommendation

Transcontinental Rum Line 2013 Rum (Guadeloupe) 43% abv, $50.

Jonquil/gold color; perfect purity. Oh my, check all preconceptions at the door as the initial sniffs encounter a dazzling, delicately spiced up-front aroma that includes seductively juicy scents of just-ripened tropical fruits, especially banana, pineapple, and guava, dried orchard fruits, namely nectarine, plus faint hints of cooking spices, in particular, carda-mom; secondary inhalations find a continuation of the tropical juiciness, but now there are gentle waves of verbena and meadowsweet. Entry highlights the delicacy of the fruitiness found in the bouquet while bolstering the garden-fresh herbaceous flavor profile, culmi-nating in a splendidly fresh midpalate that's balanced, off-dry, and crisp. Ends on a grassy, sugarcane-like note that's not sweet at all, but rather earthy and fibrous.

2018 Rating: ★ ★ ★ ★/Highly Recommended

Transcontinental Rum Line 2014 Rum (Fiji) 48% abv, $49.

Earth yellow color; flawlessly pure. An earthy, candle wax–like rum funk is appar-ent in the first whiffs, as the aroma features scents of flaxseed, textile fibers, hemp, pine resin, and decomposing vegetation; after more air contact, the bouquet maintains its earthy pong, adding back notes of lard, bacon fat, pork rind, sage, and parsley. Entry is vibrant, tongue-on-stone dry, a bit like baked brussels sprouts, highly vegetal, and flinty; midpalate reflects every single aspect identified in the entry and then introduces bigger spiciness in the forms of betel leaf, wormwood, gentian, and chamomile. Finishes desert dry, acutely bitter, and leafy/vegetal. A challenging rum, but one that demands your attention all the way through, and for that I applaud it.

2018 Rating: ★ ★ ★/Recommended

Uruapan Charanda Single Agricola Rum (Mexico) 46.5% abv, $39.

Clear as rainwater; free from any sediment or floating debris. Initially, I pick up a rustic scent that's earthy, grassy, and slightly rubber pencil eraser–like; after more aeration, the aroma turns a little mineral- and stone-like, as a flinty fragrance that reminds me of lead comes to dominate. Entry is round, matchstick-like, sulphury, and stony; midpalate features more of the grassiness found in the opening nosing passes that's vegetal and floral, as the midpalate leads into the earthy, dry, and hemp-like finish. Not my cup of rum necessarily, but I appreciate its earthy uniqueness.

2019 Rating: ★ ★ ★/Recommended

Vaval Clairin Rum (Haiti) 48.8% abv, $40.

Eggshell/pearl color; unblemished purity. Similar to the Sajous and the Casimir clairins, this opening aroma is acutely grassy, caney, and bean-like, as piquant scents of damp soil,

wet forest, paraffin, and parchment emerge; secondary inhalations encounter dry-as-a-bone fragrances that are elemental, stone/shale-like, flinty, and strikingly similar to nail polish. Entry is surprisingly fruity and semisweet, which I didn't expect; midpalate maintains the mildly fruity ripeness that's more akin to fruit peel oil than to pulp or juice. Aftertaste reflects the midpalate impressions of fruit rind oiliness and mild sweetness and takes them further into a medium-deep finish that's sap-like and eggy. A curious rum.
2018 Rating: ★ ★ ★/Recommended

Zaya Gran Reserva Rum (Trinidad) 40% abv, $30.
Brandy-like henna color; superb purity. Up front, the first nosing passes pick up ambrosial, candied fruit aromas, especially red cherry, baked peach, pear tart, and brown sugar; secondary inhalations encounter more rummy fragrances, like caramel cream, turbinado sugar, cane juice, and fudge. Entry features tastes of bittersweet cocoa powder, espresso, coffee bean, baked ham with clove studs, and cinnamon bun; midpalate returns to the cooked fruit character, which now tastes far more grilled than oven baked. Ends a bit like maple syrup. Highly stylistic in its flavor approach and, consequently, it might be too idiosyncratic for some rum lovers.
2019 Rating: ★ ★ ★/Recommended

GIN AND GENEVER—WORLD

Considered by distillers to be the most difficult spirit to produce, gin begins life most often as a distilled grain-based neutral spirit that is, in truth, vodka. The addition of botanical flavorings, most vitally juniper, makes that unflavored, colorless distillate into gin. While the juniper berry is gin's mandatory ingredient, other commonly utilized botanical flavorings include angelica root, bay leaf, cardamom, coriander, cubeb, fennel, ginger, grains of paradise, cassia, orris root, and citrus peels, pulp and/or zest from lemons, oranges, grapefruits, limes, and/or tangerines. Lesser used but still important gin botanicals include cucumber, rose petal, lavender, black and white pepper, gentian, cinnamon, caraway seeds, chamomile, clove, anise, licorice, elderflower, fennel, eucalyptus, violets, almonds, saffron, sarsaparilla, and others.

When I first started writing about spirits in 1989, there were but a handful of premium gins populating the USA marketplace: Tanqueray London Dry (still the greatest London Dry gin of them all, comprised of but four botanicals—juniper, coriander, angelica, and licorice), Beefeater London Dry, Boodles London Dry, and, on occasion, Plymouth Gin. Of course, there were any number of cheap "well" gins, such as Fleischmann's, Gordon's, and Gilbey's. But the white-collar gins were scarce as they collected dust on backbars.

Then came the 2000s with the introductions of Tanqueray No. Ten, Bombay Sapphire, and Hendrick's. These three, in particular, altered the direction for gin as they cut new and exciting pathways that offered fresh styles and vibrant sensory experiences. Today in 2021, we talk about available gins globally in the thousands, as bartenders in particular have embraced gin due primarily to it being the core ingredient of scores of classic cocktails, including the gin Dry Martini, Clover Club, Aviation, Gimlet, Negroni, French 75, Corpse Reviver No. 2, Singapore Sling, and my personal favorite, Gin and Tonic.

If I have one complaint about the current bevy of gins, it is that low-on-the-learning-curve craft distillers bury their gins beneath the crushing weight of too many botanicals. When they receive a poor score from me and ask me why they fared badly, I typically pass along six words of counsel: "Buy Tanqueray London Dry. Four botanicals." The rest I leave to them.

As far as sources for top-quality juniper go, the world's elite gin distillers universally prefer the juniper berries from Eastern Europe (Albania, Herzegovina, and Bosnia, especially), Morocco, and Tuscany. The majority of deep blue/purple juniper berries are harvested in the wild by hand in these choice regions. Juniper berries (*Juniperus communis*) are the small, round, nodule-like fruit from the cypress family of trees (genus: *cupressaceae*). This sturdy family of trees has existed at least since the Triassic period of 250 million years ago. Indeed, the Triassic era was when all the current continents were clustered together in the giant continent known as Pangaea.

Juniper's curative properties have been known since at least 1000 CE when oils from the berries were mixed with various alcohols, mostly wine, for medicinal reasons throughout

Europe. These crude, bitter-tasting beverages were viewed as curatives for people with digestive, liver, and/or kidney ailments. All the more reason to order a gin Dry Martini next time you are in your favorite watering hole.

International Varieties

Distilled Gin: A style of gin in which existing alcohol is distilled again along with juniper and possibly other botanical flavorings.

Genever: The traditional variety of malty tasting, heavy-bodied gin invented in Holland. Sometimes compared to whiskey because of the high malt content, most genevers are matured in wood barrels. Those labeled as *Jonge* are usually young, light in color, and zesty while those marked as *Oude* are matured longer in barrels, are deeper in color, and quite stout in character.

Gin: The variety of high-alcohol-degree gin that is basically vodka flavored after distillation with juniper and other botanical elements.

London Dry: The most globally preferred style of gin, which is alcohol that has been redistilled with juniper and other botanicals. This style is one in which the juniper is prevalent and is very dry to the taste.

Mahon: A Spanish variety of gin that hails from the Balearic Islands that lie off Spain's eastern coast. Typically, mahon is wine-distilled gin.

New Western/New World/International: This confounding style is ill-defined and championed mostly by North American craft distillers. It's purposely juniper "backward," allowing other botanicals, particularly citrus, angelica, orris, flower petals, cucumber, and coriander to dominate.

Old Tom: An old-fashioned sweetened variety that had its heyday in nineteenth-century England. At the present time, there is mild enthusiasm in some quarters for a comeback, but that will be short-lived as the style is overall clunky and overweight.

Plymouth: A specific variety of dry gin that hails only from the Black Friars Distillery in England's southwest city of Plymouth.

Sloe Gin

Sloe Gin (usually only 15–30 percent abv, but the European Union has ruled that it must be at least 25 percent to be labeled as such) is, in fact, not a gin at all but instead a red-colored liqueur that has gin as a base. Sloe gin is produced by macerating sloe berries (*Prunus spinosa*) in gin for from three to six months. Sloes, a member of the rose family, are also known as *blackthorn* and are native to northwest Africa, western Asia, and Europe.

1911 Premium Small Batch Gin (USA) 44% abv, $30.

Clean and transparent as rainwater. I like the fruity, tart opening aroma that hints of baked apple and juniper/pine tree; secondary inhalations after more air contact discover deeper, provocative, earthy fragrances of gunmetal, chalk, lead pencil, black pepper, and citrus that eclipse the juniper, but somehow it all works as the New Western style bouquet is pleasing. Entry is zesty due to the citrus/lemon peel that underpins the fragile juniper flavor; midpalate returns to the metallic earthiness that's prevalent in the aroma. Aftertaste sees a surge in cedar/juniper taste that earns this brisk gin a third rating star and a recommendation for gin adventurers, not necessarily for those people who are dyed-in-the-wool London Dry aficionados.

2018 Rating: ★ ★ ★/Recommended

A. Smith Bowman Rye Expectations Gin (USA) 45% abv, $35/375 ml.

Silvery clear and colorless. This curiously grainy, rye bread–like opening aroma is compelling, assertive, and smells of newly woven canvas, chickpea, and herbal ointment; the aromatic surprises continue after additional aeration as the fragrance turns more in the direction of beans/legumes, never once offering evidence of juniper. Entry features some juniper berry quality along with a fine-tuned citric acid thrust that underpins the canvas-like element; midpalate offers the most gin-like arguments of the evaluation as the juniper at last does emerge as a major player, eclipsing the rye grain/rye bread flavors that by this point have been dialed back. Finishes medium long, satiny, and full in texture, with an orange zest finale that's pleasing and satisfying. Totally different and captivating entry into the gin marathon race that's growing by the minute.

2017 Rating: ★ ★ ★ ★/Highly Recommended

Ada Lovelace California Gin (USA) 40% abv, $39.

Sediment-free and void of color. What I like about this assertive aroma is the opening burst of pine forest–like juniper that sets the tone immediately for a juniper-forward, dry-as-the-Sahara style; secondary sniffs detect more in the way of additional ingredients, including coriander, lemon zest, and angelica—highly appealing aromatics. Entry is lean, tart, deeply piney, and crisp; midpalate shows a bit more density in the texture as the juniper is allowed to run wild in a pine cone/cedar display that's astringent and marvelously tangy. Concludes dry, tart, acidic, and razor edged. A really solid, London Dry–like effort that's worth every penny.

2018 Rating: ★ ★ ★ ★/Highly Recommended

Amass Los Angeles Dry Gin (USA) 45% abv, $55.

Perfect clarity, no sediment or color. With (count 'em) twenty-nine botanicals fighting for survival like a WWE SmackDown, aromatic balance might be tricky to achieve as the initial impressions downplay the juniper to the point of near exclusion—other ingredients, especially the floral/plant elements such as bay leaf, cassia, and hibiscus, rule the early nosings; after more aeration, the bouquet squeezes out some minute measure of cedary juniper, but that's about it. Entry is jammed with an array of competing flavors that never meld into a unified flavor profile with purpose; midpalate is like a clown-filled Volkswagen. A messy,

ill-conceived textbook example of, one, when more is NOT better than less in gin and, two, embarrassingly unsophisticated amateur distilling.
2019 Rating: ★/Not Recommended

Austin Reserve Batch No. 14 Gin (USA) 50% abv, $32.
Colorless, limpid, impeccably clean and clear. There's an aggressive botanical thrust in the first nosings that highlight brambles, vegetation, moss/lichen, candle wax, dried flowers; secondary whiffs encounter less impactful scents of dried flowers (violets), sesame seed, caraway seed, peppermint, pine/cedar, coriander, angelica. Entry is highly floral, sappy, semi-sweet, herbal, sage-like, thyme-like, rosemary-like; midpalate reflects all the entry findings and adds bay leaf, cilantro. Finishes a bit too hot, but the overall impression is positive. What it lacks (substantially) in finesse and elegance, it counters with raw power and grit.
2015 Rating: ★★★/Recommended

Aviation American Gin (USA) 42% abv, $25.
Pristine, sediment-free appearance. Perhaps the quintessential, defining New Western style that led the charge a decade ago in juniper-subtle gins, the first inhalations pick up woodsy/forest floor scents of wet leaves, moss, wet sand, tree bark, and damp vegetation, along with distant scents of gunpowder and aluminum foil; later whiffs detect joss stick, green tea, chai, and candle wax. Entry contradicts the aroma by offering nuances of juniper, cassia bark, coriander, orange peel, and black pepper, which are balanced and savory; midpalate builds upon the advances in the entry, highlighting the citrus peel especially. Finishes nicely, with the flurry of citrus-fruit zestiness that wins me over once again. Well done and emblematic for the style.
2018 Rating: ★★★/Recommended

Azzurre Gin (USA) 40% abv, $33.
Bright, mineral water transparency; pure. Opening aromas are a little muted and disorganized as there's no dominant fragrance, not even juniper; in the second passes I get candle wax, vegetable oil, some minor elements of juniper, dill, anise, citrus zest; a lackluster bouquet, by all accounts. Entry echoes the bouquet as the flavor profile leans heavily on neutrality and less on meek botanical presence; midpalate shows more character as the juniper finally emerges, as does lemon peel, cardamom, black pepper that all last into the finish. Recovered somewhat in midpalate and aftertaste from the desultory aroma and entry phases. Needs work.
2015 Rating: ★★/Not Recommended

Bainbridge Heritage Organic Doug Fir Gin (USA) 45% abv, $39.
Slight pewter-like tint; clean and pure. I like the cedary/pine forest aroma that is tangy, pungent, and not a little sap-like; second passes following further air contact bring out highly perfumed botanicals, especially juniper berry, lemon peel, orange zest, and black pepper—this is a distinctive bouquet that might be too overpowering for some, but I like it. Entry is resiny, sap-like, even a bit honeyed as the juniper takes charge, leading the way for the astringent citrus thrust; midpalate features all the elements found at entry, in particular,

a bittersweet aspect that is totally influenced by the pine sap. Finishes clean, deeply zesty, and bark-like.

2018 Rating: ★ ★ ★/Recommended

Bainbridge Oaked Organic Doug Fir Gin (USA) 45% abv, $39.

Owns a straw-yellow color; excellent purity level. Opens aromatically with a velvety rush of unsalted butter and egg cream notes that are unexpected and atypical but highly appealing; second passes pick up the soft, cushiony juniper, which mingles very well with the wood resin/sappy notes, creating a unique gin bouquet. Entry is extremely resiny and bark-like as the juniper is suddenly lost amidst the pine forest; midpalate finds the juniper regaining its place as the pine resins fade, allowing the juniper berry zestiness to prevail. Concludes long in the throat, intensely piney, bark-like, and resiny.

2018 Rating: ★ ★ ★/Recommended

Barr Hill Gin (USA) 45% abv, $36.

Owns a slight pewter-like tint to its clean appearance. Yes, there's clearly juniper in the initial nosing passes, but there's also a faint hint of earthiness that's kind of waxy and floral/vine-like, which must be the honey ingredient; further inhalations following more aeration highlight the honey aspect as the juniper takes on a pine tree sappiness. Entry is amazingly forward and assertive, mostly with the honey flavor that eclipses the juniper to the degree of obliteration, making me question if this is really more a flavored vodka; midpalate finds a mild resurgence of the juniper that lifts this into two star territory. There's quality distillation here. What I question is the use of the intense honey, which blankets the juniper, ties a rope around it, then dumps it in the river.

2018 Rating: ★ ★/Not Recommended

Batch Industrial Strength Gin (England) 55% abv, $39.

Pristine clarity; colorless. The first nosings pick up ample amounts of pine-driven juniper and lemon peel while the elevated abv remains comfortably in a supporting role; later inhalations detect more serious aromatic notes of black pepper, cardamom, anise, and key lime. Entry is assertively warm due to the 110 proof, but not once does my palate flinch from the spirity warmth, plus there's the woodsy presence of the juniper that mitigates the alcohol. Midpalate brings together the various taste elements in a zesty, citrusy, piney wave of flavor impact that extends deep into the pleasantly dry and crisp aftertaste.

2019 Rating: ★ ★ ★ ★/Highly Recommended

Batch Signature Gin (England) 40% abv, $35.

Crystalline appearance and pure. First inhalations detect robust fragrances reminiscent of damp forest flora, especially wet pine/cedar trees, plus healthy doses of cardamom and clove; after more aeration, the aroma profile changes direction by adding feathery scents of lemongrass, lemon curd, and, most prominent of all, allspice. Entry, in contrast to the hearty bouquet, is gently tingling and semidry on the palate, as tastes of flower petals and cinnamon vie for attention; there's a sudden calmness at midpalate that indicates, at least to me, that there's insufficient alcohol by volume to continue pushing the flavors forward into the aftertaste. If this gin were mine, I'd hike up the abv to at least 46–47 percent to accentuate the highly pleasant botanicals.

2019 Rating: ★ ★ ★/Recommended

Batsman Small Batch Gin (France) 47.5% abv, $28.
Molasses base. Totally colorless; impeccable purity. In the opening whiffs, I detect traces of pine nut, cedar, ground black pepper, and dried citrus peel; later inhalations pick up deeper cooking spices (bay leaf, thyme, parsley) as the juniper fades to the background. Entry is tart, citrusy, and lean, then it goes vegetal and moderately oily as it passes over the palate, losing a little bit of the juniper thrust; midpalate sees the juniper regain some ground, but the dominant flavor remains the cooking spices identified in the aroma. Finish is waxy in texture, vegetal, herbal, dry, and brief to medium long. Certainly not a London Dry style; more in the International/Western style, in which the juniper plays a supporting role.

2016 Rating: ★ ★ ★/Recommended

Battle Standard 142 Navy Strength American Dry Gin (USA) 57% abv, $35.
Perfectly pure and colorless appearance. Right from the pour, the beany, junipery, piney, citrusy bouquet fills my office with succulent and zesty aromas, and while I acknowledge the 114-proof engine as the fragrance generator, I also admit to loving this early bouquet; further aeration releases more of the orange blossom scent that jibes nicely with the cooking spices, especially the cardamom and coriander—I also hasten to note that the ferocity of the abv-driven aroma settles down with air contact, leaving plenty of room for the botanicals to be appreciated. Entry is robust, to be sure, as one would expect, but it's not a four-alarm first impression either, and this measured strength allows, in particular, the non-juniper (especially citrus peel, cardamom, and grains of paradise) botanicals to shine. Midpalate continues with the abv warmth on the tongue as the juniper element, at last, emerges with vigor, bringing with it a surge of pine/cedar/minty flavor that accelerates into the citrusy medium-long aftertaste.

2018 Rating: ★ ★ ★ ★/Highly Recommended

Beefeater 24 London Dry Gin (England) 47% abv, $23.
Colorless, unflawed appearance. What I get up front on the nose are traces of green tea, parsley, mint, evergreen, and tropical fruits, like grapefruit, guava, and papaya; further time in the glass brings out much more of the juniper aspect as it lords over the supporting ingredients. Entry is minerally, chalky, earthy, and piquant, lacking in juniper push; midpalate is finer, more tangy than the entry and more texturally plush. Finishes long, tight, juniper forward, and lead pencil–like. To be candid, I've never thought Beefeater 24 to be a classic dry gin, and that impression remains almost a decade after the initial review. It's serviceable, above average, and well made, to be sure.

2018 Rating: ★ ★ ★/Recommended

Beefeater London Dry Gin (England) 47% abv, $19.
Crystalline appearance. The engaging freshness of the opening aromatics is delicate, understated, and midlevel degree juniper/sappy, and I admittedly love it for its graceful entry; later whiffs encounter zesty scents of lemon peel, chalky earth/minerals, peach pit,

lavender petal, and coriander—a textbook London Dry bouquet. Entry is refreshingly clean, astringent, and tart, yet it displays a lushness of texture that supports the botanicals stylishly; midpalate is crisp, lean, acidic, lemony/citric acid–like, and full of juniper berry oiliness. Aftertaste highlights the juniper berry tanginess. Lovely, elegant at every sophisticated turn.
2018 Rating: ★ ★ ★ ★/Highly Recommended

Beefeater London Pink Strawberry Flavored Gin (England) 37.5% abv, $20.
Rosy pink color; sediment-free. There is no doubt about the presence of strawberry as the first whiffs highlight candied strawberry fragrance and nothing resembling gin; second-level nosings do not detect any juniper existence as the candied strawberry eclipses all other aromatics. Entry is a touch sweet, very fruit/berry-like, and quite insipid; midpalate is all about strawberry compote and hard candy, as my final in-mouth impression is of strawberry-flavored vodka and nothing more. The finish echoes the midpalate, adding nothing new. I'm all for experimentation, but this one never lifts off the launching pad.
2019 Rating: ★/Not Recommended

Bloom London Dry Gin (England) 40% abv, $28.
Pristine appearance; sediment-free and colorless. First nosings pick up featherlight traces of herbal tea, pine cone, and citrus pulp—these opening aromatics are ghostlike whispers; secondary inhalations detect more substantial scents, especially the citrus peel and the tea leaf/floral elements, as the juniper, while present, plays a minor role. Entry is fragile and delicate at the 40 percent abv level, and it's here that the juniper comes alive, taking the taste profile's helm; midpalate is friendly, pleasantly piney, and velvety in texture. Concludes longer than I had anticipated and keenly pine cone–like.
2018 Rating: ★ ★ ★/Recommended

Bluecoat American Dry Gin (USA) 47% abv, $28.
Pewter-like hue to it, and I do note some, likely inconsequential, tendrils of sediment floating in the core. First nosings after the pour detect mildly pleasing scents of citrus (orange peel, especially), cardamom, and orris root—so far so good; seven minutes of added time in the glass stimulates a metallic/coin-like element as well as an herbal aspect (juniper/cedar/pine) that drown out the citrus. Entry is citrusy/orangey (again), with a nice viscosity and a low-key sweetness level; midpalate stage is notable for its citrus zestiness, as that component takes center stage and the herbal parts diminish in strength. A problem arises, to my disappointment, in the aftertaste, which turns very metallic as though you're licking a coin; this development took a third star away from it. While hardly in the ranks of Beefeater or Tanqueray or Citadelle or Plymouth, I can see why some people have become devotees.
2018 Rating: ★ ★/Not Recommended

Bobby's Schiedam Jenever (Holland) 38% abv, $35.
Spotless purity; colorless. First olfactory impressions are grainy (water crackers), spring onion–like, and a touch soapy; with more air contact the aroma turns slightly floral (lemon blossom), vine-like, and parchment-like. Entry flavor is surprisingly lemongrass-like, citrusy, and tart; midpalate is malty, citrusy to a major degree, and refreshing. Ends on a lemon peel

note that edges out all other flavor elements. Simple and not interesting enough for my liquor cabinet.

2019 Rating: ★ ★/Not Recommended

Bombay Original London Dry Gin (England) 43% abv, $25.

No color whatsoever; crystalline purity. First whiffs pick up ample amounts of juniper/pine tree, as well as lesser fragrances of cassia, angelica, and citrus, but if one's paying attention there is quite a lot happening here aromatically; second passes feature more than enough juniper to seal the deal on this being a fine London Dry. Entry is a bit disappointing in the feel of it, as the zestiness of the aroma seems missing due, in part, to the lightness of the texture and the alcohol level; midpalate regains this gin's composure as the juniper returns in its pine forest glory, but I wish nevertheless that the abv was 47 percent, not 43. Finishes a dash sweet and floral.

2020 Rating: ★ ★/Not Recommended

Bombay Sapphire London Dry Gin (England) 47% abv, $33.

Crystalline clarity; colorless. Opening nosing gets doused with heavy scents of lemon peel, lemongrass, and lemon drop candy, with only feathery traces of juniper pineyness; secondary whiffs detect more of the juniper berry, but likewise tree bark/woodsy hints of cassia and orris root. So lithe, so light, so ephemeral at entry that I want to grab it by the lapels and shake more juniper out of it to match the intensity of the alcohol; midpalate shows the woodsy/foresty aspect especially with cassia, angelica, and orris leading the flavor highlight reel—the juniper and the citrus elements are lost by this juncture, and that's precisely why I can never recommend this gin—the juniper gets trampled by the earthy botanicals and, yes, the cyan blue bottle is pretty but I want London Dry gin, and this isn't London Dry gin as I believe it to be.

2018 Rating: ★ ★/Not Recommended

Bombay Sapphire East London Dry Gin (England) 42% abv, $33.

Colorless; clean. Initial scents are of ground black peppercorn and cedar bark/juniper berry, with the ground pepper overshadowing the piney juniper; more time in the glass unleashes forest-like features like cassia bark and orris root, but also lemon zest and coriander for a pleasantly forward bouquet that I find more like London Dry than the regular Sapphire. Entry is botanically pleasing, with a feathery sweetness and fruity ripeness—it just makes a bolder statement than the regular Sapphire, which I find too ghostlike; midpalate features pine forest juniper as well as the Thai lemongrass, as the black pepper aspect fades. Finishes brisk, showing an eleventh-hour punch of juniper and anise. Solidly four stars all the way.

2018 Rating: ★ ★ ★ ★/Highly Recommended

Boodles British London Dry Gin (England) 45.2% abv, $24.

Flawless; pure and free of color and sediment. Up front, the first whiffs detect only muted juniper, as there are bigger aromas lurking such as peanut shell, limestone, burnt match, salted butter, egg cream, egg yolk, and black pepper; after more air contact, the juniper finally breaks through. Entry plays up minerality and earthiness in the initial taste and there's a bit of funkiness/mustiness/damp attic; midpalate is a little harsh and raw, to my surprise, as the juniper

element is buried beneath the crush of aggressive alcohol and unappealing botanicals that lack zest and/or freshness. A disastrous result and a severe downgrade from a once admired crisp and lively London Dry gin. Pivotal question: Why mess with the original recipe?
2018 Rating: ★/Not Recommended

Boot Hill Distillery Batch #2 Gin (USA) 43% abv, $30.
Excellent clarity; limpid appearance. This first nosing is incredibly leafy, vine-like, and vegetal, like a newly tilled garden, with nary a trace of juniper; after more air contact, I get mainly black tea, brown rice, and botanicals such as orris and angelica, but again hardly any juniper. Entry offers a flash of juniper but mostly stays the course of being intensely earthy, now almost beany/hummus/legume-like; midpalate brings with it a wave of savory, tangy, bittersweet flavor thrust that launches the juniper into the picture, thereby saving its recommendation. This is a New Western–style gin with attitude that, while not a brand that I would buy, is nonetheless a better than average example of a juniper-backward style.
2018 Rating: ★ ★ ★/Recommended

Brazos Texas Style Gin (USA) 46.25% abv, $30.
Pale, dusty-gold color; very good clarity. Initially, there's a strong odor of dried, tart citrus peel; orange pith; orange blossom; rosemary; and Earl Grey tea that keeps the juniper/pine tree buried beneath the citrus and rosemary in the opening sniffs. Second-round whiffs find that the juniper remains eclipsed by the heavy doses of citrus juice/peel/pith and the cooking spice elements of rosemary, cardamom; a questionable choice for gin. Entry is strikingly herbal/woodsy, as well as citrus peel–like now to the point where there's hardly any juniper presence, and this brings up the question as to whether or not this liquid is more a flavored vodka than a gin; midpalate is tasty, medium dense, deeply citrusy and acidic, black tea–like and slightly sweet. Concludes on the sweet side of the dry/sweet scale, herbal, orangey. Purely from the taste standpoint, this is clearly recommendable. Is it a gin, though?
2016 Rating: ★ ★ ★/Recommended

Breuckelen Distilling Glorious Gin (USA) 45% abv, $45.
Absolutely immaculate, sediment-free purity; transparent. I don't smell as much juniper-like pine at first as I do other forest and orchard botanicals, such as citrus, orris, angelica, fennel—there's a distant resemblance to gingerbread in the initial aromatic go-round; second-round sniffs encounter black pepper, coriander, ginger root, and at last low-degree juniper berry. Entry taste leans in the direction of woodsy, bark-like, citrusy, botanical flavors that are stronger than the juniper aspect, which is present but positioned more as a background note; midpalate echoes the entry in all elements except that a spiciness comes to the fore, reaching deep into the aftertaste. Dry, citrusy, rustic, fruity, yet sophisticated. Don't expect Beefeater or Tanqueray because this is no London Dry gin.
2016 Rating: ★ ★ ★ ★/Highly Recommended

Brockmans Intensely Smooth Gin (England) 40% abv, $35.
Crystalline appearance; blemish-free. This opening aroma is ambrosial and frothing with wild strawberry and wild blackberry scents that make it seem more a flavored vodka than a gin in the bouquet; further air contact sees the berry-a-thon diminish slightly, but

not enough to allow any other fragrance (like JUNIPER) to peek through the curtains. Entry is all about the tart berry flavoring and has little to nothing to do with gin; midpalate continues the berry parade as any other botanicals are swamped by the sea surge of berry fruit. What were these people thinking, calling this a gin when it is anything but? I mean, really . . . I have no patience with frivolous junk like this.
2018 Rating: ★/Not Recommended

Broker's London Dry Gin (England) 47% abv, $24.

Colorless; impeccable purity. As many times as I've evaluated this gin over the years, I always come back to liking its first aromatics after the pour for their clean crispness, citrusy freshness, and juniper-forward approach; secondary inhalations merely serve to reinforce the initial findings. Entry is zesty, spicy, lemon peel–like, and properly oily, even being in the middle range of viscosity; midpalate stage adds touches of cardamom, angelica, and orange peel that round out the in-mouth experience. Finishes medium long, citrusy, and pine needle–like. Very good value.
2020 Rating: ★★★★/Highly Recommended

Brooklyn Small Batch Gin (USA) 40% abv, $46.

Clean as rainwater, colorless. Initial whiffs pick up fiber-like scents of burlap, cotton, and uncharacteristic notes of peanut butter, peanut shell, moss/lichen, wet earth, with only a mere hint of old, moldy juniper berry; later inhalations after further air contact do little to redeem this awkward bouquet. Entry shows modest improvement over the meandering aroma as traces of juniper berry, lemon peels, angelica, and orris appear, at last; midpalate offers a modicum of grace, elegance, and a strong presence of juniper pineyness that I like. Even though this gin displayed a surge of pleasant botanical richness in the mouth, what torpedoes a recommendation from me is the unforgivably musty aroma.
2015 Rating: ★★/Not Recommended

Bulldog London Dry Gin (United Kingdom) 40% abv, $28.

Void of color; very good clarity. This opening aroma is plump, floral (orange blossom), gently sweet, and even a touch earthy, as any hint of juniper is, for the moment at least, concealed; further sniffing reveals delicate aromas of cedar forest (the juniper), rose petal, tangerine, grapefruit, and orris root. Entry is round, a little fat rather than crisp, but enjoyably smooth and easy; midpalate encounters earthy, flinty flavors of minerals, cereal grain, mild pine, and coriander. Ends brief to medium long. London Dry style shines brighter and more vividly at 47 percent abv rather than 40 percent.
2020 Rating: ★★★★/Highly Recommended

By The Dutch Distilled Dry Gin (Holland) 42.5% abv, $50.

Limpid, colorless transparency; flawless purity. The tangy aromatic attributes that stand out in the opening inhalations are the nicely merged juniper berry and lemon zest, as well as a creamy maltiness that pushes forward the botanicals; after more air contact, the second round of sniffing serves only to mirror the initial impressions with the only change being the addition of a grassiness to the bouquet's profile. Entry is firm in texture, drier than I had anticipated it would be, and focused tightly on the juniper/dried lemon peel partnership;

midpalate stage locates a few more faint traces of other botanicals, mostly angelica, orris, grains of paradise, cubeb, and cardamom. Finishes medium long, pleasantly dry.
2018 Rating: ★ ★ ★ ★/Highly Recommended

By The Dutch Old Genever (Holland) 38% abv, $50.

Good clarity; bisque/ecru color. Smells instantly of malt wine in its sour, yeasty, sourdough-like manner in the opening aromatic salvo that's almost as citrusy as it is grainy/bakery-like; more aeration really brings the citrus peel to dominance as the bouquet turns its attention to an unripened fruitiness. Entry reflects the breadiness noted in the aroma, and the citrus element develops into a featured aspect in tandem with the doughy quality; midpalate highlights the citrus tartness as well as the yeasty maltiness, both leading into the crisp, pleasantly acidic finish.
2016 Rating: ★ ★ ★/Recommended

Cadenhead's Old Raj Dry Gin (England) 55% abv, $52.

Pale, tarnished-silver color; superbly clear. The tanginess of the elevated abv is obvious from the first sniff, but there's enough background fragrance (cardamom, basil, licorice, juniper) to balance the alcohol potency; further inhalations after more aeration detect traces of lemon zest, sea salt, honeysuckle, gardenia, and bread dough to make the aromatics thrilling in their depth and latitude. Entry is round, firmly structured, fireplace warm, lightly toasted, intensely juniper-like, almost jammy, and lovely all the way; midpalate features controlled power in the taste profile that's long, deep, multilayered, and bursting with dried-fruit and black pepper character. Ends long in the throat, creamy/oily in texture, piquant, and tangy, and just plain luscious. A landmark gin that might be too much for some drinkers, but just right for others.
2019 Rating: ★ ★ ★ ★ ★/Highest Recommendation

Caorunn Small Batch Scottish Gin (Scotland) 41.8% abv, $35.

Pristine; colorless. I like the heightened fresh floral aspect of the opening aroma, which is later on buttressed by a complex web of aromas, including red berries, allspice, lemongrass, cardamom, sassafras, pine needle–like juniper. Entry is rich, layered, moderately sweet, biscuity, citrusy/lemon peel; midpalate echoes the entry, adding aspects of black pepper, cedar, cigar box. Aftertaste is lush, viscous, peppery. A worthy addition to any gin lover's collection.
2016 Rating: ★ ★ ★ ★/Highly Recommended

Catoctin Creek Watershed Gin (USA) 46% abv, $34.

Colorless appearance, with some sediment seen floating in the core. Opening nosings encounter delicate aromatic traces of limestone, minerals, moss, fading juniper, huckleberry, peanuts; secondary inhalations pick up hints of citrus peel, citrus zest, angelica, pine tar. Entry is thickly textured, rich in dried botanical flavors, especially star anise, basil, parsley, thyme, juniper; midpalate features a cacophony of vegetative flavors, from spicy rye to orange peel to angelica to cedar bark to white rice to allspice to mace. Aftertaste finds the juniper as it reemerges. A too-busy gin that would improve, I believe, with a honing down of the botanicals. As it is, it is a traffic jam at a major intersection. I'm not implying that all gins should mirror Tanqueray. What I am saying is that with gin, simpler is usually better.

Because of the intensity of most botanicals, less can be more if utilized judiciously and in the right ratios. I think that there exists a recommendable gin here, but perhaps in a succeeding generation. Not as it is right now.

2016 Rating: ★★/Not Recommended

Chase GB Extra Dry Gin (England) 40% abv, $40.

One of the few gins I know of that is made from a potato base spirit. Faint pewter tint; there're too many minuscule bubble clouds floating in the core for my comfort level. Up front aromas include lemon zest, coriander, and juniper in equal measure, making it dry but not necessarily London Dry; with more aeration, the juniper aspect fades in favor of the citrus peel, coriander, clove, and cinnamon. Entry flavor is dominated by the baking spice contingent (cinnamon, clove) as well as angelica with the juniper well hidden; midpalate shows a creamy texture (doubtless from the potato) as the flavor turns sweeter than that of the entry's and a bit floral/vegetal. Finishes soft, plump in texture, spicy, and earthy/elemental.

2018 Rating: ★★★/Recommended

Citadelle Gin (France) 44% abv, $25.

Spotlessly pure and colorless. This opening fragrance is one of gin's great aromatic moments, as the harmonious commingling of the nineteen botanicals is so meticulously managed that I don't find a single flaw; more time in the glass allows the juniper to emerge to some degree but not so much that it can be termed "dominant"; if one feels the need to utilize more than ten botanicals, this is a textbook example of how to do it. Entry is sublimely elegant, balanced, clean, and tart; midpalate echoes the entry as the taste profile is so seamlessly constructed, the botanicals seem to become one, leading to the sensationally classy, understated, sumptuous finish. I take my hat off to master distiller Alexandre Gabriel of Maison Ferrand for creating a perfect gin.

2018 Rating: ★★★★★/Highest Recommendation

Citadelle Reserve Gin (France) 45.2% abv, $45.

Immaculate clarity; shows a greenish, pale, lemon-juice-yellow color. In the first whiffs I pick up distinctive notes of red cherry, lemon zest, tangerine, juniper, almond, and coriander; then in the second passes, I find that the twenty-two botanicals have merged into a single aroma that is woodsy, floral, earthy, slightly spicy, and zesty—a lovely matured gin bouquet by any measure. Entry is soft, dry, but sap-like/resiny, full in texture, and piquant; midpalate is elegant, round, supple, earthy, dense yet creamy, and peppery/spicy. Aftertaste is a touch hot in the throat, but that is mitigated by the lushness of the texture. Not as glorious as the expression I reviewed in 2013, but still a true beauty to search out and buy.

2018 Rating: ★★★★/Highly Recommended

Copley London Dry Gin (Holland) 42% abv, $18.

Crystal clear, pure, and colorless. The evidence of pine forest/juniper/pine cone is obvious right from the initial nosing passes, then I detect an additional presence of ore/metal/shale earthiness that runs parallel to the juniper; with more air contact, the metal/coin aspect overtakes the pleasing juniper berry component, which I find disappointing. Entry goes in an entirely different direction from the bouquet as a top-heavy citrus/lemon curd flavor

makes the texture viscous and lumpy, therefore sacrificing crispness; by the midpalate stage, this gin has lost all sense of direction, freshness, and/or purpose, as the various character factions clash, leading to a befuddled aftertaste that doesn't know what it is or where it's going. A low-acid, poor-distillation mess. Avoid.
2019 Rating: ★/Not Recommended

Copperworks Gin (USA) 47% abv, $38.
Clear as rainwater; colorless. The first whiffs easily pick up strong hints of juniper/cedar/pine without breaking a sweat, but beneath the pine tree scent are other aromatic features, most clearly lemon peel, cardamom, and angelica; the juniper-forward profile in the aroma places it primarily in London Dry territory, but it does offer a thin slice of so-called New Western style in its leathery, velvet-like subtext. Entry is acutely zesty (lemon peel, lemon oil) and piney, as the juniper races forward, pushed by the totally correct abv level of 47 percent (THANK YOU, Copperworks, for deciding on the alcohol-range sweet spot for dry gin); midpalate stage echoes the entry as the juniper berry sappiness takes the helm, making it a Gin and Tonic winner from the get-go or even in a Gin Swizzle that would make nice with the club soda. This is a well-crafted dry gin that's got a wonderful future ahead of it as gin makes its move as a hot category.
2017 Rating: ★★★★/Highly Recommended

Copperworks Release No. 10 Northwest Cask Finished Gin (USA) 50% abv, $45.
Malted barley; pot still distillation. Finishing cask is new American oak. The pale topaz color is pretty, bright, and sediment-free. I smell the toasty, vanilla-like oak immediately in the initial sniffs right before I discover traces of juniper berry, black pepper, walnut oil, and dried violet fragrances; secondary inhalations pick up a dazzling aromatic display of pine forest and vanilla bean oakiness that makes this a highly memorable mature gin nosing experience. Entry is keenly sap-like, almost resiny, with large dollops of pine sap, maple, and oak resin flavors; midpalate is texturally fabulous and silky while the flavor profile features an astringent bitterness that's heavily pine-driven and woody. An example of the promise in matured gin.
2017 Rating: ★★★★/Highly Recommended

Cotswolds Dry Gin (England) 46% abv, $50.
Wheat base. Silvery and transparent but with some core sediment. Though it doesn't claim it on the label, this is a London Dry style that's intensely juniper forward in the first inhalations, but also quite waxy, herbal, and fruity; second passes pick up tiny aromatic morsels of angelica, cilantro, and coriander as the piney juniper component stays completely in command. Entry is gently sweet, pleasingly piney/cedary, delicately herbal, and oily in texture; midpalate notes highlight the juniper berry in a silky texture that's lush but neither syrupy nor fat, and the overall flavor profile is acutely dry, tart, acidic, fresh, and substantial. Aftertaste is medium long and features serious pine tree aromatics that fill the nasal cavity with cedar notes as I savor the finish. Handsome and traditional in style, but with quality all the way.
2016 Rating: ★★★★★/Highest Recommendation

D. George Benham's Barrel Finished Gin (USA) 48% abv, $43.
Owns an amber color; excellent, sediment-free clarity. The barrel influence immediately

dictates the aromatic direction by overwhelming the botanicals rather than enhancing them, and I come away from this first nosing pass underwhelmed; secondary inhalations discover a meager menu of botanical evidence, mostly of the sweet type, which leaves me dissatisfied. Entry, at least, introduces the botanical mix that cowers beneath the gustatory weight of the resiny barrel; midpalate is awkward, way too resiny/sappy/tannic, and those impressions alone are what kills this experiment for me. While I'm all for being adventurous in this wonderfully open period of modern distillation, some things just don't work, and this is one of them.

2019 Rating: ★/Not Recommended

D. George Benham's Sonoma Dry Gin (USA) 45% abv, $40.

Owns a bit of pewter/silver-like tint; overall very good purity. Initial whiffs pick up assertive first aromas of mint, orange zest, lemon drop, angelica, and faded juniper; second passes expose pungent hints of eucalyptus, grains of paradise, coriander, green tea, licorice, and star anise, which becomes a major impact player—the juniper is afforded only insignificant influence. Entry is large, open, and friendly, but perhaps a little too hung up on the non-juniper botanicals, creating a virtual free-for-all of conflicting flavors, for instance, the mint fights the citrus and the star anise dosage scraps with and eclipses everything else; midpalate is medicinal, sorely lacking in the bonding pineyness of juniper and angelica, and therefore turning its back on traditional gin character. Okay, here's the deal: As is the inherent trouble with so many scores of small-scale gins, D. George Benham's comes off more as cough syrup (the mint and eucalyptus impressions) due to too many botanicals than anything I'd want to make a cocktail with, and that is its ultimate downfall . . . like scores of other so-called "craft" or "artisanal" gins. Mind you, this gin isn't undrinkable and might even find its way into the occasional G&T, but as an ingredient for more elegant gin-based cocktails (namely, Dry Martini, Aviation), it would be way too clumsy, unbalanced, and ham-fisted. More is less, in this case.

2017 Rating: ★★/Not Recommended

Damrak Amsterdam Original Gin (Holland) 41.8% abv, $23.

Transparent as mineral water; superb purity. This first nosing is all about minerals, earth, shale, and parchment scents that are flinty and stone-like; following more aeration, the aroma goes a bit in the direction of grain kernels and dry breakfast cereal, with juniper pushed way back to the rear seating. Entry is crisp, edgy, flinty, and agile as the juniper aspect makes a bigger appearance at last, accounting for much of the flavor early on; midpalate offers a supple texture that balances the razor-edged, stony taste profile that now features intensely piney juniper. Finishes totally dry, almost arid, as the high acidity ratchets up the astringency level.

2018 Rating: ★★★/Recommended

Darnley's View London Dry Gin (United Kingdom) 40% abv, $35.

Silvery clarity; colorless and pure. The first nosings don't pick up much in the way of London Dry personality but I keep sniffing; more air contact releases faint hints of juniper, fresh flowers, and tangerine peel. Entry is refined, elegant, toasty dry, and highly floral, with the juniper underpinning the entire taste profile with subtlety; midpalate exposes a trace

more of the flowery aspect, but the show belongs to the juniper—I like the creamy texture, as well. Concludes medium long, chewy, slightly toasted, and keenly piney.
2018 Rating: ★ ★ ★/Recommended

Darnley's View Spiced Gin (United Kingdom) 42.7% abv, $34.
Silvery clear and clean in appearance. First inhalations don't get a lot of fragrance other than soft juniper and tangy baking spices, namely cinnamon, mace, and nutmeg; later passes detect hidden juniper, angelica, and coriander, but the primary thrust here is the baking-spice element. Entry is lightly toasted, dry to the point of being tart, a touch pine needle–like, and overall meandering; midpalate mirrors the entry stage, offering very little on which to grip as the flavor profile seems distracted and unfocused. Concludes short, mildly spicy, and low on flavor impact. Take a pass on it.
2019 Rating: ★ ★/Not Recommended

Deepwells Botanical Dry Gin (USA) 47% abv, $35.
Brilliantly clear, colorless, pure. I like the savory opening aromas that are slightly toasted, cedar box–like, piney, vegetal, forest floor–like, zesty; what comes out in spades with aeration is black peppercorn, cubeb, orange blossom, but frankly this is a botanical banquet of the first magnitude. Entry is clearly defined by the juniper but also by lesser flavors of orris, lemon peel, and flower petals of all sorts; midpalate is pleasantly oily and viscous, rich and piquant, piney and citrusy. Finishes long, semisweet, highly herbaceous (sage, rosemary, anise), and elegant. Nicely done.
2015 Rating: ★ ★ ★ ★/Highly Recommended

Dida's Pressed Gin (USA) 40% abv, $40.
Distilled from grapes. Clean, clear, pure, and colorless appearance. I get fragrances of fruit compote, yellow raisins, vines/brambles, dry soil, and a whisper of juniper in the opening round of sniffing; secondary passes pick up a heightened fruitiness that starts to eclipse the juniper, turning this definitively into a New Western style of gin. Entry is juicy, too sweet, and fruit salad–like, as the juniper aspect gets trampled by the marauding fruit/grape presence; midpalate is thickly textured, deeply fruity/grapy, lacking in acidity, and juicy, but just too overloaded with grape influence to be considered anything but a flavored vodka made from grapes . . . and even as that I couldn't recommend it. Understated it ain't.
2019 Rating: ★/Not Recommended

Diep 9 Old Genever (Belgium) 35% abv, $39.
Very pretty golden-yellow/brut champagne–like color; flawless clarity. Wow, the extra barrel aging (two years) brings out all sorts of intriguing aromas, including steamed white rice, fennel, dried vegetation, and egg yolk; further aeration after seven minutes brings out a buttery, eggy aroma that's nearly fruity. Entry is silky in texture, smooth, and intensely cereal-like; midpalate is dry to off-dry, mildly fruity, malty, and breakfast cereal–like. Aftertaste is grainy/malty and unsalted snack cracker–like. Good but I prefer the Young Genever.
2015 Rating: ★ ★ ★/Recommended

Diep 9 Young Genever (Belgium) 35% abv, $33.
Translucent and impeccably clean and clear. I like the opening nose quite a lot for its malty/grainy freshness, delicate dusty dryness, and its elegant spiciness; later nosings detect subtle aromatic nuances of beans, allspice, parsley, and wax paper. Entry mirrors the bouquet to a tee, offering squeaky clean and zesty flavors that are grain-driven and crisp; midpalate is stony and minerally, but also deeply malty and dusty dry. Finish is clean, smooth, and delicately malty. This is what many producers of "white whiskeys" are trying to achieve but come up painfully short. Classy and very tasty.
2015 Rating: ★ ★ ★ ★/Highly Recommended

Dingle Original Pot Still Gin (Ireland) 42.5% abv, $30.
What I like about this transparent, colorless appearance is the unmistakable presence of floating oils in the core. First whiffs encounter delicate scents of cedar, floor wax, parchment, dried flowers, orange peel, all in measured amounts that integrate by the second passes, which focus more on the dried rose petal–like perfume: a study in gin botanical understatement that makes its point with finesse rather than power. Entry is gently sweet, sap-like, highly vegetal, earthy, woodsy, peppery, anise-like, even slightly minty; midpalate stage is all about elemental integration and completion as the taste profile turns herbaceous, sap-like, green. Aftertaste is gentlemanly, composed, properly piney, citrusy, delicious.
2015 Rating: ★ ★ ★ ★/Highly Recommended

Diplôme 1945 Original 1945 Recipe Gin (France) 44% abv, $36.
More sediment seen floating about than I'd like to report on; lightly tinted, like tarnished silver in color. Initial whiffs pick up fresh, clean, crisp aromas of pine/cedar (juniper berries), orris root, coriander, citrus peel, fennel, and white pepper; secondary inhalations find that the aromatics gradually fade but the juniper core fragrance remains solidly in control, carrying the bouquet forward. Entry leans heavily in the juniper camp as the depth of the piney/berry flavor edges out virtually all other taste elements, except for angelica and woodsy flavors that are similar to cardamom and grains of paradise; midpalate echoes the entry as the profile is dominated by the pineyness of the juniper berry and what might be oil of lemon peel. An issue arises for me in the aftertaste as the flavor profile curiously turns bitter and bark-like. Texture is good and suitably oily, but the bitterness in the finish erases one rating star.
2016 Rating: ★ ★ ★/Recommended

Door County Distillery Gin (USA) 47% abv, $25.
Flawless clarity; void of color. I take to the initial aromas immediately that ripple with juniper plus forest/woodsy botanicals like moss, pine cone, tree bark, cassia, mint, and orris; further aeration brings out lemon juice/zest, menthol, and black pepper notes that integrate with the juniper, creating a highly pleasing bouquet. Entry is zesty with the citrus peel, but not so citrusy that the juniper is lost; the crispness of the midpalate is present due to the high acidity that maintains the acute freshness and structure at a solid 47 percent abv. Where I have an issue is in the slightly raw, mineral-like aftertaste, but other than that, this Wisconsin gin deserves a recommendation.
2018 Rating: ★ ★ ★/Recommended

Downslope Distilling Ould Tom Gin (USA) 40% abv, $35.

Pot still. Eleven botanicals. Base material is sugarcane as opposed to grain. Marigold/straw-yellow color; a fair amount of floating debris seen. Aromatically, a football field apart from London Dry style due mainly to the meager background presence of juniper and the in-yer-face posture of maple/sap, brown sugar (the cane influence), rosemary, and soy sauce; seven minutes later, the bouquet explodes with keenly spicy notes of nutmeg and cinnamon. Entry is zesty, grassy/caney, on the sweeter side of the scale, but pleasingly tangy; midpalate features brown sugar/cane, sap, resin, and vanilla bean. I like it for what it is—a peculiar cane-based spirit—but right now I still prefer Ransom Old Tom from Oregon. My belief is that the cane base detracts from the style, creating in the process something that I wouldn't personally classify as Old Tom gin. Therefore, I recommend it with a caveat.

2013 Rating: ★★★/Recommended

Drumshanbo Gunpowder Irish Gin (Ireland) 43% abv, $40.

Very good purity; as colorless as mineral water. I like the softness of the juniper berry and the lavender-like floral aspect found in the first nosings; secondary inhalations after more air contact find the juniper holding steady while the spring garden feature increases in intensity, but the delicate balance between the two primary fragrances remains solid. Entry is sweet, tea-like, and spicy with a big herbaceous back note that hurtles the juniper forward; midpalate is supple, lush in texture, and tangy. Finishes medium long, sweet, and tangy. I sit on the three star/four star fence with this one. Worth trying, I believe.

2018 Rating: ★★★/Recommended

Dry Fly Barrel Reserve Gin (USA) 40% abv, $35.

Citrine tint; immaculately clear. This first nosing pass discovers leathery, tree bark–like, citrusy, and sourdough aromas that remind me more of aquavit than gin; allowing for more aeration time, I then unearth soda-like, egg cream fragrances that again have nothing to do with gin and everything to do with aquavit. Entry is sickly sweet, sap-like, and lemony; midpalate doesn't help out very much in the way of improving the flavor profile, as the taste direction travels a spicy, plastic-like road that kills the chance for a second rating star. An experiment that simply doesn't pan out.

2019 Rating: ★/Not Recommended

Dry Fly Washington Dry Gin (USA) 40% abv, $30.

Sediment-free and clean appearance. Opening smells offer juniper/pine oil, orchard fruit peel, mint, beer-like, and breakfast-cereal grain scents that are nicely melded and foresty/woodsy; secondary aromas include dried flowers, honeysuckle, and graham cracker. Entry is slightly toasted, drier than I thought it would be, deeply floral, yeasty, and baked; midpalate mirrors the entry, adding meandering flavors of peppermint, rosehips, chalk, and minerals, as the juniper presence is overshadowed by more elemental/woodsy tastes. An awkward attempt at premium gin that would be helped by two things: one, a greater juniper presence and, two, an abv of 44–47 percent. As it is, I can't recommend it.

2019 Rating: ★★/Not Recommended

Dry Town Gin (USA) 46% abv, $35.

Pure as springwater; colorless. Initial nosings pick up alluring scents of lemon peel/lemon zest, piney juniper, cardamom, and orris in nearly equal dosages, though the citrus peel leads by a nose; later sniffs detect earthier elements such as sage, cucumber, elderflower, and tomato vine. Entry taste profile features the herbal earthiness found in the latter stages of the bouquet more than the cedary juniper as this gin lays out its New Western style credentials; midpalate is piquant (peppery) and tangy, somewhat prickly on the tongue, but this is all to the good as the juniper has checked out with its luggage by now. Finishes medium long, quite prickly, which is desirable for the style.

2018 Rating: ★ ★ ★/Recommended

Eau Claire Parlour Gin (Canada) 40% abv, $38.

Colorless; excellent purity. Right off the crack of the aromatic bat I detect assertive herbal fragrances of sage, cardamom, coriander, angelica, lemon drop, orange zest, and a mere hint of juniper that's tucked deep within the folds of the other botanicals; this deeply herbal bouquet stays the course after more air contact, keeping the non-juniper botanicals—sage, thyme, black pepper, citrus peel—in the crosshairs while the juniper languishes in the closet. Entry, at last, features a bit more of the juniper snappiness that was sorely lacking in the aroma, and it's also here where the citrus aspect shifts into passing gear, eclipsing the other botanicals and leading to a midpalate that is based in citric acid primarily and juniper berry oil next. Concludes pleasantly as the juniper finally comes to the fore in a pine-driven aftertaste. Touts itself as a London Dry style but I beg to differ since the juniper doesn't appreciably appear until the midpalate. If I were to categorize Eau Claire, I'd call it a New Western–style gin. If it were mine, I'd also take the abv chains off it and bump it up to a minimum of 45–47 percent alcohol to help push the juniper forward. Then it's possible that it could be viewed as London Dry. But not as it is now.

2017 Rating: ★ ★ ★/Recommended

Eden Mill Hop Gin (Scotland) 46% abv, $40.

Sports a flinty, greenish, straw-yellow color; flawless purity. Wow, I like this deeply grainy, complex opening aroma, rife with flowery/orange blossom/muscat grape notes that are almost sweet and honeyed but not quite that far on the dryness/sweetness scale. Following more aeration, the bouquet unfolds even more spring garden–like perfume, especially honeysuckle and roses, as the juniper/pine aspect emerges with a burst of cedar forest presence. Entry is sap-like, intense, oily, piney, tree bark–like; midpalate goes peppermint bark–like, deeply herbaceous, and botanical, but in a measured manner that allows all the elements to shine. Aftertaste is long, deliciously oily, supple, and memorable. Love it.

2017 Rating: ★ ★ ★ ★ ★/Highest Recommendation

Eden Mill Love Gin (Scotland) 42% abv, $40.

Owns a touch of pewter/tarnished-silver shading; superb clarity. There's an unequivocal aroma of grain spirit up front, and this bread-like/doughy fragrance is supported by more subtle scents of juniper, black peppercorn, poppy seed, anise, sage, and thyme; later inhalations after more air contact round out the bouquet with nuances of margarine, cooking oil, pecans. Entry is toasty, more spicy than herbal, piquant, and the spirit level seems higher than 42 percent and that's a plus; midpalate stage offers a taste profile that's more dry than bitter or sweet, plus it's toasty/roasted, keenly juniper-like and piney, with a background flash of citric acid. What occurs at midpalate carries over into the highly pleasant finish. A gin with personality.

2017 Rating: ★★★★/Highly Recommended

Elephant London Dry Gin (Germany) 45% abv, $35.

I notice a cream soda–like tint of pewter color; excellent in its purity. Strangely, this opening aroma is largely, inexplicably as featureless as an unflavored vodka—whither the botanicals? I ponder; second passes after more air contact fail to reveal more in the way of aromatic presence other than neutral grain spirit; HUH? Entry is tart, citrusy, lemon peel–like, and therefore at least a little zesty; midpalate features fruity tastes that remind me more of orchard fruit rather than vine fruit, and the juniper aspect is hidden in there somewhere as well as a trace of ginger. The brief, uninteresting finish reflects the general flatness and hollow nature of this gin's overall character.

2019 Rating: ★★/Not Recommended

Empress 1908 Original Indigo Gin (Canada) 42.5% abv, $30.

The indigo coloring is startling at the pour—look, it's a very pretty gem-like blue, but I find it distracting and perhaps that is my closed-minded failing. Opening nosing passes struggle to locate any scent substantial enough to identify, except for a faint pulse of juniper, but that's as clear as radio signals from outer space; more time in the glass only serves to bring out a cry of exasperation from me as I still can't locate any fragrance upon which to grip. Entry, at least, features more than ample gripable flavors in the forms of juniper, star anise, lemon peel, coriander, and angelica; midpalate is hearty, juniper-driven, yet owns plenty of woodsy botanical treats that are mossy, leafy, black tea–like, and peppery. After early misgivings, I end up thinking that this is a recommendable gin due primarily to its zesty, medium-dense flavor profile that quashed my skepticism and disappointment with the bouquet.

2018 Rating: ★★★/Recommended

ESP American Beauty Rose Ginger Cinnamon Gin (USA) 42% abv, $35.

Transparent, but both pours confirm a sediment problem that looks like tendrils of either cloth or fiber. First nosing comes across unusual aromas that are a baked, kind of rubbery combination of ginger, beeswax, plastic, and cinnamon with no trace of juniper/pine; secondary whiffs confirm all the first-round impressions and add wispy hints of green peppercorn, steamed brown rice, tofu, kale; not a gin bouquet to write home about. Moderately better in the entry as the juniper aspect finally makes a weary, mumbling appearance, but the primary flavor thrust is that awkward marriage of moldy ginger and cinnamon, a teaming that works as seamlessly as Kanye West and Taylor Swift. Finishes floral, a little juicy, but basically this gin has bought an express ticket to Nowheresville. Wave goodbye from the station platform, then buy Tanqueray or Beefeater to feel alive again.

2015 Rating: ★/Not Recommended

ESP Smoke & Mirrors Applewood Smoke Peppercorn Caraway Gin (USA) 42% abv, $35.

Crystal-clear appearance; superb purity. Clearly, the reference to "smoke" in the name identifies the applewood smoke flavoring and maybe some of the peppercorn, but already this distillate has nothing to do with gin, even in its most extreme mode, which this miserable rendering is outside of by 1,028 miles aromatically—mezcal, maybe. Secondary sniffs after further aeration find the campfire smoke a little more settled, but now that's replaced by a rancid, filled-to-capacity ashtray-like reek that's about as welcome as a buttock boil. Entry is smoky, tobacco-like, plastic-like, minerally, earthy, unpleasant; midpalate is a train wreck, possibly that same express to Nowheresville that its sibling, American Beauty, was on. Not just "Not Recommended," but Reviled.

2015 Rating: ★/Not Recommended

Farmer's Small Batch Organic Gin (USA) 46.7% abv, $30.

Limpid and clear, with a touch of pewter tint. Initial whiffs immediately identify the unmistakable lemongrass aspect that dominates the early nosings; secondary inhalations detect the cushiony softness of elderflower, yet the juniper at this point makes its presence known in an acute astringency that crackles on the palate. Entry is delicate, intensely floral, lightly citrusy, and juniper-driven right from the start; midpalate offers a clean, crisp, flowery flavor profile that's supported by a medium-weight texture and firm structure that's high in acid. Concludes crisp, fresh, and vivid in its floral aspect.

2018 Rating: ★★★★/Highly Recommended

Fenimore Gin (USA) 40% abv, $45.

Absolute clarity, with some oils seen floating in the core; colorless. The aroma that, to me, comes to the forefront is eucalyptus, followed by juniper, citrus, citric acid, and bay leaf; secondary inhalations discover sage, plastic/vinyl, and pod-like aromas. Entry features the pod-like aspect found in the aroma as the juniper fades a little; midpalate finds the juniper in the driver's seat, along with a noticeable floral element of rose and lilac. Pleasant finish is understated, a little meek, but flower-shop fresh. If it were mine, I'd raise the abv to at least 45 percent, maybe 46 percent, to put more jolt into the midpalate and finish.

2017 Rating: ★★★/Recommended

Ferdinand's Saar Dry Gin (Germany) 44% abv, $63.

Flawless purity; colorless appearance. Impressions of fresh flowers (rose petal, especially), summer garden, leafy vegetation/vines, jasmine, tropical fruit, and a low degree of juniper oil make for pleasant sniffing right after the pour; more air contact accentuates the fruit aspect, which has now turned into orange peel, as the juniper slowly diminishes. Entry offers a creamy texture upon which floats the orangey/lemony flavors of peel, zest, and juice that, to my surprise, intermingle nicely with the understated juniper; midpalate does its best to maintain the fruity/citrusy flavor but as that aspect diminishes, the juniper and other botanicals don't appear to carry enough depth to fill the growing void, and the core goes slightly hollow by the aftertaste stage. By not holding its center intact, this fruit-driven gin remains recommendable but not highly recommended.

2016 Rating: ★★★/Recommended

Ferdinand's Saar Quince Gin (Germany) 30% abv, $60.

Riesling infused. Brilliant golden/honey hue; superb clarity. The nose is pleasingly cedar-like and grapy in equal measure, plus there are delightfully nuanced elements of pumpkin seed and spiced pumpkin that make the trip worthwhile; the aroma blossoms into a bouquet of flowers after more aeration time. Entry is tart, acidic, even sour as the riesling fruit takes the lead on the flavor front; midpalate doesn't particularly echo the entry as the taste profile takes a sharp left, going severely tart but also appealingly herbal. Finishes brief, borderline astringent, nicely acidic, and therefore fresh and suddenly citrusy. A curious but wholly fun romp through Germany's idea of flavored gin . . . or flavored something.

2016 Rating: ★ ★ ★ ★/Highly Recommended

FEW American Gin (USA) 40% abv, $40.

This gin has a slight shade of pewter but is otherwise void of color; excellent clarity. Right from the opening sniffs I get lemon custard/lemon meringue pie notes that direct the aroma's course early on, not allowing much room for any other botanical; it's later in the second passes following more aeration that I detect distant echoes of juniper, almost like searching for signs of extraterrestrial life, so I move on to the gustatory phase. Entry is full-bodied, creamy, and richly textured, and it's that firm foundation of grain spirit that pushes forward the citric acid/lemony flavor that owns hints of juniper, cardamom, and tree bark; midpalate holds the line on the robust, cushiony structure upon which the lemon curd and juniper flavors play, with a fleeting nod to a curious beany taste that emerges in the aftertaste. I like this atypical gin but can't help but wonder if a higher proof of perhaps 90 or 92 wouldn't accentuate the flavor elements more and maybe even nudge it towards four star territory.

2018 Rating: ★ ★ ★/Recommended

FEW Barrel Gin (USA) 46.5% abv, $50.

Amber/old gold color; impeccably clean. I like the deeply woody initial aromas that remind me of new pine flooring, pine cones, and springtime cedar forest, though I have to believe that a good share of the pineyness is derived from the juniper element, not just the oak barrels in which this gin matured; following more air contact, the botanicals come alive, especially the juniper, black pepper, tobacco leaf, and licorice. Entry is dense and intense with succulent wood-influenced flavors that, at first, are caramel-like (caramelized onion, actually), cocoa bean–like, oaky, and creamy, then they morph into more woodsy tastes of juniper, menthol/mint, dark chocolate, and marshmallow; midpalate treats one to zesty, integrated flavors of piney juniper, cocoa bean, mint, and eucalyptus. Finishes very long, minty, and fresh. If not the best matured gin on the market, certainly in the running for that title.

2018 Rating: ★ ★ ★ ★/Highly Recommended

FEW Breakfast Gin (USA) 42% abv, $40.

As pristine and sediment-free as possible; colorless purity. Up front, I pick up modest earthy/woodsy notes of clay, earthenware, unsalted butter, cassia bark, and lavender, but the primary aromatic thrust for me is the deep graininess of the base; with more air contact, the botanicals settle in, offering very mild scents of black tea, orange zest, and baking spices (clove, cinnamon, perhaps even nutmeg) as any hint of juniper remains buried. Entry is dry, moderately tannic, and astringent, featuring a modicum of earthy botanicals, mostly black tea leaves, orange zest/peel, and toasted bread; midpalate at last exposes the low-volume juniper element as the earthiness and graininess remain the headliners. Concludes by staying the course on the grain-forward dry character that allows just enough room for the citrus/orange component to peek through. I like this well-made grain distillate easily enough for a recommendation—no hesitation there—but more as an intriguing flavored spirit than as gin in the formal sense. But then, in this remarkable era of bending the long-accepted rules, it should always just come down to the quality of the spirit.

2018 Rating: ★★★/Recommended

Fifty Pounds London Dry Gin (England) 43.5% abv, $40.

Absolutely pristine; transparent, without a hint of color. First off aromatically, the juniper softness is beguiling and understated in the initial whiffs; secondary inhalations pick up earthy aspects, mainly cement, dry sand, and dried leaves—I find myself being a little disappointed in this meek bouquet. Entry recovers significant amounts of the aroma's lost ground by offering tangy, zesty, even succulent tastes of juniper berry/cedar, lemon pulp, orange zest, angelica, and orris; midpalate features a creamy texture that provides the foundation for the piquant botanicals that are dry, tart, and yet offer enough ripeness to round off the high-acid edginess. Ends in a flurry of juniper/pine cone earthiness that's satisfying and punchy. A case of serious redemption in which the flavor profile's splendor rescued the bouquet's anemic performance.

2018 Rating: ★★★★/Highly Recommended

Foggy Harbor Distilled Gin (USA) 47.5% abv, $29.

Clean as a whistle; limpid; flawless purity. First nosing passes fail to pick up much in the way of gin fragrance except for a peanut-shell quality; secondary inhalations detect lesser scents of grass/hay, candle wax, cardamom, coriander, and barely perceptible juniper. Entry sees an obvious escalation in attributes as the taste profile comes alive in the mouth in waves of juniper, soy sauce, star anise, lychee, peanuts, tree bark; midpalate echoes much of the entry impressions, adding a pleasant texture that's oily and a bit of abv heat that I favorably respond to. Finish is long, zesty, citrusy, cedar-like, peppery—lots going on here into the conclusion.

2015 Rating: ★★★/Recommended

Fords London Dry Gin (England) 45% abv, $24.

Void of color and flawlessly pure and free of sediment. This tart, astringent, and splendidly juniper-driven and floral early aroma could only be London Dry; secondary passes unearth lovely, harmonious scents of apple blossom, angelica, coriander, cassia, and lemon zest that all orbit around the planet governed by juniper—a deliciously understated, elegant bouquet. Entry shows all the virtues found in the bouquet and adds a black pepper piquancy that sparkles on and enlivens the palate; midpalate features more of the piney juniper that clearly is the glue of this classic London Dry. Aftertaste is balanced, chewy in texture, bittersweet, tart, and completely guided by the oiliness of the juniper. One of the top ten London Drys in the marketplace.

2018 Rating: ★★★★★/Highest Recommendation

Fords Officers' Reserve London Dry Gin (England) 54.5% abv, $35.

There is a faint tint to this appearance that can best be described either as pewter or egg white; superbly clean; the slight coloring is certainly due to this gin being barrel finished. Juniper berry aroma leaps from the glass along with juicy scents of grapefruit and mandarin orange; later inhalations following more aeration highlight the citrus components, in particular, the orange and lemon peels. Entry is robust, weighty in texture, and deeply pine tree–like, as the elevated abv thrusts the opening flavors headlong into the midpalate stage, where the taste profile offers a pleasing balance of juniper, zesty citrus, and stout alcohol. Finishes a bit too hot for my taste, but the overall impression is of regular Fords London Dry but with a turbocharged engine.

2020 Rating: ★ ★ ★ ★/Highly Recommended

Four Pillars Navy Strength Gin (Australia) 58.8% abv, $45.

Crystalline clarity; colorless. Though the abv is highly elevated, the first nosing passes aren't prickly with alcohol and, in fact, what comes through more than anything else are curiously atypical and incongruous fragrances of lima beans, sour citrus, pea pods, hemp, and wet sand; secondary whiffs pick up flashes of juniper that are embedded in the scents of overripe, turning-brown limes, green vegetable, palm fronds, damp straw, and broccoli—a disappointing, misguided bouquet. Entry offers more gin-like aspects than the dismal aroma as the abv prickles on the tongue and the juniper comes on strong as does the lime juice element; midpalate reverts a bit into the vegetal quandary prevalent in the bouquet, and I'm sorry about that devolution. Concludes intensely lime-like and tart, but by this time any chance of recovery is lost.

2018 Rating: ★ ★/Not Recommended

Four Pillars Rare Dry Gin (Australia) 41.8% abv, $36.

Transparent but with a barely discernable haze; sediment-free. I like the opening aromas that include orchard fruit tartness, dry stone, cement, arid landscape, lightweight juniper, and bay leaf; more aeration brings about a bigger juniper presence as well as deft touches of lemon zest and angelica; I favorably respond to the understated, earthy nature of the bouquet. Entry is surprisingly sweet (?), ripe, juicy, and floral at first, then the juniper and leafy botanicals kick in, changing the flavor's direction to a more woodsy, earthy, drier path; midpalate sees the juniper take command with the assistance of the bay leaf and angelica, thereby creating an off-dry, moderately astringent taste profile that lasts deep into the aftertaste stage. A gin that alters its course several times but the end result is pleasing and herbaceous.

2018 Rating: ★ ★ ★/Recommended

Frey Ranch Estate Distillery Gin (USA) 45% abv, $40.

Rainwater clear, colorless, pure. Early on in the nose, I detect juniper, to be sure, but there's also a peculiar, aridly dry but appetizing aroma of dry leaves, sage, shrubbery; later sniffs encounter deeper notes of sage, along with subtler traces of orris root, angelica, and black pepper—I like this bouquet. Entry is dusty dry, densely herbal/botanical, peppery, spicy, even a touch hot/fiery on the tongue once the entry evolves into the midpalate, but the overall sense I have is that this is a well-made gin whose character is simply zesty, forward,

and a little prickly. Finishes with a full flourish of juniper oiliness that rounds out the experience. Me like, even if gin traditionalists might find fault.
2016 Rating: ★ ★ ★ ★/Highly Recommended

Garnish Island Gin (Ireland) 46% abv, $27.
Clear, void of color, and pure. The juicy, ripe, tree bark–like, and pine forest aroma in the first inhalations is peppery, zesty, and pleasant; after additional aeration, the aroma turns drier, almost arid/desert landscape–like, emitting dusty scents that are highlighted by fragrances of dried flowers, stone, and licorice. Entry echoes the latter-stage nosing impressions, as the taste profile is basically dry, but with succulent hints of rose petal, lavender, hibiscus, and rose hips that buttress the firm juniper/pine cone core flavor; midpalate is the key moment when all the components merge into a singular London Dry portrait that's herbal, floral, dry, and amiable. Medium-long aftertaste.
2019 Rating: ★ ★ ★ ★/Highly Recommended

Ginraw Barcelona Gastronomic Gin (Spain) 42.3% abv, $53.
Clear as rainwater; colorless. I take kindly to the generosity shown by the opening aromas, as vivid fragrances of pine cone, lemon peel, coriander, and orris root make their presence known immediately; secondary sniffs pick up deeper, equally enjoyable scents of licorice/anise, lavender, and rose hips. Entry is delectable, dry, delightfully piney/juniper berry–like, woodsy, and floral; midpalate stays the flavor profile course set by the entry that takes this satisfying taste experience deep into the aftertaste with a final dash of black pepper. The best Spanish gin in the marketplace by a full length.
2019 Rating: ★ ★ ★ ★/Highly Recommended

Gordon's London Dry Gin (Canada) 40% abv, $14.
Author's note: This version of Gordon's is distilled in Canada. Clean, limpid appearance. Same NGS opening aroma as from thirteen years ago, with merely a hint of juniper that's a bit lost amidst the pencil eraser, cardboard, and compost scents; later sniffs pick up odors of burnt match, hard-boiled egg, sweat, gym shoes, black pepper. Entry at last shows some juniper provenance but hardly enough to justify raising the final score; midpalate offers botanical bits of orange peel, cardamom, coriander, angelica, and licorice but too little juniper for its London Dry status. Concludes meekly and with a flurry of angelica.
2018 Rating: ★/Not Recommended

Gordon's Traveller's Edition London Dry Gin (England) 47.3% abv, $n/a.
Available in Duty Free. No color; crystalline purity. Right from the initial sniffs, I greatly appreciate the juiciness of the juniper berry that mingles perfectly with the scents of angelica, coriander, and lemon peel, all of which right from the start says with gusto, "London Dry Gin"; secondary whiffs echo and reinforce the initial impressions. Entry is highlighted by the silky texture upon which dance all the flavor elements, in particular, the juniper; midpalate is svelte, satiny, pine forest–like, citrusy, tart, piquant, and even a touch peppery. Finishes in the same dry gin pantheon as Tanqueray London Dry, Cotswolds, Beefeater, Fords, and Sipsmith.
2020 Rating: ★ ★ ★ ★ ★/Highest Recommendation

Greenall's Original London Dry Gin (England) 37.5% abv, $25.
Very good cleanliness; transparent. Once again, I detect a touch of sulfur/burnt match that seems to be a prevailing aroma in 2018, if not a pleasant one; juniper is hidden underneath the blanket of burnt match/diesel fuel. Entry does sport enough juniper to make the case for London Dry, as lesser botanicals bring up the rear; midpalate is slightly roasted/toasty (WTF?), as the licorice, anise traces push forward the juniper berry/cedary sappiness. Closes fast, loose, and uninteresting.
2018 Rating: ★★/Not Recommended

Greenhook Ginsmiths American Dry Gin (USA) 47% abv, $35.
Positively clear as rainwater and colorless. I like this aroma right from the first whiffs not because it is particularly London Dry-like, 'cause it isn't, but because it IS keenly fresh, subtle, floral, and deeply herbaceous. During the multiple second passes I pick up nuances of orange rind; fresh garden flowers (elderflower, for one); zesty, pine cone–like juniper; black pepper; and green tea. Entry shows me a new side as the taste profile offers a cinnamon-like opening flavor that crackles with spicy vibrancy and freshness; the midpalate stage is this gin's apex moment as the flavors crescendo into a melded taste experience that's tart, coyly ripe and spicy, juicy with citrus, and perfectly piney and floral all the way deep into the aftertaste. In an era of sorely inadequate craft gins by the dozens, Greenhook is a genuine standout. A definite keeper.
2018 Rating: ★★★★/Highly Recommended

Gustaf Navy Strength Gin (USA) 57% abv, $48.
Unblemished, limpid, colorless appearance. I detect in the first sniffs a surprising saltiness/salinity that then quickly fades as the tsunami of oily juniper berry takes the helm, supported by traces of cardamom, black pepper, lemon zest, vegetable oil, height-of-summer herb garden; secondary whiffs unearth floral scents that are surprisingly unaffected by any sense of alcohol, which is under tight rein. Entry is gently sweet, floral, juicy, tangy, cedary, and nicely herbal and oily/buttery; midpalate reflects the entry to a tee as the richness of the texture becomes apparent in ribbons of dense, sweetly herbal flavors that never seem too hot or spirity, but also turn brittle and acidic, almost excessively so. Aftertaste has a curious marine quality to it that's not quite salty but is briny nonetheless. Thought it to be a bit too busy for my liking, though I certainly saw some genuine quality. I prefer the Solveig (also from Far North Spirits) by a significant measure.
2015 Rating: ★★★/Recommended

G'Vine Floraison Gin (France) 40% abv, $45.
No color or tint whatsoever; pure and clean. The first sniffs detect vine-like, floral scents that are whisper light and ethereal, with no hint of juniper berry; with a touch more aeration, I can pick up a faint presence of juniper as the flower garden/climbing hydrangea aromas dominate the proceedings. Entry is very fat in texture, oily to the negative, and lumbering; midpalate stage merely echoes the un-gin-like entry, as this awkward, clumsy attempt at gin shows the subtlety of a jackhammer going off outside your bedroom window at 3:00 AM.
2020 Rating: ★/Not Recommended

G'Vine Nouaison Gin (France) 45% abv, $50.

Flawlessly clean and void of color. I immediately get a wave of pleasant juniper berry/cedar forest and white peppercorn; more time in the glass affords it a few moments to gather itself as it offers pleasant supplementary fragrances of rose petal, citrus rind, spearmint, and prickly pear. Entry is full weighted in texture but is neither too fat nor clumsy, as the flavor profile zeroes in on a whole host of woodsy/forest floor botanicals, especially angelica, orris, and very bitter tree bark; midpalate processes all the entry data and offers a flavor profile that's definitely gin-like but with a deeply earthy underpinning that's dry, herbal, leafy, and green. Nice, but it would never under any circumstances replace my London Dry favorites.
2020 Rating: ★ ★ ★/Recommended

Hendrick's Gin (Scotland) 44% abv, $43.

Pretty rainwater clarity; totally void of color. This attractive, easy as Sunday morning aroma is dappled with spring garden/florist-shop fragrances of rose petal, rose hips, honeysuckle, lemon blossom, and carnation, with subtle hints of juniper berry, angelica, and caraway seed; later inhalations unearth more of the citrus influence, especially orange peel—at the very tail end of the sniffing, I detect the cucumber, which rounds out the bouquet in style. Entry is softly floral, vegetal, a touch sweet, and not particularly juniper-like, as the woodsy botanicals and the citrus lead the taste parade; midpalate stage finds the sweet spot of the gustatory moment as the botanicals turn cushiony, plush, gently sweet, vegetal, and woodsy. Ends briefly, flower-like, and cucumber-like. I enjoy this gin enough for a recommendation, but I can't say that I'd choose it over Beefeater, Cotswolds, or any of the majestic Tanquerays.
2018 Rating: ★ ★ ★/Recommended

Hendrick's Midsummer Solstice Gin (Scotland) 43.4% abv, $35.

Colorless; impeccably free of sediment. Very floral/aromatic plant-like scents (violets, roses, lavender, hydrangea) and melon-like (watermelon) in the opening inhalations after the pour, and while I find the fragrances lovely, I also don't understand what this has to do with gin; secondary whiffs reinforce the initial impressions, adding ripe berry fruits, but the lack of juniper presence brings me to the point where I consider this a flavored vodka. Entry is intense with flower oils and dried fruit peels; midpalate offers a composed, summer flower garden flavor profile, but again I wonder why this is promoted as gin and not as a heavily floral flavored vodka, for which I'd give it a recommendation. As a gin, I can't possibly recommend it.
2020 Rating: ★ ★/Not Recommended

Hendrick's Orbium Gin (Scotland) 43.4% abv, $40.

Shows a pale, tarnished-silver/pewter tint; superb clarity. Initially, I pick up vague aromas of crushed violet petals, sorghum, and quinine; after allowing for more air contact, secondary nosing passes fail to inspire, as the bouquet remains distant, vague, and limp. Entry is semisweet, near-bitter, clumsy, and hot on the tongue; midpalate doesn't help the situation as it mirrors the entry, leading to a dismal, dead-on-arrival finish. A stunningly disastrous miscue.
2019 Rating: ★/Not Recommended

Highclere Castle London Dry Gin (England) 43.5% abv, $40.

No color; ideal transparency and clarity. The initial nosing pass is all about spring flower garden freshness and perfume, and it's this delicacy of fragrance that makes it so appealing; the juniper essence comes alive in the second passes, as does a citrus peel tartness that mingles nicely with the pineyness of the juniper. Entry shows more than enough textural grace, as the juniper/pine sap tartness is nicely bitter and mitigated by the citrus peel; midpalate highlights the crispness of the juniper and the citrus peel that all becomes wrapped in a floral package that is lavender-like. Aftertaste is elemental, pine tree–like, and compact. The rare London Dry that is actually better, I believe, by being less than 47 percent abv.
2020 Rating: ★ ★ ★ ★/Highly Recommended

Hotaling & Co. Genevieve Barrel Finished Genever Style Gin (USA) 47.3% abv, $65.

Visually, this gin sports a jonquil/maize yellow color and excellent purity. Nosewise, it opens with a brisk parchment and damp cardboard fragrance that's as much Office Depot as it is gin distillery, and from there I pick up additional odors of steamed white rice (in fact, Arborio), wet adobe/clay, pea pods, and bay leaf; after more aeration, the aromas of crayons, wax, and ginseng vie for dominance. Entry is prickly, astringent, dry as an Arizona highway in July, bread-like, citrusy, and tart; midpalate reprises all the entry findings adding hints of dry malt and breakfast cereal. Concludes zesty and citrusy sour. Not my cup of gin—or, for that matter, genever—but I applaud Hotaling for giving it a solid bash.
2018 Rating: ★ ★/Not Recommended

Hotaling & Co. Old Tom Gin (USA) 45% abv, $35.

Not as clear as I'd like as I spot some floating tendrils of sediment in the colorless appearance. The opening nose is pleasantly floral (marigold, lavender), gently sweet, and juicy/sappy from the pronounced juniper berry element; secondary inhalations detect more fruit than I found in the first passes, as I now get a lychee-like fragrance that's delectable. Entry is piquant, slightly peppery (fresh ground black peppercorn), juicy from the juniper and star anise, and succulent; midpalate mirrors the entry impressions, adding a more floral back note that harmonizes well with the juniper and the star anise. Finishes with a generous texture, a subtle hint of peppery astringency, and fruit peel tanginess. A solid example of the style.
2019 Rating: ★ ★ ★ ★/Highly Recommended

Inverroche Amber Gin (South Africa) 43% abv, $45.

A rare sugarcane-based gin. According to the back label, the pretty topaz color is naturally derived from the leeching of South African botanicals; superb clarity. Oh my, this first aroma is really attractive as scents of juniper and citrus peel mingle with floral and fruity fragrances, such as orchard fruit (pears, especially), jasmine, honeysuckle, and orange blossom; secondary inhalations bring in a delicate spiciness that's neither tangy nor peppery but more like bakery-shop spices, such as nutmeg, cinnamon, allspice, and clove. Entry is off-dry and slightly honeyed, even a touch bittersweet as the botanicals run in unison, creating a gently spiced taste profile that's delightful; midpalate stays the course set in the entry phase as the

delicate spice notes buzz around the citrus peel and juniper headlining flavors, creating a near-sumptuous finish that's long, elegant, and flat-out lovely.
2018 Rating: ★ ★ ★ ★/Highly Recommended

Inverroche Classic Gin (South Africa) 43% abv, $45.
Sugarcane-based gin. I like the pewter tint to this otherwise transparent, sediment-free appearance. Nosewise, this is London Dry in style as the juniper/cedar sap brightness dominates the initial whiffs along with an obvious lemon-twist fragrance that parallels the piney juniper with a fresh air quality that's beguiling, dry as a bone, and snappy; after more air contact, the bouquet turns more serious in the direction of earthy botanicals (grains of paradise, cubeb, angelica) and garden flowers (violets, honeysuckle). Entry is chockfull of tart, citrusy tastes that underpin the cedary piquancy of the juniper, and it's that acute, almost crackling dryness that makes me like it so much; midpalate is solid in texture, zesty with spiciness, and crisp and clean on the palate. Finishes as nimbly and cleanly as it started. A seriously good, mega-piney dry gin that deserves a big North American audience.
2018 Rating: ★ ★ ★ ★/Highly Recommended

Inverroche Verdant Gin (South Africa) 43% abv, $45.
Sugarcane-based gin. Owns a greenish/green-olive/khaki tint that's impeccably pure. Opening sniffs pick up all sorts of fresh spring garden aromas, from grapevines to jasmine to lilac to lavender and more; later whiffs detect passing scents of juniper and hydrangea—I mean, this gin's bouquet is a virtual springtime nursery. Entry is seriously "green," garden fresh, floral, shrub, and tree bark–like, but there's still ample juniper presence to let you know this spirit's gin intentions; midpalate is acutely vegetal, floral, viny, and "green." Finishes medium long, a bit peppery/piquant, flowery, to be sure, and bakery-shop spicy (nutmeg, clove, especially).
2018 Rating: ★ ★ ★/Recommended

Jaisalmer Indian Craft Gin (India) 43% abv, $50.
Ideal clarity; totally color-free. There's an intriguing India subcontinent–influenced twist to the opening aroma that's decidedly spicy and reminiscent of black pepper, cardamom, smoked paprika, and black tea; secondary inhalations unearth traces of juniper and pine tree, but the primarily aromatic thrust continues to be the natural, controlled, and pleasant spiciness. Entry takes a sudden left turn away from the bouquet as the taste profile offers high-flying, expressive flavors of juniper that are cradled in lemongrass and citrus peel; midpalate stage emphasizes the engaging harmony between the spice, juniper, and citrus, and that harmony lasts into the brief, buoyant finish.
2019 Rating: ★ ★ ★/Recommended

Journeyman Bilberry Black Hearts Gin (USA) 45% abv, $35.
Springwater clear. Smells of old woodshed, wet earth, forest floor, mushrooms, moss, with nuances of juniper; no fruitiness whatsoever, very little spice, but lots of minerals, earth notes. Entry is delicate, semisweet as some fruitiness emerges, mostly berry (I guess the bilberry); midpalate is drier than entry, woodsy, herbal (dried rosemary), floral (dried flowers),

menthol-like/minty. Didn't love or hate it, but it's well made enough to recommend for gin aficionados who like to explore. Intriguing.
2014 Rating: ★★★/Recommended

Juniper Grove American Dry Gin (USA) 46% abv, $35.
Void of color; spotless clarity. I favorably respond to the opening aromatics that are brimming with pine tree/juniper berry/alpine forest and citrus peel tartness from the very first sniff; the zestiness found in the initial inhalations continues in the second passes, though the pine tree diminishes a bit, leaving a hole that is filled by the scents of citrus peels and coriander. Entry features a viny/bramble-like opening flavor that's related to the juniper, as the citrus aspects fade; midpalate sees the coriander get top billing, as now the juniper grows pale, leading to an unpleasant aftertaste that is too metallic, coin-like, and flinty for its own good. Pleasant in the nose and at entry, then it loses the plot in midpalate and finish.
2020 Rating: ★★/Not Recommended

Junipero Gin (USA) 49.3% abv, $35.
There are tiny tendrils of sediment seen floating, but not enough to cause alarm; otherwise crystal clear and colorless. The splendid opening aroma highlights the juniper in spades, as well as earthbound botanicals, notably orris and angelica, but then in the second nosing passes other notes come alive, especially citrus peel, dried flowers, tree bark that all orbit around the high-flying sphere of juicy, sappy juniper. Entry is elegant, nearly sedate, yet there's a substantial core flavor of pristine spirit, piney juniper, and root botanicals that carry forward the taste profile to the midpalate, which highlights the juniper and flowers in a style that's graceful and powerful, but not overpowering. Finishes with a flurry of juniper, gentle heat, and honeysuckle, wrapped in a thick blanket of viscosity that is stunningly oily and lovely.
2019 Rating: ★★★★/Highly Recommended

Koval Dry Gin (USA) 47% abv, $34.
Completely color-free; excellent clarity. Wow, the beany first aromas are dry but intensely kernel-like, almost cocoa-like, and minerally/stony as the juniper fights for position among the rocky Field of Beans; secondary inhalations following more aeration encounter a sudden lack of aromatic force in the bean department, which opens the door for barely perceptible traces of juniper, angelica, and coriander. Entry features a strong measure of the beaniness that undercuts the juniper presence almost to zero, making this gin more of a flavored vodka by the midpalate stage. Finishes dry (as advertised), but the mineral and legume-like aspects trample the idea of customary gin almost entirely, except for the flare of juniper taste in the tail end. This simply doesn't work for me.
2016 Rating: ★★/Not Recommended

Litchfield Batchers' Gin (USA) 43% abv, $37.
Absolute purity, totally translucent and colorless. The first aromatic burst is mildly piney, but mostly herbal and woodsy/forest floor–like in thrust; secondary whiffs encounter a bit more of the juniper as the other botanicals suddenly blow off with further air contact. Entry is stunningly sweet at first, then goes drier as the tree sap/resiny aspect kicks in, allowing the

cedar/pineyness of the juniper to circle back; midpalate features coriander, dried citrus peel, angelica, and clove tastes that are pleasantly dry and satiny in texture. Aftertaste is medium long, nicely oily, dry, and herbal. Nice job here.
2016 Rating: ★★★★/Highly Recommended

Luxardo Sour Cherry Gin (Italy) 37.5% abv, $35.
Sports a red-cherry color; superb purity. Smells immediately of sour cherry and little else, so I move on to the second round of inhalations, finding a keen bittersweet scent that is cherry-like, to be sure, but also a deeply herbaceous/earthy quality that's very tree bark–like and appealing. Entry is bittersweet, very cherry-like and ripe; midpalate exhibits lots of cherry flavor, but also there are other botanical tastes, especially cassia, cinnamon, and juniper that come through. Finishes medium long, sour cherry–like, and pleasantly tart.
2018 Rating: ★★★/Recommended

Mahón Gin (Spain) 41% abv, $47.
Pot still. Pristine clarity; colorless appearance. Initial inhalations pick up green, raw juniper berry scents as well as sweet pea, nickel, minerals, dry earth; later nosing passes encounter cardamom, caraway seed, orris, citrus rind. Entry is highly floral (rose petals, honeysuckle), piney, juicy, semisweet, vegetal, leafy; midpalate reflects the green vegetation (brussels sprouts) noted at entry along with a peppercorn aspect that's pleasantly spicy. Finishes light weighted, citrusy, nicely floral. Liked it enough to recommend, didn't love it.
2015 Rating: ★★★/Recommended

Martin Miller's Gin (England) 40% abv, $28.
Clear and immaculate as springwater; void of color. I like the cherry blossom fragrance in the first nosing passes as well as the flinty/steely aspect that points out the aroma's stone-like dryness; further aeration stirs up more aromas, especially carnation, juniper, limestone, coriander, jasmine, and orris; a solid, sturdy gin bouquet that turns more floral with time. Entry is buttery in texture, dense, and remarkably oily, all of which I like; midpalate is prickly and astringent, piney and floral, delicately spicy and herbal. Aftertaste is medium long, but then fades quickly. My sense is that, while easily recommendable as is, I'd appreciate it more if the abv was at least 43–44 percent. The higher abv would push the juniper forward, whereas here it becomes an afterthought by midpalate.
2018 Rating: ★★★/Recommended

Martin Miller's Westbourne Strength Gin (England) 45.2% abv, $40.
Limpid appearance; sediment-free purity. I respond favorably to this vigorous first aroma that is laden with bold juniper, coriander, angelica, and lemon zest; following more air contact, the citrus/lemon peel/lemon blossom aspect picks up the baton and runs away with the second nosing passes. Entry is edgy, crisp, flinty, mineral-like, and not short of juniper berry sappiness; midpalate highlights the juniper and the lemon blossom, in particular, in a formidable display of gin brawniness. Concludes long in the throat, tart, pleasantly astringent, and keenly lemony. A dandy gin to have in your liquor cabinet.
2018 Rating: ★★★★/Highly Recommended

Master's Selection London Dry Gin (Spain) 43.9% abv, $25.

Impeccable clarity; transparent, colorless. Initial whiffs encounter crisp, desert-dry, crackling pine needle aromas that invigorate the olfactory machinery; after a few more minutes of aeration, the fresh-off-the-branch juniper berry piquancy stays the course, steering the direction of this very pleasant London Dry from Spain, a gin-loving nation. Entry is supple, nicely oily/viscous, delicately sweet, herbal/botanical; midpalate finds a fruit element emerging—orange or tangerine, I think. Aftertaste echoes the midpalate, in particular, the pleasant texture. Should rethink the cheesy-looking blue bottle.

2014 Rating: ★ ★ ★ ★/Highly Recommended

Molto Italiano Gin (Italy) 56.3% abv, $39.

Colorless; perfectly pure. Considering the elevated abv, this opening nose is delicately piney, balanced, slightly floral, and shows just a hint of citrus-peel tartness and acidity to maintain freshness; following more aeration, the bouquet turns flowery (lavender, orange blossom) and solidly juniper-like while remaining dry and focused; an impressive dry gin aroma, to say the least. Entry offers hearty but not aggressive spicy flavors of cardamom, coriander, clove, vanilla bean, and lemon zest that wrap around the juniper core taste and push it forward into the extended, warm-on-the-tongue finish. An Italian gin that deserves your attention.

2019 Rating: ★ ★ ★ ★/Highly Recommended

Monkey 47 Schwarzwald Dry Gin (Germany) 47% abv, $45/375 ml.

Bisque/tarnished-silver color; flawless clarity. Opening sniffs detect heavily floral scents that are dried out, vegetal, gamey, citrusy, fruity, piney/sappy—it's an "onion bouquet" or one that keeps revealing another layer when you think that you've arrived at the core fragrance; secondary inhalations pick up wax, camphor, eucalyptus, mint. Entry is intensely flowery, showing heightened notes of violets, rose petal, chamomile, honeysuckle blossoms—it's a florist shop in a glass; midpalate is more herbal, foresty/woodsy, with an entire orchestra of flavors, including white pepper, juniper, sage, rosemary, cumin, coriander, lemon peel, sassafras, tree bark. Intriguing, long, dry to off-dry, dense finish of multiple botanicals. I like it, but don't expect London Dry.

2015 Rating: ★ ★ ★ ★/Highly Recommended

New Amsterdam No. 485 Gin (USA) 40% abv, $15.

Limpid appearance, clean, colorless. Wow, this opening New Western nose is all about citrus (lemon, lime) pulp and zest with no room left for juniper; later sniffs after more air contact discover only heightened citrus aspects that have now become more juicy than zesty; too one-dimensional. Entry does introduce a brief glimpse at juniper, but then the avalanche of lemon and lime peels and juice obliterates any sense of juniper; midpalate stays the high-citrus direction and dominance, leaving me no choice but to dismiss it as an off-balance, plebian American gin that serves no serious purpose to the current gin conversation except to those drinkers who a) don't understand gin but like citrus-flavored vodka or b) don't know anything at all about beverage quality but like citrus-flavored vodka.

2019 Rating: ★/Not Recommended

No. 209 Gin (USA) 46% abv, $30.

Silvery/pewter tint; superb, blemish-free clarity. In the initial inhalations, I detect fresh garden herbs/plants/tree barks (clearly evident: eucalyptus, bay leaf, coriander, cassia) more than I do juniper (very soft), and for the style (New Western), that is expected; following more minutes of air contact, the aroma blossoms into a round, delicate, elegant bouquet whose primary feature remains the herbaceous aromatic backbone. Entry is classy, slightly piquant from a peppery thrust, mineral-like, and floral; midpalate features a gently sweet and ripe citrusy taste that's acutely acidic, which maintains the edgy, crisp flavor profile through to the tangy, low-key finish. Along with Junipero and Aviation, the pioneer of the New Western style that hasn't lost any of its charm along the way.

2018 Rating: ★ ★ ★ ★/Highly Recommended

No. 3 London Dry Gin (England) 46% abv, $43.

Visually, there's a faint shade of pewter to this appearance; excellent clarity. Opening nosings detect hints of grapefruit pith, coriander, and chalky minerals that buttress the head-lining pine forest–like juniper fragrance; secondary inhalations encounter deeper notes of dried citrus that couch the tangy, clearly defined juniper scent. Entry is appealingly stone dry, juniper dense, mineral-like, squeaky clean, and sharp as a razor; midpalate reflects the findings of the entry to a tee, as the juniper element soars to expected heights and the citrus-fueled acidity maintains the sturdy structure. A solid, well-crafted, traditional London Dry.

2018 Rating: ★ ★ ★ ★/Highly Recommended

Nolet's Silver Dry Gin (Holland) 47.6% abv, $50.

The white wine/pale straw color is totally sediment-free and pure. A gin aroma that smells like no other in the world marketplace and one, for me at least, that takes gin to new heights; the deeply floral/orchard fruit notes of elderflower, rose, peach, and nectarine accentuate the coyness of the juniper element, thereby creating a satisfyingly full and ambrosial gin standard; second whiffs find a greater juniper presence that mingles well with the peach aspect. Entry texture is as smooth as silk, while the flavor profile boasts the orchard fruits as well as a wild berry taste that brings more acidity to the experience; midpalate sees the various components merge into a finely tuned flavor experience that's underpinned by the creamy, lush texture. The finish is affected by the 47.6 percent abv, which adds a campfire warmth moment to crown the evaluation. I'm aware that this iconoclastic, highly controversial gin has severe critics, but I maintain that the boldness of Nolet's Silver's flavors takes gin into new territory and is one of the few gins that I'd drink straight.

2018 Rating: ★ ★ ★ ★ ★/Highest Recommendation

Notaris Bartender's Choice Rome Genever (Holland) 47% abv, $80.

Straw-yellow color; excellent clarity. I immediately am exposed to vibrant, assertive scents of malted grain, cardboard, onionskin parchment, textile fiber, and nylon in the opening inhalations; secondary sniffs pick up deeper, grainier, maltier fragrances that are pleasant and cereal-like. Entry is tasty, tangy, dense in texture, and extremely malty (malted milk balls); midpalate profile offers more unsweetened breakfast cereal and snack cracker flavors

that are dry, tangy, and biscuity. Finishes savory, slightly peppery, and reminiscent of graham crackers. I like the higher abv, which gives this genever a robust character.
2019 Rating: ★★★★/Highly Recommended

O.R.E. 118 Raw Vegan Gin (USA) 41% abv, $35.
Distilled from chardonnay grapes. There's a faint shade of tarnished silver so it is not colorless; excellent clarity. The initial inhalations totally perplex me as I think that perhaps I'm sniffing a plum brandy or a kirschwasser because this aroma in no manner resembles a gin . . . great start, eh; after more aeration I discover that additional air contact simply unleashed more of the fruit compote fragrance, bearing no resemblance whatsoever to any variety of gin. Entry is all-fruit-all-the-time with merely the faintest hints of juniper or other botanicals, and while it doesn't taste bad, I can't help but wonder the reasoning behind calling this spirit a gin when I would have labeled it as "flavored grape spirit." This is as far as I am willing to go with this.
2019 Rating: ★/Not Recommended

Old Duff Genever (Holland) 40% abv, $30.
Clear and colorless as rainwater; ideal purity. First nosing passes pick up textile-driven aromas of canvas, burlap, wool, steamed white rice, corrugated cardboard, and flint; following more aeration, the aroma turns grainier as the scent of oatmeal/porridge emerges, followed by anise/licorice and the merest whisper of juniper. Entry is cleansing, stone dry, grainy, bright, and tart; midpalate takes a left turn, offering near-succulent flavors of graham cracker, malted milk ball, and orange chocolates. Aftertaste is my favorite stage as the taste profile goes for broke with citric acid and clean tartness.
2018 Rating: ★★★/Recommended

Old Duff Maltwine Genever (Holland) 45% abv, $50.
Limpid appearance; unblemished clarity. First whiffs pick up textile-like aromas, especially cotton fiber, wool, and nylon, with background notes of yeast, ale, and dark pumpernickel bread; later stage inhalations following more air contact detect notes of sea breeze, fresh air drying linens, unsweetened breakfast cereal (shredded wheat, in particular), and oatmeal. Entry is pleasantly toasty, crisply dry, dense, and deeply grainy/malty; midpalate offers piquant flavors of black pepper, graham cracker, honey, and brown sugar. Finishes long in the throat, medium rich in texture, and deeply grainy/malty.
2018 Rating: ★★★★/Highly Recommended

OOLA Batch #32 Gin (USA) 47% abv, $45.
Clean as rainwater. Animated, herbal, flowery, spicy aromas abound in the initial whiffs to the point where I can't identify all of them as they appear; later inhalations find a calmer bouquet in which I can at least pick out juniper, citrus peel, rose petal, pine needle, coriander, black pepper. Entry is a bit plump, nicely cedar-like, deeply herbal, floral; midpalate accurately echoes the entry. Since gin is the hardest spirit to produce, I like to give a bit of leeway, and while this gin has some fine attributes on which to build, I don't see it as being more than a three star, recommendable gin of good, but not great, character.
2014 Rating: ★★★/Recommended

Opihr Oriental London Dry Gin (England) 42.5% abv, $28.

The shimmering translucent appearance is colorless and flawlessly pure. Up front, the first aromas are deeply peppery (freshly ground black pepper), piquant, and cumin seed–like, as the tangy, gunpowder-like spiciness eclipses any presence of juniper; after more aeration, secondary sniffs encounter the same level of potency from the pepperiness, which now is akin to pepper-crusted beef, while the cumin aspect fades slightly, giving way to cubeb and coriander scents. Entry is alive with acute Asian-leaning spiciness, with the juniper peeking out from behind the curtain of peppercorn and seeds; midpalate stays the zesty/tangy course as the various flavor elements merge into a single dry but not astringent taste that features the juniper only as a minor botanical ingredient. This is a pleasantly divergent, entirely recommendable gin, but not one that I'd describe as London Dry.

2018 Rating: ★★★/Recommended

Oxley Cold Distilled London Dry Gin (England) 47% abv, $39.

Clean and unblemished as rainwater. In the first inhalations after the pour, I feel a wave of prickliness in the nose from the 94 proof, and I also detect faint traces of juniper berry, angelica, and citrus zest; later inhalations after more aeration pick up nowhere near the level of low-to-moderate grade aromatic intensity discovered earlier, as I feel the bouquet shot its wad in the opening. Entry immediately features two aspects, lemon peel and black pepper, that both dominate to the point where the juniper seems relegated to the shadows; ditto in the midpalate stage, where the juniper has faded to obscurity while the citrus peel and black pepper continue their race to the finish line. Years ago, I gave this London Dry a favorable review and a recommendation but now I cannot.

2019 Rating: ★★/Not Recommended

Pine Barrens Barrel Reserve Finished Botanical Dry Gin (USA) 47% abv, $40.

Pale, harvest corn–yellow color from barrel aging; sediment-free purity. First nosings pick up piney, woody/resiny, foresty, bark-like aromas that are all over the gin map in terms of possibilities, with scant evidence of juniper, as the sheer amount of botanicals used (twenty-eight according to the label) masks the main ingredient; secondary whiffs find the same situation, with the juniper buried beneath the weight of so many other aromas. Entry is a bit more juniper forward as the taste profile, though crowded, appears to be a bit more focused than the bouquet; midpalate features a pleasant compromise between the juniper and the other botanicals as the flavor reaches a plateau, pushed forward by the 47 percent abv, which in my mind saves the day for this gin. Concludes deeply, densely herbal, dry, earthy, woodsy, crowded.

2017 Rating: ★★★/Recommended

Plymouth Gin (England) 41.2% abv, $33.

Flawless clarity; colorless. The aromas in the opening sniffs that have the biggest impact for me are the orange and the orris, as together they offer a slightly toasted, roasted, kernel-like scent that's delicate and dry; later inhalations detect the juniper, cardamom, and lemon peels as the botanical fragrances merge into one highly sophisticated bouquet that absolutely says "gin" but certainly not London Dry—one of my favorite spirit aromas due mainly to its subtlety. Entry is so supple in texture that I want to use the descriptor "plush"

so, damn it, I will—this is plush, round, dense, oily, and creamy; midpalate is where the abv comes into play as there's a campfire embers–like warmth that quietly pushes forward the juniper and the citrus elements, creating a stately, elegant flavor profile of the highest rank. Plymouth is an authentic gin classic that never ceases to bedazzle and amaze.
2018 Rating: ★★★★★/Highest Recommendation

Plymouth Navy Strength Gin (England) 57% abv, $38.
Unblemished purity; void of color. The heightened abv is immediately apparent, though it isn't in the least abrasive or burning as the kernel-like botanicals slowly emerge in the opening whiffs; allowing it more time for aeration, the aroma then offers piquant, earthy scents of cardamom, orris, and angelica, with a feathery hint of juniper. Entry is full-bodied, assertive, husky, and dry, as the juniper comes alive a bit more in tandem with the citrus rinds; midpalate presents a sensationally delicious, harmonious, and piquant taste experience that, for me at least, epitomizes what navy strength gin is all about—a truly staggeringly luscious gin experience that is unique and memorable. Concludes softly, long in the throat, and delightfully warming and amiable. The clinic, the road map, for all the wannabe navy strength gins in the world.
2018 Rating: ★★★★★/Highest Recommendation

Prairie Certified Organic Gin (USA) 40% abv, $20.
Immaculate purity; colorless. The opening nosing picks up a keen lemon zestiness that sets the dry, citrusy stage for other botanicals, namely coriander and sage, while the pine cone–like hint of juniper remains distant; another few minutes of air contact sees the juniper aspect emerge just a bit more, but mainly this bouquet is dominated by sage, lemon, and coriander. Entry is pleasant, if a touch inexplicably sharp since the abv is only 40 percent, and the juniper remains an afterthought; midpalate shows the most character identification in the green, herbaceous botanicals that call all the shots. Aftertaste is meek but all right overall, if uninspiring even as a New Western–style gin. There's no glaring flaw in this gin, which is why it scores two stars, but if it were mine I'd give it a higher abv of at least 45 percent and a bigger commitment from the herbal, non-juniper botanicals.
2018 Rating: ★★/Not Recommended

Principe De Los Apostoles Seco Gin (Argentina) 42% abv, $38.
Clear as rainwater; void of color. There're solid, if curious, opening aromatic hits of eucalyptus, sagebrush, pencil eraser, Play-Doh, pipe cleaners, coriander, menthol, Vicks VapoRub, and citrus all at the same strength, but hardly any juniper; later sniffs detect incongruous scents of menthol/mint, copy paper, and green tobacco, all in a nonsensical gin bouquet that makes me think that the distiller just threw in whatever was handy and nearby. Entry taste is bloody awful, too peppery, too minty, and without any direction or juniper quality, and therefore it's more a menthol/eucalyptus–flavored vodka than a gin; midpalate is nasty, awkwardly without purpose or direction, and a distilling mess. If it were mine, I'd change my name, head for remote Patagonia, and hope that in fifty to sixty years, all would be forgotten.
2018 Rating: ★/Not Recommended

Queen's Courage New York Old Tom Gin (USA) 45% abv, $38.
Limpid appearance; unblemished clarity. Immediately in the first sniff I get the slightly sour note of freshly baked loaves of rye bread in a paper bag, then the aroma expands to include baker's yeast, malt wine, malted milk, and honey; secondary inhalations introduce fragrances of pine cone (the juniper), gum, salted caramel, and green tea. Entry is intensely malty/grainy and delicately sweet, wrapped in a taste profile that's mildly succulent, dense in texture, and pleasingly herbaceous without being overwrought; midpalate carries on the grainy/cereal-like character of the entry along with the low-flying, now somewhat flinty, flavors of pine/cedar, cassia, lemon zest, and sage. A solidly made Old Tom style that's worthy of a look-see by anyone interested in learning about this old, historically important style of gin. Good job here.
2018 Rating: ★ ★ ★ ★/Highly Recommended

Ransom Batch #06 Dry Gin (USA) 43% abv, $23.
Barley/rye/corn base spirit. Pewter/silver crystalline appearance; limpid clarity. The opening nosing passes are treated to an integrated, delicately floral out-of-the-gate aroma that's alluringly tart/sour, citrusy, juicy, and deeply herbal, with the juniper acting as the bonding agent among the numerous botanicals; later sniffs encounter much the same in the manner of lemon peel, lemon pulp/pith, orange juice, the mild sharpness of coriander, yeast, and hoppy flowers that together form a sophisticated rather than a rustic bouquet; lovely, gentle, and polite. Entry is remarkably floral (honeysuckle), garden-like, beany, and herbal simultaneously while the juniper floats just beneath the surface flavors; midpalate continues the überfloral banquet in which the juniper is a little lost at this stage, being replaced by caraway and coriander as the midpalate turns into the aftertaste. I respond favorably to this International/Western–style gin but can't help but wonder what it would be like at 45/46 percent alcohol. Perhaps that level would be too much for the delicacy of this gin, but I'd be interested to see how that would work, and if that would earn it a fifth rating star.
2016 Rating: ★ ★ ★ ★/Highly Recommended

Ransom Batch #16 Dry Gin (USA) 44% abv, $30.
Immaculate purity; colorless appearance. I get truckloads of lemon and orange zest in the initial whiffs after the pour, then they gently dissipate, leaving the aromatic door wide open for caraway, juniper, and coriander scents that move the deeply grainy/malty bouquet forward; interestingly, following more air contact, the citrus parade resumes but with more of the juniper element leading the band. Entry is intensely malt-driven and bread dough–like, almost yeasty and sour as the botanicals give way momentarily to the base spirit attributes; midpalate is the place where the base spirit and botanicals merge, giving off pleasantly dry, mineral-like, and earthy flavors. Aftertaste is round, chewy in texture, acutely earthy, and piney.
2018 Rating: ★ ★ ★ ★/Highly Recommended

Ransom Batch #82 Old Tom Gin (USA) 44% abv, $39.
Sports an old gold color and flawless clarity. I immediately like the opening fragrance that's bread-like, malty, zesty with citrus juiciness, and sap-like from the juniper; once this Old Tom has had a chance to mingle with air, the aromatic profile shifts to a more floral/

spring garden fragrance that's delicate and gently spicy. Entry is juicy with orange and lemon and boosted by the coriander and cardamom pods, which stick out in particular; midpalate stage is pleasing for its gingery zestiness that's bready/cookie-like and deeply earthy and root-like. Finishes very long in the throat and spicy.
2018 Rating: ★ ★ ★ ★/Highly Recommended

Rehorst Premium Gin (USA) 44% abv, $30.
Shimmering, transparent brightness; sediment-free. Up front, there's a potent, welcome wave of juniper, cedar, pine plank, orange zest, angelica; with further aeration, the aroma marginally expands to include coriander, basil, and lemon zest. Entry is velvety in texture, with a noticeable orange zest underpinning that's tart and appealing, but there's also an herbal aspect that's unique; midpalate shows a tangy flavor in which the juniper suddenly takes a back seat to other botanicals, in this case, an herbaceous aspect that's leafy, fresh, and earthy. Finishes well, with a last flourish of snappy juniper. Hats off to Great Lakes Distillery.
2015 Rating: ★ ★ ★/Recommended

Rétha Oceanic Gin (France) 40% abv, $50.
Perfectly translucent; clean and clear. First whiffs detect gingerbread, juniper berry, and cedar tree, all with delicate touches of sea salt and leafy green vegetable; second nosing passes discover the juniper berry in the descent, and the sea salt and "green" element ascending. Entry, I find, is a touch soapy, salty, and vegetal while the juniper element goes largely silent; midpalate is flinty and mineral-like to a fault, as any hint of gin is obscured by the earthy, soil-like flavor. Finishes badly, with no resemblance to gin. If you're hankering for French gin, just buy Citadelle.
2020 Rating: ★/Not Recommended

Rock Rose Navy Strength Gin (Scotland) 57% abv, $50.
Owns the faintest hint of pewter shading; excellent purity. Up front in the first nosings, there's a clear-cut citrus tanginess that collaborates with garden-fresh herbs and woodsy botanicals, providing a comely herbaceous quality that's fresh and mesmerizingly floral; secondary passes detect a growing earthiness that's akin to minerals and flint. Entry is rich in texture, sweeter than I anticipated, and even more floral than the latter stages of the sniffing; midpalate settles in with the garden-fresh flavoring that is ushered forward by the high abv. Concludes a touch citrusy and piquant.
2020 Rating: ★ ★ ★ ★/Highly Recommended

Roku Gin (Japan) 43% abv, $28.
Void of color; pristine purity. Right from the first sniffs, there is an astounding menu of savory aromas, including juniper/pine tree/Douglas fir, flower petals, ripe orchard fruits (yuzu), herbs (bay leaf, hyssop), and spices (black peppercorn); later whiffs pick up less of the juniper, as the floral and herbal aspects take charge. Entry is highlighted by the yuzu and a touch of green-tea flavor that dries out the palate; midpalate is dense with herbaceous notes that are earthy, vegetal, leafy, and stone dry. Aftertaste is very long, mineral-like, dry as a bone, showing flashes of the juniper to close the circle.
2018 Rating: ★ ★ ★ ★/Highly Recommended

Russell Henry Hawaiian White Ginger Gin (USA) 41.6% abv, $38.
A touch cloudy/misty in the glass, but otherwise clear. Owns an almost identical opening aroma as the London Dry but with a higher herbal content that, to me, isn't necessarily identifiable as ginger, but is root-like and tubery, all the same—let's call it earthy and be done with it; by the time that the gin has had another six minutes of aeration, however, the ginger aspect does become more animated, but so do fragrances of marshmallow, limestone, spring flower garden, and egg white—let's just say that this is an atypical gin bouquet. Entry is delicate, gently bittersweet, herbaceous, and at last a touch juniper-like; midpalate features more of the ginger, but there is no paucity of juniper, coriander, rose petal, or angelica either. Finishes like silk in the throat. Delicious, different.
2016 Rating: ★ ★ ★ ★ ★/Highest Recommendation

Russell Henry Malaysian Limes Gin (USA) 41.6% abv, $38.
Crystalline and pure in appearance. Oh my, this opening aroma is seductively citrusy, but also offers incongruous scents of pistachio, limestone, and peach pit; after another six minutes of time in the glass, the bouquet opens up only marginally, as the baseline aroma of citrus continues, leaving room for mere traces of chrysanthemum, white pepper, and vinyl. Entry is more citrusy/lime-like than the bouquet, but remains delicate, almost fragile; midpalate is silky, oily in texture, clean, moderately sweet, and long in the throat. Concludes on a citrus-peel note that's bitter.
2016 Rating: ★ ★ ★ ★/Highly Recommended

Russell Henry London Dry Gin (USA) 45% abv, $38.
Crystalline, colorless purity. First sniffs pick up feathery echoes of juniper, angelica, cardamom, citrus zest, orris root that are all working in harmony; with further aeration, the citric acid takes the lead, leaving just enough room for pine needle and orris background fragrances to stay in the aromatic picture; elegant, refined, a fairy-dust London Dry bouquet. Entry is richly textured, sweet, keenly lemony, floral; midpalate stage takes a right turn at Pine and Juniper Streets and goes the length of the finish in grand juniper berry, London Dry style, except for an unexpected touch of coin/nickel taste in the final moments of aftertaste that prevents the bestowing of the fifth rating star.
2019 Rating: ★ ★ ★ ★/Highly Recommended

Scapegrace Small Batch Dry Gin (New Zealand) 42.2% abv, $35.
Pristine, colorless appearance. Up front, I like the sharp, citrusy/lime-like note that runs a parallel track to the pronounced juniper character; secondary inhalations pick up additional scents of dried citrus peel, coriander, and angelica that push forward the juniper pineyness. Entry is sedate, calm, and under the radar in its potency, as mellow, integrated flavors of juniper, pine tree/pine sap make their case; midpalate highlights the juniper berry as much as any other botanical and that's fine by me. Its lack of textural depth is most apparent in the finish, and that prevents the bestowing of a fourth rating star.
2019 Rating: ★ ★ ★/Recommended

Scapegrace Gold London Dry Gin (New Zealand) 57% abv, $60.
Colorless as rainwater; flawlessly pure. Initially, I pick up aromas of black peppercorn,

pumpkin seed, caraway seed, and arid landscape, with the juniper berry component kept at a distance; the reluctance of the aroma to offer anything of substance disturbs me so I decide to press forward. Entry at last touts a minor role for the juniper berry oil, but that role is as a supporting character to the lead player, the tart taste of citrus peel; midpalate is this gin's best moment as the juniper finally takes its turn at bat and gets a solid hit. Finishes medium long, neither abrasive nor hot (considering the high abv), and with a bit of finesse. Pricey, though.
2020 Rating: ★★★/Recommended

Schlichte Steinhaeger Dry Gin (Germany) 40% abv, $22.
Unblemished clarity; colorless appearance. The pine forest/pine needle first aroma is telltale and powerful in its depiction of gin, then with more time in the glass a mineral-like aromatic undercurrent takes hold, reminding me of wet cement, cement block, building materials, even plaster board—curious; second passes find the juniper berry/pine cone aspect significantly faded, leaving in its wake a dried leaf fragrance. Entry is clean, pleasingly pine-like, crisp; midpalate shows a creamy, oily texture that's very nice plus a touch of angelica. Not what I'd consider London Dry or even New World, but a solid gin whose primary virtue is its layered, satin-like texture.
2015 Rating: ★★★/Recommended

Seagram's Distiller's Reserve Gin (USA) 47% abv, $12.
This appearance shows a distinctive tarnished-silver/egg white–like tint of color; excellent purity. Up front, it smells of juniper berry, freshly ground black pepper, angelica, and grains of paradise—in other words, it smells of traditional London Dry style gin; in the later aromatic stages, a citrusy/lemony aspect comes to the forefront that mingles nicely with the juiciness/sappy character of the juniper. Entry offers a substantial, moderately creamy texture that underpins the dry, herbaceous, pine sap flavor that turns mildly sweet by the midpalate juncture, where the taste profile demonstrates that this gin deserves to be recommended. Concludes zesty, citrusy, and piney. Superb value and should not be overlooked because of its friendly retail price, as it runs rings around more than a few $20–$22 gins.
2018 Rating: ★★★/Recommended

Silent Pool London Dry Gin (England) 43% abv, $50.
Pristine appearance; colorless, except for a faint pewter-like tint. Opening whiffs detect woods-like botanicals, mainly juniper, tree bark, sap, and dry leaves; secondary inhalations get more of the juniper berry pineyness that brings it into the London Dry sector. Entry is pleasantly dry and oily, as the juniper element increases in strength with time in the glass; midpalate stays the juniper course, exhibiting a brambly, bark-like aspect that just momentarily brings my attention away from the juniper. Finishes brief, nicely sap- and cedar-like. Pricey, though, when one can buy an equivalent bottle size of Beefeater or Tanqueray for 60 percent less.
2019 Rating: ★★★/Recommended

Sipsmith London Dry Gin (England) 41.6% abv, $45.
Transparent purity; clean and clear as springwater. The lovely opening fragrances are delicate, balanced, a trifle fruity, nutty, and floral, and with just the right level of juniper

berry burst to safely call it London Dry; secondary whiffs detect a bolder presence of juniper and almond (actually, almond paste/butter) as well as cassia bark, which brings an acute tartness that I relish. Entry is creamy in texture, fruity with citrus peel, and spring garden floral with coriander and juniper/cypress; midpalate maintains that gloriously rich texture upon which the flavors dance in harmony all the way through the flowery, juicy, sappy aftertaste. Delicious and finely balanced.

2018 Rating: ★ ★ ★ ★ ★/Highest Recommendation

Solveig Gin (USA) 43.5% abv, $40.

Flawless purity; devoid of any hint of color. The aroma that leaps out at me initially and bites my face is the fresh, leafy thyme, but then juniper berry emerges along with a healthy dose of citrus to bring some order to the early fragrance; even after further aeration, the aroma remains feisty, highly herbal, and animated as the citrus now comes to dominate over the juniper and the thyme, creating a velvety bouquet that's grapefruity/citrusy/lemony, eggy, and zesty; like no other gin I've smelled in three or four years. Entry is decidedly piquant with leafy herb flavors, highlighted by thyme, bay leaf, basil, as well as black pepper, plus other flavor aspects like pine cone, mint, buttered rye bread; midpalate echoes all the entry traits, adding traces of spirit, green vegetables (asparagus, kale), and linseed oil. Finishes long, oily, silky, embers warm, herbal sweet. A very different gin.

2015 Rating: ★ ★ ★ ★/Highly Recommended

Spirit of Hven Backafallsbyn Swedish Navy Strength Gin (Sweden) 57.1% abv, $64.

Pristine and bright as rainwater and colorless. Now here, as opposed to its anemic and appallingly poor 80-proof sibling, is a ginny first bouquet that's snappily fresh, piney, woodsy-herbal, peppery, and citrusy, all in one single opening true-to-gin package; secondary whiffs discover more of the supplemental botanicals, especially grains of paradise, cardamom, orris root, and angelica, all of which unite to serve as supporting role players to the alcohol thrust, the citrus peel, and the pine cone–like juniper. Entry is broad and big in texture, nearing a stage of almost being too fat and oily, but be that as it may, this first taste profile is jam-packed with lively pine/cedar and lemon zest flavors that are pushed forward by the 57.1 percent abv; midpalate stage sees the flavor calm down a bit, allowing for a burst of herbaceous sweetness to emerge, lasting deep into the lush, prickly finish. Is this Swedish Navy Strength Gin the equal of, say, Plymouth Navy Strength from England? No, not even close. But it does show far more gin character than its deeply troubled 40 percent sibling.

2017 Rating: ★ ★ ★/Recommended

Spirit of Hven Backafallsbyn Swedish Organic Distilled Gin (Sweden) 40% abv, $43.

Void of color, but strangely milky and turbid, which leads me to think that there is a filtration issue here. First whiffs detect heavy doses of leafy botanicals, such as coriander and Norwegian angelica, that overlay more subtle flavorings like juniper, grains of paradise, orris root, and cardamom; secondary nosings after more aeration unearth a bigger role for the juniper and now a larger hit from citrus, probably lemon zest or orange peel—but this aroma is disjointed. Entry owns a fat, chunky texture that lacks the crispness that I like to find in the entry stage of a gin and that raises a red flag; midpalate is clumsy, awkward, too fat, too oily, and all this leads to a flatline finish that only serves to disappoint. A messy, poorly made spirit that is masquerading as a gin. It telegraphed production problems right from the appearance phase. Do yourself a favor and just buy that bottle of Beefeater or Tanqueray London Dry, or if you are searching for a non-mainstream gin, Cotswolds Dry Gin. But this sad offering? Nope.

2017 Rating: ★/Not Recommended

St. Augustine New World Gin (USA) 47% abv, $32.

Sugarcane base. Flawless purity; colorless. First whiffs detect generous aromas of pronounced juniper (mostly as cedar sap), tree bark (there's almost a root beer quality to it), earthy roots, and citrus zest (tangerine, lemon) that work together nicely in the early going aromatics; secondary passes after more air contact see the juniper and lemon peel fragrances take firm command. Entry is keenly zesty, tangy, herbal, astringent, bitter, piney; midpalate grows in pine needle intensity and turns slightly sweeter than the entry. While not deep on elegance or nuance, this no-holds-barred gin with a big personality is nonetheless one that's pleasing in its straightforward, rambunctious manner.

2015 Rating: ★★★/Recommended

St. George Botanivore Gin (USA) 45% abv, $29.

No tint, no color; flawless clarity. This first nosing pass is all about fresh spring herb garden, as the degrees of aromatic presence multiply by the second, including bread dough, nutmeg, mint, black peppercorn, rosemary, and coriander; later whiffs detect deeper scents, especially pine cone/tree, pine sap, lemongrass, and dried citrus peel. Entry is lush, yet crisp and intensely piney; midpalate stays the herbal/spice garden course, with the juniper/pine aspect now growing in strength and zestiness. Concludes fresh, herbaceous, leafy spice–like (parsley, perhaps), and clean.

2020 Rating: ★★★★/Highly Recommended

St. George Spirits Dry Rye Reposado Gin (USA) 49.5% abv, $50.

Rye. Aged in French and American casks that once matured syrah and grenache wines. Pretty umber/burnt-orange hue; minor sediment seen. The initial nosings are compelling because I detect a wildly incongruous mix of juniper, red wine, sweet red pepper, coriander, blueberries, dried flowers, and seedless rye bread (??); further time in the glass releases subtle notes of tangerine, sassafras, and root beer. Entry is appealing, citrusy (tangelo?), spicy, slightly tannic, and root-like; midpalate is supple, intensely earthy/minerally, oily, anise-like, and moderately herbaceous. Concludes dry to off-dry, earthy, and distantly winey. It is not really a gin, by my definition, but is more an oak-aged hybrid spirit that combines attributes of whiskey, wine, gin to a minor degree, aquavit, and herbal liqueurs.

2016 Rating: ★★★/Recommended

St. George Terroir Gin (USA) 45% abv, $29.

Rainwater clear and clean; colorless. This opening nose is atypical, woodsy, and intensely earthy, as pungent aromas of pine forest/needle, bay leaf, brambles, and orris root lead the way; secondary whiffs pick up supplementary fragrances of allspice, mace, cardamom, and angelica. Entry is fresh, stunningly herbal, and flinty/mineral-like, with tastes of eucalyptus, menthol, and pine nut; midpalate mirrors the entry findings, adding piquant flavors of sage, thyme, anise, and fennel. Its strikingly medicinal finish is unlike any other gin in the marketplace.

2020 Rating: ★ ★ ★/Recommended

Stirk's Oak Barrel Finished Gin (Scotland) 46% abv, $40.

Flax/golden hay-yellow/gold color; very good, sediment-free clarity. The subtlety of the first aromas is accentuated by the charming hint of pine forest—what it really reminds me of is Christmas morning and the first whiff of the tree; later inhalations detect more in the way of tree sap and delicate oak resins (this gin was cask matured in barrels that formerly held Speyside malt whisky). Entry does have a buttery texture that I'm certain comes from the oak barrel, but that's not to say that the cedar aspect of the juniper is drowned out by it because it's not; midpalate is creamy in the mouth, zesty, slightly acidic, and therefore fresh, a bit toasty and egg cream–like while still herbal. Finishes long, supple, piquant, peppery. Nicely done and one of the better barrel-aged gins around.

2017 Rating: ★ ★ ★ ★/Highly Recommended

Stonecutter Spirits Single Barrel Gin (USA) 45% abv, $55.

Matured in an ex-bourbon barrel. Gamboge coloring; impeccable clarity. First sniffs pick up a woody trace aroma of whiskey that eventually blows off, leaving the pathway clear for aromas of peanut shell, latent juniper, angelica, sage, and coriander; subsequent inhalations after more aeration discover a bark-like scent that interplays well with the juniper pineyness and the root-derived botanicals. Entry is sturdily firm, somewhat peppery, a little floral (orange blossom), showing at this point a mere whisper of juniper; midpalate is a little too woody for my liking, but simultaneously there is an emerging juniper core flavor that allows for other botanicals such as cassia, ginger, and cardamom, making the case for a New World gin style expression that's robust, oaky, and alluringly fruity. The brawny finish confirms all of the midpalate impressions, and I end up liking this gin more than I thought I would.

2016 Rating: ★ ★ ★ ★/Highly Recommended

Striped Pig Gin (USA) 43% abv, $27.

Excellent clarity; totally colorless. Wow, there's a big hit of lavender in the opening whiffs that dominates the aroma so I move on; the second-stage nosings pick up faint traces of juniper/pine cone and citrus peel that are folded over amidst the blankets of lavender fragrance—I love the scent of lavender but like anything, a little goes a long way. Entry is highly floral and oily from the lavender, and therefore top-heavy and off-balance; midpalate shows a mildly pleasant juiciness that's citrus in nature, but the fog of the lavender continues deep into the finish. My sense is that there is a good, recommendable gin here if the distiller's foot were to be lighter on the lavender accelerator.

2018 Rating: ★ ★/Not Recommended

Sunset Hills Virginia Gin (USA) 40% abv, $29.

Impeccably clean and clear appearance. This gin aroma is very delicate and needs time to develop in the glass; a later pass reveals very soft aromatics that include pine, leather, citrus, white rice. Entry is also meek, nicely piney, a little floral, peppery, root-like, earthy, leafy; midpalate echoes the entry but turns slightly acidic, though that's fine, as the flavor profile goes tart in the finish. A low-key gin that's quietly solid.

2015 Rating: ★ ★ ★/Recommended

Tanqueray Bloomsbury London Dry Gin (England) 47.3% abv, $33/liter.

Like every Tanqueray, pristine appearance; void of color. Opening nosing passes pick up touches of cedary juniper but not at the potency of Tanqueray London Dry (my personal all-time favorite gin), which I must believe is the point of this limited-edition gin, easing up on the juniper accelerator but neither applying the brake; more aeration brings out the other botanicals, most notably, at least to my olfactory mechanism, the savory and cassia; I like this London Dry variation. Entry is delightfully piney/cedary and almost floral in the initial tastes, then at midpalate the cassia and savory reemerge in powerful waves of intense flavor that come to dominate the taste profile by the time the aftertaste begins. This gin finishes warm, with creamy ribbons of juniper flavor that without doubt bring the focus back to London Dry territory. The only thing keeping it from a fifth rating star is the bit of raw harshness in the throat at finish. Otherwise, splendid.

2016 Rating: ★ ★ ★ ★/Highly Recommended

Tanqueray London Dry Gin (England) 47.3% abv, $24.

There's no question that this aroma belongs to Tanqueray London Dry due primarily to its exquisite harmony and its juniper forward thrust that's well-behaved and deeply earthy and vegetal; secondary inhalations after more air contact bring up the coriander snappiness and licorice bite that I admire so much and have done so for decades of spirits writing. Entry is where this classic earns all its rating stars, as the pungency of the juniper is presented in textbook form, and the creamy, rich texture provides the foundation for the flavor profile; midpalate reflects all the splendor of the entry stage and actually deepens it, especially with the juniper element as the piney/pine needle taste soars off the charts. Ends in a sumptuous, lush fashion in which the juniper is unquestionably the king, as this gin defines what London Dry gin is all about. Without any question whatsoever, one of the twenty-five greatest distilled spirits ever produced.

2018 Rating: ★ ★ ★ ★ ★/Highest Recommendation

Tanqueray Malacca Gin (England) 40% abv, $28/liter.

Flawless, translucent clarity; sediment-free. I detect scents of lead pencil, tree bark, forest floor, and moss in addition to the juniper/pine tree foundational fragrance; following another eight minutes of air contact, the juniper steps up a bit more, as does the supplemental spiciness. Entry is velvety smooth, intensely fruity, and is marginally sweeter than either Tanqueray London Dry or Tanqueray No. Ten; midpalate is delightfully citrusy, elegant, piney, and more tart than the entry. Finishes long in the throat, slightly baked, and wonderfully creamy and grapefruit tart.

2015 Rating: ★ ★ ★ ★/Highly Recommended

Tanqueray No. Ten Gin (England) 47.3% abv, $37.

Perfect clarity; colorless. I am admittedly a total fool for this citrus zest opening fragrance that screams "citrus/grapefruit," but it's also the floral, green-tea aspect that underpins

the citrus that charms me; more aeration time brings out the juniper pineyness, to be sure, but also it's the chamomile "greenness" that makes this bouquet so complete, so sublimely balanced. Entry is rich in texture (like its sibling, the London Dry) and downright juicy without being ripe or sweet—in fact, the taste profile at the entry is acutely astringent and highly acidic, making it refreshing and tart; midpalate is the place where all the components merge into one fantastically delicious flavor that has shades of London Dry, but the intensity of the citrus and flowers keeps it separate from that designation. Along with its sibling, the highest expression of what truly great gin can be.
2018 Rating: ★ ★ ★ ★ ★/Highest Recommendation

Teerenpeli PYYGin (Finland) 45% abv, $40.

Clean and clear; void of color. Oh my, what I get early on in the nose are black pepper, crushed red pepper, paprika, and fennel, which drown out any juniper aspect; the pepper-mill aroma continues with conviction after more aeration, along with a deeply fennel-like presence. Entry is all about the peppery but only slightly piquant frontline taste of the various pepper types as the juniper again is MIA; midpalate continues on Pepper Road, as now the taste profile offers a tongue-tingling piquancy. Aftertaste is long, zesty. While I'm not entirely sure if this spirit should be classified as gin, I can say without hesitation that I like its uniqueness enough to recommend it as long as one doesn't expect a London Dry gin style.
2019 Rating: ★ ★ ★/Recommended

The Botanist Islay Dry Gin (Scotland) 46% abv, $35.

Shows a shocking amount of whitish-gray floating debris; I changed my sampling glass and the second pour was identical to the first. Opening nosing passes encounter intensely beany/kernel-like aromas, plus a bevy of other botanicals, including flower petals, jasmine, apple peel, orange zest, and angelica; following another six minutes of air contact, the citrus zest emerges as the dominant feature along with juniper/pine; it's actually a lovely, expansive, and generous gin bouquet. Entry is silky, leaning to sweet, floral, and citrusy; midpalate highlights more of the juniper and other rooty things, like orris. Finishes cleanly and bitter-sweet and chewy.
2017 Rating: ★ ★ ★ ★/Highly Recommended

The London No. 1 Original Blue Gin (England) 47% abv, $32.

The pretty electric-blue/celeste color is disconcerting but pure; sorry, but I just don't take a shine to artificial coloring. Nosingwise, I pick up early, if weak, scents of orange peel, faint juniper berry, and flint; secondary inhalations following more air contact don't pick up much more in the way of overt gin bouquet. Entry is on the sweeter side of the ledger, mineral-like, mildly floral, with enough juniper showing through to call it dry gin; midpalate turns a bit fruitier than the entry and even succulent as the citrus component comes fully into play at this point. Concludes medium long, juicy, and mildly pleasing. Unimpressive overall.
2018 Rating: ★ ★/Not Recommended

The Revivalist Equinox Expression Botanical Gin (USA) 43% abv, $40.

Void of color; impeccably clean and free of sediment. I pick up trace aromas of citrus peel, pencil eraser, dried flowers in a yearbook, fresh mint, and dried cooking herbs (bay leaf, parsley) that orbit around the core fragrance of juniper—this is an exceedingly fragile aroma whose delicacy is its charm; secondary nosing passes detect a touch less of juniper, as a "green," vegetal, spring flower garden aspect overtakes the aroma. Entry is lean, elemental, and mineral-like, showing just a whisper of juniper, but enough to make the New World gin case; midpalate offers a more pronounced dose of piney juniper that acts as the bonding agent for the herbaceousness and the mintiness that both reach deep into the subtle, understated finish, which I like. A monarch butterfly of a gin, whose inherent appeal is its dainty intricacy.

2016 Rating: ★★★/Recommended

The Revivalist Solstice Expression Botanical Gin (USA) 46.5% abv, $50.
Matured in red wine barrels that explains the intriguing purple/gray/wine-stain shade; excellent clarity. Here's what I get in the first whiffs after the pour: toasted oak, brambly zinfandel, lemon peel, ginger, parchment, new leather, faint licorice, tobacco leaf, cigar box; after more time in the glass I pick up wax paper, grape skin, cinnamon, tankyness, but no juniper at all—so once again questions of true category pop up. Entry is rife with grapiness, intensely grape skin–like, and therefore tannic and drying on the tongue, with juniper providing only a sliver of contributing flavor; midpalate is nicer than the entry as the juniper kick-starts itself and mingles well with the grape peel, brambles, blackberry flavors that are tart and acutely acidic. Aftertaste showcases the juniper/grape tandem, and it works despite itself, though in the end I can't find enough attributes to recommend it. That said, I appreciate the effort to attempt something different as well as the spirit of adventure that it takes to create a controversial distillate such as this. The main problem, as I see it, is that there are limited applications for this gin.

2016 Rating: ★★/Not Recommended

The Revivalist Summertide Expression Botanical Gin (USA) 42% abv, $40.
Clean as a whistle and totally colorless. I heartily like the zesty, tangy, remarkably grassy quality of the first aromas and, in fact, completely get the Summertide moniker as a result of the opening whiffs and, most importantly, there is enough juniper presence (and peppermint) to recognize this offering as a New World–style gin. My mind ventures to the laziest days of July as the second-stage inhalations bolster the first-stage impressions, adding a marginally deeper pineyness from the juniper that mingles nicely with the mown grass, fresh flower garden, mildly fruity, and citrusy supporting fragrances—a seriously pleasant and evocative bouquet. Entry is buttressed by the juniper foundation and displays black peppercorn, peppermint in lesser amounts, lemongrass, and cilantro/coriander; midpalate is zesty, acutely New World gin–like, floral, "green," and nicely mannered. The sweet aftertaste highlights the mint and juniper in equal amounts, making for a pleasing finish.

2016 Rating: ★★★★/Highly Recommended

Thomas Dakin Gin (England) 42% abv, $31.
Copper pot still distillation in Manchester, England; founded in 1761. Pristine and sediment-free; clear-as-rainwater appearance. Opening nose is soft, delicate, and earthy, as the juniper element stays largely hidden beneath the flinty/mineral-like surface aroma; more

aeration introduces fragrances reminiscent of damp leaves, grapefruit peel, gunmetal, lime-stone, and shale. Entry shows the flash of sappy juniper, and while the taste profile is dry to the point of being astringent, I wouldn't characterize this as being London Dry since the juniper isn't the dominant flavor—perhaps it's a Manchester Dry style; midpalate is arid in its dryness and deeply mineral-like. Aftertaste dries out the throat with its acidity, and it's at this juncture that the juniper emerges in full voice. The growing intensity during the flavor stages is highly appealing. A definite keeper.

2018 Rating: ★ ★ ★ ★/Highly Recommended

Tinkerman's Citrus Supreme Gin (USA) 46% abv, $30.

Pristine clarity; colorless. The fragrant scent of citrus peel/zest abounds in the up-front aroma, and it's not a single fruit but an orchestra of citrus varieties making the noise; sec-ondary whiffs are greeted by another tier of botanicals, these being earthier in nature, such as dry sand, vanilla bean, cassia bark, and sage. Entry is ripe, fruity, pleasantly tart, and there-fore edgy, astringent, and refreshing as the palate dries out; midpalate sees the juniper/pine nut aspect grow in intensity, as does the tartness. Aftertaste is medium long, tangy, nearly piquant, and dry. I'd call it middle-of-the-road New Western style.

2018 Rating: ★ ★ ★/Recommended

Tinkerman's Curiously Bright & Complex Gin (USA) 46% abv, $30.

Flawless purity; limpid appearance. Right from the first inhalations, there's a zesty cit-rusy/citric acid crispness that's appealing, but just beyond that initial fragrance I encounter leafy/viny/vegetal aromas that are tea-like and almost maritime; later sniffs pick up more of the seaside scent that's slightly salty, peppery, kale- and ginger-like—where's the juniper? Entry is a tad sharp at first, but there's plenty of busy botanical presence as the search for juniper continues amidst the bustling crowd of flavorings; midpalate offers a bit of respite from the Macy's Thanksgiving Day parade of flavors as the juniper at last makes a brief appearance but is quickly pushed back into the throng. Concludes medium long, a little thin, green tea–like, acutely vegetal, and earthy. It's just too busy for me, as the horde of botanicals illustrates the primary fault of most contemporary gins that simply try too hard by throwing every botanical that's close at hand into the brew. Less is often more.

2018 Rating: ★ ★/Not Recommended

Tinkerman's Sweet Spice Gin (USA) 46% abv, $30.

Transparent, clean, colorless. This first nosing is all about earthbound, spicy delights, like vanilla, nutmeg, tree bark, root beer, sarsaparilla, and cola nut; secondary inhalations detect hardly any juniper amidst the forest of woodsy herbs, roots, and barks. Entry is sassy, spicy, and very soda pop–like in its rooty, bark-like flavor profile; midpalate is quite alluring as the juniper finally shows up through the throng of botanicals. Concludes dry, piquant, and spicy.

2018 Rating: ★ ★ ★/Recommended

Tommyrotter Distillery American Gin (USA) 42% abv, $35.

Springwater transparent; clean as a whistle. In the first whiffs after the pour, the early aroma features cucumber, dried violets, angelica, black pepper, and soft juniper; later inhalations encounter more of the floral scent as well as juniper but less of the other spices and botanicals. Entry is a little prickly at first, but that rounds off leaving behind tastes of pine, tree sap/resin, thyme, white pepper; midpalate sees a bit of the alcohol prickliness return to prod the taste buds awake. Finishes low-key, zesty, juniper-like, and a touch too minerally. I see potential here.

2016 Rating: ★ ★ ★/Recommended

TOPO Piedmont Gin (USA) 46% abv, $30.

Very faint pewter tint; very good purity. Opening aromas are curiously earthy, leafy, vegetal, slightly citrusy, and viny, with only the scantest trace of juniper; secondary nosings after further aeration highlight the baked earth aspect as well as bringing out other botanicals, mostly anise, black pepper, tobacco leaf, and cardamom; an intriguing, low-juniper-impact gin that has a vegetal charm. Entry taste flashes a note of cucumber, along with a deft touch of citrus oil and orange zest; midpalate is pleasantly fruity, oily, and herbal. Looking for London Dry? Pass on this because it lives in a parallel universe. Hankering for a new twist on gin? Go for it. Me like.

2015 Rating: ★ ★ ★ ★/Highly Recommended

Treaty Oak Waterloo Antique Gin (USA) 47% abv, $30.

Sandy-brown/harvest gold color; excellent purity. Wow, this assertive opening, flower shop–like nose is reminiscent of rose petals, dried violets, and lavender with potent doses of pickled cucumber and sweet relish; second inhalations pick up all the opening impressions, as well as traces of cola, pipe tobacco, brown sugar, maple, and black pepper. Entry is quite sweet, oaky, and vanilla bean–like at first, then the resiny taste of oak takes command, leading to a midpalate stage that's medium full in texture, oaky/resiny, lean yet biscuity, toasted, and supple tasting. Aftertaste is driven completely now by the oak influence, which, for me, is too woody, fat-like, and resiny as the spirit loses its gin identity. I appreciate the spirit of adventure and innovation that this gin represents, but this wood-heavy experiment doesn't work for me.

2018 Rating: ★ ★/Not Recommended

Treaty Oak Waterloo No. 9 Gin (USA) 47% abv, $25.

Colorless; impeccably clean and free of sediment. Frontline aromas focus more on floral aspects than herbal as I initially pick up subtle nuances of lavender and honeysuckle, but then the more traditional dry gin aromas emerge, especially juniper and coriander, to make for pleasing sniffing; later nosing passes detect the merging of both the floral and herbal components into a unified, harmonious, and delicate bouquet that's gentle and spring garden–like. Entry echoes all the aromatic findings, except for a heightened flowery presence, which introduces a citrusy oiliness to the texture that's becoming; midpalate harkens back to the juniper and coriander elements and the stony-dry flavor that goes mineral-like, citrusy, and flinty. Finishes in a flurry of woodsy/floral earthiness that's pleasant and suddenly off-dry rather than dry.

2018 Rating: ★ ★ ★/Recommended

Treaty Oak Waterloo Old Yaupon Gin (USA) 45% abv, $25.

The citron color is foggy/turbid and sediment-free. I like this opening aroma as it's

alluringly herbal, juicy, floral, and gently spicy, with juniper nowhere to be found, but that's fine at this point; later whiffs encounter a narrower fragrance that's delicate in its honey sweetness, feathery in its herbaceous roundness, and a bit like buttermilk biscuits and honey. Entry is pleasingly sweet and citrusy, with just a trace of juniper showing; midpalate highlights the acid-driven juiciness of the citrus aspect as well as the flowery element that's clean and delicate. Aftertaste features the Yaupon honey, flower petals, grapefruit, and citric acid in harmony. It's a technical stretch to say that this is a gin, but frankly it's so yummy and unique that I'd buy it simply to enjoy on its own, chilled with a slice of lemon.
2018 Rating: ★★★★/Highly Recommended

Tyler's Original City of London Dry Gin (England) 47% abv, $20.
Clear as springwater; sediment-free and void of color. I immediately like the deeply botanical, forest floor, cedar forest–like opening fragrance that's zesty and elegant at the same time; secondary whiffs pick up more of the black pepper, lemon rind, gravel, and floral notes that all enhance the juniper core. Entry is creamy rich in texture, dry as a bone, yet it offers multiple layers of flavor, including pine nut, juniper berry, coriander, angelica, orris, and lavender; midpalate brings the taste profile to a razor-edged crispness that's cleansing and tart. Concludes mineral-like, peppery, flowery, and crisp.
2019 Rating: ★★★★/Highly Recommended

Uncle Val's Botanical Gin (USA) 45% abv, $40.
Overall, above average clarity, with some very minor sediment tendrils seen. Highly aromatic right from the pour, this gin offers pungent, acutely herbaceous scents of thyme, sage, and dried flowers in abundance; further air contact stimulates tangy lemon peel and citrus oil fragrances that dominate the latter stages of the olfactory evaluation. Entry is gently sweet, keenly lemony, and appealingly floral, though the low degree of juniper is apparent; midpalate is sharp, crisp, acidic, and piquant. Finishes with a burst of lemon oil and high acidity that maintains the freshness. Well made in a non-London Dry profile. There's so much lemon peel/lemon zest presence in this gin that I don't feel it would jibe at all with citrus-centric gin cocktails.
2015 Rating: ★★★/Recommended

Uncle's Val's Peppered Gin (USA) 45% abv, $39.
Owns a discernible and pretty ecru/tarnished-silver tint color; unblemished clarity. Opening inhalations find prickly aromas that attack the olfactory mechanism, offering little hint of juniper pineyness or other normal gin botanicals (angelica, cassia, orris, coriander, lemon peel), and that's the idea as slight nuances of pepper grow in strength with air contact; by the second passes, the pepper influence is more apparent, but the overall fragrance flies under the radar. Entry is ashy, toasted, moderately spicy, creamy in texture, almost coffee-like, beany, smoky, tar-like; midpalate is more obvious in its pepper direction, but again it's a peppery aspect that, to me, is more ash-like/smoky/tobacco-like than actually red or green or black pepper; I'm informed that there's a hint of pimento in the mix and that becomes clear in the finish. I like this gin enough to recommend, but prefer the swank and elegant Restorative.
2015 Rating: ★★★/Recommended

Uncle's Val's Restorative Gin (USA) 45% abv, $39.
Clear and clean as rainwater. After the initial sniffs following the pour I can't help but think of one thing, "Hendrick's Gin," as Uncle Val's Restorative does a close, if not identical, job of emulation, and that's due primarily to two (apparent) ingredient botanicals, cucumber and rose petal, that are both in evidence early on; after further aeration, the juniper aspect gets itself together and shines through, beacon-like, in the latter stages of the bouquet. Entry is really yummy, in that the juniper-cucumber-rose petal troika gets amiable support from deeply herbaceous coriander while the alcohol base turns velvety smooth and viscous; midpalate is damn near unctuous and oily as the flavor profile goes for broke. Finishes long, luxuriously creamy, and a little hot, but acceptably so. This style can only be categorized as "floral."
2015 Rating: ★ ★ ★ ★/Highly Recommended

Ungava Canadian Premium Gin (Canada) 43.1% abv, $30.
Bright neon-yellow color; flawless clarity. Opening sniffs encounter lightly toasted, piney, herbal notes with deft touches of loose leaf tobacco, green tea—there's something "leafy green" about this appealing initial fragrance; air contact brings out a pod-like scent that's dry, seed-like (caraway, sesame), and black pepper–like, but the entire bouquet is based in juniper berry. Entry is delicately juicy and citrusy, with a background flavor of cedar box/sap that's refreshing and intensely herbal; midpalate focuses on the juniper, which carries forward all the other tart botanical flavors, including flowers, citrus, red berries. Finishes as delicately and piney as it started. Lovely, balanced, unique.
2015 Rating: ★ ★ ★ ★/Highly Recommended

VOR Icelandic Pot Distilled Gin (Iceland) 47% abv, $80.
Barley. Colorless, showing barely perceptible sediment that is inconsequential. I like the reined-in juniper rush in the opening inhalations as this allows for other botanicals to seep through, like dried flowers, cut grass, anise, bay leaf; after more time in the glass, the aroma rounds off nicely as the various botanicals merge into a singular bouquet, which is dry, herbaceous, woodsy, and clean. Entry is stunningly floral and almost sweet and dewy in its flower-laden manner in which the juniper is present but only as an equal contributor; midpalate brings in what tastes like citrus zest or dried lemon peel, which adds some acidity to keep the structure tight and focused on the mélange of botanicals deep into the elegant aftertaste. With all the gins flooding the marketplace, most of them subpar, it's a treat to find one of the New World style that's actually delicious due to the craftsmanship of the producer, who doesn't overplay his/her hand with the botanical mix. Well done and worth the price tag.
2016 Rating: ★ ★ ★ ★/Highly Recommended

Whitley Neill Handcrafted Dry Gin (England) 43% abv, $35.
Clear as springwater; ideal purity. First nosings pick up atypical but extremely pleasant flowery scents that are nuanced and subtle and don't interfere with the juniper presence; this fresh spring garden fragrance continues into the second nosing passes, which are moderately fruitier and riper than the first passes. Entry is delightfully fruity, but dry and zesty; midpalate highlights the juniper aspect in particular, making the gustatory stage the highlight

of the evaluation. Finishes long, wonderfully floral, crisp from the piney juniper, and well balanced.
2018 Rating: ★ ★ ★ ★/Highly Recommended

Wilds Fine American Gin (USA) 42% abv, $30.

Shows a slight pewter tinge; superb clarity. Curiously, I smell hints of salad bar and pencil eraser along with subtler scents of juniper, coriander, angelica, and orris root; second passes bring out oak plank and tree bark that mingle well with the aforementioned fragrances. Entry fails to capitalize on the fine traits of the aroma and that disappoints; midpalate picks up some of the juniper/cedar slack in this New Western gin enough to nearly make it recommendable. Waxy, soap-like finish. The breakdown of consistency between the pleasant aroma and the in-mouth stages relegate this American gin to the sidelines.
2019 Rating: ★ ★/Not Recommended

Woody Creek Colorado Gin (USA) 47% abv, $39.

Potato base. Perfect clarity; colorless. Wow, I actually detect the potato presence immediately because there's a mild sweetness that's very spud-like, but that's not to say that there isn't evidence of juniper. Second passes following more air contact find the release of botanicals, especially citrus and a pleasing floral (lavender, hibiscus) aspect, but the inclusion of cranberries comes out at the very end. This gin's botanical list includes juniper, lemongrass, coriander, hibiscus, lavender, grains of paradise, angelica, cinnamon, orange, lemon, lime; this is a very busy gin bouquet but I have to say that I like it as it comes off as a hybrid between London Dry and New World. Entry is nicely flowery (very petal-like), citrusy, and fruity, but there's still enough juniper presence to balance out the other botanicals; midpalate echoes the entry as the floral aspect remains strong and equal to the juniper and citrus peel, creating a potent, big flavor that goes deep into the creamy, oily finish. I think in the end, the New World style triumphs over the London Dry style as the robust taste rumbles along like a Harley-Davidson bike.
2016 Rating: ★ ★ ★/Recommended

AGAVE SPIRITS—MEXICO

All agave-based spirits of Mexico, including tequila, are collected beneath the categorical name known as *mezcal*. So mezcal, then, is confusingly both a spirits category associated solely with Mexico as well as a specific subcategory (agave spirits made in/around Oaxaca, Mexico) within that category. Aside from tequila and mezcal, other agave-based Mexican spirits include *sotol, raicilla,* and *bacanora*.

Mezcal, tequila, and other agave-based spirits are created in Mexico from the fermented and distilled juice of agave plants. The agave plant is not a cactus; rather, it is but one of a family of succulents thought now to be from the asparagus family under the botanical name *agavaceae*. Like any other type of botanical genus, the agave family tree includes different branches, many distinct strains. Some botanists now estimate that there are more than two hundred individual types of agave.

Farmers, who cultivate agaves over tens of thousands of acres throughout west-central and southern Mexico, collectively prefer the customary agricultural name, maguey, to agave. The term *maguey*, pronounced *meh-gay*, is derived from the indigenous Náhuatl word *maya-huel* (*my-ah-hwell*), an ancient term that was employed centuries ago when native holy men invoked the goddess of the agave plant. For our purposes, let's use the word that most consumers are familiar with: "agave."

TEQUILA—MEXICO

Tequila is a subcategory of mezcal in a similar way that Scotch whisky or bourbon are subcategories of the greater whiskey category, or cognac and armagnac are subcategories of the brandy category.

All tequila, by law, must be produced exclusively in the five west-central Mexican states of Jalisco (specifically, 124 municipalities), Nayarit (eight municipalities), Michoacán (thirty municipalities), Guanajuato (seven municipalities), and/or Tamaulipas (eleven municipalities) from but a single variety of agave, *tequiliana Weber azul*. This type was named after the German botanist F. Weber, who classified agaves at the turn of the twentieth century. Blue agave plants generally take a minimum of six to eight years to grow to the point of being ready for harvest. From the farmers' standpoint, raising agave is a long-term enterprise and investment. It is estimated that today three hundred million blue agave plants are harvested annually for tequila production.

Jalisco is home to the town of Tequila, the acknowledged epicenter of production, and is divided into two primary growing regions: the "Lowlands" are located around the town of Tequila, and "Los Altos," or the "Highlands," are located northwest of Tequila. Lowlands tequilas are depicted as being herbaceous while Highlands tequilas are bolder in flavor and texture.

In tequila production, harvested agaves are cooked to soften the *piñas* (the bulbous heart of the agave plant) so that the juice can be extracted via crushing. The juice is then fermented. The fermented juice is next distilled either in traditional pot stills or in modern, tall column stills. Some categories of tequila (reposado, añejo, extra añejo) are then matured in oak barrels.

Labeling Laws

Tequila is bottled at different classifications that are officially regulated by the Consejo Regulador del Tequila (CRT).

Tipo Uno: Blancos, Platas, Platinums, or Silvers (white) are bottled within sixty days of distillation, and therefore offer the most essential agave flavors.

Tipo Dos: Joven or Oro (gold) is immature tequila that is a blend of silver with reposado or añejo.

Tipo Tres: Reposados (rested) have been aged from two to twelve months in oak barrels and are favored by Mexican consumers.

Tipo Quatro: Añejo (old) are matured in oak barrels, with a maximum capacity of six hundred liters, for a minimum of twelve months but no more than thirty-six months.

Tipo Cinco: Extra Aged is tequila that has been matured in oak barrels, with a maximum capacity of six hundred liters, for at least three years (thirty-six months).

Mixto is low-grade tequila that by law must contain at least 51 percent of 100 percent agave tequila. The balance of spirit is usually made from sugarcane distillate.

Regulations also stipulate that every bottle of tequila must have on the label a NOM number (standing for *Norma Oficial Mexicana*) that identifies the specific distillery at which that tequila was produced. The NOM assists in keeping clear which of the approximately seventy tequila distilleries produced that brand, as now there are about five hundred individual brands. Likewise, the words "Hecho en Mexico," or "Made in Mexico," must, by law, appear somewhere on the label as another guarantee of authenticity.

1800 Reposado Tequila 40% abv, $34.

Citron color; superb clarity. Initial nosing passes detect subtle, behind-the-scenes aromas of green chili pepper, gunpowder, dill, citrus peel, and olive brine; later whiffs following more aeration encounter peppery, zesty, and mildly fat-like aromas that hint of agave, lard,

and bacon fat. Entry is slightly metallic, flinty, lead pencil–like, and chalky; midpalate offers a little more herbaceousness mostly in the forms of dill and salty pickle brine, but the core is hollow. Maturation in both American and French oak barrels doesn't accomplish the goal of added refinement. There's not enough agave character here to refine. Drinkable, but void of personality. In *Kindred Spirits 2* I rated this 1800 four stars! No excuse for this plummet in quality other than poor choices at the distillery level.
2020 Rating: ★★/Not Recommended

1800 Reserva Añejo Tequila 40% abv, $40.
    Pretty amber color; excellent purity. Up front, I get big, assertive aromas of bacon fat, burnt matchstick, charcoal briquette, pine tar, and heavily roasted agave; later sniffs go heavily salted, smoky, charred, and swampy. Entry is fat in texture, sugar sweet and syrupy, and lightly peppery; midpalate offers sweet, sap-like, and resiny tastes that have lost any sense of agave herbacousness, and that's enough for me not to recommend it. Rated four stars (!) in *Kindred Spirits 2* from 2008. What a shame that this once proud and pleasing brand has hit the quality skids.
2020 Rating: ★★/Not Recommended

1800 Silver Tequila 40% abv, $34.
    Silvery clear and sediment-free appearance. This opening fragrance is delicately sweet with agave syrup tang, and it is moderately smoky, piquant, and mineral-like; secondary passes pick up herbal/flora traits, especially prickly pear, aniseed, licorice, eucalyptus, and pine needle. Entry flavors pick up where the last sniffs left off, featuring herbaceous tastes that are mildly off-dry/medium sweet, sappy, and succulent; midpalate turns up the volume on the sweetness dial a bit too loudly and this becomes the dominant highlight of this stage, leading unfortunately to an aggressively sap-like, overly honeyed, and agave syrup–like conclusion that's simply too much. An off-balance, barely average silver that I've known in times past to be better. In *Kindred Spirits 2* I rated it three stars.
2020 Rating: ★★/Not Recommended

901 Añejo Tequila 40% abv, $50.
    Flat/dullish amber color; excellent clarity. This opening nose features black pepper in spades, malted milk, sawdust, and lead pencil; post-aeration time, there is an oaky quality that reminds me of tree sap and resin, plus there's evidence of prickly pear, anise, caraway seed, and baked apple; a complex bouquet. Entry is waxy, vegetal, and earthy/mushroomy; midpalate showcases the earthy element and a healthy dose of oak resin. Finishes softly, beeswax-like, and leaner than the reposado.
2016 Rating: ★★★/Recommended

901 Reposado Tequila 40% abv, $45.
    Oyster/tarnished-silver appearance; impeccable purity. First whiffs encounter lush and generously animated aromas of dill, pickle brine, asparagus, and white pepper; following another six minutes of air contact, the aroma expands to include orange blossom, citrus, and sand; a far above average reposado bouquet. Entry is sweet, with whispers of green vegetable, brown butter, and black pepper; midpalate shows off some tobacco and baked pear flavors

that meld nicely with the vegetal aspect. Ends on an off-dry note that's keenly peppery. It doesn't bludgeon you with the wood, leaving the agave in full display.
2016 Rating: ★ ★ ★ ★/Highly Recommended

901 Silver Tequila 40% abv, $37.

Totally colorless; limpid and clean. Right from the first whiffs, there's a lovely, slightly sweet pickle brine and green-olive fragrance that's more elegant and latent than assertive or bold; second passes after more aeration tell the tale of a slightly plump and buttery bouquet that leans away from the olive brine and moves towards bacon fat resemblance. Entry is acutely green pepper–like and is a little spiky in zestiness, and that leads to a blandness at midpalate that takes me by surprise. The taste profile recovers in the aftertaste as the pepper-iness returns with enough animation to warrant a mild recommendation.
2018 Rating: ★ ★ ★/Recommended

Astral Blanco Tequila 46% abv, $40.

NOTE THE 92-PROOF STRENGTH. Colorless and pure. Oh baby, now this is what I call old-fashioned, real-deal blanco tequila that hasn't been prettied up, primped, homogenized, or pasteurized—I like the peppery (jalapeño), no-nonsense opening aro-matic burst that yells out "Dill! Pickle brine! Salt! Limestone!"; secondary whiffs echo the findings of the initial nosing pass, adding earth notes of stone, sand, and vegetation. Entry comes on strong after a second or two to make sure you know that this isn't an 80-proof model but one with more octane; midpalate profile hinges upon the 92-proof strength, but what is supported by that abv is all-agave, all-the-time in its keenly peppery, green veggie, and dill-like flavor. Finishes long, spicy, lead pencil–like and suddenly agave-nectar sweet. WHAT A RIDE!
2016 Rating: ★ ★ ★ ★ ★/Highest Recommendation

Avión Añejo Single Origin Tequila 40% abv, $65.

Bright greenish-yellow color; impeccably clean. First whiffs pick up notes of vanilla bean, coffee bean, savory, and clove; secondary inhalations discover evolved, moderately mature scents of clay/terra-cotta, tobacco leaves, candle wax, and camphor. Entry offers a sweet-leaning first flavor that's bean-like, lemon curd–like, and zesty; midpalate taste profile goes more towards the barrel influence as the later flavors include oak resin, honey, and dill. A sound añejo that thankfully doesn't leave the agave influence behind.
2020 Rating: ★ ★ ★ ★/Highly Recommended

Avión Reposado Single Origin Tequila 40% abv, $57.

Faint tint similar to brut champagne; beautifully clean and clear. Initial aromatics include baked pineapple, tangerine, orange peel, lemongrass, and mustard seed; after more aeration, the aroma blossoms even more, adding pleasing, garden-fresh, vegetal scents of tomato vine, geranium, chamomile, and hydrangea. Entry is gently sweet, tangy, vegetal (jalapeño pepper), and herbal (sage, dill); midpalate echoes the entry and adds crisp, razor-edged flavors of green olive, green tea, bay leaf, and salted almond. Ends long, moderately salty, fresh, and with more than ample agave herbaceousness present. A deliciously clean reposado.
2020 Rating: ★ ★ ★ ★/Highly Recommended

Avión Reserva 44 Extra Añejo Tequila 40% abv, $150.
Greenish/jonquil/straw color; superb purity. Wow, there's a piquant spice-o-rama happening here in the initial whiffs, including vanilla bean, allspice, clove; later sniffs detect egg cream, vanilla soda, root beer. Entry is keenly bittersweet at first, then it turns brown-sugar sweet as it lies on the tongue; midpalate is chalky, intensely spicy (cinnamon, tree bark), sarsaparilla root–like, lightly toasted, creamy through the languid finish.
2019 Rating: ★ ★ ★ ★/Highly Recommended

Azuñia Añejo Reserved Organic Tequila 40% abv, $44.
Appearance is harvest gold in color and impeccably pure. First, I get asphalt/road tar aromas that quickly blow off, leaving behind traces of burnt vegetable, hard-boiled egg, and lavender; later whiffs find more harmonious, floral aromas that have integrated with aeration, including orange blossom, lavender, eucalyptus, and chamomile, as well as green melon, parsley, and cabbage. Ends up very nicely, as composed flavors of dried flowers, fresh garden herbs, and honey merge into a classy aftertaste.
2019 Rating: ★ ★ ★ ★/Highly Recommended

Azuñia Blanco Organic Tequila 40% abv, $35.
This tequila is as crystalline and colorless as springwater. Right from the initial sniff, I like the zesty, green pepper, jalapeño-like aroma that is as vegetal as it is textile fiber/hemp-like, but it's clean, nimble, and tight; after more aeration the bouquet shows off its razor-edged acidity, and that quality maintains the delicate crispness and deeply peppery element that I find so alluring and correct. Entry stage fires on all cylinders, as the taste profile features everything from asphalt to carbon/campfire embers to candle wax to black pepper to green vegetable (asparagus) to citrus peel; this huge mouthful of flavor continues at midpalate in the integrated, slightly burnt, and smoky forms of caramelized onion, sautéed mushroom, and grilled poblano pepper. A robust, no-prisoners-taken blanco that harkens back to the 1980s and early 1990s when 100 percent agave blancos weren't neutered and homogenized, as so many are today.
2019 Rating: ★ ★ ★ ★ ★/Highest Recommendation

Azuñia Reposado Organic Tequila 40% abv, $40.
Sunglow-yellow color; excellent clarity. I like the gently spicy and herbal opening aromas that remind me of leafy cilantro, lemongrass, and verbena; more time in the glass affords the bouquet the space to add fragrances of brown salted butter, baked pineapple, and tobacco leaf. Entry is tangy, piquant, and a touch fat-like; midpalate turns more woody/oaky, honeyed, and butterscotch-like. Pleasantly spicy and resiny/sap-like, as the vegetal agave aspect seems a bit adrift. Recommendable, to be sure, but I wish that there had been left a bit more agave character.
2019 Rating: ★ ★ ★/Recommended

Baron Platinum Blanco Tequila 40% abv, $55.
Pure as rainwater; limpid. Displays a pungent agave/fiber/saline aromatic thrust that's pleasantly alive with dill, pickle brine, saltine cracker fragrances; additional air contact stimulates more substantial scents of fennel, anise, dry pavement, hemp/rope, black pepper; I

like where this aroma is going. Entry is highly vegetal, green vegetable–like, sappy; mid-palate bursts with agave syrup taste and is leafy, resiny, but then goes bitter, chalky in the aftertaste, which took it to three stars from a potential four. Very good bouquet; solid flavor entry, then in late midpalate a creosote-like bitterness took over.
2014 Rating: ★ ★ ★/Recommended

Blue Nectar Founder's Blend Añejo Azul Tequila 40% abv, $60.

The sepia/topaz color is brilliant, shiny, and pure. The first nosing passes pick up delectable scents of sugar cookie batter, buttermilk biscuits, multigrain bread toast, toasted almond, all of which wrap around the core aroma of roasted agave—very seductive aromatically; secondary pass echoes the initial whiffs, adding light touches of bacon fat, prickly pear, black pepper, bay leaf, and dried leaves in the forest. Entry is round, chewy, silky in texture and nutty, buttery, and slightly smoked in the flavor department, which again does NOT lose sight of the agave base; midpalate is gently toasty, approaching sweet, but with enough remaining agave zestiness and earthiness to bring the taste profile to a crescendo in the delicious, satiny, long finish. Seriously tasty.
2017 Rating: ★ ★ ★ ★ ★/Highest Recommendation

Blue Nectar Special Reserve Infused with Natural Spice Flavor Reposado Tequila 40% abv, $50.

Marginally darker dry-sherry color by half a shade to the standard reposado; flawless purity. First whiffs reveal pleasing green vegetable–like agave fragrance that's dry, zesty, tangy, just gently spiced; secondary inhalations following further aeration only pick up emerging notes of black pepper. Entry is sap-like, sweeter than the standard reposado, tangy, resiny; midpalate echoes the entry to a tee but is slightly drier, adding only dry stone/minerals to the flavor mix. Concludes extended, silky, peppery. The addition of spice is hardly noticed. That's good because the agave remains in charge.
2014 Rating: ★ ★ ★ ★/Highly Recommended

Blue Nectar Reposado Tequila 40% abv, $45.

Has the same bisque/talmi gold color of Manzanilla sherry; free of sediment. I like the opening aromatics that include sea salt, textile fibers, rosemary, black pepper, dried flowers; second-stage nosings pick up deeper fragrances of gum, grass, shale, limestone, nail polish remover. Entry is refined, mildly toasted, semisweet, salty, almost cocoa-like; midpalate is roasted, vegetal, oily (positive) in texture, meaty. Finishes long, like steamed asparagus, green, keenly vegetal, utterly charming, agave forward.
2014 Rating: ★ ★ ★ ★/Highly Recommended

Blue Nectar Silver Tequila 40% abv, $35.

Faint pewter hue; crystalline clarity. Offers a lovely, elegant, dill-filled opening aroma that's equally spicy, earthy/soil-like, sandy, and vegetal (pickle); secondary whiffs encounter moderate aspects of cigarette ash, loose leaf tobacco, green olive, brine, sea salt, tree sap. Entry is peppery, spicy, moderately oily, tobacco-like; midpalate closes in on the spicy/peppery aspect, making the finish medium long, minerally, dusty dry.
2014 Rating: ★ ★ ★/Recommended

Bríbón Añejo Tequila 40% abv, $33.
Mustard color; flawlessly pure. Whoa, the seeded rye bread and sesame seed/sesame oil opening aromas are potent and piquant; second passes reveal a small amount of added scents, including textile fiber/hemp, damp vegetation, mushroom/lichen, mushroom soup, and hominy. Entry is rich in buttery/fat-like texture, which supports the semisweet flavors that boast of brown sugar, milk chocolate, light toffee, and buttercream; midpalate tastes focus on the fat aspect that's also peppery and spicy. Finishes medium long, chewy, pipe tobacco–like, and significantly drier than the entry or midpalate, and that's the pivotal aspect that pushes this añejo into recommended territory.
2018 Rating: ★★★/Recommended

Bríbón Blanco Tequila 40% abv, $25.
Clear and clean as springwater. Up-front aromas offer zesty fragrances of black peppercorn, chamomile, and gentian that work nicely together; more aeration brings out intriguing seed- and oil-like traces of sesame oil and peanut oil as well as herbaceous notes of anise, dill, olive brine, and charred agave. Entry is sweeter than the bouquet implies, featuring a taste of agave syrup along with more elemental/vegetal flavors of grilled asparagus, grilled pineapple, and roasted peppers; midpalate harkens back with accuracy to the entry impressions, adding only a light touch of burnt tobacco leaves. Finishes long, toasty, and moderately viscous in texture.
2018 Rating: ★★★/Recommended

Bríbón Reposado Tequila 40% abv, $28.
Green-tea color; superb purity. Opening inhalations encounter biscuity, bakery-shop pastry, off-dry, and salted butter–like aromas that are supple, assertive, vivid, and plump, bordering on fat; secondary whiffs pick up added scents of margarine, olive oil, green olive, roasted chili peppers, and cordite/gunpowder. Entry findings pick up where the latter aromatic stage left off, encountering dry, flinty, almost brittle, but oily flavors of dry earth, green peppers, green olive, vegetable cooking oil that come wrapped in a waxy texture; midpalate surprisingly goes a little too flat and flabby for my liking as the munitions/black powder aspect takes charge, overshadowing all other agave-based components. Aftertaste is short, narrowly focused, and oaky/vanilla bittersweet in the tail end. My guess is that, one, either the oak barrels used in maturation were untreated/unseasoned, and therefore were loaded with polymers and lipids, which would account for the flatness found in the midpalate, or, two, this reposado was allowed to linger too long in the oak barrel. One way or t'other, the wood maturation killed this tequila. Too bad because it started out nicely in the aroma.
2018 Rating: ★★/Not Recommended

Caballito Cerrero Blanco Tequila 46% abv, $77.
Harvest 2008. Batch size 984, 750 ml bottles. Translucent; colorless; some wispy sediment seen but it's nothing of consequence. There's not a great deal of early fragrance to grab on to in the initial passes other than a waxiness that's a little akin to floor or furniture polish, which for agave isn't necessarily a negative—I just wish that there was more inherent earthiness and/or spiciness to it; additional time in the glass fails to stimulate much more in

the way of aroma, so I accept the fact that it's meek and underachieving in bouquet terms and move on. Entry is oddly floral, like dried violets or carnation petals, then the flavor makes an abrupt right turn, offering more traditional tastes of chewing tobacco, vegetable cooking oil, sage, and jalapeño pepper; midpalate builds on the fetching entry, featuring a slightly smoked taste that's bitter and charcoal-like. Finishes medium long, waxy, earthy/stony, parched, and warming. Kudos for the 46 percent abv that accounts for the heft of the texture. Had the aroma offered more grabworthy virtues, this would have been a four star rating.
2017 Rating: ★ ★ ★/Recommended

Cabo Wabo Blanco Tequila 40% abv, $36.

Crystalline, silvery appearance that is sediment-free. The first whiffs detect lovely agave fragrances of dill pickle, sea salt, lemon grass, and cooked cabbage; following more aeration, the bouquet rounds out into a briny, tobacco ash, woodsmoke scent that's vibrant, clean, and crisp. Entry is lean, astringent, and clean as a whistle, offering tightly wound, integrated flavors of black pepper, jalapeño pepper, green bean, and verbena; midpalate is supple in texture, keenly piquant, and prickly on the tongue. The finish is vibrant, peppery, and salty.
2019 Rating: ★ ★ ★ ★/Highly Recommended

Cabo Wabo Reposado Tequila 40% abv, $37.

Color is citrine/lemon juice; flawless purity. I like this laid-back, easy, and approachable opening aroma as it reminds me of scallions, garden vegetables, oak resin, and even a bit of tobacco ashes; secondary inhalations detect deeper fragrances, in particular, chive, green olive, brine, cabbage, and lentils. Entry is soft, supple, and a touch burnt/smoky and wholly herbal and vegetal; midpalate features broader flavors, namely, honey, oak resin/sap, and maple, but none of those overshadow its agave core, tomato vine, green-tomato core taste. Finishes medium long, silky, and properly vegetal and peppery. Nice repo, this.
2020 Rating: ★ ★ ★ ★/Highly Recommended

Casamigos Añejo Tequila 40% abv, $55.

Flax/gold color; perfect clarity. Opening aromas include marshmallow, green grass, toffee, woodsmoke, cigar tobacco; secondary passes detect brown sugar, agave syrup. Entry features the delicate sweetness promised in the fragrance along with light touches of maple, lychee; midpalate is firm in structure, meaning it holds lots of acidity, and the taste profile is sap-like, vegetal, grassy, oaky, vanilla bean–like, with a distant trace of allspice. Ends on a moderately spicy note that's pleasant and sensuous.
2017 Rating: ★ ★ ★/Recommended

Casamigos Blanco Tequila 40% abv, $43.

A Highlands blanco. Transparent, but with minuscule tendrils of sediment seen. Offers pleasing and salty opening aromas of dill, fennel, and stone; further aeration stimulates aromas of chalk/limestone, black pepper, asparagus, green pepper, and textile fibers. Entry is sweeter and juicier than the bouquet, featuring cocoa and coffee bean richness; midpalate plays up the cocoa/dark chocolate aspect to the hilt, thereby dispensing with the saline,

vegetal, spicy aspects. Concludes medium long, more bean-like than vegetal, but the spiciness returns in the form of black pepper.
2019 Rating: ★ ★ ★/Recommended

Casamigos Reposado Tequila 40% abv, $43.
    A Highlands reposado. Pale straw/yellow color; small amount of sediment seen under the lamp. Initial inhalations highlight the cocoa bean element found in the Blanco as it eclipses much of the natural vegetal and spice aspects; secondary aromas after further air contact reinforce the oak-influenced cocoa bean/chocolate fragrance, but again this aromatic dominance overshadows much of the innate vegetable and cooking spice (dill) aromas of agave. Entry is chocolatey, smooth as satin, and shows a hint of pepperiness; midpalate showcases the oak influence, now in the form of vanilla bean. Finishes a little short, moderately beany (vanilla), and sweet.
2019 Rating: ★ ★ ★/Recommended

Cazadores Añejo Tequila 40% abv, $43.
    Bright marigold/sunflower color; clean and clear. It is now evident that the Cazadores aromatic style is meant to be ethereal and whisper thin, and this fragrance—unfortunately—takes that philosophical belief to a record level of blandness, showing zero agave presence; later sniffs offer no glimpse into what makes agave spirits so attractive to me—earthiness, herbal tanginess, brininess, and occasionally saltiness—but this bouquet gives only anemic, passive, neutral grain spirit scents that have nothing to do with tequila. Entry is . . . wait, I'm stopping this evaluation right now, as I refuse to give this neutered impostor any more of my time.
2020 Rating: ★/Not Recommended

Cazadores Blanco Tequila 40% abv, $28.
    Color, none; pristine clarity. I like this bright, keenly peppery, dill pickle–like opening bouquet because it is herbaceous and fresh as a blanco should be; secondary passes encounter a different set of underlying fragrances, including textile fiber, hemp, grass, and sealing wax that support and push forward the top-note aromas. Entry is lean, stripped down, dry, earthy, and slightly salty; midpalate features much of what is found at entry, adding bits of minerals, terra-cotta, and orchard-fruit rind. Finishes short, tangy. Its best virtues are wrapped up in the bouquet.
2020 Rating: ★ ★ ★/Recommended

Cazadores Reposado Tequila 40% abv, $37.
    Color is a faint pewter/brut champagne; excellent cleanliness. Aromatics are as faint and amorphous as the appearance, offering paper-thin scents of lemon rind, savory, and metal; later sniffs detect dry stone, cement, grain wafer, and paraffin but nothing more of any agave-influenced substance. Entry is zesty, a tad on the sweeter side of the dry/sweet scale, and prickly on the tongue; midpalate echoes the entry down to the prickliness, but there's so little agave presence here that I wonder why this exists at all. Finishes cleanly, crisply, but blandly, almost as though this is agave-based vodka.
2020 Rating: ★/Not Recommended

Cenote Añejo Azul Tequila 40% abv, $50.
Rich marigold/gamboge color; flawless clarity. Similar to the Blanco reviewed below, the initial whiffs are of heavily smoked agave so I move on; secondary inhalations after allowing for more aeration find salted fish, sea breeze, green pepper, and smoldering campfire fragrances. Entry offers deep tastes of freshly ground black pepper, creosote, seared beef, and little more pertaining to quality tequila; midpalate echoes the woeful entry stage. I'm done here. This is a step below garbage.
2019 Rating: ★/Not Recommended

Cenote Blanco Azul Tequila 40% abv, $37.
This tequila owns a hint of tarnished-silver tinting and is dazzlingly clean. Up front, I pick up vivid aromas of roasted agave, autumnal burning leaves, and chimney soot, as well as cooked vegetables, such as kale, artichoke, and eggplant; a second round of sniffing unearths deeper fragrances including pine tar, cedar forest, dill pickle, and olive brine; there's a lot happening here aromatically. Entry is richly textured, semisweet, quite smoky and tobacco ash–like, and carries a foundational flavor of charred agave hearts; midpalate continues the smoke-a-thon perhaps a bit longer than necessary as this feature now affects the latter taste stage to the point where I lop off a rating star for the smoke intensity. Finishes a little too creosote-like, and therefore off balance, in my view. The ham-fisted smoke/burnt character, which builds in the mouth, goes too far and thus I can't recommend it.
2019 Rating: ★★/Not Recommended

Cenote Reposado Azul Tequila 40% abv, $43.
Pale fourteen-karat-gold color; excellent purity. Okay, I recognize this seared, burnt match aroma immediately as a sibling of the Cenote Blanco, and I'm therefore thinking that I'm biased against it from the outset; further inhalations after more air contact find only minor mitigation of the cigarette ash, woodsmoke, charred agave heart character; I move on. Entry shows some agave pepperiness at the start, which negates at least some of the charcoal briquette/wildfire aspect; midpalate shows traces of black pepper, cooking oil, and limestone flavors that point to agave, so that's somewhat of a plus. Concludes peppery, gently sweet, slightly spicy from the oak influence (cinnamon), and just flat and uninteresting overall. It suffers what so many tequilas from 2015 forward suffer from: dullness and a lack of agave personality.
2019 Rating: ★★/Not Recommended

Chamucos Añejo Tequila 40% abv, $60.
Saffron color; shimmering purity. The first nosings are a bit muted, except for distant echoes of bacon fat, the ever-present black pepper, marjoram, and mustard seed; next-phase sniffing after more air contact locates incongruous aromatic hints of wet hay, wet grass, damp forest, and peanut oil. Entry is surprisingly delicate and understated, as the flavor profile features tastes of buttermilk, salted butter, Crisco, and Parma ham; midpalate turns away from the fat-driven tastes of the entry and goes in the vegetal/herbaceous direction in the forms of agave, allspice, mace, dill, green tea, uncured tobacco, and star anise. Concludes medium long, a touch woody/oaky/resiny, and off-dry.
2018 Rating: ★★★/Recommended

Chamucos Reposado Tequila 40% abv, $56.

Green-tea color; immaculate clarity. Immediate odors following the pour are highly vegetal and legume-like, meaning specifically, akin to scallion/spring onion, leek, soybean, pinto bean, mashed potato, and baked brussels sprouts; secondary inhalations discover notes of ground black peppercorn, crushed red pepper, gentian, and agave frond. Entry is pleasantly peppery, off-dry, moderately oily in texture, and olive brine–like; midpalate is oily, acutely vegetal, green, off-dry, acidic, and therefore fresh and loaded with agave-leaning flavors of dill, anise, licorice, chamomile, green tea, and brine. Ends up dry, tangy, and properly agave-like. Hurray, a reposado in 2018 that honors its base material, agave, by actually tasting like it. Had the in-mouth phases showed more textural complexity, this would have easily scored a fourth rating star.
2018 Rating: ★ ★ ★/Recommended

Chinaco Añejo Tequila 40% abv, $70.

Straw-yellow; fair to good clarity. I immediately pick up featherweight scents of oak resins/sap, as well as tree bark and sawdust; secondary inhalations identify tight-as-a-drum and ethereal fragrances of bay leaf and mustard seed. Entry is as contained and understated as the bouquet, emitting only a handful of parched flavors, in particular, limestone, green tea, chive, and marjoram; midpalate reinforces the entry findings, expanding them only to include gentian and black pepper. Concludes medium long, dry as the desert, and in the final burst of flavor shows a fennel-like taste that could only be derived from blue agave. Reminds me of blue agave tequilas dated from the late 1980s and early 1990s when they had authenticity and genuine character.
2019 Rating: ★ ★ ★ ★/Highly Recommended

Chinaco Blanco Tequila 40% abv, $40.

Crystalline appearance; free of sediment. Why do so embarrassingly few contemporary 100 percent blue agave blanco/silver/platinum tequilas smell as authentic as this crisp, highly vegetal, acidic, earthy, rustic, and dill-like fragrance? Second nosing passes after more aeration discover even more true agave aromas, especially green olive, sagebrush, bay leaf, and zesty dill pickle. Entry is supple in texture, flinty dry, vegetal, and dill-like; midpalate is the pinnacle moment for this blanco as all the flavor components merge into a singular taste that is deeply mineral-like, dry as the Mojave, and splendidly peppery. Flashes nuances of green chili pepper and fish oil in the piquant finish. I reviewed this groundbreaking tequila in the first *Kindred Spirits* in 1997 and rated it three stars. It deserves an upgrade to four stars.
2019 Rating: ★ ★ ★ ★/Highly Recommended

Chinaco Reposado Tequila 40% abv, $57.

Citrine; minor, inconsequential particles of sediment seen. There's a pleasing roundness to this opening aroma that is reminiscent of green-leaf tobacco, citrus rind, tangerine, and lychee; more expressive fragrances develop after additional air contact in the forms of freshly harvested hay, pistachio, lemon curd, and dill. Entry is squeaky tart, deeply earthy and stone-like, fresh and acidic, peppery and astringent; midpalate echoes all the entry

impressions, adding only a saltine cracker back note that's barely perceptible. Aftertaste is ashy, almost sooty, tangy, and as lean and lanky as a long-distance runner.
2019 Rating: ★ ★ ★/Recommended

Chinaco Ultra Cristalino Tequila 40% abv, $72.
The appearance is free of sediment and crystalline. Initially, I like the dry, leathery, vegetal aroma that's crisp, acidic, and showing a paper-thin veil of agave-driven dill spiciness and artichoke heart; further air contact releases more fragrance in the straightforward, if complex, forms of gentian, eucalyptus, and verbena. Entry is dry, salty, green vegetable–like (asparagus, spinach), high in acid, and therefore crisply clean; midpalate is the pinnacle moment for this aged then filtered tequila as the taste profile unfolds on the tongue in pleasing waves of roasted agave, peanut oil, dill pickle, and hard cheese. Aftertaste is deep and long as the roasted agave and dill pickle aspects carry the message forward with style and balance.
2019 Rating: ★ ★ ★ ★/Highly Recommended

Cierto Private Collection Añejo Tequila 40% abv, $350.
Cierto Tequila is only available to Club Cierto members. This color is closest to straw-yellow; impeccably clean. Up front, there are pleasant aromas of dill, anise, fennel, green onion, and sage; later sniffs after more air contact detect more fragrances, such as paraffin, textile fiber, lead pencil, honey, and cocoa bean. Entry offers complex, chocolatey flavors of candy bar, carob, brown butter, bacon fat, almond paste, and tree sap/maple; midpalate flavors include all of the entry stage findings, plus caramelized onion, clove, and vanilla bean. Finishes very long, buttery/creamy, oaky, and bark-like.
2019 Rating: ★ ★ ★ ★/Highly Recommended

Cierto Private Collection Blanco Tequila 40% abv, $175.
There's a slightly pewter-like tint to this blanco; flawless purity. First nosing passes pick up grassy, vegetal, herbal aromas reminiscent of thyme, sage, dry leaves, chamomile, dill, and pickle brine; secondary inhalations are more zesty and citrusy, as scents of lemon peel, kiwi, and pineapple abound. Entry is round, viscous in texture, and delicately sweet with agave sugars; midpalate is tasty and peppery, as the piquancy of freshly ground black pepper rises to the top of the flavor menu. The viscosity first noted in the entry stage plays a major role in the silky finish, as it overtakes the flavor profile a little too much for its own good. Still recommendable, however, if overpriced.
2019 Rating: ★ ★ ★/Recommended

Cierto Private Collection Extra Añejo Tequila 40% abv, $450.
Color is mustard/saffron; immaculately clear and free of sediment. First aromatic impressions are of tree bark, oak plank, wood chips, and pine/cedar; secondary inhalations after more aeration encounter spicier aspects, mostly nutmeg, cinnamon, and mace. Entry, at least, introduces a strong, pungent agave saltiness that completely enlivens the sensory experience as it accentuates the oak impact and the herbal aspects; midpalate reflects the

entry stage, adding delicate flavors of cocoa powder, carob, and caramel. Aftertaste is splendidly integrated, mellow, and like toasted marshmallow.
2019 Rating: ★★★★/Highly Recommended

Cierto Private Collection Reposado Tequila 40% abv, $250.
The pale, tarnished-silver color is similar to that of brut champagne; excellent clarity. I like the opening aroma that's tart, mildly zesty, crisp with acidity, and vegetal; further aeration stimulates fragrances of citrus peel, salted butter, tangerine, green tea, and bay leaf. Entry is quite mineral-like and flinty, as the earthiness overshadows the fruit, fats, and tea-like aspects to the detriment of the taste profile; midpalate recovers somewhat as the stone-like component fades, leaving space for the citrus fruit, walnut, hazelnut, and green pepper flavors to impress. Ends dry, astringent, clean, and just slightly oaky.
2019 Rating: ★★★/Recommended

Corazon Añejo Tequila 40% abv, $41.
Saffron color; superb purity. Offers subtle nuances of oak barrel char, vanilla bean, carob, and clove in the initial sniffs after the pour—in other words, the first aromas are totally influenced by the wood; more aeration allows for minuscule, overwhelmed scents of agave syrup and dill, but the headliner here is the charred oak barrel. Entry is mildly pleasant, a little bit piquant with agave fiber flavor; midpalate shows delicate touches of black pepper and salty olive brine, but there's no mistaking what's in charge, and that's the oak impact. The aftertaste is too resiny, waxy, and textile-like for my liking. The agave base is lost among the dense forest of oak trees, a present-day common failing of older tequilas.
2018 Rating: ★★/Not Recommended

Corazon Blanco Tequila 40% abv, $26.
Clear as rainwater; sediment-free. Whoa, there's a curious, atypical aromatic nod to tobacco leaf, tomato vine, eucalyptus, and camphor in the initial whiffs after the pour; secondary scents include candle wax, green tea, orange peel, almond, and green olive. Entry is round in texture, gently sweet, and nearly succulent, but also savory and herbaceous; midpalate highlights the herbal aspect, especially the parsley, bay leaf, and lemongrass. Finish is nimble, brief, drier than the midpalate, and keenly peppery. Deceptively intense.
2020 Rating: ★★★★/Highly Recommended

Corazon Reposado Tequila 40% abv, $26.
Khaki color; flawlessly pure. Opening nose is crisp with crackling acidity and vibrant with peppery, sagebrush-like aromas that are harmonious and clean; later sniffs pick up light touches of leather, candle wax, campfire embers, leeks, and burning leaves. Entry is sleek, intensely herbal (predominantly dill and bay leaf), acidic, and therefore clean and zesty; midpalate is dense, spirity, brisk, razor edged, desert dry, and waxy. Aftertaste integrates all of the above notables from the entry and midpalate into a creamy, viscous finish that's silky, a little smoky, and wholly satisfying.
2018 Rating: ★★★★/Highly Recommended

Década Silver Tequila 40% abv, $46.
Clean as rainwater; void of any color. Opening nosings offer pleasantly earthy (moss, mushroom, dry soil) and spicy (black pepper, sage, parsley, thyme) fragrances in equal measure, all the while maintaining the integrity of the agave; secondary whiffs pick up mildly salty nuances of baked pineapple, dill pickle, pickle brine, and cedar bark as the agave element fades a little. Entry is metallic, flinty, totally stone dry, and even a touch coin-like; midpalate primarily highlights the flint aspect, as the taste remains aridly dry and narrowly focused on dried earth component. Aftertaste is astringent, high in acidity, cleansing (a plus), keenly peppery (pasilla or serrano). There are enough positive elements (dry, clean, spicy) in this silver tequila to recommend it, but I felt that perhaps a measure of the natural agave funk had been processed out, and therefore what could have been a four star silver is, in reality, a three star silver.
2017 Rating: ★ ★ ★/Recommended

DeLeón Añejo Tequila 40% abv, $70.
Ochre/topaz color; pristine purity. This opening aroma is delicately vegetal, grassy, woody, tobacco-like, slightly leathery; additional air contact brings out an end-of-summer, exhausted flower garden/spice garden aroma that's slightly sweet, earthy, and buttery. Entry is heavily wood impacted, creamy, nutty, nougat-like, peanut butter–like, marginally salty; midpalate is resiny, off-dry, delicately grassy, semisweet, a bit honeyed through the classy aftertaste. I found more agave presence in this edition than in the reposado, strangely enough, and for that I was grateful. Hence the fourth star.
2015 Rating: ★ ★ ★ ★/Highly Recommended

DeLeón Extra Añejo Tequila 51% abv, $350.
Wheat-field/champagne color is curiously the lightest of the four; flawless clarity. First aromatics speak of cereal husk, kernels, unpopped popcorn, parchment, but no agave to pinpoint or identify as the base material; secondary whiffs pick up dried flowers, damp soil, earthy aromas that once again don't clearly point to agave. Entry is raw, harsh, aggressive, metallic, fiery, but it does showcase some agave aspect, which is welcome; midpalate settles down in the heat department as the grassy, vegetal flavor profile takes charge, but there is still a lingering flavor of metal coin that distracts one's attention away from the agave deep into the awkward, tongue-on-stone finish. An expensive mess.
2015 Rating: ★/Not Recommended

DeLeón Leona Añejo Tequila 40% abv, $850.
Pretty copper/burnt-orange color; sediment-free clarity. Opening aromas include chrysanthemum, airplane glue, roasted peppers, pipe tobacco; secondary sniffs pick up supplementary aromas of vegetable oil, candle wax, tree sap. Entry is sappy, maple-like, caramel-like, bittersweet; midpalate showcases the wood influence more than the agave, and that's where I lose interest as the flavor profile turns beany, chocolatey, over-roasted, like BBQ sauce, tomato paste. There's no sense of agave in this spirit, and that's what so blatantly wrong with it. More like an unsophisticated brandy than an oak-aged tequila.
2015 Rating: ★ ★/Not Recommended

DeLeón Reposado Tequila 40% abv, $65.

Amber/sepia color; excellent clarity. I get lots of bittersweet cocoa, nougat, black pepper nuances in the initial nosing passes with an underlying agave/vegetal aspect that maintains the direction; second inhalations unearth baked bread, dough, vanilla biscuits. Entry is toasty, nutty, semisweet, beany, adequately spicy, but along the way the agave seems lost; midpalate is rich, chewy, creamy, nearly viscous, but while it is nice tasting, to be clear, the agave has clearly been pushed to the side in favor of oak impact. Finishes very spicy (all baking spices such as cinnamon, vanilla, clove), oaky, and tree-sap sweet. Look, this tequila as a drinkable beverage is good as evidenced by the score on how it smells and tastes, but this is also a tequila that more resembles a brandy than what I think of as 100 percent agave tequila.

2015 Rating: ★ ★ ★/Recommended

Don Julio 1942 Añejo Tequila 40% abv, $125.

Attractive yellow/gold color; superb purity. Initial sniffs offer highlights of marshmallow, vanilla, oak, and sawdust; secondary sniffs following seven minutes of aeration feature the vanilla aspect as well as leafy/floral notes not noticed in the first inhalations; a smashingly lovely and elegant bouquet. Entry is firm, delightfully oily, mildly peppery, and oaky sweet; midpalate is elegant, slightly toasty, medium viscous, herbal, and delicate sweet. Finishes softly, with a sweet oak ending. Exquisitely tasty.

2018 Rating: ★ ★ ★ ★ ★/Highest Recommendation

Don Julio 70 Añejo Tequila 40% abv, $70.

Crystal clear; sediment-free clarity. For an añejo, it's surprisingly neutral in the opening whiffs, except for a peanut butter quality and maybe a bit of dill; later inhalations after another seven minutes of air contact don't produce many new results, so I move on. Entry is solid, oaky, vanilla-like, and gently sweet and creamy; midpalate is very firm in structure, more dry than sweet, slightly toasted, and rich. Ends on a cake frosting–like sweet note, then it turns herbal. I was prepared to give three stars, then the midpalate and finish pushed me to four. Not quite sure, though, why a clear añejo is necessary.

2015 Rating: ★ ★ ★ ★/Highly Recommended

Don Julio Añejo Tequila 40% abv, $55.

Straw-yellow color; ideal purity. There's an intriguing creosote aspect to the opening aroma that's almost but not quite smoky/toasted; aeration helps to bring out a roasted pineapple scent, but that's about the limit for this bouquet. Entry is dusty dry, bittersweet, and slightly metallic as the vegetal/herbal aspect ascends; midpalate is slate-like, keenly peppery, and a little short. Concludes on an herbal note of sage and bay leaf. Pleasing.

2015 Rating: ★ ★ ★/Recommended

Don Julio Blanco Tequila 40% abv, $47.

Colorless; immaculately clean and free of sediment. Immediately I smell notes of pickle brine, green olive, prickly pear, vinyl, and geranium; secondary whiffs pick up added fragrances of clay, dry sand, pencil eraser, cabbage, and mustard seed. Entry is drier than I thought it would be, slightly toasty, pleasingly herbal (sage, bay leaf), salty, waxy in texture,

and piquant; midpalate echoes the entry impressions, adding green peppercorn, green tea, and eucalyptus. Concludes medium long, silky in the mouth, dry as the Sahara, and peppery. Have always thought of this as a 100 percent de agave blanco benchmark, and while I'm reducing its rating by one star from my review in *Kindred Spirits 2*, I still think that in the "diffuser era" it is a safe bet for tequila purists.
2020 Rating: ★ ★ ★ ★/Highly Recommended

Don Julio REAL Añejo Tequila 40% abv, $350.
Pale straw/fourteen-karat-gold color; a shocking amount of floating detritus seen—not good. The opening nose is surprisingly flat, showing just a touch of herbaceous dryness; eight more minutes of air contact open up only minor scents of dill and sage, but no wood to speak of. Entry is lush, intensely dill-like, sweeter than I recall, and moderately oily; midpalate is peppery, vegetal, and mildly spicy. Don't know what's happened here but this is not the product I reviewed in 2007. Must be, I hope, a bad bottle. The sediment was actually resting on my tongue in a rather disturbing fashion.
2017 Rating: ★ ★/Not Recommended

Don Julio Reposado Tequila 40% abv, $50.
Pale-yellow/tarnished-silver color; impeccable clarity. Lovely smells of cookie batter/cake batter, salted butter, and bay leaf waft up from the glass in the first nosings after the pour; the buttery aspect builds into butterscotch, light caramel, saltwater taffy, and lightly toasted marshmallow in the latter stages. Entry is tight, firm, peppery, and dried herb–like (sage); midpalate is biscuity, spicy, and clean, with a touch of fennel. Ends on a bitter note that's a trace oaky.
2017 Rating: ★ ★ ★ ★/Highly Recommended

Don Sergio Añejo Tequila 40% abv, $25.
Attractive gamboge/gold color; sediment-free. This peculiar first aroma reminds me more of maple syrup or tree sap than agave distillate; after more time in glass, the aroma turns sweeter and more confectionery in its simplicity. Entry is too sweet for its own good as the agave is lost among the wood influences; midpalate is the same—drinkable but not distinctly agave-like.
2016 Rating: ★ ★/Not Recommended

Don Sergio Blanco Tequila 40% abv, $20.
Superb clarity; translucent. Opening whiffs detect sweet agave and black pepper notes that are clearly defined and natural; seven minutes more of air contact release pleasant vegetal/herbal scents, including dill, sage, and road tar. Entry is properly spicy, even zesty, as the black pepper aspect takes charge of the flavor profile; midpalate features baked agave notes that are bittersweet. Finishes medium long, intensely spicy, and astringent.
2016 Rating: ★ ★ ★/Recommended

Don Sergio Reposado Tequila 40% abv, $22.
Tarnished-silver/flax color; unblemished purity. Delicate aromas of marshmallow,

brown sugar, and coriander highlight the early nosings; following six more minutes of aeration, the aroma turns into a supple, integrated bouquet of merit, featuring gentle scents of bay leaf, cocoa, and oaky vanilla. Entry is alluringly tangy and beany; midpalate highlights the wood resin/oakiness as well as the vanilla aspect. Ends sweet, piney.
2016 Rating: ★ ★ ★/Recommended

el Jimador Blanco Tequila 40% abv, $20.
Pewter/silver tint; transparent, colorless. Up front, I pick up paper-like scents of wax paper, parchment, beeswax; later sniffs encounter more botanical and earthy fragrances, including wet soil, forest floor, moss, cucumber. Entry is delicately spicy, showing traces of sage, dill; midpalate is medium long, lean in texture, peppery, dry, and showing a faint hint of saltiness. Ends clean, crisp, vegetal, off-dry.
2014 Rating: ★ ★ ★/Recommended

el Jimador Reposado Tequila 40% abv, $25.
Cream color; superb clarity. First inhalations detect scents of rubber band, metal, sage, and black peppercorn; secondary whiffs pick up wafts of egg white, meringue, and almond paste; this is a simple bouquet. Entry is intriguingly minty and herb garden–like, evoking tastes of thyme, agave syrup, lavender, and lemongrass; midpalate is tightly wound, uncomplicated, off-dry, and vegetal. Finishes medium long, silky, and drier than the midpalate. First rated in 2000 and scored three stars. I still like this highly affordable reposado and, like twenty years ago, believe that its best application is in Margaritas. Remains a very good value.
2020 Rating: ★ ★ ★/Recommended

El Padrino de Mi Tierra Añejo Tequila 40% abv, $27.
Bright amber color; sediment-free. Initial whiffs detect wildly out-of-place aromas of Naugahyde (artificial leather), dried-out pine needles, and plastic; secondary inhalations are just as horrible as the first round. Entry is plastic-like, cleaning fluid–like, and just disgusting; I don't even bother with the midpalate and finish. The worst line of 100 percent agave tequila in the universe.
2017 Rating: ★/Not Recommended

El Padrino de Mi Tierra Blanco Tequila 40% abv, $22.
Pristine, flawless, totally translucent appearance. I pick up strong fragrances of lead pencil, shale, tar, soybean, lanolin, oyster shell, seaweed, and beeswax, a peculiar mix; emerging as the winner after six minutes of additional air contact is the lanolin, which is disappointing. Entry lacks a clear agave direction; midpalate features beeswax and industrial cleaning fluid flavors, which are unworthy of and unaligned with the contemporary standard of 100 percent agave spirits.
2017 Rating: ★/Not Recommended

El Padrino de Mi Tierra Reposado Tequila 40% abv, $24.
Flax/straw-yellow color; superb purity. All I smell in this opening aroma is newly tanned leather and plastic; following another seven minutes of aeration, the aroma comes

off sweet and stony/minerally. Entry is simplistic, bittersweet, and shows a strained touch of agave-like spice; midpalate is thin, hollow, lacking depth, and just plain miserable. I'm starting to hate my job.

2017 Rating: ★/Not Recommended

El Pintor Joven Tequila 41% abv, $100.

The tarnished-silver/ecru color is bright and sediment-free. I like the peppery, salty, seaweed-like, vegetal, cooking oil–like opening aromas that scream "AGAVE!!!"; following another seven to eight minutes of air contact, the aroma opens up even more, now including fragrant scents of dill, pickle brine, sage, sea salt, grilled pineapple, and dry cement. Entry is chalky, stony, pungent, and slightly prickly, but overall pleasantly herbal and vegetal; midpalate softens some of the flavor components, especially the saltiness as that aspect turns more fat-like and supple—now the flavor profile highlights the pepperiness and herbaceous qualities, making it easily recommendable. I do not think that this is a landmark for joven tequila, though it's genial and correct. As it is, I'd say that it rides the fence that divides three and four star quality. That said, I see real quality here.

2017 Rating: ★ ★ ★/Recommended

El Tesoro de Don Felipe 80th Anniversary Edition 8 Year Old Extra Añejo Tequila 41.5% abv, $200.

Buff/citrine color; perfect purity. First inhalations detect agave-fueled fragrances of dill, olive brine, verbena, green olive, onionskin, tomato vine, and salt that make my day as a veteran spirits reviewer who loves real tequila, not the insipid present-day versions; after more aeration, the aroma starts to display the effects of wood aging by emitting scents of tobacco leaf, eucalyptus, oak resin, terra-cotta, and sagebrush. Entry is intensely sap-like and resiny, yet it hasn't lost its agave connection at all as the background tastes include candle wax/paraffin, fennel, bay leaf, and lime juice; midpalate highlights the flavors identified as the entry background, especially the fennel, lime juice, tobacco leaf, and bay leaf. Concludes pleasingly agave forward in a briny, deeply herbal, green olive, lightly smoked manner. What's so impressive about this ancient (by tequila standards) extra añejo tequila is that even though it spent eight years in the barrel, it hasn't lost any of its core agave personality. A fitting tribute to El Tesoro de Don Felipe.

2018 Rating: ★ ★ ★ ★ ★/Highest Recommendation

El Tesoro Extra Añejo Tequila 40% abv, $100.

Color is beige/vanilla; flawless purity. Whoa, the opening fragrance is rife with autumn garden scents, from sunflower to dill to minerals to gourds; more aeration stimulates a whole additional menu of aromas, including honey, walnut, green olive, wet sand, sea salt, salted almond, and candle wax. Entry showcases the oak barrel influence in resiny, nutty flavors of fresh honey, salted butter, almond paste/nougat, and green chili pepper; midpalate stage mirrors the entry, and it's here that the textural viscosity comes into play as the saltiness admired in the entry stage turns into a dominant feature, similar to salted caramel. Finishes long, deeply agave-like in its vegetal element, and zesty.

2019 Rating: ★ ★ ★ ★/Highly Recommended

El Tesoro Reposado Tequila 40% abv, $50.

The color is a brut champagne–like lemon-chiffon yellow; superb purity. Opening aroma is all about green pepper and chili pepper, with side notes of almond, walnut, and terra-cotta/clay; secondary sniffs pick up traces of rubber pencil eraser, fennel, anise, parsley, and savory, but it's the cleanness of the bouquet that sets it apart. Entry shows tastes of pickle brine, charcoal, dill, sage, and tomatillo; midpalate displays a glorious menu of lean, tightly wound flavors, especially tobacco leaf, scallion, mustard seed, and chamomile. Finishes medium long, dry as a bone, and vividly carob-like.

2019 Rating: ★ ★ ★ ★/Highly Recommended

Espanita Blanco Tequila 40% abv, $28.

Silvery, but in fact colorless; impeccably pure. First off, I detect dry, crushed stone/gravel notes that are mineral-like, but the aroma profile changes quickly into a more herbal/spicy bouquet that highlights scents of dill, bay leaf, black peppercorn; secondary inhalations after more aeration pick up fragrances of dried herbs (dill, bay leaf again), but also light touches of lemongrass and sage. Entry flavor is tongue-on-stone dry, deeply peppery, and even a little prickly on the tongue due primarily to the herbaceous zestiness as much as the abv; midpalate sees the herbal aspect dominate as tastes of black peppercorn, dill, spruce, and agave fibers thrive in the medium-bodied, slightly oily texture. Finishes long, peppery, herbal, dry, with a late hint of agave syrup sweetness.

2016 Rating: ★ ★ ★ ★/Highly Recommended

Espanita Reposado Tequila 40% abv, $30.

Pretty color of bisque/electrum/Manzanilla sherry; low degree of sediment seen but inconsequential. There's an immediate thrust of egg white/egg cream aroma that's more spicy than elemental or dairy-like or herbal, but overall the initial impression is of a mildly succulent, slightly oily, creamy aroma; secondary whiffs pick up a higher degree of spiced butter (like jalapeño mixed with salted butter) fragrance that's mildly zesty, saline, and peppery. Entry is notably creamy, with attractive tastes of walnut, cacao, kola nut, and pine; midpalate stage features a wealth of flavors, such as sassafras, tobacco, hyssop that mingle nicely with the green vegetal agave. Aftertaste is medium long, drier than the midpalate, and even a touch smoky. What's so attractive about this reposado is that it's both zesty/feral and elegant/classic in equal measure, and that's the key to the puzzle. Succulent and savory, as it proves that agave accepts wood aging gracefully, but for the wood aging to be effective, it has to allow the agave to be a little bit untidy, snarly, and robust.

2016 Rating: ★ ★ ★ ★ ★/Highest Recommendation

Espolón Añejo Tequila 40% abv, $32.

Mustard color; pristinely clean. Here in the first inhalations I pick up salad bar–like aromas of vinegar, bibb lettuce, cucumber, scallions, and green pepper but nothing even remotely resembling agave; more time in the glass helps a little as the aroma turns more to textile fiber/hemp/cotton and green vegetables such as asparagus, as I at last find some agave presence. Entry is salty, resiny, eucalyptus-like, and tobacco leaf–like; midpalate goes the resiny/pine tar route as the astringency of the flavor profile turns radically dry and acidic. I taste pine in the finish as though I'm gnawing on a two-by-four, and that for me places this

stubbornly oaky añejo in the "Not Recommended" zone. Tequila producers have lost their minds with their insistence on over-oaking añejo tequila, and I'm fed up with it.
2018 Rating: ★★/Not Recommended

Espolón Blanco Tequila 40% abv, $26.
Rainwater clean and limpid. First aromatic impressions are of hemp, campfire embers, dill, sweet pickle relish; with further aeration, the bouquet takes a drier turn as the dill and textile fiber notes take charge, along with roasted agave, light sulfur, and salt. Entry is bitter, metallic, dry roasted, and like pickle brine; midpalate shows a touch of spirit-driven heat and prickliness, along with a slightly sweeter turn as the bitter flavor advances into the finish. I kept wanting to raise the score to four stars, but the bitterness noted in the entry, midpalate, and aftertaste prevented me.
2016 Rating: ★★★/Recommended

Espolón Reposado Tequila (Mexico) 40% abv, $26.
Pretty, light muscadet–like yellow/flax color; superb purity. Ripe, delicately sweet, almost pineapple-like opening fragrances are slightly peppery (green pepper), saline, dill-like; secondary scents include peanut butter, deep agave, light vanilla bean. Entry is peppery, salty, vegetal, intense; midpalate brings out the agave aspect well, but there's a sense of hollowness in the core flavor and viscosity that bring me back to a three star rating, as was given way back in 2001.
2016 Rating: ★★★/Recommended

Familia Camarena Reposado Tequila 40% abv, $20.
Pale-yellow/ecru color; excellent clarity. The two months in wood brings about a pine resin quality that reminds me of pickle brine in the opening aromatic excursion; following another few minutes of air contact, the bouquet fades a bit too much for me, becoming pulpy and oily. Entry is gently sweet and resiny but is a little fat; midpalate offers flavors that bring to mind jalapeño pepper, salt, black pepper, and milk chocolate. The flabbiness noted at entry and then again noticeable in the finish are bothersome to me and weren't present when I reviewed this tequila back in 2010.
2018 Rating: ★★/Not Recommended

Familia Camarena Silver Tequila 40% abv, $20.
Clear as rainwater; sediment-free. First nosings uncover proper agave scents of dill, brine, saltine cracker, and earth/limestone; another five minutes in the glass stimulates aromas of lead pencil, anise, black pepper, sage, and thyme. Entry features dusty-dry tastes of black peppercorn and dill; midpalate turns marginally sweeter as a pleasing flavor of milk chocolate takes charge but not so dominantly that the agave zestiness of the brine and dill are lost. Concludes spirity, medium sweet, balanced, and chewy. Good value for the money overall, but I feel that this brand has slipped.
2018 Rating: ★★★/Recommended

Fortaleza Blanco Tequila 40% abv, $48.
Pristine clarity; silvery appearance. Up-front aromas include agave syrup, grilled green

chili peppers, lead pencil, terra-cotta, and shallot; later sniffs expand the olfactory scope, adding verbena, lemongrass, parsley, and green melon; a lovely, expressive bouquet. Entry is keenly bittersweet, deeply vegetal, and vivid with tastes of agave syrup (still!), carbon/charcoal, seared meat, grilled pineapple, cabbage, and minerals; midpalate echoes much of the entry findings, throwing in traces of black pepper and carob, but the big story at this juncture is the creamy, viscous texture that coddles the palate. Aftertaste is notable for its elegance, rich feel, and its moderately spiced and zesty parting flavor. A rustic style that is straight out of the 1980s when 100 percent agave tequilas were bountiful and true in their reflection of agave, not mere paper-thin suggestions as so many are these days.
2019 Rating: ★ ★ ★ ★/Highest Recommendation

Fortaleza Reposado Tequila 40% abv, $58.
Crystalline purity; vanilla-extract color. This opening nose is hidden a bit behind a wax-like top-note scent, but if you stick with it and give it more time to aerate, you'll be rewarded with a biscuity, vegetal, delicately sweet aroma that's slightly spicy; secondary passes pick up deeper fragrances, including lemon peel, lemongrass, mustard seed, and clove. Entry is swank, elegant, oily in texture, vibrant with green vegetable tastes as well as egg cream and vanilla flavors; midpalate offers a sturdy, opulent flavor menu that's filled with tastes of charred meat, egg cream, vanilla wafer, and toasted bread. Finishes long, lush in texture, mineral-like/flinty, medium sweet, and judiciously honeyed.
2019 Rating: ★ ★ ★ ★/Highest Recommendation

Fuenteseca Reserva 12 Year Old Extra Añejo Azul Tequila 45% abv, $220.
Amber/topaz color; pristine clarity. Initial inhalations detect butcher's wax paper, vegetable oil, textile fiber; secondary whiffs pick up little that resembles agave, but instead encounter tree sap, resin, sawdust, wood plank. Entry is zesty, piquant, black pepper–like, dry to bitter, oily; midpalate is tobacco-like, sweeter than the entry, slightly caramel-like, loaded with vanilla bean, delicately smoky, even a touch salty. Lots happening here from entry point through woody/resiny aftertaste, and it is the heavy wood aspect that after a promising entry stage knocks it to three from a potential four star rating. There are good, tasty elements here, but the oak dominance obliterates any trace of agave. Price is highly prohibitive, though. Age also begs the question: Is this tequila? For half the price I can buy five star Martell Cordon Bleu Cognac.
2016 Rating: ★ ★ ★/Recommended

Fuenteseca Reserva 18 Year Old Extra Añejo Azul Tequila 43% abv, $420.
Maize/eighteen-karat-gold color; flawless purity. I smell creamy cookie dough, slightly honeyed scents in the opening whiffs; later inhalations discover oaky vanilla, new leather, canvas, mild baking spices. Entry is delicately sweet, almost sherried, moderately salty, pruny; midpalate builds well on the dried-fruit entry, introducing elements of pine tar, sap, cola nut. Finishes long, honey sweet, spicy, piquant.
2016 Rating: ★ ★ ★ ★/Highly Recommended

Fuenteseca Reserva 9 Year Old Extra Añejo Azul Tequila 43% abv, $146.
Gold/straw color; excellent purity. Smells up front of pine needle/cedar, cigar tobacco,

foundry metal; secondary whiffs feature pine forest, tropical fruit, wet vegetation. Entry is clean, sugary, confection shop–like, vaguely spicy; midpalate shows far more spice and oaky vanilla than agave flavor but is savory, delicately sweet, silky, refined right through the aftertaste.
2016 Rating: ★★★★/Highly Recommended

Gran Centenario Añejo Tequila 40% abv, $38.
   Color is old gold/mustard; superb clarity. There is some agave-driven pickle juice/brine that is noticeable in the first nosing passes, in addition to herbal scents, especially sagebrush and parsley; secondary inhalations pick up an agave syrup–like sweetness that's pleasing and plump. Entry picks up where the last inhalations left off, featuring a delightfully sweet and sappy first flavor that's equally influenced between the oak barrels and the roasted agave; midpalate highlights the oak barrel features now more than the agave, which is why I held back on a fourth rating star. Ends up plump, silky, a touch prickly, and nut-butter sweet.
2020 Rating: ★★★/Recommended

Gran Centenario Reposado Tequila 40% abv, $32.
   Green/gold color; sediment-free appearance. Right off the crack of the bat I pick up delicate, low-volume aromas of sea salt, verbena, lemongrass, and pickle barrel; next whiffs after more aeration encounter equally sedate fragrances, but this time they include green tobacco, green tea, green onion, green pepper, and lead pencil. Entry is polite, slightly nutty, dry as the Mojave Desert, and a touch "green," as in green vegetables; midpalate stage features a pleasant touch of oaky vanilla, as well as background flavors of black peppercorn and carob. Rated this tequila four stars in *Kindred Spirits 2* back in 2008, but like other tequilas, I'm knocking this reposado down one peg on the five-step ladder because it doesn't display the same agave intensity as in yesteryear.
2020 Rating: ★★★/Recommended

Herradura 2016 Port Cask Finished Reserva Reposado Tequila 40% abv, $90.
   Pretty goldenrod/harvest gold color; impeccably pure. Wow, there's a dill-a-thon happening in the opening aromatic moments as the briny, lightly salted, and comely fragrance reminds me of Polish dill pickles floating in a barrel; later inhalations pick up earthy notes of parsley, clay/terra-cotta, scallion/spring onion, and a barely perceptible trace of raisins. Entry owns a solid structure of crisp agave herbaceousness that enfolds supporting flavors of black raisins, bacon fat, carob, and walnut; midpalate features the resiny quality of the oak influence accompanied by a toasted agave heart oiliness that is seductive and satiny smooth. Ends up elegant, stately, deeply oaky, with subtle hints of dried fruits, in particular quince, yellow plum, white grapes. An experiment that works.
2018 Rating: ★★★★/Highly Recommended

Herradura Añejo Tequila 40% abv, $52.
   Aged twenty-five months. Flax color; excellent purity. Opening impressions include lemony/citrusy and quince-like notes that form the core aroma; more air contact stimulates fragrances of parsley, drying leaves, green tobacco, eucalyptus, and honeysuckle. Entry displays flashy flavors of sea-salt-sprinkled caramels, honey, agave syrup, nougat, and latte;

midpalate echoes all the entry impressions, adding nuances of toffee, malted milk ball candy, and prickly pear juice. Finishes semisweet, salty, and lush in texture, with a bite of black pepper. This was rated five stars in *Kindred Spirits 2*, but I believe this version must come in at four stars due to the obscuring of the agave a bit too much in the flavor department. That said, four stars ain't bad.
2020 Rating: ★ ★ ★ ★/Highly Recommended

Herradura Colección de la Casa Reserva 2013 Cognac Cask Finish Reposado Tequila 40% abv, $89.
Ecru/bisque/Manzanilla color; excellent clarity. I get all sorts of aromas that remind me, first, of wine grapes/wine and, second, of envelope glue; later inhalations encounter nicely integrated scents of dried flowers, allspice, vanilla wafer. Entry is supple in texture, like spice cake with brown sugar, citrus, nuts, dried fruits; midpalate is composed, spicy (baking spices), creamy, slightly doughy, biscuity. Finishes long, delicately sweet, clove-like, luscious. Builds to a sensational aftertaste.
2016 Rating: ★ ★ ★ ★ ★/Highest Recommendation

Herradura Colección de la Casa Reserva 2016 Port Cask Finished Reposado Tequila 40% abv, $90.
Old gold/amber color; pristine clarity. Opens with a lovely honeyed agave aroma that's gentle in its pungency and is almost floral and like arid landscape; secondary passes pick up moderately briny, dill-like notes that echo the agave and, last, there's a stony, wet-cement sidewalk perfume that I find lovely, evocative, and earthy. Entry remains earthy, is pleasantly prickly on the tongue, a bit syrupy, slightly winey, and off-dry; midpalate brings out a maple-like toastiness that's keenly woody/sap-like and in one word, delicious. Aftertaste highlights the vegetative agave fiber-like flavor that is mildly salty, oily in texture, and off-dry. Nice idea that's executed well.
2017 Rating: ★ ★ ★ ★/Highly Recommended

Herradura Colección de la Casa Reserva 2015 Directo de Alambique Silver Tequila 55% abv, $90.
Only thirteen thousand bottles available worldwide. Limpid, impeccable clarity; no hint at all of color or tint. This is a heady, animated opening aroma that bursts from the glass in assertive waves of rubber sole, prickly pear, sea salt, and jalapeño pepper; following additional aeration, the aromatics turn more mineral-like, gummy, and black pepper–like. Entry is dusty dry and potent, but neither fiery nor hot as the elevated abv (55 percent) advances the botanical flavors, highlighted by pickle-like brininess that I really like; midpalate goes softer (!) and more nuanced as the taste profile turns marginally sweeter and more biscuity than the entry, almost as though there's a touch of fresh honey or, better, agave syrup in it (even though I know there is not), as the midpalate effortlessly transitions to the finish that's medium long, moderately sweet, and oily in texture. This silver evolves in the glass, ending in a crescendo aftertaste of substance and charm. It's clear to me that the 110 proof makes it better than if it had been reduced to the standard 80 proof.
2016 Rating: ★ ★ ★ ★ ★/Highest Recommendation

Herradura Reposado Tequila 40% abv, $45.
Aged eleven months. Vanilla color; flawless clarity. First nosing passes pick up only the most subtle fragrances, including faint whispers of carob, egg yolk, and walnut; further aeration brings out slightly larger scents of pencil eraser, orange blossom, and parchment. Entry is more expressive than the sedate bouquet, offering brisk flavors of green tea, green tomato/tomatillo, dill pickle, and aniseed; midpalate builds upon the entry features, creating a pleasing crescendo of aridly dry, slightly salty, elemental (dry stone, dry soil, minerals), and dill-like tastes that flow freely into the medium-long, crisp, and clean aftertaste. Rated four stars in *Kindred Spirits 2* and I'm happy to say that I'm holding to that score with this Herradura edition twelve years later.
2020 Rating: ★ ★ ★ ★/Highly Recommended

Herradura Silver Tequila 40% abv, $39.
Pretty tarnished-silver/cream soda coloring; ideal clarity. Wow, the potency of the pickle brine–like opening sniffs, which quickly evolve into butcher's wax paper and mustard seed scents, is astounding in their swiftness and totality; later inhalations after the boost from aeration bring on board powerful fragrances of sawdust, pencil eraser, nail polish remover, and uncured green leaf tobacco. Entry flavors flatline a bit as the taste adjusts itself on the tongue, but then they come alive with textile fiber–like freshness, sage herbaceousness, and high-acid edginess that merge with the oily texture in the midpalate stage, where this tequila at last blossoms. Aftertaste closes the circle on the pickle brine aspect that goes more in the manner of green olive with pimento.
2018 Rating: ★ ★ ★ ★/Highly Recommended

Jose Cuervo Tradicional Reposado Tequila 40% abv, $42.
Cream-soda color; sediment-free appearance. My initial aromatic impressions are of pickle brine, salted almond, salted cod, dried herbs (especially bay leaf, thyme), and fennel; later sniffs correlate with the first inhalations but highlight the herbaceous aspect to a higher degree. Entry is gently sweet, with prickly pear elements, as well as tastes of savory and agave syrup; midpalate stays the course with the agave syrup component, and that masks any other aspect. Concludes medium long and too banal for a recommendation. I remember this as being better, a tequila with more character. This edition seems neutered.
2019 Rating: ★ ★/Not Recommended

Lunazul Double Barrel Reserva Especial 2015 Wheated Bourbon Barrel Finish Reposado Tequila 40% abv, $40.
A dark reposado by traditional standard, the color is jonquil/gamboge/young Sauternes–like, and the purity level is flawless. I really like the opening aroma that's slightly baked, roasted, nut-like, and tannic; secondary whiffs pick up under-the-radar aromas of citrus peel, textile fiber, pencil eraser, and dried sage. Entry features a sweet, grainy quality that must be from the bourbon barrel because it dominates the opening in-mouth stage as it mingles with the peppery, herbal agave essence; midpalate echoes much from the entry, but now the barrel impact becomes larger as the agave herbaceousness fades to the background in favor of the barrel influence. Aftertaste shows vanilla bean, sweetened coconut, tree sap. If it were mine (which it admittedly isn't), I'd tone down the bourbon barrel to allow the agave

to have some needed presence in the entry, midpalate, and finish stages. Like all Lunazuls, it is obviously well made. I just think it's a stylistic difference of opinion.
2016 Rating: ★ ★ ★/Recommended

Lunazul Primero Añejo Tequila 40% abv, $25.
A colorless añejo; clear and clean core. Owns a lovely agave opening fragrance that's deep into fennel and dill plus there's a vegetal sweetness that's appealing; second passes support the initial findings and add tar, tobacco, plastic, candle wax. Entry is sturdy, agave sweet/sour, steely, fibrous, slightly toasty; midpalate reaches for more herbaceousness and gets there as the late flavor profile highlights the dill, pickle brine aspects that make it all worth it. Concludes long, succulent, intensely ripe. This is a better tequila than the one I lambasted four years ago.
2015 Rating: ★ ★ ★/Recommended

Milagro Añejo Tequila 40% abv, $44.
Jonquil/mango color; impeccable clarity. This initial aroma after the pour reminds me most of baked clay/terra-cotta, as well as paraffin, sealing wax, and fennel; second passes after more aeration reveal understated fragrances of lichen/moss and mushroom. Entry features more of the woodsy/forest aspects than wax, and yet the agave element, which is slightly briny, is never out of the picture. Ends up low-key, gently sweet, vegetal, and a little like salted butter.
2019 Rating: ★ ★ ★ ★/Highly Recommended

Milagro Reposado Tequila 40% abv, $30.
Color is jasmine yellow; flawless purity. Right from the starting gate, I like this fresh, dill pickle–like opening aroma due to its lean, no-fat, no-frills character; with more air contact, the aroma turns into a bouquet, one that commands your attention due to its pleasing brininess. Entry surprises me, in that it comes off being fat and chunky in direct opposition to the tight aroma findings; midpalate stays the chunky, overstated course, as I now believe the oak influence has overshadowed the agave way too much, which I find disappointing for a reposado.
2019 Rating: ★ ★/Not Recommended

Milagro Select Barrel Reserve Añejo Tequila 40% abv, $99.
Mango/amber color; immaculate purity. The opening aromas are stone-like, arid landscape–like, dry, and yet faintly fruity (kiwi, lime); following more air contact, the aroma highlights more of the fruit aspect, primarily the kiwi, adding a background note of green melon. Entry is subtle in approach, astringent, oaky, a little bit vanilla bean–like, and toasted; midpalate highlights the toasty elements mostly in the forms of campfire embers, pipe tobacco, and black tea. Ends on a crisp, oaky note that allows in enough agave/green vegetal character to make it well worth the price.
2019 Rating: ★ ★ ★ ★/Highly Recommended

Milagro Select Barrel Reserve Reposado Tequila 40% abv, $56.
Maize color; excellent clarity. Immediately, I like this aroma, as it offers crisp, vegetal

aromas of savory, asparagus, and green bean; after more aeration, the aroma adds only minor hints of tobacco leaf, verbena, and eucalyptus. Entry is clean, creamy, and a touch sweet due to flavors of oak resin, maple, tomatillo, and coffee bean; midpalate is all about the oak and coffee bean that both compete for dominance at the expense of much of the vegetal agave aspect. Finishes toasty and semisweet, showing a deft touch of agave syrup.
2019 Rating: ★ ★ ★/Recommended

Milagro Select Barrel Reserve Silver Tequila 40% abv, $53.
Pristine appearance; totally void of color. Up front, I appreciate the semisweet aroma that's all agave, reminding me of lemon zest, lead pencil, and asphalt, but most of all pickle brine; later inhalations locate additional scents, including sagebrush, green pepper, and anise. Entry is drier than the bouquet implies, as the taste profile exhibits more mineral-like, earthy aspects than agave/vegetal; midpalate stays the earthy, leaden course a bit too firmly, as much of the agave character seems lost by the wayside. Just buy the frontline Milagro Silver.
2019 Rating: ★ ★/Not Recommended

Milagro Silver Tequila 40% abv, $25.
There's a slight pewter tint in this appearance, which is sediment-free. Initial nosing passes pick up fresh, briny agave scents that are zesty, floral, dry, coriander- and dill-like; more aeration brings out deeper fragrances, such as matchstick, campfire embers, woodsmoke, tobacco leaf, textile fiber, and tangerine. Entry is chalky, creamy, acutely pepper-like, and a touch prickly on the tongue, which I like; midpalate is toasted (akin to baked orchard fruit), slightly smoky, with background tastes of black tea and caramelized onion. Aftertaste is long, smoky, embers-like, and slightly salty. Reminds me of 100 percent agave tequila from the early 1990s when genuine agave character meant something. Outstanding value!
2019 Rating: ★ ★ ★ ★/Highly Recommended

Ocho Single Estate 2016 Los Patos Plata Tequila 40% abv, $60.
Owns a pewter/tarnished-silver hint of color; free of sediment. First sniffs encounter sedate scents of black peppercorn, stone, and dry earth/arid landscape; later nosings pick up fragrances of lots of textile/hemp/rope smells that mute the spiciness but enhance the agave pulp. Entry is dry to off-dry, with nuances of licorice, pickle brine, and green olive; midpalate highlights the brininess along with a keen black-pepper piquancy that lasts deep into the finish, which is warm, peppery, and even a touch salty. Concludes medium long, zesty, slightly citrusy, and a touch smoky.
2018 Rating: ★ ★ ★ ★ ★/Highest Recommendation

Ocho Single Estate 2016 Puerto del Aire Plata Tequila 40% abv, $60.
Crystalline, unblemished appearance. Initial aromas are front-loaded with textile fiber, nickel/minerals, damp limestone, and beeswax; more aeration unleashes more of the wet stone aspect, as the bouquet turns dense with minerals. Entry is off-dry and concentrated in its agave dillness, brininess, and baked earth; midpalate features tongue-on-stone dryness but likewise the sweet pulpy/briny agave element, as these two lead flavors merge into a

delectable aftertaste that's earthy/spicy. One of the finest remaining examples of authentic 100 percent agave tequila as rendered by a true master of the art.
2018 Rating: ★ ★ ★ ★ ★/Highest Recommendation

Olmeca Altos Lot 15207 Plata Tequila 40% abv, $25.
Silvery transparent and colorless; sediment-free clarity. The initial nosing passes detect a very ripe, sugary, *aguamiel* (translation: honey water) agave presence that's slightly spicy with white pepper and jalapeño, but simply way too sweet; secondary inhalations after more aeration discover that the agave sweetness has faded (hurray!), and this opened the door for more of the vegetal, herbal, peppery aspects to emerge, salvaging the aromatics. Entry echoes the first nosing passes as the taste profile is sweet, sappy, and resiny; midpalate mimes the entry as the aggressive overripe agave flavor overshadows any other taste possibilities. Finishes sappy sweet.
2016 Rating: ★ ★/Not Recommended

Olmeca Altos Lot 15208 Reposado Tequila 40% abv, $25.
Fino sherry–like nine-karat-gold color; superb clarity. I like the first aromas on this politely mannered reposado because they are already integrated and evolved, highlighting the ripe agave, but not to the point of being oversweet, plus there are supporting scents of black pepper and dill to round off the ripe agave; secondary passes detect the black pepper element that seems to have picked up strength with aeration. Entry is a little too sweet and honeyed for my liking, but to its credit there are other flavors to note, particularly ground black pepper, dill, and poppy seed; midpalate can't entirely shake off the overripe agave sweetness, but the spiciness does emerge a bit more to counter the sweetness.
2016 Rating: ★ ★/Not Recommended

Partida Añejo Tequila 40% abv, $50.
Champagne-like/gamboge color; superb purity. The subtlety of the first aroma is deceiving because while I know there's a lot going on, the fragrance is feathery light and ethereal, as hints of juicy agave make their selective way to the top of the glass; secondary sniffs unearth marginally more of the wood aspect as it gently pushes forward the herbaceous agave and nascent pepperiness. Entry is medium rich, sweetly ripe, pleasantly oaky, mildly spicy (clove, vanilla), and very savory; midpalate is drier than the entry as the vegetal/herbal qualities of the agave reinsert themselves into the flavor profile. Aftertaste is chewy, moderately oily, and sweet like the entry. The laid-back qualities of this añejo and perhaps a bit of plumpness has made me lower my rating of several years ago to a four star rating. I really like it but there's a difference in the intensity that I noticed immediately from the one I first evaluated in 2005.
2016 Rating: ★ ★ ★ ★/Highly Recommended

Partida Blanco Tequila 40% abv, $40.
The shimmering transparency catches the light; perfectly pure. There is nothing more sublimely suave or integrated in the blanco/silver tequila subcategory than this benchmark aroma—the slightly saline, delicately spicy scent captures all the glory of unaged agave spirit; secondary inhalations detect subtle notes of white pepper, dill, pickle brine, cigar tobacco, and dried flowers. Entry is silky smooth, harmonious, yet chewy and creamy in texture,

with the agave always guiding the direction; midpalate keys in on the elemental, aridly dry, herbal quality of agave while the underpinning texture pushes forward the array of flavors that converge in the tangy, zesty, acidic finish that's crisp, clean, and immensely satisfying. A blueprint for how to make blanco tequila.

2016 Rating: ★★★★★/Highest Recommendation

Partida Elegante Extra Añejo Tequila 40% abv, $350.

Lovely maize/old gold color; far more cork sediment seen floating about than I'd like. There's a serious aromatic leaning in the opening whiffs as the agave/dill gives way to the honey of the oak at first, but then within a minute the agave regains the upper hand and stirs the rich aroma to a place of herbal prominence. Secondary nosings unearth traces of caramel, pickle brine, sage, thyme, and brown butter; this is a deep, dense bouquet of consequence. Entry is sublimely subtle yet majestically lush and creamy, as the oaky vanilla and coconut aspects come to the fore without obliterating the agave zestiness; midpalate is keenly acidic and therefore fresh and crisp, as the agave presence remains strong and apparent through the aftertaste stage, which begs for a cigar accompaniment. Luscious, opulent, balanced.

2016 Rating: ★★★★★/Highest Recommendation

Partida Reposado Tequila 40% abv, $45.

Manzanilla sherry–like/straw-yellow color; unblemished purity. The delicacy of the initial sniffs confirms the pedigree of this tequila as the aroma unfolds in layers over the course of a minute or two, and what comes to light are scents of black pepper, dill, brine, vanilla bean, and green vegetables; after another several minutes of aeration, the bouquet turns slightly tobacco-like, woody, and densely herbal. Entry is generous in texture yet crisply clean and focused on roasted agave, but it's the sheer elegance and balance of the flavor that make it so superior; midpalate shines brightly like a constellation of brilliant stars as tastes of medium-sweet agave, light honey, toasted marshmallow, and cinnamon bun vie for attention, lasting deep into the sophisticated finish that seems fathomless. One of the best reposados available.

2016 Rating: ★★★★★/Highest Recommendation

Partida Roble Fino Añejo Sherry Oak Finish Tequila 45% abv, $125.

Author's note: There are three new Partida expressions that are each finished in casks that formerly held sherry. Goldenrod/harvest gold color; impeccably clear and clean. Oh yeah, now we're talking burnt matches, smoldering campfire embers, egg yolks/hard-boiled egg, bacon fat, lard, and shallot-like aromas that all echo earthy agave; secondary whiffs detect baked scents of pear, nectarine, and white grapes/raisins that dominate the bouquet as the herbal/vegetal/smoky aspects recede a bit. Entry owns an impactful, multilevel flavor of pickle brine/dill and baked orchard and vineyard fruits that together present the taste buds with a dramatically exciting and piquant agave flavor experience unlike and better than any other; midpalate mirrors the entry stage, adding a larger portion of mincemeat-like sherry cask flavor without sacrificing the earthy agave core taste. Finishes long, ripe, semisweet, vegetal, and dill-like. I believe that it's the 45 percent abv that makes this tequila so memorable as much as it is the sherry cask finishing.

2019 Rating: ★★★★★/Highest Recommendation

Partida Roble Fino Cristalino Sherry Oak Finish Tequila 40% abv, $100.

Crystalline, sediment-free appearance; pewter-like silvery color. Up front, I find distinctive aromatic notes of toasted hazelnut, salted butter, carob, and green tobacco leaves; after more aeration, the fragrances pick up earthy, mineral-like scents of terra-cotta, coriander, sage, lead pencil, tin can, and dill. Entry showcases more agave character than the bouquet, as dry, slightly bittersweet flavors of carbon/charcoal, black tea, caramelized onion, green olive, and grilled pineapple cover the palate; midpalate stage is where the inclusion of sherry cask emerges, and it's this pivotal addition of gentle, winey sweetness that accentuates the agave elements that last deep into the near-succulent, pleasingly pruny aftertaste.

2019 Rating: ★ ★ ★ ★/Highly Recommended

Partida Roble Fino Reposado Sherry Oak Finish Tequila 43% abv, $110.

Excellent clarity; citron color. Wow, I immediately like this laser-focused opening aroma that features keenly herbal scents of sage, fennel, anise, savory, and bay leaf (laurel), as well as green chili pepper, leather, and green tomato vine; secondary inhalations pick up subtler notes of road tar, quince, casaba melon, hard-boiled egg, brown butter, and black peppercorn. Entry flavors are grapy, winey, and berry-like, and that fruitiness dominates the early stage, except for the foundational agave vegetal/herbaceous taste; midpalate highlights the sherry cask/agave plant marriage via the succulent, semisweet flavor that's not short on agave syrup richness and tanginess; in fact, the agave presence is found mostly in the lush texture. Concludes long in the throat, moderately peppery/spicy, not as sweet as the midpalate, and therefore more herbal and green vegetable–like. This is the dawn of a promising new era for 100 percent agave tequila, one that's been needed for at least a decade. Note the abv level.

2019 Rating: ★ ★ ★ ★ ★/Highest Recommendation

Pasote Añejo Tequila 40% abv, $69.

Pale white-corn/flax color; impeccable clarity. I like the herbal, green vegetable, collected and calm opening bouquet that's far more dry and vegetal than either the Blanco or the Reposado, and therefore classier; secondary inhalations pick up more in the way of dill, pickle brine, sea salt, lard. Entry is silky to the touch, off-dry to bittersweet, moderately toasty, clean due to the high acidity, and just a tad green pepper–like; midpalate reflects the entry, adding candle wax, lanolin, but the taste profile fades markedly by the finish stage.

2016 Rating: ★ ★ ★/Recommended

Pasote Blanco Tequila 40% abv, $49.

Rainwater clear and clean. Holy mackerel, Batman, this first aroma is bursting with assertive gherkin pickle brine, hotdog relish, pickled onion, and perfumey prickly pear fragrances that are sweet/sour and, no matter their tanginess, quite attractive; secondary sniffs pick up marginally scaled-back brininess but there's still plenty of salty zest to enjoy. Entry is assertively vegetal, herbal, off-dry, and slightly like roasted chili peppers; midpalate provides the most pleasure as the various taste components combine for a real-deal, deeply vegetal agave experience. Aftertaste is medium long, keenly peppery, drier than the midpalate.

2016 Rating: ★ ★ ★/Recommended

Pasote Reposado Tequila 40% abv, $59.
Pale oyster/ecru/tarnished-silver tint; flawless purity. Unlike its rambunctious sibling, Pasote Blanco, where the brine is off the charts, this reposado is more elegant largely because the pickle brine is far more integrated with the naturally piquant taste of agave, making for a more balanced opening aroma profile; later sniffs encounter traces of beeswax, corrugated cardboard, prickly pear, latex glove. Entry is slightly toasted, caramelized sweet, a touch honeyed; midpalate seizes the agave ripeness and runs with it into the aftertaste where the profile turns gentler, a little too tame for my liking, but recommendable, nonetheless.
2016 Rating: ★ ★ ★/Recommended

Patron Añejo Tequila 40% abv, $55.
Pretty white wine/pale straw color; impeccably pure. I like this round, supple, assertive opening nose that has near-succulent aromas of honeysuckle, tobacco leaf, prickly pear, and eucalyptus as the headliners; after more aeration, the bouquet turns up the volume on lemongrass, anise, parsley, mustard seed, and pencil eraser aromas that suit me just fine. Entry features sassy flavors of black peppercorn, bacon fat, salt, and green olive; midpalate echoes the entry, adding plump flavors of vegetable cooking oil, salted butter, and a soft kiss of oaky vanilla. Ends up medium long, gently ripe but not sweet, moderately oily, and appealing. Easily the cream of the three frontline Patrons.
2018 Rating: ★ ★ ★/Recommended

Patron Reposado Tequila 40% abv, $50.
Owns a tarnished-silver/bisque shading; as clean as one could hope for. This opening aroma mirrors the qualities I found in the Silver, meaning dill and a mélange of tropical fruits; secondary inhalations pick up pleasant but delicate and narrowly focused herbal notes of sage, thyme, bay leaf, and tomato vine. Entry sports a lively, animated sour flavor of pickle brine–like agave, and that I like; midpalate shows an acidic burst that maintains the cleanness of the flavor profile, but by this point I'm looking for more dimension and layers and am not finding them in a similar manner to the vacant midpalate of the Silver. Concludes one-dimensional, sour, sap-like, and slightly resiny. The lack of character makes me yearn for my personal benchmark in this subcategory: Partida Reposado (five stars).
2018 Rating: ★ ★/Not Recommended

Patron Silver Tequila 40% abv, $45.
Pristine appearance; totally transparent and colorless. Up front, I pick up dill notes, alongside tangy fruit notes headlined by lime peel, kiwi, and underripe pineapple—I like the vivacity of this opening aroma; later inhalations offer more piquancy in the forms of scallions, verbena, sealing wax, quince, and lemon blossom. Entry is clean, but too sweet and sappy for my liking, but that said, there is substantial agave/sagebrush flavor showing through the curtain of sweetness/ripeness; midpalate echoes the entry stage, adding a sharp pepperiness that's more jalapeño-like than black pepper–like. The finish is disappointingly skimpy, toothless, and lackluster, and that ushers me to my final rating. Nowhere near the splendor of its pricier cousin, Roca Patron Silver, which I rated four stars in 2014 and is one

of my favorite silver tequilas. This silver has a hollowness that develops in the midpalate and aftertaste, the very moments when it should shine the brightest.
2018 Rating: ★★/Not Recommended

Pueblo Viejo Añejo Tequila 40% abv, $30.
Flax color; flawlessly clean. The delicacy of the opening aroma is alluring as it meanders upward from the glass in soft waves that remind me of caramelized onion, sautéed mushrooms, Saran Wrap, and dried flowers; secondary inhalations offer subtle scents of green pepper, dill, dried leaves, and sea salt. Entry tastes of vanilla initially, then that flavor fades, leaving the door open for more vegetal and kernel flavors such as tobacco and coffee bean; midpalate is gentle, off-dry, slightly resiny and woody, maple-like, and cocoa bean–like. Concludes brief, beany, and bittersweet.
2018 Rating: ★★★/Recommended

Pueblo Viejo Blanco Tequila 40% abv, $20.
Unblemished, immaculate transparency. I like the opening aromas as they remind me of textile fibers/hemp, baking soda, limestone, and dill pickle; next phase inhalations following more aeration bring out fragrances of damp earth, moss/lichen, tomatillo, tomato vines, and green coffee bean. Entry is agile, a bit thin, showing keenly vegetal flavors of snow peas and asparagus as well as black pepper, artichoke, and soy sauce; midpalate turns mineral-like, offering metallic/earthy tastes of limestone, gunmetal, and ore but, to its credit, the agave/pineapple/artichoke qualities remain vibrant. Finishes short in the throat, peppery, and green. Hardly a classic silver on the level of, say, Siete Leguas or Partida, but at the agreeable price, it is one to seriously consider as your everyday silver tequila.
2018 Rating: ★★★/Recommended

Pueblo Viejo Reposado Tequila 40% abv, $25.
Vanilla color; superb purity. Oooh my, I like the first nosing passes that feature full-out agave juice and citrus-like zestiness that are clean, fresh, and delicately spiced with bay leaf, thyme, and nutmeg; secondary inhalations accentuate the deep agave juice nectar-like aroma that's more ripe than sweet and is creamy in a salted butter–like manner that is top-notch. Entry is drier than the bouquet, more mineral- and lead pencil–like, but the agave essence never fades from view; midpalate is salty, with traces of dill, black pepper, lime zest, and green tobacco. Aftertaste is medium long, stone-on-tongue dry, jalapeño pepper–like, and minerally.
2018 Rating: ★★★★/Highly Recommended

Qui Platinum Extra Añejo Tequila (Mexcio) 40% abv, $60.
Yet another nearly colorless older tequila—what's so impolitic about amber color? There is a pewter tint to this extra añejo, and it is very clean. The nose is curiously muted in the first sniffs, except for distant traces of dill, fennel, salt; air contact stimulates a little more aroma, with the second inhalations picking up more agave/vegetal fragrance as well as black pepper, textile fiber, citrus. Entry is very bittersweet, oily in texture, mildly spicy; midpalate stage is filled with earthy flavors, like dry stone, chalk, and green vegetables (kale, asparagus). Aftertaste is medium long, drier than the midpalate, slightly salty, resiny/sap-like. I feel as

though the oak impact has stolen some of the agave charm, but there's still some appeal here. That said, if you want a colorless 100 percent agave tequila, just purchase a blanco/silver. I'm obviously missing the point of colorless añejos, and now extra añejos, in the same way that I miss the point of gorillas dancing *Swan Lake*.
2015 Rating: ★ ★ ★/Recommended

Revolución Añejo Tequila 40% abv, $60.
Color is saffron/jonquil; clarity is ideal. Wow, up-front aromas highlight biscuity fragrances including brown butter, cinnamon, vanilla-flavored coffee, hot cocoa, and egg cream; with more aeration comes the full force of roasted/toasted agave in the delectable, desserty forms of cream caramel, crème brûlée, and peach cobbler, as well as roasted asparagus. The tart, dry-as-a-bone entry tastes of cucumber, dill, fire-roasted peppers, and green tobacco; midpalate launches into a flavor flurry of green pepper, black pepper, pickles, grilled vegetables, and tomatillo. Finishes long, savory, slightly honeyed, and resiny.
2018 Rating: ★ ★ ★ ★/Highly Recommended

Revolución Añejo Cristalino Tequila 40% abv, $60.
Excellent purity; void of color. Smells curiously of overripe pineapple in the first inhalations after the pour with nary a hint of agave presence; further inhalations following more air contact fail to locate any other scent beyond the flabby pineapple—by stripping this añejo of color it appears that the distiller also stripped it of any trace of aroma. Entry is a train wreck of unintentional sweetness as the flavor profile regrettably mirrors the bouquet; midpalate is Pineapple City. This is nothing short of a disaster.
2018 Rating: ★/Not Recommended

Revolución Extra Añejo Tequila 40% abv, $80.
Buff/saffron color; impeccably clean and free of sediment. The opening nose is lightly smoky, toasted, and pickled; secondary sniffs reveal deeper, more sinewy aromas, including oak plank, light vanilla, toffee, baked coconut, maple, and brown sugar. Entry is toasty, salty, acutely resiny, and maple-like; midpalate stage features more woody oakiness than agave character and that, for me, is the sign of this tequila being left too long in the barrel, probably by at least six months. When the lipids, polymers, and acids of oak eclipse the naturally vegetal agave character in a barrel-matured tequila, I check out. So here, I am officially gone.
2018 Rating: ★ ★/Not Recommended

Revolución Reposado Tequila 40% abv, $50.
The color is vanilla; appearance is perfectly pure. This nose suffers from off odors that are industrial, chemical, flat, and flabby; secondary sniffs only pick up more unflattering smells, such as plastic, sheet metal, and plasterboard—an aromatic mess. Entry echoes the bouquet findings as the taste profile turns up dull, flabby, and industrial; midpalate is, well, so far off base as a reposado that I decide to cash in my chips and close it down. An aberration for this brand and a travesty of a reposado. It never should have been released. "Hello, is this Quality Control? Pack your bags because YOU ARE FIRED."
2018 Rating: ★/Not Recommended

Revolución Silver Tequila 40% abv, $45.
I notice a slight pewter tint to the appearance that is flawlessly pure. Right from the initial whiffs I pick up clean, dry-as-stone agave juice that is highlighted by notes of dill pickle, artichoke, soybean, and textile fiber; secondary inhalations detect more in the way of spices, namely mace, allspice, and vanilla bean. Entry is rich in texture, spicy/peppery, with hints of cucumber and coriander; midpalate stage is the apex moment of the experience as lush, gently bitter, and vegetal flavors merge into a single taste profile that's dusty dry, slightly piquant, and polished. Ends as elegantly as it began, with a lush texture that underpins the flavors. Really nice.
2018 Rating: ★ ★ ★ ★ /Highly Recommended

Riazul Añejo Tequila 40% abv, $65.
Wheat-field golden color; completely sediment-free. *This is añejo tequila?* I wonder as I sniff this highly atypical aroma that's floral (but dead flowers), dry-cleaner stinky, waxy, parchment- and airplane glue–like without the slenderest hint of agave; the second set of nosing passes following more air contact discover unappealing plastic wrapping scents along with powdered milk and powdered egg, and really I just want out of this. Entry is strangely sweet, somewhat vegetal and herbal, but also a touch smoked; midpalate is all over the flavor map as the tastes of boisé, sugar maple, burnt rubber, and road tar make for unpleasant imbibing. Steer clear.
2018 Rating: ★/Not Recommended

Riazul Premium Plata Tequila 40% abv, $50.
Pretty oyster tint; impeccable purity. I like this generous opening aroma that's rife with tropical fruits (guava and banana, especially), straw, freshly mown lawn, and salted butter; secondary passes reveal soft lactic notes of heavy cream but also desert-like notes of prickly pear and sagebrush mixed with smoldering campfire. Entry is edgy, peppery, medium full in textural weight, modestly oily, and sooty; midpalate features a solid core of carbon/charcoal, tomato vine, and honey. Finishes medium long, marginally oily, pleasantly creamy, and smooth.
2018 Rating: ★ ★ ★ /Recommended

Roca Patrón Añejo Tequila 44% abv, $90.
Bright eighteen-karat-gold color; sediment-free purity. First aromatics are delicate, gently sweet, lightly vegetal, grassy, slightly sap-like; another seven minutes of aeration bring out lanolin, candle wax, new leather aromas that are complementary to the vegetal underpinning scent. Entry is semisweet, oaky/woody, slightly resiny, piquant; midpalate highlights the spiciness/peppery quality that becomes a primary force along with the keen acidity, which maintains the balance nicely through to the chewy, semisweet finish.
2014 Rating: ★ ★ ★ ★ /Highly Recommended

Roca Patrón Reposado Tequila 42% abv, $80.
Pale-gold/ecru/tarnished-silver color; impeccable clarity. This fragrant aroma is colored initially by traces of oak influence in the form of vanilla bean; tantalizingly laced with baking spice, secondary inhalations discover additional scents of pipe tobacco, lanolin, almond

paste, lemon drop, hay. Entry is elegant, infused with oakiness but not overly so; midpalate displays a mélange of flavors including roasted green pepper, cocoa, baked pear. Concludes long in the throat, off-dry, succulent, almost honey-like. Alcohol strength is ideal.
2014 Rating: ★ ★ ★ ★ ★/Highest Recommendation

Roca Patrón Silver Tequila 45% abv, $70.
As clean and translucent as rainwater; superb purity. I respond very favorably to the biscuity opening aroma that turns slightly baked, keenly vegetal, agave syrup–like, tangy, slightly peppery in the second pass after more air contact—a graceful, elegant, but sturdy bouquet. Entry is toasty, moderately roasted, vegetal, grassy, with no evidence of salinity; midpalate is clean, acidic, edgy, minerally, prickly pear–like. Finish highlights the green-vegetable aspect without becoming sweet or sappy, thereby maintaining the agave integrity and vegetal, peppery qualities that make tequila so appealing. I applaud the bump in abv because that element keeps the focus squarely on the agave core flavor.
2014 Rating: ★ ★ ★ ★/Highly Recommended

Sauza 901 Silver Tequila 40% abv, $30.
Colorless, immaculate appearance. Features vividly herbal and vegetal first aromas of green pepper, dried sage, and cast iron/metal; additional aeration stimulates broader herbal scents of mint, dill, fennel, black pepper, and anise. Entry highlights flavors of tar, black pepper, and sweet agave juice; midpalate is mildly smoky, ashy, and drier than the entry. Finishes solidly, in a storm of grilled vegetable (eggplant) and pine/cedar.
2015 Rating: ★ ★ ★/Recommended

Savage & Cooke Ayate Añejo Tequila 40% abv, $95.
Topaz/old gold color; pristine purity. Offers high-toned aromas of new oak, maple, wood resins, and newly tanned leather in the initial whiffs after the pour—everything woody but agave; later sniffs unearth nothing new, except for a trace of black pepper, which raised my hopes of locating some agave character, perhaps in the taste profile. Entry is all wood, all the time, offering nothing in the way of agave herbaceousness, and I can only sigh; midpalate mirrors the wood-a-thon of the entry, and at this point, I throw in the towel. I'm done.
2017 Rating: ★ ★/Not Recommended

Savage & Cooke Ayate Reposado Tequila 40% abv, $65.
Gamboge color; excellent clarity. In the opening whiffs, I encounter buttery waves of agave syrup, pineapple, lemon drop, limestone chalk, and gunmetal aromas; after more air contact, further inhalations pick up brown butter, sautéed mushrooms, and mere hints of agave dill and green pepper. Entry is creamy, satiny in texture, peppery but only mildly herbal and agave-like, but the primary influence is the oak barrel, which blunts the herbal agave thrust while maintaining the viscosity and the butter taste. Midpalate reflects the entry, and this is illustrative of what is wrong with tequila in 2017: It has lost its way in terms of what the original tequila producers intended. The State of Jalisco agave distillers of the 1950s, 1960s, 1970s, and 1980s believed that the art of tequila was the enhancement of the agave plant through distillation and, if any, moderate oak maturation, not having the deeply herbal and dill-like agave element obliterated by too much oak. Tequilas like this

are why bartenders across the US have turned to mezcal and away from what has become homogenized, packaged-for-clubs tequila. Geez, and that clunky bottle on top of it. Get me out of here.
2017 Rating: ★★/Not Recommended

Siete Leguas Añejo Tequila 40% abv, $60.
Pretty citrine/maize yellow color; impeccable clarity. Ahhh, I smell delicate and delectable opening fragrances of green olive, dill pickle, bay leaf, sage, and chamomile after the pour; allowing for more aeration, I now detect more animated scents of green pepper, tomato vine, green tea, geranium, and earthy minerals. Entry is solid in structure; deep in tannic, astringent agave flavors (tea leaves, green tea, green pepper, dill, cucumber); acidic, and therefore fresh, with background flavors of fennel and salted butter. Midpalate echoes the entry findings, adding a touch more oak heft, which rounds out the supple texture. Aftertaste is long, lush, dill pickle–like, and fresh. One of the rare contemporary añejos that I could live with.
2018 Rating: ★★★★/Highly Recommended

Siete Leguas Blanco Tequila 40% abv, $42.
Silvery translucent; pristine clarity. Oh my, the acuteness and integration of the early-on pickle brine, dill, kiwi, and green-olive aromas provide a unique blanco tequila olfactory experience of the highest rank; further air contact stimulates additional delicately herbal scents, including thyme, sage, and bay leaf that mingle perfectly with the foundational briny aromas—a one-of-a-kind experience. Entry is seductively peppery, silky in texture, and herbaceous/vegetal as flavors of tobacco leaf, lemongrass, green pepper, fennel, and lead pencil can all be identified at this stage; midpalate calls a halt to the taste individuality as they integrate beautifully into a benchmark (for blanco/silver) taste profile that defines the term "harmonious." Concludes fully weighted, buttery, intensely herbal (dill, sage, thyme), leafy (green tobacco), and crisply clean. A gold standard for silver tequila.
2018 Rating: ★★★★★/Highest Recommendation

t1 Tequila Estelar Añejo Tequila 40% abv, $65.
Earth yellow/sandy-brown color; flawlessly clear and free of sediment. I immediately like this opening aroma as it's front-loaded with classic, earthy agave fragrances, such as dill, green olive, green chili pepper, aniseed, soot, and chimney; later whiffs detect broader scents, including eucalyptus, black peppercorn, and candle wax. Entry offers more woodiness than the bouquet, as oaky, tree bark–like, and resiny flavors dominate the tastes; at midpalate, the agave earthiness again surfaces, which balances and enhances the wood/oak notes. Concludes dry, resiny, and toasted. A better añejo in an age of over-wooded añejos.
2019 Rating: ★★★★/Highly Recommended

t1 Tequila Excepcional Reposado Tequila 40% abv, $50.
Straw color; impeccable purity. First nosing after the pour does not pick up much in the aromatic sense, except for subdued hints of salted butter, vegetable oil, and burnt match; secondary inhalations discover marginally deeper though still slight aromas of cement, peppermint, green tea, and eucalyptus. Entry is supple in texture, lightly roasted/baked, salty,

with flavors of green vegetable (roasted broccoli), green chili pepper, thyme, sage, and dill; midpalate reflects all of the entry findings, throwing in off-dry tastes of egg cream, green tobacco, honey, and sourdough. Showcases all of its round, toasty virtues in the long, slightly smoked finish.
2019 Rating: ★ ★ ★ ★/Highly Recommended

t1 Tequila Sensacional Extra Añejo Tequila 42% abv, $120.
Pretty bronze color; superb clarity. I like the slightly funked-up opening aroma, which features old oak, rancio, hard cheese, and butter brickle aromas; later sniffs after more aeration discover more toasted fragrances of roasted agave heart, pipe tobacco, charcoal briquette, and toasted marshmallow. Entry is clean, acidic, crisp, peppery, and woody; the midpalate stage is where this tequila stretches its legs, offering mature, harmonious, off-dry flavors of toasted wheat bread, toffee, fudge, and roasted jalapeño. Aftertaste is long in the throat, drier than the midpalate, and showing mature tastes of black tea with honey, ginger, thyme, and eucalyptus. A truly fine, subtle extra añejo that doesn't overplay its wood element as so many contemporary extras do.
2019 Rating: ★ ★ ★ ★/Highly Recommended

t1 Tequila Ultra Fino Blanco Tequila 40% abv, $45.
Pristine appearance; void of color. Opening scents speak of nothing but freshly harvested agave piñas: ripe, juicy, slightly salty, earthy, and dill-like; later inhalations after more air contact unearth deeper fragrances, such as limestone, cooking oil, lard, bacon fat, lead pencil, and arid desert. Entry features a creamy, voluptuous texture that's enhanced by tangy flavors of black peppercorn, cigarette tobacco, poppy seed, split pea, and green olive; midpalate stage affirms the entry-stage findings, adding custard/flan, sage, thyme, dill, and pickle brine. Lustrous finish flashes robust, off-dry tastes of dill, green olive, toasted agave, salted butter, green tea, and chamomile. A superb blanco of the first rank.
2019 Rating: ★ ★ ★ ★ ★/Highest Recommendation

Tapatio 110 Blanco Tequila 55% abv, $48.
NOTE THE 110 PROOF. Clean and clear as rainwater. The saline agave explosion in the first whiff staggers my olfactory bulb for a moment, but interestingly the high proof isn't as large a presence as the foundational agave fragrance and to that I say, "Hallelujah!"; secondary nosing passes after another eight minutes discover a whole other layer of aromatics, including wet stone, grain, textile fiber/hemp, rubber pencil eraser, and dried thyme. Entry is richly textured, creamy and buttery, with reined-in bacon fat/pork rind and BBQ flavors; midpalate offers expansive tastes that include tobacco leaf, tar, salt, and agave nectar. Aftertaste is as majestic, yet controlled, as the entry and midpalate. Another Tapatio triumph.
2019 Rating: ★ ★ ★ ★ ★/Highest Recommendation

Tapatio Blanco Tequila 40% abv, $34.
Clear as rainwater; flawless purity. First whiffs detect remarkably clean fragrances of dill, green olive, and brine; six minutes more of aeration stimulate deeper fragrances, including candle wax, black pepper, sage, and textile fibers, an iconic smell of agave piña fibers; a textbook bouquet for blanco tequila. Entry is agave sweet, acutely peppery (green, black, and

jalapeño), and viscous; midpalate is waxy, highly vegetal, earthy/stony, dry, and spicy, with a low-grade salinity. Finishes long, silky textured, spicy/peppery, and balanced. A superb, technically perfect blanco that ranks with the great Siete Leguas.
2019 Rating: ★ ★ ★ ★ ★/Highest Recommendation

Tattoo Organic Añejo Tequila 40% abv, $50.
Citrine color; acceptable clarity. First sniffs pick up wood-influenced aspects of vanilla, crème brûlée, oak plank, sawdust, and masquerading vanilla; further aeration unleashes timid aromas of pipe tobacco, prickly pear, honey, and salt. Entry is velvety in texture, drier than I had anticipated, woody, elemental/earthy, and just slightly spicy; midpalate echoes the entry stage, adding only bits and pieces of tobacco, pine, mint, and menthol. Finishes medium long, a touch too woody, and cedar-like.
2019 Rating: ★ ★ ★/Recommended

Tattoo Organic Blanco Tequila 40% abv, $43.
Colorless appearance; good purity level. This engaging opening aroma is intensely grassy, vegetal, dill-like, and green chili pepper–like; later sniffs pick up more subtle scents of pine forest, chamomile, eucalyptus, green tea, and freshly sawn wood. Entry is spicy, with piquant black pepper notes that drive the flavor forward to the near-exclusion of all other taste aspects; midpalate takes the flavor on a different path direction, one that's more vegetal, citrusy, and Tabasco-like. Finishes medium long, deeply peppery, orange peel–like.
2019 Rating: ★ ★ ★/Recommended

Tears of Llorona Extra Añejo Tequila 43% abv, $250.
Copper color; free of sediment. Initial whiffs pick up wood-related aromas, such as pine tar, oak resin, sawdust, plank, and tree sap; later inhalations following more aeration add spicier notes, including cinnamon, clove, nutmeg, and egg cream. Entry flavors include baking spice elements, such as nutmeg, mace, allspice, as well as candied walnut and almond paste. In the midpalate stage, I begin to wonder if I'll locate any trace of agave zest in this heavily wooded extra añejo, and finally I do find a smidgen of roasted agave heart, but the heavy-handed finish blots out any hint of agave by dropping a dense curtain of chunky oak oils, fats, and sugars. I liked the aromatic stages, but the overbearing in-mouth experience killed any chance of a recommendation.
2019 Rating: ★ ★/Not Recommended

Trianon Añejo Tequila 40% abv, $50.
Finally, an añejo that looks real, with its attractive topaz color; flawless purity. I get heavy dosage smells of tree sap and resin up front, but then those blow off, leaving behind nicely vegetal agave scents that are rooted in fennel, dill, salt, fibers; second passes encounter arid traces of cigar tobacco, sagebrush, dry earth. Entry is round, biscuity, sap-like, oaky, vanilla bean–like; midpalate is toasty, roasted, bittersweet, as in dark chocolate, and it's here where I feel the oak has eclipsed the agave. Aftertaste is oaky, pleasantly sweet, but I wish the wood would back off a little.
2015 Rating: ★ ★ ★/Recommended

Trianon Blanco Tequila 40% abv, $40.

Crystal-clear appearance; translucent; sediment-free. I like the opening aromatic sassiness that's peppery, spicy, vegetal, green, keenly agave-driven; flashes of dill, fennel, olive brine all highlight the secondary inhalations. Entry is dry, with hints of uncooked asparagus, raw green chili pepper, dry earth/sand, and is a little textile-like; midpalate maintains the vegetal aspect nicely as well as the dryness, but a measure of the agave assertiveness goes a touch flat as the midpalate stage moves into the aftertaste phase. Easily recommendable, but in the end, I wished for more complexity and depth in the later stages.

2015 Rating: ★ ★ ★/Recommended

Trianon Reposado Tequila 40% abv, $46.

Silvery/straw-yellow color; impeccable purity. The first nosing picks up trademark agave vegetal greenness, pleasing herbaceousness (dill, bay leaf), toasty oak, loose leaf tobacco, and a piquancy that's definitely similar to jalapeño pepper. Entry is peppery, salty, vegetal, herbaceous, tobacco-like, delicate; midpalate reflects the entry, but loses a bit of steam as the flavor profile turns safe and smooth, thereby losing a fragment of agave rusticity. Finishes round, gently sweet, supple.

2015 Rating: ★ ★ ★/Recommended

Tromba Añejo Tequila 40% abv, $90.

Pale-gold/flaxen color; unblemished clarity. I get peaches, pears, brussels sprouts, white pepper in the alluring initial whiffs; in later sniffs I detect rope/hemp/flax, green pepper, brown-sugar sweetness, toffee, new leather. Entry features a pleasing taste profile that has elements of textile fiber, ash, soy sauce, green vegetables; midpalate highlights the ash and adds limestone/chalkiness that dries out the flavor all the way through the tangy, briny aftertaste.

2016 Rating: ★ ★ ★/Recommended

Villa Lobos Añejo Tequila 40% abv, $60.

Paler color than one expects from añejo—ecru/talmi gold; unblemished clarity. I like the peppery, vegetable garden–like quality in the first nosings as the aroma reaches for integration and charm and easily achieves both; secondary inhalations after more air contact solidify the dry, tangy vegetal aromatics that are so appealing; what's nice about this bouquet is that even though it is an añejo, the wood isn't dominant at all and, in fact, serves to promote the herbal, cactus-like agave traits. Entry is delicately sweet, honeyed, ripe, peppery, and balanced; midpalate displays a creamy, oily texture that underscores the zestiness of the agave. A nifty añejo.

2016 Rating: ★ ★ ★ ★/Highly Recommended

Villa Lobos Blanco Tequila 40% abv, $47.

Crystal clear and flawlessly clean and free of sediment. I like the vivid agave opening fragrance that's heavily vegetal, similar to parched earth (desert-like dryness) and prickly pear, and yet is pleasingly herbaceous (dill, thyme); with more air contact, the aroma fades a bit too quickly, leaving behind delicate scents of pencil eraser, wet pavement, textile fiber, palm oil. Entry is a little raw and aggressive with heat and astringency, but the fiber-like agave aspect comes through enough to be appreciated; midpalate maintains the high degree of

astringency that keeps the flavor fresh, completely dry, and minerally. Aftertaste is medium long, dry, peppery.
2016 Rating: ★ ★ ★/Recommended

Villa Lobos Extra Añejo Tequila 40% abv, $99.
Jonquil/yellow-gold color; some minor sediment seen. There's a road tar, creosote element that leaps out in the initial whiffs that then evolves into a charcoal, charred pineapple fragrance over time; secondary inhalations find traces of chalk, toffee, brown butter, oak resins, tree sap, maple syrup; following more air contact, I detect new tanned leather, green vegetable (agave essence), cigar tobacco, mint, and limestone. Entry highlights the oak first, then the agave thrust as the flavor profile tries to balance the wood and agave influences, with the wood winning out; midpalate features little else but oaky vanilla and nutmeg flavors that eclipse the herbal agave totally, leaving me disappointed. Finishes resiny sweet.
2016 Rating: ★ ★/Not Recommended

Villa Lobos Reposado Tequila 40% abv, $49.
Faint hint of oyster/electrum color; very good clarity. The silver thread of similarity to the blanco is evident right from the first whiff, as the aromatics lean towards vegetation, arid desert, dry sand/soil and yet offer subtle traces of dried cooking herbs; later inhalations after more air contact discover that, like the Blanco, the vibrancy of the bouquet trails off. Entry is noticeably sweet and oaky vanilla-like; midpalate is toasty, tobacco-like, and slightly smoky, but there's plenty of nectar-like sweetness to savor as the midpalate moves into the succulent, bountiful aftertaste phase that might be a little too sweet for some aficionados as the agave itself becomes an afterthought. Overall, I think that this reposado is recommendable, however.
2016 Rating: ★ ★ ★/Recommended

MEZCAL—MEXICO

Generally speaking, the same fundamental process is required to create mezcal (fermentation, distillation) as tequila, though mezcal is not produced from blue agave. Mezcal, by contrast, is made from approximately thirty agave varieties rather than one, as in the case of tequila. The workhorse variety in the making of mezcal is *Agave angustifolia Haw*, which is known to Mexican farmers as *espadín*. The thirty non-blue agave types are one pivotal reason for mezcal's marked taste difference from smoother, silkier tequila.

Mezcal production originates in primitive factories, called *palenques*, that are located in the south-central Mexican states of Oaxaca, Durango, San Luis Potosí, Guerrero, Guanajuato, Puebla, Tamaulipas, and Zacatecas. Alcohol-by-volume content of mezcal ranges on average from a low of 40 percent up to a high of 52 percent in more specialized bottlings.

One more important point of difference is in the distillation method. While tequilas have nearly always been double distilled in pot stills, mezcals for decades were—and to large measure still are—distilled only once. This means that many natural chemical compounds and oils remain in the finished product. These are thought in some quarters to be negative traits that gave off musky odors reminiscent of burning tires, rotting meat, or creosote. Mezcal proponents argue that these biochemical remnants are what make mezcal so special and unique . . . and refreshingly different from tequila.

Mezcal Varieties

Mezcal: A general category of mezcal that dictates that the agaves can be cooked in any format: subterranean pits, above-ground ovens, or autoclaves. Cooked agaves can be crushed mechanically or by hand-crushing mills, fermented in any type of vessel, and distilled in either pot stills or column stills.

Artisanal Mezcal: Harvested agaves are cooked in pit ovens or masonry wells; milled with shredders but with emphasis on hand, stone, or wooden milling; fermentation occurs in wood or clay containers or animal skins or hollows of stone; distillation is done in direct-fire copper or earthenware stills, with wood, copper, or clay caps.

Ancestral Mezcal: The most rustic mezcals, whose agaves are cooked in direct-fire-pit ovens or masonry wells; hand crushed in stone or wood mills; fermented in animal hide, wood, earthen, and/or stone vats with agave fibers still unfiltered; distilled in direct-fire clay stills with wood or clay still caps.

Labeling Laws

Blanco/White: unaged mezcal

Reposado: aged for at least two months but not more than twelve months in wood barrels, including native Mexican woods

Añejo: aged for at least twelve months in wood barrels

Madurado (glass matured): refers to ancestral mezcal matured in glass vessels

Distilado con: mezcal redistilled with fruits, grains, or raw meats (chicken or turkey breast mostly) for additional flavors

Abocado con: mezcals that are macerated or flavored with essences

Alipús Eduardo Hernandez Santa Ana del Rio Oaxaca Mezcal 46.9% abv, $48.
Produced from espadín agave. Crystalline, very minor sediment seen. Big-time rubber tire/rubber band/inner tube aromas explode out of the glass in the initial inhalations; subsequent sniffs pick up baked earth/dry clay/dry riverbed, textile fiber, candle wax notes that are assertive and pungent. Entry is lead-like/metallic/nickel coin–like at first, then the flavor turns semisweet/charred sweet, smoky, roasted, BBQ; midpalate mirrors the heavily smoked/toasted entry, adding a vegetal/grilled green vegetable taste that's intensely smoked yet somewhat simultaneously graceful.
2015 Review: ★ ★ ★ ★/Highly Recommended

Alipús San Andres Ensamble Mezcal 47.2% abv, $65.
Author's note: Ensamble means blend. Dazzling clarity; colorless yet silvery somehow. Not only are there whiffs of campfire smoke, rubber pencil eraser, and burnt match in the opening nosing, but there's also an unusual presence, a nuance of ripe tropical fruit (pineapple? papaya?); more aeration accentuates the fruit aspect, which now is more like kiwi or star fruit while the tangy smokiness turns more like cigar ash; this is a mesmerizing mezcal bouquet of subtlety. Entry is keenly rubbery, vegetal, lean and acidic, astringent, and moderately smoky; midpalate echoes the entry, adding green pepper, as the fruitiness so prevalent in the bouquet vanishes. Finishes very long, mildly smoky, sooty.
2016 Review: ★ ★ ★ ★/Highly Recommended

Amarás Cupreata, Mazatlan, Guerrero Mezcal 43% abv, $58.
Silver/mercury color; spotlessly clean. Up-front aromas include sealing wax, plastic, and vinyl; after more aeration, the aroma expands only marginally to include parchment, butcher's wax paper, and seaweed. Entry is lemony/citrusy at first, then that aspect recedes, leaving the door open for flavors of ashes, burnt log, charcoal, and seared meat; midpalate highlights the charcoal/burnt elements making the flavor profile slightly sweet. Ends up gently sweet, medium weighted, mineral-like, and vegetal.
2019 Review: ★ ★ ★/Recommended

Amarás Espadín Joven Mezcal 41% abv, $50.
Glassy limpidity, colorless; some sediment seen floating. First nasal impressions are of rubber tire, pencil eraser, vinegar, fennel, aloe, dill, loose leaf tobacco—this is a virtual stampede of exotic aromatics right out of the gate; second passes after more air contact find a more settled bouquet headlined by creosote and road tar. Entry is delicately smoky sweet, kind of like pipe tobacco; midpalate is rife with vegetal, grassy agave richness and multiple levels of flavor, including charred pineapple, nectarine, lemon peel. This is a clinic on how splendid mezcal can be when a balance is struck between the fibrous quality of agave, smoking/cooking of the agave, and excellent distillation.
2015 Review: ★ ★ ★ ★ ★/Highest Recommendation

Bosscal Joven Mezcal 42% abv, $50.
Very pale pewter tint; a moderate amount of sediment seen. Opening sniffs encounter mossy/forest floor aromas that are green and earthy, but lacking a bit too much of agave-inspired dill or campfire for its own good; secondary inhalations go a little too flat for my liking. Entry shows a spirited flavor menu of bacon fat, wax candy, lead pencil, and tobacco ash; midpalate ventures more into herb territory as the headlining tastes become sage, bay leaf, verbena, and savory. Aftertaste is mild, rather brief, and mildly peppery.
2019 Review: ★ ★/Not Recommended

Bozal Ancestral Papalote o Cupreata Agave from Chilapa Pueblo Joven Mezcal 47.9% abv, $100.
Slight tarnished-silver tinge of color; impeccable purity. This aroma is a mite closed off in the very first inhalation, then with time and more air contact it grudgingly opens up featuring scents of haystack, mown grass that's been lying around for hours, model airplane glue, metal grate, and flaxseed oil; more aeration adds bits of loose leaf tobacco, old leather, tackle box, old library, and is the most multilayered and complex aroma of the Bozal roster. Entry is vibrant with almost minty agave flavor that's rich but not unctuous, zesty in a citrus peel–like manner, tannic, and therefore dry, yet creamy and supple in texture—a lovely, harmonious entry of the first rank; midpalate soars into the flavor stratosphere in waves of opulent flavors, including canola oil, pickle brine, saltine cracker, kippers, cigarette ash, and loose leaf tobacco. Aftertaste is surprisingly mellow, sturdy, buttery (salted Irish butter), eggy, and long. Top of the class.
2016 Review: ★ ★ ★ ★ ★/Highest Recommendation

Bozal Cuixe Single Maguey San Baltazar Pueblo Joven Mezcal 47% abv, $80.
Pewter tinge of color; unblemished clarity. This opening aroma reminds me of ink more than anything, including rubber tire or road tar, both of which emerge as minor hints; more time in the glass allows for hardware/paint-shop fragrances of turpentine, steel wool, fiberglass insulation as well as tobacco-shop scents of cigar box, cigar tobacco. Entry is acutely leafy and vegetal, slightly smoked/roasted, bittersweet; midpalate echoes the entry phase, adding traces of poppy seed, fresh Italian parsley, dried sage. Aftertaste is medium long, quite prickly on the tongue, lean, and austere. Really tasty.
2016 Review: ★ ★ ★ ★/Highly Recommended

Bozal Espadín-Barril-Mexicano Agaves from Ejutla de Crespo y San Baltazar Pueblos Ensamble Joven Mezcal 47% abv, $50.

Crystalline appearance; colorless; flawless purity. First sniffs get treated to classical rubber tire/inner tube, and pencil eraser frontline aromas that are more mineral-like and flinty than either smoked or roasted; the extreme, aridly dry minerality shines through even more with added aeration along with faint traces of vinegar, shoe polish, and sheet metal. Entry strikingly mirrors the aroma, especially in the rubber tire and flint departments, as the flavor profile goes bitter, dry, and astringent; at midpalate, there's a sweeping flavor of flinty stone that dries out the palate to desert-like drought status. Finishes medium long, more stone-like than metallic, vegetal, green, grassy, austere.

2016 Review: ★ ★ ★/Recommended

Bozal Tobasiche Single Maguey San Baltazar Pueblo Joven Mezcal 47% abv, $80.

Very minor tendrils of sediment seen—inconsequential; silvery, transparent appearance. Similar to the Cuixe Joven, this up-front nose offers traces of India ink, asphalt, sheet metal, nails, and insulation; secondary inhalations pick up scents that are more textile fiber–like, flaxen, reedy, green vegetation–like, road tar–like, but little or no smokiness to speak of. Entry is oily, linseed oil–like, vegetal (brussels sprouts), dry, high in acid; midpalate reflects the entry perfectly and throws in black peppercorn, burnt match/sulfur, charcoal briquette, seared ham flavors that overlap into the vibrant finish, which is salty, meat-like, oily, vegetal, peppery.

2016 Review: ★ ★ ★ ★/Highly Recommended

Del Maguey Single Village San Jose Rio Minas Espadín/Arroqueño Mezcal 50% abv, $99.

Pewter tint; sediment seen. Opening fragrance is all rubber tire and inner tube at first, then I locate a pleasing scent of New Mexico chili pepper (capsicum) that's fresh, wax-like, and green. Later sniffs pick up tantalizing aromas of burnt match; green, uncured tobacco; and wet cement. I like this bouquet because you really get a concentrated agave perfume that's highly delectable. Entry is lean, high in acid, and therefore cracking fresh and peppery; midpalate is deeply flavorful, highlighting the toastiness and dill-like nature of the agave. Finishes extra long and drier than the midpalate.

2019 Review: ★ ★ ★ ★ ★/Highest Recommendation

Del Maguey Single Village San Luis del Rio Mezcal 47% abv, $69.

Colorless; clean as rainwater. Initial sniffs detect nuanced aromas of sour apple, tin can, chamomile, green tea, and parchment; secondary sniffs pick up additional aromas of dry stone, sage, green tomato (tomatillo), and tomato vine. Entry is richly textured, deeply smoky and ash-like, and road tar–like; midpalate features subtle touches of vine fruits, especially green melon and casaba. Aftertaste is medium long, slightly smoky, and cigar tobacco–like.

2019 Review: ★ ★ ★ ★/Highly Recommended

Del Maguey Single Village San Luis del Rio Tobaziche Mezcal 47% abv, $125.

Tarnished-silver tint; minor sediment. There's a curious and wonderful opening aroma

that reminds me of pickled cucumber, borscht, dill, and pickled jalapeño pepper; secondary whiffs detect rubber pencil eraser, old smokestack/old chimney, damp wool, and marshland. Entry is riveting in its acidic freshness as it cleanses the entire palate; midpalate features a flavor menu, wrapped in a waxy texture, that includes sour apple, green pepper (poblano especially), sea salt, and toasted sourdough bread. Aftertaste is extended, tart to the point of astringency, and totally refreshing. Terrific.
2019 Review: ★ ★ ★ ★ ★/Highest Recommendation

Del Maguey Single Village Santa Catarina Minas Arroqueño Mezcal 49% abv, $125.
Pale pewter color with yellowish edge; excellent purity. First whiffs pick up pleasant aromas of nail polish, burnt lemon twist, buttermilk, green chili pepper, flapjacks, and white peppercorn; later inhalations following more air contact discover deeper scents, including white flour, baked pineapple, eucalyptus, hydrangea, and shiitake mushrooms. Entry is oddly sweet, nut-like, almost carob-like, and succulent; midpalate highlights the nuttiness found in the entry as round, supple tastes of hazelnut and nougat (!) abound. Finish is medium long, bountiful in texture, doughy, and gently sweet.
2019 Review: ★ ★ ★ ★/Highly Recommended

Del Maguey Single Village Santa Catarina Minas Pechuga Mezcal 49% abv, $199.
Slight pewter tint; clear and clean. This opening nose is subtle, tantalizing, salty, and a bit like egg yolk and/or hard-boiled egg; following more aeration, pleasant scents of carob, walnut, carbon/charcoal, and rosemary delight the olfactory sense. Entry is dry as lead pencil, mineral-like but not metallic or coin-like; midpalate is the sweet spot of the evaluation as the flavor menu includes pickle brine, cigar tobacco, lemongrass, vanilla bean, and clove. Finishes long, a touch like nougat and/or caramelized onion. Succulent and delicious.
2019 Review: ★ ★ ★ ★ ★/Highest Recommendation

Del Maguey Single Village VIDA de San Luis del Rio Mezcal 42% abv, $37.
Void of color; superb purity. This aroma is as fresh and agave-driven as you'll ever find, with subtle back notes of asphalt, matchstick, and carob; secondary inhalations pick up deeper scents of dill, thyme, sage, and lemongrass. Entry is gently sweet and fruity, but neither ambrosial or ripe, as cleansing flavors of lemon peel, lime, and tangerine vie for dominance; midpalate features green melon and quince flavors that are just a shade smoky and tar-like. Aftertaste is medium long, fruity, and touched with cigarette ash. Excellent value.
2019 Review: ★ ★ ★ ★/Highly Recommended

Don Amado Arroqueño Mezcal 46% abv, $90.
Silvery and pristine appearance. I like the initial burst of citrus peel, green pepper, and casaba melon fragrances that are slightly pickled and dill-like but not enough to make it overbearing; secondary inhalations with a touch more aeration pretty much echo the initial findings. Entry is sophisticatedly clean, piquant, and herbal, offering near-succulent tastes of quince, carob, and spring onion; midpalate sees the flavor profile deepen, becoming drier and more pickled. Finish is medium long and pleasantly as dry as lead.
2019 Review: ★ ★ ★ ★/Highly Recommended

Donaji 10 Year Old Extra Añejo Mezcal 40% abv, $79.
Espadín from Oaxaca; twice distilled in copper pot stills. Pale topaz color; excellent
clarity. Owns a peculiar initial aroma of cocoa bean, dark chocolate, glue that morphs into
stir-fried bok choy (Chinese cabbage), shoe polish, soy sauce, and wet sand in the second
passes. Entry is keenly sappy/resiny (obviously from the wood), and more distinctive than
the Joven as the taste profile surges with pipe tobacco, road tar/asphalt flavors that are tangy,
smoky, and seared; midpalate is surprisingly behaved and almost too low-key for a mezcal
this mature—what I'm saying is, I expected more agave pizzazz but I got lots of oakiness
instead. I like this mezcal and recommend it like its sibling, but they are quite reserved and
genteel compared to what one normally expects from rustic mezcal.
2016 Review: ★★★/Recommended

Donaji Joven Mezcal 40% abv, $40.
Espadín from Oaxaca; twice distilled in copper pot stills. Pale pewter tint in color; very
good purity. Offers a true mezcal first aroma of rubber tire, pencil eraser, new saddle leather,
and some but not an overabundance of green vegetable; later inhalations after more aeration
discover that the rubber tire aspect has expanded with the air contact and now dominates
the aromatic profile. Entry is softly sweet and ripe at first, then the flavor turns peppery,
tobacco-like, toasty, almost grainy; midpalate echoes the entry as the rubber tire element
returns to merge nicely with the tobacco and peppers. Finishes medium long, mildly assertive, vegetal, waxy. Not on the same quality level as the far more idiosyncratic Del Maguey
Single Village Mezcals, but tasty and easy.
2016 Review: ★★★/Recommended

El Jolgorio Americana Arruqueno Mezcal 53.7% abv, $155.
Limpid; oyster tint; unblemished clarity. Early on, disparate aromas include nail polish remover, tomato paste, violets, camphor, eucalyptus; secondary whiffs following a few
more minutes of air contact encounter additional scents of damp earth, wet grass/hay,
glue. Entry is moderately sweet in a cereal-like manner but is likewise minty, gum-like,
saccharine; midpalate unleashes toasty, vegetal, cigarette-like flavors that match up well
with the mintiness. The elevated abv also gives the flavors a foundational lift that accentuates them.
2016 Review: ★★★★/Highly Recommended

El Jolgorio Angustifolia Espadín Mezcal 47.8% abv, $80.
Slight tint of ecru; pristine clarity. Whoa, this aroma is off-the-charts citrusy,
lemongrass-like, rind-like, zesty, waxy in the initial sniffs; later inhalations discover conver-
gent scents of aloe, palm wood, fern, damiana. Entry is citrusy/lemony, zesty, tart, fruity;
midpalate continues the citrus dominance as the flavor profile shifts slightly to a vegetal
status in the aftertaste, which is slightly sweet, viscous, acutely peppery, satisfying.
2016 Review: ★★★★/Highly Recommended

El Jolgorio Karwinskii Barril Mezcal 47% abv, $115.
Transparent; tarnished-silver color; flawless clarity. Yep, there's rubber tire and pencil
eraser aromas in the first sniffs but there's also dill, fennel, bay leaf scents, which add a

pleasing earthiness; additional air contact brings out olive brine, black pepper, poppy seed, soybean. Entry is desert dry, stony, minerally, medium bodied, keenly peppery; midpalate stays the dry course, adding zesty notes of dried fruit rind, nuts. Aftertaste is very dry, mineral-driven, toasty, bare bones.
2016 Review: ★ ★ ★/Recommended

El Jolgorio Karwinskii Cuixe Mezcal 47% abv, $115.
Ecru/tarnished-silver tint; clear and clean as springwater. Nicely proportioned first aromas include dill, candle wax, new leather, flax, textile fiber, white rice; later inhalations include white pepper, bay leaf, parchment. Entry is, to my surprise, semisweet, grainy, pear-like, juicy, ripe; midpalate mirrors the entry and adds citrus rind, white grapefruit, guava flavors that meld perfectly through the near-succulent aftertaste. Atypical, savory, elegant.
2016 Review: ★ ★ ★ ★/Highly Recommended

El Jolgorio Karwinskii Madrecuixe Mezcal 47% abv, $115.
Transparent; no color tint at all; excellent purity level. At first, I find the opening aroma neutral but then with further inhalations I unearth scents of dill, chicory, artichoke, tobacco; secondary whiffs encounter green pepper, black peppercorn, hemp, flax, wax paper. Entry is metallic, lead-like, peppery, totally dry, herbaceous; midpalate is slightly sweeter than entry, offering more ripe notes that carry through nicely to the flax-like finish.
2016 Review: ★ ★ ★/Recommended

El Jolgorio Marmorata Tepeztate Mezcal 49.2% abv, $123.
Pristine as rainwater appearance; sediment-free. Wow, I really like this slightly minty, slightly peppery, mildly floral opening aroma that hints at a lot of fragrances but commits fully to none, making it ethereal, a teaser; more aeration brings out scents of toasted marshmallow, charred meat, bacon fat; an exciting, unpredictable mezcal bouquet. Entry is piquant, loaded with creosote, lead pencil flavors that are moderately toasted, smoky, rubbery, bittersweet, cocoa bean–like. Aftertaste is lean, but mildly toffee-like, salty. We have a winner.
2016 Review: ★ ★ ★ ★ ★/Highest Recommendation

El Jolgorio Pechuga Espadín Mezcal 48% abv, $130.
Pewter tint; flawless purity. Intriguingly, one of the most neutral, off-the-radar mezcal aromas I've ever sniffed; allowing for a few more minutes of air contact, the secondary whiffs encounter delicate scents of dried flowers, wet cement, damp sand, little more than can be described. Entry is surprisingly semisweet, caramel-like, ashy, yet earthy and vegetal at the same time; midpalate phase features toasted honey wheat bread, tobacco leaf flavors. Concludes oily, long, spicy, moderately smoky.
2016 Review: ★ ★ ★ ★/Highly Recommended

El Jolgorio Potatorum Tobalá Mezcal 48% abv, $115.
Tarnished-silver hue; superb purity. Opening sniffs pick up garden-like aromas of dried flowers, fallen leaves, soybean, tofu, peanuts, palm oil; secondary whiffs add traces of beeswax, textile fiber, cardboard. Entry is sweet, smoky, charred, baked cherry–like, toasty;

midpalate features buoyant tastes of baked berries, black cherry, yam, brown sugar, fennel, olive brine. Finishes long, smoky, sweet.
2016 Review: ★ ★ ★ ★/Highly Recommended

El Jolgorio Rhodacantha Mexicano Mezcal 47% abv, $115.
Nearly colorless but for a pewter tint; excellent purity level. Opening fragrance is delightfully tobacco-like, floral, earthy, coffee bean–like, espresso-like; further aeration stimulates stone-dry scents akin to pickle brine, lead pencil, nickel, granite, shale, then at the final moment, fruity/pear-like. Entry is off-dry, smoky, loose tobacco leaf–like, vegetal; midpalate echoes the entry and is squeaky clean, not as smoked as the entry, drier now as it leads into the stony, peppery, waxy finish.
2016 Review: ★ ★ ★/Recommended

Kimo Sabe Albedo Joven Mezcal 43% abv, $34.
Harvest 2014. Batch size eight hundred 750 ml bottles. Immaculately clean; void of any color. I have to continue sniffing in the opening nosings in search of any level of agave aroma—I must be dreaming because this is the least pungent mezcal fragrance I've ever experienced; obviously, this aroma requires some mingling with oxygen before it cuts loose, and indeed after another seven to eight minutes, it does begin to offer some, if meager, agave traits, mostly butcher's wax paper, plastic, floor polish, desert sand, prickly pear, and honeysuckle. Entry is pleasant, peppery, a little bit combustible (gently warming), moderately waxy, highly vegetal, with distant echoes of asphalt and road tar; midpalate highlights the agave earthiness and dill-like spice, as some of the other taste components fade away. The finish is savory, peppery, bitter, and just a touch honeyed. Far from the usual raucous, rustic, caustic in-mouth explosion one expects of mezcal, but a more stylized, if homogenized, version that might be thought of perhaps as an entry-level expression. That said, there's simply not enough grip or stuffing here to recommend.
2017 Review: ★ ★/Not Recommended

Kimo Sabe Rubedo Reposado Mezcal 41.5% abv, $44.
Harvest 2014. Batch size eight hundred 750 ml bottles. Bisque in color, meaning the color of brut champagne; clear and clean appearance. This nose is faintly buttery and even a little honeyed in the first sniffs, and it has a tomato vine–like aspect that's alluringly vegetal; further air contact does not release any discernible scents that are different from the opening impressions. Entry, not surprisingly, comes out meek, a little hollow, and a touch honeyed at first as the taste profile reaches out cautiously without conviction; midpalate is low-key, delicately sweet, a bit candied, but it's lost the agave edge that one wants in mezcal. There are no major production flaws here, and in the end it's almost recommendable, but people buying mezcal are looking for greater complexity and agave expression than this reposado offers. The most memorable mezcals are the ones that have distinctive roasted agave characters that sometimes take you by the lapels and smack you around just for the sport of it. No smacking here. It's hollow. And, really, change the name. This isn't the 1950s with us all watching *The Lone Ranger* in black and white.
2017 Review: ★ ★/Not Recommended

Los Amantes Añejo Mezcal 40% abv, $75.

Jonquil/gold color; pristine purity. Opening aromas are strikingly similar to those of the Reposado, meaning dough, pastry, yeast, and dried flowers; secondary passes encounter nearly identical odors again to those offered by the Reposado (dill, anise, white rice, etc.). Entry offers a big, substantive texture that underpins the first flavors of agave, tree sap, resin, black pepper, toasted oak, and pine nut; midpalate goes a touch sweeter than the entry as the tree sap aspect turns maple-like, sugary, and sappy. Aftertaste echoes the midpalate. I think the extra time in oak has made this mezcal a touch too candied. Otherwise, there is ample quality here for a recommendation.

2018 Review: ★ ★ ★/Recommended

Los Amantes Joven Mezcal 40% abv, $45.

Void of color; a few tendrils of sediment seen but inconsequential. Up front, I smell plastic vinyl, candle wax, paraffin, lard, corrugated cardboard, and parchment immediately after the pour; second passes detect beeswax, floor polish, car wax, and green string bean in abundance. Entry is agave syrup sweet, lightly toasted, bean-like, doughy, and viscous in texture; midpalate goes a little crisper than the entry as the acidity kicks in, bringing about a spicier, more peppery flavor profile that's supple, piquant, and zesty, without being profound. Ends off-dry, vegetal, green tea–like, green tobacco–like, and mildly toasted.

2018 Review: ★ ★ ★/Recommended

Los Amantes Reposado Mezcal 40% abv, $55.

Aureolin color; good clarity. First whiffs encounter round, buttermilk biscuit–like, cookie dough–like aromas that are akin to unbaked puff pastry, yeast, and dried flowers; the next nosing passes after more aeration pick up clear scents of baker's yeast, hops, aloe, steamed white rice, dill, and anise. Entry is viscous in texture, toasted, honey wheat bread–like, cooking oil–like, and a bit like salted fish; midpalate is the apex moment for this mezcal as the various flavors merge into a singular, green vegetable, piquant taste that comes wrapped in an oily, silky texture. Ends long in the throat, lightly smoked, salty, vegetal, herbaceous, and highly pleasant.

2018 Review: ★ ★ ★ ★/Highly Recommended

Los Nahuales Joven Mezcal 47% abv, $62.

Harvest 2014. Batch size eight hundred 750 ml bottles. Slight tarnished-silver/oyster tint; utterly clean appearance. Oh yeah, there are distinctive agave aromas here, including rubber inner tube, matchstick, tomato vine, floor polish, and green tea; additional time in the glass unleashes tidal waves of wet sand, wet cement, fennel, flint, tongue on stone, dill, and pickle brine. Entry soars immediately with earthy tastes of chickpea, coriander, dill, savory, and charcoal; midpalate features a flavor profile that's semisweet with agave syrup, carob, and cocoa bean. Finishes long, clean, crisply acidic, and moderately smoked. In the final evaluation moments I'm thinking things like *elegant*, *sophisticated*, and *classy*.

2017 Review: ★ ★ ★ ★/Highly Recommended

Los Nahuales Special No. 2 Mezcal 47% abv, $84.

Harvest 2014. Batch size eight hundred 750 ml bottles. Transparent and colorless as

gin; sediment-free. First nosings pick up textile-like aromas of nylon/synthetics, cotton fabric, arid desert, dry sand, and prickly pear; later sniffs following more air contact unearth mineral-like fragrances of limestone, flint, pencil eraser, and granite as the bouquet goes Mojave Desert–dry and sage-like. Entry is herbal, slightly less dry than the aroma, showing elemental flavors of agave fiber, hemp, seaweed, jalapeño pepper, gum; midpalate turns a corner on the dryness/sweetness scale in favor of measured sweetness as the flavor becomes more bittersweet and bean-like than sugary or chocolate sweet. Aftertaste features a succulence that is irresistibly luscious, grassy, herbaceous, and floral (carnation). A superb mezcal.
2017 Review: ★ ★ ★ ★ ★/Highest Recommendation

Los Nahuales Special No. 3 Mezcal 49% abv, $102.

Colorless; very minor sediment seen. Oh yeah, there's an abundance of rubber tire, plastic, and saddle-leather opening aromas that are dry and elemental; later inhalations detect reduced rubber tire and mineral elements and more roasted agave–related fragrances, such as black peppercorn, green chili, and olive brine. Entry is tart, citrusy, acidic, slightly ripe, and green tobacco–like; midpalate echoes the entry, throwing in additional flavors of nickel, eucalyptus, and burnt rubber. Aftertaste is smokier than the entry or midpalate, reflecting a charcoal-like finale that's highly pleasant.
2019 Review: ★ ★ ★ ★/Highly Recommended

Los Vecinos del Campo Ensamble Mezcal 45% abv, $50.

Ecru/bisque/tarnished-silver tint; unblemished clarity. Lovely opening aromas include pencil eraser, chamomile, dill pickle, and asphalt/road tar, but it's the green, vegetal agave fiber scent that's so attractive; second whiffs pick up fragrances of green tea, hemp, palm frond, and green pea in an intriguing egg-like, soy-like, astringent parting aroma that's neither aggressive nor bombastic. Entry comes off sweeter than the bouquet implies as savory scents of dry stone, chalk, honey, and soy sauce abound; at midpalate, an acute acidity takes charge as the taste profile narrows down to minerals, lead pencil, chalk, and campfire smoke. Aftertaste highlights the midpalate flavors, adding textile fiber and black pepper.
2018 Review: ★ ★ ★ ★/Highly Recommended

Los Vecinos del Campo Tobalá Mezcal 46% abv, $90.

Pewter-like tint; flawlessly pure. First nosing passes detect pleasant, arid landscape smells of dry sand, stone/granite, scallion, shallots, white pepper; secondary inhalations don't vary much from those of the initial impressions, save for a slight sweetening, which reminds me of Vidalia onion; the final deep breaths find wax paper, parchment, cardboard, and gardenia. Entry taste is of ripe agave juice, bitter cocoa bean, grain kernel; midpalate stage is densely oily in texture, providing the platform for flavors of baker's yeast, sourdough, buttered toast, popcorn, lemon curd. Finishes long, with carbonic end flavors of dying campfire smoke, cigarette ash, green tobacco, asphalt, and sassafras.
2018 Review: ★ ★ ★ ★/Highly Recommended

Los Vecinos Espadín Mezcal 45% abv, $34.

Void of color; sediment-free clarity. Up-front fragrances bedazzle me, offering hoisin sauce, tomato paste, charcoal briquette, cigar tobacco, grilled pork, and balsamic vinegar;

secondary inhalations pick up more settled, lightly toasted, off-dry, and astringent notes of vinegar, lemon oil, and charred meat. Entry features flavors of wet cement, fresh road tar, cigarette ash, black pepper; midpalate is the zenith moment for this mezcal as it highlights the merging of full-weighted, medium oily, supple, astringent, vegetal, and totally yummy flavors. Aftertaste is moderately smoky/charred, meaty, and caramelized onion–like. This wonderful mezcal is the ideal marriage of unruly, wild mezcal and distilling sophistication.
2018 Review: ★ ★ ★ ★ ★/Highest Recommendation

Marca Negra Dobadán Mezcal 48% abv, $139.
Transparent; colorless; moderate sediment seen. I like this opening aroma a lot as fruity/grapy notes emerge immediately in the vegetal, minerally, earthy, floral fragrance; secondary whiffs pick up fibrous, textile-like scents as well as subtle hints of rubber tire, asphalt, chicory, lima bean, steamed brown rice. Entry is surprisingly sweet, cane sugar–like, candied, vegetal; midpalate features the sweet, sap-like agave taste, which turns toasty, warming in the long-lasting finish. Remarkably fruity mezcal that's very different.
2014 Review: ★ ★ ★ ★/Highly Recommended

Marca Negra Ensamble Bicuixe, Espadín, Madrecuixe Mezcal 47% abv, $139.
Clear as rainwater; minor sediment present. Rubber pencil eraser, car tire notes abound in this pleasing initial aroma that's reined in, as well as peppery, vegetal, stony/chalky; the vegetal/arugula/kale fragrance is dazzling after further aeration as the aromatic direction goes deeply green vegetable–like, earthy, bitter in second-nosing pass. Entry is dry, sand- and cement-like, tongue-on-stone quality, with a background note of tropical fruit; midpalate offers slightly sappy, resinous flavors that are more off-dry than flat-out dry. Aftertaste reflects the entry mostly as the taste profile turns deeply earthy, sandy. Good, no doubt, but not as focused as Dobadán and Tobalá.
2017 Review: ★ ★ ★/Recommended

Marca Negra Espadín Mezcal 50.9% abv, $65.
Translucent; spotlessly clean and clear. Initial whiffs detect expansive, pungent scents of rubber tire, burning embers/ash, baked fruits, lead pencil, charred meat, and smoking cigar; following more time in the glass, the aroma collapses, offering only tobacco ash and rubber tire. Entry is velvety in texture, heavily smoked/ashy, and acutely peppery; midpalate mirrors the entry, adding only black pepper. Good example of quality espadín mezcal.
2017 Review: ★ ★ ★ ★/Highly Recommended

Marca Negra Tepeztate Mezcal 47.3% abv, $128.
There's the faintest tint of tarnished silver in this mezcal; very minor sediment—inconsequential. "Peculiar" doesn't begin to tell the story of this aroma that's rubbery but also floor wax–like, mildly ashy, sawdust-like, sappy/resiny; the woodsy element doesn't calm down with more air contact, in fact, it seems to accelerate as the tree sap/resin component transforms into furniture polish, glue, and asphalt/macadam. Entry goes very fruity as the waxiness and road tar depart, leaving the door wide open for the agave pulpiness to take charge and it does; midpalate stays the fruity/pulpy course as the flavor profile becomes marginally smokier, pungent, almost like charred

pineapple or charred orchard fruit (pear, peach). Finish is medium long, reserved, gently sweet, and ripe. Very nice, especially in the subtle in-mouth stages.
2017 Review: ★ ★ ★ ★/Highly Recommended

Marca Negra Tobalá Mezcal 50% abv, $139.
Pristine appearance; colorless; flawless purity. First nosings detect soaring aromas of freshly laid asphalt, creosote, tin can, nickel, dry earth; later-stage sniffs encounter desert-dry, wholly rustic aromas of plastic, kerosene, baked agave, prickly pear. Entry is intensely bitter, rubber tire–like, deeply smoky, charred, like burning tobacco; midpalate echoes the entry, especially with the bitterness, as the taste profile turns briny, salty, green olive–like. Wildly flavorful finish.
2017 Review: ★ ★ ★ ★/Highly Recommended

Mayalen Wild Cupreata Joven Mezcal 48.1% abv, $50.
Pristine, limpid, sediment-free appearance. Smells out of the gate like the dry stone, arid land, cardboard, herbal, sagebrush, prickly pear scents of the dewy morning desert; secondary sniffs pick up subtle notes of pencil eraser, asphalt, creosote, dried sage. Entry is highly viscous, green vegetable–like, sweet and sour, tart, astringent, beany; midpalate mirrors the entry profile, delving deeper into the green vegetable aspect to the point where it's charred vegetable matter by the smoky, sweet aftertaste.
2016 Review: ★ ★ ★ ★/Highly Recommended

Mezcalero No. 16 Mezcal 47.1% abv, $96.
Crystalline clarity; void of color. This linear up-front and intensely "green" aroma is all about flax, textile fibers, hemp, cigarette tobacco; secondary inhalations pick up notes of fennel, manila, green-leaf vegetable that are underlined by a core fragrance of dry earth/soil—really interesting bouquet, this one. Entry is remarkably stone-like, intensely minerally, even a touch horseradish-like, brazenly tangy, and feral; midpalate reflects the entry to a tee but expands the horseradish character that brings a zestiness that's vegetal and raw. Aftertaste is properly oily, astringent, mildly smoky, and extended.
2016 Review: ★ ★ ★ ★/Highly Recommended

Mezcalero No. 18 Mezcal 47% abv, $96.
Bicuixe, madrecuixe, and espadín agaves. Clear and as colorless as rainwater. I immediately get rubber inner tube, creosote, rubber pencil eraser, and envelope glue scents that are more fruity than spicy, more ripe than bitter or piquant, and more rubbery than herbal, but altogether exhilarating; later sniffs pick up prickly pear and kiwi scents, along with smoldering campfire notes that add a touch of charcoal/carbon. Entry is dazzlingly peppery, citrusy, dusty dry yet bittersweet simultaneously, and loaded with raw agave/vegetal thrust; midpalate takes a left turn, highlighting the sweeter side of the ripe agave in potent waves of tobacco ash, sandalwood, and tobacco chaw. Finishes blustery, smoked, salty, and ash-like. Could be nothing else but real-deal village mezcal represented by the wizards at Craft Distillers.
2017 Review: ★ ★ ★ ★/Highly Recommended

Mezcalero No. 19 Mezcal 47% abv, $95.

Clear-as-rainwater appearance; colorless. Opening sniffs detect large, assertive scents of rubber inner tube, cigarette ashes, creosote, burnt matches, oil paint, and agave frond; secondary inhalations affirm the first-stage impressions, adding jalapeño pepper, poblano pepper, ancho, glue, and seaweed. Entry tastes are sweeter, riper than I had anticipated as they reflect agave syrup, honeysuckle petals, dill, licorice, green tobacco, and black pepper; midpalate deepens the taste profile by bringing in the oily, satiny texture, which blankets the tongue in smoked pepper, olive brine, green olive, and canola oil flavors. Finishes long, campfire smoky, oily, creosote-like, and sap-like. Lovely.

2018 Review: ★ ★ ★ ★ ★/Highest Recommendation

Mezcalero No. 2 Mezcal 48.76% abv, $135.

Impeccably pure and colorless. This frontline aroma pushes pickle brine, dill, fennel, palm oil scents in your face without apology plus there's an undercurrent of spirit that's borderline piquant/prickly; following further air contact, the aroma turns vegetable garden–like, offering dry, tangy notes of textile fiber, flax, canola oil, corrugated cardboard. Entry is so smooth that it's silky and oily, mildly piquant and spicy (chili pepper), and satisfyingly elegant, yet dense; midpalate brings out more density of flavor as the taste profile steers in the vegetal directions of baked eggplant, grilled asparagus, sautéed brussels sprouts. Aftertaste remains vegetal, roasted/toasty, slightly smoky, and peppery but offers a honey-like final taste that's succulent and luscious.

2016 Review: ★ ★ ★ ★ ★/Highest Recommendation

Mezcalero No. 3 Mezcal 48.5% abv, $135.

Wild tobalá agaves. Void of color; sediment-free clarity. This oily, acutely vegetal, and floral opening nose is rife with potato skins, nails, saddle leather, carnations, orange blossom, jasmine, and honeysuckle fragrances that merge into a unified bouquet after ten minutes of air contact; secondary sniffs pick up fruity scents of kiwi, papaya, guava, poi, and banana that intermingle with the oily, leathery, and floral scents that never once let you forget what the base material is: tobalá agave. Entry is sultry, smoky, vegetal, and deeply herbal; midpalate reflects all the entry impressions and adds dill, green olive, pickle brine, and sea salt. Ends on a toasty/smoked note that's on the sweeter side of the dry/sweet scale but luscious and sensual all the way.

2017 Review: ★ ★ ★ ★ ★/Highest Recommendation

Mezcalero No. 8 Don Valente Angel, Santa Maria la Pila, Oaxaca Mezcal 47.9% abv, $84.

Produced from wild/semiwild madrecuixe, dobadán, and tobalá agaves. Translucent; colorless; inconsequential sediment seen. Opening whiffs provide major-league aromas of pickle brine, sweet pickle relish for your hot dog, plus vinegar, mustard seed, poppy seed; later on, I breathe in supplemental aromas of lacquer, floor polish, and broiled red pepper. Entry is satiny in texture, citrusy, deeply tobacco-like (pipe), mildly vinegary; midpalate features scaled-back pickle relish, caramelized onion, maple char, baked agave. Finishes

moderately, not overwhelmingly smoky or rubbery or medicinal, but rather tight, integrated, off-dry, vegetal, mildly smoked.
2014 Review: ★★★★★/Highest Recommendation

Mezcalero No. 8 Santa Maria la Pila Mezcal 47.9% abv, $84.
Tobalá, madrecuixe, dobadán agaves. Clean and clear as rainwater. This mezcal is deceptively understated as it grudgingly gives off measured opening fragrances of fresh dill, pickle brine, green olive, vinyl; following further aeration, there's a shift in focus to granite/stone, dried-earth aromas that impart a subtle rubberiness mixed with pickle brine. Entry is smoked, tobacco-like, astringent, dry as a bone, intensely phenolic; midpalate is more rubbery, baked asparagus–like, smoky. Finishes a little short, dry, toasty.
2016 Review: ★★★★/Highly Recommended

Mezcalosfera de Mezcaloteca Magueyes Bicuixe Madrecuixe y Verde Mezcal 48.9% abv, $179.
This appearance owns a faint tint of pale yellow at the edges; some minor sediment seen. I like this opening fragrance, which is green, vegetal, and slightly pickled with dill-like scents; the robust agave/vegetal aroma remains firm, vibrant, and mildly spiced with green peppers, mustard seed, shallot. Entry is on the sweeter side of the dry/sweet scale, but there's a vegetable garden vitality and heartiness to the flavor profile that's quite irresistible; midpalate echoes the entry, adding succulent tastes of chamomile, honey, green tea, and tobacco leaf that lead into a mineral-like finish. Expensive, but a dandy mezcal that runs with the best in the marketplace.
2019 Review: ★★★★★/Highest Recommendation

Miel de Tierra Añejo Mezcal 40% abv, $72.
Bright flax/gold color; flawless purity. Hello, Aroma, where are you? Virtually void of fragrance and a kind of mezcal vodka, a mezka in other words. Entry is dismally dull and blah, as scant flavor character is found; midpalate ditto. Stop wasting my time with this gutless, zero-charm garbage that has nothing to do with mezcal. So lacking in character I can't even laugh at it. If you even think of buying this, I may never speak to you again.
2016 Review: ★/Not Recommended

Miel de Tierra Joven Mezcal 40% abv, $55.
Clear and clean and colorless as springwater. There's a fresh fruitiness to this opening aroma that's void of smoke, road tar, tobacco expectations and is therefore squeaky clean if slightly oily; later sniffs detect notes of banana, soy sauce, orange blossom, fresh peas, Boston lettuce—hardly your typical mezcal bouquet, but its crisp freshness is appealing, if against assumptions. Entry is curiously sweet, then sour, then a touch mossy/white button mushroom–like in the first in-mouth stage; midpalate remains true to the fungi/mushroom-like entry as the flavor profile stays nimble, delicate in intensity but texturally oily and creamy. Finishes cleanly, crisply, and short to medium long in length. A tidied-up mezcal, dressed in a suit, and playing against type.
2016 Review: ★★★/Recommended

Miel de Tierra Salmiana Joven Mezcal 40% abv, $89.

Colorless; pristine purity. This opening aroma is keenly paper-like, parchment-like, as well as white onion–like, scallion-like, and even a bit like soybean/tofu and steamed white rice; later sniffs after more aeration discover lean, acidic, but not astringent fragrances that are reflective more of green vegetable than salt, brine, or smoke. Entry is assiduously clean, acidic, slightly rubbery, even a touch tarmac-like as the controlled smokiness builds with time and palate coverage; midpalate offers a moderately powerful smoke punch that's gently sweet, tar-like, and saline, but there's more to this flavor profile as it advances into the after-taste stage, featuring (suddenly) sweet-ish tastes of tropical fruits, agave syrup, and sugar. It's like this mezcal was designed to be well-mannered, but its naturally feral nature couldn't be reined in altogether.

2016 Review: ★ ★ ★ ★/Highly Recommended

Miel de Tierra Reposado Mezcal 40% abv, $62.

Chardonnay-yellow/gamboge color; excellent clarity. The buttoned-down opening aroma is disappointingly inexpressive and lackluster—I move on; secondary inhalations after more air contact uncover very little in the way of aromatic expansion, and except for meager notes of cotton fiber and soybean, there's not a lot happening here. Entry is medium sweet, mildly oily in texture, but like the uninspired bouquet, the first taste profile is too cleaned up and tequila-like for me; midpalate is boringly mute, void of any smoky agave thrust, and is totally oak-driven. While there are no glaring technical flaws, this is Mezcal Lite, and therefore of no interest to me.

2016 Review: ★ ★/Not Recommended

Montelobos Espadín Mezcal 43.2% abv, $40.

Crystal-clear appearance; void of color. Subtle aromas of sliced almond, textile fiber, hemp, bay leaf, and savory mingle nicely in the opening sniffs; secondary inhalations don't pick up any additional scents, as the established fragrances come together into a unified bouquet that's gentle, elegant, and slightly peach-like. Entry is chalky tasting, mineral-like, stony, and a bit like charcoal briquette/carbon; midpalate features the carbon aspect but more as cigar ash than campfire. Finishes dense with woodsmoke. I was heading to four stars in the aroma, then the taste profile diverted a bit too much from the aroma.

2019 Review: ★ ★ ★/Recommended

Montelobos Tobalá Mezcal 46.8% abv, $100.

Clean-as-springwater appearance; no color. I like this opening bouquet, which has traces of flowers, lemongrass, citrus peel, matchstick, and paraffin; following more air con-tact, an earthy quality emerges, reminiscent of arid landscape, sagebrush, and eucalyptus. Entry is silky, delicately smoked, tobacco ash–like, and mineral-like; midpalate reflects the entry aspects, adding flavors of lead pencil, textile fiber, and ore. The complex aftertaste is medium long.

2019 Review: ★ ★ ★ ★/Highly Recommended

Papá Rey Espadín Joven Mezcal 40% abv, $35.

Shows a bit of pewter tint; pristine clarity. Oh my, there're vibrant earthy scents of wax

paper, clay, campfire embers, and inner tube that leave a positive first impression; following more aeration, the bouquet takes on a waxier, textile fiber–like profile that's neither dry nor sweet but somewhere in between. Entry goes a touch sweeter than I anticipated, but the agave character remains peppery, tobacco-like, and wholly intact; midpalate shows a bit more spice than the entry stage, but overall, it remains gently sweet, green vegetable–like, and fat in texture.
2019 Review: ★★★/Recommended

Real Minero Barril Joven Mezcal 49.9% abv, $130.
Harvest 2014. Batch size eight hundred 750 ml bottles. Oyster coloring; excellent clarity. I like the seaside forest opening aromas of sea salt, fennel, spring onion, camphor, eucalyptus, and olive brine; further time in the glass allows for added elemental scents like tin can, gunmetal, pewter, and ore. Entry is succulent, fruity, especially kiwi-, pineapple-, and melon-like, and salty sweet, kind of like sea salt mixed into toffee; midpalate is more settled and refined as the taste profile features citrusy aspects (tangerine, grapefruit) as well as a grassiness that's vegetal and earthy in equal measure. Aftertaste is medium long, ripe with fruit, lemony, and vegetal. Rode the four star/five star fence—a bit more core complexity in the finish would have placed it on the five star side. As it is, this is a solid, sturdy four star mezcal.
2017 Review: ★★★★/Highly Recommended

Real Minero Espadín-Largo-Tripon-Barril Joven Mezcal 46.9% abv, $150.
Harvest 2004. Batch size 930 750 ml bottles. Oyster-like, silvery coloring; perfect purity. There's a waxy, textile fiber-like, metallic opening aroma that's fetching and elemental; secondary whiffs detect deeper fragrances of vegetation, mostly green tea, green tobacco leaf, parsley, and tomato vine. Entry is oily, buttery, tart, and slightly fruity (quince, pear); midpalate features a high degree of fruit presence, as well as a furniture polish–like aspect that's industrial and fibrous. Aftertaste is rather brief, mildly toasted, and a touch sweet. Some substantial virtues still exist here, but there's a sense that the core is becoming hollow and past its peak.
2017 Review: ★★★/Recommended

Real Minero Largo Joven Mezcal 47.8% abv, $150.
Harvest 2014. Batch size 361 750 ml bottles. Tarnished-silver tint; impeccable purity. The initial nosing brings with it a whole array of fragrances, including carob, coffee bean, hydrangea, toasted marshmallow, burnt matches, Spanish onion, and tomato vine; more aeration time brings out bigger bean-like aromas, especially coffee and cocoa, along with black tea and brown-butter scents; this is a complex bouquet. Entry is rich and oily in texture, piquant and peppery in flavors, and starchy and semisweet; midpalate features deep, tasty fruit and herb flavors of dried orange peel, honey, lavender, clove, and allspice. Concludes on a fruity note (citrus zest) that's also herbal (bay leaf, parsley, mustard seed) and rustic in character.
2017 Review: ★★★★/Highly Recommended

Real Minero Pechuga Joven Mezcal 57.7% abv, $175.
Harvest 2008. Batch size 984 750 ml bottles. Owns a pewter-like hint of color;

sediment-free. Smells politely of sandalwood, cedar sawdust, vegetable cooking oil, and peat moss in the initial whiffs after the pour; secondary inhalations pick up slightly more traditional mezcal fragrances, such as campfire embers, lead pencil, rubber inner tube, and cigarette ash but they are of the low-wattage variety. Entry flavors display the rusticity of artisanal mezcal in the forms of baked banana, seaweed, baked cabbage, and caramelized onion; midpalate shines with sharp, edgy peppery/spicy tastes of jalapeño pepper, cayenne, and olive brine. Finishes medium long, nicely peppery, yet savory. Delicious.
2017 Review: ★ ★ ★ ★ ★/Highest Recommendation

Rey Campero Cuixe Joven Mezcal 48.1% abv, $95.
Batch size 1,729 750 ml bottles. While I see some floating tendrils of sediment in the core, I don't see problematic issues; colorless. I get all sorts of wild agave smells here, from box of rubber bands to clove to mustard seed to poppy seed to hazelnut, and that's just within the first minute or two; more aeration stimulates more pungent scents, including aniseed, licorice, carnation, chamomile, and tobacco. Entry is zesty, peppery, piquant, and oily in texture while the taste profile features honeysuckle, paraffin, burnt match, and metal coin; midpalate brings all the various taste points together in a crescendo of flavor that's bittersweet, honeyed, highly vegetal, mildly herbal, and altogether lovely. Concludes medium long, moderately smoky, and ripe.
2017 Review: ★ ★ ★ ★/Highly Recommended

Rey Campero Espadín Joven Mezcal 48% abv, $60.
Batch size 1,694 750 ml bottles. There's a pale pewter tint to this appearance, which otherwise is translucent and pure. This opening nose has the gunmetal/coin smell of espadín all over it, along with tart elements, such as grapefruit and prickly pear; later sniffs following more air contact discover flowery scents, in particular of orange blossom and geranium, plus tangy notes of black pepper and eucalyptus. Entry is sharp at first as the acids and alcohol converge on the tip of the tongue, then the mild burn changes into a fireplace warmth with aridly dry, moderately herbal flavors of stone, sage, and resin taking charge; midpalate is pleasant, dry as a bone, and nicely vegetal with agave spice and tartness. Concludes herbal and leafy (tobacco, tomato vine). A solid but not spectacular espadín.
2017 Review: ★ ★ ★/Recommended

Rey Campero Jabalí Joven Mezcal 49% abv, $118.
Batch size eighty 750 ml bottles. Void of color; immaculately pure. Immediately, I get smells of paraffin, candle wax, waxy fruit peel, sawdust, tree bark, and prickly pear; later sniffs pick up leather, shoe polish, walnut paste, coriander, charcoal, and kerosene. Entry flavor is semisweet, fruity (banana), salty, and like salted butter; midpalate stage is the apex as evolved tastes of green tea, sautéed mushroom, lemongrass, and cocoa bean merge into one flavor that is mature, earthy/soil-like, and clay-like. This harmonious flavor extends deep in the aftertaste, which builds with tastes of sweet pipe tobacco smoke and charred marshmallow.
2017 Review: ★ ★ ★ ★/Highly Recommended

Rey Campero Madrecuixe Joven Mezcal 48.6% abv, $95.
Batch size 1,757 750 ml bottles. Pewter-like coloring; totally sediment-free. I get

immediate hits of terra-cotta pot, pencil eraser, asphalt, fennel, and chamomile in the zesty opening whiffs; allowing it another eight minutes to aerate, I dive in again, picking up carbon, matchstick, wet sand, seaweed, dill, and green-olive brine. Entry is sultry, tangy, a bit like jalapeño pepper, paprika, savory, and mustard seed; midpalate is toasted, briny, salty, and akin to salted toffee. Aftertaste is long, buttery, keenly vegetal, and piquant, reflecting the carbon/matchstick noted in the second inhalations.

2017 Review: ★ ★ ★ ★/Highly Recommended

Rey Campero Mexicano Joven Mezcal 48.6% abv, $95.

Batch size 1,782 750 ml bottles. Void of color; sediment-free purity. There's a whole menu of odors here, including egg white, white peppercorn, vanilla bean, savory, and verbena; more air contact makes the nose fade a bit as the piquancy element turns citrusy and zesty. Entry-taste profile features lead pencil, cactus, not so much carbon or charcoal as brown butter and tobacco leaf; midpalate sees the taste fade a little too quickly, leaving nothing much for the aftertaste, which should be a big moment for mezcal. The aroma and entry are nearly worth the experience, but many mezcal veterans might be disappointed with the lame midpalate and finish.

2017 Review: ★ ★/Not Recommended

Rey Campero Tepextate Joven Mezcal 48.27% abv, $118.

Batch size 760 750 ml bottles. As transparent and colorless as rainwater; superb clarity. At first sniff, I find incongruous, yet lovely, fragrances of dried flowers (violet and hydrangea), creosote, vinyl, chamomile, and eucalyptus; following several more minutes of air contact, the aroma stays the earthy, vegetal, spent garden route, offering autumnal scents of lichen, mushroom, peat moss, and damp compost. Entry is full-weighted, velvety in texture, sharply tangy, and peppery, yet fruity sweet and caramelized; midpalate offers evolved, mature, integrated flavors of sage, pickle brine, dill, sea salt, baked pineapple, kiwi, and black tea. Concludes very long, smoky, ash-like, and tasting of cigar. A beauty that showcases the wild tepextate agave at its briny, salty, fruity finest.

2017 Review: ★ ★ ★ ★ ★/Highest Recommendation

Rey Campero Tobalá Joven Mezcal 48.5% abv, $118.

Batch size 893 750 ml bottles. Like the Espadín, I see a faint touch of tarnished silver coloring here; perfect clarity. That hushed tobalá aroma of crushed flower petal, distant tangerine peel, lavender, verbena, and lemongrass is beguiling and fathomless; more time in the glass allows for deft touches of herbs (bay leaf, coriander) and fruit (green melon, kiwi) to emerge, creating an elegant, tangy, and iconic bouquet. Entry is ripe, fruity, and herbal, yet there's also a building oiliness to the texture that carries the flavors forward into the sensuous, rich, and peppery midpalate that is the apex moment of the evaluation. Aftertaste echoes the sublime midpalate point as the taste winds down, becoming more smoky, charred, and bittersweet.

2017 Review: ★ ★ ★ ★ ★/Highest Recommendation

Rey Campero Wild Tepextate Joven Mezcal 49% abv, $115.
Crystal clear; colorless purity. Whoa, I get vibrant jalapeño pepper, black pepper, terra-cotta, and palm tree fragrances in abundance in the initial whiffs; the highly pleasant aroma continues to impress after more air contact, releasing added scents of asphalt, lemongrass, citrus peel, and yellow onion. Entry is an eye-opening taste experience that's lightly toasted, salty, mildly smoked, and vegetal, and this all comes wrapped in a creamy texture; midpalate echoes the entry findings while throwing in the zestiness of freshly ground black pepper, poblano pepper, smoked paprika, and carbon. Finishes long, sweeter due to the increasing smokiness, and satisfying.
2019 Review: ★ ★ ★ ★/Highly Recommended

Vago Elote Espadín Mezcal 51.1% abv, $55.
Shows just a hint of pewter color; clear as rainwater. This mega-vegetal opening fragrance is all about asparagus, brussels sprouts, spinach, and leeks; secondary whiffs pick up additional herbal scents of sage, bay leaf, parsley, and fennel. Entry takes a left turn that leaves the aromatic impressions behind as it features flavors of salted butter, bacon fat, lard, hard-boiled egg, and cabbage; midpalate adds tastes of eucalyptus, tomato vine, and tomatillo. Aftertaste is medium long, vegetal.
2019 Review: ★ ★ ★ ★/Highly Recommended

Vago Jarquin Espadín Mezcal 50.6% abv, $53.
Silvery appearance; superb clarity. Up-front nosing passes pick up earthy traces of diesel fuel, lead pencil, creosote, charcoal, and campfire embers; later sniffs detect burning leaves, tobacco ashes, and baked green-vegetable scents. Entry is zesty, spicy, peppery, and mildly salty; midpalate features rubber tire, textile fiber, road tar, and nicotine flavors. Finishes smoky, burnt, and carbon filled.
2019 Review: ★ ★ ★/Recommended

Yuu Baal Espadín Añejo Mezcal 40% abv, $60.
Very pretty nine-karat-gold/gamboge color; impeccably clean and sediment-free. The fragrance is tight, austere, sappy, slightly resiny in the first sniffs; later inhalations after additional aeration uncover faint echoes of creosote, cement, asphalt, but little more. Entry is oaky, with hints of vanilla, buttercream, and nougat that all go a long way to mask the agave underpinning; midpalate is pleasingly oily in texture, slightly smoked, salty, and piney. Aftertaste is long, creamy, lightly spiced, with my only complaint being that the zesty agave aspect is eclipsed by the wood maturation, making it more tequila-like than a mezcal.
2016 Review: ★ ★ ★/Recommended

Yuu Baal Espadín Joven Mezcal 48% abv, $40.
Nearly colorless, but showing a subtle tint of tarnished-silver/pewter; excellent purity. There is naturally the surface fragrance of rubber tire/pencil eraser, which more than any other has become the hallmark scent of mezcal, but there's also an underlying aroma of

textile fiber/agave frond that's both intensely vegetal and compelling; later sniffs detect arid landscape scents of dried sage, dry earth, sandy beach, and loose leaf tobacco—I like this bouquet. Entry reflects the purity found and appreciated in the aroma as the flavor profile goes tangy, a little prickly on the tongue (me like), herbal, and spicy (freshly ground black pepper); midpalate is pleasingly oily in texture, deeply vegetal, "green," fresh, acidic, astringent, and delicious all the way deep into the aftertaste.
2016 Review: ★ ★ ★ ★ /Highly Recommended

Yuu Baal Espadín Reposado Mezcal 40% abv, $50.
Attractive pale hay/bisque yellow color; unblemished clarity. This initial aroma is exotic and invitingly pure as evocative scents of nail polish, plastic, vinyl flooring, and agave pulp vie for dominance, with faint evidence of rubber; following more air contact, there suddenly is a rubber band–like fragrance that leads to earthiness, slight herbaceousness, and green olive fragrances. Entry has more of a tobacco ash-like smokiness to it than the more agave-driven Espadín Joven; midpalate highlights the smoke in more of a road tar/asphalt manner, setting up the palate for a big textured, oily finish that's as rubbery as it is cigar-like. Finishes elegantly, sturdier than the Joven as the extra barrel time adds lushness. Nice job here.
2016 Review: ★ ★ ★ ★ /Highly Recommended

Yuu Baal Madrecuixe Joven Mezcal 48% abv, $130.
Totally transparent; crystalline appearance. Wow, I get early-stage fragrances of green peas, ink, plastic, split pea soup, navy bean that all take me by surprise for their offbeat nature, but that's not to say that I don't like them because I most certainly do; second-stage inhalations encounter more intense beaniness than anything else except for a fiber-like scent that reminds me of plastic three-ring binders. Entry is highly plastic-like and almost grain kernel–like in its resinous approach; midpalate stays the narrow resiny course as the flavor profile offers too little in the way of expansion to justify the price tag. Recommendable due to its intensity, but nowhere near the grace and character of the Tobalá and Tepeztate.
2016 Review: ★ ★ ★ /Recommended

Yuu Baal Tepeztate Joven Mezcal 48% abv, $140.
Void of color or tint; silvery clean. This subtle up-front aroma offers elemental hints of billiard ball, stone slab, slate, dry cement, river stone, clay; second-stage whiffs pick up ashtray, tobacco leaf, smoldering campfire, lightly toasted marshmallow, seared meat. Entry takes me by surprise due to an up-front sweetness that vanishes within seconds, leaving behind toasty, tobacco-like flavors that echo the bouquet; midpalate is lean, slightly smoky and sooty, with sideline tastes of rubber and agave syrup. Concludes long, spicy, burnt, and ashy.
2016 Review: ★ ★ ★ ★ /Highly Recommended

Yuu Baal Tobalá Joven Mezcal 48% abv, $130.
Colorless; limpid; sediment-free and pristine. Okay, here we go, with opening scents of rubber ball/tennis ball, agave pulp, green vegetable, green olive, olive brine, saltine cracker;

later inhalations detect dill pickle, jalapeño pepper, textile fiber, dry earth, sheet metal, patent leather. Entry is keenly rubbery, zesty, a little prickly, highly vegetal, salty, "green"; midpalate is long and more focused on the agave/vegetal flavor than the entry, which I like and applaud. Finishes clean as a whistle, prickly, peppery, and free of any wood maturation interference, for which I'm grateful. A handsome, elegant, classical mezcal of character and density.

2016 Review: ★ ★ ★ ★ ★/Highest Recommendation

SOTOL AND BACANORA-MEXICO

Other Agave Spirit Varieties

Sotol: traditional agave beverage of Durango, Chihuahua, and Coahuila states

Bacanora: agave spirit of the state of Sonora

Raicilla: agave spirit that resembles mezcal from Jalisco

Clande Sotol 48.8% abv, $80.
Pristine clarity; colorless. Initial nosings pick up dry, almost plastic-like fragrances of black pepper, creosote, lemon oil, caramelized onion, and pickled herring; secondary aromatic laps find additional scents of pipe tobacco, camphor, hemp, and terra-cotta. Entry is piquant, heavily spiced with black pepper, and more than a bit tasting like rotten onion; midpalate is awash with nasty chemical-like flavors of sulfur and carbon/charcoal briquette. Stay well clear of this one.
2019 Review: ★/Not Recommended

Rancho Tepúa Bacanora 48% abv, $50.
Void of color; small amount of floating sediment seen. First aromas are of burning rope/hemp, woodsmoke, creosote, and roasted agave; later inhalations detect lightly charred, mineral-like scents of cigarette ash, lead pipe, corrugated cardboard, pond water, and latex. Entry is strikingly sweet, tobacco-like, and sooty, with an agave nectar twang; midpalate is more mineral-like and earthy, featuring tastes of pine tar, tree resin, burnt maple, and metal. Finishes earthy, elemental, drier than the entry, and vegetal. Not my cup of tea.
2019 Review: ★ ★/Not Recommended

Santo Cuviso Joven Bacanora 45% abv, $92.
Silvery appearance; no coloration. This opening aroma is lard-like initially, then it morphs into a plastic-like scent that's lacking in agave charm; secondary whiffs after more aeration don't make any headway in the bouquet as the primary aroma of plastic furniture covering remains firmly in charge. Entry shows more elegance than found at any point in the bouquet as the flavor profile offers salty tastes of butter, spring onion, cauliflower, and lime peel; midpalate echoes the entry but fails to exhibit enough core charm and substance to warrant a recommendation.
2019 Review: ★ ★/Not Recommended

VODKA-WORLD

Modern-day vodka is produced from just about any fermentable organic material, but it is mostly the result of widely cultivated grains, such as wheat, corn, barley, sorghum, and rye. The first vodkas originated in Poland and Russia at about the same time, the fourteenth century CE, with the initial historical record being a Polish court document, dated 1405. Long perceived as a neutral spirit (clear libation) primarily from eastern and northern Europe and later Scandinavia, vodka today is made in scores of nations, in both unflavored and flavored versions.

Though erroneously depicted as being "flavorless, odorless, and colorless," especially by the United States government, vodka offers, in fact, a broad range of tastes, textures, and aromas. These distinctions depend largely upon the specific base material (grain, grape, fruit, sugar beets, potatoes, sugarcane), the variety of distillation (pot still versus column still), and the source of filtration (charcoal, quartz, compacted paper, diamonds, precious metals).

Since the 1950s, vodka has likewise been the key spirit base for myriad cocktails and thus is viewed by most bartenders around the world as an indispensable staple spirit. Vodka hit its most recent peak of popularity in the three-year period of 2010–2012. According to Statista, it is predicted to reach 578 million liters in 2021. Even accounting for the vodka segment's weird phase of laboratory-generated flavors of 2010–2015 (wedding cake, cotton candy, bubble gum, et cetera) that damaged its reputation as a serious distillate, vodka has come through the darkness of that unfortunate miscalculation in relatively good shape.

No matter what your favorite gin-smitten bartender might claim, no matter how many times its own cavalier marketers declare it's been distilled or filtered, no matter that the majority are void of color or barrel aging, vodka should not be dismissed as a lesser category to whiskey or brandy or gin. The reality, as substantiated by history, is this: vodka remains a classic and wholly relevant spirit, one with an undeniably authentic centuries-old pedigree rooted deeply in several cultures that many millions of consumers across the globe relish.

I have included in this chapter *aquavit/akvavit*, the vodka-like spirit produced mostly in Scandinavian nations. Popular since the 1400s, aquavit is made from grain or potatoes and is gently flavored with herbs and/or seeds. Aquavit, the spirit, is obviously identified with the Latin words for water of life, aqua vitae.

Absolut Citron Citrus Vodka (Sweden) 40% abv, $20.
Made from wheat. Clear and clean as rainwater; colorless. First up aromatically, I pick up nuances of lime and lemon, with the lemon leading by a full length; later sniffs encounter

ripe, fresh-squeezed lemon juice and pulp, but no zest or peel—this is a superbly defined bouquet. Entry is where the zestiness of lemon peel comes into a major role that crackles with astringency; at midpalate, the brisk, razor-edged acids smooth out somewhat, creating a mouthfeel that's round, almost chewy, yet still sharply defined by the lemon juice. Ends clean as a whistle, zesty, and trim.

2018 Rating: ★★★★/Highly Recommended

Absolut Elyx Vodka (Sweden) 40% abv, $50.

Clear and pristine. The inviting toasty opening aroma is desert dry and intensely grain-driven; additional time in the glass fires up a beany/grain kernel bitterness that's highly attractive and pungent. Smooth as silk at entry, more off-dry than dry, and wonderfully breakfast cereal–like; the flavor intensity ascends in the midpalate as the taste profile goes dusty dry, grainy, bittersweet, nutty, cocoa bean– and snack cracker–like. Robust in the aftertaste. Unflavored vodka with tons of flavor, texture, and character.

2017 Rating: ★★★★★/Highest Recommendation

Absolut Grapefruit Vodka (Sweden) 40% abv, $20.

Clear and colorless as rainwater. I like this opening fragrance a lot, as it clearly depicts the tart pith and juice of freshly sliced yellow grapefruit; secondary sniffs pick up what's already been described, especially the juice aspect more than the pulp/pith. Entry is keenly grapefruit-like, properly astringent, juicy, and tart; midpalate dutifully stays the course plotted by the entry. Aftertaste tartness makes me pucker a little. Definitely true to a very tart grapefruit strain, but I wouldn't have minded a strain with a smidgen more natural sugar to counter the severity of the acid.

2019 Rating: ★★★/Recommended

Absolut Hibiskus Vodka (Sweden) 40% abv, $21.

Flawless purity; transparent. Opening nosing passes after the pour delight in the beautifully matched fruit and floral flavorings of pomegranate and hibiscus, which are evenly proportioned; following another six minutes of aeration, the bouquet turns more flowery than fruity, and that directional change works well as the natural elegance of the hibiscus makes for pleasurable sniffing. Entry is evenly split between the fruit and floral aspects, showing plenty of acidity; midpalate stage features the two starring leads in harmony as the taste profile goes dry and quietly fruity ripe. Finish is all about the hibiscus.

2016 Rating: ★★★★/Highly Recommended

Absolut Lime Vodka (Sweden) 40% abv, $20.

Pristine clarity and void of color. Like other Absolut flavored vodkas, this comely, inviting opening aroma is a revelation of authenticity to the source and more akin to key lime than other strains of the citrus fruit; further down the aromatic road, the bouquet tones down the tartness in favor of a gentle ripeness that's totally fetching. Entry is delicate in its depiction of lime and is therefore a touch sour and zesty; midpalate features more of the lime juiciness and that's a plus, as the flavor profile sings with freshness and citrus piquancy. Finishes medium long, tart, and pleasant.

2019 Rating: ★★★★/Highly Recommended

Absolut Mandarin Vodka (Sweden) 40% abv, $20.
Made from wheat. Pristine clarity; colorless. The buoyancy of the opening aroma that screams "RIPE ORANGE!" is delightful and invigoratingly tart without being pithy or pulpy; secondary nosing passes find slightly less animated scents of orange rind along with the inherent juiciness, but there is a noticeable decrease in the aromatic luster with further air contact. Entry is pleasantly juicy, astringent, and zesty, as the flavor of orange peel moves to the forefront, bringing with it an acute tartness that I like; midpalate reflects the entry mainly in continuing with the peel-driven tartness that makes my mouth pucker. Finishes fresh, juicy, and keenly zesty. As delightful as I remembered from eighteen years ago.
2018 Rating: ★ ★ ★ ★/Highly Recommended

Absolut Vodka (Sweden) 40% abv, $21.
Impeccable purity and totally colorless. First whiffs encounter soft scents of breakfast cereal, wheat toast, and yeast; additional time in the glass brings out a cracked pepper quality that adds tanginess and spice; impressive in its razor-crisp cleanness. Entry is subtle, dry, breakfast cereal–like, and slightly spiced; midpalate is toasty, bread-like, and seed-like. Finishes moderately oily, silky, and clean as a whistle. Superb distillation.
2020 Rating: ★ ★ ★/Recommended

Ao Vodka (Japan) 40% abv, $50.
Japanese rice base. Clean and pure appearance. Smells alluringly of Arborio rice/white rice, jasmine, citrus in the initial whiffs; citric acid eclipses grain/rice element in later stages, giving it a crisp, clean bouquet that is totally dry. Entry is razor sharp and dry, with traces of lead pencil, stone, minerals; midpalate is bone-dry, refreshing, cleansing, deeply mineral-like, earthy, elemental. The aftertaste highlights the medium degree of viscosity and the acute minerality of it. Different and tangy.
2016 Rating: ★ ★ ★ ★/Highly Recommended

Ardent Union Tri-Blend Vodka (USA) 44.4% abv, $30.
Crystalline purity. The earthy, bread crumb–like or, better, panko-like winter wheat aroma catapults from the glass in the initial nosing pass, creating a pleasing first impression that demolishes the myth that unflavored vodka is featureless; later sniffs discover dry scents of cement and sand, but there are also parallel fragrances of bay laurel and Styrofoam that delight. Entry is round, keenly peppery to the point of being piquant, a touch salty, and firmly structured; midpalate provides the big prize as the 88.8 proof enters the equation, providing a robust taste component that's square jawed, hearty, and in yer face. Finishes long, dry, cereal-like, and mildly toasted. No-nonsense style is alluring and daring.
2019 Rating: ★ ★ ★ ★ ★/Highest Recommendation

Belvedere Intense Vodka (Poland) 50% abv, $55.
Ideal clarity; colorless. The opening fragrance of seedless rye bread is zesty and welcome; later whiffs after more aeration pick up nuances of clay, dry earth, and stone that underline this vodka's severe, lead pencil–like dryness. The aggression in the entry phase perks up the taste buds, but then that aspect fades, leaving in its wake a dry-cereal flavor that's one-dimensional; midpalate stage offers a trace of alcohol intensity, but not enough to push

forward the rye snack cracker and cereal tastes into the aftertaste, which comes off a little flat and banal. Good and drinkable, but I'd hoped for more pizzaz.
2019 Rating: ★ ★ ★/Recommended

Belvedere Lake Bartezek Single Estate Rye Unfiltered Polish Vodka (Poland) 40% abv, $40/liter.
Flawless purity; no color. The first whiffs pick up delicate fragrances of unseeded rye bread, lightly toasted bread, and pebbles; after more air contact, the aroma opens up slightly, allowing for greater access to scents of fresh water, rainfall, and marshland. Entry is sublime in its flavor composition, as defined tastes of minerals, stone, fresh water, and ore combine with dry cereal, unsalted snack cracker, and sourdough to create a stunningly sophisticated taste profile that runs smoothly through the midpalate and all the way into the textbook finish, in which all the moving parts dwell in complete harmony. A masterpiece of unflavored vodka majesty and elegance.
2019 Rating: ★ ★ ★ ★ ★/Highest Recommendation

Belvedere Smogory Forest Single Estate Rye Unfiltered Polish Vodka (Poland) 40% abv, $40/liter.
Exemplary clarity; void of color. Opening inhalations pick up distant aromas of unsalted snack cracker (Ryvita), wood chips, and wet stone; secondary whiffs find more ethereal scents that are elusive and therefore difficult to pigeonhole, except for a soft fragrance of limestone. Entry offers more character traits than the bouquet, as dry flavors of tongue on stone, oats, and ore are present; midpalate flavors highlight the dry cereal, bread dough aspects as well as zesty spice that float atop the creamy, viscous texture, creating an extended finish that is elegant and memorable.
2019 Rating: ★ ★ ★ ★/Highly Recommended

Belvedere Vodka (Poland) 40% abv, $40.
Made from rye. Obvious purity; colorless. The first inhalations detect fey, almost indistinguishable scents of grain, turpentine, and creosote; secondary whiffs are met with dry to off-dry fragrances of minerals, dry stone, and arid landscape. Entry offers much more in the way of definable attributes as the taste profile features desert-dry/dusty flavors of chalk, cereal grain, grain husk, and charcoal; midpalate highlights the deep graininess that, by now, has turned semisweet and almost resiny/sap-like. Concludes medium long, toasty, breakfast cereal–like, and a little raw in the throat. A disappointing super-premium vodka that doesn't match up to other rye vodkas, such as Sobieski.
2018 Rating: ★ ★/Not Recommended

Bismarck Vodka (Germany) 40% abv, $29.
Clean-as-a-whistle appearance; sediment-free and pure. I like the piquancy of the opening aroma after the pour because it's midlevel peppery and zesty and focused on grain kernel; with further aeration, the grain kernel spice is embellished in an appealing manner as the bouquet turns pleasantly bittersweet and nearly caramel-like. Entry is toasty/roasted, creamy, and alluringly oily; midpalate features all of the fine attributes of the entry and adds

breakfast cereal graininess that's clean, astringent, and substantial. Not a wallflower of a vodka, but one with a distinct and charming personality.
2015 Rating: ★ ★ ★ ★/Highly Recommended

BiVi Sicilian Vodka (Italy) 40% abv, $30.
Wheat. There's a slight haze in the core of this vodka that dissipates quickly so no issues here; transparent, colorless. Opening whiffs discover pleasant, dusty-dry, snack cracker–like aromas that are heavily reminiscent of Wheat Thins; second sniffs unearth fragrances of dry stone, limestone/chalk, minerals, charcoal briquettes. Entry is firm, beany (cocoa, vanilla), bitter, acutely mineral-like; midpalate echoes every flavor aspect found at entry and adds burnt toast, charcoal to the mix. Finishes quite long, charred, bitter.
2015 Rating: ★ ★ ★/Recommended

Bleustorm Ultra-Premium French Wheat Vodka (France) 40% abv, $30.
French wheat. Pristine, colorless appearance. Initial whiffs immediately pick up assertive, slightly bitter but alluring scents of graham cracker, lead pencil, fruit pit, dried apricot, spiced apple peel; second passes after further air contact accentuate the spiced apple-peel aspect and also shine the spotlight on the fruity wheat; this is a dazzling vodka bouquet. Entry mirrors the bouquet as the spiced fruit and fruit-stone elements remain strong amidst the grain intensity and complexity; midpalate reinforces the grain underpinning, exhibited mostly in the dry-as-stone foundational flavor and the medium oily viscosity. Finishes moderately long, earthy/stony, grainy, desert dry.
2015 Rating: ★ ★ ★ ★/Highly Recommended

Boru Vodka (Ireland) 40% abv, $19.
No color; superbly clean and clear. Aromatic highlights are the limestone/flint/earthy notes in the initial whiffs after the pour; secondary inhalations pick up a slightly seared/charred aspect that might be from the filtering process but it's pronounced, vegetal, and smoky. Entry reflects the burnt/smoldering element found in the latter stage of nosing and is an unusual vodka quality, but one that I like; midpalate echoes the entry and the aromatic stages to a tee. Ends lightly smoked, grainy, earthy, and clean. An underrated vodka, as I have thought for twenty years.
2020 Rating: ★ ★ ★ ★/Highly Recommended

Boyd & Blair Potato Vodka (USA) 40% abv, $29.
Very good clarity. Wow, this aroma comes flying out of the glass in waves of white potato, starch, and parchment; seven more minutes of aeration don't greatly alter the aromatic profile, but there is a noticeable deepening of the established scents, especially the raw white potato element. Entry is nothing short of luscious, semisweet, chewy, oily, and smooth; midpalate adds cocoa bean, maple, and honey. Aftertaste is graceful, solid, and simply delicious. So sumptuous and tasty that it's spectacular neat. The best small-scale vodka in the world and the finest potato vodka available from anywhere. BRAVO! AN AWESOME ACHIEVEMENT FROM THIS PENNSYLVANIA DISTILLERY!
2020 Rating: ★ ★ ★ ★ ★/Highest Recommendation

Broken Shed Premium Vodka (New Zealand) 40%, $35.

Perfect clarity; colorless and sediment-free. Whey. Wow, it isn't often that I smell a completely neutral vodka, but this one is virtually void of all aromatics except for a slight metallic/steely scent in the first inhalations after the pour; more time in the glass doesn't release much more in the way of fragrance so I move on. Entry is clean, crisp, and slightly biting (assertive spirit) on the tongue; midpalate is brisk, tightly wound, dry, and narrow in focus. Biscuity aftertaste is brief and featherlight. No flaws to cite and as a result recommendable for fans of featureless vodka.

2015 Rating: ★ ★ ★/Recommended

Cathead Vodka (USA) 40% abv, $20.

Pristine purity; colorless. Smells properly grainy, dry, and snack cracker–like in the opening whiffs, but overall neutral and slightly spirity; what aromatics were present in the first inhalations pretty much dissipate by the second round of nosing. Entry offers far more in the way of impressions than the bland aroma, mostly in crackling dry, acidic, brittle flavors of unsweetened cereal; midpalate mirrors the entry in that the high degree of acidity dries out the palate in this immaculate vodka that is a model of neutrality. While most twenty-first-century vodkas display varying levels of character, which are sometimes startlingly vivid, Cathead plays it straight to the US regulations for vodka as being odorless, colorless, flavorless. Its purity alone makes it worth recommending.

2016 Rating: ★ ★ ★/Recommended

Chase English Potato Vodka (England) 40% abv, $33.

Silvery clear and clean. Opening smell is dry and reminds me of white potato meat; secondary inhalations after more air contact reveal little more. Entry is sweeter than the bouquet, offering a buttery, oily texture that wraps around the potato-skin flavor; midpalate mirrors the entry impressions, adding just a little hint of starchiness. Ends sweetly, cleanly, and fully textured.

2018 Rating: ★ ★ ★/Recommended

Chopin Potato Vodka (Poland) 40% abv, $30.

Pristine, springwater appearance; impeccable clarity. The initial nosings after the pour present the olfactory bulb with an elegant, vegetal, dry, and altogether pleasant vodka fragrance; following another seven minutes in the glass, the bouquet turns a shade sweeter and far more potato-y, all the while maintaining its gracefulness. Entry is dusty dry, alluringly viscous, and is substantial in the mouth; midpalate features tastes of unsalted potato chips, potato peel, and fresh spirit. Aftertaste is brief, lightly oily, and blessedly dry and therefore superb for cocktail mixing.

2015 Rating: ★ ★ ★ ★/Highly Recommended

Chopin Rye Vodka (Poland) 40% abv, $30.

Perfect purity, translucent. Aromawise, one has to dig in and be persistent about gleaning any discernable fragrances from this stingy bouquet, but persistence does pay off by the second round of sniffing eight minutes in, as faint scents of citric acid, grain spirit, and mildly salty tartrate emerge. Entry is more animated than the aroma as the flavor shows a

low degree of sweetness and just a hint of spicy snap; midpalate phase is this vodka's best attribute as the flavor profile runs dry, slightly salty, spicy, and clean. Definitely recommendable as a cocktail ingredient.
2015 Rating: ★ ★ ★/Recommended

Chopin Wheat Vodka (Poland) 40% abv, $30.

Flawlessly clean, colorless, and sediment-free. Round, nicely grainy, snack cracker–like aromas abound in the generous opening whiffs; with further air contact, the bouquet turns biscuity, cookie batter–like, and a little maple-like; a lovely vodka fragrance. Entry is long, moderately viscous, silky, and delicately sweet and grainy; midpalate is breakfast cereal–like, drier than the entry, and generally delightful right through the sap-like finish. Serve either as a chilled shot or in a Gimlet. Though not a five star vodka, the best of the Chopins by a whisker.
2015 Rating: ★ ★ ★ ★/Highly Recommended

Cîroc Snap Frost Vodka (France) 40% abv, $40.

Made from French cultivated grapes. Excellent clarity; void of color. The grape base is apparent right from the first sniff in the ambrosial forms of ripe red grapes and red plums; secondary whiffs turn the aroma a little less ripe, therefore more piquant and tangy, and that development is a plus. Entry is slightly toasted, raisiny, ripe, and meaty; midpalate is especially spicy, almost citrusy in its bearing, but crisp and razor edged. During the olfactory stages I was thinking that Cîroc wasn't as impressive as it was in 2002, but once it hit my palate, there was no question as to its quality and individuality.
2018 Rating: ★ ★ ★ ★/Highly Recommended

Craft Distillers DSP CA 162 Citrus Hystrix Vodka (USA) 40% abv, $38.

Flavored with Malaysian limes and their leaves. Tarnished-silver color; pure. Intensely limey, more juicy than zesty/tangy in the opening inhalations; the deep lime presence permeates the secondary whiffs as the fruit aspect now turns more peel-like than pulpy with exposure to air. That said, the bouquet is the model of subtlety and understatement; though there are faint echoes, it ain't Rose's lime juice. Entry is acidic, cleansing, crisp, deeply lime-like, sweet/sour; midpalate features much of the entry-flavor qualities, adding a mild upturn on the sweetness. Does it echo key lime pie, one might ask? No, not even close, because to resemble key lime pie there needs to be a pastry/doughy note, and this core flavor is all about lime juice and lime juice only, which is what makes it such a potential mixing bonanza.
2014 Rating: ★ ★ ★ ★ ★/Highest Recommendation

Craft Distillers DSP CA 162 Citrus Medica Vodka (USA) 40% abv, $38.

Flavored with domestically grown Buddha's hand citrons. Bisque/ecru color of Manzanilla sherry—deepest tone of the three DSP flavoreds; flawless purity. Pleasingly acidic, clean, crisp in the first sniffs without being sharp or aggressive and, actually, more lemony than anything, though, it must be noted, citrons (Southeast Asia origins) and lemons are cousins, not siblings; later inhalations pick up subtle notes of lemongrass, pine. Entry is

clean, deeply earthy, acidic, waxy; midpalate showcases the pithiness rather than the juiciness of citron, and that is its core strength. Love the balance of this vodka.
2014 Rating: ★★★★/Highly Recommended

Craft Distillers DSP CA 162 Reticulata Var. Sunshine Vodka (USA) 40% abv, $38.
Flavored with sweet tangerines and tangelos. Pale oyster color; excellent clarity. First aromatic impressions include tangerine peel, to be sure, but also succulent tangelo juice; secondary passes detect ghostlike aromas of candied orange and orange soda, which add a welcome touch of low-degree sweetness. Entry features the pith of the fruits more than the juice; midpalate is tart, clean, crisp, acidic, more tangelo-like than tangerine-like. Finishes medium long, pleasingly refreshing.
2014 Rating: ★★★★/Highly Recommended

Craft Distillers DSP CA 162 Straight Vodka (USA) 40% abv, $38.
Wheat base with wine grape distillate. Rainwater clarity. Opens up with a pleasingly plump aroma of BIG BOUQUET wine grapes, almost ambrosial in its fruit-salad leaning; after more time in the glass, the bouquet takes a left turn at the intersection of Seed and Grape Skin Streets, as the aromatics go from ambrosial to seed-like, slightly bitter, pulpy. Entry is low-volume grapy, zesty, highly acidic, and therefore refreshing; the lean midpalate plays up a mild fruitiness but, to its credit, doesn't overplay that hand, leading to a stone-dry finish where the wheat emerges in a crackling manner that's pleasantly brittle. Really like this vodka because it's so focused, complex.
2014 Rating: ★★★★/Highly Recommended

Craft Distillers DSP CA 162 Vaccinium Macrocarpon Cranberry Vodka (USA) 40% abv, $38.
Tawny port/brick red color; excellent purity. Smells lusciously of fresh-picked cranberries in a piquant, tart manner that's refreshing and spicy clean; second inhalations after more air contact introduce a juicier, riper scent that's full of acidity and cranberry zest; a compelling, authentic bouquet that gets the job done. Entry flavor is vibrant, astringent, keenly tart, and genuinely cranberry-like; midpalate stays the course set at the entry as the dynamic cranberry juiciness remains firm but now more bitter than tart, more tannic skin–like than juicy/pulpy, and that direction leads into the peppery aftertaste that veers away from the fruit and turns tangy/spicy. Really different, really tasty.
2015 Rating: ★★★★/Highly Recommended

Crop Organic Harvest Earth Meyer Lemon Vodka (USA) 35% abv, $29.
Colorless, translucent, totally pure in appearance. Opening whiffs can't miss the succulence of the ripe lemon juice fragrance, which is pure, crisp, properly tart, and unmistakable in its origin; aeration deepens the citrus/lemon perfume, making the bouquet seductive. Entry is delightfully tart and lemony, without being sour or sharp; midpalate makes no bones about featuring the star player as the lemon-a-thon continues gracefully. Finishes alluringly tart and fresh.
2017 Rating: ★★★★/Highly Recommended

Crop Organic Spiced Pumpkin Vodka (USA) 35% abv, $30.

Old gold/amber color; perfect purity. Smells nicely and genuinely of spiced pumpkin right out of the aromatic gate; the dried herbal/spice (nutmeg, for me) aspect builds in the second passes. Entry is genuine spiced (now cinnamon) pumpkin flavor; midpalate is concentrated and deliciously piquant. Really tasty.

2016 Rating: ★ ★ ★ ★/Highly Recommended

Crop Organic Vodka (USA) 40% abv, $30.

Crystalline and silvery, but with minor sediment showing. I suspect that this vodka is made from a mix of corn, wheat, and barley grains; the opening nosing passes detect strong and very dry notes of snack crackers (Wheat Thins, Triscuit, and the like); another six minutes of exposure to air coax out stony/mineral-like scents that interact well with the concentrated graininess; there's some genuine substance here. Palate entry is more keenly sweet than the desert-dry aroma, and I like the unexpected switch in character; midpalate is sturdy, medium weighted in texture, a touch drier than the entry stage, and seriously tasty as a clean distillate. Ends on a grainy sweet note that's balanced and understated. Excellent job here.

2020 Rating: ★ ★ ★ ★/Highly Recommended

Danzka Apple Vodka (Denmark) 40% abv, $20.

Transparent; excellent clarity. First sniffs pick up a clean, green-apple-peel tanginess that's slightly spiced (nutmeg) but alluring; secondary inhalations detect less of the nutmeg and more of the apple pulp/meat, which curiously is cider-like, tart, and savory. Entry is sweeter (applesauce) than I'd hoped it would be, and that's an issue because the acute acidity seems to have been beaten down; midpalate mirrors the entry, and that relegates it to "Not Recommended" territory since much of the sharp freshness is now lost, and the vodka consequently turns flabby, not fresh. And what's with the keen spiciness that overshadows the apple? Bad decision-making here in the production choices.

2016 Rating: ★/Not Recommended

Danzka Citrus Vodka (Denmark) 40% abv, $20.

Colorless; very good purity. Opening aroma is juicy, pulpy, zesty, highlighting both lemon and lime; later whiffs detect more of the citrus zest and is therefore tangier and more bitter than the initial scent. Entry is ripely citric, nicely bitter, zesty, peel-like; midpalate turns sweeter than the tarter entry, but it's not enough to eclipse the citrus underpinning, which lasts deep into the acidic, sour aftertaste. Quite tasty due to its crisp freshness.

2016 Rating: ★ ★ ★/Recommended

Danzka Cranraz Cranberry/Raspberry Vodka (Denmark) 40% abv, $20.

Shimmering and colorless; impeccable purity. Pleasing first fragrances of raspberry compote and cranberry juice are properly zesty, tart, and just slightly under-ripe, which maintains the acidity; later whiffs after more air contact see the sweetness/ripeness dial go up as the bouquet turns jammy. Entry is mildly berry-like but so featherweight light that I almost forget what the flavorings are; midpalate picks up the slack left by the lackluster entry by reintroducing the tart berry element that carries the taste into the slightly sour finish. If

there hadn't been a solid recovery in the midpalate, this vodka would not have ended up being "Recommended." But the dip in the entry wasn't enough to punish it.
2016 Rating: ★ ★ ★/Recommended

Danzka Vodka (Denmark) 40% abv, $20.
Danish wheat base. Absolutely crystal clear and sediment-free; limpid translucence. Owns a pleasant, grainy, slightly spicy opening aroma that's lithe and agile, almost floral; secondary passes discover a soft ripeness that's more grain-like than fruity. Entry is reserved, sweeter than the aroma, and once again marginally spicy; midpalate is lightly toasted, and while not to be considered hearty or robust, is alluringly firm and neutral in its bearing. Finishes brief in the throat, grainy, dusty dry. I like it more than I did twenty-two years ago and am willing to bump it up by one star due to its impeccable cleanness and overall elegance.
2016 Rating: ★ ★ ★/Recommended

Dingle Pot Still Vodka (Ireland) 40% abv, $50.
Clear-as-rainwater appearance. Evidence of the charcoal filtering is unmistakable in the opening whiffs, which offer elements of burnt toast, charcoal briquette, and campfire; secondary sniffs pick up more of the grain density and aridly dry notes that say to me "clean" and "concentrated." Entry is toasted, parched in its dryness degree, and it sports a heavily roasted and bittersweet charred grain component that is front and center; midpalate echoes the entry, but in a softer tone in which the taste profile displays a mellow side that's semisweet and cocoa-like. Ends on a smoky, semisweet note. Awfully good and had it exhibited more textural layering in the mouth, I'd have given it a fifth rating star.
2019 Rating: ★ ★ ★ ★/Highly Recommended

Dixie Black Pepper Vodka (USA) 40% abv, $18.
Clean and crystalline appearance. My immediate response to this opening aroma is highly favorable, as the fragrance delivers on the promise of black pepper but does so in a measured manner that allows you to savor it without any hint of prickliness; secondary inhalations find the black pepper aspect turning mellow, steely, totally dry, and mesmerizingly lead pencil–like; I love this bouquet. Entry holds true to the black pepper flavoring in a way that's now slightly zesty but neither hot nor harsh; midpalate reflects the entry as the taste profile features but one flavor—but that's enough for total satisfaction. Concludes peppery, warming, and tangy. A superb flavored vodka suitable for your next Bloody Mary.
2018 Rating: ★ ★ ★ ★/Highly Recommended

Dixie Southern Vodka (USA) 40% abv, $18.
Clear as mineral water; sediment-free. First nosing passes pick up nuances of corn husk, tamale/polenta, and unsalted snack cracker; secondary whiffs detect deeper layers of aroma, notably unbuttered popcorn, cornmeal, and corn fritter. Entry teases the palate with off-dry to semisweet tastes of lead pencil, dry stone, and popcorn at first, then at midpalate there's a shift in direction as the taste profile goes semisweet in corn syrup and caramel corn flavors. Ends nicely in a round, supple texture that gives base to the peppery, corny, cereal flavor.
2018 Rating: ★ ★ ★/Recommended

Dry Fly Washington Wheat Vodka (USA) 40% abv, $30.

Crystalline appearance. This first nosing pass offers a wheat-driven succulence that's remarkably fruity and nutty; second passes pick up accelerated fruit salad/ambrosial notes that now are super-ripe and pulpy. Entry is stone dry, grainy, snack cracker–like, and bordering on succulent; midpalate goes drier still, providing a stony, elemental, flinty flavor profile that's clean, razor edged, and incredibly crisp. Finishes brief, desert dry, and neutral.
2019 Rating: ★ ★ ★/Recommended

Eau Claire Prickly Pear EquineOx Vodka (Canada) 40% abv, $35.

This appearance shows a pewter/silver color that has just a trace of sediment. First nosings pick up intensely ripe, waxy, and almost syrupy scents of bubble gum, baked pineapple, grilled nectarine, and the sugary liquid that you find in canned peaches; secondary inhalations are swamped by fruit salad–like sweetness; a little more subtlety would have been welcomed here. Entry shows more sophistication as the taste profile turns away from the needlessly sweet bouquet, instead going intriguingly bitter, mineral-like, and stony; midpalate stage is where this vodka shows its best qualities in the forms of flinty, chalky, spicy flavors that remind me of true prickly pear juice. Finishes medium long in the throat, delicately juicy, satiny in texture, and bittersweet. Just skip the aroma and go right to tasting it. Came from a long way back to rescue its recommendation.
2017 Rating: ★ ★ ★/Recommended

Effen Blood Orange Vodka (Holland) 37.5% abv, $30.

Clear as springwater; colorless. First aromatic impressions are of light-fingered orange peel, orange pulp, with a smidgen of juiciness; later sniffs taken after more time in the glass offer a bigger, rounder citrus/orange scent that's nicely acidic yet ripe and juicy. Entry is sharp-edged citric acid, drying in the mouth, zesty and peel-like, authentic; midpalate highlights the orange zest aspect, making the taste profile significantly more bitter than that of the entry. Ends up acutely bitter, peel-like, piquant. I like this vodka a lot.
2017 Rating: ★ ★ ★ ★/Highly Recommended

Effen Green Apple Vodka (Holland) 37.5% abv, $30.

Impeccable purity; void of color. Initial whiffs pick up very tart green-apple-skin aromas that are waxy and vinyl-like, with no hint at all of apple meat; following more aeration, the aroma turns a little more fruity while remaining pleasantly tart—hardly an applesauce-like aroma but more akin to slightly under-ripe green apple. Entry is sweeter than the aroma suggests it would be, and the texture is velvety and comforting in its thickness; midpalate highlights the tart, slightly bitter green apple flavor that's supported by the now substantially oily texture. Concludes on a fruity, nearly juicy note of ripe green apple. Nice job here of maintaining the natural acidity of green apple while providing plenty of rich flavor.
2017 Rating: ★ ★ ★ ★/Highly Recommended

Effen Raspberry Vodka (Holland) 37.5% abv, $30.

Unblemished clarity; no color whatsoever. My first inhalations detect a bramble-like/nettle aspect that's as minty as it is vine-like, verdant, and wild; after a few more minutes of air contact, red raspberry fragrance emerges, supplying the olfactory sense with a pleasant berry perfume that's true and genuine. Entry is richly textured, ripe, red raspberry–like to the nth degree yet pleasingly sour and acidic; midpalate keeps up with the intensity found in the entry, adding more powerful raspberry flavor that's fresh, clean, and alluring deep into the fabulous finish.

2017 Rating: ★★★★★/Highest Recommendation

Effen Vodka (Holland) 40% abv, $30.

Flawless purity; colorless. First nosings encounter dry, deeply grainy/kernel-like aromas that are delicate and almost fruity; additional time in the glass brings out a bit more of the beguiling citrus-like fruitiness. Entry is delightfully smooth, medium bodied, slightly oily, tongue-on-stone dry, and a touch grainy; midpalate features the creamy texture that underpins the dry flavors of grain and snack crackers. Concludes long in the throat, complex, concentrated, and refined.

2017 Rating: ★★★★/Highly Recommended

EG Windsor Earl Grey Tea & Sage Vodka (USA) 40% abv, $55.

Crystalline clarity; colorless. First inhalations definitely identify the Earl Grey tea up front due to the unmistakable perfume of bergamot, but immediately thereafter the sage aspect emerges and merges nicely with the black tea; secondary nosing passes appear to highlight the dried sage element more than the tea, creating a refined herbal bouquet of sophistication. Entry is dry, intensely minerally, herbal, and gently sweet; midpalate is charged with the black tea component as the sage withdraws only to reappear in the savory aftertaste. Superb job of blending.

2015 Rating: ★★★★/Highly Recommended

Elation Hemp Flavored Vodka (Switzerland) 40% abv, $33.

Flawless clarity; colorless. First nosing passes encounter bitter scents (that I like a lot) of caraway seeds, freshly ground black pepper, lead pipe, and coriander; later sniffs serve to reinforce the initial impressions, adding nothing except for a marginal fading of intensity. Entry is severely bitter, prickly on the tongue, stony, mineral-like, aggressive, and even a little hot; midpalate stage features more of the cereal grain than the hemp additive, and that makes for calmer enjoyment that lasts through the entire medium-long finish. The atypical bouquet and the midpalate are worth the experience.

2016 Rating: ★★★/Recommended

Elit Vodka (Latvia) 40% abv, $50.

Pristine, sediment-free appearance. Smells up front of flint/calcareous soil/limestone/ diatomaceous earth in desert-dry aromatic waves, showing just a trace of breakfast cereal; later sniffs discover a round, supple, and mineral-like bouquet that's clean, engaging, grainy, and razor crisp. Entry is lush, acutely peppery/spicy, deeply flavorful, and snack cracker–like; midpalate turns acidic, cleansing, nutty, and slightly bittersweet. Finishes medium long, luscious, oily in texture, piquant, and with a tangy snap that's undeniably terrific and, for unflavored vodka, profound. A benchmark.

2018 Rating: ★★★★★/Highest Recommendation

Frey Ranch Estate Distillery Vodka (USA) 40% abv, $40.
Grain combination of corn, wheat, barley, and rye. Pristine clarity; colorless. I like the opening aroma because it's completely dry, clean, cereal-like, almost nutty in its kernel-, husk-like manner and it works; later whiffs after more air contact pick up denser notes of snack crackers (Wheat Thins, Triscuit, especially) and dry breakfast cereal as the grain factor becaues more intense. Entry, by contrast, is bitter but still grainy, and a little nuttier than the bouquet; midpalate sees the taste profile turn bittersweet, sap-like, and resiny as this vodka keeps evolving with time in the glass. Finishes very long for an unflavored vodka, and is acutely resiny, bittersweet, vegetal, but immaculate. What's admirable about this vodka is that the grain ratios are spot on and the distillation is very good. What prevented me from bestowing one more rating star was the escalating bitterness from the entry forward to the aftertaste. Other than that, this is a solid, good quality effort.
2016 Rating: ★ ★ ★ ★/Highly Recommended

Gamle Ode Dill Aquavit (USA) 42% abv, $30.
Void of color; flawlessly clear and clean. Oh my, I really respond to the dill pickle opening burst of piquant, leathery aroma, but also the seeded rye bread fragrance that underscores the dill aspect nicely; remains vividly seed-like and herbal through the second inhalations as the bouquet components merge and fade slightly with aeration. Entry is keenly dill-like, peppery, and spicy on the tongue; midpalate sees the dill element give way a little to the caraway seed and rye bread as the taste profile goes silky, warm, and just a bit toasty and herbal. Aftertaste is pleasingly long, smooth as silk, peppery, seed-like, and quietly dill-like. Hats off to 45th Parallel for their sense of adventure and distilling skill.
2017 Rating: ★ ★ ★/Recommended

Gamle Ode Dill Celebration on Rye Whiskey Barrels Aquavit (USA) 50.09% abv, $42.
Bright amber/old gold/wheat-field color; superb clarity. This aroma has an unexpected, candy-shop grainy sweetness to it in which the herbaceousness of the aquavit is swamped a little too much by the whiskey barrel impact; later sniffs following additional aeration find a touch more of the herbal aquavit emerging as the barrel influence recedes. Entry is torched by the high abv, which obliterates the herbal thrust of the aquavit character, and then I'm forced to consider: *Why?* Midpalate doesn't really recover its footing, though the flavor profile is less abrasive as the alcohol levels off, leaving behind shallow footprints of dill, black pepper, and rye bread. I see what was attempted here, but in this case I would have lowered the abv to maybe 44–45 percent to eliminate the chance of burn.
2017 Rating: ★ ★/Not Recommended

Gera Premium Vodka (Lithuania) 40% abv, $10.
Crystalline and pure. Smells pleasantly of Wheaties cereal, doused with a dash of sugar in the opening whiffs after the pour; second-round inhalations encounter peanut, cardboard, and freshly ground black pepper. Entry is nice, in that it is clean, dry, and grainy, with a smooth, medium-weighted viscosity; midpalate mirrors the entry exactly. Aftertaste is unabashedly cereally and snack cracker–like, and by simply presenting these qualities in an honest, no-frills manner, this Lithuanian vodka won me over.
2015 Rating: ★ ★ ★ ★/Highly Recommended

Golden State California Corn Vodka (USA) 42% abv, $39.
One hundred percent California corn distilled in pot still. Clear and clean appearance. Initial whiffs pick up more of corn husk than corn kernel, but there's no mistaking the base material; secondary inhalations discover cornstarch and cornmeal aromatic leanings that are firm yet subtle and completely dry. Entry is considerably sweeter and grainier than the bouquet; midpalate accurately reflects the sweet corn entry, offering little else, except for a silky texture that wins me over for the recommendation. Aftertaste is like corn bread.
2016 Rating: ★★★/Recommended

Golia Vodka (Mongolia) 40% abv, $30.
Translucent; minor sediment seen. Toasted cereal, bread dough scents in first passes; goes neutral in later inhalations, then sweet as grain kernel—seed-like aspects appear after aeration. Entry is too sweet, grainy; midpalate is acidic, raw, unfocused. Finish turns drier than entry, but harshness in aftertaste kills any chance of recommendation. Texture is wafer thin; aroma is hollow; flavor profile lacks depth/complexity. Not undrinkable, just scattered and uninteresting.
2014 Rating: ★★/Not Recommended

Goral Vodka Master (Slovak Republic) 40% abv, $28.
Wheat. Sediment-free; shimmering brightness, colorless. Opening nose is like dry soil, fallen leaves in early autumn, and slightly fruity, which is so emblematic of wheat vodkas; secondary inhalations encounter deeper fragrances of minerals, copper wire, nickel, dried flowers, and all of these are supported by the wheat-based delicate fruitiness. Entry is almost raisiny, ripe, sweeter than the aroma, grainy in a snack cracker manner; midpalate sees some of the entry taste flurry fade into a quiet, subdued, dusty-dry aftertaste, but the ripeness keeps it intriguing throughout the entire evaluation.
2015 Rating: ★★★/Recommended

Grey Goose Vodka (France) 40% abv, $40.
Made from wheat. Pretty in its obvious purity. The delicacy of the first aromas is charming to a degree as the soft wheat snack cracker scent fills the nasal cavity, but I want a little more fragrance from this not-inexpensive vodka; aeration helps a bit as the aroma turns rounder and marginally semisweet with time. Entry is a touch fat in texture and sap-like, which I find disappointing in that I prefer my unflavored vodkas to be tight, edgy, and crisp, and GG simply is not; midpalate stays the course with the sugary fatness that now goes into cake frosting mode as the flavor profile leaves me cold. Concludes semisweet, grainy, parchment-like, and stodgy. I know this brand is popular, but it's just not a style of unflavored vodka that I like. It's too chunked up.
2018 Rating: ★★/Not Recommended

Grey Goose VX Finished with a Hint of Precious Cognac Vodka (France) 40% abv, $75.
Wheat-based vodka (95 percent) and one-year-old eau-de-vie (5 percent) from grapes grown in Cognac's storied Grande Champagne district. Limpid appearance; ideal clarity. First impressions are pleasantly fruity and snack cracker–like in equal measure, as gently

sweet wheat distillate combines well with the floral aspect of the cognac eau-de-vie; additional time in the glass brings out tropical fruit fragrances, like grapefruit and pineapple, as well as a mildly spicy, woodsy, eucalyptus-like scent. Entry is dry initially, grainy, a touch breakfast cereal–like but doesn't showcase much of the grape influence; midpalate features a minerally, lead pencil–like front taste that's supported by a medium-bodied, desert-dry texture. Finishes nicely as the dryness leads the way along with an earthiness that I can best describe as being mineral-like.
2015 Rating: ★★★/Recommended

Haku Vodka (Japan) 40% abv, $28.
Crystalline, colorless appearance. Up-front aromas after the pour are subtle and reminiscent of steamed basmati rice, plus there's a trace of campfire smoke way in the distance; secondary inhalations pick up the rice once again but in a deeper degree as well as hints of dry soil, arid landscape, limestone, and chalk. Entry is clean and surprisingly sweet; midpalate turns on the charm as the flavor profile launches into rich, toasted cereal grain tastes that are viscous in texture and intensely maple- and sap-like, almost honeyed. Finishes short in the throat, dense, and bittersweet. One of a handful of unflavored vodkas that I'd enjoy neat, chilled. High-quality distilling.
2018 Rating: ★★★★/Highly Recommended

Hangar 1 Vodka (USA) 40% abv, $29.
Mix of grapes and grain. Slightest of pewter tints; 100 percent sediment-free. First-nosing findings include a fascinating menu of aromas such as wet canvas, wet cement, white raisins, damp sand, and chalk; with more aeration, the bouquet unfolds in layers of dried vine fruits/berries, metal coin, lead pencil, grape stems, and moss. Entry is bold in its richness, bitter, and mineral-like; midpalate launches full-flight into dry, desert, arid landscape territory through mineral/dry-earth flavors of sage, dry breakfast cereal/Wheaties, grain husk, tobacco leaf, and tar. Sports this amazing array of distinctive flavors over into the dazzling finish. A sophisticated American vodka that I've admired for two decades.
2020 Rating: ★★★★/Highly Recommended

Hanson of Sonoma Grape Based Organic Small Batch Habañero Vodka (USA) 40% abv, $33.
There's a faint tinge of tarnished-silver coloring which comes from, I'm guessing, the habañero peppers; there is also seen floating widely spaced pieces of sediment. First nosings are prickly from the pepper influence, but in such a manner that is simultaneously enlivening and stimulating; the habañero impact becomes more concentrated and narrower of field with additional aeration, and that narrowing makes the second-stage inhalations all the more intense. Entry is silky smooth in texture, mildly piquant at first, then the capsaicin (inherent spiciness) kicks in, providing the taste buds with a slow burn of heat that's exceedingly pleasant; midpalate stage is even more flavor focused than the entry, as the habañero zestiness turns into genuine peppery heat that blankets the tongue all the way through the acutely peppery finish. If, like me, you relish hot peppers, try this fiery vodka that is true to the wonderfully spicy habañero pepper.
2016 Rating: ★★★★/Highly Recommended

Hanson of Sonoma Grape Based Organic Small Batch Original Vodka (USA) 40% abv, $33.
Lacy tendrils seen floating about, but inconsequential to the final rating; colorless. This first inhalation comes across as a chewing gum/gummy bear–like fragrance that's more like orchard fruit than vineyard fruit, at least to me, but it's pleasant in its understatement; the fruitiness appears to deepen with more air contact, going from fresh to ripe, even flowery. Entry is alluringly ripe, viscous, and a little piquant; midpalate echoes the entry while pushing forward the fruit complexity that accelerates in the aftertaste. My impression is that the Hanson people really understand the intricacies of distillation, and that comes across from beginning to end.
2016 Rating: ★★★★/Highly Recommended

Journeyman Red Arrow Vodka (USA) 45% abv, $30.
Pewter appearance; sediment-free. Right out of the box the elevated abv adds a piquancy as the alcohol pushes the wheat/breakfast cereal aroma forward like a fifty-foot wave propelling a surfer; aeration intensifies the abv thrust, opening up layers of fragrance, like caramelized onion, brown butter, BBQ sauce; wowwee. Entry is big, assertive, creamy in texture, charred, biscuity; midpalate is doughy/bread-like, and yeasty. Highly appealing to me as it makes the case for wheat-based vodka being sensational at a higher abv.
2016 Rating: ★★★★★/Highest Recommendation

Kalak Single Malt Vodka (Ireland) 40% abv, $30.
One hundred percent Irish malted barley. Pristine, colorless appearance. The highly distinctive opening nose hits all the right buttons—it's dry to the point of being slightly sour; it's minerally/earthy/flinty, which is unusual in unflavored vodka; and there's a kelp-like element that makes it almost maritime. Secondary sniffs detect deeper fragrances of steamed white rice, wort, yeast, scone, and grist. Entry is like no other vodka in the marketplace as the taste profile reminds me immediately of youthful malt whisky; midpalate features latent spice in the form of black pepper as well as truffle, egg white, meringue, and tofu. Aftertaste is long, toasted, dry, and mellow. A must-try vodka for anyone who loves malted barley whiskies—in other words, Kalak is the whiskey-lover's vodka.
2017 Rating: ★★★★★/Highest Recommendation

Karlsson's Gold Vodka (Sweden) 40% abv, $17.
Wonderfully clean and clear as springwater. Initial nosing passes immediately pick up the slightly sweet and earthy fragrance of potato skins (it's made from Swedish potatoes), as well as faint hints of unsalted butter; secondary whiffs offer a touch more of the buttery quality but that doesn't overshadow the firm core of potato skin essence. Entry is dry, firm in the mouth texturally, showing a hint of acidic edginess that cleanses the palate; midpalate is tart, astringent, and assertive, featuring the tangy acidity found in the entry point. Finishes quite long for a neutral spirit, and that I have to conclude is from good distillation practices. All things considered, I wanted more from this vodka than it had to offer.
2019 Rating: ★★★/Recommended

Ketel One Citroen Citrus Vodka (Netherlands) 40% abv, $29.

Made from wheat. Silvery translucent and flawlessly pure. This frontline nose is all about fresh-squeezed lemon juice plus a dash of lemon pulp, making for highly desirable inhaling; the balance found in the later nosings among the acute acidity, freshness of the lemon juice, and the pulp is nothing short of dazzling. Entry is tart, peel-like in its astringency, and mouth-puckering in its lemony nature—just about what anyone could want from lemon-flavored vodka; midpalate shines as a beacon of lemon juice purity and definition. Ends fresh, alluringly tart, and dense in its lemon character. Stunningly delicious.

2018 Rating: ★★★★★/Highest Recommendation

Ketel One Vodka (Netherlands) 40% abv, $29.

Made from wheat. Pot still distillation. I like this opening fragrance as it offers hefty aromas of Wheat Thins crackers, hemp, grain husk, and unsweetened breakfast cereal; later whiffs detect deeper, charcoal briquette–like aromas of estery flowers (carnation) and fruit (kiwi). Entry is creamy, buttery, burnt, charcoal-like, and toasty; midpalate is where this vodka shines brightest as the multiple layers of flavor and texture come together in a cushiony wave of plumpness that is impressively rich without being unctuous or cloying. Ends on a bright, almost nut-like note that is buttery and rich.

2018 Rating: ★★★★/Highly Recommended

Leaf Made from Alaskan Glacial Water Organic Vodka (USA) 40% abv, $17.

Limpid, colorless; pure. Smells lightly grainy, fresh, with a little bit of charcoal underpinning in opening inhalations; later sniffs pick up dried flowers and traces of honey and sugar water, but the char factor looms large. Entry is bittersweet, charred/seared, intensely grainy; midpalate highlights the toasty, smoky assets. Aftertaste is vividly bittersweet, piquant, full of roasted grain flavor. Who says that vodka has to be "flavorless"? Why, it's the ever-plugged-in US government!

2014 Rating: ★★★★/Highly Recommended

Leaf Made from Rocky Mountain Mineral Water Organic Vodka (USA) 40% abv, $17.

Crystal clear; sediment free. There's a solid grainy/Wheaties cereal-like aromatic core in the first whiff that's followed later on by neutral aromas of cardboard, linen, cotton fiber. Entry is mildly toasty, moderately grainy, delicate; midpalate hits a pleasant balance between delicate flavors, acidity, and abv level. Nice, but not as memorable as its Alaskan Glacial Water sibling.

2014 Rating: ★★★/Recommended

Loaded Vodka (USA) 40% abv, $20.

One hundred percent corn. Right in the core, there is an undulating wave of minuscule sediment tendrils seen hovering; colorless appearance. Opening sniffs pick up gently sweet, cornmeal aromas that are intensely cereal-like and slightly biscuity; later inhalations encounter more concentrated fragrances of cornmeal, corn husk, and creamed corn. Entry favors the creamed corn aspect as the texture adds to that impression a measure of waxiness; midpalate reaffirms the creamed corn impression as the taste profile ratchets up the sweetness a notch by the time the aftertaste kicks off. A highly likable corn vodka of substance and direction.

2016 Rating: ★★★★/**Highly Recommended**

Luksusowa Potato Vodka (Poland) 40% abv, $15.

Void of color; clean and clear of sediment. There's very little in the way of aroma in the first sniffs after the pour; more aeration can't seem to pry open the aromatic box, so I move on. Entry is gently sweet, fat in texture, starchy, and as plain as your dumb cousin Harold; midpalate merely reflects the entry findings, adding nothing more of consequence. There aren't any major flaws; it's just not an interesting unflavored vodka.

2018 Rating: ★★/**Not Recommended**

Norden Aquavit (USA) 45% abv, $30.

Void of color; flawless clarity. The first whiffs pick up lovely scents of caraway seeds, gentle citrus peel, and black peppercorn; with more aeration, the aroma takes on added scents of steel wool, rye bread with caraway, toasted oats, green vegetation, and green pepper. Entry is keenly peppery and seed-like, showing off the zesty, tangy taste of caraway seeds at their peak moment; midpalate is deliciously tangy, peppery, and citrusy. Finishes long, acutely peppery, and delicious.

2018 Rating: ★★★★/**Highly Recommended**

OOLA Batch #28 Vodka (USA) 42% abv, $38.

Colorless, inconsequential sediment. Whoa, I detect an unusual amount of citrus, kidney bean/legume, peanut butter aromas that make for compelling sniffing in the first round; later inhalations encounter baker's wax paper, steamed white rice, textile fiber. Entry is smooth, satiny in texture, concentrated, nutty, beany; midpalate reflects all the entry findings, adding dry-as-a-bone acute graininess, breakfast cereal, unsalted snack crackers. Lots going on here that is definitely worth the trip.

2014 Rating: ★★★★/**Highly Recommended**

Polugar Classic Rye Vodka (Poland) 38.5% abv, $119.

Colorless; impeccable clarity. My initial impression is one of rye bread without caraway seeds and also rye toast that's just slightly burnt at the edge, but as the aroma mingles with air, it grows in intensity; by the second passes, the aroma is keenly peppery, round, slightly fruity and ripe, and pleasantly engaging. Entry is completely dry, tightly wound, intensely grainy and rye bread–like, with sideline notes of snack cracker (Ryvita comes to mind) and rye toast; midpalate mirrors the entry, adding little more to the in-mouth phases except for a taste of freshly ground black pepper. Aftertaste is spicy, lean, desert dry, and slightly toasty.

2016 Rating: ★★★★/**Highly Recommended**

Polugar No. 1 Rye & Wheat Vodka (Poland) 38.5% abv, $45.

Perfect purity; limpid and clean. Smelling this aroma right after both the Polugar Wheat and the Polugar Rye makes the case that blending might be the way to go because this fragrance takes the finest virtues of both and transforms them into something magically enticing, grainy, floral, fruity (baked and/or dried), parchment-like, and herbal/woodsy just in the first inhalations; secondary whiffs reaffirm the majesty of the first passes and add traces of pine sap, wet leaves, moss, and lichen—a complex bouquet of the first rank. Entry is silky, smooth, acidic, but fruity and waxy if a touch lesser than the promise discovered in the supple bouquet; midpalate is round, alluringly minerally and stony, and therefore dusty dry, but I kept hoping for the fastball down the middle and it didn't come. Finishes more mineral-like than cereal-like, but with a subtle under-the-radar flurry of fruit pulp ripeness that seems to come out of nowhere. One of the best unflavored vodka aromas around.

2016 Rating: ★ ★ ★ ★/Highly Recommended

Polugar No. 2 Garlic & Pepper Vodka (Poland) 38.5% abv, $53.
I notice low-level sediment in the core, but hardly enough to be detrimental to the otherwise transparent appearance. As someone who believes in the cooking and physiological merits of garlic, this frontline aroma is heavenly in its authentic garlic depiction, but it's the combination of the garlic and chili pepper that creates an ideal flavored vodka bouquet right from the start; as time wears on, it's the chili pepper piquancy that comes to rule the aromatic day as the crushed garlic aspect becomes the underlying support player; a brilliantly conceived and executed bouquet. Entry is coyly garlicky yet there's a chili pepper flare-up from the capsaicin that's manageably warm but not fiery; midpalate is appealingly embers warm from the chili influence that pushes the garlic presence forward, sending it propelled into the aftertaste that is savory, zesty, calmer than I thought it might be, and honorably balanced in its depiction of the two flavors. A superbly crafted flavored vodka.

2016 Rating: ★ ★ ★ ★ ★/Highest Recommendation

Polugar No. 3 Caraway Vodka (Poland) 38.5% abv, $53.
Unblemished purity; sediment-free. Wow, the essence of caraway is striking in its genuineness and seed-like bitterness, hitting the right chord in the first nosing passes; secondary whiffs pick up even deeper and denser seed characteristics as the oiliness of the caraway emerges as though the seed were crushed right in the sampling glass—amazing authenticity. Entry is supple in texture, radiantly seed-like, properly and delicately bitter, lightly toasted, marginally oily; midpalate reflects the entry impressions to a tee, adding a toastier edge than noticed in the entry. Aftertaste loses the textural oiliness, but the taste remains focused entirely on the savory caraway.

2016 Rating: ★ ★ ★ ★/Highly Recommended

Polugar No. 4 Honey & Allspice Vodka (Poland) 38.5% abv, $53.
I like the faint bisque/electrum tint; flawless clarity; very pretty appearance. In the opening sniffs, the zestiness of the allspice is unmistakably present, but it's the honey component that is the foundation of this ultra-sensual early aroma; with more time in the glass, the bouquet evolves into an amaro- or a bitters-like fragrance as the allspice piquancy stimulates the olfactory mechanism; a one-of-a-kind bouquet of the highest order. Entry features more of the honey element up front than the allspice, but there's enough of the spiciness accounted for, which balances the honey impact; midpalate is

tangy as the honey fades, leaving the flavor door wide open for the bitterness of the allspice. Finishes long, bitter, spicy, herbal.

2016 Rating: ★ ★ ★ ★ /Highly Recommended

Polugar Single Malt Rye Vodka (Poland) 38.5% abv, $249.
Totally colorless; flawlessly clean and pure. Right out of the aromatic gate the scent is juicy, almost citrusy, slightly smoked, peppery, prickly high in the nasal cavity, and stony/mineral-like; second passes pick up sweet-and-sour sauce, soy sauce, pickle brine, dill, sage, bay leaf, eucalyptus, bacon fat—I mean, this could go on all day. Entry is creamy in texture, rich in candy flavors, especially malted milk ball and nougat, and is nicely baked without being burnt or sulphury; midpalate is toasty, sweeter than the entry taste, meaty, densely grainy/malty all the way deep into the finish, which is long, lush, slightly roasted/toasty, just a smidgen spicy, and plump with malted rye.

2016 Rating: ★ ★ ★ ★ ★ /Highest Recommendation

Polugar Wheat Vodka (Poland) 38.5% abv, $100.
Crystalline appearance; silvery transparent; very minor sediment—inconsequential. Oh man, the assertive breakfast cereal (Wheaties) aroma is beany (lima, soy), waxy (candle wax), and marvelously fragrant and animated in the starting point after the pour; secondary whiffs detect deft scents of apple, white grape, and yellow plum—this is an intriguing bouquet that I simply don't want to end. Entry is clean, dry, deeply grainy and breakfast cereal–like, raisiny, acutely ripe; midpalate echoes the entry findings, adding a potent, apple-like acidity that maintains the freshness well and long into the satisfying finish that is dry yet is more bountiful than austere. Simply delicious.

2016 Rating: ★ ★ ★ ★ ★ /Highest Recommendation

Portland Potato Vodka (USA) 40% abv, $23.
Pristine, unblemished, limpid appearance. Opening scents after the pour are lively, starchy, and delicately sweet—quite attractive and vivid; further aeration encourages the sweeter side of the bouquet to deepen, but there is likewise an aromatic strand of stone/mineral that complements the mild vegetal sweetness. Entry features the stone/mineral in spades while the potato sweetness diminishes significantly; midpalate is all about the stony dryness and that's about all. After the genuinely lovely bouquet of real merit, the in-mouth stages falter a little, but the overall impression is promising and recommendable.

2015 Rating: ★ ★ ★ /Recommended

Prairie Organic Vodka (Russia) 40% abv, $22.
One hundred percent organic corn. Colorless; pristine appearance. Up front in the nose, I pick up a density that is bone-dry, appealing in its assertiveness, and metallic in equal measure; further air contact unleashes vivid fragrances of cornstarch, polenta, cornmeal, and unbuttered popcorn, as well as cotton, textile fiber, and corn husk. Entry is as clean as a whistle, deeply grainy and husk-like, marginally sweeter than the aroma implies, and lush in texture; midpalate reflects all the entry findings and adds burnt flavors of caramelized onion

and charred-on-the-grill sweet corn. Concludes increasingly sweet in the finish, as the maize/corn base won't be denied.

2020 Rating: ★ ★ ★ ★/Highly Recommended

Purity Ultra 34 Premium Vodka (Sweden) 40% abv, $23.
Without any hint of color; perfect purity. First whiffs pick up grainy, delicate, cereal-like scents that are ethereal, egg white–like, coin-like/minerally, and reminiscent of parchment; secondary inhalations detect additional fragrances of damp forest, leather, and graham cracker. Entry is succulent, thickly textured, creamy, decidedly sweeter than the nose implies, and semidry; midpalate offers a highlight reel of flavors, ranging from wheat bread toast to saltine cracker to bittersweet cocoa to caramel, all wrapped in a buttery texture that cradles the tongue. Finishes long, arid in its dryness, and silky in texture. One of only a handful of perfect unflavored vodkas.

2020 Rating: ★ ★ ★ ★ ★/Highest Recommendation

Råvo Vodka (Sweden) 40% abv, $23.
Pristine clarity; colorless. I like the immediate black tea–like graininess of the first sniffs as the aroma comes off-dry, crisp, and lean; secondary inhalations discover a perceptible ratcheting up on the dryness/sweetness scale as the bouquet turns more bittersweet, akin to toasted grain and burning embers. Entry is viscous, creamy, and significantly sweeter than the bouquet led on, being almost charcoal-like; midpalate is like caramel corn, sautéed onion, hoisin sauce, soy sauce, and Assam tea. Ends tasting like sweetened breakfast cereal, caramel, and cocoa powder. Had it held back a little more on the expanding grainy sweetness, I'd have given it a fourth star.

2018 Rating: ★ ★ ★/Recommended

Reyka Small Batch Vodka (Iceland) 40% abv, $30.
Minuscule particles of tendril-like sediment seen, along with clouds of what appears to be very small effervescence. Gently sweet and kernel-like in the first engaging sniffs; added minutes in the glass arouse more aromas, including breakfast cereal and dry-roasted peanuts. Entry is round and supple, tasting of unsalted Wheat Thins and Wheaties cereal; midpalate is toasty, dry, and a touch charcoal-like. Finishes short and intriguingly biscuity, with a parting shot of vanilla bean.

2019 Rating: ★ ★ ★ ★/Highly Recommended

Rocksov Ultra Premium Vodka (USA) 40% abv, $33.
Rye. Flawless purity; colorless transparence. First sniffs detect disparate fragrances of glue, mesquite, sour apple, egg white, cooking oil, soy sauce; following another period of aeration, the bouquet adds traces of sesame oil, poppy seed, vinegar; a curious bouquet that's all over the map in terms of fragrance but the underlying scent is sour. Entry is sweeter, riper than the aroma, and that's a welcome stage of evolution for a rye-based spirit; midpalate offers a firm, sturdy texture that supports the flavor profile, which has now grown to include

buttered rye bread, peanut oil. Finishes short, off-dry, oily, spicy, and good enough for a third rating star and a recommendation.
2015 Rating: ★★★/Recommended

Russian Diamond Vodka (Russia) 40% abv, $25.
Clear as springwater; colorless. Opening bouquet is a little mute and very neutral; additional air contact doesn't raise much more in the aroma stage, so I move on. Entry is mildly charred, grainy/wheat-like, toasty; midpalate goes sweeter, more charred than the entry. Finishes cereal-like, dry, peppery.
2014 Rating: ★★★/Recommended

Russian Standard Original Vodka (Russia) 40% abv, $22.
Winter wheat. No color; flawlessly clean and pure. The first aromatic impressions after the pour are of under-the-radar scents of dry cereal, Wheat Thins snack crackers, and sagebrush; allowing for more air contact, later whiffs don't discover anything more in the way of new aromas as the bouquet actually diminishes with aeration. Entry is pleasingly crisp, lean, and only mildly grainy; midpalate sees a bit more assertiveness, as dry-as-a-bone tastes of unsweetened Wheaties cereal and wheat-based snack cracker up the flavor ante enough for a recommendation. Aftertaste mirrors the midpalate. Clean and nimble.
2020 Rating: ★★★/Recommended

SKYY Vodka (USA) 40% abv, $26.
Brilliant clarity; sediment-free. Smells up front of unsalted wheat crackers, with delicate off-dry touches of herbs (jasmine), green tea, and pine; further aeration highlights more of the wheat germ–like grain rather than pine or herbs, both of which fade. Entry approaches being sweet, yet it's crisp and intensely grainy; midpalate shows minor citrus rind/citric acid aspects that maintain the backbone well. Finishes smoothly, with an assertive vanilla bean–like roundness and spiciness.
2019 Rating: ★★★/Recommended

Smirnoff Triple Distilled 100-Proof Vodka (USA) 50% abv, $21.
Flawless purity; colorless. There's a curiously fruity/estery quality to the first inhalations that isn't quite grainy as it leans towards being sour or, better, sourdough bread–like; later whiffs pick up notes of lychee, pine nut, parchment, and minerals. Entry is a bit spiky and aggressive, but it's also deeply grainy, piquant, and cereal-like; midpalate displays an array of flavors including Wheat Thins crackers, toasted white bread, malted milk balls, and tree sap/resins as the 100 proof pushes forward any traces of taste. Concludes warm and smoldering on the tongue, prickly, and lightly peppered.
2018 Rating: ★★★/Recommended

Smirnoff Triple Distilled Vodka (USA) 40% abv, $15.
Excellent clarity; void of color. Aromawise, there's simply not a lot happening in the opening sniffs, except for desultory scents of cardboard and dry stone; later inhalations fail to bring anything more of note to the table so I move on. Entry offers more than the

ghostlike bouquet in the forms of dry cereal, grain husk, and snack cracker tastes; midpalate turns a little like graham cracker, but otherwise there's not a great deal of gustatory activity here. Concludes like the whisper it began as. While it's largely vacant of character, it isn't offensive, aggressive, or distasteful. It's just, well, meek and wholly uninteresting.

2018 Rating: ★★/Not Recommended

Smith's Vodka (USA) 40% abv, $20.

Corn. Impeccable purity; limpid. Opening sniffs pick up strong aromas of corn husk, creamed corn, toasted grain; secondary whiffs encounter off-dry aromas of cornflakes, new leather, dried parsley. Entry features stone-dry cereal tastes, with background notes of herbs; midpalate is clean, dusty dry, moderately biscuity.

2014 Rating: ★★★/Recommended

Snow Leopard Vodka (Poland) 40% abv, $35.

Spelt. Silvery, transparent, clear of sediment. Delicately sweet, earthy, buttery aromas abound in the initial inhalations as the low-level acidity acts in a supplementary way rather than being dominant, therefore providing a clear path for scents of fat, lard, vegetable oil to take charge; secondary sniffs confirm all the first findings and, in fact, turn slightly flowery/spring garden–like. Entry is silky, smooth, pleasantly oily, off-dry, chewy in texture; midpalate showcases the minerally, almost metallic graininess that's dry, toasty, nickel-like, and stony long into the finish.

2019 Rating: ★★★★/Highly Recommended

Sobieski Vodka (Poland) 40% abv, $14.

Made from rye. Immaculate purity; no color whatsoever. There's an obvious spiciness to the first nosing that's like unseeded rye bread and Ryvita crackers; the aroma builds with more air contact, releasing slightly baked aromas of toasted rye bread, charcoal briquettes, and cigarette ash. Entry is round, full weighted, semisweet, supple, and sap-like; midpalate echoes the entry, adding lush flavors of pine nuts, maple, and tree bark. Concludes medium long, satiny in texture, semisweet, and satisfying. Superb value for the money and a hidden gem of an unflavored vodka.

2018 Rating: ★★★★/Highly Recommended

Soyombo Vodka (Mongolia) 40% abv, $30.

Pewter/silver tint; pure. Notes of pineapple, banana up front; later on, the aroma picks up some low-grade sweetness and floral aspect with aeration and opens up to include black peppercorn, wheat germ, snack crackers, dry breakfast cereal. Entry offers sweetened breakfast cereal tastes that are abundant and vivid, with background citric acid notes (lemon peel); at midpalate, viscosity is a plus as the texture pushes the grain flavor forward as does the acidity, which leaves the palate dusty dry. Exhibits a sophistication that immediately points to applications as a chilled vodka shot, food accompaniment (smoked haddock, smoked salmon, in particular), and as an ingredient in minimalist cocktails such as the Gimlet, Vodka Martini.

2014 Rating: ★★★★/Highly Recommended

Spirit of Hven Backafallsbyn Swedish Organic Aquavit (Sweden) 40% abv, $53.
This aquavit's sandy-brown/ochre color is bright and sediment-free. The initial sniffs pick up only fleeting traces of caraway seed, cardamom, and perhaps a faint whisper of dill as the bouquet incrementally gains its footing; with further air contact, the aromatic characteristics emerge in the pronounced forms of caraway seed and dill, with a small dose of lemon zest—this is an elegant, restrained aquavit bouquet but one that rewards those with patience. Entry is oily and billowy in texture, giving a firm structure to the flavors of caraway seed, anise, and wheat snack cracker; midpalate shows a piquancy that's suddenly black pepper–like and dancing-on-the-tongue tangy without being prickly or hot. Concludes in a brief aftertaste that's mildly spiced and understated. Deceptively delicious due primarily to its toned-down virtues.
2017 Rating: ★ ★ ★ ★/Highly Recommended

Spirit of Hven Backafallsbyn Organic Vodka (Sweden) 40% abv, $43.
Flawlessly pure and colorless. I like the vivid grainy/breakfast cereal opening aroma that's dry, compact, and reminiscent of a white French baguette that's still warm from the oven; later whiffs pick up the mandatory scent (in unflavored vodka) of black peppercorn that adds a pleasing crackling snap to the bouquet. Entry is acutely tangy, arid in its desert-air dryness, and flinty, mineral- and stone-like as it unfolds on the tongue; midpalate highlights all the entry features, with the big part going to the flinty dryness that seems, in my mind, to be an ideal platform for a Vodka Martini. Finishes a little too chalky, but overall, I like the density and freshness of this vodka's crisp, razor-edged graininess.
2017 Rating: ★ ★ ★ ★/Highly Recommended

Square One Bergamot Orange Flavored Organic Vodka (USA) 40% abv, $30.
Colorless, but hazy right after the pour; the haze fades quickly. First inhalations confirm what's on the label, as concentrated fragrances of orange peel and fresh tangerine pulp make for pleasant sniffing in the opening round; air contact deepens the citrus/orange/tangerine/blood orange underpinnings as the bouquet goes more zesty, dried peel–like than juicy/pulpy, and therefore turns nicely (for me, at least) astringent, tart, and acidic. Entry is delightfully tart and orange peel–like, then at midpalate the taste profile leaps forward into a juicier mode that outdistances the zestiness, lasting deep into the irresistibly savory aftertaste.
2015 Rating: ★ ★ ★ ★/Highly Recommended

St. Augustine Batch #2 Florida Cane Vodka (USA) 40% abv, $28.
Sugarcane. Unblemished; colorless. Right out of the starting gate, this aroma could only be one thing, and that is sugarcane due to its sappy, maple-like surface aroma and its deeper foundational fragrance of grassy sugar; secondary whiffs serve to reinforce the findings of the initial inhalations. Entry is delicately sweet, sugary but in a controlled manner that's pleasant and easily quaffable; midpalate reflects the entry, adding perhaps a touch more sweetness, beaniness, ripeness before turning earthy and grassy in the medium-length finish.
2015 Rating: ★ ★ ★/Recommended

St. George All Purpose Vodka (USA) 40% abv, $25.
Non-GMO corn and St. George Pear Brandy. Bright, colorless appearance that is

sediment-free. I can definitely recognize the gauzy corn spirit right after the pour, but then something magical happens as the pear brandy starts to impose itself in the second pass in nuances of orchard fruit, fruit stone, then soaring scents of pear at the very end of sniffing; like no other vodka bouquet I know of and far better than the majority. Entry is intensely fruity, wonderfully so, in truth, but also viny/brambly, juicy but off-dry and profoundly zesty; midpalate carries forward all the gustatory splendor of the entry and adds a taut viscosity that ushers in the beguiling aftertaste. That rare vodka that is perfect served moderately chilled (I suggest 45 degrees Fahrenheit) and neat. All Purpose Vodka needs nothing added to it. A hands-down instant classic by the amazing St. George Spirits wizards of Alameda, California.
2015 Rating: ★ ★ ★ ★ ★/Highest Recommendation

St. George California Citrus Orange Vodka (USA) 40% abv, $30.
Absolute clarity; tint-free transparency. Up front, it smells deliciously of ripe, just-picked navel oranges and nothing else, except for a deft trace of orange peel; additional time in the glass serves to deepen the orange juice, orange zest charms, and tart, acidic freshness. Entry is pleasingly tart and deeply orangey, even showing a bit of pithy astringency, which maintains the tangy appeal; midpalate underscores the joys of the entry and adds a graceful touch of dried orange peel that makes the mouth pucker just prior to the aftertaste. Concludes as citrusy and authentic as it began. A rare gem of a citrus-flavored vodka that shows how flavoring can and should be done: with subtlety. Nothing short of brilliant.
2015 Rating: ★ ★ ★ ★ ★/Highest Recommendation

St. George Green Chile Vodka (USA) 40% abv, $30.
Jalapeño, serrano, habañero, bell peppers. Shows an oyster/electrum coloring that is really a slight tint and superb purity. As someone who perceives peppers as a sort of spiritual experience, this opening aroma is nirvana as the dominant fragrances are the serrano and habañero peppers as they should be due to their high levels of capsaicinoids (the tasteless chemical compounds in the flesh of peppers that bind to taste receptors in our mouths), producing the feeling of heat/pain; in fact, the presence of capsaicinoids is so prevalent in this vodka that their molecules prick the membranes in my nose, causing my eyes to water a bit; the second passes are even more intense and concentrated than the first. Entry profile is surprisingly mild, yet delectably zesty and tangy without being a three-alarm fire in the mouth; midpalate is delightfully oily/viscous, acutely peppery (more green bell and jalapeño) and approachable, tasty, and integrated. Finishes long, just slightly hot, actually more warm than hot, and remarkably pepper-like and real. A model of how vodka flavoring can take imbibers on a memorable journey of discovery.
2015 Rating: ★ ★ ★ ★ ★/Highest Recommendation

Stolichnaya Gluten Free Vodka (Latvia) 40% abv, $20.
Made from corn and buckwheat; thrice distilled; filtered four times through quartz sand and birch charcoal. Crystalline, pristine, and colorless appearance. The initial inhalations are pleasantly grainy and snack cracker–like, with a tinge of black peppercorn at the edges; this aroma expands with further aeration and features elegant scents of dry, unsweetened breakfast cereal, grain husk, cornmeal, lemon zest, and black pepper. Entry is keenly

piquant, even pungent with zesty black pepper, citrus zest, and cocoa powder notes that eclipse the foundational graininess; midpalate stage is where the warming, campfire-like distillate emerges as the flavor profile turns biscuit-like, buttery, yet spicy, and a touch smoky. Ends off-dry, sturdy, and alluringly smoky and roasted (maybe from the birch wood charcoal used in filtration?). Nice to review this characterful vodka again after many years.
2018 Rating: ★ ★ ★ ★/Highly Recommended

Stolichnaya Original Vodka (Latvia) 40% abv, $20.
Made with wheat. This vodka has a wild history of roller coaster–like quality. Limpid, transparent, clean and clear appearance. First sniffs pick up savory, if hazy, aromas of grain, parchment, gauze, textile fiber, and oatmeal; secondary inhalations don't detect much beyond what's already been described. Entry is pleasantly creamy, lightly spiced (black peppercorn), and muesli- and dry cereal–like; midpalate highlights the muesli aspect, in particular, as the taste profile turns left at the corner of Sweet and Bittersweet, all the while featuring deep grainy and toasted pumpernickel–like flavors that conclude bittersweet and slightly honeyed. A dazzling entry, midpalate, and finish, and deserves four stars.
2018 Rating: ★ ★ ★ ★/Highly Recommended

Stolichnaya Stoli Blueberi Blueberry Vodka (Latvia) 37.5% abv, $20.
Crystalline appearance; colorless. The blueberry flavoring in the opening nosing is a bit off-center, oddly revealing traces of mango, along with blueberry meat/pulp; later sniffs find that aeration gives this bouquet direction to Blueberry Hill as the marginally ripe blueberry essence comes through in softly succulent, ambrosial waves. Entry is convincingly blueberry-like, more dried blueberry, or rather the kind you might find in breakfast cereals, than fresh, but that is okay; midpalate reflects the entry in that the blueberry flavoring is dry, intensely acidic (hurray!), and tart. Concludes elegantly, under the radar, and subtle in its final approach. Nicely done, with understatement as all good flavored vodkas are.
2018 Rating: ★ ★ ★ ★/Highly Recommended

Stolichnaya Stoli Citros Citrus Vodka (Latvia) 37.5% abv, $20.
Void of color; sediment-free and crystalline. I need to dig a little deeper than I think is necessary to find ample aromatics in the opening pass, and what I discover is soft, slightly flabby lemon juice flavoring that's far meeker than I recall from 2003; while hoping that additional aeration will stimulate more in the way of fragrance, I am able to only discern faint traces of lemon juice and pulp even after the tenth minute of aeration—disappointing. Entry is painfully flabby, dulled out, and chunky as the lemon flavoring seems light-years from the core of the taste profile, sort of a periphery taste rather than the main event; midpalate echoes the entry findings, and I find this radical change from what I tasted in 2003 very disappointing. This vodka has lost its snap, its core strength, its direction. I hate reviews like this where former glory is dashed on the rocks of mediocrity.
2018 Rating: ★ ★/Not Recommended

Stolichnaya Stoli Hot Jalapeño Vodka (Latvia) 37.5% abv, $20.
Silvery, limpid, and pure. First whiffs pick up distant aromas of fresh-picked peppers, but not noticeable as chili peppers at this juncture; the jalapeño character needs more

aeration to emerge and emerge it does in the second passes. Entry is lightly peppery, showing just a hint of capsaicin, the chemical compound in chili peppers that is generally considered as an irritant to mammals—in this case, the dosage is low; midpalate is comfortably spicy and embers warm as the capsaicin level is kept to a low degree but there's enough zesty tang present to make you notice it. This vodka would be suitable for a spicy Bloody Mary cocktail.
2018 Rating: ★ ★ ★/Recommended

Stolichnaya Stoli Ohranj Orange Vodka (Latvia) 37.5% abv, $20.

Clean as springwater; void of color. I like the initial aromas of tart orange juice and peel that while faint offer just enough pungency to make it crystal clear as to what the flavoring agent is; there's a clear fading of aromatic intensity with more aeration so I move on. Entry shows more than ample tartness and juiciness as the orange flavoring spreads itself widely across the palate, showing good acidity and texture; midpalate is nicely juicy, crisp, acidic, and true to the fruit. Aftertaste builds upon the midpalate, ending in a crescendo of pleasant orange juice flavor.
2018 Rating: ★ ★ ★/Recommended

Stolichnaya Stoli Peachik Peach Vodka (Latvia) 37.5% abv, $20.

Crystalline, colorless appearance that is blemish-free. Wow, the fresh-peaches-right-off-the-tree opening aroma is succulent, ambrosial, and true to the fruit; a bit of aeration deepens the splendor of the fresh peach fragrance that is remarkably ripe and genuine; gets my vote as the best Stoli flavored vodka aroma. Entry flavor is good but not as vibrant as the bouquet implies, and that's a slight letdown; midpalate flavor turns a little too industrial, earthy, and mineral-like, losing much of the fresh peach attributes found in the lovely aroma. Finishes cleanly, moderately peachy, and gently sweet.
2018 Rating: ★ ★ ★/Recommended

Stolichnaya Stoli Razberi Raspberry Vodka (Latvia) 37.5% abv, $20.

Impeccably clean, void of color, and free of sediment. First nosings after the pour don't mine much in the way of aroma except for a subtle, dry, acidic trace of ripe raspberry on the vine; secondary whiffs are greeted with bigger waves of viny raspberry jam scents, as further air contact releases more juiciness. Entry is true-to-the-fruit juicy but leaning more towards acidic crispness than fat juiciness, and for me that's a huge plus; midpalate largely mirrors the entry phase, but the depth of the raspberry preserves–like flavor is genuinely tasty. Finishes lovely, stately, acidic enough to maintain the razor edge.
2018 Rating: ★ ★ ★ ★/Highly Recommended

Stolichnaya Stoli Salted Karamel Salted Caramel Vodka (Latvia) 37.5% abv, $20.

Perfectly clean and rainwater clear. Opening inhalations immediately following the pour do pick up caramel but not the salt; allowing for more air contact, I dive in again after five minutes and it's here that the saline quality appears in tandem with the light, buttery caramel—pleasantly so. Entry is true to the label identification as there indeed are caramel-like flavors that appear to be mingled with salt, but overall there's a hollow falseness to this vodka that somehow doesn't ring true with my taste buds; midpalate doesn't help

much as the taste is now coming off as manufactured, laboratory-like, and unpleasant. Ends in a mineral-like heap on my tongue. Pass on this.
2018 Rating: ★/Not Recommended

Stolichnaya Stoli Strasberi Strawberry Vodka (Latvia) 37.5% abv, $20.
Limpid; colorless; pure. Up front, it smells of fresh, just-picked, slightly under-ripe strawberries—so far, so good; I like the acidic kick that's apparent, keeping the sweetness at bay as the strawberry essence comes through, going just a shade riper than in the initial nosing. Entry, to its credit, keeps the sweetness in check and this allows the strawberry flavoring to shine in a manner that's more under-ripe and steely than juicy and sweet; midpalate turns down Juicy Street just a little way, making the finish delectably succulent.
2018 Rating: ★★★/Recommended

Stolichnaya Stoli Vanil Vanilla Vodka (Latvia) 37.5% abv, $20.
Clear and colorless as springwater appearance. Initial whiffs pick up faint hints of vanilla bean but little more; after more time in the glass the aroma builds in intensity as the vanilla essence comes to the fore, neither sweet nor dry but more zesty and tangy. Entry is leaner than I remember but still owns a solid vanilla bean core that's subtle and firmly structured; midpalate is remarkably bean-like and tasty without being a blockbuster flavor or one that's cloying. Aftertaste is cake frosting–like, beany, as the flavor now leans in the direction of vanilla extract. Even though I don't feel the same sense of wonder as I did when I reviewed it back in 1997, I still think that this is one of the premier flavored vodkas in the marketplace.
2018 Rating: ★★★★/Highly Recommended

Svedka Vodka (Sweden) 40% abv, $16.
Clean as rainwater; pewter-like hint of color. Nose in the early stages is a little muted, showing only faint scents of grain husk and cereal; further air contact does wonders for this aroma as it opens up significantly after just ten minutes of aeration with waves of dry cereal, egg white, and grain husk. Entry is firm, crisp, dry, and deeply grainy; midpalate is where most of the taste action lives, as it exhibits moderately vivid flavors of Wheat Thins crackers, unsweetened breakfast cereal, and unbuttered wheat bread toast. Finishes clean and aridly dry. In previous years I have rated this unflavored vodka four stars. In view of how far unflavored vodkas have come in two decades, I am now scoring it three stars. That said, it remains a solid value that punches far above its weight class.
2020 Rating: ★★★/Recommended

Syvä Vodka (USA) 45% abv, $31.
As transparent as springwater; sediment-free appearance. Oh my, the concentrated, pungent, slap-your-face opening aroma offers lemon curd, sawdust, sour grape, rye toast, caraway seed, grain kernel oil, haystack . . . I mean, this could go on and on; later sniffs find aromas of egg white, egg cream soda, sourdough, baker's yeast, tin can, minerals. Entry is warming, slightly smoky, viscous/deeply oily (love this aspect!), roasted, grainy, bittersweet, highly appetizing; midpalate is all about the high degree of grain oil that makes this stage rich, yet dry, toasty, sap-like, chewy, like vegetable oil, and nothing short of luscious as an intense beany

quality emerges just as the midpalate evolves into the aftertaste, creating a final phase that's sappy, resiny, beany, deep, dense, and succulent—wow, this vodka has character to spare!
2015 Rating: ★ ★ ★ ★ ★/Highest Recommendation

Tahoe Blue Vodka (USA) 40% abv, $30.
A blend of grape, corn, and sugarcane vodkas. Clean as springwater; translucent. Opening sniffs detect restrained, clean, and bone-dry aromas of fruit and grain in painfully small portions; another five minutes of air contact unleash only minor traces of cereal grain, fruit stone/pit, and soft spirit. Entry offers mildly pleasing taste notes of graham crackers and a medium-sweet sugarcane flavor that shows an oily texture; midpalate is a little all over the map but regains focus near the finish as the profile highlights both the sugarcane and corn elements far more than the grapes. This vodka's pleasant neutrality would work in cocktails more so than as a shot, where the slight lack of definition wouldn't hold up.
2015 Rating: ★ ★ ★/Recommended

Three Olives Mango Vodka (USA) 35% abv, $20.
Translucent and flawlessly clear. Gentle traces of mango fruit, very dry indeed, greet the nose in the opening inhalations; aeration adds a faint hint of baking spice to the aroma as the mango fades a bit with air contact. Palate entry is delicate and authentic, but more dry than ripe; midpalate continues the subtle approach with the flavoring, and that's a relief since delicacy with flavoring is the way to go. Finishes tart, true to the fruit, and even a touch minerally. Some mango aficionados might want bigger mango flavor, but I prefer the softer approach, especially when I'm thinking *cocktails*. I applaud the masterful and restrained blending of Three Olives.
2020 Rating: ★ ★ ★ ★/Highly Recommended

Three Olives Root Beer Vodka (USA) 35% abv, $20.
Ideal clarity. Initial aromas can't be anything other than root beer at its botanical/herbal/root-like truest; added aeration time brings out a sugary sweetness that's controlled and soda pop–like and not in the least overbearing. Palate entry is, like all Three Olives flavored vodkas, genuine and reined in; midpalate is pleasingly sweet and egg cream–like, with a background trace of vanilla. Concludes clean, plump, but not cloying. Not sure about applications, but I'll leave that to mixologists.
2020 Rating: ★ ★ ★/Recommended

Three Olives Tomato Vodka (USA) 35% abv, $20.
Silvery clear and impeccably clean. The slightly sour tomato aroma right out of the starting gate is genuine, alluringly zesty (peppery), and more like tomato paste than fresh tomato, but the authenticity is impressive and right away I'm thinking *Bloody Mary*; another seven minutes of air contact have the aroma staying the course from the opening whiffs as the astringent, unabashedly peppery tomato paste remains true and focused. Palate entry is marginally sweeter and more pulpy than the aroma and it takes the experience to the next level; midpalate serves up more of the tangy black pepper element that keeps any sweetness at bay. Concludes spicy and prickly in the mouth.
2020 Rating: ★ ★ ★/Recommended

Three Olives Triple Shot Espresso Vodka (USA) 35% abv, $20.

Looks like cola or black coffee in its deep brownness. Offers keen aromas of espresso and coffee beans in the first nosings; after another six minutes in the glass, the aroma fills out and deepens, becoming more oily and intensely beany. Palate entry is very sweet and not as fiercely espresso-like as I'd hoped it would be; midpalate flavor profile, however, is richer and deeper than that of the entry, and that's where this recommendation gets salvaged. Ends up sweet, nearly liqueur-like. Recommendable but doesn't carry the concentration of either of the two Van Gogh Espresso vodkas.
2020 Rating: ★ ★ ★/Recommended

Three Olives Vodka (England) 40% abv, $21.

English wheat. Spotless clarity; void of color. Soft aromatic eruptions of vegetable cooking oil; raw, uncooked grains; and flint make their way out of the sampling glass in the first minutes. Later passes unearth equally subtle and nuanced aromas of baked almond and unsweetened breakfast cereal. Entry is tight, clean, July-in-the-Mojave dry, and grain-driven; midpalate has more to say, especially about the graininess that now has turned husk-like and mineral-like. Aftertaste flashes potent signs of wheat bread, grain kernel, and snack cracker. This vodka builds in intensity. Lovely and bright all the way through.
2020 Rating: ★ ★ ★ ★/Highly Recommended

Three Olives Watermelon Vodka (USA) 35% abv, $20.

Clear as rainwater. Once again, the delicacy of the first aromatic encounter is a joy to behold, as juicy, slightly under-ripe watermelon fragrance wafts up from the sampling glass; six more minutes of air contact deepens the ripeness of the melon fruit, making it succulent. Palate entry is sweeter than the aroma and satisfyingly ambrosial and long; midpalate echoes all the flavor virtues found in the entry. Having such a solid distillate flavored so judiciously makes for exciting quaffing and mixing.
2020 Rating: ★ ★ ★/Recommended

Tito's Handmade Vodka (USA) 40% abv, $20.

Pristine, clean, void of color. The opening nosing sequence doesn't offer a huge amount of aroma, but there is a notable cornstarch aspect that's dry on the whole and starchy; secondary sniffs pick up additional fragrances, mostly corn husk, unbuttered corn on the cob, and canola oil. Entry is full textured, moderately oily, more bitter than sweet, cereal-like, and resiny; midpalate features highlights of cornmeal/tamale, corn syrup, and caramel corn. Aftertaste is corn sweet, sap-like, lightly toasted, and keenly starchy.
2018 Rating: ★ ★ ★/Recommended

TOPO Batch #2 Handcrafted from Organic Carolina Wheat Vodka (USA) 40% abv, $30.

Clear as rainwater. I favorably respond to the toasty, grainy smell of wheat snack crackers that greets you after the pour; the intensity of the wheat cereal aroma remains constant into the second passes as the bouquet turns more beany and kernel-like (Grape-Nuts cereal). Entry is sturdy, moderately viscous, cereal dry yet with a beany bittersweet aspect that's very charming; midpalate is long, significantly sweeter than the entry, creamy in texture, chewy, and vanilla-like. It's rare that I come across an unflavored grain-based vodka with so much layering, depth of flavor, character, and ribbony texture. Tasty enough to quaff neat and slightly chilled.

2016 Rating: ★ ★ ★ ★ ★/Highest Recommendation

Ultimat Vodka (Poland) 40% abv, $45.
Grains and potato base. Colorless, but has a minor purity issue as I see more gray tendril-like sediment than I'd like to see. First nosings are pleasingly stony, mineral-like, and neutral, with scant evidence of grain or potato; later sniffs after more aeration discover that the first-round fragrance has disappeared, leaving behind a totally neutral bouquet. Entry is delicate, slightly oily, and a little spicy and peppery, which I like; midpalate shows an oiliness that must be from the potato aspect because it's also low-on-the-scale sweet. Aftertaste reflects the findings of the midpalate and is moderately pleasing.

2016 Rating: ★ ★ ★/Recommended

Valt Vodka (Scotland) 40% abv, $49.
One hundred percent malted barley. Not as pristine as I'd like to see, with some floating particles noted; colorless. This vodka nose is so deeply earthy, botanical, and woodsy that I almost think that it's flavored, which it is not, but, man alive, the initial scent is mushroom-like, dry leaves–like, cereally, and like few other unflavored vodkas I know of; secondary whiffs now pick up a minerality that's stone-like (granite) and different than the opening aromatics. Entry provides the taste buds with a feast of breakfast cereal, snack cracker flavors that are slightly sweet, delicate in their bearing, and just a bit oily; midpalate confirms all the entry findings and goes further with the grain intensity that ushers in a muesli-like, lightly honeyed aftertaste that's delicious and almost juicy. What started as a two star vodka in the first nosing evolved in the latter nosing, entry, and midpalate into a three star vodka, and then the sterling finish earned it a fourth rating star for succulence.

2016 Rating: ★ ★ ★ ★/Highly Recommended

Van Gogh Açaí-Blueberry Vodka (Holland) 35% abv, $27.
Highly appealing amethyst/dark orchid color; transparent and pristine. Initial aroma is a mélange of berries, fragrant, moderately viny/brambly, tart, tannic; the whiffs after more air contact find the aroma turning more ambrosial, slightly candied. Entry is deliciously fruity, berry-like, delicately sweet, succulent; midpalate echoes the entry, adding a deft touch of acidity that maintains the freshness with style. Finishes elegantly, genuine, more tart than sweet. Found it more charming and balanced than seven years ago and therefore am upping the score to five stars. Seriously tasty.

2019 Rating: ★ ★ ★ ★ ★/Highest Recommendation

Van Gogh Coconut Vodka (Holland) 35% abv, $27.
Shows a faint yellowish color; perfect clarity. It's been ten years since I've smelled this vodka and reviewing it again makes me realize what gifted artisans the Royal Dirkzwager distillers are—first nosings pick up genuine aromas of unsweetened coconut meat and a delicate toastiness that make for pleasurable nosing at the highest rank; secondary sniffs bask in the splendor of real coconut magic. Entry is satiny smooth, creamy, sweeter than the

aroma, lush; midpalate is slightly toasted, delicately sweet, authentic. Finish is luscious. In my personal pantheon of greatest flavored spirits of all-time. WOOOOW!
2019 Rating: ★★★★★/Highest Recommendation

Van Gogh Cool Peach Vodka (Holland) 35% abv, $27.
Colorless; totally transparent and sediment-free. The peach ripeness leaps from the glass in big, defined aromatic waves that are fresh, real, gently sweet; secondary whiffs encounter softer fragrances of white peach, zesty spice, peach peel. Entry is succulent, ripe, peachy sweet, juicy, satiny textured; midpalate reinforces all the assets of the taste entry, adding a drier peach aspect that lasts deep into the aftertaste, which is balanced, acidic, crisp. A dandy flavored vodka of substance and grace.
2019 Rating: ★★★★/Highly Recommended

Van Gogh Double Espresso Vodka (Holland) 35% abv, $27.
Coffee-bean-brown color, nearly opaque; pure. Opening nosing passes are impressive, in that the bitter coffee bean/espresso scents are scarily accurate to the real thing without the slightest hint of sweetness; intense beaniness continues into the second stage of inhalation as the bouquet turns toastier, more roasted, keenly bitter yet scrumptious. Entry is lush, satiny in texture, and incredibly espresso-coffee-bean-like in its beany concentration; midpalate builds upon the tastes of the entry, becoming even more bitter and, therefore, genuine. Aftertaste is beany, rich, authentic. A fabulous flavored vodka . . . and I'm not even a coffee/espresso drinker.
2019 Rating: ★★★★★/Highest Recommendation

Van Gogh Dutch Caramel Vodka (Holland) 35% abv, $27.
Sepia/terra-cotta color; superb clarity. Smells seductively of toffee, caramel, nougat, butterscotch aromas in the early whiffs; later inhalations pick up butter brickle, toasted marshmallow. Entry is toasty, moderately sweet, intensely caramel-like, candy-store succulent; midpalate is richly caramel-like but is as bitter as it is sweet, reminding me slightly of maple bars from Vermont. Finishes gracefully long, chewy, moderately sweet.
2019 Rating: ★★★★/Highly Recommended

Van Gogh Dutch Chocolate Vodka (Holland) 35% abv, $27.
Ecru/talmi gold/champagne color; impeccable clarity. Smells of bittersweet chocolate, cocoa butter, lard, brown butter in the initial sniffs; later inhalations encounter more cocoa beans, milk chocolate scents rather than dark chocolate. Entry is pleasingly bittersweet, plump, creamy, beany; midpalate maintains the bittersweet aspect, lasting deep into the aftertaste.
2019 Rating: ★★★★/Highly Recommended

Van Gogh Espresso Vodka (Holland) 35% abv, $27.
Oyster/tarnished-silver color; superb purity. The delicate, almost coy opening aroma is all about freshly ground coffee beans and alluring espresso bitterness—a beguiling bouquet; secondary inhalations pick up far more roasted bean fragrance than in the first whiffs, and that deepens the experience. Entry reflects the second aroma more than the initial scents as the roasted bean aspect surges forward in tsunamis of rich, espresso taste that's supported by

a bittersweet undercurrent; midpalate mirrors the entry and adds toasted marshmallow to the taste mix. Gloriously subdued finish is the perfect way to end the experience.
2019 Rating: ★ ★ ★ ★ ★/Highest Recommendation

Van Gogh Rich Dark Chocolate Vodka (Holland) 35% abv, $27.
Chestnut/cocoa color, almost opaque. Offers dark, bittersweet aromas in the first passes that are cacao-like, concentrated, beany; second-stage inhalations build upon the first impressions turning slightly sweet. Entry is rich but not in the least unctuous or cloying as the taste profile remains true to the source and intensely beany; midpalate sports a satiny texture that alone is worth the bottle price, but in the end it's the bittersweet chocolate flavoring that makes this medium-bodied vodka so pleasurable.
2019 Rating: ★ ★ ★ ★/Highly Recommended

Van Gogh Vanilla Vodka (Holland) 35% abv, $27.
Shiny, impeccable clarity. Opening nose is all about vanilla bean, vanilla extract, cake frosting aromas that are charming because they are not sweet, but, in fact, bittersweet and intensely beany; secondary whiffs buttress the first impressions with toasty vanilla, marshmallow fragrances that are inviting. Entry is silky, creamy, pleasingly warm, and bittersweet, focusing solely on vanilla bean spiciness; midpalate echoes the entry stage entirely, offering gentle but substantial vanilla bean essence at its purest. Remains one of my all-time favorite flavored vodkas (the list is short) due to its restraint, high degree of elegance, and authenticity. Masterful blending.
2019 Rating: ★ ★ ★ ★ ★/Highest Recommendation

Van Gogh Vodka (Holland) 40% abv, $29.
Clear as rainwater; sediment-free. Opening nose is whistle clean, sleek, elegant, desert dry, dusty, almost coy; secondary whiffs detect deeper notes of nuts (peanuts), black pepper, candle wax. Entry is slightly toasty, marshmallow-like, grainy, opulent, breakfast cereal–like, just plain tasty; midpalate envelops the palate in a blanket of toasted grain that's seductively plump, bacon fat–like, bittersweet, scrumptious. Textbook aftertaste that's integrated, drier than the midpalate, roasted, grainy, flat-out luscious. A clinic on how delicious unflavored vodka could be.
2019 Rating: ★ ★ ★ ★ ★/Highest Recommendation

Van Gogh Wild Appel Vodka (Holland) 35% abv, $27.
Flawless purity, limpid appearance. Green apple fragrance is rife in this tantalizing first nosing that's equal parts spicy, apple-like, peel-like, pulpy, almost cider-like; secondary inhalations pick up more of the spiced, baked, green apple essence and that's what's so appealing about this bouquet. Entry is lusciously tart, more pulpy than juicy, and loaded with baked apple/apple pie flavors; midpalate is long, sweetly ripe, dense, better than I recall, zesty, cinnamon-like. Aftertaste is infinitely long, like apple pie, and spicy.
2019 Rating: ★ ★ ★ ★/Highly Recommended

Van Hoo Vodka (Belgium) 40% abv, $25.
Crystalline appearance; sediment-free and limpid. The initial nosings need to be

repeated and frequent in order to ascertain any substantial fragrance other than a dullish grainy component that is one rung from the bottom on the neutral scale; in the second passes I get a curious pea-like scent that, while pleasant, seems incongruous for grain vodka. Entry reveals a bland taste profile that is modestly grainy, with deft touches of cereal sweetness but is overall quite neutral; midpalate doesn't unearth anything further in the way of notable flavor impact. Finishes dusty dry. There's no major flaw (stinky, too sweet, biting, etc.), and it would probably rate three stars except for its lack of grip and its parchment-thin character. Just as unexciting as it was back in 1998. Today, vodka can be so much more than, well, what vodka has always been perceived to be.

2016 Rating: ★ ★/Not Recommended

Veil Vodka (USA) 40% abv, $13.

Beautifully crystalline appearance. Nicely animated aromatics include cracked wheat, Wheat Thins snack crackers, and dry breakfast cereal; additional time in the glass brings out faint traces of citrus peel and black pepper. Entry highlights the peppery aspect; midpalate is silky smooth, clean, and acutely spicy/peppery. Aftertaste follows the midpalate in spiciness.

2015 Rating: ★ ★ ★/Recommended

Vikingfjord Vodka (Norway) 40% abv, $15.

Potato base. Column still. Void of color and flawless purity. First inhalations after the pour fail to encounter much aromatic thrust and, in fact, as the vodka sits aerating in the glass, it fades even more except for a timid earthiness that actually reminds me of potato peel; so much for the nosing exercise and for ten minutes of my life that I won't get back. Entry does offer a little more character than the vacuous bouquet in the form of grain kernel; midpalate pushes the flavor ball forward, to its credit, as the profile turns gently sweet and mildly oily in texture. Finishes semisweet and more grainy than potato-like.

2016 Rating: ★ ★/Not Recommended

Víti Icelandic Aquavite (Iceland) 47% abv, $80.

One hundred percent malted barley. Translucent and clean. The caraway seed influence is unmistakably evident right from the first whiffs as I envision rye bread laced with caraway seeds from my childhood in Chicago; without getting carried away by nostalgia, I find the second round of inhalations is varied in character as the caraway fades slightly, leaving the door open for dry fragrances of breakfast cereal, toasted grain, and shredded wheat. Entry is intensely seed-like, a bit rustic, and pleasantly prickly on the tongue as the 47 percent abv comes into play; midpalate is smoother than the entry, moderately sweeter, more complex in its grain intensity, biscuity, dense, and just overall tasty and mouthfilling. Finishes long, caraway-like, peppery, zesty, and prickly. An aquavit that deserves your attention.

2016 Rating: ★ ★ ★ ★/Highly Recommended

VOO Ultra Premium Vodka (USA) 40% abv, $55.

Clean and clear appearance. There's a slight sweetness to this grainy/mashy opening nose that's pleasant and welcoming; second inhalations detect more intense and dense scents of cereal grains, as well as subtler notes of estery ethyl acetate, almost tropical fruit–like.

Entry is bittersweet, chewy, fat in texture, loaded with glycerin-like attributes that lend a white sugar/vanilla bean cake frosting flavor that is forceful enough to last unabated straight through the midpalate stage and into the finish. A vodka designed for consumers who prefer their beverages sweet.

2016 Rating: ★★★/Recommended

Western Son Texas Vodka, Batch No. 001-01012 (USA) 40% abv, $18.

One hundred percent yellow corn. Flawless purity; colorless. Opening nose is a little muted, so I dig deeper to find distant, aridly dry aromas of candle wax, parchment, and cornstarch; later passes show just a hint more sweetness as the corn element begins to emerge; overall a lackluster unflavored vodka bouquet. Entry barely registers any taste profile as the neutrality commands the helm; midpalate is acceptably appealing and offers a bit more corny sweetness that's kind of baseless and drifting due to the skimpy texture. Finishes grainy, kernel-like, acidic enough to be described as clean, but is too lean and austere to be recommended.

2016 Rating: ★★/Not Recommended

Woody Creek 100% Potato Vodka (USA) 40% abv, $32.

Ideally pristine and without any color shading whatsoever. The sweet, earthy, potato peel–like opening aroma could be from nothing but potatoes; with further aeration, the bouquet turns more sour and vegetal adding even a mild floral/florist-shop note that makes for appealing sniffing. Entry screams "POTATO" immediately and while the opening taste is hardly nuanced, it is full in its volume and intention; midpalate stays the Potato Highway course as the flavor becomes enveloped in a silky cloak of oily texture that I find very nice. Is Woody Creek from Colorado in the same North American league as Pennsylvania's brilliant Boyd & Blair Potato Vodka (five stars)? Not just yet, but give it time in the form of several more batches. I'll be watching with interest.

2016 Rating: ★★★★/Highly Recommended

Woody Creek Reserve Vodka (USA) 40% abv, $79.

Made from one hundred percent Stobrawa potatoes. Impeccable purity; colorless. The opening aroma can be nothing but potato, as there is a sweet/sour tandem fragrance occurring that is compelling and inviting; secondary sniffs after more aeration discover that the sour aspect, which I find starchy and biscuity, comes to dominate. Entry is full in texture, mild sweetness but mostly is vegetal, pasty, and starchy; midpalate reflects the entry as the potato presence continues to dominate (but why shouldn't it?), the texture builds in perceived mass, and the core flavor becomes sweeter. Aftertaste is medium long, clean, rich in texture, gaining in sweetness, and is just plain pleasing.

2016 Rating: ★★★★/Highly Recommended

Zodiac Potato Black Cherry Vodka (USA) 35% abv, $26.

Pewter/tarnished-silver/gray color; clean and pure. Wow, ripe black cherry perfume wafts up from the copita in rich waves of real just-picked fruit; aeration only bolsters the impressions from the initial nosing as the fruit aspect drifts up from the glass in a charming display of authenticity. Entry is tart, astringent, acidic, and genuinely tasty; midpalate goes a touch sweeter and riper, and that makes for satisfying imbibing. Fruity and tart finish closes the circle. Nice to see a judicious use of flavoring for a change rather than the usual overkill. Well done.

2015 Rating: ★ ★ ★ ★/Highly Recommended

Zodiac Potato Vodka (USA) 40% abv, $26.

Distilled in Rigby, Idaho. Pristine appearance. Displays some earthiness in the opening whiffs after the pour, along with a parchment aspect; time in the glass stimulates little except for a beeswax component and a dash of potato peel; a clean, wispy bouquet. Entry is really pleasant and near-robust in taste as the potato element comes alive by comparison to the low-key bouquet; midpalate highlights the chewy texture and the buttery flavor. Concludes semisweet more than sweet, a little brittle in the throat, but acceptably hearty, which, for me, makes the experience worthwhile.

2015 Rating: ★ ★ ★/Recommended

LIQUEURS, APERITIFS, AMARI, AND BITTERS—WORLD

I won't lie to you. Liqueurs, critical as they may be to the greater spirits category and to the creation of cocktails, aren't my favorite potables to evaluate. I don't respond well to icky-sticky sweetness overall, and I therefore find many liqueurs not to my liking, as scores register off-the-charts levels of sugar. That said, as a professional critic, it is incumbent upon me to perform my level best in their analyses.

The historical record concerning liqueurs is long, colorful, and diverse. The first were likely created as medicinal remedies as far back as the late Middle Ages, primarily in the Christian monasteries, abbeys, and convents that dotted western and central Europe. Traditional herbal liqueurs such as Chartreuse and Bénédictine D.O.M. bear witness to this legacy. The growth of mixed drinks in the nineteenth and twentieth centuries boosted the profile of liqueurs, as they became staple ingredients in many classic and contemporary cocktails.

Since liqueurs are produced the world over from myriad ingredients and base distillates, there is no set of regulatory or production standards that apply to all. I therefore break them down into easily understood subcategories, such as herbal/mint, nut (hazelnut, almond, walnut), fruit (including berry, tropical, and orchard fruits), and bean (meaning coffee, cocoa, et cetera) liqueurs. Each of these subcategories generates numerous sub-subcategories, which for the sake of my sanity and your time I will not elaborate upon.

Since *Kindred Spirits 2*, there has been an explosion of interest in bitters, aperitifs, and amari (plural of *amaro*) as they form a whole other subcategory of herb/botanical-linked cocktail ingredients that add tang, an herblike earthiness, and piquancy to mixed drinks. Many are accounted for here, tasted on their own.

Still, for all of my mild reservations, there exist more than a few liqueurs and amari that stand out from the pack. The ratings will speak for themselves on those.

1889 by Geijer Glogg Liqueur (USA) 20% abv, $32.
Amber color; clean and pure. Wow, I like the gingerroot powder and tuber notes that are pungent and accented by supplemental aromas of brown rice, nutmeg, and clove; secondary passes after eight minutes of further aeration encounter more vigorous gingerroot powder presence as well as cardamom. Entry is (thankfully) moderately sweet, delectably herbal, and lightly spiced; midpalate is fresh, deeply herbal, and zesty/tangy more in a spice

manner than a citrusy way. Ends on an off-dry note, herbaceous and supple. Well done. Traditionally served warm.
2015 Rating: ★ ★ ★ ★/Highly Recommended

Alberti Strega Limoncello Liqueur (Italy) 30% abv, $20.
Attractive, misty lemon-juice-yellow color; good purity. I like the juicy, tart, lemony fragrance that is both zesty and tangy; secondary whiffs after six minutes of further air contact reveal nothing new as the aromatic profile remains vibrantly juicy, sweet/sour, and citrusy. Entry is tart, acidic, lemony, and yet is pleasantly sweet; midpalate is a trace sweeter than the entry but neither cloying nor syrupy like some lesser limoncellos. Ends lemon-drop sweet.
2014 Rating: ★ ★ ★/Recommended

Alberti Strega Sambuca Liqueur (Italy) 42% abv, $20.
Translucent and clear, but with minuscule, inconsequential sediment seen under the lamp. Initial inhalations after the pour lead directly to vivid aniseed/anise/licorice tastes that explode in the tasting copita; after seven minutes of additional aeration, the bouquet turns alluringly beany and kernel-like, highlighting the legume effect of chickpea and lentil—I like this no-nonsense sambuca fragrance. Entry is creamy in texture, intensely licorice-like, beany, and only moderately sweet; midpalate is less sweet than the entry but even more licorice- and bean-like. Finishes like liquid satin and is medium sweet. A very good, best-kept-secret sambuca.
2014 Rating: ★ ★ ★ ★/Highly Recommended

Aperol Aperitivo (Italy) 20% abv, $22.
Neon-orange color; flawless clarity. The orange, tangerine, and rhubarb opening aromas had me from the first whiff; further aeration brings out the earthiness of the herbs and dried spices, but also introduces a fresh garden-like scent that's vine-like, grassy, and a bit like dried orange peel. Entry comes off sweet at first but then turns drier and keenly fruity/citrusy; midpalate introduces a bittersweet aspect that counters the fruit intensity, and the entire exercise ends on a refreshing, crisp, razor-edged note that's gently orangey and ripe. The mixing aperitif of the moment and deservedly so.
2020 Rating: ★ ★ ★ ★/Highly Recommended

Artez ArVani Vanilla Liqueur (France) 40% abv, $35.
Mahogany color; very good clarity. Smells very nicely of Madagascar vanilla bean, honeysuckle, and brown sugar in the first sniffs; the roundness of the initial aromatic impressions remains as a primary feature in the secondary inhalations, turning more vanilla extract–like as the influence of air contact grows. Entry is dense, intensely vanilla bean–like, and yet there is clear evidence of the spirit base; midpalate is rich but not unctuous, beany without being metallic, and balanced. Aftertaste is long, bittersweet, and honeyed.
2017 Rating: ★ ★ ★ ★/Highly Recommended

Bailey's The Original Irish Cream Liqueur (Ireland) 17% abv, $29.
Opaque, sandy/khaki color. First sniffs detect lovely, delicately spiced aromas of cinnamon, nutmeg, and cream, akin to eggnog but clearly its own ilk; secondary whiffs pick up

much more of the rich creaminess. Entry is smooth on the tongue, creamy without being unctuous, and with enough spice snappiness to keep the taste buds intrigued; midpalate turns on the spiciness with zesty notes of the nutmeg and now even clove. Ends long, cushiony, creamy, and savory.

2018 Rating: ★★★★/Highly Recommended

Bailoni Wachauer Gold-Apricot Liqueur (Austria) 30% abv, $40.
Pale amber/old gold color; superb purity. Subtle nose offers understated apricot fragrance that's ripe, peel-like, fruit stone–like, mildly sweet; after more air contact, the bouquet opens up slightly, emitting sophisticated, genteel aromas of, first, dried apricot, then apricot preserves. Entry is sublimely sweet, fruity, ripe, balanced; midpalate is lush, silky, viscous, and strikingly true to the source. An excellent expression of tart apricot fruit in liquid form.

2014 Rating: ★★★★/Highly Recommended

Bärenjäger Honey & Bourbon Liqueur (Germany) 35% abv, $32.
Amber/topaz color; unblemished purity. The opening aroma is anything but bashful as potent notes of dark honey and vanilla-laced bourbon rise from the sampling glass in sustained waves; extra air time sees the aroma turn slightly burnt and toasty, which gives it another level of perfume. Entry is sweet, woody, resiny, more honeyed than whiskey-like; midpalate goes all out with the honey element, but intriguingly the profile isn't what I'd describe as sweet as much as it is elemental, woodsy, rustic, and frankly, tasty as a shot at the bar.

2015 Rating: ★★★/Recommended

Barrow's Intense Ginger Liqueur (USA) 22% abv, $32.
Hazy, lemon yellow color; lots of sediment seen, which is normal for this type of libation. Gee willikers, this opening nose is zesty, gingery, piquant, citrusy, and very friendly; secondary nosings encounter a slightly subdued ginger aspect, but that allows the spiciness to dominate. Entry is juicy, citrusy, gingery, simple; midpalate reflects the entry impressions as the taste profile goes tangier, more herbaceous. Finishes long, like ginger snaps, ripe, delicately sweet, tangy. Good product whose affability doesn't mask the quality.

2014 Rating: ★★★★/Highly Recommended

Barsol Perfecto Amor Aperitif Wine (Peru) 17% abv, $20.
Amber/sandy-brown color; very good clarity. First inhalations pick up intense grape pulp, stemmy aromas that are top-heavy with bramble, viny scents reminiscent of grape harvest and early stage winemaking; secondary sniffs after more air contact find that the grape intensity hasn't waned one iota. Entry is pleasantly grapy, ripe, and almost pear-like in its flavor profile; the midpalate stage features a slight drying out of the flavor as the acidity now takes charge, providing a clean, tangy, near plum-like taste. Finishes brief in the throat, agile in its grapiness/fruitiness, and concentrated suddenly in its ripe sweetness.

2019 Rating: ★★★/Recommended

Bäska Snaps med Malört Bitters (France) 40% abv, $33.
Burnt-orange color; owns a gauzy haze. Opening nosings pick up an understated

licorice/anise fragrance that dances above background scents of parsley, bay leaf, burlap, hemp, lemon peel; secondary sniffs unearth nothing more. Entry is pungently bitter, creamy in texture, metallic; midpalate features a bitter caraway seediness that lasts deep into the aftertaste. Well made.
2014 Rating: ★ ★ ★/Recommended

Belle de Brillet Originale Poire William with Cognac Liqueur (France) 30% abv, $45.
Brilliant gold/harvest yellow color; flawless purity. One of the best fruit liqueur opening aromas of any, offering crisp acidity that maintains the aromatic integrity perfectly; secondary whiffs encounter rich, ripe pear notes that are supported with class by the sterling Brillet cognac—one of a kind. Entry is lusciously ripe yet also refreshingly tart; midpalate is medium long, juicy, but neither cloying nor unctuous, with the pear flavor and cognac in harmony. Finishes as gracefully as any liqueur available today, ripe, fruity, and remarkably elegant. A classic liqueur that would be impossible to improve upon.
2018 Rating: ★ ★ ★ ★ ★/Highest Recommendation

Berentzen Apple Liqueur (Germany) 20% abv, $20.
Bright flax/pale gold color; excellent purity. Opening aroma is strikingly like apple peel, tart, and fresh; second passes find that the crisp acidity of the first sniffs carries over following further aeration, creating a pleasurable walk-in-the-orchards fragrance of moderate impact and authenticity. Entry is nicely sour at first, then the taste profile turns riper and juicier as it leads into the midpalate stage that's properly tart and acidic. Finishes brief, crisp, apple-like. I'm raising the star rating to three stars/recommended. Can't say for sure why I didn't like this liqueur more back in 1998. It is perfectly serviceable, though not as charming as the Pear Liqueur or Wild Cherry.
2015 Rating: ★ ★ ★/Recommended

Berentzen Icemint Schnapps (Germany) 50% abv, $20.
Clear as mineral water; average purity. The peppermint aromatic thrust is all-encompassing, potent, true, and actually quite alluring because the elevated abv never steps in the way of the peppermint enjoyment. This bouquet reminds me of Christmas tree peppermint candy canes, and therefore brings up happy thoughts; neither cloying nor unctuously overpowering. Entry is sweet, true to peppermint all the way through the midpalate and finish. Yes, one can quibble about it being a one-note melody, but in this case it works. Astoundingly, the 100 proof is never an issue.
2015 Rating: ★ ★ ★ ★/Highly Recommended

Berentzen Peach Liqueur (Germany) 20% abv, $20.
There's a slight pewter-like quality to the appearance that doesn't allow me to describe it as colorless; perfect clarity. The softness of the peach perfume is pleasing because its delicacy makes it more a nuance than a typical liqueur aroma bomb; with more air contact, the peach aspect deepens and ripens, but that's what is to be expected, and therefore is acceptable. Entry is intensely peach-like, slightly under-ripe, nicely acidic, and clean in the mouth; midpalate stays the course of featuring the peach flavor in understated form while keeping

the acid level relatively high. Finish comes off a bit flinty and thin, but otherwise I think the producer did right by keeping the main flavor component subtle and a touch sour.
2016 Rating: ★ ★ ★/Recommended

Berentzen Pear Liqueur (Germany) 15% abv, $20.
Very pale bisque/pewter/brut champagne color; minor floating sediment in core. Pear aroma is evident right from the initial sniffs after the pour, but there are also traces of wet cement, pear peel, and butcher's wax paper; second passes detect mostly the juicy, ripe, pulpy pear aspect, which lasts the entire second stage; a pleasingly delicate bouquet. Entry is ethereal, alluringly tart, moderately juicy, subtle yet steady and focused; midpalate plays the tart juiciness to the hilt, leading into the slightly sour, refreshing, acidic but not astringent finish. The strength of this elegant liqueur is its nuanced bouquet, which sets the stage for a delightful flavor profile that delivers the lightweight goods in style.
2015 Rating: ★ ★ ★ ★/Highly Recommended

Berentzen White Apple Liqueur (Germany) 25% abv, $23.
According to the label, it's made with calvados and "premium wheat spirit." Clear, transparent, and immaculate-as-rainwater appearance. Smells up front of neutral grain spirit, cardboard, parchment, beeswax before it gets around to apple or calvados, which I find confusing since calvados typically provides a prominent apple orchard bouquet; on the second lap, I discover waxy apple-peel fragrance but not enough apple juice or apple pulp. Entry is flat tasting, stunningly manufactured, and inauthentic in its "apple-ness"; midpalate recovers a little respectability as a more appley flavor arrives on the scene, if tardily so. Finish better than the entry or midpalate, but there remains this awkward ersatz apple flavor that I can't get beyond. Missed opportunity, this one.
2015 Rating: ★ ★/Not Recommended

Berentzen Wild Cherry Liqueur (Germany) 15% abv, $20.
Looks just like cherry juice in its ruby port–like/crimson color; above-average clarity. First inhalations pick up black cherry, cassis, boysenberry fragrances that are properly bitter and peel-like and not in the least cloying or sugar chubby; second whiffs pull out traces of cherry pit, cherry jam, or compote in measured, alluringly fruity manner; good job here aromatically. Entry is nicely sweet, no—check that, maybe more ripe than flat-out sweet, and that translates to a tart juiciness that is appealing, slightly astringent; midpalate seizes the tart orchard-fruit advances made in the entry and propels them forward into a lean, ripe, but not sweet aftertaste, which caps this lovely liqueur experience. The juicy freshness wins the day.
2015 Rating: ★ ★ ★ ★/Highly Recommended

Bigallet China-China Amer Liqueur (France) 40% abv, $38.
Color is a chestnut-brown/molasses/espresso lookalike. Wow, the first nosing is treated to a zesty, citrusy mélange of aromas, everything from rhubarb to celery to aniseed to bitter orange to tangerine to blood orange, then all these attributes remain deep into the secondary whiffs. Entry is keenly citrusy, peel-like, orangey, piquant, bittersweet, then the midpalate

stage echoes all the findings of the entry. Aftertaste highlights the orange peel. Delicious, unique aperitif.
2014 Rating: ★ ★ ★ ★ ★/Highest Recommendation

Bitter Truth Apricot Liqueur (Germany) 22% abv, $32.
Eighteen-karat-gold color; flawless clarity. Apricot fragrance is expansive, expressive in the first nosings after the pour; the "juicy" factor grows with added air contact, making the secondary sniffs more pleasing than the initial nosings. Entry owns all the correct apricot credentials as the taste profile goes sweet/sour, tangy, ripe; to my surprise, midpalate goes a little flat as the apricot flavor turns more sour than sweet or ripe, but overall, the effect is still positive, acidic, astringent. Aftertaste highlights the astringency, which is why the finish is so clean.
2014 Rating: ★ ★ ★/Recommended

Bitter Truth Elderflower Liqueur (Germany) 22% abv, $32.
Sauvignon blanc–like straw-yellow color; superb purity. I really like the floral/fruity opening aroma, which is rich, minerally, ripe, without being cloying or overblown; secondary inhalations detect deeper layers of spring garden–like freshness and almost lychee-like fragrance—an excellent bouquet. Gently sweet, tangy entry flavors greet the taste buds in soft waves of floral, quince-like flavors; midpalate highlights a fruit peel–like zestiness that nicely complements the elderflower pineyness. Finish is seriously tart, fresh, cleansing, finely proportioned.
2014 Rating: ★ ★ ★ ★/Highly Recommended

Bitter Truth Pimento Dram Allspice Liqueur (Germany) 22% abv, $32.
Mahogany-brown color; very good purity. Lovely, delicately bitter opening aroma is pleasingly tangy, bark-like, botanical, spicy, peppery, piquant, keenly allspice-like; secondary sniffs following another few minutes of aeration largely echo the initial findings, adding chalk, gum, road tar. Entry is sweet/sour, caraway seed-like, citrus rind–like, fresh; midpalate goes acutely bark-like, sappy, spicy, earthy, botanical, medicinal. Like nothing you've tried before.
2014 Rating: ★ ★ ★ ★/Highly Recommended

Bitter Truth Violet Liqueur (Germany) 22% abv, $32.
Appearancewise, BT Violet is more bluish than violet/purple and is, for all intents and purposes, opaque. The opening aromatics are lovely, delicately floral, a touch pine-like/cedary, with subtle traces of citrus peel; with further aeration, the bouquet settles in as the flowery aspect fades substantially. Entry is sweet but not syrupy, floral/botanical in nature, with that deft hint of citrus again; midpalate flavor profile loses a little momentum from the entry. Finishes pleasantly, moderately flowery, medium sweet.
2014 Rating: ★ ★ ★/Recommended

Bittermens Amère Sauvage Liqueur (USA) 23% abv, $25.
Pretty topaz/black-tea color; flawless clarity. Right out of the aromatic gate, I like the deeply botanical/herbal fragrance that features tangerine zest, chamomile, green tea, chalk, dry earth/clay; secondary whiffs confirm all aromas discovered in initial nosings, adding

only linseed oil. Entry is pleasantly bittersweet, with layers of tea leaf, chamomile, sage, lemongrass flavors; midpalate is like forest floor, moss, leaves, tea, refined sugar. Tasty digestif liqueur for sensitive stomachs.
2014 Rating: ★★★★/Highly Recommended

Bittermens New Orleans Coffee Liqueur (USA) 24% abv, $24/375 ml.
Mahogany/nut-brown color; opaque; lots of coffee bean sediment. Crazy intensity of the coffee bean as the first inhalations pick up roasted bean, roasted nuts, and chicory; second whiffs after aeration encounter tightly wound, bitter aromas of coffee bean, tree bark, resins, and oils. Entry is off-the-charts concentrated, almost like sucking coffee beans, and is therefore wildly bitter but astoundingly authentic; midpalate mirrors the entry and adds more espresso-like concentration. Even though I'm not a coffee drinker, I appreciate what distiller Avery Glasser has done with this unique liqueur. My only concern centers on whether or not this degree of coffee bean power can be appreciated by a wide commercial audience. I say, buy it for an experience like no other in the ranks of coffee liqueurs.
2015 Rating: ★★★★/Highly Recommended

Black Note Amaro (Italy) 21% abv, $33.
Mahogany/walnut-brown color; superb clarity. Smells right out of the aromatic gate of damp earth, fennel, anise, tree bark, nutshell, and mushrooms—seriously lush and foresty; second whiffs pick up gentian, angelica, coriander, bay leaf, sage. Entry is supple, reined in, earthy but not rustic, slightly peppery, finely textured; midpalate reflects all the entry findings and adds citrus peel, cinchona, tree sap, tree resins. Concludes long in the throat, gently bittersweet, and piney. Liked it from start to finish and would serve it with one ice cube and an orange peel.
2016 Rating: ★★★★/Highly Recommended

Bruto Americano (USA) 24% abv, $30.
The very pretty color is brick red/cardinal; purity is fine and without sediment issues. Opening whiffs are confronted with feral aromas of dried orange peel, cardamom, cigar box, cedar/pine, Chinese herbs, and a woodsy rootiness that brings to mind Asian cuisine; further air contact serves to bolster the intense foresty/rootiness that now is the dominant aromatic feature. Entry is clean, with a monster bitterness that is totally derived from the root botanicals (St. George Spirits website says gentian root), but I also pick up aniseed and tree bark qualities. Finishes long, tangy, slightly citrusy, clean, and begging for a slice of orange. America's elegant answer to Italy's Campari.
2016 Rating: ★★★★/Highly Recommended

Bushmills Irish Honey Whiskey Liqueur (Ireland) 35% abv, $25.
Pretty marigold/oak-aged chardonnay-gold color. Soft opening nose is juicy, malty, tropical fruity, and delicately sweet; secondary nosings after another six minutes of air contact reveal nothing new. Entry is very ripe and juicy, but not cloying in the least; midpalate focuses on the malt whiskey more than the honey, and that's where it wins me over completely. Elegant, fruity finish. One of the best of the world's honey-whiskey marriages.
2015 Rating: ★★★★/Highly Recommended

Clear Creek Distillery Cherry Liqueur (USA) 19.01% abv, $22/375 ml.

Opaque black color. Oh my, this complex first aroma reminds me as much of cigar tobacco as it does of black cherry juice; what's so intriguing about it is that the bouquet is one-dimensional but is so genuine that you can't stop sniffing it. Entry is keenly jammy, ripe, cherry-like; midpalate is silky in texture, dense, complex, creamy to the point of almost being like a Crème de Cerise. Extended aftertaste is concentrated, fresh, showing plenty of foundational acidity. A clinic on how to carry out the making of cherry liqueur.

2015 Rating: ★ ★ ★ ★ ★/Highest Recommendation

Clear Creek Distillery Marion Blackberry Liqueur (USA) 19.19% abv, $22/375 ml.

Inky black/purple color. Initial nosing passes reveal deep, dense aromas of blackberry ripeness, moderate brambles-like vegetation, berry seeds, blackberry preserves—lovely and true to the fruit; second inhalations find an emergence of acute jamminess that is highly desirable without being unctuous or cloying, just fresh, juicy, acidic. Entry is sublimely ripe without being sugary sweet because there's so much inherent acidity to keep the structural focus on harmony and balance; midpalate is juicy, fresh without being jammy. Aftertaste is medium long, juicy, pleasantly tart. Seriously tasty.

2015 Rating: ★ ★ ★ ★ ★/Highest Recommendation

Clear Creek Distillery Pear Liqueur (USA) 23.1% abv, $22/375 ml.

Bright burnished-copper color; excellent purity. This is an elegant aromatic tribute to the glory of ripe pears; what I like so much is the balanced way this liqueur brings the pear essence to you without clubbing you with sweetness or sugar bombs; there is obvious acidity that maintains the structure without eclipsing the subtle ripe-pear fragrance; terrific, understated bouquet. Entry is divinely ripe and almost a little like spiced, baked pear due to the nuanced presence of cinnamon; midpalate is deeply flavorful, true to pear, mildly spicy, zesty, medium bodied, satiny in texture. Finishes long, intensely pear-like, more off-dry than sweet, elegant, supple.

2015 Rating: ★ ★ ★ ★/Highly Recommended

Clear Creek Distillery Raspberry Liqueur (USA) 20.56% abv, $22/375 ml.

Dense, inky black color. As a lover of raspberry, this initial inhalation is pure heaven for me, aromatically speaking; with further aeration, the aroma builds to a stunning crescendo where the brambly raspberry fruit is perfectly juicy, jammy, ripe; a textbook raspberry liqueur bouquet. Entry is medium bodied, acutely viny/bramble-like, juicy, preserves-like, concentrated, fresh; midpalate echoes entry totally, adding a little seed-like tanginess that accentuates the deep fruitiness well into the fabulous finish. A benchmark for American-made berry liqueurs.

2015 Rating: ★ ★ ★ ★ ★/Highest Recommendation

Cointreau Liqueur (France) 40% abv, $45.

Cointreau is without question the finest, most versatile liqueur ever made and one of the world's top two greatest spirits. Not only is Cointreau the triple sec backbone of countless classic cocktails, such as the Margarita, Cosmopolitan, Sidecar, Brandy Crusta, Corpse

Reviver #2, Mai Tai, Seelbach, and Pegu Club, but it is luscious on its own, slightly chilled. There, this is all you'll ever need to know about it. Now, go buy a case.
2020 Rating: ★ ★ ★ ★ ★/Highest Recommendation

Disaronno Originale Amaretto (Italy) 28% abv, $28.
Lovely chestnut/henna color; flawless purity. The first whiffs of sweet almond paste are luscious and inviting and, to the producer's credit, not overly sweet; second whiffs highlight not only the intense nuttiness of this classic liqueur but also its subtle fruitiness, which reminds me of stone fruits. Entry is supple, medium bodied, lush, and elegant; midpalate is rich in almond/nuttiness, with the sweetness factor always in check. Aftertaste features the almond paste flavor and, hey, this is amaretto as it should be.
2016 Rating: ★ ★ ★ ★/Highly Recommended

Disaronno Riserva Liqueur (Italy) 40% abv, $349.
Only ten thousand bottles available worldwide of this onetime blend of amaretto and blended Scotch whisky. First new expression of Disaronno in five centuries. Gorgeous topaz/saffron color; excellent purity. I detect easily identifiable scents of almond paste and nougat in the initial inhalations; after more time in the glass the aroma dives deeper into the almond foundation, but there isn't really a significant change from the first sniffs. Entry is where the first trace of slightly salty blended Scotch appears, even if it seems buried beneath the weight of sugary sweetness; midpalate sees the fleeting impact of the Scotch vanish as the sweetened almond intensity swamps all other taste possibilities. Aftertaste is singularly candied almond and nothing else. This is a very tasty amaretto but the price tag is ridiculous.
2015 Rating: ★ ★ ★ ★/Highly Recommended

Drambuie Liqueur (Scotland) 40% abv, $39.
Straw/sauternes color; excellent purity. Smells of salty maritime single malt whisky immediately; more air content enhances the earthiness of the aroma as the layers of fragrance unfold, including pine needle, thyme, rosemary, honey, heather, and eucalyptus that mingle harmoniously with the single malts. Entry is firm, thick, and gently sweet and finely balanced by a staunch herbaceous aspect; midpalate plays up the dried herbs, spices (especially nutmeg, allspice, cinnamon), and honey, leading to the big-hearted, robust finish that's singularly spectacular.
2018 Rating: ★ ★ ★ ★ ★/Highest Recommendation

Drambuie 15 Liqueur (Scotland) 43% abv, $60.
Made exclusively with Speyside single malts that are at least fifteen years old. Pretty, pale topaz color; flawless clarity. Wow, I can really smell the heathery/floral malt whisky in the first inhalations more than the honey, herbs, and spices, and this me like very much; after another seven minutes of air contact, the bouquet at last does show some of its heather honey and green-leaf herbaceousness, all of which add up to an understated, highly sophisticated aroma of the first rank. Entry features honey flavor first, then substantial layers of Speyside malts vigorously come on that are refined, floral, and cereal dry; midpalate is noticeably drier than the entry taste as the single malt aspect kicks in fully, guiding the flavor profile to a dusty, dry finish that merely hints of spice and honey. Ultra-complex, significantly drier

than the original Drambuie, and I think better suited to contemporary taste leanings. This is not to say that I don't still admire and love the original because I do. This version hits the sweet spot.
2016 Rating: ★ ★ ★ ★ ★/Highest Recommendation

Elation Nectar de Poire Liqueur (France) 30% abv, $40.
Cognac base. Pretty terra-cotta/old gold color; flawless purity. Initial nosings detect slightly ripe pear (yellow, not red or bosc) aromas that are simultaneously spicy, moderately juicy, and clean; later sniffs pick up more of the pear skin and pulp than the juice, and that makes for a drier, leaner bouquet. Entry is crisp, pleasingly tart, but neither astringent nor mineral-like; midpalate is sweeter, creamier in texture than the entry is, and this leads to a silky, ambrosial, chewy aftertaste. The use of the word "Nectar" in the name is appropriate due to the fact that it does exhibit a nectar-like quality in the midpalate and finish.
2015 Rating: ★ ★ ★/Recommended

Fernet dei Fratelli Loreto Liqueur (USA) 40% abv, $34.
An American-made fernet-style amaro. Maroon/russet color; excellent clarity. The unusual opening bouquet is highly floral (honeysuckle), seed-like (poppy, pumpkin), and earthy/woodsy (peat moss, mushrooms, dried leaves) as the various aromatics vie for dominance; secondary whiffs detect cola nut, sarsaparilla, mothball, menthol, peppermint, and cotton fiber. Entry is very bitter, foresty, leafy, earthy, herbal, and dried fruit–like (apricot); midpalate remains on the bitter course, with elemental tastes of flint, metal coin, bramble. Can see cocktail applications here. Overall, good quality.
2017 Rating: ★ ★ ★/Recommended

Fratelli Vergnano Arancino Organic Blood Orange Artisanal Liqueur (Italy) 17% abv, $30.
Appearance is turbid/cloudy/opaque rose/orange color; cannot determine purity through the milkiness. The first inhalations detect the innately juicy, zesty, bitter, and sour fragrance of blood orange, making the case that liqueurs don't always have to be sweet; secondary whiffs pick up orange soda–like and orange zest scents that are fresh and tart. Entry seems a little bit watered down as the blood orange flavor is more diffused than the aroma, which while light was appealingly tangy; midpalate is again more akin to orange soda than what I'd consider to be a liqueur, and it's this lack of flavor intensity and core substance that knocks off a rating star—that said, there is enough crisply acidic blood orange taste to recommend it.
2017 Rating: ★ ★ ★/Recommended

Fratelli Vergnano Limonino Organic Lemon Artisanal Liqueur (Italy) 17% abv, $30.
As clear and pristine as rainwater; void of color. I like the fresh lemon juice scent that rises from the copita in assertive waves in the opening inhalations; the lemoniness turns more to zestiness/lemon peel as the aroma mixes with oxygen, and that's what maintains such a razor-edged freshness to the bouquet. Entry flavors are acidic/citric, cleansing, deeply lemon juice–like, and remarkably fresh and vivid; midpalate features juicy, zesty,

ripe, but not sweet flavors of freshly cut lemon, and it's the balance between the lemon pulp and the acid that keeps the in-mouth stage so invigorating. Yes, this is a liqueur, but what makes it so attractive is the distiller's astute decision to highlight and define the lemon juice not by sweetness, ripeness, or added cane sugar but rather by its naturally tart crispness.
2017 Rating: ★★★★/Highly Recommended

Fratelli Vergnano Maraschino Liqueur (Italy) 30% abv, $30.
Spotlessly clear and pure in appearance. First nosing brings with it loads of intense marasca cherry ripeness and tartness as the nose goes in the direction of cherry pit more than cherry meat, and that explains the deep-seated bitterness; further nosing after more time in the glass doesn't reveal anything new, and so I move on. Entry is pleasantly bitter and acutely cherry-like, with a background taste of minerals; midpalate turns slightly toasted, deeply minerally, and like cherry compote. Ranks in the same league for a cocktail as Luxardo Il Maraschino Originale Cherry Liqueur (four stars) and Maraska Maraschino Liqueur (three stars).
2017 Rating: ★★★/Recommended

Gabriel Boudier Dijon Crème de Cassis de Dijon Liqueur (France) 20% abv, $25.
Opaque, purple/black color. Gloriously sublime bittersweet opening aroma is all-cassis all-the-time and wonderfully brambly and leafy and viny and viscous and . . . utterly beguiling; aroma is so firmly entrenched in concentrated juiciness that even seven more minutes of aeration don't subvert or alter the path of its mission. Entry is intensely sweet, black-curranty, and creamy, but also deeply brambly/viny. Delicious, all the way. Think Kir Royales.
2015 Rating: ★★★★/Highly Recommended

Gabriel Boudier Dijon Crème de Fraises a La Fraise des Bois Liqueur (France) 20% abv, $25.
Brown/reddish/chestnut color; excellent purity. The slightly overripe strawberry fragrance leaps from the sampling glass in graceful, jammy waves in the initial inhalations after the pour; following additional air contact time, the bouquet settles down into a preserves-like profile that is more ripe than flat-out sweet. Entry is intensely strawberry-like, unabashedly sweet, but neither syrupy nor cloying. Concludes on a mellow, jammy note that's harmonious in its sweetness/acidity balance.
2015 Rating: ★★★★/Highly Recommended

Gabriel Boudier Dijon Crème de Framboises Liqueur (France) 20% abv, $25.
Auburn/henna color; flawless purity. This first aromatic burst could only be raspberry due as much to its viny/leafy aspect as to the ripe berry jam component; the preserves quality grows with aeration, making for pleasant sniffing. Entry is fundamentally jammy and incredibly juicy; midpalate shows more than ample acidity to maintain the focus of the fruit source, and that's the winning ticket in the crème liqueur sweepstakes. Ends on a bramble and berry note that closes the circle elegantly.
2015 Rating: ★★★★/Highly Recommended

Gabriel Boudier Dijon Crème de Mûres Sauvages Liqueur (France) 20% abv, $25.

Caramel, cola-brown color; excellent clarity. First whiffs detect waxy, viny, leafy scents that aren't berry- or bramble-like at all but far more dusty, stony, plastic, rubbery, and minerally; mineral aspect actually ascends while the leafy/vegetal side descends; what's sorely missing is much evidence of blackberry. Entry is sweet, sugary, and moderately blackberry-like but somehow misses the mark; midpalate is viny and waxy but not fruity enough to convince me that this is recommendable.

2015 Rating: ★★/Not Recommended

Gabriel Boudier Dijon Crème de Pêches Liqueur (France) 18% abv, $25.

Golden honey color; superb clarity. The ripe peach perfume is radiant and vivid in the first nosing passes after the pour; in the second passes after further aeration, the aromatic focus shifts slightly to peach-stone bitterness that nicely balances out the ripe peach sweetness. Entry is ideally balanced between acid, fruit, and spirit; midpalate features the ripe white peach meat and a juicy back note that lasts well into the aftertaste. Textbook fruit liqueur.

2015 Rating: ★★★★★/Highest Recommendation

Galliano L'Aperitivo (Italy) 24% abv, $17/375 ml.

Cherry juice/brick red color; superb clarity. Smells pleasantly of fennel, sagebrush, Earl Grey tea, cardamom, and lavender in the first whiffs after the pour; secondary inhalations highlight more citrus, primarily grapefruit and tangerine that underscore the mineral-like spices that are dry and nicely astringent and peppery. Entry is dry, tart, intensely mineral-like and herbal, with the headliners being sandalwood, cinnamon, and sage; midpalate is brisk, crisp, clean, and zesty. A classy bitter alternative to Aperol or Campari that works well in all-season cocktails such as Negroni, citrusy spritzers, and sparkling wine cocktails.

2017 Rating: ★★★★/Highly Recommended

Giffard Abricot du Roussillon Liqueur (France) 25% abv, $32.

Orange/old gold color; excellent clarity. Aroma is full of apricot snap and zestiness right from the first whiffs after the pour, plus a slight nuttiness; later inhalations detect more of the ripe apricot meat as the fragrance turns dense and deeply fruity and ripe. Entry features tart to sour flavors of apricot, nuts, fruit stone, then the midpalate stage highlights the apricot juiciness in a near-tart display of acid/ripeness balance that plays deep into the aftertaste.

2016 Rating: ★★★★/Highly Recommended

Giffard Banane du Brésil Liqueur (France) 25% abv, $32.

Pretty gold/marigold color; excellent clarity. Smells delicately of banana peel/pulp, spiced banana, hemp/fiber in the opening nosings; later inhalations detect softly fruity aromas of ripe banana that are not in the least sweet. Taste profile is more ripe than sweet but fully realized in banana flavor. Elegant, sweetest in the aftertaste.

2016 Rating: ★★★★/Highly Recommended

Giffard Cassis Noir de Bourgogne Liqueur (France) 20% abv, $32.

Opaque, inky black color. Deep, resinous, brambly, bittersweet aromas of black currant

and vines abound in this lovely opening scent; air contact releases more fruitiness in the second passes as the fragrance turns slightly sour and very tart. Entry is dense, intensely sweet, and berry-like; midpalate features the concentrated berry tartness and the texture is creamy. Finishes long, intense, sour, viny.
2016 Rating: ★ ★ ★ ★/Highly Recommended

Giffard Crème de Fraise des Bois Liqueur (France) 16% abv, $25.
Cheerful strawberry/rose/orange color, with superb clarity. Smells of fresh strawberries in the berry patch in the initial sniffs after the pour; secondary aromas are sweeter, juicier than the opening scent. Entry is properly juicy, ripe, slightly sour, berry-like; midpalate leans towards being sweet/sour and a bit brambly/earthy. Taste fades a little in the finish, but there's still ample juiciness and ripeness.
2016 Rating: ★ ★ ★/Recommended

Giffard Crème de Framboise Liqueur (France) 16% abv, $25.
Blood red color; almost opaque in appearance density. Initial fragrance is intensely ripe, genuinely raspberry-like, more tart than sweet, a touch brambly, very compelling; secondary passes unearth a faint spiciness that nicely supplements the fruitiness. Entry is keenly raspberry-like, juicy, perfectly sweet without being cloying or syrupy; midpalate highlights the acidity that maintains the structure well. Finishes long, ripe, gently sweet and juicy. Very good indeed.
2016 Rating: ★ ★ ★ ★/Highly Recommended

Giffard Crème de Mûre Liqueur (France) 16% abv, $25.
Jet black, opaque appearance. The rich, luxuriant aroma is all about blackberries, ripe and sweet, through all stages of inhaling, adding a deft touch of waxiness in the secondary sniffs. Entry is creamy, fat with plummy/berry lushness; midpalate mirrors the entry to a tee, throwing in a tiny bit of brambles, green vegetation. Finishes more bittersweet than sweet and immensely satisfying. A textbook blackberry liqueur.
2016 Rating: ★ ★ ★ ★ ★/Highest Recommendation

Giffard Crème de Pamplemousse Rose Liqueur (France) 16% abv, $25.
The pale pink/rose color is attractively eye-catching; perfect, oily purity. First whiffs pick up undeniable pink grapefruit tartness and piquancy, with sideline scents of grapefruit pulp and peel; secondary sniffs, which are deeper due to more air contact, highlight the grapefruit juiciness. Entry taste is true to the fruit source, deeply citrusy; midpalate is calmer, more ripe than juicy, more bittersweet than sweet. Aftertaste is long, acidic, fresh.
2016 Rating: ★ ★ ★ ★/Highly Recommended

Giffard Crème de Pêche de Vigne Liqueur (France) 16% abv, $25.
Shows a peachy gold/tarnished-silver color; superb purity. Opening nosing detects just barely ripe yellow peach (not white), peach skins, sugared peach slices; later sniffs pick up more of the peach skins and even a touch of peach pit as the aroma goes all out to please. Entry flavor is intensely peach-like, very ripe, borderline sweet/sour, lovely and full-bodied;

midpalate is a touch syrupy, acutely peachy, pleasingly ripe, with the finish leaning towards a peel-like bitterness that nicely counters the juicy midpalate.
2016 Rating: ★★★★/Highly Recommended

Giffard Crème de Violette Liqueur (France) 16% abv, $25.
Deep, inky, very pretty purple color is nearly opaque. Gentle floral scent of violets and fresh spring garden are compelling and genuine; secondary inhalations find the floral fragrance goes deeper and richer as the aroma grows in intensity with further aeration. Taste profile at entry is more earthy and flowery than sweet or lush, and that's a credit to the distiller for maintaining that level of authenticity; midpalate and finish echo the entry, providing a satisfying taste experience. A subtle, classy ingredient for Aviation cocktails.
2016 Rating: ★★★★/Highly Recommended

Giffard Ginger of the Indies Liqueur (France) 35% abv, $32.
Pale straw/oyster color; ideal clarity. Smells pleasantly of gingerbread, with delicate supplemental traces of citrus peel, pine needle, fennel, coriander in the initial whiffs; with additional aeration, the pine forest/cedar/alpine fragrances become bolder as the ginger recedes. Entry is sweeter than I expected, resiny, sap-like, mildly ginger-like; midpalate highlights the zesty ginger nicely. Aftertaste is dominated by the pine needle. I see mixing possibilities here, as the comparison to New World gin is unmistakable.
2016 Rating: ★★★/Recommended

Giffard Lichi-Li Liqueur (France) 18% abv, $25.
Cherry/rose-pink color is pretty; clarity is excellent. Opening fragrance of lychee is spot-on, flower shop–like (rose, especially), slightly fruity, almost nutty; secondary sniffs detect a gentle sweetness that's understated, peachy, candied. Entry is featherlight in its sweetness, fruity, lychee-like, delicate; midpalate features the lychee flavor in spades, as the sweetness dials back. Finishes ripe, fruity, moderately nutty. A whisper-like liqueur that's tasty, savory, mixable.
2016 Rating: ★★★★/Highly Recommended

Giffard Menthe-Pastille Liqueur (France) 24% abv, $30.
Clear as rainwater. Bold, nose-tingling scents of menthol, peppermint lead this aromatic parade like drum majors in the opening sniffs; later inhalations encounter intense, minty aromas that remind me of York Peppermint Pattie candies since now with aeration there's a sweet tanginess to the aroma. Entry is intensely minty, spicy, candy-like, but just gently sweet; midpalate echoes the entry. Finishes cleanly, extra minty, agreeably sweet.
2016 Rating: ★★★/Recommended

Giffard Muroise du Val de Loire Liqueur (France) 18% abv, $32.
Muroise is a cross between raspberry and blackberry. Dense purple color; opaque. First inhalations are greeted with deeply ambrosial, jammy scents of blackberry, raspberry, loganberry, black plum—let's just say that it's berry heaven. Entry is luxuriously viscous, sweet/sour, ripe, intensely berry-like, preserves-like; midpalate mirrors the entry stage, adding a bit

of black pepper spiciness for good measure. Remarkable concentration and intensity in the finish, along with late tastes of seeds, peel.

2016 Rating: ★★★★/Highly Recommended

Giffard Triple Sec Liqueur (France) 40% abv, $32.

Produced from Curaçao oranges. I notice a little bit of core haze that remains throughout the entire visual stage; colorless. Initial whiffs pick up the pulpy astringency of tart oranges, in which any trace of ripeness is purely accidental; secondary stage inhalations accentuate the opening stage, remaining acutely dry and zesty. Entry is keenly dry, acidic, astringent, pulpy rather than juicy, and wholly in keeping with true triple sec; midpalate features more of an orangey flavor profile. Finish is viscous, tart, moderately oily. Cocktail ready, willing, and able.

2016 Rating: ★★★★/Highly Recommended

Giffard Vanille de Madagascar Liqueur (France) 20% abv, $32.

Old gold/maize color; superb purity. Heavy, bean-like vanilla extract aromas waft from the sampling glass as the message of vanilla bean is unequivocally clear; secondary sniffs encounter unexpected touches of cardboard, fiber. Entry taste is thick, ultra-sweet, gummy, vanilla frosting–like; midpalate reflects the entry phase. I love vanilla but this is simply too much of a good thing. The deficit of subtlety sinks it, which is surprising since most of the Giffard liqueurs scored points through understatement.

2016 Rating: ★/Not Recommended

GM Titanium Liqueur (France) 40% abv, $45.

GM Titanium is an expression of legendary and venerable Grand Marnier, which includes, according to them, a unique combination of "wild tropical orange essence" and "Asian Calamansi citrus with a dash of spices" with their fine cognac. Asian calamansi is native to Southeast Asia and is a hybrid cross of mandarin orange and kumquat. Pretty amber color; flawless purity. I like the first scents of orange zest, lemon peel, and baking spice (vanilla, cinnamon, allspice) that waft gently out of the evaluation glass; additional time in the glass encourages more of the cognac to emerge, adding a lovely substance to the bouquet. Entry is semisweet, amazingly citrusy, and therefore clean and lithe, and once again I'm aware of the cognac foundation for which I'm very happy; midpalate is silky smooth, spirity, citrusy, and more bittersweet than sweet, which to me is a huge plus in maintaining the flavor focus of citrus/cognac. A delicious new expression that accentuates the fabled portfolio.

2015 Rating: ★★★★/Highly Recommended

Grand Marnier Cordon Rouge Triple Orange Liqueur (France) 40% abv, $40.

Bright copper color. Perhaps the most easily identifiable aroma in the greater liqueur category; has a luscious sweet/sour, tangerine/mandarin orange perfume that never stops enchanting. Entry is lovely, balanced, and creamy, as the orange zest's acidity mingles well with the cognac's alcohol, making for exquisite drinking through the midpalate stage. Finishes like liquid satin. If this were the sole GM expression, I'd give it five stars, but because of the sublime existence of the Centenaire and the Cinquantenaire, it must be rated four.

2019 Rating: ★★★★ /Highly Recommended

Grand Marnier Cuvée du Centenaire Triple Orange Liqueur (France) 40% abv, $100.
Looks very close in appearance to the coppery/ochre Cordon Rouge; superb purity. Initially smells of cognac as much as it does of orange zest, and that's a major difference with the Cordon Rouge, which focuses more on the zest; second sniffs discover a slight bittersweet aspect that is tangy and piquant. At entry, there's the ideal balance between the citric acid, alcohol, cognac, and wood, with the essence of the cognac always prevailing. Concludes with sheer finesse, sweet/sour presence, and that incredibly lush texture. Never ceases to amaze me for its perfection as a Grand Cru Classe liqueur.
2019 Rating: ★ ★ ★ ★ ★ /Highest Recommendation

Grand Marnier Cuvée du Cent Cinquantenaire Triple Orange Liqueur (France) 40% abv, $190.
Dark amber/bronze color; pristine purity. Opening perfume is intensely brandy-like, but balanced through the ten minutes of sniffing; the triple orange acts as the ideal companion to the old cognac, making the bouquet a classic. Entry tastes wonderfully of orange zest and tangerine, as well as very old cognac; midpalate shines a light on the dried citrus peel. Ends up remarkably mellow and textured. Couldn't possibly be better than it already is.
2019 Rating: ★ ★ ★ ★ ★ /Highest Recommendation

Grand Marnier Cuvée 1880 Liqueur (France) 40% abv, $350.
Made from XO Grande Champagne cognac. Attractive bronze/henna color; perfect purity. The orange zest takes a back seat to the cognac essence in the opening nosing phase after the pour; after another eight minutes of time in the glass, the bouquet rounds out to a deeply complex, sweet/sour, orangey mélange of aromas. Entry is perfectly balanced between the orange peel, sweetness factor, acidity, and cognac; midpalate provides an awesome flavor experience of the first rank, one in which all the taste elements are in ideal precision. If we gave six rating stars, GM Cuvée 1880 Liqueur would be so rated. Timeless elegance. Worthy of the name Grand Marnier.
2015 Rating: ★ ★ ★ ★ ★/Highest Recommendation

Grand Marnier Signature Collection № 2 Raspberry Peach Liqueur (France) 40% abv, $40.
Lovely rubious, rose/gold/brut rosé champagne–like color; impeccable clarity. Wow, the opening aroma is ambrosial, ripe, and tantalizingly berry- and peach-like; another six minutes of air contact stimulate deeper aromas, in particular the white peach aspect. Entry is ripe and sweet, but neither cloying nor lumpy because the acidity level remains high, maintaining the freshness; midpalate accentuates the strawberry initially, then the peach element reemerges as the taste stage heads into the fruit salad/fruit compote finish, which nicely closes the circle. In a word, luscious.
2014 Rating: ★ ★ ★ ★/Highly Recommended

HPNOTIQ Liqueur (France) 17% abv, $30.
Cyan/electric-blue color, opaque. The overwhelming first impression, which is immensely pleasing, is of a large bowl of ripe and just-picked tropical fruits, in particular, banana, pineapple, guava, mango, and, most predominant, passion fruit; the next

inhalations following more air contact unearth a ripe juiciness that is more integrated than in the first go-round, in which the fruits stood out. Entry is delightfully sour and tart, as the acidity maintains the freshness of the fruit; midpalate echoes the entry, with the passion fruit being the only element that seems to radiate. Ends juicy, snappily astringent, and very tasty.
2018 Rating: ★★★★/Highly Recommended

Iris Liqueur (USA) 35% abv, $48.
Pretty yellow/green appearance, superb clarity. Starts out aromatically herbal/herb garden–like and engagingly floral, with a solid presence of moderately spicy sweetness; following another eight minutes of air contact, little changes in the aromatic profile. Entry is unabashedly sweet, but is spicy and floral enough to balance the sugary aspect; midpalate showcases more of the iris/floral show element, after which it is named, and turns concentrated and, for me, a bit too sugar-intense in the finish.
2015 Rating: ★★★/Recommended

Jacquiot Crème de Cassis Liqueur (France) 18% abv, $16/375 ml.
Opaque, deep purple color. Initial whiffs detect wonderfully complex, astringent, and überberry fragrances that are concentrated and delicate; second passes after another eight minutes merely reinforce the first impressions, adding brambles, vegetation/leaves, and black pepper notes. Entry is tangy, deeply sweet and jammy, and complex; midpalate features the black-currant acidity, which makes it fresh and not in the least cloying. Concludes viscous, intensely rich, but still holding enough acidity in its core to maintain the integrity of the black currants. WOW.
2015 Rating: ★★★★★/Highest Recommendation

Jacquiot Crème de Pêche Peach Liqueur (France) 18% abv, $18/375 ml.
The saffron color is clean and clear of sediment. First nosing passes discover a tangy aroma of peach peel that is almost more floral than fruity, but whatever the case it's appealing and fresh, not in the least sugary sweet; later sniffs following more time in the glass heighten the peachy element now in the form of pulp rather than peel. Entry is pleasantly sweet but neither cloying nor unctuous as the acidity level remains high enough to keep the structure from collapsing in on itself; midpalate mirrors the entry, but the peach ripeness becomes more dense and weighty on the tongue. Concludes long, intensely peach-like but not too sweet, as once again the inherent acidity keeps the sweetness from dominating.
2015 Rating: ★★★★/Highly Recommended

Jägermeister Liqueur (Germany) 35% abv, $24.
Burnt umber/black-coffee color; looks clean through the near opacity. First whiffs encounter a full orchestra of herbal aromas, starting with star anise, fennel, and licorice, most prominently, but likewise offering delicate notes of cardamom, basil, lemongrass, lavender, and black peppercorn—a welcoming bouquet of high herbal density; with more aeration, the intensity does noticeably smooth out, leaving behind a nicely integrated bouquet of spicy (thyme, rosemary, spearmint), woodsy (angelica, pine, eucalyptus), forest floor piquancy that I find to this day appealing. Entry is piercingly herbal and bitter, but it's the

acute spiciness from what seems like black peppercorn and mint that maintains the freshness; midpalate is more decidedly woodsy/forest floor–like as the bark-like and root-like botanicals take command, leading to the zesty, citrusy aftertaste.
2018 Rating: ★★★/Recommended

Journeyman Humdinger Jalapeño Spirit (USA) 45% abv, $30.

Pewter/silver tint; pure. I get the jalapeño aspect immediately in the first whiffs; beyond that, there's not a lot happening aromatically other than a concentrated waxiness. Entry is piquant, mildly spicy, moderately pleasant; midpalate brings the base spirit more into play as the 90 proof becomes more evident on the lips, but still there's a lack of defining character that leaves this spirit wandering aimlessly.
2015 Rating: ★★/Not Recommended

Journeyman Snaggle Tooth Coffee Liqueur (USA) 40% abv, $30.

Attractive chestnut/mahogany color; excellent clarity. Wow, the initial aromas are all about coffee bean and espresso, plus there's an intriguing splash of peanut butter that's hidden away. Entry is concentrated, near cloying, viscous, and beany; midpalate is so fat and thick in texture that it loses my interest in the cascades of enveloping sugar sweetness. Started out well, concluded like a clunker.
2015 Rating: ★★/Not Recommended

Killepitsch Krauter Liqueur (Germany) 42% abv, $25.

Deep mahogany/dark brown color. Smells of equal parts dried fruit and fresh herbs in the first sniffs after the pour; turns kind of beany in the second passes as the fruit fades and the herbs come on in strength. Entry is herbal bittersweet, astringent, and chunky/chewy in texture; midpalate spotlights the herbaceous flavors of roots, leaves, and bark to a high degree of sophistication and pleasure. Ends on a tree bark note that's sappy and tart.
2015 Rating: ★★★★/Highly Recommended

Kleos The Mastiha Spirit (Greece) 30% abv, $37.

Clear and clean-as-rainwater appearance. Wow, I like the opening aroma immediately as it reminds me of uncooked asparagus, spinach, drying autumn leaves, fennel, and damp cork; secondary nosing passes detect deeper terrestrial scents, especially wet sand, damp earth, rainfall, and rain forest. Entry flavors focus on the uncooked vegetable aspect, in particular, the asparagus, but now it's more white asparagus than green; midpalate is earthy, agile, and vegetal. Ends on a softly sweet note that maintains the earthiness and spring garden freshness so appreciated in the bouquet and in-mouth phases. Excellent job here of clean distillation and flavor management.
2020 Rating: ★★★★/Highly Recommended

Koval Chrysanthemum & Honey Liqueur (USA) 20% abv, $24.

Turbid, flax, talmi gold color. Okay, I get the honey element in the opening nosing, but beyond that??? Following a bouquet that is a dead end, the entry features a modicum of fruitiness amidst the halo of honey, but there's simply not enough charm or balance here to make a go of it as a viable product for the general public. AGAIN: Just because it's "craft" doesn't automatically mean it's up to the standards of quality that we go by. In fact, a poor, ill-defined product like this does more harm than good to the craft distilling movement because newcomers to spirits might take away that this type of messy liquid is what craft distilling is all about when it isn't.

2015 Rating: ★/Not Recommended

Koval Organic Ginger Liqueur (USA) 20% abv, $24.

Hazy, cloudy, hazel swamp-water appearance. First sniffs detect unmistakable ginger presence, but there's also a cardboard, warehouse fragrance that undercuts the natural snap and earthy vividness of fresh ginger; later inhalations are unpleasantly soapy. Entry is, well, not very tasty, as the ginger is overwhelmed by the detergent aspect; midpalate is dismal. Should not be available to the public since it is an experiment that went wildly astray.

2014 Rating: ★/Not Recommended

Kringle Cream Liqueur (USA) 15% abv, $20.

Rum based. Pure milk-white color; opaque. I like the buttery, peanut-like, butter brickle–like, candy bouquet that's zesty and understated. Even better in the mouth as the candied, toffee, nougat, almond paste flavors integrate perfectly. A must buy for cream liqueur fans.

2015 Rating: ★★★★/Highly Recommended

Lejay Crème de Cassis Liqueur (France) 18% abv, $30.

Opaque purple/Concord grape juice color. Smells true-to-source bittersweet, brambly, leafy in the opening whiffs; intense, concentrated, juicy, preserves-like aromas in second passes. Entry is creamy/silky in texture, bittersweet, acidic and therefore fresh; midpalate features the tart black-currant bramble aspect that comes out like this only in the best crème de cassis. A gold standard.

2015 Rating: ★★★★★/Highest Recommendation

Lo-Fi Aperitifs Gentian Amaro (USA) 16% abv, $26.

Black cherry/maroon color; excellent clarity. The opening aroma is delightfully fragrant, juicy without being overly ripe, herbal, bark-like, exotic, winey but not sweet, fruity (citrus, tropical), gingery, and pleasingly floral; second passes encounter more of the earthy, botanical depth as the aroma turns into a supple bouquet, offering hints of grapefruit rind, anise, gentian, and mace; I couldn't stop sniffing it. Entry is fruity in a citrusy/grapefruit manner; midpalate is as fruity as it is herbal and crackling fresh, almost peppery from the various herbs, roots, and barks in the recipe. Finishes cleanly, more tart than anything else, fresh, and luscious. A perfect before-dinner treat served moderately chilled (50–55° F), with a half rind of sliced grapefruit.

2016 Rating: ★★★★/Highly Recommended

Lucano Amaro (Italy) 28% abv, $30.

The cola-brown color is as near opaque as possible. First nosing passes detect gentle aromas of aniseed, licorice, gentian, orris root, sour apple; second inhalations, following further aeration, pick up scents of poppy and sesame seeds, soybeans, soy sauce, kale. Entry is light, astringent, pleasantly bitter, and deeply herbaceous; midpalate highlights the entry impressions, adding nuances of black peppercorn, basil, sage, thyme that last deep into the delicate finish.

2015 Rating: ★★★★/Highly Recommended

Luxardo Abano Amaro (Italy) 30% abv, $26.

Opaque, jet-brown/black color. First aromatic impressions, which are scrumptious, are laced with properly herbaceous/botanical scents of orange peel, cardamom, and baking spices, in particular, cinnamon and nutmeg—an aromatic banquet; later sniffs encounter more narrowly focused herbal/earthy traces, especially roots and tubers. Entry features the moderately bitter taste of the orange peel and cardamom as they tango on one's tongue in a dance of seduction all the way through the midpalate and well into the aftertaste. What's so appealing to me about this world-class amaro is its choice of the middle road path in terms of bitterness. So many other notable amaros club you into submission with bitterness while Luxardo lulls you with its restrained bitterness. Beautifully done.

2016 Rating: ★★★★★/Highest Recommendation

Luxardo Amaretto di Saschira Liqueur (Italy) 28% abv, $28.

Nut-brown color; impeccable clarity. The laser beam–like intensity of the almond aspect is focused, deep, gently candied, and even a little fruity; further air contact brings out more of the almond layering. Entry is rich, but neither cloying nor syrupy, and the initial taste is of almond paste that's more nutty than sweet or nougat-like; midpalate mirrors the entry and the flavor's richness accelerates as the profile turns ultra-elegant, harmonious, sinewy in texture, completely integrated. Long, definitive finish. For me, the prototypical amaretto.

2016 Rating: ★★★★★/Highest Recommendation

Luxardo Apricot Albicocca Liqueur (Italy) 30% abv, $27.

Bronze/copper color; flawless clarity. First sniffs detect delicate apricot aromas, mostly peel; after another seven minutes of aeration, the aromatic profile turns maderized (oxidized), delicately sweet, and more herbal than fruity or ripe. Entry is bittersweet, apricot intense, and ripe; midpalate highlights ripe, candied apricot and turns a little syrupy in the finish. Aftertaste is pleasingly sweet, woody, raisiny, and ripe.

2016 Rating: ★★★★/Highly Recommended

Luxardo Bitter (Italy) 25% abv, $26.

Cherry red color; excellent clarity. Right out of the gate the nose smells of citrus peel, cooking spice, and dried fruits; another six minutes bring out additional scents of rhubarb and fennel; a lovely fragrance. Entry is delicately fruity, medium sweet, pleasantly bitter, creamy in texture, and nicely herbal; midpalate features the rhubarb, candied walnut, bitter orange, and seeds (caraway?). Aftertaste is sublimely zesty and mildly bitter. Serve before dinner on the rocks with a twist of lemon or bitter orange. Elegant and savory.

2016 Rating: ★★★★★/Highest Recommendation

Luxardo Fernet Amaro (Italy) 45% abv, $28.
Dark brown/mahogany color. Wow, this initial nosing gets my attention as the aromatic profile features piquant and spicy notes of cola nut, candle wax, damp earth/rain forest, and moss/mushrooms/truffles—YEE-HAH; following another seven minutes of air contact, the bouquet blossoms into an herbal/earthy/vegetal bomb that features clay, stone, roots, dried herbs, and cooking spices. Entry is keenly bitter, ashy, tobacco-like, vegetal, and mossy in flavor; midpalate offers intriguing vegetal tastes of asparagus, kale, spinach, along with rooty/earthy flavors that somehow all work. Finishes calmly and acutely bitter.
2016 Rating: ★★★★/Highly Recommended

Luxardo Sangue Morlacco Liqueur (Italy) 30% abv, $28.
Cherry liqueur. Deep mahogany/reddish-brown/henna color. Oh my, the black cherry perfume ascends from the copita in subtle waves of dried fruit and fruit pit in the initial inhalations after the pour; the aroma dries out as it aerates, creating a bouquet that reminds me of old leather, library, and fruitcake. Entry is sweet, concentrated, and extremely cherry-like, but it's not cloying; midpalate is incredibly sweet and ripe without being bombastic about the sweetness due primarily to the high acidity, which keeps the sweetness in check. Succulent and luscious.
2015 Rating: ★★★★/Highly Recommended

Luxardo Triplum Triple Sec Orange Liqueur (Italy) 39% abv, $28.
Clear as rainwater; impeccable clarity. Opening smells are of sweet oranges and tangerines, but with plenty of zest notes that showcase the oils of the skins more than the pulp; the secondary sniffs are juicy, fruity, and ripe. Entry is delicately sweet, oily, and orangey; midpalate is long, lush, and properly citrusy.
2015 Rating: ★★★/Recommended

Maraska Original Maraschino Cherry Liqueur (Croatia) 32% abv, $20.
Clean and pure as rainwater. The first aromatic impressions are impressively cherry-like, tart, fruity but not cloying or overripe, earthy, elemental, fruit stone–like; by the time that further air contact becomes an influence, the bouquet has softened and rounded off, which leaves the door open for the cherry core to turn juicier than in the first pass, and more complex as a result. Entry is serenely succulent, eminently cherry-like, and genuine in its juiciness and preserves-like bearing; midpalate reflects the entry to a tee, adding a rush of acidity.
2015 Rating: ★★★★/Highly Recommended

Maraska Pelinkovac Bitter Liqueur (Croatia) 28% abv, $20.
A digestif meant to be served neat. Shows an ochre/deep amber color; excellent purity. I kept hoping that I'd detect more herbaceousness in the first nosing of this ancient herbal bitter; all I seem to encounter though are drifting, unfocused, light scents of dry stone, minerals, limestone/chalk. After another ten minutes of aeration, the bouquet turns slightly herbal, offering ethereal fragrances of dried leaves, diatomaceous earth, caraway seed, poppy seed. Entry is astringent, deeply leafy, herbal, earthy, bitter; midpalate adds traces of black

peppercorn, mace, sarsaparilla, root beer, grain husk, brown rice. Lots going on in the flavor profile that isn't detected in the bouquet.
2015 Rating: ★ ★ ★/Recommended

Marolo Milla Grappa & Camomile Liqueur (Italy) 35% abv, $55.
The opening aromatics are deeply herbal, earthy, leafy, green, woodsy, slightly briny, and neither dry nor sweet; in the second nosings I recognize the grappa base that underpins all the green tea, vegetal, chamomile features that make this liqueur so subtle yet quietly luscious. Entry is far more animated than the nuanced bouquet as the green tea flavor especially takes charge; midpalate is tangy, earthy, acutely vegetal/leafy, gently sweet, and suddenly fruity/grapy. One of the most understated, deceptively complex, and delicious liqueurs in the marketplace.
2015 Rating: ★ ★ ★ ★ ★/Highest Recommendation

Mathilde Cassis Liqueur (France) 16% abv, $28.
Inky, opaque, black color. Smells up front of very ripe black currants, brambles/leaves/vegetation; second passes reveal as much of the green, earthy vegetation as the berries, and that's what is so special about this first-rate cassis bouquet. Entry highlights the berries more than the vines/bramble aspect, and that shows how skillfully produced this liqueur is since at this stage, the black currant is the motivating force, not the vines it was grown on; midpalate is the picture of perfection for cassis as it mirrors the entry but with greater depth and jammy concentration. Aftertaste is long, juicy, ripe, preserves-like. A classic.
2015 Rating: ★ ★ ★ ★ ★/Highest Recommendation

Mathilde Framboise Liqueur (France) 40% abv, $28.
The redbrick/henna color is stunning; perfect clarity. One of the great berry liqueur bouquets of all time: fresh, ripe, acidic, true to the fruit, luscious, bittersweet, leafy, viny, perfect; second sniffs reinforce the opening stage impressions, even heightening them. Entry is sublimely raspberry-like, authentic, like biting into fresh fruit; midpalate mirrors the entry stage, adding a touch of spiciness. Amazing finish that's tart, razor edged with acid, lush.
2015 Rating: ★ ★ ★ ★ ★/Highest Recommendation

Mathilde Orange XO Liqueur (France) 40% abv, $28.
Color is a burnt-orange/amber hue; excellent clarity. Sports a pleasingly orangey first aroma that's tart, zesty, a touch on the marmalade side; second whiffs pick up more of the orange pulp element. Entry is acidic, tart, citrusy, substantial; midpalate offers a foundational flavor of cognac that nearly balances with the orange presence, but not quite. Finishes with a cognac flourish that minimizes the orange aspect a bit too much. Good and recommendable, to be clear, but not the type of orange liqueur that works especially well in cocktails because it is too dominant and not a team player.
2015 Rating: ★ ★ ★/Recommended

Mathilde Pêche Liqueur (France) 18% abv, $28.
Ecru/champagne-yellow color; pristine clarity. Opening aroma is quintessential ripe,

yellow peach in its juicy, fragrant manner; second-stage inhalations offer succulent, almost chewy scents that accurately reflect the splendor of ripe yellow peaches. Entry is intensely peach-like, sweet without being cloying, ripe without being unctuous; midpalate carries the succulence mantle ably as the peach flavor seems to get more concentrated and spicy, and this acceleration lasts deep into the elegant, fresh aftertaste.
2014 Rating: ★★★★★/Highest Recommendation

Mathilde Poire Liqueur (France) 18% abv, $28.
Flax/bisque color; perfect purity. Pear fruit is ripe, juicy, fresh in the first burst of aromatics; aroma gains traces of spice, seeds, minerals with further air contact wherein there is no obvious sweetness. Entry is fat, creamy in texture, unabashedly sweet, intensely ripe; midpalate is ambrosial and juicier than the entry. Aftertaste is concentrated, juicy, succulent, ripe.
2015 Rating: ★★★★/Highly Recommended

Merlet C2 Cassis & Cognac Liqueur (France) 33% abv, $35.
Opaque black/purple color. The perfume of black currant/cassis is piquant but not overpowering and is bitter and tartly alluring in the first inhalations after the pour; further aeration doesn't change anything as the cassis remains firmly in charge. Entry is zesty, tangy, bittersweet, and yet I taste the cognac through the blizzard of cassis; midpalate is tart, fruity/berry-like, and generally yummy though I prefer the Citron & Cognac. Ends on a softer note than the entry and midpalate.
2016 Rating: ★★★/Recommended

Merlet C2 Citron & Cognac Liqueur (France) 33% abv, $35.
Yellow/greenish color; flawless purity. Initial whiffs encounter deeply citrusy up-front aromas that are more peel/zest-like than pulpy or juicy, and I don't pick up any cognac at all; additional time in the glass doesn't alter the aroma very much except to heighten the citrus peel/oil presence. Entry is very tart but not sour and is deliciously balanced and harmonious, and I actually do taste the cognac base; midpalate is zesty, acidic, tart, and savory, and the cognac comes out even more at this stage. Aftertaste highlights the citrus peel and oil, making my mouth pucker. Man, this is tangy and tasty!
2016 Rating: ★★★★/Highly Recommended

Merlet Lune d'Abricot Liqueur (France) 25% abv, $35.
The jonquil/deep straw color is flawlessly pure. Opening nosing passes unearth scents of ripe apricot, apricot preserves, and fruit skin; second passes don't reveal much more than what was found in the first impressions other than a deepening of the apricot core aroma. Entry is unabashedly sweet yet there's a counterbalance in the tartness, which features acidity; midpalate echoes the entry, adding a larger portion of acidity that keeps the freshness vividly alive through the ambrosial aftertaste.
2015 Rating: ★★★/Recommended

Merlet Trois Citrus Liqueur (France) 40% abv, $38.
Maceration and distillation of blood orange, lemon, and bitter orange. As translucent

and transparent as springwater, though I can see oils in the core; immaculately clear. There are oodles of citrusy odors in the opening sniffs as the bitter orange element takes the lead in the early phase, followed by the lemon and blood orange; the citrus-a-thon continues aromatically in the second inhalations after further aeration, but here the blood orange charges to the front in tart, almost astringent waves of orangey bliss. Entry is austere, minerally, and heavily dried orange peel–like as the bitter orange reemerges as the dominant factor. Finishes long, moderately oily, very clean, zesty, and acidic, but most of all genuinely luscious.
2015 Rating: ★★★★★/Highest Recommendation

Molinari Caffe Liquore (Italy) 36% abv, $26.
Opaque brown/black color. Opening aromas are spicy, intensely bean-like, black Colombian coffee prone, rich, heavily roasted; second pass reflects the findings on the opening nosing. Entry is rich, smoky, ash-like, espresso-like; midpalate deepens the coffee bean aspect (if that's possible) and spans far into the lush, chewy aftertaste, which is keenly bittersweet. A really good, genuine coffee liqueur.
2015 Rating: ★★★★/Highly Recommended

Molinari Limoncello di Capri Lemon Liqueur (Italy) 32% abv, $26.
Frosty/hazy lemon yellow appearance is spot on. Aroma is zesty, tangy, citrusy, tart, and nicely piquant with lemon zest throughout both nosing passes. Entry is a bit syrupy, but the flavor profile is acidic, tart, properly sour, juicy. Finishes lemony, clean. Recommendable, but would have liked to have seen less textural bulk and more zesty snap, which would have earned it a fourth star. Serve chilled.
2015 Rating: ★★★/Recommended

Molinari Sambuca Extra Liqueur (Italy) 36% abv, $26.
Brilliant, transparent, oily core; superb purity. The tantalizingly botanical aroma of anise entices the taste buds as the deeply herbal, forest-like/woodsy fragrances keep unfolding through both rounds of sniffing, providing a textbook sambuca bouquet that is not too sweet but intensely herbaceous. While the sweetness held off in the aroma, it comes on with a full-frontal barrage in the entry; midpalate echoes the entry. Aftertaste is delicately sweet, concentrated, sugary, seed-like. Lovely.
2015 Rating: ★★★★/Highly Recommended

Montenegro Amaro (Italy) 40% abv, $45.
Very pretty persimmon/tea-rose orange color; superb clarity. I get lively, animated aromas in the first sniffs of wet cement, tangerine peel, marshmallow, lavender, and jasmine; secondary inhalations discover additional aromas of pecan pie, berry tart, red cherry juice, and menthol. Entry is herbaceous, pruny, sweet but not cloying, and with enough acidity to carry the flavors forward into the nutty, nougat-like midpalate, which also features flavors of dried citrus peel, sesame seed, soy sauce, vinegar, and cherry pit. Finishes long, fruity, nutty, and herbal. Really tasty, even on its own. Excellent substitute for vermouth in a Manhattan cocktail.
2017 Rating: ★★★★/Highly Recommended

Okanagan Spirits Blackcurrant Liqueur (Canada) 24% abv, $35.

Opaque, black/deep purple color. I detect lots of juicy, sour berry tanginess in the opening whiffs; later sniffs find that there's an additional fragrance of soil, vines, brambles that make the fruitiness work. Entry is keenly sour, incredibly tart; midpalate holds on to the mega-tartness, and that's a positive since the whole in-mouth experience hinges on the high acidity, which gives structure, freshness, and authenticity. Very nice indeed.

2015 Rating: ★ ★ ★ ★/Highly Recommended

Okanagan Spirits Sea Buckthorn Liqueur (Canada) 24% abv, $35.

Orange color is marred badly by masses of sediment that kill the visual appeal instantly. Initial whiffs encounter unpleasantly rancid, barnyard, livestock, cow pie aromas that spell disaster; later inhalations prove just as malodorous and putrid. Entry makes a weird right turn, coming up fruity, ripe, sweet; midpalate retains the fruity/sweet aspect but by this time all hope is lost on this one. I know things are bad when I don't want to take a sip.

2015 Rating: ★/Not Recommended

PAMA Pomegranate Liqueur (USA) 17% abv, $20.

Color of cherry juice; pure. Lovely, zesty, ripe, tart aromas of pomegranate, cherry, cranberry all explode from the glass in the first inhalations; the ambrosial secondary sniffs are juicy, ripe, intensely berry-like. Entry reflects all the tart juiciness found in the initial nosing and builds upon that; midpalate ripples with delightfully sour pomegranate juice taste. The producers could easily have made PAMA sweet, but instead they wisely maintained the natural tartness, which is what makes this a sterling liqueur.

2020 Rating: ★ ★ ★ ★/Highly Recommended

Pavan Liqueur de France (France) 18% abv, $32.

Pretty pale-green/tarnished-silver appearance. Lovely first scents of dried orange peel, white grapes, summer flower garden, delicate spice make the headlines aromatically. Entry is intensely fruity/grapy/citrusy, ripe, sweet, satiny; midpalate is juicy, sweet, ambrosial. Long finish, concentrated, shows increased acidity in concluding stage, which brings a three star liqueur into four star territory.

2016 Rating: ★ ★ ★ ★/Highly Recommended

Pierre Ferrand Dry Curaçao (France) 40% abv, $30.

Sun-glow yellow color; flawlessly pure. Right from the first whiffs, the crackling snap of dried orange peel mesmerizes the olfactory mechanism with its freshness and authenticity; later inhalations dig a bit deeper with the assistance of aeration and discover a whole other level of fragrance that showcases the positive effects of the cognac base that mingles so nimbly and seamlessly with the dried orange peel; the only triple sec subcategory bouquet that rivals that of Cointreau. Entry is lush, silky smooth, deeply citrusy, and orange peel–like, with a background note of smoky spice that disguises the sweetness; midpalate echoes the entry findings, adding just a brief burst of alcohol warmth to the tongue. Aftertaste is very long, drier than the midpalate (thank you to the cognac for this feature), and supple. In 2012 I rated this outstanding triple sec from the genius of Alexandre Gabriel four stars, and

I feel that as it has now stood the test of time, it's totally correct to bump it to five star status. One of the top five entries in the liqueur category of the past two generations.
2020 Rating: ★ ★ ★ ★ ★/Highest Recommendation

Plymouth Sloe Gin (England) 26% abv, $28.
The maroon/aged tawny port–like color is dazzling under the examination lamp; immaculate purity. Opening whiffs detect intensely bramble-like, thistle-like, tart, and astringent aromas of ripe sloe berries; secondary inhalations find that the tart, almost waxy, viny-ness of the sloe berry aspect is enhanced with further air contact. Entry is sweet/sour, dense in its ripeness, crisply acidic and therefore fresh on the tongue, and gloriously delicious; midpalate highlights the razor-edged sloe berry acidity that keeps the freshness at a high degree, thereby maintaining the integrity of the sound structure all the way through the sumptuous, crackling, bittersweet finish. There's simply none better.
2018 Rating: ★ ★ ★ ★ ★/Highest Recommendation

Priqly Prickly Pear Liqueur (Malta) 21% abv, $33.
Flax/cream color; excellent sediment-free clarity. The intriguingly spicy opening nose offers an almost white grape–like juiciness that's pleasantly ripe and peel-like; further air contact assists in the stimulation of an earthiness that's both fibrous and viny, and this understated aromatic development acts as a background to the delicate fruitiness—unlike any liqueur aroma I've come across previously and one that I like. Entry is lithe and vivid with intensely ripe muscat grape–like flavor that is slightly spiced (nutmeg?) and delightfully ambrosial; midpalate features more of the skin/peel astringency that keeps the dryness/sweetness level markedly on the off-dry degree. Concludes gently ripe and spicy. Unique. Lovely.
2018 Rating: ★ ★ ★ ★/Highly Recommended

Rivulet Pecan Liqueur (USA) 30% abv, $35.
The bright copper color is attractive and sediment-free. The nose is as advertised and awash in pecan fragrance that is acutely authentic, dry, and, well, nutty/pecan-like; second passes merely reflect the opening aromatic salvo. Entry is delightfully sweet and pecan real, with side notes of candied pecan and pecan pie; midpalate mirrors the entry, but offers deeper, more substantial pecan flavors that are lip-smacking and genuine. Finishes long, intensely nutty, only moderately sweet (this liqueur's strong point), and toasty. Excellent job here.
2015 Rating: ★ ★ ★ ★/Highly Recommended

RumChata Rum Cream Liqueur (USA) 13.75% abv, $21.
Looks like whole milk in its beige-like whiteness. Smells of vegetation, damp forest, rum, powdered milk, steamed white rice, and egg yolk in the initial inhalations; second passes note scents of under-ripe tropical fruits (guava, papaya), rice pudding, and sour milk. Entry is startlingly sweet, like ripe fruits, but also milky and creamy, almost like whipped cream as the rum breaks into the open more; midpalate highlights the milky rum aspect, with the supporting role falling to the hint of spice. Finishes cleanly, creamy, and tasty.
2018 Rating: ★ ★ ★/Recommended

Schladerer Edel-Kirsch Cherry Liqueur (Germany) 28% abv, $29.
Attractive plum-purple color; not quite opaque. First sniffs pick up brambly/viny, cherry compote lushness in the opening aromas; secondary inhalations after more aeration time detect a lush red-cherry scent that lasts long. Entry is sedate, understated, sweet/sour, tart, and just barely juicy/jammy; midpalate is very viny/bark-like, but also richly fruity and like cherry preserves. Concludes long, jammy, and like brandied cherries. Pretty darn delicious in a quiet manner that's appealing.
2015 Rating: ★★★★/Highly Recommended

Sorel Liqueur (USA) 15% abv, $33.
Cassis-like coloring; excellent purity. BOFFO AROMATICO! My goodness, I detect major clove, nutmeg, and ginger right out of the aromatic gate; this feisty bouquet is laden with zesty spice that lasts long into the secondary passes. Entry is—to my complete surprise—gently sweet, fruity, floral, and spicy; midpalate is succulent, piquant, peppery, zesty, and totally beguiling. Aftertaste brings all the various components together in a rush of elegant juiciness. Perfectly rendered in terms of spice, floral aspect, acid freshness, and fruitiness. All the flavors are pulling the wagon in unison. Love it. Unlimited cocktail potential.
2015 Rating: ★★★★★/Highest Recommendation

Spring 44 Fortify Bitter Liqueur (USA) 30% abv, $34.
Brick red color; excellent clarity. Initial inhalations after the pour encounter incongruous aromas of brown rice, dried cherry, duct tape, envelope glue, stone fruits (plum, in particular), Jolly Rancher hard candies—I mean, this bouquet is all over the aromatic map but I like it; more air contact appears to settle down the aromatics as the primary focus becomes botanical, especially forest floor after rain, tree bark, wet leaves, black pepper, flax, pumpkin seed, textile fiber. Entry reflects the bouquet to a degree, but the taste profile borders on being sour/tart, acidic, fresh, herbal, woodsy; midpalate echoes the entry as the herbaceousness kicks into high gear, as do the sour fruit and astringency that direct the finish.
2016 Rating: ★★★/Recommended

St. George Raspberry Liqueur (USA) 20% abv, $35.
Opaque, deep eggplant color. Smells heavenly of freshly picked raspberries, in which you can actually still detect the bitter seeds as well as the berry pulp; later whiffs focus primarily on the berry astringency and acid, which keeps the bouquet tight and fresh. Entry is sublimely raspberry jam–like, sweet but tart, silky, creamy; midpalate echoes the splendor of the entry and features incredibly tart and true flavors of fresh raspberry fruit. Genuine and luscious beyond words.
2016 Rating: ★★★★★/Highest Recommendation

St. George Spiced Pear Liqueur (USA) 20% abv, $35.
Jonquil/yellow-gold color; flawless purity. Up front, I pick up intense clove, cinnamon, pear juice scents that are already high flying and assertive—no waiting needed; later inhalations encounter tangy, fruity, almost pastry-like odors that are in harmony. Entry is medium viscous, pleasingly tart, juicy, spicy in equal measures; midpalate advances the entry

impressions well and in tart-to-sour fashion, which wins me over. Ends more spicy than juicy.
2016 Rating: ★ ★ ★ ★/Highly Recommended

St-Germain Liqueur (France) 20% abv, $33.
Flax/straw color; impeccably pure. The first nosings are treated to elegant, integrated aromas that are distinctly herbal, floral, hay-, parchment-, and green tea–like; following more aeration, there's a soft push towards the floral aspect, which speaks softly but carries the moment as the other ethereal fragrances give way. Entry turns up the dial on sweetness, but it's the variety of sweetness that's sweet and sour, and that's what makes this initial in-mouth impression so outstanding; midpalate is memorable for its flowery taste framed by ripe fruit, especially white grapes. Released in 2007, St-Germain has become the finest, most admired, and widely utilized liqueur of the twenty-first century. Just look on any backbar and you'll see it somewhere, since bartenders now consider it an essential ingredient. All this aside, it's a superbly rendered, understated liqueur that is a model for any liqueur producer.
2018 Rating: ★ ★ ★ ★ ★/Highest Recommendation

Tempus Fugit Crème de Banane Liqueur (Switzerland) 26% abv, $35.
Deep tawny port–like auburn/henna color; flawless purity. Smells initially like chocolate-covered banana or a classic "banana split" dessert (ice cream, halved banana, whipped cream, chocolate syrup); after more aeration, the banana aspect turns riper and more like banana-nut bread—a yummy bouquet. Entry is crazily rich, thick, viscous, honeyed, and rife with baked banana flavor; midpalate provides the highlight reel for this liqueur as the banana-nut flavor reaches stratospheric levels on the pleasure meter in seductive waves of baked banana, banana-nut bread, and banana sorbet. Finishes baked, significantly drier than either the entry or midpalate (hurray!), and dazzlingly succulent. An amazing liqueur achievement of the top rank.
2017 Rating: ★ ★ ★ ★ ★/Highest Recommendation

Tempus Fugit Spirits Crème de Noyaux Liqueur (Switzerland) 30% abv, $40.
Bright cherry/raspberry color; impeccable purity. The initial sniffs are treated to stone-dry, cherry-pit fragrance, then with more aeration the aroma turns into a drier black-cherry perfume that's regal, tart, and deeply jammy and preserves-like. Entry is dense, ripe, and black-cherry sweet; midpalate gets the full effect of the texture's lush, creamy viscosity that supports the rich cherry taste. Aftertaste is infinitely long, super-ripe, but neither cloying nor syrupy.
2017 Rating: ★ ★ ★ ★/Highly Recommended

Th. Kramers Aromatique Bitter (Germany) 40% abv, $35.
Black walnut color. Initial whiffs detect deeply herbaceous aromas/ of damp woods/forest, anise, tree bark, cardamom, cinnamon, bay leaf, eucalyptus, ginger; secondary sniffs encounter a fragrance that isn't as assertive as in the first nosing, but one that's settled down, offering deeply botanical, some might say, medicinal scents that are compelling. Entry highlights the woody/bark-like aspects but then turns bittersweet, sap-like, smoky, toasty, black

tea–like; midpalate is really the best phase as the flavors meld into one unified taste that's bittersweet, pleasantly viscous, and silky.
2016 Rating: ★ ★ ★ ★/Highly Recommended

The Bitter Truth E**X**R Bitter Liqueur (France) 30% abv, $35.

Opaque, jet-black color. First nosing passes discover very little as the aroma is closed for business, except for a subtle citrus-peel fragrance that could best be described as "ethereal"; additional air contact stimulates some other faint aromas that are herbal, woodsy, fruity, earthy, but neither distinctive nor generous. Entry is mildly piquant, with low-flying astringent flavors of black currant, dates, figs, leafy herbs, rooty herbs; midpalate is moderate, yet deceptively potent in its herbal presence, but there's still not enough flavor impact in total to make a definitive statement. What could be perceived by some as elegance is viewed by me as being too meek, too cautious. That said, I certainly see quality here and believe that it's well made. I'd just like to see more animation.
2015 Rating: ★ ★ ★/Recommended

Tia Maria Liqueur (Italy) 26.5% abv, $23.

Beautiful espresso-brown color; perfect clarity. The coffee bean fragrance right from the start is elegant and lovely and true to coffee, and even though I am not a coffee drinker, this has always been a favorite coffee liqueur of mine; with aeration, the beaniness builds in the second stage of nosing. Entry is bittersweet, intensely beany, espresso-like, and clean; midpalate mirrors all the entry findings, adding for good measure a bit of cocoa/mocha, especially in the medium-long finish. A beauty of a liqueur that deserves the spotlight once again.
2016 Rating: ★ ★ ★ ★/Highly Recommended

Torres Gran Torres Orange Liqueur (Spain) 39% abv, $20.

The lovely topaz/amber color is totally sediment-free and clean. The first nosing passes offer crisp, tart, and zesty orange-pulp aromas that, to me, are close to the Valencia variety of orange and, to lesser degree, blood orange; secondary inhalations deepen the orange-pulp perfume that's lovely in its authenticity. Entry is pleasingly acidic and therefore fresh and crisp at first, then the sweetness enters, underscoring the orange-peel zestiness; the intensely sweet midpalate is within acceptable bounds and is engagingly like orange peel. Ends on a subdued orange zest note that quietly sums up the analysis. Had the sweetness level encountered in the midpalate been turned down a couple of notches, I would have without hesitation bestowed a fourth rating star. The quality is there.
2018 Rating: ★ ★ ★/Recommended

Tuaca Cinnaster Cinnamon & Vanilla Liqueur (USA) 35% abv, $24.

Brandy-like topaz/brown color; excellent clarity. I like the initial smells after the pour, which feature both the vanilla and cinnamon elements in balance; the second nosing passes after further aeration don't accomplish much as the vanilla/cinnamon tandem stays the course. Entry is crisp, piquant, pleasantly spiced, and not only sweet; midpalate is nicely spicy as the cinnamon aspect takes the lead. Alluring finish. A well-made shooter for the younger demographic.

2016 Rating: ★★★/Recommended

Tuvè Fernet Amaro (Italy) 35% abv, $35.

Cinnamon/ginger color; unblemished purity. This initial nosing packs a prickly punch to it, which I like, but also offers subtle traces of anise, cinchona, plastic, beeswax, linseed oil; second inhalations pick up more earthiness, forest floor, mintiness, cinnamon, ginger, black peppercorn. Entry is sharply defined, narrow in focus, metallic, lead pencil–like, nutty, minerally, flinty, dry; midpalate is more herbal than minerally, offering crisply bitter tastes of lime zest, peppermint, orange peel, coriander, cardamom, fennel. Aftertaste is bittersweet, spicy, deeply flavorful, and tobacco-like.

2016 Rating: ★★★★/Highly Recommended

Zwack Unicum Herb Liqueur (Hungary) 40% abv, $26.

Mahogany/chestnut-brown color; nearly opaque but not quite 100 percent. First whiffs detect nuances of forest herbs and botanicals, especially dried leaves, grains of paradise, fennel, vinyl; secondary inhalations feature anise, onion grass, chives, coriander, dried basil, carob . . . this can go on forever. Entry is patently bitter, dense, deeply herbal, woodsy, earthy, mushroomy; midpalate features carob, dried parsley, black pepper, grape seed oil. Finish is deeply astringent, unabashedly herbal.

2018 Rating: ★★★★/Highly Recommended

ABSINTHE-WORLD

Absinthe (a.k.a. Green Fairy) is the world's most curious and misunderstood spirit by a long shot. Its story is a three-act saga of meteoric, nineteenth-century success, fueled by its enthusiastic use by the French army and the day's artistic luminaries. Act Two, set in the early twentieth century, included condemnation by various governments and its commercial banishment for absinthe's inclusion of wormwood, fennel, and hyssop. Then, in Act Three, in the late twentieth century, absinthe experienced redemption and a dramatic return around the world as governments, led by France, Switzerland, and eventually the United States (2007) enabled production to resume by allowing the inclusion of the three chemical compounds in question.

But along the way, absinthe's Act One was filled with wild and often unfounded misconceptions of hallucinatory experiences upon consumption, poisoning by the wormwood, hyssop, and fennel seed components rather than by sheer overconsumption, and an entire battery of far-fetched fantasies that contributed to its formal dismissal in Europe and America prior to the outbreak of World War I. These extreme actions were in large measure directed by an appalling lack of scientific fact and evidence and by the period's small-minded, we-know-best prejudices. Keep in mind that legislated Prohibition in the United States was just a few years away, beginning in 1920.

Now, some have argued that absinthe has been its own worst enemy because of its unusual array of herbal ingredients, its extraordinarily high abv rate, which is typically north of 60 percent, its own set of service tools, and even its ghostly green appearance, which turns hazy (called the *louche*) when drops of water are added. Is there a grain of truth to that position? No. The reality is that absinthe, when consumed with thoughtful care, can be a wonderful, uplifting, and unique experience, one that should not be missed by spirits enthusiasts.

Germain-Robin Absinthe Superieure (USA) 45.15% abv, $50.

Pewter/tarnished-silver tint; very good clarity. Lots of menthol, woodsy, forest floor, earthy appeal in the opening nosing passes, plus ethanol, furniture polish, makeup remover, plastic, deeply herbal fragrances; secondary sniffs echo the findings of the early round, adding only candle wax, kiwi, lychee. Entry is zesty, keenly peppery, tangy, herbaceous; midpalate highlights soybean, black pepper, spearmint, dill, basil, parsley, grassy tastes. I like this absinthe's manageable abv level, which I acknowledge is well below the traditional 65–68 percent level.

2015 Rating: ★ ★ ★ ★ ★/Highest Recommendation

Jade 1901 Absinthe Supérieure (France) 68% abv, $99.

Pretty yellow/green/pistachio color that's a touch hazy; otherwise pure. First nosings pick up soaring scents of mint plus underlying aromas of honeysuckle, orange blossom, lemon balm, coriander, fennel; the aromatic banquet continues in the second inhalations as waves of nutmeg, clove, aniseed, and poppy seed vie for prominence without stepping all over each other. Entry, which is hot, is minty, astringent, mineral-like on the tongue, then it turns softly herbal in the midpalate as the flavors meld into one entity: oily, viscous, green, vegetal, deeply herbaceous, grassy. Aftertaste reflects all the joys of the entry and midpalate in softer tones. Very tasty.

2015 Rating: ★ ★ ★ ★ ★/Highest Recommendation

Jade C.F. Berger Absinthe Supérieure (France) 65% abv, $99.

Pale key-lime green/yellow tint; flawlessly pure. This opening aroma is intensely waxy, piquant, legume-like (peas, beans), and loaded with dried herbs, alfalfa, grain, forest floor; second sniffs, following more aeration, find the licorice/fennel and star anise elements finally gathering steam as the alcohol remains flying under the radar. Entry is aggressively fiery, then quickly turns embers warm and friendly as the herbaceous flavors take charge, especially the star anise, lemon balm, and angelica; midpalate is harmonious, balanced, gently warming, lusciously oily, delicious. Aftertaste is moderately hot, intensely sage-like, grassy, creamy.

2015 Rating: ★ ★ ★ ★ ★/Highest Recommendation

Jade Esprit Edouard Absinthe Supérieure (France) 72% abv, $99.

Camouflage-green/green-olive color; superb clarity. There's a meaty, substantial foundational aroma of dried flowers (carnations, roses, honeysuckle, jasmine) that carries the bouquet forward in the initial whiffs after the pour; second-time nosings discover deeper scents, in particular, walnut oil, tropical fruits, star anise, lemon zest, lemon balm, hyssop, limestone/chalk. Entry features some of the chalkiness of the aroma but also fragrances of aniseed, licorice, thyme, fennel; midpalate is juicy, fruity, ripe, astringent, bitter, minty, with supporting flavors of chamomile, eucalyptus. Concludes long, bittersweet, oily, floral once again, with delicate touches of orchard fruits. Really luscious.

2015 Rating: ★ ★ ★ ★ ★/Highest Recommendation

Jade Nouvelle-Orléans Absinthe Supérieure (France) 68% abv, $99.

Brilliantly bright apple-green/chartreuse color; impeccable clarity. This curiously reticent opening aroma highlights the spiciness of absinthe in a way that's unusually sedate and laid-back—there's no alcohol burst, very little in the way of deep herbal thrusts and parries, and even less play on star anise, fennel, or wormwood; additional aeration wakes up this bouquet as the anise/licorice team gets working, and the dried-flower contingent adds its two cents, and the peppermint, angelica, and coriander all make worthy contributions that matter. Entry is the sweetest of the Jades, and for that I'm grateful; midpalate stage is alive with sugar, warming but not blistering heat, and rife with complex botanical flavor layers that alternately sear and soothe. Finish is sophisticated, green, highly astringent, cleansing in the throat and on the palate.

2015 Rating: ★ ★ ★ ★ ★/Highest Recommendation

Lucid Absinthe Supérieure (France) 62% abv, $60.

Color is misty yellow/green; impeccably sediment-free. First whiffs detect an entire warehouse of exotic aromas, including bison grass, wormwood, spring onion, candle wax, glue, hyssop, lemon balm, and star anise fruit; after another seven-minute span of air contact, the bouquet turns as mineral-like as it is herbal/woodsy. Entry is concentrated, highly complex, searing on the tongue at first, yet agile and focused as the alcohol heat fades, leaving behind layers of fennel, licorice, coriander, and mint; midpalate mirrors the entry but maintains a lower profile heatwise, allowing the botanical mix to shine unencumbered. Finish is long, peppery, zesty, deeply herbaceous.

2015 Rating: ★ ★ ★ ★/Highly Recommended

Pernod Original Recipe Absinthe Supérieure (France) 68% abv, $68.

Pale tea-green color; superb purity. The anise/licorice dominance is real from the first whiffs, but later on there are other aromatic aspects, including cardamom, green tea, fennel, stone, cement, wood plank, sawdust. Entry is bitter, leafy, earthy, woodsy, herbal, dry; midpalate is spicy/peppery, warming, sweeter than the entry, concentrated, acutely herbal.

2014 Rating: ★ ★ ★ ★/Highly Recommended

Vieux Pontarlier 65º Française Absinthe Superiéure (France) 65% abv, $75.

Pretty aqua/green color; ideal purity. Initial nosing after the pour detects keenly brisk yet deep herbal/botanical notes combining with an unexpected, almost hidden seaside/fishy/sardine (!?) note that creeps up on the botanicals but never overtakes them; seven more minutes in the glass doesn't do this bouquet justice because it likely needs at least an hour of further exposure to air to stretch out completely but, that said, the second stage of inhalations substantiates the sea air/fish/botanical marriage in spades; like no other absinthe bouquet I've encountered. Entry is incredibly vibrant and teasing and bursting with flavors of sage, fennel, dill, sea salt, green olive, white pepper . . . man, this is what I've always looked for in absinthe that the others, to date, haven't delivered; midpalate is astringent, cleansing, acutely peppery/spicy, and yet oddly well-behaved and highly palatable straight. Ends with a cherry bomb of exploding herbal flavors that nicely sum up the experience. The best absinthe in the world.

2019 Rating: ★ ★ ★ ★ ★/Highest Recommendation

APPENDIX

F. PAUL PACULT'S LIST OF THE THIRTY GAME-CHANGING FIVE STAR SPIRITS, 1989-2021

I'm including this roster of exceptional spirits that either changed my viewpoint or, better, opened my eyes to the hidden virtues of a category as never before. These spirits were as much my personal instructors to categorical excellence as all the distillers and master blenders I've encountered. They provided indelible touchstones to which I've referred thousands of times over the past three decades of reviewing spirits. Alas, many of these iconic spirits are available only in my memory bank and not necessarily reviewed in this book.

AB Collection (Antonella Bocchino) Fiore di Rosa Grappa (Italy)

You won't find this treasure anymore, but it remains in my experience the most eye-opening spirit from Italy and helped shape my understanding of the modern grappa industry. Created by grappa distiller Antonella Bocchino, Fiore di Rosa was spirit made from rose petals. It was and still is unlike any other top-drawer spirit I've ever tasted.

Asbach 1952 Goethe Cask #1 Brandy (Germany)

Rarely in all my years of evaluating spirits in my home office did I actually speak out loud as to how delicious a spirit was. I did so with this ancient brandy from Germany. So rare, as to be virtually nonexistent. What was it that I exclaimed? I think it was, "I'm drinking eternity."

Bailie Nicol Jarvis Blend of Old Scotch Whisky

This discontinued blended Scotch (originally blended by The Glenmorangie Company) had one of the highest ratios of malt whisky to grain whisky at 60 percent malt/40 percent grain for blends. I first tasted it sometime between 1995–1998 while in the midst of my busiest period of writing about Scotch whisky for the *New York Times Magazine*. BNJ provided an extraordinary elegance and majesty rivaled only in my experience by Chivas 18. Can't find it now except perhaps at auction.

Black Bowmore 1964 1ˢᵗ Edition 29 Year Old Single Malt Scotch Whisky

I first tasted this legendary Islay Scotch (the first American to be so honored) in a Glasgow bar courtesy of master distiller of Bowmore (at the time) Jim McEwan and former owner Brian Morrison. Most of all, I recall the midnight-black color (What? It's not amber?) as well as the heavenly, raisiny, pruny aroma that was so much the antithesis of single malt Scotch at that time. (Maybe 1993?) I still have a few ounces of it, and memories of Jim and Brian smiling when I was rendered speechless.

Booker's "The Center Cut" 2015–03 Straight Kentucky Bourbon Whiskey

The stories I could tell you about traveling around America with Booker Noe in the early 1990s . . . wait. I did in *American Still Life*. Be that as it may, while I might think now that Beam Suntory has watered down Booker's with too many annual releases (for a few years SIX per year/now FOUR), this one from 2015 stands out as perhaps the finest Booker's of all time.

Boyd & Blair Potato Vodka (USA)

In a small distillery located just outside of Pittsburgh, Pennsylvania, distiller Barry Young makes the finest potato vodka in the world. Wait, let me amend that . . . Barry makes the best vodka in the world, period.

BRN Sea Wynde Pot Still Rum (Jamaica and Guyana)

No longer in production, BRN Sea Wynde came courtesy of Mark Andrews, former owner of Castle Brands and the person behind Knappogue Castle Irish whiskeys. The BRN stands for British Royal Navy, the inspiration for Sea Wynde. This seductive blend of five pot still rums elevated my understanding of what rum could achieve when placed in the right hands.

Buffalo Trace Antique Collection 2012 George T. Stagg Kentucky Straight Bourbon Whiskey

To this day, I consider this full-throttle KSB to be the finest American whiskey I've ever tasted. It was part of the now iconic Antique Collection 2012 from Buffalo Trace Distillery that blew my mind. Proves the point that "cask strength" can indeed be majestic AND elegant.

Bush Pilot Private Reserve Single Cask 13 Year Old Canadian Whisky

One of the great whisky stories of the 1990s is Bush Pilot. Made at the Hiram Walker Distillery in Ontario, BP was a delicious 100 percent unblended corn whisky that was bottled by spirits pioneer Robert Denton for his wife Marilyn Smith in honor of her father who had owned a small bush airline. It's no longer available because of a frivolous and petty lawsuit brought by Anheuser-Busch, who took umbrage to the name. Showed me early on what Canada can produce in terms of superlative quality.

Chivas Regal 18 Year Old Gold Signature Blended Scotch Whisky

Always my swift and convincing answer when someone of low understanding says to me, "Scotch blends never measure up to single malts." Try this, dummy. Among a litany of triumphs, CR18 is master blender Colin Scott's enthralling, legendary masterpiece.

Clear Creek Distillery Eau-de-Vie-de-Pomme Apple Brandy (USA)

As one more prime example of how far American craft distilling came in the last quarter of the twentieth century, Clear Creek's Eau-de-Vie-de-Pomme remains the front-runner in domestic non-grape pot still brandy for me, perhaps rivaled only by the same distillery's Pear Brandy. The vision of legendary master distiller Steve McCarthy, now retired, lives on.

Cointreau Liqueur (France)
Cointreau is the spirit on this list that I've consumed more than any other due to its inclusion in so many cocktails that I personally prefer, starting with the original Margarita and Sidecar. A visit to the distillery some years ago is forever etched in my memory for the unforgettable aroma of orange peel. I pour it over fresh fruit. Sue and I use it in baking. Nothing ranks close to it.

Dartigalongue Vintage 1984 Bas-Armagnac
If any armagnac would make a believer of Bas-Armagnac's virtues out of any doubter, this would be the one. The regal air of this brandy, so refined and earthy at the same time, is nothing short of breathtaking. You want to teach someone about armagnac's magical side, here you go.

Del Maguey Single Village Wild Jabalí
There are few descriptors that are grand enough to adequately characterize this fabled mezcal, made in the village of Santa Maria Albarradas from the challenging wild jabalí agave in Oaxaca. The jabalí agaves that made up this classic mezcal ranged in age from eighteen to twenty years old, grown at an elevation of 5,577 feet. It won the Ultimate Spirits Challenge Chairman's Trophy as Best Mezcal in 2018.

Domaine Charbay Distillery Nostalgie Black Walnut Liqueur (USA)
Me not being a lover of liqueurs, Charbay's Nostalgie opened up doors that I never thought possible in sweet libations. The distilling skill it takes to produce a sweet potable that doesn't lose its base material identity is to be admired and revered. A milestone moment for master distiller Miles Karakasevic.

Francis Darroze Domaine de la Post 1980 Ténarèze-Armagnac
That milestone experience that made me a true devotee of Ténarèze-Armagnac, a much ignored AOC brandy district in Gascony that I think bests Bas-Armagnac for both longevity and grace.

Germain-Robin Old & Rare Riesling Single Barrel V320 Alambic Brandy (USA)
My choice for the greatest American pot still brandy of all time. Whoever claims that legendary grape brandy can't be produced outside of France hasn't experienced this singular masterpiece. The memory of it still thrills me.

Glenmorangie Nectar D'Or Sauternes Cask Finish Highland Single Malt Scotch Whisky
In my view, the greatest single malt Scotch to be treated in any type of "finishing" oak barrel. While sherry, port, Madeira, and other barrel types have now been widely used as finishing touches to scores of whiskeys, Glenmorangie master blender Dr. Bill Lumsden's genius came to full fruition with this supple, luscious expression.

Highland Park 18 Year Old Viking Pride Orkneys Single Malt Scotch Whisky
The most complete distilled and matured grain-based spirit I've reviewed over three decades. HP18, which I have evaluated many times, crystallizes and defines what "Five

Stars" epitomizes. It is that ultra-rare expression of perfection, year after year. It continues to be in my view the world's greatest spirit and my go-to desert island staple.

Jean Fillioux Réserve Familiale Grande Champagne Cognac

This supple, magnificent, estate-grown cognac will always be the foremost member of my brandy pantheon. This rare gem encapsulates the district's unique soil and environment, grapes, perfect alembic distillation, and oak barrel maturation, thereby creating the most eloquent expression of Grande Champagne that I know of.

Macallan M Speyside Single Malt Scotch Whisky

While I've loved many Speyside single malts over the last three decades, none tops this rare and excruciatingly expensive offering from The Macallan. Makes the case for instituting a sixth rating star.

Michter's 20 Year Old Kentucky Straight Bourbon Whiskey

All I can say about this spectacularly luscious whiskey is . . . oh, I just said it. SPEC-TACULARLY LUSCIOUS. A bona fide legend in American whiskey lore.

Midleton Very Rare 2006 Irish Blended Whiskey

I rated this blended Irish whiskey wonder 96/100 points when I was spirits editor for *Wine Enthusiast* magazine. I still consider this expression the finest Midleton to date. The creation of master distiller Barry Crockett in 1984, Midleton VR is a yearly release of twelve to twenty-five-year-old whiskeys that are matured in ex-bourbon and ex-sherry casks. The annual amount is small as the volume is limited to a mere fifty barrels.

Neisson Blanc Rhum Agricole (Martinique)

Neisson Blanc taught me to appreciate rhum agricole for all its mineral-like, vegetal, grassy splendor in one sitting. Not only did the Blanc express the zesty caney grassiness in spades, it also featured an integrated core flavor experience that illustrated the skill of the master distiller.

Nonino Cru Grappa di Monovitigno Picolit (Italy)

The redoubtable quality of this magical elixir is what makes grappa in the twenty-first century so lovely. Two things in my opinion make this spirit so exquisite: the genius of the Nonino family, and the delicacy and floral nature of the picolit grape variety. These factors collaborate in the creation of one of Italy's most memorable distillate experiences.

Partida Reposado Tequila

While I recall with fondness the first times I sipped Chinaco and the old, original Herraduras in the early 1990s, nothing prepared me for this 100 percent agave classic. Partida Reposado is an ideal combination of agave richness and zest, superb distillation, and the judicious perfection of wood aging.

Redbreast 21 Year Old Single Pot Still Irish Whiskey

Close on the heels of the Midleton Very Rare 2006 is this blustery beauty of a single pot still whiskey from Ireland. Its premise is to take no prisoners with a robust style that's brash and unapologetic. It remains one of only two spirits that earned a perfect score of 100 points at Ultimate Spirits Challenge 2014.

Tanqueray London Dry Gin (England)

This is all I have to say about the world's best gin: juniper + angelica root + licorice + coriander = TANQUERAY. Four ingredients, masterfully blended. Peerless gin. I hope that the hundreds of well-meaning but woefully inept craft distillers around the world who are flooding the marketplace with poorly made, fat-in-the-gut gins get the message.

Tesseron Trésor Grande Champagne Cognac

Here is a brandy that can eloquently make the case for *terroir* occurring in distilled spirits. A hallmark Grande Champagne that showcases this district's chalky soil by being the earthiest, flintiest cognac I've ever evaluated. The depth of character is nothing short of astounding.

Vieux Pontarlier 65º Française Absinthe Superiéure (France)

While I am not a fan of absinthe in general, and while there are several fine ones in the current marketplace, this spectacular rendering came close to converting me as a regular imbiber. There simply is no equal. Thanks to John Troia of Tempus Fugit Spirits.

ACKNOWLEDGMENTS

Organizing, editing, and designing such a massive compilation takes an enormous amount of expertise. To shine a spotlight on those talented people most responsible, I would first like to thank our good friends at BenBella/Matt Holt Books, including Matthew Holt, Alexa Stevenson, Monica Lowry, Jay Kilburn, Mallory Hyde, and Alicia Kania for their enthusiastic support and insightful guidance. My appreciation roster also includes my colleague and friend Sarah Tirone, who assisted by conducting a thorough examination of the raw manuscript, review by review, and Scott Calamar, the book's impossibly patient copy editor. My wife and partner, Sue Woodley, directed all the lanes of traffic, which were at times bumper-to-bumper for this book project. To all, my deepest gratitude.

ABOUT THE AUTHOR

F. PAUL PACULT has been hailed as "... an all-knowing spirituous oracle, a J.D. Power of liquor" by *Imbibe* magazine and "America's foremost spirits authority" by Forbes.com. He is the author of seven books and a contributor to two other books, all on beverage alcohol. From 1991 to 2019, he was the editor and sole reviewer of the quarterly, advertising-free, subscription-only newsletter, *F. Paul Pacult's Spirit Journal*. Beginning in 1989, his writings have been published in the *New York Times Magazine*, *Wine Enthusiast*, Delta Air Lines SKY magazine, *Playboy* magazine, *Cheers*, *Beverage Dynamics*, *MarketWatch*, and scores of other publications. Pacult has been honored multiple times in Scotland, France, and the United States for his contributions to beverage alcohol journalism and education. He has also acted since 1995 as a consultant to large and small beverage companies both on the creation of new spirits brands and the refreshing of established brands. As an educator, he is a cofounder of the award-winning company Beverage Alcohol Resource, and along with Sue Woodley created the trade education "Authority" series. In 2010, along with David Talbot and Sue Woodley, he established the beverage competition company *Ultimate Beverage Challenge*, where he is Judging Director. Pacult is also serving as Master Blender for the American whiskey brand Jacob's Pardon. He resides in New York's Hudson Valley with his wife and partner, Sue Woodley.